COMPARATIVE
POLITICS TODAY

Principal Contributors

Gabriel A. Almond	Stanford University
Frederick C. Barghoorn	Yale University
Wayne A. Cornelius	University of California, San Diego
Ann L. Craig	University of California, San Diego
Russell J. Dalton	University of California, Irvine
Henry W. Ehrmann	Dartmouth College
Scott C. Flanagan	Florida State University
G. Bingham Powell, Jr.	University of Rochester
Austin Ranney	University of California, Berkeley
Thomas F. Remington	Emory University
Bradley M. Richardson	Ohio State University
Richard Rose	University of Strathclyde, Scotland
Martin A. Schain	New York University
James R. Townsend	University of Washington
Brantly Womack	Northern Illinois University
Crawford Young	University of Wisconsin, Madison

COMPARATIVE
POLITICS TODAY

A WORLD VIEW

FIFTH EDITION

GENERAL EDITORS

GABRIEL A. ALMOND
Stanford University

G. BINGHAM POWELL, JR.
University of Rochester

HarperCollinsPublishers

Photo Credits

Page 8, AP/Wide World; 14, AP/Wide World; 20, Robert Frerck/ Odyssey Productions, Chicago; 23, Tass from SOVFOTO; 25, AP/Wide World; 34, Paul Conklin; 38, Giani Giansanti/Sygma; 43, Mary Ellen Mark; 48, UPI/Bettmann; 55, AP/Wide World; 59, UPI/Bettmann; 64, Les Wilson/Photri, Inc.; 69, Balder/Sygma; 72, Patrick Forester/Sygma; 78, Reuters/UPI/Bettmann; 87, AP/Wide World; 95, Paul Conklin; 101, AP/Wide World; 102, AP/Wide World; 108, Jay Lurie/Black Star; 117, Michel Philippo/Sygma; 120, Reuters/UPI/Bettmann; 141, Courtesy of British Information Services; 149, UPI/Bettmann; 158, Reuters/UPI/Bettmann; 195, Courtesy of the French Embassy Press and Information Division; 223, Jean-Claude Francalon/Gamma-Liaison; 232, Courtesy of the Constitutional Council; 246, AP/Wide World; 252, Reuters/UPI/Bettmann; 308, Reuters/UPI/Bettmann; 317, AP/Wide World; 339, AP/Wide World; 355, Reuters/Bettmann; 376, Reuters/UPI/Bettmann; 384, AP/Wide World; 410, Agence Vu, Paris; 424, Eastfoto; 443, Reuters/UPI/Bettmann; 456, Eastfoto; 465, Courtesy of Francisco Mayo/Mayocolor; 474, Courtesy of Roberto Cordova Studio C and KPBS Television, San Diego; 483, Courtesy of Partido Revolucionario Institutional; 505, Wayne Cornelius; 529, Courtesy of the Tanzania Information Service; 543, Reuters/UPI/Bettmann; 550, Cilo/Gamma-Liaison; 557, Verges/Sygma; 569, J. P. Laffont/Sygma; 574, Christina Thomson/Woodfin Camp & Associates; 588, Steven Folk/Gamma-Liaison.

Sponsoring Editor: Lauren Silverman
Development Editor: Susan Mraz
Project Editor: Ellen MacElree
Assistant Art Director: Lucy Krikorian
Text Design: Keithley and Associates, Inc.
Cover Design: Jan Kessner
Photo Researcher: Kathy Smeilis
Production Manager/Assistant: Willie Lane/Jeffrey Taub
Compositor: Digitype, Inc.
Printer and Binder: R. R. Donnelley & Sons Company
Cover Printer: The Lehigh Press, Inc.

Comparative Politics Today: A World View, Fifth Edition

Copyright © 1992 by Gabriel A. Almond and G. Bingham Powell, Jr.

Library of Congress Cataloging-in-Publication Data

Comparative politics today : a world view / general editors, Gabriel
   A. Almond, G. Bingham Powell, Jr. — 5th ed.
        p.   cm.
   Includes bibliographical references and index.
   ISBN 0-673-52029-3
   1. Comparative government.   I. Almond, Gabriel Abraham, 1911 –
II. Powell, G. Bingham.
JF51.C62 1992
320.3 — dc20

91-27867
CIP

91 92 93 94   9 8 7 6 5 4 3 2 1

BRIEF CONTENTS

DETAILED

CONTENTS

PREFACE

The fifth edition of *Comparative Politics Today* is a "post–cold war" edition with an up-to-date treatment of the transformation of Soviet politics and society (Chapter Thirteen), and of postunification Germany (Chapter Eleven). We have added the United States (Chapter Seventeen) and Japan (Chapter Twelve) to our country studies. It is no longer justifiable to exclude the American case from a text in comparative politics, if it ever was defensible. As a reflection of the historic decline in American hegemony in the last decades and the swiftly growing interdependence of the world, we now need to place the United States in a perspective that explicitly includes other nations and cultures and employs common categories in their analysis. Similarly, the inclusion of Japan among our country studies gives us the case of an advanced democracy with one of the most powerful economies in the world, rising swiftly from strikingly different historical and cultural premises than those of the Western world, with its own versions of democratic political culture and political institutions, and its own versions of value change and transitions.

The work as a whole takes into account the ways in which the political world has changed in the crucial few years that have elapsed since the publication of the fourth edition. The theme of the comparative politics of the 1990s is change, transformation, transition, with democratization and economic liberalization as the major trends. The transformations began in the mid-1970s with the collapse of the authoritarian regimes of Southern Europe — Greece, Portugal, and Spain — and the reinstitution of democratic regimes in those countries. They spread to Latin America — Argentina, Brazil, and Chile, among others; and to East Asia — South Korea, Taiwan, and the Philippines. Then, most dramatically of all, in the 1980s the Eastern European countries and the Soviet Union began to change themselves, moving at different paces in the direction of democratic governments and market economies.

The most interesting questions have to do with the ways in which different structural and cultural starting points and different strategies of democratization and economic growth policy affect subsequent development. For the bureaucratic and military authoritarian regimes of Southern Europe and Latin America, it appears that successful democratization was preceded by economic crisis tending to discredit the authoritarian ruling groups, and a moderate strategy of democratization involving bargaining and accommodation between the authoritarian elites and the oppositional movements. In the Latin American countries such an accommodative strategy has made it easier for them to democratize than to free their economies from protectionism and state subsidization.[1] Mexico is an interesting reversal of this situation (see Chapter Fifteen). It has experienced substantial economic liberalization and less democratization.

For the East Asian countries of South Korea and Taiwan, rapid development led by successful export growth policies, along with incremental, accommodative strategies of democratization, seems to explain these movements toward democratic market societies. The kind of variety in these democratic transitions, in historical background, culture, economic development, and political structure, as well as in the strategic decisions of elites, can enhance our understanding of effective developmental policies.

The transition from communist authoritarian regimes has begun more recently, and consequently there has been little experience to evaluate in exploring favorable conditions and effective strategies. From what has happened so far we observe again that the movement to democratization and to market economies has been through bargaining and coalition making between old

1 – See Nancy Bermeo, "Rethinking Regime Change," *Comparative Politics*, April 1990, 359 ff.; and Guillermo O'Donnell and Phillippe Schmitter, *Transitions from Authoritarian Rule: Tentative Conclusions about Uncertain Democracies* (Baltimore: Johns Hopkins University Press, 1986); Seymour Martin Lipset, "Political Renewal on the Left: A Comparative Perspective" (Washington, D.C.: Progressive Policy Institute, January 1990).

and new elites, rather than through violent mass movements destroying authoritarian institutions.[2]

The striking aspect of these transitions is that, with one or two exceptions such as Rumania, there has been so little blood shed in this devolution of power. Where there has been violence it has not been in the arena of struggle between reactionaries and the new leaderships, but in the primordial arenas of ethnicity and religion. Here weakening of government authority in the Soviet Union and Eastern Europe has made possible the rise to the surface of long smouldering grievances and violent angers in multicultural and multireligious societies. Georgia, Armenia and Azerbaijan, Slovenia and Croatia are cases in point.

For the advanced democratic capitalist countries this has also been an era of transition. The trend toward rising levels of taxation and expenditure since the early decades of the present century came to a halt in the early 1980s. Throughout the capitalist world beginning in these years and regardless of whether governments have been conservative or social democratic, there was a mood of "deregulation," "denationalization," and tax reduction. The politics of the 1980s was concerned with the relative size and structure of the public sector in democratic market economies — the scope and direction of regulatory penetration, and the scale and composition of the "welfare net." The most interesting questions in the democratic market societies are concerned with the ways prior structural and cultural conditions, as well as reform strategies, affect politics and policy outcomes. Rich historical studies and well-conceived research programs can be drawn upon in trying to explain the past and anticipate the future.[3] Clearly, the comparative politics of the 1990s must emphasize the theme of change and transition to complement the comparative institutional and process themes of the structural functional approach. And while the global pattern has clearly been toward democratization and market economics, we need to avoid becoming intellectually captive to these contemporary trends. Failed efforts at democratization and marketization may reverse the trend back toward military and technocratic regimes for some countries in the years ahead. Deregulated and "tax-reformed" economies may result in costs and inequities that only governmental regulation and income transfers can remedy. Tight-fisted budgets may result in neglect of infrastructural maintenance — roads, bridges, school buildings, and the like — and exact higher costs at a later time.

Issues having to do with the essence of democracy, its varieties, the conditions that foster it, the shortcomings to which it is prone, the relations between democratic politics and economic markets, are treated in a contemporary literature that has engaged the efforts of our ablest political theorists.[4] Indeed, the classic welfare and distributive issues of nineteenth- and twentieth-century politics have now been overtaken by new issues, and old ones long thought resolved have resurfaced. The new ones have to do with quality of life and environment as summarized in the symbolism of "greening." Environmentalism and postmaterialism have entered into the politics of most advanced industrial societies as strong and widely distributed opinion trends, as organized and powerful pressure groups or in the form of political parties represented in parliaments, or as powerful factions of major parties. There is a growing literature on postmaterialist political culture and its impact on political organization and process.[5]

The old issues — the primordial and parochial ones of ethnicity and religion — thought to have been subordinated and tamed by the nation-state and by the triumph of science and technology, turn out to have ex-

2 – See, among others, Timothy Garton Ash, *The Magic Lantern* (New York: Random House, 1990); Archie Brown, *Political Leadership in the Soviet Union* (Bloomington: Indiana University Press, 1989); George W. Breslauer, *Can Gorbachev's Reforms Succeed?* (Berkeley-Stanford Program in Soviet Studies, Center for Slavic and East European Studies, 1990).

3 – Hugh Heclo, *Modern Social Politics in Britain and Sweden* (New Haven, Conn.: Yale University Press, 1974): Peter Flora and Arnold Heidenheimer, *The Development of Welfare States in Europe and America* (New Brunswick, N.J.: Transaction Books, 1981); Arnold Heidenheimer, Hugh Heclo, and Carolyn Teich Adams, *Comparative Public Policy: The Politics of Social Choice in America, Europe, and Japan*, 3rd ed. (New York: St. Martin's Press, 1990); Francis G. Castles, ed., *The Comparative History of Public Policy* (Cambridge, England: Polity Press, 1989).

4 – See, for example, Giovanni Sartori, *The Theory of Democracy Revisited* (Chatham, N.J.: Chatham House Publishers, 1987); Robert A. Dahl, *Dilemmas of Pluralist Democracy* (New Haven, Conn.: Yale University Press, 1982); Dahl, *A Preface to Economic Democracy* (Berkeley, Calif.: University of California Press, 1985); Dahl, *Democracy and Its Critics* (New Haven, Conn.: Yale University Press, 1989); Charles E. Lindblom, *Politics and Markets* (New York: Basic Books, 1977); Arend Lijphart, *Democracies* (New Haven, Conn.: Yale University Press, 1984); G. Bingham Powell, *Contemporary Democracies* (Cambridge, Mass.: Harvard University Press, 1982).

5 – See, for example, Samuel Barnes and Max Kaase, *Political Action: Mass Participation on Five Western Democracies* (Beverly Hills, Calif.: Sage Publications, 1979); Russell J. Dalton, Scott Flanagan, and Paul Allen Beck, *Electoral Change in Advanced Industrial Democracies: Realignment or Dealignment?* (Princeton, N.J.: Princeton University Press, 1984); Kay Lawson, and Peter Merkl, eds., *When Parties Fail: Emerging Alternative Organizations* (Princeton, N.J.: Princeton University Press, 1988); Ronald Inglehart, *Culture Shift in Advanced Industrial Society* (Princeton, N.J.: Princeton University Press, 1990).

traordinary vitality. The cohesion of nation-states has been undermined by the resurfacing of subnational ethnic identities. And scientific and rational thought, tarnished by the nuclear threat and environmental deterioration, has been challenged by revitalized religious movements.

The rise of religious fundamentalisms around the world, the conditions associated with their emergence, and their impact on politics and public policy are described in a series of studies under the editorship of Martin Marty and Scott Appleby, and under the auspices of the American Academy of Arts and Sciences.[6] The rise of ethnic movements and conflicts in the last years is reported in a growing literature describing its extent and analyzing its causes and consequences.[7]

The autonomy and integrity of the modern nation-state are also under pressure from the international side, where regional and global interests in economic welfare have been creating regimes and institutions at the supernational level. Two developments have been of particular importance: the move toward integration in Western Europe with the adoption of a common European economy as of 1992,[8] and the increased power and legitimacy of the United Nations following the termina-

tion of the cold war, and the successful collective security effort under the auspices of the United Nations in the Persian Gulf in 1991. Discussions of some of these trends are to be found in Chapter 2 and in the chapters on Britain, France, and Germany.

The authors of the fifth edition of *Comparative Politics Today* owe a debt of gratitude to a number of anonymous readers who carefully corrected our prose and protected us from serious errors. A devoted and resourceful HarperCollins team, led by its political science editor, Lauren Silverman, and consisting of Ellen MacElree, Susan Mraz, and Betty Pessagno, who oversaw the manuscript as it passed through the evaluating, editing, and publishing process, should have a share of the credit for whatever distinction this edition earns. In addition, a number of reviewers provided useful suggestions: Stephen Douglas, University of Illinois; Joe Hagan, University of Wyoming; David Keithly, Lynchburg College; Fred Kramer, University of Massachusetts, Amherst; and David Luchins, Touro College.

Gabriel A. Almond
G. Bingham Powell

6—They include Martin Marty and Scott Appleby, eds., Vol. I, *Fundamentalism Observed*; Vol. II, *Remaking The World: The Fundamentalist Impact*; Vol. III, *The Character of Fundamentalism*, all based on recent research, and are to be published by the University of Chicago Press in 1991–1993; see also Bruce Lawrence, *Defenders of God: Fundamentalism in Christianity, Judaism, and Islam* (San Francisco: Harper & Row, 1989).

7—See, for example, Joseph Rothschild, *Ethnic Politics* (New York: Columbia University Press, 1981); Nelson Kasfir, *The Shrinking Political Arena* (Berkeley: University of California Press, 1975); Crawford Young, *The Politics of Cultural Pluralism* (Madison: University of Wisconsin Press, 1976); Donald Horowitz, *Ethnic Groups In Conflict* (Berkeley: University of California Press, 1985); Bohdan Nahaylo, *Soviet Disunion* (London: Hamish, 1990).

8—Robert O. Keohane and Stanley Hoffman, *The New European Community: Decision-making and Institutional Change* (Boulder, Colo.: Westview Press, 1991).

PART ONE

INTRODUCTION

GABRIEL A. ALMOND
G. BINGHAM POWELL, JR.

CHAPTER 1

THE STUDY OF
COMPARATIVE POLITICS

THIS QUOTATION from the French social philosopher Alexis de Tocqueville tells us that comparison is fundamental to all human thought, as well as being the methodological core of the scientific method. Comparing the past and present of our nation and comparing our experience with that of other nations deepen our perspective on our own institutions. Examining politics in other societies permits us to see a wider range of political alternatives and illuminates the virtues and shortcomings in our own political life. By taking us out of the network of assumptions and familiar arrangements within which we usually operate, comparative analysis helps expand our awareness of the possibilities of politics.

Without comparisons to make, the mind does not know how to proceed.

Alexis de Tocqueville

Comparative political analysis also helps to develop explanations and to test theories of the way in which political processes work and in which political change occurs. Here the logic and the intention of the comparative methods used by political scientists are similar to those used in more exact sciences. The political scientist cannot design experiments to manipulate political arrangements and observe the consequences. But it is possible to describe and explain the different combinations of events and institutions found in the politics of different societies. Two thousand years ago, Aristotle in his *Politics* contrasted the economies and social structures of the many Greek city-states, in an effort to determine how the social and economic environment affected political institutions and policies. A modern political scientist, Robert Dahl, in his studies of democracy, compares the economic characteristics, cultures, and historical experiences of many contemporary nations in an effort to discover the combinations of conditions and characteristics that are associated with that form of government.[1] Other theorists, in their attempt to explain differences between the processes and performance of political systems, have compared constitutional regimes with tyrannies, two-party democracies with multiparty democracies, and stable governments with unstable regimes.

In the 1990s as the cold war comes to an end the world is engaged in vast experiments in alternative approaches to economic growth, alternative strategies for transitions to democracy, alternative forms of controlling and using the powers of government. All governments are grappling with new issues of preserving our environment, old issues of opportunity and economic security for citizens, and ancient issues of conflicts of ethnic identities and religious values. In a world made ever smaller by instantaneous communication and interdependent economies, these problems and achievements spill across national boundaries.

Comparative analysis is a powerful and versatile tool. It enhances our ability to describe and understand political processes and political change in any country by offering concepts and reference points from a broader perspective. The comparative approach also stimulates us to form general theories of political relationships. It encourages and enables us to test our political theories by confronting them with the experience of many institutions and settings. The primary goal of this text is to provide the reader with access to this powerful tool for thought and analysis.

COMPARATIVE SYSTEMS: STRUCTURE AND FUNCTION

We use three concepts throughout this book — system, structure, and function. *System* implies an organization that interacts with an environment, influencing it and being influenced by it. The word also suggests that there are many interacting internal parts. The *political system* is one important set of social institutions concerned with formulating and implementing the collective goals of a society, or groups within it. The decisions of the political system are normally backed up by legitimate coercion, and obedience may be compelled. Realistically, legitimacy may vary a good deal. For example, the legitimacy of the American system was quite high in the decade after World War II; it declined substantially during and after the Vietnam War. Low legitimacy may be the reason for breakdowns in political organization and failures in public policy. Policy failures in turn can be the cause of declining legitimacy. The transformation of the Soviet system in recent years came after a failed and costly war in Afghanistan, a nuclear power disaster in Chernobyl, and an apparently irreversible decline in economic productivity.

Political systems do many things. They wage war or encourage peace; cultivate international trade or restrict it; open their borders to the exchange of ideas and artistic experiences or close them; tax their populations equitably or inequitably; regulate behavior strictly or less strictly; allocate resources for education, health, and welfare, or fail to do so; pay due regard to the interdependence of humanity and nature, or permit nature's capital to be depleted or misused. In order to carry on these many activities, political systems have institutions, agencies, or *structures*, such as political parties, parliaments, bureaucracies, and courts, which carry on specific activities, or perform *functions*, which in turn enable the political system to formulate and enforce its policies. System, structure, and function are concepts essential to our understanding of how politics is affected by its natural and human environments, and how it affects them.

Figure 1.1 suggests that a political system exists in both a domestic and an international environment, molding these environments and being molded by them. The system receives *inputs* of demands and supports from these environments and attempts to shape them through its *outputs*. In the figure, we use the United States as the central actor, and we include the countries studied in this book for our environmental examples — the Soviet Union, China, Britain, France, Germany, Japan, and Mexico. Figure 1.1 is quite schematic and oversimplified. Exchanges among countries may vary in many ways. For example, they may be dense or "sparse"; U.S. – Canadian relations exemplify the dense end of the continuum, while U.S. – Nepalese relations would be at the sparse end. The United States has substantial trade relations with some nations and relatively little trade with others. Some countries have an excess of imports over exports, whereas others have an excess of exports over imports. With such countries as the NATO nations, Japan, South Korea, Israel, and Saudi Arabia, military exchanges and support are of great importance.

The interdependence of nations — the volume and value of imports and exports, transfers of capital, the extent of foreign travel and international communication — has increased enormously in the last decades. We might represent this process as a thickening of the input and output arrows in Figure 1.1. Fluctuations in this flow of transactions and traffic attributable to depression, inflation, protective tariffs, war, and the like may work havoc with the economies of the nations affected.

The interaction of the political system with its domestic environment may be illustrated by the emergence of the so-called *postindustrial society* in the United States. The composition of the American labor force has

FIGURE 1.1
THE POLITICAL SYSTEM AND ITS ENVIRONMENTS

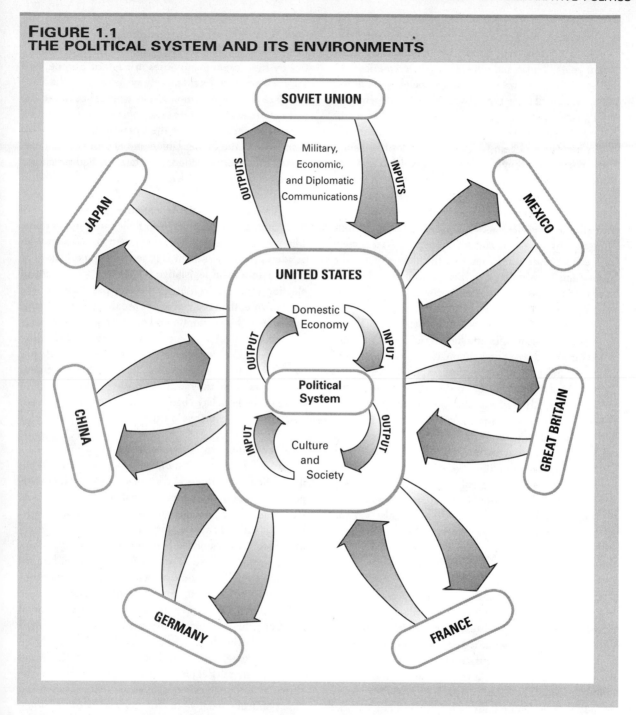

changed dramatically in the last half century. Agricultural employment has declined to a relatively small percentage, employment in heavy extractive and manufacturing industries has decreased substantially, and the newer, high-technology occupations, the professions, and the service occupations have increased sharply as a proportion of the labor force. The last half century has also witnessed significant improvements in the educational level of the American population, although the quality of education particularly at the primary and secondary levels has come in for very serious criticism in recent years. These and other changes in American social structure have transformed the social bases of the party system. There are now as many independents among American voters as loyal Democrats and Republicans. Workers of the older, primarily European ethnic stocks have ceased being a solid support for the Democratic party, and they now tend to divide their votes almost equally between the two parties. On the whole, these changes in the labor force have been associated with a more conservative trend in economic policy and with efforts to cut back welfare and other expenditures. A more educated and culturally sophisticated society has become more concerned with the quality of life, the beauty and healthfulness of the environment, and like issues. In input–output terms, socioeconomic changes have changed the political demands of the electorate and the kinds of policies that it supports. Thus, a new pattern of politics results in different policy outputs, different kinds and levels of taxation, changes in regulatory patterns, and changes in welfare expenditures.

The advantage of the system–environment approach is that it directs our attention to the interdependence of what happens within and between nations and provides us with a vocabulary to describe, compare, and explain these interacting events. If we are to make sound judgments in politics, we need to place political systems in their environments, recognizing how these environments both set limits on and provide opportunities for political choices. The internal organization and procedures of a political system need to be understood within the framework of a basic question: what structures are most suitable for the policies pursued by that system?

The system–environment approach keeps us from reaching quick and biased political judgments. If a country is poor in natural resources and lacks the skills necessary to exploit what it has, we cannot fault it for having a low industrial output or poor educational and social services. Similarly, a country dominated and exploited by another country with a conservative policy cannot be condemned for failing to introduce social reforms.

The policies that leaders and political activists can follow are limited by the system and its institutions. However, in this era of rapid change, if the goals of the leadership and the political activists change, one set of political institutions may quickly be replaced by another. One of the most dramatic illustrations of such an institutional transformation was the breakdown of control by the Communist parties in Eastern Europe, and their replacement by multiparty systems, once the leadership of the Soviet Union lost its confidence in the Soviet system and the future of socialism. Once the Soviet leadership decided to give the Communist party power monopoly in the Soviet Union and accept political pluralism and internal economic reform, it had no choice but to adopt a permissive and conciliatory policy toward its former satellites.

The notion of interdependence goes even further than this relationship between policy and institutions. The various parts of a political system are also interdependent. If a government is based on popularly elected representatives in legislative bodies, then a system of election must be instituted. If many people enjoy the right to vote, then the politicians seeking office will have to mobilize the electorate and organize political parties to carry on election campaigns. As the policymaking agencies of the political system enact laws, they will need administrators and civil servants to implement these laws, and they will need judges to determine whether the laws have been violated and to decide what punishments to impose on the violators.

Political Structures or Institutions

Figure 1.2 locates within the political system the familiar political institutions and agencies — interest groups, political parties, legislatures, executives, bureaucracies, and courts. The difficulty with this sixfold classification is that it will not carry us very far in comparing political systems with each other. Britain and China have all six types of political institutions, at least in name, but not only are they organized differently in the two countries but they also function very differently indeed. Britain has a monarch — a queen — who performs ceremonial functions, like opening Parliament, conferring knighthoods and other honors. China does not have a specialized ceremonial executive. There is a president, elected by the National People's Congress, who performs the ceremonial functions as well as some political functions. The political executive in Britain consists of the prime minister, the ministers assigned to the Cabinet, and the larger ministry which consists of all the heads of departments and agencies. All these officials are usually selected from Parliament. There is a similar structure in China, called the State Council, headed by a premier

FIGURE 1.2
THE POLITICAL SYSTEM AND ITS STRUCTURES

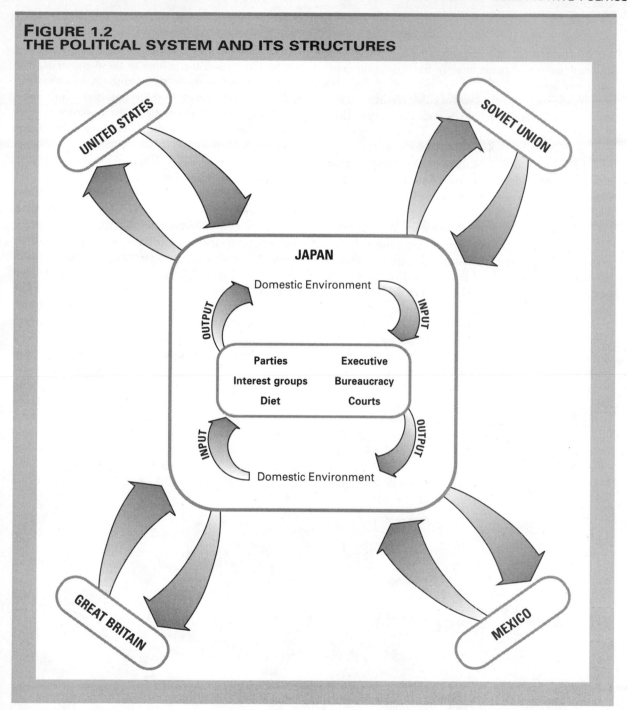

and consisting of the various ministers and ministerial commissions. But while the British prime minister and Cabinet have substantial policymaking power, the State Council in China is closely supervised by the general secretary, the Politburo, and the Central Committee of the Chinese Communist party. Both Britain and China have legislative bodies—the House of Commons in Britain and the National People's Congress in China.

But while the House of Commons is a very important institution in the policymaking process, the Chinese Congress meets for only brief periods, legitimating and ratifying decisions made mainly by the Communist party authorities.

When we get to the level of political parties in the two countries, the differences become even larger. Britain has a competitive party system. The majority in the House of Commons and the Cabinet are constantly confronted by an opposition party or parties, competing for public support and looking forward to the next election when they may unseat the incumbent majority. In the Chinese case the Communist party is the dynamic and controlling political force in the whole political process. There are no other political parties. The principal decisions are taken in the Politburo and to some extent in the Central Committee of the Communist party. The governmental agencies implement the policies, which have to be initiated and/or approved by the top Communist party leaders. British interest groups are autonomous organizations that play important roles in the polity and the economy. Chinese trade unions and other professional organizations have to be viewed as parts of the official apparatus, dominated by the Communist party, that perform mobilizing, socializing, and facilitating functions.

Thus, an institution-by-insti-tution comparison of British and Chinese institutions that did not spell out functions in detail would not bring us far toward understanding the important similarities and differences in the politics of these countries. It is only when we separate structure from function, and trace these activities through the inputs, the conversion processes, and outputs of the political system, that we can arrive at judgments of the significance of the various political institutions.

Structure and Function

Only when we begin to ask questions about process and performance can we attach meaning to structural characteristics. Only when we can say that specific institutions perform specific functions with specific consequences does our comparative analysis begin to make some sense. Figure 1.3 shows how we relate structure to function and process to policy and performance. (The functions and processes shown in the figure are discussed in greater detail in Chapters Three through Eight, and in each of the country studies in Part Three.)

In the center of Figure 1.3 under the heading "process functions" are listed the distinctive activities necessary for policy to be made and implemented in any kind of political system. We call these *process functions* because they play a direct and necessary role in the process of making policy. Before policy can be decided, some individuals and groups in the government or the society must decide what they want and hope to get from politics. The political process begins as these interests are

Similar structures, different functions. This photograph of the April 4, 1989 meeting of the Chinese National Congress shows the delegates voting on a resolution. Since there is only one political party in China, voting is an act of regime support rather than political choice.

FIGURE 1.3
THE POLITICAL SYSTEM AND ITS FUNCTIONS

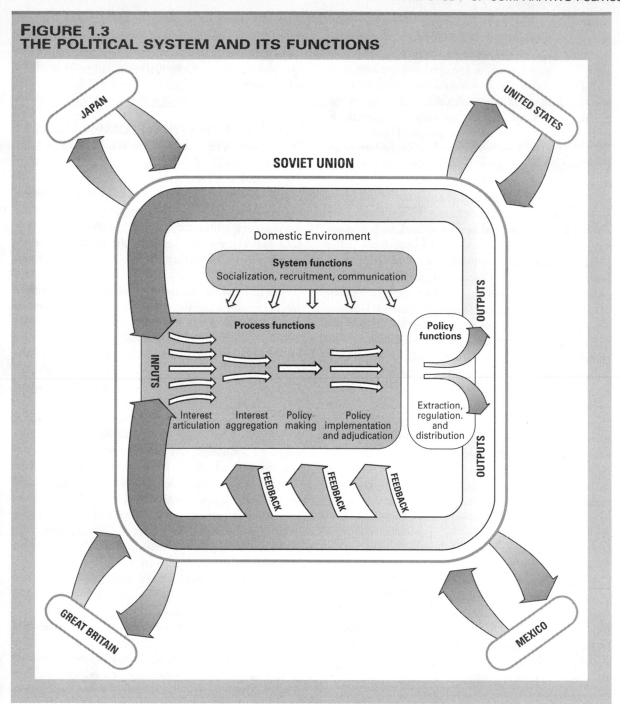

expressed or articulated. The many arrows on the left of the figure show these initial expressions. To be effective, however, the inputs of interests must be combined into policy alternatives—such as higher or lower taxes or more or less social security benefits—for which substantial political support can be mobilized. Thus, the arrows on the left are consolidated as the process moves from *interest articulation* to *interest aggregation*. Alternative policies are then considered. A coalition that commands substantial political resources such as votes backs one of them, and authoritative *policymaking* takes place. The policy must be enforced and implemented, and if it is challenged or violated there must be some process of *adjudication*. Each policy may affect many different aspects of a society, as reflected in the many arrows for the *implementation* phase. These process functions that we have been describing are performed by such political structures as parties, legislatures, political executives, bureaucracies, and courts.

The three functions listed at the top of the figure —socialization, recruitment, and communication— are not directly involved in making and implementing public policy but are of fundamental importance to the political system. The arrows leading from these three functions to all parts of the political process suggest their crucial role in underpinning and permeating the political process. *Political socialization* involves families, schools, communications media, churches, and all the various political structures that develop, reinforce, and transform attitudes of political significance in the society. *Political recruitment* refers to the selection of people for political activity and government offices. *Political communication* refers to the flow of information through the society and through the various structures that make up the political system. We refer to these three functions as *system functions*, because they determine whether or not the system will change or be maintained, whether, for example, policymaking will continue to be dominated by a single authoritarian party or military council, or whether competitive parties and a legislature will replace them.

The third set of functions, listed at the right of the figure, treats the outputs, the implementations of the political process. We call these the *policy functions*, the substantive impacts on the society, the economy, and the culture. These functions would include the various forms of regulation of behavior, extractions of resources in the form of taxes and the like, and distribution of benefits and services to various groups in the population. The outcomes of all these political activities, in a cyclical fashion, result in new inputs, in new demands for legislation or for administrative action, and in increases or decreases in the amount of support given to the political system.

These functional concepts describe the activities carried on in any society regardless of how its political system is organized, or what kinds of policies it produces. Using these functional categories, we can determine how institutions in different countries combine in the making and implementation of different kinds of public policy.

AN ILLUSTRATIVE COMPARISON: THE SOVIET UNION IN 1985 AND 1990*

Figures 1.4 and 1.5 offer a simplified graphic comparison of structures and functions in the Soviet political system before and after the sweeping reforms of the political system initiated by Mikhail Gorbachev. The contrast between the two highlights the significant decentralization of power that has occurred in the Soviet Union.

The most immediate visual impression we receive from comparing the two figures is the heavier shading throughout the figure for 1990. In contrast to 1985, when the Communist party and the state bureaucracy monopolized or dominated many political functions, the figure for 1990 shows that the range of governmental, political, and social institutions performing political functions has increased significantly.

These figures also reveal several specific changes. In 1985 the Communist party of the Soviet Union dominated all political functions, while preventing independent parties and interest groups from organizing, but in 1990 numerous new independent parties and pressure groups were active in articulating and aggregating demands: strike committees and new trade union federations voiced workers' interests; groups of deputies in the Supreme Soviet were formed to draft alternative versions of legislative acts; owners of cooperative businesses formed associations to lobby government and seek protection for their enterprises. At the same time, the power of the Communist party had significantly weakened, and several prominent political leaders had left it.

Still another important change affected the power of the governments of the country's union republics. Under the old system, the republics' rights were largely nominal and were contradicted in fact by the strong centralizing power of the Communist party and the state

*This comparison of the Soviet Union in 1985 and 1990 was written by Thomas Remington.

FIGURE 1.4
THE SOVIET POLITICAL SYSTEM IN 1985

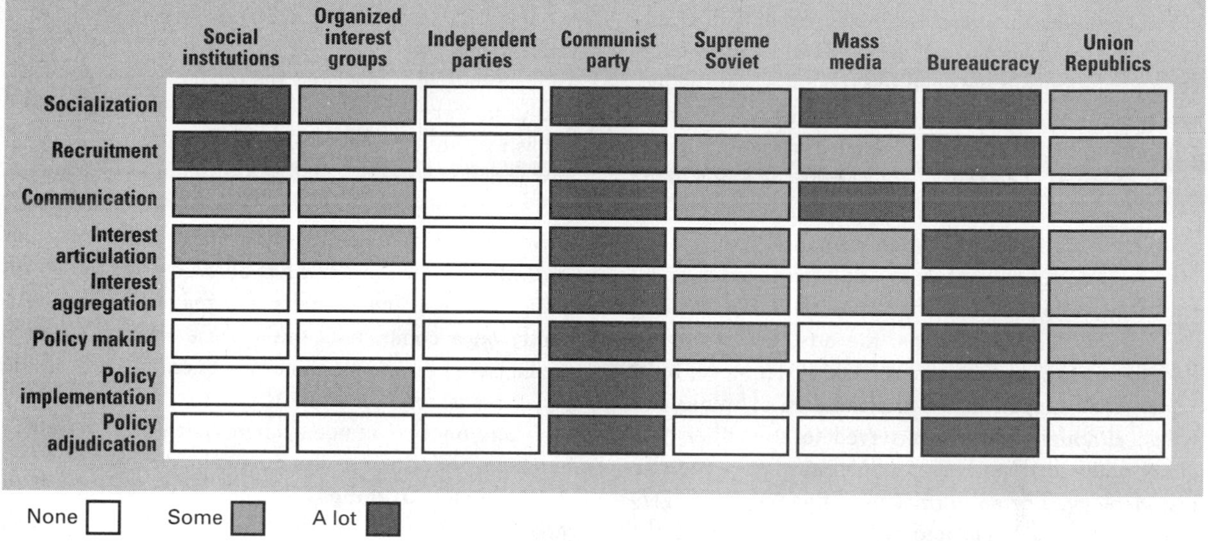

	Social institutions	Organized interest groups	Independent parties	Communist party	Supreme Soviet	Mass media	Bureaucracy	Union Republics
Socialization	A lot	Some	None	A lot	Some	A lot	A lot	Some
Recruitment	A lot	Some	None	A lot	Some	Some	A lot	Some
Communication	Some	Some	None	A lot	Some	A lot	A lot	Some
Interest articulation	Some	Some	None	A lot	Some	Some	Some	Some
Interest aggregation	None	None	None	A lot	Some	Some	A lot	Some
Policy making	None	None	None	A lot	Some	None	A lot	Some
Policy implementation	None	Some	None	A lot	None	Some	A lot	Some
Policy adjudication	None	None	None	A lot	None	None	A lot	None

None ☐   Some ▨   A lot ▦

FIGURE 1.5
THE SOVIET POLITICAL SYSTEM IN 1990

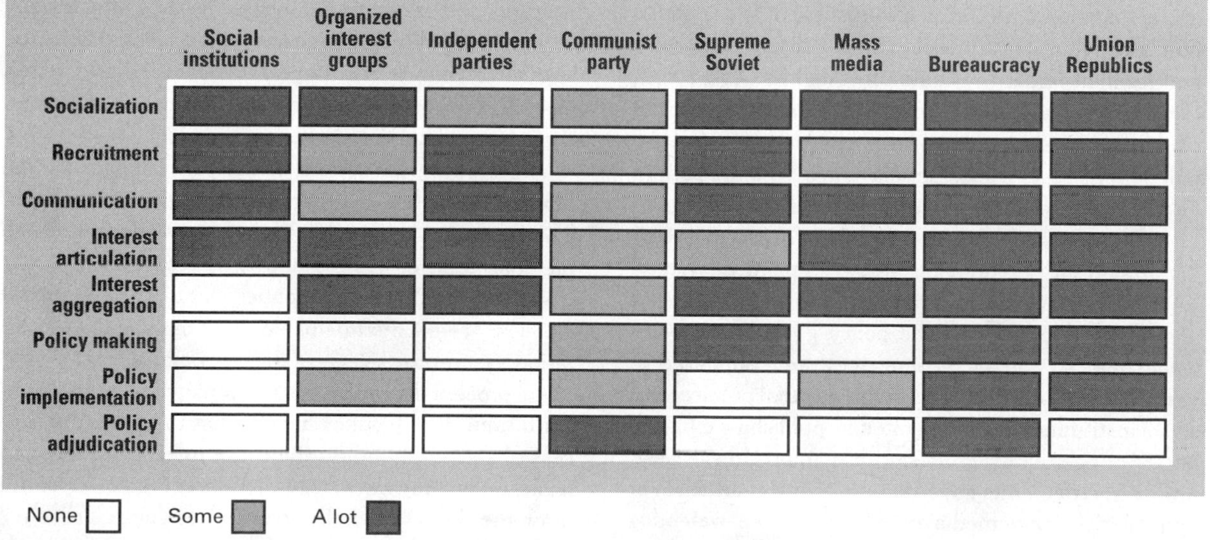

	Social institutions	Organized interest groups	Independent parties	Communist party	Supreme Soviet	Mass media	Bureaucracy	Union Republics
Socialization	A lot	A lot	Some	Some	A lot	Some	Some	Some
Recruitment	A lot	Some	A lot	Some	A lot	Some	A lot	A lot
Communication	A lot	Some	A lot	Some	A lot	A lot	A lot	Some
Interest articulation	A lot	A lot	A lot	Some	Some	A lot	A lot	A lot
Interest aggregation	None	A lot	A lot	Some	A lot	A lot	A lot	A lot
Policy making	None	None	None	Some	A lot	None	A lot	A lot
Policy implementation	None	Some	None	Some	None	Some	A lot	A lot
Policy adjudication	None	None	None	A lot	None	None	A lot	None

None ☐   Some ▨   A lot ▦

bureaucracy. As a consequence (perhaps unforeseen) of the liberalizing changes introduced by Gorbachev, republican governments declared their autonomy and control over the territories and resources of their republics. Some republics, in fact, declared full independence. A new relationship between the republics and the federal union was being hammered out, with the republics demanding significantly expanded rights under a new treaty of union. The shift of power from the union to the republics is reflected in the darker shading of the column in Figure 1.5 marked "'union republics."

In the political system in 1985 there was room for social institutions such as the family, churches, schools, occupations and professions, the arts, hobby groups, and so on, to perform certain basic system-level functions. They helped in the transmission of values and ideas, although they often served to strengthen religious, nationalist, and other influences alien to communist ideology. The authorities used some of these agencies, such as schools and workplaces, to direct the socialization and recruitment function. But there is no doubt that as institutions linking people in relations of trust, they also exerted an independent influence on citizens' political outlooks and behavior. They were also an important but unofficial channel for communication, as they enabled people to discuss ideas and form opinion independently of the state-run media. With the liberalization of the political system new, organized groups have been able to form, mobilize support, and develop leadership. In many cases, they have developed out of the social institutions of family, friendship, professional and occupational ties, ethnic solidarity, religious affiliation, and cultural institutions, which had proven durable and resilient under the communist regime. As a result, the ability of society to develop its own independent channels for influencing government has expanded significantly. This is a substantial change from the pattern in the past, when the state dominated society.

The mass media were traditionally assigned several important functions in the Soviet political system. They were expected to propagate and interpret Soviet ideological doctrine and the policy goals of the party leadership. At the same time, they were supposed to vent concerns and problems in the way that political and social institutions operated, often by publishing citizens' letters of complaint, criticism, or opinion. In the past, however, strict limits governed what kind of criticism or opinion the mass media could voice. The watchdog function that the media served was intended mainly to

aid in the implementation of policy. These roles are reflected in Figure 1.4 by the heavy shading in the cells for socialization and communication and the light shading for interest articulation and aggregation and policy implementation.

Since 1985, however, the media have been given vastly greater freedom to explore sensitive topics and publish without political censorship. Gorbachev's *glasnost* (openness) policy has made many media organs into champions of reform and has given them much greater opportunity to articulate and aggregate popular interests. A new press law has allowed individuals and groups to found newspapers and magazines independently on a commercial basis. As a result, the mass media have become much more influential actors in the policy processes.

Still another major change concerns the shift in functions performed by the national legislature, the Supreme Soviet. In the past the Supreme Soviet served largely as a forum for ratifying decisions that had been made by the party and the state bureaucracy. It met for a few days two times a year. Its members performed their duties on a spare-time basis; there were no professional legislators. It was convened to hear government reports and to approve the national budget, the national plan, and a small number of legislative bills, which it invariably adopted with a minimum of debate. At the same time, a large number of administrative acts with the force of law were adopted without debate or publicity by bureaucratic agencies, over which the Supreme Soviet had no effective means of oversight or control. Deputies were elected in single-candidate races to which most voters attached little importance. As a result, the entire legislative branch was largely a façade behind which party leaders and the state bureaucracy controlled all important policy decisions.

Following the reform of the political system, the Soviet Union has restructured its legislative branch. The Supreme Soviet is smaller (542 as opposed to the previous total of 1,500) and is elected from a larger Congress of People's Deputies. The 1989 national elections were a mixture of elements of the old, authoritarian system for selecting deputies and a free, democratic process of nominations, campaigns, and election. With time, the deputies have begun to undergo a process of socialization into their new roles as full-fledged legislators. They have begun to assert the power of the Supreme Soviet in challenges to President Gorbachev and the Council of Ministers. They have formed specialized committees that initiate and deliberate on legislative bills, and hold hearings on the performance of government. In short, while the final outcome of the process of transition is still not visible, the outlines of a parliamentary system have begun to take shape in the Soviet Union.

One other significant change in the political system is not shown in the figures but deserves a comment. As part of the package of changes in 1990 which ended the Communist party's constitutional monopoly on a leading role in society, Gorbachev pushed through another constitutional change creating a strong executive presidency. The powers of the Soviet president are potentially very broad, much like the powers of the French, Mexican, or U.S. presidents. As soon as the legislature approved Gorbachev's proposal for a state presidency, Gorbachev was immediately elected to fill it. It is important to bear in mind that, while the Communist party has given up a great deal of its power over major policy decisions in foreign and domestic affairs, the new presidency has an extremely broad mandate and very limited accountability either to the legislature or the populace at large. This comparison only brings us to Soviet politics as of 1990. More recent developments are treated in Chapter Thirteen.

The brief comparison presented here is meant to illustrate the use of the structural-functional approach. This approach enables us to examine how similar functions are performed in different countries, or in the same country at two different points in time. Similarly, we may examine changes or contrasts in the functions performed by the same structures over time or across different political systems. In a country undergoing a rapid and dramatic transition, this framework helps us to analyze changes in the distribution of power among the major institutions making up the political system. Neither the analysis of structures nor that of functions is complete without the other. A structural analysis tells us the number of political parties, or the organization of the legislature, and how the executive branch, the courts, the bureaucracy, the mass media, interest groups, and other elements of the political system are set up and by what rules or standards they operate. A functional analysis tells us how these institutions and organizations interact to produce and implement policies. In Parts Two and Three of this book we deal more specifically with the functions of the various social institutions, with the variety of interest groups and their functions, and with the structural-functional properties of party systems, legislatures, executives, and cabinets. Here we illustrate the method and its advantages.

THE POLICY LEVEL: PERFORMANCE, OUTCOME, AND EVALUATION OF POLITICAL SYSTEMS

The important question is, what do these differences in structure and function do for the interests, needs, and aspirations of people? Figures 1.1 and 1.3 suggest the relationship between what happens in politics and in the society, and between what happens in the society and the international environment. The structural-functional differences we have been discussing determine the give-and-take between polity and environment, and the importance of that give-and-take for such values as welfare, justice, freedom, equality, peace, and prosperity. At the left of Figure 1.3 are arrows signifying inputs —demands and supports from the society and the international system and inputs from the independent initiatives of political leaders and bureaucrats. At the right are arrows signifying outputs and outcomes, the end-products of the political process, the things a government does for and to its people.

We have to distinguish between the efforts, the things a government does, and the actual outcome of these efforts. Governments may spend equal amounts on education or health, or defense, but with different consequences. Not only government efficiency or corruption, but also where a country starts from in terms of cultural, economic, and technological level, as well as changes in its environment, play a role in the effectiveness of performance. Americans spend more per capita on education than any other people in the world, but their children perform less well in important subjects than do children in some other countries that spend substantially less. The United States and the USSR spent enormous sums on defense in the last decades, and yet both countries were held at bay by small countries resolved to resist at all costs, and because of these failed efforts they were weakened internally. The outcome of public policy is never wholly in the hands of the people and their leaders in the various nations of the world. Conditions in the internal environment, conditions and events in the larger external world, and simple chance may frustrate the most thoughtfully crafted programs and plans.

Finally, we must step even further back to consider

Modern governments provide for the safety, welfare, and well-being of their citizens. Here in the center of London with Big Ben dominating the scene are the Houses of Parliament where policies are debated and decided. In back of Big Ben and out of view is the Whitehall District where tens of thousands of civil servants implement these policies.

the whole situation of political system, process, and policy, and the environment, to evaluate what political systems are doing. Evaluation is complex because people value different things and put different emphasis on what they value. We will refer to the different things people may value as political *goods*. In Chapter Eight we discuss goods associated with the system level, such as the stability or adaptability of political institutions; goods associated with the process level, such as citizen participation in politics; and goods associated with the policy level, such as welfare, security, and liberty. To evaluate what a political system is doing, we must look at each of these areas and assess *performance* and *outcomes*. We must also be aware of how outcomes affect individuals and subgroups in the society, effects that may often be overlooked in presenting averages, and of the continuing problem of building for the future as well as living today. This last problem affects both poor nations, which wish to survive and alleviate suffering today, but also improve their children's lot of tomorrow; and rich nations, which must deal with the costs to their children of polluted and depleted natural resources as the result of careless consumption patterns of the past.

THE APPROACH TO COMPARATIVE POLITICS IN THIS BOOK

We approach the problem of comparison in this book in three ways. In the present chapter we have discussed comparative political analysis in general terms and have introduced the three levels of study: system, process, and policy. In Chapter Two we continue our introductory remarks by discussing the main issues and problems of politics in the world today, problems established or shaped in the environments in which political systems operate. In Part Two of this book we identify and analyze the processes and functions found in all political systems, thus making it possible to compare nations with one another and to evaluate their special features. We also introduce the principal varieties of political systems in the world today and discuss their policies and performance.

Part Three contains studies of eight countries, and one analysis on a regional scale of sub-Saharan Africa that includes many countries. The countries included in Part Three represent the variety of systems and environments in the world today. Britain, France, Germany, and Japan are industrialized democracies; China is a communist nation in the early stages of industrialization; Mexico is a partially industrialized, partially democratic nation; and the African nations are new countries embarking on economic and political development. The USSR, formerly the dominant power of the Soviet bloc, is engaged in a major restructuring in the direction of a democratic, market society. Here we seek to capture its structure and process in midcourse, uncertain of what the future will hold. The United States appears as the final chapter, since it is our purpose to compare it with the other countries in our book in order to bring out the common and unique properties of our own system of government, as well as the common and unique properties of the other major types of political systems in the world today.

KEY TERMS

adjudication
function
implementation
inputs
interest aggregation

interest articulation
outcomes
outputs
performance
policy functions

policymaking
political communication
political recruitment
political socialization
political system

postindustrial society
process functions
structure
system functions

END NOTE

1. Robert A. Dahl, *Polyarchy: Participation and Opposition* (New Haven, Conn.: Yale University Press, 1971); see also Dahl, *Democracy and Its Critics* (New Haven, Conn.: Yale University Press, 1989).

CHAPTER 2

THE ENVIRONMENT

OF THE

POLITICAL SYSTEM

THE DOMESTIC and international environments of nations shape the issues of their politics. These environments confront the political system with sets of problems, such as unemployment, inflation, economic growth, ethnic conflict, and threats from foreign enemies. The resources that are available may be more or less adequate to cope with these problems. Large, industrial, wealthy societies such as Japan, the members of the European Common Market, and the United States have problems and levels of resources that are very different from those of a smaller agricultural society such as Tanzania or an oil kingdom such as Saudi Arabia. We may think of a nation's structural-functional arrangements as a basic organization for dealing with these issues. In this chapter we want to outline some of the most important contextual features that shape political issues.

OLD NATIONS, NEW NATIONS

Almost the entire land surface of the globe today is divided into independent national territories. Two centuries ago, at the time the United States was gaining its independence, most of the independent nations were in Europe (see Figure 2.1). Much of the rest of the world had been parceled out as colonies to one or another of the European empires. Figure 2.1 shows the explosive growth in the number of nations that took place in the nineteenth century, principally in Latin America when the Spanish and Portuguese empires broke up into twenty independent nations. Europe also experienced some of this movement toward national separation and independence as the Turkish empire gave up Greece, Bulgaria, and Albania, and Scandinavia and the Low Countries divided into their present form. During the period between the two world wars, the national explosion extended to North Africa and the Middle East, and Europe continued to fragment as the Russian and Austro-

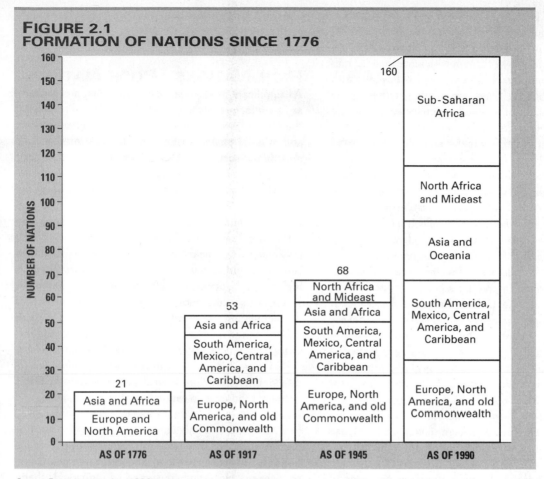

FIGURE 2.1
FORMATION OF NATIONS SINCE 1776

Source: For contemporary (1990) members of the United Nations, *World Almanac and Book of Facts* (New York: Pharos Books, 1990), p. 777. Data to 1945 from Charles Taylor and Michael Hudson, *World Handbook of Political and Social Indicators* (New Haven, Conn.: Yale University Press, 1972), pp. 26ff.

Hungarian empires gave up Poland, Finland, Czecho-slovakia, and Yugoslavia. There was a brief period of independence for the three Baltic countries — Lithuania, Latvia, and Estonia, countries that have again broken free from the Soviet Union.

But it was in the period since World War II that the national explosion really took off, with the addition of some forty-five countries in North Africa and the Middle East, a doubling of the Asian and Oceanian quota of nations, and the attainment of independence by nine Caribbean island countries. Most of the additions to na-tionhood in the last decade are relatively small in area, population, and resources.

More than half of the present membership of the United Nations (UN) came into existence in the dec-ades since World War II. The newest (160th) member of the UN is the Principality of Liechtenstein, a tiny coun-try of 60 square miles, nestled in the Alps. All these nations — new as well as old — share certain character-istics. They have legal authority over their territories and people; they have armies, air forces, and in some cases navies; they send and receive ambassadors; they belong to the United Nations; they collect taxes; they seek to regulate their economies and maintain order through parliaments, ministries, departments, courts, police, and prisons, but they also vary enormously.

BIG NATIONS, SMALL NATIONS

One of the many ways in which nations vary is territorial size. Another is population size. The country with the largest area is the Soviet Union with more than 22 million square kilometers. China has the most people, with more than a billion. There are many countries at the other extremes, but the smallest independent political entity in both respects is Vatican City, with an area of less than half a square kilometer and under a thousand residents.

The political implications of these striking contrasts in population size and geographic area are not obvious or easily evaluated. It does not follow that only big countries are important and influential. Cuba successfully challenges the United States; Israel stands off the Arab world; tiny Vatican City has enormous power and influence. Nor does it follow that area and population size determine a country's political system. Both Luxembourg and the United States are democracies. Authoritarian regimes can be found in countries that are small, medium, or large. These enormous contrasts in size show only that the nations now making up the world differ greatly in their range of physical and human resources. Although area and population (as well as geographic location) do not strictly determine politics, economics, or culture, they are important factors, affecting economic development, foreign policy and defense problems, and many other issues of political significance.

The geostrategic location of nations has been of great importance in their development. A nation located in the center of Europe in the sixteenth through nineteenth centuries could not avoid building a large land army to protect itself from the predatory action of its neighbors. Such a nation would be unlikely to develop free political institutions, since it would have to extract resources on a large scale, and keep its population under control. England in the course of its development was protected by the Channel; it could defend itself through its navy. It could do with a smaller army, lower taxation, and less centralization of power. The United States was a similar case. The Atlantic Ocean and the relatively open continent were of crucial importance in shaping U.S. political institutions. Far removed from the centers of Western development, the peoples of Asia, Africa, and Latin America were colonized by the more powerful Western nations. Only in recent decades, having won their freedom, are these nations developing their econo-

mies and modernizing their societies, catching up and, in the case of Japan, overtaking the Western pacesetters.

RICH NATIONS, POOR NATIONS

As significant as physical size, population, and location are such factors as the availability of natural resources, the level of economic and social development, ethnic and cultural characteristics, and the rate of economic growth and social change. Furthermore, it may be misleading to distinguish among nations on the basis of total mineral resources, gross national production, and the like. Wealth, income, opportunity, and even historical memories and language are not evenly distributed within a nation. A high *gross national product (GNP)* may conceal significant inequalities in the distribution of economic and social amenities and opportunities. A high rate of national growth may benefit only particular regions or social groups, leaving large areas or parts of the population unrewarded or even less well off than before. These regional, class, ethnic, religious, and historical differences may have great political significance.

Figure 2.2 gives the gross national product per capita for thirteen nations from all parts of the world. Gross national product is an estimate of the value of goods and services produced by the people in a country in a given year. Because it is only an estimate, the figure must be used cautiously. The figure for the GNP of poorer nations, for instance, tends to underestimate goods and services produced and consumed by individuals themselves, particularly when they are engaged in subsistence agriculture. Although we must be cautious in using these figures, there can be no question that the difference between the GNP of rich nations and poor nations is enormous. Here is Japan with an average product per capita of more than $21,000 per year in 1985 and Tanzania with $160. The United Arab Emirates, awash in oil, averages more than $13,000 per capita.

Let us compare Figure 2.3, which measures the proportion of the working population engaged in agriculture, with Figure 2.2, measuring GNP per capita. We find that the United States, with the second highest per capita national product in Figure 2.2, has the second smallest proportion of the workforce in agriculture, and that China, the second lowest in per capita national product, has more than 60 percent of its workers in agriculture. On the whole, the rich countries prove

FIGURE 2.2
PER CAPITA GROSS NATIONAL PRODUCT FOR SELECTED NATIONS, 1988 (IN U.S. DOLLARS)

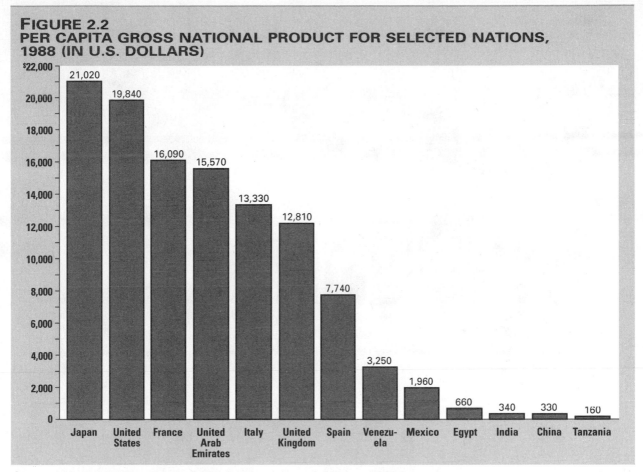

Source: World Bank, *World Development Report* (New York: Oxford University Press, 1990), pp. 178–179.

to be predominantly industrial, commercial, and urban, whereas the poor countries are predominantly agricultural and rural.

To be rich and industrialized also means to be literate and educated and to have access to the larger world of complex events, activities, and values. In the six most industrialized countries in our list — Britain, France, West Germany, the United States, the USSR, and Japan — practically everyone over the age of fifteen years can read and write. In India, Tanzania, and Egypt only one-half the population or less has this minimal degree of education. Moreover, the countries with the fewest literate citizens are also most lacking in radios and other communication devices that do not require *literacy*.

Industrialization, education, and exposure to the communications media are associated with better nutrition and medical care. In the economically advanced countries, fewer children die in infancy, and people on the average live longer. In recent years the average citizen of Britain, France, West Germany, Israel, Japan, and the United States has had a life expectancy at birth of about seventy-five years. The average Soviet or Chinese citizen, however, has had a life expectancy of around seventy years; the average Mexican, sixty-six years; the average Egyptian, around sixty years; and the average Indian or Tanzanian, little more than fifty years (see Table 8.3).

These characteristics — material productivity, education, exposure to communications media, longer and

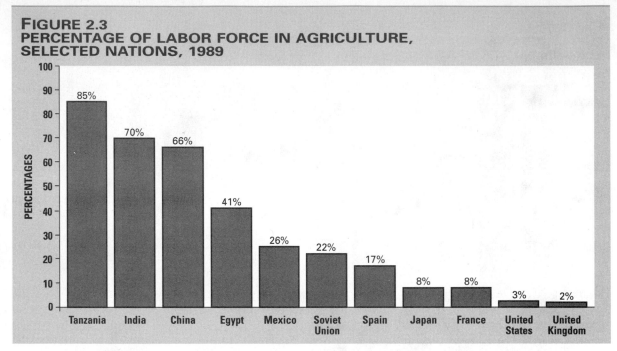

FIGURE 2.3
PERCENTAGE OF LABOR FORCE IN AGRICULTURE,
SELECTED NATIONS, 1989

Source: Countries of the World and Their Leaders Yearbook, 1991; A Compilation of U.S. State Department Reports (New York: Yale Research Inc., 1991), Vol. 1.

A watercart drawn by bullocks providing irrigation for farmland in Mexico illustrates the problem of agricultural modernization.

healthier lives — are closely interconnected. Only when a country becomes economically productive can it afford better education, communications media, and nutrition and health care. In order to become more productive, it needs the resources to develop a skilled and healthy labor force and build the factories, productive farms, and transportation systems that material welfare requires. Preindustrial nations face most urgently the issues of economic development: how to improve the immediate welfare of their citizens, yet also build and invest for the future. Typically, these are also newer nations, and they also face the challenge of creating national awareness and building effective political institutions.

ECONOMIC INEQUALITY WITHIN NATIONS

The political processes of a country may be affected sharply by internal divisions of income, wealth, and occupation, as well as by economic dependence or poverty. Table 2.1 compares wealth and *income inequality* for those countries for which we have data. The former communist countries included are Yugoslavia, Hungary, and Poland. (Unfortunately, no data were available for the USSR or China.) The table makes the point that there tends to be a positive association between economic development and equality of income, at least past a certain stage in economic growth. Wealthy nations like the United States, Japan, and the European nations tend to have more equitable income distributions than poorer countries like Brazil and Mexico. In the advanced industrial nations the wealthiest 10 percent of the households receive about one quarter of the national income, while the poorest 40 percent receive around 20 percent. In the United States the poorest 40 percent get only 15 percent of the national income. In a middle-income country like Brazil, the wealthiest 10 percent get 46 percent of the national income, and the poorest 40 percent get only 8 percent.

The association of industrialization and high productivity with more equal distribution of income has been true historically and tends to be true today. The trend toward greater equality in industrial societies is more marked with respect to income — that is, wages, salaries, and the like — than to wealth — ownership of land or other forms of property. The first stages of indus-

TABLE 2.1
SELECTED NATIONS' WORLD RANKING BY PER CAPITA GNP AND INEQUALITY OF INCOME DISTRIBUTION, 1979–1982

Country	Date	% of national income to wealthiest 10%	% of national income to poorest 40%	GNP per capita (1988)
Japan	1979	22.4	21.9	21,020
United States	1985	25.0	15.7	19,840
West Germany	1984	23.4	19.5	18,480
France	1979	25.5	18.4	16,090
United Kingdom	1979	23.3	17.3	12,810
Yugoslavia	1987	26.6	17.1	2,520
Hungary	1983	18.7	26.2	2,460
Poland	1987	21.0	23.9	1,860
Brazil	1983	46.2	8.1	2,160
Malaysia	1987	34.8	13.9	1,940
Mexico	1986	38.8	11.6	1,690
Ivory Coast	1986	36.3	13.0	770
India	1987	26.7	20.4	340
Bangladesh	1982	24.9	22.4	170

Source: World Bank, *World Development Report, 1990* (New York: Oxford University Press, 1990), Table 30, pp. 236–237, Table 1, pp. 178–179.

trialization and modernization may actually *increase* inequality in the distribution of income by creating a dual economy and society — a rural sector, with wide variation of landholding and status, and an urban industrial commercial sector, with its own differentials in income and consumption patterns. These inequalities, already present in most preindustrial societies, tend to increase at the same time as education and communication are spreading; this pattern helps explain the political instability of many developing countries. It also helps explain their susceptibility to egalitarian political movements. Inequality, then, is an issue all developing nations must face. We will examine strategies applied to that problem later.

The fact that inequalities are often less extreme in the advanced industrial nations does not mean that the issue of inequality is unimportant there. Britain, among the countries with a more nearly equal distribution of income, is frequently agitated by intense conflicts between industry and labor over the distribution of wealth, income, and opportunity. The failure of British industry to grow rapidly has compounded these problems. In the United States in the last decade, income inequality has increased substantially, as taxation has become more regressive and more favorable to the rich.

CULTURAL HETEROGENEITY WITHIN NATIONS

Nations are divided not only horizontally according to differences in income, wealth, and opportunity, but also vertically by language, culture, and religion. One of the most culturally fragmented countries is Tanzania, with more than a hundred tribal groups speaking different languages and dialects, although Swahili is commonly spoken throughout the country. The largest tribal group contains less than 10 percent of the population. India is also divided into many linguistic-cultural groups, but a dominant language — Hindi — is spoken by almost 40 percent of the population. India has an acute conflict today between the Sikhs and the dominant Hindu majority in the state of the Punjab. There is a strong secessionist movement among the Sikhs.

Since the adoption of *perestroika* and *glasnost*, the Soviet Union seems to have been coming apart at the seams. The Soviet Union includes some fifteen major nationalities which are represented in the republics and another thirty-eight smaller ethnic groups which are represented in administrative subdivisions. As of this writing, it appears probable that some of these nationality-based republics, such as the Baltic countries, will secede and become independent. Where more than one nationality disputes a particular territory as, for example, Armenia and Azerbaijan, there is the prospect of continued conflict and bloodshed.

South Africa presents another case of acute racial-ethnic conflict. Seventy-one percent of the population is black, consisting of ten distinct linguistic-tribal groups. The whites, divided mainly into the dominant Afrikaner and a smaller English group, make up about 17 percent of the population. In addition, coloureds (mulattos) number some 9 percent and Asians around 3 percent. The system of Afrikaner–white dominance protected by apartheid (segregation) legislation and governmental arrangements that give the whites complete legal and political control is now in process of being modified. Whatever arrangements come out of the present negotiations, it is clear that South African politics for the foreseeable future will be heavily burdened by ethnic conflict.

Racial conflict has agitated American politics since the founding of the Republic. Most recently in the 1960s, these tensions erupted into violence. Although the conflict is less violent today, race continues to be a serious political problem in the United States. Even a country as homogeneous as Japan has an "untouchable" minority — the Burakumin — who number about 2 million and who are confined to lowly occupations and segregated in ghettos. If we add to these problems the bitterness and irreconcilability of the Israeli–Arab confrontation in the Middle East and the Catholic–Protestant conflict in Northern Ireland, it is evident that ethnicity and religion are the most divisive and seemingly unresolvable causes of internal political conflict in the contemporary world.

INTERNATIONAL INTERDEPENDENCE*

Although the size of the globe is fixed, the distance between nations is variable. In the twentieth century technological, economic, and political changes have drawn the nations closer to each other, sometimes for better (rising living standards in the world economy) and sometimes for worse (war). As we approach the year 2000, the effects of international *interdependence* will

*This section has been written by Richard Rose

The high cost of a divided political culture is reflected in the grief of these women mourning a young man killed in ethnic conflict in Azerbaijan in the USSR.

be increasingly felt in rich nations and poor, in democracies and dictatorships.

The logic of interdependence is simple: what one nation does also affects others in the same system.[1] The term *hegemony* describes an international system in which there is a fundamental asymmetry in the power of nations in relation to each other. In a hegemonic system, interdependence takes the form of one nation being dominant, and other nations having to follow. For decades after World War II the United States was such a leader. Europeans described having Americans as an ally as akin to being in bed with an elephant; when the elephant rolled over, everyone felt it.

Today, the United States is not the only dominant nation in the international arena.[2] Germany has recovered its earlier economic strength; it has replaced the United States as the world's largest exporter. Japan has been transformed from a rural society producing toys and handicrafts to a high-technology economy exporting money and products throughout the globe; the United States annually runs a trade deficit with Japan of tens of billions of dollars. The used car lots of the United States are a tangible example of interdependence, for Ameri-

can, Japanese, and European cars compete there for consumer dollars.

The end of the cold war has removed the Soviet Union as a major military threat to Europe and the United States, but it has not removed all military threats. China, with a population more than four times that of the United States, has the capacity to mobilize far larger armed forces than the United States. The Vietnam War showed that on home ground a foreign army could defeat the United States in the field. Iraq thought itself sufficiently strong militarily in August 1990 to occupy its oil-rich neighbor Kuwait. It took a major military effort under UN auspices to deprive it of its conquest. The United States remains a dominant country because it is both a major military and a major economic power. By contrast, Germany and Japan are major economic powers, but they are minor military powers, compared to Britain and France, because of their disarmament after their defeat in World War II. The Soviet Union has had a massive military force, but its centrally planned economy has proved so weak that the cost of sustaining such a force has proved too much for the administration of Mikhail Gorbachev.

National Security in an Interdependent World

Securing national borders against foreign attack or to protect other national interests abroad is a primary concern of every government; it is also a classic example of the importance of interdependence. The force that any one nation must mobilize depends on the forces that can be mobilized by nations that it perceives as threatening it.

For four decades after the end of World War II, the United States perceived the Soviet Union as the major threat to its national security, and the Soviet Union perceived the United States as its major threat. The United States formed the North Atlantic Treaty Organization (NATO) alliance to deter Soviet aggression in Western Europe, and the Soviet Union formed the Warsaw Pact alliance to defend communist regimes in Eastern Europe. Because modern military strength depends on advancing technology, there was continuous competition in developing armaments at a cost of hundreds of billions. More and more sophisticated weapons systems were developed — but there was no armed conflict between NATO and Warsaw Pact nations.

In the 1980s, the logic of interdependence was demonstrated in a novel way: agreement on arms control between the United States, under the leadership of President Ronald Reagan, and the Soviet Union, under Mikhail Gorbachev. As long as both sides reduced their military capability simultaneously, then the balance of power remained the same between them.

At the same time, the Soviet Union found that it could no longer maintain hegemony over Warsaw Pact countries in Eastern Europe. Communist regimes in the German Democratic Republic, Czechoslovakia, Poland, Hungary, and Bulgaria were based on the presence and readiness to use Soviet troops, not on the support of national populations. But the Soviet Union could not use military force to crush opposition to communist dominance in these countries as it had done after 1945, without risking the recommencement of the cold war and another military arms race with NATO. In 1989 one East European country after another regained its independence of the Soviet Union. Constitutions were revised to end the Communist party's monopoly of power, free elections were held placing noncommunist parties in office, and agreements were negotiated for the withdrawal of Soviet troops. Moscow accepted these changes; a Soviet spokesperson even proclaimed the Sinatra doctrine (after singer Frank Sinatra's song about

each person doing it his or her way); each country was free to govern itself in its own way.

The removal of the wall dividing East and West Berlin illustrates how events in an interdependent system can be linked in a chain reaction. The collapse of the Iron Curtain dividing Eastern and Western Europe led to the collapse of the German Democratic Republic; its people and territory became united as part of an enlarged Federal Republic of Germany. The addition of 18 million people makes Germany the most populous country of Europe (78 million) and the dominant country economically. Germany's central geographical position between Poland on the east and France on the west adds to its strategic importance.

Within each Eastern European country politicians have to create, more or less from scratch, new political institutions to maintain order, allow for popular representation, and introduce a market economy in place of a centrally planned economy. In most countries the transition from a Soviet regime was bloodless, but in Romania the fall of the communist dictator, Nicolae Ceausescu, was achieved only after a short but bloody internal rising.

The persistence of nationality differences within Eastern European countries is one threat to national security and public order. In Romania there were conflicts between those who identified themselves as Hungarians and Romanians. In Yugoslavia, formed as a federation of ethnic groups after World War I, multiple ethnic tensions have already led to the secession of the Slovenes and perhaps the Croations as well.

The Middle East also demonstrates the importance of interdependence. At the end of the 1970s, the rise of the Ayatollah Khomeni in Iran raised the prospect of Islamic fundamentalism and destabilized a region that was the major source of oil for many Western nations. Western nations thus backed Iraq, led by General Saddam Hussein, in a war against Iran that lasted from 1980 to 1988. Iraq's unsuccessful effort to annex oil-rich Kuwait has already been mentioned.

As a global power, the U.S. government sees national security affected by any major change in a region that is deemed to be important to American interests. If a small Central American state acts in ways that Washington deems threatening to security in the Western Hemisphere, it may send troops there, as it did in the 1980s in Grenada and Panama. It has troops permanently stationed in Asia and Europe as well as North America, and now the Middle East.

Every phase of national security policy and implementation is affected by international interdependence: by the production of weapon systems as these are stimulated by military technological developments elsewhere in the world; by the deployment of military forces and material in different areas, or by the actual use of military force in the form of maneuvers or combat.

Economic Interdependence

The international economy today is far removed from the traditional marketplace in which producers and buyers worked and lived close at hand. Europeans watch American films on a Japanese television set after driving home in a German or an Italian car; Japanese teenagers may walk down the street wearing American blue jeans while listening to Beatles songs on their Sony Walkman; and an American may wear Italian-styled clothes while driving a Japanese car to a baseball game.

Money, manufactured goods, services, and people all move across international borders. A strong currency makes imports cheaper, thus lowering prices for domestic consumers, but it will make it harder for its manufacturers by raising its export prices. If a government wants to stimulate consumption to gain electoral popularity, this may lead to an increase in imports and a trade deficit. A company that is in the business of making money does not need to manufacture goods where its headquarters is located. It can operate as a multinational company employing people in other continents to make the goods it sells to earn profits.

The growth of national economies in the postwar era has been fueled by a growth in international trade, for no nation can or would want to produce everything that its people need. Middle Eastern countries can export oil to meet the cost of importing foreign cars, and Japan can export manufactured goods in order to meet the cost of importing petroleum. Because of its diverse natural resources and large population, the United States has exported less than a tenth of its national product; by contrast, France and Germany export a quarter of their national product, and a small country such as Austria exports more than a third of its national product.

The development of the European Community illustrates the way in which politics and trade go together. The first step toward economic integration was the European Coal and Steel Community, founded in 1951 by

United States and South Korean soldiers in June of 1990 patrolling the Demilitarized Zone on the border between South and North Korea illustrate the problem of national security in modern international relations.

France, West Germany, Italy, Belgium, the Netherlands, and Luxembourg. The political objective was to integrate Germany's capacity for producing military materials into a supranational European framework. In 1957 these six countries also created a European Economic Community, popularly known as the Common Market. Britain, Ireland, and Denmark joined the Community in 1973. After replacing their dictatorships with democratic governments, Spain, Portugal, and Greece joined in the 1980s. Southern European nations have been motivated not only by economic advantage, but also by the hope that the Community will promote political stability where democratic institutions are still relatively youthful.

In 1992 the European Community is completing the creation of a single European market with free movement of goods, services, and people throughout its twelve member states. To achieve a single market, the Community has had to develop some supranational political powers. In addition to removing tariffs, member states must agree not to adopt industrial policies that will give one nation's manufacturers a competitive advantage. In agriculture, where subsidies are the norm, member states must accept Community regulations that keep food prices above world market levels. Increasingly, European countries are also coordinating monetary policies in order to reduce inflation and wide fluctuations in exchange rates between currencies.

Collectively, the member states of the European Community are a major economic and political power by comparison with the United States and Canada, now joined in a free trade agreement, and with Japan (Figure 2.4).

Politically, the European Community is not a su-

perpower but an alliance of states, with each state retaining its own national government, national armed force, and national Parliament. The multinational European Commission in Brussels proposes policies for the Community, but decisions must be approved by the Council of Ministers of the national governments of the member states. On most major issues the decision must be unanimous. The directly elected Parliament of the European Community does not exercise significant legislative powers; it questions and advises the commission.

The Community relies heavily on legal regulations because it obtains very little revenue from national governments. Rich Northern European countries such as Germany, Denmark, and the Netherlands are not prepared to be taxed to bring up living standards in the poorer Mediterranean countries such as Portugal and Greece.

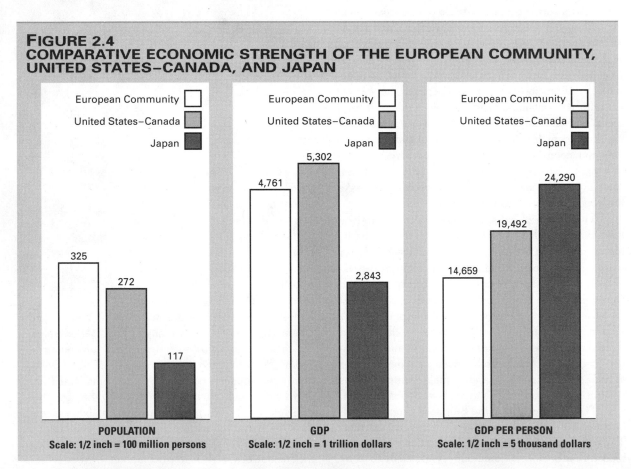

FIGURE 2.4
COMPARATIVE ECONOMIC STRENGTH OF THE EUROPEAN COMMUNITY, UNITED STATES–CANADA, AND JAPAN

Source: OECD in Figures, OECD Observer #164, June–July 1990, Data 1988.

With the collapse of the Soviet model of centrally planned economies, Eastern European countries are turning to the European Community for technical assistance, financial aid, and political support. To admit more nations into membership into the Community would extend the geographical scope, but increase the diversity of its members, thus reducing the already weak level of political cohesion.

Viewed from inside Europe, the Community appears to be about as weak as the confederation of separate American states was before the adoption of the United States Constitution in 1787. Proponents of a United States of Europe would like to see a constitution adopted for a popularly elected government that would have more authority. The alternative vision is of a *Europe des Patries* (Europe of Nations), in which the Community would represent the lowest common denominator of agreement between member states.

Viewed from the outside, the European Community is important because it already has the power to exclude other nations from trading within a market of 325 million people. This power does not worry American multinational firms such as Ford Motor Company and IBM, which are already well established in Community countries. But it does worry Japanese manufacturers, who have only recently begun to assemble or manufacture products in Europe. It also concerns American farmers who see their cheaper products excluded by Community barriers to free trade in agriculture.

The freer movement of money, goods, and services brings with it many problems. The free movement of people across national boundaries has increased the level of international terrorism. Planes can be blown up by bombs planted by terrorist groups or highjacked by armed passengers. The free movement of goods and services can be exploited by traders in illegal products, such as narcotics. In Latin America drug dealers have amassed billions of dollars and financed illegal armies by producing hard drugs for export to the United States, where their sale and use exacerbates drug problems in American cities.

The free movement of capital has enabled Third World countries such as Argentina, Brazil, and Mexico to amass tens of billions of dollars of debt from international lending agencies and from commercial banks in the United States and elsewhere. When these countries lack the money to pay interest on loans, this creates a financial crisis for major banks as well as for the debtor countries. The problem exists in Eastern Europe too,

most notably in Poland, where a communist regime borrowed large sums from European and American banks which it spent in an unsuccessful effort to buy popular support.

Every nation both exports and imports goods and services. The global total of imports and exports between countries balances out. However, individual countries can run a trade surplus or a trade deficit. Germany and Japan have had big trade surpluses for more than a decade. France and Italy tend to have balanced trade, with substantial imports and exports almost equal in size. For decades after 1945 the American economy generated a large trade surplus, because there was little competition for manufactured goods produced in the United States. However, economic growth on other continents led to a reversal of this pattern in the 1980s. The trade deficit makes possible a more rapid increase in consumption by Americans, but it also means paying more in the future to finance the deficit.

National governments enjoy the benefits of an increasingly interdependent international economy, but they dislike the costs, and a government has the power to erect trade barriers designed to help one or more sectors for its national economy. European Community barriers to the import of cheap food are a benefit that it provides to agricultural interests. The structural barriers to the low-cost distribution of American consumer goods in Japan are a benefit the Japanese Liberal Democratic party produces for the various pressure groups that support it. The large contracts that the Department of Defense gives American aircraft manufacturers help subsidize the cost of developing planes for sale abroad.

The Organization of Petroleum Exporting Countries (OPEC) demonstrates how national governments can band together to produce the benefits of an international cartel. Instead of oil producers competing against each other in a free market, which would drive down the price of oil, OPEC countries agree to set the price of oil much higher than in a free market. When the cartel is successful, it drives up the cost of imports for countries without oil, and it boosts the income of oil-producing nations.

The Constraints of Interdependence

Interdependence imposes constraints on every government in the world. Leaders of small countries have always known that they depend on what larger nations do militarily; governments in countries that depend on exports for their well-being have always known that world market conditions are a major determinant of national prosperity.

The growth in international economic interdependence today means that even rich countries cannot dominate the world economy. The dollar is no longer the sole currency of international importance. Europeans look to the German Deutsche mark as a more reliable and less inflation-prone standard of value than the dollar. The Japanese are constrained by the large American trade deficit to their country, for American success in reducing imports from Japan would threaten a major reduction in Japanese exports.

In a world of interdependence, popularly elected democratic politicians cannot simply do what the people want or even what they themselves want to do, if these wishes go against strong international pressures. An incumbent government cannot easily stimulate a preelection boom if the result will be a rapid depreciation of its currency internationally, with unwelcome domestic consequences shortly afterward. Constraints affect dictators as well as democrats. Since the Gulf War, countries will think twice before embarking on aggressive military action against its neighbors.

Of course, nations are constrained by their own history as well as by their international interdependence. The governments of Eastern European countries would like to achieve a West European standard of living as fast as they can. But it is far easier to change political institutions than to overcome the handicaps of more than forty years of a centrally planned economy that sacrificed economic growth to the dictates of communist ideology.[3]

The growing importance of transnational influences also places constraints on the study of national political systems through comparative politics.[4] When countries are no longer completely insulated from each other, we must keep an eye out for what happens abroad as well as what happens at home. For example, the strength of a national economy, which is often reckoned an important influence on voting behavior, depends on whether there is a boom or recession in the world economy as well as on what national governments do. We can no longer compare the governments of Europe as if they were completely separate; membership in the European Community provides tangible institutional evidence of interdependence.

Modern weaponry, the independence of the world economy, the international character of problems of environmental pollution and conservation, and the internationalization of the media of communication—all challenge the autonomy and viability of the nation-state, at least as it has functioned historically. No one doubts the absurdity of a nuclear war in which universal destruction may be accomplished by a few simple operations, in which protectionist measures in one country can produce economic disaster in another, in which waste dropped in the Rhine River by a Swiss factory poisons German and Dutch water, or in which acid rain produced by American factories destroys Canadian forests. The modern media have turned humankind into what almost amounts to a single audience where all these absurdities play out and where it may be hoped, if not presumed, that some learning process is going forward. These international challenges may in time lead to a further development of international problem-solving mechanisms and even of international law. The rise of the nation-state, after all, was a response to challenges beyond the problem-solving capacity of petty principalities and kingdoms. The ending of the cold war encourages hopes that these urgent problems will no longer be obscured by the politics of international confrontation and stalemate.

KEY TERMS

agricultural labor force	European Community	income inequality	literacy
cultural heterogeneity	foreign trade dependence	industrialization	multinational corporations
developmental goals	gross national product	interdependence	wealth inequality
economic development	(GNP)		

END NOTES

1. See Robert Keohane and Joseph S. Nye, *Power and Interdependence* (Glenview, Ill.: Scott, Foresman/Little, Brown, 1989).

2. For different views of hegemony, compare Robert Keohane, *After Hegemony* (Princeton, N.J.: Princeton University Press, 1984); Robert Gilpin,

The Political Economy of International Relations (Princeton, N.J.: Princeton University Press, 1987); Bruce Russett, "The Mysterious Case of Vanishing Hegemony. Or, Is Mark Twain Really Dead?," *International Organization*, 39: 1 (1987), pp. 207–31; Susan Strange, "The Persisting Myth of Lost Hegemony," *International Organization* 41: 4 (1987), pp. 551–74; and Joseph Nye (New York: Basic Books, 1990). The best-known historical discussion is the final chapter of Paul Kennedy's *The Rise and Fall of Empires* (New York: Random House, 1987).

3. See John Clark and Aaron Wildavsky, *The Moral Collapse of Communism: Poland as a Cautionary Tale* (San Francisco: Institute of Contemporary Studies, 1990).

4. See Richard Rose, "Changing Forms of the Study of Comparative Politics," *Political Studies* (1991).

PART TWO

SYSTEM, PROCESS, AND POLICY

GABRIEL A. ALMOND
G. BINGHAM POWELL, JR.

CHAPTER 3

POLITICAL
SOCIALIZATION AND
POLITICAL CULTURE

POLITICAL SOCIALIZATION

W E USE the term *socialization* to refer to the way children are introduced to the values and attitudes of their society. *Political socialization* is the part of this process that shapes political attitudes. Most children acquire elementary but distinctive political attitudes and behavior patterns at a relatively early age.[1] While some of these attitudes will be elaborated and revised as the child develops, others may remain parts of the political self throughout life.

At any time an individual's *political self* will be a combination of several feelings and attitudes in varying proportions. At the deepest level there are general identifications and beliefs such as nationalism, tribal or class self-images, ideological commitments, and a fundamental sense of one's rights and duties in the society. There are also less emotional commitments to and knowledge about political and governmental institutions, such as the electoral system, the structure of the legislature and the court system, and the power of the executive. Finally, there are more fleeting views of current events, policies, issues, and personalities. All these attitudes change, but those in the first group have often been acquired earliest and tend to be more durable.

Political socialization never really ceases; therefore, the political self is always changing. Many of life's most common experiences — becoming involved in new social groups and roles, moving from one part of the country to another, shifting up or down the social and economic ladder, becoming a parent, finding or losing a job — modify our political perspective. More dramatic experiences, such as immigration to a new country or suffering through an economic depression, can sharply alter political attitudes.

Two general points about political socialization need to be emphasized. The first is that political socialization can take the form of either direct or indirect transmission and learning. Socialization is direct when it involves the

Political socialization begins as children become aware of politics. Here, American Girl Scouts have come to Washington to see their government and meet Congresswoman Claudine Schneider of Rhode Island.

explicit communication of information, values, or feelings toward politics. Civics courses in public schools are *direct political socialization*, as are the efforts by Communist parties to inculcate the ideas of "the Soviet man" or the "Cuban socialist man."

Indirect political socialization occurs when political views are inadvertently molded by our experiences. Such indirect political socialization may have particular force in a child's early years. For example, the child's development of either an accommodating or an aggressive stance toward parents, teachers, and friends is likely to affect the adult's posture toward political leaders and fellow citizens in later life. Or, growing up in a time of deprivation and hardship may leave the future adult with a more materialistic set of value priorities.

The second major point is that socialization continues throughout an individual's life. Attitudes established during childhood are always being adapted or reinforced as the individual passes through a variety of social experiences. Early family influences can create a favorable image of a political party, but subsequent education, job experience, and the influence of friends may dramatically alter that early image. Furthermore, certain events and experiences — a war or an economic depression — may leave their mark on the whole society. Such events seem to have their greatest impact on young people just becoming involved in political life, such as first-time voters, but most people are affected to some degree. When experiences bring about drastic changes in the attitudes of older members of the society, we speak of *political resocialization*.

Political socialization transmits and transforms a nation's political culture. It is the way one generation passes on political standards and beliefs to succeeding generations, a process called cultural transmission. It transforms the political culture when it leads the citizens, or some of them, to view and experience politics in a different way. In times of rapid change or extraordinary events, such as the formation of a new nation, political socialization may even create a political culture where none existed before.

Few societies have been exposed to more dramatic forces for political resocialization than Germany. The governments in both East and West Germany made massive efforts after World War II to shape the political culture through direct political socialization. In both East and West even larger transformations have been wrought by experiences of indirect socialization. A brief discussion of socialization and German political culture can illustrate these processes. (For a more extensive discussion of Germany, see Chapter Eleven.)

POLITICAL RESOCIALIZATION IN GERMANY

In post–World War II Germany those in authority deliberately sought to transform the national political culture. In West Germany the occupation forces of the victorious Allies and, over a longer period, the postwar government sought to alter German political values and behavior to make them more supportive of the democratic political structures created for the postwar era. They made deliberate efforts to use schools, political parties, and civic organizations to inculcate citizens in democratic values. Participation in competitive elections was encouraged, though not required.

In East Germany the Soviet-dominated communist regime used the typical socialization techniques of modern authoritarian societies to inculcate values of obedience, communist ideology (including acceptance of a one-party state and centrally controlled economy), equality, and support for the Soviet bloc in international affairs. Their approach involved coordinated control of the mass media and the school system. They also used the party and its linked organizations, such as the trade unions, to mobilize citizens into symbolic support activities such as demonstrations and voting in noncompetitive elections.

In West Germany the transformation of political culture over four decades has been remarkable. Extraordinary changes have been documented, including greatly increased trust in government, commitment to democratic processes, and readiness to participate in politics. In addition, the Germans have exhibited increasingly moderate partisanship, and a consensus has emerged on the political and economic organization of society. Government efforts at direct political socialization have no doubt played a role, but students of contemporary German politics[2] attribute most of the change to four factors that are primarily indirect.

The first factor involves generational replacement rather than individual resocialization. Over the past forty years the older generations, who had retained some identification with the prewar German regimes and whose political experiences had been largely disastrous, have been increasingly outnumbered by the younger age groups. These younger groups have been socialized in the peace and prosperity of the postwar period, as well as exposed to deliberate efforts to inculcate democratic attitudes.

The second factor shaping the political culture is said to be the absence of a credible alternative to the democratic Bonn regime. The experience of Hitler's Third Reich discredited fascism; the example of East Germany discredited communism. In the post–World War II world, Germany was militarily powerless and unification of East and West appeared impossible.

The third factor has been the postwar modernization of West Germany. With the loss of the eastern part of the country, West Germany became more homogeneously urban and industrial. The rapid rate of growth in this period accentuated these tendencies. The German family became more egalitarian and parent–child relations more permissive. The educational level of the population increased. In most countries these changes are associated with a more attentive and participatory political culture.

Finally, the West German political and economic systems have performed successfully. Early legislation equalized the burdens of defeat and helped integrate the refugees from the eastern territories. Economic reconstruction rapidly turned West Germany into the leading European industrial power. Fiscal and social policies were effectively employed to maintain economic growth and stability, high levels of employment, and relatively high standards of education, health care, housing, and recreation. The political system has usually been able to combine fairly equitable representation, stable governments, responsiveness to popular pressures, and negotiated policymaking. Several smooth transitions of power have now taken place. These successes have built a reservoir of confidence in the political system and its institutions.

We know less about the course of political socialization in East Germany. Public opinion poll data tracing attitude changes are not available. Political education was heavily stressed, and the education system was closely intertwined with political organizations. However, the family and various informal networks continued to function independently, and some observers saw a large gap between verbal acceptance of the official political culture and actual behavior.[3] Sporadic expressions of discontent were quickly and brutally suppressed.

East Germany was generally considered one of the most successful of the Eastern European regimes under Soviet domination, achieving the highest level of economic development, remarkable successes in international athletic competition, and impressive levels of education and health. But in the end the regime's efforts to build a legitimacy that could carry it through hard times were outweighed by reports of the freedom and prosperity in the West, distaste for repression, and growing economic difficulties. When other Eastern European nations opened their borders to the West in the Spring of 1989, hundreds of thousands of East Germans took advantage of the opportunity to flee the country. As the Soviet Union withdrew its backing from hard-line leaders and encouraged reform instead of repression as a response to the drain of citizens, the internal support for the communist regime seemed to vanish. When the freer press revealed abuses of power and privilege by the leadership (such as private hunting lodges), citizen anger was intensified.

In the first free elections parties with ties to West Germany dominated the results, and the (reformed) communists were routed. Despite some fears about the changes, support for reunification of the two Germanies in a context of democracy seemed overwhelming. It remains to be seen, of course, if the East Germans' distinctive socialization experiences will leave their mark as a subculture within a reunited Germany. It seems likely that it will be so, but we cannot yet say what form it will take.

AGENTS OF POLITICAL SOCIALIZATION

Political socialization is accomplished through a variety of institutions and agents. Some, like civics courses in schools, are deliberately designed for this purpose. Others, like play and work groups, are likely to affect political socialization indirectly.

The Family

The direct and indirect influences of the family — the first socialization structure that an individual encounters — are powerful and lasting. The most distinctive of these influences is the shaping of attitudes toward authority. The family makes collective decisions, and for the child these decisions may be authoritative — failure to obey may lead to punishment. An early experience with participation in family decision making can increase the child's sense of political competence, provide him with skills for political interaction, and make him more likely to participate actively in the political system as an adult. By the same token, the child's pattern of obedience to decisions can help to predispose his future performance as a political subject. The family also shapes future political attitudes by locating the individual in a vast social world; establishing ethnic, linguistic, and religious ties and social class; affirming cultural and educational values and achievements; and directing occupational and economic aspirations.[4] An increasing interest in politics and in political activism among women has profoundly affected the family's function as a socializing agent. Education reduces the rate of political apathy among women in all countries, but in the United States — and to a lesser extent in Great Britain — even less educated women tend to be politically informed, observant, and emotionally involved in the political life of their communities.

The School

Educated persons are more aware of the impact of government on their lives and pay more attention to politics. They have more information about political processes and undertake a wider range of activities in their political behavior. These effects of education have appeared in studies of political attitudes in many nations.[5]

Schools provide adolescents with knowledge about the political world and their role in it. They provide children with more concrete perceptions of political institutions and relationships. Schools also transmit the values and attitudes of the society. They can play an important role in shaping attitudes about the unwritten rules of the political game, as the traditional British public schools instill the values of public duty, informal political relations, and political integrity. Schools can reinforce affection for the political system and provide common symbols for an expressive response to the system, such as the flag and pledge of allegiance. Teaching cultural history can serve a similar function in a new nation.

In contrast, the educational system in South Africa has had as its main goal the development and perpetuation of differences between the races. The apartheid culture was supported both by inculcating attitudes of separateness and by providing different skills and knowledge. There was no mixing of white and black children. White children learned early that their parents and other siblings treated blacks as inferior people. As they grew older they learned that whites were different and superior to blacks. White children in South Africa are required by law to attend primary and secondary school, where the environment has been exclusive as it was at home. The school experience usually confirms and strengthens the attitudes acquired by white children at home.

Education for the black majority has been different. After forcing most of the private mission schools to close, the government dealt with black education through a separate government department that provided segregated elementary education for most African children, and secondary education for a few. In 1979, after several years of improvement, the government still spent more than ten times as much per student on white education as on black African education.[6] Black dissatisfaction with the quality of education, as well as with the unsuccessful government efforts to force the use of Afrikaans as the language of instruction in the mid-1970s, has been one of the major sources of continuing black unrest in South Africa.

Religious Organizations

The great religions of the world are carriers of moral values, which inevitably have political implications. The great religious leaders have seen themselves as teachers, and their followers have usually attempted to shape the socialization of children through schooling and to socialize converts of all ages through preaching and religious services. While the frequency of church attendance varies greatly in different societies and religions, the presence of religious organizations is felt in many political systems. Where the churches systematically teach values that are at least in part at odds with the controlling political system, as in the years of tensions between the communist regime and the Catholic Church in Poland, the struggle over socialization can be of the greatest significance in the society. The reemergence of vigorous religious fundamentalism has had a major impact in the Muslim world and in recent times has been a shaping factor in the politics of the Middle East.

Peer Groups

Although the school and family are the agents most obviously engaged in socialization, several other social units also shape political attitudes. One is peer groups, including childhood play groups, friendship cliques, and small work groups, in which members share relatively equal status and close ties. Individuals adopt the views of their peers because they like or respect them or because they want to be like them. A peer group socializes its members by motivating or pressuring them to conform to the attitudes or behavior accepted by the group. An individual may become interested in politics or begin to follow political events because close friends do so. High school seniors may choose to go on to college because other students with whom they identify have chosen to do the same. In such cases, the individual modifies his or her interests and behavior to reflect those of the group in an effort to be accepted by its members.[7]

Occupation

Jobs and the formal and informal organizations built around them — unions, professional associations, and the like — are also channels for the explicit communication of information and beliefs. Individuals identify with a group, such as a union, and use that group as a political reference point. They become sensitive to the group's norms and evaluate its actions according to their sense of what is best for the group and what it stands for. Participating in collective bargaining or a strike can be a powerful socializing experience for worker and employer alike. Striking laborers learn that they can shape decisions being made about their future, and also gain knowledge of specific skills, such as demonstrating and picketing, which may come in handy as they participate in other political activity.

Occupational and professional associations such as the American Medical Association are among the most universal and influential secondary groups affecting political attitudes in modern and modernizing societies. They enlist large numbers of trained professionals, and ensure their loyalty by defending their members' economic and professional interests. Because these associations relate to occupational strata, they promote and intensify occupational and class-related political values.

Mass Media

Modern societies cannot exist without widespread and rapid communication. Information about events occurring anywhere in the world becomes general knowledge in a few hours. Much of the world, particularly its modern parts, has become a single audience, moved by the same events and motivated by similar tastes. In 1989 the movements for democracy throughout Eastern Europe fed on the knowledge of each others' tactics and successes, given extra impact by newspapers, television, and radio newly free to report these exciting events in and beyond their own nation. We know that the mass media — newspapers, radio, television, magazines — play an important part in transmitting modern attitudes and values to the new nations. In addition to providing specific and immediate information about political events, the mass media also convey, directly or indirectly, the major values on which a society agrees. Certain symbols are conveyed in an emotional context, and the events described along-side them take on a specific emotional color. Controlled mass media can be a powerful force in shaping political beliefs, although citizens will soon ignore reports that are inconsistent with their personal experiences.

Political Parties

Specialized political structures, such as interest groups and parties, play a deliberate and important role in political socialization. Political parties attempt to mold issue preferences, arouse the apathetic, and find new issues as they mobilize support for candidates. Political parties —such as the Republicans and Democrats in the United States or Labour and Conservatives in Britain —typically draw heavily on traditional symbols of the nation or a class and reinforce them. A competitive party system may focus criticism on the government's *incum-*

Use of the mass media to attempt to shape public opinion is dramatically illustrated in the confrontation between General Jaruzelski, head of the military government, and Pope John Paul in Warsaw in June 1983, as each in turn reads a statement appealing to the Polish people. Their respective staffs stand behind them.

bents (officeholders), but it often reinforces support for the basic structures and processes. Parties also keep citizens in contact with the political structures. Most individuals are concerned with politics only in a limited way, but a steady flow of party activities, culminating in an election every few years, keeps citizens involved in their citizenship, their participant roles.

In competitive party systems, party socialization activities can also be divisive. In their efforts to gain support, leaders may appeal to class, language, religion, and other ethnic divisions and make citizens more aware of these differences. In the 1960s in Belgium, the small Flemish and French separatist parties emphasized language differences and split the traditional Belgian party system, which had been stable for fifty years; aroused massive political conflict; and brought about major policy changes, including constitutional revisions. Many leaders in preindustrial nations

oppose competitive parties because they fear such divisiveness in their new nations.

In communist nations until recently and in many preindustrial nations, governments have used a single party to attempt to inculcate common attitudes of national unity, support for the government, and ideological agreement. The combination of a single party and controlled mass media is potent: The media present a single point of view, and the party activities reinforce that perspective by involving the citizen more directly and personally. Yet, as demonstrated recently in Eastern Europe and the USSR, years of directed socialization by media and party cannot compete with citizens' personal experiences in shaping underlying attitudes.

Direct Contact with Governmental Structures

In modern societies, the wide scope of governmental activities brings citizens into frequent contact with various bureaucratic agencies. A study found that 72 percent of adult Americans had interacted with at least one government agency in the preceding year; about a third had interacted with more. The most frequent contacts were with tax authorities, school officials, and the police.[8] The scope of government intervention in daily life, and hence the necessity for contacts with government, is greater in many Western European nations than in the United States, and it is greater still in many communist countries.

These personal experiences are powerful agents of socialization, strengthening or undercutting the images presented by other agents. No matter how positive the view of the political system that has been taught in school, a citizen who is harassed by the police, ignored by welfare agencies, or unfairly taxed is unlikely to feel much warmth toward the authorities.

In their study of citizen attitudes in five nations, Almond and Verba found marked differences across countries in the expectations that citizens had of their treatment by police and bureaucrats.[9] Italians, and particularly Mexicans, had quite dismal expectations as to equality and responsiveness of treatment. American blacks also reported quite negative expectations in these 1960 interviews. It is quite likely that these expectations were in large measure a response to actual patterns of treatment by government.

The Social and Cultural Environment

We have emphasized that specific events, such as war, depression, or prosperity, can be powerful socialization influences. Fundamental cultural style, expressed in a consistent manner through many socialization agents, can also have great effect. An important example is the implicit message of modern technology and scientific culture. Alex Inkeles and David Smith's study of the development of modern attitudes in six nations emphasizes how factory experience can create an awareness of the possibilities of organization, change, and control over nature. They report how one Nigerian worker replied to a question about how his new work made him feel.

> Sometimes like nine feet tall with arms a yard wide. Here in the factory I alone with my machine can twist any way I want a piece of steel all the men in my home village together could not begin to bend at all.[10]

They found that factory work, education, and mass media exposure all contributed in major ways to information on national issues and leaders, openness to new experiences, appreciation of technical skill, readiness for social change, and personal and political self-confi-

dence. For almost two centuries now the secularizing influences of science and control over nature have shaped political cultures, first in the West and increasingly throughout the world.

POLITICAL CULTURE

A *political culture* is a particular distribution of political attitudes, values, feelings, information, and skills. As people's attitudes affect what they will do, a nation's political culture affects the conduct of its citizens and leaders throughout the political system. We can compare aspects of political culture in different nations, and so understand the propensities for present and future behavior. In approaching any specific political system it would be useful to develop a map of the important contours of its political culture, as well as a corresponding map of its structures and functions.

System Propensities

One way of mapping a nation's political culture is to describe citizens' attitudes to the three levels of the political system: system, process, and policy. At the system level we are interested in the citizens' and leaders' views of the values and organizations that hold the political system together. How is it and how should it be that leaders are selected and citizens come to obey the laws? At the process level we are interested in individuals' propensities to become involved in the process: to make demands, obey the law, support some groups and oppose others, and participate in various ways. At the policy level we want to know what policies citizens and leaders expect from the government. What goals are to be established and how are they to be achieved?

Perhaps the most important aspect of system propensities is the level and basis of *legitimacy* of the government. If citizens believe that they ought to obey the laws, then legitimacy is high. If they see no reason to obey, or if they comply only from fear, then legitimacy is low. Because it is much easier to get compliance when citizens believe in the legitimacy of the government, virtually all governments, even the most brutal and coercive, try to make citizens believe that their laws ought to be obeyed and that it is legitimate to use force against those who resist. A government with high legitimacy will be more effective in making and implementing policies and more likely to overcome hardships and reversals.

Citizens may recognize a government as legitimate

for many reasons. In a traditional society, legitimacy may depend on the ruler's inheriting the throne and on the ruler's obedience to religious customs such as making sacrifices and performing rituals. In a modern democracy, the legitimacy of the authorities will depend on their selection by citizens in competitive elections and on their following constitutional procedures in lawmaking. In other political cultures, the leaders may base their claim to legitimacy on their special grace, wisdom, or ideology, which they claim will transform citizens' lives for the better, even though they do not respond to specific demands or follow prescribed procedures.

Whether legitimacy is based on tradition, ideology, citizen participation, or specific policies has important implications for the efficiency and stability of the political system. These bases of legitimacy set the rules for a kind of exchange between citizens and authorities. Citizens obey the laws, and in return the government meets the obligations set by its basis of legitimacy. As long as the obligations are met, citizens should comply and provide support and appropriate participation. If customs are violated — the constitution subverted, the ruling ideology ignored — then authorities must expect resistance and rebellion.

In systems in which legitimacy is low and bases for legitimacy are not accepted, citizens often resort to violence as a solution to political disagreement. Three serious problems for legitimacy are the following: (1) failure of all citizens to accept the national political community, as in Northern Ireland; (2) lack of general acceptance of the current arrangements for recruiting leaders and making policies, as in South Africa; and (3) loss of confidence that the leaders are fulfilling their part of the bargain of making the right kinds of laws or following the right procedures.

The Soviet Union's current difficulties in restructuring its political system are so serious because all three kinds of legitimacy problems have appeared. Many of the republics are seeking some form of independence from the USSR; there is no consensus on either a communist state or what type of democratic competition to introduce; shortages of food and consumer goods are causing citizens to lose faith in the government's economic and political policies. The Gorbachev leadership must try to deal with all three problems at the same time, to limit and forestall chaotic violence.

Process Propensities

As shown in Figure 3.1, in a hypothetical modern industrial democracy a sizable proportion (60 percent) of

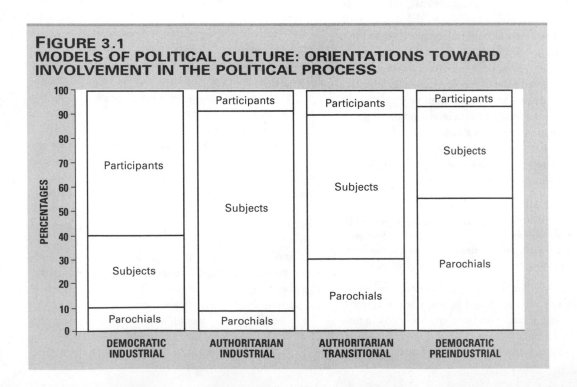

**FIGURE 3.1
MODELS OF POLITICAL CULTURE: ORIENTATIONS TOWARD INVOLVEMENT IN THE POLITICAL PROCESS**

adults may be involved as actual and potential participants in political processes. They are informed about politics and can and do make political demands, giving their political support to different political leaders. We call these people *participants*. Another 30 percent are simply *subjects*; they passively obey government officials and the law, but they do not vote or involve themselves in politics. A third group (10 percent) are hardly aware of government and politics. They may be illiterates, rural people living in remote areas, or older women unresponsive to female suffrage who are almost entirely involved in their families and communities. We call these people *parochials*.

Such a distribution would not be unusual in modern democracies. It provides enough political activists to ensure competition between political parties and sizable voter turnout, as well as critical audiences for debate on public issues and pressure groups certain to propose new policies and protect their particular interests.

The second column in Figure 3.1 depicts a largely industrialized authoritarian society, such as the Soviet Union has been. A rather small minority of citizens becomes involved in the huge one-party system, which penetrates and oversees the society, as well as deciding its policies. Most of the rest of the citizens are mobilized as subjects by the party, the bureaucracy, and the government-controlled mass media. Citizens are encouraged and even coerced to cast a symbolic vote of support in elections, and to pay taxes, obey regulations, accept assigned jobs, and so forth. Thanks to the effectiveness of modern societal organization and communications, and to the efforts of the authoritarian party, few citizens are unaware of the government and its influence on their lives. Hence, we see that most of the society is made up of subjects, rather than parochials or participants. If such a society suddenly attempts democratization of its politics, many citizens must learn to become participants as well as subjects.

The third model is of an authoritarian system that is partly industrial and partly modern, perhaps a country such as Chile or Taiwan. In spite of an authoritarian political organization, some participants — students and intellectuals, for example — would oppose the system and try to change it by persuasion or more aggressive acts of protest. Favored groups, like businessmen and landowners, would discuss public issues and engage in lobbying. But most people in such a system would be passive subjects, aware of government and complying with the law, but not otherwise involved in public affairs.

The parochials, peasants, and farm laborers working and living in large landed estates would have little conscious contact with the political system.

Our fourth example is the democratic preindustrial system, perhaps one like India, which has a predominantly rural, illiterate population. In such a country there would be many fewer political participants, chiefly educated professionals, businessmen, and landowners. A much larger number of employees, workers, and perhaps independent farmers would be directly affected by government taxation and other official policies. But the largest group of citizens would be illiterate farm workers and peasants, whose knowledge of and involvement with the public sector would be minimal. In such a society it is a great challenge to create a more aware citizenry that can participate meaningfully and shape public policies through democratic means.

Another relevant feature of process culture is people's beliefs about other groups and themselves as group members. Do individuals see the society as divided into social classes, regional groups, or ethnic communities? Do they identify themselves with particular factions or parties? How do they feel about groups of which they are not members? The question of political trust of other groups will affect the willingness of citizens to work with others for political goals, as well as the willingness of leaders to form coalitions with other groups. The governing of a large nation requires forming large coalitions, and there must be substantial amounts of trust in other leaders to keep bargains and be honest in negotiations. Beyond the question of trust, but related to it, is the question of hostility, an emotional component to intergroup and interpersonal relations. The tragic examples of ethnic, religious, and ideological conflict in many nations show how easily hostility can be converted into violence and aggressive action. One need only think of the terrible toll of civil war in Nigeria, Lebanon, Northern Ireland, or El Salvador.

Policy Propensities

If we are to understand the politics of a nation, we must understand the issues people care about and the underlying images of the good society and how to achieve it that shape their opinions. Citizens in different nations attach different importance to various policy outcomes. In some societies private property is highly valued; in others communal possessions are the rule. Some goods are valued by nearly everyone, such as material welfare, but societies differ nevertheless: some emphasize equality and minimum standards for all, while others emphasize the opportunity to move up the economic ladder. Some cultures put more weight on welfare and security, and others value liberty and procedural justice. Moreover, the combination of learned values, strategies, and social conditions will lead to quite different perceptions about how to achieve desired social outcomes. One study showed that 73 percent of the Italian Parliament strongly agreed that a government wanting to help the poor would have to take from the rich in order to do it. Only 12 percent of the British Parliament took the same strong position, and half disagreed with the idea that redistribution was laden with conflict.[11] Similarly, citizens and leaders in preindustrial nations disagree about the mixture of government regulation and direct government investment in the economy necessary for economic growth.

Consensual or Conflictual Political Cultures

Political cultures may be consensual or conflictual on issues of public policy and on their views of legitimate governmental and political arrangements. In a *consensual political culture*, citizens tend to agree on the appropriate means of making political decisions and tend to share views of what the major problems of the society are and how to solve them. In more *conflictual cultures* the citizens are sharply divided, often on both the legitimacy of the regime and solutions to major problems.

In the United States, Britain, and Germany many citizens place themselves at the center of the ideological spectrum, with most of the rest at the moderate left or right. Very few place themselves at the extreme left or extreme right.[12] The more conflictual distributions in the political cultures of such countries as France, Italy, and Greece both encourage and reflect the more intense political debates in these countries. Such debates have been associated with disputes over a regime's legitimacy, as well as disagreements on political issues. In all three countries, however, the divisions seem to have gradually become less conflictual over the last twenty years. (See Chapter Ten for a more detailed discussion of events in France.)

When a country is deeply divided in political attitudes and values, we speak of the distinctive groups as *political subcultures*. The citizens in these subcultures have sharply different points of view on at least some critical political issues, such as the boundaries of the nation, the nature of the regime, or the correct ideology. Typically, they affiliate with different political parties

and interest groups, read different newspapers, and even have separate social clubs and sporting groups. Thus, they are exposed to quite distinctive patterns of socialization. Such organized differences once characterized the electorates in France and Italy, contrasting communist and Catholic subcultures, but these cleavages have declined substantially. Where political subcultures coincide with ethnic, national, or religious differences, as in Northern Ireland and Lebanon, the divisions can be very enduring and threatening.

Figure 3.2 reflects the sharpness of subcultural division in Northern Ireland. In 1983 and 1987 five parties contested the national elections in Northern Ireland. Two of these parties appealed mainly to Protestants and stood above all for regaining Protestant domination over Northern Ireland politics that had prevailed from 1922 until direct British intervention in the early 1970s. The Democratic Unionist party, in particular, stood for direct resistance to any compromises. Two of the parties appealed mainly to Catholics. Sinn Fein called for both armed and electoral struggle leading to union with the Republic of Ireland, while the Social Democratic and Labour party (SDLP) called for negotiated compromises of Ireland, Britain, and the two communities in Northern Ireland. One party, the Alliance, tried to rally moderate forces in both Protestant and Catholic communities against continuing conflict.[13]

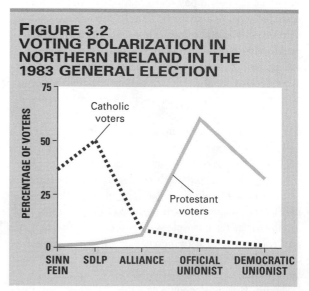

**FIGURE 3.2
VOTING POLARIZATION IN
NORTHERN IRELAND IN THE
1983 GENERAL ELECTION**

Source: Calculated from data in Ian McAllister and Richard Rose, based on a 1983 election survey. The parties received very similar rates in 1983 and 1987.

The parties are shown across the bottom of the figure, with the cross-community moderate party in the center and the most extreme parties at the respective far left (Sinn Fein) and far right (Democratic Unionist). The choices of Protestant voters are shown with an unbroken line, while the Catholic voters' choices are shown with a dotted line. The clarity of division between the Catholic and Protestant subcultures is dramatized by the huge gap in the center — neither community supported the only party appealing for support across religious lines. Protestants voted overwhelmingly (91 percent) for the two Protestant parties, and Catholics voted almost as overwhelmingly (87 percent) for the two Catholic parties. The citizenry is not quite perfectly polarized, for the more moderate of the two community parties won more support within each community. But a third or more of each community did support the most extreme party available to it. Conflictual subcultures of this kind pose very difficult problems for any political system. In Northern Ireland the conflicts between subcultures have destroyed local democratic politics, driven thousands from their homes, and cost nearly 3,000 lives in the last 20 years.

CHANGE IN POLITICAL CULTURE

A nation's political culture affects the behavior of citizens and leaders as they perform political actions and respond to political events. The system, process, and policy propensities are essential guidelines to understanding past and future political actions. The presence of more conflictual distributions of policy propensities, or even intensely divided political subcultures, indicates possible problems in resolving policy differences. Where these differences are

Children in Northern Ireland take occupation forces nearly for granted: the religious ethnic conflict between Catholics and Protestants has cost more than three thousand lives and much hardship.

firmly incorporated into the political self in many individuals, it may be difficult to overcome them. On the other hand, a strong and widely shared sense of legitimacy of the political regime may sustain the political system through hard times and help leaders to overcome policy divisions.

We end this chapter as we began it, by emphasizing that attitudes can be changed by experiences, that socialization takes place throughout life, and that the formation and reformation of political culture is a continuing process. Not only the exposure of citizens to new experiences, but also the gradual change of generations means continuing modification of the political culture as new groups of citizens have different experiences on which to draw.

Recent studies of political culture in the United States and Western Europe report a number of significant changes in attitudes toward politics and public policy.[14] One of the most significant of these changes is characteristic of the groups that came of age in the 1960s and 1970s, which tend to be less materialistic and less oriented to the work ethic than the earlier generations. This trend seems to have been slowed by the more recent economic recessions, but it continues to alter the value priorities of the political agenda. Issues of the environment and equal opportunity for self-expression for all individuals grow in importance, although traditional economic issues remain salient. Another change is a general propensity to engage in previously unconventional types of political activity such as demonstrations, sit-ins, and the like.

Of course, the legitimacy of any government rests on a complicated mixture of procedure and policy. In traditional societies the time frame is a long one. If crops fail, enemies invade, and floods destroy, then, eventually, as in Imperial China, the emperor may lose the mandate of heaven, or the chiefs their authority, or the feudal lords their claim to the loyalty of their serfs. In modern secular societies there is a more direct and explicit connection between acceptable policy outcomes and the granting of legitimacy to the government. The belief that human beings can shape the environment puts pressure on political leaders to perform well. If they do not, they will lose legitimacy, and their ability to govern will be undermined; perhaps the regime will even be threatened if the incumbents are not replaced. The ease with which communist governments were swept away in Eastern Europe in 1989 shows how deeply their legitimacy had been undermined by their own performance, despite the efforts at direct socialization from above.

These events and studies reporting significant changes in basic political and cultural attitudes in the United States and Western Europe make it clear that political culture is not a static phenomenon. Although the evidence we have is insufficient to justify predicting fundamental changes in the political cultures of advanced industrial societies, it does remind us that our understanding of political culture must be dynamic.

KEY TERMS

agents of political
   socialization
conflictual political culture
consensual political
   culture

direct and indirect
   socialization
legitimacy
parochials

participants
political culture
political resocialization
political self

political socialization
political subcultures
subjects

END NOTES

1. See, for example, Gabriel A. Almond and Sidney Verba, *The Civic Culture: Political Attitudes and Democracy in Five Nations* (Princeton, N.J.: Princeton University Press, 1963), ch. 12; M. Kent Jennings, Klaus R. Allerbeck, and Leopold Rosenmayr, "Generations and Families," in Samuel H. Barnes, Max Kaase, et al., *Political Action: Mass Participation in Five Western Democracies* (Beverly Hills, Calif.: Sage Publications, 1979), chs. 15, 16.

2. For a thorough analysis of these changes in German political culture in West Germany, see David P. Conradt, "Changing German Political Culture," in Gabriel A. Almond and Sidney Verba, eds., *The Civic Culture Revisited* (Boston: Little, Brown, 1980); Kendall L. Baker, Russell J. Dalton, and Kai Hildebrandt, *Germany Transformed: Political Culture and the New Politics* (Cambridge, Mass.: Harvard University Press, 1981); and Chapter Eleven of this book.

3. See Christiane Lemke, "Political Socialization and the 'Micromilieu': Toward a Political Sociology of GDR Society," *International Journal of Sociology*, 18 (Fall 1989), pp. 59–76.

4. Richard E. Dawson, Kenneth Prewitt, and Karen Dawson, *Political Socialization*, 2nd ed. (Boston: Little, Brown, 1977), ch. 7.

5. For example, see Sidney Verba, Norman H. Nie, and Jae-on Kim, *Participation and Political Equality: A Seven-Nation Study* (New York: Cambridge University Press, 1978); Almond and Verba, *The Civic Culture*; Barnes and Kaase et al., *Political Action*, ch. 4.

6. Leonard Thompson and Andrew Prior, *South African Politics* (New Haven, Conn.: Yale University Press, 1982), p. 119.

7. Dawson, Prewitt, and Dawson, *Political Socialization*, ch. 9.

8. Robert G. Lehnen, *American Institutions: Political Opinion and Public Policy* (Hinsdale, Ill.: Holt, Rinehart & Winston, 1976), p. 183.

9. Almond and Verba, *Civic Culture*, pp. 108–109. And see Dwaine Marvick, "The Political Socialization of the American Negro," *Annals of the American Academy* No. 361 (September 1965), pp. 112–127.

10. Alex Inkeles and David H. Smith, *Becoming Modern* (Cambridge, Mass.: Harvard University Press, 1974), p. 158.

11. Robert Putnam, *The Beliefs of Politicians* (New Haven, Conn.: Yale University Press, 1973), p. 108.

12. See, for example, the data reported in Zentralarchiv fur empirische Sozialforschung, *Political Action: An Eight Nation Study 1973–1976* (Cologne, Germany: University of Cologne, 1979), pp. 35–36; and in Jacques-Rene Rabier, Helene Riffault, and Ronald Inglehart, *Euro-Barometer 28: Relations with Third World Countries and Energy Problems, November 1987* (Ann Arbor, Mich.: Inter-University Consortium for Political and Social Research, 1989), pp. 325–326.

13. More detailed discussion of the positions offered by the parties, and of the fears and hopes of each community and its leaders, can be found in Padraig O'Malley's *The Uncivil Wars: Ireland Today* (Boston: Houghton Mifflin, 1983).

14. Ronald Inglehart, *The Silent Revolution* (Princeton, N.J.: Princeton University Press, 1977); Barnes and Kaase, et al., *Political Action*; Ronald Inglehart, *Cultural Shift in Advanced Industrial Societies* (Princeton, N.J.: Princeton University Press, 1990).

CHAPTER 4

POLITICAL
RECRUITMENT AND
POLITICAL STRUCTURE

P OLITICAL structures are the organized ways that people carry out political activities. The most obvious structures are familiar political institutions, such as parties, elections, legislatures, executives, and bureaucracies. The function of *political recruitment* determines which people are selected to become active members of these structures and how long they remain there.

The political election is one of the most common political structures in the modern world. Nations that hold no elections (such as Saudi Arabia) are unusual. The election's most obvious component, the act of voting by the individual citizen, is one of the simplest and most frequently performed political actions. The citizen enters a voting booth and indicates support for a political candidate or party. The number of voters can easily be counted and the votes determined.

Most elections are apparently about recruitment of political leaders, the incumbents of policymaking structures. Yet, elections vary greatly in the functions they perform in the political system. Few structures illustrate so clearly the need for a structural-functional approach to describing political systems. A brief discussion of contemporary elections can usefully introduce our treatment of political recruitment and political structures.

Figure 4.1 shows levels of voter participation in elections from the late 1970s to the present in several countries. As we see, in most of these countries most of the time, half to nearly all the citizens actually voted. In Britain, Germany, and the United States, as in most of the world's democracies, most citizens could participate, and they could choose between competing political parties and candidates. In the Western European democracies at least three-quarters of the citizens usually voted; in the United States about half the electorate went to the polls in presidential elections. Citizens' choices affected the recruitment of leaders to the top offices of government. Shifts in citizen support brought to power new coalitions committed to new policies. Moreover,

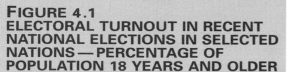

FIGURE 4.1
ELECTORAL TURNOUT IN RECENT NATIONAL ELECTIONS IN SELECTED NATIONS — PERCENTAGE OF POPULATION 18 YEARS AND OLDER

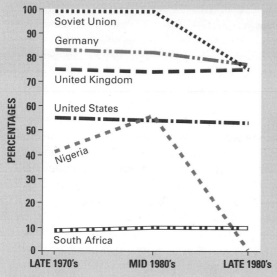

Sources: Turnout estimates calculated by the authors, using voter participation data from Thomas Mackie and Richard Rose, *The International Almanac of Electoral History,* 2nd ed. (New York: Free Press, 1982), *The European Journal of Political Research,* and *Keesing's Contemporary Archives*; and population of voting age calculated from United Nations *Demographic Yearbooks.* USSR 1990 turnout estimate generously made available from a survey conducted by Raymond M. Duch and James L. Gibson in conjunction with the Institute of Sociology, USSR Academy of Sciences, in European USSR in May 1990. Estimates for Germany are for West Germany only in 1976 and 1983; combined Germany in 1990.

the desire for office, to attain or retain political power, encouraged leaders to modify policies to meet citizen expectations. Despite its simplicity the implications of the vote can be profound.

In the other countries in the table the implications were somewhat different. In South Africa *competitive elections* gave white voters the opportunity to shape recruitment and policies to some extent. In contrast, the large black majority had no voting rights at all. Total participation of about 10 percent of the adult population reflected about average participation by whites (around 70 percent), but no participation at all by blacks. In Nigeria in the late 1970s and early 1980s all citizens had the opportunity to shape recruitment and policy through competitive elections. Participation increased to include around half the citizens by 1983. Elections did not remain a significant recruitment structure for long. The new president elected in 1983 was in office

only a few months before being deposed by a military coup. No new national elections have yet been permitted.

In the Soviet Union until 1990 the people were able to vote for only one candidate, who was always a nominee of the Communist party. The very high levels of voter participation reflected government-pressured expressions of symbolic support for the regime. Elections and voting in that system, as in China and Eastern Europe, played a role in socialization. They had little to do with recruitment. In Mexico elections have been more significant. More than one party is allowed to compete, and elections have been important in recruitment at the local level. But the dominant party, the Partido Revolucionario Institucional (PRI), has controlled the national election process through a variety of means, and elections have not been important in the recruitment of top leaders. However, competition has become more serious, and the next elections in Mexico may play a different role.

In most of the countries, the average levels of voter participation are fairly stable over time. The two dramatic changes noted above — those in Nigeria and the Soviet Union — are both important but in opposite ways. In Nigeria the decline of voter participation signified the replacement of elections by military control. The dramatic decline in voter participation in the USSR in 1990, on the other hand, was actually a positive sign vis-à-vis the meaningfulness of Soviet elections in recruitment. It signified the withdrawal of coercion to show symbolic support for the one Communist candidate, and it went hand in hand with genuine opportunities for choosing between candidates. Although non-Communist parties were still not allowed to organize and compete, the choices did shape the balance of preferences in the newly significant Soviet legislature.

Even this brief consideration of electoral structures and voting participation underlines three points. First, we must take a structural-functional perspective and look at what elections actually do, which depends on who is allowed (or compelled) to participate and what sort of competition is permitted for what offices. Second, the political system is a system, and the implications and workings of election structures depend on other structures and functions as well. Is there freedom to communicate new information and to organize new parties? How are public policies actually made — are the elections for positions that are important in policymaking? Third, recruitment is a system function that in many

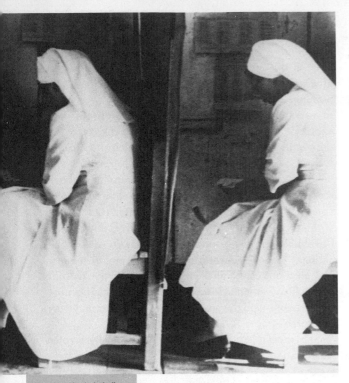

Nuns mark their ballots in the legislative elections in May 1987, participating in the return of democracy to the Philippines after fifteen years of authoritarian rule. Such competitive elections are a major feature of the decade's trend to democratization.

Citizens as Participants

In the next three chapters we will discuss the input functions of interest articulation, interest aggregation, and policymaking. As we can see in Table 4.1, citizens can become involved in each of these functions. In interest articulation, citizens make requests, demands, and pleas for policies. Some interest articulation involves only a citizen and his family, as when a veteran writes to his congressman for help in getting his benefits approved, or when a homeowner asks the local party precinct leader to see if she can have her driveway snowplowed regularly. These narrow, personal demands on the political system are called *parochial contacts*. Citizens become involved in politics in this way in all political systems, even the most repressive. In the vast bureaucracies of contemporary communist systems citizens may be almost continually involved in trying to get improvement in their conditions and treatment within the bounds of official policy. Citizens may also become involved in politics as members of interest groups (discussed in detail in Chapter Five). They may include formal groups organized for interest articulation, such as professional groups like the American Medical Association, or they may be informal local groups, like the signers of a petition submitted to a city council, or they may even be the spontaneous gathering of outraged ghetto dwellers, whose smoldering resentment of poverty and injustice erupts in a sudden riot over an accusation of police brutality. In authoritarian systems, interest group activities are much more carefully limited and regulated than in democratic systems.

Interest aggregation activities are those in which the citizen provides active political support — commits political resources — to a political leader or faction. The two major categories of citizen interest aggregation activities are voting and campaign activity in competitive elections. The great and ingenious invention of representative democracy makes these activities possible for the average citizen. By allowing freedom to organize and communicate and to form political parties, and by making the recruitment of top policymakers dependent on winning elections, the structures of democracy allow citizens to affect policies. Citizens affect policies not merely by making requests or appealing to the conscience of leaders, but by being counted in the choice of leaders. Where citizens can take part in choosing leaders, other input activities, such as demands made by interest groups, will also receive more attention. A citizens' action group, labor union, or business lobby that can offer

ways affects the working of the political process and the resulting public policies. Recruitment can directly bring to office policymakers committed to different policies. Competitive elections can also affect policy indirectly as elites work to build election support or avoid election losses in their day-to-day policymaking.

THE RECRUITMENT OF CITIZENS

Citizens become involved in the political process in two ways. *Participant activities* are those in which the average citizen makes some attempt to influence policymaking. She may write a congressman to urge passage of fair-housing legislation, or she may work to help a candidate favoring industrial development rather than environmentalism. *Subject activities* are those in which the average citizen is involved in policy implementation. Laws have been made, and the citizen responds to them, whether as taxpayer, welfare recipient, or simple law abider. Table 4.1 shows the major types of citizen involvement in politics and some examples of each type.

TABLE 4.1
TYPES OF CITIZEN INVOLVEMENT IN POLITICS

Participant activities	Subject activities
Interest articulation	Resource provider
Parochial contacting	Taxpayer
Informal group activity	Military draftee
Formal group activity	Juror
Protest activity	Resource receiver
Interest aggregation	Social security recipient
Voting in competitive elections	Welfare recipient
Party work in competitive elections	Veterans' benefit recipient
Policymaking	Behavior regulatee
Voting in referendum	Obeyer of laws
Member of town meeting, workers' council	Parent sending child to school
	Manufacturer obeying safety regulations
	Symbol receiver, provider
	Giver of pledge, loyalty oath
	Listener to political speeches
	Voter in noncompetitive election

the votes of many members, or that can contribute money or stuff envelopes before election day, will receive serious attention when it raises policy issues.

Even in democratically oriented nations, of course, it is difficult for citizens to be very involved in direct policymaking. The average citizen, by definition, does not make his living in politics, and his time is therefore somewhat limited. And apart from an occasional referendum, most national policies cannot be fruitfully decided with mass participation. Drafting legislation is a complicated process. But at the local level citizen involvement is somewhat more feasible, because citizens are better informed about issues and events. On one hand, there are some special forms of local self-government in which very broad participation does take place, including the New England town meeting and Yugoslavian forms of self-government, such as apartment and house councils and workers' councils. On the other

hand, there are local policymaking roles that are part-time elite roles. American city council members, as well as many other local officials in many societies, are not full-time officials. They just cross the borderline between citizen and elite activity.

Who Participates?

Participation by citizens varies greatly across types of activities and types of political systems. Table 4.2 shows some types of citizen participation in five of the countries studied in this book: the United States, Britain, Germany, France, and the Soviet Union. At the top of the table we see the most ordinary and the most dramatic forms of citizen involvement in interest articulation: contacting officials and participating in lawful protest demonstrations. As already suggested, contacting local officials for help is found in all types of countries. In both the United States and the USSR nearly a third of the electorate does this at least sometimes; in the German and British democracies the degree of local activity is slightly less; higher proportions approach regional or national officials.

Participation in political protests, on the other hand, varies greatly within and across countries, depending on the types of issues, the skills of the organizers, and the acceptability of this type of action to citizens and governments. Peaceful protests have become an increasingly acceptable form of action to many citizens in the Western democracies over the past thirty years, although older citizens are still more inclined to view them suspiciously. By now 10 to 15 percent of the citizens in the United States, Britain, and Germany have at some time participated in such demonstrations. Although these protests have become increasingly a conventional form of participation, they are still more attractive to the young, the better educated, and the politically dissatisfied.[1] As shown in Table 4.2, France has had far more protest involvement than the other three democracies, with over a quarter of the population reporting having participated at some points. These numbers reflect both French traditions of popular protest and the difficulties citizens have often found in getting the attention of majoritarian governments of both right and left under the Fifth Republic. The final column shows that only 4 percent of Soviet citizens report having participated in protests, reflecting the strong government repression of such activities until very recently. Given their current circumstances of serious discontent, substantial education, the absence of regularized party

TABLE 4.2
CITIZEN PARTICIPATION IN FIVE NATIONS (PERCENTAGE)

Type of participation	Nation				
	West Germany	United Kingdom	France	United States	USSR
INTEREST ARTICULATION					
Ever contact local officials	13	21	NA	34	27
Ever participate in peaceful protest demonstration	14	10	26	12	4
INTEREST AGGREGATION					
Average national voter turnout in competitive elections	85	75	78	54	76
Ever persuaded others how to vote	45	17	NA	40	31
Ever worked for party on candidate	21	8	NA	30	9

Sources: All USSR data were generously provided by Raymond M. Duch and James L. Gibson based on their survey in conjunction with the Institute of Sociology, USSR Academy of Sciences, in European USSR in May 1990. Local contacting estimates in other countries are based on data reported in Norman H. Nie, Sidney Verba, Henry E. Brady, Kay L. Schlozman, and Jane Junn, "Participation in America: Continuity and Change," paper presented at the Annual Meeting of the Midwest Political Science Association, Chicago, 1988; George Moser, Geraint Parry, and Neil Day, "Political Participation in Britain," paper presented at the Annual Meeting of the American Political Science Association, Washington, D.C., 1986; M. Kent Jennings, Jan W. van Deth, et al., *Continuities in Political Action*, p. 55. Protest estimates from Russell J. Dalton, *Citizen Politics in Western Democracies*, p. 65. Voter turnout from G. Bingham Powell, Jr., "American Voter Turnout in Comparative Perspective," p. 38. Estimates for persuasion and party work from Barnes and Kaase, et al., *Political Action*, pp. 541–542.

competition, and much looser government controls, we may expect to see dramatic increases in Soviet protest actions.

Much harder to measure by a single statistic than local contacting or protest participation is the vast range of citizen involvement in formal and informal groups, which in turn undertake various forms of interest articulation activities in many countries. Most studies suggest, however, that Americans are particularly likely to be active members of formal and informal groups.[2] These activities, which for most citizens represent indirect forms of interest articulation, are discussed at greater length in Chapter Five.

Table 4.2 also shows direct citizen involvement in several forms of interest aggregation. Democracies are remarkable in that competitive elections offer important political resources to all citizens. First, we see the average turnout of citizens in competitive national elections, which was also shown for some specific elections in Figure 4.1. Among the democracies the United States stands out for its rather low levels of national voting participation: only around half of the potential electorate, rather than three-fourths or more as in the average democracy, votes. The last two lines of the table show, however, that this comparatively poor American performance in voting does not simply reflect relative

apathy. Americans are much more likely to try to persuade others how to vote than are their British counterparts, and they are much more likely to work for a party or candidate than either British or German citizens.

The Soviet Union just had its first semicompetitive national election in the Spring of 1990, and even here competition was allowed between candidates but not in a multiparty context. So the Soviets have little experience with the broad opportunities for citizen involvement in interest aggregation. Nonetheless, turnout was a healthy 76 percent, nearly a third of the electorate reported trying to persuade others how to vote, and 9 percent reported helping to prepare or distribute materials for candidates.

The paradox of American political participation, which contrasts low turnout in elections with heavy involvement in other forms of political activity, results from the interaction of the two major factors that shape individual political involvement: the institutional setting and the resources of individuals. Voting participation is sharply affected by eligibility requirements and registration laws, by the organizational pervasiveness and mobilizing activities of political parties, and by the sharp contrast in party and candidate choices. In all these ways the American voting environment is less conducive to citizen turnout. Registration requirements mean that citizens who change addresses must make a new effort to reestablish their eligibility, while registration is automatic in many European nations. Party organizations are more centralized in Europe and are more extensive in many nations than in the United States. Traditionally, ideological contrasts between parties have been more dramatic in Europe, and parties often have strong, specialized links to economic or religious groups. For voting, such institutional factors outweigh the levels of citizen education and general interest, which are higher in the United States than in much of Western Europe.[3]

For other forms of activity, the citizen resources of education and interest, as well as the extensive networks of organizations, tend to pull Americans into politics at a higher rate than citizens in most democracies.[4] In the case of campaign activity, the looser American electoral organizations, which are now centered on candidates more than parties, create both opportunities and needs for involvement by the general public. The rather low levels of campaign activity in Britain (8 percent in Table 4.2, as compared to 30 percent for the United States) reflect short campaigns, dominated by nationally linked party organizations, as well as lower levels of education and general political interest.

Citizen participation reflects, then, the way citizens with various participant attitudes utilize opportunities offered by institutions and issues. Citizens who are well informed, confident of their ability to influence others, or attentive to political affairs, or who think it their duty to get involved, will make use of opportunities for participation. Skill and confidence are especially important in complicated activities like organizing new groups or rising to be a leader in an organization. Much cross-national research has shown that better educated, wealthier, and occupationally skilled citizens are more likely, on average, to develop the attitudes that encourage participation.[5] The personal resources and skills that such people develop in their private lives can be easily converted into political involvement when duty calls or need arises. Consequently, these studies have shown that the better-off citizens in a society tend to be more active in politics than the less well-off. This tendency is least pronounced in the easiest activities, such as voting participation and personal contacting, and most pronounced in forming groups.

The tendency for the better-off to dominate in the arenas of participation is also more pronounced in societies such as the United States with weak party orga-

nizations, weak working-class groups (such as labor unions), and without parties appealing distinctively to the interests of the lower classes. In nations with stronger working-class parties and labor unions, organizational networks may develop which to some extent counterbalance the greater information and awareness of the more affluent citizens.

Citizens as Subjects

One of the most pervasive of all citizen roles is that of taxpayer. This role has probably generated more citizen resistance to the efforts of authorities to promote compliance than any other. Tax revolts are a recurrent feature of political history in many nations and cultures. The demand of taxpayers to have greater voice in policymaking in return for their assent to increased taxes is a prominent theme in the history of democracy. The American and French revolutions were in part precipitated by their governments' efforts to raise taxes. Antitax movements, antitax campaign promises, and even antitax parties were a regular feature of politics in many democracies in the 1970s and 1980s.

Resources must be extracted from the society for a wide range of government activities. Modern nonsocialist societies extract from a quarter to half of the national income in taxes and levies of various kinds. Communist political systems in the Soviet Union and Eastern Europe extract from half to three-quarters of the national income through taxation and profits on nationalized industries (see Chapter Eight). Many devices are used to compel citizens to become obedient providers of the necessary resources. The United States relies heavily on direct income taxes. The government withholds the income of individual earners, as well as corporations, who must file annual statements to request refunds when they have overpaid or must make additional payments when they have underpaid. An agency of the government, the Internal Revenue Service, monitors citizen taxation. Many state and local governments also tax incomes or use a host of indirect taxes, such as sales taxes. Although the primary sanction for compliance is coercion, with severe penalties provided for tax evasion, a normative emphasis on obedience to the law and good citizenship supplements coercion. In fact, some European nations have much higher levels of tax evasion than the United States. In France, tax evasion is virtually a time-honored custom, and government budget forecasters always anticipate a substantial shortfall.[6]

Citizen roles as receivers of governmental benefits

are assumed much more readily, although here too government agencies must typically engage in substantial public education campaigns to inform citizens of the availability of benefits and how to receive them. Aid to the handicapped, to war veterans, to the aged, to the poor, and to various special groups takes a great variety of forms. Patterns of bureaucratic implementation typically require citizens to register or to make special applications for the benefits in question, whether these are welfare benefits, medical care, or loans to small business or for disaster relief. The agency must then monitor the system to see that only eligible citizens receive the benefits.

Modern societies are also covered by networks of regulations. Parents are commonly required to send children of certain ages to school for specific periods of the year. Compliance is achieved by a combination of incentive and coercion. On one hand, education is emphasized as a positive benefit to children and families. On the other hand, penalties are provided for failure to comply, unless educational requirements are met otherwise. It is, indeed, difficult to think of occupational and other major social and economic roles in modern societies that are not somehow linked to a form of government regulation. From traffic regulation to antitrust laws, the citizen in a complex society faces regulatory action. Yet, here too there is variation. In authoritarian political systems the regulation is usually more pervasive and often more arbitrary, and it extends to the control of internal travel, public gatherings, and public speech.

A final form of citizen subject role is of particular interest: the symbolic involvement role. Most political systems attempt to involve citizens with symbols of the community, regime, and authorities. In some countries, schoolchildren must learn and recite a pledge of allegiance; complex legal battles have been fought in the United States over the efforts of citizens to resist this requirement for religious or ethical reasons. The mass media are filled with efforts by political leaders to invoke and reinforce symbols of national history and unity.

Contemporary authoritarian systems, particularly the one-party states, press the symbolic involvement of citizens much further. In major efforts to socialize citizen attitudes through symbolic role playing, these systems typically mobilize every citizen to cast a vote for the single party's candidate on election day and to participate in parades, work groups, and the like. For the same purpose, many have instituted vast recreational programs, particularly to further the involvement of the young. The penetrative party and bureaucratic organizations in these regimes usually are highly effective in mobilizing citizens to perform these symbolic roles, although the effect on attitudes would seem to fall short of the expectations of the rulers.[7] Recent events in the Soviet Union and Eastern Europe suggest that decades of symbolic participation did not build a strong belief in the legitimacy of these regimes.

HOW MUCH PARTICIPATION?

One aspect of the participation explosion is a widespread belief, particularly among younger people, in *participant democracy*. The main thrust of this belief is that even in democratic countries political decisions are made by the establishment — the economically privileged and the politically powerful. The solution to this problem, claim the proponents of participant democracy, is to bring decision making down to the level of the community and small groups, back to the people. As a result, citizens would be able to grasp the issues and act politically in their own interest.

Other political theorists maintain that even in democracies there must be a division of political labor and influence, and that a country in which most people would be politically active much of the time would be impossible to govern.[8]

The fundamental question is whether a direct, participant democracy is possible in modern nations confronted with contemporary conditions and problems. Robert Dahl has faced this question and presented an analysis that merits some attention.[9] His argument starts with the idea that the preferences, values, and interests of all members of political communities should be taken into account in the decisions of democratic political systems. If all or most members of the community have the same interests and preferences, then there is no problem. But since this unanimity never occurs, some kind of rule of decision is essential. The majority principle would seem to be an ethically acceptable solution, but in some cases majority rule may be impossible, because the interests of some minority may be so important that its members would not tolerate rule by majority. Language, religion, and property rights are examples of issues over which the application of majority rule may result in civil war, national fragmentation, and the destruction of democracy. In democracies majority rule is normally limited in some areas, either through the acceptance of mutual guarantees protecting the interests of minorities (permitting free practice of religion, the right to speak and be educated in minority languages, and so forth), or through a reserved area of autonomous decisions in which government is prohibited from interfering (freedom of speech, press, assembly, petition, and so forth). But these limits on majority rule are only the beginning of sound democratic logic.[10]

Dahl argues that the ideal of participant democracy must confront the sheer numbers of people involved, the differences in interests and preferences, and the need for competence. It must also confront the economic aspects of participation — that is, what people must forgo in the way of time, energy, and money if they are active in politics. He concludes that its cost to the individual limits the role that direct participation can play in democratic government. Delegation of power to representatives (held accountable, to be sure, through elections) and to nonelected professionals and specialists is a necessary and desirable alternative.

Dahl concludes his discussion of the limits of participant democracy with the metaphor of Chinese boxes, the ancient toy consisting of a large box that contains smaller and smaller boxes. Just as there is a range of box sizes, political problems occur in all dimensions and at all levels. Problem-solving organizations must exist at each level if the problems are going to be solved at all. The big box is analogous to the international level, where, it becomes increasingly evident, problem-solving apparatus and capacity will have to develop if the human race is to survive. The tiny box is analogous to the local community, where direct participation of individuals in local political decisions like sewage disposal, education, and road maintenance is both possible and feasible, because many individuals not only want to solve these problems but are competent to judge the effectiveness of alternative solutions and are motivated to pay the costs of participating. As one moves from the tiniest box to the largest one, specialized competence becomes more important and the costs of participation become greater, necessitating reliance on elected representatives and appointed professionals.

None of this, however, argues that the ideal of participation has been fully realized in the contemporary nations characterized (properly) as democracies. Recent experiments in local community participation and in participation by workers and their representatives in the decision making of economic enterprises suggest that there are still opportunities for democratic creativ-ity. And the recent mobilization and politicization of members of underprivileged minority groups, women, and young people in industrial democracies show that there are still bastions of privilege and inequality to conquer.

THE RECRUITMENT OF ELITES

Becoming Eligible:
Bias Toward the Better Off

Every political system has procedures for the recruitment, or selection, of political and administrative officeholders. In democracies such as the United States, Britain, and France, political and administrative positions are formally open to any candidate with sufficient talent. But political recruits, like political participants, tend to be people of middle- or upper-class background or those coming from the lower classes who have been able to gain access to education.[11] Of course, this somewhat overstates the case. The trade unions or leftist political parties in some countries may serve as channels of political advancement for people lacking in economic advantage or educational opportunity. Thus, the Labour party delegation in the British House of Commons and the Communist party delegation in the French National Assembly include a substantial number of workers. The workers have usually acquired political skills and experience, however, by holding offices in trade unions or other groups.

There is a reason for this bias in political recruitment. Political and governmental leadership, particularly in modern, technologically sophisticated societies, requires knowledge and skills hard to acquire in any way other than through education and training. Natural intelligence and experience in a trade union or cooperative society may, to a limited degree, take the place of substantial formal education. Even in leftist parties, however, the higher offices tend to be held by educated professional people rather than by members of the working class.

Communist countries, despite their ideologies of working-class revolution, have not been able to avoid this bias. As they advance into industrialism, or as they seek to do so, they depend increasingly on trained technicians. Even the running of an effective revolutionary party calls for technical competence and substantial knowledge. In the Soviet Union, the Central Committee of the Communist party has increasingly been composed of persons with higher education who are recruited from the regional party organizations, the army, and the bureaucracy. The emergence in communist countries of an educated, technically competent, and privileged ruling class violates their revolutionary populist ideology, and some friction has resulted. Thus, we observe a cycle of recruitment of the technically competent followed by ideological and populistic attacks on bureaucracy and privilege. Nowhere has this been more marked than in China, where the Great Proletarian Cultural Revolution of the late 1960s sought to destroy the powers and privileges of the party leadership and the governmental bureaucracy and bring power back to the people. Yet if the communist countries are to make and implement developmental programs, they cannot escape this dependence on education and competence. In recent years China has returned to an emphasis on education and technological development and even experimented with encouraging greater individual initiative. (See Chapter Fourteen for more detailed discussion of recent Chinese reforms.)

Selection of Elite Policymakers

From among those who have been recruited to lower levels of the political elite, a much smaller number must be selected for the top roles. Historically, the problem of selecting the individuals to fill the top policymaking roles has been critical for maintaining the internal order and stability of government. Monarchs, presidents, generals, and party chairmen exercise great power over policy directions. A major accomplishment of stable democracies has been to regulate the potential conflict involved in succession and confine it to the mobilization of votes instead of weapons. When we refer generally to "recruitment structures," we are thinking of how systems choose the top policymakers and executives.

Table 4.3 shows these recruitment structures in a number of contemporary nations. The most familiar structures in the table are the presidential and parliamentary forms of competitive party systems. In the presidential form, as in the United States and France, parties select candidates for nomination, and the electorate more or less directly chooses between these. The Mexican system is similar, but the Partido Revolucionario Institucional (PRI) has such control over the electoral process that for half a century the electorate has merely ratified the party's presidential nominee. That nomination itself has been achieved after complex bargaining between party factions and other powerful groups.

In the parliamentary form, the chief executive is not selected directly by popular election. Rather, the parties select leaders, and the electorate votes to determine the strength of the party in the assembly. If a party

TABLE 4.3
RECRUITMENT OF CHIEF EXECUTIVE IN SELECTED CONTEMPORARY NATIONS, 1990

Country	Chief executive structure[a]	Recruitment structures[b]	How often has type of government survived succession[c]
United States	President	Party and electorate	Very often
Germany	Prime minister	Party and assembly	Often
Japan	Prime minister	Party and assembly	Often
France	President	Party and electorate	Often
Great Britain	Prime minister	Party and assembly	Very often
USSR	President	Assembly	None
Mexico	President	Elites and party	Very often
Nigeria	President	Military	No experience
China	Party secretary	Party and military	Twice
India	Prime minister	Party and assembly	Often-(one interruption)

[a]"Party secretary" refers to that position or a similar one as head of party in communist regime.
[b]"Party and assembly" refers to the typical parliamentary system.
[c]"Often" means that at least three successions have taken place; that is, a new individual has assumed the chief executive role three times under that type of government.

or coalition of parties wins a majority, its leader becomes prime minister. Such elected assembly majorities usually support stable and effective governments, as in Britain and West Germany, and thus recruitment is tied directly to interest aggregation and policy creation. But in these systems party defections or a changing coalition can force a change in government if the assembly majority becomes too dissatisfied, as in Germany in October 1982.

If no party or coalition wins a majority in the election, bargaining takes place in the legislative assembly to enable some prime minister to emerge who can command a majority of assembly seats — or who can at least receive passive support for the moment. Where the legislature does not include strong extremist or antidemocratic representation such negotiated coalitions can also be quite stable.[12] Deeply conflictual party divisions can, however, lead to frequent changes in government in multiparty systems. In Italy, for example, the average prime minister has been able to govern for less than a year before being replaced. In both the competitive presidential and parliamentary systems the tenure of the chief executive is periodically renewed, as new elections

are held and either the incumbent is retained or a successor is chosen.

Table 4.3 also illustrates the role of noncompetitive parties. In Mexico, as we have seen, selection takes place through a rather open process of oligarchic bargaining within and around the PRI and the incumbent president, who cannot succeed himself (see Chapter Fifteen). Despite the somewhat closed recruitment process, the rule of no reelection forces periodic change in personnel, and often in policy, and the party and the semicompetitive elections do bring about popular involvement.

In the USSR, as in the other communist regimes, the Communist party long selected the first secretary or its equivalent, who was in effect the controlling force in the executive. Individual succession was not a simple matter. These systems provided no limited term for incumbents and no clear means of regularly assessing political support. The incumbents were difficult to oust once they had consolidated their supporters into key party positions, but they always had to be aware of the possibility of a party coup of the type that ousted Nikita Khrushchev from the Soviet leadership in 1964. As

In parliamentary democracies the head of government's power depends on legislative support. Prime Minister Nakasone sat alone after accepting the loss of his proposed sales tax in the struggle to pass the 1987 Japanese budget.

systems, however, the hierarchical party-selection structures seemed quite successful in maintaining themselves until recently. The dramatic changes in the Soviet Union raise many uncertainties about recruitment and stability. As discussed more fully in Chapter Thirteen, Gorbachev has attempted to move away from the Communist party as the sole channel of elite recruitment. The new position of president that Gorbachev occupies has many formal powers and is selected, at least formally, by the Congress of Deputies. As indicated in Table 4.3, however, these new arrangements have not yet survived even their first transition. Their future stability remains undecided. Nor has the influence of the party in recruitment to lower level positions been settled.

The poorer nations, moving down the column of Table 4.3, show substantially less stability, and the regimes have usually had less experience at surviving succession crises. The regime in Nigeria is typical of governments in many nations not shown in the table. It experienced military rule from the civil war in the 1960s until 1979, then introduced a competitive presidential system, which was overthrown by a military coup shortly after its second free election in 1983. As discussed in Chapter Sixteen, many African nations are under military governments, some of which have experienced repeated coups against incumbent leaders. Military governments, stable or unstable, have also been common in Latin America and the Middle East. In China the Communist party has remained in power but has suffered several periods of internal strife, and the army has been involved in recruitment at all levels. India's democracy was interrupted by authoritarian emergency rule that postponed elections for several years in the 1970s.

It is indicative of the great need to mobilize broadly based political resources behind the selection of chief executives in contemporary political systems that political parties are important selection structures in so many cases. The frequent appearance of parties also reflects, no doubt, the nature of legitimacy in secular cultures: the promise that the rulers' actions will be in the interest of the ruled.

Control of Elites

Performance of the system functions is crucial for the stability of a political system. Elite recruitment is one of the most essential system functions. Traditional empires and dictatorships, in which self-perpetuation was a major goal of the rulers, seem to have focused on recruitment as the system function to be most carefully regulated. Lesser elites were controlled through the careful selection of loyalists to fill the supervisory roles in the military and civilian bureaucracies and through the provision of powerful inducements for continuing loyal performance. The conquering general or authoritarian dictator mixes rewards to favorites with severe penalties for failure or disloyalty.

Modern authoritarian systems have discovered that more efficient and effective control is achieved by simultaneous manipulation of political socialization, political recruitment, and political communication. Socialization efforts are made to instill loyalty, to recruit loyal activists, and to limit and regulate the flow of information.

But if recruitment is made a part of a larger pattern of control, it is hardly neglected. Selection in the USSR has been accomplished through a device called *nomenklatura*. Under this procedure important positions are kept under the direct supervision of a specific party agency whose officials have the final word on the advancement of anyone to such an office (see Chapter Thirteen). Moreover, a complicated set of inducements is offered to make sure that chosen officials perform as they are supposed to. These inducements make it difficult for any but the topmost officials to have much freedom of action. Maximum control is ensured with normative incentives, such as appeal to party, ideology, and national idealism; financial incentives, such as better salaries, access to finer food and clothing, better housing, and freedom to travel; and coercive control, such as reporting by policy, party, and bureaucrats. Demotion or imprisonment are penalties for disapproved actions. To avoid that bane of authoritarian systems, the coup by police or military forces, the varied layers of command and inducement structures are interwoven.

Democratic systems, too, use selection and regulation to attempt to control the performance of government officials. As we have emphasized, periodic renewal of the tenure of elected officials is a fundamental device for ensuring the responsiveness of democratic elites. But other recruitment and expulsion structures also exist. In many parliamentary systems the prime minister and Cabinet can be replaced without a national election if they lose the confidence of a majority of members of a Parliament. An example in Germany was the replacement of Socialdemoktratische Partei Deutschlands

(SPD) Chancellor Helmut Schmidt by Helmut Kohl of the Christlich Demokratische Union (CDU) in October 1982. In the American system the Supreme Court has the authority to declare congressional or presidential actions unconstitutional, and impeachment procedures can be used against the incumbents in top roles, even the president (as seen in the events forcing President Nixon from office) or a Supreme Court justice, if their activities stray too far beyond permissible bounds. Military officers and civil servants are also subject to removal from office or demotion for violating their oaths of office or for failing to perform their duties. These devices to ensure that the powerful perform their duties as expected are an essential part of political recruitment.

DEMOCRATIC AND AUTHORITARIAN POLITICAL STRUCTURES

The most important structural-functional distinction in classifying political systems is between *democratic* and *authoritarian systems*. Other important distinctions can be made at other levels, as between nations in preindustrial and industrial environments, or between nations with conservative or change-oriented policy tendencies. But in describing structures and functions we stress initially the degree of democratization. At the level of nation-states, democracy consists of political structures that involve citizens in selecting among competing political leaders. The more citizens are involved and the more meaningful their choices, the more democratic the system.

No simple criterion of democracy exists. The sheer number of citizens voting is no guide. Both citizen participation and meaningful choices between competing elites are essential. As political systems become larger, more complex, and more capable of penetrating and shaping the society, the probability of some form of citizen involvement increases, but the question of the meaningfulness of participation also becomes more serious. In a modern society it is possible for the government to control and shape the flow of information and communication, the formation of attitudes and culture, and the recruitment of elites at all levels. On the other hand, it is also possible for independent social and political subsystems to exert autonomous influence on politics. High levels of education and information can build a participant political culture. Specialized social, economic, and political groups of all kinds can be springboards for the average citizen to make political demands and mobilize other people into political activity, even to build new political parties and support new alternatives in leadership. Thus, more developed political systems, especially in industrial societies, have greater potential for authoritarian control of citizens on a mass scale, as well as for democratic control by citizens on a mass scale.

Figure 4.2 illustrates the democratic-authoritarian distinction in national political structures. The placement of the nations shows how that distinction becomes more dramatic and clear-cut as a national political system develops more specialized and inclusive organizations for controlling the society. At the top right and top left of the figure are Britain and the USSR; both systems have many specialized structures for shaping their societies, including schools, mass media, party systems, and vast bureaucracies, and both are able to draw on literate and skilled populations. But in Britain and the other modern democracies these many structures and the involved population give citizens substantial ability to control their leaders. In the USSR and East Germany the policies made by the top leaders controlled citizens, whose sources of information, freedom to form groups, and patterns of involvement with the government were carefully directed from above. As suggested by the arrows for both countries, the late 1980s and early 1990s saw important shifts toward democracy. East Germany has been incorporated into a democratic united Germany. The USSR has introduced much more local autonomy, more freedom of information and activity, and a degree of electoral competition. It remains to be seen if the USSR will shift further toward the democratic system it could achieve, revert to authoritarianism, or remain in a mixed situation, as Mexico has been.

In such systems as India, China, Egypt, the Philippines, Tanzania, and Nigeria, the development of specialized and integrated structures is much less complete. They show significant democratic or authoritarian leanings, but both the citizens' capacity for input and the leaders' capacity for manipulation and control are less. The democratic opportunities or authoritarian constraints in such systems are often very meaningful to educated elites or to those living in areas near the bureaucratic centers, but less relevant to the average citizen in the countryside.

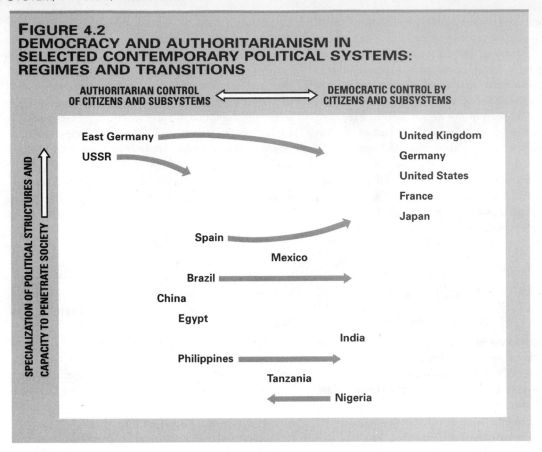

FIGURE 4.2
DEMOCRACY AND AUTHORITARIANISM IN SELECTED CONTEMPORARY POLITICAL SYSTEMS: REGIMES AND TRANSITIONS

Transitions toward democracy have been a major feature of world politics in the last fifteen years, beginning with the collapse of authoritarian regimes in Southern Europe, extending to regimes in Latin America and Asia, and most recently culminating in the dramatic democratization of Eastern Europe. The generally democratic direction of the arrows of transition in Figure 4.2 reflects those trends with some specific examples (Spain, Brazil, the Philippines, East Germany, and the USSR). Many of those transitions have been relatively peaceful and reflect a negotiated response of authoritarian rulers to citizen pressures. Military forces have frequently stood aside or even supported the citizens against the dictators. The legitimacy of authoritarian regimes has been undermined everywhere, especially since the collapse of the model (and support) of the Soviet Union.

Yet the table also shows us the case of Nigeria, where a democratic-leaning regime installed in 1979 was overthrown by a military coup shortly after its second competitive national election in 1983. The arrows of transition can move in either direction. It can be difficult to consolidate stable regimes, especially in the less economically developed societies. Immediately after World War II many of the newly independent colonial nations set up the formal institutions of democracy; only a few of these survived as long as a decade. The fate of the most recent wave of transitions may tell us much about the possibilities and problems of efforts at democratization.[13]

A rebel Civil Guard captain and his men held the Spanish Parliament and Cabinet at gunpoint on February 23, 1981, threatening the new democracy. Determined resistance by the King and all the democratic parties discouraged further support for the coup, and the rebels surrendered peacefully.

KEY TERMS

authoritarian system	interest aggregation	participant activities	subject activities
competitive elections	interest articulation	participant democracy	transitions toward
democratic system	nomenklatura	political recruitment	democracy

END NOTES

1. Samuel H. Barnes, Max Kaase, et al., *Political Action: Mass Participation in Five Western Democracies* (Beverly Hills, Calif.: Sage Publications, 1979); Russell Dalton, *Citizen Politics in Western Democracies* (Chatham, N.J.: Chatham House, 1988), ch. 4; M. Kent Jennings and Jan W. van Deth et al., *Continuities in Political Action* (New York: Walter de Gruyter, 1990).

2. Gabriel A. Almond and Sidney Verba, *The Civic Culture* (Princeton, N.J.: Princeton University Press, 1963); Sidney Verba, Norman N. Nie, and Jae-on Kim, *Participation and Political Equality* (Cambridge: Cambridge University Press, 1978); Barnes and Kaase, et al., *Political Action*.

3. See G. Bingham Powell, Jr., "American Voter Turnout in Comparative Perspective," *American Political Science Review*, 80 (March 1986), pp. 17–44; and Robert Jackman, "Political Institutions and Voter Turnout in Industrial Democracies," *American Political Science Review*, 81 (June 1987), pp. 405–424.

4. See Verba, Nie, and Kim, *Participation and Political Equality*; Barnes, Kaase, et al., *Political Action*.

5. In addition to the references in the previous notes

in this chapter, see Robert Lane, *Political Life* (Glencoe, Ill.: Free Press, 1959); and Alex Inkeles and David H. Smith, *Becoming Modern* (Cambridge, Mass.: Harvard University Press, 1974).

6. See High Heclo, Arnold Heidenheimer, and Carolyn Teich Adams, *Comparative Public Policy*, 3rd. ed. (New York: St. Martin's Press, 1990), p. 191.

7. Archie Brown and Jack Gray, *Political Culture and Political Change in Communist States* (New York: Holmes & Meier, 1977), passim.

8. See, for example, Seymour Martin Lipset, *Political Man* (London: Mercury Books, 1963); Harry Eckstein, *A Theory of Stable Democracy* (Princeton, N.J.: Center of International Studies, Princeton University Press, 1961); Almond and Verba, *Civic Culture*.

9. Robert A. Dahl, *After the Revolution*, 2nd ed. (New Haven, Conn.: Yale University Press, 1990). Also see his *Democracy and Its Critics* (New Haven, Conn.: Yale University Press, 1989).

10. For a description of the majoritarian and nonmajoritarian practices, see Arendt Lijphart, *Democracies* (New Haven, Conn.: Yale University Press, 1984). For some evidence of the advantages of nonmajoritarian constitutions and party systems in inhibiting violence and channeling participation through legitimate political channels in democracies, see G. Bingham Powell, *Contemporary Democracies* (Cambridge, Mass.: Harvard University Press, 1982), chs. 4, 6, 10.

11. See the general review of many studies by Robert Putnam, *The Comparative Study of Political Elites* (Englewood Cliffs, N.J.: Prentice–Hall, 1976).

12. See Powell, *Contemporary Democracies*, ch. 7; and Lawrence C. Dodd, *Coalitions in Parliamentary Governments* (Princeton, N.J.: Princeton University Press, 1976).

13. There is a fascinating variety in the democratic transitions, in historical background, culture, economic development, political structure, and the strategic decisions of elites. For some of the emerging analyses of these trends by political scientists, see Nancy Bermeo, "Rethinking Regime Change," *Comparative Politics* (April 1990), pp. 359 ff; Guillermo O'Donnell and Philippe Schmitter, *Transitions from Authoritarian Rule: Tentative Conclusions about Uncertain Democracies* (Baltimore: Johns Hopkins University Press, 1986); Robert A. Pastor, ed., *Democracy in the Americas* (New York: Holmes & Meier, 1989); Seymour Martin Lipset, "Political Renewal on the Left: A Comparative Perspective" (Washington, D.C.: Progressive Policy Institute, January 1990). Also see the essays in Myron Weiner and Ergun Ozbudun, *Competitive Elections in Developing Countries* (Durham, N.C.: Duke University Press, 1987).

CHAPTER 5

INTEREST GROUPS
AND INTEREST
ARTICULATION

E VERY POLITICAL system has some way of formulating and responding to demands. As we saw in Chapter Four, the simplest form of *interest articulation* is the individual making a plea or request to a city council member, legislator, tax or zoning officer, or, in a more traditional system, village head or tribal chieftain.

Interest groups have been organized on the basis of tribal membership, race, national origin, religion, and policy issues. Usually the most powerful, largest, and financially strongest groups are those based on occupation or profession, because the livelihoods and careers of men and women are affected most immediately by governmental policy and action. Most countries that permit their foundation have labor unions, manufacturers' associations, farm groups, and associations of doctors, lawyers, engineers, and teachers.

During the last hundred years or so, as societies have industrialized and the scope of government activity has widened, the quantity and variety of interest groups have grown proportionately. Interest group headquarters, sometimes numbering in the thousands, are to be found in capitals like London, Washington, Paris, Bonn, and Rome. Some of these headquarters are in buildings as imposing as those housing major governmental agencies. In countries with powerful local governments, interest groups will be active at the provincial or local level as well.

TYPES OF INTEREST GROUPS

Interest groups vary in structure, style, financing, and support base, among other things, and the variation for any nation may greatly influence its politics, its economics, and its social life.

Individual Contactors and Patron–Client Networks

Individuals may act alone in contacting political officials, and under some conditions these activities may be quite important. We have seen in Table 4.2 that contacting officials about narrow personal or family matters remains common in the modern world. Indeed, it has probably increased in complex industrial societies with large government bureaucracies. So, too, there may be an increase in individuals' efforts to articulate their opinions on broader issues, as when they write to their Senator on foreign policy or approach their local zoning board about neighborhood improvement. Purely personal efforts may become important when many people act on the same type of problem or when an individual contactor is too influential to be ignored, as when a wealthy campaign contributor brings a personal problem to the attention of a politician or when the dictator's minister asks a favor for his child. Individual efforts to articulate interests on broader issues, however, become closely intertwined, typically, with group awareness and intermittent group activities, which we will discuss in the following sections.

More interesting is the creation of networks of individual supporters by political leaders, who try to build followings by exchanging favors and support with each citizen in the network. The politician provides benefits, such as cutting red tape or securing government loans or services, in return for the citizen's votes, campaign activities or contributions, or personal favors. Such networks, often called *patronage networks* or *patron–client networks*, may be especially prevalent in societies where many individuals survive on a narrow economic margin and where formal organizations to sustain them are not effective.[1] The existence of a large number of sets of personal arrangements between politicians and individual followers may make it hard to build broad and stable organizations, because leaders may move from one organization or party to another, taking their followers along.

In authoritarian societies, where a small elite makes most decisions, and in all societies where bureaucracies have much power, personal networks built by individual leaders take on importance. Students of Soviet politics have written of the patronage followings established by Josef Stalin, Nikita Khrushchev, Leonid Brezhnev, and other leaders in their rise to power and the effects of these networks on the careers of both leaders and followers.[2] Networks of personal supporters are a special kind of political structure, because their members are not drawn together by a shared interest in making policy demands, but are held together by the skill and resources of the leader in satisfying the needs of the followers.

Anomic Groups

Anomic interest groups are the more or less spontaneous groups that form suddenly when many individuals respond similarly to frustration, disappointment, or other strong emotions. They are flash affairs, rising and subsiding suddenly. Without previous organization or planning, individuals long frustrated may suddenly take to the streets to vent their anger as a rumor of new injustice sweeps the community or news of a government action touches deep emotions. Their actions may lead to violence, but not necessarily.

Particularly where organized groups are absent or where they have failed to obtain adequate representation in the political system, smoldering discontent may be sparked by an incident or by the emergence of a leader. It may then suddenly explode in unpredictable and uncontrollable ways. After a long period of domestic quiet, Egypt was swept by riots in 1977 as people protested an increase in government-regulated food prices. In the communist countries of Eastern Europe violent, generally spontaneous protest occurred in East Berlin and Hungary in the 1950s, in Czechoslovakia in 1968 during the period of Soviet occupation, and in Poland in the 1980s when the free trade union Solidarity was formed and then suppressed by the government.

Some political systems, including those of the United States, France, Italy, India, and some Arab nations, report a rather high frequency of such violent and spontaneous anomic behavior. (See Table 8.8.) Other countries are notable for the infrequency of such disturbances. Traditions and models of anomic behavior help turn frustration into action. In France protestors draw on two centuries of street barricade experience since the great Revolution of 1789. In the United States, rioting and protests gathered momentum in the 1960s, and a decade of reported rioting and protests offered models for spontaneous political action that occurred in many black areas after the assassination of Martin Luther King in 1968 and on many college campuses after the American invasion of Cambodia in 1970. Wildcat strikes, long a feature of the British trade union scene, also occur frequently in such Continental European countries as France, Italy, and Sweden.

In 1988 and 1989 pro-democracy rallies, protests, and riots spread rapidly across Eastern Europe. The long-suppressed discontents burst forth in many places as citizens realized that the Soviet Union would no longer support repressive local regimes and that many of these had lost the will and military support to crush dissent. News of other protests stimulated efforts and provided a model for similar action; each new success provided further encouragement.

We must be cautious, however, about characterizing as anomic political behavior what is really the result of detailed planning by organized groups. The farmers' demonstrations in France and Britain and at the European Community headquarters in Brussels have owed much to indignation, but little to spontaneity.

Nonassociational Groups

Like anomic groups, *nonassociational groups* rarely are well organized, and their activity is episodic. They differ from anomic groups because they are based on common interests of ethnicity, region, religion, occupation, or perhaps kinship. Because of these continuing economic or cultural ties, nonassociational groups have more continuity than anomic groups. Subgroups within a large nonassociational group (such as blacks or workers) may, however, act as an anomic group, as in the spontaneous 1986 boycotts, protests, and riots in many black South African townships growing out of anger at the government's education policies. Similarly, in 1986 riots broke out in Kazakhstan in the USSR when the provincial Muslim party leader was replaced by an ethnic Russian.

There are two especially interesting kinds of nonassociational groups. One is the very large group that has not become formally organized, although its members perceive, perhaps dimly, their common interests. The best example may be the consumer interest group, such as all coffee drinkers, but many ethnic, regional, and occupational groups also fit into this category. The problem in organizing such groups is that with so many members sharing a rather small problem, it is difficult to find leaders who are willing to commit the effort and time needed to organize.

A second type of nonassociational group is the small village, economic, or ethnic subgroup, whose members know each other personally. Thus, in the Italian labor disorders of the 1960s and 1970s southern Italian migrants in northern Italian factories were often deployed as pickets in groups based on the villages of their origin.[3] The small, face-to-face group has some important advantages and may be highly effective in some political situations. If its members are well connected or its goals unpopular or illegal, the group may prefer to remain informal, even inconspicuous. Examples of the action of such groups include work stoppages and petitions demanding better wages and hospital conditions by doctors in Mexico City in the 1960s,[4] requests made by large landowners asking a bureaucrat to continue a grain tariff, and the appeal of relatives of a government tax collector for favored treatment for the family business. As the last two examples suggest, personal interest articulation may often have more legitimacy and be put on a more permanent basis by invoking group ties and interests. Leaders similarly invoke such connections in building personal support networks.

Institutional Groups

Political parties, business corporations, legislatures, armies, bureaucracies, and churches often support *institutional groups* or have members with special responsibility for lobbying. These groups are formal and have other political or social functions in addition to interest articulation. But either as corporate bodies or as smaller groups within these bodies (legislative blocs, officer cliques, higher or lower clergy, religious orders, departments, skill groups, and ideological cliques in bureaucracies), such groups express their own interests or represent the interest of other groups in the society.

In France as in most societies civil and military bureaucracies do not simply react to pressures from the outside; in the absence of political directives they often act as independent forces of interest representation. In Italy, groups formed especially for interest articulation are forced to compete with many institutional groups. The Roman Catholic Church, especially, has used its influence in Italian politics, even if much of its intervention has taken the form of religious education. In 1948 the pope and bishops repeatedly admonished Catholics, under penalty of sin, to use their votes to defeat socialists and communists. In 1978 the Permanent Council of the Italian Bishops' Conference denounced "Marxists and Communists" in a warning against allowing the Communist party to become a member of the governing coalition. Less overtly, the church seeks influence by having members of the clergy call on officeholders.

Where institutional interest groups are powerful, it is usually because of the strength provided by their organizational base. In authoritarian regimes, which prohibit or at least control other types of groups, institutional groups play a very large role. Educational officials, party officials and factions, jurists, factory managers, officers in the military services, and groups composed of many other institutionally based members have had significant roles in interest articulation in communist regimes.[5] In preindustrial societies, which usually have few associational groups and where such groups usually fail to mobilize much support, the prominent part played by military groups, corporations, party factions, and bureaucrats is well known. We pointed out the frequency of military coups in such societies (see Chapter Four), but even where the military does not seize power directly, the possibility of such action forces close government attention to military requests. In industrial democracies, too, bureaucratic and corporate interests use their great resources and special information to affect policy. In the United States the military-industrial complex consists of the combination of personnel in the Defense Department and defense industries who join in support of military expenditures.

The British Society of Civil Servants, a well-organized and usually effective associational interest group, assembles for an orderly meeting in a London hall to plan a 24-hour work stoppage.

Associational Groups

Associational groups include trade unions, chambers of commerce and manufacturers' associations, ethnic associations, religious associations, and civic groups. These organizations are formed explicitly to represent the interests of a particular group. They have orderly procedures for formulating interests and demands, and they often employ a full-time professional staff.

In Great Britain, for example, the British Iron and Steel Federation, composed of directors of leading companies, negotiates with the government on matters affecting the steel industry. The chief political work of the Federation involves bargaining outside the channels of party politics. The Federation representatives meet with civil servants about regulations and legislative proposals. They also try to influence public opinion through advertising campaigns, like one mounted against nationalization of the steel industry.[6]

Associational interest groups — where they are allowed to flourish — affect the development of other types of groups. Their organizational base gives them an advantage over nonassociational groups, and their tactics and goals are often recognized as legitimate in society. By representing a broad range of groups and interests, they may effectively limit the influence of anomic, nonassociational, and institutional groups.

Some democratic theorists have been suspicious of associational "pressure" groups, stressing that the special demands and advantages of such groups may be contrary to the public interest or the interests of the less well-organized citizens. Students of American politics have sometimes emphasized the "business or upper-class bias of the pressure group system" in the United States.[7] Surveys of citizen behavior support this argument of a bias in American group activity, but they also show that associational groups in the United States and in other countries can be an important route into politics for citizens with fewer individual resources.[8] Even if initially organized for other purposes, the presence of associational groups can solve many of the problems of organization and mobilization faced by discontented, but scattered, individuals.[9] Moreover, associational group activity can help citizens to develop and clarify their own preferences, provide important information about political events, and articulate the interests of citizens more clearly and precisely than parties and elections.[10]

In short, associational interest groups have an important role to play in democratic societies. One of the problems to be faced by the newly democratized nations of Eastern Europe is how to build a rich associational group life in societies in which organized groups have long been suppressed or controlled. These societies have long been shaped by institutional interest groups operating within the Communist party and the bureaucracies. With the collapse of the Communist party institutions, the bureaucratic groups could dominate interest articulation, with only sporadic input from anomic and nonassociational groups and within loose constraint from the new parties and legislatures. The process of building new, independent associational groups to articulate the specialized interests of different citizens is already underway and will be important to the democratic process.

Interest Group Systems

Research in comparative politics has drawn attention to systematic connections between interest groups and be-

tween the group and the government policymaking institutions. The differences in types of connections allow us to talk of different interest group systems in modern societies. All the modern societies have large numbers of interest groups, but the patterns of relationship differ. It is useful to distinguish between *pluralist, democratic corporatist,* and *controlled interest group systems.*

Pluralist interest group systems are characterized by many kinds of autonomous associational groups. Not only are there different associational groups for different interests, such as labor unions, business associations, and professional groups, but also articulation is fragmented within each type of interest. Many different labor unions, many different employer and business associations, many different ethnic, professional, and local groups — all simultaneously press demands on policymakers and on the implementing bureaucracies. Typically, some sectors and segments of society are more densely organized and more coordinated than others, but extensive coordination between groups is fairly rare. The United States is the best known example of a strongly pluralist interest group system; Canada and New Zealand are also typically cited as examples. Despite its greater labor union membership and somewhat greater coordination of economic associations, Britain tends to fall on the pluralist side in most analyses, as do France and Japan.

Democratic corporatist interest group systems are characterized by much closer coordination between organizations making demands for groups in a particular sector of society. Moreover, these densely and centrally organized groups are systematically involved in making and implementing policy. They regularly and legitimately work with the government agencies and, usually, with political party organizations as partners in negotiating solutions to policy problems. The best studied democratic corporatist arrangements have been in the area of economic problems. Countries with large and unified "peak" associations of business and labor that negotiated with each other and the government had better records than more pluralist countries in sustaining employment while restraining inflation in the 1970s and early 1980s. The most thoroughly corporatist countries are found in Austria, the Netherlands, and the Scandinavian nations of Norway and Sweden. Substantial tendencies of democratic corporatism are also found in such countries as Germany and Denmark.[11]

Because different sectors of a society may vary in their organized interest groups and in their government relations, we must be cautious about generalizing too much about interest group systems. However, Table 5.1 shows the striking differences in organization of the labor movement in some of the nations in this book, as well as a more purely corporatist example. The countries are ranked by the average percentage of the total labor force that are members of unions. That percentage is shown in column 3. We see that in Sweden about 70 percent of the labor force is organized into unions. These unions have close ties with the Social Democratic party. Moreover, as shown in column 4, the labor movement in Sweden is relatively unified, scoring 8 on a ten-point scale. (Such countries as Norway, Denmark, and Austria also have half or more of their labor forces organized into highly centralized unions.)

In Britain about 45 percent of the labor force is unionized, but these unions are not as highly coordinated as those of the corporatist countries. The member unions in the British Trades Unions Congress have strong traditions of individual autonomy and are themselves relatively decentralized. Partially for that reason corporatist-type agreements to control wages and prices negotiated in the mid-1970s in Britain were not long sustained. The central negotiators could not get the local union organizations to honor the agreements, especially as real incomes fell. (West) Germany had a somewhat lower level of union membership, around a third of the labor force, but the German unions are relatively well coordinated and have been able to negotiate national wage policies with representatives of business and government.

Table 5.1 shows that union membership in the United States, France, and Japan is relatively low, with less than one worker in four belonging to a union. Moreover, the union movements themselves are relatively fragmented and decentralized. In these countries there are few traditions of "social partnership" between government, unions, and employer associations. In the area of labor policy, at least, these are highly pluralist, not corporatist, interest group systems. However, corporatist-type arrangements may well be found in Japan in the case of other group interests. (See Chapter Twelve.)

In some democratic systems, such as France and Italy, many associational interest groups, such as trade unions and peasant associations, have been controlled by the Communist party or the Roman Catholic Church. Usually, these groups tended to mobilize support for the political parties or social institutions that dominated them. This lack of autonomy had serious consequences for politics. Denial of independent expression to interest groups may lead to outbreaks of violence. Subordination of interest groups by parties may limit the adaptability of the political process. However, these structures of subordination seem to be breaking down.

Finally, in thoroughly controlled interest group systems, the organized groups are penetrated and dominated by other institutions, such as parties and bureaucracies. The best examples are the traditional communist systems in which the dominating party organizations penetrate all levels of society and exercise close control over all such associational groups as are permitted to exist. Unions and youth associations, for example, are completely subordinated to the Communist party, and only rarely are they permitted to articu-

TABLE 5.1
INTEREST GROUP SYSTEMS OF LABOR UNIONS

Type of system	Country	Average percent of labor force unionized, 1965–1980	Organizational unity of labor — ten-point scale
Democratic Corporatist	Sweden	70	8
	Austria	50	10
Mixed	West Germany	32	8
	Britain	45	4
Pluralist	France	24	2
	United States	21	4
	Japan	16	2

Source: Adapted from David R. Cameron, in John Goldthorpe, ed., *Order and Conflict in Contemporary Capitalism* (Oxford: Oxford University Press, 1984), p. 165.

late autonomous interests of their members. This control was exercised in the Soviet Union and Eastern Europe; it continues in China and Cuba. The authoritarian corporatist systems found in noncommunist nations like pre-democratic Spain, Brazil, and Mexico also encouraged highly controlled interest groups. Interest articulation was limited to the official group leaders, who could use their positions in political institutions as a base from which to express their demands. As we have already noted, numerous institutional interest groups do emerge in these societies, especially from parts of the party and bureaucracy, such as the military, as do informal nonassociational groups.

ACCESS TO THE INFLUENTIAL

To be effective, interest groups must be able to reach key policymakers. Groups may express the interests of their members and yet fail to penetrate and influence policymakers. Political systems vary in the ways they organize and distribute political resources. Interest groups vary in the tactics used to gain access to the resource holders. Their tactics are shaped in part by the opportunities offered by the structure of policymaking, as well as by their own values and preferences.

It is useful to distinguish between legitimate or constitutional *channels of political access* (such as the mass media, parties, and legislatures) and illegitimate, *coercive access channels*. These channels correspond to the two major types of political resources that can be used in trying to get elites to respond. One type is established by the legitimate structures of the government, which designate the resources to be used in policymaking. In a democratic political system, the appropriate resources may be votes in the national assembly. Various groups may attempt to gain control of these legislative votes by influencing the parties that win elections, or the voters who choose them, or through bargaining, persuasion, or promises of support to incumbents. However, direct violence remains as a second type of resource, a coercive channel of access for individuals and groups who feel that they are otherwise powerless.

If only one major legitimate channel of political access is available, as in a political system dominated by a single party, it becomes difficult for all groups to achieve access. Demands transmitted though that channel may be distorted as they work their way to key decision makers. The leadership thus may be prevented from getting information about the needs and demands of important groups. Over the long run, such misperceptions can easily lead to miscalculations by the leadership and to unrest among the dissatisfied groups, who may turn to violence.

Legitimate Access Channels

One important means of access to political elites in all societies is through *personal connections* — the use of family, school, local, or other social ties. An excellent example is the information network among the British elite based on old school ties originating at Eton or Harrow, or in the colleges at Oxford and Cambridge universities. Similarly, in Japan many alumni of the University of Tokyo Law School hold top positions among the political and bureaucratic elites and are able to act in concert because of these personal ties.

Although personal connections are commonly used by nonassociational groups representing family or regional interests, they serve other groups as well. Face-to-face contact is one of the most effective means of shaping attitudes and conveying messages. Demands communicated by a friend or neighbor carry much more weight than a formal letter from a stranger. Even in a very modern political system, personal connections are usually cultivated with care. In Washington, D.C., the business of advising interest groups and individuals on access problems has become a profession, involving the full-time efforts of individuals with personal contacts who are influential in government.

The *mass media* — television, radio, newspapers, and magazines — constitute an important access channel in democratic societies. Many interest groups spend a great deal of effort trying to see that their interests receive favorable attention in the media. Interest groups such as the organizations of senior citizens encourage background reports on their needs, as well as coverage of their views on specific policies. When a cause receives national media attention, the message to policymakers has added weight because they know that millions of voters have been sensitized to the issue. Moreover, groups believe that in an open society, "objective" news coverage will have more credibility than sponsored messages. However, the confusion created by the number of messages and by their lack of specific direction can limit the effectiveness of the mass media for many less important groups.

The mass media can play an important part in mobilizing support for interest group efforts, leading to donations of time and money, as well as spontaneous expressions of similar demands from sympathizers. The loosening of government control from the media in the communist regimes of Eastern Europe and the Soviet Union gave a huge boost to the democracy movement. Reports of policy failures in economic policy, the environment, and social services helped undermine the legitimacy of the incumbent regimes. Reports of successful protests and demonstrations in other parts of the country, or in other countries, enhanced the confidence of demonstrators everywhere. The multitude of spontaneous, as well as coordinated, actions encouraged by mass media reports helped convince the incumbents that their support had vanished.

Political parties can be an important legitimate channel of access, but a number of factors limit their usefulness. Highly ideological parties with a hierarchical structure, such as most Communist parties, are more likely to control affiliated interest groups than to communicate the interest groups' demands. Decentralized party organizations, like those in the United States, whether inside or outside the legislative organization, may be less helpful than individual legislators or blocs would be. In a nation like Great Britain, on the other hand, the various components of the party organization, particularly parliamentary committees, are important channels for transmitting demands to the Cabinet and the party in power. In nations like Mexico, where one loosely structured party dominates the political system, the party provides a vital channel for the articulation of many interests.

Legislatures are a common target of interest group activities. Standard lobbying tactics include appearances and testimony before legislative committees, providing information to individual legislators and similar activities. In the United States political action committees raise campaign contributions for individual members of Congress and can usually be sure of some political attention. In Britain and France the strong party discipline in the legislature and in its committees lessen the importance of members of Parliament (MPs) and parliamentary committees as access channels for interest groups. In Germany and many other European democracies the presence of strong committees and/or power divided among multiple parties encourage interest groups to use them as access channels. The combination of loose party discipline and decentralized committees as a source of much legislation makes the U.S. Congress a major target of group efforts.

Government bureaucracies are major access chan-nels in most political systems. Contacts with the bureaucratic agencies may be particularly important where the bureaucracy has policymaking authority, where the group is more interested in shaping procedures than policy content, or where interests are narrow and directly involve few citizens. A study of access channels used by groups in Birmingham, England, for example, showed that on broad issues involving class, ethnic, or consumer groups, the associations tended to work through the political parties. On the many narrower issues, involving few other groups and less political conflict, the associations tended to turn to the appropriate administrative department.[12]

Protest demonstrations, strikes, and other forms of nonviolent but dramatic and direct pressure on government may be legitimate or illegitimate tactics, depending on the political systems involved. Such demonstrations may be either spontaneous actions of anomic groups or, more frequently, an organized resort to less conventional channels by organized groups. In democratic societies, protest demonstrations may be efforts to mobilize popular support—eventually electoral support—for the group's cause. The civil rights and anti-Vietnam War demonstrations in the United States were examples of such activity. In nondemocratic societies such demonstrations are more hazardous and represent perhaps more extreme dissatisfaction with alternative channels. As we saw in Chapter Four, the use of peaceful protest is more frequent in democratic societies, no doubt because of the greater control on activity and on reporting about it in authoritarian systems.

Protest demonstrations have been aptly described as a tactic of society's powerless, those who do not have access or resources to influence policymakers through conventional channels of party, legislature, and bureaucracy.[13] As a tactic of the powerless, protest activity is especially attractive to young people and minority groups, who are not among the elite. Protests have also been a favored tactic of groups whose ideological commitments focus on challenging the established social and political order.[14] Yet, since the 1970s protest demonstrations have increasingly been accepted as legitimate and used as a conventional channel for interest articulation by those who feel that disciplined parties and bureaucratic agencies are deaf to their complaints. Protests can supplement other channels, especially in gaining the attention of the mass media in an age when television comes to every household. Thus, we find doctors in Paris, civil servants in Sweden, and "gray panthers" in America using a tactic once limited to students and minorities.

Coercive Channels and Tactics

Most scholars who have written on the subject see acts of collective violence as closely associated with the character of a society and the circumstances that prevail there. In his studies of civil strife, Ted Robert Gurr has developed the concept of relative deprivation to explain the frustration or discontent that motivates people to act aggressively. Gurr defines relative deprivation as a "discrepancy between people's expectations about the goods and conditions of life to which they are entitled, on the one hand, and, on the other, their value capabilities — the degree to which they think they can attain these goods and conditions."[15] The sense of relative deprivation leads to frustration and anger; aggressive violence releases those feelings.

Feelings of relative deprivation are only a source. Of course, the more such discontent and anger persist, the greater the chance of collective violence. But other conditions are important also. People will tend to turn to violence if they believe it is justified and if they believe it will lead to success. If they believe that their government is illegitimate and the cause of their discontent, they will readily turn to political violence if there are no other means of bringing about change. To this end, it is the responsibility of the government and its institutions to provide peaceful alternatives to violence as a means of change.

This general analysis of violence should not blind us to the differences between types of violent political activity. A *riot*, for example, involves the spontaneous expression of collective anger and dissatisfaction by a group of citizens. Though riots have long been dismissed as aberrant and irrational action by social riffraff, modern studies have shown that rioters vary greatly in their motivation, behavior, and social background.[16] Most riots in fact seem to follow some fairly clear-cut patterns, such as confining destruction or violence to particular areas or targets. Riots are often directed against property rather than persons, as seen in most American ghetto riots, where the overwhelming majority of deaths were caused by untrained troops attempting to restore order, not by rioters. Relative deprivation seems to be a major cause of riots, but the release of the frustrations is not as aimless as is often supposed.

And while deprivation may help fuel the discontent, *strikes* and *obstructions* — as well as many violent

Standing before a portrait of Sun Yat-sen, founder of the Republic of China, a student leader speaks to more than 300,000 Chinese students gathered in Tiananmen Square in Beijing on May 4, 1989, to call for greater democracy and freedom. The protest was later crushed by government forces.

demonstrations that are called riots but should not be — are typically carried out by well-organized associational or institutional groups. According to Ann Wilner, for example, public protests in Indonesia during the rule of Sukarno were largely stage-managed, "instigated, provoked, and planned by one or several members of a political elite," in order to test their strength, gain support from the undecided, frighten others from joining the opposition, and challenge higher authorities.[17] James Payne suggests that in Peru, violent demonstrations and riots under the civilian regimes of the early 1960s were "fully a part of the

Peruvian pattern, not merely distasteful, peripheral incidents." The labor unions, in particular, found such tactics crucial to their survival.[18]

The influence of strikes and obstructions has varied, depending on the legitimacy of the government and coercive pressure from other groups. General strikes in Belgium were instrumental in bringing about expanded suffrage early in the twentieth century, but were disastrous failures for the sponsoring organizations in Italy in 1922 and Britain in 1927. Like the massive truckers' strike that helped bring down the government in Chile in 1972–1973, these unsuccessful actions left deep bitterness in the societies. The peasant farmers' tactics of seizing public buildings, blocking roads, and the like won major concessions from the French government in the early 1960s, in part because the government was threatened by terrorism from right-wing army groups and discontent elsewhere and badly needed peasant support. By the late 1960s, a stronger regime was able to ignore or suppress peasant obstructions,[19] but had to yield major concessions to the strikes by workers that virtually shut down France for a month in 1968. Most spectacularly, the strikes and obstructions and demonstrations in Eastern Europe in 1989 and 1990, like the earlier people's power movement in the Philippines, had massive success against regimes that had lost legitimacy.

Finally, *terrorism*, including deliberate assassination, armed attacks on other groups or government officials, and provocation of bloodshed has been used as an interest articulation tactic in some societies. The use of terrorism typically reflects the desire of some groups to change the rules of the political game. The tragedies in Northern Ireland, the frequent kidnappings and attacks by groups in the Middle East seeking to dramatize the situation of the Palestinians, and the surges of terrorist action in Italy in the 1970s demonstrate the continuing use of such tactics.

The use of *political terror tactics* has seldom been successful without large-scale backing of terrorist groups from many citizens, as in some independence movements. Massive deadly violence may destroy a democratic regime, leading to curtailment of civil rights or even military intervention when many citizens and leaders come to feel that any alternative is preferable to more violence. But small-group terrorism usually fails when confronted by united democratic leadership,[20] and such violence often forfeits the sympathy that is needed if the group's cause is to receive a responsive hearing.

POLICY PERSPECTIVES ON INTEREST ARTICULATION

As we pointed out in Chapter One, we need to look at the structures performing political functions from both a process and a policy perspective. If we are to understand the formation of policies, we need to know not merely which groups articulate interests, but what policy preferences they express. Many associational interest groups specialize in certain policy areas. The concerns of other interest groups, such as anomic or institutional groups, may be less easily discerned, but they are equally important for the policy process.

Table 5.2 provides an overview of interest articulation. The far left column indicates the types of groups that commonly articulate interests in modern societies. The next columns provide examples of interest articulation by each type in respective policy areas: extractive, distributive, and regulative policies in the domestic arena, and a few examples of international policies. Another dimension is provided by the symbols, which indicate when coercive, illegitimate channels were used, rather than constitutional ones. Careful examination of each case will provide a more precise classification of the access channels, such as elite representation by American black congressmen, use of party channels by the Italian Catholic Church, and use of terror by the French OAS. In this table we have used examples from many nations in order to suggest the varied possibilities, as well as to fill in all the categories with reasonably obvious cases. If we were studying interest articulation patterns in one nation, of course, we should attempt to build up the table showing the structures, policies, and channels involved during a particular period.

Although we have focused on relatively specific policy articulations, expressions of discontent can be much more vague and diffuse. Another distinction to make is the level at which the demand is made. Rather than distinguishing between requests for different policies, we might distinguish between demands for minor policy changes, for changes in the processes of decision making and implementation, and for changes in the basic system itself, particularly in elite recruitment. Students of the Soviet system have used terms such as sub-

TABLE 5.2
PROCESS AND POLICY PERSPECTIVES ON INTEREST ARTICULATION

Types of interest groups	Examples of Interest Articulation in Various Policy Areas			
	Domestic extractive policy	Domestic distributive policy	Domestic regulative policy	International policy
Individual	Peasant family seeks patron's aid with tax law.	Austrian worker asks party official for housing aid.	U.S. family business seeks relief from pollution standards.	British worker writes MP against Common Market.
Anomic groups	Nigerian women riot over rumor of taxes (1950s).[a]	Polish workers strike to protest bread prices.	Venezuelan citizens strike against dictatorship, 1958.[a]	U.S. students demonstrate against South African policy, 1986.
Nonassociational groups	Mexican business leaders discuss taxes with president.	U.S. Black Caucus in Congress calls for minority jobs.	Soviet Jewish citizens demand freedom to emigrate from USSR.	Saudi Arabian royal family factions favor oil embargo.
Institutional groups	American universities urge that charitable contributions remain tax deductible, 1986.	U.S. Army Corps of Engineers proposes new river locks.	Anglican church leaders ask an end to racial oppression in South Africa, 1986.	USSR Politburo faction favors withdrawal from Afghanistan, 1986.
Associational groups	French student groups protest government-imposed tuition increases, 1986.[b]	British Medical Association negotiates salaries under Health Services.	U.S. retail druggists lobby to pass fair trade laws.	Middle Eastern groups launch terror attacks to protest U.S. and Israeli Lebanon policies.[a]

[a]Use of coercive, unconstitutional access channels and tactics.
[b]Use of coercion by some elements or subgroups.

versive or integral opposition to refer to actions calling for basic change in the communist system,[21] as opposed to factional or sectoral interests articulated by institutional groups on policy questions.

INTEREST GROUP DEVELOPMENT

One of the consequences of modernization is a widespread belief that the conditions of life can be altered through human action. Modernization also usually involves education, urbanization, radical growth in public communication, and in most cases improvement in the physical conditions of life. These changes are closely related to increases in political awareness, participation, and feelings of political competence. Such participant attitudes encourage more diverse and mass-based interest articulation.

At the same time that participant attitudes emerge in the political culture of societies undergoing modernization, the specialization of labor, as people become involved in many types of work beyond agricultural production, leads to the formation of large numbers of special interests. The complex interdependence of modern life, the exposure provided by mass communications, and the wide-ranging role of government further multiply political interests. The processes by which these interests and attitudes are organized into associational interest groups are complex. The barriers to coordination and cooperation are overcome in many different ways. The emergent interest group systems, pluralist or corporatist, autonomous or controlled, dominated by the better-off or more equally mobilized, are shaped by the history of interest group development during modernization.

Successful political development requires that complex interest group systems emerge to express the needs of groups and individuals in complex modern societies. Yet, this process is by no means automatic. Societies vary widely in the extent to which people engage in associational activity. One element is the trust that is generally shared among members of the society. Edward Banfield pointed to the extreme case of an Italian village within which almost no associational activity occurred, with people unwilling to trust anyone outside their immediate family.[22] Robert Putnam and his colleagues found evidence that such

Demolition of a giant statue of Lenin in Romania reflects and symbolizes the success of the massive popular demonstrations against communism and for democracy that swept across Eastern Europe in 1989–1990.

attitudes show continuity over long time periods and were strongly related to political successes of regional governments in Italy.[23] Ronald Inglehart has shown similar continuity in political trust levels over a decade in the national political cultures of Western Europe.[24] Thus, in some societies, modernization may weaken traditional structures but fail to foster the development of effective associational groups because of the inhibition of social attitudes. Their ability to achieve either stability or democracy will be hindered as a result.

In other cases, as we have noted, authoritarian parties and bureaucracies may control and penetrate associational groups and choke off the channels of political access. Eastern Europe offers a situation in which forty years or more of authoritarian domination suppressed autonomous interest groups. On one hand, the processes of economic modernization had put great pressure on these authoritarian systems to allow more open organization and expression of political interests. On the other hand, the opening of these societies has led to an explosion of interest articulation activity and a great need for associational groups to provide regular and organized expression for citizens' interests. They are also needed to counterbalance the demands from institutional groups in the civilian and military bureaucracies.

The English publicist and scholar, Timothy Garton Ash, has captured the mood and flavor of the emergence of "civil society" in Eastern Europe in the late 1980s. In October 1988, as movements and associations began to bubble up in such countries as Poland and Hungary, he wrote:

> A comprehensive map of the opposition in East Central Europe today would resemble nothing so much as one of those kaleidoscopic multicolored maps of ethnic groups in this region before the war. In both Poland and Hungary, groups or grouplets whose identities or programs arise from specific postwar realities overlap or combine with groups raising almost every flag, slogan, aspiration, or prejudice of the prewar political spectrum (except communism): populists, reform economists, radical sociologists, Smallholders, Lutherans, Catholic "base groups," Evangelical sects, democratic opposition, democratic youth, democratic academics, Solidarity, Fighting Solidarity, national Democrats, liberal democrats, Christian democrats, social democrats, liberal Catholics and conservative Catholics, Christian socialists, Jews, anti-semites, advocates of workers' self government, apostles of free enterprise, "Neo-realists," "neopositivists": you name it, we have it. And this is merely the surface of the explicit opposition. One could produce

another rich catalogue of official or semiofficial projects for "reform." Hungarian political scientists have coined the delightful term "paradigm ecstacy."[25]

Some observers have argued that even the free postindustrial societies of Western Europe and North America need more innovation among interest group organizations.[26] Many interests may be based on social values or on material interests that no longer correspond to occupational categories. Citizens interested in the environment, peace, consumer protection, and participatory values may be too scattered and too mobile to be easily mobilized by traditional associational groups. Some of these citizens believe that the challenge they want to pose to society cannot be expressed through ordinary associational organizations using conventional channels of access. On the organizational side, the new social movements in Western Europe have sought more fluid and dynamic organizations, with constantly changing leadership and members who move in and out of organizational involvement. Some of the parties and organizations have made great efforts to ensure continuing turnover of leaders to avoid becoming like the bureaucratic society they wish to alter. Where participation and self-expression are themselves among the most important values being articulated, the group structure must be always in change.

On the tactical side, the new social movements have used a wide range of approaches and often disagreed over the value of partisan campaigning, conventional lobbying, and radical protest. The "green" movements in several nations, especially West Germany, have sometimes acted as or sponsored political parties, if only to gain a better forum for protest. Some of these parties have had striking success. It is too soon to say if the new social movements will add a new category, with elements of anomic, nonassociational, and associational groups all intertwined, to our classification of interest groups. But their efforts remind us that political change is the theme of our time.

KEY TERMS

anomic interest groups
associational groups
channel of political access
coercive access channels
controlled interest group systems

democratic corporatist interest group systems
institutional groups
interest articulation
legitimate access channels

nonassociational groups
patron–client networks
pluralist interest group systems

political terror tactics
relative deprivation
riots
strikes

END NOTES

1. These clientelist or patronage structures are discussed further in Chapter Six in terms of their role in interest aggregation.

2. See the essays in G. F. Skilling and F. Griffiths, eds., *Interest Groups in Soviet Politics* (Princeton, N.J.: Princeton University Press, 1971).

3. See Charles Sabel, *Work and Politics* (New York: Columbia University Press, 1982), p. 162.

4. Evelyn P. Stevens, "Protest Movements in an Authoritarian Regime," *Comparative Politics*, 7:3 (April 1975), pp. 361–382.

5. See Skilling and Griffiths, *Interest Groups*; the essays by Frederick C. Barghoorn and Skilling in Robert A. Dahl, *Regimes and Oppositions* (New Haven, Conn.: Yale University Press, 1973); Roman Kolkowicz, "Interest Groups in Soviet Politics," *Comparative Politics*, 2:3 (April 1970), pp. 445–472; and Chapter Thirteen of this text.

6. Richard Rose, *Influencing Voters* (London: Faber & Faber, 1967), pp. 110–114. On associational group activity in Britain more generally, see J. J. Richardson and A.F.G. Jordan, *Governing under Pressure* (Oxford: Martin Robinson, 1979).

7. E. E. Schattschneider, *The Semi-Sovereign People* (Hinsdale, Ill.: Dryden Press, 1960), p. 30; also see Grant McConnell, *Private Power and American Democracy* (New York: Alfred A. Knopf, 1966).

8. Sidney Verba and Norman H. Nie, *Participation in America* (New York: Harper & Row, 1972), ch. 11; Sidney Verba, Norman H. Nie, and Jae-on Kim, *Participation and Political Equality: A Seven-Nation Study* (New York: Cambridge University Press, 1978), chs. 6, 7.

9. Mancur Olson, *The Logic of Collective Action* (Cambridge, Mass.: Harvard University Press, 1965).

10. Gabriel A. Almond and Sidney Verba, *The Civic Culture* (Princeton, N.J.: Princeton University

Press, 1963), pp. 300–322; William Kornhauser, *The Politics of Mass Society* (Glencoe, Ill.: Free Press, 1959).

11. For cross-national comparisons, see the essays by Gerhard Lembruch and by David R. Cameron in John Goldthorpe, ed., *Order and Conflict in Contemporary Capitalism* (Oxford: Oxford University Press, 1984); Peter J. Katzenstein, *Small States in World Markets* (Ithaca, N.Y.: Cornell University Press, 1985); Philippe Schmitter, "Interest Intermediation and Regime Governability," in Suzanne Berger, ed., *Organizing Interests in Western Europe* (New York: Cambridge University Press, 1981), ch. 12.

12. K. Newton and D. S. Morris, "British Interest Group Theory Reexamined," *Comparative Politics*, 7 (July 1975), pp. 577–595; also see Richardson and Jordan, *Governing under Pressure*.

13. James Q. Wilson, "The Strategy of Protest," *Journal of Conflict Resolution*, 5:3 (September 1961), pp. 291–303; Michael Lipsky, "Protest as a Political Resource," *American Political Science Review* 62:4 (December 1968), pp. 1144–1158.

14. See the essays in Russell J. Dalton and Manfred Kuechler, *Challenging the Political Order: New Social and Political Movements in Western Democracies* (New York: Oxford University Press, 1990).

15. Ted Robert Gurr, "A Comparative Study of Civil Strife," in Hugh David Graham and Ted Robert Gurr, eds., *The History of Violence in America* (New York: Bantam Press, 1969), pp. 462–463; more generally, see Ted Robert Gurr, *Why Men Rebel* (Princeton, N.J.: Princeton University Press, 1970).

16. See James F. Short and Marvin E. Wolfgang, eds., *Collective Violence* (Chicago: Aldine–Atherton, 1972); and see Anthony Oberschall, *Social Conflict and Social Movements* (Englewood Cliffs, N.J.: Prentice–Hall, 1973).

17. Ann Ruth Wilner, "Public Protest in Indonesia," in Ivo K. Feierabend, Rosalind Feierabend, and Ted Robert Gurr, eds., *Anger, Violence, and Politics* (Englewood Cliffs, N.J.: Prentice–Hall, 1972), pp. 355–357.

18. James Payne, "Peru: The Politics of Structured Violence," in Feierabend, Feierabend, and Gurr, eds., *Anger, Violence, and Politics*, p. 360.

19. Suzanne Berger, *Peasants Against Politics* (Cambridge, Mass.: Harvard University Press, 1972).

20. On violence and democratic survival, see G. Bingham Powell, Jr., *Contemporary Democracies: Participation, Stability and Violence* (Cambridge, Mass.: Harvard University Press, 1982), ch. 8, and the contributions to Juan J. Linz and Alfred Stepan, eds., *The Breakdown of Democratic Regimes* (Baltimore: Johns Hopkins University Press, 1978).

21. See Barghoorn and Skilling in Dahl, *Regimes and Oppositions*.

22. Edward C. Banfield, *The Moral Basis of a Backward Society* (New York: Free Press, 1958).

23. Robert Putnam, Roberto Leonardi, Raffaella Y. Nanetti, and Franco Pavoncello, "Explaining Institutional Success: The Case of Italian Regional Government," *American Political Science Review*, 77 (March 1983), pp. 55–74.

24. Ronald Inglehart, *Culture Shift in Advanced Industrial Societies* (Princeton, N.J.: Princeton University Press, 1990), pp. 34–36. Also see Almond and Verba, *The Civic Culture*, ch. 11.

25. Timothy Garton Ash, "The Opposition," in *The New York Review of Books*, October 13, 1988, p. 3. For a broader and more comprehensive treatment of the emergence of interest groups and political movements in Eastern Europe in 1988–1989, see his *The Magic Lantern* (New York: Random House, 1990).

26. This discussion of the new social movements and the issues they raise draws heavily on Dalton and Kuechler, *Challenging the Political Order*.

CHAPTER 6

INTEREST
AGGREGATION AND
POLITICAL PARTIES

NTEREST aggregation is the activity in which the demands and resources of individuals and groups are combined into significant policy proposals. The proposals become significant as they gain the backing of substantial political resources. Political parties are particularly adept at interest aggregation. They nominate candidates who stand for a set of policies, and then they try to build support for those candidates. Modern political parties first took shape as excluded groups strove to compete for power and dominant groups sought public support to sustain themselves.

In a democratic system a number of parties compete to mobilize the backing of interest groups and voters. In authoritarian systems one party tries to mobilize citizens' support for its policies and candidates. In both systems interest aggregation may well take place within the parties, as party conventions or party leaders hear the demands of different groups — unions, consumers, party factions, business organizations — and create policy alternatives. In authoritarian systems, however, the process is more covert and controlled.

Taking the structural-functional approach draws our attention to the fact that parties may perform many different functions and that many different structures may perform interest aggregation. Parties frequently affect political socialization, shaping the political culture as they organize thinking about political issues and strive to build support for their ideologies, specific issue positions, and candidates. Parties affect political recruitment as they mobilize voters and are involved in selecting would-be officeholders. They articulate interests of their own and transmit the demands of others. Governing parties are also involved in making public policy and even overseeing its implementation and adjudication. But the distinctive and defining goal of a political party, its mobilization of support for policies and candidates, is especially related to interest aggregation.

Even a single individual can evaluate a variety of claims and considerations in adopting a policy position. If he or she controls substantial political resources, as an influential party leader or a military dictator, his or her personal role in interest aggregation may be considerable. But large national political systems usually develop more specialized organizations for the specific purpose of aggregating interests and resources behind policies. Political parties are just such organizations. In this chapter we compare the role of parties with that of other structures in interest aggregation.

INTEREST GROUPS AND INTEREST AGGREGATION

A well-nigh universal political structure is clientelism, or patron–client relations. It was the defining principle of feudalism. The king and his lords, the lord and his knights, the knight and his serfs and tenants, all were bound by ties of personal dependence and loyalty. The political machines of Boss Tweed of New York, John F. ("Honey Fitz") Fitzgerald of Boston, Richard Daley of Chicago, and the like were similarly bound together by patronage and loyalty. But patron–clientelism is not confined to relationships cemented by patronage only. Every president of the United States has had his circle of personal confidants, his "brain trust," his "California mafia," bound to their chief by ideological and policy propensities as well as by interests in jobs and power.

Kremlinologists — those scholars and journalists who follow shifts in personnel in Soviet politics — have identified for us the personal networks of the various Soviet leaders, showing us how the rise of a Khrushchev, a Brezhnev, or a Gorbachev is accompanied by the rise of a personal network from the same region or the same governmental agency. Using the analogy of mountain climbing for the rise (and fall) of political leaders in the Soviet Union, some Soviet specialists have referred to these personal networks as *Seilschaften* ("roped parties of climbers").

Contemporary patron–client theory was pioneered by students of East, Southeast, and South Asia, where this phenomenon seems to dominate the political processes of such countries as the Philippines, Indonesia, Thailand, Japan, and India. It is related to recruitment to political office, interest aggregation, policymaking, and policy implementing. Indeed, it would seem to be like the cell in biology or the atom in physics — the primitive structure of all politics, the human interactions out of which larger and more complicated political structures are composed.[1]

Domination of interest aggregation by patron–client ties, however, typically means a static pattern of overall policy formation. In such a political system, the ability to mobilize political resources behind unified policies of social change or to respond to crises will be difficult, because doing so depends on ever-shifting agreements between many factional leaders. In modern societies, as citizens become aware of larger collective interests and have the resources and skills to work for them, personal networks are regulated, replaced, and incorporated within broader organizations. As we see in Table 6.1 extensive performance of interest aggregation by such personal networks is confined mainly to the least economically developed countries.

The subtle dividing line between interest articulation and aggregation can easily be crossed by organizations with powerful resources. Although often operating merely to express demands and support major political contenders, such as parties, associational groups can occasionally wield sufficient resources to become contenders in their own right. The power of the labor unions within the British Labour party, for example, has rested on the unions' ability to develop coherent policy positions and mobilize the votes of their members to support those positions. In many European nations, national decision-making bodies have been set up outside the normal legislative channels, bodies with substantial authority to make national policies in special areas, such as the Dutch Social and Economic Council or the Austrian chamber system. These bodies incorporate labor unions' and employer associations' representatives.

As we discussed in Chapter Five, the set of arrangements called democratic corporatism has in some countries been especially effective in aggregating the interests of both labor and business groups into economic policies controlling unemployment and inflation. These arrangements include continuous political bargaining between large, relatively centralized labor and business interest groups, political parties, and state bureaucracies. They have often been closely linked to political domination by a democratic socialist political party. Such corporatist systems then, include and link organizations that in other political systems play very different, often-antagonistic, roles.[2]

Institutional groups like bureaucratic and military factions can also be important interest aggregators. Indeed, the bureaucracy acts as a kind of interest aggrega-

TABLE 6.1
STRUCTURES PERFORMING INTEREST AGGREGATION IN SELECTED CONTEMPORARY NATIONS[a]

Country	Extensiveness of Interest Aggregation by Actor				
	Patron–client networks	Associational groups	Competitive political parties	Noncompetitive parties	Military forces
United States	Low	Moderate	High		Low
West Germany	Low	High	High		Low
Japan	Moderate	High	High		Low
France	Low	Moderate	High		Low
Great Britain	Low	High	High		Low
USSR	Low	Low	Low	Moderate	Moderate
Mexico	Moderate	Moderate	Low	High	Low
Nigeria	High	Low	Low		High
Egypt	High	Low	Low	Moderate	Moderate
China	Low	Low	Low	High	Moderate
India	High	Moderate	Moderate		Low
Tanzania	High	Low	Low	High	Low

[a]Extensiveness of interest aggregation rated as low, moderate, or high only. Rating refers to broad-level performance and may vary in different issue areas and at different times.

tor in most societies. Although established primarily for the implementation of policies whose broad outline is set by higher authorities, the bureaucracy may negotiate with a variety of groups to find their preferences or mobilize their support. Agencies may even be "captured" by interest groups and used to support their demands. The desire of bureaucrats to expand their organizations by the discovery of new problems and policies, as well as to increase their ability to solve problems in their special areas, often leads them to create client support.

Military interest groups, with their special control over the instruments of violence, have great potential power as interest aggregators. If the legitimacy of the government breaks down and all groups feel free to use coercion and violence to shape policies, then the united military can usually be decisive. One study showed that in the 1960s almost 40 percent of nations were confronted with military coup attempts, and these were at least partially successful in changing leaders or policy in about a third of the nations. Less than half of these coup attempts, however, were concerned with general political issues and public policy. Most military coups seem motivated by grievances and the military's fears that their professional or career interests will be slighted or overlooked by civil authorities.[3]

COMPETITIVE PARTY SYSTEMS AND INTEREST AGGREGATION

In analyzing parties it is especially important to keep in mind the sharp distinction between *competitive party systems*, seeking primarily to build on electoral support, and noncompetitive or authoritarian parties. This distinction does not depend on the closeness of electoral victory, or even on the number of parties. It depends on the primacy of winning votes as a prerequisite for control of policymaking, on one hand, and on the possibility for several parties to form and organize to seek those votes, on the other. Thus, a party can win most of the votes in a given area or region, or even a given national election, but nonetheless be a competitive party. Its goals involve winning elections, either as a primary objective or as a means for policymaking; its dominance at the polls is always subject to challenge by other parties; its organization thus involves arrangements for finding out what voters want and getting supporters involved.

In analyzing the role of competitive parties in interest aggregation, we need to consider not only the individual party, but also the structure of parties, electorates, electoral laws, and policymaking bodies that interact in a competitive party system. Typically, interest aggregation in a competitive party system takes place at one or more levels: within the individual parties, as the party chooses candidates and adopts policy proposals; through electoral competition, as voters give varying amounts of support to different parties; and through bargaining and coalition building in the legislature or executive.

Competitive Parties and Elections

At the first level, individual parties develop a set of policy positions. Typically, these positions are believed to have the backing of large or cohesive groups of voters. In systems with only two parties, it is important for a party to win a majority, so targeting the "center" of the electorate is crucial strategically.[4] In systems with many political parties, where none has much chance of winning a majority, it may be more valuable to seek a distinctive and cohesive electoral base. Party policy positions may well reflect the continuing linkages between the party and interest groups, such as labor unions, business associations, or religious and ethnic groups.[5] Historical issue commitments and ideological traditions also play a role.

The procedure for developing policy positions varies greatly from country to country and from party to party. In the United States the national party conventions are the focus of developing policy positions, both through the formation of party platforms and, perhaps more importantly, through the selection of candidates committed to certain policies. In other countries, more often party platforms or manifestos are issued by centralized party program committees or in speeches by party leaders.[6] Whatever the procedure, the final party position is usually a mixture of strategic electioneering and aggregation of interests expressed within the party.

The parties then offer their chosen candidates and policies to the electorate. They not only present candidates, but they also attempt to publicize them and mobilize electoral support through rallies, mass media promotion, door-to-door campaigning, and systematic efforts to locate sympathetic voters and get them to the polls. In the elections citizens directly participate in interest aggregation by voting for different parties. Such votes are converted into legislative seats and, in presidential systems control of the chief executive, by the electoral rules. In the last thirty years political scientists have done a great deal of research on the dynamics of citizens' voting decisions, including the role played by issue and ideological positions, group–party connections, learned "identification" with parties, and evaluations of the performance of the current incumbents.[7]

Figure 6.1 offers a comparative "snapshot" of interest aggregation by parties and voters in several democratic countries. It uses the device of the left–right scale, which in many countries and for many voters acts as a kind of summary of the issues that voters find most important. Voters are shown a scale of numbers, with 1 identified as left (or liberal in the U.S.) and 10 identified as right (or conservative in the U.S.). They are then asked to place the parties and themselves on this continuum. In Figure 6.1 we see the left–right scale and where the voters for each party placed themselves on the scale. The height of the column above the scale shows what percentage of the electorate voted for that party.

Several interesting differences between *party-electoral aggregation* in different party systems are illustrated by Figure 6.1. First, we can see that in the countries at the top of the figure, especially in the United States, most voters support only a few parties. Moreover, those parties are close to the center of the continuum, where the bulk of voters place themselves. The left–right "gap" between the average party supporters is rather small. Democrats are somewhat to the left and Republicans somewhat to the right, but on average they are not far apart. If we saw the full distribution of voters, rather than just the averages, we would see that there is a lot of overlap between the self-placement of voters supporting the respective parties. This aggregation implies concentration of political resources behind the

Competitive election campaigns draw citizens into the process of interest aggregation in democracies. In Nicaragua opposition presidential candidate Violete Chamorro rallies her supporters during the 1990 campaign, eventually won by her party.

FIGURE 6.1
INTEREST AGGREGATION BY COMPETITIVE PARTIES AND VOTERS:
PERCENT OF VOTERS FOR EACH PARTY AND THEIR AVERAGE
SELF-PLACEMENT ON LEFT–RIGHT SCALE IN LEGISLATIVE ELECTIONS
IN FIVE COUNTRIES

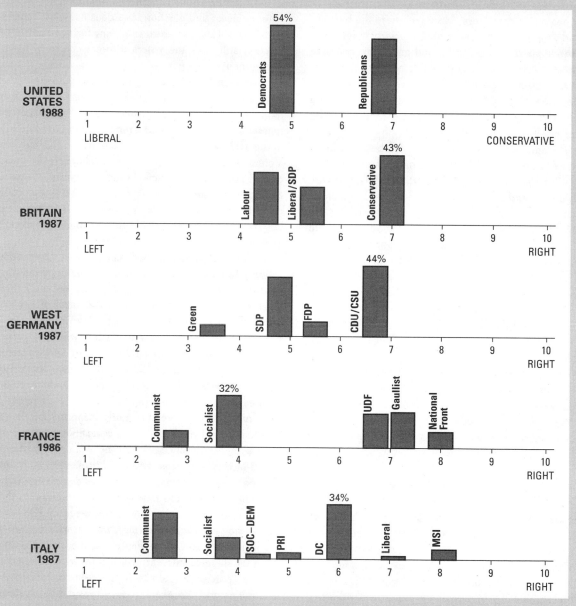

Source: Surveys of voters in Britain, Germany, France, and Italy from *Eurobarometer 25,* April 1986. USA from 1986 Gallup Survey reported in Harold W. Stanley and Richard G. Niemi, *Vital Statistics on American Politics* (Washington, D.C.: CQ Press, 1988), p. 131; USA uses Liberal and Conservative Instead of Left and Right; adjusted 9 point scale.

"centrist" policies of both parties.

In the countries toward the bottom of the figure, especially in Italy, many parties receive support from voters. The Communist and the Christian Democrat parties have the most support; many other parties receive significant voting support as well. The figure for Italy has many short bars. Moreover, here the bars are spread well across the spectrum. Each party is aggregating the support of a more limited and more cohesive group of voters. The ideological gap between the rightmost and left-most parties is quite great. The dispersed aggregation of the party-electoral system means that a much more diverse range of ideological interests will be represented in the legislature.

Britain, Germany, and France fall between these more extreme cases. Britain looks more like the United States in its pattern of voter support, but the parties are further apart and the smaller Liberal/Social Democratic Alliance falls between them. Germany looks rather like Britain, except that the center party is smaller and there is a notable Green party on the left. France looks more like Italy. But France has one interesting feature that sets it apart from other countries: there is no party whose supporters' average position is near the middle. There are still substantial numbers of French voters whose position is toward the center, although fewer than in the United States, Germany, and Britain, but the party offerings pull them sharply to the right or the left. If we were to look at the offerings of the parties as placed by expert observers on a similar scale, we would see that they gave voters no option of center choice.[8] This aggregation reflects and encourages the confrontation between coalitions of right and left that has been typical of Fifth Republic France.

Competitive Parties in Government

If a competitive party wins control of the legislature and the executive, it will be able to pass and implement its policies. Sometimes this control will emerge directly from the electoral process, as a single party wins a majority of the vote. Far more often, no party wins a majority of votes. In many countries the working of the election laws benefits some parties at the expense of others. If these distortions are sufficient, less than 50 percent of the vote may be converted into more than 50 percent of the legislative seats. In Britain, none of the legislature majorities won by either the Labour party or the Conservatives in the 1970s and 1980s were based on support of a majority of voters. For example, Mrs.

Thatcher's Conservative party won a solid majority of legislative seats in 1983 and 1987 with the backing of only about 42 percent of the voters. The quarter of the electorate supporting the center parties received only a handful of legislative seats.[9]

In other countries, the combination of parties, voter choices, and election laws does not create single-party majorities, but *party coalitions* formed before the election still offer the voters a direct choice of future governments. The parties in alliance encourage mutual support from the electorate, often taking advantage of special provisions of voting laws, and agree that if they jointly win a majority of legislative seats they will govern together. In Germany and France, many governments in the 1970s and 1980s came to power in this fashion. Voters are thus given a major role in choosing the direction of government policy through party and electoral aggregation. Single-party and, sometimes, preelection coalition governments also provide voters rather clear targets if they choose to hold the incumbents accountable for their performance in office.

The importance of such majoritarian aggregation through the election process has been demonstrated by studies showing that very often parties do fulfill their electoral promises when they gain control of government. For example, British parties take pride in their record of manifesto implementation while in office. When Socialist and Social Democratic governments have come to power in Europe, they have tended to expand the size and efforts of the governmental sector. Studies also suggest that Republicans and Democrats in the United States have been fairly responsible in keeping their promises.[10] However, opposition parties that have been out of office a long time and developed programs of radical change often find these difficult to implement when they come to power, as demonstrated by the experiences of the new left-wing governments that came to power in France and in Greece in 1981.

If no party or preelection coalition wins control of the legislature and the executive at the election, then the final stage of interest aggregation by parties takes place as parties bargain to form coalitions within the assemblies and the executive. In presidential systems this bargaining between parties may arise when one party gains control of the executive and the other gains control of the legislature, as has been true in the United States in most of the years since 1968. In the United States, as in Japan, the complexity of the bargaining is enhanced by the lack of internal cohesion or discipline of the parties. Aggregation must take place between party factions within and across party lines.

In parliamentary systems, when no party wins a majority, the result is either a minority government or a majority coalition of several parties. In the minority case, the executive must continually bargain with other parties to get policies adopted, and even to remain in office.[11] In the case of majority coalitions, the bargaining will be focused primarily on coalition partners, who may divide up the policy areas or develop some other processes of aggregation. Such coalitions tend to be fairly stable in some countries, such as the Netherlands, and much less so in others, such as Finland and Italy, depending on the party makeup of the legislature and other factors.[12] In any case the process of interest aggregation continues through the parties in the legislature and executive. The continuation of interest aggregation at this stage is also enhanced when different parties gain control of different houses of the legislature (as in the United States in 1980–1986 or frequently in Germany in the 1970s and 1980s), or when parties share power in strong legislative committees, or when internal party factions limit party discipline.

The factors that encourage less decisive electoral aggregation and more aggregation within the legislature and the executive have both costs and benefits.[13] On one hand, the connection between voter choice and government policy is made less direct, which can be frustrating and disillusioning to voters. Moreover, the fact that interest aggregation is still going on so "late" in the political process, that new coalitions of interests and resources are constantly emerging on different issues, is confusing to citizens (and even informed observers). It is difficult to assign clear responsibility for government policy when power to shape it is shifting and widely shared. Thus, the value of the vote is lessened as an instrument either directly to shape policy through electing future governments or to punish parties clearly responsible for undesirable policy. Elections as instruments of accountability and manifesto choice are diminished by shifting coalitions after the election.

On the other side, this continuing aggregation can mean that voters for *all* parties, not only the election winners, will have their elected representatives taking part effectively in interest aggregation and policymaking. Such a representative connection can be especially important for citizen minorities. All citizens are minorities on some issues, and some are notable minorities on many issues. If the rules of election and representation are fair, the possibility of continuing influence on interest aggregation between elections is a valuable protection for minority interests. Finally, even elected governments that won a majority of votes, which few elected governments have, will typically not have majority support for their policy proposals on all issues. British politics offers a number of examples (such as the Labour party's renationalization of the steel industry in 1966) of majority parties implementing manifesto promises that public opinion polls showed were not supported by a majority of voters. So a more flexible pattern of interest aggregation at the legislative level, if based on fair representation, may be helpful to many, and not just the minorities. Bargaining between equitably represented groups may even enhance the possibility that policies will reflect different citizen majorities on different issues. Elections as instruments of representation may be enhanced by postelection aggregation, even though they are diminished as instruments of accountability.

Classifying Competitive Party Systems

In Figure 6.2 competitive party systems are classified by type, with examples given for each type. We distinguish between *majoritarian* and multiparty systems and rate them according to the relative antagonism between parties.[14] The number and strength of parties influences legislative activity and the business of forming government. The majoritarian systems either are dominated by just two parties, as in the United States, or they have two substantial parties and election laws that usually create legislative majorities for one of them, as in Britain and New Zealand. The purely *multiparty systems* have combinations of parties, voter support, and election laws that virtually ensure that no single party will win a legislative majority. Interest aggregation by party bargaining after the election will be critical for shaping policy directions. Germany and France, as we have already mentioned, are multiparty systems in which voter support of party coalitions at the electoral level has major impact on forming governments and policies.

A large number of parties does not itself cause government instability. More important is the degree of antagonism or polarization among the parties. We refer to a system as *consensual* if the parties commanding most of the legislative seats are not too far apart on policies and have a reasonable amount of trust in each other and in the political system. These are typically party systems like those shown toward the top of Figure 6.1. If the legislature is dominated by parties that are very far apart

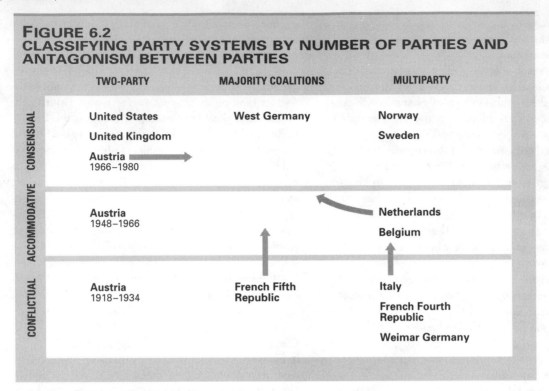

FIGURE 6.2
CLASSIFYING PARTY SYSTEMS BY NUMBER OF PARTIES AND ANTAGONISM BETWEEN PARTIES

on issues or are highly distrustful and antagonistic toward each other and the political system, we would classify that party system as *conflictual*. If a party system has mixed characteristics — that is, both consensual and conflictual — we classify it as *consociational* or *accommodative*. Arend Lijphart in particular used those terms to describe party systems in which political leaders are able to bridge the intense differences between antagonistic voters.[15]

The United States and Britain are contemporary examples of consensual majoritarian systems, although they differ in the degree of consensus. They are not perfect two-party systems. Britain, in addition to the Labour and Conservative parties, has several parties of the center, the Scottish Nationalist party, and a smaller Welsh party. However, in Britain a single party usually wins a legislative majority and controls the legislature and the executive with disciplined party voting. The United States has had third-party movements and candidates intermittently. Shifting orientations of presidential party candidates alter the degree of consensus somewhat from election to election. Moreover, the loose cohesion of American parties and the frequently divided control of legislature and executive lead to postelection

bargaining that is in some ways similar to consensual multiparty systems. Germany has two large parties, and an alliance between one of those parties and the Free Democrats has usually won legislative control. Good examples of consensual multiparty systems have been found in Norway and Sweden. In these countries there are four or five parties — socialists, agrarian/center, liberals, conservatives, small communist movements. The three or four larger parties have usually been able to construct long-lived governments, singly or in coalition.

Austria between 1918 and 1934 is the best example of a majoritarian conflictual system. Antagonism between the Socialist party and the other parties was so intense that in the mid-1930s it produced a brief civil war. This conflict resulted in suppression of the Socialist party, the collapse of democratic government, and the creation of an authoritarian one-party system. The case of Austria also illustrates how change can take place in party systems over time. After World War II the leaders of the two major parties negotiated an elaborate coalition agreement of mutual power sharing — and mutual checks and suspicion — as the country sought to control its conflicts while rebuilding its economy and seeking freedom from occupying Soviet forces in the Eastern regions. After some twenty years of the consociational "Grand Coalition," party antagonism had declined to the point that more normal majority politics could be tolerated, although some consociational elements remained. In recent years the Austrian party system has appeared to be closer to the more ordinary consensual system, with some single-party majorities and some coalitions.

France, Italy, and Weimar Germany have been good examples of conflictual multiparty systems, with powerful Communist parties on the left and conservative or fascist movements on the right. Cabinets had to be formed out of centrist movements, which were themselves divided on many issues, thus making for instability, poor government performance, and loss of citizen confidence in democracy. These factors contributed to the overthrow of democracy in Weimar Germany and the collapse of the Fourth French Republic. More recently, the French and Italian party systems have become somewhat less antagonistic. Some signs of accommodation appeared in Italy in the 1970s when the Communists rallied together with other parties against Red Brigade terrorism, and in France when the Communist party lost ground to the more moderate Socialist party.

The mixed system we call consociational arises in countries in which considerable conflict and antagonism exists on the basis of religion, ethnicity, or social class. Through historical experience the leaderships of competing movements in such countries as the Netherlands have found bases of accommodation that provide mutual guarantees to the various groups. In the consociational systems of Austria and Lebanon after World War II, groups — the socialists and Catholics in Austria, and the Christians and Muslims in Lebanon — worked out a set of understandings making it possible for stable governments to be formed. Austria's accommodation was based on a two-party system, and Lebanon's on many small, personalistic religious parties. These two examples have gone in opposite directions in recent years. Since 1966 Austria has begun to move toward a consensual two-party system, while since 1975 Lebanon has been penetrated and fragmented by the Middle Eastern conflict and fallen victim to civil war.

All this suggests that, although the number of parties is of some importance in relation to stability, the degree of antagonism among parties is of greater significance. Where multiparty systems consist of relatively moderate antagonists, stability and effective performance seem possible. Where systems consist of highly antagonistic elements, collapse and civil war are ever-present possibilities, regardless of the number of parties. When crises develop, the commitment of the leaders of major political parties to work together to defend democracy can be critical for its survival. It may be easier to arrange such commitments in a multiparty, representational setting.[16] Prewar Austria, Chile, and the Weimar Republic of Germany are tragic examples of the absence or failure of such cooperation. Some of the new democracies of Eastern Europe and Latin America and Asia, especially those divided by language or ethnicity, face similar challenges.

AUTHORITARIAN PARTY SYSTEMS

Authoritarian party systems are also specialized interest aggregation structures. They deliberately attempt to develop policy proposals and to mobilize support for them, but they do so in a completely different way from the competitive party systems we have been discussing. With authoritarian party systems, aggregation takes place within the ranks of the party or in interactions with business groups, landowners, and institutional groups in the bureaucracy or military. The citizens have no opportunity to shape aggregation by choosing between party alternatives.

Authoritarian party systems can be distinguished on a range of exclusiveness, according to the tightness of control from the top down within the party and the degree of control over other groups by the party. At one extreme is the *totalitarian party*, which insists on total control over political resources by the party leadership. It recognizes no legitimate interest aggregation by groups within the party, nor does it permit any free activity by social groups, citizens, or other government agencies. As we discussed in Chapter Five, even interest groups are totally controlled. The totalitarian party tries to preempt any autonomous interest articulation by social groups. It penetrates the entire society and mobilizes support for policies developed at the top. These policies are legitimated by an encompassing political ideology that claims to know the true interests of the citizens, whatever their immediate preferences.[18]

Exclusive Governing Parties

Few parties have long maintained the absolute central control, penetration, and ideological mobilization of the totalitarian model. However, the ruling Communist parties of the USSR before 1985, of Eastern Europe before 1989, and of China and Cuba today certainly fall toward that end of the authoritarian party scale. The Chinese regime, for example, has not typically recognized the legitimacy of any large internal groups. Interest articulation by individuals, within bounds, may be permitted; the mobilization of wide support before the top elite has decided on policy is not permitted.[18]

Even at early stages of totalitarian mobilization, the exclusive governing party may be the focus of more internal aggregation at various levels than is commonly recognized or legitimately permitted. Internally, various groups may coalesce around such interests as region or industry, or behind leaders of policy factions. Generational differences or differences of temperament may distinguish hard-liners and soft-liners on ranges of policy. Either openly or covertly, beneath the supposedly united front power struggles may erupt in times of crisis, with different leaders mobilizing backing for themselves and their positions. Succession crises are particularly likely to generate such power struggles, as demonstrated at the death of Stalin in the USSR and at the death of Mao Zedong in China.

Whether thoroughly "totalitarian" or merely as *exclusive governing parties*, the penetrative and controlling single parties can play important roles in mobilizing support for policies. An unchallenged ideological focus provides legitimacy and coherence; the party is used to penetrate and organize most social structures in the name of that ideology and in accordance with centralized policies. As these parties have aged, many have seemed to enter a stage of more "mature" totalitarianism that maintains penetration and control, but places less emphasis on mobilization. Finally, as shown by events in the Soviet Union and Eastern Europe, if and when the party leaders lose faith in the unifying ideology, it may be difficult to maintain party coherence.

As an instrument designed for unified mobilization, the exclusive governing party has seemed attractive to many leaders committed to massive social change. The party that successfully mobilized a colonial people behind independence, for example, might be used to penetrate and change an underdeveloped society. As the experiences of many new nations have shown, however, the creation of an exclusive and penetrating governing party that could be used for social transformation is extremely difficult. The protracted guerrilla warfare that contributed to the development of the Chinese and Cuban parties is not easily replicated.

The exclusive governing parties attempted in some African states have had limited penetrative capacity. Kwame Nkrumah's widely publicized effort in Ghana was easily toppled by a military coup. By 1990 the loss of confidence in Marxist-Leninist ideology and in the Soviet model of totalitarian development led all eight of the African regimes that had once invoked it to abandon that approach.[19] Even in China the party has been forced several times to rely on the army, even on coalitions of regional army commanders, to sustain its control.

Inclusive Governing Parties

Throughout the Third World, especially in nations with notable ethnic and tribal divisions, the more successful authoritarian systems have seemed to be *inclusive authoritarian party systems*, rather than exclusive. That is, they have recognized the autonomy of social, cultural, and economic groups and have tried to incorporate them or bargain with them, rather than penetrate and remake them. In the more successful African one-party systems, such as Kenya and Tanzania, aggregation around personalistic, factional, and tribal-oriented groups has been permitted within decentralized party organizations.[20] Even before the current crisis of international communism, the indigenous communism in Yugoslavia had taken a more decentralized and corporatist form, as a matter of policy and in recognition of the party's linkage to peasant supporters.[21]

These types of party systems are sometimes called authoritarian corporatist systems. Like the democratic corporatist systems (see Chapter Five), they encourage formation of large organized interest groups whose representatives can bargain with each other and the state. Unlike the democratic corporatist systems, however, these authoritarian party systems provide no political resources directly to the citizens. Efforts at independent protest and mobilization outside the official channels are suppressed. They do permit some autonomous formation of demands within the ranks of the party and by groups associated with it.

The degree of legitimate aggregation permitted below the top leadership in the inclusive authoritarian systems may be substantial and take many forms. The party will typically try to gather various social groups under the general party umbrella and also negotiate with more or less autonomous groups and institutions outside the party. Some of these inclusive parties have attempted aggressive programs of social change. Others have been primarily arenas for aggregating various social and institutional interests. At the extreme of loosest and least exclusive control, such parties may even permit other parties to offer candidates in elections, as long as they have no real chance of winning.

The oldest and one of the most elaborately inclusive authoritarian parties has been the Partido Revolucionario Institucional (PRI) in Mexico. The PRI dominated the political process and gave other parties no realistic chances of winning elections for over fifty years. The PRI maintained general popular support after the creation of a broad coalition within the party by Lazaro Cardenas in the 1930s; it was also careful to control the counting of the ballots. Its actions were not shaped by electoral competition, at least until the late 1980s. But the party incorporated many associational groups within it, with separate sectors for labor, agrarian, and popular interests. While some discontent was suppressed, other dissatisfied individuals were deliberately enticed into the party. The party also gave informal recognition to rather distinct and well-organized political factions grouped behind such figures as some of the ex-presidents.

Various Mexican leaders mobilized their factions within the PRI and in other important groups not directly affiliated with it, such as big business interests. Bargaining was particularly important every six years when the party chose a new presidential nominee. The legal provision that the incumbent president could not succeed himself guaranteed some turnover of elites and may have facilitated more legitimate and open internal bargaining. Recently, however, rising discontent has emphasized the difficulties in coordinating all interests through the party. Those of the urban and rural poor who have not shared in Mexico's general growth have joined with others who want a more fully democratic system. Mexico seems at long last to be moving toward genuine party competition. (See Chapter Fifteen.)

The relative stability of some inclusive authoritarian party systems does not hide the frequent failures to build stable authoritarian party systems. In many countries the governing authoritarian party coexists in uneasy and unstable coalition with the armed forces and the civilian bureaucracy. In some countries the party has become relatively unimportant window dressing for a military regime or personal tyranny.[22] The loss of confidence in authoritarian party solutions to problems of economic development and ethnic conflict has seriously weakened their ability to aggregate interests. As the memories of a unifying struggle against colonialism have faded, and the leaders of independence movements have departed or been forced from office, the ties of ideology and experience that held such parties together have unraveled. This trend has been encouraged by the general loss of legitimacy of the single-party model. In some cases the failure of authoritarian parties has permitted the emergence of party competition. In others the consequence has been enhanced resort to naked coercion by government agencies or private forces, with the military serving as final arbiter.

MILITARY FORCES AND INTEREST AGGREGATION

We cannot leave our consideration of structures performing interest aggregation without discussing *military governments*. The last decades have seen the overthrow of many of the single-party and multiparty regimes established in the new nations after independence. In some cases one party regime was replaced with another. More frequently, the new regime was based on the military as the final policymaker, or at least as one of the most important interest aggregators. Even where civilian rule was later reestablished, the experience of successful military intervention seems to interject the military as a long-time contender. In Brazil the military played a crucial interest aggregation role in the democratic processes before 1964 and played the dominant aggregating and policymaking roles for twenty years after. In Nigeria, the collapse of democracy into civil war resulted in military rule until 1979. In 1983 another military coup deposed a democratically elected Nigerian president. In Ghana the overthrow of Nkrumah was followed by military rule interspersed with experimentation with competitive parties. In Chile military government was the rule for fifteen years. And in many other nations, including Syria, Pakistan, Indonesia, Guinea, Ethiopia, Paraguay, Haiti, and Argentina, the military has been the dominant, or at least a major interest aggregator. In fact, the armed forces are the dominant interest aggregation structure in about one quarter of the world's regimes, including about half of those in Africa. (See Figure 6.3 and Chapter Sixteen below.)

The military's virtual monopoly of coercive resources gives it great potential power as a political contender. Thus, when agreement fails on aggregation either through democratic or authoritarian party systems, the military may emerge by default as the only force able

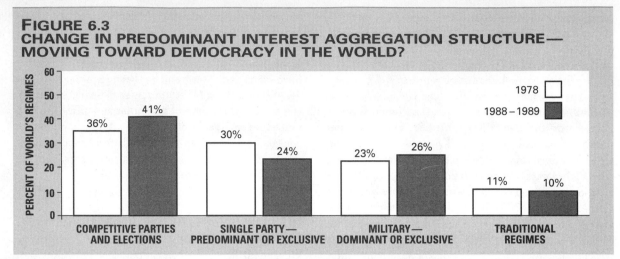

FIGURE 6.3
CHANGE IN PREDOMINANT INTEREST AGGREGATION STRUCTURE—
MOVING TOWARD DEMOCRACY IN THE WORLD?

Source: Adapted from Raymond D. Gastil, *Freedom in the World 1979* (New York: Freedom House, 1979), pp. 40–41; and Raymond D. Gastil, *Freedom in the World 1988–1989* (New York: Freedom House, 1989), pp. 70–71. To reflect events in late 1989, East Germany, Poland, Czechoslovakia, Hungary, and Yugoslavia were moved from single-party to competitive party-election regimes.

to maintain orderly government. The soldiers then remain the basic force underpinning the personal tyranny of a civilian president or a military council. Or the armed forces may use coercive power to further institutional or even ideological objectives. Military rulers may use control of the state to attempt to create military and/or bureaucratic versions of authoritarian corporatism, linking organized groups and the state bureaucracy with the military as final arbiter of disagreement. They may undertake "defensive" modernization in alliance with business groups or even undertake more radical restructuring modernization.[23] In Latin America almost all the corporatist versions of authoritarian aggregation have had a strong military component and only rarely a dominating role for the authoritarian party.

The major limitation on the armed forces in interest aggregation is that their internal structures are not designed to mobilize support across a range of issues or outside the coercive arena. The military is primarily organized to facilitate downward processing of commands involving the implementation of coercion. It is not set up to aggregate internal differences and affect a compromise, or to mobilize wide support of all components behind policy. Moreover, military organizations are not easily adapted to rally or communicate with social groups outside the command hierarchy. Thus, the military lacks those advantages in mobilizing support held by party systems. These internal limitations may be less serious when the military is dealing with common grievances and putting pressure on—or seizing power from

—incumbent authorities. These limitations become a major problem, however, when a military government needs to mobilize backing for, say, economic development policy. Legitimate authority and communication of the regime's political and ideological goals to many social sectors are then needed. For these reasons military governments frequently prove unstable, are forced to share power with other institutions, or encourage the formation of cooperating authoritarian parties.

TRENDS IN INTEREST AGGREGATION

We have noted in Chapter Four and elsewhere the *democratic trend* that began in the mid-1970s and gained important momentum with the collapse of authoritarian regimes in Eastern Europe at the end of the 1980s. While the importance of this trend cannot be denied, we do not want to overstate it either. Figure 6.3 attempts to classify the world's regimes by the predominant interest aggregation structure at two points: the end of the 1970s and the end of the 1980s. The percentages we report have to be viewed as estimates, often based on limited information. But the figure provides a rough idea of the frequency of the three major forms: competitive parties and elections, single-party regimes, and military-dominated regimes. The "residual" category of traditional governments consists mostly of small kingdoms in the Middle East, South Asia, and the Pacific.

The lightly colored bars show the situation in the

late 1970s. About one-third of the world's 154 independent countries were reported to have competitive party and electoral systems as their predominant interest aggregation structures. These regimes were the main form in Western Europe and North America (including the Caribbean), not uncommon in Latin America and Asia, but rare in Africa and the Middle East. Nearly as many countries had one of the versions of single-party regimes. They were the main form in Eastern Europe and relatively common in Africa and Asia, though rare in the Western Hemisphere and Western Europe. In slightly less than a quarter of the countries the armed forces dominated interest aggregation, either formally (military governments) or in practice (military-dominated civilian governments). The military-dominated regimes accounted for about a third or more of the countries in Africa and Latin America.

A decade later, as shown by the dark-colored bars, the trend is obviously away from single-party governments. Across the world these have declined from 30 to 24 percent of the regimes, although they still account for nearly 40 percent of African nations. As we already know, the decline of exclusive governing party regimes is even more striking. The majority of the remaining single-party systems are loosely corporatist, with a few exceptions such as China and Cuba. The decline of ideological underpinnings for authoritarian governments, as well as the withdrawal of support from the Soviet Union, has contributed to this trend. As expected, the democratic trend toward competitive party and electoral systems is notable, with an increase from 36 to 41 percent of the world's political systems (and more experimenting with some competition).

We must note, however, that the proportion of military governments has actually increased slightly, from 23 to 26 percent of the world's countries. Perhaps in deference to the decline in the legitimacy of authoritarianism, the military is now more likely to dominate from behind the scenes than through direct rule, especially in Latin America. Latin America also saw the genuine replacement of military regimes by competitive party regimes in such important countries as Argentina, Brazil, and Uruguay. But the proportion of military-dominated governments has increased notably in Africa (from 36 to 46 percent of the total) and the Middle East, while remaining about the same in Asia and the Pacific. The recent casualties to military intervention include competitive governments in Fiji in the South Pacific (1987) and Suriname in South America (1991). Although the

Romanian citizens fighting with the army against the supporters of the Ceausescu dictatorship board an armored personnel carrier in December 1989.

era of confidence in military government as a solution to development seems to have passed, military domination remains a likely outcome when other types of government are unable to solve internal conflicts. Such is now the challenge facing the new experimentally competitive regimes of Eastern Europe and the Soviet Union, as well as the Third World.

SIGNIFICANCE OF INTEREST AGGREGATION

How interests are aggregated is an important determinant of what a country's government does for and to its citizens. The factors that most interest us about government and politics — stability, revolution, participation, welfare, equality, liberty, security — are very much a consequence of interest aggregation. Through interest aggregation the desires and demands of citizens are converted into a few policy alternatives. In terms of policy, the consequence is that many possible policies have been eliminated and only a few remain. In terms of process, the consequence is that political resources have been accumulated in the hands of relatively few individuals, who will decide policy. The remaining policy alternatives are serious or major alternatives, because they have the backing of numerous political resources. Policy alternatives such as the government taking over all heavy industrial production in the United States are not serious, because no set of leaders commanding major political resources favors them, even though these policies are implemented in other countries.

Narrowing and combining policy wishes can be seen easily in the working of competitive party systems. Of the many possible policy preferences, only a few are backed by parties, after the parties choose leaders and establish platforms to run on. In the elections, voters give backing to some of these parties and thus shape the strength of party representation in the legislature. Even at the legislative stage, some further consolidation and coalition building takes place between party factions or party groups. At some point, however, the majority of policy possibilities have been eliminated. Either they were never backed by parties, or parties supporting them did badly in the elections. In noncompetitive party systems, military governments, and monarchies, aggregation works differently, but with the similar effect of narrowing and combining policies and resources. It may be that on some issues, aggregation will virtually determine policy, as when power is held by a military government, a faction of an authoritarian party, or a disciplined party majority in a competitive system. In other cases the legislative assembly, military council, or party politburo may contain several factions of similar strength.

One characteristic of interest aggregation in all systems is its degree of polarization. In Chapter Three we discussed consensual and polarized political cultures. We mentioned that the United States, West Germany, and Britain were consensual, with most citizens preferring moderate positions. Italy, France, and Greece were more polarized cultures, with larger concentrations of citizens on the left and fewer in the center.

Polarization in the policymaking body should look pretty much like polarization in the political culture. In a consensual society, like Germany, the Bundestag is made up of mainly moderate and tolerant parties. In conflictual Italy, the stalemated Parliament is dominated by deeply divided parties — the Communists and the Christian Democrats.

But politics shapes its environment as well as reflecting it. Interest aggregation often alters the amount of polarization that the political culture might be expected to project into policymaking. That is one reason politics is so fascinating. Well-organized and well-led political parties might, at least for a while, be able to dominate politics and limit the strength of extremist groups in the legislature, as in the consociational model we mentioned earlier. Conversely, well-organized extremists might be able to appeal to the fears and prejudices of some groups and get them more effectively to the polls, thus gaining more legislative strength in an otherwise consensual country.

Of course, authoritarian interest aggregation structures tend to create a political power balance that is far from reflecting popular opinion. In a highly divided and conflict-ridden society, such unrepresentativeness may be viewed as a great virtue. Leaders of military coups in many nations have justified their overthrow of party governments by claiming to depolarize politics and rid the nation of conflict it cannot afford. Similarly, heads of authoritarian parties typically claim that their nation must concentrate all its energies and resources on common purposes and that to allow party competition would be too polarizing. One justification for democracy is that it leads political leaders to act as the people wish. In a polarized political culture, the cost of interest aggregation that reflects division and uncertainty may be seen as too high a price to pay for citizen control. As the frequent instability in authoritarian and military governments indicates, however, it may be easier to do away with the appearance of polarization than the reality. Cultural divisions may end up being reflected through military factions or intraparty groups, instead of through party competition, and the citizens may end up without either freedom and participation or stability.

KEY TERMS

authoritarian party systems	consociational party systems	interest aggregation	party-electoral aggregation
competitive party systems	democratic trends	majoritarian party systems	party-governmental aggregation
conflictual party systems	exclusive governing party	military government	totalitarian party
consensual party systems	inclusive governing party	multiparty systems	
		party coalitions	

END NOTES

1. Steffan Schmitt, James Scott, Carl Lande, and Laura Guasti, *Friends, Followers and Factions* (Berkeley, Calif.: University of California Press, 1977); S. Eisenstadt and Rene Lemarchand, *Political Clientelism, Patronage and Development* (Beverly Hills, Calif.: Sage Publications, 1981); John W. Lewis, *Political Networks and the Chinese Policy Process* (Stanford, Calif.: Northeast Asia Forum, 1986); Lucian W. Pye, *Asian Power and Politics* (Cambridge, Mass.: Harvard University Press, 1985); T. H. Rigby and Bokdan Harasimin, *Leadership Selection and Patron Client Relations in the USSR and Yugoslavia* (Beverly Hills, Calif.: Sage Publications, 1981).

2. See Philippe Schmitter, "Interest Intermediation and Regime Governability," in Suzanne Berger, ed., *Organizing Interests in Western Europe* (New York: Cambridge University Press, 1981), ch. 12; David Cameron, "Social Democracy, Corporatism and Labor Quiescence: The Representation of Interests in Advanced Capitalist Society," in John Goldthorpe, ed., *Order and Conflict in Contemporary Capitalism* (Oxford: Oxford University Press, 1984), ch. 7; and Peter J. Katzenstein, *Small States in World Markets* (Ithaca, N.Y.: Cornell University Press, 1985).

3. William Thompson, *The Grievances of Military Coup-Makers* (Beverly Hills, Calif.: Sage Publications, 1973).

4. The large literature on party strategies owes its largest debt to Anthony Downs, *An Economic Theory of Democracy* (New York: Harper & Row, 1957). More generally, see Dennis C. Mueller, *Public Choice* (Cambridge: Cambridge University Press, 1979).

5. Seymour Martin Lipset and Stein Rokkan, eds., *Party Systems and Voter Alignments* (New York: Macmillan, 1967); Richard Rose, ed., *Electoral Behavior: A Comparative Handbook* (New York: Free Press, 1974); Russell J. Dalton, Scott C. Flanagan and Paul Allen Beck, eds., *Electoral Change in Advanced Industrial Societies* (Princeton, N.J.: Princeton University Press, 1984).

6. Ian Budge, David Robertson, and Derek Hearl, *Ideology, Strategy and Party Change: Spatial Analyses of Post-War Election Programmes in 19*

7. In addition to the references in note 5 above, see Michael Lewis–Beck, *Economics and Elections: The Major Western Democracies* (Ann Arbor: University of Michigan Press, 1988); Ian Budge, Ivor Crewe, and Dennis Farlie, *Party Identification and Beyond* (London: John Wiley, 1976); Russell J. Dalton, *Citizen Politics in Western Democracies* (Chatham, N.J.: Chatham House, 1988).

8. For example, the survey of "experts" by Castles and Mair in 1982 shows a center gap of over three points between the Socialist party and the nearest conservative party (UDF), although between a quarter and a third of voters regularly place themselves at the center. See Francis G. Castles and Peter Mair, "Left–Right Scales: Some 'Expert' Judgments," *European Journal of Political Research*, 12 (1984), pp. 73–88. Also see Dalton, *Citizen Politics in Western Democracies*, p. 196.

9. For analyses of the implications of election laws for party representation and government majorities, see Douglas Rae, *The Political Consequences of Election Laws* (New Haven, Conn.: Yale University Press, 1967, 1971) and Arend Lijphart, "The Political Consequences of Electoral Laws, 1945–1985," *American Political Science Review*, 84 (June 1990), pp. 481–496.

10. For Britain, see Richard Rose, *Do Parties Make a Difference?* (Chatham, N.J.: Chatham House, 1984), ch. 5; also see Colin Rallings, "The Influence of Election Programmes: Britain and Canada, 1945–1979," in Budge, Robertson, and Hearl, *Ideology, Strategy, and Party Change*, pp. 1–14. More generally, see David R. Cameron, "The Expansion of the Public Economy," *American Political Science Review*, 72 (December 1978), pp. 1243–1261; and Francis G. Castles, ed., *The Impact of Political Parties* (Beverly Hills, Calif.: Sage Publications, 1982). For the United States, see Gerald Pomper, *Elections in America* (New York: Dodd, Mead, 1968), chs. 7–10.

11. See Kaare Strom, *Minority Government and Majority Rule* (New York: Cambridge University Press, 1990).

12. On cabinet stability, see Lawrence C. Dodd, *Coalitions in Parliamentary Government*

(Princeton, N.J.: Princeton University Press, 1976); G. Bingham Powell, Jr., *Contemporary Democracies* (Cambridge, Mass.: Harvard University Press, 1982), ch. 7; Gary King, James E. Alt, N. E. Burns, and Michael Laver, "A Unified Model of Cabinet Dissolution in Parliamentary Democracies," *American Journal of Political Science*, 35 (1991).

13. On these issues of citizen control, see G. Bingham Powell, Jr., "Constitutional Design and Citizen Electoral Control," *Journal of Theoretical Politics*, 1 (April 1989), pp. 107–130; G. Bingham Powell, Jr., "Holding Governments Accountable," Paper presented to the American Political Science Association Annual Meetings, San Francisco, 1990.

14. This classification is adapted from Arend Lijphart's *Democracy in Plural Societies* (New Haven, Conn.: Yale University Press, 1977) and *Democracies* (New Haven, Conn.: Yale University Press, 1984). Also see Powell, *Contemporary Democracies*, and Powell, "Constitutional Design and Citizen Electoral Control."

15. Lijphart, *Democracy in Plural Societies*.

16. On the role of parties in the defense of democracy, see Powell, *Contemporary Democracies*, chs. 8, 10; and the contributions in Juan J. Linz and Alfred Stepan, eds., *The Breakdown of Democratic Regimes* (Baltimore: Johns Hopkins University Press, 1978).

17. On totalitarian parties see, for example, C. F. Friedrich and Z. K. Brzezinski, *Totalitarian Dictatorship and Autocracy* (Cambridge, Mass.: Harvard University Press, 1956); Juan Linz, "Totalitarian and Authoritarian Regimes," in Fred Greenstein and Nelson Polsby, eds., *Handbook of Political Science* (Reading, Mass.: Addison–Wesley, 1975), Vol. 3, pp. 175–412; Amos Perlmutter, *Modern Authoritarianism: A Comparative Institutional Analysis* (New Haven, Conn.: Yale University Press, 1981), especially pp. 62–114.

18. See Chapter Fourteen; see also Franz Schurman, *Ideology and Organization in Communist China* (Berkeley: University of California Press, 1966).

19. On the efforts in Africa, see Crawford Young, *Ideology and Development in Africa* (New Haven, Conn.: Yale University Press, 1982), ch. 2. On recent events, see Chapter Sixteen below.

20. See Henry Bienen, *Kenya: The Politics of Participation and Control* (Princeton, N.J.: Princeton University Press, 1974); and Chapter Sixteen below.

21. See Bogdan Denis Denitch, *The Legitimation of a Revolution: The Yugoslav Case* (New Haven, Conn.: Yale University Press, 1976).

22. See Robert H. Jackson and Carl G. Rosberg, *Personal Rule in Black Africa* (Berkeley: University of California Press, 1982); Young, *Ideology and Development in Africa*; and Chapter Sixteen below.

23. Perlmutter, *Modern Authoritarianism*, pp. 114 ff.; see also Alfred Stepan, *The State and Society: Peru in Comparative Perspective* (Princeton, N.J.: Princeton University Press, 1978) and the essays in David Collier, ed., *The New Authoritarianism* (Princeton, N.J.: Princeton University Press, 1979).

CHAPTER 7

GOVERNMENT
AND POLICYMAKING

OLICYMAKING IS the pivotal stage in the political process. The lineup of political forces has taken shape, and now authoritative policies must be enacted: bills proposed and passed by the legislature or edicts issued by the ruling council. Later, policy goals must be implemented, their consequences reviewed.

To understand how policies are made, we must know what the decision rules are. What kind of power is effective and legitimate in different political systems? Is it a simple majority vote in the legislature or such a vote plus approval by an independently elected executive? Or is it a decree issued by the monarch, a signed unanimous agreement by military field commanders, or the official backing of the politburo? Or is it merely the whim of the military dictator?

We must also recognize the governmental agencies' leading position in policymaking. The demands of interest groups for tax decreases or for the protection of endangered species cannot become effective unless they are transformed into laws by policymaking institutions and implemented by government officials according to some accepted decision rule. Economic, societal, and personality influences become important when they impinge on or manifest themselves within the institutions of government: parliaments, cabinets, ministries and executive departments, and courts. Much of public policy is initiated within government agencies, by department ministers or secretaries, by powerful senators or congressmen, and even by judicial authorities. The picture of government as a flow from society to government and then from government back to society is oversimplified. The process may begin from within the government itself.

This chapter focuses on decision rules and on the policymaking role of such governmental structures as legislatures, executives, and bureaucracies. Many scholars feel that in the 1960s and 1970s political science neglected these issues while concentrating on citizen attitudes and party politics. Their movement to reaffirm the centrality of institutions has now gained wide recognition. We draw here on many of their insights.[1]

DECISION RULES
FOR POLICYMAKING

All governments must have some set of working rules for making decisions. They must have a working constitution. Even a military government or a dictatorship based on coercion attempts to have a working set of arrangements for having decrees proposed, considered, and adopted. *Decision rules* are the basic rules governing how decisions are made, spelling out the policymaking roles, dividing them territorially and functionally, and the like.

The decision rules set the terms of the political contest. Individuals and groups seeking to influence policy have to operate within the framework of these rules. If a nation decentralizes policymaking authority, so that to preserve the environment it is necessary to get majority votes in many state legislatures, a great effort will be needed for groups to initiate new conservation measures. If the working constitution merely requires a formal decree from the commander of the armed forces, or a declaration by the politburo, a different approach will be needed to influence these crucial policymakers. The decision rules shape political activity because they determine what political resources to seek — whether legislative seats or the support of regional military commanders — and how to acquire and use them.

The importance of the stability of a nation's basic decision rules was suggested by Thomas Jefferson in his introduction to the first Manual of the House of Representatives: "A bad set of rules is better than no rules at all." In the absence of a legitimate set of arrangements for formulating issues, deliberating and debating them, and deciding among points of view, government may break down and issues may be decided by force.

Making Constitutions

Constitution making is a fundamental political act: it creates or transforms the decision rules. Basic changes in constitutional rules tend to take place in the aftermath of defeat in war, the success of independence movements, or significant social or revolutionary change. Thus, the defeated powers and the successor states of World Wars I and II all adopted new constitutions or had new constitutions imposed on them.

Most of the constitutions that are in force today were formed as the result of some break, often violent, with the past — war, revolution, colonial rebellion. In these situations decision rules have to accommodate new internal power distributions or external power con-

texts. Britain is unusual in not having a formal written constitution, but rather only a long-accepted and highly developed set of customs, buttressed by major statutes. This practice reflects the gradual, incremental, and, on the whole, peaceful history of Britain. Nevertheless, the major changes in British decision rules, such as the shifting of power from the Crown to Parliament in the seventeenth century, and the Reform Acts of 1832 and 1867, which established party and cabinet government based on broad electorates, followed on periods of civil war, mass mobilizations, and disorder. Perhaps the greatest exception to the association between disruptive upheavals and constitution creation is the peaceful development over the last thirty years of the constitution of the European Community, an emergent political unit whose growing powers are altering the decision rules affecting 250 million Europeans. But while there has been no violence associated with the formation of the European Community, its origins cannot be separated from World War II.

The decades since World War II have seen much constitutional experimentation. Japan, Germany, and Italy — the defeated powers — introduced new political arrangements that have proven durable. France has had two constitutions in this period, and it appears that its second effort — the Fifth Republic — will be successful. Both Germany and France have undertaken some interesting constitutional engineering intended to overcome the weaknesses of their earlier constitutional arrangements — the Weimar Republic and the Fourth Republic. The German constitutional framers sought to overcome the political fragmentation and instability of the Weimar Republic by combining proportional representation with single-member district plurality voting and by eliminating splinter parties with less than 5 percent of the vote. These arrangements encourage the German voters to make their choices among the larger political parties, hence reducing party fragmentation. They also introduced a novel arrangement intended to cope with problems of Cabinet instability. A government may be overthrown after the loss of a vote of confidence in the Bundestag only if it is a "constructive" vote of no confidence. That is, a vote of nonconfidence in the incumbent government must be accompanied by presentation of an alternative majority in the Bundestag. (See Chapter Eleven.) The French experiment is a combination of parliamentary and presidential government. The Fifth Republic has introduced a separately elected powerful presidency, along with the normal prime minister and Cabinet responsible to the National Assembly. (See Chapter Ten.)

Despite the success of the most recent German and French experiments, it is difficult to determine political processes by reshaping decision rules according to rational plans and intentions. As March and Olsen have argued, "[T]he contemporary record with respect to intentional change does not encourage boundless confidence in the possibilities for deliberate controlled change."[2] They point out that it is possible to "shock" institutions into change, but the outcome of the shocks may turn out to be quite different from what was intended.

The 1990s are an important period of constitutional experimentation that will test to the utmost the ability of constitution framers to engineer political processes. The Soviet constitution is being revised by eliminating the monopoly power of the Communist party and by establishing a powerful presidency, a representative Supreme Soviet, and a decentralized federal system. (See Chapter Thirteen.) The Eastern European communist constitutions have been replaced by democratic parliamentary constitutions, providing for competitive electoral and party systems. The South African constitution is in process of being revised in the direction of equality regardless of race. The Gulf crisis of 1990–1991 has produced cracks in the patrimonial monarchic constitutions of the Arabian Peninsula. In all these cases the outcome of constitutional change is far from certain.

Geographic Distribution of Government Power

The basic decision rules or constitutions of political systems differ along three dimensions: (1) geographic distribution of authority; (2) structural separation of authority; and (3) limitations on governmental authority.

Classifying systems according to the geographic division of power gives us *confederal systems* at one extreme, *unitary systems* at the other extreme, and *federal systems* in the middle (see Table 7.1). The United States under the Articles of Confederation was a confederal system. The central government had power over

TABLE 7.1
DIVISION AND LIMITATION OF GOVERNMENTAL AUTHORITY

Geographic distribution of authority			
Centralized ←			→ Decentralized
Unitary	**Federal**	**Confederal**	
France	United States under Constitution	United States under Articles of Confederation	
Japan	Germany	European Economic Community	
Great Britain	India		
China			

Structural separation of authority			
Concentrated ←			→ Separated
Authoritarian	**Parliamentary**	**Mixed[a]**	**Presidential**
China	Mexico	Germany	France	United States
Egypt	Tanzania	Great Britain		Venezuela
Iraq		Japan		
Saudi Arabia		India		

Judicial limitations on governmental authority		
Unlimited ←		→ Limited
Nonindependent courts	**Independent courts**	**Power of judicial review**
China	France	United States
Egypt	Great Britain	Germany
Iraq	India	Japan
	Tanzania	

[a]Parliamentary and presidential.

foreign affairs and defense, but it had to depend on financial and other support from the states to implement this power. Under the Constitution, adopted in 1787, the American government changed from confederal to federal; that is, both central and state governments had spheres of authority and the means to implement their power. Today, the United States, Germany, India, and Tanzania are federal systems in which central and local units each have autonomy in particular spheres of public policy. These policy areas and powers are, however, divided among central and local units in varying ways.

The United Kingdom, France, China, and Japan are unitary governments with power and authority concentrated at the center. Regional and local units have those powers specifically delegated to them from the central government, which may change or withdraw the powers by central decision.

In comparing confederal, federal, and unitary systems, however, we must keep in mind the distinction between formal and actual distribution of power. In unitary systems, in spite of the formal concentration of power at the center, regional and local units may acquire authority that the central government rarely challenges. In the American federal system over the last century power has steadily moved from the states toward the center. Thus, the real differences between federal and unitary systems may be considerably less significant than their formal arrangements suggest. An extreme example of the discrepancy between formal and actual federalism was the Soviet Union in the pre-Gorbachev era. It consisted of some fifteen republics, each of which had substantial formal authority. In practice the governing apparatus was the Communist party, a highly centralized body that exercised authority at both the center and the periphery. The federal distribution of power in the Soviet Union between the central government and the republics is still an undecided issue of great importance.

Separation of Governmental Powers

Comparing governments according to the structural concentration or separation of policymaking authority reveals several types. These are illustrated in Table 7.1. In *authoritarian regimes*, such as China, Iraq, and Saudi Arabia, there is no fully settled delegation of authority to legislatures, courts, or similar structures outside the office of chief executive. In such systems, power may either be concentrated in a political bureau or military council, or, typically, it may consist of an uneasy balance of military factions, bureaucrats, and party leaders. But none of these groups, as they bring their political resources to bear on policymaking, is faced with an accepted need to compete for citizen support. Such systems vary greatly in the extent to which they attempt to regulate all aspects of social and economic life. They also vary in the amount of debate and even in contestation allowed within the party or military. Mexico and Tanzania, as shown in Table 7.1, are relatively more open in this respect. In all the authoritarian systems, however, the rules of governmental policymaking involve a concentration of power at one point.

Parliamentary regimes, such as those of Germany, Great Britain, Japan, and India, are characterized by a combination of the political executive and the assembly. However, prime ministers and cabinets in parliamentary governments do not lack settled spheres of authority and power. Rather, the executive (usually called a cabinet or council of ministers) is selected from the assembly and holds office only as long as it can command the support of a majority in the assembly.

Policymaking authority is most sharply separated in the *democratic presidential regime*, of which the United States is the outstanding example. The principal characteristics of this regime are that the political executive is independently elected, holds office for the entire term whether or not he or she has the legislature's support, and has substantial authority in policymaking, as in the American president's veto power. At the same time, the executive must deal with an independently elected legislature that also has policymaking authority; this factor distinguishes the democratic presidential regime from many authoritarian regimes called presidential. Of course, if the same party controls both presidency and legislature and if the party has internal agreement, this effective aggregation of political resources will create a situation much like that in parliamentary regimes with stable party governments or coalitions (Chapter 17).

France under the Fifth Republic (since 1959) is an interesting example of a *mixed parliamentary-presidential regime*. The president of France, who has substantial power, is elected by popular vote and holds office for a seven-year term, whether or not he is supported by the National Assembly, which is reelected every five years. The French premier and Council of Ministers, on the other hand, depend on a majority in the National Assembly. For the first time in the life of the Fifth Republic, the 1986 election gave France a National Assembly, and consequently a premier and Council of Ministers, controlled by political parties different from the party of the president. This situation in which the president of the republic and the Council of Ministers were of different political parties (called cohabitation) lasted two years and was viewed as a successful test of the viability of the constitution of the Fifth Republic. (See Chapter 10.)

It should be noted that the USSR does not appear in Table 7.1. The present governing arrangements in the USSR are in the process of moving from a centralized "party–state," with a command economy to a federalized, separation of powers system with independent courts and a private economy. It is too soon to assert that genuine equilibria on these dimensions have been reached (see Chapter Thirteen).

Limitations on Government Powers

Unlike the authoritarian regimes, parliamentary, presidential, and parliamentary-presidential regimes are characterized by some form of legal or customary limitation on authority. Systems in which the powers of various government units are defined and limited by a written constitution, statutes, and custom are called *constitutional regimes*. Constitutional regimes typically restrict government power. Citizens' rights — such as the right to a fair trial and freedom to speak, petition, publish, and assemble — are protected against government interference except under unusual and specified circumstances. The courts are crucial institutions in the limitations of governmental power.

Governments may be divided into those, at one extreme, in which the power to coerce citizens is relatively unlimited by the courts, and those, at the other extreme, in which the courts not only protect the rights of citizens but also police other parts of the government to see that their powers are properly exercised. The United States is the best example of a system in which political power is limited by the courts. Its institution of *judicial review* allows federal and state courts to rule that other parts of the government have exceeded their powers. Most other constitutional regimes have independent courts that can protect citizens against the improper implementation of laws and regulations but cannot overrule the assembly or the political executive. The substantive rights of citizens in these systems are protected by statute, custom, self-restraint, and political pressure. The constitutional courts of Germany and Japan have limited powers of judicial review of the decisions of other agencies of government.

All written constitutions provide for amending pro-

President Bush delivering his State of the Union message to both Houses of Congress, suggests a form of government in which power is shared between a president and a legislature.

cedures, since it is generally recognized that there must be some adaptability and flexibility in basic decision rules, as problems arise with existing institutions, or as social structure changes and new groups demand access. Those procedures can be an important limitation on governmental power. Many constitutions provide that certain arrangements may not be amended, as, for example, the provision in the U.S. Constitution granting each state equal representation in the Senate.

Amending procedures vary widely, ranging from the complex to the simple. Perhaps the simplest case is that of New Zealand where an act of Parliament can change the New Zealand Constitution Act of 1852. Some constitutions prescribe an absolute majority of all legislators, rather than the majority of a quorum which is sufficient for ordinary statutes. Others require that an amendment be approved twice with an interval of time between passages. In some cases a popular referendum is added on to the legislative action. The U.S. Constitution has the most difficult formal procedure, requiring initiation by two-thirds of both houses of the Congress (or by the never employed procedure of a national convention called by two-thirds of the states); and approval by three-fourths of the state legislatures, or three-fourths of specially elected conventions held in the states.

Constitutions that have more complicated amending procedures such as the American are called "rigid" constitutions; the simpler ones are said to be "flexible." Here again, however, we have to distinguish between law and practice. Some flexible constitutions such as those of Norway and Denmark have rarely been amended, while rigid ones like the American and Swiss have frequently been changed.[3]

Table 7.1 emphasizes very general differences, and tends to obscure significant differences within categories, as, for example, among democratic political systems. Arend Lijphart, in an important recent study of types of democracy, divides democratic regimes into two major categories: majoritarian and consensual.[4] The institutions of the majoritarian type of democracy are relatively simple, designed to give power to the representatives of the majority of the voters. The political executive — the cabinet — is chosen from among the leaders of a unicameral legislature, or from the dominant of two chambers in a bicameral legislature. Hence, power is concentrated at a single point, not divided as in a *separation of powers* system. The party systems of these majoritarian democracies tend to follow a simple left – right division, and their electoral arrangements are of the single-member district, plurality variety.

According to Lijphart, consensual democracies are designed to break up and limit the exercise of power. They typically provide for power sharing in the executive, often requiring that ethnic and religious groups be represented in the cabinet. They are also characterized by bicameral legislatures in which one of the chambers is representative of regional and ethnic groups. Switzerland, Belgium, and the Netherlands are good examples of consensual democracies; New Zealand, Britain, and Sweden are good examples of majoritarian systems. The United States falls in between with a majoritarian electoral and party system, a majoritarian executive, a federal distribution of power among the central government and the states, and a consensual bicameral legislature with a powerful Senate, representative of the states.

Clearly, majoritarian systems are typical of homogeneous, culturally unified societies, as in Britain, New Zealand, and Sweden, while consensual democracy is more typical of religiously and linguistically heterogeneous societies such as Switzerland, Belgium, and the Netherlands.

The Democratizing Trend in Decision-Rules

In the last decades there has been a trend toward democratization outside the North American-European area. In some of these new and transitional democracies the changes may be more formal than real. Neither our Table 7.1 nor Lijphart's distinctions captures the differences. They have to be compared according to the extent to which basic civil liberties are accorded, elections are genuinely free, the media of communication are open to competition, and the like.

In a recent paper surveying the democratic trend around the world, Larry Diamond offers a sevenfold typology of regimes according to the extent to which they accord the rights and permit the institutions that make genuine pluralism and effective participation possible. At the extreme nondemocratic level Diamond includes such countries as China, Cuba, Libya, and Iraq. In the middle categories are such countries as Egypt, Yugoslavia, Chile, and Mexico. Among the countries in the category of not fully institutionalized democracies are Brazil, Venezuela, Israel, and Argentina. The stable liberal democracy group includes the countries of Western Europe and North America, as well as Australia, New Zealand, Japan, and one or two others.

In the almost two decades between 1972 and 1989, according to Diamond, the percentage of countries falling into the democratizing or the democratic categories has increased from roughly 40 to 50 percent. This is hardly a landslide. (Compare Figure 6.3.) It is good to remember these figures when we speak of global democratization. While democratic progress has taken place, as of 1989 more than 40 percent of the nations included in Diamond's calculation (130) were still in the two least democratic categories.[5]

ASSEMBLIES

In addition to political parties, which we discussed in Chapter Six, three important types of institutions are involved in policymaking: the executive, whether elective or appointive; the higher levels of bureaucracy; and the assembly. Political executives—presidents and their appointees in presidential systems; prime ministers and cabinets in parliamentary systems; and politburos or presidia in communist systems—tend to be the main formulators of public policy. But the distribution of policymaking predominance among the three institutions varies from country to country and from issue area to issue area.

Almost all contemporary political systems have assemblies, variously called chambers, senates, diets, soviets, and the like. Today more than 80 percent of the one hundred and sixty odd independent countries belonging to the United Nations have such governmental bodies. Assemblies are generally elected by popular vote and hence are accountable at least formally to the citizenry. Thus, they are legitimating agencies. The almost universal adoption of legislative institutions suggests that in the modern world a legitimate government must formally include a representative popular component.

The Functions of Assemblies

All assemblies[6] have many members—ranging from fewer than a hundred to more than a thousand—who deliberate, debate, and vote on policies that come before them. Most important policies and rules must be considered and at least formally approved by these bodies before they have the force of law. Although legislative approval is needed to give authority to policy, in most countries legislation is actually formulated elsewhere, usually by the political executive and the upper levels of the bureaucracy.

When we compare assemblies on the basis of their importance as political and policymaking agencies, the American Congress, which plays a very important role in the formulation and enactment of legislation, is at one extreme. The other extreme is represented by the National People's Congress of the People's Republic of China, which meets infrequently and does little more than listen to statements by party leaders and legitimize decisions made elsewhere. Roughly midway between the two is the House of Commons in Britain. There legislative proposals are sometimes initiated or modified by ordinary members of Parliament, but public policy is usually made by the Cabinet or ministers (who are, to be sure, chosen from the members of the parliamentary body). The typical assembly primarily provides a debating forum, formally enacts legislation, and sometimes amends it.

A recent study of European legislatures classifies them according to power in the decision-making process and popular perception of their importance. The judgment of power is that of academic experts; estimates of citizen perception are based on samples of popular opinion made through recent surveys. It is of interest that, while the Italian legislature is rated first in terms of expert estimates of power (see Table 7.2), among the European populations surveyed, popular Italian opinion rates its legislative body lowest in importance. Britain, on the other hand, is third from the bottom in expert judgment of influence in the policymaking process, but comes out on top in terms of "importance" in popular opinion. Ireland moves from the lowest expert evaluation to high public ranking. The legislature's prestige in a nation does not accurately reflect its policymaking influence; it is more a reflection of the general esteem in which governmental institutions are held. Thus, frequent Cabinet crises and changes in Italy reduce popular respect for government in general, but they create opportunities for policy initiatives by groups in the legislature and a more important role in the making and unmaking of Cabinets.

Assemblies perform a wide variety of functions other than policymaking. Debates in assemblies can contribute to the socialization process, shaping citizens' and elites' perceptions not only of political issues, but also of the appropriate norms and procedures of the political system. Assemblies can also play a major role in elite recruitment, especially in parliamentary systems where prime ministers and cabinet members typically serve their apprenticeships in the assembly. The com-

TABLE 7.2
THE ROLE OF LEGISLATURES IN SELECTED EUROPEAN COUNTRIES

Policy influence ranking	Importance to citizens ranking
Italy	Britain
Holland	Ireland
Sweden	West Germany
West Germany	Holland
Britain	France
France	Italy
Ireland	

Source: Adapted from Philip Norton, "Conclusion: Legislatures in Perspective," *West European Politics,* 13 (July 1990), p. 146; and *Eurobarometer,* 19 (April 1983), p. 110.

mittee hearings and floor debates in legislative assemblies may be important sites for interest articulation and interest aggregation, especially if majority party control is absent or loosely exercised.

However, as in policymaking, the assemblies of different nations play very different roles in their respective political systems. The British House of Commons is ordinarily of little importance in policymaking, because it is controlled by the ruling party's majority, but the Commons and its debates are central to socialization and elite recruitment. The American Congress and its committees play a major role in interest aggregation and policymaking; they must share other functions with many other institutions in the decentralized American system. Thus far, at least, the People's Congress in China has played only a limited socialization role in China's political process.

This brief comparison of the functions performed by assemblies should set to rest the simplified notion that assemblies legislate. All assemblies in democratic systems have an important relationship to legislation, but not a dominant one. Their political importance lies not just in this relationship, but also in the great variety of other political functions they perform.

Differences in Structures of Assemblies

Assemblies differ in their organizational patterns as well as in their powers and functions. About half the parliaments or congresses consist of two chambers, which have different powers and different ways of selecting members.

In Europe, parliaments developed out of "estates," bodies representing different sociopolitical groups intermittently called together by kings or other hereditary rulers for consultation and gathering revenue. In France there were three estates: the clergy, the higher aristocracy, and the so-called third estate, representing other classes. In England in the early period, estates were organized in two chambers — the lords spiritual (the bishops) and temporal in the House of Lords, and knights and burgesses elected from the counties and boroughs to the House of Commons. Today this basis of parliamentary organization persists only in England, where the House of Lords (its powers greatly diminished) is still dominated numerically by the hereditary aristocracy.

Most of the democratic countries, and some of the authoritarian ones, have bicameral (two-chamber) assemblies. Federal systems provide simultaneously for two forms of representation: one chamber for constituencies based on population, and the second for constituencies based on federal units. Even in unitary systems such as France *bicameralism* is a common practice, but the purpose of the second chamber is to break up the process of policymaking and provide for longer and more cautious consideration of legislation. The emphasis in these systems is on separation of power rather than distinct representation of special geographic entities.

The formation of the American Congress reflected a desire for both federalism and separation of powers. The House directly represents the citizens, with districts made up of roughly equal numbers, giving a voice to various local interests and, in the aggregate, the popular majority. The fifty American states are equally represented in the Senate; thus, federal units have special access to one of the two legislative chambers and are in a position to protect their interests. The American congressional system is also connected with the other branches in the federal separation of powers and checks and balances. Thus, the Senate must approve treaties and executive appointments as a way of checking the executive, and all measures involving taxation and appropriations must be initiated in the House.

The American system, in which the two chambers seem practically equal in power, is unusual. In most bicameral systems one chamber is dominant, and the second (the British House of Lords and the French Senate) tends to play a primarily limiting and delaying role. As we have pointed out, cabinets in parliamentary systems are usually chosen from the majority party or parties' leadership in the more popularly representative chamber. Governments in parliamentary systems depend on majority support to continue in office. If the cabinet is chosen from among the majority party in one of the chambers, then the cabinet is responsible to that chamber, which will consequently acquire a more important position in policymaking than the second chamber.

Assemblies also differ in their internal organization, in ways that have major consequences for policymaking and implementation. There are two kinds of internal organization in assemblies and parliaments: party organization and formal organization (presiding officers, committees, and the like). A party system in a presidential government may function differently from that in a parliamentary government. Parliamentary parties in Britain, as in most parliamentary systems, are disciplined in that members of Parliament rarely vote in opposition to the instructions of party leaders. Because cabinets generally hold office as long as they can command a majority of the assembly, deviating from party discipline means risking the fall of the government and new elections.

In presidential systems, the executive and members of the assembly are elected for definite terms of office, and the fate of the party and of its members is less directly and immediately involved in voting on legislative measures. In American legislatures, party discipline operates principally with respect to procedural questions, like the selection of a presiding officer or the appointment of committees. On substantive legislative and policy issues, Democratic and Republican legislators, federal and state, are freer to decide whether or not to vote with party leaders. A comparison of roll-call votes in the American Congress and the British House of Commons would show much more consistency in party voting among British members of Parliament.

All assemblies have a committee structure, some division of labor permitting specialized groups of legislators to deliberate on particular kinds of issues and recommend action to the whole assembly. Without such a sublegislative organization, it would be impossible to handle the large flow of legislative business. As we have seen, however, the importance of committees varies. The committee systems of presidential regimes such as the American tend to be very influential in the legislative process, highly specialized and matching the executive departments in subject matter, and tending to dominate the legislative process. In parliamentary regimes the situation varies. Countries such as Germany, Norway, Sweden, Belgium, and Italy have specialized committee systems that match the ministries and exert some influence over the legislative process. The United Kingdom, Ireland, and France committees are less developed and influential.[7]

POLITICAL EXECUTIVES

Political executives have many names and titles, and their duties and powers also vary enormously.[8] Even the functions and authority of the world's few remaining monarchs are strikingly different. Some political executives are called presidents, but their powers and functions may differ substantially. Some political executives are called prime ministers or premiers, and others chairmen. Political executives can also be collective, with

such titles as cabinet, council of ministers, politburo, or presidium.

Titles do not specify the functions these officials perform, but executives may be distinguished as shown in Table 7.3. Political executives are *effective* only if they have genuine powers in the enactment and implementation of laws and regulations. If they do not have these powers, they are symbolic or *ceremonial*.

Individual effective executives include the American presidency, an office with very substantial powers affecting all processes of government. Although the American executive includes collective bodies such as the Cabinet and the National Security Council, they advise the president instead of acting as collective decision makers. The French president is also a powerful individual executive, who appoints the premier and may dissolve the Assembly and call for new elections.

Saudi Arabia is a surviving traditional kingship in which a large concentration of power is regulated and limited by custom and tradition. Ministerial councils or cabinets may be part of these systems, but they tend to be dominated by the monarch. The first secretary of the Central Committee of China's Communist party is also

---

TABLE 7.3
TYPES OF POLITICAL EXECUTIVES: EXAMPLES FROM SELECTED COUNTRIES

Effective	Ceremonial
Individual	
President of the United States	Swedish king
Prime minister of Sweden	President of Germany
	British queen
President of France	Japanese emperor
Chancellor of Germany	President of India
British prime minister	President of the PRC
General secretary of the Central Committee, PRC	
President of Mexico	
Prime minister of India	
President of Tanzania	
Collective	
British Cabinet	British royal family
Japanese Cabinet	
Politburo, China	
Swiss Federal Council	

an individual political executive, and he tends to be an important political figure.

Sorting out political systems on the individual-collective scale is a bit more complicated. In Britain the prime minister tends to dominate the Cabinet in time of war or emergency. Strong prime ministers even in less troubled times may dominate their Cabinets, but for the most part the British executive is a collective unit. The Cabinet meets regularly, makes important decisions, and acts on the basis of group deliberation. The Federal Council of Switzerland is an extreme example of a collective executive. The chairman of the Federal Council is elected annually and seems to be little more than a presiding officer.

Although we may speak of the political executive as being individual or collective, we are talking about the distribution of power and authority in it, not simple numbers. All executives have many members. They consist of elective and appointive officials who have policymaking power. A British prime minister makes some 100 ministerial and junior ministerial appointments; a German chancellor may make a similar number. In the United States, on taking office an incoming president may have to make as many as 2,000 political appointments, of which 200 are key policymaking positions in the executive branch.

A word or two about ceremonial executives is appropriate. Monarchs like the British queen and Scandinavian kings are principally ceremonial and symbolic officers with very occasional political powers. They are living symbols of the state and nation and of their historical continuity. Britain's queen opens Parliament and makes statements on important holidays and anniversaries. When there is an election, or when a government falls, the queen formally appoints a new prime minister. She is the symbol and the transmitter of legitimacy. Normally she has no choice in selecting a prime minister, since she picks the candidate likely to have a majority in the House of Commons, but if there is doubt about which leader has a majority or who leads the party, the queen's discretion may be an important power.

In republican countries with parliamentary systems, presidents perform the functions that fall to kings and queens in parliamentary monarchies. German and Italian presidents issue statements, make speeches on important anniversaries, and designate prime ministers after elections or when a government has resigned.

A system in which the ceremonial executive is separated from the effective executive has a number of advantages. The ceremonial executive tends to be above politics and symbolizes unity and continuity. The American presidency, which combines both effective and ceremonial functions, risks the likelihood that the president will use ceremonial and symbolic authority to enhance political power or that involvement in politics may hamper presidential performance of the symbolic or unifying role. Communist countries have tended to separate the ceremonial and the effective executives. The president of the People's Republic of China, elected by the Congress, is a ceremonial officer. He greets distinguished visitors, and opens and presides over meetings of the People's Congress.

Britain's royal family is an example of a collective *ceremonial executive.* So many occasions call for the physical presence of the monarch that members of the royal family share appearances. The activities of the royal family are reported daily in the press, giving legitimacy to a great variety of events. There is much riding in carriages, parading, and ritual in British public life. In contrast, the Scandinavian monarchies are more humdrum, and the Scandinavian countries are sometimes called bicycle monarchies.

Functions of the Executive

Political executives typically perform important system functions. The executive is the locus of leadership in the political system. Kemal Ataturks, Roosevelts, de Gaulles, Reagans, and Adenauers may hold the chief executive positions, and their energy, ideas, imagination, and images may provide stabilizing and adaptive capacity to the political system.

Studies of childhood socialization show that the first political role perceived by children tends to be the top political executive — the president, prime minister, and king or queen. In early childhood the tendency is to identify the top political executive as a parent figure; as the child matures he or she begins to differentiate political from other roles, as well as to differentiate among various political roles (see Chapter Three). The conduct of the political executive affects the trust and confidence that young people feel in the whole political system and that they carry with them into adulthood. People who experienced Roosevelt, Churchill, de Gaulle, or Adenauer in their childhoods bring expectations into their adult political lives that are different from those of people who were children under Johnson or Nixon, Macmillan or Thatcher.

The role of the political executive in recruitment is

obviously important. Presidents, prime ministers, and first secretaries have large and important appointive powers, not only of cabinet and politburo members and government ministers, but of judges as well. Typically, the political executive is the source of honors and distinctions to members of the government and private citizens — they give distinguished service medals, knighthoods and peerages, and prizes of various kinds.

The political executive plays a central role in political communication, the top executive having the crucial one. Presidents' press conferences, prime ministers' speeches in parliaments, cabinet members' testimony in committees, and the party leaders' speeches at the party congress may communicate important information about past, present, and future trends of domestic and foreign policy. These high-level communications may be appeals for support or for improved performance in various sectors of the society and economy, or they may outline new policies.

The executive is of primary significance in the performance of the process functions. The executive may serve as an advocate of particular interests, as when a president supports the demands of minority groups or the business community or a prime minister supports the interests of pensioners or depressed regions. Cabinet members typically speak for particular interests, such as labor, business, agriculture, children, and minority groups. They may play a crucial role as interest aggrega-

tors as they seek to build coalitions favoring legislation. Typically, the executive is the most important structure in policymaking. The executive normally initiates new policies and, depending on the division of powers between the executive and the legislature, has a substantial part in their adoption. The political executive also oversees the implementation of policies and can hold subordinate officials accountable for their performance.

Whatever dynamism a political system has tends to be focused in the executive. The central decisions in a foreign policy crisis are generally made by the top executive: the president (George Bush in the Gulf Crisis) or the prime minister (Margaret Thatcher in the Falklands Crisis). In domestic policy too, a bureaucracy without an executive tends to implement past policies, rather than to initiate new ones. Without the direction of politically motivated ministers, bureaucracies tend toward inertia and conservatism. The decision of a president, prime minister, cabinet, or politburo to pursue a new course in foreign or domestic policy will usually be accompanied by structural adaptations — the appointment of a vigorous minister, an increase in staff, the establishment of a special cabinet committee, and the like. Where the political executive is weak and divided, as in Fourth Re-

In modernized nations monarchs are usually ceremonial executives, living symbols of political legitimacy. Here, Sweden's King Carl Gustaf conducts Spain's King Juan Carlos on a tour of Stockholm.

The making of foreign policy is illustrated by this scene from the economic summit meeting of July 1990, where President Bush is welcoming his distinguished guests to a Bayou dinner in Houston, Texas.

public France or contemporary Italy, this dynamic force is missing. Initiative then passes to the bureaucracy, legislative committees, and powerful interest groups, and general needs, interests, and problems may be neglected. In a separation of powers system when the presidency and the Congress are controlled by different parties, even a strong president may be hampered in carrying out an effective policy.

Although the executive consists of the cabinet heads for all the policy areas, its policy thrust will be reflected by its composition. New departures in foreign policy or welfare policy may be reflected in new appointments or rearrangements, and sometimes by the direct assumption of responsibility for a policy area by the chief political executive.

THE BUREAUCRACY

Modern societies are dominated by large organizations, and the largest organizations in these societies are the government *bureaucracies*. As governments increase efforts to improve the health, productivity, welfare, and security of their populations, the size of government organizations keeps increasing.

Structure of the Bureaucracy

Of course, not all government employees are equally significant in the political process. Most important are the highly trained expert personnel of the top civil service. In his analysis of policymaking in Britain, F.M.G. Wilson argues that the British government consists of some one hundred frontbench members of Parliament, some twenty of whom serve in the Cabinet, and the remainder of whom serve as ministers, junior ministers, and parliamentary secretaries in charge of the government departments. This relatively small group of political policymakers confronts some 3,000 permanent higher civil servants largely recruited as young men from the universities directly into the *higher civil service*. They spend their lives as an elite corps, moving about from ministry to ministry, watching governments come and go, and becoming increasingly important as policymakers as they rise into the top posts.[9]

The importance of the permanent higher civil service is not unique to Britain, though perhaps it has been most fully institutionalized there. In Sweden and France, too, the higher civil service is filled with powerful generalists who can bring long tenure, experience, and technical knowledge to their particular areas. In the United States, many top positions go to presidential appointees rather than to permanent civil servants. Despite this difference and despite a greater emphasis on technical specialization, there are permanent civil servants in the key positions just below the top appointees in such agencies as the Internal Revenue Service, the Central Intelligence Agency, the National Institutes of Health, and all the Cabinet departments. These people tend to be specialists, such as military officers, diplomats, doctors, scientists, economists, and engineers, and they exert great influence on the formulation and execution of policies in their specialties.

Bureaucracies may present special problems in revolution and in counterrevolution. When the Bolsheviks originally took power in Russia in 1917, they had to depend on some of the military officers and officials of the Czarist regime until they could train their own. The secretariat of the Communist party attempted to oversee their loyalty. In the 1990s with the disestablishment of the Communist parties in the Soviet Union and the Eastern European countries, bureaucratic resistance and inertia have hampered the implementation of new policies. Although bureaucracies are supposed to be politically and ideologically neutral agencies, in fact they are influenced by the dominant ideologies of the time and tend to have conservative propensities and institutional interests of their own.

Functions of the Bureaucracy

A functional analysis of the bureaucracy may suggest why this governmental organization has acquired such enormous significance in most contemporary societies. We have often stressed that most political agencies and institutions perform a number of functions. The bureaucracy is almost alone in carrying out its function — enforcement or implementation of laws, rules, and regulations. In a sense bureaucracies monopolize the output side of the political system. (Occasionally, of course, policymakers take the law into their own hands. The establishment of the "Plumbers" unit in the Nixon White House, the Colonel Oliver North operations in the Reagan White House, and their performance of what are normally policy, security, and other operational functions are examples of policymakers attempting directly to control implementation.)

In addition to this near monopoly of enforcement, bureaucracies greatly influence the processes of policymaking. Most modern legislation is general and can be effectively enforced only if administrative officials work out regulations elaborating the policy. The extent to which a general policy is carried out usually depends on

bureaucrats' interpretations of it and on the spirit and effectiveness with which they enforce it. Moreover, much of the adjudication in modern political systems is performed by administrative agencies with power to hold hearings and enforce regulations whether organized as independent regulatory bodies or as units in regular operating departments.

In Chapters Five and Six we discussed how bureaucratic agencies may serve as articulators and aggregators of interests. Departments like those for agriculture, labor, defense, welfare, and education may be among the most important voices of interest groups. And when an agriculture department obtains agreement on policy among different agricultural interest groups or a labor department draws together competing trade unions around some common policy, bureaucrats are performing a significant interest-aggregating function.

Finally, bureaucracies are instrumental in performing the communication function. Even in democratic systems, the bureaucracy is one of the most important sources of information about public issues and political events. News reporters are constantly knocking at the doors of administrative officials in search of the latest information on all spheres of foreign and domestic policy. Although an aggressive press in a modern democracy may force considerable information out of the bureaucracy, bureaucrats clearly have some control over the amount of information they divulge and the way it is interpreted. The decisions made by political elites, whether executives or legislators, are also based to a considerable extent on the information they obtain from administrative agencies. Similarly, interest groups, political parties, and the public depend on the information transmitted by administrative officials.

The truth of the matter is that modern, complex societies cannot get along without bureaucracies, and it also seems to be practically impossible to get along with them. The title of a book, *Implementation: How Great Expectations in Washington Are Dashed in Oakland*, and the development of a new field of research — implementation studies — express this dilemma.[10] Public policies are statements of intent enacted by the executive and the assembly. They allocate resources and designate responsibility for the realization of these goals. But realization depends on the bureaucracy and the responsiveness of the groups affected by the policies. Policies may be lost in the thicket of bureaucratic misunderstanding or opposition.

Creating and maintaining a responsive and responsible bureaucracy is one of the intractable problems of modern and modernizing society — capitalist or socialist, advanced or backward. It is a problem that can never be solved thoroughly, but only mitigated or kept under control by a variety of countervailing structures and influences.

Mark Nadel and Frances Rourke suggest the variety of ways that bureaucracies may be influenced and controlled externally or internally, through government and nongovernment agencies and forces (see Table 7.4).[11] The major external government control is, as we have suggested, the political executive. Although presidents, prime ministers, and ministers formally command subordinate officials and have the power to remove them for nonperformance of duty, there is actually mutual dependence and reciprocal control between executives and bureaucracies. The power of the executive is typically expressed in efforts at persuasion; rarely does it take the extreme form of dismissal or transfer. Centralized budgeting and administrative reorganization are other means by which the executive controls bureaucracy. The reallocation of resources among administrative agencies and changing lines of authority may bring bureaucratic implementation into greater conformity with the aims of the political executive.

Assemblies and courts also exercise significant external controls over the bureaucracy. Committee investigations, questions put to administrative agencies by assembly members, judicial processes controlling administrative excesses — all may have some effect on bureaucratic performance. The invention and rapid diffu-

sion of the institution of the *ombudsman* is another indication of the problem of controlling the bureaucracy from the perspective of injury or injustice to individuals.[12] In the Scandinavian countries, Britain, Germany, and elsewhere the ombudsman investigates claims of injury or of damage made by individuals as the result of government action, offering a procedure more expeditious and less costly than court action. Ombudsmen report to the legislative body for remedial action.

Among the extragovernmental forces and agencies that attempt to control bureaucracies are public opinion and the mass media; interest groups of various kinds, particularly public interest groups (like "Nader's Raiders"); and the constituencies of bureaucratic agencies, such as business, labor, farmers, and minority groups.

Bureaucratic responsiveness and responsibility are affected by internal controls, such as advisory committees formed by people representing many parties and many interest groups, and decentralization, which brings the bureaucracy closer to the groups it affects. Finally, the attitudes and values of the bureaucrats themselves affect their responsiveness and responsibility. Different bureaucracies have different attitudes toward public opinion, the media, and political parties. The norms and values that bureaucrats bring as they are recruited into public service, and the standards and obligations they are taught to respect within public service, have an important bearing on bureaucratic performance.

The variety and kinds of controls we have been

TABLE 7.4
TYPOLOGY OF CONTROLS FOR BUREAUCRATIC RESPONSIBILITY

	Formal	Informal
External	Directly or indirectly elected chief executive: president, prime minister, governor, etc.	Public opinion
		Press
	Elected assembly: congress, parliament, city council, etc.	Public interest groups
		Constituencies
	Courts	Competing bureaucratic organizations
	Ombudsman	
Internal	Representative bureaucracy where legally required	Perception of public opinion (anticipated reaction)
		Professional standards
	Citizen participation where legally required	Socialization in the norms of responsibility
	Decentralization	

Source: Taken from Mark V. Nadel and Frances E. Rourke, "Bureaucracies," in Fred I. Greenstein and Nelson W. Polsby, eds., *Handbook of Political Science*, vol. 5. © 1975, Addison–Wesley, Reading, Mass., p. 416. Reprinted with permission.

discussing operate in the advanced industrial democracies. Authoritarian systems lack many of these controls, particularly the external ones of elected political executives and legislators, independent courts, mass media, and interest groups. Authoritarian systems are particularly prone to bureaucratic inefficiency and conservatism in the absence of free and competitive elections, autonomous interest groups, and a free press.

"Bureaucracy," in the sense of inefficiency and inertia, is pandemic. It is truly a dilemma because we are unlikely to invent any schemes for carrying out large-scale social tasks without the organization, division of labor, and professionalism that bureaucracy provides. Its pathologies can only be mitigated. The art of modern political leadership consists not only in the prudent search for appropriate goals and policies, but also in the attempt to learn how to interact with the massive and complex bureaucracy—how and when to press and coerce it, reshuffle it, terminate its redundant and obsolete parts, flatter and reward it, teach it, and be taught by it.

KEY TERMS

authoritarian regime
bicameralism
bureaucracy
ceremonial executive
civil service

confederal systems
constitutional regime
decision rules
democratic presidential regime

federal systems
higher civil service
judicial review
ombudsman

parliamentary regime
policymaking
separation of powers
unitary systems

END NOTES

1. As March and Olsen put it: "Political institutions simplify the potential confusions of action by providing action alternatives: they simplify the potential confusions of meaning by creating a structure for interpreting history and anticipating the future; and they simplify the complications of heterogeneity by shaping the preferences of participants." James G. March and Johann P. Olsen, *Rediscovering Institutions: The Organizational Basis of Politics* (New York: Free Press, 1989), pp. 171–172. See also Alfred Stepan, *State and Society: Peru in Comparative Perspective* (Princeton, N.J.: Princeton University Press, 1978); and Peter Evans, Jurgen Rueschemeyer, and Theda Skocpol, *Bringing the State Back In* (Cambridge: Cambridge University Press, 1985).

2. March and Olsen, *Rediscovering Institutions*, p. 58.

3. On comparative constitutions, see Ivo Duchacek, *Power Maps: Comparative Politics of Constitutions* (Santa Barbara, Calif.: ABC Clio Press, 1973), pp. 210 ff.

4. Arend Lijphart, *Democracies: Patterns of Majoritarian and Consensus Government in Twenty-One Countries* (New Haven, Conn.: Yale University Press, 1984), chs. 1 and 2. Also see Robert A. Dahl, *Democracy and Its Critics* (New Haven, Conn.: Yale University Press, 1989).

5. Larry Diamond, "The Globalization of Democracy: Trends, Types, Causes, Prospects," unpublished paper, Stanford, California, Hoover Institution, 1990. In making this classification and classifying countries, Diamond draws on the work of Robert A. Dahl, *Polyarchy: Participation and Opposition* (New Haven, Conn.: Yale University Press, 1971); Michael Coppedge and Wolfgang Reinicke, "Measuring Polyarchy," *Studies in Comparative International Development*, 25:1 (Spring 1990), pp. 51–72; and Raymond D. Gastil, ed., *Freedom in the World: Political Rights and Civil Liberties, 1988–1989* (New York: Freedom House, 1989).

6. On functions of legislatures, see Robert Packenham, "Legislatures and Political Development," in Arthur Kornberg and L. D. Musolf, eds., *Legislatures in Developmental Perspective* (Durham, N.C.: Duke University Press, 1970); Jean Blondel, *Comparative Legislatures* (Englewood Cliffs, N.J.: Prentice-Hall, 1973), pp. 144 ff.; Gerhard Loewenberg and Samuel Patterson, *Comparing Legislatures* (Boston: Little, Brown, 1979), ch. 2; Michael Mezey, *Comparative Legislatures* (Durham, N.C.: Duke University Press, 1979); Philip Norton, "Parliaments: A Framework for Analysis," and "Legislatures in Comparative Perspective" in

West European Politics, 13 (July 1990), pp. 1–9, 143–155.

7. See Kaare Strom, *Minority Government and Majority Rule* (Cambridge, England: Cambridge University Press, 1990), pp. 72 ff.

8. For detailed information about the organization and recruitment of the modern political executive, see Jean Blondel, *World Leaders: Heads of Government in the Post War Period* (Beverly Hills, Calif.: Sage Publications, 1980); Jean Blondel, *The Organization of Governments: A Comparative Analysis of Governmental Structures* (Beverly Hills, Calif.: Sage Publications, 1982); Jean Blondel, *Government Ministers in the Contemporary World* (Beverly Hills, Calif.: Sage Publications, 1985).

9. F.M.G. Wilson, "Policymaking and the Policymakers" in Richard Rose, ed., *Policymaking in Britain* (New York: Free Press, 1969), pp. 360–361.

10. Jeffrey Pressman and Aaron Wildavsky (Berkeley and Los Angeles: University of California Press, 1973).

11. Mark V. Nadel and Frances E. Rourke, "Bureaucracies," in Fred I. Greenstein and Nelson W. Polsby, eds., *Handbook of Political Science*, vol. 5 (Reading, Mass.: Addison–Wesley, 1975), pp. 373–440.

12. See Frank Stacey, *The British Ombudsman* (Oxford: Clarendon Press, 1971); and Roy Gregory and Peter Hutchesson, *The Parliamentary Ombudsman; A Study in the Control of Administrative Action* (London: Allen & Unwin, 1975).

CHAPTER 8

PUBLIC POLICY

I N THE past century Western nations have been transformed from authoritarian or oligarchic regimes with limited suffrage to democratic systems. The power of the state has increasingly been used to meet popular needs and demands. The democratic political process has produced *welfare states* with programs of social insurance, health, public education, and the like. As the level of expenditures has grown to between one-third and one-half of the national product in most industrialized democratic countries, a number of problems have arisen. The increasing cost of the welfare state in taxes has produced a welfare backlash or tax rebellion in some countries, efforts to prevent further increases in welfare programs and to roll back those already in effect. The size of the government budget, and its effects on savings, investment, inflation, and employment, has been the central issue in the politics of advanced industrial societies in recent years.

Thus, the simple relationship between democratization and welfare characteristic of the earlier decades of the twentieth century has given way to a more problematic situation. The study of public policy has become a growth industry in the social sciences. Among the interesting themes being explored in this growing field of study are the varieties of welfare states and their causes. The United States is an example of a welfare pattern that stresses equality of opportunity through public education, in contrast to the European continent, where social security and health programs have taken precedence over educational programs.[1]

The crisis of the welfare state has provoked a conservative reaction that stresses setting limits on public expenditures and labor costs.[2] An alternative corporatist approach, which has had some success in small European countries, involves regular bargaining relationships among labor, business, and government over issues of wage, price, and investment policies.[3]

The data we present in this chapter are intended to provide background for understanding these and other contemporary controversies over public policy. We will compare in general the policy performance of countries with differing characteristics in different parts of the world. The public policies of nations may be summarized and compared according to their *outputs*, that is, the kinds of actions governments take in order to accomplish their purposes. We can classify these actions or outputs under four headings. First is the extraction of resources from the domestic and international environments:

How important are the welfare outputs of the state? A homeless man on a cold night in Seattle.

mediate or direct benefit. Figure 8.1 shows the revenue extracted by the central government as a percentage of gross national product (GNP) for a selection of nations in North and Latin America, Western and Eastern Europe, the Middle East, Africa, and Asia. We have included Hungary as reflecting the communist pattern of Eastern Europe. The data reported in the figure are for 1988, hence predating the economic reform of Hungary and the other Eastern European countries. (Comparable data for surviving communist countries — China, Cuba, and Vietnam — were not available.) Hungarian central government revenues as a proportion of GNP in 1988, the last year of the communist regime, were the largest for our selection of countries. The state extracted 58.2 percent of gross national product from its economy. It is of interest that the size of government revenue in the advanced capitalist world is not radically smaller than that of Hungary and other Eastern European countries when they were under communist control. Thus, the Swedish central government extracted almost 43 percent of its GNP; Israel more than 41 percent; and the United Kingdom more than 36 percent.

We should observe that Figure 8.1 reports *central government* revenues only. In such federal systems as the United States and Germany we would have to add the state and local revenues to the central revenues to get an accurate picture of the extractive burden borne by these countries. A substantial proportion of government revenue in the United States is collected by states and localities. The total for all revenues for the United States would run to more than 30 percent. Similarly for Germany, the *länder* and municipalities collect substantial amounts of revenue, which would raise the total to more than 40 percent. Even unitary countries such as Britain and Sweden collect some of their revenue through local governments. British total revenue would come to more than 45 percent, and Sweden would reach a total of over 50 percent. The difference in revenue as a proportion of GNP between command socialist economies and advanced welfare economies has been one of degree.[4]

Outside the European – North American area the size of central government revenue rarely exceeds 20 percent. Syria's revenues amount to 22.6 percent of its GNP, but more than half of this total takes the form of income from government-owned property and facilities, and grants from Arab oil countries. The central government revenues of Nigeria, Korea, and Mexico are all in the 18 percent of GNP range. Revenue levels are high in Nigeria and Mexico because both countries have large

money, goods, persons, and services. Second is distributive activity: what money, goods, and services are distributed, and to whom? Third is the regulation of human behavior — the use of compulsion and inducement to enforce extractive and distributive compliance or otherwise bring about desired behavior. Last is symbolic performance, the political speeches, holidays, rites, public monuments and statues, and the like used by leaders to exhort citizens to desired forms of conduct, to provide inspiring examples, to edify the population, and to socialize the young.

EXTRACTIVE PERFORMANCE

All political systems, even the simplest, extract resources from their environments. When primitive peoples go to war, specific age groups may be called on to fight. Such direct extraction of services is still found in the most complex of modern states, in the form of military duty, other obligatory public service like jury duty, or compulsory labor imposed on those convicted of crime.

The most common form of resource extraction in contemporary nations is taxation. Taxation is the extraction of money or goods from members of a political system, in consideration for which they receive no im-

FIGURE 8.1
CENTRAL GOVERNMENT REVENUE AS A PERCENTAGE OF GNP AND BY SOURCE OF REVENUE FOR SELECTED COUNTRIES, 1988

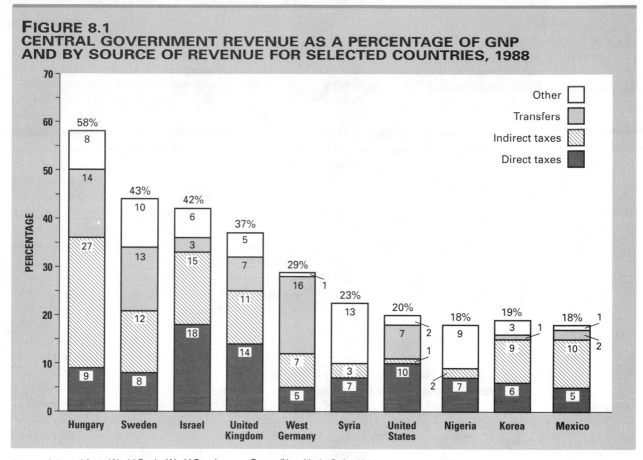

Source: Adapted from World Bank, *World Development Report* (New York: Oxford University Press, 1990), Table 12, pp. 200–201. Percents are rounded off.

government-owned oil sectors, and income from these sectors is reported as revenue. Bangladesh has a total central government revenue of 8.6 percent of GNP; India 14.2 percent; Uganda 8.2 percent; Ghana 13.8 percent; and the like.[5]

We have not included Japan in Figure 8.1 since the *World Development Report* only gives a total revenue number for Japan and does not break it down according to type of revenue which we discuss generally below. Japan is the least heavily taxed of all developed countries, with a proportion of central government revenues to GNP of only 13 percent and an expenditure level of 17 percent.[6]

Figure 8.1 also reports the sources of revenue as a proportion of GNP for each country. Sources of revenue are important because they determine who pays how much of the taxes. Personal and corporate income taxes, and taxes on capital gains and wealth are called *direct*

taxes, in that they are directly levied on persons and corporations. They generally tend to be *progressive* in character; that is, the tax rates are higher for richer than for poorer citizens. *Indirect taxes* such as sales and value added taxes, excise taxes, and customs duties are levied on transactions, or services, and their welfare distributive effects depend on who purchases the commodities and services. Thus, direct taxes on luxury goods may not be regressive, since the poor rarely purchase them. But general sales taxes or value added taxes that affect necessities such as food and clothing are *regressive;* that is, those who are less able to afford them share an equal burden with those who can.

In 1988 Hungary received almost half of its revenue in indirect taxes — taxes on turnover in the process of manufacture, sales, excises, and customs duties. Nine percent of its GNP was extracted in direct taxes primarily on income; and 14 percent was taken in transfers from firms and employees for social services. In Germany and the United Kingdom most of the revenue comes from transfer payments and income taxes, but Germany relies far more heavily on transfer payments and Britain more on income taxes. Countries such as Mexico and Korea obtain most of their revenue from indirect taxes, which has the effect of burdening the poor more substantially.

The composition of the revenues of nations is quite complex, depending on the kinds of taxes imposed, the distribution of income and wealth, the consumption patterns of different strata of the population, and deliberate government efforts at distributive equity. Heidenheimer, Heclo, and Adams classify the tax systems of *OECD* (the Organization for Economic Cooperation and Development, which includes some twenty-six free-market economies, primarily in Europe and North America) countries into the following groupings. Heavy social security tax systems include Germany, Austria, the Netherlands, France, and Italy which receive one-third to one-half of their revenue from social security, which is imposed more or less equally on both employers and employees. The United States and Japan are farthest below average in total tax burden, but they rely more heavily on direct taxes and transfers rather than on sales and consumption taxes. Finally, countries such as Sweden and Norway impose the highest tax burdens of all the OECD countries, and they rely on all three types of taxation — direct, indirect, and transfer payments. Both countries impose the greatest burden of social security payments on the employers, with Sweden levying the entire social security tax on employers and Norway taking three-quarters of it.[7]

Tax rates have been decreasing in all Western countries in the last decade, and there has been a shift from the more visible direct income taxes to less visible indirect consumption taxes and a sharp decrease in higher income tax rates. From 1975 to 1990 British top marginal rates declined by 43 percent, the U.S. by 42 percent, Swedish by 35 percent, and Japanese by 25 percent. The average decline in top tax rates for all OECD countries in the last fifteen years has been 18 percent.[8] These trends in revenue policy have been associated with the spread of monetarist and supply-side economic ideology, stressing the importance of entrepreneurial incentives for productivity. This change in patterns of taxation has increased income inequality in the advanced industrial countries.

DISTRIBUTIVE PERFORMANCE

The distributive performance of the political system is the allocation by governmental agencies of various kinds of money, goods, services, honors, and opportunities to individuals and groups in the society. It can be measured and compared according to the quantity of whatever is distributed, the areas of human life touched by these benefits, the sections of the population receiving these benefits, and the relationship between human needs and governmental distributions intended to meet these needs. Government expenditures do not measure all these distributions, but they give us a quantitative measure of this distributive effort. Although these figures are drawn from a variety of sources especially from data released by the governments, and their accuracy cannot be guaranteed, they are rough indicators of the countries' efforts.

Figure 8.2 reports central governmental expenditures as a percentage of GNP as a total, and as percentages for defense, welfare, and other purposes, for a selection of nations roughly representative of areas and levels of development. As we glance across the figure, it is clear that the level of central government expenditures varies substantially from country to country — depending primarily on level of economic development and political ideology. Central government expenditure accounts for more than 58 percent of Hungary's GNP, more than 50 percent of that of Israel, over 40 percent of Swedish GNP, and so on down to 22 percent of the U.S. and almost 18 percent of the South Korean. Again state and local expenditures create a problem. If we were to add them to central figures, the total for the United States would rise to more than 30 percent and that for Germany to more than 40 percent. They would also raise the total for such countries as Sweden and the United Kingdom, for even in these unitary systems local governments have some expenditures based on their own revenues.

The cross-hatched sections of the bars represent the proportion of GNP spent by central government on welfare. The size of the cross-hatching for Israel, Sweden, the United Kingdom, Germany, and relatively for the United States justifies our calling these countries welfare states. More than 17 percent of GNP for Israel, 26 percent for Sweden, over 17 percent for the United Kingdom, more than 20 percent for Germany, and 11 percent (more than half of total central expenditures) for the United States, represent expenditures for education,

FIGURE 8.2
CENTRAL GOVERNMENT EXPENDITURE AS A PERCENTAGE OF GNP AND BY OBJECT OF EXPENDITURE FOR SELECTED COUNTRIES, 1988

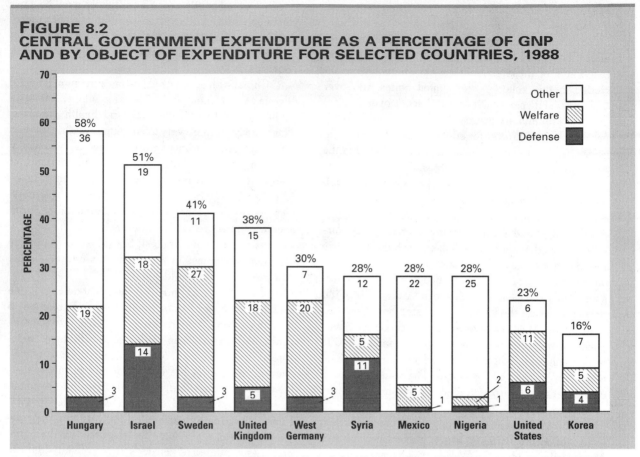

Source: Adapted from World Bank, *World Development Report* (New York: Oxford University Press, 1990), Table 11, pp. 198–199. Percents are rounded off.

health, social security, housing, and the like. If we were to add state and local expenditures to these central figures, the welfare proportion would be even greater, since state and local functions generally include, in addition to public safety, roads, and transportation, such welfare functions as education, health, and sanitation. In Third World countries such as Syria, Mexico, and Nigeria, while welfare needs are great, the welfare effort of central governments is relatively small. Korea, a rapidly modernizing country, also has a growing welfare sector, principally in education — one-third of its expenditures are for welfare purposes. Chapter Twelve describes the increasing welfare effort in Japan over the last several decades.

The solidly colored sections of the bars in Figure 8.2 represent the defense and military efforts of these countries in 1988 as percentages of GNP. Israel was the

most burdened of these countries, spending 14 percent of its GNP for military purposes in 1988. It is interesting that this total did not come at the expense of welfare expenditures. Despite its heavy military loading, Israel maintained its membership among the welfare democracies. Syria spent more than 11 percent of its GNP for military purposes and only 4.7 percent for welfare in 1988. The United States spent 5.6 percent of GNP for defense in 1988 and twice that amount for welfare at the federal level. South Korea spent almost equal amounts for defense and welfare. Japan, not listed in the figure (but see Chapter Twelve), spends very little for defense but an increasing amount for welfare.

Figure 8.2 fails to capture the actual magnitude of the effort made by government for defense and welfare purposes. With a large GNP per capita, a country like the United States spends substantially more on military, educational, and health purposes, even though this represents less of a burden on the economy as a whole. Table 8.1, showing expenditures per capita on military, educational, and health purposes, displays the dollar magnitude of these expenditures for the countries included in this volume. The United States with over $15,000 GNP per capita in 1984 spent over $1,000 per capita for military purposes and also had the highest per capita expenditures for education and second highest for health. Still it was not as heavily burdened as the other advanced industrial countries. In that same year Japan spent only $103 per capita for defense but $529 per capita on education, an amount roughly equal to per capita educational expenditures for the United Kingdom, France, and West Germany. In the light of more reliable data that are now available, questions have been raised about the accuracy of such statistics as we report on the Soviet economy, even though our figures were estimates of the Central Intelligence Agency (CIA). It is now argued that the CIA overestimated Soviet productivity in the last decade or so. Table 8.1 shows the Soviet Union with a GNP per capita of approximately $7,000 in 1984 and expenditures of $816 for defense, $332 for education, and $227 for health. The leading socialist country at that time was trailing the Western countries in welfare expenditures.

The vicious circle affecting the poorer nations is suggested by the figures for China, Mexico, and Nigeria. Mexico, classified by the *World Development Report* as "a lower middle income economy" with a GNP per capita in 1984 of a little over $3,000, only spent $79 per capita on education (less than one-fifth of what France, Britain, and Germany spent), and $48 per capita on health (about one-tenth that of the Western European countries).

China, with seven or eight times the population of Nigeria, spent about the same amount per capita in 1984 on military, educational, and health purposes. The tragedy for these very low-income countries is that, while they are confronted with the urgent challenge of upgrading the skills and improving the performance of their workforces, their resources are insufficient to make rapid headway. The striking differences in these rankings and in the economic and governmental performance which they reflect are not reported in the mood of winners or losers in a contest, but rather to emphasize the great differences in the conditions of material life that prevail in the world today.

Table 8.1 and Figure 8.2 show that defense is one area in which per capita wealth has little relation to spending efforts. Nations locked in tense international confrontations or those undertaking efforts at widespread influence, make extraordinary defense efforts, even at the cost of the education and health of their inhabitants. Education, health, and welfare expenditures, on the other hand, are affected by levels of wealth. Poor nations, with their limited budgets and many demands, cannot easily spare the resources for these programs (see Harold Wilensky's study of sixty-four nations).[9] In both absolute and relative terms expenditure

TABLE 8.1
EXPENDITURES PER CAPITA FOR DEFENSE, EDUCATION, AND HEALTH FOR SELECTED COUNTRIES IN 1984

Country	GNP per capita	Military expenditures per capita	Education expenditures per capita	Health expenditures per capita
United States	15,541	1,002	771	674
United Kingdom	8,616	470	447	470
France	10,152	421	537	676
West Germany	10,985	359	506	891
Japan	10,300	103	529	474
Soviet Union	7,095	816	332	227
China	307	21	8	4
Mexico	3,027	20	79	48
Nigeria	767	14	15	5

Source: Ruth Leger Sivard, *World Military and Social Expenditures 1987–88* (Washington, D.C.: World Priorities, 1988).

on social security in poor nations tends to be limited. This limitation is due in part to their rather youthful populations and the role of the extended family in caring for the elderly and infirm. All the wealthier nations make efforts to assist the aged and unemployed; however, differences in expenditures reflect policy and historical experience. The United States made a much greater effort, and much earlier, in mass education than did most European nations; on the other hand, Americans began spending on social insurance and public services much later, and still do less in this area. Americans have historically put much more emphasis on equality of opportunity and less on welfare obligations than Europeans. Wilensky also found that centralized governments, well-organized working-class parties and movements, and low military expenditures were all associated with stronger efforts in welfare.

Prior to the watershed year of 1989, the communist countries of Eastern Europe were spending less on education, health, and welfare than the democracies of Western Europe. As Table 8.1 shows, the Soviet Union was also substantially behind in education and health expenditures. In addition, in the last decades their growth rates fell substantially behind. It is easy to see how confidence in the future of socialism dissipated in these countries even within the inner circles of the Communist parties. It is impossible to predict the rates and patterns of change among these countries, but in all of them we observe the emergence of larger private economic sectors. We can also anticipate that levels of revenue and expenditure will become more similar to Western patterns.

REGULATIVE PERFORMANCE

Regulative performance is the exercise of control by a political system over the behavior of individuals and groups in the society. Although we usually associate regulation with legal coercion or its threat, political systems commonly control behavior by exhortation and by material or financial inducements as well.

The regulative activities of modern political systems have proliferated enormously over the last century or so. Industrialization and urban concentration have produced interdependence and problems in traffic, health, and public order. Growth in industry has created problems with monopolies, industrial safety, and labor exploitation. At the same time, the growth of science and the development of the attitude that humanity can

harness and control nature have led to increased resort to governmental action. Recent history has been marked by the proliferation of regulatory activities.

The pattern of regulation varies not only with the broad socioeconomic and cultural changes associated with industrialization and urbanization, but also with changes in other cultural values. Thus, in recent years regulation in the United States has extended to include protection of voting rights, correction of racial segregation, prohibition of discrimination against minority groups and women in employment, control of pollution, and the like. At the same time, in most modern nations regulation of birth control, abortion, divorce, and sexual conduct has lessened.

In characterizing the regulative performance of a political system, we answer these questions:

1. What aspects of human behavior and interaction are regulated and to what degree? Does the government regulate such domains as family relations, economic activity, religious activity, political activity, geographic mobility, professional and occupational qualifications, and protection of person and property?
2. What sanctions are used to compel or induce citizens to comply? Does the government use exhortation and moral persuasion, financial rewards and penalties, licensing of some types of action, physical confinement or punishment, and direction of various activities?
3. What groups in the society are regulated, with what procedural limitations on enforcement and what protections for rights? Are there rights of appeal? Are these sanctions applied uniformly, or do they affect different areas or groups differently?

All modern nations use these sanctions in varying degrees. But the variety of patterns is great and reflects values, goals, and strategies. Governments have taken over various industries in many nations, but the range is very different. In 1960, one study shows, government in the United States employed only 1 percent of the persons engaged in mining and manufacturing and 28 percent of those working for public utilities supplying gas, water, and electrical power; in France, the corresponding figures were 8 percent and 71 percent.[10]

Although we must treat the critical area of regulative performance briefly, one more aspect must be emphasized: government control over political participation and communication. We saw in earlier chapters that the presence or absence of political competition was an essential structural feature of political systems. Political systems vary all the way from authoritarian regimes that prohibit party organization, the formation of voluntary associations, and freedom of communication, to democratic systems, where such rights are protected. Government regulatory performance in this area has a crucial effect on political processes.

Table 8.2 shows the political rights and civil liberties ratings for a selection of countries for the year 1988. Political rights refer to the opportunities people have to participate in the choice of political leaders—voting rights, the right to run for office, and the like. Civil liberties refer to the substantive areas of human behavior such as freedom of speech, press, assembly, and religion as well as procedural protections, such as trial by jury, against arbitrary governmental action. Those countries receiving rankings of 6 or 7 in the second column are assumed to exercise complete control over the communications media and to set no limits on government regulatory activity vis-à-vis the individual. The rankings are based on indicators evaluated by a number of referees.

There is an important correspondence between rankings for political and civil rights. No country that scores high on participatory rights is very low on civil liberties, and no country low on participatory rights is high on civil liberties, suggesting that there is a strong relationship between popular participation and the rule of law and equitable procedure. The evaluations range from a high of 1 on both aspects of rights for the United Kingdom, Japan, and the United States to the lowest possible scores of 7 and 7 for Iraq. These rankings, of course, vary over time. Nigeria's rose with the reestablishment of democracy in 1980, but plummeted after the military coup in 1985. Ratings for the United States have improved since the civil rights movement of the 1960s. The ratings for Israel depend on whether the occupied territories are included. These ratings are for 1988 and so were compiled before the onset of the Palestinian disorders.

Lest the impression be given that regulation is only negative in value, as in the suppression of rights, we should be reminded that our civilization and our amenities are dependent on governmental regulation. Such matters as safety of persons and property, prevention of environmental pollution, provision of adequate sanitation, safe disposal of toxic wastes, maintenance of occupational safety, and equal access to housing and education are commonly covered by governmental regulation and implementation. The revolt against overregulation in the last decades should not be permitted to obscure this fundamental point.[11]

SYMBOLIC PERFORMANCE

A fourth category of political system outputs is symbolic performance. Much communication by political leaders takes the form of appeals to history, courage, boldness, wisdom, and magnanimity embodied in the nation's past; or appeals to values and ideologies, such as equality, liberty, community, democracy, communism, liberalism, or religious tradition, or promises of future accomplishment and rewards. Political systems differ in citizens' confidence in their leaders and faith in their political symbols. Symbolic outputs are also intended, however, to enhance other aspects of performance: to make people pay their taxes more readily and honestly, comply with the law more faithfully, or accept sacrifice, danger, and hardship. Such appeals may be especially important in times of crisis. Some of the most magnificent and most successful examples are to be found in Winston Churchill's stirring speeches to the British people during the dangerous moments when Britain stood

TABLE 8.2
POLITICAL RIGHTS AND LIBERTIES RATINGS FOR SELECTED COUNTRIES, 1988

Country	Political rights[a]	Civil liberties[b]
United States	1	1
West Germany	1	2
Japan	1	1
France	1	2
United Kingdom	1	1
Israel	2	2
Soviet Union	6	5
Mexico	3	4
Nigeria	5	5
Iraq	7	7
China	6	6

[a]Ratings range from the highest of 1 to the lowest of 7. Political rights here refer to the right to participate in determining who will govern one's country.
[b]Civil liberties refer to those freedoms that make it possible to mobilize new opinions and to the rights of the individual vis-à-vis the state.
Source: Raymond D. Gastil, ed., *Freedom in the World* (New York: Freedom House, 1989), pp. 50–56.

alone after the fall of France in World War II, but symbolic performance is also important in less extreme circumstances. Political leaders seek to influence citizens' behavior in energy crises or in times of drought, famine, and disaster. "Jawboning" — exhorting business executives and labor leaders to go slow in raising prices and wages — is a frequently employed anti-inflation measure. Public buildings, plazas, monuments, holidays with their parades, and civic and patriotic indoctrination in schools all contribute to the population's sense of governmental legitimacy and its willingness to comply with public policy.[12]

OUTCOMES OF POLITICAL PERFORMANCE

Our comparisons of the levels and composition of taxation, governmental expenditures, and regulation in different countries do not tell us how these measures affect welfare and order. The functioning of the economy and the social order as well as international events may frustrate the purpose of political leaders. Thus, a tax rebate to increase consumption and stimulate the economy may be nullified by a rise in the price of oil. Increases in health expenditures may have no effect because of rising health costs; or health services may be so distributed as not to reach those most in need.

DOMESTIC WELFARE OUTCOMES

In Tables 8.3 and 8.4, we compare nations on a number of welfare, health, education, and equity indicators. The first three columns of Table 8.3 record GNP per capita, and growth rates for the almost quarter century from 1965 until 1988 and for the period 1980–1988. Then we attempt to show the connection between these economic patterns and health conditions reflected in life expectancy, infant mortality, and the daily per capita caloric intake. Table 8.4 compares education policy and level in different kinds of countries in terms of educational aspirations, the effort expended, and the educational level attained including the educational status of women. Our purpose in presenting these socioeconomic data is to show how governmental and private efforts in different kinds of societies affect human life chances — the availability of economic opportunity, the equity of income distribution, the health and longevity, the skill and creativity of their populations. Although the natural resources, the socioeconomic structure, and the cultural and historical backgrounds of these countries constitute constraints and opportunities, politics and government are the purposive and collective goal-setting and problem-solving institutions in the pursuit of economic growth, social welfare, and equity.

The range in per capita GNP reported in Table 8.3 staggers the imagination. Japan's GNP is more than one

TABLE 8.3
WELFARE OUTCOMES IN SELECTED COUNTRIES, 1988

Country	GNP per capita 1988	GNP growth 1965–1988	GNP growth 1980–1988	Life expectancy at birth	Inf. mortality per 1000 live births	Daily calories
Japan	21,020	6.5	3.9	78	18	2,864
United States	19,840	2.7	3.3	76	25	3,645
West Germany	18,480	3.3	1.8	75	24	3,528
France	16,090	4.0	1.8	76	22	3,336
United Kingdom	12,810	2.4	2.8	75	20	3,256
Hungary	2,460	5.6	1.6	70	16	3,569
Mexico	1,760	6.5	0.5	69	46	3,132
Egypt	660	6.8	5.7	63	83	3,342
India	340	3.6	5.2	58	97	2,238
China	330	6.4	10.3	70	31	2,630
Nigeria	290	6.9	−1.1	51	103	2,146
Tanzania	160	3.7	2.0	53	104	2,192

Source: World Bank, *World Development Report, 1990* (New York: Oxford University Press, 1990), Tables 1 & 2, pp. 178–181, Table 28, pp. 232–233.

TABLE 8.4
EDUCATION POLICY IN SELECTED COUNTRIES: EFFECT, OUTPUT, AND OUTCOMES (1980s)

Country	Goal and Output				Outcomes (percent)		
	Years of required education	Percent GNP for public education	Exp. $ mil.	Exp. per cap. $	15–19 year-old, in school	Literacy	Women's share in university enrollment
Japan	9	5.0	63,550	529	76	99	24
United States	11	6.7	182,520	771	77	99	50
France	10	5.7	29,507	537	66	99	51
West Germany	12	4.4	30,953	506	60	99	38
United Kingdom	11	5.0	25,260	447	75	99	40
Soviet Union	10	7.3	91,800	332	62	99	50
Hungary	10	5.6	3,130	293	62	99	50
China	9	—	8,720	8	55	69	28
India	8	3.4	6,280	8	46	44	26
Mexico	6	3.4	6,160	79	69	90	34
Egypt	9	5.5	1,480	31	52	44	33
Nigeria	6	1.4	1,510	15	46	42	16
Tanzania	7	4.1	235	11	44	46	18

Sources: Columns 1 and 2, UNESCO *Statistical Yearbook, 1989* (Paris: UNESCO, 1989), pp. III–1 ff.; columns 3, 4, 5, 6, Ruth Leger Sivard, *World Military and Social Expenditures* (Washington, D.C.: World Priorities, 1987–1988), pp. 43 ff.

hundred times that of Tanzania. The United States, Germany, and France also have per capita GNPs that are more than one hundred times larger than that of Tanzania. The economy of Hungary, the only then socialist country included in the table, is a little more than one-tenth that of Japan and about the same fraction of American productivity. While the economies of Nigeria, China, India, and Egypt are more productive than that of Tanzania, there is an enormous economic asymmetry between all the advanced and developing societies. Household services, subsistence agriculture, and other forms of household productivity do not get properly included in national income accounting, so that the figures for the lower income economies are somewhat exaggerated — but only somewhat.

Part of the explanation for these disparities is reported in columns 2 and 3 of Table 8.3, which give the rate of growth in GNP over the last twenty-three years, and for the first eight years of the 1980s. Japan has been running a strong and steady economic development race since its rise from defeat in World War II. While its rate of growth receded somewhat in the 1980s, it still has the highest rate of growth among all the advanced industrial societies listed in the table. Along with this pattern of

growth goes the best record in life expectancy and infant mortality. It is intriguing that with the highest GNP per capita, the average caloric intake of the Japanese is substantially lower than that of all the other advanced industrial countries, and the medium-income developing societies as well. The difference is a dietary-cultural one —South Korea, Hong Kong, and Singapore, all East Asian, have similarly low caloric intakes.

Comparison of rates of growth over the period 1965–1988 and the more recent 1980–1988 period reveals a number of interesting differences. The United States and the United Kingdom, respectively, under the conservative Reagan and Thatcher regimes, increased their economic momentum somewhat during those years, in contrast to all the other advanced market economies. Hungary's decline was precipitous from 5.6 percent over the whole 1965–1988 period to 1.6 percent in the 1980s. Mexico and Nigeria also experienced radical declines in rates of growth, explained by the fall in oil prices. China and India showed strong growth rates during the 1980s.

The relationship between economic level and health is dramatically demonstrated in the figures for Nigeria and Tanzania where life expectancy is in the low

fifties and one out of ten infants fails to survive the first year of life. The importance of culture and public policy is suggested by the figures for China and India. With the same GNP per capita, Chinese life expectancy is seventy years and infant mortality is thirty-one per thousand live births, while those of India are fifty-eight years and ninety-seven, respectively. China has a much larger number of physicians per capita than India and a larger per capita caloric intake.

Other kinds of data also demonstrate the strong effect of economic level on health expenditures, health facilities, and sanitation. One authority reports that in the 1980s the average public expenditure per capita for health for the economically developed countries was $469 and compared with $11 for the developing countries. The average number of persons per physician in the developed world was 398, as compared with 2,043 for the developing world. While 97 percent of the people of the developed world had access to safe water, this was true for only 53 percent of the population of the less advantaged areas.

Gross national product per capita figures are averages; they do not tell us how the economic product is distributed in different societies. Data on income distribution are not easy to come by, but the data in Table 2.1 in Chapter 2 gave us some impression of how income distribution varies in four kinds of nations: (1) advanced market societies, (2) socialist (ex-communist) societies, (3) medium-income developing societies, and (4) low-income developing societies. Looking back at Table 2.1, we can see that in advanced capitalist societies the top 10 percent of households get around one-fourth of the income and the bottom 40 percent get about 15 to a little more than 20 percent. For the three socialist countries included in Table 2.1 — Yugoslavia (1987), Hungary (1983), and Poland (1987) — the data are rather surprising. Yugoslavia turns out to have a more unequal distribution than Japan, while Hungary has the most equalitarian distribution of all — more than one-fourth of the income goes to the poorest 40 percent of the households and only 18.7 percent to the top tenth of the households. Poland's figures are nearly as equal as Hungary's. All three countries have a wealth level well below that of the advanced market societies.

The two Third World patterns are particularly interesting and illustrate the operation of the well-known Kuznets curve. In his studies of European economic history, Simon Kuznets pointed out that in the early stages of industrialization income distribution became more unequal as the more advanced industrial sector outpaced the rural agricultural sector. In the later stages of industrialization, income distribution came closer to equality. The data in Table 2.1 tend to support this theory. Brazil, Malaysia, and Mexico with GNPs per capita between $2,160 and $1,690, at a midpoint in economic developmental level, have the most unequal income distribution among the countries in the table. India and Bangladesh, lower down, have more equal distributions, while the Ivory Coast with a GNP of $770 has a distribution pattern much like that of Mexico.

The Kuznets curve is explained by the common trends of economic and political modernization. In the early stages of modernization the large, traditional rural sector is left behind as industry and commercial agriculture begin to grow. At higher levels of economic attainment, the rural agricultural sector is penetrated and reduced in size by comparison with the growing industrial and service sectors of the economy. In addition, the development of trade unions and political parties in democratic countries results in legislation that affects income distribution through taxation, wage policy, and social security, health, and other benefits.[13]

The data in Tables 8.3 and 2.1 show how public policies affect welfare in some respects. A more thorough picture of the way policy may affect outcomes is shown in Table 8.4, which focuses on education, an important aspect of welfare. In the first column we see each country's educational goals — the number of years children are required to attend school. The next three columns describe performance in educational policy. First, we see the expenditure on public education as a percentage of GNP, a rough measure of proportional effort. The next column shows how that effort translates into actual dollars. Then we see those dollars relative to population size, a crude measure of the amount avail-

able for the children who must be educated. Countries such as Tanzania and Egypt devote similar percentages of the GNP to education as do the advanced industrial societies. If you examine the per capita expenditure column, however, you will see that the differences in dollar expenditures are enormous.

The fifth and sixth columns show the policy outcomes in the short run and the long run. The short-run effort is the percentage of the five to nineteen year olds in school. This percentage is greatly affected by the dollars actually spent, although differences in efficiency and emphasis on mass or elite education also shape this outcome. Then, we see the long-term outcome measured in literacy. Literacy is affected by education programs, but slowly, unless very substantial adult education programs are undertaken. In countries like India and Nigeria most of the older people are illiterate, and it will take a long time for the education of the younger generation to have its effects. China has made more of an effort in adult education, although these data must be treated with caution, because they are merely estimates. The figure of 99 percent literate in the United States conflicts with studies showing substantial functional illiteracy among American adults. The final column tells us something of the status of women in these societies — what proportion of university students are women. The range is from approximately half in the United States, the Soviet Union, and France to less than one-fifth in such countries as Nigeria and Tanzania.

Table 8.4 reveals the sobering difficulties of trying to change societies, even in an area such as literacy, where modern methods and technology are available. It is hard for a poor country to spend a high percentage of its GNP on education, because to do so means that sacrifices must be made elsewhere. In any case, the country's revenue is probably limited, because much of its productive effort simply goes to feed the producers. No matter how large the country's percentage of effort may be, it does not translate into much per child, because the resource base is small and the population is growing rapidly, pouring children into the new schools. The older population in mostly illiterate, so that the net effect on literacy is slow.

DOMESTIC SECURITY OUTCOMES

Maintaining order and national security and protecting persons and property are the government's most fundamental responsibilities. Despite the general rise of crime in many modern societies, we have relatively little in the way of comparative data. Statistics are more reliable and up to date for the United States, which is by far the most crime-prone country of all. While the increase in crime has been worldwide, in 1989 the crime rate in the United States was 15 percent over the 1980 level.[14] Murder rates are usually considered the most reliable statistics. Table 8.5 shows a great variation in murder rates for countries for which we have data, but the United States and Mexico have much larger murder rates than other countries. The United States was also highest in the proportion of criminal offenders (these data are for the mid–1970s), having more than 4,000 criminals per 100,000 population compared with under 1,600 for West Germany, around 1,300 for France, and around 750 for the United Kingdom. We do not know much about the causes of these differences, though the greater availability of hand guns in the United States is surely part of the explanation for its particularly high increase in violent crime.

Column 3 shows the number of incidents of riots in a selection of countries from 1948 to 1977. The ab-sence of riots indicates the ability of groups in society to resolve issues short of violence and the degree of satisfaction with government. It also reflects the extent to which nations successfully impose discipline on their populations, the amount of freedom they accord them, and the amount and incidence of policing. All these data must be viewed with great caution, because they are taken from the public press, which is more reliable in some nations than others.

The figures for the United States are relatively high, reflecting the disturbances of the 1960s and early 1970s over civil rights and the Vietnam War. The high figures for the United Kingdom are mostly for Northern Ireland, but racial disturbances in other parts of Britain also helped push the figures up. The large number of riots in India reflects the high level of ethnic-linguistic conflict in that subcontinent.

OUTPUTS AND OUTCOMES IN THE INTERNATIONAL ARENA

Nations typically engage in a great variety of international activities in order to enhance their welfare and security — economic, diplomatic, and military — and these activities affect prosperity and depression, war and peace, stability and change in the international political economy. These developments in turn affect the internal politics and policies of nations in a never-ending process. The interplay of international political and economic conditions and the political processes and public policy outputs of nations has been described and analyzed in a recent series of studies by Peter Gourevitch. He traced the political and policy responses of five Western industrial nations — Great Britain, France, Germany, Sweden, and the United States — to the three world depressions of 1870–1890, 1930–1940, and 1975–1985. Gourevitch also shows how these crises affected business, labor, and agriculture differently in each country, tracing the preferences and responses of interest groups, their interaction with political parties in each country, through to changes in political structure and policy. These changes in political structure and policy in individual countries are attributable to the impact of international depression and can be seen as creating the basis for equilibrium or breakdown in the last century of Western international relations. Thus, the world depression of the 1930s produced a conservative reaction in England, a moderate left reaction in the United States, a polarization and paralysis of public policy in

TABLE 8.5
CRIME AND DISORDER IN SELECTED COUNTRIES

Country	Murders per 100,000 (mid-1980s)	Criminal offenders per 100,000 (mid-1970s)	Riots, 1948–1977
United States	8.9	4,251	861
West Germany	1.1	1,597	143
Japan	0.8	519	195
France	1.2	1,358	207
United Kingdom	0.7	762	372
Mexico	17.0	ND	177
Egypt	0.5	19	99
Hungary	2.5	ND	32
Czechoslovakia	1.1	ND	68
Poland	1.7	ND	92
Nigeria	2.8	80	194
India	3.4	216	678

Sources: Column 1, United Nations; *Demographic Yearbook, 1988* (New York: United Nations, 1989); column 2, Interpol Crime Statistics reported in George T. Kurian, *The New Book of World Rankings* (New York: Facts in File Publications, 1984); column 3, Charles Taylor and David Jodice, *World Handbook of Political and Social Indicators,* 3rd ed., Vol. 1, chs. 2–4 (New Haven, Conn.: Yale University Press, 1983).

Will the threat of war decline? Reagan and Gorbachev congratulate each other on the signing of the Intermediate and Shorter Range Missile Treaty at the White House in January of 1988. Another major step was taken at the signing of the START Treaty in Moscow in 1991 by Presidents Bush and Gorbachev.

France, and a radical polarization, a breakdown of democracy, and the emergence of an aggressive nationalism in Germany. While the causes of World War II were complex and in considerable part generated from within the international system, the pacifism of Britain, the demoralization and defeatism of France, the isolationism of the United States, and the nihilism and aggression of Germany were fed by the economic devastation of the world depression of the 1930s.[15]

The most important and most costly outcome of the interaction among nations is warfare. Table 8.6 reports the incidence of warfare for a variety of nations since the conclusion of the Napoleonic wars in 1816 — reporting the number of wars and battle deaths incurred by each country. Russia has averaged more than 50,000 battle deaths per year in the last century and a half, and Germany more than 30,000. These costs of international warfare have gradually escalated. Most of the deaths are concentrated in the twentieth century, and civilian deaths (which the table does not show) have risen even more rapidly. According to one authority, more than 90 percent of the deaths in war since 1700 have occurred in our century. Wars have occasioned as many civilian as military deaths. As of 1987 some twenty-two wars were underway, with a death toll in these wars as of that date of over 2 million, more than 80

percent of them civilian. These included the wars in Afghanistan, Angola, Cambodia, Colombia, El Salvador, Ethiopia, Guatemala, India, Iran, Iraq, Lebanon, Nicaragua, Sri Lanka, the Sudan, Vietnam, and others.[16]

As nuclear weapons are developed, large-scale war threatens to become far more destructive to lives and property and far more random in its choice of victims, threatening the very survival of humankind and life on our planet. Until 1914 the incidence and magnitude of war seemed to bear some relationship to public policy; at least leaders of nations acted as though these costs in human and material destruction were appropriate and acceptable. The alliance that defeated Napoleon in 1815 viewed the Europe which the Treaty of Vienna newly constituted as an outcome worth the cost in blood and treasure of the long Napoleonic wars. Victorious Prussia under Bismarck could view the Austrian and French wars of the midnineteenth century as reasonable costs for German unification under Prussia. It is well to recognize, however, that the Franco-Prussian War was a prelude to World War I, as World War I was a prelude to World War II. The relationship between war as a means and the importance of its objectives began to grow apart in the twentieth century. With the creation and use of nuclear weapons at the end of World War II, and the accumulation of enormous nuclear arsenals in the last decades, leaders of nations and "security professionals" have come to the conclusion that there would be no victors in such a war and that the sole purpose of a nuclear arsenal is to deter an antagonist.

The Gorbachev revolution has led to significant steps in the reduction of nuclear arsenals and of armaments generally. The number of wars in the Third World — in Africa, the Middle East, and Latin America, in which the United States and the USSR confront each other through client states, has also rapidly declined. There has been a similar abatement of confrontation between China and capitalist countries. But while the sharp bipolar capitalism – communism tension in international relations has abated, and the deliberative and authoritative role of the United Nations Organization in international disputes has been enhanced, warfare and even large-scale warfare, as the Gulf War demonstrates, is an expected feature of international relations. The Gulf War involved a coalition of thirty-two countries, organized by the United States to enforce United Nations Security Council resolutions ordering Iraq to withdraw from Kuwait after it had invaded and

TABLE 8.6
INTERNATIONAL SECURITY OUTCOMES IN SELECTED NATIONS, 1816−1980

Country	Years in international system	Number of wars[a]	Battle deaths[a]	Battle deaths per year
Russia	165	19	9,731,211	58,977
Germany[b]	156	6	5,353,500	34,317
China	121	11	3,128,499	25,855
France	163	22	1,965,128	12,056
Japan	114	9	1,371,447	12,030
United Kingdom	165	19	1,295,230	7,850
United States	165	8	664,816	4,029
Egypt	44	5	25,000	568
India	34	5	14,000	412
Mexico	150	3	19,000	127
Tanzania	20	1	1,000	50

[a]Does not include civil wars.
[b]Figures are for Prussia before unification in 1871.
Source: Calculated from data made available by the Inter-University Consortium for Political and Social Research. The data up to 1980 were collected by J. David Singer and Melvin Small for their book, *The Wages of War 1816−1965* (New York: John Wiley & Sons, 1972), pp. 275 ff.

annexed that country in early August 1990. The Security Council imposed sanctions, embargoing all exports and imports out of and into Iraq. It also authorized the use of all means (including force) to implement its order to withdraw. The coalition forces under United States Command, consisting of more than half a million troops, thousands of aircraft, tanks, armored vehicles, and hundreds of naval vessels, started aerial bombardment of Iraqi forces on January 17, 1991. After a brief campaign of only 100 hours the Iraqi forces were defeated and compelled to withdraw from Kuwait. Whether this first-time experience of successful military action under UN auspices leads to a new collective security order preventing military aggression, as President Bush declared, remains to be seen.

For the foreseeable future substantial budget allocations for armaments, the design, production, and sale of more versatile weapons, and the deployment and use of such military means will no doubt continue to be a crucial component of international relations.

POLITICAL GOODS AND POLITICAL PRODUCTIVITY

Our approach to political analysis leads us from process to performance to evaluation. If we are to compare and

evaluate the working of different political systems, we need a checklist to direct our attention to the variety of desired goals that can be implemented by political action. One society or one group of citizens may value order and stability; another may value participation and liberty. They may value these political "goods" with different intensity, and their preferences and the intensity of their preferences may change with time and circumstances.

Evaluation of political performance is inescapable, even when we think we are being completely unbiased. A long tradition in political analysis has emphasized the system goods of order, predictability, and stability. Political instability—constitutional breakdowns, frequent cabinet changes, riots, demonstrations, and the like—upset most people. Another school of thought has emphasized goods associated with process—citizens' participation and freedom of political competition. Democracy is good and authoritarianism is bad, according to this school of thought, which directs research to maintaining democracy. Systems rejecting it or failing to sustain it are considered unsuccessful. Recent interest in human needs, in the quality of life, and in the tremendous problems of economic development has led to concentration on policy goods, such as economic welfare, quality of life, and personal security. A political system that improves welfare, decreases inequalities, enhances public safety, or cleans up its environment becomes the model.

All these schools of thought are preoccupied with important practical goods valued by most people in varying degrees and under varying circumstances. Without accepting any particular theory about basic human needs and values, we can say that each of these goods, and others listed here, have been valued by many people in many societies. Table 8.7 draws on our three-level analysis of political systems and on the work and thought of a number of scholars and thinkers to present a checklist of goods or values that are produced by political systems.

We cannot deal with these items at great length, but we can emphasize a few of the ideas involved. *System* goods have to do with the regularity and predictability with which political systems work and with the ability of systems to adapt to environmental challenges and changes. Regularity and adaptability are typically somewhat in conflict. On the one hand, most people feel anxiety if serious interruptions and changes affect the routine and behavior of political life. Successions of military coups or continuing collapses of cabinet governments or resignations of presidents create unease and unpredictability. On the other hand, as conditions change—as

wars, rebellions, and economic disasters occur—or as aspirations change, people feel that the political system needs to adapt.

At the *process* level, we identify such goods as effective, satisfying participation, which most citizens typically desire if given a choice, and which produces generally positive views of the political system. Participation is not merely valued instrumentally, as a means to force political elites to respond, but for its own sake, because it increases the individual's sense of competence and dignity. Compliance can also be a good, as individuals seek to avoid penalties or to respond to the powerful impulse to serve others, which can be one of humanity's most gratifying experiences. President John F. Kennedy in his inaugural address called on such impulses to serve and sacrifice when he said, "Ask not what your country can do for you, but what you can do for your country." Winston Churchill's homage to the Royal Air Force in the "Battle of Britain" similarly appealed to nobler human instincts: "Never have so many owed so much to so few." In national crises in many countries, young people especially have almost always volunteered their services with an enthusiasm that cannot be explained by simple calculation of the individual benefits from increasing effectiveness of policy. Procedural justice (trial by jury, habeas corpus, no cruel and unusual punish-

TABLE 8.7
PRODUCTIVITY OF POLITICAL SYSTEMS

Levels of political goods	Classes of goods	Content and examples
Systems level	System maintenance	Regularity and predictability of processes in domestic and international politics
	System adaptation	Structural and cultural adaptability in response to environmental change and challenges
Process level	Participation in political inputs	Instrumental to domestic and foreign policy; directly produces a sense of dignity and efficacy, where met with responsiveness
	Compliance and support	Fulfillment of citizens' duty and patriotic service
	Procedural justice	Equitable procedure and equality before the law
Policy level	Welfare	Growth per capita; quantity and quality of health and welfare; distributive equity
	Security	Safety of person and property; public order, national security
	Liberty	Freedom from regulation, protection of privacy, and respect for autonomy of other individuals, groups, and nations

ment) is another crucial process value, whose deprivation is a severe blow to citizens and without which other goods may be impaired.

At the *policy* level we come to the values of welfare, its quantity, quality, and equity; personal and national security; and freedom from interference in a life of reasonable privacy. We have discussed, indirectly, some of the welfare and security goods, but more must be said about liberty, which is sometimes viewed only as a purely negative good, a freedom from governmental regulation and harassment. Freedom is more than inhibition of government action, because infractions of liberty and privacy may be initiated by private individuals and organizations. In fact, liberty may be fostered by government intervention, when private parties interfere with the liberty of others. Much recent legislation on racial segregation may be understood as impelled by this purpose. Here, of course, different groups and perspectives may come to conflict over liberty, and liberty feeds back into many other goods. Liberty to act, organize, obtain information, and protest is an indispensable part of effective political participation. Nor is it irrelevant to such policy goods as social, political, and economic equality. Prior to the recent breakdown of communism in Eastern Europe and the Soviet Union, it was a common view that the communist countries were trading liberty for equality, by contrast with capitalism which was said to trade off equality for liberty. It will take historians and social scientists a long time to digest and evaluate the communist experience, but what has come to light in the aftermath of "1989" is the extent of corruption and privilege in communist societies, and the relatively low level of productivity of these countries in the last decades. It does not appear to be an exaggeration to say that, while they had surely traded off liberty and had provided a basic security of employment, it was primarily the failure of their economies to enhance productivity and welfare that led to the ideological demoralization.

STRATEGIES FOR PRODUCING POLITICAL GOODS

A Typology of Political Systems

All political systems embody strategies for producing political goods. The strategies may be oriented to goods on one level or another, or to goods intended for the few or the many. The strategies may be shaped primarily by challenges imposed from the environment, by inheritance from the past, or by the self-conscious efforts of present-day politicians. We can in any case classify political systems by policy strategies. We saw in Chapter Two that the major environmental feature of the political system was its economy, either preindustrial or industrial. All preindustrial nations face a host of similar problems, the most challenging being increasing welfare goods. Because of similarities in challenges, resources, and goals, we usually treat the preindustrial nations as a major category for study, further subdividing them by the political structures and strategies they adopt in their effort to increase welfare goods.

The industrial nations face a somewhat different set of problems. One of the major questions they must consider is how to handle process goods, particularly participation. We saw in Chapters Three, Four, and Five that socioeconomic development brings increased citizen awareness of and participation in politics. In the industrial nations political input structures must be developed to deal with this potential for citizen participation on a large scale. One major strategy is to introduce a single authoritarian party to contain, direct, and mobilize citizens under government control. The other is to permit competing parties that mobilize citizens behind leaders representing different goods and strategies. We refer to the first of these strategies as authoritarian and to the second as democratic. Within these major classifications, we further classify systems by the conservatism of their policy, the degree to which they limit the role of the political system in relation to the economy. This approach, then, distinguishes these varieties of political systems:

I. Industrial nations
  A. Democratic
    1. Conservative Democratic
    2. Social Democratic
  B. Authoritarian
    1. Conservative
    2. Radical
II. Preindustrial nations
  A. Neotraditional
  B. Populist Democratic
  C. Authoritarian
    1. Technocratic
    2. Technocratic-distributive
    3. Technocratic-mobilization

INDUSTRIALIZED DEMOCRATIC NATIONS

The industrialized democratic nations must reconcile pressures to maintain or increase government services and personal income with the need to accumulate resources for investment in economic growth. In varying degrees all contemporary democratic industrial nations suffer from unemployment, powerful inflationary tendencies, and relatively slow rates of growth. The classic capital–labor confrontation in these countries has been complicated by the emergence of the environment as a salient issue. Industrial pollution of air and water, the problem of the disposal of nuclear and toxic waste, divides nations differently, with a substantial part of the middle classes opposing growth that does not take into careful account environmental consequences, and a substantial part of the working classes favoring growth and employment even at the cost of some environmental danger.

These dilemmas — both the old classical capital and labor issues, and the newer environmental issues —facing all industrial democracies may be dealt with conservatively as in the United States in the Reagan–Bush era, or in social democratic fashion as in Norway and Sweden, where social programs have been maintained, and the environment largely protected. But as we have shown above, in both types of democratic regimes in the last decades levels of taxation and welfare expenditure have declined. The environmental issue tends to divide both conservative and left parties. In some European countries "Green" ecologically oriented parties have emerged, which typically form coalitions with the larger social democratic movements.

INDUSTRIALIZED AUTHORITARIAN NATIONS
It is possible to classify industrial authoritarian nations into radical and conservative varieties. Prior to the collapse of communism in Eastern Europe such regimes as the Soviet Union, the German Democratic Republic, Poland, Czechoslovakia, and Hungary were examples of the radical variety of industrialized authoritarian regime. Poland, Czechoslovakia, and Hungary are now in transition, moving in the direction of market economies and democratic polities. If disappointment and failure should undermine their recently established and still fragile democratic institutions, it is unlikely that these regimes would return to their socialist pasts. What is more likely is a resort to a technocratic authoritarian approach with the containment of popular pressure and protest by repressive means, and the management of investment and distribution in the interest of economic growth. For the Soviet Union, however, we cannot rule

out the possibility that given the continuation of ethno-national disintegration and economic failure, the groups controlling the old coercive institutions and organizations may have sufficient vitality to reinstitute the repressive politics and preserve much of the command economy of the pre–"1989" era.

Franco's Spain, the Greece of the Colonels, perhaps the Chile of Pinochet, and the Brazil of the generals are examples of the second, conservative variety of authoritarianism, although the last two were at a lower level of industrialization. The military authoritarian regimes of Southern Europe and Latin America of the 1960s and 1970s followed policies of suppressing popular political organization, controlling welfare expenditure, and granting considerable freedom to private enterprise, in the interest of fostering economic growth, though at the expense of increasing inequality of wealth and income. In general, and across the board without regard to regime type, the credibility of socialism and of high welfare expenditures has declined in the last decades, while that of capitalism and democracy has risen. It would be wrong, however, to assume that this is more than the move of a pendulum. A decade of conservative democratic policy in the United States has accentuated inequality and has produced a growing stratum of "children in poverty," the neglect of a deteriorating infrastructure (roads, bridges, public buildings, schools), and the like. The democratization of the Latin American and Eastern European countries will be held hostage to the success of efforts to free and vitalize their economies. Thus, while the category of the industrialized, authoritarian regime in both its radical and conservative varieties is relatively empty at the moment, it would be a mistake to discard the category as no longer relevant.

PREINDUSTRIAL NATIONS
The preindustrial nations face common problems posed by the challenge of modernization. We classify these nations by the strategy they adopt to meet these challenges. *Neotraditional political systems* emphasize the system good of stability. Many of the regimes of sub-Saharan Africa are in this category. These mainly static systems are characterized by low growth rates, low literacy, and low rates of industrialization. They have survived into the modern era with their traditional social structures and cultures mostly unchanged. Their primary modern development has been modern military institutions and technology, which in many cases has enabled groups of officers to

seize and keep power. Where these systems stabilize, the elite maintains cohesion through a system of police suppression, patronage, spoils, and privileges distributed through urban interest groups and tribal elites. A good many systems that began as democracies have reverted to this strategy of merely maintaining their power and privileges, with generally low productivity.[17]

In the early years of colonial emancipation, in the 1950s and early 1960s, a kind of populistic democracy was established in many of the new nations of Asia, Africa, as well as in Latin America. The tremendous strains of competitive politics in a preindustrial setting soon became apparent. With the emergence, sooner or later, of leaders appealing to the poorest members of the society, policy demands for more equitable material distribution, as well as for growth, became difficult to resist. Conflicts between growth and equity became difficult to resolve, and also, once participation was mobilized, ethnic and tribal differences came to the fore. Such ethnic conflicts are difficult to manage stably even in industrial systems, but with the limited resources of preindustrialized societies the problems are more severe. The result has been that the postcolonial, democratic systems have disappeared. The African populist regimes fell in the 1960s, either to military coups or to one-party machines, themselves often swept away later by coups. In Latin America the much older democratic systems in Uruguay and Chile were also overwhelmed by internal pressures for welfare under conditions of low growth and high inflation. Many of the countries that turned authoritarian in the 1960s and 1970s have now reverted to democracy, but still must stand the test of effective economic and social policy.

The other three categories of preindustrial nations reflect various authoritarian strategies. They sacrifice competitive participation, to greater or lesser degree, in trying to achieve stability and economic growth. The authoritarian *technocratic* approach was successful in part in Brazil, where a coalition of military and civilian technocrats and middle-class business interests suppressed participation and kept distribution unequal. Income inequality increased markedly, but economic growth was rapid. South Korea followed an authoritarian technocratic-distributive strategy, which suppressed participation but encouraged some income distribution as well as growth. Early land reforms, rapid development of education, labor-intensive, export-oriented industrialization, and substantial American advice, sup-

port, and pressure have marked the Korean experiment. Its economic success seems to be leading to effective democratization.

The last category, the authoritarian technocratic-mobilizational strategy, has been exemplified primarily by preindustrial communist countries, and in a less aggressively mobilizing form in such countries as Taiwan, Tanzania, and Mexico. This approach is distinguished by a single political party mobilizing and involving citizens in the political process. Competitive participation is suppressed or limited. This category has rapidly emptied in the last few years as the Soviet Union and the Eastern European countries have rejected Marxism–Leninism in favor of more democratic–free market strategies. China, Vietnam, North Korea and Cuba are the last remaining communist societies, dominated by single mobilizing political parties.

The noncommunist mobilizational systems vary substantially in success and in their emphasis on growth and distribution. Taiwan has been successful in combining growth and distributive equity under the domination of the Kuomintang (KMT) party. In recent years the monopoly of the KMT party has been challenged, and politics has become increasingly competitive. Mexico has been dominated by the Institutional Revolutionary party (PRI) which incorporated the major interest groups of labor, business, and agriculture into its internal structure, and which governed the Mexican economy in a relatively effective and stable way until the collapse of oil prices. There is a threat to the domination of the PRI both from the right and left, and a more competitive party system is likely to emerge in the next few years (see Chapter Fifteen).

Tanzania is at the very beginning of economic development. The Tanzania African National Union controls political competition, permitting multiple candidates for election to the Parliament, and attempting to transform and modernize the economy. Government intervention in the economy has not been successful, and there has been a return to private agriculture. Growth has been very slow. (See Chapter Sixteen.)

The problems of the preindustrial nations are so different and formidable that no one strategy is sure to achieve even the goals of growth. One tragic aspect of efforts to increase productivity is that a nation can sacrifice liberty and competition, but still not achieve even the goals of growth or equity. South Korea and Taiwan are examples of Third World nations that have achieved the goals of growth and distribution by authoritarian political means and that are now in process of democratizing. But they are still exceptional cases. Some of this Third World record of success and failure is reported in Chapter Fourteen on China, Chapter Fifteen on Mexico, and Chapter Sixteen on the politics of Africa.

TRADEOFFS AND OPPORTUNITY COSTS

One of the hard facts about political goods is that all are desirable but cannot be pursued simultaneously. A political system has to trade off one value to obtain another. Spending funds on education is giving up the opportunity to spend them on welfare, or to leave them in the hands of consumers for their own use. These *tradeoffs* and *opportunity costs* are found not only in simple decisions about giving up education for better health care, but also in complicated decisions about investment for the future as opposed to consumption today. Even more difficult are the tradeoffs between security and liberty, or stability and adaptation, where the very concepts imply giving up some of the one for some of the other. The extreme of liberty, wherein each person is totally free to act, would make a highly insecure world where the strong would bully the weak and it would be difficult to arrange collective action. Yet, without some liberty to act, security is of little value, as the prisoner is too well aware.

Not only do goods have negative tradeoffs, but the tradeoffs are not the same under all circumstances. Under some conditions increasing liberty somewhat will also increase security, because riots against censorship will end. Under some conditions investment in education will be paid back many times in health and welfare, because trained citizens can care better for themselves and work more productively. One of the important tasks of social science is to discover the conditions under which positive and negative tradeoffs occur. If a system beset with coups and violence, disease and physical suffering, suppression and arbitrary rule can be replaced with a more stable, more participatory system that makes some progress in economic development, few will doubt that the tradeoff is positive.

We stress, however, that analogies from economics are no more than analogies. Political science has no way of converting units of liberty into units of safety and welfare. And because politics may involve violence on a large scale, we must acknowledge that we can never calculate the value of a political outcome gained at the cost of human life. People act as though they know how to make such conversions, but political scientists can only point to values that people have emphasized at different times and places, and indicate the range and variety of values considered. The weight given to various goods will vary in different cultures and contexts. The advantage of a clear-cut ideology is that it provides people with logical schemes for telling how much one value should be traded against another, and thus offers orderly sequences of action leading to the outcome that is viewed as best. Such schemes may be invaluable for those pressed to action in the terrible circumstances of war, revolution, and famine. But there is no ideology, just as there is no political science, that can solve all these problems objectively.

KEY TERMS

command economy	indirect taxes	outputs and outcomes	regulative policies
direct taxes	neotraditional political	political performance	symbolic policies
distributive policies	system	progressive taxes	technocratic
extractive policies	OECD	public policies	tradeoff
feedback	opportunity cost	regressive taxes	welfare state

END NOTES

1. See, among others, Peter Flora and Arnold Heidenheimer, *The Development of Welfare States in Europe and America* (New Brunswick, N.J.: Transaction Books, 1981); Arnold Heidenheimer, Hugh Heclo, and Carolyn Teich Adams, *Comparative Public Policy*, 3rd ed. (New York: St. Martin's Press, 1990). See also Francis G. Castles, *The Comparative History of Public Policy* (Cambridge, England: Polity Press, 1989).

2. See, for example, Samuel Brittan, *The Economic Consequences of Democracy* (London: Temple Smith, 1977); Michael Boskin, *The Crisis in Social Security* (San Francisco: Institute for Contemporary Studies, 1978); Mancur Olson, *The Rise and Decline of Nations* (New Haven, Conn.: Yale University Press, 1982).

3. See, for example, Philippe Schmitter and Gerhard Lehmbruch, eds., *Trends Toward Corporatist Intermediation* (Beverly Hills, Calif.: Sage Publications, 1979); Suzanne Berger, ed., *Organizing Interests in Western Europe: Pluralism, Corporatism, and the Transformation of Politics* (Cambridge: Cambridge University Press, 1981); John Goldthorpe, ed., *Order and Conflict in Contemporary Capitalism: Studies in the Political Economy of Western European Nations* (Oxford: Clarendon Press, 1984); Peter Katzenstein, *Small States in World Markets* (Ithaca, N.Y.: Cornell University Press, 1985); Heidenheimer, Heclo, and Adams, *Comparative Public Policy*, p. 360.

4. See Heidenheimer, Heclo, and Adams, *Comparative Public Policy*, p. 198.

5. World Bank, *World Development Report* (New York: Oxford University Press, 1990), pp. 200–201.

6. See Heidenheimer, Heclo, and Adams, *Comparative Public Policy*, p. 198. (For an in-depth discussion of Japanese extractive and distributive patterns, see Chapter Twelve.)

7. Ibid., pp. 196–197.

8. Ibid., p. 211.

9. Harold Wilensky, *The Welfare State and Equality* (Berkeley: University of California Press, 1975); also Harold Wilensky, Gregory Luebbert, Susan Hahn, and Adrienne Jamieson, *Comparative Social Policy: Theories, Methods, Findings* (Berkeley, Calif.: Institute of International Studies, 1985).

10. Fredrick L. Pryor, *Property and Industrial Organization in Communist and Capitalist Nations* (Bloomington: Indiana University Press, 1973), pp. 46–47.

11. For an excellent discussion on all aspects of regulation in the United States, see James Q. Wilson, ed., *The Politics of Regulation* (New York: Basic Books, 1980).

12. Ruth Leger Sivard, *World Military and Social Expenditures, 1987–88* (Washington, D.C.: World Priorities, 1987–1988), p. 47.

13. Simon Kuznets, "Economic Growth and Income Equality," *American Economic Review*, 45 (1955), pp. 1–28; Hollis Chenery et al., *Redistribution with Growth* (New York: Oxford University Press, 1974), pp. 17 ff.

14. U.S. Department of Justice, FBI, *Uniform Crime Reports for the United States* (Washington, D.C.: U.S. Government Printing Office 1990), p. 48.

15. Peter Gourevitch, *Politics in Hard Times* (Ithaca, N.Y.: Cornell University Press, 1986).

16. Sivard, *World Military and Social Expenditures*, p. 28.

17. See Robert H. Jackson and Carl G. Rosberg, *Personal Rule in Black Africa* (Berkeley: University of California Press, 1982).

PART THREE

COUNTRY STUDIES

THE UNITED KINGDOM

(Standard Statistical Regions)

ATLANTIC

OCEAN

SCOTLAND

Aberdeen

Glasgow Edinburgh

North Sea

NORTHERN
Belfast
IRELAND

Irish Sea

Newcastle

Tyne R.

NORTH

ENGLAND

REPUBLIC

OF

IRELAND

Dublin

YORKSHIRE

Leeds

AND

Liverpool Manchester

Mersey

Sheffield

HUMBERSIDE

NORTH
WEST

EAST MIDLANDS

WEST

Birmingham

MIDLANDS

ENGLAND

EAST ANGLIA

WALES

Cardiff

Severn R.

Bristol

Thames

SOUTH

Greater
London R.

EAST

SOUTH WEST

English Channel

Scale of Miles

0   100

CHAPTER 9

RICHARD ROSE

POLITICS IN ENGLAND

ENGLAND IS DIFFERENT

UNDERSTANDING ENGLAND is important in the study of politics because England is a deviant case. Violence and revolution are common features of twentieth-century domestic politics throughout the world. From time to time violence has also been a feature of American political life. Yet for the past three centuries within England domestic political differences have been settled without resort to revolution or civil war. Just as Alexis de Tocqueville traveled to America in 1831 to seek the secrets of democracy, so one might journey to England to seek the secrets of stable representative government.

Modern societies with stable representative governments are rare in the world today. Many nations with representative government have been influenced by England. This is especially true of the United States, the first British colony. As Bernard Bailyn, the author of *The Origins of American Politics*, notes: "The pattern of political activity in the colonies was part of a more comprehensive British pattern and cannot be understood in isolation from that larger system."[1]

Wherever there are representative institutions of government, they are likely to have been influenced by England. Its Parliament has been a model for institutions of democratic government in places as far-flung as India, Australia, and Canada. Comparison implies contrasts too. The distinctiveness of politics in England is evident in the failure of attempts to transplant its institutions wholesale to other countries. Dozens of former British colonies were given constitutions based on the British model at the time they obtained independence. In most cases, these institutions have been replaced by dictators or have been very much altered. The distinctiveness of England is made even more evident by the failure of its institutions in Northern Ireland.

While England has ties with many different countries, it does not resemble any other nation. In the days of the British Empire, it maintained close relations with the old dominions of Canada, Australia, New Zealand, and South Africa, and with subject colonies. These ties have not survived the evolution of Empire into Commonwealth. Today, it is linked by treaty with other member nations of the European Community, but most English people do not think of themselves as European.

In addition to representativeness, effectiveness is desirable too; here the record of contemporary British government is checkered. As the homeland of the Industrial Revolution, England was the richest nation in the world in the nineteenth century. In the era since World War II, the economy has grown slowly but surely; government has had more money to spend on programs for health care, education, and social security; and ordinary families have had more money to spend on consumer goods, housing, and foreign travel.

But the progress of the economy has been accompanied by many setbacks; the British economy has grown more slowly than that of the United States or its European competitors. In the 1960s a Labour government under Harold Wilson argued that socialism promised higher rates of economic growth — but growth did not come. In the 1980s Conservative Prime Minister Margaret Thatcher argued the need for radical change. Paradoxically, efforts to reduce government influence require more government action to set changes in motion.

More than half a century ago, the distinguished French writer, André Siegfried, diagnosed England's position thus: "To turn the corner from the nineteenth into the twentieth century; there, in a word, is the whole British problem."[2] Since then, England has achieved great change. In the turbulent world of today, it faces a new challenge: to prepare for entry into the twenty-first century.

THE CONSTRAINTS OF HISTORY

Every country is constrained by its history. Past actions limit present alternatives. Compared to other countries, England has been fortunate in solving many of the fundamental problems of governing before the onset of industrialization. The Crown was established as the central political authority in late medieval times. The supremacy of secular power over spiritual power was settled in the sixteenth century, when Henry VIII broke with the Roman Catholic Church to establish the Church of England. The power struggle between Crown and Parliament in the civil war of the 1640s was resolved by the Restoration of 1660 and the Glorious Revolution of 1688; the monarchy continued but with less power than before. At the start of industrialization in

the eighteenth century, authority was divided between the Crown and Parliament in a system of limited representative government.

The continuity of England's political institutions is remarkable. Prince Charles, the heir to an ancient Crown, pilots jet airplanes and a medieval-styled chancellor of the Exchequer pilots the pound through the deep waters of the international economy. Former Labour Prime Minister Clement Attlee summarized the interpenetration of different periods of the past in a tribute to Winston Churchill: "There was a layer of seventeenth century, a layer of eighteenth century, a layer of nineteenth century and possibly even a layer of twentieth century. You were never sure which layer would be uppermost."[3] Symbols of continuity often mask great changes in English life. Parliament was once a supporter of royal authority; then it was a restraint on it, deposing monarchs; next it became a lawmaking body. Today Parliament is primarily an electoral college deciding which party leader controls the government.

The Making of Modern England

Industrialization, not political revolution, created the great discontinuity in modern English history. There is no agreement among social scientists about when England developed a modern system of government. A constitutional historian might date the change at 1485, an economic historian from about 1760, and a frustrated egalitarian reformer might proclaim that it hasn't happened yet.[4] It is simplest to say that modern government came in the reign of Queen Victoria from 1837 to 1901. During this era the principal features of the old unwritten constitution were altered, so that government could cope with the problems of a society that was increasingly urban, literate, industrial, and critical of unchanged traditions.

The 1832 Reform Act started a process of enfranchising the masses that led to the granting of the vote to a majority of English males by 1885. Concurrently, party organization began to develop along recognizably modern lines. Innovations promoted by rationalist reformers led to the development of an effective civil service. Before the end of the nineteenth century, England had a constitutional bureaucracy capable of everything from economically saving candle ends to enacting laws that provided safe water and sewers for booming cities.

The nineteenth-century transformation was great. From 1800 to 1900 the population of the United Kingdom increased from 16 to 41 million. The gross national product (GNP) increased more than eleven times in total, and increased per capita by more than four times. Government spending as a share of GNP grew by only 2 percent in the century, because of the fiscal dividend of economic growth. In 1900 public expenditure was equal to 14 percent of the national product.[5]

The creation of a modern system of government did not make the problems of governing disappear, but it did create institutions useful for responding to the challenges that have confronted twentieth-century England.

The first challenge has been national defense. In World War I, Britain and France held Germany at bay, winning in 1918 with latter-day American support. In 1940 under the leadership of Winston Churchill, Britain stood alone against Nazi Germany until the war broadened to include Russia, Japan, and the United States. Britain again emerged on the winning side in 1945.

The second great challenge, granting the working class the full rights of citizenship, was met gradually. The supremacy of the elected House of Commons over the aristocratic and hereditary House of Lords was established by legislation in 1911. In 1918 the right to vote was granted all adult men aged twenty-one or more and all women aged twenty-eight; women were given the right to vote at the same age as men in 1928. The Labour party, founded in 1900 to secure the representation of manual workers in Parliament, first briefly formed a minority government in 1924.

The third challenge concerned the distribution of the fruits of economic growth through tax-financed social welfare, policies benefiting the mass of citizens. Compulsory primary education was introduced in 1870. The Liberal government of 1906–1914 introduced old-age pensions and unemployment insurance. Interwar governments expanded welfare services. The British government was relatively well placed to increase public spending, for the country's GNP doubled between 1913 and 1938, a rate of growth faster than that of France, Germany, or Sweden.

World War II brought about great changes within England. The wartime all-party coalition government of Winston Churchill provided "fair shares for all" while mobilizing the population for all-out war. From this coalition emerged the Beveridge Report on Social Welfare, John Maynard Keynes's Full Employment White Paper of 1944, and the Butler Education Act of 1944. These three measures — the first two named after Lib-

erals and the third after a Conservative — remain landmarks of the welfare state today.

The fair shares policy was continued by the Labour government of Clement Attlee elected in 1945. The National Health Service was established in 1948, providing medical care for all without charge. Coal mines, gas and electricity, railways, and the steel industries were nationalized (that is, taken into government ownership). By 1951 the Labour government had exhausted its catalog of agreed changes, but its economic policies had yet to produce prosperity. A much reformed Conservative party under Winston Churchill returned to power.

Since that time, successive Conservative and Labour governments have sought economic prosperity, good social welfare services, and increased take-home pay for ordinary citizens. The 1950s saw a marked rise in living standards. Consumer goods once thought to be the privilege of a few, such as automobiles and refrigerators, became widely distributed, and new products, such as television, were successfully marketed. Some observers interpreted the boom in mass consumption as the start of a classless society.

The Conservatives won reelection in 1955 and 1959. Prime Minister Harold Macmillan summarized the economic record of the 1950s by saying, "Most of our people have never had it so good." But Macmillan was also cautious about the future. In 1957, he warned:

> What is beginning to worry some of us is, "Is it too good to be true?" or perhaps I should say, "Is it too good to last?" Amidst all this prosperity, there is one problem that has troubled us — in one way or another — ever since the war. It's the problem of rising prices.[6]

Inflation has remained a problem, especially when it has coincided with rising unemployment and low rates of economic growth.

The 1960s saw the beginning of publicly expressed disillusionment with British government. Past continuities were attacked as the dead hand of tradition. A stream of books was published on the theme "What's wrong with Britain?" Official inquiries proposed reforms of the civil service, local government, Parliament, education, and industrial relations. New titles were given government department offices, symbolizing a desire for change for its own sake. Behind the entrance to these restyled offices, however, the same people went through the same routines as before.

The experience of Conservative government

under Edward Heath from 1970 to 1974 and Labour government under Harold Wilson and James Callaghan from 1974 to 1979 demonstrated that difficulties of governing are not the fault of particular individuals or parties. In trying to limit unprecedented inflation by controlling wages, Heath risked his authority in a confrontation with the National Union of Mineworkers. The impasse was broken by the election of February 28, 1974, which returned a vote of no confidence in both major parties. The Conservative share of the vote dropped to 38 percent and Labour's to 37 percent. The Liberal vote more than doubled, rising to 19 percent.

A minority Labour government under Harold Wilson won a bare parliamentary majority with only 39 percent of the vote in the October 1974 general election. The Labour government maintained political consensus. Instead of confrontation with the unions, it proclaimed a social contract intended to limit wage increases in return for increased public spending on social welfare benefits. In 1975 this policy collapsed. By the beginning of 1979, the economy had gone from bad to worse. Unemployment stood at 1.5 million, the highest since the 1930s; prices had doubled since 1974; real wages had fallen, and the economy had contracted in two of the preceding four years.

The British general election of May 3, 1979, saw the two major parties reversing roles. The Labour government under James Callaghan argued against change. The nominally Conservative party led by Margaret Thatcher called for radical change in the country's economic policy. The Conservatives won a majority in Parliament with 44 percent of the popular vote; Labour's share of the popular vote fell to 37 percent. Thatcher thus became the first woman prime minister of a major European country.

Thatcher was determined to make a break with the past in both style and substance. She regarded the economic failures of past governments as arising from too much consensual compromise and too little conviction. "The Old Testament prophets did not say 'Brothers, I want a consensus'. They said: 'This is my faith. This is what I passionately believe. If you believe it too, then come with me'." [7]

Thatcher's conviction was that the market offered a cure for the country's economic difficulties. Her views were not those of a conventional Conservative, who accepts a mixed-economy welfare state. Instead, as Milton Friedman, the Nobel Prize-winning monetary economist, noted: "Mrs. Thatcher represents a different tradition. She represents a tradition of the nineteenth-century Liberal, of Manchester Liberalism, of free market free trade." [8]

Margaret Thatcher is unique among twentieth-century prime ministers in giving her name to an ism, Thatcherism. Although in principle opposed to government intervention in society, she believed in strong government as long as she was in charge, supporting more spending on the police and a strong defense force and showing undiplomatic toughness in negotiations in the European Community. She was also quick to assert her personal authority against colleagues in the Cabinet and civil servants. But strongly held views do not constitute a logical political philosophy.

> There has been a tendency, particularly on the left, to make Thatcherism seem more clear-cut than it is — to devise an ideology from what is in practice a series of values and instincts and a political alliance. Both opponents and supporters of the Thatcher Administration have created more of a pattern from the disconnected events and policies than is warranted. [9]

For a decade Thatcher enjoyed unprecedented good fortune electorally. Her first term was difficult. Unemployment doubled to more than 12 percent, and instead of growing faster, in some years the economy contracted. The chief positive achievement was to cut inflation. The 1982 Argentine invasion of the sparsely populated Falkland Islands, a remote British colony in the South Atlantic, led to a brief, virtually bloodless war that Britain won.

The Conservatives won a landslide election victory in 1983 as a result of divisions among opponents. The Labour party shifted to the left under the leadership of Michael Foot. In protest against this shift left, in 1981 four former Labour Cabinet ministers formed a new Social Democratic party (SDP) with Roy Jenkins as leader. The SDP concluded an electoral alliance with the Liberal party, a third party whose vote had risen in the 1970s. The new Alliance favored social policies espoused by Labour and market-oriented economic policies endorsed by the Conservatives. Labour won 27 percent of the vote, and the Alliance won 25 percent.

Continued divisions among opponents gave Thatcher an unprecedented third election victory in 1987 with 42 percent of the vote. The Labour party under Neil Kinnock won 31 percent, and the Alliance, 23 percent of the vote. Immediately after the election the Alliance split. The majority of the SDP voted to join with the Liberals in a new merged party, the Liberal Democrats, and elected a Liberal MP, Paddy Ashdown, as leader. Labour leader Neil Kinnock launched a major policy review that reduced Labour's commitment to traditional socialist principles and seized on U.S.–Soviet disarmament measures to proclaim that a British nuclear deterrent was no longer of major importance.

In eleven years in office, the Thatcher administration experienced both achievements and frustrations. Industrial relations acts reduced the legal immunities of trade unions and gave union members the right to vote on whether to hold a strike. Local government was curbed by central government legislation that abolished metropolitan-area government in London and other large cities, and replaced residential property taxes with a community charge or poll tax on each adult. The central government imposed changes in schools and universities. It privatized formerly state-owned industries such as British Telecommunications, British Petroleum, and British Gas, selling shares to investors through the stock market.

Overall, the Thatcher administration's economic record was uneven (Figure 9.1). Twice the economy grew at a rate above 4 percent a year, and in two years it contracted; the average rate of economic growth in the 1980s was slightly below that of the United States. Unemployment rose to the highest level in half a century and then fell sharply; for more than half the period, unemployment was above 10 percent, higher than in the United States. Inflation fell from its peak in the 1970s, but it has remained high by comparison with the rates in Europe and the United States.

The force of political inertia frustrated Thatcher's hope of making big cuts in public expenditure. Upon taking office her administration immediately became responsible for high-cost social security, health, and education programs that are electorally popular. Because of this inheritance, during Thatcher's term of office public expenditure remained around 40 percent of the national product.[10]

Nor did Margaret Thatcher win the hearts and minds of the electorate. Confronted with the consequences for public services of cuts in taxation and public spending, a majority of public opinion came to support more public spending financed by higher taxes. When voters were asked on the tenth anniversary of her period in office whether or not they approved of "the Thatcher revolution," less than one-third responded yes.[11] Within the Conservative party, too, there was opposition to her autocratic and bossy treatment of Cabinet colleagues. Thatcher's opposition to European integration isolated her from influence in the European Community.

At the start of the Autumn 1990 session of Parliament, disgruntled Conservative members of Parliament (MPs) led by Michael Heseltine forced an unprece-

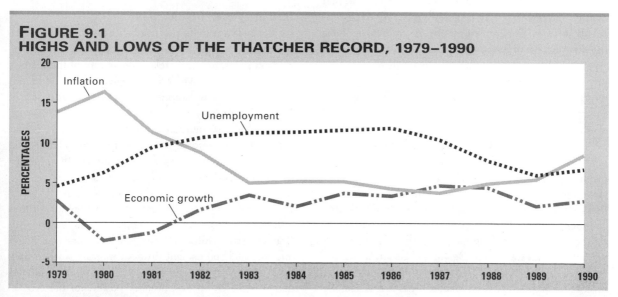

FIGURE 9.1
HIGHS AND LOWS OF THE THATCHER RECORD, 1979–1990

Source: OECD, *Economic Outlook,* June 1990, Tables R1, R11 and R19; *Economic Trends,* July 1990.

dented ballot for party leadership. In the first round, the prime minister won just over half the votes of Conservative MPs. Under the party's complicated rules for electing a leader, this was not enough to confirm Thatcher in office, and she resigned rather than risk a humiliating defeat on a second ballot. Conservative MPs then elected John Major, the chancellor of the Exchequer (minister in charge of the Treasury), as party leader and thus prime minister.

The forty-seven-year-old Major had only entered Parliament in 1979. He won the party leadership with the support of Conservative MPs favoring Thatcherite views. However, in an interview just before becoming prime minister, Major indicated a pragmatic rather than an ideological approach to politics: "The most important thing in negotiations is to obtain a satisfactory outcome. This sometimes makes it difficult to determine with quite the clarity one would wish precisely what one's position would be." [12]

A Mixed Inheritance

Political achievements come first when Britons are asked to say how proud they are of their country. The proportion expressing pride in being British is 86 percent, second highest among a range of major Western nations. National pride is achieved without the aggressive promotion of patriotism in schools and in the media. Britons are proud of their country, but they are not bellicose. [13]

England's present is not to be compared with that of other nations, but with England's past. Given historical advantages, the implicit premise of political action is the assimilation of past and present; it is not the radical rejection of the past for an unknown and untested future, recommended by Labour's hard left and by the most ideological of the Thatcherites. The spirit is summed up in the motto of Lord Hugh Cecil: "Even when I changed, it should be to preserve." [14]

The greatest political asset is England's centuries-old heritage of representative government. The early resolution of fundamental political issues means that no violence is committed against the state as it is in revolutionary countries. The early creation of national identity confines nationalist breakaway movements to the periphery of the United Kingdom, rather than at the center of politics, as in Canada or Belgium. The government's acceptance of the rule of law makes the English secure against authoritarian rule. Because parties peacefully exchange roles as government and opposition, citizens

have an effective choice about who governs, a democratic prerogative denied by most member states of the United Nations.

Although past success is a great source of confidence, it cannot guarantee the future. The fact that Victorian leaders successfully modernized their institutions may encourage their heirs but cannot resolve today's problems. Future historians will not characterize the present by what went before but by what it is a prelude to.

THE CONSTRAINTS OF PLACE

Great Britain's island position is its most significant geographic feature; insularity is one of its most striking cultural characteristics. Even though there is no other continent to which the island could conceivably be assigned, the English Channel has for centuries maintained a deep gulf between England and continental Europe. In the words of a French writer, "We might liken England to a ship which, though anchored in European waters, is always ready to sail away." [15] The construction of the Channel Tunnel between England and France will not close the gap between England and the Continent. Past links with Commonwealth countries on other continents further reduce the significance of distance. Politically, England may claim to be equally close to or distant from Europe, North America, and the nations of the global Commonwealth.

Insularity and Involvement

Insularity is not to be confused with isolation. The British Empire covered territories as scattered as India, New Zealand, Nigeria, and Ireland. The end of the Empire began with the grant of independence to India and Pakistan in 1947. The Empire has been replaced by a free association of forty-six sovereign states, the Commonwealth. The independent status of its chief members is shown by the removal of the word "British" from the title of the Commonwealth. Commonwealth countries today are divided politically and socially.

British foreign policy since 1945 is a story of contracting military and diplomatic commitments. Britain retains one of the five permanent places in the Security Council of the United Nations, and it is a member of 126 international bodies. But Britain's military power is now limited. Victory in the 1982 Falklands War did not demonstrate front-rank military power, for the Argentine military force was not well organized or equipped.

Moreover, only 1,800 people live in the Falkland Islands. Britain sent troops to fight in the Persian Gulf in 1991, but its force was much smaller than that of the United States.

Most citizens accept Britain's decline as a world power. When the Gallup Poll asks whether people would rather Britain were a leading world power or a small neutral country like Sweden or Switzerland, 53 percent endorse the status of the small countries as against 33 percent who want Britain's restoration to major world power status.[16]

Whereas Britain uses force only occasionally, its economic transactions are continuous. The British economy depends for success on trade in the world economy. England must export to live, for it imports much of its food, and many raw materials for industry. To pay for the imports, England exports a wide range of manufactured goods, as well as "invisible" services produced by the financial institutions of the city of London. The value of the pound (£) against the dollar since 1972 has fluctuated from above $2.50 to less than $1.25.

The influence of international market forces on the British is substantial. To meet balance-of-payments problems, Britain required International Monetary Fund (IMF) loans in 1967 and 1976. To secure IMF loans, the government had to adopt unpopular economic measures, such as squeezing consumption and increasing unemployment, in order to forestall other difficulties, such as inflation. James Callaghan, who was in charge of the Treasury when Britain went cap in hand for its first IMF loan and was prime minister during the second loan, has explained Britain's difficulties below:

> No one owes Britain a living, and may I say to you quite bluntly that despite the measures of the last twelve months we are still not earning the standard of living we are enjoying. We are keeping up our standards by borrowing, and this cannot go on indefinitely.[17]

As England's world position has declined, government has increasingly looked to Europe. In a jet age, the English Channel is no longer a barrier to travel to the continent of Europe. Television carries news, sports, and entertainment across national boundaries. Economic links have grown; for example, a multinational corporation such as the Ford Motor Company links its factories from Britain to Spain, just as it links Ford factories in different American states.

When the European Community was established in 1957, Britain did not join, considering its position superior to that of continental neighbors ravaged by war. It joined in 1973 under the leadership of Edward Heath; political controversy on the issue cut across party lines. A 1975 national referendum on membership voted 67 to 33 percent in favor of remaining a member. Public opinion and politicians continue to be divided about what role Britain can or should play in the European Community. A dispute among Cabinet ministers about linking the British pound with other European currencies helped trigger Margaret Thatcher's exit from office. The link was established.

Critics have objected to the Community's power to make regulations about trade, employment, and consumer products that are binding on British firms without approval by Parliament, and to prevent Parliament from enacting laws inconsistent with Community membership. Opponents have also complained about the cost of Community membership, for Britain pays more in subsidies to inefficient farmers on the Continent than its farmers receive in return. Yet another criticism is that the political interests of the Community, which stretches from Portugal to Greece and thence to Germany and Denmark, are not the same as those of Britain.

Events are transforming the significance of the Community. It is committed to a single European market in 1992 with free movement of goods, services, and workers. No agreement has been reached about whether the Community should be a free market with a minimum of economic regulation or a social market with regulations advocated by trade unions. Differences between left and right can be found throughout the Community.

If a political community is defined as a system sharing common rights and obligations, then the European Community remains on the periphery of British politics. Of all tax revenues collected in Britain, only 1 percent are devoted to Community purposes, and virtually all laws in force are acts of Parliament, not directives from the Community. The Community has virtually no impact on the daily operation of social security, health, and education policies. Although Community policies do have some economic effect, Britain's economy is also sensitive to outside forces from the United States to the Persian Gulf and Japan.

The constraints of history and place limit the extent to which British government can insulate the country from international economic trends. Today, the effective choice is not between England being populous and rich or small and rich, but between England being a big, rich country or a populous, relatively poor country.

In failing to resolve this choice satisfactorily, England's leaders demonstrate the aptness of the judgment of the American diplomat, Dean Acheson: "Great Britain has lost an empire and has not yet found a role."[18]

One Crown and Many Nations

The English Crown is the oldest and best known in the world, yet there is no such thing as an English state. In international law as in the title of the queen, the state is the United Kingdom of Great Britain and Northern Ireland. The island of Great Britain, the principal part of the United Kingdom, is divided into three parts: England, Scotland, and Wales. England, smaller in area than Alabama or Wisconsin, constitutes 55 percent of the land area of Great Britain. The other part of the United Kingdom, Northern Ireland, consists of six counties of Ulster that have remained under the Crown rather than join the independent Irish Republic ruled from Dublin.

The United Kingdom is a multinational state.[19] The great majority of English people think of themselves as English, Welsh people think of themselves as Welsh, and Scottish people think of themselves as Scots. In Northern Ireland there is no agreement about national identity; Catholics tend to see themselves as Irish, and Protestants see themselves as British or Ulster. Except in Northern Ireland, these distinctive identities can be harmonized with British identification (Table 9.1).

Scotland was once an independent kingdom, linked with England by an accident of dynastic succession in 1603 and governed under a common Parliament since 1707. The Scots have retained separate legal, religious, and educational institutions. In 1885 a separate minister for Scottish affairs was appointed. The Scottish Office gradually accumulated administrative responsibilities for health, education, agriculture, housing, and economic development. Its policies have remained consistent with those applied in England, for the head of the Scottish Office is a Cabinet minister bound to the collective decisions of a British Cabinet, and all laws affecting Scotland are made by Parliament in London.[20]

The most distinctive feature of Wales is its language, but the proportion of Welsh-speaking people in its population has declined from 53 percent in 1891 to 20 percent today. Within Wales there are very sharp contrasts between the English-speaking industrial, more populous south, and the Welsh-speaking rural, less populous northwest. Since the sixteenth century, when Wales was amalgamated with England, it has almost invariably been governed by the same laws as England. In 1964 a separate Welsh Office was established for administrative purposes; its head was made a Cabinet minister. The laws that the Welsh Office administers have normally been acts of Parliament that apply equally to England and Wales.[21]

Northern Ireland is the most un-English part of the United Kingdom. Formally, Northern Ireland is a secular polity, but in practice, differences between Protes-

TABLE 9.1
NATIONAL IDENTITY IN THE UNITED KINGDOM (PERCENTAGE)

	England	Scotland	Wales	N. Ireland Prot.	N. Ireland Catholic
THINKS OF SELF AS:					
British	38	35	33	67	15
English	57	2	8	—	—
Scottish	2	52	—	—	—
Welsh	1	—	57	—	—
Ulster	—	—	—	20	6
Irish	1	1	—	8	69
Other, don't know	1	10	2	5	10
Total	100	100	100	100	100

Source: Richard Rose, *The Territorial Dimension in Government: Understanding the United Kingdom* (Chatham, N.J.: Chatham House, 1982), p. 14.

tants and Catholics dominate its politics. Protestants, who represent two-thirds of the population, maintain that they are British, and wish to be under the Crown. Until 1972 the Protestant majority exercised extensive local powers, including police powers, with a home-rule Parliament at Stormont, a suburb of Belfast. Many Catholics did not support this regime, wishing instead to leave the United Kingdom and join the Republic of Ireland.[22]

Since the start of civil rights demonstrations by Catholics in Northern Ireland in 1968, the land has been in turmoil. Demonstrations turned to street violence in August 1969, and the British Army intervened. The illegal Irish Republican Army (IRA) was revived and in 1971 began a military campaign to remove Northern Ireland from the United Kingdom. In retaliation, Protestants have organized illegal forces, too. Since August 1969, more than 2,800 people have been killed in political violence, equivalent to 100,000 political deaths in Britain or 450,000 in America.

British policy in Northern Ireland has been erratic and unsuccessful. In 1971 the British Army helped to intern hundreds of Catholics without trial in an unsuccessful attempt to break the IRA. In 1972 the British government abolished the Stormont Parliament, placing government in the hands of a Northern Ireland Office under a British Cabinet minister. In 1974 the government created a short-lived Northern Ireland executive, sharing power between one faction of Protestant Unionists and the Catholic Social Democratic and Labour party. The executive collapsed in the face of a general strike organized by Protestant workers. The Northern Ireland Office has since administered Ulster by procedures described as temporary direct rule.

In 1985 the British government signed an accord with the Irish government creating a joint committee to discuss arrangements for governing Northern Ireland. Protestants have regarded this agreement as an infringement on British sovereignty. They reject the British Parliament's right to allow the Republic of Ireland to be involved in their affairs — especially as the Republic's government has the goal of making Northern Ireland part of an enlarged Republic of Ireland.

For generations differences between nations within the United Kingdom were confined to differing levels of support for the Conservative and Labour parties. In the 1970s the party system was temporarily destabilized by the challenge of nationalist parties. The challenge has been most successful in Northern Ireland, where the Conservative and Labour parties have stopped contesting seats. In Scotland the Scottish National party came in second in October 1974, with 30 percent of the Scottish vote. In Wales, Plaid Cymru, a nationalist party, usually polls less than one-tenth of the Welsh vote. The most distinctive feature of Welsh politics is the disproportionately high Labour vote.

In response to the rise in nationalist votes in Scotland and Wales, in August 1974 the Labour government pledged to devolve limited government responsibilities to popularly elected assemblies in Scotland and Wales. In 1978 Parliament approved devolution acts. The measures were put to a referendum in Scotland and Wales in 1979. Welsh voters rejected the devolution of authority to a Welsh Assembly, 80 percent voting against.

In Scotland, a narrow majority of Scots voting gave approval to devolution; 51.6 percent voted yes, and 48.4 percent voted no. But Parliament stipulated that if fewer than 40 percent of those eligible to vote approved devolution, Parliament should reconsider the issue. The proportion of voters endorsing devolution was 32.8 percent of the Scottish electorate. The House of Commons decided that this was insufficient to justify a separate Scottish legislative assembly, and voted not to put devolution into effect.

Three general elections since the 1979 devolution referendum have shown support for pro-United Kingdom sentiments in both Scotland and Wales. In 1987 the vote of the Scottish National party dropped to 14 percent, and it won only three seats in Parliament. The vote of the Welsh Nationalists dropped to 7.3 percent, and they had three MPs. But the fall of the Conservative vote in Scotland to 24 percent meant that the great majority of Scottish voters endorsed parties that advocate devolution of powers to a quasi-federal Parliament in Edinburgh.

The United Kingdom is a union, that is, a political system that has only one source of authority: Parliament. It thus differs from a federal system, which divides powers. The institutions for governing the United Kingdom are not uniform. Some special arrangements are made for government in Scotland and Wales, and many more in Northern Ireland. Yet the extent of differences can easily be exaggerated. A 15 percent vote for a Nationalist party means that 85 percent have voted for parties favoring the United Kingdom. Social differences are limited, too. Divisions within each nation — class in England, Scotland, and Wales, and religion in Northern

Ireland — are more important than differences between nations.[23]

Politics in England is the subject of this chapter because England dominates the United Kingdom. Its people constitute five-sixths of the total population, and the remainder are divided among three noncontiguous nations. No United Kingdom government will ever overlook what is central to England, and politicians who wish to advance in British government must accept the norms of English society.

A Multiracial England?

Through the centuries England has received a small but noteworthy number of immigrants from other lands, principally Europe. The present queen is descended from German royalty, who came from Hanover in 1714 to assume the English throne in succession to the Scottish Stuarts. Until the outbreak of anti-German sentiment in World War I, the surname of the royal family was Saxe–Coburg–Gotha. By royal proclamation, King George V changed the family name to Windsor in 1917.

In the late 1950s immigrants began to arrive in England from the West Indies, Pakistan, India, and other parts of the new Commonwealth. Most immigrants have been attracted to England by jobs. Census estimates of the nonwhite population of the United Kingdom have risen from 74,000 in 1951 to upwards of 2.5 million today, just under 5 percent of the total population. This total includes people born in Britain of immigrant parents, as well as those born in Asia or the West Indies.

Immigrants have little in common upon arrival: they are divided by culture, religion, and class. West Indians speak English as their native language. Many immigrants from India and Pakistan are not fluent in English, and Muslims and Sikhs follow distinctive practices. The small number of African immigrants are divided among themselves by nationality. Some immigrants from Africa are Asians who have abandoned businesses there under pressure from black nationalist politicians. Within each national group, some immigrants are educated and are anxious to improve their income, while others have less education and lower aspirations.[24]

Public opinion has opposed the immigration of nonwhites. Conservative and Labour governments passed laws in 1962, 1968, and 1971 limiting the number of nonwhite immigrants. Laws to encourage better race relations and antidiscrimination measures have also been enacted. The policies are often modeled on American legislation, except that judicial enforcement is much weaker. This follows from the absence of a British Bill of Rights and of courts with the powers of American courts. In combating discrimination the government-sponsored Commission for Racial Equality relies primarily on investigation and conciliation rather than on prosecution.

Today, the important issues of race relations center on the treatment of British-born offspring of immigrants who are not white. A melting pot theory assumes that British-born children of immigrants will integrate with the host society. Another theory predicts that nonwhite youths will come to have more in common with each other, insofar as they share discrimination because of color.

Immigrants and their offspring are gradually becoming integrated into electoral politics. Because nonwhite electors tend to be concentrated in about sixty constituencies, immigrant pressure groups can organize to make local parties sensitive to their pressures. There are now hundreds of nonwhite councillors elected in local government. At the 1987 general election twenty-eight nonwhite candidates were nominated, and four, all Labour, were elected. The MPs' origins reflect the diversity of immigrants to Britain; one was born in the South American ex-colony of Guyana, another in Aden, a third in Ghana, and a fourth in London.

THE CONSTITUTION OF THE CROWN

Before examining what government does, we must understand what government is. The normal approach in describing a government is to refer to its constitution. However, England has no written constitution. At no time in the past was there a break with tradition, forcing politicians to think about the basis of authority and write down how the country should be governed.

The unwritten constitution of England is a jumble of acts of Parliament, judicial pronouncements, customs, and conventions about the rules of the political game. The vagueness of the constitution makes it flexible, but it also gives few ironclad guarantees to citizens, in the way that the American Bill of Rights does. In the words of a constitutional lawyer, J. A. G. Griffith, "The Constitution is what happens." People who do not like what happens when British government uses its authority have called for a written constitution with an effective Bill of Rights for individuals.[25]

Comparing the written American and the unwritten English constitutions emphasizes how few constraints are placed on government by an unwritten constitution (Table 9.2). The U.S. Constitution gives the Supreme Court the final power to decide what the government may or may not do. By contrast, Parliament, where the government of the day commands a majority of votes, is the final authority in England. The Bill of Rights in the American Constitution allows anyone to seek redress in the courts for infringement of personal rights, whereas in England an individual who believes his or her personal rights are infringed by an act of Parliament has no redress through the courts. Whereas amendments to the U.S. Constitution must receive the endorsement of well over half the states and members of Congress, in England the unwritten constitution can be changed by an act of Parliament, or simply by the government of the day acting without precedent.

In everyday political conversation, English people do not talk about the constitution but about government. They use the term *government* in many senses. They may speak of the queen's government, to emphasize enduring and nonpartisan features, use the name of the current prime minister to stress personal and transitory features, or refer to a Labour or Conservative government to emphasize partisanship. The term *government officials* usually refers to civil servants.

Collectively, the executive agencies of government are often referred to as Whitehall, after the London street in which many major government offices are located. Downing Street, the home of the prime minister, is a small lane off Whitehall, and Parliament — the

The continuity of the British royal family is illustrated by this photograph, which shows those who can expect to be on the throne over more than a century: Elizabeth, the Queen Mother; her daughter, Queen Elizabeth II; the immediate heir to the throne, Charles, the Prince of Wales; and his son and heir, the infant Prince William.

home of both the House of Commons and the House of Lords — is at the bottom end of Whitehall.

The Crown symbolizes government power. However, the monarch does not personally determine the major activities of Her Majesty's Government. Queen Elizabeth II is concerned with the ceremonial aspects of government. The Queen gives formal assent to laws passed by Parliament; she may not publicly state an opinion about leg-

TABLE 9.2
COMPARING AN UNWRITTEN AND A WRITTEN CONSTITUTION

	England (unwritten)	United States (written)
Origins	Medieval customs	1787: Constitutional Convention
Form	Unwritten, indefinite	Written, precise
Final power to interpret	Majority in Parliament	Supreme Court
Bill of individual rights	No	Yes
Amendment	Ordinary vote in Parliament; unprecedented action by government	More than majority vote in Congress; states
Centrality in political debate	Low	High

islation. The Queen is also responsible for inviting the leader of the party with the largest number of seats in the House of Commons to become prime minister and for dissolving Parliament before a general election. The Queen is expected to respect the will of Parliament, as communicated to her by the leader of the majority party.[26]

The question thus arises: What constitutes the Crown? No simple answer can be given. The Crown is a symbol to which people are asked to give loyalty. It is a concept of indefinite territory; it does not refer to a particular primordial community of people. The idea of the Crown confuses the dignified parts of the constitution, which sanctify authority by tradition and myth, with the efficient parts, which carry out the work of government.

What the Prime Minister Says and Does

Within the Cabinet the prime minister occupies a unique position, sometimes referred to as *primus inter pares* (first among equals). But as Winston Churchill once wrote, "There can be no comparison between the positions of number one, and numbers two, three or four."[27] The preeminence of the prime minister is ambiguous. A politician at the apex of government is remote from what is happening on the ground. The more responsibilities attributed to the prime minister, the less time there is to devote to any one task. Like a president, a prime minister is the prisoner of the political law of first things first. The imperatives of the prime minister are as follows:

1. *Party management.* A prime minister may be self-interested, but he or she is not self-employed. Before becoming prime minister, a politician must normally spend a quarter-century in party activities in and out of Parliament. To remain prime minister, a politician must retain the confidence of the parliamentary party as well as that of the electorate. Failure to maintain the confidence of Conservative MPs led to Margaret Thatcher's resignation from office as party leader and prime minister.

To manage the party in Parliament, the prime minister can wield patronage. The prime minister determines which of several hundred MPs receive appointment as one of about twenty Cabinet ministers. In addition, there are up to one hundred other variously titled subordinate posts within departments as ministers, under secretaries, or parliamentary secretaries. Patronage appointments are thus held by almost a third of the governing party in the House of Commons. Collectively, ministers in patronage posts fill the frontbench seats of the governing party in the House of Commons. Those in the party without any job in government constitute backbenchers; many of them aspire to become frontbenchers.

In making ministerial appointments, a prime minister can use any of four different criteria: personal loyalty (rewarding friends); co-option (bribing critics by giving them an office that obliges them to support the government); representativeness (for example, appointing a Scot or a woman); and competence in giving direction to a government department.

2. *Parliamentary performance.* The prime minister speaks in parliamentary debates about major foreign or economic issues. In addition, twice a week the prime minister appears in the House of Commons at question time, engaging in rapid-fire repartee with a highly partisan audience. Unprotected by a speechwriter's script or by television editing, the prime minister must show that he or she is a good advocate of the government's policies or suffer loss of support.[28]

3. *Media performance.* Publicity is thrust on any incumbent of Downing Street; so, too, are unthinking adulation and criticism. Unlike the Queen, the prime minister is the object of partisan controversy. Journalists tend to reflect the opinion of MPs; hence, a prime minister who is effective in the Commons will usually be reported positively in the media.

Television enables a politician to speak directly to the electorate. Television success is affected by personal qualities, but media advisers have difficulty in making significant changes in the personality of a fifty-year-old politician.

4. *Winning elections.* The only election a prime minister must win is election as party leader. Six of the ten persons who have held the office since 1945 — Winston Churchill, Anthony Eden, Harold Macmillan, Sir Alec Douglas–Home, James Callaghan, and John Major — first entered Downing Street during the middle of a Parliament.

Once in office, a prime minister must pay attention to weekly public opinion polls. In a parliamentary system, party is more important than personal appeal in determining how people vote. While the personality of a prime minister remains relatively static, his or her popularity fluctuates greatly with the fortunes of government policies. Even though Margaret Thatcher had led her party to three election victories, when opinion polls and byelection results indicated that she would lead the party to defeat at the next election, Conservative MPs voted for a change. In the thirteen elections since 1945, the prime minister of the day has seven times led the governing party to victory and six times to defeat.

5. *Policy leadership.* Leading government is a political rather than a managerial task. The prime minister is responsible for maintaining an overall sense of direction in the actions taken by Cabinet ministers, and works closely with a few ministers on policies of central importance. Margaret Thatcher was unusual in going further; she often gave orders to Cabinet members or vetoed their proposals as if she were a directly elected president rather than the captain of a Cabinet team with responsibilities to colleagues. In the end, her unwillingness to share responsibility with colleagues led to resignations that helped bring about her downfall.

A prime minister is ex officio involved in international affairs, dealing with the heads of other governments around the world. In doing so, the prime minister must balance the competing demands of foreign governments and domestic politics. Within government, there is often a difference of opinion between the Treasury and the Foreign Office. The prime minister is uniquely placed to see the interconnections between economic issues and other political objectives, and to ask questions and give advice that the Treasury's chief minister cannot ignore. The prime minister's involvement is not proof of power, for in international affairs and economic policy the influence of British government on outcomes is often limited.

In Whitehall, the prime minister's authority derives from chairing Cabinet meetings and being its authorized spokesperson in the Commons, on television, and to foreign governments. Votes are rarely taken in Cabinet. As chair of the Cabinet, the prime minister sums up the discussion. In Clement Attlee's words:

The job of the Prime Minister is to get the general feeling — collect the voices. And then, when everything reasonable has been said, to get on with the job

and say, "Well I think the decision of the Cabinet is, this, that or the other. Any objections?" Usually there aren't.[29]

While formal powers remain constant, the influence of an individual prime minister varies with political circumstances and with how the incumbent defines the role. Individual prime ministers set very different sights (see Figure 9.2). Clement Attlee, Labour prime minister from 1945 to 1951, was a nonassertive spokesman for the lowest common denominator of views within the Cabinet, keeping himself above the clash of ministerial personalities. When Winston Churchill succeeded in 1951, he concentrated on foreign affairs, exerting little influence in domestic policy. Anthony Eden failed to define a role for himself in domestic politics. In foreign affairs Eden took the initiative leading to Britain's unsuccessful Suez War of 1956. As a result, Eden's health broke and his resignation followed.

Harold Macmillan was ready to intervene in policy, but his directives were not so frequent as to cause friction with his Cabinet. Macmillan was exceptional in that he had previously held major posts concerned with both the economy and foreign affairs. After seven years in office, however, political setbacks and ill health caused the party to welcome his resignation on health grounds in October 1963. Sir Alec Douglas – Home had good health, but he lacked any knowledge of economic affairs, the chief problem at the time. In addition, many Cabinet ministers opposed Sir Alec because of the way a party caucus had secured him the post. He lasted only a year as prime minister and less than two years as Conservative party leader.

Both Harold Wilson and Edward Heath assumed office committed to an activist definition of the prime minister's job. But Wilson's fondness for publicity led critics to describe him as being more interested in public relations than in policies. In reaction, Edward Heath entered office in 1970 with the declared intention of action, not words. Heath pursued major domestic and foreign policy objectives. However, in 1974, the electorate rejected Heath's aggressive direction of the economy, and Harold Wilson reappeared as political conciliator promoting consensus in place of confrontation. James Callaghan, who succeeded Wilson in 1976, also avoided aggressive leadership. Emollient words replaced the promise of action as the dominant image of a prime minister.

The election of Margaret Thatcher brought to 10

FIGURE 9.2
BRITISH PRIME MINISTERS AND GOVERNMENTS SINCE 1940

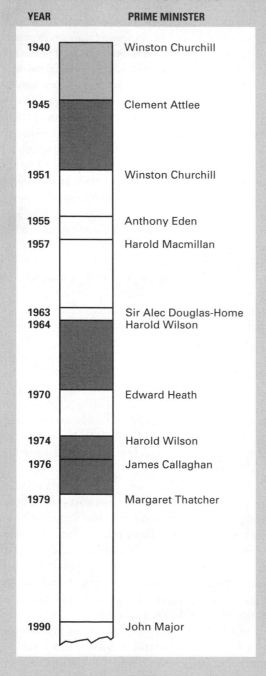

YEAR	PRIME MINISTER
1940	Winston Churchill
1945	Clement Attlee
1951	Winston Churchill
1955	Anthony Eden
1957	Harold Macmillan
1963	Sir Alec Douglas-Home
1964	Harold Wilson
1970	Edward Heath
1974	Harold Wilson
1976	James Callaghan
1979	Margaret Thatcher
1990	John Major

Coalition: Conservative, Labour, and Liberal   Labour   Conservative

Downing Street a politician with distinctive attributes. First, she had strong views about many major policies and was ready to assert them, even if they contradicted the views of her Cabinet colleagues. Second, she was no respecter of protocol, being prepared to push her views against the wishes of Cabinet colleagues and civil service advisers by any means necessary. By winning three elections, Mrs. Thatcher had eleven years in office to promote her views about the substance and style of government.

John Major became prime minister in 1990 in difficult circumstances. He was expected to reverse the fortunes of a party that was much behind Labour in the opinion polls. At the same time he was expected to continue the policies of the Thatcher administration in which he had served. The presence in Parliament of the candidates he defeated in the race for the leadership makes it much harder for him to assert his personal views. Nor do his colleagues want him to do so after eleven years of unusually aggressive leadership by Margaret Thatcher.

The Thatcher administration illustrates both the strengths and limits of a prime minister who seeks to act like a president. She succeeded in imposing economic policies that many colleagues disliked. Her readiness to give orders rather than consult meant that many colleagues were prepared to leak unfavorable stories about her to the press. The result was a Cabinet in which dissension and low morale intermittently erupted in public view, and eventually contributed to her downfall without a general election being held.

As an individual politician, a British prime minister has less formal authority than an American president. The president is directly elected by the nation's voters for a fixed four-year term. A prime minister is chosen by colleagues for an indefinite term. The president is thus more secure in office than a prime minister. The president is the undoubted leader of the federal executive and can dismiss Cabinet appointees with little fear of the consequences; by contrast, senior colleagues of a prime minister are potential rivals for leadership.

Collectively, however, the British government is more powerful than the administration of an American president. Armed with the authority of the Cabinet and support from the majority party in the Commons, a prime minister can be certain that virtually all legislation introduced by Cabinet ministers will be enacted into law. By contrast, congressional opposition defeats many legislative proposals of a president. The prime minister is at the apex of a unitary government, embracing local as well as central government, with powers not limited by the courts or by a written constitution. Although the president is the leading person in the executive branch of the federal government, he or she is without authority over Congress, state and local government, and the judiciary.

The Cabinet and Cabinet Ministers

The Cabinet mobilizes the collective authority of government because its members are the heads of Whitehall departments, as well as representing the majority party in Parliament. Walter Bagehot described the Cabinet as securing "the close union, the nearly complete fusion of the executive and legislative powers." [30]

Each Cabinet minister is responsible for a particular government department, and his or her political reputation depends on the skill with which its cause is advanced in Whitehall, in Parliament, with pressure groups, and the media. Each minister is inclined to see issues from the perspective of a department rather than the government as a whole. Ministers compete with each other for scarce resources, and oppose each other when issues arise that put departmental interests in conflict. To advance a cause, a minister will lobby in Cabinet and in the governing party, and sometimes use leaks to the press. One minister's loyalty to a cause may look like disloyalty to colleagues.

The convention of Cabinet responsibility requires that all ministers, including dozens too junior to sit in the Cabinet, give public support to a Cabinet decision, or at least refrain from making public criticism. Cabinet ministers usually go along silently with their colleagues' proposals, to ensure that their colleagues will endorse their own measures. If a minister does not wish to go along, it is conventional for the minister to resign. Such is the political pain of giving up office that only a dozen members of the Cabinet have resigned on political grounds since 1945.

Notwithstanding the Cabinet's formal importance, it normally ratifies rather than makes decisions. One reason is the pressure of time. A second reason is that the great majority of matters that go up to the Cabinet have normally been discussed in great detail beforehand, for ministers meet in Cabinet committees to review the preliminary reports of civil servants. Whenever possible, Cabinet ministers prefer to resolve their differences in a committee or by informal negotiations. By so doing they can enter full Cabinet meetings with a recommendation that it is difficult to challenge. [31]

What the government as a whole can do is determined by the departments headed by individual members of the Cabinet. If the Cabinet is the keystone in the arch of central government, the departments are the building blocks. Every Cabinet decision must be administered by a department or by interdepartmental collaboration. The great bulk of decisions are taken within departments.

Unlike the American Cabinet, the size of the British Cabinet is not fixed. The prime minister decides which departments are included in the Cabinet, and the number varies. In every Cabinet some departments are organized primarily in terms of clients and others by services. The Cabinet that John Major created upon becoming prime minister in 1990 had departments for

1. Economic affairs — treasury; trade and industry; employment; energy; transport; agriculture.
2. External affairs — foreign and commonwealth office; defense.
3. Social services — health; social security; education and science.
4. Environmental and territorial — environment (including English local government and housing); the Scottish Office; the Welsh Office; the Northern Ireland Office.
5. Law — lord chancellor's office; Home Office; the attorney-general and the solicitor-general for England and Wales; the lord advocate and the solicitor-general for Scotland.
6. Managerial and nondepartmental — leader of the House of Commons; leader of the House of Lords; chancellor of the Duchy of Lancaster, chief whip in the House of Commons.

Departments are not single-purpose institutions with a clear hierarchy of tasks; each is an agglomeration of administrative units brought together by government expansion, fusion, and fission. [32] Since 1964 responsibilities for trade, industry, and technology have been placed in departments labeled Technology, then Trade and Industry, then separated into two departments for Trade and for Industry, and once again reunited as a single Trade and Industry department. Each time that the title on the front door of the department was changed, most officials and programs continued as before.

The Treasury and the Home Office illustrate differences among Whitehall departments. The Home Office has a staff approximately ten times larger than the Treasury. Because of the importance of the economy, however, the Treasury has more senior civil servants than the Home Office. The Home Office has more staff at lower levels because of the number and scale of its routine tasks involving supervision of police, fire, prison, drugs, cruelty to animals, control of obscene publications, race relations, and so on. The Treasury, by contrast, has a few major and interrelated tasks. The job of home secretary is much more varied. More paperwork is required, and the home secretary is always vulnerable to adverse publicity if, for example, a convicted murderer escapes from prison. But the job of the chancellor of the Exchequer, the minister in charge of the Treasury, is more important politically, for the future of the governing party is influenced by the performance of the economy.

Every minister has many roles.[33] When policies are discussed, a minister may initiate measures, select among alternatives brought forward from within the department, or avoid making any decision at all. A Cabinet minister is also the executive head of a large bureaucracy, formally responsible for all that is done by thousands of civil servants. In addition, a minister is a department's ambassador to the world outside, representing the department in the Cabinet and the Commons, in discussions with pressure groups, and in the mass media.

The Civil Service

Although government could continue for months without new legislation, it would collapse overnight if hundreds of thousands of civil servants stopped administering laws. Because British government is big government, even a civil servant who rarely sees a minister can be responsible for a staff of several thousand people or spending tens of millions of pounds. Only if these duties are executed routinely will ministers have the time and opportunity to make new policies.

Civil servants are divided into a variety of groups unequal in size and political significance. The largest group (about 200,000) consists of clerical staff, with little discretion doing routine tasks that are the stuff of bureaucracy. The job of delivering services to the general public is left to local government, the National Health Service, and public corporations such as the Post Office.

The most important group of civil servants is the smallest: the few hundred people in the open class who advise ministers and oversee work of the departments. Top civil servants deny they are politicians because of the partisan connotations of the term. However, their work is political because they are concerned not with management details but with what government ought to do, formulating, reviewing, and advising on broad policies.[34]

An official publication seeking to recruit bright graduates for the higher civil service declares: "You will be involved from the outset in matters of major policy or resource allocation and, under the guidance of experienced administrators, encouraged to put forward your own constructive ideas and to take responsible decisions."[35] Civil servants are not apolitical; they are bipartisan, prepared to work for whichever party is the winner of an election.

The first responsibility of higher civil servants is to look after their departmental minister. A Cabinet minister spends as much time with civil servants as with partisan colleagues. A minister wants civil servants to assist in formulating and evaluating policies. A busy politician simply does not have time to go into details about the problems facing a department; he or she wants a "brief" (that is, a carefully judged summary) about problems. Second, a minister expects civil servants to protect him from mistakes. Third, a minister needs the help of officials to market policies to other departments, to pressure groups and the media.

Civil servants prefer to work for a minister who will make decisions and stick to them, and respect their expertise and listen to their views before a decision is taken. Civil servants also value the good opinion of their colleagues. Their style is not like that of the professional American athlete; English civil servants tend to believe that winning is less important than how one plays the game.

The Thatcher government introduced a new phenomenon in Whitehall: a prime minister who distrusted the civil service, believing it inherently inferior to business. The government's privatization campaign was one way of removing responsibilities from civil servants. In addition, Thatcher sought to promote officials whom she believed shared her vision of the virtues of managerial efficiency and the market. Because the Thatcher administration was the duly elected government of the day, civil servants could not argue in principle against accepting its policies.[36]

Critics of the Thatcher style of governing accused

her of failing to respect conventions, which higher civil servants are meant to protect. Some even challenged the doctrine that a civil servant must support a minister, whatever the official's personal opinion. In one well-publicized case, a Ministry of Defense official, Clive Ponting, leaked to the House of Commons evidence that questioned the accuracy of government statements about the conduct of the Falklands War, and was indicted for violating the Official Secrets Act. The judge told the jury that the issue was: "Can it then be in the interests of the state to go against the policy of the government of the day?" The jury concluded that it could be; Ponting was acquitted.

Government as a Network

Policymaking is the joint product of the actions of Cabinet ministers and civil servants. The ship of state has only one tiller — but two pairs of hands give it direction. Thus, anything that affects one part affects the whole system. If the caliber of the civil service deteriorates, this reduces the performance of the Cabinet. If a prime minister or Cabinet ministers are unrealistic or uncertain in setting policy objectives, civil servants cannot act to their full potential.[37]

In an era of big government, power cannot reside within a single individual; it is manifest in a network of relations within and between institutions. A network is not a pyramid leading to a single peak. British government is a mountain range with a number of peak institutions and individuals. Politics is about the relationship between prime minister, ministers, and their departments, and leading civil servants.

The prime minister is the single most important person in government but not all-important. R.H.S. Crossman, a former Labour minister, has argued that departmental ministers make "primary decisions" in consultation with the Cabinet; any decision taken solely by a minister becomes, by definition, "not at all important."[38]

There are a number of weaknesses in this argument, the first of which is vagueness. To say that the prime minister makes the most important decisions and departmental ministers the secondary decisions, begs the question: What is an important decision? The distinction between important and unimportant decisions is never defined. The decisions in which the prime minister is not involved, such as routine spending on social security and health, are more numerous and affect more public spending than matters that receive his or her at-

tention. Describing the prime minister as at the apex of government aptly symbolizes how far the person on top is from events on the ground.

Second, the time of a prime minister is scarce. The more attention given to international affairs and the economy, the less time there is for all the everyday domestic concerns of Cabinet ministers. As one Downing Street official has described policymaking: "It's like skating over an enormous globe of thin ice. You have to keep moving fast all the time."[39] Trying to do everything risks imposing self-inflicted wounds; a case in point is Thatcher's personal decision to impose an unpopular and administratively costly poll tax.

A small staff is a third limitation on the prime ministerial directives. Only half a dozen civil servants and ten political appointees work on the prime minister's behalf in Downing Street — a far cry from the hundreds who work for the U.S. president. None of the prime minister's staff can issue orders to a Cabinet minister, as a White House staffer can, for British ministers are not subordinates as Cabinet secretaries are in Washington.

Fourth, the issues that immediately concern the prime minister, such as foreign affairs and the international dimension of the economy, are fields where the power of British government has declined in the postwar era. The prime minister must concentrate on these issues because they involve exchanges between heads of government. But as Britain is no longer the world power that it once was, these activities indicate the limited influence of a prime minister.

The prime minister has the opportunity to intervene selectively in a variety of issues of importance to the government as a whole. A prime ministerial intervention can take the form of a question to a minister: What is your department doing about X? Why doesn't the department prepare plans to do Y? Such questions cannot be ignored. But a prime minister who promotes policies that split the governing party risks loss of party confidence and office, as Margaret Thatcher found out in 1990.

Within the government network, a small number of very senior ministers are important in determining policies. The chancellor of the Exchequer, in charge of the Treasury, has a threefold importance: he or she is immediately responsible for managing the economy; oversees a large number of civil servants expert in the economy; and is a substantial political figure in the governing party. A few ministers will exercise influence because of their personal or political relationship with the prime minister.

A handful of leading civil servants are also central in the network. The Cabinet Office has a staff that serves all Cabinet committees, tracking developments throughout government. The secretary of the Cabinet writes the minutes of Cabinet and sees that appropriate followup measures are taken. He is in daily contact with the prime minister about what is happening within Whitehall and disseminates requests from the prime minister to departments. Within a department, the permanent secretary is the highest ranking civil servant, usually having much more experience and knowledge of a department's problems than a transitory Cabinet minister.

A network is much more than a few persons; it is a system that links dozens of ministries with each other, and ties ministers with civil servants. Within a network, many different officials can deal simultaneously with problems in many different places. It is not necessary for one person to be responsible for all that is done in the name of British government. Nor is it impossible for one person to determine everything that government does.

THE ROLE OF PARLIAMENT

In its ceremonial role, Parliament is very impressive.[40] In terms of efficient power, however, Parliament is not so impressive, because its influence on policy is strictly limited. The government controls its proceedings. The prime minister can be sure that any government proposal will be promptly voted on in Parliament, for the executive drafts legislation and controls amendments. Furthermore, the government enjoys the power of the purse: the budget it prepares is debated in Parliament but rarely altered.

In the United States, by contrast, each house of Congress controls its own proceedings independent of the White House, and when Republicans control the presidency and Democrats Congress, party loyalty reinforces the independence of each. An American president may ask Congress to enact a bill, but he or she cannot compel a favorable vote. The president's budget is not a final document but an attempt to persuade Congress to tax and spend as the White House wants. Parliament lacks each of these powerful checks on the executive.

In a year's parliamentary business, the government can secure the passage of every bill it introduces.

The government's ability to get its way reflects the fact that if it makes a measure a vote of confidence, then MPs in the majority party must vote for the bill or risk their government losing office. The bills the government promotes are often criticized in the House of Commons, but the government almost invariably determines whether or not proposed amendments will be enacted. The government may introduce amendments to improve a bill or placate critics. Of the amendments moved without government backing, 95 percent are defeated.[41]

The House of Commons

The principal division in central government is between the majority party, which controls the Commons *and* Cabinet, and the opposition party in the Commons. The government consistently wins votes in the House of Commons because it has a majority there that votes on party lines stated in a weekly memorandum issued by the party's chief whip. MPs almost always accept the whip's instructions because they recognize that only by voting as a bloc can their party continue to control government. The government falls if it loses a vote of confidence on a major issue.

In nine-tenths of all votes in the Commons, voting is strictly along party lines; not one of over six hundred Conservative or Labour MPs votes with another party. When an MP does break ranks, such rebel votes rarely influence the verdict of Parliament. The government's state of mind was expressed by a Labour Cabinet minister as follows: "It's carrying democracy too far if you don't know the result of the vote before the meeting."[42]

Within the governing party, backbench MPs have opportunities to influence government, individually and collectively. The whip is expected to listen to the views of dissatisfied backbench MPs and to convey their concerns to ministers. In the corridors, dining rooms, and committees of the Commons, backbenchers can tell ministers what they think is wrong.

The opposition party cannot expect to alter major government decisions because it lacks a majority of votes. The opposition accepts the defeat of its motions for up to five years, the maximum life of a contemporary Parliament, because it hopes for victory in the next election. As long as the two major parties alternate in winning a parliamentary majority, each can expect to enjoy all the power of government part of the time.

In a typical year, the Commons spends more of its time in debating the principles or implications of policies than in discussing legislation. Many ministerial deci-

sions are statements of intent, since the government cannot unilaterally determine the state of the economy or international events. In advance of government action, parliamentary debates register the mood of the House, indicating what decisions or statements of intent would be popular. After the event, MPs debate the wisdom and effectiveness of the government's decisions.

The Commons' first function is weighing the reputation of men and women.[43] MPs continually assess their colleagues as ministers and potential ministers. A minister may win a formal vote of confidence but lose status if his or her arguments are demolished in debate. The clublike atmosphere of the Commons permits MPs to judge their colleagues over the years, separating those who merit trust from those who do not.

Second, MPs scrutinze the administration of laws. An MP may write to a minister, questioning a department decision called to his or her attention by a constituent or pressure group. If the MP is not satisfied with the answer, the issue can be raised at question time in the Commons. An MP can also raise administrative issues in the adjournment debate during the last half hour of every parliamentary day. The knowledge that dissatisfaction with a private reply can lead to public debate ensures that correspondence from backbench MPs is given special attention within the minister's office.

MPs can request the parliamentary commissioner for administration (also known as the ombudsman, after the Scandinavian prototype) to investigate complaints about maladministration by government departments. Because many areas are excluded from the commissioner's inquiry, complaints are often rejected as being outside the commissioner's jurisdiction. The commissioner has no power to order reversal of a government decision.

The design of the House of Commons reflects the British Constitution: MPs in the government party sit on one side of the House, and all the Opposition MPs face them from the opposite side. This differs from legislatures such as the U.S. Congress. There members sit together in a semicircle, and there is no clearcut division between Government and Opposition as in the House of Commons.

The House of Commons uses committees to scrutinize administration. A small group of MPs can give more time to an issue than can the whole house. Moreover, committees can interview civil servants and other experts, question ministers, and publish reports. Parliamentary committees have little political influence, however. As committees move from discussions of detail to questions of political principle, they raise questions of confidence in the government. Party loyalty usually secures the government against losing votes in committees.

Talking about legislation is a third function of the House of Commons; it does not actually write laws. Ministers decide on the general principles of bills, which are written by specialist lawyers acting on instructions from civil servants who spell out a minister's intentions. Particular details are discussed at length with affected and interested parties before being introduced in the Commons. Such influence as the Commons exerts on legislation is felt during drafting, when Whitehall seeks to anticipate what MPs will choose to attack in debate. Laws are described as acts of Parliament, but it would be more accurate if they were stamped "Made in Whitehall."

A fourth function of MPs is to voice ideas and opinions outside as well as inside the House of Commons. An MP has much more access to the mass media than an ordinary citizen. However, Parliament cannot sway mass opinion, because the mass of the electorate is not as interested in the work of Parliament as are MPs or professors of politics. Only the quality newspapers read by one-tenth of the electorate report speeches made in the Commons. Television has access to Parliament, but news programs usually show only sound bites, not full speeches or debates. The public's lack of interest in debate is matched by that of MPs. Only one-sixth of backbenchers regularly listen to their colleagues' speeches in the House of Commons.

A newly elected MP contemplating his or her role as one among 650 members of the House of Commons is faced with many alternatives. An MP may decide to be a party loyalist, voting as the leadership decides, without participating in deliberations about policy. The MP who wishes to be more than a name in a division list must decide whether to make a mark by brilliance in debate, attending routine committee meetings as an acknowledged representative of a pressure group, or in a nonpartisan way, for example, as a wit. An MP is expected to speak for constituency interests, but constituents accept that their MP will not vote against party policy if it is in conflict with local interests. The only role that an MP will rarely undertake is that of legislator.

The House of Lords
The House of Lords is unique among the upper chambers of modern Western parliaments because it has a hereditary basis. Although hereditary peers constitute the majority, they do not dominate its proceedings. Beginning in 1958, distinguished men and women have been appointed to life peerages. Many peers are retired members of the House of Commons; they find the more relaxed pace of the Lords suited to their advancing years.

Like the Commons, the Lords weigh men and women as fit or unfit for ministerial office. Because of the high average age of peers, few expect office; only in the Conservative ranks are there younger peers seeking to establish themselves politically. Since 1963, politically ambitious heirs to peerages have been able to disclaim their hereditary status and stand for election to the Commons.

The Lords' power to reject bills passed by the Commons was formidable until the Parliament Act of 1911 abolished its right of veto, substituting the power to delay the enactment of legislation. The power of delay is especially significant in the year before a general election. Occasionally, the Lords delays the passage of a major government bill or forces the government to accept amendments against its wishes.

The Lords avoids rejecting measures from the Commons, because doing so would raise questions about its own status. The Lords cannot claim to represent the nation, because its members are neither popularly elected nor representative of a cross-section of the population. Moreover, the Lords has had a Conservative majority, albeit a majority that is declining.

The government often introduces relatively noncontroversial legislation in the Lords if it deals with technical matters. The government can use the Lords as a revising chamber to incorporate amendments. In addition, the Lords can discuss public issues without reference to legislation. The government or opposition may initiate a debate on foreign affairs, or individual peers may raise such topics as pornography or the future of hill farming. Peers can also question ministers.

The Influence of Parliament
Parliament influences government in two major ways. First, backbench MPs, especially in the governing party, can demand that the government do something about an issue or voice opposition to a proposed government action. Second, the procedures of the Commons make introduction of a major bill a lengthy and tiring effort for a minister, who must be prepared to explain

and defend it as the Commons discusses it in principle and in detail.

The limited influence of both houses of Parliament encourages proposals for reform, particularly from younger MPs who wish to make their jobs as interesting and important as possible. Proposals to reform the Commons have languished because proponents of reform disagree about the part Parliament should take in government. Some reformers believe that Parliament should be able to prevent executive actions; others simply wish for increased influence over what the executive does. One group wants to transfer power from Whitehall to the Commons; the other wants to improve the work of Whitehall by correcting its errors.

The most important obstacle to reform reflects the great grievance of backbench reformers: the power of decision rests with the Cabinet and not with the Commons as a whole. Whatever MPs say as members of the opposition or on the backbenches, once in the Cabinet they think that the present limited influence of Parliament is all the executive can allow or afford.

POLITICAL CULTURE AND AUTHORITY

The political culture of England consists of values, beliefs, and emotional attitudes about authority. Because of the continuity of political institutions, many contemporary cultural outlooks reflect past values transmitted to today's citizens through an intergenerational process of political socialization.

Allegiance to Authority: The Legitimacy of the System

Of all attitudes affecting government, the most important concern allegiance to political authority. The government can claim full legitimacy only if its citizens support authority and favor compliance with basic rules. Support for a regime is not a judgment about the effectiveness or efficiency of government. English people simultaneously value their form of government, while making many specific criticisms of how it works.

The continuity of authority in England makes the idea of overthrowing the existing regime inconceivable to many people. When public opinion polls ask what people think of government by elected representatives, 94 percent support it as a good way of governing. Surveys consistently show that only about 5 percent believe that society must be radically changed by revolutionary action. MPs give almost unanimous support to the established system.[44]

The political difficulties arising from Britain's persisting economic troubles have reduced confidence in the effectiveness of government. Even so, the people have faith in the legitimacy of parliamentary institutions. Even Nationalist parties in Scotland, Wales, and Northern Ireland, while rejecting government by a Parliament in London, do not reject parliamentary government within their own territory. Except in Northern Ireland, extremist parties of the right and left receive derisory votes.

The legitimacy of government is also evidenced by the readiness of the English people to comply with laws. Law enforcement does not require large numbers of armed police or undercover agents. In proportion to its population, England's police force is one-third smaller than that of America, West Germany, or France. Street violence, kidnappings, and assassinations have not become facts of English political life. The crimes that are committed are considered antisocial rather than crimes against the state.

The very concept of political crime is unknown in England. Only in Northern Ireland have politically motivated violations of the law frequently been directed at undermining authority. It is a reminder that the authority of Westminster institutions rests on customs and traditions that cannot easily be exported.

The rise of unorthodox methods of political activity — protest marches, rent strikes, sit-ins at public buildings, and violence to property and persons — has reaffirmed the commitment of most English people to the conventional rules of the political game. Surveys show that there is little support for political action outside the law. A majority disapprove of eight forms of political protest ranging from boycotts to painting slogans on walls. Only one-sixth approve unconventional but legal protest action, such as unofficial strikes or measures that are illegal but well publicized, such as occupying buildings.[45]

The English commitment to lawful political action reflects values about how people ought to act, not simply calculations about what will work as the minority believing unorthodox measures are effective is larger than the group approving such measures. Since most people disapprove of unorthodox political behavior and do not believe it to be effective, it follows that very few engage in such protests; 6 percent report involvement in boycotts and 5 percent in unofficial strikes.

The commitment of the English people to established authority is also shown by their readiness to support the government in taking strong measures when its authority is challenged. Surveys show that 80 percent approve the courts giving severe sentences to protesters who disregard the police, and 73 percent approve the police using force against demonstrators. Only a minority go so far as to endorse government actions that would conflict with individual rights, such as declaring all protest demonstrations illegal. While most English people reject unorthodox political action, they also reject bending the law to repress lawful disagreement with government policy.

The legitimacy accorded to government in England is not the result of carefully calculated policies. Officeholders try to avoid raising constitutional issues, because they are so difficult to resolve in the absence of a written constitution.

English political philosophers have speculated for centuries about the causes of allegiance to authority. They offer conflicting explanations which are over the heads of the great mass of the population, who have never read their arguments. The political outlook of the mass of English people is derived from experience far more than from books.

The symbols of a common past, such as the monarchy are sometimes cited as a major determinant of legitimacy. But surveys of public opinion show that the Queen is of little political significance; she is viewed as a nonpolitical figure. The popularity of a monarch is a consequence not a cause of political legitimacy.[46] Moreover, in Northern Ireland, the Queen is a symbol of divisions between Protestants proclaiming loyalty to the British Crown and Republicans who reject the Crown.

In a survey asking people why they support the government, the most popular reason (77 percent) was: "It's the best form of government we know." Authority is not said to be perfect, or even trouble free: it is valued on the basis of experience. Popular endorsement of government—"It's the kind of government the people want"—is also viewed as a justification by 66 percent. A total of 65 percent also regard authority as inevitable: "We've got to accept it whatever we think."[47] Contrary to what economic determinists sometimes argue, popular allegiance is not bought by the provision of public benefits, for the economic difficulties since 1975 have not caused the rise of antidemocratic parties, and the same is true of earlier periods.

The Role of Law

Courts and police are relatively unimportant in the political culture; the role of law is narrow. Whereas judges once proclaimed the doctrine of the rule of law to restrain royal absolutism, today English judges have adopted a self-denying view of their role.

Unlike American courts, English courts claim no power to declare an act of Parliament unconstitutional. Nor will they set aside an act because it conflicts with what claimants describe as natural rights. English judges believe that an unwritten constitution can be altered, but they want no part of the job. That is for Parliament and the electorate.[48] *Final court of appeal is political, not judicial*

Instead of reviewing constitutionality, English courts determine whether the executive acts within its statutory powers. If an action of the central government or a local authority is *ultra vires* (outside its powers), the courts may order the government or authority to desist. The courts may also quash an action undertaken in a procedurally improper manner. But if a statute delegates discretion to a public authority, the courts do not question how the executive exercises its discretion. Even if the courts rule against the executive, the effect of such a judgment can be annulled by a subsequent act of Parliament retroactively authorizing an action.

An English person who believes that the government has denied his or her basic rights will find it difficult to get English courts to redress the grievance. There are no primary rules in the unwritten constitution or in legal documents that the citizen may invoke against an act of Parliament. The American Bill of Rights holds that some individual rights are superior to statute. In England, the court will uphold the actions of a government as long as there is statutory authority, and it is also very ready to trust police evidence.

Today, some politicians and lawyers argue that there ought to be an English Bill of Rights that would protect individual rights against actions that might even be sanctioned by Parliament. The "un-Britishness" of such a proposal is made evident by the fact that the simplest way in which it could be done would be to incorporate guarantees currently laid down in the European Convention on Human Rights.

In practice, the powers of British government are limited by cultural norms about what government should and should not do. In the words of one High

Court judge: "In the constitution of this country, there are no guaranteed or absolute rights. The safeguard of British liberty is in the good sense of the people and in the system of representative and responsible government which has been evolved."[49]

The role of the police illustrates the importance of mutual trust between governors and governed. In England, police operate on the assumption that their authority will usually be accepted and that those they seek to apprehend will be shunned by society at large. Police patrol unarmed; criminals are expected to be unarmed too. To a remarkable extent the police are respected. This does not mean that they are never criticized. However, most people think that police officers who abuse their authority are atypical of the police force.

Today, trust between police and citizens is subject to erosion on four fronts. First, the police are becoming more remote. A generation ago policemen patrolled on foot or on bicycle, maintaining close contact with the community. Today they patrol in cars or keep areas under electronic surveillance. Second, illegal acts by the police are increasing, including abuse of police powers to secure wrongful convictions. Third, left-wing groups have sought physical confrontations with the police in demonstrations and illegal picketing. Fourth, in immigrant areas of cities there is ambivalence. Many immigrants desire protection against crime, but there is concern that some law enforcement officials do not enforce the law fairly when immigrants are involved.[50]

England has no paramilitary security force to compel obedience to the law, or anything like the American National Guard for use in the event of domestic political disorder. The navy is England's major armed service; the navy goes into action at sea, away from the mass of the urban population. The army is virtually never used to enforce public order within England; it is occasionally a source of ready manpower to help deal with a flood.

The importance of English attitudes in maintaining law and order is demonstrated by a comparison with Northern Ireland. Parliament has never been successful in efforts to export English institutions of police or courts there, because these institutions can operate only with the full consent of the population, and both Protestants and Catholics have withheld this consent. Westminster's first reaction to civil rights disorders in Ulster was to encourage the Northern Ireland government to imitate English procedures. But violence followed and "un-English" emergency measures have been used instead.[51]

The gradual increase in crime; the use of police to enforce controversial industrial relations laws; and sporadic disturbances in inner-city areas largely inhabited by nonwhite Britons have demonstrated the practical limits of police authority. Right-wing groups ask for more power to be given to the police; left-wing groups criticize the police for enforcing laws limiting picketing that they dislike; and the majority of the population is disturbed by rising crime rates. Nonetheless, the police still retains major reserves of popular support.

Whose Authority?

Those who govern make up a small select fraction of the population; their authority is justified because they are believed to represent the country as a whole. The three major justifications for authority exercised by representatives are trusteeship, collectivist ideologies, and individual choice.

In the *trusteeship* theory, leaders take the initiative in determining what government does. MPs and Cabinet are not expected to ask what people want, but to use their independent judgment to determine what is in the best interests of society. In the words of L. S. Amery, a Conservative Cabinet minister writing after World War II, England is governed "for the people, with, but not by, the people."[52]

The trustee view of government is summed up in the epigram, "the government's job is to govern." The outlook is popular with the party in office, because it justifies doing whatever it wishes. The opposition party rejects this theory because it does not exercise the power of government. Civil servants find the doctrine congenial because they permanently serve the governing party, and see themselves as permanent (albeit nonelected) trustees of the public interest.

In predemocratic times, government by trustees was justified on the grounds that ordinary people should defer to their betters, who were defined by aristocratic birth or gentlemanly manners. Today, only a very small and aging proportion of English people are prepared to defer to others on grounds of social status.[53]

Right and left can see representation in *collectivist* terms, with major socioeconomic groups rather than individuals as the constituent units of politics. Collectivists argue that the aggregation of individual preferences by groups is inevitable in making decisions in a country with more than 56 million citizens. From a collectivist perspective, parties and pressure groups advocating group economic interests are more authoritative than individual voters.[54]

Conservatives have historically emphasized an organic harmony between different economic groups. All parts are meant to be linked, like the parts of the human body, each with a different function. Those who are better off are expected to help those who are less well off by supporting public services and voluntary activities.

The socialist vision of group politics emphasizes economic divisions, with trade unions the chief representative of employed people, bargaining collectively about wages with employers and with government about national economic policy. However, less than one-quarter of the electorate and less than two-fifths of the labor force now belong to a trade union. Under Neil Kinnock the Labour party has loosened rather than strengthened its ties with unions, voicing an electoral appeal aimed at individuals and families.

Individualist theories of representation emphasize the importance of each citizen in the political process. The Liberal Democrats argue that political parties should not represent organized group interests but individuals. However, individuals very rarely have the opportunity to vote directly on what government does. Only once has Britain held a nationwide referendum.

Margaret Thatcher appealed to the values of economic individualism, with each person being responsible for his or her welfare, rather than the government taking that responsibility. However, when she declared — "There is no such thing as society" — this statement was discounted as ideological hyperbole, for it denied the existence of schools, hospitals, social security benefits, and other social institutions that government collectively provides for individuals.

Because a multiplicity of cultural outlooks coexist within England, the political culture is a composite. Leading Cabinet ministers and civil servants often claim they are trustees for the nation, acting as they think best. Lesser ministers tend to be caught up in collectivist politics, negotiating to reconcile conflicts between and within parties and pressure groups. At election time, the votes of millions of individual English people decide who governs.

Although both MPs and civil servants recognize the significance of individual voters, MPs see their primary role as representing collective groups or as trustees for the nation. In the words of a Labour MP: "The essential thing in a democracy is a general election in which a government is elected with power to do any damned thing it likes and if the people don't like it, they have the right to chuck it out."[55] A Conservative member with an aristocratic background endorses the same view with characteristic mock diffidence:

> I personally consider myself capable of coming to decisions without having to fight an election once every four or five years, but on the other hand, the people must be allowed to feel that they can exercise some control, even if it's only the control of chucking somebody out that they don't like.[56]

Culture as a Constraint on Policy

The diffuse legitimacy that the English people confer on government does not allow government to do anything or everything. The norms of the political culture include a set of dos and don'ts about the scope of political authority. In theory, Parliament can enact any policy that the government recommends; in practice, the government is limited by what people will stand for.

Liberty is chief among the things that government cannot interfere with. Cultural norms about freedom of action and speech prevent political censorship. In the 1960s laws against sexual relations between consenting male adults were repealed, and censorship of books, films, and plays was virtually abandoned. Abortion was legalized in 1968, further reducing the scope of legislation affecting private morality.

Cultural expectations also influence what politicians must do. Regardless of party preference, nearly everybody believes the government ought to provide education, health services, and social security. In both Conservative and Labour governments disputes are about how much money the government should spend, which social programs should have priority, and how they should be financed.

The significance of cultural norms is illustrated by comparing British and American expectations of what government ought to do (Figure 9.3). In Britain a majority of people think government ought to provide health care for the sick and a decent living standard for the old, keep prices under control, and help industry grow. A majority of Americans do not support these views. Whereas Americans overwhelmingly reject the idea that government ought to reduce income differences between rich and poor, Britons are divided, and the division is also reflected in party politics. Overall, 57 percent of Britons expect government to promote social policies, more than twice the average of 23 percent of Americans.

FIGURE 9.3
ANGLO-AMERICAN DIFFERENCES ABOUT GOVERNMENT'S ROLE

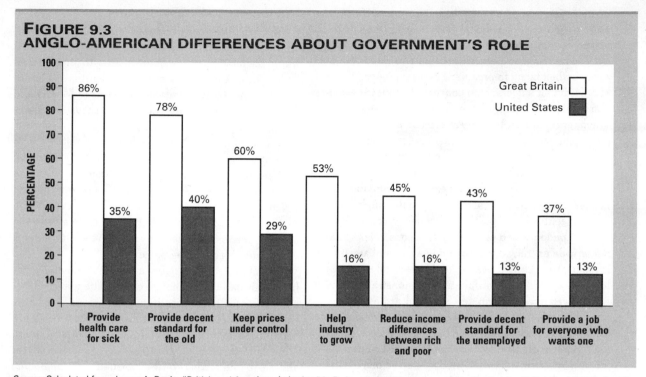

Source: Calculated from James A. Davis, "British and American Attitudes," in R. Jowell, S. Witherspoon, and L. Brook, eds., *British Social Attitudes: The 1986 Report* (Aldershot: Gower, 1986), p. 102.

Today, the most significant limits on the scope of government policy are practical, not cultural. This is most evident in the government's efforts to manage the economy. Government can influence the economy through its monetary policies, by legislation and public expenditure, exhortation, offering incentives to business and unions, and sometimes by passing temporary legislation to regulate wages or prices. However, in a mixed economy the actions of business, unions and the international economy influence outcomes too.[57]

MASS PARTICIPATION AND SOCIALIZATION

Socialization influences the political division of labor. At an early age children learn about social differences with political salience, about political parties and about the political roles that he or she may take. The adult population then divides into a small number who actively participate in politics and a large mass who only intermittently participate.

Popular Participation

If participation is defined as paying taxes and drawing benefits from public programs, then everyone participates in government. The mixed-economy welfare state provides benefits at every stage of life, from maternity and children's benefits, to health care and pensions in old age. A majority of the population lives in a household drawing a weekly cash benefit from government, and 90 percent are part of a family that annually enjoys such major benefits as health care, education, or a pension.

An election is the one opportunity people have to influence government directly. Every British citizen aged eighteen or over is eligible to vote. Local government officials undertake the burden of registration, and registration lists are revised annually to maintain accuracy. The wide dispersal of voting stations, a high density of population, and a widespread sense of civic duty result in a turnout that has averaged 77 percent since 1950, which is very high by comparison with an American presidential election.

Voting, however, is the only political activity that most people undertake. Only 7 percent of the electorate can be classified as activists, engaging in at least five of ten common political activities: voting, helping in fund-raising efforts, urging others to vote, holding office in an organization, and presenting their views to an MP.[58] For most members of a political party, paying dues is the extent of their involvement.

Many English people participate in politics indirectly by belonging to organized interest groups. These range from an anglers' club concerned about the pollution of a local stream to the Automobile Association, which represents motorists. An estimated 61 percent of the population belongs to at least one organization (Figure 9.4). A total of 14 percent are officers or committee members of a voluntary organization.

Ad hoc protest groups appear in local and national politics. Many reflect local concern about a single issue. The concentration of politics in London makes it possible for London-based protest organizations to appear as nationwide organizations, by hiring a hall and advertising a meeting. Only 6 percent of the electorate say they have taken part in a lawful street demonstration, and even fewer have participated in illegal protests.[59]

The majority of English people are not regularly active in politics; depending on the measure used, only 3 to 14 percent of the electorate can be described as regular participants in politics. If holding elected office is the measure of political involvement, the proportion drops below 1 percent.

Socialization Influences

FAMILY The family's influence comes first chronologically in the child's life; political attitudes learned within the family become intertwined with primary family loyalties. A child may not know what the Labour or Conservative party stands for, but if it is Mom's and Dad's party that can plant the seeds of party identification.

The influence of family is, however, limited, for 36 percent of the electorate do not know how one or both of their parents usually voted, or else their parents voted for opposing parties. Among those who report knowing which party both parents supported, just over half vote as their parents have done. In the electorate as a whole, only 35 percent say that they know how both parents voted and voted for the same party.[60]

Children also acquire a religious identification from their parents. Although church attendance is low and parties are secular institutions, religion retains a residual influence on party loyalties. Persons who have been raised as members of the state-supported Church of England are more likely to support the Conservatives, and those in nonconformist Protestant denominations, Catholics, or without a religion are more likely to vote Labour. Except in Northern Ireland, religion no longer

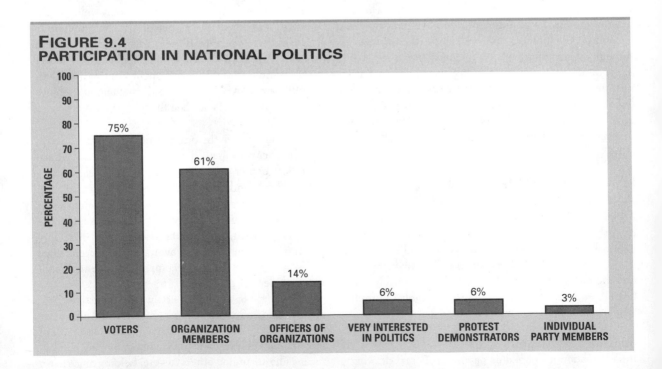

FIGURE 9.4
PARTICIPATION IN NATIONAL POLITICS

has a substantial influence on voting, and there are no groups comparable to the American religious right.

GENDER: SIMILARITIES AND DIFFERENCES

In childhood boys and girls learn different social roles according to gender, but as adults they have an equal right to vote and participate in politics.

Today all political parties do their best to avoid offending women, for they constitute more than half the electorate; nor do parties offend men, for they constitute 48 percent of the electorate. Parties emphasize issues that appeal to both sexes. When a party addresses foreign policy or the economy, it does so by stressing common concerns of both genders. The 1976 Sex Discrimination Act, prohibiting discrimination in employment, was enacted by a Labour government but followed a report issued by a Conservative government.

At each general election, women divide between parties in much the same way as men do. Class differences are much more important than gender in determining how people vote. For example, even though Margaret Thatcher is a woman, she did not attract a disproportionate amount of votes from women. Moreover, her "tough" approach to economic and foreign policy issues and her lack of interest in feminist issues constituted a rejection of conventional thinking about gender roles in politics.

Men and women tend to have much the same political attitudes (Table 9.3). On major national issues such as unemployment, wages and prices, and housing, no statistically significant difference is found between men and women. On the issue of troops in Northern Ireland, women are almost evenly divided in their views, and so too are men. The issue that registers the biggest difference, the display of sex and nudity in the media, divides both men and women, and the issue that shows the second biggest difference, the regulation of labor unions, has no gender connotations.

Gender differences do lead to differences in political participation. Whereas women constitute more than half the electorate, less than one-third of elected councillors in local government are women. A record number of women—forty-one—was elected to the House of Commons in 1987, but given the size of the House, it remains 94 percent male. At Cabinet level, women are scarce. Thatcher's Conservative Cabinet was typical in having only one woman member; the unusual feature was that this lone woman was the prime minister.

EDUCATION
English schools teach "life adjustment" as well as academic subjects, emphasizing behavior and attitudes appropriate to different levels of achievement. Schools also give instruction in citizenship. Youths learn that when a vote is taken, each person has only a single vote, rather than votes weighted according to IQ.

In England education has always assumed inequality. The majority of the population has been con-

---

TABLE 9.3
SIMILARITY OF POLITICAL ATTITUDES OF MEN AND WOMEN

Political attitude	Men	Women	Difference between men and women
	(% ENDORSING)		%
Increase public spending to reduce unemployment	80	80	0
Take Britain out of Common Market	34	34	0
Withdraw troops from Northern Ireland now	48	49	−1
Send colored immigrants home	47	46	1
Spend more money on health service	96	94	2
Government should influence wages and prices	74	76	−2
Introduce stricter laws to regulate unions	42	53	−11
Reduce sex and nudity on television, films, magazines	40	64	−24
Average difference			5

Source: Calculated by the author from Gallup Poll survey, November 12–17, 1986.

Youthful enthusiasm has a place alongside staid institutions. Here casually dressed strollers enjoy themselves at a street festival in London's Notting Hill Gate area, with two helmeted "bobbies" (that is, policemen) looking on. Although youth culture is always in search of new fashions, the political behavior of youths reflects much continuity with the past.

sidered fit for only a minimum of education. Until the end of World War II, the majority left school at fourteen; today, the minimum age for leaving school is sixteen, and half of all students end their education at this age. The highly educated are a small fraction of the population; they expect and are expected to play a leading role in politics.

Within the state system the great majority of pupils now attend comprehensive secondary schools, which recruit students of all levels of ability. Within these schools, pupils are usually divided into a very academic stream headed for university, a stream heading for a good set of examination passes at advanced level (equivalent to up to two years of an American university education), and those who leave at sixteen with only a basic education.

Public schools — that is, private, tuition-charging, and sometimes boarding institutions such as Eton and Harrow — accept pupils with a wide range of intellectual abilities. These pupils have one characteristic in common: their parents pay high tuition fees. In boarding schools young people can be raised in a homogeneous class environment rather than in the mixed-class environment found in many cities and towns. Approximately 6 percent of young persons attend public schools. The great majority of ex-public school pupils seek careers in industry or in the professions. Today, less than half of all MPs have attended public schools. Top jobs in politics often go to those who have a common touch, as indicated by attendance at a state secondary school; both

John Major and Neil Kinnock attended state secondary schools, and so did the four previous prime ministers, Margaret Thatcher, James Callaghan, Harold Wilson, and Edward Heath.

Approximately one young person in ten enters higher education; tuition is paid by government grant and students whose parents are not well off receive grants from public funds for living expenses. Historically, England has had few universities. In 1956 half of all English university students attended either Oxford, Cambridge, or the University of London. In the 1960s many new universities were created; sixteen of the thirty-four English universities were launched between 1961 and 1967.

The stratification of English education suggests that the more education a person has, the more likely a person would be to favor the Conservatives as the party of merit and of persons in middle-class jobs. In fact, this is not the case. People with a university degree or its equivalent are actually *less* likely to vote Conservative than people with a minimum of education. The most pro-Conservative groups are those with an intermediate education and a middle-class job, not the best educated graduates.

Education is most strongly related to active participation in politics. The more education a person has, the greater the possibility of climbing the political ladder. People with a minimum of education constitute more than three-quarters of the electorate but less than half of all local government councillors and less than 2 percent of all MPs. The relatively small percentage of university graduates in the country constitutes 65 percent of all MPs. Insofar as state grants permit young people to go to university regardless of parental income, the concentration of graduates in top political jobs reflects the creation of a meritocracy (that is, rule by people with demonstrated intellectual merit).

CLASS   The concept of class in England can refer to one socioeconomic characteristic, such as occupational status, income, or education, or it can be a shorthand term summarizing many socialization influences. Occupation is the most commonly used indicator of class in England. To group people together by occupation does not mean, however, that they are identical in every other respect.

Nearly every definition of occupational class places three-fifths of English people in the working class and more than two-fifths in the middle class. Since 1918 party competition has been interpreted in class terms; the Conservative party is described as a middle-class party, and Labour as a working-class party. But the links are limited. If class completely determined voting, then Labour would win every election, for a majority of the electorate is working class.

The links between class and party (Figure 9.5) are limited for three principal reasons. First, almost half the electorate do not think of themselves as belonging to either the middle class or the working class. Furthermore, less than one in seven conforms to the stereotype of a middle-class person (nonmanual occupation, above-average education, homeowner, no trade union membership, and subjective identification with the middle class), or its counterpart working-class stereotype. Most Britons have a mixture of middle-class and working-class attributes.

Second, class is no longer perceived as very important in social relations. When the 1987 British Election Survey asked people if they thought it would be difficult to have friends in other classes, 67 percent said it would make no difference. Even when there is an awareness of class differences, this is not normally translated into a sense of class grievances or conflict. Only 6 percent said everyone should have much the same wage regardless of their skill or responsibility.

Third, the relationship between class and party is not symmetrical. The middle class is more strongly Conservative than the working class is Labour. In 1987 the Conservatives won more than half the middle-class vote, whereas Labour won only 39 percent of the working-

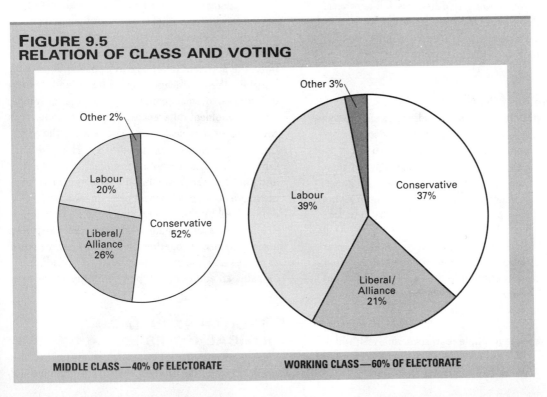

**FIGURE 9.5
RELATION OF CLASS AND VOTING**

MIDDLE CLASS—40% OF ELECTORATE

Other 2%
Labour 20%
Liberal/Alliance 26%
Conservative 52%

WORKING CLASS—60% OF ELECTORATE

Other 3%
Labour 39%
Conservative 37%
Liberal/Alliance 21%

class vote. The Liberal and Alliance parties draw votes almost in proportion to the class structure of the electorate.

Less than half the electorate votes consistent with their class: 22 percent of voters are middle-class Conservatives, and 24 percent are working-class Labour voters. When the majority of voters do not act the way theories of class determinism predict, the theories must be rejected.

Socioeconomic experiences other than occupation also influence voting. At each level of the class structure, people who belong to trade unions are more likely to vote Labour, but the difference is limited in degree. Among manual workers belonging to trade unions, a majority did *not* vote Labour in 1987, and two-fifths of union members have middle-class jobs, for example, teachers.

Housing creates neighborhoods with political relevance, for one-fifth of the electorate lives in houses owned by the municipal council. Council houses are usually clustered together, creating a sense of identification among council tenants. Among working-class council tenants, Labour secured 59 percent of the vote in 1987; among working-class homeowners it won only 34 percent of the vote. The Conservative party won 58 percent of the vote among middle-class homeowners. The Conservatives benefited most from this, for 73 percent of the electorate live in owner-occupied homes, more than three times the proportion living in council houses.

The Cumulative Effect

The most distinctive feature of political socialization in England is the existence of relatively few social divisions that are politically salient. There is nothing in England comparable to the political division between races in the United States or to differences of language found in countries such as Canada. Nor is there a parallel to the intense religious division in Northern Ireland.

Political socialization is a lifetime learning process in which a multiplicity of influences accumulate. What comes first in time, learning in the family, is important for a child, but it is very distant from the current performance of the parties (Figure 9.6). The relative importance of different stages of political socialization can be tested by a stepwise multiple regression analysis, which shows how much of the variance in voting is accounted for by each stage in the socialization process.[61]

1. *Family loyalties.* The most important family influence is the parents' party loyalty, when that is known. The parents' class is second in importance, and religion, third. Age, gender, and education differences have no independent influence. Although family comes first in time, it is second to political values as an influence on the voting of adults, explaining 20 percent of the total variance.

2. *Socioeconomic interests.* Adult socioeconomic interests account for an additional 9 percent of the variance in voting. Material standards of living, as indicated by homeownership and a higher income, are more important than trade union membership or occupational class.

3. *Political values.* In the course of a lifetime, an individual develops lasting values concerning the goals of government and the way people ought to behave in society. These values are independent of family and socioeconomic interests. Economic values concerned with trade unions, the welfare state, business, and privatization together account for nearly 25 percent of the variance in voting. "New" noneconomic values concerned with such matters as protecting the environment and morality account for only 3 percent of the vote, for each party is divided on such values.

4. *Spatial context.* Where a person lives affects who a person talks to and what is said. But the great part of political conversation reinforces already held views, because it occurs between likeminded people. Similarly, the apparent difference in Conservative voting between the south and north of England reflects differences in socioeconomic interests and values, not geographical differences. Contextual influences therefore explain less than 2 percent of the vote.

5. *Current performance of the parties.* How the government handles current issues affects the economy and public expenditure, but the judgments that people make about government performance are largely determined by their preexisting values. This is particularly true of popular evaluations of party and leader images. Altogether, the current performance of parties and leaders during the life of a Parliament explains an additional 10 percent of the variance in voting.

RECRUITMENT INTO POLITICAL ROLES

We may view recruitment into political roles in two very different ways. Tasks can be defined, and then individ-

FIGURE 9.6
POLITICAL SOCIALIZATION AS A LIFETIME LEARNING PROCESS

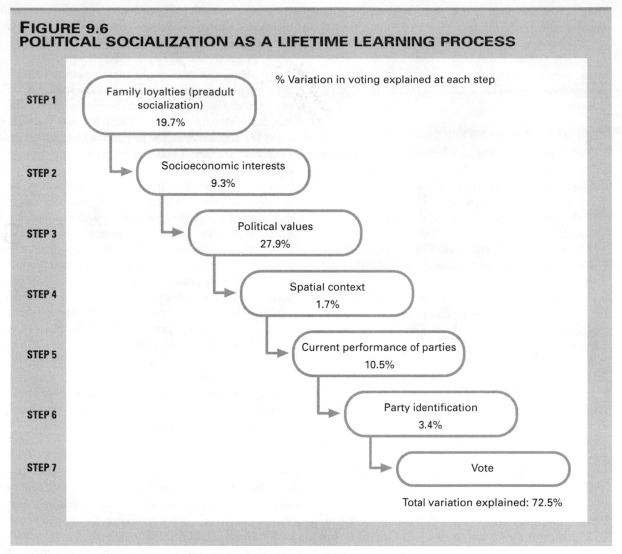

% Variation in voting explained at each step

STEP 1 — Family loyalties (preadult socialization) 19.7%

STEP 2 — Socioeconomic interests 9.3%

STEP 3 — Political values 27.9%

STEP 4 — Spatial context 1.7%

STEP 5 — Current performance of parties 10.5%

STEP 6 — Party identification 3.4%

STEP 7 — Vote

Total variation explained: 72.5%

Source: Adapted from Richard Rose and Ian McAllister, *The Loyalties of Voters* (Newbury Park, Calif.: 1990), pp. 36, 152.

uals with appropriate skills can be recruited. This is the approach of management consultants. Alternatively, it is possible to analyze inductively the attributes that lead people to seek political roles and ask: given their skills, what kind of job can these people do? The constraints of history, institutions, and socialization make the inductive approach more suitable.

The most important political roles in Britain are: Cabinet minister, higher civil servant, or intermittent public person. Their recruitment patterns differ greatly. To become a Cabinet minister an individual must first be elected to Parliament. Individuals gain entry to the civil service shortly after leaving university by passing a very competitive entrance examination. Promotion follows by a process of achievement and approval by seniors. Intermittent public persons depend on patronage for appointment to public bodies, or they are leaders of major interest groups in society.

In all political roles, experience is positively valued. Starting early on a political career is almost a precondition of success. Those who seek leading roles are not expected to begin in local politics and work their way gradually to the top in Westminster. Instead, at an early age an individual becomes a "cadet" in a position qualifying for a central political role, and then gradually accumulates skill and seniority.

Geography is another influence on recruitment. Ministers, higher civil servants, and most intermittent public persons spend their working lives in London. Jobs outside London are miles from the centers of political power.

Cabinet Ministers

For a person ambitious to be a Cabinet minister, becoming an MP is the first step. Nomination for a winnable or safe seat in the House of Commons is in the hands of local party selection committees. There are no popular primaries in the American style, and a parliamentary candidate does not have to live in the constituency in which he or she is nominated. Once nominated and elected, an MP is not usually threatened with defeat in a general election.

Once in the House of Commons, an MP seeks to get noticed. Some ways of doing so — for example, grabbing headlines by questioning the wisdom of the party leadership — make it difficult to gain promotion to ministerial rank. Other approaches, such as successfully attacking opposition leaders in the cut and thrust of debate or being well informed about a politically important topic, assist promotion.

Experience in the Commons does not prepare an individual for the work of a ministry. An MP's chief concerns are dealing with people and talking about ideas. A minister must also be able to handle paperwork, appraise policy alternatives, and relate political generalities to specific technical problems facing a ministry.[62] The recruitment process ensures that ministers have had ample experience in the House of Commons, but not that politicians understand their department's tasks.

A prime minister's discretion in recruiting ministers is limited by the fact that he or she must distribute about one hundred jobs among approximately two hundred governing party MPs eligible for office, since many backbenchers are ruled out on grounds of parliamentary inexperience, old age, political extremism, personal unreliability, or lack of interest in office. A majority of MPs elected three times or more are given a ministerial post. The restriction of appointments to established MPs prevents a nationwide canvass for expert ministers.

A minister learns about a department's work on the job. The amount of time required to learn the ropes varies with a department's complexity. Anthony Crosland, a Labour minister, reckoned: "It takes you six months to get your head properly above water, a year to get the general drift of most of the field, and two years really to master the whole of a department."[63]

Cabinet ministers are frequently reshuffled from department to department. The average minister can expect to stay in a particular job for only two years. The rate of ministerial turnover in Britain is one of the highest in Western nations. The prospect of change encourages backbenchers to hope for inclusion in the government at the next reshuffle, and it spurs existing ministers to work for promotion to a higher status job or be dropped from office. When a minister gets a new job as the result of a reshuffle, he or she usually arrives at a department with no previous experience of its problems.

The recruitment of ministers has come under criticism from reformers. Industrialists argue the need for more businesslike ministers, and economists the need for more economic expertise. Some praise the American system of recruiting political executives from state government, universities, profitmaking companies or the ranks of experts in a department's field.

Higher Civil Servants

Whereas MPs come and go from ministerial office with great frequency, civil servants have a job in Whitehall for the whole of their working lives.

British higher civil servants are recruited without any specific professional qualifications or training. They are meant to be the "best and the brightest"; this usually means getting a very good degree in medieval or modern history or ancient or modern languages at Oxford or Cambridge. When the Fulton Committee on the Civil Service recommended that recruits should have "relevant" specialist knowledge, members could not decide what kind of knowledge was relevant to the work of government.[64] The Civil Service Commission now tests candidates for ability to summarize lengthy prose papers, to resolve a problem by fitting specific facts to general regulations, to draw inferences from a simple table of social statistics, and to perform in group discussions of problems of government.

Because bright civil service entrants lack specialized skills and need decades to reach the highest posts, role socialization into Whitehall by senior civil servants is especially important. The process thus makes for continuity. For example, the current head of the civil service, Sir Robin Butler, entered government in 1961, under a head who had entered the civil service in 1925.

Seniors determine the promotion of their juniors, transmitting established assumptions about how government works. In the course of a career, civil servants become specialists in the difficult task of managing political ministers and government business. As the TV series, "Yes, Minister" shows, they are adept at saying "yes" to a Cabinet minister when they mean "really?" and "up to a point" when they mean "no."[65]

The Thatcher era altered the career expectations of higher civil servants, because she had a very different view of their work than that of her predecessors. The making of policy was deemed the task of Cabinet ministers and, above all, Downing Street, and not of civil servants.[66] Higher civil servants were expected to become managers of other civil servants, increasing the efficiency of government programs to help cut public expenditure. The "next steps" initiative is intended to separate the day-to-day delivery of such central government services as automobile licenses, patents, and social security benefits from the working of policymaking agencies.[67] It assumes that policy and administration can be divorced from each other, an assumption that most political scientists reject.

Intermittent Public Persons

Many individuals are only intermittently involved in politics; they are appointed by government to jobs defined as public service rather than public sector, and often financed with public funds. This group includes individuals as diverse as the archbishop of Canterbury, the chairman of the British Broadcasting Corporation, the chairman of the Horserace Totalisator Board, and the regius professor of Greek at Oxford. If challenged, each would deny being a politician, yet claim to be carrying out duties in the public interest.

Thousands of people are recruited into part-time public service, mostly without salary, through appointments to more than 300 bodies concerned with public policy. An official tabulation of public boards staffed by intermittent public persons found that more than ten thousand full-time and part-time members had been appointed by the Whitehall departments sponsoring the bodies. Most individuals hold only one appointment, and it is without any salary. Rewards may take the form of a royal honor, ranging from the lowly rank of OBE (Order of the British Empire) up to a knighthood, or even membership in the House of Lords. Committees staffed with such appointees have been attacked as *quangos* (quasi-nongovernmental agencies). In fact,

they do not govern Britain but offer advice to those who choose to listen.[68]

Intermittent public persons usually are not candidates for elective office and are not established civil servants. Notwithstanding a lack of conventional public office, they are as heavily involved in the policy process as the average MP.

Selective Recruitment

The extent to which political recruitment is regarded as open or closed depends on links between those in political roles and those without a role. Nothing could be more selective than a parliamentary election that results in one person becoming prime minister of a country with 56 million people. Yet nothing is more representative, because an election is the one occasion on which every adult can participate in politics with equal effect.

Traditionally, leaders simultaneously enjoyed high rank in politics and the economy, and high social status. However, the twentieth century has witnessed the rise of the full-time professional politician, just as professionalization has come to other social roles from sports to scholarship. Aristocrats, businesspeople, or trade union leaders can no longer expect to translate their high standing there into an important post in politics. Since the end of World War II, no business leader has been a senior Cabinet minister, and only two leading trade union officials have made this transition.

As careers become more specialized, a professional politician gains an increased understanding of his or her own sphere, at the price of becoming increasingly remote from other spheres. After years of interviewing persons in leading positions in many areas of English life, Anthony Sampson concluded: "My own fear is not that the Establishment in Britain is too close, but that it is not close enough, that the circles are overlapping less and less and that one half of the ring has very little contact with the other half."[69]

The greater the scope of activities defined as political, the greater the number of people actively involved in government. Government influence on the economy has transformed company directors and union shop stewards into intermittent politicians. Yet their economic position gives them freedom to act independently of government. Workers can vote with their feet by going on strike for higher pay, and businesspeople can vote with their pocketbooks by investing money outside the United Kingdom.

Like success in polo, success in politics is due to

skill and experience. But the opportunity to play polo is determined by family circumstances, too. Intense socialization into a political role in early adulthood is the best way to gain high office, overriding other socialization influences. Once in office, new Cabinet ministers are powerful, but accession to office also alters politicians. Lord Balniel, the heir to one of the oldest titles in Britain, has noted that existing patterns of politics are preserved "not so much by the conscious efforts of the well established, but by the zeal of those who have just won entry, and by the hopes of those who still aspire." [70]

POLITICAL COMMUNICATION

The liberal model of English politics demands a great flow of information between governors and governed. The greater the supply of information, the better informed the public is meant to be, and the better the policies of government. In the liberal model, the public has the right to know.

The Whitehall model is very different: information is regarded as a scarce commodity, and it is not freely exchanged. Publicity is considered costly because it may upset private negotiations with interest groups. Whitehall conventions assume that publicity is not in the public interest. While both views have adherents, in government the Whitehall model predominates. [71]

The chief means of political communication, the mass media, are large and complex industries constrained by their audiences. Newspapers with well-educated readers write about politics differently than mass-circulation tabloids. Broadcasting by law is meant to be politically impartial, whereas newspapers are often very partisan.

Broadcasting

Television and radio are highly centralized but competitive. The British Broadcasting Corporation (BBC) maintains two television networks, four radio networks, and local stations throughout the United Kingdom. The Independent Television Commission licenses more than a dozen regional companies forming a popular commercial TV network and Channel 4 for specialist television programs. Commercial local radio stations operate under the auspices of a Radio Authority.

The BBC's board of governors is appointed by the government of the day, as are members of the ITC. The BBC does not sell advertising; it derives much of its revenue from an annual license fee paid by each household that owns a television set. The government of the day determines how much the license fee is; in 1991 it was £100, or about $175. Independent television company revenues come primarily from advertising; profits are greatly affected by the charges that government imposes on holders of commercial television franchises.

Because broadcasting authorities can never be sure which party will be in office when their license is up for renewal, they have a strong incentive not to take sides between parties. In the 1987 election campaign, broadcasting devoted a third of the time to covering each of the three main contending parties. Parties cannot purchase time to advertise themselves; each party is allocated free time for party political broadcasts prepared by themselves.

Broadcasters disagree about how they ought to cover politics. The traditional BBC view was a sacerdotal (priestly) one, seeing public affairs as important and politicians as deserving respect. Younger broadcasters tend to view themselves as public watchdogs guarding against politicians manipulating the media. They are ready to cross-examine government ministers and run exposés of actions that government has tried to keep quiet. This leads the government, whether Conservative or Labour, to accuse such television journalists of being biased against their party. [72]

Most television viewers regard television as politically impartial. Only 26 percent consider the BBC as biased, and only 17 percent believe independent television companies are biased. The minority who say that television is biased disagree about the direction of alleged favoritism, about half seeing bias favoring the Conservatives and half seeing it favoring Labour. [73]

The Press

The English press is centralized in London, unlike the decentralized press in the United States, Canada, and many European countries. Morning newspapers edited in London circulate throughout England and account for the great bulk of newspaper circulation. Except for Scotland and Northern Ireland, papers printed outside London concentrate on local news; politics is treated as an event that happens in London. Centralization is intensified by the fact that some publishers own more than one newspaper or have multinational media interests. For example, Rupert Murdoch owns both the down-market *Sun* and the up-market *Times*, in addition to his American and Australian media interests.

National newspapers are sharply divided between the popular and the quality press. England has five quality daily papers: *The Times, The Guardian, The Telegraph, The Independent,* and *The Financial Times.* By contrast, the United States has only three nationally read quality papers: the *New York Times, Washington Post,* and *Wall Street Journal.* However, the British quality papers are read by only one-sixth of the electorate.

Britain's popular papers are entertainment media more than they are papers reporting news. Stories about television celebrities, sports, sex, and crime receive more prominence than the actions of government and Parliament. The *Sun* became the biggest selling daily paper in Britain by introducing photographs of bare-breasted models on page three. Anyone who reads only the popular press will be ill informed about politics in England, and the great majority of the electorate reads only a popular paper.

Correlation between how people vote and the political outlook of the paper they read is not proof that papers determine how their readers vote. Political socialization not only shapes political loyalties, but can also influence the choice of newspapers on nonpolitical as well as political grounds. When television is the primary source of political news, no paper can be a monopoly source of political information.

Communication and Noncommunication

Communicators and politicians need each other. Journalists need politicians as news sources, and politicians need journalists to publicize their views, even though ordinary people may not notice what they say.

Journalists define news as something that was not previously known; shining a spotlight into the dark corners of government is one way to discover news. Competition among papers makes it virtually impossible today for the government to repress news.

The media encourage politicians to make newsworthy comments; the reward is having their face on television or their name in print, and a sense of national celebrity. A few politicians can have their views printed because of their high status. In the words of a political journalist, "You may not believe what a man is saying, but if he or she is Prime Minister, that person has a right to have those views known."[74]

Many conventions of English political life emphasize noncommunication. Politicians often hide their deliberations behind the veil of collective Cabinet responsibility. Civil servants dislike public discussion when it involves controversy. The 1911 Official Secrets Act very strictly limited what politicians and civil servants could divulge about discussions in Whitehall. The 1989 Official Secrets Act reduces the scope of official information that cannot be published without authorization to such matters as national security, defense, and international relations.

The Whitehall view remains restrictive; *"the need to know still dominates the right to know."*[75] Government documents are shown to the press only when a politician wants to influence events by leaking them. Senior public officials can be very selective in what they say and do not say. When accused in court of telling a lie about the British government's efforts in 1987 to suppress an embarrassing memoir by a retired intelligence officer, the then head of the civil service, Sir Robert Armstrong, replied: "It is a misleading impression, not a lie. It was being economical with the truth." A tendency to secrecy remains strong because it meets the interests of the most important people in government — Cabinet ministers and civil servants.

Noncommunication between government and governed is sometimes a handicap in Whitehall. Such are the obstacles that the prime minister may not learn about difficulties within a department until an embarrassing question is asked in the House of Commons. The lack of informed public discussion of policy alternatives in advance of a final decision may result in the government making up its mind in ignorance of public reaction.

Busy policymakers want help, not information for its own sake. Whitehall departments will encourage discussion of an issue if they are uncertain about what they want to do. They will discourage discussion if they feel confident about a policy. A policymaker's readiness to engage in a public dialogue does not reflect a desire for knowledge, but a desire to advance political goals.

ARTICULATING GROUP PRESSURES

Organization is necessary to give voice to political views. Without organization, people of the same political mind would have no means of representing their opinions to government. With organization, officials can lobby government to act, and government can consult with an institution about problems of mutual concern.

Unlike political parties, interest groups do not seek to control government by contesting elections. Instead, they seek to influence government decisions regardless of the party in office. The links between interest groups and political parties vary between left and right. Trade unions are institutionally part of the Labour party, providing nearly all the money and most of the votes in the party's formal governing body. Thus, the link is much closer than it is in the United States, where the AFL–CIO has no institutional voice in the Democratic party. Although the private enterprise philosophy of the Conservative party is congenial to business, the party existed long before Britain was industrialized. There is no formal institutional connection between business groups and the Conservatives; the principal links are a common ideology and a readiness of business to give the Conservatives money.

What Interest Groups Want

The scope of demands articulated by interest groups varies enormously from the very narrow concerns of an association for wounded ex-servicemen, to the encompassing concern with the economy of organizations such as the Confederation of British Industries and the Trades Union Congress. Groups also differ in the nature of their interests; some are concerned with material objectives, whereas others deal with causes such as capital punishment or race relations.[76]

In articulating interests, groups usually seek four goals:

1. Information about government policies and changes in policies.
2. Influence on policymaking.
3. Sympathetic administration of established policies.
4. Symbolic status, such as being given the prefix "Royal" in their title.

For the most part, Whitehall departments are happy to consult with interest groups, because they can provide government officials with

1. Practical information about what is happening in their field.
2. Opinions about policies under consideration.
3. Cooperation in the administration of existing policies.
4. Assistance in implementing new policies.

Since most of these needs are complementary, interest groups and government usually find it easy to negotiate. Negotiations proceed with few threats of coercion. When each needs the other, bargaining partners can operate on the principle of exchange. Public officials and group spokespersons know that if there are many interests and points of view, some compromises will be necessary. The object of negotiation is agreement. Agreement is convenient for participants because it avoids decisions being made by politicians who know and care less about details than interest group officials and civil servants in ministries.

Organizing for Political Action

The ability of interests to exert pressure on government depends on their organizational capacity. Workers in a one-industry town are easily organized. Because they are in frequent contact with each other away from work as well as on the job, they are a social group as well as a political group. By contrast, consumers are more difficult to organize because they are a categoric group; customers in a shop are interested in goods and services, not their relations with other customers.

The more committed members are to a pressure group's goals, the more confident its leaders can be that they speak for a united membership. In the absence of commitment, a group can be ineffective. The Confederation of British Industries represents the lowest common denominator of views among its members; major manufacturers and retailers independently press their views on government. When the leader of the National Union of Mineworkers (NUM), Arthur Scargill, called a year-long strike against the government-owned National Coal Board in 1984, he refused to allow union members to vote on the action. Denied a strike ballot, many members felt no commitment to obey the strike order. As a result, the NUM lost its strike and its membership split into two separate unions.

Whitehall finds it administratively convenient to deal with united interest groups, because they are best able to implement an agreement. But decades of attempts to plan the British economy demonstrate that leaders of business and unions cannot guarantee that a bargain they make will be carried out, for there is limited solidarity between leaders and those whom they claim to represent. Individuals usually have a multiplicity of identities, which can be in conflict, for example, as workers desiring higher wages and as consumers wanting lower prices. Group members who care about an issue may also disagree about what their leaders ought to do.

Interest group leaders can articulate demands, but

they cannot force their members to accept a bargain. As one experienced British economist writes:

> Neither the trade unions nor management have systems of private government that can send plenipotentiaries to negotiate on their behalf and commit them to settlement, save on limited issues and particular occasions, when the negotiators can keep in touch with their constituents as the negotiations proceed.[77]

The Thatcher administration demonstrated that a government that is clear in its own policy and faced with conflicting views from pressure groups can ignore demands and instead lay down its own pattern of policy.

Political Values as Constraints

Interest groups must accept the values of the government of the day as given; the likelihood of achieving group aims depends on the relationship between the group's and the government's respective values. The more values are shared between a pressure group and a political party, the greater the prospect of harmony when that party is in office — and the greater the prospect of a pressure group being excluded from influence when the party's opponents are in office. The more a group's values are consistent with the cultural norms of society as a whole, the easier it is to equate its interest with the national interest.

Differences in values divide interest groups into insiders and outsiders.[78] *Insider* groups advance their case in quiet negotiations with Whitehall departments. The demands made are adapted so that they are within the realm of what is politically possible, given the values and commitments of the government of the day. By contrast, *outsider* groups are unable to negotiate with government because their demands are inconsistent with the government of the day. If they are inconsistent with the views of the opposition as well, then outsider groups are completely marginalized. Excluded from influence in Whitehall, they often turn to the media to seek publicity for their causes.

The permanent insiders' positions are invariably in harmony with the government of the day. These groups are often noncontroversial, such as the Royal National Institute for the Blind. The primary concern of permanent insiders is to negotiate on details of administration and finance, and to press for the expansion of programs benefiting the group.

Groups that advocate demands that are the subject of partisan controversy must be prepared to see their status rise and decline. Trade unions, for example, expect to see their influence rise when a Labour government is in office, and business groups expect a better hearing in Whitehall when the Conservatives are in office.

Pressure groups created or financed by government risk becoming its prisoners when they are not in agreement with government policies. A nationalized industry such as British Rails will want to press certain of its interests on the Ministry of Transport, yet it is also very vulnerable to pressure from that ministry. A not-for-profit social welfare agency that receives a substantial amount of its income from a government grant, for example, to help those with AIDS, may jeopardize the grant if it publicly campaigns against government.

Aspiring insider groups would like to become part of the Whitehall community but have not yet had their interests so recognized. They therefore advance demands in a form that can be written into an act of Parliament, and they ask for funds that are within the realm of credibility, in hopes that their proposals will be adopted and they can then operate as insiders.

Complete outsiders are excluded from Whitehall, whatever the government of the day, because their demands go against prevailing cultural norms. Whatever the party in office, the Ministry of Defense does not consult pacifist groups, for nothing can be negotiated between two groups whose principles are mutually exclusive.

From Pluralism and Corporatism to Dealing at Arm's Length

For two decades after the end of World War II, interest groups and government cooperated in a pluralistic process of policymaking, in which there was competition between a multiplicity of groups. Government usually acted as a broker seeking agreement; occasionally, ministers imposed their own pattern of policy.

From the early 1960s to 1979 corporatism was popular, as government sought to bring together business, trade union, and political interests in tripartite institutions, intending to reach consensus on such controversial issues as wages, prices, and industrial policy. Corporatist bargaining assumed a political consensus as to the specific actions that should be taken on inflation and unemployment. It also assumed that the leaders of each group could secure the cooperation of those whom they represented.

In practice, neither Edward Heath's Conservative administration nor Labour governments were able to achieve a sustained consensus, nor were interest group leaders able to deliver their nominal followers. By 1979 tripartite corporatist institutions showed that they were inadequate to promote economic growth and fight inflation.

The Thatcher administration adopted a strategy of arm's-length dealing with both trade unions and business groups. Instead of making the state a central actor in negotiations with interest groups, it followed a *state-distancing* strategy, trying to keep the government from involvement in the everyday activities of the marketplace such as wage bargaining, investment decisions, and pricing policies.

A state-distancing strategy concentrates on policies that government can put into effect without agreement from interest groups. It emphasizes legislation to achieve goals, for no interest group can defy an act of Parliament. Laws have reduced the capacity of trade unions to frustrate government policies through industrial action. State-distancing is also reflected in the privatization of state-owned industries. Money supply is also a measure that government can control to a significant extent.[79]

State-distancing places less reliance on negotiations with interest groups and more on the independent authority of the Crown. Business and labor are free to carry on as they like — but only within the pattern imposed by the government's macroeconomic policy and legislation. Most unions and some businessmen do not like this pattern, which tolerates high unemployment as the price of fighting inflation. The government can ignore their criticisms as long as it has a majority in Parliament.

THE PARTY SYSTEM: CHOICE AND AGGREGATION

British government is party government. Voters determine not who governs but which party will govern. Parties organize the selection of candidates, election campaigns, and the preparation of policies. An individual does not vote for particular policies or for a personality but for the party that is deemed best at aggregating the interests and values of millions of citizens.

Each party is one element in a party system; the term *system* emphasizes the interdependence of parties competing with each other for votes. What happens to one party affects what happens to others. If the Labour party becomes very unpopular, then the Conservatives are likely to win an election, and if a Conservative government then becomes unpopular, this makes it easier for its opponents to gain votes.

For most of the postwar era, Britain was said to have a two-party system, for government was in the hands of either the Conservatives or Labour. Growing dissatisfaction with both parties led to the rise of support for the Liberals and then the Alliance parties, and in Scotland and Wales for nationalist parties. The Alliance further destabilized the system by collapsing after the 1987 election.

Electoral Choice

A general election must occur at least once every five years; within that period the prime minister is free to call an election at any time. Although every prime minister tries to pick a date when victory is certain, often this does not happen. The party in office has lost six of thirteen postwar elections.

The ballot offers a British voter a very simple choice between three or four candidates seeking to become the sole member of Parliament from the constituency. No other office is at stake in a parliamentary election. The outcome is determined by adding together the results of the contests in each of the 650 parliamentary constituencies. The party that secures the most MPs (which in 1951 and February 1974 was not the party with the largest share of the popular vote) is declared the election winner.

A lifetime of political socialization leads to relatively stable political outlooks among voters (Figure 9.6). But for the past two decades the Conservative and Labour parties have veered to and from extremes, and an Alliance party has risen and collapsed in the center. Party-led instability forces people to think afresh about how to vote. Even though individuals may still vote for the same party as in the past, their identification with a party is weakening; less than a quarter now strongly identify with a political party.[80]

The two-party system emerged following a period of considerable instability involving the Conservatives, Liberals, Labour, and Irish parties, with many coalition governments between 1910 and 1945. Between 1945 and 1970 the Conservative and Labour parties together took an average of 91 percent of the popular vote and in 1951 as much as 97 percent (Figure 9.7). The Liberals had difficulty finding candidates to contest most seats

FIGURE 9.7
VOTES CAST IN GENERAL ELECTIONS SINCE 1945

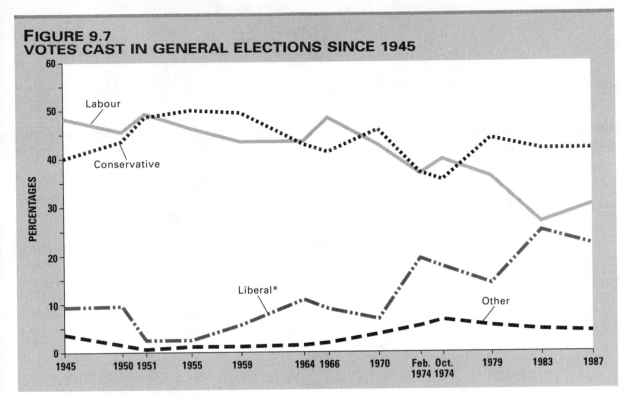

*In 1983–87, Liberal–SDP Alliance.

and even more difficulty winning votes. Support for the two largest parties was very evenly balanced; Labour won four of these contests and the Conservatives won four.

A new multiparty system emerged in 1974. In the February "Who governs?" election, the electorate responded with a plague on the houses of both major parties. The Liberals won nearly one-fifth of the vote, and the Nationalists also did surprisingly well in Scotland and Wales. The result was that the Labour government lacked a working majority in the Commons. The 1980s saw spectacular disarray among the Conservatives' opponents, as the Labour vote plummeted and the Alliance vote rose to within a few percentage points of Labour's.

The breakup of the Alliance after the 1987 election did not end multiparty politics, for the Liberal Democrats were formed in succession to the Liberals and the Social Democrats. At the 1989 European Parliament election, Green party candidates won 15 percent of the British vote in an election in which turnout was well below half the electorate. In 1990 the Conservatives

experienced their biggest upheaval in decades by forcing Margaret Thatcher to resign as prime minister and replacing her with John Major.

The unexpected emergence of an Alliance and then a Green vote is a reminder that in a multiparty system the position of the Conservative and Labour parties is always vulnerable to challenge. Most voters are also aware of this vulnerability. In the 1990s all electors under the age of forty will have voted only in a multiparty election.

Britain definitely has a multiparty system for electoral competition. First, three candidates—Conservative, Labour, and now Liberal Democrat—normally contest seats, and in Scotland and Wales, Nationalist candidates are also present. Second, the two largest parties do not monopolize the popular vote; they have not won 90 percent of the vote since 1959. Third, the two largest parties nationally are often not the front-running parties at the constituency level. In 1987 the Alliance parties were more often the second-place challenger to Conservative MPs than was the official opposition party, Labour. Fourth, more than half a dozen par-

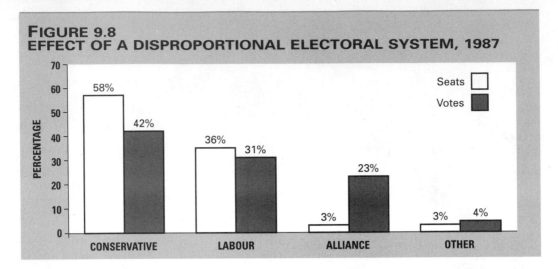

FIGURE 9.8
EFFECT OF A DISPROPORTIONAL ELECTORAL SYSTEM, 1987

ties consistently win seats in the House of Commons. Fifth, significant shifts in votes usually are not between the two largest parties. In 1987, nine-tenths of voters changing their behavior either moved between the Alliance and a party of the right or left, or in and out of abstention rather than switching from Conservative to Labour or vice versa.

In terms of government, Britain can be said to have a two-party system, since control has alternated since 1945 between two parties, the Conservatives and Labour. But the party winning a majority of seats in the House of Commons does so without winning an absolute majority of the popular vote. No party has won half the popular vote since 1935. Since 1974 the election winner's share of the vote has averaged 41 percent, less than what the losing candidate in an American presidential election normally gains.

The first-past-the-post electoral system is a system of *dis*proportional representation, manufacturing a majority in the House of Commons from a minority share of the popular vote. The party with the most votes in a constituency wins the seat. As long as only two parties contested a constituency, then one candidate had to win an absolute majority. In a multiparty system this is not the case. In 1987 the winning candidate had half the vote in only 43 percent of all constituencies.

To win seats in the House of Commons, a party must either win one-third of the popular vote nationwide or concentrate votes in a limited number of constituencies. Nationalist parties in Scotland, Wales, and Northern Ireland do concentrate their strength in one part of the United Kingdom. However, the Alliance parties and

Liberal Democrats spread their support nationwide, as a result of which their candidates much more often finish second. Labour concentrates its vote in industrial, working-class areas; it comes in first where its support is strong, and third where its support is weak.

The 1987 election result illustrates the disproportionality between votes and seats in the House of Commons. In three-way fights, the strongest party, the Conservatives, did best, because it often won constituencies with less than half the vote. The second largest party, Labour, did better than strict proportionality would dictate. The Nationalist parties won seats almost in proportion to their share of the United Kingdom vote, but the Alliance parties won very few seats because their support tended to be evenly spread. In a proportional representation system, the Alliance parties would have claimed 147 seats, not 22, and would have held the balance of power in a coalition with one of the two largest parties (Figure 9.8).

Control of Party Organization

Political parties are often referred to as machines, a word that is very misleading. Parties cannot manufacture votes, nor can a party organization mechanically convert the preferences of voters into government policy. Least of all can a political party be controlled in the way that an army can be commanded. Parties are like universities; they are inherently decentralized, and people belong to them for a variety of motives.

Much of the effort devoted to party organization is concerned not with winning votes but with keeping together three disparate parts of the party: the mass party in the constituencies; party headquarters; and the party in Parliament. Constituency parties have the most members, but the party in Parliament has the greatest political importance.

In addition to campaigning at election time, constituency parties are nationally significant because each selects its parliamentary candidate. At no stage in the selection of parliamentary candidates are the voters consulted, as in an American primary. Internal divisions in the Labour party have encouraged hard left groups in constituencies to adopt candidates whose far left views are out of sympathy with the Labour leadership. In the Conservative party, personality factors tend to be more important. The decentralization of the selection process allows for the choice of parliamentary candidates with a wide variety of political outlooks and abilities.

The headquarters of each party in London is an imperfect link between the party in the constituencies and the party in Parliament. Headquarters staff provide more or less routine organizational and publicity services to constituency parties and to the party in Parliament. The Conservative Central Office has a clear line of authority, for its chair is appointed by the party leader in Parliament. By contrast, the staff at Labour party headquarters serves under a National Executive Committee whose members are elected primarily by trade unions. Each party has an annual conference to debate policy and to vote on some policy resolutions.

The party in Parliament declares party policy in the conduct of daily business at Westminster. Events and issues often arise quickly, and pressures of time greatly limit consultation between the party inside the House of Commons and outside. Once a party's leadership has made a commitment in Parliament, this is an important political fact; other sections of the party are expected to go along with its decisions or foment disunity.

Members of Parliament are the legitimate representatives of tens of millions of people who vote for the party but are not dues-paying party members. Hence, when a dispute arises about which segment of the party is best qualified to articulate policy, MPs can claim to represent the largest, though unorganized part, those who vote for a party.

The party leader is strongest when he or she is also prime minister. Constitutional principles and Cabinet patronage strengthen a prime minister's hand. Moreover, an open attack on a prime minister threatens electoral defeat as a result of intraparty conflict. Lacking the power of patronage, the opposition leader is more vulnerable to critics. The opposition leader's influence depends on whether he or she is expected soon to be prime minister or to lose in the next election.

A Conservative leader is independent of constituency associations, which are separately organized from the centralized campaign group, the Conservative Central Office. A leader remains vulnerable to the loss of support from MPs. The rules allow a ballot to be held for the leadership at the start of each year's session of Parliament. In 1990 dissatisfaction was so widespread that Margaret Thatcher could not win 57.5 percent of the votes of Conservative MPs, the proportion needed for victory on the first ballot. The rules allow new candidates to enter the second ballot, and John Major, then chancellor of the Exchequer, did so successfully.

The Liberal Democratic leader has inherited the shambles of two party organizations, the Liberals and the Social Democrats. The Liberal Democratic organization depends on the leader making the party appear credible in Parliament and the media, in order to have a chance to attract popular support, which activates more candidates, constituency organizations, and financial support.

The Labour leader's position is ambiguous. He or she is elected by an electoral college in which 40 percent of the votes are cast by trade unions, 30 percent by constituency parties, and 30 percent by MPs. The election manifesto is meant to be subject to consultation between the parliamentary leadership and extraparliamentary institutions of the party. Sitting Labour MPs are subject to pressure from their constituency party, which can decide not to renominate them if it does not like what the MPs have been doing in Parliament.

Labour's eleven years in government between 1964 and 1979 gave the party's extraparliamentary left an opportunity to exploit these ambiguities for its own ends. The actions of the Wilson and Callaghan governments disappointed left-wing adherents of socialist ideals. Whereas Labour leaders could ignore criticisms in office, in opposition the left took control of the party organization. Labour's lengthy 1983 left-wing election manifesto, described by a Labour MP as "the longest suicide note in history," led to the party's worst electoral defeat since 1918.

In reaction, the major trade unions supported the election of Neil Kinnock as party leader, who has moved the party from the left to the center and has promoted changes in party organization that place more power in the leader's hands. After more than a decade out of office, Labour politicians have supported moving to the political center, the position occupied by the majority of voters. Nonetheless, tensions remain within the party.

Policy Preferences

The extent to which parties do or should stand for conflicting policies is disputed. The Conservative party does not have any statement of goals in its constitution. The Liberal Democrats and their predecessors usually endorse goals that are so broad that almost any party could agree with them. Traditionally, the Labour party has been committed to socialism, but its leaders prefer to appeal to the voters with ideologically vague slogans such as "Let's Go with Labour."

When voters are asked to place themselves on a left-right scale, 44 percent reject both categories, they place themselves in the center or are don't knows. The next largest groups place themselves slightly to the right or slightly to the left. Thus, three-quarters of the electorate is at or very near the political center. Only 11 percent see themselves as moderately or substantially to the right, and 9 percent are far to the left.[81]

When public opinion is examined across a range of twenty issues, such as rising prices, protecting the environment, spending money on the health service, the place of nonwhite immigrants in British society, foreign aid, and trade union legislation, *most Conservative, Labour, and Alliance voters agree with each other on three-quarters of the issues.*[82] How a person votes is thus a poor guide to what a person thinks about issues.

The most common form of political disagreement today is within parties. Traditionally, the Labour party has had the most aggressive form of factional politics, with a hard left attacking a leadership committed to the achievements of past Labour governments and seeking to govern again. Center parties appeal to voters from both the Conservative and Labour ranks; hence, their supporters tend to divide on issues. Margaret Thatcher divided Conservatives between those who shared her views about the superiority of the market, and "wets," those who had more sympathy for government-sponsored social policies.[83] In each party there are many supporters who have few clearcut views on policy; they often are decisive in intraparty disputes.

Faced with an electorate that is dominated by middle-of-the-road consensual views, political parties respond by presenting election manifestos that have a very broad appeal. The titles of manifestos are virtually interchangeable between the Conservative and Labour parties (Table 9.4). The cover of the 1987 Labour manifesto even abandoned the traditional party color of red. The yuppie designer socialists, noting that a red background would clash with the photograph of the ginger-haired, freckled-faced party leader, Neil Kinnock, made the background color brown.

Once in office, the governing party has the authority to enact any legislation it wants. But it is constrained from doing so by its lack of knowledge, by programs and pressures inherited from its predecessors, and by electoral calculations.[84]

In opposition, politicians have no opportunity to come to grips with the problems of government departments, for opposition MPs cannot cross-examine minis-

---

TABLE 9.4
CONSENSUAL TITLES OF PARTY ELECTION MANIFESTOS

Year	Conservatives	Labour
1964	Prosperity with a Purpose	Let's Go with Labour
1966	Action, not Words	Time for Decision
1970	A Better Tomorrow	Now Britain's Strong— Let's Make It Great to Live In
1974	Firm Action for a Fair Britain	Let Us Work Together
1974	Putting Britain First	Britain Will Win with Labour
1979	The Conservative Manifesto	The Labour Way Is the Better Way
1983	The Challenge of Our Times	The New Hope for Britain
1987	The Next Moves Forward	Britain Will Win

ters as American members of Congress do. Opposition MPs have disincentives to work out programs in detail, for this may lead to disputes within the party or expose their ideas to criticism by ministers backed by the civil service. Opposition MPs tend to overestimate the ease with which changes can be made. Sometimes they also underestimate the "mess" left behind by the party that has performed so badly that it loses an election.

Once in office, ministers find that much has *not* changed. All the laws enacted by their predecessors must be enforced, even if the government of the day would not have enacted them. A newly elected government also inherits many commitments to foreign countries and to the European Community. Civil servants point out that any big change also faces big difficulties. As a former Conservative minister said of his Labour successors, "they inherited our problems and our remedies."[85]

A party can consistently use its majority in the House of Commons to force through controversial legislation, or it can enact laws that reflect the broadest consensus that Whitehall civil servants can achieve. A review of government bills introduced in the House of Commons from 1964 to 1983 shows that on average the governing party proposes three consensus bills for every one that the opposition party will vote against on principle. In the case of the 1964–1970 Labour government, six of every seven bills that it introduced to Parliament were not opposed by the Conservative opposition.[86]

Even though the procedures and conventions of the House of Commons encourage the opposition to vote against government legislation, there is usually agreement across party lines. Most bills become law without partisan divisions of principle. The bills that create controversy are newsworthy because they are out of the ordinary; the majority of government measures are acceptable to the leaders of all parties.

MAKING AND DELIVERING GOVERNMENT POLICIES

Making and delivering public policies are like the two sides of the moon; they belong together, but each must be seen from a different perspective. Because Britain is a unitary state, making policy is the prerogative of the government at Westminster. Decisions taken there are binding on local government and functional agencies such as the National Health Service.

From the perspective of the ordinary citizen, the actions of government are evident only when services are delivered locally. The speeches that government ministers make in praise of their achievements will be credible to ordinary people only if they can see the results in their home, in the actions of teachers at the local primary school, in the services of doctors, or in the way the police respond to an emergency call in their community.

So numerous are the organizations involved in making and delivering policies that policymaking involves much intragovernmental politics. Westminster provides the legal authority and the money for public programs, but institutions separate from Whitehall, such as local government, the health service, and nationalized industries, deliver most services. The significance of service delivery limits centralization, just as the authority of the Crown in Parliament limits decentralization.

The Limits of Centralization

Making policy is far more difficult than stating policy intentions. To translate a statement of good intentions into a concrete program requires running what one former minister has described as "the Whitehall obstacle race."[87] A minister must first win approval for a new measure from Cabinet colleagues whose departments are affected; from the Treasury, which will be asked to authorize money; and from the prime minister, who judges how particular measures fit into the government's overall political strategy. Once these obstacles are overcome, a minister must then negotiate details within the department, with other agencies of government, and with affected interest groups.

The Cabinet is constitutionally the chief mechanism for coordinating government policy. In practice, however, as one Cabinet minister learned to his surprise, "The only thing that is hardly ever discussed is general policy."[88] If every minister spoke about every issue on the Cabinet agenda, there would only be time to discuss a few topics at a meeting. On matters outside their departmental responsibility most Cabinet ministers remain silent.

As the activities of government expand, interdepartmental committees multiply, because what one ministry does affects the interests of another. The typical Cabinet committee includes the ministers whose departments are most affected by an issue, and a senior chairperson. The prime minister can use Cabinet committees to exclude critics from discussions. The committees have the time and political authority to settle most disputes between departments.

Civil servants, rather than ministers, are the most important coordinating personnel in Whitehall. Every Cabinet committee is shadowed by a committee of civil servants from the same departments. Because civil servants are more numerous, they can devote more time to interdepartmental negotiations. As permanent officials, civil servants are prone to seek agreement.

The limits on central direction to government led Edward Heath to establish a Central Policy Review Staff (CPRS) in 1971 to provide a comprehensive view of government strategy. With a staff of fifteen, less than one person for each department, the CPRS could not be compared with the Executive Office of the President in Washington. When asked to name the CPRS's major achievements, its first head, Lord Rothschild, said:

> I don't know that the government is better run as a result of our work. I think the highest compliment I ever got paid was from a Cabinet minister who said: "You make us think from time to time." I thought that was a great achievement, considering how much ministers have to do. They don't have much time to think.[89]

In 1983 Margaret Thatcher abolished the CPRS.

The Growth of Government Nationwide

Government was created by concentrating authority at the center, and Westminster has been the seat of government since early medieval times. However, the authority of the Crown was largely isolated; its impact did not extend far beyond Westminster.

The growth of government has caused a shift from government at the center to government nationwide.[90] The development of the Post Office in the nineteenth century was an initial landmark in the centralized organization of services delivered nationwide. Government on the scale that we know it today could not exist if all its activities were still concentrated in London, for only a small portion of the British population lives there.

The expansion of education, social security, health, and other programs has created many public agencies that deliver public policies from one end of Britain to another. For example, education is authorized by an act of Parliament, principally financed by central government revenue, and the minister in charge of the Department of Education and Science is answerable to Parliament for what is done in local schools. However, the delivery of primary and second education is in the hands of local government authorities or even local schools, and universities and polytechnics are separately organized. As the department employs only 1 percent of the people working in education, the success of its policies depends on actions taken by other agencies.

Whitehall ministries are most important in setting the legal framework for public programs. An act of Parliament is needed to justify any program, including measures undertaken by local government, and government controls a majority in Parliament. Money is the second major resource; Whitehall ministries largely determine the tax revenue available to other public sector agencies. But only two of the four biggest spending programs — social security and defense — are directly administered from Whitehall.

Most goods and services produced by public agencies are not delivered by Whitehall ministries. Nearly two-fifths of public expenditure is in the hands of local government, the health service, or nationalized industries, and 86 percent of public employees work for these non-Whitehall agencies.[91]

Local government is the principal institution for delivering services. One reason is that it is local; police protection, refuse collection, planning permissions, and primary schooling are all services that must be delivered where people live. Another reason is that local councils are multipurpose authorities; a local council runs libraries and crematoria as well as schools and the police. Collectively, local government accounts for more than one-quarter of total public expenditure; a large fraction of this money is obtained from central government in the form of grants to finance programs required by acts of Parliament.

Nationalized industries are important to the economy, providing such major services as railways and coal. Even after the major privatization initiatives of the Thatcher administration, nationalized industries continue to employ one-sixth of all public workers. The economic importance of nationalized industries is understated by expenditure figures, which only report the subsidy an industry receives from the Treasury. Most of the revenue of nationalized industries comes from selling goods in the market.

The National Health Service (NHS) is headed by an official appointed by Whitehall but outside the ministries and local government. The NHS is not a single organization but a complex of different institutions. Hospitals are directly administered by the service and consume the largest portion of its funds. Medical and dental care are the responsibility of self-employed physicians and dentists. Altogether, people working for the National Health Service constitute one-fifth of all public employees and account for more than one-eighth of total public expenditure.

There are many reasons why ministers are not in charge of delivering the services for which they answer to the House of Commons. Ministers may wish to avoid charges of political interference (the Board of Inland Revenue). They may also want to allow flexibility in commercial operations (the Bank of England), lend an aura of impartiality to quasi-judicial activities (the Monopolies Commission), show respect for the extragovernmental origins of an institution (Oxford and Cambridge universities), allow qualified professionals to regulate technical matters (the Royal College of Physicians and Surgeons), or remove controversial matters from Whitehall (Family Planning Association).

The Limits of Decentralization

Decentralization involves complementary decisions about territory and function. Typically, an agency that is characterized in territorial terms, such as the Scottish Office, has multiple program functions. An agency defined by a particular function, such as the National Coal Board, operates within specified boundaries, whether they be the nation of England or the whole of Britain.[92]

LOCAL GOVERNMENT Constitutionally, local government is limited because its functions, its taxing powers, and its territorial boundaries are all defined by acts of Parliament. In the United States the federal system entrenches many powers of state and local government, but in Britain central government can and does alter boundaries, taxing powers, and functions of local authorities. The statement — "Local councillors are not necessarily political animals; we could manage without them"[93] — was made by a left-wing law professor; it could as easily have come from a Thatcherite.

Westminster politicians argue that it is important to maintain the same standards of public policy nationwide. The doctrine of *territorial justice* prescribes that schools in inner cities and rural areas should have the same standards as those in the suburbs. Conservative politicians want the national standard to be economy and efficiency, minimizing expenditure; Labour politicians want a different national standard, high spending on locally provided public services.

Ministers emphasize that they are accountable to a national electorate of tens of millions of people, whereas local councillors are accountable only to an electorate numbered in tens or hundreds of thousands. Instead of small being beautiful, bigger electorates are assumed to be better. The reorganization of local government in the early 1970s in pursuit of efficiency created fewer and more populous local authorities. Since electors usually identify with a smaller unit, a neighborhood or a district, local government is no longer local.

The structure of English local government differs with the level of urbanization. A total of 59 percent live in shire counties, which combine cities, suburbs, and countryside. Shire counties are responsible for delivering education, land-use planning, roads and transport, and personal social services. Each shire is divided into districts with its own elected council responsible for housing and minor services. In populous metropolitan areas the Thatcher administration abolished the two-tier system of metropolitan and district councils; all metropolitan responsibilities are now concentrated in a single tier of district councils. One-sixth of England lives in Greater London, where the London boroughs or adjacent district councils and shire counties are responsible for delivering services.[94]

An elected council is responsible for each local authority. Councillors are unpaid and are usually part-time representatives. Disciplined parties contest council elections. Low voter turnout has made it possible for some local Labour councils to be taken over by extreme left wingers characterized as the "loony left" by their critics. As a result of the role of the Liberal Democrats, no party has a majority in many councils, and various experiments are being made with open or tacit coalitions.[95]

The crucial political relationships within a local authority are those between councillors who chair the most important council committees such as finance, education, housing, and so forth, and the professional officials delivering the programs that the committees supervise. Unlike higher civil servants in Whitehall, local government chief officers are specialists appointed on grounds of expertise, merit, and seniority. They enjoy influence through their specialist knowledge, their control of day-to-day operations, and their commitment to professional values. For example, teachers want more spending on schools, and architects want to build more and more houses.

The aims of central-local finance have always been

in conflict. Local authorities would like to spend more on their programs — if only Whitehall would increase its cash grant to them. In turn, the Treasury thinks local authorities spend too much and looks for ways to keep the central grant from growing. The Thatcher administration first cut the central government grant to local authorities. Since local spending was not cut in proportion, local property taxes (rates) skyrocketed. In response, it abolished local property taxes on residences, introducing instead a community charge or poll tax on every adult living in a local authority. Whereas property taxes increase with the value of a house, the poll tax charge is the same for everyone. The change produced great political controversy. One of the first decisions of the government of John Major was to announce in 1991 the replacement of the poll tax by a property tax on residential housing.

Because central government depends on local authorities to deliver programs and local authorities depend on Westminster to obtain legal authority and money, the two groups cannot ignore each other. However, when they negotiate, they are unequally matched, for the center's control of legislation and finance gives it the power to impose its way.

THE NATIONAL HEALTH SERVICE The directors of the National Health Service are appointed by the central government. The goals of the health service are consensual: to prevent disease and to provide health care to everyone. Because the health service claims more than one-eighth of total public expenditure, its costs are a perennial concern of the Treasury and the minister of health.

Hospitals treat people with many acute illnesses, employ most of NHS personnel, and consume the largest portion of the health service budget. A hospital is a large organization employing nonmedical personnel to provide meals, laundry, and other services. It can be subject to many bureaucratic procedures and administrative controls.

Health care given outside hospitals by doctors, dentists, and others is not as easily subjected to bureaucratic controls. Doctors are professionals who expect and are expected to recommend treatment according to their own judgment, and not according to administrative regulations. The NHS method of payment discourages unnecessary treatment, for a doctor is paid a fixed annual rate for each person registered with a physician rather than on a fee-for-service basis, as is normal in the United States.

Health care provided without charge is costly to produce. The central government meets the bill for nearly seven-eighths of all forms of medical treatment in Britain. Yet public finance also tightly controls total expenditure. Britain spends about half as much of its national product on health care as does the United States.[96]

Queuing is the chief means by which the health service controls the use of medical and hospital facilities, for access free of charge does not mean instant access. Patients requiring hospitalization may wait weeks or months if facilities are in short supply. Since less than 10 percent of the population is covered by private health insurance, waiting in a queue or doing without health treatment are the only alternatives for the great majority of British people. There is always tension between medical doctors and nurses, who want more spent on health services, and the Treasury.

A BASIC DILEMMA Central authority in decision making and decentralized responsibility for delivering services are meant to be complementary, but they can be contradictory. The center's power to set minimum standards and place a ceiling on costs is balanced by local control over the delivery of services. Lord Hailsham, a minister with experience in many departments, describes the difficulties Cabinet ministers have with exercising authority at a distance:

> In the Admiralty you are a person having authority. You say to one person "come" and he cometh, and to another "go" and he goeth. It is not so in the Ministry of Education. You suggest rather than direct. You say to one man "come" and he cometh not, and to another "go" and he stays where he is.[97]

The Mix of State and Market

Although people speak of government managing the economy, the metaphor is misleading, for the economy is not an hierarchical organization. The economy is a market; the gross national product is the sum of activities of tens of millions of producers and consumers. The difficulties of government in producing economic growth, stable prices, and full employment show the limits of government influence on the market.

The British economy is a mixed economy. The great bulk of firms are profitmaking, consumers can spend as they like what money they have, and, except in emergencies, wages and prices are decided independently of government. Government influences the market through taxing and spending policies, interest rates, and policies for growth and unemployment. In turn, the market affects government, for the greater the level of prosperity, the greater the tax revenue flowing into the Treasury; the less satisfactory the state of the economy, the greater the public deficit is likely to be.

NATIONALIZATION AND PRIVATIZATION

Nationalized industries are an extreme example of the mixed economy: they are owned by government, yet they sell their products in the market. Nationalized firms are run as public corporations separate from Whitehall, selling goods in the market, and their employees are not civil servants. Investment decisions, however, are subject to political influence, and so, too, are pricing policies and wage negotiations. Some nationalized industries have made a profit, while others have consistently lost money.[98]

Every nationalized industry has had a common problem: a lack of clear and consistent priorities. The initial Labour hope that nationalized industries could be the primary instruments of a planned economy was abandoned when planning failed. After a long period of neglect in the 1950s and 1960s, the government exploited the industries for short-term advantage as the economy deteriorated in the 1970s.

The Conservative government of Margaret Thatcher promoted privatization, selling nationalized industries on the stock market. Profitmaking industries selling telephone services, oil, or gas, were sold without difficulty. Industries that were losing money, such as British Airways and British Steel, had to be reorganized and to shed unprofitable activities before they could be privatized.[99] Nationalized industries that have needed large annual subsidies such as British Rail and the National Coal Board are especially difficult to privatize. Selling council houses to tenants at prices well below the market price is popular with buyers.

Privatization has been justified on grounds of economic efficiency (the market is deemed to work better than government in determining investment, production, and prices); ideology (the power of government is reduced); and short-term financial gain (revenue from the sale of public assets reduces the annual budget deficit). Although the Labour party initially opposed privatization, the sale of tens of billions of pounds of public assets makes it very costly financially to repurchase all the industries. In the case of council houses or shares

bought by people at bargain prices, it would be electorally counterproductive as well.[100]

Privatization leaves unresolved the extent of the public interest in companies now in the private sector. For a firm sold as a monopoly or a virtual monopoly, such as British Telecommunications, the government set up a new regulatory authority, OFTEL (the Office of Telecommunications) to regulate prices. Privatization of the water industry also raises issues of public health. In a mixed economy, the roles of the government and the private sector can change, but the two remain interdependent.

THE TREASURY BALANCING ACT

When money is involved, the Treasury is important. Before the Cabinet considers a new policy, the Treasury must be consulted about its cost, and before a bill is put to Parliament, the Treasury must approve its cost as being consistent with overall public expenditure commitments. The annual budget cycle provides another opportunity for the review of policies; ministers in charge of spending departments try to extract more money for their programs, and the Treasury tries to keep down spending.

The Treasury is responsible for policies affecting economic growth, prices, and wages. It is the government's chief link with the Bank of England, which oversees the money supply and finances government deficits. The Treasury also negotiates with foreign governments about the international economy and stabilizing the exchange rate of the pound with foreign currencies, such as the Deutsche mark and the dollar.

Whatever the issue, the Treasury is at hand to remind the Cabinet of the economist's proposition that every policy conferring benefits also has costs. Politicians tend to dislike this, and many attack the Treasury for articulating such a view. But a veteran Treasury official argues that the Treasury view simply reflects "the force of circumstances"; a prime minister cannot ignore the Treasury "because the Treasury stands for reality."[101]

A former chancellor, Denis Healey, has ruefully noted, "Running the economy is more like gardening than operating a computer."[102] A Bank of England economist, C.A.E. Goodhart, concludes:

> Looking at exactly the same economy and even using on occasion very similar structural equations, different modelers come to totally different policy conclusions because of their fundamental perceptions about the work-

ing of the economy. Econometrics has not, at least so far, provided any alternative for basic judgment.[103]

The centrality of economics to party values, to interest groups, and to the government's electoral strategy makes decisions on major economic issues of pervasive concern to politicians. When economists disagree in their advice, politicians are then free to choose between alternatives, each supported by some professional economists and scoffed at by others.[104]

The Contingency of Influence

In a complex political system, we cannot expect all types of policies to be decided in the same way. Decisions about war and peace tend to be centralized, whereas decisions about whether a particular piece of land should be used for housing or whether it should remain a meadow are usually made by local authorities. Any model of the policy process is likely to fit some issue areas but not others.

Cabinet ministers and civil servants are important politically because they are consistently involved in the policy process. By contrast, functional agencies and interest groups concentrate on one limited subject, and local government has a limited territorial competence.

The making of policy is constrained by disputes within government as much as by differences between government and its opponents. The public sector is an arena of competition in which the many tentacles of the octopus of government sometimes work against each other. Independent of party, disputes can arise between agencies of government. The greater the government's concerns, the more likely controversies are to be interorganizational but intragovernmental; the public sector contains within itself most of the political conflicts found in English society.

THE PROOF OF POLICY

The outputs of government are influential but not all important in achieving government's intentions. The proof of policy is whether these outputs produce the outcomes that policymakers desire. Even more important in a democracy is the ordinary person's evaluation of government's capacity to deliver goods and services, and popular commitment to the British system of government.

Problem Outputs

Programs unite what analysis separates. The institutions and resources of government are not administered apart from each other. Program outputs are produced by public sector organizations together mobilizing the resources of law, money, and public employees for a specific purpose such as teaching children in schools or providing military defense.

The tremendous growth of government in the twentieth century has not been produced by a growth in institutions; there is still only one prime minister and one Parliament. This growth is the product, rather, of a great increase in the number of government programs and, even more, in the resources claimed by long-established programs, as more people claim welfare state benefits, and the value of education, health, and social security benefits increases too.[105]

When we ask which programs of government are most important, the answer depends on the criterion we use to measure importance. If we think of the programs necessary by definition to maintain an independent state, these are very few. To continue in existence, a government must maintain law and order domestically and protect its national security through diplomacy and military force. It must also collect taxes and pay interest on past debts.[106] The Crown performed these functions successfully for centuries before the mixed-economy welfare state ever developed.

The resources mobilized by British government to meet its minimum *defining concerns* account for about one-tenth of the national product and one-quarter of public expenditure (Table 9.5). Defense claims the largest share of personnel in this sector. The police and tax administration are labor-intensive, whereas a small professional elite deals with diplomacy. Tax administration is also law-intensive, for people would not pay taxes if they were not compelled to do so; the police is law-intensive too. If British government were concerned only with maintaining its existence, it would be a small, not a big government.

Today *social programs* concerned with health, education, and social security and personal social services claim more than half of public expenditure and half of all public employees. The payment of social security benefits is money-intensive but not labor-intensive, for it is administratively easy to transfer tens of billions of pounds from the public purse to retired people. Education and the National Health Service are labor- as well as money-intensive. The great bulk of money spent on these services pays the salaries of teachers, doctors, nurses, and employees involved in maintaining schools, hospitals, and clinics.

TABLE 9.5
PROGRAM OUTPUTS

	Money (£ bn)	Employees (000)	Laws (% total)
SOCIAL PROGRAMS			
Social security	44.4	224	⎫
Health	18.8	1,538	⎬ 7.9
Personal social services	3.4	376	⎭
Education	20.1	1,281	2.0
	£86.7	3,419	9.9%
ECONOMIC PROGRAMS			
Housing and environment	8.7	195	8.3
Transport	5.7	401	4.4
Employment	3.7	54	2.8
Trade, industry, energy	3.5	985	13.3
Agriculture	2.5	20	5.0
	£24.1	1,655	33.8%
DEFINING CONCERNS			
Defense	18.1	521	2.4
Foreign affairs	3.4	11	9.3
Law and order	6.9	285	17.2
Tax administration	1.3	100	12.3
Debt interest payments	17.8	n.a.	n.a.
	£47.5	917	41.2
Miscellaneous	3.8	889	15.1[a]
	£162.1	6,880	100%

[a]Includes 9.9 percent of legislation accounted for by the Scottish Office, paralleling the laws of many Whitehall departments.
Source: Compiled principally from tables in Chapter 3 of Richard Rose, *Ministers and Ministries* (Oxford: Clarendon Press, 1987) and *The Government's Expenditure Plans 1988–89 to 1990–91* (London: HMSO, Cm. 288–I), principally Chapter 2.

Social programs do not depend on the enactment of new laws. Social programs are big because they depend on old laws enacted long before any current member of Parliament entered office. For example, compulsory free education dates back to 1870, social security to 1908, and the National Health Service to 1948. Each new administration inherits major social commitments from its predecessor, commitments to provide services that affect families throughout the life cycle. To stop spending money on health care, social security, and education might reduce taxes, but it would also disrupt the lives of the great majority of British people.[107] Government has grown greatly because the social programs it produces, such as health care, education, and social security, are regarded as "good" goods and services.

Programs to *mobilize economic resources,* such as energy and transport, involve large numbers of public employees but do not make large claims on the public purse because they are nationalized industries, selling services. Altogether, economic programs account for less than 15 percent of total public expenditure. Economic programs do involve a large amount of legislation, because a market economy needs a firm base of company and property law. The broadest measure of the impact of government economic policy is found in the national income accounts of society as a whole.

Policy Outcomes

In the past quarter-century domestic and foreign commentators have often complained about the state of

England, invoking evidence of economic decline relative to Germany or Japan. But ordinary people do not compare their lives with people on the other side of the earth. The most important comparison is with their own past. Moreover, many changes in an individual's life reflect personal circumstances, such as children growing up and leaving home, or people having more problems with their health when they grow older.

The maintenance of security at home and abroad is the first concern of both governors and governed. In an interdependent world, the British government alone cannot guarantee national security, but it can and does contribute to international actions to deter aggression. It is a founder member of NATO, and it has sent troops to fight alongside American forces in support of UN-endorsed actions against aggressors, as in Korea in 1950 and the Gulf War in 1991.

The security of the individual against crime has declined in postwar England, as it has in other advanced industrial nations. Most of the increase in deviant behavior has involved theft and burglary. Crimes of violence are relatively few, and the police normally patrol unarmed. English society has a much lower level of violence than most Western nations; its murder rate, for example, is less than one-quarter that of the United States. (Northern Ireland is an exception.) Courts are used much less in Britain than in the United States, and lawyers are fewer. The avoidance of courts to settle disputes is a sign of greater trust as well as less crime than in the United States.

In each decade since World War II, the British economy has grown significantly. Compounding a small annual rate of economic growth over many decades results in a major change in the economy overall. Per capita national income in real terms has increased by more than two and one-half times since 1945. Many consumer goods that were once classified as luxuries, such as owning a home, an automobile, a refrigerator, and a washing machine, are now mass consumption goods. Things that were unknown in 1945, such as foreign jet holidays or color television, are now common in most households.

Analyzing household incomes by the socialist criterion of income equality shows that inequality remains in Britain, as it does in every other advanced industrial society. At some periods of the postwar era the income of the well-to-do has grown more rapidly than that of people with below-average incomes, thus increasing *relative* inequality. At other times, income differentials have narrowed. If statistics about income are examined in terms of the *absolute* standard of living, they show a long-term rise in absolute income in all groups in society.

On all the major indicators of social well-being, the British people enjoy a higher standard of living today than they did a generation or two ago.[108] Health has improved greatly during the era of the National Health Service. Infant mortality has declined by two-thirds, from thirty-one deaths per thousand in 1951 to less than nine today. Life expectancy at birth has risen by seven years for women and for men.

In the area of education the postwar expansion of schools has improved the ratio of pupils to teachers in elementary schools from thirty in 1951 to twenty-two today. The proportion of sixteen and seventeen year olds staying on in school has risen from 11 percent to 50 percent. After leaving secondary school, a quarter of British youths go on to further education in institutions that often did not exist in 1945.

Housing has expanded greatly in both quantity and quality. Nearly all the millions of substandard pre-1914 houses without an indoor toilet or bath have been razed. More than half the houses in England have been built since the end of World War II. While the floor space and conveniences of a modern English house or council flat are often not equal to those of American houses, they are far superior to what was previously available to the average English family.

The longer the time span, the greater the improvement in the material conditions of English life. Total welfare in society is the sum of services provided by the government, the market, and the individual household. In the past half century, both public *and* private provision of the major services that make up welfare in society has increased greatly. Economic growth has financed the expansion, and the welfare state has played a major part in the distribution of the expanded welfare.[109]

POPULAR EVALUATION In a modern democracy, the government's underlying aim is to maintain popular commitment to the constitutional regime. Without popular confidence, government is ineffective, repressive, or repudiated.

Many of the activities of government, such as national defense and protection of the environment, are addressed to society as a whole. Other program outputs are part of the everyday lives of millions of households; these include health care from birth to old age, educa-

TABLE 9.6
FAMILIES RECEIVING A MAJOR SOCIAL BENEFIT (PERCENTAGE)

Benefit	Receive	Do not receive
Dependent on public transport	38	62
Pension	36	64
Regular treatment doctor	35	65
Education	34	66
Housing	30	70
Hospital care in past year	29	71
Unemployment benefit	23	77
Personal social services	5	95
Percent of all families	89	11

Source: Calculated by the author from data reported in *Gallup Political Index*, No. 285 (May 1984), pp. 22–35.

tion, a pension, and a host of other social services. These programs are so taken for granted that people often think of them as nonpolitical. A child at school or an elderly person visiting a doctor does not think of himself or herself as participating in politics. Yet the services received are authorized and paid for by government.

Nearly nine-tenths of all families currently receive at least one major benefit regularly from government, benefits that would cost weeks or months of wages if purchased in the market (Table 9.6). The average household receives 2.3 welfare benefits, for example, drawing a pension and receiving National Health Service treatment, or having a council house and children at school. Although no one service at any one point in time affects a majority of families, in the course of a lifetime everyone is likely to make major use of these programs. The small minority not currently benefiting from social programs, for example, a young single person in good health living in a privately rented flat, is likely to marry, start a family, and rely on public education, health services, and a social security pension in old age.

The economic ups and downs of government in the past two decades have led some analysts to forecast the collapse of democracy in Britain if the economy fails to grow steadily.[110] Expecting economic difficulties to cause political collapse betrays ignorance of British history. In the years between the two world wars, when economic depression was widespread, politics in England avoided the extremism that was widespread on the European continent.

Frustration with the shortcomings of government presupposes a prior expectation of success. In fact, most English people usually do not expect government to succeed in dealing with rising prices, unemployment, and economic growth. A government responsible for a deteriorating economy would actually be meeting widespread pessimistic expectations! When people expect the economy to deteriorate, there is a "revolution of falling expectations." Thus, if the economy does not deteriorate, then this is good news considering what had been expected. For example, a 10 percent inflation rate can be heralded as a big fall, if the rate had earlier been above 20 percent, as was once the case in the 1970s.

The unexpected and rapidly rising inflation and unemployment in the 1970s created the circumstances for a politics of reprieve. As economic conditions worsened, expectations declined. The response was not protest politics but "a politics of quiet disillusion, in which lack of involvement or indifference to organized party politics was the most important feature."[111]

Even though the media often highlight the problems of the unemployed and the disadvantaged, the great majority of English people report that they are getting by with what they have, without having to draw on savings or run into debt. Means-tested welfare state benefits provide a floor for people who would otherwise be destitute.

Most people do not evaluate their personal circumstances in the same way as they evaluate their economic circumstances. When the Gallup Poll asks people whether they think next year will be better or worse for them than this year has been, nine-tenths of the time a majority say that they expect the coming year to be all right for them, even though many simultaneously anticipate economic difficulties. Economic prosperity is thus a desirable but not a necessary condition for personal well-being.

The English attitude toward democracy is both moderate and stable. In opinion surveys, a clear majority consistently give a positive evaluation of democracy, and satisfaction is usually above the average for European Community countries. The minority who show a degree of dissatisfaction are not in favor of radical change; they prefer gradual reform. Only a tenth report that they are not at all satisfied and want wholesale change.

Time and again, when people are asked to evaluate their lives, the same pattern recurs. People are most satisfied with their family, friends, home, and job, and least satisfied with the major institutions of society. Individuals generalize their view of life primarily from face-to-face experiences, and not from the actions of distant political institutions.[112]

KEY TERMS

Alliance (Liberals and Social Democrats)
Cabinet
centralization
class
collective responsibility
Conservative party
cumulative effect of socialization
decentralization
defining concerns
economic programs
first-past-the-post electoral system
industrialization
insider and outsider groups
insularity
intermittent public persons
Labour party
legitimacy of authority
Liberal Democrats
middle-of-the-road consensus
modernization
monarchy
multiparty system
noncommunication
Northern Ireland
party discipline
popular evaluation
prime minister
privatization
program outputs
service-delivery
social programs
state-distancing
Thatcherism
trusteeship
United Kingdom
unwritten constitution
Whitehall

END NOTES

1. Bernard Bailyn, *The Origins of American Politics* (New York: Vintage, 1970), p. ix.
2. André Siegfried, *England's Crisis* (New York: Harcourt, Brace, 1931), p. 13.
3. Clement Attlee, *The Guardian* (Manchester), April 21, 1963.
4. Cf. Richard Rose, "England: A Traditionally Modern Political Culture," in Lucian W. Pye and Sidney Verba, eds., *Political Culture and Political Development* (Princeton, N.J.: Princeton University Press, 1965), pp. 83–129.
5. See Jindrich Veverka, "The Growth of Government Expenditure in the United Kingdom since 1870," *Scottish Journal of Political Economy*, 10:2 (1963), pp. 114 ff.
6. Quoted in Dennis Kavanagh and Richard Rose, eds., *New Trends in British Politics* (Beverly Hills, Calif.: Sage Publications, 1977), p. 13.
7. Quoted in Richard Rose, *Do Parties Make a Difference?*, 2nd ed. (Chatham, N.J.: Chatham House, 1984).
8. "Thatcher Praised by Her Guru," *The Guardian* (London), March 12, 1983.
9. Peter Riddell, *The Thatcher Government* (Oxford: Martin Robertson, 1983), pp. 15–16. See also Dennis Kavanagh, *Thatcherism and British Politics*, 2nd ed. (Oxford: Oxford University Press, 1990), Hugo Young, *Thatcher* (London: Macmillan, 1989); and Peter Jenkins, *Mrs. Thatcher's Revolution* (Cambridge, Mass.: Harvard University Press, 1987).
10. "Inheritance before Choice in Public Policy," *Journal of Theoretical Politics*, 2:3 (1990), pp. 263–291.
11. See *Gallup Political Index* (London, 1989).
12. Quoted by Joe Rogaly, "Major Adopts a Pragmatic Approach to Tory Election Issues," *Financial Times* (London), November 28, 1990.

13. See "Pride in Nation," Chapter 2 of Richard Rose, *Ordinary People in Public Policy* (Newbury Park, Calif.: Sage Publications, 1990).

14. Lord Hugh Cecil, *Conservatism* (London: Williams & Norgate, c. 1912), p. 243.

15. Siegfried, *England's Crisis*, p. 303.

16. *Gallup Political Index*, London, No. 276 (August 1983), p. 14.

17. Prime Ministerial broadcast, April 5, 1976.

18. Dean Acheson, "Britain's Independent Role about Played Out," *The Times* (London), December 6, 1962.

19. See Richard Rose, *The Territorial Dimension in Government: Understanding the United Kingdom* (Chatham, N.J.: Chatham House, 1982), and P. Madgwick and R. Rose, eds., *The Territorial Dimension in United Kingdom Politics* (London: Macmillan, 1982), pp. 100–136.

20. See James Kellas, *The Scottish Political System*, 3rd ed. (New York: Cambridge University Press, 1984).

21. See P. Madgwick and P. Rawkins, "The Welsh Language in the Policy Process," in Madgwick and Rose, eds., *The Territorial Dimension in United Kingdom Politics*, pp. 67–99, and Ian C. Thomas, "Giving Direction to the Welsh Office," in Richard Rose, *Ministers and Ministries* (Oxford: Clarendon Press, 1987), pp. 142–188.

22. See Richard Rose, *Governing without Consensus* (Boston: Beacon Press, 1971); Padraig O'Malley, *The Uncivil Wars: Ireland Today* (Boston: Houghton Mifflin, 1983); and Paul Arthur, *Government and Politics of Northern Ireland* (London: Longman, 1984).

23. Compare Richard Rose and Ian McAllister, *United Kingdom Facts* (New York: Holmes & Meier, 1982), ch. 9.

24. See Mohammed Anwar, *Race and Politics* (London: Tavistock, 1989). Z. Layton-Henry, *The Politics of Race in Britain* (London: 1984); Nathan Glazer and Ken Young, eds., *Ethnic Pluralism and Public Policy* (London: Heinemann, 1983).

25. Quoted in Peter Hennessy, "Raw Politics Decide Procedure in Whitehall," *New Statesman & Nation* (London), October 24, 1986, p. 10. Cf. Philip Norton, *The Constitution in Flux* (Oxford: Martin Robertson, 1982); J. Jowell and D. Oliver, eds., *The Changing Constitution* (Oxford: Clarendon Press, 1985); and Richard Holme and Michael Elliott, eds., *1688–1988: Time for a New Constitution* (London: Macmillan, 1988).

26. See Richard Rose and Dennis Kavanagh, "The Monarchy in Contemporary Political Culture," *Comparative Politics*, 8:3 (1976), pp. 648–576.

27. Winston Churchill, *Their Finest Hour* (London: Cassell, 1949), p. 14. For an overall picture, see Richard Rose, "British Government: The Job at the Top," in R. Rose and E. Suleiman, eds., *Presidents and Prime Ministers* (Washington, D.C.: American Enterprise Institute, 1980), pp. 1–49.

28. See P. Dunleavy, G. W. Jones, and B. O'Leary, "Prime Ministers and the Commons: Patterns of Behaviour, 1868 to 1987," *Public Administration*, 68:1 (1990), pp. 123–140.

29. Quoted in Francis Williams, *A Prime Minister Remembers* (London: Hutchinson, 1961), p. 81.

30. Walter Bagehot, *The English Constitution* (London: World's Classics edition, 1955), p. 9.

31. See Peter Hennessy, *Cabinet* (Oxford: Basil Blackwell, 1986); T. T. Mackie and B. W. Hogwood, eds., *Unlocking the Cabinet* (Beverly Hills, Calif.: Sage Publications, 1985).

32. See Richard Rose, *Ministers and Ministries: A Functional Analysis* (Oxford: Clarendon Press, 1987).

33. See Bruce W. Headey, *British Cabinet Ministers* (London: George Allen & Unwin, 1974).

34. Richard Rose, "The Political Status of Higher Civil Servants in Britain," in E. Suleiman, ed., *Bureaucrats and Policy Making* (New York: Holmes & Meier, 1984), pp. 138–173.

35. *Careers in the Civil Service — An Alternative View* (London: First Division Association, 1987), p. 12.

36. See Richard Rose, "Loyalty, Voice or Exit? Margaret Thatcher's Challenge to the Civil Service," in T. Ellwein, J. J. Hesse, R. Mayntz, and F. W. Scharpf, eds., *Jahrbuch zur Staats- und Verwaltungswissenschaft* (Baden–Baden: Nomos, 1988), pp. 189–218.

37. See Richard Rose, "Steering the Ship of State: One Tiller but Two Pairs of Hands," *British Journal of Political Science*, 17:4 (1987), pp. 409–433.

38. Crossman, "Introduction" to Walter Bagehot, *The English Constitution* (London: Fontana, 1963), pp. 51ff. See also J. P. Mackintosh, *The British Cabinet* (London: Stevens, 1968).

39. Quoted in R. Rose, "British Government: The Job at the Top," p. 43.

40. The term *Parliament* can refer to the House of Commons or to both the House of Commons and the largely hereditary House of Lords.

41. See Denis Van Mechelen and Richard Rose, *Patterns of Parliamentary Legislation* (Aldershot: Gower, 1986).

42. Eric Varley, quoted in A. Michie and S. Hoggart, *The Pact* (London: Quartet Books, 1978), p. 13. See also Richard Rose, "Still the Era of Party Government," *Parliamentary Affairs*, 36:3 (1983), pp. 282–299.

43. On MPs and Parliament, see Philip Norton, *The Commons in Perspective* (Oxford: Martin Robertson, 1981), and S. A. Walkland and M. Ryle, eds., *The Commons Today* (London: Fontana, 1981).

44. See Committee on the Management of Local Government, *The Local Government Elector*, vol. 3 (London: Her Majesty's Stationery Office, 1967), pp. 66ff; semiannual Euro-Barometer surveys of the Commission of the European Communities, Brussels, and Robert D. Putnam, *The Beliefs of Politicians* (New Haven, Conn.: Yale University Press, 1973).

45. See Alan Marsh, *Protest and Political Consciousness* (Beverly Hills, Calif.: Sage Publications, 1977), Table 3.2. For more recent but less detailed data, see A. Heath and R. Topf, "Political Culture," in Roger Jowell et al., *British Social Attitudes: the 1987 Report* (Aldershot: Gower, 1987), pp. 52ff.

46. Richard Rose and Dennis Kavanagh, "The Monarchy in Contemporary Political Culture," *Comparative Politics*, 8:3 (1976), pp. 548–576.

47. See Richard Rose and Harve Mossawir, "Voting and Elections: A Functional Analysis," *Political Studies* 15:2 (1967), pp. 182ff.

48. For Anglo-American comparisons, see Richard Hodder–Williams, "Courts of Last Resort," in Hodder–Williams and James Ceaser, eds., *Politics in Britain and the United States* (Durham, N.C.: Duke University Press, 1986), pp. 142–172.

49. Lord Wright, in *Liversidge v. Sir John Anderson and Another, 1941*, quoted in G. Le May, *British Government, 1914–1953* (London: Methuen, 1955), p. 332.

50. For criticisms, see, for example, John Benyon and Colin Bourn, eds., *The Police: Powers, Procedures and Properties* (Oxford: Pergamon, 1986); Maurice Punch, *Conduct Unbecoming* (London: Tavistock, 1985); and Robert Reiner, *The Politics of the Police* (Brighton: Wheatsheaf, 1985).

51. See Richard Rose, "On the Priorities of Citizenship in the Deep South and Northern Ireland," *Journal of Politics*, 38:2 (1976), pp. 247–291.

52. L. S. Amery, *Thoughts on the Constitution* (London: Oxford University Press, 1953), p. 21.

53. See Dennis Kavanagh, "The Deferential English: A Comparative Critique," *Government and Opposition*, 6:3 (1971), pp. 333–360, and Samuel H. Beer, *Britain Against Itself* (London: Faber, 1982).

54. For collectivist interpretations, see Samuel H. Beer, *Modern British Politics*, 3rd ed. (London: Faber & Faber, 1982), and Peter Hall, *Governing the Economy* (London: Polity, 1986), pp. 268ff.

55. Quoted from Putnam, *Beliefs of Politicians*, p. 172.

56. Ibid., p. 173.

57. See, for example, Wyn Grant and Shiv Nath, *The Politics of Economic Policymaking* (Oxford: Blackwell, 1984) and Paul Mosley, *The Making of Economic Policy* (Brighton: Wheatsheaf, 1984).

58. Robert M. Worcester, "The Hidden Activists," in Rose, ed., *Studies in British Politics*, 3rd ed. (New York: St. Martin's Press, 1976), pp. 198–203, and David Phillips, "Participation and Political Values" in M. Abrams, D. Gerard, and N. Timms, eds., *Values and Social Change* (London: Macmillan, 1985).

59. Heath and Topf, "Political Culture," p. 56.

60. See Richard Rose and Ian McAllister, *The Loyalties of Voters* (Newbury Park, Calif.: 1990), ch. 3, and subsequent chapters, for details of data cited here on social influences and the vote in Britain.

61. The figures here are derived from a hierarchical stepwise multiple regression analysis of the choice of voters between Conservative, Alliance, and Labour parties at the 1987 British election. For full details, see Rose and McAllister, *Loyalties of Voters*.

62. See Rose, *Ministers and Ministries*, especially Chapter 4, and Kevin Theakston, *Junior Ministers in British Government* (Oxford: Basil Blackwell, 1987).

63. Quoted in Maurice Kogan, *The Politics of*

Education (Harmondsworth: Penguin, 1971), p. 135.

64. See the Fulton Committee, *Report*, Vol. 1, pp. 27ff, and Appendix E, especially p. 162.

65. See Hugo Young and Anne Sloman, *No, Minister: An Inquiry into the Civil Service* (London: BBC Publications, 1982).

66. See Peter Hennessy, *Whitehall* (London: Fontana, 1990), chs. 14–15; Richard Rose, "Loyalty, Voice or Exit? Margaret Thatcher's Challenge to the Civil Service," in Ellwein et al., eds., *Jahrbuch zur Staats- und Verwaltungswissenschaft*, pp. 189–218.

67. See Efficiency Unit, *Improving Management in Government: The Next Steps* (London: HMSO, 1988), and more generally, Les Metcalfe and Sue Richards, *Improving Public Management*, 2nd ed. (London: Sage Publications, 1990).

68. Cf. Peter Hennessy, *The Great and the Good* (London: Policy Studies Institute Research Report No. 654, 1986); Cabinet Office, *Public Bodies 1984* (London: HMSO, 1984); and Anthony Barker, ed., *Quangos in Britain* (London: Macmillan, 1982).

69. Anthony Sampson, *Anatomy of Britain* (London: Hodder & Stoughton, 1962), pp. 222–223.

70. Lord Balniel, "The Upper Classes," *The Twentieth Century*, No. 999 (1960), p. 432.

71. Cf. Colin Bennett, "From the Dark to the Light: The Open Government Debate in Britain," *Journal of Public Policy*, 5:2 (1985), pp. 187–214.

72. Cf. Jay G. Blumler, "Producers' Attitudes towards Television Coverage of an Election Campaign," in R. Rose, ed., *Studies in British Politics*, 3rd ed. (New York: St. Martin's Press, 1976), pp. 266–291, and Godfrey Hodgson, *Cut! The BBC and the Politicians* (London: Macmillan, 1988).

73. See Martin Harrop, "Voters," in Jean Seaton and Ben Pimlott, eds., *The Media in British Politics* (Aldershot: Avebury, 1987), pp. 45–63; *Gallup Political Index*, No. 329 (January 1988), p. 17.

74. Private conversation of the author with a well-known parliamentary reporter.

75. Bennett, "From the Dark to the Light," p. 209; italics in the original.

76. For studies of pressure groups, see, for example, J. J. Richardson and A. G. Jordan, *Governing under Pressure* (Oxford: Martin Robertson, 1979); David Marsh, ed., *Pressure Politics* (London: Junction Books, 1983); and Wyn Grant with Jane Sargent, *Business and Politics in Britain* (London: Macmillan, 1987).

77. E. H. Phelps–Brown, "The National Economic Development Organization," *Public Administration*, 51 (Autumn 1963), p. 245.

78. Cf. Wyn Grant, "Insider and Outsider Pressure Groups," *Social Studies Review*, 1:1 (1985), pp. 31–34.

79. See Jim Bulpitt, "The Discipline of the New Democracy: Mrs. Thatcher's Statecraft," *Political Studies*, 34:1 (1986), pp. 19–39.

80. On the interaction between changes in parties and voters, see Rose and McAllister, *Loyalties of Voters*.

81. *Gallup Political Index*, No. 323 (July 1987), p. 16.

82. For details, see Richard Rose, *Politics in England*, 5th ed. (New York: Harper Collins, 1989), pp. 261ff.

83. Ivor Crewe, "Has the Electorate Become Thatcherite?," in Robert Skidelsky, ed., *Thatcherism* (Oxford: Basil Blackwell, 1989), pp. 25–49.

84. See Rose, *Do Parties Make a Difference?*, especially Chapter 8, "Something Stronger Than Parties," and Rose, "Steering the Ship of State."

85. Reginald Maudling, quoted in David Butler and Michael Pinto–Duschinsky, *The British General Election of 1970* (London: Macmillan, 1971), p. 62. On institutionalized factors, see Rose, "Inheritance before Choice in Public Policy," pp. 263–291.

86. For details, see Denis Van Mechelen and Richard Rose, *Patterns of Parliamentary Legislation* (Aldershot: Gower, 1986), Table 3.

87. Hugh Dalton, *Call Back Yesterday* (London: Muller, 1953), p. 237.

88. L. S. Amery, *Thoughts on the Constitution* (London: Oxford University Press, 1953), p. 87.

89. "Thinking about the Think Tank," *The Listener* (London), December 28, 1972. See also Tessa Blackstone and William Plowden, *Inside the Think Tank: Advising the Cabinet, 1971–1983* (London: Heinemann, 1988).

90. See Richard Rose, "From Government at the Centre to Government Nationwide," in Yves Meny and Vincent Wright, eds., *Centre-Periphery Relations in Western Europe* (London: George Allen & Unwin, 1985), pp. 13–32, and Richard Parry, "Territory and Public

Employment: A General Model and British Evidence," *Journal of Public Policy*, 1:2 (1981), pp. 221–250.

91. See Rose, *Ministers and Ministries*, especially Chapter 3.

92. See Rose, *The Territorial Dimension in Government*, chs. 5–6.

93. J.A.G. Griffith, *Central Departments and Local Authorities* (London: George Allen & Unwin, 1966), p. 542.

94. For an overview, see Tony Byrne, *Local Government in Britain*, 4th ed. (Harmondsworth: Penguin, 1986).

95. See W. L. Miller, *Irrelevant Elections? The Quality of Local Democracy in Britain* (Oxford: Clarendon Press, 1988); Colin Mellors, "Coalition Strategies: The Case of British Local Government," in V. Bogdanor, ed., *Coalition Government in Western Europe* (London: Heinemann, 1983), pp. 231–247.

96. OECD, *Health Care Systems in Transition: The Search for Efficiency* (Paris: OECD, 1990), p. 14.

97. Quoted in Maurice Kogan, *The Politics of Education* (Harmondsworth: Penguin, 1971), p. 31.

98. See, for example, Robert Millward and D. M. Parker, "Public and Private Enterprise," in R. Millward et al., *Public Sector Economics* (London: Longman, 1983), pp. 199–274.

99. See, for example, John Vickers and George Yarrow, *Privatization: An Economic Analysis* (Cambridge: Mass.: MIT Press, 1988); Ellen M. Pint, "Nationalization and Privatization: A Rational Choice Perspective on Efficiency," *Journal of Public Policy*, 10:3 (1990), pp. 267–298, and Richard Rose, "Privatization as a Problem of Satisficing and Dissatisficing," *American Review of Public Administration*, 19:2 (1989), pp. 97–118.

100. See Ian McAllister and Donley Studlar, "Popular Versus Elite Views of Privatization: The Case of Britain," *Journal of Public Policy*, 9:2 (1989), pp. 157–178.

101. Sir Leo Pliatzky, quoted in Peter Hennessy, "The Guilt of the Treasury 1000," *New Statesman*, January 23, 1987. See also Hugo Young and Anne Sloman, *But Chancellor: An Inquiry into the Treasury* (London: BBC Publications, 1984).

102. Denis Healey, quoted in Paul Mosley, *The Making of Economic Policy* (Brighton: Wheatsheaf, 1984). Cf. Peter Hall, *Governing the Economy: The Politics of State Intervention in Britain and France* (Cambridge: Polity Press, 1986).

103. "Monetary Policy," in Michael Posner, ed., *Demand Management* (London: Heinemann, 1978), p. 188.

104. See Richard Rose, "Political Economy and Public Policy: The Problem of Joint Appraisal," in Warren J. Samuels, ed., *Fundamentals of the Economic Role of Government* (Westport, Conn.: Greenwood Press, 1989), pp. 157–166.

105. See Richard Rose, "The Programme Approach to the Growth of Government," *British Journal of Political Science*, 15:1 (1985), pp. 1–28.

106. See Richard Rose, "On the Priorities of Government," *European Journal of Political Research*, 4 (1976), pp. 247–289.

107. See Rose, "Inheritance before Choice in Public Policy."

108. For up-to-date statistics, see the annual government publication, *Social Trends* (London: HMSO), and for long-term measures, see A. H. Halsey, ed., *Social Trends since 1900*, 2nd ed. (London: Macmillan, 2nd ed. 1988).

109. For full historical details, see Richard Rose, "The Dynamics of the Welfare Mix in Britain," in Richard Rose and Rei Shiratori, eds., *The Welfare State East and West* (New York: Oxford University Press, 1986), pp. 80–106.

110. See, for example, Samuel Brittan, "The Economic Consequences of Democracy," *British Journal of Political Science*, 5:2 (1975), pp. 129–159.

111. James Alt, *The Politics of Economic Decline* (Cambridge: Cambridge University Press, 1979), p. 270. On the politics of reprieve, see Richard Rose, "Misperceiving Public Expenditure — Feelings about 'Cuts'," in Charles H. Levine and Irene Rubin, eds., *Fiscal Stress and Public Policy* (Beverly Hills, Calif.: Sage Publications, 1980), p. 228.

112. See Rose, *Ordinary People in Public Policy*, chs. 9 and 10.

FRANCE
(Regional Organization)

North Sea

ENGLAND

BELGIUM

GERM

English Channel

LUX.

Lille •
NORD

PICARDIE

HAUTE

LORRAINE

Seine R.

NORMANDIE

★ Paris
Paris

CHAMPAGNE

ALSACE

Rhine R.

Stra

BASSE

RÉGION
PARISIENNE

BRETAGNE

SWIT

PAYS
DE LA LOIRE

Loire R.

CENTRE

BOURGOGNE

FRANCHE-
COMTÉ

• Nantes

Bay of Biscay

POITOU-
CHARENTE

LIMOUSIN

Clermont-
• Ferrand

AUVERGNE

Lyon •

• St. Étienne

RHÔNE-ALPES

Grenoble
•

• Bordeaux

Garonne R.

Rhône R.

AQUITAINE

MIDI-PYRÉNÉES

LANGUEDOC

PROVENCE-
CÔTE D'AZUR

N

Toulouse •

• Marseilles

Toulon •

SPAIN

Mediterranean Sea

0   100
Scale of Miles

CHAPTER 10

Henry W. Ehrmann
AND
Martin A. Schain

POLITICS IN FRANCE

INTRODUCTION

FRANCE IS one of the most perplexing countries to judge and interpret. The French Enlightenment made an enormous contribution to what was later termed the "world revolution of the West" on both sides of the Atlantic. The overthrow of the French monarchy was motivated by many of the same ideas that led to the American Revolution. But if the American Revolution rapidly became a symbol of unity during the nineteenth century, the French Revolution became a symbol of sharp, and often violent, division about the proper organization of government. Political scientists whose task it is to explain the rise and the demise of political institutions have found in the record of past French regimes ample material for study and reflection.

The stability of the present French republic has surprised many Frenchmen as well as the outside world. The student of comparative politics also recognizes that by combining two models of democratic government, the presidential and the parliamentary, the Fifth Republic is engaged in a constitutional experiment that has not been successful in other countries but so far has served France well since its adoption.

The Frenchman Montesquieu remarked that those nations are happy whose history is boring to read. To the extent that this is true, France is an unhappy country, for its history has been fascinating and turbulent, not boring. No wonder its political systems have invited unending and frequently passionate comments from French and foreign observers alike.

A HISTORICAL PERSPECTIVE

One of the oldest nation-states of Europe, France has had a remarkably stable population mix, and the French have a strong sense of national identity. The period of unstable revolutionary regimes that followed the storming of the

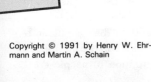

Bastille in 1789 and the fall of the monarchy three years later ended in the seizure of power by Napoleon Bonaparte, who proclaimed himself first consul and, later, emperor. The other European powers formed an alliance and forced Napoleon's surrender as well as the restoration of the Bourbon monarchy. Another revolution in 1830 drove the last Bourbon from the French throne and replaced him with Louis Philippe of the House of Orléans, who promised a more moderate rule bounded by a new constitution.

Growing dissatisfaction among the rising bourgeoisie and the urban population produced still another Paris revolution in 1848. With it came the proclamation of the Second Republic (1848–1852) and a promise of universal suffrage. Conflict between its middle-class and lower class components, however, kept the republican government ineffective, and out of the disorder rose another Napoleon, nephew of the first emperor. Louis Napoleon, crowned Napoleon III in 1852, brought stability to France for more than a decade, but his last years were marked by growing indecision and ill-conceived foreign ventures. His defeat and capture in the Franco-Prussian War (1870) began another turbulent period: France was occupied and forced into a humiliating armistice; radicals in Paris proclaimed the Paris Commune, which held out for two months until crushed by the conservative French government forces. In the commune's aftermath, the struggle between republicans and monarchists led to the establishment of a conservative Third Republic in 1871 and to a new constitution in 1875. In the words of one of the leading politicians of the time, it was "the Republic which divides us least." In spite of such inauspicious beginnings, the Third Republic proved to be the longest regime in modern France, surviving World War I and lasting until France's defeat and occupation by Nazi Germany in 1940.

General Charles de Gaulle entered liberated Paris in 1944 with the hope that sweeping reforms would give France the viable democracy it had long sought. After less than two years, he resigned as head of the Provisional government, impatient as he was with the country's return to traditional party politics. In fact, the Fourth Republic (1944–1958) disappointed earlier hopes and proved unable to cope with the tensions created by the cold war and the anticolonialist uprising in Algeria. When a threat of civil war arose over these issues in 1958, General de Gaulle was invited to return to power and help the country establish more stable institutions. Since then France has lived under the constitution of the Fifth Republic, enacted by a referendum in 1958.

The commemoration of the two hundredth anniversary of the French Revolution in 1989 was marked by a reinterpretation of what had been in past centuries divisive events through the prism of current political concerns. Instead of seeing the revolutionary events as reinforcing present political divisions in France, influential scholars (and the government itself) emphasized that, at long last, the revolution was "over" and that 1989 was a festival of national reconciliation. By this, they meant that the issues that emerged from the revolution no longer divided France and that France was no longer at war with itself about an acceptable regime.

ECONOMY AND SOCIETY

Geographically, France is at once Atlantic, Continental, and Mediterranean; hence, it occupies a unique place in Europe. In 1990 a total of 56.3 million people, about one-fourth as many as the population of the United States, lived in an area one-fifteenth the size of the United States. It is estimated that more than 4.5 million foreigners live in France, more than half of whom come from outside of Europe, mostly from North Africa and Africa. One and a half million Frenchmen are foreign-born. Thus, at least 10 percent of the French population is foreign-born, a far higher proportion than in the United States.

Urbanization has come slowly to France, in contrast to its neighbors, but it is now highly urbanized. Before World War II, 48 percent of the population lived in rural communities of fewer than 2,000 inhabitants; only 26 percent do so at present, although this population has stabilized since 1975. In 1936 only sixteen French cities had a population of more than 100,000; they now number thirty-six. Five cities have a population of more than 300,000. Compared with European countries with similar population (Britain and Germany), France has relatively few large cities. (Only Paris has more than a million people). Nevertheless, today France is highly urbanized. In 1975, three quarters of the population lived in urban areas; this percentage has diminished slightly since then.

More than one-fourth of the urban population — one-fifth of the entire nation — lives in the metropolitan region of Paris. This concentration of people creates staggering problems, as it does in other metropolitan areas of the world. In a country with centuries-old traditions of administrative, economic, and cultural centralization, it has also produced a dramatic gap in human and material resources between Paris and the rest of the country. With more than one-fourth of French industrial production, the Paris region supports a per capita income about 45 percent higher than the national average.

Overall, French economic development has been more than respectable in the recent past. In per capita gross domestic product (GDP) France ranks among the wealthiest nations of the world (only slightly behind what was West Germany and well ahead of Britain and Italy). (For further comparison, see Figure 2.2.) Among European countries, only in France did the GDP more than double between 1960 and 1982. France fared somewhat worse than some other industrialized countries during the recession of the 1980s. By 1989 there were clear signs that the economy was once again expanding, although unemployment continued to remain at about 10 percent.

The labor force has changed drastically since the end of World War II in ways that have made France similar to other industrialized countries. Between 1970 and 1986 an additional 3 million people entered the labor force, a larger increase than that in other countries. Some of this growth was due to the larger number of women remaining employed for a longer period of time. For over a century, the proportion of employed women had been higher in France than in most European countries, mostly in agriculture, artisan shops, and factories. Today, most women work in offices in the service sector of the economy. In 1954 women comprised 35 percent of the labor force; today, they make up 42 percent of a much larger labor force. The proportion of French women working (46 percent) is slightly lower than that of the United States but among the highest in Western Europe.

In 1938, 37 percent of French labor was employed in agriculture; the proportion was down to 6 percent in 1988, and it is still declining. The proportion employed in industry has remained more or less constant at about 30 percent (although the number of workers in smokestack industries has declined considerably), but employment in the service sector has risen from 33 percent in 1938 to 62 percent today, reaching about the same level as in the United States, and slightly above the average for the European Community.

By comparison with other highly developed industrial countries, the agricultural sector of France remains important both economically and politically. (For comparisons between the agricultural labor force in France and other countries, see Figure 2.3.) France has slightly more cultivated acreage (34 percent of the total acreage of the country) than other countries in the European Community. In spite of the population shift to the cities, agricultural production has not declined, and the increase of productivity is far higher in farming than in the rest of the economy. France remains the top producer of key agricultural products in Europe. But this impressive performance hides the fact that, although the income of farmowners is, on the average, about equal to that of a middle-level executive, the disparity of income between the smallest and largest farms is greater than in any other country in the European Community. Because the political stability of the Third Republic depended on a large and stable peasantry, French agriculture was supported with protective tariffs that helped French farmers (and small businessmen) cling to their established routines. Only since 1945 have serious efforts been made to modernize agriculture. More attention is being paid to the possible advantages of farm cooperatives; marginal farms are being consolidated; technical education has been vastly improved; and further mechanization and experimentation are being used as avenues for long-range structural reforms. Consolidation of farmland has proceeded rapidly, and by 1983 the mean size of a French farm was larger than that of any country in Europe except Britain and Luxembourg. Even so, subsidies to the agricultural sector still cost the government almost as much as its total revenue from income taxes.

The business counterpart of the family farm is the family firm. Well over half of the 2.7 million industrial and commercial enterprises in France belong to individuals, and half of these are classified as *entreprises artisanales* (craftsmen). Of the 537,000 industrial and commercial firms with the largest volume of business in 1983 (which employed over 11 million people), only 25 percent employed more than ten workers, and fewer than 0.3 percent are large enough to employ more than 500 workers. About 60 percent of salaried wage-earners in France work in firms with fewer than 500 employees, but this percentage is comparable to that in Germany and in other industrialized countries, where employment in small firms has been growing in recent years.

Some of the most advanced French industries are highly concentrated, and the few firms at the top account for most of the employment and business turnover. Even in some of the older sectors (such as automobile manufacture, ship construction, and rubber), half or more of the employment and business turnover is concentrated in the top four firms.

What remains unusual in an advanced "managerial" economy such as France is that more than half of the top 200 industrial concerns were still family controlled in the early 1980s. However, the importance of family firms has been declining. Pressures for change are emerging from the modernized sectors of the economy, from growing competition within the European Community, and from younger members of the business community and the bureaucracy. The values of stability and privilege are everywhere in conflict with arguments in favor of competition and innovation.

CONSTITUTION AND GOVERNMENTAL STRUCTURE

The constitution of 1958 is the sixteenth since the fall of the Bastille in 1789. Past republican regimes, known less for their achievements than for their instability, were invariably based on the principle that Parliament could overturn a government no longer backed by a majority of the elected representatives. Such an arrangement can work satisfactorily, as it does in most of Western Europe, when the country (and Parliament) embrace two or a few well-organized parties. The party or the coalition that has gained a majority at the polls forms the government and can count on the almost unconditional support of its members in Parliament until the next elections. At that time, it is either kept in power or replaced by an equally disciplined party or coalition of parties.

Why France never had the disciplined parties necessary for such a system will be explained below. The point for now is that the constitution that General de Gaulle submitted for popular approval in 1958 offered to remedy previous failings. In preceding republics the president has been little more than a figurehead. According to the new constitution, the president was to become a visible chief of state. He was to be placed "above the parties" to represent the unity of the national community. As guardian of the constitution he

was to be an arbiter who would rely on other powers — Parliament, the Cabinet, or the people — for the full weight of government action. He would have the option of appealing to the people in two ways. With the agreement of the government or Parliament, he could submit certain important pieces of legislation to the electorate as a referendum (Article 11); and, after consulting with the prime minister and the parliamentary leaders, he could dissolve Parliament and call for new elections. In case of grave threat "to the institutions of the Republic," the president also had the option of invoking emergency powers (Article 16).

Virtually all of the most powerful constitutional powers of the president — those that give the president formal power — have been used sparingly. Emergency powers were used only once (by General de Gaulle) in 1961, when the rebellion of the generals in Algiers clearly justified such use. The mutiny collapsed after a few days, not because a constitutional provision provided residual powers but because de Gaulle's authority was unimpaired and hence left the rebels isolated and impotent. President de Gaulle dissolved Parliament twice (in 1962 and 1968), both times to exploit a political opportunity to strengthen the majority supporting presidential policies. Parliament was not dissolved by a president again until 1981, as a consequence of Mitterrand's first election. Mitterand dissolved Parliament once more in 1988, to profit from the political momentum of his second victory.

The legitimacy and political authority of the president was greatly augmented by popular election. According to the 1958 constitution, the president was to be elected indirectly, by a college comprised mostly of local government officials. In 1962, however, a referendum replaced the original design with a system of popular election of the president for a renewable term of seven years. At present, France is the only country in Western Europe to select its president by direct popular vote.

President de Gaulle outlined his view of the office when he said that power "emanates directly from the people, which implies that the Head of State, elected by the nation, is the source and holder of this power."[1] Every president who has succeeded De Gaulle has maintained the general's basic interpretation of the office, but there have been some changes in content as well as style (for details, see pp. 222–224).

The prime minister has been responsible for the day-to-day running of the government (Articles 20–21), but the division of responsibility between the president and "his" prime minister varies not only with the personalities of those who hold each of the executive offices, but also with the conditions under which the prime minister serves.

Parliament is composed of two houses: the National Assembly and the Senate. The National Assembly is elected directly for five years by all citizens over eighteen; it may be dissolved at any time, though not twice within a year.

The instability of previous regimes had been attributed mostly to the constant meddling of Parliament with the activities of the executive. The constitution of 1958 strove to put an end to the subordination of government to Parliament. It imposed strict rules of behavior on each deputy and on Parliament as a body. These requirements, it was hoped, would ensure the needed equilibrium.

Now the Cabinet, rather than Parliament, is in control of proceedings in both houses and can require priority for bills it wishes to promote. The president rather than the prime minister chooses the Cabinet members (Article 8). Parliament still enacts laws, but the domain of such laws is strictly defined. Many areas of modern life that in other democracies are regulated by laws and debated and approved by Parliament are turned over to rule making by the executive in France (Articles 34–37).

The nineteen standing committees of the National Assembly under the Fourth Republic have been reduced to six, and the committees were enlarged — from 60 to 120 members — to prevent interaction among highly specialized deputies or senators who could become effective rivals of the ministers.

It is not surprising that the new constitution spelled out in detail the conditions under which the National Assembly could overthrow a government. An explicit motion of censure must be formulated and passed by more than one-half of the house. Even after such a motion of censure, the government might resist the pressure to resign: the president can dissolve the Assembly and call for new elections. During the first year after these elections a new dissolution of Parliament is prohibited by the constitution. Hence, the president would have to appoint a government that has majority support in Parliament, even though the president might disapprove of its policies. The vote of censure is the only way Parliament can criticize the conduct of government, but no government has been censured since 1962. Since that time every government has had a working (if not always friendly) majority in the National Assembly.

The National Assembly, whose members are elected for five years, shares legislative functions with the Senate. Not only in France but in all countries without a federal structure, the problem of how to organize a bicameral legislature is complex. How should the membership be defined if there are no territorial units to be represented? Making it an appointed rather than an elected body removes democratic legitimacy. If for that reason it is denied powers equal to those of the popularly elected Parliament, how is it possible to avoid having it slighted, as the British House of Lords is? In the Fifth Republic, as in previous regimes, the Senate is elected indirectly for a term of nine years by an electoral college in which rural constituencies are overrepresented. The Upper House has the right to initiate legislation and must approve of all bills adopted by the National Assembly. If the two houses disagree on pending legislation, the government can appoint a joint committee. If the views of the two houses are not reconciled, the government may resubmit the bill (either the original bill or as amended by the Senate) to the National Assembly for a definitive vote (Article 45). Therefore, unlike the United States, the two houses are not equal (see Figure 10.1).

Until the Fifth Republic, France had no judicial check on the constitutionality of the actions of its political authorities. The Constitutional Council (articles 56–62)[2] was originally conceived primarily as a safeguard against any legislative erosion of the constraints that the constitution has placed on the prerogatives of Parliament. Nevertheless, the council has played an increasingly important role in the legislative process (see page 227). Since a 1974 amendment to the constitution which permits sixty deputies or senators to bring cases before the council, it has now become almost routine for the council to examine important bills passed by the majority in parliament, generally on petition by the opposition. Laws (or parts of laws) that are declared contrary to the constitution cannot be promulgated.

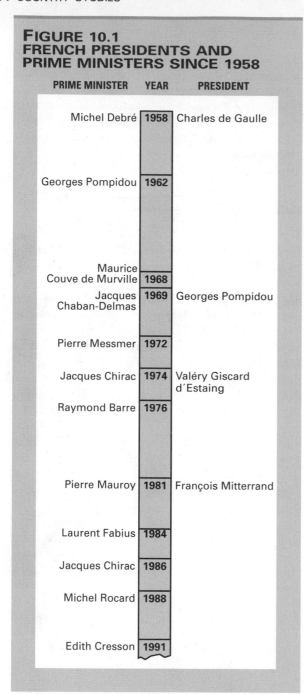

FIGURE 10.1
FRENCH PRESIDENTS AND
PRIME MINISTERS SINCE 1958

PRIME MINISTER	YEAR	PRESIDENT
Michel Debré	1958	Charles de Gaulle
Georges Pompidou	1962	
Maurice Couve de Murville	1968	
Jacques Chaban-Delmas	1969	Georges Pompidou
Pierre Messmer	1972	
Jacques Chirac	1974	Valéry Giscard d'Estaing
Raymond Barre	1976	
Pierre Mauroy	1981	François Mitterrand
Laurent Fabius	1984	
Jacques Chirac	1986	
Michel Rocard	1988	
Edith Cresson	1991	

POLITICAL CULTURE AND SOCIALIZATION

Themes of Political Culture

THE BURDEN OF HISTORY Historical thinking can prove both a bond and — as the American Civil War demonstrates — a hindrance to consensus. The French are so fascinated by their own history that feuds of the past are constantly superimposed on the conflicts of the present. This passionate use of historical memories, resulting in seemingly inflexible ambitions, warnings, and taboos, complicates political decision making. In de Gaulle's words, France is "weighed down by history."[3]

ABSTRACTION AND SYMBOLISM In the Age of Enlightenment the monarchy, in an effort to compensate for the severity it imposed on the educated classes, left them free to voice their views on many topics, provided the discussion remained general and abstract. The urge to discuss a wide range of problems, even trivial ones, in broad philosophical terms has hardly diminished. The exaltation of the abstract is reflected in the significance attributed to symbols and rituals. Rural communities that fought on opposite sides in the French Revolution still pay homage to different heroes, nearly two centuries later. They seem to have no real quarrel with each other, but inherited symbols and their political and religious habits have kept them apart.[4] This tradition helps explain why a nation united by almost universal admiration for a common historical experience holds to conflicting interpretations of its meaning.

DISTRUST OF GOVERNMENT AND POLITICS The French have long shared in the widespread ambivalence of modern times that combines distrust of government with high expectations from it. The French citizen's simultaneous distrust of authority and craving for it fed on both his individualism and his passion for equality. This attitude has produced a self-reliant individual convinced that he was responsible to himself, and perhaps to his family, for what he was and might become. Obstacles were created by the outside world, the "they" who operate beyond the circle of the family, the family firm, the village. Most of the time, however, "they" were identified with the government.

Memories reaching back to the eighteenth century justified a state of mind that was potentially, if seldom overtly, insubordinate. A strong government was considered to be reactionary by nature, even if it pretended

The National Assembly (Parliament) in session. The speaker (in traditional tails) is reading a presidential message to the deputies. The first benches facing the dais are occupied by members of the government.

to be progressive. When a citizen participated in public life, he hoped to weaken governmental authority rather than encourage change, even when change was overdue. At times this individualism was tainted with anarchism. Yet the French also accommodated themselves rather easily to bureaucratic rule. Since administrative rulings supposedly treat all situations with the same yardstick, they satisfy the sharp sense of equality possessed by a people who have felt forever shortchanged by the government and by the privileges those in power bestow on others.

Even though the Revolution of 1789 did not break with the past as completely as is commonly believed, it conditioned the general outlook on crisis and compromise, continuity and change. Sudden change rather than gradual mutation, dramatic conflicts couched in the language of mutually exclusive, radical ideologies —these are the experiences that have excited the French at historical moments when their minds were particularly malleable. At the end of the nineteenth century, history itself appeared to an illustrious French historian, Ernest Renan, as a "kind of civil war." In fact,

what appears to the outsider as permanent instability is a fairly regular alternation between brief violent crises and prolonged periods of routine. The French had become accustomed to thinking that no thorough change can ever be brought about except by a major upheaval. Since the great revolution, every French adult has experienced — usually more than once — occasions of political excitement followed by disappointment. This process led at times to moral exhaustion and widespread skepticism about any possibility of change.

Whether they originated within the country or were brought about by international conflict, each of France's emergencies has resulted in a constitutional crisis. Each time, the triumphant forces have codified their norms and philosophy, usually in a comprehensive document. This history explains why constitutions have never played the role of fundamental charters. Prior to the Fifth Republic, their norms were satisfactory to only one segment of society and hotly contested by others.

In the years immediately following 1958, the reaction to the constitution of the Fifth Republic resembled that to other constitutions in France. Support for its institutions was generally limited to voters who supported the governments of the day. This began to change after 1962, with the popular election of the president. The election of Mitterrand to the presidency in 1981, and the peaceful transfer of power from a right to a left majority in the National Assembly, laid to rest the 200-year-old constitutional debate among French elites, and proved to be the capstone of acceptance of the institutions of the Fifth Republic among the masses of French citizens. Indeed, most French citizens accepted the institutional arrangements of the republic long before their political leaders.

Confidence in institutions has tended to vary with the perceived closeness of institutions to the daily lives of people. When French people are asked in which institutions they have the most confidence, they invariably give the highest ratings to local officials and professional organizations (such as trade unions), rather than to political parties or national representatives. However, the one national official that receives ratings as high as local mayors is the president of the republic.[5]

RELIGIOUS AND ANTIRELIGIOUS TRADITIONS

France is at once a Catholic country — 82 percent of the children born in 1982 were baptized into the Catholic faith (92 percent in 1958) — and a country that the church itself considers as "dechristianized." Of the 81 percent of the population who describe themselves as Catholic, only 14 percent (by some estimates, 10 percent) attend Mass regularly, and 61 percent either never go to church at all or go only for such ceremonies as baptism or marriage.

Until well into the present century, the mutual hostility between believers and nonbelievers was one of the main features of the political culture. Since the Revolution, it has divided society and political life at all levels. Even now, there are important differences between the political behavior of practicing Catholics and nonbelievers.

French Catholics viewed the Revolution of 1789 as the work of satanic men, and enemies of the church became militant in their opposition to Catholic forms and symbols. This division continued through the nineteenth century. With the establishment of the Third Republic in 1875, differences between the political subcultures of Catholicism and anticlericalism deepened further. After a few years militant anticlericalism took firm control of the republic. Parliament rescinded the centuries-old compact with the Vatican, expelled most Catholic orders, and severed all ties between church and state, so that "the moral unity of the country could be reestablished." Hostility between Catholics and anticlericals almost broke out into generalized violence. In rural regions, where Catholic observance had become a matter of habit rather than of genuine faith, dechristianization spread, spurred on by new legislation that deprived the church of all official prestige.[6]

The militancy of the republican regime was matched by the pope, who excommunicated every deputy voting for the separation laws. Faithful Catholics were driven to the view that only the overthrow of the regime could overcome their isolation.

As in other European Catholic countries, the difference between the political right and left was largely determined by attitudes toward the Catholic Church. In those rural regions where religious practice continued to be lively and where the voters listened to the local clergy, conservative candidates carried the vote. Nonetheless, for a total of sixty years (1879 to 1939), with rare exceptions, no practicing Catholic obtained Cabinet rank in any of the numerous ministries.

The situation began to change during the interwar period and especially after Catholics and agnostics found themselves side by side, and sometimes joined together, in the resistance movement during World War II. Leftist movements and, more recently, the Socialist party have attracted a large number of young Catholics, even though the depth of religious practice continues to be the best predictor of whether a voter will support a party of the right.

Much of the electoral success of the left in recent years can be attributed to the decline in church attendance. Nevertheless, one study shows that children who are brought up in an observant environment may stop attending church without moving politically to the left.[7]

Religious practice has been declining in all industrialized countries since the 1950s, and, in France, the space of the Catholic "world" has been shrinking, in some ways quite dramatically, since the 1960s. However, there are enormous regional differences, as well as important differences among socioeconomic groups. In one rural and poor department in the center of France in the 1970s regular attendance was down to 6 percent of the Catholic population, but it was as high as 68 percent in one of the Alsatian departments of the east. Comparisons between departments of similar structure and located in the same region seem to indicate that historical rather than socioeconomic factors determine the degree of dechristianization.

Farmers are, by far, the most observant group in France, but their numbers are declining rapidly. Blue-collar workers, for most of this century, have been the least observant: only 8 percent of workers who claim to be Catholic admit to attending church regularly (compared with 22 percent of farmers). The estrangement between the working class and the church, which occurred in France as in other countries of Continental Europe during the early stages of industrialization, contributed to the class consciousness of the workers. It made a majority of them into followers of radical rather than conservative parties. The legacy of this estrangement remains a central fact of French religious, cultural, and, to a considerable extent, political life.

The difference between the religious attitudes of men and women has been more pronounced in France than in other countries of similar development. A far higher proportion of women describe themselves as Catholics than men and attend church regularly. Moreover, fewer women, compared with men, declare themselves to be without religion. But this masks a dramatic and continuing generational change among women. Regular church attendance of women below the age of forty declined to about the level of men in the late 1960s and has continued to diminish since then along with that of young men. As a result, women now vote for the left in about the same proportions as men do: a higher proportion of women than men have voted socialist, though not communist, in the 1980s. There is some evidence that the integration of more women into the workforce is the principal cause of both changing religious practice among women and changing political behavior.[8]

What we have presented so far does not convey the important changes that have taken place within the Catholic subculture. Today, the vast majority of those who identify themselves as Catholics reject some of the most important teachings of the church, including the church's positions on abortion, premarital sex, and marriage of priests. Even among regularly practicing Catholics, there is considerable support for these positions.

"In the nineteenth century," one social scientist has argued, "Public opinion accepted the interference of the church in private life, but not in public affairs. Today, it is the reverse." Catholicism no longer functions as a well-integrated community, with a common view of the world and common social values.[9] This may help explain why the number of priests in France declined by 25 percent between the mid-1960s and the mid-1980s, to about 30,000 in the entire country.

Most private schools in France are Catholic parochial schools, which have been subsidized by the state since the Fourth Republic. The status of these schools (in a country in which state support for Catholic schools, attended by 16 percent of French students, coexists with the separation of church and state) has never been fully settled.

In 1984 the Socialist government introduced legislation that would maintain subsidies, in return for the equalization of standards between the public and private school systems, and that would give parochial school teachers official status, without infringing on their teaching. But the legislation provoked public opposition by merging new concerns with the quality of education (and therefore the need to maintain an independent choice) with the old church – state issue. The result was massive mobilization on behalf of church schools. In the spring of 1984, when the bill was close to being voted into law by the socialist majority in Parliament, more than 1 million partisans of the private schools gathered in Paris in a symbolic demonstration for "freedom" against the government, whereupon President Mitterrand withdrew the bill and his minister of education resigned. The "street" had won. The episode showed that ideological conflicts, grounded in the past and seemingly overcome by a change in attitudes, can still be revived and used for political ends.

For many reasons, French Jews (numbering about 700,000 since the exodus that followed Algerian independence) have been so integrated into French society that they do not need to be discussed as a separate element of political culture. Accordingly, there has rarely been a "Jewish vote," except when the government voiced open criticism of Israel or manifested pro-Arab sympathies. Terrorist attacks against the Jewish population, however, have revived bitter memories of the war years when French public authorities became willing tools of Nazi extermination policies. They also have resulted in stronger Jewish ethnic consciousness.

In contrast to the traditional attitude of the Jewish population, the Protestants (just under 1 million or 1.7 percent of the population and growing) have, at least until recently, lived somewhat apart, with heavy concentrations in Alsace, in the Paris region, and in some regions of central and southeastern France. About two-thirds of Protestants belong to the upper bourgeoisie. The proportion of Protestants in high public positions was and is very large. Until recently, they usually voted more to the left than others in their socioeconomic position or in the same region. Since the liberation of 1944, however, their electoral behavior, like their activities in cultural and economic associations, has been determined by factors other than religion. They too have been fully integrated into the mainstream of French political culture.

Muslims are probably the fastest growing religious group in France today. One scholar has estimated that there are now as many as 3 million Muslims in France, two-thirds of whom are immigrants from Muslim countries.[10] The emergence and growth of Islamic institutions in France has been part of a larger phenomenon of the integration of the "new" immigration into France. In the 1970s and 1980s the affirmation of religious identification coincided with (and to some extent was a part of) the social and political mobilization and organization of immigrants from Muslim countries, especially of North African assembly-line workers.

The emergence of Islam has also challenged the traditional French view of the separation of church and state. Unlike Catholics, who have insisted on the right to maintain their own schools, or Protestants, who have supported the principle of secular state schools, some Muslim groups have insisted both on the right to attend state schools and, while attending them, to conserve practices (especially with regard to dress and similar matters) considered contrary to the French tradition of secularism by state education authorities. There is little doubt that the adjustment of Islam to life in France has also meant a rethinking, and some reluctant readjustment, of French values to the pressures of Muslim practice.

CLASS AND STATUS Feelings about class differences shape a society's authority pattern and the style in which authority is exercised. The French, like the English, are very conscious of living in a society divided into classes. But since quality is valued more highly in France than in England, deference toward the upper classes is far less developed, and resentful antagonism is widespread.

The number of those who are conscious of belonging to a class has been relatively strong in France, particularly among workers. One important study, for example, found a far greater intensity of spontaneous class consciousness among French workers in the 1970s than among comparable groups of British workers.[11] While class identity has been strong among workers, it has been as strong (and in some cases stronger) among other occupational groups.

Spontaneous class identity has been declining since the 1970s. In 1987, 56 percent of respondents felt that they belonged to a class, compared with 68 percent eleven years earlier. Moreover, the decline in class identification has been more notable among some groups than among others.[12] By 1987, although class commitments had generally declined, they had declined most among blue-collar workers (down to 50 percent) and less among white-collar employees and executives (59 and 60 percent, respectively). Among middle managers, feelings of class identity had actually increased (to 63 percent). Thus, by the late 1980s French workers identified themselves as belonging to a class less frequently than any other major salaried group.

But with which class do respondents identify? In general, there has been a decline in working-class identification (among all groups), and a small increase in middle-class identification. While the declining number of blue-collar workers, as well as executives and businesspeople, are generally clear about their class identification, white-collar workers and middle management are more divided. About as many white-collar workers think of themselves as working class as those who think of themselves as middle class.

Existing evidence indicates that economic and social transformations have reduced the level of class identification but have not eradicated subjective feelings about class differences and class antagonism. Indeed, as the number of immigrant workers among the least qualified workers has grown, traditional class differences have been reinforced by ethnic differences.

Political Socialization

The attitudinal patterns that we have analyzed here have been shaped through experience with the political system, as well as through some key institutions and agents. Some agents, such as political associations, act to socialize political values quite directly, while others, such as the family and the media, tend to act in a more indirect manner.

In an old country like France, agents of political socialization change slowly, even when regimes change rapidly. Socializing agents are carriers of a broader cultural tradition. Like any other teaching process, political socialization passes on from one generation to the next "a mixture of attitudes developed in a mixture of historical periods." But "traditions, everyone agrees, do not form a constituted and fixed set of values, of knowledge and of representations; socialization never functions as a simple mechanism of identical reproduction. . . . [but rather as] an important instrument for the reorganization and the reinvention of tradition."[13]

FAMILY For those French who view their neighbors and fellow citizens with distrust, and the institutions around them with cynicism, the family is a safe haven. At least in the past, the French were always sociable to outsiders whom they met on neutral ground, such as cafés or clubs. But distance was otherwise maintained and intimacy rarely granted. Concern for stability, safe income, property, and continuity were common to bourgeois and peasant families, though not to the urban or agricultural workers. The training of children in bourgeois and peasant families was marked by close supervision, incessant correction, and strict sanctions.

Since the war, and particularly during the last twenty years, the life of the French family, the role of its members, and its relationship to outsiders have all undergone fundamental, and sometimes contradictory, changes. More than in any other European country, there continues to be almost universal support for the ideal of the traditional family. On the other hand, very few people condemn the idea of couples living together without being married. In 1985, 20 percent of all births were to unmarried couples. This percentage, though slightly lower than that in the United States, is three times higher than it was twenty years before. As births among married couples have declined, births among unmarried couples have increased. The number of divorces each year is now about 40 percent the number of marriages, and divorce has almost doubled since 1976, when new and more flexible divorce legislation came into effect.[14] Moreover, there is more justification now than in the past to draw a picture of "the typical" French family. Class distinctions have not vanished, but a greater similarity of life-styles, family "togetherness" (however silent it may be in front of the television set), and altered views on the exercise of authority within the nuclear family have modified cultural traits.

Legislative changes have modified only gradually the legal incapacities of married women which the Napoleonic Code had stipulated. Not until 1970 would a law proclaim the absolute equality of the two parents in the exercise of parental authority and for the moral and material management of the family. Because women have insisted on labor-saving devices for house and farm, they have been described as the "secret agents of modernity" in the countryside.[15] The idealized image of the "woman at home" has been challenged by the continuous increase of married "women at work." Almost half of all women over the age of fifteen are now employed, and more than 80 percent of French women between the ages of twenty-five and forty-five are now working continuously during their adult years.

The employment of a greater number of married women has had an impact on the role of the family as a vehicle of socialization. Working women differ from those who are not gainfully employed in regard to moral concepts, religious practice, political interest, electoral participation, party alignment, and so on. In their general orientations employed women are far closer to the men of the milieu, the class, or the age group to which they belong, than to women who are not employed.[16] The evolution of attitudes in France is comparable to that in other European countries.

Although family values and behavior have changed, the family remains an important structure through which political values — broadly conceived — are transmitted from generation to generation. Several studies have demonstrated a significant influence of parents over the general left – right political choices made by their children.[17] Families also play an important role in the religious socialization of children, which, in turn, is linked to political orientations. Moreover, as children grow older, they resemble their parents' patterns even more.

The effectiveness of the family as an agent of socialization for general religious and ideological orientations does not mean that succeeding generations do not have formative experiences of their own or that there are no significant differences in the political commitments of different age cohorts. Therefore, political socialization is a product not only of the family experience, but also of childhood experiences with peers, education, and the changing larger world.[18]

ASSOCIATIONS AND SOCIALIZATION

The French bias against authority might have encouraged association if the egalitarian thrust and the competition between individuals did not cast suspicion on those who recommended that efforts be combined. The ambivalence toward participation in group life was not merely negativistic apathy but was related to a lack of belief in the value of cooperation.[19] This cultural ambivalence has been reinforced by legal restrictions on associational life, as well as by a strong republican tradition hostile to groups serving as intermediaries between the people and the state.

Nevertheless, after World War II, overall membership in associations in France was comparable to that of the United States. As in most European countries, organizational membership was highly politicized and tended to reinforce, rather than cross, political divisions.[20]

During the past decade some have spoken about an association explosion. Has there been a parallel growth of group membership? There is evidence that it has doubled in recent years, but that as more middle-class people have joined associations, working-class people have dropped out: almost half of male professors and high school teachers belonged to an association, compared with 4.6 percent of unskilled female workers in 1983.[21] On the other hand, there is considerable evidence that by the late 1980s membership in organizations and groups that were either directly political, or advocated political issues, had diminished considerably.

There are uncertainties about the role of associations, old and new, in the socialization process of individuals. Some observers seem to confirm that membership in French organizations involves less actual participation than in American or British organizations and hence has less impact on social and political attitudes. The cultural distrust noted above is manifest less in lower membership than in the inability of organizational leaders to relate to their members and to mobilize them for action. Other research indicates that some organizations have had considerable influence over social and political attitudes (trade unions, for example) by their very presence, even where membership is low.[22]

EDUCATION The most important way a community preserves and transmits its cultural and political values is through education. Napoleon Bonaparte recognized the significance of education, and well into the second half of the twentieth century the French educational system has remained an imposing historical monument, in the unmistakable style of the First Empire. The edifice Napoleon erected combined education at all levels, from primary school to postgraduate professional training, into one centralized corporation: the imperial university. Its job was to teach the national doctrine through uniform programs at various levels.

The strict military discipline of the Napoleonic model has been loosened by succeeding regimes, but each has discovered that the machinery created by Napoleon was a convenient and coherent instrument for transmitting the values — both changing and permanent — of French civilization. The centralized imperial university has therefore never been truly dismantled, and the minister of education, who presides over a ministry that employs almost a million people, continues to control curriculum and teaching methods, the criteria for selection and advancement of pupils and teachers, and the content of examinations.

Making advancement at every step depend on passing an examination is not peculiar to France. What is distinctly French is not so much the widespread cult of competitive examinations (shared by Japan among others), but an obsessive and quite unrealistic belief that everybody is equal before an examination. Success or failure in the examination shapes not only the candidates and their families, but also the milieu to which they will belong. The idea that education is an effective weapon for emancipation and social betterment has had popular as well as official recognition. Farmers and workers regard the instruction of their children, a better instruction than they had, as an important weapon in the fight against the "others" in an oppressive world. The movement of rural youth into the ranks of elementary school teachers has been of great importance for a two-step social promotion.

The *baccalauréat* — the certificate of completion of the secondary school, the *lycée* — has remained almost the sole means, and until recently also a guarantee, of access to higher education. But such a system suits and profits best those self-motivated bourgeois children for whom it was designed. The distance between teacher and pupil, the absence of good teaching methods, and the emphasis on the cultivated use of language widen the cultural gap further.

During the Fifth Republic, the structure of the French educational system at every level has undergone significant change. The increase in the number of students at the secondary level and in higher education has been phenomenal. The secondary schools, which trained only 700,000 students as late as 1945, now provide instruction for more than 5 million. Between 1958 and 1988 the number of students in higher education rose from 170,000 to 1.4 million. By 1988 the proportion of seventeen to twenty-four year olds in school (42 percent) was higher than that of the United States, and higher than that of any other European country. The proportion of university students was also the highest in Europe but lower than that of the United States.[23]

Educational reforms during the past twenty-five years have altered the traditional structure of French education. The introduction of a comprehensive middle school with a common core curriculum in 1963 basically altered the system of early academic selection, and other reforms eliminated rigid ability tracking. However, implementation of reforms, whether passed by governments of the right or the left, has often been difficult because of the opposition from middle-class parents and teachers unions of the left.[24]

The effects of these reforms have altered only slightly the impact of class differences in academic success. There are still vast differences in the success of children from different social backgrounds in the *baccalauréat* examination, which is the gateway to university education.[25]

Because of the principle of open admission, every holder of the *baccalauréat* can theoretically gain entrance to a university. But there is, as in some American state universities, a rather ruthless elimination at the end of the first year and sometimes later. Here again students of lower class background fare worse than the others. In addition, the number of students from such backgrounds is disproportionately great in fields whose diplomas have the lowest value in the professional market and where unemployment is greatest.

The most ambitious attempt ever made to reform a university system at one stroke was made in the wake of the student rebellion of 1968. Other endeavors at undoing the Napoleonic structures were undertaken in the 1970s and 1980s by conservative as well as by socialist governments. They strove, by different means, to encourage the autonomy of each university, the participation of teachers, students, and staff in the running of the university, and the collaboration among different disciplines. Some of the reforms, though duly enacted, were withdrawn by the government because of massive protest demonstrations in the streets, similar to those that had prevented the settlement of the controversy between public and parochial schools in 1984 (see above). Others failed of implementation because of the wide-spread resistance by those concerned. Administrative autonomy remains fragmentary as long as the ministry holds the financial pursestrings, as well as the right to grant degrees. The widely lamented crisis of the university system has hardly been alleviated, while the size of the student population continues to increase.

An additional problem of the university system is the parallel system of *grandes écoles*, a sector of higher education that functions outside of the network of universities under very different rules. Until recently, these schools have escaped much of the criticism directed against the universities; at any rate they have not been subjected to large-scale reforms. At a time when universities have seen their enrollment multiply (by more than 400 percent since 1960), the more prestigious *grandes écoles* have hardly increased the number of students admitted upon strict entrance examinations.[26]

For more than a century the best of the *grandes écoles* have been the training ground of highly specialized elites. The schools prepare for careers in engineering of various kinds, in business management, and in the top ranks of the civil service. Their different recruitment of students and of teaching staffs as well as their teaching methods reflects on the outlook and even on the temperament of many of their graduates. In contrast to university graduates, virtually all graduates of the *grandes écoles* are immediately placed and often assume positions of great responsibility.[27]

SOCIALIZATION AND COMMUNICATION

The mass media of modern society do not necessarily displace other channels; rather, they link existing networks and frequently transform their product. In a country such as France, the political effectiveness of the mass media is often determined by the way in which the people appraise the integrity of the instrument, whether they believe that it serves or disturbs the functioning of the political system.

In the past, business firms, tycoons, political parties, and governments (both French and foreign) have habitually backed major newspapers. Today, the press operates under the same conditions as it does in other Western democracies, except that for the daily press revenue from advertising remains comparatively low. Most newspapers and magazines are owned by business enterprises, many of them conglomerates that extend into fields other than periodical publications.

In spite of a growth in population, the circulation of daily newspapers in France has been declining since the war. The decline in readership, a common phenomenon in most Western democracies, is due, among other factors, to competition from other media such as television and radio. It has been accompanied by a decline in the number of newspapers.

By the 1970s television had replaced all other media as a primary source of political information, and to a greater extent in France than in Germany, Britain, or the United States.[28] At the approach of the 1988 presidential elections, only 37 percent of the respondents in a public opinion poll believed that the daily press would influence their choice, against 62 percent (up from 46 percent in 1981) who attributed such a role to television.

Almost all French households now own a radio and television; about 80 percent of the population spend three hours a day in front of the TV. There has been, especially over the last years, a steady increase in current affairs programs. In normal times — that is, with no elections on the horizon — such programs occupy about a third of the total output of all TV channels.

During the Fifth Republic television has increasingly become the primary mediator between political forces and individual citizens, and, as in other countries, it has had an impact on the organization and substance of politics. First, a personality that plays well on television (not just a unique personality such as Charles de Gaulle) has become an essential ingredient of politics. As in other countries, image and spectacle have become important elements of politics. Second, television has helped set the agenda of political issues, by choosing among the great variety of themes, problems, and issues dealt with by political and social forces, and by magnifying them for mass publics. Finally, television has become the arena within which national electoral campaigns take place, largely displacing mass rallies and meetings.

From the end of the war until the government of the left introduced changes in 1982, all broadcasting and television stations that originated programs on French territory were owned by the state and operated by personnel whom the state appointed and remunerated. For the unstable Cabinets of the Fourth Republic, not less than for the forceful presidents of the Fifth, telecommunications were the voice of France and that voice was identified with the government in power.

Beginning in 1981, and by successive steps, the basic system of state monopoly has been dismantled. As a first and quite important step, in 1982 the (socialist!) government introduced legislation authorizing private radio stations to operate in France. The move was an attempt to regularize and regulate more than a thousand pirate radio stations already in existence. Inevitably, this vast network of 1,600 stations is becoming increasingly consolidated — not by the state this time, but by private entrepreneurs who provide programming services, and who in some instances are effectively buying control of a large number of local stations.

The 1982 legislation also reorganized the public television system. It granted new rights of reply to government communications and allotted free time to all political parties during electoral campaigns. During the following years, however, these changes were dwarfed by a process of gradual privatization, begun under the socialists and continued by the conservatives after 1986. Today, only two of the seven French television channels are still publicly controlled.

RECRUITMENT AND STYLE OF ELITES

Mass values are the environment within which government functions, but the value patterns of leading political and administrative decision makers are often quite different from those of ordinary citizens, including those who share their general political orientation. Therefore, we need an analysis of the socialization and recruitment of elites, of their background, of their style of action, and of their values in order to understand how they exercise and maintain power.

Until the Fifth Republic, Parliament provided the nucleus of French decision makers.[29] Besides members of Parliament, elected officers of municipalities or departments, some local party leaders, and a few journalists of national renown were counted among what is known in France as the political class, altogether comprising not more than 15,000 or 20,000 persons. All gravitated toward the halls of the National Assembly or the Senate, the lower and upper houses of Parliament.

Compared with the membership of the British House of Commons, that of the lower house of the French Parliament has always been of more modest social origin. From about 1879 on, professional people (lawyers, doctors and journalists) increasingly dominated the Chamber of Deputies, now called the National Assembly; the vast majority were local notables, trained in law and experienced in local administration.

A substantial change in political recruitment occurred during the Fourth Republic, when for the first time the percentage of self-employed became a minority. The percentage of lawyers was cut in half, and the proportion of blue- and white-collar workers increased to almost 20 percent (which reflected the rise in the electoral strength of the Communist party). The percentage of teachers also continued to grow.[30] Nevertheless, the number of deputies with working-class backgrounds has always been smaller than in the House of Commons and other European parliaments, partly because the syndicalist tradition of the French labor movement frowned on the assumption of parliamentary seats by trade union leaders.

The professional background of today's deputies and the changes that have taken place since the war generally reflect both the waxing and waning strength of the parties at a given election, as well as more general trends to be observed in the parliaments of other democracies. The steady decline in the number of farmers is, of course, in part the consequence of the general decline of the farming population. The steadily diminishing share of blue- and white-collar workers is at least in part to be explained by the professionalization of parliamentary personnel, as well as by the decline of the Communist party in the 1980s.

What is most striking about the professional background of deputies under the Fifth Republic has been the number who come from the public sector: almost half the deputies in the 1980s. The number of top civil servants in the National Assembly has risen constantly since 1958, and the left landslide of 1981 only accentuated this process. Although high civil servants have tended to represent parties of the right, a third of those who sat in the 1988 Assembly were part of the socialist group. Even more important than their number is the political weight that these deputy-bureaucrats carry in Parliament. Some of the civil servants who stand for election to Parliament have previously held positions in the political executive, either as members of the ministerial staffs or as junior ministers. Not surprisingly, in Parliament they are frequently chosen for a post in the Cabinet.

More than in any other Western democracy, the highest ranks of the civil service are the training and recruitment grounds for top positions in both politics and industry. Among the high civil servants, about 2,300 are members of the most important administrative agencies, the *grands corps*, from which the vast majority

of the roughly 500 administrators engaged in political decision making are drawn.[31]

The recruitment base of the highest levels of the civil service has been and remains extremely narrow. The knowledge and mentality required to pass the various examinations have given clear advantages to the children of senior civil servants. As a result, the ranking bureaucracy has formed something approaching a hereditary class.[32]

Several important attempts have been made to develop a system of more open recruitment into the higher civil service, but all of them have been only marginally successful.

The Ecole Nationale d'Administration (ENA) and the École Polytechnique, together with the other *grandes écoles*, (see p. 201), play an essential role in the recruitment of administrative, political, and business elites. Virtually all the members of the most important *grands corps* (the most important administrative agencies mentioned above) are recruited directly from the graduating classes of the ENA and the Polytechnique (most of whose graduates have also attended other *grandes écoles*). What differentiates the members of the *grands corps* from other ranking administrators is their general competence and mobility. At any one time as many as two-thirds of the members of one of these *corps* might be on detached service or on special missions to other administrative agencies or special assignments.

But they might be, and frequently are, engaged in politics, either as parliamentarians or as members of the executive: eight of the eleven prime ministers who have served since 1959 have been members of a *grand corps* who attended a *grande école*, and the percentage of ministers in any given government who are members of one of the *grand corps* has varied between 10 and 60 percent.[33] Thus, the *grande école–grands corps* system, with its small number of members, has produced, and continues to produce, a remarkable proportion of the country's political elite.

The same system has also become increasingly important for recruitment of high business executives. Movement from the public sector to the private sector (*pantouflage*—one puts on the "soft slippers" of jobs outside the civil service) is facilitated by the fact that members of the *grands corps* can go on leave for years, while they retain their seniority and pension rights, as well as the right to return to their job. (Few who leave do in fact return.)

Thus, the relationship between the *grandes écoles*

and the *grands corps*, on one hand, and politics and business, on the other, is the structure of a powerful elite system that the changes of government in the 1980s did not touch. While this system is hardly monolithic politically, the narrowness of recruitment does contribute to a similarity of style as well as to some similar value orientations.

INTEREST GROUPS

The Expression of Interests

Political participation in France has been generally structured by organized groups and political parties, and, as in many other European countries, the organization of political life has been largely defined within the historical cleavages of class and religious traditions that we analyzed above. Interest groups have, therefore, frequently shared ideological roots and commitments with political parties, with which they have occasionally had organizational connections.

Actual memberships in almost all groups organized to defend the interests of a specific economic or social sector have varied considerably over time by sector, but they are generally much smaller than comparable groups in other industrialized countries. In the late 1980s no more than 13 percent of potential membership belonged to trade unions, and about 50 percent of French farmers and approximately 75 percent of large industrial enterprises had joined their respective organizations.[34] There never has been a steady, if slow, progression of membership. Many of the important groups have experienced a mass influx of new members at dramatic moments in the country's social or political history. But as soon as conditions become normal, "normal" individualism reasserts itself and leaves many associations with too small a membership to justify their claims of representativeness. The treasuries of groups are often so depleted that they are unable to employ a competent staff. The modern interest group official is a fairly recent phenomenon to be found only in certain sectors of the group system, such as business associations.

Interest groups are also weakened by ideological division. Many of the same groups that in other systems defend the interests of workers, farmers, veterans, schoolchildren, and consumers are divided in France by ideological preferences. The result is that even established French interest groups exhibit a radicalism in action and announced objectives which has become rare in

countries of similar development and is more generally found in an early industrial era. They want to demonstrate their militancy when the plurality of ideologically divided organizations forces each of them to compete for the same clientele in order to establish their representativeness.[35] Organizations suffering from internal conflicts and membership fluctuations try to mobilize potential members and marginal groups by inflated demands and by boldness of action. For groups that lack the means of using the information media, such tactics also become a way to put their case before the public at large. In such a setting, even the defense of purely economic, social, or cultural interests takes on a political color.

The French labor movement is divided into national confederations of differing political sympathies.[36] The anticapitalism of most of them has fed on many sources, among others on Marxist concepts of the class struggle, and on Christian or personalist indignation about the inequities of the existing system. Historical experiences have driven French labor, unlike other European trade unions, to avoid direct organizational ties with political parties.

Membership in the French labor movement has declined steeply in the 1980s, unaffected by the political victory of the left in 1981. Although union membership has been declining in every industrialized country (except Sweden), membership in France is now the lowest. Surveys show that the youngest group of salaried workers has virtually deserted the trade union movement.[37] In fact, unions have been losing members and support at the very time when the trade union movement has become more institutionalized at the workplace and better protected by legislation than at any other time in its history.

French labor has been the sector that has had the most difficulty dealing with ideological fragmentation. One result has been union pluralism (which means that workers may be represented by several union confederations in the same plant), and constant competition among unions for membership and support. Even during periods when the national unions have agreed to act together, animosities at the plant level have sometimes prevented agreement.[38] Moreover, the weakness of union organization at the plant level—which is where most lengthy strikes are called—means that unions are difficult bargaining partners. Union organizations at this level maintain only weak control over the strike weapon. Although union militants have become quite adept at "sensitizing" workers, and in this sense at engendering many of the preconditions for strike action, as well as channeling strike movements once they have begun, they have considerable difficulty in effectively calling strikes and effectively ending them. Thus, unions are highly dependent on the general environment, what they call the social climate, in order to support their positions at the bargaining table. Their ability to represent workers is frequently in question, and their ability to mobilize workers at any given moment is an essential criterion of their representativeness.

Legislation passed by the government of the left in the 1980s was meant to strengthen the union's position at the plant level. By creating an "obligation to negotiate" for management and by protecting the right of expression for workers, the government hoped to stimulate collective negotiations.[39]

In fact, this "Wagner Act" of French labor has brought about some important changes in industrial relations and has stimulated collective negotiations. However, given their increasing weakness, unions have been poorly placed to take advantage of the potential benefits of the legislation, which has refocused French industrial relations on the plant level, without necessarily increasing the effectiveness of unions. Numerous agreements have been reached with local plant committees, while others have reflected the domination of management.

The oldest and by some measures, the largest of the union confederations is the *Confédération Générale du Travail* (CGT—the General Confederation of Labor). Since the war the CGT has been identified closely with the Communist party: its secretary-general belongs to the Politburo of the party, half of the members of its executive are also prominent party members, and the others have always hewed closely to the party line. Yet by tradition and by its relative effectiveness as the largest labor organization, it has enrolled many noncommunists among its members. Surveys indicate that in recent national elections about half its members have voted noncommunist.

The second strongest labor organization is the *Confédération Française Democratique du Travail* (CFDT). In many ways the CFDT is the most original and the most interesting of all labor movements in Western Europe.[40] An offshoot of a Catholic trade union movement, it promoted a program in the 1970s that called for worker self-management (*autogestion*), many of the ideas of which were integrated into the labor legislation passed in 1982. The leaders of the CFDT see the policy of the confederation as an alternative to the oppositional stance of the CGT, as well as to that of the reformists of the Force Ouvrière, who in principle refuse to share management responsibility. In fact, the CFDT offers itself as a potential partner to "modern" capitalist management. The political sympathies of its members have always been divided, but since the mid-1970s a growing majority of its members have identified with the Socialist party.

The third major labor confederation, *Force Ouvrière* (FO), was formed at the beginning of the cold war in 1948 in reaction to the communist domination of the CGT. It is the only major trade union organization that claims to have gained membership in recent years and to have surpassed the CGT in membership. Although the claims are probably exaggerated, the trend seems to be well founded. It is certainly connected with the steady decline of the Communist party. The FO adheres to a position that is close to the traditions of American trade unionism and has focused on collective bargaining, as a "counterweight" to employers and the state.

Since the end of World War II, French business has been able to keep trade associations and employers' organizations, large and modern as well as many small and traditional firms, within one rather imposing and exceptionally well-staffed confederation, the *Conseil National du Patronat Français* (CNPF). Not that divergent interests, differing economic concepts, and indeed conflicting ideologies have not clashed. Frequently, internal divergences have prevented the national organization from acting forcefully and at times have hampered its representativeness in negotiations with government or trade unions. After the events of 1968 new bylaws strengthened the hand of the national leadership. The employers' organizations weathered the difficult years of the nationalization introduced by the socialists and the restructuring of social legislation and industrial relations without lessening their status as influential interest groups.

Since the CNPF is dominated primarily by big business, shopkeepers and the owners of many small firms feel that they are better defended by more movement-oriented groups than by the streamlined modern lobby that the CNPF has become.[41] The result has been a succession of small business movements and groups that have challenged the more established organizations more or less successfully for some period of time. This gives us some indication of the kind of organizational instability that exists in the business sector as well as other sectors that are fighting for their survival.

The defense of agricultural interests has a long record of internal strife. However, under the Fifth Republic, the Fédération Nationale des Syndicats Agricoles (FNSEA — the National Federation of Agricultural Unions) became the best organized sector and served as the government's instrument for modernizing French agriculture. The rural reform legislation of the 1960s provided for the "collaboration of the professional agricultural organizations." From the outset, this collaboration was offered only to the FNSEA. From this privileged position the federation was able to gain both patronage and control over key institutions through which agriculture was being transformed, and it was able to use these instruments to organize a large proportion of French farmers. The first socialist minister of agriculture, Edith Cresson, challenged this relationship, but the FNSEA was able to mobilize formidable support among farmers which resulted in the minister's resignation and the reestablishment of close collaboration between the government and the federation. Thus, having established its domination over the farming sector with the support of a succession of governments, it was then able to demonstrate its opposition to government policy with the support of the vast majority of a declining number of farmers.

In general, organized interests in France are expressed through an impressive range of different kinds of organizations: from the weak and fragmented trade union movement, to the explosive movements of small business and commerce, to the better organized and well-financed CNPF, to the well-organized FNSEA that strongly influences the development and implementation of agriculture policy. What seems to differentiate France from other industrial countries is neither the organization of interests nor their style of expression, but the range of organization and style.

Means of Access and Styles of Action

In preceding regimes, organized interests found Parliament the most convenient means of access to political power. During the Third and Fourth republics the highly specialized and powerful committees of both houses of Parliament were little more than institutional facades for interest groups. Quite frequently, groups substituted bills of their own design for those submitted by the government.

Among the reasons given in 1958 for reforming and rationalizing Parliament was the desire to reduce the role of organized interests in the legislative process. By and large this has been accomplished, but interest groups have not lost all influence on rule making and policy formation. To be effective, groups now use the channels that the best equipped have long found most rewarding, channels that give them direct access to the administration.

The indispensable collaboration between organized private interests and the state is institutionalized in advisory committees that are attached to most administrative agencies and composed mainly of civil servants and group representatives. When civil servants merely take into account the opinions and documentation presented to them before deciding, the effect is beneficial. But often decision makers defer to group suggestions, so that administrative functions are parceled out to socioeconomic groups. Nonetheless, these tendencies toward privileged access, sometimes called neocorporatist, and prevalent in some other European countries have, with the possible exception of agriculture, remained weak in France. The weak organization of the labor and small business sectors means that organizations in these sectors are unreliable partners.

Organized interests also bring pressure to bear on the political executive. For a long time the ministerial staffs, the circle of personal collaborators who support every French minister, have been an important target. Inasmuch as the present regime has strengthened the position of the political executive, it has also enabled both the prime minister and the president to function more effectively as arbiters between competing claims and to exercise stricter control over many agencies and ministries.

It is not astonishing that some interests have easier access to governmental bureaus than others. An affinity of views between group representatives and public administrators might be based on common outlook, common social origin, or education. The official of an important trade association or of their peak association, the CNPF, who has already sorted out the raw demands of his constituents and submits them in rational fashion, easily gets a more sympathetic hearing in the bureaus than an organization that seeks to defend atomistic interests by mobilizing latent resentment. Since it is now far more advantageous to impress two well-placed administrators than twenty deputies, the impact of the best organized interests, equipped with qualified staff and useful documentation, has undoubtedly increased. Both style and staff carry weight. This also holds true for non-associational interests defended by business firms or some prominent families.

High civil servants tend to distinguish between professional organizations, which they consider serious or dynamic enough to listen to, and interest groups, which should be kept at a distance.[42] The perspectives of interest representatives tend to reflect their own strength, as well as their experience in collaborating with different parts of the state and government. Trade union representatives acknowledge their reliance on the social climate at large (the level of strike activity) to determine their ability to bargain effectively with the state. Representatives of business claim to rely more on contacts with civil servants, compared with those of agriculture who say that they rely more on contacts at the ministerial level.[43]

Some of these realities and perceptions changed after 1981, when the socialists came to power. Farm groups and some business groups turned increasingly to action in the streets to test the social climate and the will of the government, while unions found a more receptive audience in government ministries. In part, this was related to the placement of relatively large numbers of trade unionists in key positions within the ministries. However, after 1984, and especially after the election of a conservative government in 1986, most of the pre–1981 patterns were reaffirmed.

Central to the kind of state interest group collaboration described as neocorporatism is the notion that the state plays a key role in both shaping and defining the legitimacy of the interest group universe, and in establishing the rules by which the collaboration takes place. The French state, at various levels, has strongly influenced the relationship among groups and even their existence in key areas, through official recognition and subsidization. Although representative organizations may exist with or without official recognition, this designation gives them access to consultative bodies, the right to sign collective agreements (especially important in the case of trade unions), and the right to certain forms of subsidies. Therefore, recognition is an important tool that both conservative and socialist governments have used to influence the group universe.

The French state has subsidized interest groups for many years, both indirectly and directly. Trade union organizations were indirectly subsidized by local governments even before the turn of the century by being given access to meeting rooms in labor meeting halls. Since the 1930s the state has required employers to effectively underwrite the time of many union militants by requiring that shop stewards, members of plant committees, and union delegates be given time off to meet their official responsibilities. Officially recognized organizations have also received direct subsidies to carry out programs of education and training, subsidies that basically support the organizations themselves.[44] This money provides a substantial part of the budgets of the poorer interest groups (especially trade unions), many of which would find it difficult to maintain their organizations without it.

Thus, by favoring some groups over others through recognition and subsidization, the role of the state seems to conform to neocorporatist criteria. However, in other ways the corporatist model is less applicable in France than in other European countries. Corporatist policymaking presumes close collaboration between the state administration and a dominant interest group (or coalition of groups) in each major socioeconomic sector (agriculture, labor, and employers). This group (or coalition) should be able to speak with authority for those people it represents and should be capable of making binding commitments on their behalf. What stands out in the French case, as we noted above, is the unevenness of this pattern of corporatist policymaking.

If neocorporatist policymaking tends to be controlled by interest group leaders, we have noted that for interest groups in France, mass action ("social climate"), often poorly controlled by leaders, can be quite important. This is generally true for trade unions but has been periodically true in every sector.

During the years of socialist government, more and more people took to the streets to protest impending legislation or just out of fear for their status: artisans, small businessmen, truckers, doctors, medical students, all of them organized either by old-established or by newly formed interest groups. In quite a few cases the demonstrations led to violence and near-riots. Ironically, the apex of this form of pressure politics was the peaceful march of 1 million who scuttled the planned reforms of the parochial schools.

The same scenario took place under the Chirac government when demonstrations by university and high school students forced the withdrawal of a planned university reform. This time, however, there was no clash of conflicting ideologies and very little influence by any organized group, but rather a spontaneous expression of anxiety about the future. The result was the same. Indeed, it can be argued that group protest has been more effective in France (at least negatively) than in other industrialized countries because it is part of a pattern of group–state relations, in which protests remain limited in scope and intensity, but government recognizes them as a valid expression of interest. Only in this way can we understand why "strong" governments seem to concede so easily to protests by weakly organized groups.

POLITICAL PARTICIPATION AND VOTING

In most democracies, no form of political participation is as extensive as voting. Although France is a unitary state, elections are held with considerable frequency at every territorial level. Councillors are elected for each of more than 36,000 communes in France, for each of 100 departments (counties), and for each of twenty-six regions. Deputies to the National Assembly are elected at least once every five years, and the president of the Republic is elected (or reelected) at least once every seven years. In addition, elections for representatives to the European Parliament have been held in France, as well as every other country in the European Community, every five years since 1979.

The French Electorate

France was the first European country to enfranchise a mass electorate, and France was also the first European country to demonstrate that a mass electorate did not preclude the possibility of authoritarian government. The electoral law of 1848 enfranchised all male citizens over the age of twenty-one, but, within five years, this same mass electorate had ratified Louis Napoleon's coup d'état and his establishment of the Second Empire. Rather than restrict the electorate, Napoleon perfected new modern techniques for manipulating a mass electorate by gerrymandering districts, skillfully using public works as patronage for official candidates, and exerting pressure through the administrative hierarchy.

From the Second Empire to the end of World War II, the size of the electorate remained more or less stable, but suddenly more than doubled, when women twenty-one years of age and older were granted the vote in 1944. After the voting age was lowered to eighteen in 1974, 2.5 million voters were added to the rolls, and by 1988, there were about 40 million voters in France.

Electoral Participation and Abstention

Surprisingly, in both the Third and the Fourth republics general disenchantment with parliamentary institutions never prevented a high turnout at national elections. Since the consolidation of republican institutions in 1885 (and with the one exception of the somewhat abnormal post–World War I selection of 1919), electoral participation never fell to less than 71 percent of registered voters, and in most elections participation was much higher.[45] Constituency interests and an individualized appeal to the voters kept tension and hence interest high.

Beginning with the elections of 1946, the women's vote, doubling the electorate, was bound to have short-term and long-term effects on both voting and the distribution of party support. The two most obvious short-term effects in the early years of the Fourth Republic were the increase of abstention (since a smaller proportion of women voted than men) and a tilt toward the political right. However, by the 1980s, these differences between men and women had disappeared. Abstention levels were about the same, and women showed slightly more preference for the left than men.

Voting participation in elections of the Fifth Republic appears to have undergone a significant change and has fluctuated far more than during previous republics. Abstention has tended to be highest in referendums and European elections, and lowest in presidential contests, with other kinds of elections falling somewhere in between. (See Table 10.1.)

During the 1980s, the normal level of abstention increased substantially. In the 1988 legislative election, an abstention rate of 34.3 percent set a record for any of the French republics. The European elections had always attracted relatively few voters, but in 1989 over half the registered voters stayed home. Finally, the referendum on a new government for New Caledonia, in November 1988, set a new record, with almost 63 percent of the registered voters not voting.

These high and growing levels of abstention, which are such a striking departure from what had come to be regarded as the norm, are not equally distributed among the electorate. They have been growing faster among voters of the left than among voters of the right, and faster in working-class constituencies than in more middle-class constituencies. Rising abstention seems to be linked to a larger phenomenon of change in the party system. Since the late 1970s, there has been a trend of

TABLE 10.1
FRENCH REFERENDUMS (R) AND SECOND BALLOTS OF PRESIDENTIAL ELECTIONS (P), 1958–1988 (VOTING IN METROPOLITAN FRANCE)

Date	Registered voters (millions)	Abstentions (% registered)	"Yes" votes + votes for winning candidate		"No" votes + votes for losing candidate	
			% reg	% cast	% reg	% cast
9/28/58(R)	26.6	15.1	66.4	79.2	17.4	20.7
1/8/61(R)	27.2	23.5	55.9	75.3	18.4	24.7
4/8/62(R)	27.0	24.4	64.9	90.7	6.6	9.3
10/28/62(R)	27.6	22.7	46.4	61.7	28.8	38.2
12/19/65(P)	28.2	15.4	44.8	54.5	37.4	45.5
4/18/69(R)	28.7	19.4	36.7	46.7	41.6	53.2
6/15/69(P)	28.8	30.9	37.2	57.5	27.4	42.4
4/23/72(R)	29.1	39.5	36.1	67.7	17.2	32.3
5/19/74(P)	29.8	12.1	43.9	50.7	42.8	49.3
5/10/81(P)	35.5	13.6	43.8	52.2	40.1	47.8
5/8/88(P)	38.2	15.9	43.8	54.0	37.3	46.0
11/6/88(R)	37.8	63.0	26.1	80.0	6.5	20.0

declining confidence by voters in all political parties, some of which is expressed through growing abstention rates among voters who formerly voted for both right and left. Abstention from voting is one aspect of the major structural change that the French party system is undergoing.[46]

As in other countries, age, social class, and education were and remain important factors in determining the degree of electoral participation, both registration and voting. The least educated, the lowest income groups, and the youngest and oldest age groups vote less frequently.

Voting in Parliamentary Elections: Voting, Parties, and Electoral Systems

Throughout the Third and Fourth republics, with the exception of a short interlude between 1945 and 1947 when a modern party system seemed to be in the making, the French voters looked on representatives in Parliament as personal "ambassadors" in Paris. Through the vote the citizen entrusted the deputy with the defense of constituency interest, caring little as to how a coherent national policy could emerge when the cleavages of society were faithfully reproduced in Parliament.

In other Western parliamentary systems structured and disciplined parties emerged along with a mass electorate and modified the earlier system of representation. Binding instructions from party or parliamentary groups leave the representatives little room for independent decisions based on constituency considerations, but instead determine the course of action for government or opposition. In the United States, where the parties wield far less power to discipline, constituency considerations are far more important in the decision-making process of Congress, but the presidential elections permit the electorate to influence the general orientation of government by deciding who should govern and who should be replaced at the helm of the government. In the French republics of the past, there were neither disciplined parties nor popular elections of the executive.

This lack explains the traditional ambivalence of the French voter toward the parliamentary system. As guardians of constituency interests, deputies and senators still commanded respect. But when the deputies engaged in what de Gaulle called the "games, poisons and delights" of the system — when they made and unmade governments, seemingly without regard for the popular verdict in the preceding election — popular contempt engulfed both the representatives and the system.

Since the early days of the Third Republic, France has experimented with a great number of electoral systems and devices without obtaining more satisfactory results. The increased stability of the Fifth Republic cannot be attributed to the method of electing National Assembly deputies, for the system is essentially the same one used during the most troubled years of the Third Republic: As in the United States, rather small electoral districts (almost 600 of them in continental France) are represented by a single deputy. On the first election day only those candidates are elected who obtain a majority of all votes cast; this is a relatively rare occurrence because of the abundance of candidates. In runoff elections the choice is narrowed to the two or three top candidates, and a plurality is sufficient for election.

A well-known effect of this electoral system is the advantage which the leading party reaps in the runoff election: It usually ends up with a larger number of seats than is justified by its share in the popular vote. As a result, the electoral system, from 1962 on, has encouraged political parties to reach electoral agreements in order to maximize their chances of runoff victories. For reasons of political tactics (to be explained below) the Socialist party shifted to a modified form of proportional representation shortly before the election of 1986. The new conservative majority returned promptly to the older system that had served it so well in so many elections.

Voting in Referendums and Presidential Elections

As we have seen, French traditions of representative government frowned on any direct appeals to the electorate, mainly because the two Napoleons had used the referendum to establish or extend their powers. After the liberation from the Nazis, General de Gaulle held the reins of government and showed an inclination to obtain legitimacy for a new constitution by consulting the people directly.

Nonetheless, the 1958 constitution of the Fifth Republic made only modest departures from the classic representative model. Although the constitution was submitted to the electorate for approval, the direct appeal to the voters that it permitted under carefully prescribed conditions was hedged by parliamentary con-

trols. Between 1958 and 1972 the French electorate voted six times on a referendum, several of which transformed political institutions. Actually, all the referendums organized by de Gaulle should be qualified as plebiscites rather than referendums. A referendum, in the American states and the Swiss cantons, is an invitation to the voters to approve or disapprove a legislative or constitutional measure. A plebiscite usually requires voters to approve or reject an established policy, in circumstances such that a return to the prior system is either impossible or can be obtained only at an exorbitant price.

In 1958 a vote against the new constitution might have involved the country in a civil war, which it had narrowly escaped a few months earlier. The two following referendums ambiguously endorsed the peace settlement of the Algerian War, successfully isolating the rebellious diehards who threatened order and prosperity. Only six months after the second referendum on peace in Algeria, General de Gaulle asked the electorate to endorse a constitutional amendment of great significance: to elect the president of the republic by direct popular suffrage. Since then public opinion polls have revealed that both popular election of the president and consultation of the electorate by referendum on important issues are widely approved.

Favorable attitudes toward the referendum and the popular election of the president did not prevent the electorate from voting down, in 1969, another proposal submitted by de Gaulle, thereby causing his resignation. The legislation would have reformed the Senate and given new power to regional government. Because he wished his leadership affirmed by another plebiscite, de Gaulle declared in the midst of the campaign that he would resign if there was not a majority of yes votes. But the electorate judged the proposals on their merits. Nothing in the constitution compelled de Gaulle to resign, but his highly personal concept of his role, no longer accepted by a majority of the electorate, made his resignation inevitable.

Since 1969 there have been only two referendums. De Gaulle's successor Georges Pompidou called for a referendum only once and without the dramatic appeal with which de Gaulle had launched his plebiscites. In 1972 he obtained a plurality of votes for admission of Great Britain to the Common Market; but almost 40 percent of the eligible voters abstained. (For the results of referendums and presidential elections between 1958 and 1988, see Table 10.1.) During the presidency of Valéry Giscard d'Estaing not a single referendum was held.

Upon assuming the presidency, François Mitterrand declared that the only form of popular consultation he found suitable was the method used by the Swiss (and he could have said, the American states) to bring important questions of public concern before the electorate. In 1984, when the socialist government was in difficulties over the proposed private school legislation that we have already discussed, Mitterrand did indeed announce he would settle the conflict by an appeal to the electorate, which should decide on an appropriate reform bill. But such a procedure would first have required an amendment to the constitution enlarging the possibilities for calling a referendum. When the Senate balked at such a change and when it turned out that the electorate was at best indifferent to the entire proposal, the plan for a referendum was abandoned.

The only referendum during the Mitterrand period, in 1988, dealt with approval for an accord between warring parties on the future of New Caledonia; the referendum had been a condition of the agreement. Sixty-three percent of the voters stayed home. Therefore, although 80 percent of those who voted approved the accord, they represented only 26 percent of the electorate.

Therefore, it seems that the usefulness of the referendum as a tool of executive authority was limited to the Gaullist experience, and its usefulness as a tool for passing policy is limited by constitutional restrictions. By the 1980s the referendum as a form of public participation was still regarded favorably by 76 percent of the electorate. It ranked just behind the popularly elected presidency and the Constitutional Council, among the most highly approved institutional innovations of the Fifth Republic. Yet voters are obviously not inclined to cast their ballots in referendums on foregone conclusions (1972) or on questions that deal with remote problems (1988).

Whatever the future use of the referendum, at present the presidential elections by direct popular suffrage are for French voters the most important expressions of the "general will."

Ever since the presidential elections of 1965, it had become evident that French voters derived great satisfaction from knowing that, unlike past parliamentary elections, national and not parochial alignments

were at stake, and that they were invited to pronounce themselves effectively on such issues. The traditional and once deeply rooted attitude that the only useful vote was against the government no longer made sense when almost everybody knew that the task was to elect an executive endowed with strong powers for seven years. Accordingly, turnout in presidential elections has been the highest of all elections. The one exception, the Pompidou election in 1969, when abstentions reached 31 percent, was due not to indifference but to the abstention of communist voters obeying a directive from the leadership.

The nomination procedures for presidential candidates reflect de Gaulle's dislike for giving any role to political parties and make it very easy to put a candidate on the first ballot, even easier than on the presidential primaries in the United States. So far, however, no presidential candidate, not even de Gaulle in 1965, has obtained the absolute majority needed to ensure election on the first ballot. In runoffs, held two weeks after the first ballot, only the two most successful candidates face each other. All serious candidates have been backed by a party or a coalition of parties, the provisions of the law notwithstanding. The French understood soon what the citizens of the United States learned during the seedtime of their republic: It is impossible to mount a national political campaign without the support, skill, and experience of a political party.

If all the presidential campaigns have fascinated French voters and foreign observers, it is not only due to the novelty of a nationwide competition in a country accustomed to small constituencies and parochial contests. Style and content of campaign oratory have generally been of high quality. Because the formal campaigns are short and concentrated, radio, television, and newspapers are able to grant candidates, commentators, and forecasters considerable time and space. The televised duels between Valéry Giscard d'Estaing and François Mitterrand in May 1974 and in 1981 and between Mitterrand and Chirac in 1988, patterned after debates between presidential candidates in the United States but of far higher quality, were viewed by at least 50 percent of the population.

In addition to use of the mass media, impressive mass meetings were held throughout the country, attended mostly, but not exclusively, by young voters. Campaign literature, issued by hastily improvised headquarters, was abundant. Any direct election of a chief executive must personalize issues, and for this very reason it was enjoyed by the French voters.

Informal campaigns, however, are long and arduous. For example, later in this chapter we will see that turmoil and conflict have surrounded the designation of candidates within each of the major political parties since the 1988 elections. The fixed terms of the French presidency mean that, unless the president dies or resigns, there are no "snap" elections for the chief executive as there are from time to time in Britain and Germany. As a result, even in the absence of primaries, the informal campaign begins to get quite intense a full year to two years before the election. The long term in office can give even an unpopular president (as Mitterrand was just two years before 1988) a great deal of time to remake his image, as Mitterrand did between 1986 and 1988.

Just as in the United States, social coalitions that produce presidents are different from those that produce majorities in the legislature. For example, what seems to distinguish the voters who voted for Mitterrand in the first round of the presidential elections in 1988 from those who voted for the socialists in the first round of the legislative elections a month later is that a higher percentage of those who think of themselves as being of the left (80 percent versus 71 percent), and of people "without religion" (54 versus 41 percent) voted socialist than voted for Mitterrand. Although they were ideologically more committed to the left, the socialist voters came from higher income groups, had higher status jobs, and were generally younger than the Mitterrand voters. What this means is that presidential candidate Mitterrand must appeal to a broader audience than party leader Mitterrand did before he was president. In fact, Mitterrand's success in establishing a political distance between his socialist origins and his presidential position in the 1980s explains a great deal about his political success in 1988. He is the first president in the history of the Fifth Republic to have been elected twice in popular elections.

The process of coalition building around presidential elections has probably been the key element in political party consolidation and in the development of party coalitions. The prize of the presidency has become so significant, as we will see, that it has preoccupied the parties of both the right and the left since the 1960s and has influenced their organization , their tactics, and their relations with one another.

POLITICAL PARTIES

The Traditional Party System

Some analysts of election data see a chronic and seemingly unalterable division of the French into two large political families, each motivated by a different mood or temperament and usually classified as the right and the left. If we view elections from this perspective, political alignments have remained surprisingly stable over long periods of history. As late as 1962, the opposition to de Gaulle was strongest where for more than a century republican traditions had a solid foundation. The alignments in the presidential contest of 1974 and the parliamentary elections of 1978 mirrored the same divisions. Soon thereafter, however, the left's inroads into formerly conservative strongholds had changed the traditional distribution of votes.

The electoral systems of the Third and Fifth republics apparently favored a simplification of political alignments. In most constituencies runoff elections result in the confrontation of two candidates, each more or less representing one of the camps. A simple and stable division could have resulted long ago in a pattern of two parties or coalitions alternating in having power and being in opposition, and hence giving valid expression to the voters' options. Why has this not occurred?

Except for the Socialists and the Communists, French party organizations have mostly remained as skeletal as the parties were in other countries at the time of their nineteenth-century beginnings. French parties developed in a mainly preindustrial and preurban environment, catering at first to upper middle-class and later to middle-class elements. Their foremost and sometimes only function was to provide an organizational framework for selecting and electing candidates for local, departmental, and national offices. Party organization tended to be both fragmentary at the national level, and local in orientation below the national level, with only modest linkage between the two levels.

Slow and irregular industrialization hampered the formation of a disciplined working-class party that would have challenged the bourgeois parties to overhaul their structures. The electoral system and a powerful upper house of Parliament, with its heavy overrepresentation of the rural population, kept the workers in a position of electoral inferiority.

French parties that have represented the majority of the electorate throughout long periods were internally created; that is, they gradually emerged from groups inside the legislature. Political organization at the local constituency level aimed mainly at assuring election or reelection of members belonging to various legislative blocs or factions in Parliament.

An internally created party is almost always less disciplined and ideologically less coherent than one that has begun outside the legislature. During election campaigns the candidates of legislative parties could expect little financial support from the organization. Between elections, those representing the traditional party formations were not responsive to any party directives coming from outside Parliament. Even within a parliamentary group or faction the formal institution of a whip, who maintains party discipline, was unknown. In most cases representatives voted solely in accordance with the commands of "career, conscience, and constituency."[47]

This form of representation and party organization survived largely because voters preferred it. An electorate that distrusts authority and wants representation to protect it against arbitrary government is likely to be suspicious of parties organized for political reform. For all their antagonism, the republican and antirepublican traditions had one thing in common: their aversion to well-established and strongly organized parties. Party membership has always been low, except during short and dramatic situations. As late as the 1960s no more than 2 percent of registered voters were known to be party members; in other European democracies, particularly Great Britain and Germany, some parties have a following of more than a million members.

Organizational weakness contributed to the endurance of a multiparty system. But the primary cause of such division has been past conflicts over interests and values, many of them dimly remembered except for the resentments they caused, which have persisted. Historical traditions have determined whether constituencies are regularly on the right or the left of the political spectrum.

The endurance of a weak multiparty system, in turn, fed into the abstract and ideological style of French politics. To avoid the suggestion that they represented no more than limited interests or personalities, these weak parties phrased even the narrowest political issues in lofty ideological terms.

The costs of the French multiparty system were especially high during the Third and Fourth republics. Parliamentary majorities consisted to a large extent of temporary coalitions whose cohesion or disruption depended on whatever problem was under consideration. As different problems arose, governments toppled or were condemned to immobility.

Neither the right nor the left could govern by itself for any length of time, because both lacked a permanent majority and included extreme groups that contested the legitimacy of the political order. As a normal consequence of this party system, an unstable center coalition was in control of the government most of the time, no matter what the outcome of the preceding elections. Between 1789 and the advent of the Fifth Republic, republican France was ruled by governments of the center for all but thirty years. In a two- or three-party system, major parties normally move toward the political center in order to gain stability and cohesion. But where extreme party plurality prevails, the center is a "morass" of political factions instead of a political force. In France, centrist coalitions were an effective, if limited, means of maintaining a regime, but an ineffective means of developing coherent policy.

In 1958 the problems introduced by the Algerian War and decolonization and by France's entrance into the Common Market culminated in a major political crisis that the party system lacked the resilience to resolve.

The new republic created a new political framework that had a major, if gradual and mostly unforeseen, influence on all parties and on their relationships to each other. The emerging party system, in turn, had an important impact on the functioning of the institutions of the system.

Present-Day Parties:[48] The Right and Center

THE RALLY FOR THE REPUBLIC (RPR) The RPR is a direct lineal descendant of the Gaullist party, thrown hastily together after de Gaulle's return to power in 1958. Only weeks after its birth, it won more than 20 percent of the vote and almost 40 percent of the seats in the first Parliament of the new republic. (See Table 10.2.)

For the next ten years the Gaullists increased their share of the vote in each parliamentary election, until in the first ballot of the landslide elections of 1968 they won over 37 percent of the votes cast, enabling Gaullist deputies alone to hold a majority in the National Assembly — a record never until then attained under a republican regime in France.

TABLE 10.2
FIRST BALLOT OF FRENCH PARLIAMENTARY ELECTIONS IN THE FIFTH REPUBLIC AND SEATS WON IN THE NATIONAL ASSEMBLY IN BOTH BALLOTS[a] (VOTING IN METROPOLIAN FRANCE)

Party	1958 % of votes cast	1958 Seats in Parliament	1962 % of votes cast	1962 Seats in Parliament	1967 % of votes cast	1967 Seats in Parliament	1968 % of votes cast	1968 Seats in Parliament	1973 % of votes cast	1973 Seats in Parliament	1978 % of votes cast	1978 Seats in Parliament	1981 % of votes cast	1981 Seats in Parliament	1986[a] % of votes cast	1986[a] Seats in Parliament	1988 % of votes cast	1988 Seats in Parliament
Registered voters (in millions)	27.24		27.53		28.3		28.3		29.9		34.4		35.54		36.61		37.95	
Percentage of abstentions	22.9		31.3		19.1		19.9		18.7		16.6		29.13		21.5		34.3	
Communists (PC)	19.1	10	21.8	41	22.5	73	20.0	34	21.2	73	20.5	86	16.2	44	9.7	35	11.3	27
Socialists (PS)	15.5	47	12.5	66	19.0	121	16.5	57	18.9	89	22.6	107	37.6	267	31.6	208	34.8	274
Left-Radicals	—	—	—	—	—	—	—	—	1.5	12	2.1	10	—	14	.25	2	1.1	2
Radicals	7.3	33	7.8	39	}	}	}	}	—	—	—	—	—	—	—	—	—	—
Center outside government majority	22.1	118	9.6	—	12.6	41	10.3	33	12.4	31	—	—	—	—	—	—	—	—
MRP	11.6	64	9.1	55	—	—	—	—	—	—	—	—	—	—	—	—	—	—
UDF (RI and other centrists in government majority)	—	—	4.4	36	}	42	}	61	10.6	77	21.4	119	19.2	63	}	129	18.5	130
Gaullists	17.6	212	32.0	233	37.7	200	43.65	293	23.9	184	22.5	155	20.8	87	42	145	19.2	128
National Front	—	—	—	—	—	—	—	—	—	—	—	—	—	—	9.9	35	9.8	1
Others	6.8	0	2.8	—	8.2	10	9.5	—	11.5	24	10.9	14	6.2	16	6.6	23	5.3	15

[a] The 1986 election was by proportional representation.

Sources: 1986——Les Elections législatives du mars 1986 (Paris: Le Monde/Supplément aux dossiers et documents du Monde, 1986); 1988——Les Elections législative du 5 juin et 12 juin 1988 (Paris: Le Monde/Supplément aux dossiers et documents du Monde, 1988).

De Gaulle himself, preferring the methods of direct democracy, had little use for any party including his own.[49] But while he was still de Gaulle's prime minister, Georges Pompidou saw the need for a better organized party if future elections were to be won and an orderly succession of the charismatic leader was to ensure a Gaullism *sans* de Gaulle. New bylaws gave muscle to the party organization at all levels and from not more than 24,000 in 1959, claimed party membership increased to almost 200,000 by 1972.[50] While leaders tended to be drawn from the administrative elite, members were generally lower middle class and distrusted the "technocrats in Paris." The role of the party's membership and of its activists remained generally limited to appearing at mass meetings and to assisting in propaganda efforts at election time. After de Gaulle's departure in 1969, however, electoral support for the party began to decline, and by the late 1970s the Gaullists were no longer the dominant party of the Fifth Republic. Nor did they attract even a majority among the voters of the right. The structure of party support also changed: it lost a quarter of its vote, but its working-class vote (blue- and white-collar workers) fell by a third.

There had been no need for a party program or even platform as long as de Gaulle was the leader. When the leader's mantle fell on different shoulders, the identification of governmental policy and the party's objectives continued in much the same way. However, by the 1973 legislative elections, pressure generated by the Common Program of the Left, by the aggressive program of the reformist center, and by indications in the polls that voters were unresponsive to the usual Gaullist slogans, induced the Gaullists to state their own objectives in a more programmatic way. As a result, they published a detailed program for government for the first time in their brief history.

As long as both the presidency and the premiership were in Gaullist hands (from 1958 to 1974) the predominance of the party in the political and administrative life of the country was assured. With the election of Valéry Giscard d'Estaing, never a Gaullist, to the presidency in 1974 and with the forced resignation in 1976 of Gaullist Jacques Chirac from the post of prime minister, the power of the Gaullist movement seemed seriously threatened. Its members no longer held any important ministerial posts. Polls revealed that voters' sympathies had fallen to between 13 and 17 percent, which augured defeat in the next elections.

The decline of the party was turned around by the energy of Chirac, whose career had been typical of the young generation of French political leaders. A graduate of the ENA, he entered on a political rather than a bureaucratic career. He was elected to Parliament at thirty-four years of age and had occupied important Cabinet posts under Pompidou. After the elections of 1974 he transformed the old Gaullist party into the Rally for the Republic. In the important election to the position of mayor of Paris the new-old party was able to ensure Chirac's election against a candidate supported by Giscard. Only a year after its reorganization the party claimed to outrank the communists, not only by its membership but also by the solidity of its nationwide organization. The leadership was thoroughly renewed and mostly handpicked by the Rally's president, Chirac.

Enmity between the two leaders of the right, Giscard and Chirac, contributed to their defeat in 1981. Chirac had entered the first ballot of the presidential election but obtained a mere 18 percent of the votes. In language lacking conviction he asked his voters to line up behind Giscard, whom the RPR had bitterly criticized in the preceding campaign. At least one-fourth of his voters ignored Chirac's appeal. These events might have sealed Giscard's defeat, in turn aggravating the rift among the parties of the right during the ensuing years of conservative disarray. In the parliamentary elections of 1981 the RPR lost heavily, though it remained the second strongest party.

By the 1980s, the RPR was quite different from its Gaullist predecessors. It was a solidly organized mass party: its claimed membership in 1986 was 850,000 (although better scholarly estimates were about 330,000).[51] Its predecessors had furnished the model for what had been described as a novel form of political organization: the "catch-all party" that appeals to a broad coalition of groups and classes. Although Chirac frequently invokes Gaullism as his inspiration, the RPR no longer has the characteristics of a catch-all party. Its appeal is directed quite clearly to a more restricted, well-defined constituency of the right that had emerged in the 1970s. In 1988 the RPR electorate, among the three parties of the right, was the closest to the classic conservative clientele: its electorate overrepresented older, wealthier voters, as well as farmers (see Table 10.3); its voters were most likely to define themselves as being on the "right," were most antileft, were most positive toward business and parochial schools, were most likely to vote for personality rather than ideas, and were least supportive of a woman's right to abortion.[52]

TABLE 10.3
SOCIOLOGICAL ANALYSIS OF THE ELECTORATE IN THE FIRST BALLOT, PRESIDENTIAL ELECTIONS OF 1988 (PERCENT OF CATEGORY)

	PCF (Lajoinie)	PS/MRG (Mitterrand)	UDF (Barre)	RPR (Chirac)	FN (LePen)	Misc.
Sex						
Men	7	32	15	20	18	8
Women	6	36	18	20	11	9
Age						
18–24	9	35	17	14	16	9
25–34	7	38	15	11	17	12
35–49	8	29	16	20	17	10
50–64	5	35	19	24	11	6
65+	7	33	15	29	12	4
Occupation						
Farmers & agricultural workers	1	19	20	40	13	7
Shopkeepers, craftsmen, and business	2	19	17	29	27	6
Executives, professionals, and intellectuals	3	19	22	24	19	13
Middle management and white collar	8	39	15	13	13	12
Workers	12	42	9	9	19	9
Inactive	7	34	18	23	12	6
Religion						
Practicing Catholic	0	18	31	38	7	6
Nonpracticing Catholic	6	39	14	16	17	14
No religion	19	41	8	9	9	14

Source: SOFRES, *Les Elections du printemps 1988.*

As party leader and presidential candidate in 1981, Chirac did not show any of the earlier concerns of Gaullism for the role of the state in modernizing the economy and society; his campaign for the presidency was clearly addressed to those who feared change. Opposition to big government, to budget deficits, and to bureaucracy were the main topics of a colorful campaign carried to big audiences.

As prime minister between 1986 and 1988, Chirac presided over a coalition government of the right that dubbed itself neoliberal and that privatized enterprises that had been nationalized under the previous government of the left, as well as banks and television channels that had been state owned for many years. Much of this was quite different from the policies de Gaulle had pursued immediately after the war and later as president of the Republic. A study that compared RPR activists in 1978 and 1984 revealed that the movement of the party toward neoliberalism corresponded to the orientation of its activists.

As mentioned before, the party's electoral record had become quite mediocre. Between 1973 and 1988 it declined from one election to the other, both in the number of votes and in seats in Parliament, except for the elections in 1986, when the RPR benefited from popular disenchantment with the socialist record. That victory, which brought to Chirac a short-lived premiership, turned into a new defeat two years later when Mitterrand badly defeated Chirac for the presidency. As a result of the 1988 elections for the National Assembly, the number of seats won by the RPR fell below those held by the Union for French Democracy (UDF) for the first time.

The frustrations of successive electoral defeats have contributed to repeated challenges to the party leadership after the 1988 elections by prominent RPR deputies on both the right and the less conservative wings of the party. The impact of the challenge was solidified in 1990, when the most powerful party factions were allotted seats on the national executive roughly proportional to their support at the congress.

Thus, the RPR is a long way from the party once dominated with a firm hand by Gaullist "barons." Its top leadership is both fractionalized and without clear purpose. The organizing discourse of Gaullism is long gone, and the RPR has not been able to replace it with an ideologically based unity. The situation is aggravated by the fact that the RPR, like the UDF, has not been able to deal effectively with the dilemma posed by the rise of the National Front.

THE UNION FOR FRENCH DEMOCRACY (UDF)

As early as 1971–1972 Giscard d'Estaing and his closest collaborator, Michel Poniatowski, had launched their programmatic slogan: "France wants to be governed from the center." We have seen that France had in fact been so governed during much of the Third and Fourth republics. To prevent the center's exclusion from power in the Gaullist republic had been Giscard's foremost concern.

By origin and nature Giscard's party, the Republican party (PR), has been the typical party, or rather nonparty, of French conservatism. It came into existence in 1962, when Giscard and a few other conservative deputies found it inopportune to heed the injunction of their party to leave the government and to join the opposition because of de Gaulle's strictures against European unity and his referendum on direct elections for the presidency. From that time on the group provided a small complement of the majority in Parliament and furnished some ministers to each of the governments that succeeded each other.

Giscard's election to the presidency in 1974 seemed to offer an opportunity to turn the Republicans into a strong presidential party. By 1978 the Republicans claimed only 90,000 members, but the strength of the party derived from its representatives in Parliament, many of whom moved in and out of Cabinet posts, and from local leaders who occupied fairly important posts in municipal and departmental councils.

With the approach of the parliamentary elections of 1978, a better organization seemed necessary not only because of the threat from the left, but also because the RPR under Chirac had given Gaullism a new elan. The way chosen was the one that parties of the right and

center have always found opportune: a heterogeneous alliance among groups and personalities.

The Union for French Democracy (UDF) included, in addition to Giscard's Republicans, remnants of a Catholic party, the *Centre des Democrates Sociaux* (CDS), and the once militant anti-Catholic Radicals. It also included former socialists who balked at their party's temporary alliance with the communists, as well as extreme rightists. The ideological battles of the past within the center have become meaningless, but the parties that formed the UDF found it inopportune to abandon their own weak organizational structures. To do so would diminish the relative influence of their leaders within the UDF and possibly be detrimental to their positions in local government.

The centrist federation was reasonably successful in determining at election time who would be the best placed conservative candidate and in providing, wherever possible, a counterweight to the better organized RPR. Since 1978 parties combined in the UDF have generally run neck to neck with Chirac's party in popular vote, although until 1988 the Gaullists usually won more seats than the UDF. Both parties combined, however, were incapable of increasing the percentage of their vote beyond 42 percent in the 1980s.

Shortly after the 1988 elections, almost a third of the deputies elected on the UDF label decided to break away and form their own parliamentary group, the UDC. The dissidents, most of whom were affiliated with the CDS, acted out of discouragement with the repeated defeats of the right and out of concern for their survival in the next elections. Moreover, their decision coincided with the socialists', and especially President Mitterrand's, expressed willingness to extend their narrow majority toward the center. In Parliament, the new centrist faction either abstained from voting or supported the socialist government on some key votes. Officially, it remained a member of the opposition, and it continued to participate in the deliberations of the UDF; in fact, the UDC retained considerable flexibility. However, the momentum of this centrist faction was slowed down considerably when their list attracted less than 9 percent of the vote in the elections for the European Parliament in 1989.

In spite of repeated calls for greater unity among the component parties of the right, and within these parties, the reform and dissident movements have weakened voting discipline among all deputies of the opposition. These divisions, to some extent, have resulted from different reactions to the rise of the National Front (FN). They have also contributed to a spreading malaise among voters of the right, who have expressed their sense of protest by voting for the National Front.

THE NATIONAL FRONT Until the 1980s, the *Front National* (FN), founded by Jean–Marie Le Pen in 1972, was one of a number of relatively obscure parties of the far right. In none of the elections prior to 1983 did the National Front attract more than 1 percent of the national vote.

By 1983 the National Front's ability to mobilize an electoral following had improved. Le Pen ran for the city council in a working-class district of Paris with a high number of immigrants and gained 11.5 percent of the vote on the first ballot (compared with 2 percent by the FN list in 1977). In the 1984 elections for the European Parliament, the National Front list headed by Le Pen attracted, to the consternation of the established parties of the right and the left, almost 10 percent of the vote.

In the parliamentary elections of 1986 the FN again won almost 10 percent (about 2.7 million votes) of the total vote (and in metropolitan France, more votes than the communists), and established itself as a substantial political force. Two-thirds of these votes came from voters who had previously voted for established parties of the right, but the remainder came from former left voters (mostly socialists). Profiting from the change to proportional representation in 1986, which Mitterrand had introduced partly in order to divide the right, thirty-five FN deputies entered Parliament. In the first ballot of the presidential elections in 1988, where their candidate clearly had no chance of being elected, 90 percent of those who had voted National Front in 1986 remained loyal to Le Pen. This time 1.7 million additional votes gave the National Front candidate 14.4 percent of the total.

Over the years, the FN vote has changed in important ways. The social composition of the 1988 presidential electorate was considerably more populist than that of 1984, with FN attracting almost 20 percent of the working-class vote compared with 10 percent four years earlier. It was also younger, with 15 percent of the voters between eighteen and twenty-four, compared with 11 percent in 1984. Its sociological makeup became increasingly differentiated from that of the traditional right, at the same time that the ideological identity of its voters, who defined themselves more and more as belonging to the extreme right, moved further to the right.

What most distinguishes the voters for the National Front from those of other parties of the right is their issue orientation. For FN voters the national issues of law and order and immigration are the issues of highest priority, which is not true for voters of any other political party.[53] Voters have been less attracted by Le Pen's anti-Semitic outbursts, but these do not appear to have lost him electoral support.

It is not "immigration" alone against which FN supporters are reacting, since immigration was generally halted in 1974. As immigrants of the 1960s have become the ethnically different groups of the present, reaction to them has grown more intense, and now more political. This political reaction has been fed by a coincidental rise in unemployment in the 1980s, by the reaction against socialist policy between 1981 and 1984, and by a more general loss of confidence in political parties and established political leaders. Thus, the same man, the same party, and the same issues that attracted less than 1 percent of the vote in the 1970s were attracting 10 percent or more in the 1980s.

The National Front has often been compared to the Poujadist shopkeeper movement that attracted 2.5 million votes in the legislative elections of 1956 and then faded from the scene. FN draws its electoral and organizational support from big-city, rather than small-town, France, and its supporters come more from the right than those of Pierre Poujade. Moreover, the National Front has been far more successful than the Poujadist movement in building a strong organizational network.

Support has also been built by Jean–Marie Le Pen's ability to use the media, especially national television, effectively. He projected the image of a straight-talking populist, who "said what everyone else was thinking," who was able to put Parisian intellectuals in their place, and who carefully differentiated himself from other party leaders, "the gang of four."

Because of the abandonment of proportional representation, there is now only one FN deputy in the National Assembly. Nonetheless, there are altogether hundreds of elected representatives on the regional, department, and local levels (as well as in the European Parliament). In 1990 the National Front claimed to have 100,000 members (compared with 30,000 in 1986). Two years after Le Pen attracted 14.4 percent of the vote, polls indicated that 17 percent of respondents would vote FN.

The emergence of the National Front has had an impact on voters of all parties, especially on those who would normally vote for the right. Concern for the issues favored by the FN increased dramatically among all voters in the 1980s, and through the dynamics of party competition, the National Front has forced other political parties to place the very issues high on their political agenda. The established parties of the right have been caught in a serious dilemma. On one hand, they are unwilling to accept the definition of the immigration issue in the racist terms used by the National Front; on the other hand, they have been unable to bring FN voters back to the fold with their own more modest programs. Indeed, as the party became better established, its challenge became more difficult to ignore and more divisive when the right tried to meet it.

The Left

THE SOCIALIST PARTY In comparison with the solid social-democratic parties in other European countries, the French Socialist party (PS) lacked muscle almost since its beginnings in 1905. Slow and uneven industrialization and reluctance to organize have not only clogged the development of labor unions, but also deprived the PS of the base of working-class strength that accrued to other labor parties from their affiliation with a trade union movement.

Unlike the British Labour party, the PS also failed to absorb middle-class radicals, the equivalent of the Liberals in England. Its program, formulated in terms of doctrinaire Marxism, prevented inroads into the electorate of the left-of-center middle-class parties for a long time. The party was never strong enough to assume control of the government by itself. Its weakness reduced it to being at best one of several partners in the unstable coalition governments of the Third and Fourth republics. The role it played in such governments was usually neither conspicuous nor brilliant. Most of the working-class following of the Socialist party was concentrated in a few regions of traditional strength, such as the industrial north and urban agglomeration in the center, but the party had some strongholds elsewhere. It had a large following among the winegrowers of the south, devotees of republican ideals, of anticlericalism, and of producers' cooperatives. The proportion of civil servants, especially teachers, and of people living on

fixed income has at all times been far higher among socialist voters than in the population at large. This support made for a stable but not particularly dynamic following, especially since the young were no longer attracted by the party. In one respect only, albeit an important one, the Socialist party outshone other parties: its positions in local government remained strong, because of experienced personnel and honored traditions.

The party encountered considerable difficulties under the changed conditions in the Fifth Republic. To be condemned to a permanent and increasingly impotent opposition was unappealing. After several false starts, the old party dissolved and a new Socialist party saw the light in the Summer of 1969.

The party's early success in acquiring a new image, in attracting new members, and in reversing its electoral decline came about as a surprise. Incipient public disenchantment with conservative governments and assumption of the socialist leadership by François Mitterrand at the party congress of 1971 combined to bring about this reversal in the party's fortunes. Ten years later it led to victory at the polls. Before he joined the Socialist party Mitterrand had been in public life for twenty-seven years. In the Fourth Republic he had been a deputy for many years, mayor of a small town in the center of France, and a sometimes controversial minister in eleven short-lived Cabinets. In 1958 he was one of the few noncommunists who voted in Parliament against the Gaullist constitution. He opposed General de Gaulle in the presidential election of 1965 with the support of the socialists and the communists.

After he had imposed his leadership in the PS, his most notable achievement was holding together a party that was rent by internal tensions while it was steadily rising in public favor. Mitterrand's own anticapitalism was often strident, yet concern for justice clearly outweighed interest in economic blueprints for a socialist future. But even as late as 1979 the party's annual convention put a "break with capitalism" on its banner. The preamble of the party's program stated, "Because socialists are convinced democrats, they believe that no genuine democracy can exist in a capitalist society. In that sense the Socialist Party is a revolutionary party" —slogans to which the voters who ensured the party's victory in 1981 probably paid little attention.

If Mitterrand strove for a common program with the communists, he did so because only a coalition of the parties on the left offered a believable alternative to the right and center – right governments that had ruled the country since the advent of the Fifth Republic in 1958. But such an alternative was suspect to the voters as long as the communists were stronger and better organized than the PS. Hence, Mitterrand pledged that he would win for the socialists millions of voters who had traditionally voted the communist ticket. Such frankness promoted the very goals that it announced: the growing organizational and electoral strength of the PS. By 1978 the socialists outpolled the communists for the first time since the war.

Compared with the past, the party membership reached respectable heights (about 200,000 by 1981), though it was still not comparable to that of the large labor parties of Great Britain and the continent. In social origin the new membership comes predominantly from the salaried middle classes, the professions, the civil service, and especially the teaching profession. Workers are still represented rather sparsely, particularly in the party's leadership. But the PS did what other European socialist parties were unable to do: it became a pole of attraction to leaders of some of the new social movements that had emerged out of the activism of the late 1960s, among them ecologists and regionalists, as well as leaders of small parties of the noncommunist left.[54]

Socialist victories in municipal and cantonal elections during the 1970s were the first signal that voters' sympathies were shifting from right to left. In both the presidential and the parliamentary elections of 1981 the PS and its leader, Mitterrand, reaped the benefits of their long and patient efforts.

With 37.6 of the popular vote on the first ballot, the socialist electorate extended to the entire country and included groups that traditionally had leaned to the right. Forty-four percent of the working-class voters cast a socialist ballot, as did 46 percent of those under age thirty-four. With the party's leader as president of the republic and a socialist majority in Parliament, the PS found itself in a situation it had never known — and for which it was ill-prepared.

The following years of undivided power were bound to have an impact on the party's image and outlook. The extent of the Socialist party's reforms and the consequences of their partial failure will be discussed below. Disappointment among the party militants was a natural consequence of the socialist government's inability to live up to expectations and electoral promises.

In a party in which factional discussions had always been rampant, the exercise of power led to conflicts on desirable strategies within the government and between party and government. But they did not impair Mitterrand's authority or his ability to impose his decisions on the party leadership.

The years in office between 1981 and 1986 were an intensive, and painful, learning experience for the PS at all its levels. Under pressure from Mitterrand and a succession of socialist governments, the classical socialist ideology, which had become rather empty sloganeering even before 1981, was dismantled. What the German Social Democrats had done by adopting a new program at Bad Godesberg in 1959 the French PS did in the early 1980s by its daily practice. An at least implicit belief that a more just society can and must be achieved by reforms rather than by revolutionary action is now the party's credo.

The defeat of the PS in the parliamentary elections of 1986 turned out to be less catastrophic than expected. Its popular vote declined by a mere 6 percent, allowing it to retain its status of the strongest party. In the legislative elections of 1988 socialist support increased to almost 35 percent, enough to give them a plurality (though not a majority) in the National Assembly and to restore them to government.

Indeed, by most measures, the Socialist party has become what the Gaullists were in the 1960s, a party of government, with broad support among most social groups throughout the country. (See Table 10.3.) In the second round of the presidential elections of 1988, Mitterrand carried seventy-seven of the ninety-six departments of metropolitan France. In the 1980s the socialists have held on to most of their areas of traditional (geographic) strength and have won by making some of their strongest gains in the traditionally conservative areas in the west and east of the country.

Social trends have also favored the left. The decline of religious observance, urbanization, the growth of the salaried middle classes (technicians, middle management, etc.) and of the tertiary sector of the economy, the massive entry of women into the labor market — all these developments tore at the groups that had provided stable strength to the right: farmers, small businesspeople, the traditional bourgeoisie, and the nonemployed housewives. A strong and organized Socialist party emerged in the 1970s, just in time to take advantage of the moment when these trends formed the basis for a shift in voter loyalties, and (as we will see below) to take advantage of the decline of the legitimacy of the Communist party.

The emergence of the PS as a party of government has also exposed its Achilles heel: its organizational divisions. For socialist leaders who have occupied power since 1981, the ideological differences among the various intraparty factions have become relatively meaningless and have deteriorated into personal rivalries. Shorn of ideological pretensions, these rivalries have sharpened as the end of Mitterrand's second term in 1995 draws near and has opened, quite prematurely, the question of his succession.

At the 1990 party congress seven rival factions engaged in a struggle designed mostly to position themselves favorably for the greatest possible influence in the next administration. The public display of acrimony and opportunism was clearly discrediting the PS in public opinion. The cohesion of a party, which was still the strongest in France, appeared as fragile as it had been at the moment of its founding in 1969. Mitterrand was forced to impose a compromise that, at least momentarily, removed the rivalry from the public eye. When, a year later, he removed, in a surprise move, Michel Rocard from the prime minister's office, and replaced him with Edith Cresson, he did so in the hope of improving the party's chances for victory in the parliamentary elections to be held before June 1993.

THE COMMUNISTS   Until the late 1970s the Communist party (the PCF) was a major force in French politics, despite the fact that, except for a short interlude after the war, the party had been excluded since its beginning in 1920 from any participation in the national government. During most of the Fourth Republic it received more electoral support than any other single party (with an average of just over 25 percent of the electorate). During the Fifth Republic, the party remained, until 1978, electorally dominant on the left, although it trailed the Gaullists on the right (see Table 10.2). In addition to its successes in national elections, the party commanded, until the early 1980s, significant strength at the local level. Between 1977 and 1983, communist mayors governed in about 1,500 towns in France, with a total population of about 10 million people.

Over several decades, the party's very existence constantly impinged, nationally as well as locally, on the rules of the political game and thereby on the system itself. This was particularly true for the left, where the

hegemony of the PCF was evident not only in the contest for votes, but also in the political agenda of the left and in the ideological expression of that agenda. Until the late 1970s the communists defined (more or less) what "left" meant, while the socialists debated the acceptability of that definition. For the parties of the right, the hegemony of the PCF provided an issue (anticommunism) around which they could unite and on which they could attack both the socialists and the communists.

Compared with other Communist parties in democratic countries, the French PC began very late to free itself from Stalinist dogmatism and the tutelage of the Soviet Union. What never changed was the structure of the party, the French translation of the Leninist principle of democratic centralism.

The seemingly impressive edifice of the PC and of its numerous organizations of sympathizers was badly shaken after the rejuvenation of the PS under Mitterrand's leadership. Having repudiated the alliance with the socialists which they had signed in 1972 (the Common Program), the PC fielded its leader Georges Marchais as a candidate in the first ballot of the presidential election of 1981 with disastrous results: With only 15 percent of the vote, the party lost one-fourth of its electorate. In the parliamentary elections that followed, the number of its deputies was about halved.

When Mitterrand, in order to forestall communist criticism from the outside, invited four communists to join the first socialist Cabinet, the PC did not dare refuse for fear of being isolated at a moment of triumph for the left. Although they lacked real influence, the communist ministers were involved in policies that soon became unpopular; they resigned three years later. The electorate reacted negatively to whatever policy the PC followed.

It turned out that the defeats that the party had suffered in 1981 were only the beginning of a tailspin of electoral decline.[55] The voters who left the party in 1981, by and large, never came back. In the 1986 elections, the party vote (9.7 percent) was reduced to less than half of what it had been only eight years earlier; in the 1988 legislative elections, the party increased its proportion of the vote by almost 2 percent, but the actual number of votes remained about the same. Far more troubling, every election demonstrated that the stability of its core electorate was largely gone. In the working-class suburbs of Paris, where the PCF was attracting huge majorities as late as the 1970s, its electorate had declined to less than 30 percent, and less than 20 percent for its presidential candidate in 1988. By that time, nationally the PCF attracted not more than 15 percent of the working-class vote and less than 10 percent of the vote of those under twenty-four years of age (see Table 10.3). To win any elections at all, it has grown increasingly dependent on continued (and often difficult) cooperation with the socialists in most localities, as well as the personal popularity of some of its long-established mayors. One half of the twenty-four communist deputies elected in 1988 were mayors.

Loss of party membership went apace with electoral decline. Between 1979 and 1987 the party lost 40 percent of its membership. Although party membership remains large by French standards (perhaps 300,000), its organization has been increasingly divided, ineffective, and challenged by successive waves of dissidence from within.

What has remained stable, amidst the loss of strength and prestige, has been the party's top bureaucracy. Georges Marchais, surrounded by a group of loyal lieutenants, has been party general secretary since 1970. By 1986 surveys revealed that dissident factions within the party were supported by two-thirds of the communist electorate and that there was support for their case in at least fifteen departmental federations of the party. But the repeated efforts to renew the party have at most led to the expulsion or marginalization of the critics and the reconfirmation of the holders of power.

The rapid evolution of *perestroika* and *glasnost* in the Soviet Union, and then the collapse of communist regimes in Eastern Europe, have created an apparently hopeless dilemma for the PCF leadership. The dissidents have now evoked the changing Soviet model in support of change, while the embattled orthodox leaders have insisted on their independence(!) from Moscow.

What does the marginalization of the PCF mean for the French party system? It has healed the division that had enfeebled the left since the split of the Socialist party in 1920, in the wake of the Bolshevik seizure of power in Russia. But a price has been paid: the political representation of the French working class has been weakened. Although the fortunes of the PCF have fallen in inverse relation to the rise of the electoral strength of the PS, the proportion of workers actually voting for both parties combined has declined by 4 percent since the 1970s. In terms of membership, the representation of workers within the PS has always been feeble, com-

pared to their strong representation within the PCF (about half the membership). Moreover, while virtually no workers have risen to the leadership ranks of the PS, the majority of the communist leadership positions of the PCF have always been filled by workers. As a result, almost all the workers ever elected to the French National Assembly have been communists (ten of the eleven deputies from a working-class background elected in 1988). As the PCF has declined, so has the direct representation of workers in Parliament. It is quite clear that a traditional means of social mobility for ambitious workers is now being closed off.

Since the decline of the PCF has been paralleled by a shift of the PS toward the political center, the options of French politics have, in general, moved further to the right. Altogether, the fate of the French Communist party in the 1990s, in the smaller arena of French politics, is a momentous event, no less momentous than the collapse of communism in Eastern Europe.

POLICY PROCESSES
The Executive

As we have seen, the French constitution has a two-headed executive: as in other parliamentary regimes, the prime minister presides over the government but unlike other parliamentary regimes, the president is far from being a figurehead. It was widely predicted that such an arrangement would almost necessarily lead to constitutional crisis. None has come to pass. During the first twenty-eight years of the Fifth Republic, four presidents, for all their differences in outlook and style, and each of the prime ministers who have served under them, left no doubt that the executive had only one head, the president. (see Figure 10.1.)

The exercise of presidential powers in all their fullness was made possible not so much by the constitutional text as by a political fact: Between 1958 and 1986 the president and prime minister derived their legitimacy from the same majority in the electorate — the president by direct popular elections, the prime minister by the support of a majority of deputies in the National Assembly. In 1981 the electorate shifted its allegiance from the right to the left, yet for the ensuing five years president and Parliament were still on the same side of the political divide. The long years of political affinity between the holders of the two offices solidified and amplified presidential powers and shaped constitutional practices in ways that appear to have had a lasting impact even after political conditions changed.

From the very beginning of the Fifth Republic the president not only formally appointed the prime minister proposed to him by Parliament (as the presidents of the previous republics had also done, and as the queen of England does), but he also chose the prime minister and the other Cabinet ministers. In some cases the president also dismissed a prime minister who was clearly enjoying the confidence of a majority in Parliament.

Hence, the rather frequent reshuffling of Cabinet posts and personnel in the Fifth Republic was different from similar happenings in the Third and Fourth republics. In those systems the changes occurred in response to shifts in parliamentary support and frequently in order to forestall, at least for a short time, the government's fall from power. Now the president decides to appoint, move, or dismiss Cabinet officers on the basis of his own appreciation of the worth (or lack of it) of the individual member. This did not mean that presidential considerations were merely technical. They might have been highly political, but they were exclusively his own.

Since all powers proceed from the president, the government headed by the prime minister became essentially an administrative body, despite constitutional stipulations to the contrary. Its chief function is to provide whatever direction or resources are needed to implement the policies conceived by the chief of state. This means primarily that it must develop legislative proposals, and present an executive budget. In many respects the government's position resembles that of the Cabinet in a presidential regime such as the United States, rather than that of a government in a parliamentary system such as Great Britain and the earlier French republics. Weekly meetings of the Cabinet are chaired by the president, and are officially called the Council of Ministers. They are a forum for deliberation and confrontation of different points of view, but remain purely advisory, as they have always been.

The prime minister, in relation to Cabinet colleagues, has always been more than first among equals. Among his many functions was the harnessing of a parliamentary majority for presidential policies, since according to the constitution the government must resign when a majority in Parliament adopts a motion of censure or rejects the governmental program. This provision distinguishes France from a truly presidential regime such as the United States or Mexico.

The relationship between president and prime minister operated quite differently during the period of cohabitation from 1986 to 1988, after the election of a conservative government, while a socialist president was still in office. Without claiming any domain exclusively as his own, the president continued to occupy the foreground in foreign and military affairs, in accordance with his mandate under the constitution. The prime

President Mitterrand likes to relax near his country home a few hours south of Paris. Here, he is accompanied by friends, family and some Cabinet ministers on his annual mountain hike.

minister pursued his government's objectives but avoided interfering with presidential prerogatives, even when delays were involved. In effect, both men were conscious of setting precedents for the future.

In part as a result of the experience of cohabitation, the role of the president after the elections of 1988 was far more detached than it had been before 1986. The socialist prime minister was largely responsible for the main options that were slowly developed for governmental action, with the president setting the limits and the tone. With the appointment of a new prime minister in the spring of 1991, the president once again asserted his prerogative to set government options.

Since the early days of the de Gaulle administration, the office of the chief of state has been organized so as to maximize his ability to initiate, elaborate, and frequently execute policy. In terms of function, the staff at the Elysée Palace, the French White House, composed of a general secretariat and the presidential staff, had become somewhat similar to the Executive Office of the American president. Yet it is much smaller, comprising only forty to fifty persons.

As the president's eyes and ears, his staff members are indispensable for the exercise of presidential powers. They are in constant contact not only with the prime minister's collaborators, but also directly with individual ministries. Through these contacts the president can initiate, impede, interfere, and assure himself that presidential policies are followed.

The prime minister has a parallel network for developing and implementing policy decisions, the most important of which are the so-called interministerial meetings, frequent meetings of high civil servants attached to various ministries. The frequency of these sessions, chaired by a member of the prime minister's personal staff, reflects the growing centralization of administrative and decision-making authority within the office of the prime minister, and the growing importance of the prime minister's policy network in everyday policymaking within the executive.

When the presidential and parliamentary majorities are identical (as was the case between 1962 and 1986), the prime minister is clearly subordinate to the president.[56] Even in this case, however, the president's power is always limited by the fact that he does not control the administrative machinery directly and must work through the prime minister's office and the ministries; and cooperation between the two is essential for effective government. Under cohabitation, the prime minister clearly gains significant authority at the expense of the president. The power to set the political agenda and to command within the executive is largely transferred to the prime minister. But the president retains the power to bargain, based on his prerogatives to make appointments, to sign ordinances, and to participate in decisions on defense and foreign policy.

Since 1988, we can see the outline of yet a third intermediary pattern. As a result of the establishment of a government generally supportive of the president, but without a clear majority in the National Assembly (see Figure 10.2), the president has become increasingly dependent on the prime minister's ability to develop parliamentary majorities for a legislative agenda.

Parliament

The constitution has severely curtailed the powers of Parliament both as a source of legislation and as an organ of control over the executive. The mere fact that both houses of Parliament are now confined to sessions of regulated length (a maximum of six months in every calendar year) has resulted in so much time pressure that effectiveness is impeded.

Despite restrictions on parliamentary activity, the legislative output of the parliaments in the Fifth Republic has been quite respectable. The average of only ninety-eight laws per year enacted during the first thirty years of the Fifth Republic (125 per year during the reform period 1981–1986) was much lower than that during the Fourth Republic. However, it is double the British average for the first thirty-five years after World War II.[57] Although either the government or Parliament may propose bills, almost all legislation is in fact proposed by the government.

The government is effectively in control of proceedings in both houses and can require priority for those bills which it wishes to see adopted (see Figure 10.3). Article 44 empowers the government to force Parliament by the so-called blocked vote to accept a bill in its entirety with only the amendments agreed to by the government. In recent years the blocked vote has been used to maintain discipline within the majority, rather than to impose the will of the executive over a chaotic Parliament. Its use became an index of conflict within the governing party or coalition. After 1986, both the conservative government of Jacques Chirac and the socialist government of Michel Rocard were tempted to use the blocked vote more often and for the same rea-

FIGURE 10.2
POLITICAL REPRESENTATION IN THE NATIONAL ASSEMBLY AFTER THE ELECTION OF 1986 AND 1988

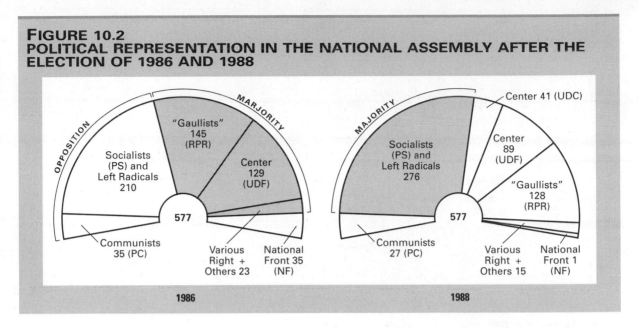

1986

1988

son: to make up for their weak support in the National Assembly.

Article 38 invites Parliament to abandon "for a limited time" its legislative function to the government if the government wishes to act as legislator "for the implementation of its program." Once Parliament has voted a broad enabling law, the government enacts legislation by way of so-called ordinances. Governments of the Fifth Republic made use of this possibility of executive lawmaking twenty-two times between 1958 and 1986, and often for important legislation, sometimes simply to expedite the legislative process. But its use has now been limited by decisions of the Constitutional Council, which requires that the enabling act spell out the limits of executive lawmaking with some precision. During the period of cohabitation, Mitterrand refused to permit the government to rule by ordinances that would have permitted it to avoid parliamentary debate.

Another constitutional provision has given the government a unique tool to ensure parliamentary support among its divided supporters. According to Article 49, section 3, the prime minister may pledge the "government's responsibility" on any bill (or section of a bill) submitted to the National Assembly. In such a case, the bill is automatically "considered as adopted," without further vote, unless the deputies succeed in censuring the government according to the strict requirements discussed earlier (see p. 193). The success of the censure motion would likely result in new elections, but no gov-

ernment has failed to have its legislation adopted under these circumstances during the Fifth Republic.

For many years, little use was made of this provision. But since 1979 various governments have resorted to it with some frequency. Between 1981 and 1986, the governments of the left used it for various reasons of expediency; it permitted them to enact important legislation quickly, without laying bare conflicts within the ranks of the governing majority. Both Chirac and Rocard (1988–1991) resorted to this procedure numerous times in order to overcome the precariousness of their majorities in Parliament. Thus, it appears that, despite the strength of the party system, this method of virtually excluding Parliament from meaningful participation in the legislative process has become a permanent fixture of governance. It has been used for adopting some of the most important pieces of legislation: France's nuclear strike force, nationalization under the socialists, and privatization under the conservatives, as well as annual budgets, military planning laws, social security legislation, economic plans — all have become law in this manner.

Other devices of exercising parliamentary control over the executive have become somewhat more effective over the years. In the 1970s, when earlier tensions started to give way to a new outlook on the role of Parliament, the National Assembly made room for a weekly session devoted to a new kind of question period that is far more like the British (and German) version. Two

FIGURE 10.3
A BILL BECOMES A LAW

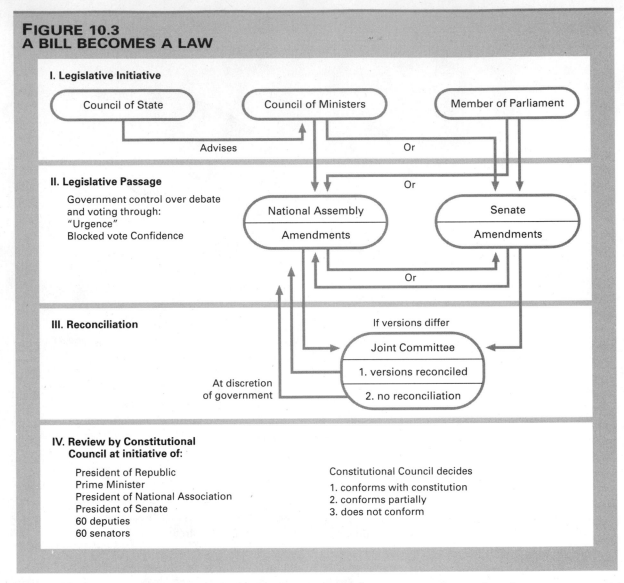

I. Legislative Initiative

Council of State   Council of Ministers   Member of Parliament

Advises   Or

II. Legislative Passage

Government control over debate
and voting through:
"Urgence"
Blocked vote Confidence

Or

National Assembly   Senate

Amendments   Amendments

Or

III. Reconciliation

If versions differ

Joint Committee

1. versions reconciled

2. no reconciliation

At discretion
of government

IV. Review by Constitutional
Council at initiative of:

President of Republic
Prime Minister
President of National Association
President of Senate
60 deputies
60 senators

Constitutional Council decides

1. conforms with constitution
2. conforms partially
3. does not conform

days a week, the party groups select and submit a dozen or more written questions an hour in advance, in rough proportion to membership of each group, and then the relevant minister answers them. Added interest is provided by the presence of television cameras in the chamber (since 1974), which record the dialogue between the government representatives and the deputies.

By using its power to amend, Parliament has vastly expanded its role in the legislative process during the past decade. In an average session the parliamentary committee principally concerned with a bill, together with individual deputies, often moves ten times as many amendments as the government. During the 1980s

amendments averaged more than 5,000 per year, and during the socialist reform period it was double that figure. These increases coincided with a significant extension of the hours devoted to legislative debate each year, which almost doubled compared to the first twenty years of the Fifth Republic.

In the 1980s the government used Parliament not only to win approval for proposed legislation, but also to shape its content, by encouraging parliamentary committees to introduce appropriate amendments. About 80 percent of these amendments were generally adopted in the final legislation. The opposition, in turn, proposed numerous amendments that would never be adopted, but that served to harass or even to obstruct the government. The dramatic increase in the number of amendments moved and the significant increase of those adopted indicate that the governments have all but abandoned their prerogative to declare amendments out of order.[58]

Finally, the role of Parliament has been enhanced by the general support French citizens give their elected deputies. Better organized parties have both added to the deputy's role as part of a group and diminished his or her role as an independent actor, capable of influencing the legislative process. Nevertheless, individual deputies still command a considerable following within their constituencies. French deputies have always had a special place in the hearts of French citizens, and public confidence has always been far stronger in them than in the parties that organize them. Two-thirds of French respondents in the 1980s knew who their deputy was, proportionately far more than those respondents in the United States who claim to know their congressman's name.

Because the electoral college that elects the members of the Senate is composed almost entirely of people selected by small-town mayors, the parties of the center, which are most influential in small towns, have been best represented in the upper house. At a time when the Gaullists held the absolute majority of seats in the National Assembly, their representation in the Senate amounted to not more than 12.7 percent of the total. The UDF still holds a plurality in the Senate, but the RPR has translated its advances at the local level (at the expense of the UDF) into more than about 27 percent of the seats.

Nevertheless, the Senate has not invariably been found on the right of the political spectrum. Its hostility to social and economic change has been balanced by a forthright defense of traditional republican liberties and by a stand against demagogic appeals to latent antiparliamentary feelings.

The Senate, in general, can do little more than delay legislation approved by the government and passed by the National Assembly. There is, however, one constitutional situation in which a majority in the upper house cannot be overruled: any constitutional amendment needs the approval of either a simple or a three-fifths majority of senators (Article 89).

Some legislation of great importance, such as the atomic striking force, the organization of military tribunals in cases involving high treason, and statutes regulating municipal elections and strikes in public services, was enacted in spite of senatorial dissent. Nonetheless, until 1981 relations between the Senate and the National Assembly were relatively harmonious. The real clash with the Senate over legislation came during the years of socialist government between 1981 and 1986, when many key bills were passed over the objections of the Senate. However, bills proposed by the government of the left that dismantled some of the "law and order" measures enacted under de Gaulle, Pompidou, and Giscard were supported by the Senate, and the upper house played a more active role when it modified the comprehensive decentralization statute passed by the socialist majority in the Assembly. Most of the changes were accepted in joint committee.

Nevertheless, criticism of the Senate and proposals for its thorough reform have come from Gaullists and socialists alike. When de Gaulle decided that the time had come for another "revolution from above," his design, incorporated into the referendum proposal of 1969, included a thorough renovation of the upper house, transforming it into a body that would represent major economic and social interests, as well as local governments. The referendum failed, as have subsequent proposals for reforming the Senate.

Checks and Balances

France has no tradition of judicial review. As in other countries with civil law systems, and in Great Britain as well, the sovereignty of Parliament has meant that the legislature has the last word and that a law enacted in constitutionally prescribed forms is not subject to further scrutiny. This principle seemed to be infringed upon when the constitution of 1958 brought forth an institutional novelty, the Constitutional Council (articles 56–62). The council in certain cases must, and in other cases may upon request, examine legislation and decide whether it conforms to the constitution. A legal provision declared unconstitutional may not be promulgated.

Each of the presidents of the two houses of Parliament chooses three of the council's members, and the president of the republic chooses another three for a (nonrenewable) nine-year term. Those who nominate the council's members were until 1974, together with the prime minister, the only ones entitled to apply to the council for constitutional scrutiny. In 1974 an amendment to Article 61 of the constitution made it possible for "sixty deputies or sixty senators" also to submit cases to the Constitutional Council. Since then appeals to the council by the opposition have become a regular feature of the French legislative process.

Whichever side is in opposition, conservative or socialist, routinely refers all major (sometimes minor as well) pieces of legislation to the council. Not all the appeals lead to a declaration of unconstitutionality: the number of successful appeals since 1981 has varied between 40 and 50 percent of all appeals filed. Few decisions declare entire statutes unconstitutional, and those that declare parts of legislation unconstitutional (sometimes trivial parts) effectively invite Parliament to rewrite the text in an acceptable way.

The impact of the Constitutional Council's decisions has been considerable and has modified short-term, and occasionally long-term, objectives of governments. Originally conceived as not more than an auxiliary institution, indeed a helpmate of the executive in its efforts to police parliamentary behavior, the council has assumed in its practice the role of a constitutional court. By doing so, it has placed itself at the juncture of law and politics.

In a landmark decision, rendered in 1971, the council had declared unconstitutional a statute, adopted by a large majority in Parliament, authorizing the prefects to refuse legislation (needed under the Law on Associations of 1901) to any association which in their opinion was likely to engage in illegal activities. To require any advance authorization violated, according to the decision, the freedom of association, one of "the fundamental principles recognized by the laws of the Republic and solemnly reaffirmed in the *preamble* of the Constitution." The invocation of the preamble greatly expanded the scope of constitutional law, since the preamble incorporated in its wording broad "principles of national sovereignty" as well as the "attachment to the Rights of Man," and an extensive Bill of Rights from the Fourth Republic constitution. For introducing judicial review into French constitutional law, the decision has been greeted as the French equivalent of *Marbury v. Madison*.

Some of the Constitutional Council's most important decisions, such as those on the nationalization of private enterprises (under the socialists), on the privatization of parts of the public sector (under the conservatives), or on government control over the media (under both), conform, by and large, to an attitude which in the United States is called judicial restraint. A few can be qualified as "activist," since they directly alter the intent of the law. But, as a nonelected body, the council

has generally avoided interference with the major political choices of the governmental majority. In a period in which alternation of governments has often resulted in sharp policy changes, the council decisions have helped define an emerging consensus. By smoothing out the raw edges of new legislation in judicial language, it has often made changes ultimately more acceptable.

Judicial review has become part of the French legislative process, but in a way that is still quite different from the United States.[59] Access remains limited, since citizens have no right to bring complaints before the council. The Constitutional Council, unlike the Supreme Court, considers legislation *before* it is promulgated. Since 1981, virtually all constitutional challenges have been initiated by legislative petition, a process that does not exist in the United States. A time element precludes the possibility of extensive deliberation: rulings must be made within a month, and in emergency situations, eight days. This is surely speedy justice, but the verdicts cannot be as explanatory as those rendered by constitutional courts in other countries. Dissenting opinions are never made public.

The judicial check on policymaking has enhanced the role of the much older Council of State; in its present form it dates back to 1799. The government now consults this council more extensively on all bills before they are submitted to Parliament, and, as it has always done, on all government decrees and regulations before they are enacted. The council also gives advice on the interpretation of constitutional texts. While its advice is never binding, its prestige is so high that, now more than before, its recommendations are seldom ignored.

Unlike the Constitutional Council, the Council of State provides recourse to individual citizens who have claims against the administration. The judicial section of the Council of State, acting either as a court of appeal or, in more important cases, as the court of first instance, is the apex of a hierarchy of administrative tribunals. By an extensive body of case law, the council has become "the great protector of the rights of property and of the rights of the individual against the State, the great redresser of wrongs committed by the State." Whenever official acts are found to be devoid of a legal basis, whether those of a Cabinet minister or a village mayor, the council will annul them and grant damages to the aggrieved plaintiff. The council has steadily broadened its criteria of legality included in the "general principles of law": equality before the law, freedom of speech and association, the right to natural justice, the right to be heard, the right not to be subjected to retroactive legislation, and other similar privileges.

The State and Territorial Relations

Since the time of the First Republic, when the Jacobins controlled the revolutionary National Assembly, the French state has been characterized by a high degree of centralized political and administrative authority. Although there have always been forces that have advocated decentralization (of political authority), as well as deconcentration (of administrative authority), the French unitary state remained (formally) "one and indivisible."[60] Essentially, this has meant that subnational territorial units (communes, departments, and regions) have had little formal decision-making autonomy, and have been dominated by political and administrative decisions made in Paris. Both state action and territorial organization in France have depended on a well-structured administration, which during long periods of political instability and unrest can be relied on to keep the machinery of the state functioning.

Since the Revolution, France has been divided into 100 departments, each about the size of an American county, each under the administrative control of a prefect, and (since the Third Republic) with a directly elected general council. Since 1955, departments have been grouped into 22 regions, each with its own prefect and, since 1986, with an elected assembly (Figure 10.4).

Centralization has always been more impressive in its formal and legal aspects than it has been in practice, and the practical and political reality has always been more complex. Although France is renowned for its centralized state, what is often ignored is the political localism that has diluted centralized decision making.

One manifestation of the political importance of local government in France has been the ability of local units to endure. It is no accident that even after recent consolidations there are still 36,433 communes (the basic area of local administration), or about as many as in the original five Common Market countries and Great Britain together. Almost 33,000 French communes have fewer than 2,000 inhabitants, and of these more than 22,000 have fewer than 500. What is most remarkable, however, is that since 1851 the number of communes in France has been reduced by only 400. Thus, unlike every other industrialized country, the consolidation of population in urban areas has resulted in virtually no consolidation of towns and villages.

The process of decentralization initiated by the government of the left in 1982–1986 was undoubtedly the most important and effective reform passed during

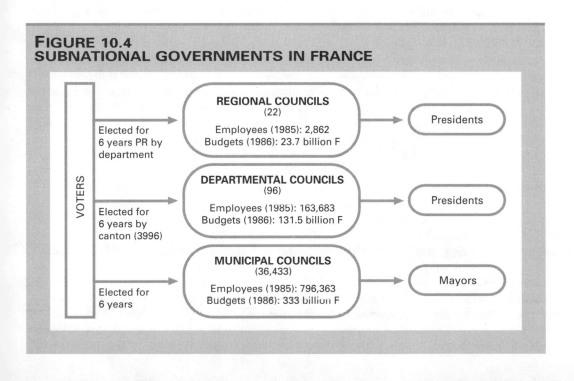

FIGURE 10.4
SUBNATIONAL GOVERNMENTS IN FRANCE

VOTERS

Elected for 6 years PR by department →
REGIONAL COUNCILS (22)
Employees (1985): 2,862
Budgets (1986): 23.7 billion F → Presidents

Elected for 6 years by canton (3996) →
DEPARTMENTAL COUNCILS (96)
Employees (1985): 163,683
Budgets (1986): 131.5 billion F → Presidents

Elected for 6 years →
MUNICIPAL COUNCILS (36,433)
Employees (1985): 796,363
Budgets (1986): 333 billion F → Mayors

that period. The strength of the reform was that it reaffirmed, reinforced, and built on the long-established system of a complicity, between central and local authorities, as well as on the patterns of change during the past twenty-five years. To be sure, the formal roles of all the local actors were altered, but the greatest change was that the previously informal power of these actors was formalized.[61]

The informal power of local officials had been based on a system of mutual dependency between them and the prefects, as well as the field services of the national ministries, which has existed since the Third Republic and endured until the 1980s. Although the administrators of the national ministries had the formal power to implement laws, rules, and regulations at the local level, they needed the cooperation of local officials, who had the confidence of their constituents, to facilitate the acceptance of the authority of the central state and to provide information that enabled the administration to operate effectively at the local level. Local officials, in turn, needed the resources and aid of the administration to help their constituents and keep their political promises.[62] As in any relationship based on permanent interaction and on cross-functioning controls, it was not always clear who controlled whom.

Both the autonomy and the relational power of municipalities were conditioned by the extent of the mayor's contacts within the political and administrative network. These contacts were certainly reinforced by the linkage to national decision making that mayors had established through their ability to hold several offices at the same time (*cumul des mandats*). Traditionally, the combining of the functions of a deputy or senator with those of a mayor or of a member of a departmental council (or both) has been a goal of a political career. Similarly, a government minister may be, and usually is, a local official as well. This sometimes meant that a mayor's influence in Paris was greater than that of the prefect who held formal administrative authority over him. There has been a consistent growth in the percentage of mayors of larger towns serving in Parliament. In the 1980s two-thirds or more of deputies and 95 percent of senators were, at the same time, local officeholders.

The decentralization legislation transferred most of the formal powers of the departmental and regional prefects to the elected presidents of the departmental and regional councils. In March 1986 regional councils were elected for the first time (by a system of proportional representation). In one stroke, the remnants of

formal administrative control over the decisions by local government were abandoned in favor of *a posteriori* review by the courts of the actions of local officials. The department presidents, elected by the department councils themselves, are now the chief departmental executive officers, and they, rather than the prefects, control the department bureaucracy.[63] This has accentuated the power of mayors of small and middle-size towns who control the departmental councils. Their enhanced political power will enable them to continue to protect the interests of diverse French communes. The representation of the interests of larger French cities has also been enhanced by the establishment of elected regional councils, within which big-city mayors have considerable influence. More broadly, decentralization has set in motion changes that seem to be replacing the old complicity and dependency between prefects and mayors, with a new interdependency — this time among elected officials. But interdependence has also grown, because there is almost no policy area over which one level of government has complete control.

What, then, is left of the role of the central bureaucracy in controlling the periphery? The greatest loss of authority has probably been among prefects. Their role now seems to be limited to security (law and order) matters and to the promotion of the government's industrial policies.

In matters of financing, the principal mechanisms through which the state has kept its hand in local government decisions (financial dependency and standards) have been weakened but have not been abandoned. There is still overall financial dependence of subnational governments on the state. Particularly at the commune level, well under half the annual budget is raised through taxes. The price that is paid for financial assistance from above is enforced compliance with standards set by the state. In areas in which the state retains decision-making power — police, education, a large area of welfare, and social security, as well as a great deal of construction — administrative discretion and central control remain important.

There is now a consensus in France that the great project of decentralization has indeed been a success. The changes legislated and decreed between 1982 and 1986 have been accepted across the political spectrum, notwithstanding the fact that they have altered some of the elements of relations between center and periphery in ways that also have political consequences. Despite overlap, the efficiency of services at the communal, departmental, and regional levels appears to have increased, and the health of local economies has been strengthened by local initiatives.

PERFORMANCE AND PROSPECTS

A Welfare State

An important measure of performance that is regularly applied to Western democracies has been their commitment and ability to distribute the benefits of economic growth. France has a mediocre record for spreading the benefits of the postwar boom and prosperity among all its citizens. In terms of income and of wealth, discrepancies between the rich and the poor remain greater in France than in other countries of equal development. However, some important changes have taken place. The income gap narrowed significantly between 1976 and 1981, and then even more during the first year of socialist government. Yet, with austerity measures after 1982, especially the government's successful effort to hold down wages, the gap began to grow once again. The emergence of long-term unemployment has resulted in an increase in the number of the new poor, who are younger than those in the past and often belong to single-parent families (30 percent of people receiving welfare support, according to one study!), as distinguished from the older retired people and the heads of household with marginal jobs who were the most frequent recipient in the past.

Since large incomes permit the accumulation of wealth, the concentration of wealth is even more conspicuous than the steepness of the income pyramid. In the 1970s it was estimated that the richest 10 percent controlled between 35 and 50 percent of all wealth; the poorest 10 percent owned not more than 5 percent. This pattern had not changed in the 1980s. In 1982 the tax authorities estimated that the richest 10 percent of the families in the country owned 51 percent of the wealth, while the richest 20 percent owned 67 percent. Because of the notorious unreliability of tax declarations, these figures probably underestimate existing inequalities.

In spite of some assertions to the contrary, it is not true that the French economy as a whole is burdened with higher taxes than other countries of similar development. What is special about France is the distribution of its taxes: the share of indirect taxes remains far higher in France than in other industrialized countries. Indirect taxes not only drive up prices but also weigh most heavily on the poor. The percentage of revenue collected

through regressive indirect taxation was the same in 1986, after five years of socialist government, as it had been in 1980. It is still about the same, although the completing of the Common Market by 1992 will require that France lower its most important indirect tax, the value added tax.

The French welfare state has been most effective in the field of social transfers. Their total amount has risen from 19 percent of GDP in 1970 to 29 percent in 1988, which puts France at about the same level as (West) Germany and Denmark, but ahead of Sweden, Britain, and most other European democracies, and far ahead of the United States. A comprehensive social security system, established in its present form after the war but extended since then, and a variety of programs assisting the aged, large families, the handicapped, and other such groups, disburse substantial benefits. When unemployment benefits, the cost of job training programs, and housing subsidies are added, total costs are as high as the entire public budget, but three-fourths of them are borne by employers and employees.

In contrast to the United States, there have been no major cutbacks in welfare state programs in France, and financing for these programs has been generally stabilized. Furthermore, as a percentage of GDP, spending on social programs has remained stable (at about 28 percent of GDP) since 1984. Thus, in the 1980s, through socialist change and the neoliberal reaction, the welfare state has remained healthy and intact. Its objectives and ground rules have found general acceptance.

NATIONALIZATION AND REGULATION

Government-operated business enterprises have long existed in France in fields that are under private ownership in other countries of Western Europe. After the nationalization at the end of World War II, the government owned and operated all or part of the following: railroading; almost all energy production (mining, electricity, nuclear energy) and much of telecommunication (radio and television); most air and maritime transport; most of the aeronautic industry; 85 percent of bank deposits; 40 percent of insurance premiums; one-third of the automobile industry; one-third of the housing industry—in addition to the old state monopolies of post, telephone, telegraph, tobacco and match manufacture, and sundry less important activities.

By the 1970s public concerns accounted for about 11 percent of the gross national product. Fifteen percent

The Constitutional Council: informality in palatial surroundings. The nine Council members, assisted only by a skeleton staff, deliberate and reach their decision in closed sessions without hearing appellants.

of the total active population, or 27 percent of all salary and wage-earners (excluding agricultural labor), were paid directly by the state either as civil servants as salaried workers or on a contractual basis. Their income came close to one-third of the total sum of wages and salaries.

To enlarge the public sector in both industry and banking had been the core of the common program of the left. Further nationalizations were considered a vehicle for modernizing a country with uneven development, as well as for effective planning. The legislation enacted in 1981–1982 completed the nationalization of the banking sector. At that point the state owned thirteen of the twenty largest firms in France, and had the controlling interest in many others. Five large-scale industrial groups that passed into public hands were leaders (not all of them prosperous) in such fields as machine tools, chemistry (including pharmaceutical products), glass, metals, and electrical power. In addition, the government obtained majority control of two important armaments firms and several ailing steel companies. About 33 percent of all salary and wage-earners received their checks from the French state in 1986. While this was high compared with the U.S. percentage, it was not out of line when compared with other European countries. If one out of nine French citizens depended on the state for their paychecks, so did one out of thirteen Italians and one out of eight Germans.

The conservative government that held power between March 1986 and May 1988 substantially altered, in line with its electoral promises, the structure of the nationalized sector in France. But its ambitious privati-

zation plans were halted (40 percent completed) only a year after their implementation began, in part because of the collapse of the stock market in 1987. Thus, some, but not all, of the companies that were nationalized by the socialist government in 1982 were returned to private stockholders. On the other hand, the conservative government also privatized some companies that had long been controlled by the state. Altogether, only 18 percent of the over 2 million workers in nationalized enterprises were "privatized" in 1986–1987 (333,000 workers). However, both the companies that were returned to private hands and those that remained in the hands of the state were quite different from what they had been a few years before. Recapitalized, restructured, and modernized, for the most part they were, in 1988, the leading edge of the French industrial machine.[64]

For the actual operation of French business, the move begun by the socialists and continued by the conservative government toward deregulation of the economy was probably more important than privatization. The deregulation of the stock market, the banking system, telecommunications, and prices has fundamentally changed the way business is conducted in both the private and public sectors.[65] The combination of budgetary rigor and state disengagement meant a real reduction of aid to industry. Sectors in difficulty, including steel, chemicals, shipbuilding, and automobile manufacturing, were therefore forced to accelerate their rationalization plans and their cutbacks in workers.

The socialist parliamentary victory in June 1988 effectively halted further privatization but did not alter the main lines of industrial and economic policy. Given substantial opposition in public opinion against further privatization, as well as the absence of political support for further nationalization, it is not likely that the structure of the nationalized sector will soon be changed by any government of the left or right. As a result, the interventionist and regulatory weight of the state is less important now than it was a decade ago, before the socialists came to power.

In other areas, the regulatory weight of the state has not diminished but has changed during the past twenty years. During the 1970s France expanded individual rights by fully establishing the rights to divorce and abortion. Under the socialist governments of the 1980s, capital punishment was abolished, the rights of those accused of crimes were strengthened, and detention without trial was checked by new procedures. Moreover, individual rights in France must now conform to the decisions of the European Court under the general umbrella of the European Community.

The media have been largely denationalized but not deregulated. A decade ago, there were no private radio and television stations in France. The socialist government first authorized private radio and television before 1986. As of 1991 private radio stations proliferate, and only two of the seven television channels are state owned. State regulation, however, remains intact, although the airwaves are far more difficult to control in the age of communications satellites.

In still other areas, the regulatory weight of the state has increased. One of the most obvious is environmental controls, which began to grow in the 1970s. By 1990 the French state was making its first significant efforts to regulate individual behavior that has an impact on the environment: the first limitations on smoking, for example, came into effect in the late 1980s.

Outlook: France and the New Architecture of Europe

The main concerns that dominated French politics a decade ago have changed dramatically. Ten years ago, a coalition of socialists and communists was promising a "rupture" with capitalism, and the ideological distance between left and right appeared to be enormous. Today, none of the major parties is presenting any proposal for dramatic change, and, like American political parties, all the parties are making their commitments as vague and as flexible as possible. After five years of socialism, and two of neoliberalism, political parties seem to be out

of fresh ideas on how to deal with the major problems of the French economy and society. The transition away from a smokestack economy has been difficult and painful, and the resulting unemployment continues to dominate public concerns. But, as in most of the rest of Europe, no one seems to have any idea about how to deal with these concerns, and the public has stopped holding governments responsible for solutions.

Political cleavages based on new conflicts are emerging, even if their outlines are still unclear. Indeed, the issues of the last decade of the twentieth century may very well be more profound and untenable than those of the past. The political stakes have moved away from questioning the nature of the regime, but they have become focused much more intensely on the nature of the political community. Between 1986 and the present, this has become evident in a variety of ways.

Immigration has given way to ethnic consciousness, particularly among the children of immigrants from North America. Unlike most of those in the past, these immigrant communities have been more reluctant to assume French cultural values as their own. This, in turn, has led to questioning the rules of naturalization for citizenship, integration into French society, and (in the end) what it means to be a Frenchman. During the 1980s growing ethnic tensions were given a political voice by the National Front, which has mobilized voters and solidified support on the basis of racist appeals. Regardless of the specific fate of the FN, ethnic consciousness and diversity is likely to grow in France because of the rapidly changing context of French politics.

A decade ago, the cold war and the separation of Europe was a fact of life, and was the basis for much of French foreign, defense and, to some extent, domestic policy. In the 1990s the cold war has been declared to be over. As a result, East European ethnic consciousness and conflicts previously held in check by Soviet power and, in any case, insulated from Western Europe by the Iron Curtain have been suddenly liberated. The disintegration of the Soviet communist experiment has also had the broader impact of undermining the legitimacy of classic socialism and has thus removed from French (and European) politics many of the issues that have separated left from right for a hundred years. Parties of the right have lost the anticommunist glue that has contributed to their cohesiveness, but parties of the left have lost much of their purpose.

Coincidentally, this process of East European disintegration has accelerated at the same time that the countries of the European Community have agreed to reinvigorate the process of West European integration, with France in the lead. Membership in the European Community has shaped almost every aspect of policy and policy planning, and has provided the context for the expansion and restructuring of the economy during the Fifth Republic.

At the beginning of his presidency in the early 1980s, Mitterrand expressed his satisfaction with the existing structures of the Common Market. But, having experienced their weakness, he was increasingly attracted to the view that some form of federalism — a "federalist finality" — would be necessary to enable Western Europe to use its considerable resources more effectively. Thus, during the Mitterrand presidency, France began to move in the direction of supporting a larger and a more tightly integrated Europe, including efforts to increase the powers of European institutions and the decision to establish a single European market by January 1993.

The opening of French borders, not only to the products of other countries, but increasingly to their peo-ple and values, may very well feed into the more general uneasiness about French national identity and support the emergence of ethnic politics. The growing integration of French economic and social institutions with those of its neighbors will continue progressively to remove key decisions from the French government acting alone. In the past, the French economy has been forced to react to joint decisions made in Brussels. In the future, a broader range of institutions will be forced to do the same. At the moment, rumblings of resistance are limited to the fringe parties (the National Front and the communists), but there is also opposition within the Socialist party and the RPR. Here, too, there is considerable potential for new political divisions.

This chapter, written at the beginning of the last decade of the twentieth century, presents a story of a strong and stable political system, in which political divisions have narrowed during the past ten years. Nevertheless, what we may be witnessing is a reordering of political divisions that will dominate in the twenty-first century.

KEY TERMS

baccalauréat
blocked vote
Napoleon Bonaparte
Cabinet (government)
cabinet (staff members of public officials)
Jacques Chirac
communes
Communist party (PCF)
Confédération Française Democratique du Travail (CFDT)
Confédération Générale du Travail (CGT)
Conseil National du Patronat Français (CNPF)
Constitution of 1958

Constitutional Council
Council of State
cumul des mandats (accumulation of electoral offices)
decentralization
Charles de Gaulle
departments
Ecole National d'Administration (ENA)
Ecole Polytechnique
Economic and Social Council
European Community
Events of 1968
Fédération National des Syndicats Agricoles

(FNSEA)
Fifth Republic
Fourth Republic
grandes écoles
grands corps
Jean-Marie Le Pen
François Mitterrand
Moslems
motion of censure
National Assembly (deputy)
National Front (FN)
nationalization
neocorporatism
ordinances
prefects
president of the Republic

prime minister
privatization
Rally for the Republic (RPR)
referendum
regions
representative democracy
Michel Rocard
Senate
Single European Act
Socialist party (PS)
the political class
the "new" immigration
Union for French Democracy (UDF)
Union of the Center (UDC)

END NOTES

1. William G. Andrews, ed., *European Political Institutions* (Princeton, N.J.: Van Nostrand, 1966), pp. 56–60.
2. In English, the best recent articles on the Constitutional Council are: John T. S. Keeler and Alec Stone, "Judicial-Political Confrontation in Mitterrand's France," in George Ross, Stanley Hoffmann, and Sylvia Malzacher, *The Mitterrand Experiment* (New York: Oxford University Press, 1987); and Stone, "Legal Constraints to Policy-

making: The Constitutional Council and the Council of State," in Paul Godt, *Policy-making in France from de Gaulle to Mitterrand* (London: Pinter Publishers, 1989).

3. Charles de Gaulle, *War Memoirs III: The Salvation* (New York: Simon & Schuster, 1960), p. 330).

4. Laurence Wylie, "Social Change at the Grass Roots," in Stanley Hoffmann, Charles P. Kindleberger, Jesse R. Pitts, et al., *In Search of France* (Cambridge, Mass.: Harvard University Press, 1963), p. 230.

5. This subject is dealt with in some detail by John Ambler in "Trust in Political and Nonpolitical Authorities in France," *Comparative Politics*, 8:1 (October 1975). Also see *Le Nouvel Observateur* March 28, 1991, p. 53.

6. These and many other interesting data on religious practice were revealed in an extensive opinion poll published in *Le Monde*, October 1, 1986.

7. Annick Percheron, "Religious Acculturation and Political Socialization in France," *West European Politics*, 5:2 (April 1982), p. 29.

8. See Nancy J. Walker, "What We Know about Voters in Britain, France and West Germany," *Public Opinion* (May–June 1988).

9. René Rémond in the article by Guilaume Malaurie and Jean-Sébastien Stehli, "Les Cathos," *l'Express*, December 9, 1988, p. 65.

10. See Gilles Kepel, *Les Banlieues de l' Islam: naissance d'une religion en France* (Paris: Seuil, 1987), pp. 9–19.

11. Duncan Gallie, *Social Inequality and Class Radicalism in France and Britain* (London: Cambridge University Press, 1983), p. 34.

12. Sofres, *L'Etat de l'opinion: clés pour 1988* (Paris: Seuil, 1988), p. 208.

13. Annick Percheron, "Socialization et tradition: transmission et invention du politique," *Pouvoirs*, 42 (1988), p. 43.

14. Ronald Inglehart, *Cultural Change* (Princeton, N.J.: Princeton University Press, 1989), Table 6–13. The figures on divorce and out-of-wedlock children are from *Données sociales 1987*, pp. 480 and 523, and *Tableaux de l'économie 1990* (Paris: INSEE, 1990), p. 21.

15. See Morin, *The Red and the White*, Ch. 8, remarking on the noisy revolution of the teenagers and the silent one of women.

16. This is the amply documented thesis of Janine Mossuz–Lavau and Mariette Sineau, *Les Femmes françaises en 1978: Insertion sociale, Insertion politique* (Paris: Centre de Documentation Sciences Humane de CNRS, 1980). The authors also found that women who were no longer working but had been employed previously were likely to express opinions closer to those of working than of nonworking women.

17. See Annick Percheron and M. Kent Jennings, "Political Continuities in French Families: A New Perspective on an Old Controversy," *Comparative Politics*, 13:4 (July 1981).

18. See Inglehart, *Cultural Change*, chs. 1–3 and Table 2.4.

19. The best developed case for French aversion to organization is in Arnold M. Rose, "Voluntary Associations in France," in Rose, ed., *Theory and Method in the Social Sciences* (Minneapolis: University of Minnesota Press, 1954). A somewhat different formulation of this case is presented by Michael Crozier, *The Stalled Society* (New York: Viking, 1973), pp. 63–74.

20. See Duncan MacRae, Jr., *Parliament, Parties and Society in France: 1946–1958* (New York: St. Martin's Press, 1967), pp. 28–32.

21. *Le Monde*, May 31, 1988.

22. Richard F. Hamilton, *Affluence and the French Worker in the Fourth Republic* (Princeton, N.J.: Princeton University Press, 1967), p. 233.

23. Data on education are taken from *Données sociales 1990*, pp. 322–355, and *Tableaux de l'économie française 1989*, p. 51.

24. John Ambler, "Constraints on Policy Innovation in Education: Thatcher's Britain and Mitterrand's France," *Comparative Politics*, 20:1 (October 1987). Also see Ambler, "Educational Pluralism in the French Fifth Republic," in James Holifield and George Ross, eds., *In Search of the New France* (New York: Routledge, 1991).

25. A recent article gives interesting details on the movement of students from different classes through the school system. The study documents the importance of class origins, but notes that, especially among lower class children, girls succeed at higher rates than boys. See Christian Baudelot and Roger Establet, "Les Filles et les garçons dans l compétition scholaire," in *Données Sociales 1990* (Paris: INSEE, 1990), pp. 344–347.

26. Which institutions qualify as *grandes écoles* is controversial. But among the 140 or so designated as such in some estimates, only 15 or 20, with an enrollment of 2,000 to 2,500, are considered

236 COUNTRY STUDIES

important, prestige schools. The number of engineering and business schools that are generally considered to be *grandes écoles* has increased in recent years. Therefore, the total enrollment of all these schools has increased significantly, to well over 100,000.

27. By far, the best book in English on the ability of the *grandes écoles* to continue to produce personnel for elite positions in France is Ezra Suleiman, *Elites in French Society* (Princeton, N.J.: Princeton University Press, 1978).

28. These results are taken from various sources and have been compiled by Russell J. Dalton in *Citizen Politics in Western Democracies* (Chatham, N.J.: Chatham House Press, 1988), p. 21.

29. For interesting studies on the origins and power of French political elites, see Jolyon Howorth and Philip G. Cerny, eds., *Elites in France: Origins, Reproduction and Power* (New York: St. Martin's Press, 1981), and Pierre Birnbaum, *The Heights of Power* (Chicago: University of Chicago Press, 1982).

30. See Roland Cayrol and Pascal Perrineau, "Governing Elites in a Changing Industrial Society: The Case of France," in Moshe M. Czudnowski, ed., *Does Who Governs Matter?* (DeKalb: Northern Illinois University Press, 1981).

31. There is no legal definition for any of these terms (nor is there any legal definition for a *grande école*), although they are widely used by citizens, journalists, and scholars. Thus, the figures given here for the early 1980s are approximations, based on positional and reputational definitions given by J-T Bodiguel and J-L Quermonne in *La Haute fonction publique sous la Ve Republique* (Paris: PUF, 1983), pp. 12–25 and 83–94.

32. Jean-Yves Potel, *L'Etat de la France et ses habitants* (Paris: Editions de la Découverte, 1985), p. 85.

33. Pierre Birnbaum, "The Socialist Elite: 'les Gros' and the State," in Philip G. Cerny and Martin A. Schain, eds., *Socialism, the State and Public Policy in France* (New York: Methuen, 1985), pp. 130–132; and Monique Dagaud and Dominique Mehl, *L'Elite Rose, Qui Gouverne?* (Paris: Ed. Ramsay, 1982), Annex VII.

34. These percentages are only approximations, since interest groups in France either refuse to publish membership figures or publish figures that are universally viewed as highly questionable. These figures are derived from Frank L. Wilson, *Interest-Group Politics in France* (New York:

Cambridge University Press, 1987), p. 143 (industrial enterprises), John T. S. Keeler, *The Politics of Neocorporatism in France* (New York: Oxford University Press, 1987), p. 109 (agriculture) and *Le Monde*, December 5, 1989 (trade unions).

35. For an analysis of the impact of this phenomenon in the trade union movement, see Martin Schain, "Relations between the CGT and the CFDT: Politics and Mass Mobilization," in Mark Kesselman, ed., *The French Workers' Movement* (London: George Allen & Unwin, 1984).

36. See Mark Kesselman, "The New Shape of French Labor and Industrial Relations: Ce n'est plus la meme chose," in Godt, *Policy-making in France from de Gaulle to Mitterrand.*

37. The most recent studies are reported in *Le Monde*, May 31, 1988, p. 42, December 5, 1989, p. 27; and *Libération*, December 13, 1988, p. 12.

38. On the importance of interunion rivalry, see W. Rand Smith, *Crisis in the French Labor Movement: A Grassroots Perspective* (New York: St. Martin's Press, 1988).

39. See the discussion of the legislation in Duncan Gallie, "*Les Lois Auroux:* The Reform of French Industrial Relations?," in Howard Machin and Vincent Wright, eds., *Economic Policy and Policy-Making under the Mitterrand Presidency 1981–1984* (London: Frances Pinter, 1985).

40. The most recent book on the CFDT is Guy Groux and René Mouriaux, *La C.F.D.T.* (Paris: Economica, 1989).

41. The most recent serious study of the CNPF and its affiliates by Henri Weber, *Le Parti des patrons: Le CNPF 1846–86* (Paris: Editions du Seuil, 1986), analyzes various trends within the *patronat*, and is based on much detailed inside information. Henry W. Ehrmann, *Organized Business in France* (Princeton, N.J.: Princeton University Press, 1957) presents case studies about the contacts between the administration and the employers organizations, but it is now dated.

42. Ezra N. Suleiman, *Politics, Power, and Bureaucracy in France: The Administrative Elite* (Princeton, N.J.: Princeton University Press, 1974), pp. 323–351.

43. See Wilson, *Interest-Group Politics in France*, pp. 151, 153, 162, and 164.

44. See John T. S. Keeler, "Situating France on the Pluralism-Corporatism Continuum," *Comparative Politics*, 17:2 (January 1985), pp. 229–249.

45. It must be noted—and this is true for all figures on electoral participation throughout this chapter—that French statistics calculate electoral participation on the basis of registered voters, while American statistics take as a basis the total number of people of voting age. About 9 percent of French citizens entitled to vote are not registered. This percentage must therefore be added to the published figures when one wishes to estimate the true rate of abstention and to compare it with the American record.

46. See Martin Schain, "Politics at the Margins: The French Communist Party and the National Front," in Godt, *Policy-Making in France.*

47. Philip M. Williams, *Crisis and Compromise in the Fourth Republic* (New York: Anchor, 1964), p. 348.

48. For a good survey of party developments between 1958 and 1981, see Frank L. Wilson, *French Political Parties under the Fifth Republic* (New York: Praeger, 1982).

49. See Jean Charlot, *The Gaullist Phenomenon: The Gaullist Movement in the Fifth Republic* (New York: Praeger, 1971).

50. As with most party claims in France, these figures are certainly exaggerated, but the trend remains significant.

51. Most of this material is taken from a landmark study by Pierre Bréchon, Jacques Derville, and Patrick Lecomte, *Les cadres du R.P.R.* (Paris: Economica, 1987), some of the findings of which are summarized by the authors in "RPR Officials: A Report on an Inquiry into the Neo-Gaullist Party Elite," *European Journal of Political Research,* 15 (1987), pp. 593–607.

52. See Gérard Grunberg, Pierre Giacometti, Florence Haegel, and Béatrice Roy, "Trois candidats, trois droites, trois électorats," *Le Monde,* April 27, 1988, p. 12.

53. See Martin Schain, "Immigration and Politics," in Peter Hall, Jack Hayward, and Howard Machin, *Developments in French Politics* (London: Macmillan, 1990). ch. 15.

54. D. S. Bell and Byron Criddle, *The French Socialist Party: The Emergence of a Party of Government,* 2nd ed. (Oxford: Clarendon Press, Oxford, 1988).

55. For an analysis of the decline of the communist vote, see Martin Schain, "The French Communist Party: The Seeds of Its Own Decline," in Peter Katzenstein, Theodore Lowi, and Sidney Tarrow, *Comparative Theory and Political Experience* (Ithaca, N.Y.: Cornell University Press, 1990). For additional insights into the decline of the PCF electorate, see Jenson and Ross, *View from the Inside: A French Communist Cell in Crisis* (Berkeley: University of California Press, 1984), Part V.

56. This analysis is taken from Oliver Duhamel's article, "President and Prime Minister," in Godt, *Policy-Making in France,* pp. 9–10.

57. For the best recent examination of legislative patterns in France and Britain, see John Keeler, *The Limits of Democratic Reform* (New York: Oxford University Press, forthcoming).

58. See Didier Maus, "Parliament in the Fifth Republic: 1958–1988," in Godt, *Policy-Making in France,* p. 17.

59. See Alec Stone, "In the Shadow of the Constitutional Council: The 'Juridicization of the Legislative Process in France," *West European Politics,* 12:2 (April 1989).

60. This phrase refers to the first article of the constitution of 1793, which proclaims that "The French Republic is one and indivisible." The constitution of the Fifth Republic repeats it.

61. See Vivien Schmidt, *Democratizing France* (New York: Cambridge University Press, 1990).

62. The now classic statement of this relationship was written by Jean–Pierre Worms, who, years later, had major responsibilities for developing the decentralization reforms for the government of the left. See "Le Préfet et ses notables," *Sociologie du Travail,* 8:3 (1966), pp. 249–275.

63. Mark Kesselman, "The Tranquil Revolution at Clochemerle: Socialist Decentralization in France," in Philip G. Cerny and Martin A. Schain, *Socialism, the State and Public Policy in France* (New York: St. Martin's Press, 1985), p. 176.

64. They were also controlled by the same people as when they were nationalized. None of the newly privatized firms changed managing directors. See Michel Bauer, "The Politics of State-Directed Privatization: The Case of France 1986–88," in *West European Politics,* 11:4 (October 1988), p. 59.

65. See Philip G. Cerny, "From *Dirigism* to Deregulation? The Case of Financial Markets," in Godt, *Policy-Making in France.*

CHAPTER 11

RUSSELL J. DALTON

POLITICS IN GERMANY

OLITICAL SCIENTISTS often talk of revolutionary thought and revolutionary action, even though revolutionary change is really quite rare—but it occurred in Germany in 1989.

With the opening of the Berlin Wall on the night of November 9, 1989, Germany's future took a new course that few anticipated and no one had predicted. This was a "people power" revolution. The East Germans' willingness to take a stand against the state, and the state's unwillingness to suppress its people with force, brought the system to its end. The once formidable East German government collapsed into a vacuum at the center of the power structure. The East German economy was generally considered the showcase of the Eastern bloc nations, but it, too, ground to a halt. All eyes turned West, toward the Federal Republic of Germany as a source of stability and political reform. German unification, an issue for the next century as a Russian spokesperson had described it in midsummer, suddenly appeared a real possibility. Protesters in Leipzig who had chanted "we are the people" when opposing the East German government in October took up the call for unification with a new refrain: "we are *one* people." The whole of 1990 was a series of accelerated elections, East/West negotiations, and international treaties that pushed the process of unification forward at a breathtaking pace. In less than a year, the unimaginable was a reality. Two German states—one democratic and one communist, one with a market economy and one with a socialist planned economy—were united.

German unification has reshaped the map of Europe, but it has also reshaped how we think about Germany and the lessons we are to draw from the German experience. In one sense, this change repeats the pattern of Germany's discontinuous political development. Within a century the political system has changed from the authoritarian state of the Second Empire (1871–1918), to the democratic system of the Weimar Republic (1919–1933), to the fascist Third Reich (1933–1945), to a postwar division of two Germanies (1945–1990), to the new unified Federal Republic of Germany. The rebuilding of West Germany from the postwar ashes provided important lessons on how a society could change and a new political system could develop. Today Germany again confronts the task of building a new nation uniting East and West, and this effort revives ongoing questions about the political identity of the Germans. Will the Federal Republic be able to successfully integrate the new residents from the East, Germans who were raised under a much different social and political system? How will the new Germany differ as a result of unification; will the Western orientation in the Federal Republic's values and international ties shift as it turns its attentions eastward? Unification carries a substantial price tag in the costs of modernizing the economy and social system of the East, and many ask whether the average citizen in the West will bear this load. The political challenges of unification nearly rival the task of building a new democratic West German republic in the aftermath of World War II.

But this German revolution takes place in a different setting than past changes in regime. This is the first time the Germans themselves have successfully led a revolution for a democratic form of government. In addition, West Germany was the political and economic success story of postwar Europe, and these strengths carry over to the present. Unification means that 16 million more people will now be able to live in a free and democratic state. A free and democratic Germany with a vibrant economy can act as a source of economic and political stability within the West, as well as fostering political reform throughout Eastern Europe.

Concern about the "German question" — the uncertainty about the German national identity and political values — is again a matter of great interest to Germans and non-Germans alike. But there are reasons to hope that this question will finally be answered in the affirmative if the new Germany accomplishes the goal that its president set out on the day of unification: "we want to serve the cause of freedom in the world within a united Europe."

THE HISTORICAL LEGACY

The German historical experience differs substantially from the experiences of most other European democracies. The social and political forces that modernized the rest of Europe came much later in Germany and had a less certain effect. For some time after most national borders had been relatively well defined, German territory was still divided among dozens of political units. Although a dominant national culture had evolved in most European states, Germany was torn by the Reformation and continuing conflicts between Catholics and

Protestants; sharp regional and economic cleavages also polarized society. Industrialization generally was the driving force behind the modernization of Europe, but German industrialization came late and did not overturn the old feudal and aristocratic order. German history, even to the present, represents a difficult and protracted process of nation building.

The Second German Empire

Through a combination of military and diplomatic victories, Otto von Bismarck, the Prussian chancellor, enlarged the territory of Prussia and then established a unified Second German Empire in 1871. The empire was an authoritarian state, with only the superficial trappings of a democracy. Political power flowed from monarch (*Kaiser*), and potential opposition groups — especially the Catholic Church and the Social Democrats — were bitterly suppressed at times. The citizen's role was to be a law-abiding subject, obeying the commands of government officials.

The strong central government made substantial progress in national development during this period. Industrialization proceeded rapidly, and German influence in international affairs grew steadily. The force of industrialization was not sufficient to modernize and liberalize society and the political system, however. Economic and political power remained concentrated in the hands of the aristocracy and traditional elites. Democratic reforms were thwarted by an authoritarian state strong enough to resist the political demands of a weak middle class. The state was supreme; its needs took precedence over those of individuals and society.

Failures of government leadership, coupled with a blindly obedient public, led Germany into World War I (1914–1918). The war devastated the nation. Almost 3 million German soldiers and civilians lost their lives, the economy was strained beyond the breaking point, and the government of the empire collapsed under the weight of its own incapacity to govern. The war ended with Germany a defeated and exhausted nation.

The Weimar Republic

In 1919 a popularly elected constitutional assembly established the new democratic system of the *Weimar Republic*. Citizens were granted universal suffrage and provided with constitutional guarantees of basic human rights. Political power was vested in a directly elected Parliament and president. Political parties organized across the full spectrum of interests and became legitimate actors in the political process. Belatedly, the Germans had their first real exposure to democracy.

From the outset, however, the Weimar government was plagued by severe problems. In the peace treaty following World War I, Germany lost all its overseas colonies and a substantial amount of European territory; it was further burdened with large reparation payments owed to the victorious Allies. A series of radical uprisings from both left and right extremists threatened the political system. Wartime destruction and the reparation payments produced continuing economic problems, finally leading to economic catastrophe in 1923. In less than a year the inflation rate was an unimaginable 26 billion percent! Ironically, the Kaiser's empire was not blamed for the wartime defeat and its consequences. Instead, many people censured the empire's liberal-democratic successor — the Weimar Republic.

The fatal blow came with the Great Depression in 1929. Almost a third of the labor force was soon unemployed, and the public was frustrated by the government's inability to deal with this crisis. Political tensions increased, and parliamentary democracy began to fail. Adolf Hitler and his National Socialist German Workers' party (the Nazis) were the major beneficiaries; their vote increased from a mere 2 percent in 1928 to 18 percent in 1930 and 33 percent in November 1932. Increasingly, the machinery of the democratic system malfunctioned or was bypassed. In a final attempt to restore public and political order, President Paul von Hindenburg appointed Hitler chancellor of the Weimar Republic in January 1933. Democracy soon came to an end.

Weimar's failure resulted from interaction among complex factors.[1] A basic weakness was the republic's lack of support from political elites and the general public. The elite class of the empire had retained control of the military, the judiciary, and the civil service. Democracy thus depended on an administrative elite that often longed for a return to a more traditional political order. Even before the onset of the depression, many leading political figures worked for the overthrow of the Weimar system. Elite criticism of Weimar encouraged similar sentiments among the public, many of whom shared these views. Many citizens retained strong emotional ties to the German Empire and questioned the basic legitimacy of Weimar. Germans still lacked a commitment to democratic principles that could unite and guide the nation. The fledgling state then faced a series of severe economic and political crises; such excessive strains might have overloaded the ability of any system to govern effectively. These crises further eroded public support for the republic and opened the door to Hitler's authoritarian and nationalistic appeals. The political institutions of Weimar also contributed to its vulnerability through the unclear division of political authority between Parliament and the president. Furthermore, the constitution granted the president broad emergency powers that eventually were abused. Finally, most Germans drastically underestimated Hitler's ambitions, intentions, and political abilities. This, perhaps, was Weimar's greatest failure.

The Third Reich

The Nazis' rise to power reflected a bizarre mixture of ruthless behavior and a concern for legal procedures. Hitler called for a new election in March 1933 and then suppressed the opposition parties. Although the Nazis still failed to capture an absolute majority in the election, their subsequent control of the Parliament was used to enact unconstitutional legislation granting Hitler dictatorial powers. Democracy was replaced by a new authoritarian "leader state."

Once entrenched in power, Hitler pursued the extremist policies that many of his moderate supporters had assumed were mere political rhetoric. All aspects of society were "coordinated" with Nazi goals. Social and political groups that might challenge the government were destroyed, taken over by Nazi agents, or co-opted into accepting the Nazi regime. The arbitrary powers of the police state grew and choked off nearly all opposition. Attacks on Jews and other minorities steadily became more violent. Massive public works projects lessened unemployment, but also built the infrastructure for a wartime economy. The military was expanded and rearmed in violation of World War I treaties, and the Reich's expansionist foreign policy challenged the international status quo.

Hitler's unrestrained political ambitions finally plunged Europe into World War II in 1939. After initial victories, a series of military defeats from 1942 on led to the total collapse of the Third Reich in May 1945. Sixty million lives were lost in the war, including 6 million European Jews who were murdered in a Nazi campaign of systematic genocide.[2] Germany lay in ruins: its industry and transportation systems were destroyed, its cities were rubble, millions were homeless, and even food was scarce. Hitler's grand design for a new German

Reich had instead destroyed the nation in a Wagnerian *Götterdämmerung*.

The Occupation Period

The political division of postwar Germany began with the advance of foreign troops on to German soil. At the end of the war, the Russians occupied the Eastern zone, and Allied forces—the United States, Britain, and France—controlled the Western zone. This was intended as an interim division, but increasing frictions between Western and Soviet leaders lessened cooperation in the administration of both regions.

In the West, the Allied military government began a denazification program to remove Nazi leaders and sympathizers from the economic, military, and political systems. Under the supervision of the occupation authorities, new political parties were established and democratic political institutions began to evolve. The economic system was reorganized along capitalist lines; the creation of a new currency and market economy in the Western zone in 1948 revitalized the economic system but also deepened the division of Germany.

Political reform followed a much different course in the Eastern zone. The new *Socialist Unity party (SED)* became a mechanism for the communists to control the political process, and the party gradually adopted a Stalinist ideology. Since the Soviets saw the capitalist system as responsible for the Third Reich, their economic policies sought to destroy this capitalist structure and construct a new socialist order in its place. By 1948 the Eastern zone had essentially become a copy of the Soviet political and economic systems.

As the distance between occupation zones widened, the Allies came to favor creation of a separate German state in the West. In Bonn, a small university town along the banks of the Rhine, the Germans began their second attempt at democracy. A Parliamentary Council met in 1948 to draft a constitution to organize the West German political system until the entire nation should be reunited. In May 1949 the state governments agreed on a *Basic Law (Grundgesetz)* to create the *Federal Republic of Germany (FRG)*, or West Germany, as a parliamentary democracy.

The Soviets watched these developments with great concern. The Soviet blockade of Berlin in 1948, for example, was partially an attempt to halt the formation of a separate German state in the West—though its result was to strengthen Western resolve. Once it became apparent that the West would follow its own course, preparations began for the creation of a separate German state in the East. A week after the formation of the Federal Republic, the People's Congress approved a draft constitution; on October 7, 1949, the new East German state was created, the *German Democratic Republic (GDR)*. As had happened in earlier periods of German history, a divided nation was again following different paths (see Figure 11.1). It would take over forty years before these paths would again converge.

FOLLOWING TWO PATHS

Although they had chosen different paths (or had them chosen for them), the two German states faced many of the same challenges in their initial years. The most immediate challenge was to resolve the pressing economic problems that left the publics in both parts of Germany struggling to survive. Despite the progress that had been made by the late 1940s, the economic picture was still bleak on both sides of the border. Unemployment remained high in the West and the average wage-earner received less than $60 a month. In 1950 almost two-thirds of the West German public felt they had been better off before the war, and severe economic hardships were still common. The situation was equally severe in the East, where a strong agricultural base was undermined by a struggling industrial sector weakened by reparation payments to the Soviets.

West Germany achieved phenomenal success in meeting this economic challenge.[3] Relying on a free enterprise system championed by the Christian Democratic party (CDU/CSU), the country experienced a period of sustained and unprecedented economic growth. By the early 1950s incomes reached the prewar level, and growth had just begun. Over the next two decades per capita wealth nearly tripled, average hourly industrial wages increased nearly fivefold, and average incomes grew nearly sevenfold. By almost all economic indicators the West German public in 1970 was several times more affluent than at any time in prewar history. This phenomenal economic growth came to be known as West Germany's *Economic Miracle (Wirtschaftswunder)*.

East Germany experienced its own economic miracle that was almost as impressive as the one in the West. Economic reform in the East was based on a system of collectivized agriculture, nationalized industry, and centralized planning.[4] In the two decades after the formation of the GDR, industrial production increased

FIGURE 11.1
THE TWO PATHS OF POSTWAR GERMANY

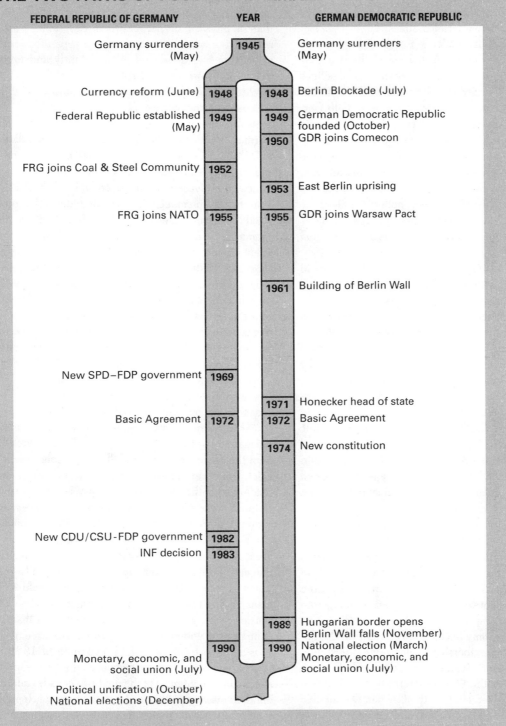

FEDERAL REPUBLIC OF GERMANY	YEAR	GERMAN DEMOCRATIC REPUBLIC
Germany surrenders (May)	1945	Germany surrenders (May)
Currency reform (June)	1948	Berlin Blockade (July)
Federal Republic established (May)	1949	German Democratic Republic founded (October)
	1950	GDR joins Comecon
FRG joins Coal & Steel Community	1952	
	1953	East Berlin uprising
FRG joins NATO	1955	GDR joins Warsaw Pact
	1961	Building of Berlin Wall
New SPD–FDP government	1969	
	1971	Honecker head of state
Basic Agreement	1972	Basic Agreement
	1974	New constitution
New CDU/CSU-FDP government	1982	
INF decision	1983	
	1989	Hungarian border opens / Berlin Wall falls (November)
	1990	National election (March) / Monetary, economic, and social union (July)
Monetary, economic, and social union (July)	1990	
Political unification (October) National elections (December)		

nearly fivefold and per capita national income grew by nearly equal measure. Although still lagging behind their more affluent relatives in the West, the German Democratic Republic became the model of efficiency and prosperity among socialist states.

Another political challenge was the problem of nation building. The uncertain division of the two German states became a major issue of international politics during the postwar period. The Federal Republic initially was viewed as a provisional state until both Germanies were reunited. The GDR struggled to develop its own identity in the shadow of the West, with its own commitment to eventual reunification. In addition to the problems of division, the occupation authorities retained the right to intervene in the domestic affairs of the two Germanies even after 1949. Thus, both states faced the challenge of defining their identity — as separate states or as parts of a larger Germany — and regaining national sovereignty.

The Federal Republic's first chancellor, Konrad Adenauer, steered the nation on a course toward gaining its national sovereignty by integrating the Federal Republic into the Western Alliance. By cooperating with its Western allies, West Germany was slowly able to improve its international standing. The Western powers would grant greater autonomy to the Federal Republic so long as it was exercised within the framework of an international body. For example, economic redevelopment was channeled through the European Coal and Steel Community (ECSC) and the European Economic Community (EEC), and military rearmament occurred within the North Atlantic Treaty Organization (NATO). Virtually full national sovereignty was gained in 1955, with the Allies retaining residual rights on the final resolution of the "German question."

The communist regime in the East countered the Federal Republic's integration into the Western alliance with calls for German reunification. And yet at the same time, the GDR went about establishing itself as a separate German state. In 1952 the regime transformed the demarcation line between East and West Germany into a fortified border and restricted access to the East. The East German economy became integrated with the Soviet bloc through membership in the Council for Mutual Economic Assistance (Comecon), and the GDR was a charter member of the Warsaw Pact. The Soviet Union recognized the sovereignty of the German Democratic Republic in 1954. The practical and symbolic division of Germany became real with the GDR's construction of the Berlin Wall in August 1961. The wall was intended to stem the tide of emigration from the East, though Eastern propaganda claimed it was to protect the GDR from Western exploitation and contamination. More than a physical barrier between East and West, it marked the formal existence of two separate German states that had developed independently and existed within their own political spheres.

Intra-German relations took a dramatically different course once the *Social Democratic party (SPD)* won control of the national government in the 1969 West German elections. The Federal Republic's relations with Eastern Europe had been marked by confrontation and hostility since the onset of the cold war. For instance, the *Hallstein Doctrine* committed the FRG to renouncing diplomatic relations with nations that recognized the German Democratic Republic. The new SPD chancellor, Willy Brandt, proposed a fundamentally different Eastern policy (*Ostpolitik*). Brandt was willing to accept the postwar political situation within Europe and sought reconciliation with the nations of Eastern Europe, including the GDR. West Germany signed treaties with the Soviet Union and Poland to resolve disagreements dating back to World War II and to establish new economic and political ties. In 1971 Brandt received the Nobel Peace Prize for his actions. The following year a Basic Agreement with East Germany formalized the relationship between the two Germanies as two separate states within one German nation.

East Germany was originally very skeptical of rapprochement with the Federal Republic, but prodding from the Soviets and Walter Ulbricht's replacement by Erich Honecker as head of the SED led to serious negotiations with the West. To the East German regime, Ostpolitik was a mixed blessing. On the positive side, it legitimized the GDR through its formal recognition by the Federal Republic and a normalization of East — West relations. On the negative side, mutual recognition and subsequent exchanges among the two German states increased the exposure to Western values and ideas among the East German population. The initial worries of many conservative GDR politicians that Ostpolitik would undermine their closed system seem to be substantiated by the eventual revolution of 1989.

After reconciliation between the two German states, both spent most of the next two decades addressing their internal policy needs. In the Federal Republic, the Social-Liberal government instituted a series of domestic policy reforms in the early 1970s that aimed at expanding social services and equalizing access to the benefits of the Economic Miracle. The SPD-led government passed measures to expand and equalize access to higher education and generally improve the quality of instruction. Social programs were broadened; new benefits were enacted in old age security, health insurance, and social services. Total social spending nearly doubled between 1969 and 1975.

The pressure for political reform in the Federal Republic slackened in the mid-1970s mainly as a result of the economic problems that confronted all of Western Europe. Worldwide recession cut sharply into West Germany's export-oriented economy. The previous trend of continually increasing affluence was replaced by slow and unsteady economic growth. In 1974 Helmut Schmidt replaced Brandt as chancellor. Schmidt successfully moderated the effect of hard economic times. There was necessary retrenchment on the domestic policy reforms; government deficits rose with the economic slowdown, and little money was available for new social programs. The Federal Republic remained an affluent nation, even if the prospects for further increases in prosperity were less certain.

The problems of unrealized reforms and renewed economic difficulties continued into the 1980s. After the 1980 election, the West German government struggled with several seemingly intractable domestic and foreign policy issues. These policy strains eventually became too great for the governing coalition to manage, and moved the economically conservative *Free Democratic party (FDP)* closer to the CDU/CSU. At the same time, voter dissatisfaction with the government increased support for the opposition Christian Democratic Union. In mid-1982 the Christian Democrats finally enticed the FDP to break with the socialists and form a new government under the leadership of Helmut Kohl, head of the CDU. The coalition called for new elections to legitimize the new government and won a sweeping victory in the 1983 poll.

The new government's mandate was to restore the Federal Republic's economy while continuing to provide for social needs. On the economic side, Kohl presided over a dramatic change in fortunes; inflation dropped sharply, interest rates plummeted, business investment grew, the trade balance moved sharply in West Germany's favor, and the stock market shot upward. While a large part of this recovery resulted from changes in the international economic climate, the conservative policies of the Kohl government contributed to the upturn in economic conditions. Public spending was held in check, and the annual federal deficit was cut. To accomplish these objectives, the government enacted some cuts in virtually all social programs, including unemployment compensation, retirement benefits, and student loans. The government also demonstrated its strong commitment to the Western defense alliance by accepting the deployment of new intermediate-range nuclear forces (INF). Public support for the government's conservative program returned the CDU-led coalition to office after the January 1987 elections.

During the 1970s the GDR adapted to its new international status.[5] East Germany established ties with nations that were now willing to grant it recognition and expanded its international presence through activities ranging from the Olympics to its new membership in the United Nations. At the same time, the GDR sought to insulate itself from Western influences that followed Ostpolitik through a conscious policy of demarcation from the West (*Abgrenzung*). A revision of the constitution in 1974 strengthened the emphasis on a separate, socialist East German state that was no longer tied to the ideal of a reunified Germany. Socialism and the fraternal ties to the Soviet Union became the basis of defining the GDR's national identity. While trade with the West expanded, other policies restricted Western influences in culture, society, and politics.

The East German economy was also buffeted by the fallout from the worldwide economic recession in the late 1970s. The trading strength of the GDR economy was based on its relative efficiency compared to that of other communist systems and the reliable flow of inexpensive raw materials from the Soviet Union, especially oil. A variety of factors diminished the cost competitiveness of East German products in international markets, and trade deficits with the West steadily grew throughout the 1980s. Moreover, the consequences of long-delayed improvements in the economic infrastructure began to manifest themselves in a deteriorating highway system, a rapidly aging housing stock, and an outdated communications system. Although the East Germans heard frequent government reports about the successes of the economy, their living standards displayed a widening gap between official pronouncements and reality.

As East German government officials grappled with their own problems, they were also disturbed by the winds of change that were blowing from the East. A bulwark of the East German system was its loyalty to the Soviet Union and its commitment to communist orthodoxy. Gorbachev's reformist policies of *perestroika* and *glasnost* in the Soviet Union seemed to undermine the pillars on which the East German system was built. At one point, the official East German newspaper even censured political reports from the Soviet Union to downplay the extent of Gorbachev's reforms. Indeed, the stimulus for political change in East Germany came not from within but from the events sweeping across the rest of Eastern Europe.

In early 1989 the first cracks in the communist system began to appear. In April the outlawed Polish Solidarity trade union was legalized; Poland soon became the first European nation to have a noncommunist head of government, and the Russians did not object. At the same time, the Hungarian Communist party endorsed the idea of free democratic elections and introduced market forces into the Hungarian economy. The liberalization in Hungary proved to be a decisive factor when it began dismantling its border with neutral Austria. A steady stream of East Germans began leaving for the West. East Germans were voting, with their feet. Almost 2 percent of the total East German population emigrated to the Federal Republic over the next six months. The growing exodus also stimulated public demonstrations within East Germany against the regime.

The East German government struggled to deal with this problem, and Gorbachev played a crucial role in directing the flow of events. He first signalled the Soviets' willingness to see Honecker replaced as head of state by Egon Krenz, who was considered a moderate by East German standards. Gorbachev informed the East German leadership that Soviet assistance would not be available to suppress the demonstrations (as it had in 1953), and encouraged them to undertake a process of internal reform with the cautious advice that "life itself punishes those who delay." Without Soviet support, the death of the GDR regime became inevitable.

Rapidly growing public protests increased the pressure on the government, and the continuing exodus to the West brought the economy to a near standstill. The nation that was once known for its efficiency and order was plunged into political and economic chaos. The government did not govern; it barely existed, struggling from crisis to crisis. In early November the government and the SED Politburo resigned. The GDR was now a country without even a government. On the evening of November 9, a GDR official announced the opening of the border between East and West Ger-

many;[6] in the former no-man's land of the Berlin Wall, Berliners from East and West joyously celebrated together.

Once the euphoria of the opening of the Berlin Wall had passed, East Germany had to address the question of "what next?" The GDR government initially followed a strategy of damage control, appointing new leaders and attempting to court public support. But the damage to the legitimacy of the state and the vitality of the economy was too great. The only apparent source of stability was a policy of unification with the Federal Republic, and the rush toward German unity began.

In March 1989 new leadership for the GDR was chosen in the first truly free elections there since 1932. The Alliance for Germany, including the eastern branch of the CDU, won control of the East German government. Both Kohl and Lothar de Maiziere, the new East German leader, forcefully moved toward unification. A currency union was accomplished on July 1, giving the two nations one currency and essentially one economy. When Kohl won Soviet concessions on the terms of unification and Germany's continued membership in NATO, the road to complete unification was opened. On October 3, 1990, after a generation of separation, the two German

Young people from East and West Berlin celebrate the opening of the Wall in November 1989.

paths again converged — but where would this new path lead?

SOCIAL FORCES

Popular accounts of unification sometimes refer to the new Germany as the fourth and richest Reich. The state has nearly 80 million people, 62 million from the West and 16 million from the East, located in the heartland of Europe. The combined economies of West and East Germany (using mid-1980s statistics) dwarf most of the neighboring economies, its size creates new imbalances in the distribution of power within Europe, and some observers even note that the combined German medal total in the 1988 Summer Olympics would best the two superpowers' performance. The combined territory of the new Germany is also large by European standards, even though it is small in comparison to the United States — about the size of Montana. But the merger of two societies and economies is more complex than the simple addition of two columns of numbers on a balance sheet. Although unification creates new strengths, it also redefines and potentially strains the social system that underlies German society and politics.

Germany historically has been marked by sharp social cleavages that structured political conflict. The nation was often torn by deep social divisions: urban interests against the landed estates, working-class people against industrialists, Protestants against Catholics. The Federal Republic experienced a gradual restructuring, diversification, and decline in these social conflicts, but the merger of East and West German societies holds the potential for reviving some of these historical social divisions.

Although both East and West Germany experienced their own economic miracles, the advances in the East were less dramatic than those in the Federal Republic. In the mid-1980s the West German standard of living ranked among the highest in the world (see Table 8.3). At the same time, the real purchasing power of the average East German's salary amounted to barely half the income of his or her West German counterpart. While basic staples were inexpensively priced in the East, most consumer goods were more expensive than in the West, and so-called luxury items (color televisions, washing machines, and automobiles) were often beyond the reach of normal families. In 1985 about a third of the dwellings in East Germany still lacked their own baths and toilets. Citizens of the GDR lived a comfortable life by East European standards, but it fell far short of Western standards.

Economic growth also transformed the economies of both the East and West. One characteristic they shared in common was a decline in the size and economic importance of the agricultural sector; between the 1950s and the 1980s the percentage of workers employed in agriculture decreased to 4 percent of the labor force in the FRG and 11 percent in the GDR. In the West, the size of the industrial sector held fairly constant, accounting for about 40 percent of the workforce. Economic expansion came in the service and technology sector, and government employment more than doubled during this period. The largest occupation category now is composed of salaried white-collar workers and civil servants. Economic growth in the East was fueled by government investments in heavy industry and manufacturing. In the mid-1980s about half of the economy was concentrated in these areas, and the service–technology sector represented a far smaller share of the national economy.

German unification has meant the merger of these two different economies and social systems: the affluent West Germans and their poor cousins from the East, the sophisticated and technologically advanced industries of the West, and the aging rust-belt factories of the GDR. At least in the short run, unification is not moderating these economic differences but is actually exacerbating them. Salaries have not equalized between both systems; civil servants in the East (if they retain their job) are paid a smaller salary than Western officials, and Eastern pensioners receive a smaller monthly check than retirees in the West. Moreover, unification was accompanied by the virtual collapse of the East German economy. Companies sustained by the closed system of the communist planned economy struggled unsuccessfully to compete with their modern West German competitors. In early 1991, nearly 3 million workers were unemployed or on short working hours in the East (out of a labor force of roughly 8.5 million), and some economists forecast that only a quarter of formerly East German companies will survive in the new unified German market.

Citizens on each side of the former border expected that such economic problems would accompany unification, and they are prepared to accept these problems at least in the short term. But if the economic development of the East proceeds more slowly than people expect or if the costs of assimilating the East German economy exceed what the majority of citizens are willing to bear, the economic aspects of unification may emerge as a politically divisive issue with both a regional and a class basis.

Religion has provided another sharp basis of social cleavage in German politics ever since the Reformation. One of the distinctive features of postwar West German politics was the moderation of this social division. Catholics, who had been a minority in prewar Germany, found themselves at parity with Protestants in West Germany because the postwar division of Germany included the heavily Catholic regions in the Federal Republic. The Christian Democratic Union also changed the traditional religious alignment that pitted Catholics against Protestants by uniting both denominations within one religious party. The historical conflicts between Protestants and Catholics mostly were replaced by differences between religious and nonreligious groups. The general secularization of society further eroded the role of religion in West German politics.

German unification may upset the delicate religious balance of politics in the Federal Republic. Catholics comprise 42 percent of the West German public, but only 7 percent in the East. Thus, unification significantly changes the religious composition of the Federal Republic, with Protestants now outnumbering Catholics by nearly 5 million people. Parity encouraged harmony that a new religious imbalance will test. A more Protestant (and working-class) electorate should also change the balance of policy preferences among the West German public and may potentially reshape electoral alliances. In addition, the integration of East German religious organizations into the Western church structure may stimulate internal changes in the nature of the religious movement in the Federal Republic.

Gender roles are another traditional source of social differentiation in German society. In the past the woman's role was defined by the three K's — *Kinder* (children), *Kirche* (church), and *Küche* (kitchen) — while politics and work were male matters. Attempts to lessen role differences have met with mixed success. The FRG's Basic Law guarantees the equality of the sexes, but the specific legislation to support this guarantee often has been lacking. Gradually, more women have entered politics and the labor force in West Germany, although women remain underrepresented within higher status professions. Cultural norms have also changed only slowly; cross-national surveys indicate that West German males are more chauvinist than

the average European, and West German women feel less liberated than other Europeans.[7]

The GDR constitution also guaranteed the equality of the sexes, and the East German government was more aggressive in protecting this guarantee. For instance, women's share of seats in the East German People's Congress was nearly twice the proportion of women in the West German Parliament. A larger percentage of East German women were employed in the labor force, although they were still underrepresented in careers with high status or authority. Maternity benefits were more generous in the East, *and* women had the unlimited right to abortion.

East German women have been one of the first groups to suffer as a result of the unification process. The proportion of women deputies decreased by nearly half in the first popularly elected East German Parliament. Eastern women have also mobilized to oppose the loss of rights and benefits that they held under East German law. In fact, the unification process was temporarily halted by the protests of women's groups in the GDR who feared the loss of abortion rights under more restrictive West German legislation. The reconciliation of conflicting abortion legislation remains an unresolved aspect of the unification process, and the higher expectations of East German women may act to remobilize the women's movement in the new unified Germany.

Another newly developing social cleavage involves Germany's growing minority of *guest workers* (*Gastarbeiter*).[8] The Economic Miracle produced a severe West German labor shortage in the 1960s, and the government responded by recruiting foreign workers from Southern Europe. Several million workers — from Turkey, Yugoslavia, Italy, Spain, and Greece — came, worked long enough to acquire skills and some personal savings, and then returned home. Many guest workers chose to remain in West Germany, however, and brought their families to join them. A similar migration of foreign workers occurred in East Germany, with Vietnamese, Angolans, and other Third World peoples relocating to the GDR. This new social stratum appears to be a permanent aspect of German society. About 6 percent of the population and 10 percent of the workforce are now foreigners.

From the beginning, the guest-worker situation has presented several potential political problems. These workers are concentrated at the low end of the economic ladder, often performing jobs that native Germans do not want. Guest workers are culturally, socially, and linguistically isolated from German society. The problems of social and cultural isolation are especially difficult for the children of guest workers. Although raised in Germany, they are not integrated into German society and do not possess the rights of German citizenship; their homeland, too, is a foreign country to them. Because of these cultural differences, social tensions often exist between native Germans and guest workers. This factor contributed to the unexpected strength of an extreme right-wing party (the Republican party) in the Spring 1989 Berlin elections. Popular reports claim that tolerance for guest workers is even lower in the East. Many analysts are concerned about the social and economic pressures that might be placed on guest workers if the costs of unification place an undue strain on the German economy.

Finally, regionalism potentially represents another strong force of social and political division in contemporary Germany. The Federal Republic is divided into sixteen states (*Länder*), ten states in the West and six new states created out of East Germany, including a new city-state of Berlin. Unification has substantially increased the cultural, economic, and political variations between the various states. Many of the Länder in the West are distinguished by their own historical traditions and social structure. The urban and liberal city-states of Hamburg and Bremen are clearly different from the surrounding rural and conservative states of Lower Saxony and Schleswig–Holstein, which in turn stand in marked contrast to the province of Mecklenberg–Vorpommerania to the East. At least for now, the language and idioms of speech help to differentiate residents from the eastern and western halves of the nation. And no one would mistake a northern German for a Bavarian from the south — their manners and dialects are too distinct.

These regional differences are reinforced by the decentralized structure of society and the economy. Economic and cultural activities are dispersed throughout the nation rather than being concentrated in a single national center. The Federal Republic's heavy urbanization has produced several dozen major metropolitan areas that function as regional economic centers. Economic activity is distributed among cities such as Frankfurt, Cologne, Dresden, Munich, Leipzig, and Hamburg. The mass media are organized around regional markets, and there are even several competing "national" theaters throughout the country.

The economic and social tensions of German unifi-cation will undoubtedly reinforce the importance of regional differences within the new German state. It is already common to hear of two German nations — one East and one West — residing within the new single state. Individuals from the East will continue to draw on their separate traditions and experiences when making political decisions, just as citizens will in the West. Similarly, even deputies in the newly elected all-German parliament openly comment on how their regional ties have become more prominent in defining their own political status and policy viewpoints. At least in the short term, therefore, regional considerations will become a more important factor in German society and politics.

INSTITUTIONS AND STRUCTURE OF GOVERNMENT

The Basic Law was intended to create a political system that could temporarily serve the Federal Republic until both halves of Germany were reunited; the preamble states this intention "to give a new order to political life for a transitional period." The final article of the Basic Law looked forward to the eventual reunification of Germany under a new political system: "This Basic Law shall cease to be in force on the day on which a constitution adopted by a free decision of the German people comes into force." In actuality, the rapid political and economic disintegration of East Germany in 1990 led to the incorporation of the GDR into the existing political, legal, and economic systems of the Federal Republic. In September 1990 the Federal Republic and the German Democratic Republic signed a treaty agreeing to unify their two states, and the Basic Law was amended to accommodate the accession of the GDR. Thus, the political system of the unified Germany functions within the procedures spelled out in the Basic Law.

When the Parliamentary Council originally framed the Basic Law in 1949, its goal was to construct a stable and effective democratic political system.[9] One specific objective was to maintain some historical continuity in political institutions. Most Germans were familiar with the workings of a parliamentary system, and there was also an interest in maintaining a federal structure of government. Both the empire and the Weimar Republic had contained federalist structures. The Allied powers saw this as a means of preventing the emergence of a strong centralized German government that again might marshal the power of Hitler's Reich.

A second objective was to design a political system

that would avoid the institutional weaknesses underlying the collapse of the Weimar democracy. The framers of the constitution wanted to establish clearer lines of political authority and responsibility. At the same time, the new system should contain more extensive checks and balances to avoid the usurpation of power that occurred in the Third Reich. Finally, the need was obvious for institutional limits on extremist and antisystem forces that might attempt to destabilize and subvert the democratic political order.

The Basic Law is an exceptional example of political engineering — the construction of a political system to achieve specific goals. The authors of the Basic Law designed a parliamentary democracy that would involve the public, encourage responsibility among political elites, disperse political power, and limit the possibility that extremists might cripple the state or illegally grasp political power.

A Federal System

Germany has one of the few federal political systems in Europe (see Figure 11.2). As noted earlier, the nation is organized into sixteen states (*Länder*), each with its own government. The state governments are important institutions in the political system created by the Basic Law. Political power is divided between the federal government (*Bund*) and the state governments. In most policy areas the federal government holds primary responsibility for policy. The states, however, are granted jurisdiction in education, culture, law enforcement, and regional planning. In several other policy areas the states and federal government share concurrent powers, although federal law takes priority in case of conflict. Furthermore, the states retain residual powers to legislate in those areas that the Basic Law has not explicitly assigned to the federal government.

The structure of state governments is based on a parliamentary system. A unicameral legislature, normally called a *Landtag*, is directly elected by popular vote. The party, or coalition of parties, which controls the legislature selects a minister president to head the state government. Next to the federal chancellor, the minister presidents may be the most powerful political offices in the Federal Republic. The minister president selects a cabinet to administer the state agencies and perform the executive functions of the state government.

Although the federal government is the major

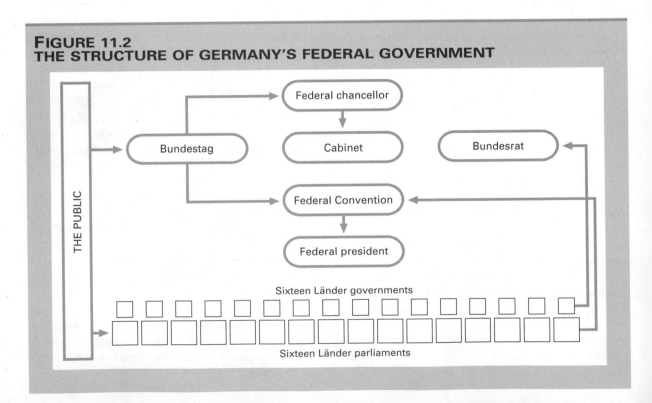

FIGURE 11.2
THE STRUCTURE OF GERMANY'S FEDERAL GOVERNMENT

force in the legislation of policy, the states hold primary responsibility for implementation and administration of policy. The states enforce their own regulations as well as most of the domestic legislation enacted by the federal government. The state governments also oversee the operation of local governments.

The political powers of the state governments extend beyond their legislative and administrative roles at the state level. One house of the federal legislature, the Bundesrat, is comprised solely of representatives appointed by the state governments. State government officials also participate in selecting the federal president and the justices of the major federal courts.

In addition to these formal institutional arrangements, extensive informal channels for policy consultations exist between state and federal officials. Intergovernmental committees and planning groups coordinate the different interests of federal and state governments. These organizations practice a style of "cooperative federalism" whereby Länder governments can coordinate their activities at a regional level or work together with federal officials.

Parliamentary Government

The central institution of the federal government is the Parliament. It passes legislation, elects the federal chancellor, debates government policies, and oversees the activities of the federal ministries. Parliament is bicameral: the popularly elected *Bundestag* is the primary legislative body; the *Bundesrat* represents the state governments at the federal level.

THE BUNDESTAG   The 656 deputies of the Bundestag are the only government officials who can claim to represent the German public directly. Deputies are selected in national elections every four years, unless the Bundestag is dissolved prematurely. The formal norms of the Bundestag encourage deputies to evaluate issues from a national perspective. The Basic Law even states that deputies serve as representatives of the whole people, and not as delegates for specific interests or political movements. In practice, however, the behavior of deputies clearly reflects their group ties.

The Bundestag's major function is to enact legislation; all federal legislation must receive its approval. The initiative for most legislation, however, lies in the executive branch. Like other modern parliaments, the Bundestag focuses on evaluating and amending the government's legislative program.

Another function of the Bundestag is to provide a forum for public debate. The plenary sessions of the Parliament consider the legislation before the chamber. Debating time is allowed to all party groupings (*Fraktionen*) according to their size; both party leaders and backbenchers normally participate. Because party members already have caucused and agreed on their voting positions, these plenary sessions serve primarily as a means of publicly expressing the party's views. During the 1970s the Bundestag began to televise important plenary sessions, thus expanding the public audience for these policy debates.

The Bundestag also scrutinizes the actions of the government on both policy and administrative issues. The most commonly used method of oversight is the "question hour," adopted from the British House of Commons. An individual deputy can submit a written question to a government minister: questions range from broad policy issues to the specific needs of one constituent. These queries are answered by government representatives during the question hour, and deputies can raise supplementary questions at that time. More than 20,000 questions were posed during the 1987–1990 term of the Bundestag. A group of deputies can also submit a written question to the government that requires a more formal written or oral reply; 400 to 500 such questions are submitted during a Bundestag session.

In addition to these formal questions, deputies can petition for a special debate on a contemporary policy problem. These debates tend to be more genuine than the plenary sessions, perhaps because debate is not limited to a specific legislative proposal. Finally, the committees of the Bundestag hold special hearings to investigate the actions of the government in their area of specialization.

The opposition parties normally make greatest use of the question and debating opportunities of the Bundestag; about two-thirds of the questions posed during the 1987–1990 term came from the small Green party. Backbenchers of the governing parties also use these devices to make their own views known. On the whole, the Bundestag's oversight powers are considerable, especially for a legislature in a parliamentary system.

THE BUNDESRAT   The second chamber of the Parliament, the Bundesrat, is a consequence of Germany's federal system. Its sixty-nine members are appointed by the state governments to represent their interests in

The beginning of a new nation: Chancellor Helmut Kohl addresses the first meeting of the all-German Parliament (Bundestag) held in the Berlin Reichstag building in October 1990.

tive process, although its legislative authority is secondary to that of the Bundestag. The federal government is required to submit all legislative proposals to the Bundesrat before forwarding them to the Bundestag. Bundesrat approval is required, however, only in policy areas where the states hold concurrent powers or where the states will administer federal regulations.

In the early years of the Federal Republic, the Bundesrat focused on the administrative aspects of federal legislation. Civil servants from the state governments examined the technical language of proposals and their potential effect on the states. Beginning in the 1960s, the Bundesrat broadened its definition of state-related policy. This expansion of the Bundesrat's involvement means that about two-thirds of legislative proposals now require its approval. More and more often, too, the chamber's deliberations are guided by political considerations rather than administrative details. This is especially true for periods when one coalition controls the Bundesrat, while another coalition holds a majority in the Bundestag.

In sum, the Parliament is mainly a body that reacts to government proposals rather than taking the initiative. In comparison to the British House of Commons or the French National Assembly, however, the Bundestag probably exercises more autonomy from the government. Especially if one includes the Bundesrat, the Parliament in Germany has more independence and opportunity to criticize and revise government proposals.

The Federal Chancellor and Cabinet

One of the weaknesses of the Weimar system was the unclear division of executive authority between the president and the *chancellor*. The Basic Law resolved this ambiguity by substantially strengthening the powers of the federal chancellor (*Bundeskanzler*). Moreover, in practice the incumbents of this office have dominated the political process and symbolized the federal government by the force of their personality. The chancellor plays such a central role in the political system that some observers describe the German system as a "chancellor democracy."

The chancellor is elected by the Bundestag and is responsible to it for the conduct of the federal government. This process grants the chancellor substantial authority. He represents a majority of the Bundestag and normally can count on their support for his legislative proposals. The chancellor usually heads his own party,

Bonn. The state governments normally appoint members of the state cabinet to serve jointly in the Bundesrat; the chamber thus can act as a permanent conference of minister presidents. Bundesrat seats are allocated to each state in numbers roughly proportionate to the state's population: six seats for the most populous states to three for the least. The votes for each state delegation are cast in a block, according to the instructions of the state government.

The Bundesrat is directly involved in the legisla-

directing party strategy and leading the party at elections.

A unique feature of the German system is the way it provides for a separation of legislative and executive power but still retains a parliamentary framework. For instance, the chancellor lacks the discretionary authority to dissolve the legislature and call for new elections, something that is normally found in parliamentary systems. The Bundestag and Bundesrat also possess an unusual ability to criticize government actions and revise government legislative proposals.

Equally important are the provisions of the Basic Law which limit the legislature's control over the chancellor and his Cabinet. In a parliamentary system the legislature normally possesses the authority to remove a chief executive whom it initially elected. During the Weimar Republic, however, extremist parties of the right and left used this device to destabilize the democratic system by opposing incumbent chancellors. The Basic Law modified this procedure and created a *constructive no-confidence vote*. In order for the Bundestag to remove a chancellor, it simultaneously must agree on a successor. This ensures a continuity in political leadership and an initial majority in support of a new chancellor. The constructive no-confidence vote means that a chancellor is not dependent on maintaining a majority on all legislative proposals. It also makes removing an incumbent more difficult; opponents cannot simply disagree with the government — a consensus must exist on an alternative.

The constructive no-confidence vote has been attempted only twice in the history of the Federal Republic — and succeeded only once. In 1982 a new CDU/CSU – FDP coalition replaced Chancellor Schmidt with a new chancellor, Helmut Kohl.

A second type of no-confidence vote allows the chancellor to attach a no-confidence provision to a government legislative proposal. If the Bundestag defeats the proposal, the chancellor may ask the federal president to call for new Bundestag elections. This no-confidence procedure provides the chancellor with the means either to test the government's voting support or to increase the incentive for the Bundestag to pass legislation that is crucial to the government.

Another source of the chancellor's authority is his control over the Cabinet. The federal government today consists of eighteen departments, each headed by a minister. The Cabinet ministers are formally appointed, or dismissed, by the federal president on the recommen-

dation of the chancellor — Bundestag approval is not necessary. The Basic Law also grants the chancellor the power to decide on the number of Cabinet ministers and their duties.

The functioning of the federal government follows three principles laid out in the Basic Law. First, the *chancellor principle* holds that the chancellor alone is responsible for the policies of the federal government. The Basic Law states that the formal policy guidelines issued by the chancellor must be followed by the Cabinet ministers; these are legally binding directives. Ministers are expected to suggest and implement policies that are consistent with the chancellor's guidelines. The chancellor is aided in these activities by the large staff of the Chancellor's Office (*Bundeskanzleramt*) which supervises the ministries and formulates the government's broad policy goals. Thus, in contrast to the British system of shared Cabinet responsibility, the German Cabinet is formally subordinate to the chancellor in policymaking.

The second principle of *ministerial autonomy* gives each minister the authority to conduct the internal workings of the department without Cabinet intervention as long as the policies conform to the government's broad guidelines. Ministers are responsible for supervising the activities of their departments, guiding the department's policy planning, preparing and overseeing the administration of policy within their jurisdiction. These duties involve managing the relevant activities of the federal ministry in addition to supervising the implementation and administration of federal laws by the state bureaucracies.

The *cabinet principle* is the third organizational guideline. When conflicts arise between departments over jurisdictional or budgetary matters, the Basic Law calls for them to be resolved in the Cabinet.

The actual working of the federal government tends to be more fluid than the formal procedures spelled out by the Basic Law.[10] In a coalition government the number and choice of ministries to be held by each party is a major issue in building the coalition. Similarly, intraparty tensions may necessitate certain Cabinet assignments in the interest of party unity. Cabinet members also display considerable independence on policy despite the formal restrictions of the Basic Law. Ministers normally are appointed because they possess expertise or interest in a policy area. In practice, they identify more with their roles as department heads than with their roles as agents of the chancellor. Ministers become spokespersons and advocates for their departments; their political success is judged by their representation of department interests.

The Cabinet thus serves as a clearinghouse for the business of the federal government. Specific ministers present policy proposals originating in their departments in the hope of gaining government endorsement. In practice, the chancellor seldom relies on formal policy instructions to guide the actions of the government. The chancellor defines a government program that reflects a consensus of the Cabinet and relies on negotiations and compromise within the Cabinet to maintain this consensus.

The Federal President

During the Weimar Republic, executive authority was divided between two offices—the chancellor and the president. Both offices were retained by the Federal Republic, but the Basic Law clearly concentrates executive authority in the chancellorship. The *federal president* (*Bundespräsident*) is a mostly ceremonial post. The president's official duties involve greeting visiting heads of state, attending official government functions, visiting foreign nations, and similar tasks.

The federal president is also removed from the competition of the political system and supposedly remains above partisan politics. The present officeholder, Richard von Weizsäcker, stepped down from his positions in the Christian Democratic Union when he became federal president in 1984. Also, the president is not selected by popular election but by a Federal Convention composed of all Bundestag deputies and an equal number of representatives chosen by the state legislatures.

This reduction in the president's formal political role does not mean that an incumbent is entirely uninvolved in the political process. The Basic Law assigns several ceremonial functions to the president, who appoints government and military officials, signs treaties and laws, and possesses the power of pardon. In these instances, however, the president is merely carrying out the will of the government, and even these actions must be countersigned by the chancellor. The president also nominates a chancellor to the Bundestag and dissolves Parliament if a government legislative proposal loses a no-confidence vote. In both instances, the president's ability to act independently is limited by the Basic Law.

Potentially more significant is the constitutional ambiguity over whether the president *must* honor requests from the government, or may refuse. The president may have the constitutional right to veto legislation by refusing to sign it, and refuse the chancellor's recommendation for Cabinet appointments, or even a request to dissolve the Bundestag. These constitutional questions have not been tested by past presidents, and thus have not been resolved by the courts. Most analysts see these ambiguities as another safety valve built into the Basic Law's elaborate system of checks and balances.

The political importance of the federal president is also based on factors that go beyond the articles of the Basic Law. An active, dynamic president, such as von Weizsäcker, can help to shape the political climate of the nation through his speeches and public activities. He is the one political figure who can rightly claim to be above politics and who can work to extend the vision of the nation beyond its everyday concerns.

The Judicial System

Despite the federal basis of the German political system, the various levels of the courts are integrated into a unitary system (see Figure 11.3). The three lowest levels of the system are administered by the states, and the highest court is at the federal level. This one court system hears both civil and criminal cases, and all courts apply the same national legal codes.

Another branch of the judicial system deals with court cases in specialized areas. One court deals with administrative complaints against government agencies, one handles tax matters, another deals with labor–management disputes, and still another resolves claims involving government social programs. Like the rest of the judicial system, these specialized courts are integrated into one system including both state and federal courts.

The Basic Law created a third branch of the judiciary. An independent Constitutional Court reviews the constitutionality of legislation, mediates disputes between levels of government, and protects the constitutional and democratic order.[11] This is an innovation for the German legal system because it places one law, the Basic Law, above all others; it also implies limits on the decision-making power of the Parliament and the judicial interpretations of lower court judges. Because of the importance of the Constitutional Court, its members are selected in equal numbers by the Bundestag and Bundesrat and can be removed only for abuse of the office.

The Federal Republic's judicial system is based on Roman law principles that are fundamentally different

FIGURE 11.3
ORGANIZATION OF THE COURTS

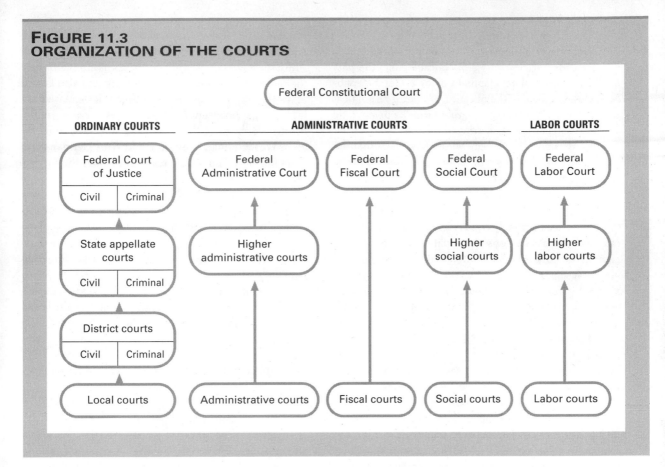

from the Anglo-American system of justice. Rather than relying on precedents from prior cases, the legal process is based on an extensive system of legal codes. The codes define legal principles in the abstract, and specific cases are judged against these standards. The system is based on a rationalist philosophy that justice can be served by following the letter of the law.

The German system also emphasizes society's rights and the efficient administration of justice over those of an individual defendant. The judicial system, for example, gives equal weight to the evidence of the prosecution and the defense. Similarly, the rules of evidence are not as restrictive as those in American courts.

Because the goal of the system is to uncover the truth within a complex web of legal codes, the judge pursues an activist role in the court. Cross-examining witnesses, determining what is acceptable as evidence, and generally directing the course of the trial are among the duties. Furthermore, in some instances the judge (or panel of judges) votes along with lay jurors in deciding a case. Naturally, the judge's opinion can easily sway the votes of the jury. A unanimous decision is not required; a majority is sufficient. In the higher courts, lay jurors are not even used. Justice is to be rational, fair, and expedient; presumably this goal requires the expertise that only judges possess.

REMAKING POLITICAL CULTURES

The history of Germany's political systems is intertwined with its cultural development. The negative aspects of past regimes were mirrored in the political beliefs of the public. Under the Kaiser, citizens were expected to be subjects, not active participants in the political process; the style of politics nurtured feelings of cynicism and intolerance. The interlude of the Weimar Republic did little to change these values. The polarization, fragmentation, and outright violence of the Weimar Republic taught people to avoid politics, and not become active participants. Moreover, democracy eventually failed, and national socialism arose in its place. The Third Reich then raised yet another generation of Germans under an intolerant, authoritarian system.

Because of Germany's historical legacy, the past and future political development of the Federal Republic is closely linked to the question of whether a political culture exists that is fully congruent with its democratic system of government. During the initial years of the Federal Republic, there were widespread fears that the nation lacked a democratic political culture, thereby making it vulnerable to the same types of problems that undermined the Weimar Republic. Public opinion polls in West Germany presented a negative image of public beliefs that was probably equally applicable to both Germanies.[12] West Germans were politically detached, acceptant of authority, and intolerant in their political views. A significant minority were unrepentant Nazis, sympathy for many elements of the Nazi ideology was widespread, and anti-Semitic feelings remained commonplace.

Perhaps even more amazing than the Economic Miracle was West Germany's success in remaking its political culture in little more than a generation. Confronted by an uncertain public commitment to democracy, the government undertook a massive program to reeducate the German public. The schools, the media, and political organizations were mobilized behind the effort. And the citizenry itself was changing — older generations raised under authoritarian regimes were being replaced by younger generations socialized exclusively during the postwar democratic era. These efforts created a new democratic political culture congruent with the political institutions and process of the Federal Republic.

Now, a second cultural question faces the nation. As the FRG sought to remake the political culture in the West, so too did the GDR in the East. Only the communists tried to create a rival culture that would support their new state and its socialist economic system. Indeed, the efforts at political education in the East were more intense and extensive, and aimed at creating a broader "socialist personality" that reached into nonpolitical attitudes and behavior.[13] Through a variety of governmental agents, young people were taught to develop a collective identity with their peers, to nurture a love for the GDR and its socialist brethren, to accept the guidance of the SED, and to understand history and society from a Marxist-Leninist perspective.

German unification means the blending of these two different political cultures, and the nature of this mixture is uncertain. In the absence of scientific social science research in the GDR, analysts could never be sure if the government's propaganda was internalized by the public. Influences from West Germany also flowed eastward, and two decades of Ostpolitik increased the interchange between East and West. Furthermore, nearly two-thirds of the East German public could receive West German television, and West German news programs garnered a larger audience than the GDR's own broadcasts. Thus, there is considerable uncertainty about how much the cultures of East and West really differ. In addition, the revolutionary political events leading to German unification represent the type of experiences that can reshape even long-held political beliefs. What does a communist think after attending communism's funeral?

The future of the Federal Republic is again dependent on a question of the compatibility of the culture and the political system. The citizens in the West are deeply committed to Western values and the democratic process, but can this culture assimilate 16 million new citizens with potentially different beliefs about how politics and society should function?

Nation and State

An essential element of the German culture has been a strong sense of German identity. A common history, culture, territory, and language created a sense of national community long before Germany was politically united. Germany was the land of Schiller, Goethe, Beethoven, and Wagner, even if the Germans disagreed on political boundaries. The imagery of a single *Volk* bound Germans together despite their social and political differences.

Previous regimes had failed, however, to develop a sense of political community as part of the German national identity. Succeeding political systems were relatively short-lived and were unable to develop a popular consensus on the nature and goals of German politics. Postwar West Germany faced a similar challenge: building a political community in a divided and defeated nation.

In the early 1950s large sectors of the West German public still were committed to the symbols and personalities of previous regimes.[14] Most citizens felt that the German Empire or Hitler's prewar Reich represented the best times for Germany. Substantial minorities also favored a return to the Imperial flag, restoration of the monarchy, or a one-party state. Almost half the population believed that if it had not been for World War II, Hitler would have been one of Germany's greatest statesmen.

Over the next two decades these ties to earlier regimes gradually weakened, and the bonds to the new institutions and leaders of the Federal Republic steadily grew stronger (Figure 11.4). The number of citizens who believed that Bundestag deputies represent the public interest doubled between 1951 and 1964; public respect shifted from the personalities of prior regimes to the chancellors of the Federal Republic. By the 1970s an overwhelming majority of the public felt that the present was the best time in German history; West Germans became more politically tolerant, and feelings of anti-Semitism declined sharply. Various other measures displayed the public's growing esteem for the new political system. For example, in 1959 very few people saw the political system as a source of national accomplishment; by 1978 almost a third of the public was openly proud of the political system and its democratic institutions.[15]

Yet even while West Germans developed a new acceptance of the formal institutions and symbols of the

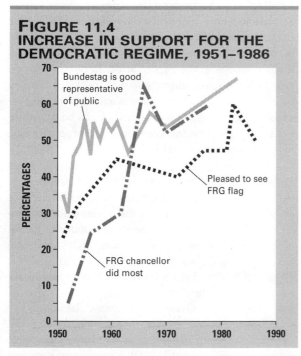

**FIGURE 11.4
INCREASE IN SUPPORT FOR THE
DEMOCRATIC REGIME, 1951–1986**

Source: Russell J. Dalton, *Politics in West Germany* (Glenview Ill.: Scott Foresman, 1989), p. 105.

Federal Republic, something was still missing, something that touched the spirit of their political feelings. There was always a tentativeness about the West German state; it was a provisional entity, and "Germany" meant a reunified nation. Were citizens of the FRG to think of themselves as Germans, West Germans, or some mix of both? In addition, the trauma of the Third Reich burned a deep scar in the West German psyche, making citizens hesitant to openly express pride in their nation or a sense of German national identity. Because of this political stigma, the Federal Republic avoided many of the emotional national symbols that are common in other industrialized nations. There were few political holidays or memorials; the national anthem was seldom played; and even the anniversary of the founding of the Federal Republic received little public attention. The uncertain national identity of the West Germans represented an unfinished element in their cultural transformation.

The quest for a national identity was even more difficult in the East. The leadership of the GDR claimed that it represented the "pure" elements of German history, while the Federal Republic was portrayed as the successor to the Third Reich. The prospect of eventual reunification also made East Germany a provisional state, at least until they abandoned the concept of a single Germany in the wake of Ostpolitik. Socialism became the basis of the East German identity. Thus, a 1990 study found that youth in the East identify Karl Marx as the figure they most admire (followed by the first president of the GDR), while Western youth are most likely to name Konrad Adenauer.

Most analysts believe that the GDR succeeded in creating at least a sense of resigned loyalty to the regime through its political and social accomplishments, but the government was never able to develop a popular consensus in support of the state.[16] The first decade of the GDR's existence was marked by repeated purges against those who might oppose the state, punctuated by the 1953 uprising of workers in East Berlin and its suppression by force. The secret police (*Stasi*) kept files on over 6 million people, government informers seemed omnipresent, and the Berlin Wall stood as a constant reminder of the nature of the East German state. The government found it necessary to use coercion and the threat of force to sustain itself, and once socialism failed, the basis for a separate East German political identity also evaporated.

Unification has begun a process whereby the German search for a national political identity might finally be resolved. The opening of the Berlin Wall created a feeling of euphoria and political excitement that was quite alien to earlier political norms. This feeling has carried forward. Most East Germans have quickly adapted themselves to the political system of the Federal Republic, a situation that is far different from West Germany in the 1950s. The celebration of unification, and the designation of October 3 as a national holiday, finally gives Germans something political to celebrate. Earlier efforts in the East and West to rekindle a historical consciousness are now proceeding with greater energy. For the first time in over a century, nearly all Germans agree where their borders begin and end. Germany is now a single nation — democratic, free, and looking toward the future.

Democratic Norms and Procedures

A second important element of the political culture involves citizen attitudes toward the system of government. In the early years of the West German state, the rules of democratic politics — majority rule, minority rights, individual liberties, and pluralistic debate — were new concepts that did not fit citizens' past experiences. In German political theory the state was traditionally viewed in an idealistic, almost mystical way. Progress, stability, order, and well-being came by subordinating individual interests to the general interests represented by the state. Political power was absolute and flowed from the state rather than from the people. This model of the authoritarian state (*Obrigkeitsstaat*) was basic to the political regimes of the Kaiser and the Third Reich.

To break this model and develop experience with democracy, the West German government drew on another traditional aspect of the political culture. Germans were used to a state based on legal principles, clearly defined authority relationships, and comprehensive codes of political conduct (*Rechtsstaat*). Authoritarian governments had used these legal formalities to legitimize their power. The leaders of West Germany constructed a system that formalized democratic procedures. Citizen participation was encouraged and expected; policymaking became open, involving all legitimate interest groups.

The West German public gradually learned democratic norms by continued exposure to the new political system. Political leadership provided a generally positive example of competition in a democratic setting. When political crises occurred, they were resolved with-

out resort to nondemocratic rhetoric and actions (by either elites or the public) and with little challenge to the basic principles of the Federal Republic. As a result, a popular consensus slowly developed in support of the democratic political system. By the mid-1960s agreement was nearly unanimous that democracy was the best form of government, and to the present day nearly all West Germans are satisfied with the basic functioning of democracy. More importantly, the West German public has displayed a growing commitment to democratic procedures — a multiparty system, conflict management, minority rights, and representative government.

Events of the past two decades have tested the long-term growth in system support and democratic norms in West Germany. The most severe challenge came from the attacks of antisystem terrorist groups in the 1970s. A small group of extremists attempted to topple the system through a guerrilla warfare campaign. Although numbering only a few hundred individuals, their violent actions put the political culture to a severe test.[17] The government had to walk a fine line in dealing with terrorism, between guaranteeing the public order and protecting civil liberties. Many observers believe that the SPD-led government erred toward the side of securing the public order by enacting excessive antiterrorist legislation. Similar controversies arose when the CDU-led government proposed restrictions on protest in response to the violent activities of anarchic and radical ecology groups in the early 1980s. In both instances, however, the basic lesson was that the West German political system could face the onslaughts of urban guerrillas and extremists, and survive with its basic institutions and procedures intact and without the public losing faith in their democratic process.

The propaganda of the East German government also stressed a democratic creed. The Communist party's first public declaration in 1945 rejected the idea of a political system based on the Soviet model and instead called for the establishment of a democratic parliamentary system with full democratic rights and freedoms for the populace. In its first constitution the GDR presented itself as a democratic state, with a multiparty system and constitutional protection of civil rights. It was, after all, the German *Democratic* Republic.

But while government propaganda stressed democracy, the reality of politics sought to create a political culture that was compatible with a communist state and socialist economy. The culture drew on traditional Prussian values of obedience, duty, and loyalty: People were again told that obedience was the responsibility of a good citizen, and support of the state (and the party) was an end in itself. The East German state depended on the continued acceptance of an authoritarian system that was more akin to the Third Reich and Second Empire than to the democratic system of the Federal Republic. Periodically, political events — the 1953 Berlin uprising, the construction of the Berlin Wall, the suppression of the Czechoslovakian reform government in 1968, and the ongoing expulsions of political dissidents — reminded East Germans of the gap between the democratic rhetoric of the regime and reality.

Perhaps one reason why the popular revolt grew so rapidly in East Germany in 1989 was that the regime had convinced the public of the value of democratic ideals, while also showing them the incompatibility of communism and these ideals. At the least, the revolutionary changes that swept through East Germany as the Berlin Wall fell nurtured a belief in democracy as the road to political reform. In a Spring 1990 public opinion survey, for example, the basic tenets of democracy received nearly universal support from both West and East Germans (Table 11.1)! Nearly all West Germans *and* East Germans endorsed the concepts of political

opposition, citizen protest, minority rights, and free speech. For example, 93 percent of West Germans believed that it was not conceivable to have a democracy without a viable opposition; 95 percent of the East Germans shared these views. Moreover, East Germans were actually more tolerant than West Germans toward conflict in a democratic setting (the lower half of the table), because GDR citizens had recently won their freedom through the public protests that challenged the communist regime. Given their democratic norms, it follows that only 38 percent of East Germans were satisfied with the workings of the political process in the GDR, even after their first free election in over fifty years, compared to 85 percent in West Germany. Rather than remaking this aspect of the East German culture, the greater need is to transform Eastern enthusiasm for democracy into a deeper and richer understanding of the workings of the process and its pragmatic strengths and weaknesses.

Social Values and the New Politics

A third area of cultural change in Germany involves a shift in public values that followed from the social and

TABLE 11.1
SUPPORT FOR DEMOCRATIC PRINCIPLES IN WEST GERMANY AND EAST GERMANY (PERCENTAGE DISTRIBUTION)

	West Germany	East Germany
Satisfied with democracy in their nation	85	38
DEMOCRATIC VALUES		
Percentage agreeing		
Democracy requires a political opposition.	93	95
Every citizen has the right to demonstrate.	90	90
Every democratic party should have the chance to govern.	91	88
Public interests should have priority over individual interests.	89	85
All people should have the right to express their opinion.	92	90
CONFLICT VERSUS ORDER		
Percentage disagreeing		
A citizen forfeits the right to protest if he threatens order.	28	50
The political opposition should support the government.	39	53
Conflicts between interests are inimical to the public interest.	47	74
In a democratic society, some conflicts require violence.	79	81

Source: German Identity 1990 Study conducted by Prof. Rudolf Wildenmann, Research Unit for Societal Developments, Mannheim (April 1990). I would like to thank Prof. Wildenmann for graciously providing access to these data.

economic accomplishments of the nation. Once substantial progress was made in developing system support and addressing traditional social needs, citizens in the West broadened their interests to include a new set of societal goals. During the past decade new issues such as pollution, women's liberation, and participation at the workplace have become more prominent. In the early 1980s a vibrant peace movement rekindled the debate on the FRG's international role. Rather than consensus and moderation, new bases of political polarization and competition emerged.

The development of these new political orientations in the West is generally explained in terms of a broad theory of value change proposed by Ronald Inglehart.[18] Inglehart maintains that a person's value priorities reflect the family and societal conditions that prevail early in life. Thus, the tremendous social, economic, and political trends that have restructured West German society could be expected to alter public preferences about what values are important and what social goals should be pursued. Older generations socialized before World War II lived at least partially under an authoritarian government, experienced long periods of economic hardship, and felt the destructive consequences of war. These older individuals remain preoccupied with so-called materialist goals — economic security, law and order, religious values, and a strong national defense — despite forty years of the Economic Miracle and political stability. In contrast, younger generations have grown up in a democratic political setting during a period of unprecedented economic prosperity, relative international stability, and now the collapse of the Soviet Empire. Given these experiences, younger generations are shifting their attention toward *postmaterialist values* or New Politics goals. Many young West Germans place a higher priority on self-expression, personal freedom, social equality, self-fulfillment, and maintaining the quality of life.

These new value orientations among the young and better educated became a cultural force through the creation of a distinct milieu where individual values were translated into social norms. Natural food stores, cooperative businesses, leftist bookstores, vegetarian restaurants, and bio-bakeries offer a life-style attuned to the new values. Small firms emphasize employee management of the company and a more humane working environment, rather than just making a profit. Day-care centers and job-sharing arrangements explore ways of allowing women to participate more fully in the labor force. This network of people and groups provides an environment in which an alternative culture could develop. The support of intellectuals, academics, and an alternative press helped diffuse these new norms so that they are no longer isolated in alternative districts but are now spread throughout society. Although still a minority of the population, these new values represent a "second culture" embedded within the dominant culture of West German society. To a much more modest extent, a similar counterculture also developed among young people in the East.

A major consequence of these changing values is the addition of new issues to the Federal Republic's political agenda. Environmental protection, including opposition to nuclear energy, has attracted widespread public attention; Germany is now one of the "greenest" of all European societies. There is renewed interest in extending the democratization of society through increased citizen participation in the political process and greater worker participation in company management (*Mitbestimmung*). In foreign policy, citizens are more interested in foreign aid for less developed countries and the general problems of North–South relations. In short, West German politics broadened its interests beyond traditional economic or security concerns to a group of New Politics interests.

The clash between New Politics groups and the political establishment is now a common aspect of West German politics. Older people, including politicians, often have difficulty communicating with youth who seem to criticize their elder's life-style and basic values. The New Politics movement also speaks about politics in a different language, because they view the world from a different perspective. For instance, instead of praising economic growth as the source of prosperity, postmaterialists criticize unplanned growth as a major source of society's problems and call for a more sustainable society. Moreover, the demands of New Politics groups occasionally lead to confrontations with the political authorities, as when an environmental group attempts to occupy a nuclear power plant or a peace group blocks the entrance to a military installation. Accommodating and managing this clash of values within the democratic process remains a major political challenge for the Federal Republic.

Two Peoples in One Nation?

Although citizens in the East and West share a common German heritage, forty years of separation have created cultural differences that now must be integrated into a single national culture. Until very recently, soldiers in the East German and West German armies viewed each other hostilely across the border; now they are comrades in arms. Bureaucrats raised in the communist system are suddenly asked to become civil servants. And citizens in the East need to adjust to their new roles in a free and democratic state.

Some aspects of these cultural differences present a potential source of division and polarization in a unified Germany. For instance, although residents in both the West and East endorse the tenets of democracy, it will be harder to reach agreement on how these ideals translate into practical politics. The open, sometimes confrontational style of Western politics will require a major adjustment for citizens raised under the closed system of the GDR. And as has happened in other recently democratized European nations, such as Spain and Portugal, initial enthusiasm for democratic politics might moderate if the system's performance does not meet popular expectations.

The life-styles and social relations of Easterners and Westerners illustrate another gap in cultural and social norms. The popular press overflows with accounts of Westerners complaining about the backwardness of people from the East (*Ossis*) — "Germany's Appalachia" is a typical description. Easterners counter with claims that West Germans (*Wessis*) are too self-centered and are slaves of a consumer society; they also sense a condescending attitude in Western actions toward the East. Even as they were celebrating unification, the former residents of the GDR openly worried about becoming second-class citizens in their new nation.

A potential cultural gap exists for attitudes toward work and the economy. When the first refugees began to move westward in 1989, they were much sought after by West German businesses, because East German workers were highly trained and reputedly firm believers in the German traits of hard work and industriousness. With unification the predominant image in the West has changed to a worry about the lack of ambition and competitiveness that a communist economy fostered. Western businesspeople seeking cooperative ventures in the East lament the lack of entrepreneurs who understand capitalist economics; instead, they deal with people socialized by years of dealing with the communist bureaucracy. It will be difficult for many Easterners to adjust to the idea of unemployment and the competitive pres-

sures of a market-based economy. This cultural gap may actually grow and become more politicized unless the economic differences between East and West begin to narrow.

Finally, unification may heighten material/postmaterial conflicts within German society. East Germany was struggling to become a materialist success, while West Germany was enjoying its postmaterial abundance. Consequently, materialist values such as higher living standards, security, hard work, and better living conditions are given greater weight in the East.[19] Most East Germans want first to share in the affluence and consumer society of the West, before they begin to fear the consequences of this affluence. Some Easterners therefore worry that the pro-environment and nonmaterial goals of New Politics groups from the West could undermine the economic development of the East. The clash of values within West German society has now been joined by East–West differences.

Germans share a common language, culture, and history — and a common set of ultimate political goals — but the strains of unification may magnify and politicize the differences between East and West rather than narrowing this gap. Germany could become two peoples within one nation. Whether the nation is able to blend these two cultures successfully will be a major factor in determining the fate and course of the new Germany.

POLITICAL LEARNING AND POLITICAL COMMUNICATION

If political systems require congruent political cultures, as many political experts maintain, then one of the basic functions of the political process is to create and perpetuate these citizen attitudes. The process of developing the beliefs and values of the public is known as *political socialization* (see Chapter 3). Political socialization is normally viewed as a source of continuity in a political system, with one generation transmitting the prevailing political norms to the next. As the preceding discussion of political cultures shows, socialization has been an agent of political change in Germany (and will again be so with unification). The development of a new democratic system in the West and a communist system in the East produced a break in past socialization patterns and a dramatic shift in the content of socialization. These resocialization efforts focused on the young, but political learning continues through the life cycle as new attitudes are formed and old attitudes are influenced by new experiences. Once these new beliefs take root, the objective of the socialization process shifts to perpetuation and deepening of these values. In addition, other elements of the socialization process, such as the media, perform a crucial communication function between citizens and political leaders. Political socialization in Germany thus involves both change and continuity.

Family Influences

Parents generally are seen as the major influence in forming the basic values and attitudes of their children. During their early years children have few sources of learning comparable to their parents. Family discussions can be a rich source of political information; children often internalize their parents' attitudes; and many of the basic values and beliefs acquired during childhood persist into adulthood.

In the early postwar years, family socialization did not function smoothly on either side of the German border. Many adults were hesitant to discuss politics openly because of the depoliticized environment of the period. Then, too, many parents were hesitant to discuss politics with their children for fear that the child would ask: "what did you do under Hitler, Daddy?" Furthermore, the political values and experiences of parents were minimally relevant to the new political orders. Parents in West Germany were ill prepared to tell their children how to be good democrats, and East German parents were equally uncertain of the new communist system. Adults learned the norms of the new political systems at almost the same time as their children.

The potential for parental socialization has grown steadily since the years immediately after the war.[20] Changing political norms increased the frequency of political discussion in the West, and family conversations about politics became commonplace. Moreover, young new parents were themselves raised under the system of the Federal Republic. These parents can pass on democratic norms and party attachments they have held for a lifetime.

The family also played an important role in the socialization process under the East German state. Researchers found that family ties were especially close in the East. Parents were an important source of political and social cues, and most young people claim to have the same political opinions as their parents. At the same time, the family provided one of the few settings where people could openly discuss their feelings and beliefs.

The family setting created a private sphere where individuals could be free of the watchful eyes of others. Here the state could be praised, but doubts could also be expressed.

Despite the growing openness within the family, both Germanies have experienced a widening generation gap in recent years. Youth in the West are more leftist than their parents, more oriented toward noneconomic goals, more positive about their role in the political process, and more likely to challenge prevailing social norms.[21] These differences between parent and child values are generally larger in the Federal Republic than in other Western European democracies. East German youth are also a product of their times; an autonomous peace movement and other counterculture groups flourished as part of the youth culture of the 1980s. The state even used once-banned Western rock music in attempts to reintegrate young people into GDR society. The youthful faces of the first refugees exiting through Hungary or the democracy protests in Leipzig and East Berlin attest to the importance of the youth culture within East Germany. The generation gap in East and West is another sign of a shift in young people's values and the adoption of goals that conflict with those of their elders.

Education

During the years when parental socialization often was lacking, the German governments used the educational system to fill some of this void.[22] In the West, the school system was enlisted in the government's program of re-educating the public to accept democratic norms. Instruction was aimed at developing a formal commitment to the institutions and procedures of the Federal Republic. Civics classes stressed the benefits of the democratic system, drawing sharp contrasts with the communist model. The educational system was crucial in remaking West German political culture.

Growing public support for the West German political system gradually made this program of formalized political education redundant. The content of civics instruction changed to give more emphasis to understanding the dynamics of the democratic process — interest representation, conflict resolution, minority rights, and the methods of citizen influence. Education in the West also adopted a more critical perspective on society and politics. A more pragmatic view of the strengths and weaknesses of democracy was substituted for the idealistic textbook images of the 1950s. The intent of the present system is to better prepare students for their adult roles as political participants.

The school system also played a key role in the political education program in the East, although the content was much different. Civics courses and the educational environment stressed the importance of the collective over the individual. The schools attempted to create a socialist personality that encompassed a devotion to communist principles, a love of the GDR, and participation in the activities of the state. Yet again, the rhetoric of education conflicted with reality. Government publications claimed that "education for peace is the overriding principle underlying classroom practice in all schools." But paramilitary training was a regular part of the curriculum and became compulsory for ninth and tenth graders in 1978. Students were told that the GDR was a state free of oppression, and then stared from their school buses at the barbed-wire strung along the border. Many young people certainly accepted the rhetoric of the regime, but the reeducation efforts remained incomplete.

Another important effect of education involves the sociological consequences of the structure of the system, which differs in fundamental terms between West and East. The secondary school system in the West generally follows the traditional European model of elitist education. The system is stratified into three distinct tracks. One track provides a general education that normally leads to vocational training and working-class occupations. A second track mixes vocational and academic training. Most graduates from this program are employed in lower middle-class occupations or the skilled trades. A third track focuses on purely academic training at a *Gymnasium* (an academic high school) in preparation for university education.

This system of educational tracks reinforces social status differences within society. Students are directed into one of the three tracks after only four to six years of primary schooling, based on their school record, parental preferences, and teacher evaluations. At this early age family influences are still a major factor in the child's development, which means that most children assigned to the academic track come from middle-class families, and most students in the vocational track are from working-class families.

Sharp distinctions separate the three tracks to reinforce the division. Students attend different schools, minimizing social contact. The curricula of the three tracks are so varied that once a student has been as-

signed, he or she will find it difficult to transfer between tracks. Fewer resources are invested in educating students in the vocational track; the *Gymnasia* are more generously financed and recruit the best qualified teachers. Every student who graduates from a *Gymnasium* is guaranteed admission to a university, where tuition is free.

Numerous attempts have been made to reform the West German educational system to lessen its elitist bias.[23] A single comprehensive secondary school that all students would attend was suggested as an alternative to tracked schools, but few state governments have been receptive to this idea; only about 5 percent of the secondary school students are enrolled in comprehensive schools. Reformers have been more successful in expanding access to the universities. In the early 1950s only 6 percent of college-aged youths attended a university; today this figure is nearly 20 percent. The West German educational system retains an elitist accent, though it is now less obvious.

The socialist ideology of the East German regime led to a different educational structure. A system of comprehensive schools was first introduced in the 1950s, and by the 1960s it had expanded to the ten-year comprehensive polytechnical schools that form the core of the educational system. Students from different social backgrounds, and with different academic abilities, attend the same school—much like the structure of public education in the United States. The schools emphasize practical career training, with a heavy dose of technical and applied courses in the later years, but a variety of courses are available to all students. Those with special academic abilities can apply to enter the extended secondary school during their twelfth year, which leads on to university training.

The differences between the educational systems of the two states illustrate the practical problems posed by German unity. Beyond the important differences in the content of education, the West lags behind in equalizing access to higher education. The Western educational system perpetuates social inequality and thus conflicts with the stated social goals of the Federal Republic. In contrast, the formal structure of the East German comprehensive schools is actually closer to the educational system of other European democracies, such as Britain or France, and highlights the elitist nature of the West German educational system. The unification treaty calls for the gradual extension of the West German educational structure to the East, but the dissolution of comprehensive schools might ironically lead to new pressures for liberal reform within the Federal Republic's educational system.

State Actions

Although the governments of both Germanies actively worked to reshape the political values of their citizens, the role of each state in the socialization process was sharply different. With the exception of the school system, the reeducation efforts in the West largely occurred through indirect mechanisms, relying on autonomous media, social groups, and the powers of persuasion; explicit political education by the government decreased as the new system took root. The East German government, in contrast, took a very active and direct role in the socialization process that even went beyond the factors we have already discussed. In contrast to the West, this role remained constant or even increased over time.

A cornerstone of the East German resocialization process was a system of government-supervised youth groups. Nearly all primary school students were enrolled in a Pioneer group. The Pioneers combined normal social activities, such as one might find in the Boy Scouts or Girl Scouts, with a basic dose of political education. At age fourteen, about three-fourths of the young graduated into membership in the Free German Youth (FDJ) group. Politics was central to the activities of the FDJ, and the organization served as a training and recruiting ground for the future leadership of East Germany. Membership in the FDJ provided entrée to the Communist party and important professions for which party membership was a prerequisite.

The East German government also attempted to institutionalize a secular alternative to the Christian confirmation (*Jugendweihe*) in order to undermine the social role of the churches. Eighth graders participated in a ceremony that intermixed political indoctrination and the rites of passage to adulthood. The ceremonies espoused themes of partriotism, civic virtue, and brotherhood with the Soviet Union — linking adulthood to the development of a socialist personality. In the 1980s up to 90 percent of all fourteen year olds participated in this ceremony.

The politicization of social life even extended to sports. The state encouraged sports as a way to keep people socially involved while promoting the value of physical fitness that drew on the traditions of the socialist working-class movement. But like other communist states, the East German government was also fond of staging mass sporting events that could include an opportunity for political indoctrination. In addition, the famous East German Olympic sports machine provided a source of national pride and became a basic tool of GDR foreign policy. The government used the medal count at the summer Olympics as an indicator of the internal accomplishments and new international stature of the GDR.

These different examples illustrate the reality of life in East Germany. Most aspects of social, economic, and political relations came under the direction of party and state institutions. From a school's selection of texts for first grade readers to the speeches at a sports awards banquet, the values of the regime touched everyday life. For those who accepted the values of the regime, these efforts at political socialization were unnoticed because they were merely an expression of values they already shared. But despite these extensive efforts, the remaking of the East German culture remained incomplete, in part because of the public's awareness of a different way of life in West Germany.

Mass Media

The mass media have a long history in Germany: the first newspaper and the first television service both appeared on German soil. Under previous regimes, however, the media frequently were censored or manipulated by political authorities. National socialism showed what a potent force for socialization the media could be, if placed in the wrong hands.

The mass media of West Germany were developed with this historical legacy in mind.[24] Immediately after the war, the Allied occupation forces licensed only newspapers and journalists who were free of Nazi ties. The Basic Law also guaranteed freedom of the press and the absence of censorship. Two consequences followed from this pattern of press development. First, a conscious effort was made to create a new journalistic tradition, committed to democratic norms, objectivity, and political neutrality. This new media style marks a clear departure from past journalistic practices, and it has contributed to the remaking of the political culture. A second consequence is the regionalization of newspaper circulation. The Federal Republic lacks an established national press like that of Britain or France. Instead, each region or large city has one or more newspapers that circulate primarily within that locale. Of the several hundred daily newspapers, only a few — such as the *Frankfurter Allgemeine Zeitung, Welt, Süeddeutsche*

Zeitung, or *Frankfurter Rundschau*—have a national following. Newspapers in the East are in the process of transition. The established East German dailies had functioned as indirect agents of the state, and the largest paper, *Neues Deutschland,* was the official organ for government policy pronouncements. New independent papers have now sprung up to compete with the older papers, and Western media sources are also freely available. This is injecting a new pluralism into the media environment of the East.

The electronic media in the Federal Republic follow a pattern of regional decentralization that now extends to the East. Radio and television networks are managed by public corporations organized at the state level. In December 1990 both West German TV networks expanded their programming to the East, supplanting the earlier East German networks. In addition, a new network, OST3 will be developed among the Eastern states to retain some autonomy from the Western networks.

Although the members of the public broadcasting corporation are appointed by the respective state governments, the media are intended to be free of governmental and commercial control. To ensure independence from commercial pressure, the media are financed mostly by taxes assessed on owners of radio and television sets. The expansion of privately owned cable and satellite television is gradually eroding the government's control of the media, but so far access to these media is still relatively limited.

During the early postwar years the mass media had an important part in the political education of the West German public. Newspapers and radio helped mold public images of the new political system and develop public understanding of the democratic process. Today that political education function is less obvious, though still present. The primary role of the contemporary media is to provide a source of information and communications linking political elites and the public. The higher quality newspapers devote substantial attention to domestic and international reporting, even though the mass-circulation daily newspapers are lacking in serious political content. The television networks are also strongly committed to political programming; about one-third of their programs deal with social or political issues. Furthermore, West German television reached eastward even before unification. When one traveled through East Germany, it was obvious that the TV antennae were pointed toward the Western stations. The

East German television news came on after the Western news instead of the same timeslot; otherwise, no one would have watched it, admitted one East German TV official. In terms of the electronic media, both Germanies have been unified for decades.

Public opinion surveys indicate that Germans have a voracious appetite for the political information provided by the mass media. A 1983 poll found that 88 percent of the West German public claimed to watch television news programs frequently. Newspapers are the second most common source of political news; 79 percent of the public read a newspaper regularly. Early survey results from the East uncover equally high levels of media usage. Except in times of dramatic events— such as the opening of the Berlin Wall—the mass media have a minor part in socializing new beliefs; this is the domain of family, school, and peers. These high levels of usage indicate, however, that the Germans are attentive media users and well informed on the flow of political events.

CITIZEN PARTICIPATION

Developing public understanding and acceptance of democratic rules was an important accomplishment for the Federal Republic. But postwar public opinion surveys found that citizens were not participating in the new process; citizens acted as political spectators, as if they were following a soccer match from the grandstand. The final step in remaking the political culture was to involve citizens in the process—to have them come onto the field and become participants.

Certainly, German history was not conducive to developing widespread public involvement in politics. Not only had three regimes failed since the turn of the century, but supporters of the previous regime had also suffered after the establishment of each new political order. These experiences probably convinced many Germans, in both the East and West, that political participation was a questionable, if not risky, pursuit.

Both German states tried to engage their citizens in politics, though with different expectations about the citizen's appropriate role. The democratic procedures of the FRG induced many citizens to become at least minimally involved in politics. Turnout in national elections was uniformly high. West Germans became well informed about the democratic system and developed an interest in political matters. After continued experience with the democratic system, citizens began to internalize their role as participants. Surveys in the late 1960s found that the public no longer was hesitant to discuss politics. Feelings of political effectiveness and civic competence also increased substantially since Almond and Verba's classic *Civic Culture* study.[25] The majority of West Germans thought their participation could influence the political process — people believed that democracy worked.

Changing perceptions of politics led to a dramatic increase in involvement. In 1953 almost two-thirds of the West German public never discussed politics; by the 1987 election about three-quarters claimed they talked about politics regularly. This expansion in citizen interest created a participatory revolution in West Germany. Participation in campaign activities and political organizations increased over time. Citizens became more open in displaying their party preferences during election campaigns, and American-style campaign paraphernalia became a common feature of West German elections.

Perhaps the most dramatic evidence of rising participation levels has been the growth of *citizen action groups* (*Bürgerinitiativen*).[26] Citizens interested in a specific issue form an ad hoc group to articulate their political demands and influence decision makers. These political groups often resort to petitions, protests, and other direct-action methods to dramatize their cause and mobilize public support. Parents organize for school reform, homeowners become involved in urban redevelopment projects, taxpayers complain about the delivery of government services, or residents protest against environmental problems in their locale. These action groups expand the means of citizen influence significantly beyond the infrequent and indirect methods of campaigns and elections.

Because the East German government considered citizen participation to be an essential feature of socialist democracy, citizen involvement was as widely encouraged as it was in the West. But individuals and groups were allowed to be politically active only in ways that would reinforce their allegiance to the state, not in ways that would question or challenge state authority. Therefore, the government organized and controlled participation. For example, elections were not measures of popular representation, but instead offered the SED an opportunity to educate the public politically. Over 90 percent of the electorate cast their ballots, and the government parties always won over 95 percent of the votes. Many citizens worked within the SED or with SED-affiliated political groups at election time. The gov-

ernment organized its own peace marches to protest the Intermediate-range Nuclear Forces (INF) decision and arranged rallies of workers to demonstrate their support of the government's economic plans. Individuals were encouraged and expected to participate in government-approved unions, social groups (such as the FDJ or the German Women's Union), and quasi-public bodies such as parent-teacher organizations. Hundreds of thousands of East Germans participated in government advisory bodies and representative committees.

Participation thus became widespread and regularized in East Germany. Some observers claimed that the extensive opportunities for citizen involvement and public discussion actually tempered public dissatisfaction with the regime. However, participation was used not as a method for citizens to influence the government, but as a method for the government to influence its citizens.

Although they draw on much different experiences, Germans from both the East and West have been socialized into a pattern of high political involvement. This can be illustrated with data on the participation patterns of East and West Berliners from a survey conducted in mid-1990 (Figure 11.5). Berlin has been a center of political activity for several years, because of the vigorous New Politics movement in the West and the activities of a capital city in the East. What is striking from these statistics is the high levels of participation on both sides of the city. Voting levels in national and state elections are among the highest of any democratic system. Roughly 78 percent of Westerners turned out at the polls in the 1990 Bundestag elections, as well as 74 percent of voters from the East. This level of participation is high by American standards, but over the preceding decade turnout in the Federal Republic had averaged nearly 90 percent. High turnout levels partially reflect a popular belief that voting is part of a citizen's duty. In addition, the electoral system is structured to encourage a big turnout: Elections are held on Sunday when everyone is free to vote; complete voter registration lists are constantly updated by the government; and the ballot is always simple — there are at most two votes to cast.

Beyond the simple act of voting, a large number of Germans participate in other aspects of politics. Three-quarters of West Berliners have signed a petition, as have a majority of East Berliners. Many individuals have participated in political demonstrations, been active in citizen action groups, or worked for a political

FIGURE 11.5
PARTICIPATION LEVELS IN EAST AND WEST BERLIN

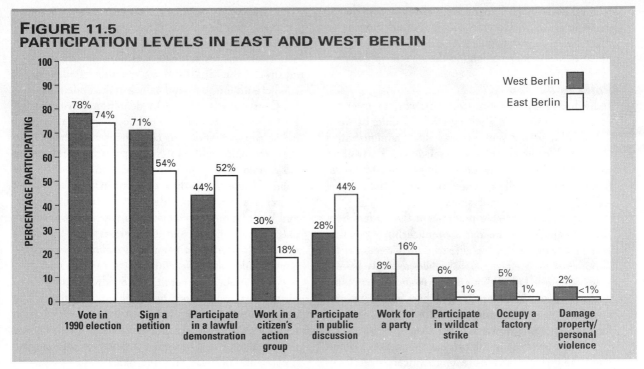

Source: Berlin Survey 1990, conducted by the Institut für Kommunikations-soziologie und Psychologie, and the Zentralinstitut für sozialwissen-schaftlicher Forschung at the Free University, Berlin; the Wissenschaftszentrum, Berlin; and the Akademie der Wissenschaften der DDR. I would like to thank Prof. Hans-Dieter Klingemann for granting me access to these data.

party. Indeed, one consequence of the participatory revolution was to add techniques of protest and direct action to the repertoire of citizen politics. These techniques are a common tool of political action in both Germanies.

Beyond the high levels of political involvement in both halves of Berlin, and we would assume in both halves of Germany, there are also distinct traces of the different contexts for political action in the FRG and the GDR. East Berliners have been more active in the examples of government-mobilized participation, such as lawful demonstrations, participating in public discussions, and working for a party (mostly the SED and other bloc parties). Despite the fact that the GDR was overthrown by a people's revolution partially centered in East Berlin, the levels of protest and antisystem actions are actually higher in the West. West Berliners are more likely to have participated in an unlawful demonstration, a boycott, a wildcat strike, or political violence. It is only within the Western democratic system that such extreme forms of political action could be tolerated.

The traditional characterization of the German citizen as quiescent and uninvolved is no longer appropri-

ate in either the West or the East. Participation has increased dramatically over the past forty years, and the public is now involved in a wide range of political activities. The spectators have become participants.

POLITICS AT THE ELITE LEVEL

The Federal Republic is a representative democracy. Above the populace is a group of a few thousand political elite who manage the actual workings of the political system. Some elites, such as party leaders and parliamentary deputies, are directly responsible to the public through elections. Civil servants and judges are appointed to represent the public interest, and they are at least indirectly responsible to the citizenry. Leaders of interest groups and political associations also are in the group of top elites, and they participate in the policy process as representatives of their specific clientele groups.

Although the group of politically influential elites is readily identifiable, they do not constitute an elite class; that is, they do not share distinct and common interests as elites in traditional or authoritarian societies often do.

Rather, elites in the Federal Republic represent the diverse interests in German society. Often there is as much heterogeneity in policy preferences among the political elites as there is among the general public.

Paths to the Top

Individuals may take numerous pathways to enter the ranks of the FRG elite. Pathways to office differ between various elite groups such as party elites, administrative elites, and leaders of interest associations. Party elites may have exceptional political abilities, and administrative elites are initially recruited because of their formal training and bureaucratic skills.

One feature of elite recruitment that differs from American politics is the long apprenticeship period that precedes entry into the top elite stratum. Candidates for national or even state political office normally have a long background of work for the party and officeholding at the local level. Similarly, researchers find that senior civil servants spend nearly all their adult lives working for the national government.

The biography of the present chancellor, Helmut Kohl, is a typical example of a long political career. At an early age Kohl became an active CDU party member; in 1959 he was first elected to the Rhineland-Palatinate state parliament; he became minister president of the state in 1969; four years later he was named national chairman of the CDU; he was the CDU/CSU chancellor candidate in the 1976 elections; and he became chancellor of the CDU/CSU–FDP coalition in 1982. Not all political careers are as illustrious as Kohl's, but they often are as long.

A long apprenticeship means that political elites have considerable experience before attaining a position of substantial power; elites also share a common basis of experience built up from interacting over many years. National politicians know each other from working together at the state or local level; the paths of civil servants cross during their long careers in the bureaucracy. These experiences tend to incorporate a sense of responsibility and regularity into elite interactions, as well as limiting the number of career shifts between different elite sectors. For instance, members of a chancellor's Cabinet are normally drawn from among party elites with extensive experience in state or federal government. Very seldom can top business leaders or popular personalities use their outside success to attain a position of political power quickly. This also contributes to the cohesion of elite politics.

Unification has created a new problem of elite recruitment for Germany. Access to elite positions, of course, followed a much different pattern in the East.[27] The prerequisites for elite positions in the GDR — loyalty to the SED and its communist ideology — conflict with the goals and values of the Federal Republic. Consequently, almost by definition, anyone in the East who is experienced in political decision making or public administration was compromised by their ties to the communist state. Thus, most political elites from the old regime have gone into political exile, and the new political leadership in the East is drawn from the ranks of church leaders, the dissident intellectual community, and West German politicians. Similarly, many individuals in the judiciary and civil service were laid off or given early retirement to allow new elites to enter positions of administrative authority.

The process of recruiting individuals with the requisite skills and without ties to the old regime will be difficult. Already many politicians have resigned when their secret ties to the GDR government or secret police were made public. The cleansing of elite positions is also problematic because only the older elites possess the experience in administering public policies or managing large firms that is required for political and economic recovery in the East. Elites in the West also are hesitant to open the political, administrative, and military systems to former residents of the East. What, for example, should the FRG's army do with the former East German generals? Questions about the competency and legitimacy of Eastern elites are likely to be a reoccurring aspect of politics in the new Germany.

Elite Orientations

The political leadership of postwar West Germany marked a sharp break from Germany's previous pattern of authoritarian orientations among elites. As noted earlier, the Allied occupation forces pursued a denazification campaign to remove Nazi and antidemocratic elites from positions of authority. Later, court decisions disbanded antisystem parties on the extreme right and left. More important in the long run, however, was the new internal consensus among West German elites. Authoritarian politics were delegitimized by the Third Reich, and the option of a communist system was discredited by developments in East Germany. The political leadership became virtually unanimous in support of a democratic political order. From nearly the start of the Federal Republic, its democratic institutions and procedures have commanded the allegiance of political elites.

Eastern Germany is now reliving this same process of creating a new elite culture. The recruitment and training of a democratic and capable new elite in the East is a vital step in rebuilding the political and economic systems. With the fall of the communist state, there apparently exists a consensus in support of the democratic process. Thus, most Easterners in elite positions, though not all, should quickly come to share the norms and political style of the West. Still, a small number of adherents to the old SED regime will participate in the political system of the Federal Republic and harbor hopes for a different political order.

INTEREST GROUPS

Interest groups are an integral part of the German political process, even more than such groups are in the United States. Compared to French interest groups, German groups are widely organized and tightly structured, and they command a favored position in the political process. The legitimacy of interest group participation in politics is generally acknowledged. Some specific interests may be favored more than others, but in general interest groups are welcomed as a necessary element in making the process work.

A close relationship connects interest groups and the government. In some occupations (doctors, lawyers, and other self-employed professions) professional associations are established by law. These associations, which date back to the medieval guilds, enforce professional rules of conduct. At the same time, these associations receive government authorization of their professional activities, making them quasi-public bodies.

The German system of formally involving interest groups in the policy process reaches further. Government officials are encouraged to contact interest groups when new policies are being formed. These consultations ensure that the government can benefit from the expertise of interest group representatives. Moreover, political norms require that all relevant interest groups be consulted before policy is made. In many cases this pattern of close interaction between the government and interest groups is legally established. Administrative regulations encourage direct contact between interest group representatives and government officials. Some laws even require that interest groups be consulted as part of the policymaking process.

In some instances the pattern of interest group activity approaches the act of governance. For example, during the mid-1970s the top representatives of government, business, and labor met in regular conference ("Concerted Action") to discuss economic issues. Officials from the three sectors attempted to reach a consensus on wage and price increases and to negotiate government economic policies. The participants in these negotiations then implemented the agreements, sometimes with the official sanction of the government.

This general pattern of cooperation between government and interest groups is described as *neocorporatism*.[28] Social interests are organized into tightly knit hierarchic associations. These interest groups then participate directly in the policy process. Policy decisions are reached in discussions and negotiations among the relevant groups, and are then implemented by government action.

This neocorporatist pattern solidifies the role of interest groups in the policy process. Governments feel that they are responding to public demands when they consult with these groups, and the members of interest groups depend on the organization for the representation of their views. Thus, the leaders of the major interest groups are important actors in the policy process.

A major advantage of neocorporatism is that it makes for efficient government; the relevant interest groups can negotiate on policy without the pressures of public debate and partisan conflict. Efficient government is not necessarily the best government, however, especially in a democracy. Decisions are reached in conference groups or advisory commissions, outside of the representative institutions of government decision making. The "relevant" interest groups are involved, but this assumes that all relevant interests are organized, and only organized interests are relevant. Decisions affecting the entire public often are made beyond the public's eye. At the same time, democratically elected representative institutions — state governments and the Bundestag — are sidestepped as interest groups deal directly with government agencies. Consequently, interest groups are playing a diminishing role in electoral politics as they concentrate their efforts on direct contact with government agencies.

A close relationship between interest groups and the government occurs in all modern democracies. Apparently, however, the bonds are stronger in Germany than in most other systems. Continued growth in neocorporatist policymaking may be an unwelcome trend if it undercuts the democratic principles of the Federal Republic.

Although interest groups come in many shapes and sizes, we focus our attention on the large associations that represent the major socioeconomic forces in society. These associations aggregate groups with similar interests into one national organization, a so-called *peak association* that can speak for its members.

Business

Two major organizational networks represent business and industrial interests within the political process. The *Federation of German Industry (BDI)* is the peak association for thirty-nine separate industrial groupings. Nearly every major industrial firm is represented within the BDI-affiliated associations. This united front enables industry to speak with authority and force on matters affecting their interests.

The *Confederation of German Employers' Associations (BDA)* includes an even larger number of business organizations. Virtually every large or medium-sized employer in the nation is affiliated with one of the fifty-six employer associations that comprise the BDA.

Although the two organizations have overlapping membership, they exercise different roles within the political process. The BDI is active primarily at the national level in lobbying decision makers on political matters of concern to business interests. Industry representatives participate extensively in government advisory committees and planning groups. The BDI assembles expert witnesses to testify before Bundestag committees on pending legislation, and BDI leaders present the view of business to government officials and Cabinet ministers. The BDI has been very effective in influencing government actions through this involvement in the policy process.

In contrast, the BDA concerns itself primarily with representing business on labor and social issues. The individual employer associations negotiate with the labor unions over employment contracts. At the national level, the BDA is the official representative of business on legislation dealing with social security, labor legislation, and social services. The BDA also nominates business representatives for a variety of government committees, ranging from the media supervisory boards to social security committees.

Business interests have a long history of close relations with the CDU/CSU and conservative politicians. Companies and their top management provide signifi-

cant financial support for the Christian Democrats, and a sizable number of Bundestag deputies have strong ties to business. Yet the legitimate role of business interests within the policy process is readily accepted by SPD and CDU politicians alike.

Labor

The German labor movement is also highly organized.[29] More than half of the active labor force belong to a union. The *German Federation of Trade Unions* (DGB) is the peak association that incorporates seventeen separate unions—such as metalworkers, building trades, the chemical industry, and postal workers—into a single organizational structure. The individual union organizations in the East are merging with their comparable Western unions and will be included within the DGB structure; at the end of 1990 the DGB included about 11 million workers. This broad-based membership includes almost all organized industrial workers and large numbers of white-collar and government employees.

As a political organization, the DGB has close ties to the Social Democratic party, although there is no formal institutional bond between the two. Most SPD deputies in the Bundestag are members of a union, and about one-tenth are former labor union officials. The DGB represents the interests of labor in government conference groups and Bundestag committees. The large mass base of the federation also makes union campaign support and the union vote an essential part of the SPD's electoral base.

In spite of their differing interests, business and unions have shown an unusual ability to work together in the FRG. The Economic Miracle was possible because labor and management implicitly agreed that the first priority was economic growth, from which both sides would prosper. Work time lost through strikes and work stoppages is consistently lower in the Federal Republic than in most other Western European systems.

This cooperation is encouraged by joint participation of business and union representatives in government committees and planning groups. Cooperation also extends into industrial decision making through the policy of *co-determination* (*Mitbestimmung*). Federal law requires that half of a large corporation's board of directors be elected by the employees. The system was first applied in the coal, iron, and steel industries in 1951; in 1976 it was extended in modified form to large corporations in other fields. When co-determination was first introduced, there were dire forecasts that it would destroy German industry. The system generally has been successful, however, in fostering better labor–management relations and thereby strengthening the economy. The Social Democrats also favor codetermination because it introduces democratic principles into the economic system.

Church Interests

Religious associations constitute the third major organized interest in German politics. Rather than being separated, church and state are closely related. The churches are subject to the rules of the state, but in return they receive formal representation and support from the government.

The churches are financed mainly through a church tax collected by the government. A surcharge (about 10 percent) is added to an employee's income tax, and this amount is transferred to his or her church. Citizens can officially opt out of the tax, but social norms discouraged this step. Similarly, Catholic primary schools in several states receive government funding, and the churches are granted government subsidies to support their social programs and aid to the needy.

In addition to this financial support, the German system of formal interest representation directly involves the churches in governing. Church appointees regularly sit on government planning committees that deal with education, social services, and family affairs. By law, the churches are represented on the supervisory boards of the public radio and television networks. Members of the Protestant and Catholic clergy occasionally serve in political offices, as Bundestag deputies or as state government officials.

Although the Catholic and Protestant churches receive the same formal representation by the government, the two churches differ in how they attempt to influence policy. The Catholic Church has close ties to the CDU and CSU, and at least implicitly encourages its members to support these parties and their conservative policies. The Catholic hierarchy is not hesitant to lobby the government on legislation dealing with social or moral issues. With its considerable resources and tightly structured organization, the Catholic Church often wields an influential role in policymaking.

The Protestant Church is a relatively loose association of regional Lutheran churches. The level and focus of the church's political involvement vary with the preferences of local pastors and bishops, and their respective congregations. In the West, the church has minimized its involvement in partisan politics, although it is seen as favoring the SPD. Instead, Protestant groups work through their formal representation on government committees or function as individual lobbying organizations.

The Protestant Church in the GDR played a more significant political role because it was one of the few organizations that retained its autonomy from the state. The church thus could serve as a meeting place for citizens who wanted to discuss freely the social and moral aspects of contemporary issues. In many congregations, religious activities furnished an outlet for political expression and an opportunity for dissident groups to coalesce. For instance, many churches organized "peace services" during the INF controversy in the early 1980s and provided a meeting point for the autonomous East German peace movement. As the German revolution gathered force in 1989, churches in Leipzig, East Berlin, and other cities granted sanctuary for citizens' groups; weekly services acted as a rallying point for opposition to the regime. Religion was not the opiate of the people, as Marx had feared, but one of the forces that swept the communists from power.

Despite their institutionalized role in the Federal Republic's formal system of interest group representation, the influence of both the Catholic and Protestant churches has gradually waned over the past several decades. Declining church attendance in both West and East marks a steady secularization of German society; about one-tenth of Westerners claim to be nonreligious, as are nearly half the residents in the East. It is possible that the politicization of the eastern churches will revitalize the churches' role in the politics of the Federal Republic, but the gradual secularization of German society suggests that the churches' popular base will continue its slow erosion.

New Politics Movements

In recent years, a new set of political interests have arisen to challenge business, labor, religion, agriculture, and other established socioeconomic interest groups. These new groups focus their efforts on the life-style and quality-of-life issues facing Germany.[30]

Environmental groups are the most visible part of the movement. Following the flowering of environmental interests in the 1970s, antinuclear groups popped up like mushrooms around nuclear power facilities, local environment action groups proliferated, and new national organizations were formed. These groups both mobilized the public's latent concern for environmental protection and translated this concern into a new force within the political process. Another part of the New Politics network is the women's movement. Women's groups first began to form in the early 1970s, and the women's movement has developed a dualistic strategy for improving the status of women: changing the consciousness of women and reforming the laws. A variety of associations and self-help groups at the local level nurture the personal development of women, while other organizations focus more on national policymaking.

These political movements, and other New Politics groups, have distinct issue interests and their own organizations, but they also can be seen as elements of a single movement. Their concerns show a common interest in the quality of life for individual citizens, whether it is the quality of the natural environment, the protection of human rights, or peace in an uncertain world. They draw their members from the same social base: young, better educated, and middle-class citizens. These groups emphasize decentralized decision making within the organization and a reliance on unconventional political tactics, such as protests and demonstrations.

The New Politics movement does not wield the influence of the established interest groups, although their membership now exceeds the size of the formal membership in the political parties. In a few short years these groups have become important and contentious actors in the political process. Moreover, the reconciliation of women's legislation in the united Germany and the resolution of the nearly catastrophic environmental problems in the East are likely to keep these concerns near the top of the political agenda.

PARTY SYSTEM AND ELECTORAL POLITICS

Parties and electoral politics present one of the clearest examples of the political contrasts between West Germany and East Germany. Following the war, the Western Allies created a democratic, competitive party system to guide the new political process in the West. The Allies licensed a broad diversity of parties as long as they were free of Nazi ties and committed to democratic procedures. The Basic Law further requires that parties support the constitutional order and democratic methods of the Federal Republic.

As a result of these provisions, West Germany developed a strong system of competitive party politics that became a mainstay of the new democratic order. Elections were structured around the competition between the conservative *Christian Democrats* (CDU/CSU) and the liberal *Social Democrats (SPD)*, with the small *Free Democratic party (FDP)* often holding the balance of power. Elections were meaningful; control of the government shifted between the left and right as a function of election outcomes. When postmaterial issues entered the political agenda in the 1980s, a new political party, *the Greens*, emerged to represent these concerns.

Although the GDR ostensibly had a multiparty system and national elections, this presented only the illusion of democracy — political power was firmly held by the Socialist Unity party (SED). In advance of an election, the SED would work with the other parties and various social groups (such as the trade unions, women's groups, and youth groups) to assemble a National Front list of candidates. The SED determined the members of this list and each party's allocation of parliamentary seats *before* the poll. Thus, the Christian Democratic, Liberal, and other parties in the East were mere extensions of the SED, and the elections themselves were largely symbolic acts.

When the East German political system collapsed, its party system was drawn into this void. Support for the SED plummeted, and the party sought to distance itself from its own history by changing its name to the *Party of Democratic Socialism (PDS)*. Many of the antigovernment opposition groups tried to develop into parties in order to compete in the first democratic elections. New political parties represented interests ranging from the Beer Drinkers Union to a women's party. As the election progressed, however, it became evident that the parties allied to the West German parties were usurping the electoral process, taking over the financing, tactics, organization, and substance of the campaign. Helmut Kohl made whistlestop tours for the conservative parties of the Alliance for Germany, while Willy Brandt and other SPD politicians campaigned for the eastern SPD. This was a West German election that took place on East German soil, and the parties with Western ties emerged as the major actors after the March 1990 elections. Ironically, the citizen groups and political movements that produced the East German revolution nearly faded from existence. In the end, the party system of the new Germany represents an extension of the West German system to the East.

Christian Democrats (CDU/CSU)

The creation of the Christian Democratic Union (CDU) in postwar West Germany signified a sharp break with the tradition of German political parties. The party was founded by a heterogeneous group of Catholics and Protestants, businesspeople and trade unionists, conservatives and liberals. Rather than representing narrow special interests, the party wanted to appeal to a broad segment of society in order to gain government power. The party's unifying principle was that West Germany should be reconstructed along Christian and humanitarian lines. Konrad Adenauer, the party leader, sought to develop the CDU/CSU into a conservative-oriented catch-all party (*Volkspartei*)—a sharp contrast to the fragmented ideological parties of Weimar. This strategy succeeded; within a single decade the CDU/CSU emerged as the largest party, capturing 45 to 50 percent of the popular vote (Figure 11.6).

The CDU operates in all states except Bavaria, where it allies itself with the *Christian Social Union (CSU)*, whose basic political philosophy is more conservative than the CDU. These two parties generally function as one in national politics, forming a single parliamentary group in the Bundestag and campaigning together in national elections.

The CDU/CSU's early voting strength allowed the party to control the government first under the leadership of Adenauer (1949–1963) and then under Ludwig Erhard (1963–1966), as shown in Table 11.2. In 1966, however, the party lost the support of its coalition partner, the FDP, and was forced to form a Grand Coalition with the Social Democrats. This sharing of power contributed to the CDU/CSU's downfall by improving the public's image of the SPD. Following the 1969 election, the SPD and FDP formed a new government coalition; for the first time in the history of the Federal Republic, the CDU/CSU became the opposition party.

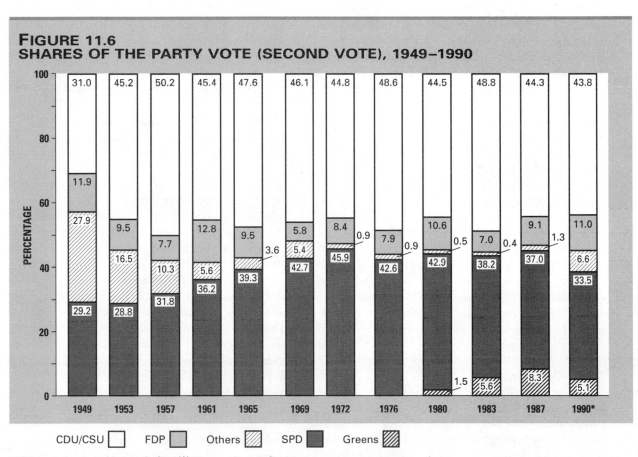

FIGURE 11.6
SHARES OF THE PARTY VOTE (SECOND VOTE), 1949–1990

Legend: CDU/CSU, FDP, Others, SPD, Greens

* 1990 percentages combine results from Western and Eastern Germany.

The Christian Democrats had a difficult time adjusting to the opposition benches. The party maintained its emphasis on Christian values and conservative economic principles, but party members could not always agree on how these goals should be translated into specific policies. Party leadership changed with each election, as the party searched for a winning theme.

In the early 1980s the strains of a weak economy increased public support for the party and its conservative economic program. In 1982 the Christian Democrats joined with the FDP to form a new conservative government through the first successful constructive no-confidence vote. The CDU-led government implemented its conservative foreign policy and domestic agenda. While ties with Eastern Europe were continued, the nation's military defense was also strengthened. One key act was the 1983 decision to station new NATO nuclear missiles in West Germany, ending a long political debate between the government and the peace movement. The CDU's major domestic goal was to restore the vitality of the economy, which it pursued through a combination of budgetary restraint and economic incentives for business. Public support for these policies returned the CDU/CSU–FDP coalition to power following the 1983 and 1987 elections.

The collapse of the East German regime provided a historic opportunity for the CDU and its leader, Helmut Kohl. While others looked on the events with wonder or uncertainty, Kohl quickly embraced the idea of closer ties between the two Germanies, leading to eventual confederation or unification. Thus, when the March 1990 GDR election became a referendum in support of German unification, the Christian Democrats were assured of victory because of the party's early commitment to German union. Helmut Kohl emerged victorious from the 1990 Bundestag elections, but with a vote total that was very close to the party's 1987 poll; there was surprisingly little to show for Kohl's historic accomplishments. Still, the CDU/CSU is seen as the party that constructed the new Germany, and the party's fate in the future is inextricably tied to the success of the unification process.

Social Democrats (SPD)

The postwar Social Democratic party in West Germany was constructed along the lines of the SPD in the Weimar Republic. The new SPD was an ideological party, primarily representing the interests of unions and the working class. In the early postwar years the Social Democrats espoused strict Marxist doctrine and consistently opposed Adenauer's Western-oriented foreign policy program. The SPD's image of West Germany's future was radically different from that of Adenauer and the Christian Democrats.

The SPD's poor performance in early elections (see Figure 11.6) generated internal pressures for the party to broaden its appeal to a wider spectrum of the electorate. At the 1959 Godesberg conference the party finally abandoned its traditional role as ideological voice of the working class. In a single act, the party renounced its Marxist economic policies and generally moved to the center on domestic and foreign policies. The party continued to represent working-class interests, but by shedding its ideological banner the SPD hoped to attract new support from the middle class. The SPD began to transform itself into a progressive catch-all party that could compete with the Christian Democrats.

An SPD breakthrough finally came in 1966 with the formation of the Grand Coalition (see Table 11.2). By sharing government control with the CDU/CSU, the Social Democrats alleviated lingering public uneasiness about the party's integrity and ability to govern. Political support for the party also grew as the SPD played an active part in resolving the nation's problems.

The SPD share of votes nearly reached parity with that of the CDU/CSU in the 1969 election. More importantly, the small FDP decided to align itself with the SPD. A new government coalition was formed with Willy Brandt as chancellor and Walter Scheel, the FDP leader, as minister of foreign affairs. For four or five years the liberal SPD–FDP coalition pursued a range of progressive new policies.[31] Then the OPEC price increase and ensuing recession severely damaged the economy. In 1974 Helmut Schmidt replaced Brandt as chancellor, and the SPD turned its attention toward the faltering economy.

Although the SPD retained government control in the 1976 and 1980 elections, these were trying times for the party. The SPD and FDP frequently disagreed on how the government should respond to continuing economic problems. Political divisions also developed within the SPD. For example, the SPD's traditional union and working-class supporters favored nuclear energy and renewed emphasis on economic growth. At the same time, many young middle-class SPD members opposed nuclear energy and large-scale economic development projects that might threaten environmental quality.

TABLE 11.2
COMPOSITION OF COALITION GOVERNMENTS

Date formed	Source of Change	Coalition Partners*	Chancellor
September, 1949	Election	CDU/CSU, FDP, DP	Adenauer (CDU)
October 1953	Election	CDU/CSU, FDP, DP, G	Adenauer (CDU)
October 1957	Election	CDU/CSU, DP	Adenauer (CDU)
November 1961	Election	CDU/CSU, FDP	Adenauer (CDU)
October 1963	Chancellor retirement	CDU/CSU, FDP	Erhard (CDU)
October 1965	Election	CDU/CSU, FDP	Erhard (CDU)
December 1966	Coalition change	CDU/CSU, SDP	Kiesinger (CDU)
October 1969	Election	SPD, FDP	Brandt (SPD)
December 1972	Election	SPD, FDP	Brandt (SPD)
May 1974	Chancellor retirement	SPD, FDP	Schmidt (SPD)
December 1976	Election	SPD, FDP	Schmidt (SPD)
November 1980	Election	SPD, FDP	Schmidt (SPD)
October 1982	Constructive no-confidence	CDU/CSU, FDP	Kohl (CDU)
March 1983	Election	CDU/CSU, FDP	Kohl (CDU)
January 1987	Election	CDU/CSU, FDP	Kohl (CDU)
December 1990	Election	CDU/CSU, FDP	Kohl (CDU)

*DP is the German party; G is the All-German Bloc/Federation of Expellees and Displaced Persons.

These policy tensions eventually led to the breakup of the SPD-led government. Unable to reconcile the conflicting policy goals of Old Left and New Left groups, and unable to resolve the nation's persisting economic problems, the SPD was forced out of the government in 1982. The SPD's heavy losses in the 1983 election inflicted a further blow on the party. Once again in opposition, the SPD faced an identity crisis. The party was challenged on the left by the Greens and on the right by the Christian–Liberal government. The question before the party was whether it should attempt to accommodate the Greens or adopt a centrist program in competition with the government. In 1987 the SPD followed a centrist strategy but was unable to make any significant improvements in its vote share. In 1990 it nominated Oskar Lafontaine as candidate for chancellor, someone who appealed more to liberal, middle-class voters, but the SPD campaign was overtaken by events in the East.

Perhaps no one (except perhaps the communists) was more surprised than the SPD by the course of events in the GDR. The SPD had been normalizing relations with the SED as a basis of intra-German cooperation, only to see the SED ousted by the citizenry. The SPD and its chancellor candidate, Oskar Lafontaine, were ambivalent about German unification and stood by quietly as Kohl spoke of a single German *Vaterland* to crowds of applauding East Germans. The SPD expected the East to be a bastion of socialist support because of Weimar voting patterns, and saw the Christian Democrats capture the votes of this new constituency. The party's poor performance in the 1990 national elections thus reflects the SPD's inability either to lead or to follow the course of the unification process.

Free Democrats (FDP)

Although the Free Democrats are far smaller than the two major parties, they wield considerable influence in the political system. Government control in a multiparty parliamentary system normally requires a coalition of parties, and the FDP often holds enough seats to have a pivotal role in forming government coalitions.

The FDP was created to continue the liberal tradition from the prewar German party system. The party initially was a strong advocate of private enterprise and drew its support from the Protestant middle class and farmers. Its economic policies made the FDP a natural ally of the CDU/CSU. From 1949 until 1956 and from 1961 until 1966, the FDP was the junior coalition partner of the CDU/CSU. In the mid-1960s the Free

Democrats sought to broaden their electoral base by downplaying their conservative economic policies and emphasizing their liberal foreign and social programs. These changes distanced the FDP from the Christian Democrats and opened the way for the SPD–FDP coalition that began in 1969. With a worsening of economic conditions in the early 1980s, the Free Democrats reasserted their conservative economic values. This led to a new coalition with the CDU/CSU that began in October 1982 and has continued through three subsequent elections.

Because of the FDP's pivotal role in forming coalitions, the party tends to have disproportionate influence on its larger coalition partners. The FDP generally acts as a moderating influence, limiting the leftist leanings of the SPD or the conservative tendencies of the CDU/CSU. This places the party in a precarious position, however, because if it allies itself too closely with either major party it may lose its political identity. The party struggled with this problem at the beginning of the 1980s, but its fortunes have improved in recent years. Many voters apparently appreciate the FDP's moderating role, and the party improved its showing in state and national elections through the later half of the decade. The FDP has also benefited from the international changes occurring in Europe. The foreign minister, Hans Dietrich Genscher of the FDP, played a leading role in negotiating the international agreements that allowed the two Germanies to unite. The FDP emerged as the big victor in the 1990 election with 11 percent of the vote.

The Greens

Environmental issues began attracting wide public attention in the 1970s, and environmentalists pursued a course of political action by organizing citizen action groups to lobby on environmental issues. Since the established parties generally were unresponsive to environmental concerns, the environmental movement started to develop its own party representatives. Small, locally based ecology parties appeared in state elections during the later 1970s, and in 1979 they won their first seats in a state legislature. In 1980 a new political party, the Greens, was created to unite the various local environmental parties under one national banner.[32] The party program included a broad range of New Politics issues: opposition to nuclear energy and Germany's participation in the arms race, commitment to environmental protection, women's rights, and further democratiza-

CDU/CSU supporters display a campaign poster of their chancellor candidate during the election campaign in November 1990.

zation of society. The Greens differed so markedly from the established parties that one Green leader described them as the "antiparty party."

The Greens quickly became successful at the state level and extended this success to national politics. In the 1983 election the party won its first representation in the Bundestag, becoming the first new party to enter Parliament since the 1950s. Using the legislature as a political forum, the Greens have campaigned vigorously for an alternative view of politics. The Greens were at the forefront of efforts in the early 1980s to block the stationing of new NATO missiles in West Germany. The party has called for much stronger measures to protect the environment and has shown staunch opposition to the government's nuclear power program. At the same time, the Greens have added a bit of color and spontaneity to the normally staid procedures of the political system. The normal dress for Green deputies is jeans and a sweater, rather than the traditional business attire of the established parties; their desks in Parliament sprout flowers and greenery, rather than folders of official-looking documents. The decentralized and participatory nature of the party's internal structure also stands in sharp contrast to the hierarchic and bureaucratized structure of the established parties.

Many political analysts initially expressed dire concerns about the impact of the Greens on the governmental system, but most now agree that the party was instrumental in bringing necessary attention to political viewpoints that previously were overlooked.

The Greens were at first ambivalent in responding to the German revolution in the East because they opposed the simple eastward extension of the West German economic and political systems. Even worse, some Green party leaders advocated an alliance with the recently dethroned communists in the East. The party leadership was out of step with the German public and their own electorate. Furthermore, to stress their opposition to the fusion of both Germanies, the West German Greens refused to develop a formal electoral alliance with any eastern party in the 1990 elections, and separate Green slates ran in the West and in the East. The Eastern alliance of the Greens and Alliance '90 won enough votes to gain eight seats in the new Bundestag, but the West German Greens fell under the 5 percent threshold and failed to win any parliamentary seats on their own. The Greens' unconventional politics had finally caught up with them, at least temporarily.

The 1990 election results were a major setback for the party. However, the Greens are still represented in the Bundestag and state governments. This continuing presence will ensure that questions about environmental quality, women's rights, and other New Politics issues will not be ignored in the unification process.

Communists to Democratic Socialists (PDS)

The Communists were one of the first political parties to form in postwar Germany, and the party's history reflects the two paths Germany followed. In the West, the Communist party (KPD) suffered because of its identification with the Soviets and the communist regime of the GDR. The party garnered a shrinking sliver of the vote in the early parliamentary elections, and then in 1956 the party was declared unconstitutional by the courts because of its undemocratic principles. A reconstituted party, now labeled the DKP, began contesting elections again in 1969 but was never able to attract a significant following.

Even before the war had ended in the East, Walter Ulbricht traveled from Moscow to Berlin and began reorganizing the Communist party in the Soviet military zone. In 1946 the Soviets forced a merger of the Eastern KPD and SPD into a new Socialist Unity party of Germany (SED) which became the ruling institution in the East. The SED and its leadership controlled the government apparatus and the electoral process; party agents were integrated into the military command structure; the party supervised the infamous state security police (*Stasi*); and party membership was a prerequisite to positions of authority and influence in the government and society. The state controlled East German society, and the SED controlled the state.

The SED's power collapsed in 1989 along with the East German regime. Party membership plummeted, and whole local and regional party units abolished themselves. The omnipotent party suddenly seemed impotent. In an attempt to save the party from complete dissolution and remain competitive in the new democratic environment in the East, the party changed its name in February 1990 and became the Party of Democratic Socialism (PDS). The old party guard was ousted from positions of authority, and new moderates took over the leadership.

The PDS has campaigned as the representative of those who feel threatened by the potential economic and social costs of German unity. The party gained a significant share of the vote in the March 1990 election (16 percent), but this support has steadily eroded. A temporary change in the electoral law enabled the PDS to win representation in the 1990 Bundestag elections, even though it captured only 2 percent of the national vote. However, the party's electoral base is limited to the East, especially areas with large numbers of former SED members. The PDS will be an advocate for their communist values and a vocal critic of the Bonn government, but without a broader base of popular support it is uncertain whether the party can establish itself as a permanent feature of the German party system.

Electoral System

The framers of the Basic Law had two goals in mind when they designed the electoral system. One was to reinstitute the proportional representation (PR) system that was used in the Weimar Republic. A PR system allocates legislative seats on the basis of a party's percentage of the popular vote. If a party receives 10 percent of the popular vote, it should receive 10 percent of the Bundestag seats. Other individuals saw advantages in the system of single-member districts used in Britain and the United States. It was thought that this system would avoid the fragmentation of the Weimar party system and ensure some accountability between an electoral district and its representative.

To satisfy both objectives, a hybrid was developed with elements of both systems. On one part of the ballot citizens vote for a candidate to represent their district. The candidate with a plurality of votes is elected as the district representative. Half the members of the Bundestag are directly elected in this manner.

On a second part of the ballot voters select a party. These second votes are added nationwide to determine each party's share of the popular vote. A party's proportion of the second vote determines its total representation in the Bundestag. Each party is then allocated additional seats so that its percentage of the combined candidate and party seats equals its share of the vote. These additional seats are distributed according to lists prepared by the state parties before the election. Half of the Bundestag members are elected as party representatives.

One major exception to this proportional representation system is the 5 percent clause. The electoral law stipulates that a party must win at least 5 percent of the national vote (or three constituency seats) to share in the distribution of party-list seats. The law is designed to withhold representation from the type of small extremist parties that plagued the Weimar Republic. In practice, however, the 5 percent clause has handicapped all minor parties and contributed to the consolidation of the party system.

This unique system has several consequences for electoral politics. In general, the party-list system gives party leaders substantial influence on who will be elected to Parliament by the placement of candidates on the list. The PR list system also ensures fair representation for the smaller parties. The FDP, for example, won a direct candidate mandate in 1990 for the first time since 1957, and yet it received Bundestag seats based on its national share of the vote. In contrast, Great Britain's district-only system discriminates against small parties; in 1987 the Liberal–SDP Alliance won 23 percent of the national vote, but only 3 percent of the parliamentary seats.

The West German two-vote system also affects campaign strategies. Although most voters cast both their ballots for the same party, the FDP traditionally encourages supporters of its larger coalition partner to "lend" their second votes to the Free Democrats. In recent federal elections these split ballots were instrumental in keeping the FDP above the 5-percent hurdle. Finally, research has shown that district and party representatives behave differently in the Bundestag. District candidates are more responsive to their constituents' needs and are more likely to follow their district's views when voting on legislation.

The Electoral Connection

One of the most essential functions of political parties in a democracy is interest representation. Elections provide individuals and social groups with an opportunity to select political elites who share their views. In turn, this choice leads to the representation of group interests in the policy process because a party must be responsive to its electoral coalition if it wants to retain the support of its voters.

Group differences in party support had gradually narrowed in the Federal Republic, as both the CDU/CSU and SPD become broad catch-all parties.[33] Citizens now apparently vote more on the basis of individual issue beliefs or family conditions than membership in social groups.

Voting alignments in the 1990 elections also shifted from historical patterns for several reasons. Unification added several million new voters to the electoral rolls and changed the composition of the electorate, and the prospects for unification overwhelmed other issues in the election and led many voters to deviate from their normal party preferences. Furthermore, the social basis of politics was still in transition in the East; class identity took on a new meaning with the transition from a socialist to a capitalist economy, and most interest groups were themselves redefining their political identity. Thus, the voting patterns for the combined German electorate in 1990 represent a mix of past voting practices in the West and a party system being formed in the East (Table 11.3).

The Christian Democrats have successfully con-

TABLE 11.3
ELECTORAL COALITIONS OF THE PARTIES IN THE 1990 FEDERAL ELECTIONS

	CDU/CSU	SPD	FDP	Greens	PDS	Total public
Region						
East	20.6	14.6	21.0	31.9	80.9	20.6
Northwest	26.8	26.7	24.8	28.2	5.2	25.5
Rhineland	24.5	33.4	27.0	22.4	0.0	28.0
Southern	28.1	25.3	27.2	17.5	13.9	25.9
Occupation						
Worker	17.7	24.8	11.7	12.8	21.5	19.5
Self-employed	10.8	4.4	13.8	7.5	4.9	8.6
White collar/government	42.1	44.7	48.9	48.7	50.5	44.2
Student	4.1	5.6	5.9	18.6	10.7	5.7
Other	25.3	20.3	19.7	12.4	12.4	22.0
Religion						
Catholic	48.2	32.7	40.1	30.5	8.3	40.0
Protestant	35.0	42.4	36.6	29.3	5.2	36.6
Other, none	16.8	24.9	23.3	40.2	86.5	23.4
Size of town						
Less than 5,000	25.1	17.8	16.4	20.4	12.4	21.6
5,000–20,000	26.2	25.8	16.8	18.2	13.3	23.0
20,000—100,000	24.5	25.3	28.7	23.2	39.0	25.9
More than 100,000	24.0	29.9	38.1	37.9	35.3	28.8
Age						
Under 40	27.8	43.9	39.9	66.0	61.9	39.8
40–59	38.5	33.1	32.8	25.9	19.1	33.6
60 and over	33.8	23.0	27.3	8.1	19.0	26.9
Gender						
Male	46.4	45.4	59.9	47.8	60.6	46.7
Female	53.6	54.5	40.1	52.2	39.4	53.3

Source: November 1990 German Election Study, conducted by the Forschungsgruppe Wahlen (N = 1239). I would like to thank Wolfgang Gibowski and Dieter Roth for providing access to these data.

verted the formerly socialist region in eastern Germany into a new source of support for the party. Approximately 20 percent of the total electorate resides in the former territories of the GDR, and these voters account for 20 percent of the CDU/CSU electorate. More generally, the Christian Democrats draw disproportionate support from the conservative sectors of society. Catholics, the self-employed, and residents of rural areas represent a substantial portion of the party's electoral coalition.

The SPD's base is almost a mirror image of the CDU/CSU's voters. A large share of the Social Demo-cratic voters come from working-class households. The party's strength is concentrated in central and north Germany, especially in the cities, and the SPD is under-represented among voters from the East. Protestant and nonreligious voters also give disproportionate support to the party.

The merger of East and West produced, at least temporarily, some anomalies in traditional voting patterns.[34] For instance, the SPD is generally the party of the working class, but in the East the CDU actually receives a larger share of the working-class vote, and the Eastern middle class disproportionately supports the leftist parties. Similarly, because there are few Catholics in the East, the CDU electorate in the five new Länder are heavily drawn from Protestant voters. The blending of these different voting patterns from East and West acted to narrow social group voting differences in the 1990 election.

One party with a distinct electoral base is the Greens. Party voters are heavily drawn from the groups identified with the New Politics movement. The party is a representative of the new middle-class, nonreligious, and urban voters. Even more striking are the age differences in party support; most (66 percent) Green voters are under forty.

The PDS also has a distinct voter clientele. The party's support is limited almost entirely to the East, where it received nearly 10 percent of the vote. The PDS electorate draws heavily on the young and the middle class — the party of the proletarian revolution actually was a party benefiting the East German intelligentsia and party faithful.

The incorporation of the new voters from the East will force the parties to rethink their political identities and electoral strategies. Thus, the first all-German election in 1990 may be only a tentative sign of what to expect from the party system in the future.

Party Government

Political parties deserve special emphasis in Germany, because parties are such important actors in the political process. Some observers describe the political system as government *for* the parties, *by* the parties, and *of* the parties.

The Basic Law is unusual in that it makes specific references to political parties (the American Constitution does not). Because parties were suppressed during the German Empire and the Third Reich, the Basic Law guarantees the legitimacy of parties and their right to exist — if they accept the principles of democratic government. Parties are also designated as the primary institutions of representative democracy. The parties are to act as intermediaries between the public and the government, and there are no provisions for direct citizen input such as initiatives and referendums. The Basic Law takes the additional step of assigning an educational function to the parties. Political parties are directed to "take part in forming the political will of the people." In other words, the parties should take the lead and not just respond to public opinion.

The centrality of parties in the political process appears in several ways. There are no direct primaries that would allow the public to select party representatives in Bundestag elections. Instead, district candidates are nominated by a small group of official party members or by a committee appointed by the membership. The selection of party-list candidates is made at state party conventions. The average voter is normally unaware of the composition of these party lists. Thus, the leadership has considerable discretion in selecting list candidates and their ordering on the list. This power can be used to reward faithful party supporters and discipline party mavericks; placement near the top of a party list virtually assures election, and low placement carries little chance of a Bundestag seat.

The dominance of party also is evident throughout the election process. Most voters view the candidates merely as party representatives rather than as autonomous political figures. Even the district candidates are elected primarily because of their party ties. Election campaigns are generously financed by the government. But again, government funding and access to public media are allocated to the parties and not the individual candidates. Government funding for the parties also continues between elections, to help them perform their informational and educational functions as prescribed in the Basic Law.

Within the Bundestag, the parties are even more influential. As noted earlier, the elected deputies are organized into strict party groups (*Fraktionen*). Organizationally, the Bundestag is structured around these *Fraktionen* rather than individual deputies. The key legislative posts and committee assignments are restricted to members of a party *Fraktion*. The size of a *Fraktion* determines its representation on legislative committees, its share of committee chairmanships, and its participation in the executive bodies of the legislature. Government funds for legislative and administrative support are distributed to the *Fraktion* and not the deputies.

As a result of these forces, the cohesion of parties within the Bundestag is exceptionally high. Parties caucus in advance of major legislation to decide the party position, and most legislative votes follow strict party lines. This is partially a consequence of a parliamentary system and partially an indicator of the pervasive influence parties have throughout the political process.

THE POLICY PROCESS

The policymaking process may begin from any part of society—an interest group, a political leader, an individual citizen, or a government official. Because all these elements interact in making public policy, it is difficult to trace the true genesis of any policy idea. Moreover, once a new policy is proposed, other interest groups come into play and become active in amending, supporting, or opposing the policy.

The pattern of interaction among policy actors varies with time and policy issues. One set of groups is most active on labor issues, and they use the methods of influence that will be most successful for their cause. A very different set of interests may assert themselves on defense policy and use far different methods of influence. This variety makes it difficult to describe policymaking as a single process, although the institutional framework for evaluating formal policy proposals is relatively uniform in all policy areas. A brief discussion of this framework will describe the various political arenas in which policy actors compete, and also clarify the balance of power between the institutions of government.

Policy Initiation

Most legislation reaches the formal policy agenda through the executive branch. One reason for this predominance is that the Cabinet and the ministries manage the affairs of government. They are responsible for preparing the budget, formulating revenue proposals, and the other routine activities of government.

The nature of a parliamentary democracy further strengthens the policymaking influence of the chancellor and the Cabinet. The chancellor acts as the primary policy spokesperson for the government and a majority of the Bundestag deputies. In speeches, interviews, and formal policy declarations, he sets the policy agenda for the government. It is the responsibility of the chancellor and Cabinet to propose new legislation that will implement the government's policy promises. Indeed, most federal ministries are so small that they cannot hope to oversee the administration of policy; primarily they are policymaking institutions. Interest groups realize the importance of the executive branch, and they generally work with the federal ministries—rather than Bundestag deputies—when they seek new legislation.

This focus on the executive branch means that two-thirds of the legislation considered by the Bundestag is proposed by the Cabinet. Thirty members of the Bundestag may jointly introduce a bill, but only about 20 percent of legislative proposals begin in this manner. Most of the Bundestag's own proposals involve private-member bills or minor issues. A majority of state governments in the Bundesrat also can propose legislation, but they do so infrequently.

The Cabinet attempts to follow a consensual decision-making style in establishing the government's policy program. Ministers seldom propose legislation that is not expected to receive Cabinet support. The chancellor has a crucial part in ensuring this consensus. The chancellor's office coordinates the legislative proposals drafted by the various ministries. If the chancellor feels that a bill conflicts with the government's stated objectives, he may ask that the proposal be withdrawn or returned to the ministry for restudy and redrafting. If a conflict on policy arises between two ministries, the chancellor may mediate the dispute. Alternatively, interministerial negotiations may be used to resolve the differences. Only in extreme cases is the chancellor unable to resolve such problems; when such stalemates occur, policy conflicts are referred to the full Cabinet.

In Cabinet deliberations the chancellor also has a major part. The chancellor is a fulcrum, balancing conflicting interests in order to reach a compromise that the government as a whole can support. His position as government and party leader gives him considerable influence as he negotiates with Cabinet members. Very seldom does a majority of the Cabinet oppose the chancellor.

When the chancellor and Cabinet agree on a legislative proposal, they occupy a dominant position in the legislative process. Because the Cabinet also represents the majority in the Bundestag, most of its initiatives are eventually enacted into law. In the tenth Bundestag 1983–1987, about 85 percent of the government's proposals became law; in contrast, only 30 percent of the Bundestag's own proposals became law.

The government's legislative position is further strengthened by provisions in the Basic Law that limit the Bundestag's authority in fiscal matters. The Parliament can revise or amend most legislative proposals. It cannot, however, alter the spending or taxation levels of legislation proposed by the Cabinet. The Parliament cannot even reallocate expenditures in the budget without the approval of the finance minister and the Cabinet.

Legislating Policy

The normal legislative process begins in the Cabinet. When a majority of the Cabinet approves a legislative proposal, it is sent to the Bundesrat for review (Figure 11.7). After receiving the Bundesrat's comments, the Cabinet formally transmits the government's proposal to the Bundestag. The bill is given a first reading, which places it on the agenda of the chamber, and the proposal is assigned to the relevant committee.

Much of the Bundestag's work takes place in these specialized committees. The committee structure generally follows the divisions of the federal ministries, such

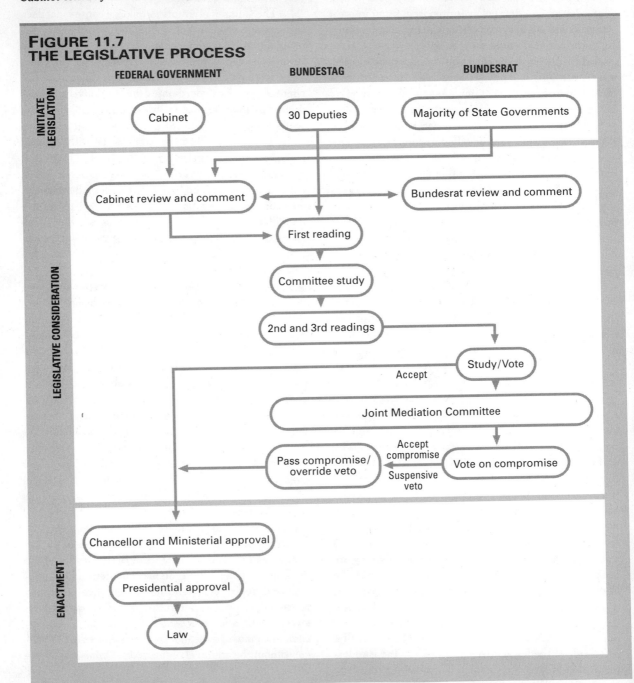

FIGURE 11.7
THE LEGISLATIVE PROCESS

as transportation, defense, labor, or agriculture. Because bills are referred to committee early in the legislative process, committees have real potential for reviewing and amending the content of legislation. Committees are expected to evaluate proposals, consult with the relevant groups, and then submit a revised proposal to the full Bundestag. Research staffs are small, but committees also make use of investigative hearings. Government and interest group representatives testify on pending legislation, and committee members themselves often have considerable expertise in their designated policy area. Most committee meetings also are held behind closed doors. The committee system thus provides an opportunity for frank discussions of proposals and negotiations among the political parties before legislation reaches the floor of the Bundestag.

When a bill is reported out of committee, it is examined by the full Bundestag and is subject to further revision. By this point in the legislative process, however, political positions already are well established. Leaders in the governing parties participated in the initial formulation of the legislation. The party *Fraktionen* in the Bundestag have caucused to determine the official party position. Major revisions during the second and third readings are infrequent; the government generally is assured of the passage of its proposals as reported out of committee.

Bundestag debate on the basic merits of government proposals is thus mostly symbolic. It allows the parties and political leaders to present their views to the public. The successful parties explain the merits of the new legislation and advertise their efforts to their supporters. For the opposition parties these debates are a means for placing their objections in the public record. Although these debates may seldom influence the outcome of a vote, they are nevertheless an important part of the Bundestag's information function.

A bill that is successful in the Bundestag is transmitted to the Bundesrat. The Bundesrat's function is to institutionalize involvement of state governments in the federal policy process. As we have seen, the legislative authority of the Bundesrat is equal to that of the Bundestag in policy areas where the states share concurrent powers with the federal government or administer federal policies. In these areas the approval of the Bundesrat is necessary for a bill to become law. In the remaining policy areas that do not involve the states directly, such as defense or foreign affairs, the chamber's approval of legislation is not essential.

This sharing of legislative power between the state and federal governments is a mixed political blessing. The system introduces flexibility into the policy process. Through their influence on policymaking and policy administration, state leaders can adapt legislation to local and regional needs. This division of power provides another check in the system of checks and balances. With strong state governments it is less likely that one leader could control the political process by usurping the national government.

The division of power between the two parliamentary bodies also presents problems. The Bundesrat's voting procedures give disproportionate weight to the smaller states. Half the votes in the Bundesrat are controlled by states that represent only a third of the population. Thus, the Bundesrat cannot claim the same popular legitimacy as the proportionally represented and directly elected Bundestag. The Bundesrat voting system may encourage parochialism by the states. The states vote as a bloc; therefore, the impetus is to view policy from the perspective of the state, rather than the national interest or party positions. The different electoral bases of the Bundestag and Bundesrat make such tensions over policy an inevitable part of the legislative process.

During the late 1980s the control of both legislative bodies was split between the CDU/CSU – FDP majority in the Bundestag and the SPD majority in the Bundesrat. In one sense, this division strengthened the power of the legislature, because the governing parties often were forced to negotiate with the opposition in the Bundesrat, especially on the sensitive issues of German union. After a brief hiatus, the SPD again won control of the Bundesrat in early 1991. This pattern of divided government will strengthen the Social Democrats' influence within the policy process.

As in the Bundestag, much of the Bundesrat's work is done in specialized committees. State leaders or state civil servants scrutinize bills for both their policy content and their administrative implications for the state governments. After committee review, a bill is submitted to the full Bundesrat. If the Bundesrat approves of the measure, it is transmitted to the chancellor for his signature. If the Bundesrat objects to the Bundestag's bill, the representatives of both bodies meet in a joint mediation committee and attempt to resolve their differences.

The results of the mediation committee are submitted to both legislative bodies for their approval. If the proposal involves the state governments, the Bundesrat may cast an *absolute* veto and the bill cannot become a law. In the remaining policy areas, the Bundesrat can cast only a *suspensive* veto. If the Bundestag approves of a measure, it may override a suspensive veto and forward the proposal to the chancellor. The final step in the process is the promulgation of the law by the federal president.

Throughout the legislative process, the executive branch is omnipresent. After transmitting the government's proposal to the Bundestag, the federal ministers begin working to support the bill. Ministry representatives testify before Bundestag and Bundesrat committees to present their position. Cabinet ministers are actively involved in lobbying committee members and influential members of the Parliament. Ministers may propose amendments or negotiate policy compromises to resolve issues that arise during parliamentary deliberations. Government representatives also are allowed to attend meetings of the joint mediation committee between the Bundestag and Bundesrat; no other nonparliamentary participants are allowed. As a result of their deliberations, the Parliament may substantially revise the government's proposals or even defeat them. The government frequently is forced to make compromises and accept amendments. The executive branch, however, retains a dominant influence on the policy process.

Policy Administration

Very few federal agencies have the resources to implement and monitor the policies enacted by the federal government. In any case, most domestic administrative responsibilities are assigned to the states by the Basic Law. As one indicator of the states' central administrative role, more civil servants are employed by the state governments than by the federal and local governments combined.

Because of the delegation of administrative responsibilities, federal legislation normally is fairly detailed to ensure that the government's intent is followed in the actual application of a law. Federal agencies also may supervise state agencies, and in cases of dispute they may apply sanctions or seek judicial review.

Despite the control exercised by the federal government, the states retain considerable discretion in applying most federal legislation. In part, they do so because the federal government lacks the resources to follow state actions closely. Federal control of the states also requires Bundesrat support, where claims for states'

rights receive a sympathetic hearing. This decentralization of political authority provides additional flexibility for the political system.

Judicial Review

As in the United States, legislation in Germany is subject to judicial review. A *Constitutional Court* has the authority to evaluate the constitutionality of legislation and to void laws that violate the provisions of the Basic Law.

Constitutional issues are brought before the court by one of three methods. The most common pattern involves constitutional complaints filed by individual citizens. When citizens feel that their constitutional rights have been violated by a government action, they may appeal directly to the court. More than 90 percent of the cases presented to the court arise from citizens' complaints. Moreover, cases can be filed without paying court costs and without a lawyer. The court is thus something of an ombudsman, assuring the average citizen that his or her fundamental rights are protected by the Basic Law and the court.

The Constitutional Court also hears cases based on "concrete" and "abstract" principles of judicial review. Instances of concrete review involve actual court cases that raise constitutional issues. Appeal to the Constitutional Court is not automatic; the case must be referred by a judge in the lower courts.

The court also can be asked to rule on legislation in the abstract, that is, as a general legal principle without reference to an actual case. The federal government, a state government, or one-third of the Bundestag deputies can request review of a law. This procedure is most often used by groups that fail to block a bill during the legislative process. During the 1970s the CDU/CSU used its control of state governments to challenge the constitutionality of the Basic Treaty with East Germany (upheld), an abortion reform law (overturned), a new co-determination law (upheld), and several other important pieces of legislation. Judicial review in the abstract expands the constitutional protection of the Basic Law. At the same time, however, it directly involves the court in the policy process and may politicize the court as another agent of policymaking.

POLICY PERFORMANCE

By most standards, the two Germanies could both boast of their positive records of government performance. The Federal Republic's economic advances of the

1950s and the early 1960s were truly phenomenal, and the progress in the East was nearly as remarkable. By the 1980s West Germany had one of the strongest economies in the world, its living standard was among the highest in any nation, and nearly all indicators of material well-being had followed an upward trend. Other government policies improved the educational system, increased workers' participation in industrial management, extended social services, and improved environmental quality. East Germany was the corresponding success story of Eastern Europe. The GDR's economy ranked among the top twenty in the world, and advances over the past generation had substantially improved the living standard of the average East German.

Despite the policy advances of the GDR, the political and social systems in the East crumbled when the opportunity for change became apparent. The collapse of the East German political regime was accompanied by a free-fall of its economy; the social and economic infrastructure of the East seemed to disintegrate overnight. Thus, the policy accomplishments of the past will not necessarily carry over to the future.

The next decade will be a time of tremendous policy change and innovation as the Federal Republic adjusts to its new domestic and foreign policy circumstances. At this point, the final outcomes are still very uncertain. The integration of two different welfare systems, two different legal systems, two different military systems, and two different social systems cannot simply be resolved by the decision to unify. Moreover, in this ever-changing environment policymakers cannot even acquire the simple factual information on which decisions should be made. The head of the Federal Republic's statistical office cautioned that it will take several years before Germany has reliable estimates of its capital stock, net worth, and other basic statistical measures.

Perhaps the best forecasts we can make for the future are based on the present policy programs and outputs of the Federal Republic, since these systems will be gradually extended to the East. Then after discussing the Federal Republic's policy record, we can consider the special policy challenges posed by German unification.

The Federal Republic's Policy Record

The West German government has grown substantially throughout the entire postwar period. Even after the explosive advances of the Economic Miracle, public expenditures for social services, education, and environ-

mental protection nearly doubled during the 1970s; spending on universities increased nearly fivefold. The 1980s are often described as a period of retrenchment, but the scope of government continued to increase both in terms of total public spending and in new policy responsibilities, albeit at a slower pace than in the past. Total public expenditures — federal, state, local, and the social security system — increased from less than DM 100 billion in 1960 to DM 741 billion in 1980 and over DM 1 trillion in 1989.

It is difficult, however, to describe the activities of government in precise terms of revenue and budgets. A major complicating factor is Germany's extensive network of social services. Social security programs are the largest component of public expenditures; however, most of their revenues and expenses are managed in separate insurance programs that are kept apart from the government's normal budgetary process.

Another complicating factor is Germany's federal system. The Basic Law distributes policy responsibilities among the three levels of government. Local authorities provide utilities (electricity, gas, and water), operate the hospitals and public recreation facilities, and administer youth and social assistance programs. The states manage educational and cultural policies; they also hold primary responsibility for public security and the administration of justice. Policies that are best handled at the national level are assigned to the federal government, which includes foreign policy and defense, transportation, and communications. Consequently, public expenditures are distributed fairly evenly over the three levels of government. In 1989 the federal budget was DM 293 billion, the combined state budgets were DM 266 billion, and local authorities spent more than DM 167 billion.

The major policy activity of government overall involves the provision of social services. In fact, the Federal Republic is often described as a welfare state, or more precisely a social services state, because of its extensive social services programs. A compulsory social insurance system includes nationwide health care, accident insurance, unemployment compensation, and retirement benefits. These insurance programs protect members of the labor force against temporary or permanent loss of earnings. A second set of programs provides financial assistance for the needy and individuals who cannot support themselves. Finally, a third set of programs spread the benefits of the Economic Miracle to all families regardless of need. For instance, the government provides financial assistance to families with children, and has special tax-free savings plans and other savings incentives for the average wage-earner. For much of the history of the Federal Republic, politicians competed to extend the coverage and benefits of such programs. As a result, public spending on social programs amounted to DM 464 billion in 1987, nearly as much as was spent on all other government programs combined (Figure 11.8).

The socioeconomic protections of the German welfare state provide generous benefits to those who need them. The unemployment program is a typical example of the range of benefits available. An unemployed worker receives insurance payments that provide about 68 percent of normal pay (63 percent for unmarried workers) for up to a year. After a year, unemployment assistance continues at about half of normal pay. Government labor offices will help the unemployed worker find new employment or obtain retraining for a new job.

If a job is located in another city, the program partially reimburses travel and moving expenses. This is not an atypical example; benefits in most other programs are equally generous.

In one way or another, the welfare state has a direct effect on almost every family. By one account, 80 percent of all families receive some type of direct financial payment from the state, either as retirement benefits, a family allowance, unemployment compensation, educational grants, or other benefits. Jens Alber has calculated that in 1980 almost 12 million citizens drew the major part of their income from social security programs, making this group even larger than the blue-collar workers in West Germany.[35]

For most of the 1980s the Germans debated whether they could afford the generous benefits of their social programs, especially when faced by problems of slow economic growth. Kohl's government entered office in 1982 with a promise to strengthen the German economy by limiting the further expansion of government, especially the welfare state.[36] Yet, Kohl's efforts to cut various social programs were constrained by a broad political consensus in support of the basic provisions of the welfare state. Despite real cuts in every single social program, social spending still accounts for about 30 percent of the gross national product, and Kohl's budgets in 1988 and 1989 called for new increases in social spending. The basic structure of the German welfare state has endured. Now, unification will likely put this consensus and the federal budget to a new test, as unemployment, welfare, and health benefits for the East place a new strain on these programs.

The government is, of course, involved in a range of other policy activities. Education, for example, is an important concern of all three levels of government, accounting for about one-tenth of all public spending (Figure 11.8). The federal government is also deeply involved in communications and transportation. The electronic media, television and radio, are owned by the government and managed by government-appointed supervisory bodies; the postal and telephone systems are government monopolies. The federal government also owns and operates the railway system. In addition to these activities, the government owns over a 25 percent share of more than 500 German companies, including Lufthansa, the VEBA energy conglomerate, and a large block of Volkswagen stock.

In recent years, the government's policy agenda has expanded to include a range of new issues, and envi-

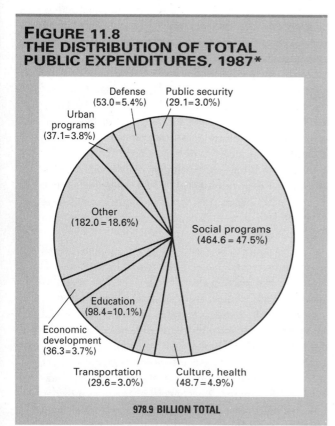

FIGURE 11.8
THE DISTRIBUTION OF TOTAL PUBLIC EXPENDITURES, 1987*

Defense (53.0 = 5.4%)
Public security (29.1 = 3.0%)
Urban programs (37.1 = 3.8%)
Other (182.0 = 18.6%)
Social programs (464.6 = 47.5%)
Education (98.4 = 10.1%)
Economic development (36.3 = 3.7%)
Transportation (29.6 = 3.0%)
Culture, health (48.7 = 4.9%)

978.9 BILLION TOTAL

*In DM billions.
Source: Statistisches Jahrbuch für die Bundesrepublik Deutschland 1990, p. 443.

ronmental protection is the most visible example. To cope with the worsening problem of acid rain, the Kohl government initiated new regulations to reduce air pollution from conventional power stations; another program offers tax incentives for automobiles that use lead-free gasoline. In 1986 Kohl created a new Ministry of the Environment, although the Federal Republic was one of the last West European nations to do so. Several basic indicators of air and water quality showed substantial improvements through the 1980s, but many pressing environmental questions, such as nuclear power and the disposal of toxic wastes, remain unresolved. Environmental protection represents a policy area requiring further government action.

Defense and foreign relations constitute another important policy activity of the government. More than for most other European nations, the German economy and security system are based on international interdependence. The Federal Republic's economy depends heavily on exports and foreign trade; in the mid-1980s over one-fourth of the West German labor force produced goods for export, a percentage much higher than that for most other industrial economies.

The Federal Republic's international economic orientation has made the nation's membership in the European Community (EC) a cornerstone of its economic policy. The FRG was an initial advocate of the EC and has benefited considerably from its EC membership. Free access to a large European market was essential to the success of the Economic Miracle, and it is a continuing basis of West Germany's export-oriented economy. Participation in Community decision making gives the Federal Republic an opportunity to influence the course of European political development.

The Federal Republic is also militarily integrated into the Western alliance through its membership in the North Atlantic Treaty Organization (NATO). Following the Korean War, the United States persuaded other Western governments to rearm the West Germans as part of the international NATO force. Since then, West German troops have been a mainstay of Western European defenses. Among the Europeans, the Federal Republic makes the largest personnel and financial contribution to NATO forces, and the West German public strongly supports the NATO alliance. Furthermore, Allied forces from six nations are permanently stationed on West German soil as NATO's front line of defense. In the event of war, these troops — including all West German combatant forces — would be under the direction

of NATO commanders. Over time, however, defense and security spending has decreased from about 13 percent of all public expenditures in the early 1960s to today's level of about 6 percent of total public spending (or about 3 percent of the gross national product).

Public expenditures indicate the policy efforts of the government, but the actual results of this spending are more difficult to assess. Most indicators of policy performance suggest that the Federal Republic has been fairly successful in achieving its policy goals. Standards of living have improved dramatically, and health statistics show similar improvement. Although localized shortages of housing still appear in the West, overall housing conditions have steadily improved. Even in new policy areas such as energy and the environment, the government has made substantial progress. The opinions of the public reflect these policy advances. In 1988 most West Germans were satisfied with their job (92 percent), housing (89 percent), living standard (83 percent), social security benefits (77 percent), and crime prevention measures (58 percent).[37] In fact, only one policy item in the survey failed to elicit satisfied responses from a majority of those interviewed: only 30 percent are satisfied with environmental protection policies. Although there is much room for improvement, the Federal Republic's past policy record is marked by considerable success.

Paying the Costs

The generous benefits of government programs are not, of course, due to government largess. The taxes and financial contributions of individuals and corporations provide the funds for these programs. Therefore, large government outlays inevitably mean an equally large collection of revenues by the government. These revenues are the real source of government programs.

Three different types of revenue provide the bulk of the resources for public policy programs.[38] Contributions to the social security system represent the largest source of public revenues (Figure 11.9). The health, unemployment, disability, retirement, and other social security funds are primarily self-financed by employer and employee contributions. For example, contributions to the pension plan amount to about 18.5 percent of a worker's gross monthly wages, half being paid by the employee and half by the employer. All the various insurance contributions combined account for about a third of the average worker's income, which is roughly

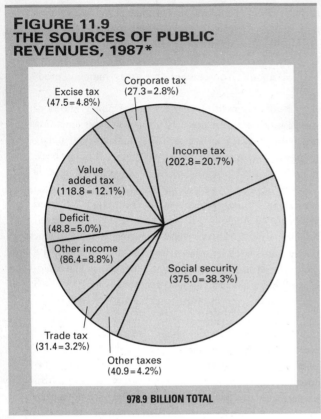

**FIGURE 11.9
THE SOURCES OF PUBLIC
REVENUES, 1987***

Corporate tax
(27.3 = 2.8%)

Excise tax
(47.5 = 4.8%)

Income tax
(202.8 = 20.7%)

Value
added tax
(118.8 = 12.1%)

Deficit
(48.8 = 5.0%)

Other income
(86.4 = 8.8%)

Social security
(375.0 = 38.3%)

Trade tax
(31.4 = 3.2%)

Other taxes
(40.9 = 4.2%)

978.9 BILLION TOTAL

*In DM billions.
Source: Statistisches Jahrbuch für die Bundesrepublik Deutschland 1989,
p. 438.

divided between contributions from the worker and from the employer.

The next most important source of public revenues are direct taxes, that is, taxes that are directly assessed by the government and paid to a government office. One of the largest portions of public revenues comes from a personal income tax that is shared by the federal, state, and local governments. The rate of personal taxation rises with income level, from a base of 22 percent to a maximum of 53 percent. After deductions and other allowances, the average worker pays about 18 percent of wages in direct income taxes. Corporate profits also are taxed but at a much lower rate than personal income. This policy encourages business to be profitable and to reinvest their profits in further growth.

The third major source of government revenues are indirect taxes. Like sales and excise taxes, indirect taxes are based on the use of income rather than wages and profits. The most common and lucrative indirect tax

is the *value added tax (VAT).* A VAT charge is added at every stage in the manufacturing process that increases the value of a product. Between the raw lumber and a completed piece of furniture, the VAT may be assessed several times. The cumulated VAT charges are included in the price of the final product, but are not separately listed on the price tag. The standard VAT is 14 percent for most goods, with lower rates for basic commodities such as food. Other indirect taxes include customs duties, an energy tax, and liquor and tobacco taxes. Altogether, indirect taxes account for about two-fifths of all public revenues.

Indirect taxes are one of the secrets to the dramatic growth of government revenues. Indirect taxes normally are "hidden" in the price of an item, rather than explicitly listed as a tax, so people are not reminded that they are paying taxes every time they purchase a product. Because these taxes are hidden, it is also easier for policymakers to raise indirect taxes without evoking citizens' awareness and opposition. Revenues from indirect taxes automatically rise with inflation, too. Indirect taxes are regressive, however; they weigh more heavily on low-income families because a larger share of their income is used for consumer goods.

The average West German obviously has deep pockets to fund the extensive variety of public policy programs; U.S. taxation levels look quite modest by comparison. The marginal tax rate for the average German worker, including taxes and social security contributions, was 63 percent in 1986, compared to a marginal rate in America of just over 40 percent. When a German goes to the corner kiosk to buy a pack of cigarettes, 73 percent of the cost goes to taxes; taxes account for 66 percent of the cost of liquor and gasoline, 28 percent of the cost of a can of coffee, and 19 percent on a package of light bulbs.

Even with these various revenue sources, public expenditures repeatedly have exceeded public revenues in recent years. To finance this deficit, the government draws on another source of "revenue"—loans and public borrowing—to maintain the level of government services. One of the initial goals of the CDU/CSU–FDP government was to halt this drain on the economy and bring the federal budget into balance (while maintaining government programs as much as possible). The growth in federal spending was held to under 3 percent per annum during the 1983–1986 term. This budgetary restraint and new taxes sharply reduced the federal deficit in the mid-1980s, but by 1988 the deficit had creeped back to its pre-CDU level of about DM 40 billion a year.

The German taxpayer seems to contribute an excessive amount to the public coffers, and Germans are no more eager than other nationalities to pay taxes. Still, the question is not how much citizens pay, but how much value is returned for their payments. In addition to normal government activities, Germans are protected against sickness, unemployment, and disability; government pension plans furnish livable retirement incomes. Moreover, the majority of the public expects the government to take an active role in providing for the needs of society and its citizens.

The Policy Challenges of Unification

Although economic and social development in East Germany lagged behind that of the West, the GDR had its own impressive record of policy accomplishments. The GDR developed a broad network of social programs, which in several areas were even more extensive than those in the West. East Germany was the economic miracle of the Eastern bloc and the strongest economy in Comecon. The East Germans were one of the few socialist nations that tried to develop new technologies, such as robotics and computers. Even though the bright lights of West Berlin shone over the Berlin Wall, East Berlin itself was an economic showplace that impressed visitors from Poland, the Soviet Union, and other East European states.

Given this positive history of policy performance, most observers were surprised by the sudden and dramatic collapse of the East German economic and social systems in the wake of the November 1989 revolution. Most analysts expected that a new form of a "socialist state with a human face" would emerge from the communist system, but before that could happen the entire socioeconomic structure fell apart. During the first half of 1990 the gross national product of the GDR decreased by nearly 5 percent, unemployment skyrocketed, and industrial production fell off by over 40 percent. As was noted above, these developments were the stimulus for East Germans to look toward the Federal Republic and German unification as a solution to their situation.

The major policy goal for the new Germany will be to resolve the problems that arise from German unification and to show that the Western system will improve the quality of life for its new residents. The most immediate challenge involves the need to rebuild the econ-

omy of the East, integrating Eastern workers and companies into the social market economy of the West. The breakdown of the East German economy was precipitated by the events of the revolution: the exodus of skilled workers to the West, the disruption in production caused by political instability, and the enticing economic promises of West German politicians. But the root causes of the GDR's economic woes go much deeper. The GDR economy looked strong in the sheltered environment of the socialist economic bloc, but it could not compete in the international marketplace once its borders were opened. The impressive growth statistics and production goals often papered over a decaying economic infrastructure and outdated manufacturing facilities. A system that guaranteed everyone a job and had no real cost accounting method produced companies that were overstaffed, inefficient, and undercapitalized by Western standards. Similarly, East Germany's positive trade balance was the product of the artificial accounting practices of the Comecon nations; moreover, many of these products were below the quality standards expected on the world market. In short, the East German regime was effective and successful only as long as it stayed within the closed economic system of the Comecon bloc. Matching the West German economy against that of the East is like racing a Porsche against the GDR's antiquated two-cylinder Trabant — in such a race the outcome is foreordained.

A number of steps are being taken to rebuild the economy of the East and then raise it to Western standards. The first step toward reconstruction was the currency union that preceded political unification. In July 1990 the East German mark (*Ostmark*) was replaced by the West German Deutsche mark as the single currency of the two states. This was an experience in "cold turkey capitalism" — overnight the East German economy had to accept the economic standards of the Federal Republic. Wages and prices were converted to West German DM, and the productivity of East German firms could be directly compared to those in the West; the gaps between the two economies were now clear. Even with salaries one-third lower in the East, productivity was even further out of balance. In order to become more competitive, Eastern firms reconfigured their cost structures and reduced their labor force as a cost-cutting measure. While this action increased the competitiveness of some firms and may enable them to survive in a single German market, the consequence was a dramatic rise in unemployment, which was especially shocking in a nation accustomed to guaranteed employment. Unemployment was further increased by cuts in the size of the Eastern civil service and other public sector employment that accompanied political unification. More than old Stasi agents were out of work; there were layoffs in the GDR's foreign service, military personnel, economic managers, public administrators, and even the famed Olympic sports coaches.

Another step in the conversion process was the creation of a trust agency (*Treuhandanstalt*) charged with privatizing the 8,000 or more firms that were owned by the GDR government. More than 80 percent of the GDR's economy was run by nationalized enterprises, the most prominent being the large state-owned cartels (*Kombinate*) that employed over a third of all East German workers. The trust is dissolving these cartels, converting individual enterprises into corporations, and selling them off to private buyers, presumably West German or other Western companies.

The privatization program confronts some of the deep structural problems of economic reconstruction. Because of the antiquated capital stock and outdated technologies of many Eastern factories, Western firms often find that it would be more cost effective to upgrade their existing facilities in the West than to rebuild an outdated factory in the East. In addition, Western firms seeking joint ventures in the East are often discouraged by the lack of economic expertise and entrepreneurial spirit among Eastern managers. Consequently, some of the supposedly most competitive Eastern firms have not attracted any Western buyers, even when factories were offered for free to companies that would undertake the necessary renovation.

The economic byproducts of German unification affect other policy areas as well. The massive unemployment that accompanied the transition from a communist to a capitalist economic system creates new demands on the welfare system of the Federal Republic. Unemployed Eastern workers draw unemployment compensation, retraining benefits, and relocation allowances. Pensions and health insurance systems in the East are also being integrated into the Western system. The Federal Republic was already debating the limits to their welfare state before German unification; as the social services costs of unification escalate, this debate will continue with new vigor.

Nobody really knows what it will cost to rebuild the East and to subsidize the economy through the recon-

struction process, but it is certain that the costs will be staggering. It is equally clear that economic change cannot occur without substantial financial backing from the government. Transportation exports estimate that it will require up to DM 200 billion in new investment to create a transportation system in the East that can sustain a modern economy. Western postal authorities calculate that over DM 50 billion is needed to upgrade the Eastern telephone system to international standards. The expense of maintaining government services in the East during this transition period may initially add another DM 100 billion annually. The first estimates of the 1991 federal budget project a deficit of over DM 140 billion, up from less than DM 30 billion in 1989, largely because of the costs associated with German union. The costs of renovating Eastern industry and agriculture are incalculable. Moreover, this renovation is likely to occur only with the protection of government financial subsidies and guaranteed loans. One attempt to estimate the total costs of reunification calculated that DM 3 trillion in government and private funds would be required over the next ten years.

It is hoped that government-backed improvements in the East's economic infrastructure will be the catalyst for a new German *Wirtschaftswunder* that will produce a positive return on the Federal Republic's investment. Development projects will lower unemployment and encourage private businesses to invest in the East. Rising private incomes will spur the growth of an underdeveloped service sector, ranging from banking services to McDonald's franchises. Its crash course in capitalism should produce new entrepreneurs who will take advantage of the economic opportunities in Eastern Germany and the other liberalizing economies of Eastern Europe. If this strategy succeeds, from the turmoil will emerge a stronger and richer new Germany.

German unification also creates new challenges for noneconomic policy areas. For example, the Federal Republic's enthusiasm for environmental protection will be tested in the new Germany. The GDR had model environmental laws, but these laws were never enforced. Consequently, many areas of the East resemble an environmentalist's nightmare: untreated toxic wastes from industry are dumped into rivers, emissions from power plants poison the air, many cities lack treatment plants for sewage, and nuclear power plants use the technology of the Soviet Union's Chernobyl reactor. Some East German rivers have pollution levels over 200 times above EC environmental standards, and the GDR government covered up the deleterious health effects of these environmental conditions.

The unification treaty calls for the development of a common environmental law between East and West, but this will be a difficult and expensive task. For example, several nuclear reactors have already been closed for safety reasons, but this only places a higher burden on the East's polluting, coal-fired power plants. The DM 200–400 billion that will be required to correct the GDR's environmental legacy will compete with economic development projects for government funding. At least in the short term, unification is likely to intensify the ongoing political debate on the tradeoffs between economic development and environmental protection.

Paralleling its domestic policy challenges, the new Germany is also undergoing a process of redefining its international identity and its foreign policy goals. The Federal Republic's role in international politics has been closely linked to its participation in the NATO alliance and the European Community, and both of these relationships may change substantially as a result of German unity.

The Federal Republic's commitment to remain within NATO initially was an impediment to German unity that threatened to evoke a Soviet veto of any unification proposal. But with the collapse of the GDR Gorbachev heeded his own advice to respond to "life itself." Kohl traveled to the Soviet Union in July 1990 and stunned most foreign observers by winning Soviet approval for a unified Germany within the NATO alliance. In return, Gorbachev gained concessions on the reduction of combined German troop levels to a total of 370,000, the definition of the GDR territory as a nuclear-free zone, and Germany's continued abstention from the development or use of atomic, biological, and chemical weapons. The Federal Republic further assumed financial responsibility for maintaining and relocating the Soviet troops over a three-year phased withdrawal. In September 1990 the four World War II allies — the United States, Britain, France, and the Soviet Union — endorsed these agreements, granting Germany its sovereignty and in essence ratifying the peace treaty that finally ended World War II.

The new Germany will likely play a much different military and strategic role as a result of these agreements. NATO existed as a bulwark of the Western defense against a Soviet threat from the East; the decline of

this threat will ameliorate the military role of the alliance. Moreover, Germany seeks to be an active advocate for peace within Europe, further developing its bridging role between East and West begun with Ostpolitik. Thus, the Federal Republic will likely press for further troop reductions within Europe and other measures to normalize East–West relations. At the same time that its citizens and allies are asking Germany to contribute to a European peace, the new Germany will also be called on by its Western allies to shoulder a larger responsibility in international disputes outside of the NATO region, such as the Persian Gulf War.

German unity will also reshape the Federal Republic's relationship to the European Community. The new Germany outweighs the other EC members in both its population and gross national product; thus, the parity that underlies the consensual nature of the Community will change. Moreover, Germany will have to walk a narrow line between being too active and too inactive in EC affairs. Some of Germany's economic partners worry that it will attempt to become a hegemon within the Community, pursuing its own national interests more aggressively; other nations worry that Germany will turn its attentions eastward, diminishing its commitment and involvement in the Community's ambitious 1992 project. Chancellor Kohl has attempted to assuage these fears, but they can only be addressed by actions and not just words. At the least, it is clear that a united Germany will approach the process of European integration based on a different calculus than that which guided German actions for the past forty years.

AFTER THE REVOLUTION

Revolutions are unsettling, both to the participants and the spectators. And this has been the case with the German revolution of 1989. The Federal Republic is forging a new social and political identity that will shape its domestic and international policies. Many Germans on both sides of the former border are hopeful, but uncertain, of what the future holds for their nation. The Federal Republic's neighbors wonder what role the new Germany will play in European and international affairs. Addressing these questions will test the strength of the Federal Republic and its new residents in the East.

On the one hand, Germans finally may be able to answer the question of their national identity. Unification has created a new German state linked to Western political values and Western social norms. Equally important, unity was achieved through a peaceful revolution (and the power of the DM), and not blood and iron. The trials of the unification process will test the public's commitment to these values. The fate of the CDU/CSU rests heavily on its ability to guide the unification process to miraculous achievements. More importantly, the government's ability to show citizens in the East that democracy and the social market economy can improve the quality of their lives may be necessary to solidify their democratic aspirations. If the revolution succeeds, this aspect of the German question may finally be answered.

The solution to the question of the German national identity raises new questions of the German national interest in international affairs. Until now, the Federal Republic knew that its national interest was based on a close attachment to the Western alliance and the economic system of the European Community. The new Germany will feel pressures to change its international role — balancing expectations for detente within Europe, calls for closer economic and political ties with Eastern Europe, and a larger role in global affairs. Germany seems unsure about expanding its international activity. In late 1990 Kohl's foreign policy adviser was prominently quoted in the European press as saying the Germans now *want* to lead. This attitude would make many of Germany's neighbors nervous because it is Germans who are saying this and because they are unsure where the Germans want to lead them. But Germany's indecisive behavior during the Persian Gulf War also makes it uncertain whether the nation is ready and willing to assume a larger international role.

The ultimate success of the 1989 revolution depends on how Germans answer these domestic and international questions.

KEY TERMS

Basic Law
Bundesrat
Bundestag
chancellor
Christian Democratic Union (CDU)
Christian Social Union (CSU)
citizen action groups
co-determination
Confederation of German

Employers' Associations (BDA)
constructive no-confidence vote
Constitutional Court
Economic Miracle
Federal president
Federal Republic of Germany (FRG)
Federation of German Industry (BDI)

Free Democratic party (FDP)
German Democratic Republic (GDR)
German Federation of Trade Unions (DGB)
The Greens
guest workers
neocorporatism
Ostpolitik
Party of Democratic

Socialism (PDS)
peak associations
postmaterial values
Social Democratic party (SPD)
Socialist Unity party (SED)
Third Reich
value added tax (VAT)
Weimar Republic

END NOTES

1. Karl Dietrich Bracher, *The German Dictatorship* (New York: Praeger, 1970); Martin Broszat, *Hitler and the Collapse of Weimar Germany* (New York: St. Martin's Press, 1987).
2. Raul Hilberg, *The Destruction of the European Jews*, revised ed. (New York: Holmes & Meier, 1985); Sarah Gordon, *Hitler, Germans and the "Jewish Question"* (Princeton, N.J.: Princeton University Press, 1984).
3. Karl Hardach, *The Political Economy of Germany in the Twentieth Century* (Berkeley: University of California Press, 1980); Eric Owen Smith, *The West German Economy* (London: Croom Helm, 1983).
4. Gregory Sandford, *From Hitler to Ulbricht: The Communist Reconstruction of East Germany, 1945–1946* (Princeton, N.J.: Princeton University Press, 1983).
5. James McAdams, *East Germany and the West: Surviving Detente* (New York: Cambridge University Press, 1985); Stephen Larrabee, ed., *The Two German States and European Security* (New York: Macmillan, 1989).
6. Egon Krenz has quickly adjusted to the Western marketplace by writing an insider's account of the fall of the GDR government, *Wenn Mauern Fallen: Die Friedliche Revolution* (Vienna: Neff Verlag, 1990).

7. Commission of the European Communities, *Eurobarometer 19* (Brussels: Commission of the European Communities, 1983); also see Eva Kolinsky, *Women in West Germany* (London: Berg Publishers, 1989).

8. Ray Rist, *Guestworkers in Germany* (New York: Praeger, 1978).

9. The Allied occupation authorities oversaw the drafting of the Basic Law and held veto power over the final document. See Peter Merkl, *The Origins of the West German Republic* (New York: Oxford University Press, 1965).

10. Nevil Johnson, *State and Government in the Federal Republic of Germany*, 2nd ed. (New York: Pergamon Press, 1983).

11. Donald Kommers, *Constitutional Jurisprudence of the Federal Republic* (Durham, N.C.: Duke University Press, 1989).

12. Anna Merritt and Richard Merritt, *Public Opinion in Occupied Germany* (Urbana: University of Illinois Press, 1970); Ralf Dahrendorf, *Society and Democracy in Germany* (New York: Doubleday, 1967).

13. Christiane Lemke, "Political Socialization and the 'Micromilieu'," in Marilyn Rueschemeyer and Christiane Lemke, eds., *The Quality of Life in the German Democratic Republic* (New York: M. E. Scharpe); Archie Brown and Jack Gray, eds., *Culture and Political Change in Communist States* (London: Macmillan, 1979).

14. Gabriel Almond and Sidney Verba, *The Civic Culture* (Princeton, N.J.: Princeton University Press, 1963); David Conradt, "Changing German Political Culture," in Gabriel Almond and Sidney Verba, eds., *The Civic Culture Revisited* (Boston: Little, Brown, 1980).

15. Conradt, "Changing German Political Culture," pp. 229–231; Kendall Baker, Russell J. Dalton, and Kai Hildebrandt, *Germany Transformed: Political Culture and the New Politics* (Cambridge, Mass.: Harvard University Press, 1981).

16. Henry Krisch, *The German Democratic Republic: The Search for Identity* (Boulder, Colo.: Westview Press, 1985); Gebhard Schweigler, "German Questions of the Shrinking of Germany," in Larabee, ed., *The Two German States and European Security.*

17. Gerald Braunthal, *Political Loyalty and Public Service in West Germany* (Amherst: University of Massachusetts Press, 1990).

18. Ronald Inglehart, *Culture Shift in Advanced Industrial Society* (Princeton, N.J.: Princeton University Press, 1990); Ronald Inglehart, *The Silent Revolution* (Princeton, N.J.: Princeton University Press, 1977).

19. Rudolf Wildenmann, German Identity 1990 survey, conducted by the Research Unit for Societal Developments, Mannheim, April 1990.

20. Russell J. Dalton, *Politics in West Germany* (Glenview, Ill.: Scott, Foresman, 1989), ch. 5; Marilyn Rueschemeyer. "New Family Forms in a State Socialist Society," *Journal of Family Issues*, 9 (1988), pp. 354–371.

21. M. Kent Jennings, Leopold Rosenmayer, and Klaus Allerbeck, "Generations and Families," in Samuel Barnes et al., *Political Action* (Beverly Hills, Calif.: Sage Publications, 1979), pp. 449–486.

22. Arthur Hearnden, *Education in the Two Germanies* (New York: Oxford University Press, 1974); Gert Glaessner, "The Education System and Society," in Klaus von Beyme and Hartmut Zimmerman, eds., *Policymaking in the German Democratic Republic* (New York: St. Martin's Press, 1984).

23. Max Planck Institute, *Between Elite and Mass Education* (Albany, N.Y.: State University of New York Press, 1982).

24. Peter Humphreys, *Media and Media Policy in West Germany* (London: Berg Publishers, 1989).

25. Almond and Verba, *The Civic Culture*; Dalton, *Politics in West Germany*, ch. 6; Baker, Dalton, and Hildebrandt, *Germany Transformed*, pp. 27–30.

26. Jutta Helm, "Citizen Lobbies in West Germany," in Peter Merkl, ed., *West European Party Systems* (New York: Free Press, 1980), pp. 576–596.

27. Thomas Baylis, *The Technical Intelligentsia and the East German Elite* (Berkeley: University of California Press, 1974).

28. Claus Offe, "The Attribution of Political Status to Interest Groups," in Suzanne Berger, ed., *Organizing Interests in Western Europe* (New York: Cambridge University Press, 1981), pp. 123–158; Peter Katzenstein, *Policy and Politics in West Germany* (Philadelphia: Temple University Press, 1987).

29. Andrei Markovits, *The Politics of the West German Trade Unions* (Cambridge: Cambridge University Press, 1986).

30. Russell Dalton and Manfred Kuechler, ed., *Challenging the Political Order: New Social and Political Movements in Western Democracies* (New York: Oxford University Press, 1990); Karl

Werner Brand et al., *Aufbruch in eine andere Gesselschaft*, 2nd ed. (Frankfurt: Campus Verlag, 1986).

31. Gerard Braunthal, *The West German Social Democrats* (Boulder, Colo.: Westview Press, 1983).

32. Werner Huelsberg, *The German Greens* (New York: Verso, 1988); Eva Kolinsky, ed., *The Greens in West Germany* (London: Berg, 1989).

33. Baker, Dalton, and Hildebrandt, *Germany Transformed*, ch. 7; Russell Dalton, *Citizen Politics in Western Democracies* (Chatham, N.J.: Chatham House Publishers, 1988), ch. 8.

34. Dieter Roth, "Die Wahlen zur Volkskammer in der DDR," *Politische Vierteljahresschrift*, 31 (1990), pp. 369–393; Forschungsgruppe Wahlen, *Bundestagswahl 1990: Eine Analyse der ersten gesamtdeutschen Bundestagswahl* (Mannheim: Forschungsgruppe Wahlen, 1990).

35. Jens Alber, "Germany," in Peter Flora, ed., *Growth to Limits* (Berlin: deGruyter, 1988), pp. 42–47.

36. Ibid.; Arnold Heidenheimer, Hugo Heclo, and Carolyn Adams, 3rd ed., *Comparative Public Policy* (New York: St. Martin's Press, 1990), ch. 10.

37. Statistiches Bundesamt, *Datenreport 4: Zahlen und Fakten üeber die Bundesrepublik Deutschland 1989/90* (Bonn: Aktuell, 1989), pp. 384–385.

38. Heidenheimer, Heclo, and Adams, *Comparative Public Policy*, ch. 6; also see Chapter Eight of this volume.

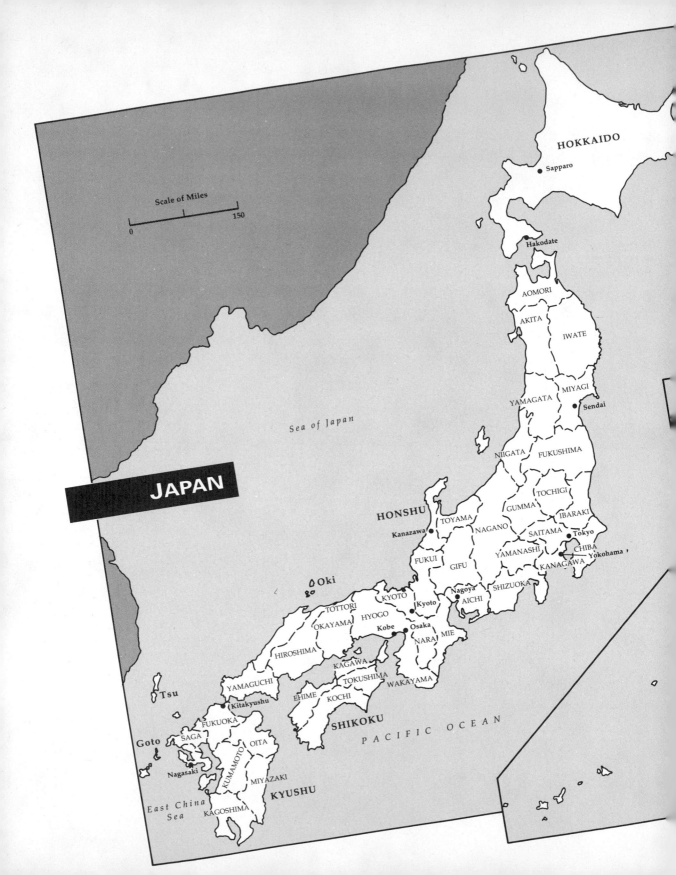

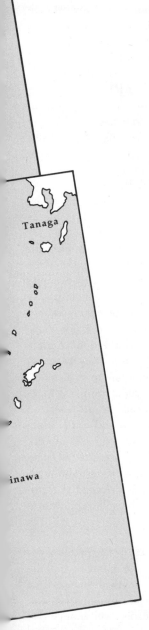

CHAPTER 12

Tanaga

inawa

SCOTT C. FLANAGAN
AND
BRADLEY M. RICHARDSON

POLITICS IN JAPAN

INTRODUCTION

THE LAND area of Japan is smaller than the American state of Montana. Moreover, much of that area is mountainous, so that the populated regions are roughly equivalent to the size of the state of Connecticut. By 1990 nearly 124 million people resided within that space, ranking Japan as the seventh largest country in the world behind China, India, the Soviet Union, the United States, Indonesia, and Brazil. More importantly, with a population of roughly half that of the United States, Japan has created the second largest economy in the world. In economic terms Japan's size is enormous.

The tale of Japan's economic development is a brilliant success story, the implications of which Americans are only recently beginning to grasp. In 1868 at the time of the Meiji Restoration, Japan was a feudal society of samurai swordsmen and peasant farmers, with 80 percent of the population engaged in agriculture, placing it roughly at the same stage of socioeconomic development as the Tudor England of 400 years before. The Restoration, which ended the Tokugawa Shogunate and symbolically returned power to the emperor, ushered in a seventy-year period of rapid modernization that transformed Japan from an agrarian, feudal society to a major industrial and military power by the late 1930s. Following Japan's expansionist military policies in the 1930s and defeat in World War II, the nation rapidly rose from the ashes and by 1990 had emerged as an advanced industrial power with an economy almost as large as that of Britain, France, and West Germany combined. Having surpassed the economy of one superpower, the Soviet Union, the Japanese economy has grown to over one-half that of the United States.[1]

While the Japanese example of sustained rapid economic growth is perhaps unparalleled in human history, its political development prior to World War II was less successful. A trend from oligarchic government toward the gradual democratization of the Meiji political structure, which began with the opening of the Diet in 1890 and flowered in 1918–1936, was followed by authoritarian militarism and ultranationalism in the middle and late 1930s. In the postwar period Japan's "American-made" democratic institutions quickly became firmly established. However, Japan's democracy has been somewhat unusual in that one party (or its pre–1955 predecessors) by itself has held power for essentially the entire post–World War II period. Some Japanese critics see this perpetual Liberal Democratic party dominance as evidence of lagged democratic development. Their views are sustained by perceptions of the ruling party as corrupt, self-serving, and responsive mainly to special interests. On the other side of the political fence, Japan's "permanent" opposition remains fragmented, ideologically divided, and largely ineffective. Balanced against these perceptions, however, is the recognition that it has been the ruling party's pragmatism and flexibility in adapting to a changing environment and providing access to a growing number of interests that has keep it in public favor while successfully presiding over a rapid march toward unprecedented prosperity for the entire nation.

As we explore politics in Japan in the sections ahead, we will turn first to a discussion of the structural changes instituted by the postwar American occupation. These radical social and structural reforms of the occupation permitted leftist parties and unions to organize and participate more freely than at any other time in Japanese history. But they also led to divisions in Japanese society between conservative and progressive camps which defined the early postwar party system. This discussion will be followed by an analysis of the political context and major political actors and periods since the occupation. We will then turn to the topics of political culture, parties and elections, political recruitment, interest groups, policymaking, and government performance. These sections will highlight the ways in which politics in Japan has changed over the last four decades as we explore the major outlines of the adaptive and pluralistic coalitional system that has kept the ruling party in power.

THE OCCUPATION REFORMS AND THE POSTWAR POLITICAL STRUCTURE

On September 2, 1945, the Japanese government formally surrendered to the Allies aboard the U.S.S. *Missouri.* Thus began a unique experiment in social engineering that lasted slightly over six and one-half years. Japan's "American interlude" was nothing short of a massive attempt to transform not only Japan's political institutions but its society as well.[2] In developing the guidelines for the occupation of Japan prior to the surrender, the American planners sought to eliminate any future Japanese threat by attacking the perceived social and political roots of ultranationalism and militarism that had spawned Japan's aggressive expansionist policies during the 1930s. The American government identified the *demilitarization* and *democratization* of Japan as the two primary goals of the occupation and installed General Douglas MacArthur as the Supreme Commander of the Allied Powers (SCAP).[3]

The first goal, that of demilitarization, was by far the easiest to accomplish and was completed rather early in the occupation. Japan was stripped of its overseas holdings, following the abrupt collapse of the Japanese Empire, and 6 million military and civilian personnel were repatriated from North and Southeast Asia. All military personnel were disarmed and demobilized, the military services were disbanded, and the armaments industry was destroyed or converted. Finally, the controversial Article 9, the so-called peace clause, was written into Japan's new constitution, declaring that "the Japanese people forever renounce war as a sovereign right of the nation" and that "land, sea and air forces, as well as other war potential, will never be maintained."[4]

The second of the occupation's two major goals, the democratization of Japan, was clearly a much more vaguely defined concept and, because of its sweeping implications, a much more difficult one to implement. Here the occupation's most pressing concern was to reconstruct fundamentally Japan's political institutions in order to remove the authoritarian aspects of the Meiji constitution and establish a sound structural framework for democracy. The more sweeping aspect of the occupation's democratization program, however, was to institute a broad set of social reforms designed to transform the socioeconomic structure and political culture of Japan.

The New Constitution

SCAP was convinced that the imperial system and the national superiority implied in the myth of divine origins were in part responsible for the rise of militarism and ultranationalism in Japan. The Meiji constitution, based as it was on the principle of imperial sovereignty, had created a political structure of transcendental authority and transcendental institutions that were above the people and inherently antidemocratic. When it became clear that in its revision efforts the Japanese government was seeking only minor changes in the Meiji constitution, MacArthur decided to take matters into his own hands. On February 3, 1946, he directed General Courtney Whitney, chief of SCAP's Government Section, to prepare a new constitution for Japan. Within ten days, Whitney's section had prepared a full draft of the new constitution. The occupation authorities exerted considerable pressure to force the Japanese Cabinet's endorsement of the new constitution, and finally, the Japanese Cabinet accepted the draft and publicly released its text on March 6, along with an imperial rescript showing the emperor's support for the document. After several months of deliberation over the constitution in the Diet, during which a number of additional minor changes were made, nearly unanimous majorities in both Houses approved the constitution. The emperor duly promulgated the new constitution on November 3, 1946, and it went into effect six months later on May 3, 1947.[5]

The Emperor
Perhaps the most profound change brought about by the new constitution was the change in the status of the emperor. According to mythology, the Japanese emperors trace their lineage to Emperor Jimmu, who was said to have been a direct descendant of the Sun Goddess, Amaterasu, and to have established the imperial dynasty with his coronation on National Foundation Day, February 11, 660 B.C. According to this accounting, the present emperor, Akihito, is the 125th monarch in a single unbroken dynastic line beginning with Jimmu. Historical records show that the dynasty can be traced back at least to the early sixteenth century A.D., making it by far the oldest surviving monarchy in existence today.

The occupation authorities decided to spare the imperial institution, because the emperor had proven to be very cooperative and useful in gaining the compliance of the military and the general populace with the surrender and demobilization orders and the reform programs. However, they determined that, while the imperial institution would survive, it would be in a very different form. The occupation attack on the status of the emperor was twofold. First the occupation sought to divest the throne of its divine trappings and to separate the emperor from all religious beliefs, rituals, and institu-

tions by abolishing state Shintoism, which was based on emperor worship, and by writing the principle of the separation of church and state into the new constitution. The second major change was the divestment of imperial sovereignty and authority. The new constitution states that the emperor is "the symbol of the State and of the unity of the people, deriving his position from the will of the people with whom resides sovereign power." Hence, sovereignty was explicitly transferred from the emperor to the people. Moreover, the constitution clearly states that the emperor shall have no powers related to government and that all acts of the emperor in matters of state require the advice and approval of the Cabinet with whom responsibility resides.[6]

The National Diet
The legislative branch of the Japanese government is composed of the two Houses of the Diet: the House of Representatives, which was carried over from the Meiji constitution, and the House of Councillors, which replaced the prewar House of Peers as the Upper House. Under the Meiji constitution, the emperor and the Cabinet enjoyed extensive decree powers, thus sharing the lawmaking role with the Diet. In order to give substance to the principle of popular sovereignty and to ensure that the responsibility for enacting legislation rests squarely with the elected representatives of the people, the new constitution states that the Diet is the "highest organ of state power" and the "sole law-making organ of the state."[7]

At present there are 512 members of the House of Representatives (HR) which are elected from 130 medium-sized electoral districts to a maximum four-year term of office. In practice, HR members rarely complete a full four-year term because the Cabinet can dissolve the Lower House at any time, and the prime minister generally times the dissolution so as to optimize his party's chances of electoral success in the ensuing election. A new election must be held within forty days of a Diet dissolution, and the new Diet must be convened thirty days following the election.[8] Following the opening of the first Diet under the new constitution in 1947, there have been sixteen HR elections up through the 1990 election, and they have been spaced at an average interval of 2.7 years between elections.

The 252 members of the House of Councillors (HC) are elected for six-year terms, with half the membership standing for election every three years. Unlike the prewar Upper House that enjoyed coequal powers with the Lower House, the House of Councillors has a clear junior partner status in the legislative process. For example, the budget must be submitted to the Lower House first, and if the House of Councillors fails to approve or reach a compromise on either a Lower House budget or treaty within thirty days of the original passage of these measures in the Lower House, the decision of the Lower House becomes the decision of the Diet.[9] During the postwar period, a distinct role for the Upper House was largely vitiated by the fact that the ruling Liberal Democratic party (LDP) has held a majority of the seats in both houses since its inception in 1955. While the LDP lost control of the Upper House for the first time in the July 1989 election, it remains to be seen whether an extended period of divided control may result in the evolution of an important independent role for the House of Councillors.

The role and workload of the Diet in the postwar period has greatly expanded over that in the prewar period, when the Diet was typically open only two months out of the year. Presently the Diet is in session the greater part of the year. However, the Diet Law distinguishes between three different types of sessions. The "ordinary" session is convened every year during the final ten days of December, lasts 150 days, and may be extended only once. "Extraordinary" sessions may be called at any time by the Cabinet or by a petition of one-fourth of the membership of either House. "Special" sessions are those that are constitutionally required to be opened thirty days following an election. The length of such extraordinary and special sessions is determined by the concurrent vote of both houses, and both types of sessions may be extended only twice. The length of the sessions and the limitations on the number of times they may be extended are important, because legislation may not be carried over from one session to the next. Hence, measures that cannot be moved through the entire legislative process before the session ends are effectively killed and must begin the long process anew when the next session begins. In the context of a longstanding conservative majority, the leftist parties, as the permanent opposition, have found the tactic of delay to be one of their most potent weapons.[10]

The occupation authorities basically modeled the Japanese parliamentary system after the British model and the *fusion of powers* concept — that is, a system in which the executive and legislative branches of government are interdependent, with the executive branch dominant. At certain points, however, the authorities were clearly influenced by the American doctrine of a separation of powers, in which the major branches of government are more independent and coequal. It is unclear whether they expected the Diet to function as a weak legislature on the British model, where Parliament's role is primarily one of interpellation, or as a strong legislature on the American model based on the committee system. As a result, the Japanese Diet emerged as a hybrid of the two models. On the one hand, both houses of the Diet have the right to interpellation, that is, the power to require the prime minister and any Cabinet ministers to come before the house or its committees to answer questions concerning government policy and draft legislation. The opposition parties use this right as a weapon primarily to criticize, and on occasion to embarrass, the government and to bring their own views before the people. On the other hand, the members of both houses were organized into sixteen standing committees that parallel the Cabinet ministries and conduct most of the important work of the Diet. As in the United States, the standing committees enable Diet members to specialize in particular substantive areas and gain expertise, making it more possible for them to propose counter-legislation or important amendments to government-sponsored bills.[11] However, given the domination of the Diet by the majority party and the rigidly enforced principle of strict party discipline in Diet voting, the Japanese Diet much more closely approaches the weak parliament and fusion of powers model than the American separation of powers and checks and balances model.

The Executive

The prewar Cabinet system was based on the Prussian model — that is, the Cabinet was not responsible to the legislature, and the legislature had no power either to select a prime minister or dissolve the Cabinet. The postwar constitution introduced two major kinds of changes in the Cabinet system. First, executive power was vested solely in the prime minister and his Cabinet.[12] Most of the Cabinet's prewar competitors for executive power were abolished — the *genro* and *jushin* councils, the Privy Council, important court offices, the Army and Navy chiefs-of-staff, and the Supreme War Council. As a further guarantee against any military resurgence, the constitution requires that all Cabinet members be civilians. The prime minister has the authority to appoint and remove all Cabinet ministers at will, to control and supervise all the various administrative branches of the government, and to submit bills and reports on national affairs and foreign relations to the Diet. In addition, the constitution specifically authorizes the Cabinet to prepare the budget, administer the civil service, conduct the affairs of state, manage foreign affairs, and, with Diet approval, conclude treaties. In short, the postwar constitution centralizes supreme executive authority in the prime minister and his Cabinet.[13]

The second major change in the Cabinet system introduced by the postwar constitution is the clear establishment of Cabinet responsibility to the elected representatives of the people. First, the prime minister is elected by the Diet among the members of the Diet. In this selection process, as in other Diet decisions, the role of the Lower House is dominant. Second, not only the prime minister but also a majority of the Cabinet members must be members of the Diet. In practice, nearly all Cabinet members have been drawn from the Diet, and generally all but two or three are members of the Lower House. Third, as noted above, the Diet can command the prime minister and his Cabinet ministers to attend sessions of both houses and their committees to reply to questions on government policy. In addition, either House of the Diet may adopt a resolution of impeachment against any individual Cabinet member. Finally, if the Lower House passes a nonconfidence resolution, rejects a confidence resolution, or fails to support any major Cabinet bill, the Cabinet must either resign en masse within ten days or dissolve the Lower House, call an election, and resign following the opening of the new Diet. In the period following a Cabinet resignation, the old Cabinet continues to function until the Diet has elected a new prime minister and he is officially installed.[14]

New official Cabinets come into being following the selection of a new prime minister and after each election of the House of Representatives, regardless of whether or not the occupant of the office of prime minister changes. In practice, however, Cabinet posts are reshuffled much more frequently, with virtually annual major reconstructions of the Cabinet in which over half of its personnel are changed. This frequent turnover can be attributed to the demands of factional politics within the ruling Liberal Democratic party. The rapid rotation of Cabinet offices makes it extremely difficult for a Cabinet minister to make a significant policy impact on his ministry or to guide a program to completion. Continuity, however, is maintained by the bureaucracy. In contrast to American practice, few offices are open to political appointments in the Japanese executive branch. Rather, the ministries and other executive agencies are staffed by career civil service bureaucrats who have generally spent their whole careers within the same ministry, gradually moving up in rank and position through some combination of seniority, personal ability, and internal politics.

The Judiciary

Under the Meiji constitution, the courts lacked any real independence from the executive. The Ministry of Justice was responsible for the administration and supervision of the courts and was empowered to appoint and dismiss judges. The postwar constitution completely transformed the judiciary into an independent, coequal branch of the government. The Japanese court system is a unitary one, highly centralized under the Supreme Court. There is, then, no separate system of local or prefectural courts, such as we find with the state court system in the United States. The Supreme Court is the final arbiter in all matters related to interpreting the law and administering the court system. In an effort to insulate further the judiciary from the executive branch and partisan political controversy, the constitution provides that all judges below the Supreme Court will be appointed by the Cabinet from a list of persons nominated by the Supreme Court for ten-year terms with the privilege of reappointment until retirement age. The judges of the Supreme Court are in essence appointed for life, but in an unusual move, the drafters of the constitution provided for a popular referendum on their appointment every ten years.[15] Borrowing from the American practice of judicial review, the Supreme Court was also explicitly given the power to rule on the constitutionality of any law, order, regulation, or official act, but to date it has exercised this power rather conservatively.

Local and Intermediate Government

Below the national level, there are two levels of government in Japan: an intermediate prefectural level and a local municipal level. Through their democratization program, the American occupation authorities tried to increase the power and autonomy of these subnational administrative levels. With this objective in mind, the new constitution called for popularly elected governors and mayors, respectively, for each of Japan's forty-seven prefectures and 3,254 cities, towns, and villages.[16] Popularly elected unicameral legislatures were also established on the prefectural and municipal levels. In all cases, the term of office for these chief executives and assemblymen on both subnational levels of government was set at four years.[17]

In spite of these and other occupation reforms aimed at decentralizing political authority, it has commonly been perceived that the intermediate and local levels of government have exercised only limited local autonomy across the postwar period. Since Japan has a unitary system, as in Britain and France, rather than a federal system, as in the United States and Canada, a narrower range of autonomy for prefectural and municipal governments is to be expected. In the Japanese case, the dominant role of the national government has been enhanced by a long bureaucratic tradition of centralized administration, the heavy postwar financial and administrative dependency of prefectures and municipalities on the national government, and the ministries' practice of directing the policies of prefectural and municipal governments through such procedures as administrative guidance and the drafting of model laws. While several studies over the past two decades have suggested that the exercise of local initiatives in the policymaking process is broader than had previously been believed, the autonomy of subnational governments in Japan is quite limited in comparison with that found in the United States.[18]

The Occupation's Socioeconomic Reforms

Beyond reforming Japan's political structure, the occupation authorities were concerned that democracy might not flourish in Japan unless the structural reforms were accompanied by a thoroughgoing transformation of Japanese society. Thus, the occupation conducted large-scale resocialization campaigns and completely overhauled the curriculum in Japan's educational system to popularize the values of democracy and individualism. Practices that instilled emperor worship were expunged, textbooks were rewritten, and the education system was restructured along the lines of the American model. To extend the liberalizing effects of education, compulsory education was increased from six to nine years and new policies were adopted that set in motion a vast postwar expansion of opportunities for higher education.

Such efforts aimed at transforming Japan's political culture require fundamental changes in political attitudes and values and typically are accomplished only with considerable time, often one or two generations.

Thus, at the same time, the occupation sought to involve broad sections of the population in a variety of reform programs in an effort to establish new clientele groups that would defend the constitution and the new rights it guaranteed after the occupation ended. SCAP planners assumed that the groups that gained new rights and benefits from one or another program would rally to the defense of the new political system as a whole and view an attack on any part of the new order as a potential attack on their own interests.[19] The principal beneficiaries of the *occupation's reforms* were women, youth, workers, tenant farmers, small businessmen, and a new generation of political and business leaders. The gains they achieved were realized through the occupation's reform of the family system, encouragement of a strong union movement, implementation of a bold land reform program, breakup of the great family-dominated holding companies (*zaibatsu*), and purge of thousands of wartime government officials, politicians, and businessmen.[20]

On the whole, the occupation reforms were quite successful. Ironically, however, one reason for their success can be attributed to SCAP's abandonment of a reformist role midway through the occupation. As the cold war set in, SCAP became apprehensive of the growing influence of the communist movement in Japan and shifted its emphasis from reform to the rebuilding of the Japanese economy. This change in course coincided with the consolidation of conservative political power in Japan, so that, instead of working at cross-purposes, SCAP and the Japanese government increasingly shared common goals. From roughly the end of 1947, the reforms were consolidated and their excesses moderated. As a result, the support of the Japanese government was won, and authority was increasingly passed back to the Japanese leadership until the termination of the occupation in April 1952.

THE PARTY SYSTEM AND THE CHANGING CONTEXT OF POLITICAL COMPETITION

One of the less propitious legacies of the occupation and its zigzag course — moving from an emphasis on reform and democratization to one of consolidation and economic growth — was the division of Japanese politics into two ideologically polarized political camps. During the first phase of the occupation, political prisoners were released from jail, and communist as well as socialist activists were freely permitted to organize political parties and mass movements. The faculties of many universities quickly became dominated by Marxist intellectuals, a vigorous student movement emerged on many university campuses, and labor unions, which were closely identified with Japan's rising leftist parties, organized over six and a half million workers by the end of 1948.[21] This collection of leftist forces — centering around the Socialist and Communist parties, labor unions, mass movements, students, and intellectuals — came to be labeled the progressive camp and rallied around the issues of protecting the new constitution and the occupation reforms.

The radical nature of many of the occupation reforms, however, ensured that they would meet with opposition among both conservative elites and the society in general. Many Japanese still revered the emperor and felt that his relegation to only a symbol in the constitution was inappropriate. Others questioned the wisdom of constitutionally denying Japan any military capability. Still more saw the occupation measures aimed at reforming the family and educational systems as attacking basic cultural values and openly worried about placing the education of Japan's next generation in the hands of the militant Marxist Japanese Teachers Union (*Nikkyoso*). Moreover, many found the strident tone of leftist protest movements and street demonstrations alien and jarring to the Japanese tradition of consensus and harmony within all social groups. Drawing on these traditional cultural themes and a sound program of economic reconstruction, the conservative parties and politicians put together a powerful counter-coalition of social forces built around big and small business and agricultural interests.

With the onset of the cold war, the occupation began to rein in the leftist forces in Japan through restrictions on strikes and union activities in the public sector in 1947–1948 and the "red purge" of communist activists and the establishment of a paramilitary National Police Reserve in 1950. By 1948 the occupation had ended its efforts to break up Japanese monopolies and had refocused its energies on strengthening Japanese business and stabilizing the Japanese economy. These efforts to control leftist influences, rebuild the Japanese economy, and secure Japan within the free world alliance as part of a global U.S. effort to contain the spread of communism were redoubled with the communist victory in China in 1949 and the onset of the Korean War in 1950. The 1951 *U.S.–Japan Security*

Treaty, which with the San Francisco Peace Treaty ended the occupation in April 1952, symbolized and consolidated this alliance between American policymakers and Japanese conservatives. In what has become known as the Yoshida Doctrine, Prime Minister Shigeru Yoshida (1946–1947, 1948–1954) set the parameters for Japan's postwar foreign policy, a policy that committed Japan to the Western alliance and the passive support of American foreign policy in return for favorable treatment in economic relations, security guarantees, and the shielding of Japan from active involvement in potentially costly and divisive international issues.[22] This foreign policy, based on a partial peace treaty that ended the war only with the Western Allies and a security treaty that aligned Japan with the capitalist West against the socialist East, raised another set of value issues that was to become one of the most central points of division between the progressives and conservatives.

In short, the two "monuments" of the occupation — the constitution and the security treaty — polarized Japan's political forces and set the tone for postwar political competition.[23] Although these legacies of the American interlude defined the contours of political competition during the 1950s and beyond, politics has not remained static. Rather, we can detect three distinct periods in the development of the post–occupation Japanese party system and politics.

The Reverse Course Period — 1952–1960

The *reverse course* period was clearly the most turbulent and conflictual period in postwar Japanese politics. What made it so explosive was that the left–right political polarization was based on cultural or value differences rather than class or economic differences.[24] Whereas issues involving class or economics may often be managed and pacified through distributive policies, there is little room for compromise where sharp differences in values divide the combatants' policy preferences. What was missing was a consensus on the constitution and a number of related issues, including the role of the emperor, the status of the military, Japan's cold war alignment with the United States, and the legitimacy of dissent and protest activities. The shock of defeat and the occupation's radical reform and resocialization policies, coupled with the changes in the education system and the re-education efforts of the progressive parties and unions, were stimulating rapid changes in values. This process of value change, however, was a very uneven one, affecting mainly the younger, more educated, urban, and unionized sector. This unevenness created a sharp value cleavage that defined a set of "cultural politics" issues, revolving around the above kinds of constitutional and foreign policy disputes. These issues lay at the base of the progressive – conservative divide and attracted the older, less educated, rural, and nonunionized to the conservative side. Throughout the period, the conservatives moved to cement Japan's alignment with the United States and to roll back a substantial number of the occupation reforms, especially in the fields of labor legislation, police powers, and education, over the shrill and sometimes violent opposition of the progressive forces.

This period saw the establishment of the *1955 system*. The amalgamations on the right and left in that year brought the two conservative parties together to form the Liberal Democratic party (LDP) and the various socialist splinters into the Japan Socialist party (JSP). Following these mergers, the only other significant party beyond these two was the Japan Communist party (JCP), which was gaining only 2 percent of the vote and less than one-half of 1 percent of the seats. At the time some saw this development as the beginning of a two-party system. In reality, it was the inauguration of a one-party dominant system, with the LDP continuously remaining in control of the government thereafter, down to the present day.

The establishment of the 1955 system ended a period of great fluidity in party labels and factional alignments on the right and left, and eliminated the need and potential for cross-camp party coalitions.[25] This "system" established a pattern of polarized social coalitions. The centers of power were dominated by an alliance between the LDP, the bureaucracy, and big business. This alliance was mobilized to tie two key interest groups, agriculture and small and medium business, directly into the ruling party's social coalition. The ministries promoted and served the interests of these groups while the ruling party, working through the bureaucracy, sought to reward them with subsidies and public works projects. Big business provided LDP politicians with the necessary funds to build candidate-centered local electoral machines based on constituency service and personal benefits and favors, and the local organizations of these interest groups mobilized blocs of votes for LDP candidates. We will call this interlocking system of interest group support, electoral mobilization, and interest

group representation the LDP system. The opposition had a separate network of fixed party – interest group alliances centering on the Socialist party and its direct ties to labor through the largest union federation, Sohyo. In an atmosphere of ideological polarization and distrust, the system operated largely to isolate the Socialists and labor from influence in the policymaking process.[26] Instead, the Socialists were relegated largely to exercising a veto power over some government measures in rare and emotionally explosive situations through delay and obstructionist tactics in the Diet, and to mobilizing their interest group allies to stage massive protest demonstrations in the streets.

Throughout the 1950s, the Socialists saw themselves as the protectors of the new constitutional order, for many in the conservative camp wanted to increase the political role of the emperor, further centralize state power, abolish the peace clause of the constitution, reinstate the military, and generally reform the political system in line with traditional values. The conservatives were largely unable to institute this agenda of reactionary measures, because in the 1955 election, the Socialists successfully crossed the one-third barrier (one-third of the Diet seats), thereby blocking any conservative efforts to revise the constitution.[27] Nevertheless, in the late 1950s the conservatives intensified the thrust of their reverse course policies under the leadership of Prime Minister Nobusuke Kishi, a former member of the Tojo War Cabinet who had been purged by the occupation and charged with Class A war crimes. Kishi's efforts to ram a number of measures through the Diet, aimed at weakening the power of the left, further antagonized and mobilized the progressive forces, and the tempo of street demonstrations and clashes with the police increased. These clashes culminated in the violent May – June mass demonstrations of 1960, revolving around the revision of the U.S. – Japan Security Treaty and the arbitrary methods the conservatives employed to secure its passage.

The High-Growth Period — 1960–1973

The year 1960, with the replacement of the highhanded Nobusuke Kishi with the more conciliatory Hayato Ikeda as the LDP prime minister, signaled a major turning point for the development of the Japanese party system. In the late 1950s observers were predicting, based on the trend lines of the rates of LDP losses and JSP gains at the polls, that the Socialists would overtake the conservatives and come to power by the late 1960s or early 1970s. The fact that this did not happen can be attributed to the strategic choices and policy directions adopted by these two parties during this period. For its parts, the LDP made a direct about-face in a flexible and pragmatic response to the failed policies of Prime Minister Kishi. Those reverse course policies had been enhancing the Socialists' image as the protectors of democracy and fostering a popular perception of the ruling party as reactionary, high-handed, and authoritarian. Under Ikeda's leadership, the conservatives shelved sensitive political issues and turned their emphasis more fully to economic growth policies. Ikeda's income-doubling plan, designed to double Japan's GNP in ten years, was immensely popular. Even more welcomed were the annual double-digit increases in real growth achieved under LDP administrations throughout the middle and late 1960s that were in effect doubling Japan's GNP every seven years. This change in policy direction eroded the salience of the cultural politics issues, while increasing affluence weakened the appeal of the Socialists' class rhetoric and their posture of unyielding, principled opposition to the ruling party on all fronts.

Ironically, the very success of the ruling party's economic programs was associated with a long-term decline in its support at the polls. This was because the processes of social change stimulated by these growth policies were shrinking the relative size of the principal groups within the LDP's social coalition. The most dramatic example of this effect is seen in the rapid decline of the farm population from nearly 50 percent of the labor force in 1950 to around 10 percent by 1980. With the rapid growth of blue- and white-collar employees, the occupational category of self-employed small merchants, manufacturers, and service providers, the LDP's other principal source of votes, also began to decline in relative terms. The effect of these changes on LDP fortunes was being augmented by the rapid expansion of secondary and higher education and the emergence of a younger postwar generation that was shedding its parents' traditional values in favor of more modern orientations. The younger generation was more inclined toward a number of the policy preferences espoused by the progressive parties, especially in regard to the set of cultural politics issues. These changes combined to produce a steady and gradual long-term decline in the LDP vote, falling from 63 percent in 1955 to a low

point of 42 percent in 1976.[28] Indeed, in the last *high-growth* period HR election held in 1972, for the first time the combined opposition party vote (48 percent) surpassed that of the ruling party (47 percent).

This gradual but cumulatively dramatic long-term shift in popular support did not result in a Socialist victory because of the JSP's response to the LDP's change in the policy agenda. In short the LDP's move away from the ideological right toward more pragmatic, centrist issues was matched by the Socialists' inflexible and ineffective adaptation to the new policy environment of the 1960s. In response to these changes, the Socialists should have moderated their revolutionary rhetoric and moved from a Marxist class party to a catch-all party. In the German case, it was this kind of divorce from Marxist ideology by the SPD in the late 1950s that enabled the party to expand its support base and ultimately come to power a decade later. In Japan, the right wing of the JSP made similar efforts to reformulate the party's ideological foundations along more moderate lines, but these attempts failed to recast the Socialist party in the social democratic mold.[29] The failure of these intraparty reform efforts can, on one level, be attributed to the legacy of the cultural politics issues that shifted the focus away from economic issues, where Marxist explanations were most vulnerable and anachronistic. Instead, the cultural politics issues focused attention on the fear of a reactionary LDP-led resurgence of militarism, imperialism, ultranationalism, and emperor worship. Here Marxist theories of capitalist regimes seemed more relevant and were reinforced by periodic reactionary statements by one conservative politician or another that would draw extensive media coverage. On an organizational level, the failure to reform can be traced to the dependency of the left wing of the JSP on the radical public sector Sohyo union federation. The effectiveness of the union's vote mobilization drives among its members ensured that the party's left-wing Diet members would always outnumber the right wing, and the union's militancy ensured that the party would remain wedded to Marxism.[30]

The repeated frustration of the right wing's efforts to moderate the JSP policy line ultimately led to the formation of splinter parties, with several right-wing groupings leaving to form the Democratic Socialist party (DSP) in 1960 and still others the Social Democratic Federation (SDF) in 1977. At the same time, the declining relevance of Marxist rhetoric to an increasingly affluent Japanese society led the growing numbers of voters that were disenchanted with the ruling party to seek alternatives to both of the two major parties. These conditions, coupled with the fact that several social groupings and organizations felt largely excluded from either the established LDP or JSP party – interest group networks, provided the opportunity for three significant minor parties to emerge and gain support during the 1960s. These parties were successful mainly in the urban areas, where the DSP drew support from the Domei private sector union federation; the Communist party (JCP), with a more moderate, pragmatic policy line, gained new supporters by organizing and serving the interests of small businessmen and new suburban communities; and the new Buddhist Clean Government party (CGP) championed the cause of many of the most disadvantaged and overlooked elements of Japanese society that had been drawn into its affiliated religious movement, the Soka Gakkai. As these three minor parties emerged and gained ground during the 1960s, the combined minor party vote rose steadily from 3 percent in the 1958 HR election to 26 percent in the 1972 election. This minor party trend meant that the declines in the ruling party's vote were matched by declines in the JSP vote, such that the relative strength of these two major parties remained at roughly a 2 to 1 ratio across the 1960s. The resulting fragmentation of the opposition vote transformed the Japanese party system into a multiparty system. This allowed the LDP to stay in power long after its vote had fallen below the 50 percent mark, because the Japanese electoral system penalizes small parties in favor of large ones and overrepresents the LDP's rural constituencies.

More Modest Growth — 1973 – 1990

The emergence of this third period in party system development was inaugurated by the LDP's second flexible and pragmatic adaptation to the changing context of political competition. By the early 1970s it had become clear to the ruling party's leadership that its traditional bases of support, by themselves, could not indefinitely sustain LDP majorities. Although the party had instituted various subsidies and protective measures to shelter farmers, small retailers, and other small enterprises from being driven out of business, the growing expense of supporting these most inefficient sectors of the Japanese economy simply to secure large voting blocs for the ruling party could not be sustained indefinitely. At best these measures were only retarding

rather than arresting the decline of these economic sectors. Therefore, while continuing to reward its traditional constituencies, the LDP also begin to reach out to other groups by addressing pollution, welfare, and other quality-of-life issues in Japan's congested urban environments and broadening its social coalition to include professional, educational, and local government associations.[31]

This change shifted the issue context once again. While the LDP's policy change in 1960 had begun to eclipse the cultural politics issues, the value cleavage that had given rise to these issues was further reinvigorated by a new set of issues that arose in the mid-1960s. These new issues posed the conservatives' growth-at-any cost economic policies on one side against growing concerns about pollution, environmental destruction, and the conservatives' neglect of welfare, recreational, and other quality-of-life concerns. Indeed, in many cases by allying themselves with local citizens' movements that emerged to protest government growth policies, the opposition parties continued to gain new supporters. When the LDP moved to co-opt these issues in the early 1970s by legislating stringent pollution standards, dramatically increasing welfare spending and addressing other urban concerns, the power of these issues to further erode support for the LDP was greatly diminished. Following the emergence of the energy crisis, with the Arab oil boycott in 1973 and one very damaging year of negative economic growth and runaway inflation in 1974, Japan entered a prolonged period of low growth that substituted modest growth rates in the 3 to 5 percent range for the 10 to 11 percent annual growth rates achieved during the 1960s. This development shifted the policy debate from quality of life to management of the economy issues, an area in which the ruling party held a substantial advantage over the opposition parties in public perceptions.

These changes arrested the long-term decline in the ruling party's vote and ushered in a period of relative stability in electoral outcomes. In Figure 12.1, the vote shares for the LDP, JSP, and the minor parties are plotted for all HR elections from 1952 through 1990. Two distinct patterns are shown. The pattern for the period up through the mid-1970s is one of very small changes from election to election that move in a continuous direction and cumulate into large long-term changes. If instead we focus on the 1972 – 1990 period, the pattern is one of lower short-term stability, with greater changes from election to election, and higher long-term stability,

FIGURE 12.1
PERCENTAGE OF POPULAR VOTE BY PARTY IN THE JAPANESE HOUSE OF REPRESENTATIVES ELECTIONS, 1952-1990

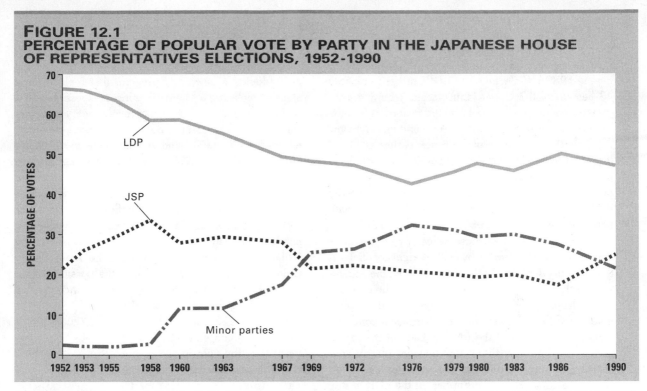

Note: The minor party vote includes votes for the JCP, DSP, CGP, NLC, and SDF during those years when the parties stood for election. The vote totals do not add to 100 percent due to the exclusion of the votes for independents and other minor parties.

with little significant cumulative direction of change. The slight resurgence in the LDP vote during the 1980s can be attributed both to the broadening of the LDP coalition and to the effect of lower growth rates on dampening the rate of further decline of the ruling party's traditional constituencies.

The visible increase in short-term electoral volatility during this period is a function of the change in the issue environment. The ruling party's co-optation of many of the opposition's welfare and quality-of-life issues has narrowed the government-opposition gap on most economic issues and has created more of an issue-less political context in which elections have become referendums on the LDP's performance. As a result, election outcomes are increasingly being influenced by short-term factors, such as scandals, the popularity of recent government actions, and the current state of the economy, which temporarily alter party images and drive voters toward or away from the ruling party. The major constraint on this volatility to date appears to be a public reluctance to turn the government over to the opposition parties that are widely perceived as being di-

vided and incapable of effectively managing the economy. The result has been a period of remarkable long-term stability in HR races over the last two decades in both the parties standing for election and their relative support levels. While some further fragmentation did occur in the 1970s, with the emergence of the New Liberal Club (NLC) in 1976 and the Social Democratic Federation (SDF) in 1977 as a result of defections from the LDP and JSP, respectively, these developments proved to be largely superficial. The NLC merged back into the LDP in 1986 after a decade of very small and declining support levels, while the SDF, though surviving, has as yet failed to attract even 1 percent of the national vote.

This period also saw a further move away from the polarization of the 1950s owing to two important new dynamics in the Japanese party system. First, the more nearly equal balance between the government and opposition seats in the Diet required the LDP to forge a broader consensus and cooperate more fully with the opposition parties in sheperding legislation through the Diet. Indeed, in three of the six HR elections during this period, the LDP achieved only razor-thin majorities that fell well below the number of seats that is needed to control both the chairmanships and majorities on all the Lower House standing committees. Moreover, following the 1989 HC election, the LDP emerged with only 43 percent of the Upper House seats, requiring even greater conciliation efforts to secure majorities for government-sponsored legislation. A second new dynamic has been the emergence of the center parties as a third force in a key balance-of-power position. In local level politics, this new swing role was witnessed in the rise of progressive governors and mayors in most of the heavily urbanized areas supported by center–left party coalitions between the mid-1960s and the mid-1970s and the retaking of most of these offices by conservative chief executives supported by center–right coalitions in the following decade. On the national level, the appearance of the center parties further reduced the polarization of the party system and increased coalition opportunities. To date, however, the divisions among the opposition parties and the unwillingness of the center parties to join any coalition that includes the communists means that the new group of swing parties in the center provides more opportunities for the LDP to stay in power should it lose a Lower House majority than openings for the emergence of a Socialist-led governing coalition.

Today, although Japan is still a one-party dominant system with the LDP remaining in control of the Lower House and the Cabinet, the 1955 system has been substantially altered. The ruling party's social coalition has been broadened, and it has become more of a "catch-almost-all" party. While some interests are being better served than others, the system no longer operates to exclude certain interests. Even labor can exercise meaningful policy inputs, not only through the opposition parties in a more balanced and rejuvenated Diet, but also through accessible points of contact in the decision-making process with the bureaucracy, advisory committees, and even LDP Dietmen. Although some groups are better positioned to get the government to do something new that benefits them, almost all groups are now able to prevent the government from doing something that would attack their vital interests without having to take to the streets.[32]

Will this form of inclusiveness and representation continue to satisfy the Japanese people in the indefinite future or will one-party dominance come to an end in the next decade? The answer to that question would seem to rest heavily with the Socialist party and whether or not it can finally transform itself from a narrow class and special interest party into an inclusive catch-all party. Recently, there have been some positive signs. In 1986 the JSP adopted a new party program that took the first steps in replacing a Marxist-Leninst perspective with a social democratic one, rejecting revolutionary and class concepts and expressing a desire to represent the entire nation.[33] A dynamic and popular new party leader emerged in the person of Chairwoman Takako Doi with a pragmatic orientation that is focused on the general citizen's livelihood concerns rather than narrow group or ideological issues. The recent unification of the labor movement, bringing Sohyo, Domei, and some other public and private sector unions together to form Rengo (Nihon Rodokumiai Sorengokai, or the Japan Trade Union Confederation), also opens the possibility that the DSP and SDF might ultimately be reincorporated into the JSP. Finally, in the 1989 Upper House election the JSP realized major gains, emerging with 35 percent of the vote in the proportional representation race compared to only 27 percent for the LDP. On the down side, the Socialists' popularity boom in 1989 quickly evaporated after the election, and the party's gains in the 1990 HR election, as shown in Figure 12.1, were much more modest

Takako Doi meets the press following the 1986 announcement of her selection as the leader of the Japan Socialist party, making her the first woman to attain such an important leadership position. Her clean, reformist image helped to lift her party's fortunes in the 1989 and 1990 general elections.

and came mainly at the expense of the minor parties rather than the LDP. Clearly, before we witness the demise of one-party dominance in Japan, more changes will have to take place within the party to build public confidence in a Socialist alternative.

POLITICAL CULTURE

When the civic culture survey was undertaken in Germany in 1959, the picture that emerged was one of a detached, passive citizenry that had recently emerged from a harsh authoritarian political system, not as yet fully committed to their new democratic institutions nor competent in exercising their rights relative to the input side of their system. Beginning in the mid-1960s and beyond, however, we have repeatedly heard about the transformation or democratization of the German political culture.[34] Our early picture of Japan's postwar political culture was quite similar. Japanese culture was seen as hierarchic and authoritarian, citizens were viewed as passive and detached from politics, and concerns were expressed as to how durable Japan's new "American-made" institutions would prove to be and how democratic its politics would become. At the time, a number of Japanese intellectuals were greatly concerned over the feudalistic attitudes that prevailed which prolonged undemocratic practices despite Japan's new political structure.[35] What differentiates the Japanese case from the German one is that expressions of concern about the flawed or immature character of democracy in Japan have persisted far longer. Well into the 1970s fears of a right-wing coup and the resurgence of militarism and ultranationalism continued to be voiced. Even today amidst Japan's spectacular economic development, concerns continue to be expressed over certain aspects of the political system, leading to images of lagged political development.

We would argue that it is time, perhaps long past time, to begin talking about the transformation of the Japanese political culture. This reassessment is the product of two kinds of changes. The first is born of a belated recognition that much has actually changed in Japan over the postwar period.[36] Western observers are often struck with how different Japanese society was and continues to be; hence, their attention tends to be drawn to what is different and the traditional sources of those differences. In addition, the Japanese reverence for tradition and their distaste for rapid and dramatic change, coupled with the slow, incremental pace of change, tends to obscure the fact that substantial cumulative changes have taken place during the postwar period.

A second change prompting this reassessment is simply a change in the way we perceive Japanese society and its persisting traditional norms and practices. Some traditional patterns that were originally viewed as premodern and dysfunctional are now seen as more suitable for and supportive of advanced industrial societies than the more "modern" organizations and practice found in the West.[37] What is non-Western and has traditional origins, then, is not necessarily incompatible with modern contexts. This is not to say that the Japanese political system doesn't have its flaws and failings. All systems do, for no system achieves the ideal standards set forth in democratic principles. The bottom line is that Japanese democracy is performing well and, based on system performance and output criteria, arguably better than many Western democracies.

What is puzzling, then, is, why the view has persisted so long that Japan's political culture is in some ways premodern and its democratic development immature. If this view had been developed and disseminated primarily by Western observers, we might attribute it to ethnocentrism. In fact, however, it is primarily Japanese observers who have perpetuated this view.

There would seem to be at least three domestic sources or purveyors of Japan's immature democracy image. One is the opposition parties. The opposition has been perpetually frustrated by the staying power of the ruling party. They have viewed one-party dominance as the most visible indicator of Japan's incomplete democratic development. They attribute this staying power to the persistence of feudalistic practices born out of the traditional norms of conformity, particularism, and hierarchy. Conformity ensured that communities, interest groups, and other organizations could deliver blocs of votes in exchange for government benefits. Particularism dictated that each group primarily sought only tangible community or group benefits rather than national policies with broad class or redistributive implications. Thus, they could usually be satisfied through subsidies, specific grants, public works projects, and other distributive policies. Hierarchy guaranteed the willingness of citizens to entrust politics to "big men" and created a pattern of the vertical integration of virtually all communities and interests into the central sources of government largess that were controlled by the LDP. The left saw these norms, then, as creating a false consciousness that obscured class politics and frustrated the horizontal mobilization of class interests.

A second and quite different source of this view has been the Japanese bureaucracy, especially the Home Ministry that supervises Japanese elections. Its election laws and documents continue to reveal a paternalistic attitude that regards the electorate as politically immature and hence constantly in need of education, guidance, and cajoling to get them to perform their democratic duties.[38] A third source would be found in the media which have gone to great lengths over the last three decades to portray the seamier side of Japanese politics. The most extreme examples here are the almost daily menu of corruption stories for virtually an entire year following both the breaking of the Lockheed Scandal in February 1976 and the Recruit Scandal in June 1988.

After a variety of sources have said for decades that there is something wrong with Japanese politics, it is not surprising that many Japanese subscribe to this view. We hear such terms as "big money politics," "structural corruption," and the "politics of local benefits" to describe some of these perceived problems. The fact that a series of reforms implemented in the 1970s to attack such perceived evils have not had the intended remedial effect, as discussed below, has only reinforced public cynicism. Why do the Japanese have such a pessimistic view of their own political system, when there is so much that they could take pride in? Gerald Curtis finds the cause of this pessimism in an unrealistic view of the Western model of democracy. He argues in essence that the Japanese have taken too literal a view of the textbook model of how a democracy is supposed to perform and as a result are frustrated by their inability to replicate the form correctly in their society.[39]

Contrary to this perception, we would argue that this pessimistic view is not the result of an infection by Western ideals but, rather, of a contradiction in Japanese cultural norms. The strong particularistic strain in Japanese culture stresses the importance of personalistic face-to-face relationships, the exchange of special favors and indulgences to strengthen these relationships, and the development of durable networks of contracts and acquaintances as a means of getting things done and ensuring that a person will be protected and treated flexibly should circumstances turn for the worse. On the other hand, Japan's holistic or group-centered norms stress the importance of group solidarity and harmony and work to ensure that result through established

consensual norms of decision making which require that all affected parties be consulted and their views integrated and reconciled with the final decision. In small group settings these two sets of cultural norms do not conflict. Rather, they reinforce each other and build great strength into Japanese social organization, which is the precise reason why they are not being attacked and displaced.

It is in large, public, political settings, however, where the exclusive tendencies of particularism come in conflict with the incorporative tendencies of holism. While holistic norms required that all should be mutually benefited, particularistic tendencies, when they become visible in a national, political setting, create the impression that politics is being run through secret deals for special interests. When others engage in the politics of particularistic benefits, and especially when they do it to excess, they are loudly, even emotionally, criticized. Yet many of these same critics will line up at the public trough to get theirs and rush to attach themselves to a powerful benefactor or, to use the Japanese metaphor, a politician with a large pipeline to the center (i.e., a well-connected man of influence who can deliver the goods). In other words, politics is good and legitimate when it benefits us, but immoral and illegitimate when it benefits others, or at least when it appears that others are being benefited more than we are.

The Japanese resolve the inherent contradiction between particularistic and holistic norms through the principle of fair share. In a particularistic setting, competition is inherently unfair. Free unrestrained competition will only ensure that the few benefit at the expense of the many. The important thing then, is not how the game is played but the results. These Japanese practices contrast sharply with the American principle of fair play. To Americans the important thing is not that the results be fair but that the rules that structure competition be fair, so that all have an equal opportunity to "win" and to the winner goes the spoils. Winning usually requires coalition building so that no one wins completely, and today's losers may become tomorrow's winners as long as the rules remain fair. This clash of cultures is very apparent in the dispute over American rights to bid on Japanese construction jobs. The U.S. government objects to the Japanese practice of designated bidding, which allows only government-approved companies to bid on public projects, and to the common *dango* practice of collusive bidding, whereby the designees get together and divide up the project prior to turning in their bids. From the Japanese perspective these practices ensure a fair outcome in which all parties get their fair share. From the American perspective it violates basic norms of fair competition. As a result, the Americans keep asking the Japanese to change their rules to make them fair to outside bidders, while the Japanese keep asking how big a piece of the market the Americans want, that is, what do they see as their fair share.

In Japanese-style democracy, then, majority rule is inherently unfair because it tends to trample and ignore the interests of the minority. Since all views and interests must be incorporated into the final consensus, decision by simple majority is viewed as being autocratic and self-seeking. One further problem here is that in order to achieve a consensus, participants in the process must be limited and negotiations must be held in strict privacy. Consensus formation is a long arduous process that can easily be derailed by public scrutiny. This leads to a privatization of conflict rather than to a socialization of conflict as we find in the United States. In the American case, an easy majority decision rule encourages combatants to go public and mobilize additional support to try to sway the balance in their favor. That would only lead to immobilism and stalemate in Japan.

How are decisions legitimated in Japan, then, if the rules do not ensure free competition and if consensus building often requires that the public be left in the dark? The answer would seem to be the outcome of the decisions, whether the outcomes provide all their fair share. Unfortunately, outcomes, though certainly more important, are more ambiguous than the rules that structure competition, especially since some outcomes remain private and hidden. Therefore, it becomes more difficult to judge fairness, and suspicions abound that some individuals or groups are "doing better than we are." Evidence that some groups are getting more than their fair share, therefore, delegitimates the decision-making process, which explains the outbursts of emotion that accompany corruption scandals and the revelations that some individuals or groups have been getting excessively large payoffs. In addition, fair does not mean equal, so disputes can arise as to what is one group's appropriate share. The Japanese try to settle such disputes by applying objective criteria, such as size, seniority, or proportionality.

If we were to judge this model of Japanese-style democracy by its results, we would have to conclude that it has been very successful. Not only has it brought government and business together in a cooperative drive for economic growth and prosperity, but it has also created one of the most equal income distributions in the world. Some analysts have labeled the resultant pattern of policymaking *patterned pluralism*, a structured competition in which no interest is excluded but some benefit more than others.[40] The contradictions between particularistic and holistic norms, therefore, are being successfully reconciled in Japan through the application of the principle of fair share. While the result has been high system performance, the ambiguities in the application of this principle breed cynicism and political dissatisfaction.

The Japanese, then, have an inherently pessimistic view of their own system. Japan's prolonged high performance, however, is forcing several reassessments. First, if the input institutions were weak during the early postwar period in Japan, that has proved to be more of an asset than a liability; it was their weakness that enhanced the stability of the system and allowed the government to focus its energies and resources on economic growth without being overwhelmed by consumer demands. Second, what may have been true then is less and less true today. If the LDP could be arrogant, unresponsive, and corrupt in the 1950s and 1960s and go largely unpunished for any malfeasance in office, that is changing. The 1960 May–June Security Treaty demonstrations that brought hundreds of thousands of Japanese into the streets to protest the LDP's breach of democratic principles was followed by an HR election in November of the same year in which the party lost only 0.2 percent in the national vote. Conversely, the 1989 HC election following the Recruit Scandal resulted in an 11 to 14 point drop. The point is that the public is increasingly punishing the ruling party for perceived wrongdoing and is thereby forcing it to be more responsive to public opinion, concerning itself with identifying more attractive leaders and taking seriously the issues of reform.

POLITICAL CULTURE AND POLITICAL CLEAVAGES

Both Japanese and foreign observers view Japan as perhaps the very essence of a homogeneous society. Foreigners are often struck by how quickly their Japanese companion will say "we Japanese" think this or "we Japanese" do that. Indeed, the Japanese seem to be convinced of the uniqueness of their own culture and often become self-absorbed in studies of what it means to be Japanese (Nihonjinron). There is a tribal quality about Japanese culture that glories in the uniqueness of the in-group and its differences from all other similarly organized out-groups. This inside/outside distinction applies to all levels of Japanese society, from the smallest group to the nation as a whole. It explains both the severity of competition and conflict in Japanese society and the ability of groups to set aside their differences and unite for a common purpose when faced with a higher level common enemy. The sense of solidarity within each in-group is intensified by exaggerating the threat from the outside. Thus, Toyota workers will unite and struggle mightily to meet the threat from Nissan. However, when the threat is perceived as coming from American automobile makers, all Japanese car companies and even the entire nation will unite to parry the challenge. The effect of these cultural norms is that competition and conflict are identified and perceived largely in horizontal rather than vertical terms.

One reason for this horizontal perspective on competition is that the social cleavages of language, race, and religion, which are so common in other societies, are largely absent in Japan. These kinds of social cleavages typically divide a society into different strata, leading to a competition between the more advantaged and the less advantaged. In the Japanese case, however, regional and linguistic differences are extremely minor and politically inconsequential. Japan has only small ethnic communities—over 600,000 Koreans and roughly 2 million *burakumin* (the descendants of an outcast group). These groups are discriminated against, but they are too small to be politically significant. Interestingly, the *burakumin* solution is to deny the distinction exists rather than publicizing and drawing attention to their plight. Religion also does not serve as a basis of social cleavage owing to eclectic Japanese attitudes toward religious beliefs and their failure to distinguish clearly between them. Instead, they typically practice a number of customs and beliefs drawn from several different religious traditions.

While the absence of the above social cleavages is readily understandable given Japan's historical pattern of isolated development for many centuries, the weak expression of class cleavages in Japanese society is harder to explain. True, economic development came more recently in Japan than in the West, resulting in a less conflictual transition that avoided the worst horrors of exploitation that occurred in the Industrial Revolution in the West. Nevertheless, Japan did industrialize, a large urbanized working class emerged, and in the

postwar period, a large union movement and two socialist parties arose to socialize workers into the ideology of class struggle. The problem for a class cleavage model of politics is that support for the socialist parties, from the early postwar period on, has been a function of organizational solidarity, not class. Nearly equal proportions of the blue- and white-collar classes are unionized; nearly equal large majorities of the unionized blue- and white-collar workers support the opposition parties; and nearly equal small majorities of the nonunionized blue- and white-collar workers support the LDP.

How do we account for the intensity of horizontal conflict in Japanese society but the muting of vertical conflict? Several explanations are possible. First, Japan's authoritarian tradition took the form of a benevolent paternalism. Hierarchic relations developed in a way that was both materially and psychologically satisfying to both partners in the relationship. Nakane's description of Japanese society as vertically organized, with emphasis being placed on cultivating feelings of oneness and solidarity across all status levels located within a particular frame or setting, be it a village or company, also applies here.[41] John Campbell provides a second perspective on the muting of conflict in Japanese society. He argues that Japan is "a profoundly conflict-oriented society, one that assumes that any human endeavor is likely to be fatally disrupted by clashes or interests or individual temperament, so that extraordinary care must be taken to preserve a semblance of 'harmony' by manipulating social relationships."[42] In other words, the Japanese are so preoccupied with conflict and preventing its disruptive effects that they have gone to unusual lengths to develop a set of social norms and practices designed to obscure and contain conflict. Finally, leftist critics view Japan's traditional cultural norms as an elaborate elite conspiracy designed to create a false consciousness and a dutiful and pliable workforce. If there is any truth to this latter view, the conspiracy seems to have worked, at least to some extent.

POLITICAL ATTITUDES AND POLITICAL INVOLVEMENT

Enormous changes across the postwar period have reshaped the Japanese citizen and with it Japan's political culture. The dramatic decline in the farm population from nearly 50 percent of the workforce in the early postwar years to less than 10 percent today has been matched by the rapid rise of the new middle class of professionals and white-collar employees. The expansion of the educational system from one of only six years of compulsory education in the prewar period to one where nearly everyone completes twelve years of schooling and roughly 40 percent go on to college ranks the Japanese population among the most highly educated in the world, perhaps the most highly educated if the quality of education and achievement levels are counted and not just years in school. These changes have been reinforced by an expanding media saturation of Japanese society and in most categories — per capita newspapers, magazines, books, hours of television viewing, and the like — Japan ranks cross-nationally either at the top or near the top. All these changes have combined to greatly expand the informed, sophisticated, politically competent portion of the electorate.

The Japanese people also participate in politics in large numbers. Roughly 70 percent of the electorate regularly turns out to vote in national elections, a far higher proportion than that found in the United States. Japanese are also more likely to attend political meetings, especially those associated with election campaigns. High numbers of Japanese citizens are also mobilized to solicit the votes of others. While the activity levels seem quite high, the levels of psychological and emotional involvement in politics appear to be significantly lower than in the American case. Japanese continue to be more detached from politics than their American counterparts, although the growing levels of cynicism in the United States over the past three decades have done much to lessen the differences between the two countries. In the Japanese case, levels of political cynicism have been high across the entire postwar period. Large majorities of Japanese feel that government leaders do not understand the people's wishes, are unresponsive to their needs, and run the government for the benefit of big business and other special interests. Socialization studies reveal that negative images of political leaders and politicians in general are acquired at an unusually early age in Japan. As those studies show, politics is not viewed as a desirable profession. Few Japanese children grow up aspiring to be politicians. Politics seems to be regarded as a necessary evil, a dirty business that requires politicians to soil their hands.

While political dissatisfaction is widespread, it does not threaten the stability of the system for several reasons. First, cynicism is an appropriate response for an electorate that is disenchanted with the corruption and money politics of the LDP but lacks confidence in the ability of any opposition coalition to manage the economy and maintain prosperity. This is a realistic cynicism, but one that is tempered by the politics of particularistic benefits discussed above. Most may grumble that they are not getting all that they should, but no one is shut out in the distribution of benefits. Second, while support for political parties and politicians is low, support for the institutions of democracy remains quite high. Finally, most Japanese have more positive perceptions of local politics, which to some extent compensates for the more negative images of national politics.

Although the high levels of cynicism diminish the levels of psychological involvement in Japan, levels of actual participation in politics vary widely across the electorate. Survey findings have shown that voting, campaign activities, and other forms of conventional political participation are related most strongly to an individual's level of psychological involvement and integration into various kinds of social networks, including community, informal small group, and formal organizational networks. The only exception here is voting, where psychological involvement has a weaker but still substantial effect as the third most important predictor after network involvement and age. Those occupational categories that score high on both network and psychological involvement — executives, professionals, owners of retail and other small enterprises, blue- and white-collar unionists, and farmowners — exhibit the highest participation levels. Conversely, those groups with low scores on both types of involvement — blue-collar nonunionists, their wives and families, and the unemployed — have the lowest participation levels. Interestingly, when we compare those that are high on one type of involvement and low on the other, network involvement appears to be more important than psychological involvement in stimulating political participation, suggesting that networks often provide both the means (channels) and the motivation (group solidarity) to participate.[43]

PARTIES AND ELECTIONS

Japan's two major parties — the Liberal Democratic party (LDP) and the Japan Socialist party (JSP) — and three important minor parties — the Democratic Socialist party (DSP), the Clean Government party (CGP), and the Japan Communist party (JCP) — differ dramatically from each other in terms of their size, organization, and electoral success. Nevertheless, they share a number of similarities. Historically, political parties in Japan developed largely as elite, cadre parties;[44] that is, the parties emerged first as parliamentary parties, alliances of politicians, and incumbent Dietmen who had to rely on their own personal election machines and their linkages to local nonparty organizations to secure election to the Diet. While this pattern was typical for the early European parties, in Japan the pattern has in many ways persisted, in part perhaps because of the more recent origins of political parties in Japan, but most importantly for structural and organizational reasons. As a result, the strongest expression of party organization has always been at the national level among the top party elite. This has led some observers to view Japanese parties as resembling small, exclusive, private clubs. Clearly, they have not developed into either decentralized, open structures that encourage the penetration of amateurs, as found in the United States, or mass membership parties as found in Western Europe.

Most Japanese parties, therefore, can be characterized as elitist organizations with limited memberships and weakly established organizations on the local, grass-roots level. Even the socialist parties, the JSP and DSP, have not succeeded in modeling themselves on the mass membership parties of Western Europe.[45] Rather, like most Japanese parties, they are most strongly organized on the national level and are controlled by small national elites. Japanese parties do differ, however, in regard to the degree to which their power structures are centralized, largely as a function of how factionalized they are. The JCP and CGP are the most centralized and have the most stable leaderships. In contrast, power is distributed among a number of competing factions within the LDP and JSP, resulting in recurrent power struggles and the frequent rotation of high party office among the factions. Indeed, in the 1950s these latter parties were often described as simply loose coalitions of factions, and, up through the 1970s, the departure of factional splinter parties or the threat of such secessions remained a serious concern.

Reflecting this pattern of top-heavy, national level organization, Japanese parties have frequently been referred to as ghost parties, that is, parties with no feet or organizational base at the grass-roots level.[46] While most parties maintain a branch headquarters in each of Japan's forty-seven prefectures, local party organization on the municipal level is much more spotty and ad hoc in nature, especially for a smaller party like the DSP. This

is not to say that the LDP, JSP, and DSP are totally lacking in local party organization, but in the less urbanized areas, the party headquarters is often a one-man operation located in the home of a prominent local politician, and performs few activities distinguishable from that politician's own personal support organization.

The reasons for this persisting pattern of organization can be traced to the rules that structure competition in Japan. First, Japan has no primary election system for the selection of Diet candidates. That coupled with a parliamentary form of government, which requires strict party discipline in Diet voting to ensure the stability of the Cabinet, has placed the control of major party decisions in the hands of a small national elite and created a centralized organizational structure, which provides little opportunity for local elites to impact on party policies. The JSP experiment with decentralizing and democratizing party decision-making structures to broaden participation beyond its parliamentary members to include rank-and-file branch activists at the prefectural level was largely a failure. The rule change between 1962 and 1977 that shifted to the prefectural branches the selection of JSP delegates to its national Congress allowed more radical ideologues to supplant the more pragmatic Diet members in directing the party program, further weakening the party's appeal to the general public.[47]

The second and most important source of the enduring weakness of local party organization is the electoral system. Following a prewar tradition, the Japanese Diet in drafting the election law selected neither the single-member district system found in the United States and Britain nor the large-district PR systems found in many European countries. Instead, two to six HR members are elected from each of the 130 Lower House districts, with each voter casting a single nontransferable ballot for only one of the candidates. The Upper House electoral system is more complex, with one to four HC members elected in each contest from each of forty-seven local constituencies, coterminous with Japan's forty-seven prefectures, for a total of seventy-six seats. At the same time, each voter casts a second ballot to fill an additional fifty Upper House seats. Up through 1982, this second ballot was cast for one of the one hundred or so candidates competing in a single nationwide constituency. Since then, these fifty seats have been filled through a PR system in which voters cast their second ballot for a party and the seats are apportioned according to party vote totals. In the local municipal and prefectural assembly elections, district size is even greater than in the HR case, as for most municipalities the whole entity serves as one large election district, while on the prefectural levels the cities, towns, and villages are the election districts. Except for the Upper House PR race, the principal feature of all these electoral systems is that they combine the *multi-member districts* of PR systems with the vote by candidate rather than party of the single-member district systems, resulting in competition not only between parties but within them. For example, in the typical five-seat HR district, eight to ten candidates may compete. Since the five highest votegetters are declared the winners, 15 percent of the vote is generally sufficient for victory. To optimize their chances of victory, the major parties may need to put up two or three candidates per district. This has meant that LDP and JSP candidates are often running first and foremost against other candidates from within their own parties who are competing for the same votes from the same supporting social strata, occupational groups, and organizations. That fact has forced party organizations to sit out the elections in a neutral, bystander role, while candidate-centered personal machines and intraparty factions provide the support for these candidates' election campaigns.

Many Japanese observers have criticized the above features of Japanese parties — their closed elitist organizations, small memberships, personal factionalism, and weak local level organization. They rue the fact that Japanese parties are based largely on candidate-centered personal machines that tie voters to candidates based on casework, local benefits, and personal favors rather than through party identifications and party principles as is perceived to be the case for many Western parties. They explain these persisting features of Japanese parties by raising the theme of the immaturity of Japanese politics as discussed above, and they view Japanese parties as premodern and based on the residual influence of traditional attitudes and practices. As Gerald Curtis argues, however, there is no reason to view contemporary Japanese patterns as premodern given the facts that (1) Western parties themselves are now moving away from the "modern" ideal in many respects; (2) the high levels of education and political sophistication found among both Japanese elites and masses make it unlikely that anachronistic and dysfunctional practices would endure; and (3) the long postwar period of evolution and testing of Japan's democratic institutions and practices suggests that what has endured has done so because it works in a modern set-

ting.[48] As discussed above, we can explain the features of Japanese parties based on the rules that structure political competition in Japan and without resort to cultural explanations. On the other hand, the rules were originally devised to conform to certain cultural parameters. Moreover, simply changing the rules does not easily create Western-style parties and politics, as can be seen from the reform movements in the Diet and within the LDP during the 1970s and 1980s. Neither the shift from the HC national constituency to a PR race in 1982 nor the reform of the campaign fund-raising laws and the establishment of an LDP presidential primary in the 1970s had the intended consequences, but rather most often exacerbated many of the negative features of Japanese politics that they were trying to correct.[49] Here we find evidence of the importance of culture and the difficulty of engineering away established patterns of behavior.

As a result of these features of Japanese parties, the linkage between parties and the masses in Japan typically is not performed by ideology, affective party attachments, or even class representation. Rather, it is accomplished either by the candidates' personal support organizations (*koenkai*) or by interest groups. Most Japanese parties have close exclusive ties with one or more large interest groups. These interest groups carry out many typical party functions. For example, on the local level most JSP organizational units (*shibu*) are located in local member unions of the Rengo federation, and the JSP membership is made up mostly of officials of those unions.[50] Similarly, the DSP has also relied on labor organizations, while the CGP draws strength from the Soka Gakkai religion's organizational networks. With these nonparty organizations often providing their affiliated party with staff and sometimes even office space, collecting political funds, socializing their own members, and mobilizing support for party candidates, there is little incentive for the parties to develop strong grassroots organizations based on attracting members from the general public on an individual basis. The major exception to this pattern is the Communist party (JCP) which does not enjoy the support of any large interest group, but rather has had to create a large associated network of front organizations to serve as its base of electoral mobilization, such as the Democratic Students' Association, the New Japan Women's Association, the Democratic Merchants and Manufacturers' Association, and other organizations of doctors, lawyers, and tax accountants.[51] All the major opposition parties, therefore, can be characterized as niche parties that enjoy the secure backing of some organized sector of Japanese society. The LDP follows a similar pattern, except instead of relying on one major associational group for organization support, it relies on a broad variety of commercial, farm, and professional associations. Many of these LDP-affiliated groups have geographically based community associations that are often drawn into the *koenkai* of a district's LDP politicians (Dietmen, governors, mayors, and assemblymen).

In addition to these similarities in organizational patterns, the formal structures of the Japanese parties bear a close resemblance to each other, at least at the national level. Each party has an executive. In the Liberal Democratic party, the executive is the president, supplemented by an executive top leadership group that includes the secretary-general and two chairmen. These chairmen preside over the party's two most important committees — the executive committee, a kind of party cabinet that addresses itself to both organizational and policy matters, and the Policy Affairs Research Council (PARC), the party's main policymaking organ comprised of seventeen divisions that correspond to the ministries and Diet standing committees and a much larger number of commissions that formulate broad policy proposals within specific issue areas.[52] The Socialist, Communist, Clean Government, and Democratic Socialist parties each have a chairperson plus collective executives, that is, central executive committees. Each party also has a "representative" institution, typically a national congress or convention that meets annually (triannually in the case of the Communist party), as well as a cluster of important national committees that perform different intraparty functions such as policy development or selection of election candidates. Each party also has a parliamentary group or caucus.

The procedures for electing the LDP president merit particular attention because, given the Liberal Democrats' continuous majority control of the Diet, their party president has always been selected as prime minister. According to the party constitution, LDP presidents are to be chosen for a two-year term to which they may be reelected only once by the party convention, with voting delegates limited primarily to the LDP Diet members. However, during periods of transition from one president to another, senior party leaders most often have selected the new party president through an informal consultation process, with the choice simply being "ratified" by a convention election. The negotiated

consensus procedure is preferred because it avoids the divisive after-effects of hotly contested party elections and averts the spectacle of massive amounts of money being passed around among the LDP Diet members to line up votes behind the leading candidates.

In an effort to reform the system and open it up to broader popular participation, outgoing Prime Minister Takeo Miki succeeded in introducing a two-stage primary system in 1977 as the method for selecting the party president. Under this system, all party members were eligible to vote in a primary election, and the two candidates receiving the highest vote in the primary faced a runoff election via the former party convention election process. Shortly after the first presidential race to be contested via a primary was held in 1978, the future of the primary system became clouded, because the primary election system not only failed to democratize the selection process and reduce the costs of presidential elections, but also unintentionally caused an increase in the severity of factional infighting within the party. As a result, another rule change in 1981 weakened the impact and likelihood of future primaries by requiring that at least four candidates be nominated by fifty LDP Diet members each in order to call a primary, with the top three primary winners standing in the runoff at the party convention.[53] Indeed, since then, there has been only one primary, in 1982, and it appears that the negotiated selection procedure among the party's top leadership is still the preferred means of selecting the LDP president/prime minister.

Campaigns and Voting Behavior

Today Japanese voters go to the polls and by and large still cast their secret ballot by writing in the name of their chosen candidate on a blank piece of paper. While the names of the candidates appear on posters around the polling place, they are not written on the ballots. That exercise of writing in names would seem a daunting task to most Americans who are used to long ballots with many offices and races to decide. Japanese voters, however, usually are faced with only one or two races in any one election. The Upper House election held at fixed intervals every three years requires one vote for a candidate running in a local constituency and a second vote, which since 1982 has been for a party in a PR race. Voters make only one choice in the Lower House election, which typically is scheduled at the convenience of the prime minister and the ruling party within a maximum four-year term. They make two choices, for a governor and prefectural assemblyman or for a mayor and municipal assemblyman, in each of the two waves of the unified local elections that are held every four years several weeks apart. These are the only electoral decisions the Japanese voters are called on to make.

Given the importance of name recognition associated with the form of balloting in Japan, great emphasis is placed on communicating the candidates' names in election campaigns. The campaign focuses on this task by plastering neighborhoods with candidate posters and cruising endlessly throughout the district in sound trucks blaring out the candidate's name over and over again, stopping occasionally for impromptu sidewalk speeches. The candidate also engages in a large number of private meetings that are organized in the neighborhoods by his or her *koenkai* members; typically, the candidate and a number of speakers on his behalf move from neighborhood to neighborhood, parading through these meetings sequentially. In addition, the candidates participate in a large number of joint candidate speech meetings organized throughout their district by the Election Management Committee of the Home Ministry. The candidate's name and statement are also included in an election brochure that the government sends to each household in the district.

These activities take on great importance owing to the candidates' very limited access to the media in Japan. Candidates are totally prohibited from buying time or space in the electronic or print media. Since 1975, the parties have been allowed unrestricted access to the media, but only to publicize their policies, not their candidates' names. While candidates are provided some free media time and space, it is so limited and constrained in regard to what is acceptable as to make it virtually worthless as a means of mobilizing support. Indeed, candidates are faced with a baffling array of legal restrictions on their activities which cover such things as the number of offices, campaign cars, and car occupants they may have, the size and number of signs, handbills, postcards, and other written material, how and where such materials may be distributed, and the number and format of speeches they can deliver. In addition, campaign funds are strictly limited, and door-to-door canvassing is totally prohibited. These regulations are so detailed that even a conscientious candidate would have great difficulty abiding by all of them. The ostensible reason for this pattern of overregulation is to make Japanese elections inexpensive, to control corrupt practices, and to provide all candidates with equal resources. They accomplish none of these objectives, however, and in fact are honored more in the breach. This raises the question of why they are kept in place. The best answer

Prime Minister Toshiki Kaifu paints in the second eye of the huge daruma doll at LDP party headquarters signifying the Liberal Democrats' victory and continued hold on power following the 1990 Lower House election.

would seem to be that these regulations help the incumbents fend off challengers by creating numerous obstacles for the uninitiated and by pushing much of the most effective campaigning up to the largely unregulated precampaign prior to the beginning of the short, usually fifteen-day official campaign period. A negative aspect of these excessive regulations, however, is that they make politics a legally marginal activity and thus discourage citizen participation.[54]

In the past, the highly restricted access to the media was not a problem because of the importance of the less publicly visible covert campaign. Much of this activity involved passing large sums of money to local politicians and other local influentials. The idea was not to buy votes, but to conduct those kinds of activities (parties, banquets, and the distribution of gifts and favors) necessary to mobilize the local politician's core supporters not only to vote for the Diet member but also to exploit their own contacts and networks to collect other votes. Voting, then, was based on patron – client pyramids that tied the Diet member to the voter through hierarchic networks of face-to-face relations. The captains and lieutenants or the big and little bosses in these chains of relationships were drawn into the Diet member's machine on the basis of longstanding personal loyalties and/or the exchange of blocks of votes for concrete benefits for their communities, usually in the form of public works projects. This voting pattern was based on community solidarity, the willingness of the residents of a village or urban neighborhood to cast their votes largely in a bloc. Their vote was either an expression of community loyalty or a favor exchanged for past or anticipated benefits received either from the candidate or the person requesting one's vote. This type of voting, typically for the candidate whose hometown is closest to one's community, was reflected in a distinct pattern of areal voting, particularly in rural areas, such that a candidate's share of the vote in Japan's multimember districts tended to peak in his or her hometown and fall off steadily as the distance from that community increased. In urban areas, companies or enterprises often substituted for the community as the basis of loyalty and the mobilizer of votes, leading to less distinct geographic peaks and troughs in the vote, since workplace does not necessarily define the boundaries of residence.[55]

These patterns of vote mobilization are prevalent even today. Attesting to this prevalence is the fact that parties that have tried to appeal directly to the voters on the basis of policy appeals, without strong organizational ties to communities, enterprises, or some other organized interest, have fared very poorly in Japan. Two parties that emerged in the 1970s, the New Liberal Club (NLC) and Social Democratic Federation (SDF), applied this new direct model of voter support. The NLC has since disappeared, and the SDF has yet to poll even 1 percent of the national vote. The opposition parties in Japan, therefore, have only been able to grow and expand their support as far as their organizational networks extend into the electorate. Conversely, this type of voting behavior is a great advantage for the ruling party because it is organizationally tied to the old middle class (farmers, merchants, and other small businessmen) which traditionally has held leadership positions in community organizations and hence is in a position to recommend candidates. Equally important is the fact that the LDP, as the ruling party, has more tangible benefits to offer communities and organized interests in exchange for support. These traditional patterns of voting behavior have helped perpetuate one-party dominance in Japan.

Two kinds of changes have been undermining this pattern of communal voting mobilized through interpersonal social networks, thereby threatening the LDP's hegemony. First, as noted in the party system section above, the rapid pace of socioeconomic development, urbanization, and occupational mobility across the first three postwar decades in Japan had the effect of shrinking the ruling party's traditional constituencies. Those groups most susceptible to mobilization by the LDP — farmers and small merchants and manufactures — declined dramatically as a proportion of the electorate. This change was associated with a long-term gradual decline in the conservative vote of about 20 percentage points between the early 1950s and the mid-1970s. Beginning in the 1970s, signs of a second and more subtle change appeared — changes in the Japanese voters themselves. Not only were the voters changing, but more importantly the kinds of influences that shape voting decision were becoming modified. On the one hand, the sociological influences of social context and social networks have been weakening. With urbanization and increased geographic mobility, Japanese communities have been becoming less bounded, integrated, and contained. As residents interact less with their neighbors and spend more of their time outside their communities, they are exposed to a growing heterogeneity of voting cues and influences, which are increasing their autonomy in selecting which influence to credit. At the same time, we find a weakening in loyalties to communities, companies, and interest associations, making it harder for all groups to enforce conformity on their members. Finally, higher levels of education, media exposure, and political sophistication are reducing the voters' dependency on social groups for voting cues.[56]

The declining power of external, sociological influences has been accompanied by a rise in internal, psychological influences on shaping voting decisions. Partisanship has been increasing in Japan, in the sense that partisan attitudes are becoming deeper and more widespread in response to the stabilization of the party system across the postwar period and the growing levels of political information among the electorate. Because of the high level of political cynicism among the Japanese electorate, however, positive affective attachments to the parties have not been rising. The trend instead has been toward an increase in *cognitive* rather than *affective* partisans, voters whose developed images and evaluations of the parties and their relative attractiveness and merits guide their voting decisions in the absence of any positive feelings of attachment or identification with the chosen party. At the same time the short-term influences of issues, the media, and candidate images have been gaining force. The long-term cultural politics issues that originally defined the party system and divided the electorate into fixed camps across the 1950s and 1960s have been declining in salience and increasingly replaced by valence issues that pose positive versus negative outcomes and focus on performance and corruption concerns. Such issues have a greater potential impact on election outcomes because they line the entire electorate up on one side of the issue (no one supports corruption) and thus may greatly penalize any party identified with the negative side of the issue. At the same time, they are inherently short term in nature and tend to fade with time as they depend on public outrage and emotion for their importance. In regard to the media, their use by individual candidates is still highly restricted. Nevertheless, elections over the past two decades have demonstrated the media's power to affect election outcomes by setting the issue agenda and projecting valence issues to the center of the political stage. There are also increasing signs that the prime minister's popularity relative to that of the leaders of the opposition parties can significantly raise or lower levels of support for the ruling party, pointing to a "prime ministerization" of election campaigns.[57]

These changes have been associated with a clear shift in voting patterns. Through the early to mid-1970s, election outcomes seemed largely impervious to short-term influences but rather, were driven by long-term forces. The changes in party vote shares between successive elections were extremely small (see Figure 12.1), as if the different parties' mobilization networks were only capable of collecting the same proportions of votes. What was changing was that voters were moving out of social networks in which conservative voting cues predominated and into social networks in which opposition party cues prevailed. Thus, small changes from election to election were cumulating into significant long-term shifts.

Since the early 1970s, all candidates have had to reach out increasingly to voters who are less organizationally linked to either their party or their own personal election machines. The result has been a shift to campaign practices that more strongly resemble Western tactics. Although still technically illegal, house-to-house canvassing is now routine, and increasingly phone banks are being installed in campaign headquarters to contact tens of thousands of voters during the last few days of the campaign. Even here, however, an effort is made to maintain some kind of personalistic or group attachment as, for example, employee lists of parent companies and their many subcontracting companies are often used.[58]

These changes in voting behavior and campaign practices have resulted in greater volatility in party vote shares from election to election but more long-term stability in the relative strength of the respective parties. More than anything else, what seems to have arrested the long-term decline in the LDP vote is the voter's reluctance to transfer power to an opposition party coalition government that is widely perceived to be divided and incompetent and likely to squander away the nation's prosperity. Nevertheless, one-party dominance seems less assured in Japan today, for it depends decreasingly on firm organizationally mobilized support and increasingly on the inability of the opposition parties, as yet, to present a credible alternative to continued LDP rule.

POLITICAL RECRUITMENT IN JAPAN

Most of Japan's local and national political elites are chosen in popular elections. Prime ministers and their Cabinets, Japan's top political elite, are selected through parliamentary processes much like those in Europe. Because the Liberal Democrats and earlier conservative parties have dominated Japanese parliaments for four decades, recruitment to Cabinet and prime ministerial positions are essentially intra-LDP (up until 1955 intraconservative) matters. Within the party, the Liberal Democratic factions dominate recruitment processes, so that interfactional negotiations and coalitions look much like Cabinet selection processes in Europe's multiparty systems. Moreover, reflecting Japan's long tradition of bureaucratic dominance, *ex-bureaucrats* have until recently been the major force among conservative party elites. However, this system is changing as the result of the growing institutionalization of purely party-based elite recruitment.[59] Finally, most persons who reach the top level of the government bureaucracy have been graduates of the top schools in Japan's educational system. This gives the ruling party's and Japan's postwar leadership a special elitist tenor.

Recruitment to the Japanese Diet

The National Diet, consisting of the House of Representatives and the House of Councillors, is Japan's most important legislative institution. As is shown in Table 12.1, five kinds of persons more commonly become members of the Lower House of the Japanese Diet than any others. These include persons who had earlier careers in local or prefectural politics, former government bureaucrats, officials of groups like labor unions and farmers' cooperatives, former secretaries to Diet members, and a general category of persons, including those with business ties, ex-journalists, and professional persons such as doctors and lawyers.

Four kinds of occupational backgrounds are present in significant proportions in the Liberal Democrats' House of Representatives contingent (Table 12.1). The largest group is former bureaucrats. Roughly one-third of the recent HRs' Liberal Democratic membership is made up of people who had formerly been employed in administrative positions in national government. The predominance of former bureaucrats in the Liberal Democratic ranks reflects, among other things, that party's long rule and proximity to the leading elements of the civil service.

Like other Diet members, former bureaucrats have considerable political resources that lead them to consider political careers or that make them attractive to political parties as candidates. Many bureaucrats form close relationships with particular interest groups with which their ministry is connected, and they can count on support from local affiliates of the group in elections. Some members of the civil service also develop close ties with business leaders, which may mean access to sources of financial support if a political career is chosen. It is also said that a bureaucratic title sits well with the electorate, whose members are motivated to choose people with "experience," according to many opinion surveys.

Many former local and prefectural political officeholders — local assemblymen, mayors, or prefectural assemblymen — also become members of the National Diet under Liberal Democratic colors. Persons with backgrounds as local politicians perform extremely important linkage or representation functions in the Japanese political system. Their political roots are close to the lives of the people they represent, given the small

TABLE 12.1
OCCUPATIONAL BACKGROUNDS OF MEMBERS OF JAPAN'S HOUSE OF REPRESENTATIVES, 1986—1989 (PERCENTAGE)

Occupation	Liberal Democrats	Japan Socialists
Ex-local/prefectural politicians	25%	30%
Ex-bureaucrats	32	0
Group officials (union, etc.)	3	54
Diet member secretaries	14	5
Other (businessmen, journalists, lawyers)	27	12

Source: Compiled from data in Seiji Koho Senta, *Seiji Handobukku* (Tokyo: 1988) and Nihon Seikei Shimbunsha, *Kokkai Benran* (Tokyo: 1989). Only percentages for Japan's two largest parties are shown for the sake of simplicity of presentation.

size of Lower House election districts and the even more compressed "base areas" (*jiban*) in which many candidates choose to focus their electoral efforts.[60]

The third largest single group of persons in the Diet's Liberal Democratic ranks are persons who were formerly personal secretaries to Diet members. In many instances these former secretaries are also sons of former Diet members and have inherited their father's name and support base upon his retirement from politics or his death. Officials of private groups represent a fourth important occupational background for Diet members. This tendency, however, has more often been the case for parliamentarians from the opposition parties such as the Japan Socialists. The Socialist party has been closely allied with the public sector unions, and many Socialist members in the Diet have come from the ranks of union leadership at the national or regional level.

Recruitment to Japanese Cabinets

Since Japan has a parliamentary system, it is natural that the occupational backgrounds of Japan's Cabinets and other top political elites would be pretty much like those found in the Diet. Moreover, given conservative dominance of parliamentary politics, intraconservative recruitment patterns should be especially important. Up until recently, ex-bureaucrats by and large dominated Japan's conservative elite politics (Table 12.2). Thus, the proportions of former bureaucrats holding ministerial positions were higher even than their representation in the House of Representatives.

The most dramatic example of bureaucratic dominance of top elite positions has been the prime ministership. Ten of the fifteen post–1948 prime ministers have been former bureaucrats. More tellingly, former bureaucrats were in power as prime ministers for longer periods of time than persons of other backgrounds. Former civil servants held the prime ministership in two-thirds of the years since 1948, the year in which postwar politics began to stabilize. More recently, persons from other kinds of backgrounds have more often become Japan's top executives. But former ex-bureaucrats still led Japan 60 percent of the time in the 1970s and 50 percent of the time in the 1980s. More than anything else, these trends indicate that ex-bureaucrats have a disproportionate amount of political skills and resources relevant to those at the national level of politics. They also indicate the strong influence of the bureaucratic ministries on Japanese political life, even under postwar constitu-

TABLE 12.2
OCCUPATIONAL BACKGROUNDS OF CABINET MEMBERS, 1963–1990

Prime Minister	Bureaucrats	Politicians	Other
Ikeda (1963–1964)	7	1.6	3.4
Sato (1964–1972)	6	1.9	4.1
Tanaka (1972–1974)	6	1.5	4.5
Miki (1974–1976)	4	1.5	6.5
Fukuda (1976–1978)	3	3	6
Ohira (1978–1980)	6	3	3
Suzuki (1980–1982)	5.5	1.5	5
Nakasone (1982–1987)	4.3	3.3	4.4
Takeshita (1987–1989)	1.5	5.5	5
Kaifu (1989–)	5	4	3

Source: Asahi Shimbunsha, *Asahi Nenkan* and the Liberal Democratic party's English language organ, *The Liberal Star*, for various years. Figures are averages for all Cabinets during each prime minister's period of power.

tional arrangements. Even as more persons from outside of the ranks of the bureaucracy gain greater representation in the Japanese Cabinet, the prime ministership has yet to be the sole domain of persons with mainly political as contrasted with bureaucratic backgrounds.

Educational Elitism and Japanese Political Life

Despite the employment of meritocratic criteria for selecting students entering leading universities, Japan has long had an *elitist educational system*. Before the war, most Japanese tended to rank their nation's educational institutions hierarchically, granting Tokyo and Kyoto Imperial universities the top position, followed by private schools like Keio and Waseda and the other national public universities (such as Kyushu, Tohoku, and Hokkaido). The hierarchical ranking system continued in the postwar era, with only some minor changes. Tokyo and Kyoto universities, as well as elite private schools like Keio and Waseda, are still the leading schools in the country by far, and to graduate from these schools clearly confers top elite status.

The elitism of the educational system is reflected in Japanese politics. Japan ranks with Britain and France in the degree to which its most senior political leaders have graduated from a very small number of schools. Only two of Japan's post–1946 prime ministers were not college graduates. More importantly, all but one of the premiers holding college degrees were graduates of elite public or private universities; most in fact came from Tokyo University's law faculty.

A high ratio of Cabinet ministers have also been leading public and private university graduates. These tendencies reflect in part educational elitism in the bureaucracy, where roughly 80 percent of the members of the upper level of the administrative service have in recent years been Tokyo University graduates.[61] The Diet itself is somewhat more egalitarian, in part because of the presence of parties that mobilize from within the trade union movement. But 94 percent of Liberal Democratic members in the House of Representatives were university graduates in 1986–1989. Within their ranks, 32 percent were elite Tokyo or Kyoto University graduates, and an additional 28 percent came from three top private schools: Keio, Waseda, and Doshisha! The proportion of university graduates and the ratio of elite public university graduates both fall off dramatically in the case of most of the opposition parties. The ironic exception is the Communist party, quite a few of whose leaders went to prestigious schools. The most egalitarian major party has been the Japan Socialists, since only 58 percent of its Diet contingent in 1987 was university educated. While the Diet shows a strong trend toward educational elitism in some instances, obviously there are also major exceptions to this rule.

INTEREST ARTICULATION AND AGGREGATION

The interest group environment in Japan is a vast landscape of literally thousands of small and large groups. Business is represented by four major groups: *the Federation of Economic Organizations*, the Federation of Employers Organizations, the Japan Chamber of Commerce and Industry, and the Keizai Doyukai. These groups have different constituencies. The Federation of Economic Organizations represents large businesses, the Federation of Employers Organizations represents big companies as employers, the Chamber of Commerce represents businesses of all sizes, and the Keizai Doyukai is a small group of policy-oriented business leaders. Trade associations like those representing iron and steel makers and automobile manufacturers are also very active in making demands to government. Other sectors like labor and agriculture are also represented by multiple groups, among them the large government employees' unions, industrial unions, and the large Central Association of the *Federation of Agricultural Coopera-*

tives. Many other functional interests have representation in Japan, such as doctors in the form of the Japan Medical Association, and small businessmen through the Medium and Small Business Political League. Even local government officials are represented in such groups as the National Governors Association and the National City Mayors Association.

Japan's political system is highly pluralistic. Hundreds of important organized interest groups regularly petition national government for consideration of their needs. In addition, thousands of local interests sporadically place demands on government for some form of assistance. Many of these groups are linked to the *Liberal Democratic party* (LDP) and support its candidates in elections as well as seeking largess through these relationships. The most prominent groups in this electoral coalition are farmers' and small business organizations, but many other groups are involved at both the national and the local level.

We call this broad network of relationships between the ruling party and its many interest group clients the Liberal Democratic "system" since it encompasses so many different kinds of political processes. Interest groups within the LDP's wide-ranging coalition support the party and its candidates in elections; in exchange, they expect LDP support within the policymaking process. Interest group demands are processed within the LDPs Policy Affairs Research Council (PARC), which itself operates much like an internal party legislature. PARC's enormous array of committees and subcommittees duplicate the organizational divisions of the Diet and actually exceed them in number. This complexly structured internal party legislature also overshadows the Diet as a center of interest group-based interest articulation and aggregation. The LDP relationships with interest groups and the resulting policy activities they engender make this a political system within a political system.

Broad Principles as Political Interests

Advocacy of broad *social principles* and *goals* is characteristic of some interest groups in Japan. Business groups like the large Federation of Economic Organizations argue that the role of government in Japan should be constrained relative to the initiatives of the private sector. They have at times opposed bills that would extend ministerial powers to intervene in industrial decisions, even though they also believe the government should promote economic stability and growth. In contrast, some of Japan's labor unions would have preferred a more socialist form of society and economy wherein government would have broad powers. The union movement has also defended other broad principles, including the postwar constitution's guarantees of civil rights and local autonomy. A few conservative religious groups have taken broad positions on the constitution and related issues.

THE QUEST FOR GOVERNMENT ASSISTANCE

A highly visible and recurring type of political interest in Japan consists of demands by organizations and communities for some kind of direct *governmental help*. Intervention in economic markets is one kind of support these groups have sought. Japan's leading agricultural organizations have wanted government to guarantee farm income equal to that of urban workers. As a result, the Japanese government has supported artificially high rice and other farm commodity prices.

A second form of government assistance that interest groups have widely advocated has been provision of special credit facilities for firms in particular economic sectors. Agricultural and small-enterprise groups like the Medium and Small Business Political League repeatedly have sought this kind of governmental help. Reflecting the especially large size of the small business sector in Japan's economy, government loans to small businesses have recently been four times as large as support for large industries. Because Japan has a tradition of centralized public finance and administration, thousands of local interest groups or coalitions also regularly turn to Tokyo for aid to finance school and road construction projects or other local public works.[62]

Interests as Demands for Regulation of Behavior

Some Japanese interest groups have asked political authorities to *regulate* the behavior of others in order to achieve some desired state of affairs. One such example has been the fight against environmental pollution. Hundreds, and perhaps even thousands, of local neighborhood and community groups in the 1970s asked local, prefectural, and national authorities to regulate the pollution-creating practices of industrial plants or to abandon plans to create new industrial zones. Groups of local residents have also asked for noise control at major airports, or for regulation of the noise and vibration from the Japan National Railway's high-speed "bullet" trains routed through their neighborhoods. At times particular Japanese industrial and agricultural organizations have

also urged market intervention through protectionist policies toward foreign imports, a policy requiring regulation of foreign trade.

Many other national and local groups have regularly petitioned the government for regulation of social and moral behavior. Women's and community groups, like the Federation of Women's Clubs and the Japan Mothers' League, have often tried to control prostitution and licentiousness. Women's groups have also opposed sales of toy weapons as part of their general opposition to war. Groups such as the labor unions and the Soka Gakkai have often denounced corruption in politics and have endorsed anticorruption legislation, another kind of regulation. The Buraku Liberation League has defended the interest of persons in traditional outcast occupations by urging an end to discrimination in employment and other areas of behavior.

Interest Group Resources: Members, Organization, Money

Interest groups have a variety of resources that are mobilized in the search for access to politicians and officials. Groups with large memberships can offer support from blocs of voters in exchange for reciprocal support for their interest claims. Quite a few important Japanese groups have mobilized voting blocs with varying degrees of success.

Japan's largest mass groups, that is, groups with large memberships, have traditionally been in the agricultural sector. In the past the federation of Agricultural Cooperatives was one of the largest mass interest groups in the world. Traditionally, the farm cooperatives have leaned more toward the Liberal Democrats in both national and prefectual elections (although opposition party connections have also existed more often than is usually acknowledged). Like other peak associations, the cooperative movement is also not a monolith with regard to the interests of its component groups and sectors. Since many farmers now work in regional industries and come under the influence of the opposition parties and labor unions, the cooperatives have had to assume an increasingly independent political posture in some places, reflecting the increasing political diversity of its own membership. The farm group's membership has also declined because of substantial decreases in the farm population beginning in the 1960s, which further qualifies its importance in politics. Finally, divisions on important agricultural policies, such as those regarding support for rice farmers, have existed over time and produced splits within the agricultural movement itself, as well as resulting in divisions within the LDP's own internal farmers' interest support groups.[63]

Japan's largest and best organized labor unions have themselves often been effective in using their memberships as a political resource. Various government employee unions have typically been successful in having at least one and sometimes several of their officials elected to the Upper and/or Lower Houses of the Diet under Japan Socialist party banners. Some industrial unions have also had success in having favored candidates elected, even though they are considerably smaller than the very large government employee unions. Unions such as the auto workers, electric power workers, and textile industry workers regularly have sent winning candidates to the House of Councillors on the Democratic Socialist ticket. Some industrial unions have also been important in the smaller House of Representatives district contests where their support was concentrated, as in the case of the Toyota auto workers in Toyota City.

The relationships between labor unions and between unions and politics are currently undergoing some change. A large umbrella labor organization called Rengo was formed in 1987 and has successfully sought affiliations from many union groups, as was mentioned above. Public sector unions joined this federation in 1989. The newly created federation accounts for 65 percent of organized labor. Rengo is expected to exercise continued political influence, including mobilizing political support for the JSP and DSP.

In addition to the large groups we have described, Japan has a number of smaller "semi-mass" interest groups that occasionally have mobilized sufficient votes to succeed at the polls. Included in this category have been the Medium and Small Business Political League (said to have 300,000 members); the Democratic Merchants and Manufacturers Association (200,000 members) oriented to the Japan Communist party; groups of farmers specializing in one type of product, such as the Association of Citrus Fruit Producers; and professional groups such as the Japan Medical Association and the Japan Dental Association. These groups were sometimes successful in the old House of Councillors' national constituency and were also important elements in coalitions of groups electing candidates in the House of Councillors local districts and House of Representatives constituencies.

Money is an important category of political re-

sources for certain Japanese interest groups. Some Japanese interest groups make heavy monetary investments in candidates and parties to try to safeguard their interests. The most important examples of the use of money in Japanese politics have been the large, regular transfers of funds from big business to the Liberal Democratic party and its factions. Political contributions are typically made on the industry association (*gyokai*) level, such as the Japan Iron and Steel Association or the Japan Automobile Manufacturers Association, and by individual corporations. The peak business associations themselves do not give money. Organizations like the Federation of Economic Organizations are said to assess the contributions of the business community among their different industrial organization members.

Other interest groups that provide political funds for the parties of their choice include the large government and industrial labor unions, which normally have given money to Japan's socialist parties. In some years the contributions from union federations equaled those from some of the top business groups that gave to the Liberal Democrats. Still, the socialist parties receive much less outside support than the Liberal Democrats, partly because there are fewer well-to-do labor union federations than wealthy industrial groups and corporations. Other interest organizations also contribute to party campaign funds or have done so in the past.

Direct Group Representation in the Diet and Advisory Councils

Interest groups seek access to decision-making centers in a variety of ways. Unlike the United States where professional lobbyists operate outside of Congress, *direct interest group representation* in legislative bodies is an accepted mode of interest group participation in Japanese politics. As pointed out above, a substantial number of Diet members are normally officials or exofficials of large interest groups.

The Japanese labor union movement has been heavily represented in the Diet and remains so today. Eighteen of twenty-five Japan Socialist party members of the Upper House from the national constituency in 1990 were union officials, in addition to many union officials from local districts in both houses (see Table 12.1). In the past many farm and other group officials also became members of the Diet under Liberal Democratic colors. At present, there are still many former group officials within the Liberal Democratic party's Diet contingent. Even though conversion of the House of Councillors national district to proportional representation would seem to have made running candidates from large organizations less obligatory than in the past, the numbers of Liberal Democrats in the Upper House representing interest groups is virtually the same now as it was a decade ago.

Membership in the Diet gives former group officials inside access to the upper level policymaking councils of their parties. Diet membership also provides added access to "policy community" communication channels that exist on a permanent basis between parliamentarians and their counterparts in particular government ministries. Some symbolic legitimacy or credibility for group interests may also have accrued from Diet membership. These and other advantages of Diet membership were probably much more important to group officials affiliated with the Liberal Democrats than to former group officers attached to other parties, which is another example of the LDP system at work.

Many Japanese interest groups and corporations also have had direct political representation through their officials' membership on advisory councils (*shingikai*) which are attached to government ministries and agencies. Every ministry of central government has at a minimum several advisory councils. At present 213 advisory councils are connected with different ministries and various agencies within the Japanese government. Each of the many advisory councils typically has several interest group representatives in addition to other members from the academic world, corporations, and other kinds of backgrounds.

In addressing the importance of advisory council membership, we must recognize that advisory councils vary in influence. Some councils, like the Agricultural, Fisheries, and Forests Ministry's Rice Price Advisory Council, have assumed an important role in political debate and have provided a point of access in the interest articulation process. But other councils apparently exist mainly to legitimize positions already adopted by the relevant ministries and agencies themselves. In the most minimal sense, membership on one of the many advisory councils attached to the Japanese government provides some kind of symbolic access and official role for the participating group.

Clientelism and Representation of Interests

Interest groups are often seen as acting in a one-way direction to "pressure" parties and government officials. In reality, groups and parties become interdependent through exchanges of electoral support and funds for advocacy of group causes. Similarly, interest groups and ministries or governmental agencies may become interdependent through use of advisory councils both for group access and for legitimization of ministry policies. Political officials also look to groups for information about sector needs as they seek to predict and understand their own political environment.

To perceive the interest group–government relationship as simply confrontational is therefore oversimplified. Nowhere is the potential for cooperative relationships between groups and government more apparent than in the clientelistic relationships that develop between particular ministries and interest groups that fall under their jurisdiction. Each bureaucratic ministry in Japan has a responsibility for supervising some broad economic sector or area of activity. The Ministry of Agriculture, Forestry, and Fisheries is concerned with problems in the farm sector and the forestry and fisheries industries; the Ministry of International Trade and Industry is responsible for both large- and small-scale manufacturing and foreign trade; and the Finance Ministry supervises the banking, insurance, and securities industries. Each of these ministries, as well as most of Japan's other bureaucratic organs, regulates behavior in its area of jurisdiction. Each ministry also typically promotes governmental assistance programs designed to help firms, groups, and citizens within its area of responsibility. In the process of regulating and serving particular economic, occupational, or welfare sectors, the ministries often take positions that are similar to those of the interest groups operating in their areas of responsibility. Close working relationships between groups and relevant ministries, such as the administration of numerous farm programs by the agricultural cooperatives, can also cement clientelistic relationships. In Japan, tendencies toward *ministerial clientelism* induced by common interests and close ties are enhanced by exchange of leading personnel between the ministries and the groups they supervise. Many bureaucrats go to work in interest groups and corporations after they retire from public service, thus becoming human bridges between organized interests and their former employers.

Petitions and Public Activities

In addition to other routes of access to the policymaking centers in Japanese politics, interests are articulated in Japan through more public modes of communication, including public statements, petitions, rallies, and demonstrations. The use of petitions (*chinjo*) is probably the most common public form of interest group communications with government organs and political parties. Tens of thousands of petitions are submitted each year to government officials, political parties, and Diet members. Petitions range from requests for minute adjustments in ministerial regulation of gasoline station operations to expressions of broad ideological views on Japan's foreign policies. In 1962 alone members of the National Farm Cooperatives Federation sent an estimated 4 million postcards and petitions to government offices and members of the Diet! The targets of petitions to national government range from the prime minister and Cabinet members to specific units of particular ministries and rank-and-file members of the Diet. Most large interest groups also express their demands via other public channels such as statements in the media, annual policy papers and resolutions, and organization publications. The Federation of Economic Organizations, for example, contributes a steady stream of suggested remedies for Japan's general economic problems similar in content and scope to the government's own broad policy statements.

Many Japanese interest groups utilize public rallies and marches to underscore their claims for political consideration. Labor unions and student groups have been noted for the frequency and occasionally the violence of their demonstration activities vis-à-vis both national and local authorities. Their struggle against ratification of the U.S.–Japan Security Treaty in May and June of 1960 was the largest public demonstration in postwar Japanese history, while later leftist groups and local farmers battled against the development of a new international airport for Tokyo for over a decade.[64] Many other interests participate in demonstrations and rallies. Long lines of flag and poster-bearing demonstrators are a frequent ritual in Tokyo's governmental district.

Interest Aggregation in Japan

A multitude of interest groups in Japan have approached government through different channels with a large number and variety of requests for help. Interests may be aggregated in the political system at many decision points. Requests for local financial support are usually dealt with by prefectural governments or in sections within particular ministries, or even by means of agreements involving several ministries, such as between the Construction and Education ministries when school construction projects are the concern. The amount of support allocated will then be added to the project list submitted with a particular ministry's annual budget request. This is an example of fairly low-level aggregation. In other instances, aggregation decisions may be made at higher levels of the bureaucracy and government. For example, the positions of national business groups on tax policy matters may be discussed in advisory councils, at the ministerial level, or in Cabinet meetings where decisions on tax and fiscal policy are considered from the point of view of their macroeconomic consequences. Other interests have been processed at the highest levels within the political system. The demands of farm groups for farm price supports have on quite a few occasions been debated at the Cabinet level, and in some instances have required interventions by the prime minister himself. In each case, aggregative decisions may be made as the proposals of groups are weighed against other alternatives on the basis of their objective or political merits.

One feature of Japanese politics is the apparent frequent inability of the ruling Liberal Democratic party to aggregate effectively interest demands within normal party channels. Where substantial pressure comes either from the rank-and-file members of the parliamentary party on behalf of different interests, or from the various party policy subcommittees, which are often de facto captives of particular interests, the ruling party submits unaggregated lists of demands to the relevant ministries and the party's executives.[65] The party's internal decision-making bodies are unable to make effective compromises on budget issues in such situations. In these cases, the party's internal organs and leadership become a transmission belt for the articulation of interests, rather than vehicles for interest aggregation.

Conclusions: Interests in Japan—Corporatism Versus Pluralism

Recent political research on Japan has fiercely debated whether interest articulation under LDP dominance in Japan is corporatist or pluralist in nature. The *corporatism–pluralism* controversy is relevant to the question of who wins in Japanese interest politics, as well as to understanding the role of private interests in that country's policymaking processes. Corporatism implies the incorporation of relationships between government and private interests. A popular version of these ideas is symbolized by the term *Japan Incorporated*. Proponents of the corporatist theory of Japanese interest politics argue that close relationships between Japan's ministries, the Liberal Democratic party, and private interests such as business and agriculture have enhanced representation of these interests while inhibiting consideration of the views of other sectors such as labor. Only interests that have close ties with the bureaucracy and ruling party are seen as successful. The corporatist "school" also views Japan's ministries as being able to impose controls on business and other groups as the result of the intimate relationship.

Other students of Japanese politics support a pluralist interpretation. As evidence, they describe the proliferation of interest groups in Japan and frequent sharp differences of opinion between different interests or between special interests and government. They note that many of these differences take place within what we have described as the LDP system of interest-linked relationships and processes. The dramatic struggles between farm groups and the government over farm prices in some years seem to indicate a degree of independence that is more characteristic of pluralism than corporatism. So does the resistance by automobile and computer corporations to MITI pressures to join in mergers and the many struggles between different business interests, such as highly visible conflicts between producers and consumers of, respectively, electric power, naptha, and aluminum ingots.[66] Pluralism can also be seen in the conflicts between different ministries over desired policies that espouse the claims of different groups. Struggles when the money demands of one ministry acting on behalf of an interest group client conflict with the views of the fiscally conservative Finance Ministry are one such example.

In reality, like many other political systems, Japanese politics includes elements of both corporatism and pluralism.[67] A kind of structural corporatism can be seen in the close ties that exist between some private interests and specific bureaucratic ministries, and between these and the relevant policy groups within the ruling party.[68] Participation in advisory councils, employment of former bureaucrats as group officials, and other kinds of clientelistic relationships and informal policy community linkages all indicate a high level of institutionalization of government–interest group relationships. The social coalition involving farmers, small and big business, other sectors of society, and the Liberal Democratic party is itself an example of linkages based on institutionalization of interest viewed broadly.

On the other hand, the frequency and assertiveness of interest demands by opposing interest groups and by private groups opposing the government, even those operating within the LDP system, are convincing evidence for the pluralist view. The LDP social coalition is a corporatist shell within which examples of pluralism abound in actual policymaking scenarios. Similarly, although many groups "win" recognition for their demands, the composition of the winning coalitions varies depending on the time and the issue. More than just a few privileged groups are represented in these processes. Much pluralism exists in Japanese politics. The question then becomes that of how to reconcile the presence of both corporatist and pluralist elements of policymaking. We would suggest that the institutionalized policy group – government – party relationships to which we have already alluded constitute policymaking channels within which pluralistic conflict takes place. Interest group – party – ministry relationships are organized, often on a relatively permanent basis. But conflict still occurs within these parameters.

An additional reason why Western observers are reluctant to see pluralism in Japanese policy processes is certainly the narrowness of the ideological or value spectrum within which pluralistic interests compete. Japan generally lacks the vibrant and highly adversarial conflict between noneconomic reform groups characteristic of American politics, and in varying degrees that of Europe as well. Japanese interest politics is mainly economic interest politics. Except for the activities of pollution and antidevelopment groups in the 1970s, a handful of groups that take positions on constitutional reform and groups representing Korean and *burakumin* minorities, the struggles of interest groups are mainly over such "goods" as price subsidies, protection of industries, and the availability of loans. What is more, Japanese society also lacks the deep class and religious value cleavages characteristic of many other industrialized countries. All these qualities make pluralistic competition between interests in Japan seem less visible.

Finally, much of the Japanese interest policymaking is also "segmented." Decisions on group interests are made at middle levels of the bureaucracy and the Liberal Democratic party, where large groups and social sectors do not visibly compete for the same resources in the manner of the larger scale political donnybrooks characteristic of traditional European and American social cleavage politics. Much of the political process involving private interests thus takes place within a semi-encapsulized process. The coal industry fights the power industry, or a single farm sector, such as lemon growers, requests protection from American imports. In most of the postwar era, however, organized labor has not fought organized business over nationalization of industry, as in Britain in some periods. Nor are there nationwide conflicts over abortion or divorce, as in Italy. Although there is group conflict in Japan, the stakes are smaller than in those countries where nationwide social class or religious groups and their party allies or sponsors fight over high-profile issues involving zero-sum issues concerning societal wealth or values. Japanese interest politics are simply not as visibly redistributional as interest politics in other more heterogeneous societies. Japanese interest politics may therefore be described as distributive pluralism.

POLICYMAKING

Public Policymaking in Japan: The Core Questions

The institutions of government are central structures in Japanese policymaking processes. The constitution gives the national political executive, the prime minister and his Cabinet, important grants of authority. The constitution also empowers the National Diet with the critical lawmaking function. The Diet is expected to debate, amend, and pass bills proposed by the Cabinet or suggested by members within the parliamentary body itself. The Diet is therefore supposed to have the last word in all policy decisions that result in passage of legislation. The main role of the national bureaucracy, including the twelve line ministries and the many agencies and commissions, is to implement public policy. Reflecting this philosophy, the bureaucracy has no assigned role in the Japanese constitution.

The reality of policymaking departs substantially from the general model implied in the formal documents. The formal institutions of government are important in Japan. But political parties and interest groups that are not mentioned in Japan's basic institutional documents also play important roles in political processes. Policymaking is profoundly affected by the presence of a dominant party, supported by and responsive to a broad internally pluralistic social coalition. The weight and strategies of the different components of the Liberal Democratic "system" profoundly influence governmental policy. Finally, Japan's traditionally strong bureaucracy is also important. Initiation of legislative

proposals is diffused throughout the administrative bureaucracy, and ministries supply many of the ideas that lead to legislation passed by the Diet.

The presence of these important political forces calls our attention to the less formal side of politics, in effect the arenas of power that are shaped by the twin forces of political tradition and ongoing political competition. How Japanese policy is made and what role different institutions and groups play in the process is the question to be addressed in the following discussion. Like the politics of other industrialized countries, there are many checks and balances in the political system. Interestingly, they are found in different places in Japan than in some other countries.

The Central Executive Elite: Powers, Vulnerability, and Policy Role

Although Japan's prime minister is not as independently powerful as an American president, in theory he does have substantial political powers. He appoints the members of his Cabinet, is empowered along with the Cabinet to propose legislative bills, and heads the enormous administrative branch of 2 million persons in its task of implementing legislation. He also leads in foreign policy formation.[69] At the same time, he is responsible to the National Diet. He can be removed from office by the lower house, if his political support in that body wanes. The chief executive of Japan must maintain a viable base of political support at all times. During the Liberal Democratic party's hegemony, this has meant intraparty support. Because the prime minister is chosen mainly by a coalition of Liberal Democratic party factions, his freedom of action is restricted by factional politics. The vulnerability of the prime minister and of his Cabinet to being pushed out of office in the factional game is sufficient to restrict considerably their freedom of choice in policy matters.[70]

The prime minister's freedom to initiate policy is also limited by the presence of numerous policy-oriented opinion groups within the Liberal Democratic party itself. In the past, "hawk" and "dove" groupings within the majority party have constrained prime ministerial initiative in decisions on defense and foreign policymaking. Groups of Liberal Democratic Diet members affiliated with institutionalized interests in agriculture and other areas also potentially restrict the prime minister and his Cabinet.[71]

Groups outside the Liberal Democratic party also potentially limit the prime minister's and his Cabinet's range of alternatives. One of these groups is the governmental bureaucracy. While the prime minister and his members are nominally heads of the administrative branch, they are still dependent on the bureaucracy for information, advice, and cooperation in handling the details involved in policymaking and implementation. The bureaucratic ministries in Japan are also a rich source of policy ideas and proposals. Other groups, including powerful interest groups and the opposition parties, also exercise important checks on the policymaking initiative of the Japanese central executive elite.

The central executive elite serves, among other roles, as *policy broker*. If the bureaucratic ministries disagree, or if the policy organs in the Liberal Democratic party oppose solutions advanced by a bureaucratic ministry, as frequently occurred in conflicts about rice price supports, the prime minister or some small group within the central executive elite typically acts as broker, or arbiter, in the policymaking process.[72]

The central executive elite also ratifies decisions made elsewhere. This elite approves decisions made by other groups (including the LDP's own Policy Affairs Research Council) when decisions fall clearly within the jurisdiction of a particular ministry or agency, when major policy initiatives are taken by especially powerful ministries, or when decisions are not highly politicized. The Finance Ministry's typical domination of national budget formulation is one such example of the first and second of these conditions.[73] In such situations the prime minister and his Cabinet follow the policy set by the ministry in question rather than independently creating policy directions. De facto central elite ratification of major interest group proposals that work their way "upward" through the party's Policy Affairs Research Council may also occur.

In some situations Japan's prime ministers have provided strong and positive executive leadership. Most of the postwar prime ministers have at some time committed themselves to a major foreign or domestic policy goal. Examples include Kishi's plan to amend the U.S.–Japan Security Treaty, Hatoyama's search for a rapprochement with the Soviet Union, and Sato's desire to normalize postwar relationships with South Korea and have Okinawa revert to Japanese control. Ikeda's resolve to double incomes and Tanaka's proposal to remodel the Japanese archipelago also reflected strong commitment to a particular policy goal. Where strong leadership is present, even strong ministries like Finance or MITI have had to be more flexible. Thus, on certain occasions, postwar Japanese prime ministers have exhibited strong leadership on major policy issues despite the many constraints on their leadership.

Bureaucratic Dominance?

Bureaucratic ministries have many sources of strength, in addition to their legislatively assigned functions. Administrative bureaucracies are relatively permanent organizations with low rates of turnover of personnel, in contrast with the impermanent careers in the political branches of government. Bureaucracies also develop highly valuable, specialized competence in particular areas of governance. The knowledge required to regulate the aviation industry (in Japan the job of the Transportation Ministry), plan multibillion dollar budgets (supervised by the Ministry of Finance), and develop high-technology defense systems (the responsibility of the Defense Agency) is an example of the expertise that civil servants must develop to carry out their jobs. In contrast, members of legislatures and central executive groups have much less opportunity to develop expert knowledge on complex aspects of the economy or technology. Staff support of legislators is also very limited in Japan (unlike the American Congress). Both the politicians' vulnerability in elections and the perhaps inevitable gap in expertise between elected officials of government and bureaucrats frequently result in de facto dependence of the elected officials on the bureaucrats for advice on complex technical issues.

Tradition enhances the Japanese tendency toward comparatively strong bureaucratic influences. The bureaucracy has been a major influence in government more or less continuously since its formal inception in the late nineteenth century. A strong administrative branch was anticipated in the Prussian-inspired constitution of 1889. The Japanese bureaucracy was especially dominant in the early development of the country's modern economy and military establishment and during the late 1930s and World War II. As a result, the ministries are accustomed to leadership. Recruitment of the top products of an elitist educational system has both reflected and reinforced the influence and status of the bureaucracy during the prewar period and today.

The Japanese bureaucratic ministries dominate policymaking through their role in initiating and drafting proposals for new laws.[74] A substantial part of the legislation considered by the Parliament in fact originates in the ministries, and is submitted via the Cabinet, rather than being formulated on the floor of the National Diet.

Other proposed laws are drafted within the ministries in response to Cabinet or Liberal Democratic party inputs. Even though the proportion of Cabinet bills has declined over time, over the past three and a half decades Cabinet bills have consistently accounted for three-fifths to two-thirds of all bills dealt with by the national Parliament. Their role in drafting legislative proposals gives ministerial officials a great deal of influence in shaping policy alternatives based on their own perceptions of complex problems and solutions. However, where proposed bills affect major ruling Liberal Democratic party concerns, opposition party commitments, group interests, consumer problems, or important macroeconomic decisions, some or all stages of decision processes are more often highly politicized. The ministries have only a qualified influence over process outcomes in these instances.

The function of delegated "legislation" is another example of the ministries' influence. The Japanese ministries formulate rules as a result of their more general responsibility for policy implementation. The major economic ministries, for example, "legislate" extensively through their formulation of ministerial ordinances and other kinds of rules; the Cabinet collectively performs a similar legislative function, utilizing Cabinet ordinances and rulings. The ministries also use an even more subtle device for enforcing ministerial policies, called *administrative guidance*. Administrative guidance refers to practices through which national ministries persuade the private sector to comply with policies by the use of explicit or implicit threats of sanctions based on the broad grants of authority by empowering legislation.[75]

The volume of direct ministerial "legislation" is substantial. Comparison of the ratio of the numbers of Diet laws with those of administrative ordinances shows that the latter has increased from roughly 1.5 times the number of Diet laws in the first postwar decade to three to four times the number in recent years.[78] These administrative "laws" do not necessarily violate the spirit of related empowering Diet legislation. But the relative scope of bureaucratic lawmaking through the ordinance power is very great in Japan.

Because of the bureaucracy's broad influence, some observers of Japanese politics ascribe almost monolithic power to it. Actually, the ministries are far from a monolithic unity, and, though very powerful, their influence is circumscribed. Interministerial differences of opinion on issues are numerous and are one of the forces that effectively limit the power of the bureaucracy as a collective entity. These differences occur when ministerial "ideologies" clash, as frequently happens when cautious Ministry of Finance bureaucrats have to deal with the more free-spending officials of other ministries. Intense debates also occur when new policies infringe on traditional ideas about which ministry should control a specific sector of economic activity. Similar long-term differences in basic attitudes have at times existed within ministries as well as between ministries. These differences and other qualifications on the independence of the bureaucracy have led to a recent view that Japan is an example of bureaucratic primacy but not bureaucratic dominance.[77]

The Japanese Diet

The 1946 constitution granted Japan's National Diet the power to make all final decisions on legislation in its capacity as the highest organ of the state. However, the strength of the administrative bureaucracy and the dominant position of the Liberal Democratic party within the Diet have meant that in many cases bills submitted by the ministries and Cabinet and also supported by the Liberal Democratic party were passed more or less automatically. As a result, many observers have felt that the Diet's main function has been to "ratify" without amending proposals initiated and decided by the Cabinet and the bureaucracy. This view was especially prominent until the 1970s.

In reality, the roles played by the Diet and its members have been much more substantial than this version of Japanese politics has argued. First, while the rate of passage of member bills has been much lower than that for Cabinet bills (15 versus 80 percent), the number of member bills relative to Cabinet bills has increased substantially over time. Moreover, their low success rate hides the fact that opposition parties sponsor member bills to present their versions of desired legislation, and even if these don't pass, they often pave the way for amendments of government bills. Finally, since the early 1970s the Diet has taken significant action on as many as four-fifths of the major bills submitted to it by the Cabinet and ministries.[78] Even if we look at all Cabinet bills rather than just major bills, we find that only 56 percent of those submitted to the Diet between 1960 and 1980 passed without being amended, postponed, or shelved. These data, which look beyond the mere fact of "passage" or "failure," confirm the image of the Diet as something more than a passive body. The evidence contradicts the idea that the Japanese Diet is merely a rubber-stamp Parliament.

Diet members as individuals also have multiple opportunities to make inputs into policymaking even before bills get to the Diet. Interest articulation involves Diet members as representatives of group demands in meetings with ministerial officials, who then incorporate some of these demands in subsequent legislative (including budget) proposals. Informal "subgovernments" or policy community coalitions that cross institutional boundaries and involve Diet members, government officials, and interest group personnel in relation to particular policy interests also exist and are said to play an especially important role in Japanese policymaking. Where present, they provide opportunities for Diet member inputs into the prelegislative drafting process that goes on within the ministries. Finally, through open debates and interpellation both on pending bills and on other important policy issues, members of the executive elite and leading bureaucratic officials are regularly pressed to defend their policy positions and decisions in the forums of the Diet.

The Liberal Democratic Party

Political parties themselves play important roles in policymaking. Parties and their internal organs perform policymaking roles at a variety of points and in different forms. Because the Liberal Democratic party and its predecessors have dominated Japanese politics for so long, such intraparty groups as the party's executive elite, the formal party policymaking organ (the very large Policy Affairs Research Council), intraparty policy groups, and *zoku* ("tribes" of like-minded LDP members who favor farmers, small businessmen, or some other interests), the intraparty factions, and rank-and-file Diet members have *each* made important inputs into policymaking processes, depending on the issue and the phase of those processes.

As leaders of a permanent majority party, the Liberal Democratic elite typically has interacted very closely with the central executive elite, that is, the prime minister and his Cabinet. The party elite also has been subject to some of the same political pressures that affect the central executive group, particularly those originating within the party, which is above everything else a catch-all party including and representing many diverse opinions and interests. For this reason, the policymaking roles of the party elite and the central elite have been similar, in that intraparty pluralism has often constrained their freedom of action.

Intraparty pluralism has also affected the efforts of the policy councils of the Liberal Democratic party to promote specific policy stands and aggregate different positions. A great diversity of interests is represented within the party and in its main policy organ, the Policy Affairs Research Council. Many of these interests have had strong rank-and-file and PARC subcommittee support. Indeed, quite a few policy communities consider important PARC subcommittees as parts of their institutionalized coalitions. Because of diverse interests and pressures from strong groups, the party's leaders often could not make decisions on which proposals merited higher and lower priorities and still preserve their positions and the party's organizational integrity. Thus, the prescribed decision-making and interest-aggregating processes of the party's PARC have been influenced by pressures from below which seek to get the upper level officials and organs of the party to accede to rank-and-file demands. Organized in support of agriculture, small business, and other interests, the party rank-and-file have succeeded in raising rice prices to a point dramatically above world market levels; thwarted efforts to liberalize farm imports from America and elsewhere; and promoted the interests of such groups as former landlords and repatriates.[79]

Informal policy groups, such as the Asian Problems Research Association and the Afro-Asian Problems Research Association, the now defunct Seirankai, the Hirakawakai, and other groups have been important elements in intra-Liberal Democratic party policy pluralism in the past. Many internal policy groups, or loose groupings such as the policy *zoku* (tribes) remain influential today. In contrast, the Liberal Democratic party factions have only occasionally participated in policymaking. The Liberal Democratic party factions generally do not have a strong ideological coloring, despite their general importance in other areas including personnel recruitment. Lacking cohesive opinions on most issues, the factions refrain from involvement in policy matters, or otherwise are indifferent *qua* factions because of other kinds of preoccupations. Occasionally, faction leaders adopt a policy position to try to unseat the incumbent prime minister. This practice is not a constant in Japanese policymaking, however, and it is more a part of the political recruitment "game" than typical policymaking scenarios.

The influence of the Liberal Democratic party on national policymaking has been derived from its status as a permanent majority party. As such, the party's parliamentary group has been able to dominate Diet processes in many instances since the party's rank-and-file parliamentarians almost always voted as a bloc. But intraparty pluralism was so great on some issues that it took a long time for the necessary unity to be achieved to make bloc voting possible.

The LDP's power also derives from its close ties with ministries, a product of the party's long-term hegemony and its recruitment of former bureaucrats to high party positions. The financial ties existing between the party and business interests might be viewed as another source of party power. Indeed, an earlier generation of Japanese studies described Japanese politics as a power triad made up of the conservative party, the bureaucracy, and big business.[80]

The Opposition Parties

The Liberal Democratic party dominated Japanese parliamentary politics throughout the late 1950s and the 1960s by maintaining a substantial, though slowly declining, majority in the Diet. Only in the 1970s did the opposition parties in the Diet collectively approach parity with the ruling Liberal Democrats. Until that time, Japan's opposition parties' junior status often reduced their impact on policy outcomes. As a result, many observers of Japanese politics have argued that until recently the role of the opposition was confined to a ritualistic expression of opposing opinions, rather than being a meaningful political force.

Actually, the opposition parties or their members were sometimes important participants in policymaking processes even before legislative parity. Individual opposition parliamentarians participated as members of Diet committees specializing in specific functional areas much as did rank-and-file Diet members from the Liberal Democratic party. Opposition party leaders and even rank-and-file parliamentarians also debated issues and shared opinions behind the scenes with their counterparts in the majority party, even when their parties' formal stands were rigidly oppositional.[81] In addition, policy community coalitions involved interest groups, ministries, or their internal divisions, and opposition parties' Diet members along with their LDP counterparts.

Claims about the opposition parties' impotence before the mid-1970s also ignore the importance of the *de facto veto* power that the opposition camp and its allies exercised over some government policy initiatives. When the opposition parties were strongly opposed to a particular proposal, they would filibuster or otherwise obstruct Diet processes and so bring normal parliamentary procedures to a standstill. As also occurred repeatedly, on many occasions the Liberal Democratic party or government wanted to get other legislation through the Diet and were prevented from doing so by opposition party blockage of normal legislative processes. Often the impasse was broken by negotiations between the governing and opposition parties, which resulted in an interparty agreement by which bills objectionable to the opposition camp were withdrawn in favor of opposition party support for normalizing Diet procedures. This power of the opposition parties to frustrate and block the LDP's legislative projects is what is meant by the de facto veto.

The de facto veto occurred on many occasions in the 1950s and early 1960s, and occasionally since then. Once this exception is noted, we can view much of the opposition party activity in the 1950s and 1960s as ritualistic opposition, in the sense that it was ultimately ineffective. In contrast, the reduction of the Liberal Democratic party majority to a very narrow margin in the mid-1970s and intermittently since then has resulted in important changes in the style of national policymaking. The political clout of Japan's opposition parties has been significantly enhanced. The result of these changes has been a continuing trend in which many important legislative bills have been amended within the Diet and more bills objectionable to the opposition have been withdrawn or postponed. Interparty coalitions also have become more common. Thus, some of the opposition parties have crossed over to support government bills on a number of important issues. In a few cases, even Japan's Socialists and Communists have joined in the passage of important legislation. As conditions have increasingly favored the softening of conflict and cooperation between parties, the frequency of intraparty compromise and agreement has increased.[82]

Patterns of Policymaking and Conflict

The variety of Japanese politics can be described by three modal patterns of policymaking. Each one of these patterns is an ideal type, and as such, they seldom appear in pure form in reality. Each represents a certain clustering of political actors, decision-making roles, patterns of conflict, and webs of influence.

The first of these patterns — the *intercamp mode* —involves the bipolar conservative-progressive confrontation. The conservatives and progressives have differed over such issues as the postwar constitution, the role of business, the autonomy of local entities and university faculties, the rights of citizens and unions, the nature of international conflict and related security arrangements, the rights of the consumer in a postindustrial society, and the welfare obligations of the state. Thus, these two major ideological camps have often confronted each other in the definition of governmental policies. As noted in our discussion of the reverse course period, intense confrontations between ideological camps in the Diet and in the streets were common in the 1950s and into the 1960s. The themes of intercamp conflict were a dominant thread in Japan's political life in the first two decades of the postwar era. Thereafter, this pattern of policymaking continued in a much qualified and less intense form owing to the shift in the issue agenda and the approach to parity in Diet seats between the Liberal Democrats and the opposition parties and the hope (at least in the early 1970s) by the middle of the road parties for participation in the government.

The second pattern in Japanese policymaking is the *interest-group mode*. By and large this is the politics of the Liberal Democratic system within a system to which we have already referred. The politics of interest-linked policymaking in Japan focuses on policy communities or "subgovernments" that link interest group representatives, members of the national Diet, many of whom are from the Liberal Democratic party, and officials from the ministries.[83] Liberal Democratic parliamentarians are also frequently members of Diet member *zoku* and leagues dedicated to advance the cause of a particular policy sector, a practice that presumably helps them gain leverage over the senior elements of their party. Interest groups and related policy communities have tended to push their causes upward through the Liberal Democratic hierarchy in the case of mass groups like farmers, former landlords, and repatriates. They may also attempt to influence the party's elite "laterally" in the case of more elite groups like big business. In contrast with the fairly dominant role of the central executive elite in intercamp policymaking processes, the central elite was typically much more reactive where interest politics were concerned. Moreover, while the stakes for groups and their members in these

processes are often great, the other actors in the process, such as the central executive elite and the "camps" in the Diet, are typically much less committed than in the case of intercamp processes. As a result, in this interest mode of policymaking we usually find a lower political profile and less conflict between the parties in the Diet.

Intrabureaucratic policymaking is the third modal pattern in contemporary Japanese policymaking. It has been both a separate policymaking pattern and often a component, sometimes at an early stage, of both intercamp and interest group policymaking. On occasions, several ministries or even one ministry has tended to be so important in a policymaking process, or in some phase of it, that the bureaucratic dominance theory could be seen as applicable. The budget is a case in point. Various ministries and agencies, especially the Ministry of Finance, have always played a big role in budget initiatives and decisions, and have actually dominated budgetmaking much of the time.

POLITICAL PERFORMANCE IN JAPAN

What the Japanese Government Does

Japanese government output can be classified into certain general themes: institution building and maintenance; provision of services; regulation of economic and social activity; assistance to specific economic groups or social sectors; and formulation of economic and other societal goals. Postwar governmental performance in these different areas can be divided into two distinct periods: (1) an era of political consolidation and high economic growth in the 1950s and 1960s; and (2) an era of infrastructural adjustment amidst more modest growth in the 1970s and 1980s. Within these two periods a kind of cyclical pattern emerged as problems generated responses in the form of governmental outputs, which in turn generated more problems. In the early postwar period the government encouraged economic development, which led to rapid industrial growth, urbanization, pollution, and increased life expectancy, which in turn generated needs addressed by quality-of-life programs in the 1970s. Later, in the 1970s, governmental commitments to social welfare, the environment, and expanded infrastructure, as well as antirecession pump-priming, themselves helped create budget deficits. These same deficits later became part of the "needs" addressed by administrative reform in the 1980s.

Japanese Political Outputs, 1952–1969: Consolidation and High Growth

Japan's economy was heavily damaged during World War II: plants and facilities were damaged or destroyed, and work was disrupted by personnel mobilization and population flight from the cities. Much of the Japanese government's initial output after the end of the war in 1945 was concerned with repairing the economy. The subsequent 1950s witnessed the beginning of a sustained period of government-encouraged economic growth, which continued and even accelerated in the 1960s.

"Cheap Government" in Japan

One of the government's major decisions to support economic development during this period was its commitment to "*cheap government.*" In the 1960s Japan had the lowest level of taxation of any major industrial power. In 1965 total taxation (excluding social security contributions) amounted to 18 percent of gross domestic product, a sharp contrast with the United States, Britain, Germany, and France, where taxes amounted to between 27 and 35 percent of GDP. Public expenditures from the annual budgets in Japan carried out the same theme of cheap government. In the 1950s and 1960s Japanese government outlays on current account represented only 13 to 14 percent of gross domestic product. In other major industrialized countries they ranged as high as 30 percent. One major reason for these differences was the lower Japanese outlay on social programs and defense. Lower outlays on these two main items, social welfare and defense, were a sizable component of the total difference between Japanese government expenditures and those of other large, industrialized countries in the relevant periods.

Japan's economic policy during the early postwar era was directed toward encouraging high levels of savings and investment. Low government overhead was one way to facilitate this goal, since less was extracted from national income and allocated to public expenditures than in other industrialized nations. The government also encouraged low interest rates in most periods, which was another factor favoring high levels of investment. A popular disposition to save was further encouraged by some tax exemptions for savings deposits. As a result of these supportive policies and social habits, savings and investment in Japan ran substantially higher than their counterparts in other industrialized nations. By the late 1960s, the Organization for Economic Co-

operation and Development (OECD) estimated that gross fixed investment in Japan averaged 38 percent of gross domestic product each year; the comparable figures for other major industrialized countries ranged between 16 percent for the United States and 26 percent for France.

High-Growth Policies

In the early postwar era, the Japanese government endeavored to promote economic growth through a variety of mechanisms in addition to cheap government. Economic plans and programs aimed at the development of specific industries were a major part of this effort. The Economic Planning Agency created five major plans between 1955 and 1967, which was approximately the period of Japan's greatest economic growth. While the plans only "indicated" desired directions, both the lengthy discussions of goals and the information about the economy that was accumulated and published to support the planning activity raised consciousness about economic goals in both the public and private sectors.[84] Economic planning continues in Japan today, as does strategic planning in all sectors of government and private sector activity.

Industry Plans

The Japanese government also used specific industry "rationalization" and development plans and related foreign trade policies to promote economic growth. In a battery of special programs aimed at Japan's steel, electrical power, shipbuilding, machinery, petrochemical, and electronics industries, the Ministry of International Trade and Industry provided incentives to encourage rapid development and competitive viability in international markets. Government bank loans using off-budget funds were part of this effort, and provided support in the 1950s and early 1960s for the electric power, shipping, coal, and iron and steel industries. Accelerated depreciation allowances for equipment purchases, special reserve funds for export market development, and deductions from income earned overseas were also employed to foster growth and strong exports. Controls over raw materials and technology imports also permitted allocation of critical materials and processes to industries slated for development.

The government role in industry development declined steadily from the early 1950s onward in terms of the share of public resources actually allocated to industry support. Interestingly, despite the belief outside

Japan that all industrial plans were successful, not all the industrial supports can be seen as rational and successful from an economic point of view. Politics more than economics lay behind heavy funding provided the coal and shipping industries in some periods, while highly successful industries like optical goods, consumer electronics, and automobiles were given very little support. More recently, the government has played a direct role in technology development, although actually at a lower rate than occurred in most other major industrialized countries.[85]

Institutional Consolidation

In addition to promoting economic growth, the Japanese government followed policies of institutional and foreign policy consolidation in the first decade of the postwar era. As one example of consolidation, the 1946 occupation-inspired constitution withstood onslaught by revisionist forces from within the conservative camp. Beginning in the late 1950s, the constitution was gradually accepted, even within the conservative forces that had sought its revision (although some revisionist sentiment remained unchanged even into the 1980s).

Japan's foreign policies during the 1950s and 1960s also stressed resolution of the problems left over from the country's defeat in World War II. Reparations agreements were signed with countries in Southeast Asia which had been invaded by Japan. Japan also became a member of the United Nations Organization in 1956. It subsequently became a nonpermanent member of the UN Security Council in 1958 and joined other international organizations like the General Agreement on Tariffs and Trade (GATT) in the 1950s and 1960s. Each of these events was hailed in Japan as a symbol of the country's reentry as a legitimate member of the international community.

Security and Limited Defense

National security was a major concern of Japan's political leaders in the 1950s. Anticommunism was rife in some circles within the conservative movement. For this reason, some conservative leaders favored an expanded domestic defense effort, although others opted for economic development. Rearmament in any form was also total anathema to the opposition forces. The outcome of the struggle over security options was a decision to establish a limited defense force backed up by mutual security arrangements with the United States. Arms budgets were eventually restricted to around 1 percent or less of the gross national product, the total force size was to be under 300,000 persons, and over time the main emphasis was placed on technological improvements in arms through a series of defense plans. In contrast, the United States spent around 6 percent of its GDP on defense in this period, while European members of the NATO alliance spent between 3 and 6 percent on military efforts.

The limited defense concept developed in the 1950s is still viable today, even though very recently there have been some expansions of defense budget outlays. Currently, Japan ranks third in the world in absolute military expenditures because of its considerable wealth as a nation. Still, defense budgets are modest relative to Japan's GDP, as are recruitment levels. In the 1960s, for example, Japan had just under four persons per one thousand in the working-age population in its military forces, in contrast with eleven and twelve persons, respectively, in Germany and Britain and twenty-five persons in the United States.[86]

The Performance of the Japanese Economy

Japan's economic performance since World War II is one of the truly dramatic trends in recent world economic history. Starting with an economy drastically disrupted by World War II and more dependent on foreign raw-material sources than any other major power, Japan in some postwar years registered the highest annual growth rates ever experienced by the world's major industrial nations. In 1960 (more or less the beginning of the high-growth period), Japan's estimated GNP was $39 billion. By 1987 the GNP figure had reached $2.3 trillion, a twenty-four-fold increase over the 1960 figures. By 1990 Japan's estimated nominal GNP was slightly over $3 trillion.

When the Japanese figures are compared on a per capita basis with those from other industrialized countries, the country's economic success can be seen even more clearly. In 1952 Japan's per capita GNP was $188, roughly one-twelfth that of the United States and one-half that of West Germany. By 1975 Japanese per capita GDP had grown to nearly two-thirds that of the United States and Germany, while by 1987 it was above American and German levels.[87]

Japanese High-Growth and Structural Change

Economic development and the high-growth experience in Japan had profound consequences for its social structure. As the economy grew in the industrial and service sectors, the population of the major urban areas expanded. In 1950 only 25 percent of the population lived in cities of over 100,000; by 1975 the figure had grown to 55 percent through emigration to both regional and large cities. In a related trend, the proportion of people in agriculture declined from 45 percent in 1950 to 12 percent in 1975. By the mid-1970s Japan had thus followed the trend in other major industrialized nations toward urbanization and abandonment of agricultural occupations.

A second major consequence of high economic growth could be seen in the labor market. Japan had traditionally been an economy with surplus labor in the rural and small business sectors. High growth changed the labor market dramatically and produced a labor shortage by the late 1960s, which continues as an even greater problem for Japanese policymakers today. The effects on wages and incomes induced by growth and labor shortages were also dramatic. Average wages in Japan, which were roughly one-ninth of those in the United States in the early 1950s, were approximately 105 percent of the American levels by the late 1980s. Wages in Japan were already higher than those in France, Italy, and Britain by the late 1970s.

The result of changes in wage levels, as well as of profit sharing through annual bonuses by major companies, was a dramatic increase over time in average family incomes in the employed sector in Japan. Farm families also prospered through price supports based on income parity formulas.[88] As general income levels moved upward, more people at the lower levels of the income scale did better. By the 1970s Japan therefore became one of the most egalitarian of the industrialized countries with regard to income distribution.[89] This pattern continues today, although inflated land values have made a few persons billionaires and raised farm prosperity above urban levels.[90]

The Benefits of Early Postwar High Growth and Affluence

High growth and increased household affluence had dramatic effects on consumption and on some aspects of the quality of life in Japan. A series of what the Japanese called booms in purchases of new automobiles, homes, and appliances swept the nation as a result of the increases in incomes and purchasing power. By the mid-1970s Japan had achieved higher rates of diffusion of some appliances and home electronic equipment than even the United States and most of Europe. More Japa-

nese homes had color television sets than any other country in the world. The same was true for washing machines. And more Japanese homes than British had refrigerators. All of these first-time large purchases became one of the driving motors for the continuing boom in the economy. Unlike most popular conceptions of Japan as being primarily dependent on exports for its economic success, the high-growth period was actually more the result of internal demand creation.

The growing consumer affluence was also reflected in the field of culture and education. More newspapers are published per population in Japan than in the United States and most other industrialized nations. Magazine publication rates are also high in Japan relative to those of many countries, as are the publication of books.[91] While Japan has long had a highly developed education system, postwar high growth and affluence produced a sharp increase in the number of students attending high school as well as a virtual explosion of matriculation in junior colleges and colleges. As a result, Japan now ranks third after Canada and the United States in the proportion of the population with a college education. Japan also has twice as many young people in universities as any European country.[92]

High growth and affluence also had some profound effects on health care, mortality, and the proportion of older people in the Japanese population. The number of health care facilities increased significantly during the high-growth period, as did the number of doctors. Qualitative improvements in diagnosis and treatment were also made. These and other effects of affluence, such as more heat in homes, improved diets, and better access to medical facilities, led to an increased life expectancy in Japan. In the mid-1950s life expectancy for males was sixty-four years and for females sixty-eight years; in 1988 the figures had jumped to seventy-six for males and eighty-one for females. As a result of these changes, the proportion of the population over sixty years of age grew from 8 percent in 1950 to 16 percent by 1988. Forecasts for the future call for substantially higher proportions of older people in Japan's population than in any other industrialized country by 2015.[93]

Negative Consequences of Growth and Related Immutable Conditions

Not all of the spinoffs of high growth in Japan in the 1960s were positive. Japan is a crowded nation with extremely little space. According to the most recent figures, it has 306 persons per square kilometer, and ranks with Korea, Indonesia, the Netherlands, and Belgium as one of the most heavily populated places on earth. Population movement to the cities and development of regional industrial centers in the 1950s and 1960s brought further concentration to already overcrowded urban areas. Figures for population concentration per square kilometer are as high as 1,700 persons for Japan's metropolitan areas. Increased crowding placed growing pressure on urban transportation facilities and on social capital, both of which were already inadequate by comparative standards, while also contributing to widespread pollution problems and housing shortages.

While Japan has one of the best urban rapid transit systems in the world and made many improvements in train lines in the 1960s and 1970s, urbanization and growth meant overcrowding of trains and long commuting times. Roads were much like urban transit. As people moved to the cities and suburbs, Japan's waste disposal and utilities systems were also hard put to keep up with demand. Compared with other industrialized countries, Japan lagged in sewage disposal facilities: in 1973 only 31 percent of Japanese homes had flush toilets, in contrast with figures above 90 percent in Britain, the United States, France, Sweden, and West Germany. Moreover, only 27 percent of homes in Japan were connected to sewer lines, whereas the figures for other countries were substantially higher.[94] Japan's cities also had little space for parks, and the growth of urban populations resulted in even lower ratios of park land per capita than had been the case previously. In 1976 there were only 1.6 square meters of park space per resident in Tokyo, compared to 80 in Stockholm, 464 in Washington, 30 in London, and 19 in New York.[95]

Few of the figures we have cited have stood still. Nonetheless, Japan still lags behind most industrialized nations in provisions of relevant services and social infrastructure. Moreover, the pressure of population and affluence has been so great that in a few areas conditions actually have declined despite absolute improvements. For example, the amount of road space available per automobile declined in some periods owing to the extremely rapid expansion in the number of vehicles. Since space is a fundamental problem especially in the cities, these conditions are not likely to change drastically in the future.

Deficiencies in transport and social capital were matched by a growing pollution problem in the late 1960s. With most of its population and all of its industrialized centers concentrated on only 20 percent of its land, Japan by the early 1970s had the highest concentration of industrial output and energy use per kilometer in the industrialized world. High-growth brought more factories, cars, and homes to the country's most heavily populated areas and even began to spread pollution to remote parts of the islands through regional industrialization and growth. As trees died and as birds fled the cities and as people suffered from air, water, noise, and even "sunshine pollution" — the shutting off of direct sunlight by construction of high-rise apartments — a myriad of local citizen movements opposed to pollution and regional growth sprang up around the country.

One of the immutables of Japan's physical setting is the shortage of usable land and space. The unfortunate land–population ratio is reflected very directly in pollution problems. It is also at the root of severe overcrowding and astronomical land prices. Neither of these problems was new to Japan, but during the high-growth period they became much more acute. In 1963 the average dwelling had just under four rooms and a total area of roughly 650 square feet. Twenty-seven years later in 1990 there have been only minor increases in the size of homes. Population pressure on housing is a constant problem. In the early 1970s and again in the 1980s, land price inflation became an additional problem. In comparative terms, both land and housing prices were and are extremely high in Japan. In 1990 an average home in Japan cost 6.3 times an average salaried employee's annual income, whereas in the United States the ratio was only 3 : 1.[96]

Recent Japanese Political Outputs: Recession Policies and Infrastructure Development

In the 1970s Japan continued to have "cheap government" in comparative terms. Yet a shift in emphasis toward greater public fiscal involvement also occurred. A 6 percent increase in the ratio of taxes to GNP could be seen between 1965 and 1978 as the Japanese government sought to cope with the problems of "structural depression," pollution, urban housing shortages, social capital inadequacies, and a rapidly aging population.

Japan's Growing Social Support System

Nowhere were the changes in fiscal priorities more evident than in outlays on social security and related programs. Whereas the Japanese budget itself increased thirty-four-fold between 1955 and 1978, outlays on social security and welfare programs increased nearly seventy-fold in the same period.[97] The share of social security and welfare programs in the total budget itself doubled. The ratio of social security and welfare outlays to gross domestic product in Japan also roughly doubled to 13 percent by 1978, in comparison with figures for the 1950s and 1960s. The changes in emphasis on social security and welfare programs in Japan were further reflected in comparative figures on social welfare commitments. As a result, by the late 1970s combined taxes and social security contributions had reached 24 percent of GDP in Japan. The Japanese figures were still lower than those elsewhere, specifically 34 percent in the United States, 38 percent in Germany, and 40 percent in France.[98] So, Japan continued to have cheap government in comparative terms. Nevertheless, the gap between Japan's social programs and those of some other major industrial nations was rapidly vanishing.[99]

Environmental and Quality-of-Life Policies and Anti-Recession Measures

Pollution policy was another example of quality-of-life concerns in reaction to the negative spinoffs of high growth. In a series of major antipollution laws passed in 1970, the government sought to implement pollution standards that were among the highest in the world. Quality-of-life problems were further addressed through expanded outlays on public works, which also served as pump-priming to combat a major recession in the mid-1970s. The high cost of oil and growing competition from newly industrializing countries resulted in a structural recession in Japan's iron and steel, shipbuilding, petrochemicals, aluminum smelting, and textiles industries at this time. Public works projects were used to relieve local unemployment and economic downturns which resulted from these changes. Some of the public works projects also supported further industrial expansion via development of needed infrastructure.

Inflation, Government Budget Deficits, and Administration Reform

Inflation was a problem in Japan in the 1970s much as it was elsewhere in the world, and concern for dampening rising prices augmented other forces for change in government economic priorities. Government economic policy outputs in this period shifted away from primary concern for long-term growth to a much greater preoccupation with management of business cycles. Indicative economic planning continued, but economic plans from the mid-1960s on came to emphasize economic stability and quality of life as much as or more than

absolute economic growth. While growth rates in the 1970s and the 1980s were considerably lower than those of the 1960s, Japan has continued to be one of the most successful economies in the world. One measure of its success has been its current position as the world's leading creditor nation.

One of the outcomes of changing fiscal priorities in the 1970s was deficit spending. In the late 1970s and for some years thereafter, Japan's budget deficit considerably exceeded that of the United States as a share of GDP. The budget deficit resulted in two major policy concerns in the government's agenda in the 1980s. The first was tax reform. A proposed tax reform remained in limbo throughout much of the 1980s until a value added tax was finally legislated in early 1989. This decision was a major factor in the LDP's defeat at the polls in that year's midsummer House of Councillors election (in addition to a major corruption scandal). Since that time the unpopular tax was removed from some food items but otherwise remains in force.

The second response to Japan's large budget deficit was a major reform of the national public administration. The ruling party's conservative attitudes toward spending and strong support from the party's business constituency contributed to this commitment. An advisory group appointed to examine administrative practices recommended, among other things, privatization of the country's publicly run national railway system, telephone and telegraph services, national airline, and government salt and tobacco monopoly. Privatization was accomplished in the mid-1980s amidst considerable political debate and sharp opposition from government employee labor unions and their political party allies.

Foreign Trade: Necessity, Success, and Source of Problems

Japan's foreign trade, which prospered during the high-growth period, continues to flourish. In 1955 the nation's total foreign commerce was just over $4 billion. By 1988 the figure was $452 billion. Its share of total world trade simultaneously increased from around 3 percent in 1960 to 15 percent in 1988. The long-term growth of Japan's foreign trade was a mixed blessing. Trade expansion permitted the nation to import the raw materials necessary to fuel high growth, satisfy new food preferences within the population, and pay huge oil bills in the 1970s. But the enormous overseas success of Japanese products produced trade imbalances and ad-

The slogan, "import raw materials, export finished goods," has helped to guide and fuel Japan's spectacular economic growth across the postwar period. As these exports have become increasingly high value and hi-tech, as in the case of the luxury cars pictured above, they have spawned growing trade friction with the United States.

verse reactions in other countries and created problems for the national government. Japan has been repeatedly involved in intense disputes with the United States and other countries as businesspeople and politicians abroad accused Japan of maintaining import barriers. While Japan had reduced or eliminated most of its formal import quotas and tariff barriers by the 1970s, critics from abroad still accused Japan of unfair trade practices. At present, this is Japan's biggest foreign policy concern.

Japan has always been heavily dependent on foreign raw materials to supply its industries. Many have marveled at its economic success in the face of such a pronounced native shortage of industrial minerals and energy sources. In recent years, for example, Japan has imported 99 percent of its iron ore needs, 92 percent of copper requirements, 78 percent of the lead needed in manufacturing, and 99.8 percent of its oil needs, which supplied about three-fourths of the country's overall energy requirements.[100] Japan's foreign trade policy has long been oriented toward securing stable sources of foreign raw materials and maintaining exports at levels sufficient to pay for these needed imports. In the 1970s oil crises brought further realization of the importance of secure sources of supply, and in a symbolic as well as real shift in priorities the Ministry of Foreign Affairs announced in 1973 that henceforth a stable raw materials supply would be a guiding force in Japan's overall diplo-

macy. The quest for resources and trade motivated closer economic ties with oil- and gas-producing nations, and led to exploration of mutual economic interests between Japan and its communist neighbors, the People's Republic of China and the USSR. Domestically, a variety of programs were established as a response to the energy crises and rise in oil prices. Like other countries Japan began to explore alternative energy possibilities, as well as domestic conservation, through the customary instruments of long-term planning and government-led research. Japan today uses substantially less energy than most other industrialized countries — it used roughly three-quarters as much energy per capita in 1988 as did Britain and France, one-half as much as West Germany, and one-third as much as the United States. Nevertheless, its energy dependence will continue to strongly influence economic trends and government policy outputs for the foreseeable future, just as it has in the recent past and in earlier periods of Japan's modern century.

CONCLUSION: MACRO-PERFORMANCE UNDER LIBERAL DEMOCRATIC HEGEMONY

Japan is one of a handful of democratic governments that have experienced one-party hegemony for a long period of time, and its politics has been profoundly affected by this fact. The Liberal Democratic party and its supportive social coalition have been a dominant force in Japan's elections, elite political recruitment, processing of group and local interests, and determination of government policy outputs for thirty-five years. This Liberal Democratic system of electoral mobilization, interest representation, and policy formulation has in turn been closely linked with, and partially dependent on, the policy primacy of the Japanese administrative bureaucracy. Furthermore, the Liberal Democrats co-opted the social and environmental policies of the opposition at critical points, as well as expanding the interest group sectors represented in its "social coalition." All of this helped keep the conservative party in power and transformed it into a more catch-all party in the process.[101] In addition to performance in specific policy areas, Liberal Democratic hegemony was displayed in three broad domains of "macro-performance": the government's general ability to extract resources, resolve conflicts, and provide for political stability.

Extractive Performance

The Liberal Democratic "system," buttressed by an activist bureaucracy, has usually demonstrated adequate levels of extractive capability during its nearly four decades in power. Japan was able to extract enough resources from the private sector in the form of taxes to support governmental commitments in the 1950s and 1960s, and again by the late 1980s. Early decisions to limit expenditures on defense and social programs were particularly important in this regard, as was a rapidly expanding revenue base resulting from high growth. Both factors contributed substantially to Japan's fiscal viability once economic growth began to accelerate.

Yet the record of the Japanese government is not completely unblemished. The scenario just described came to an end in the 1970s. Economic growth slowed down after the 1973 oil shock, and the government was faced simultaneously with a much slower expansion of its tax base and with decisions to increase expenditures on public works and social security programs. The Japanese government needed substantially more revenue by the mid-1970s than it was receiving. Rather than raise taxes, a short-run solution was found in deficit financing through sales of government bonds to financial institutions.

By the end of the 1970s deficit financing was itself becoming increasingly costly to the Japanese govern-

ment in terms of both current and anticipated interest payments. However, Japanese governments were unable for nearly a decade to make adjustments to tax laws sufficient to prevent continued heavy deficit financing of budgetary outlays. Deficits of as much as 30 percent of the budget in several years were the result. Many governments of industrialized countries have experienced similar fiscal problems in recent years. For a decade, however, the Japanese case was an especially extreme example of an "extraction crisis." Ruling party governments were unable to face the political costs of imposing new taxes until recently.

Problem-Solving Performance

The ability of governments to resolve problems and conflict is also a measure of their performance and capability. Although Japan is not a society affected by social cleavages to the degree found in early twentieth-century Europe, there still have been many areas of conflict between parties and groups. Some of these conflicts and the problems they raised were of relatively short duration. Other issues related to systemwide patterns in disagreement, or broad common problem areas have persisted across substantial time periods. These more basic problem areas include such issues as institutional consolidation, economic and infrastructure development, prolonged fiscal deficits, quality-of-life problems, foreign economic competition, national security and inter-bloc relations, and resource and energy dependency.

Profound ideological divisions, such as those over constitutional revision and national security policy, were the most difficult issues to resolve. Problems linked with Japan's deep scarcity of land relative to its population size and concentration posed similar challenges, even though the relevant political debates were not as ideological as those over security and constitutional reform issues. While many issues were resolved over time, substantially different scenarios could be seen in different policy arenas. Overall, three kinds of outcomes typically prevailed: (1) many issues were resolved; (2) quite a few issues and problems were partially but not completely resolved; and (3) action on some problems was delayed for long periods of time, and/or solutions were not found in the period under consideration. This is the nature of political decision making in all governments. But it does suggest areas of limitations in governmental performance and ability to resolve problems and issues completely.

Stability as Political Performance

Ideally, democratic governments should be stable as well as able to resolve conflict. By and large, Japan's postwar political system has been remarkably stable. By most of the measures of stability — institutional continuity, stable and institutionalized succession, effective and stable leadership coalitions, nonimmobilist and reasonably viable legislative processes, stable voting patterns, and generally low levels of mass violence and terrorism — Japan's postwar experience has been salutary. This was especially true after the mid-1950s, which marked the turning point in the development of the postwar system. Postwar Japan was actually much more stable than 1930s Japan.

The first prominent area of stability in postwar Japanese politics has been the basic governmental institutions themselves. A general cultural tendency toward institutionalization of processes and a conventionalist attention to precedent, detail, and protocol may contribute to this stability. A more central and political explanation of the success of postwar institutions lies in the simple fact that all political parties and most groups have accepted the new institutions. However much some conservatives in the 1950s argued for constitutional revision, conservative leadership generally followed the rules. Despite temporary breakdowns and unseemly behavior in the Diet, both the government parties and the opposition groups kept parliamentary government going.

The long-term dominance of Japanese politics by the conservative movement and its associated social coalition(s) were a second source of stable government. Liberal Democratic and conservative dominance carried Japan through a period of critical institutional development and transition in the 1950s and at least partially insulated the political process during this era from the potentially destabilizing effects of ideological polarization. The Liberal Democrats' ability over time to adapt and co-opt or preempt opposition party policies enhanced their hold on power, as did the conservative party's careful courting of the votes of its traditional farm and small business constituency. At the same time, the Japan Socialist party's inability to develop programs that would help it do better at the polls, and the inability of the opposition parties to present themselves as credible participants in a workable coalition government, also helped the Liberal Democrats maintain power at various points of time.

The economic well-being and growth achieved through conservative hegemony was an added factor in political stability. Despite strident leftist opposition and protest to conservative highhandness and reactionary principles in the 1950s, Japan's masses have generally been quiescent, law abiding, and supportive of the political status quo even while deploring at times its tendency to corruption. Isolated attacks were made on leaders of the right and left in the 1950s, and a brief period of political terrorism followed. But Japan's political extremists have actually been much smaller in number, less well organized, and less violent than their counterparts in the major European countries.

The most prominent source of incipient instability in Japanese politics over the past three decades has been intra-Liberal Democratic factionalism itself. On several occasions, factional infighting has brought the ruling movement to the brink of rupture and the government to the brink of collapse. The Liberal Democratic tendency toward factional squabbles over internal party matters, including succession to the prime ministership, has also added to corruption to become a de-legitimizing force in shaping a political culture of distrust. Stable conservative dominance has thus had some blemishes.

The Future

Japan's postwar political system has been an unusual one compared to the experience of most industrialized democracies. Only Norway comes close to the Liberal Democratic party's period of long-term dominance, although Sweden, Denmark, and Italy have all had long periods of dominance by a major party, either ruling alone or in coalition with much smaller groups, which approached the LDP record. Because of one-party dominance, intra-Liberal Democratic political recruitment, interest articulation and aggregation, and policymaking processes have been of overwhelming significance to Japan's political processes in general. Since 1955 Liberal Democratic party presidents have always been prime ministers, the Liberal Democratic interest group coalition has been the dominant source of interest group-related policy demands, and the policy processes within the LDP Policy Affairs Research Council have been as important in some instances as decisions within the Diet itself. Indeed, without much exaggeration PARC can be said to resemble a parliament in its internal complexity of policymaking and external importance.

We have called the sectors of the Japanese political system dominated by the Liberal Democratic party and its related internal processes the LDP system. Internal processes within the LDP are extremely important, as are the party's roots in its supportive social coalition, by which we mean the array of interest groups that support the party in elections and ask the party for supportive policies afterward. Liberal Democratic dominance has led some observers of Japanese politics to assert that the Japanese system is operated by an elitist triad of business, the bureaucracy, and the Liberal Democratic party. Others have argued that Japan's political arrangements constituted a "corporatism without labor." More recent scholarship has asserted the prominence of pluralistic tendencies within the sectors of society and interest group activity dominated by the Liberal Democrats. Some scholars feel that early postwar relationships were less pluralistic than those at present, although recent scholarship on business interest group relationships with the LDP and the bureaucracy even challenge the "change over time" hypothesis by showing evidence of widespread pluralism since the Meiji period.

Whichever interpretation of Japanese politics is asserted, it is clear that postwar Japan has been a democratic society. The constitution has been honored to the letter, even by elites and groups that favored revision. Elections have been frequent and free, while articulation of the interests of local communities, farmers, and small businesspersons has been so vibrant and the policy response thereto so comprehensive, that some observers have called Japan a special kind of interest group "welfare state." According to some analysts, the LDP system has left out the labor groups. Others, however, note that even labor is represented in policy processes addressed to conditions in recessed industries, while other constituencies, such as social welfare and health care-oriented groups, have themselves been accommodated over time by the ever-adaptive LDP. Consumers, who are not well represented in many societies, probably have fared less well on issues like food prices, where

their concerns were opposed to those of the powerful farmers' lobby. But consumers' wants have been central in determining transit and railway fares and in concessions in 1989–1990 regarding an unpopular 3 percent "sales" tax.

As we have already noted, political stability has been the hallmark of Japan's postwar experience and certainly a major factor in its high economic growth in some periods. How Japan, the Liberal Democratic party, and the four opposition parties will fare in the future, and whether Japan will remain as politically stable as it has been in the past is somewhat problematic. On one hand, there is no reason to expect that the LDP will lose the support of its social coalition. Nor is it likely that the opposition in its present form will become more credible in the near future, and therefore be able to mount a major challenge to Liberal Democratic dominance. Nevertheless, the Liberal Democrats' sudden loss of their Upper House majority in the 1989 summer election was clearly an indication that anti-LDP protest votes can be expected in great numbers when elites are irresponsible and interest groups feel they have not been represented. The suddenness of the temporary collapse of the LDP system in that one election is all the more foreboding, given Japan's looming areas of very severe economic problems. Competition from the overseas newly industrializing countries and related moves by the production facilities of some Japanese companies to "offshore" locations does not necessarily bode well for Japan's continued economic growth. At the same time the burden of supporting rapidly increasing numbers of older people via higher pension and tax contributions further threatens the nation's future economic well-being, as well as its political and social fabric. Generally, Japan's economy has grown steadily for four decades. Liberal Democratic dominance has both profited from this growth and been one of the factors supporting it. Future economic trends could finally derail the LDP coalition and produce a Japan very different from the one we have described. At present, however, that outcome seems remote.

KEY TERMS

administrative guidance
administrative reform
bureaucratic dominance
"cheap government"
corporatism

de facto veto
direct interest group
  representation
elitist educational system
ex-bureaucrats

Federation of
  Agricultural
  Cooperatives
Federation of Economic
  Organizations

fusion of powers
high growth
interbureaucratic
  policymaking
intercamp mode

interest-group mode
Liberal Democratic party
ministerial clientelism
ministerial "legislation"

multimember districts
The National Diet
1955 system
occupation reforms

parliamentary ritualism
pluralism
policy broker
quality-of-life policies

reverse course
U.S.–Japan Security
Treaty

END NOTES

1. IMF Bureau of Statistics, *International Financial Statistics*, 43 (Washington, D.C.: International Monetary Fund, 1990).

2. Kazuo Kawai, *Japan's American Interlude* (Chicago: University of Chicago Press, 1960).

3. Soon the initials SCAP came to stand both for MacArthur and the American occupation authorities in general. Theodore McNelly, *Politics and Government in Japan* (Boston: Houghton Mifflin Co., 1972), pp. 22–25; Robert E. Ward, "Presurrender Planning: Treatment of the Emperor and Constitutional Changes," pp. 1–41, in Robert E. Ward and Yoshikazu Sakamoto, eds., *Democratizing Japan: The Allied Occupation* (Honolulu: University of Hawaii Press, 1987).

4. While Article 9 has subsequently been reinterpreted to allow Japan to develop a defensive military capability, the peace clause has been effective in applying significant constraints on the growth and power of the military in postwar Japan. For the full English text of the constitution, see Robert E. Ward, *Japan's Political System* (Englewood Cliffs, N.J.: Prentice–Hall, 1978).

5. Theodore H. McNelly, "Induced Revolution: The Policy and Process of Constitutional Reform in Occupied Japan," in Ward and Sakamoto, *Democratizing Japan*, pp. 76–106.

6. Theodore McNelly, "The Role of Monarchy in the Political Modernization of Japan," *Comparative Politics* 1 (April 1969), pp. 266–381.

7. Constitution, Article 41.

8. Constitution, Article 54.

9. Constitution, Articles 59–61.

10. Hans H. Baerwald, *Japan's Parliament: An Introduction* (London: Cambridge University Press, 1974), pp. 74–102; Baerwald, *Party Politics in Japan* (Boston: Allen & Unwin, 1986).

11. Hans H. Baerwald, "Early SCAP Policy and the Rehabilitation of the Diet," in Ward and Sakamoto, *Democratizing Japan*, pp. 133–156.

12. Constitution, Article 65.

13. Constitution, Articles 66, 72–74.

14. Constitution, Articles 67–71.

15. Constitution, Articles 76–79. In practice, all justices have been approved by overwhelming majorities to date.

16. Bureau of Statistics, Office of the Prime Minister, *Japan Statistical Yearbook* (Tokyo: Japan Statistical Association, 1990).

17. Akira Amakawa, "The Making of the Postwar Local Government System" in Ward and Sakamoto, *Democratizing Japan*, pp. 253–283.

18. Kurt Steiner, *Local Government in Japan* (Stanford, Calif.: Stanford University Press, 1965); Kurt Steiner, Ellis Krauss, and Scott Flanagan, eds., *Political Opposition and Local Politics in Japan* (Princeton, N.J.: Princeton University Press, 1980); Steven Reed, *Japanese Prefectures and Policymaking* (Pittsburgh, Pa.: University of Pittsburgh Press, 1986).

19. Steiner et al., *Political Opposition*, pp. 444–448; Robert E. Ward, "Reflections on the Allied Occupation and Planned Political Change in Japan," in Robert E. Ward, ed., *Political Development in Modern Japan* (Princeton, N.J.: Princeton University Press, 1968), pp. 528–532.

20. Hans Baerwald, *The Purge of Japanese Leaders Under the Occupation* (Berkeley: University of California Press, 1959).

21. Solomon B. Levine, *Industrial Relations in Postwar Japan* (Urbana: University of Illinois Press, 1958), pp. 66–88.

22. Kenneth B. Pyle, "In Pursuit of a Grand Design: Nakasone Betwixt the Past and the Future," *Journal of Japanese Studies*, 13 (Summer 1987), pp. 243–270.

23. Junnosuke Masumi, "The 1955 System in Japan and Its Subsequent Development," *Asian Survey*, 28 (March 1988), pp. 286–306.

24. Joji Watanuki, "Patterns of Politics in Present-Day Japan," in Seymour M. Lipset and Stein Rokkan, eds., *Party Systems and Voter Alignments* (New York: Free Press, 1967), pp. 447–466.

25. Steven R. Reed, "Factions in Japanese Conservative Politics," presented at the Southern

Regional Japan Studies Seminar, Edgewater Beach Resort, Panama City Beach, Florida, October 20, 1990.

26. Takeshi Ishida, *Gendai Soshiki-ron* (Tokyo: Iwanami Shoten, 1961); Masumi, "The 1955 System in Japan"; T. J. Pempel, *Policy and Politics in Japan* (Philadelphia: Temple University Press, 1982), pp. 3–45, 296–300.

27. Constitutional amendments require a two-thirds majority vote in both houses of the Diet.

28. The 1955 percentage represents the combined vote of the two conservative parties just prior to their merger into the LDP.

29. For example, the JSP continued to call for a "dictatorship of the proletariat" up through the mid-1980s. Pempel, *Policy and Politics in Japan*, p. 35.

30. Hideo Otake, "Defense Controversies and One-Party Dominance: The Opposition in Japan and West Germany," in T. J. Pempel, ed., *Uncommon Democracies: The One-Party Dominant Regimes* (Ithaca, N.Y.: Cornell University Press, 1990).

31. Michio Muramatsu and Ellis S. Krauss, "The Dominant Party and Social Coalitions in Japan," in Pempel, ed., *Uncommon Democracies*, pp. 282–305.

32. Ibid.

33. Otake, "Defense Controversies and One-Party Dominance."

34. Gabriel A. Almond and Sidney Verba, *The Civic Culture* (Princeton, N.J.: Princeton University Press, 1963); Sidney Verba, "Germany: The Remaking of Political Culture," in Lucien W. Pye and Sidney Verba, eds., *Political Culture and Political Development* (Princeton, N.J.: Princeton University Press, 1965); David P. Conradt, "Changing German Political Culture," pp. 212–272, in Gabriel A. Almond and Sidney Verba, eds., *The Civic Culture Revisited* (Boston: Little, Brown, 1980); Kendall L. Baker, Russell J. Dalton, and Kai Hildebrandt, *Germany Transformed: Political Culture and the New Politics* (Cambridge, Mass.: Harvard University Press, 1981).

35. Hisao Otsuka, "The Formation of Modern Man: The Popular Base for Democratization," *The Japan Interpreter*, 6 (Spring 1970), p. 2.

36. See symposium by Steven R. Reed, Scott C. Flanagan, and John C. Campbell on "The Evolution of Postwar Japanese Politics: Changing Perceptions and Changing Realities," *SRJSS*, Panama City Beach, October 20, 1990.

37. For example, Ronald Dore argues that a combination of the advantages of late development and elements of Japan's Confucian tradition have combined to provide Japan with a more humanistic, community model of the company that provides Japan with competitive advantages in the areas of economic efficiency, social justice, social cohesion, worker dedication and morale, making the Japanese model or some elements of it a trend toward which other systems (such as the British) are likely to evolve. Dore, *Taking Japan Seriously: A Confucian Perspective on Leading Economic Issues* (Stanford, Calif.: Stanford University Press, 1987); Dore, *British Factory–Japanese Factory: The Origins of National Diversity in Industrial Relations* (Berkeley: University of California Press, 1973). See also John C. Campbell, *Politics and Culture in Japan* (Ann Arbor: University of Michigan, CPS/ISR, 1988).

38. Jichisho Senkyobu, *Kaisei Seiji Shikin Kisei Ho Kaisetsu* (Tokyo: Chiho Zaimu Kyokai, 1976), p. 624, as cited in Gerald L. Curtis, *The Japanese Way of Politics* (New York: Columbia University Press, 1988), p. 172.

39. Curtis, *The Japanese Way of Politics*, pp. 157–191.

40. In defining *patterned pluralism*, Muramatsu and Krauss distinguish it from classical pluralism in which policy is "merely the outcome of open-ended, competitive lobbying by pressure groups on a relatively weak government." Policymaking in Japan is characterized by a strong state with its own autonomous interests. The system is pluralistic in the sense that it provides fairly wide access to a wide variety of competing and influential actors and a fair degree of government responsiveness to social interests. It is patterned in the sense that this competition is structured by "relatively fixed and institutionalized party, bureaucratic, and ideological ties," which prevent alliances from becoming as fluid as those associated with classical pluralism. Not only have ideology and organizational history fixed patterns of party/interest group alliances, but also jurisdictional assignments of policy issues to specific ministries which themselves have specific sets of established ties to interest groups "procedurally structure the types of possible alliances and

policymaking patterns." Muramatsu and Krauss view Japan, then, as a "hybrid state" containing elements of several policymaking models. We find corporatist elements in that interest groups sometimes have cooperative relations with government and each other and in that advisory commissions (*shingikai*) are frequently used to bring competing interests directly together to hammer out acceptable solutions. The elitist aspects of the policy process no longer are as prominent as during the 1950s when the "ruling triad" of bureaucracy, business, and LDP were seen as running the show and virtually excluding labor and many other interests. Nonetheless, some elitist elements remain. Although a much broader set of interests are now organized and influential, we can still detect a hierarchy in terms of their access to and impact on the policy process. Michio Muramatsu and Ellis S. Krauss, "The Conservative Policy Line and the Development of Patterned Pluralism," in Kozo Yamamura and Yasukichi Yasuba, eds., *The Political Economy of Japan: The Domestic Transformation* (Stanford, Calif.: Stanford University Press, 1987), pp. 537–543.

41. Chie Nakane, *Japanese Society* (Berkeley: University of California Press, 1970).

42. Campbell, *Politics and Culture in Japan*, p. 7.

43. Bradley M. Richardson and Scott C. Flanagan, *Politics in Japan* (Boston, Little, Brown, 1984), pp. 229–240.

44. Duverger contrasts cadre parties, the loosely organized liberal and conservative parties that emerged in nineteenth century Europe, with mass parties, the highly structured socialist and Christian democratic parties that emerged in the early twentieth century. Maurice Duverger, *Political Parties* (New York: John Wiley, 1954).

45. The JSP and DSP actually have the smallest memberships, standing at around 50,000 members each through much of the 1970s, but rising thereafter to 127,000 and 108,000 respectively, by 1989. The CGP and JCP, which are more strongly organized at the grass-roots level, claim memberships of around 200,000 and 500,000, respectively. Only the LDP seems to have a large membership, fluctuating between 1 and 3 million over the last decade, but standing very close to the later figure by the end of the 1980s. Most of these LDP members, however, might be characterized as indirect members in the sense that they typically have become members of the party as a consequence of first becoming members of an LDP candidate's personal support organization. *Asahi Nenkan (Tokyo: Asahi Shimbunsha, 1990),* pp. 97–100.

46. James J. Foster, "Ghost-Hunting: Local Party Organization in Japan," *Asian Survey,* 22 (September 1982), pp. 843–857.

47. J. A. A. Stockwin, "The Japan Socialist Party: A Politics of Permanent Opposition," in Ronald J. Hrebenar, ed., *The Japanese Party System* (Boulder, Colo.: Westview Press, 1986).

48. Curtis, *The Japanese Way of Politics,* pp. 157–191.

49. The 1982 change in the HC electoral system, which replaced the candidate voting method for electing the national constituency seats with a proportional representation system, was designed to induce voters to focus on parties and platforms rather than candidates and their local benefits and personal favors. In the short term, however, the within-party competition for a high position on their party's list has only increased the negative "money politics" aspects of Japanese politics. The revision of the fund-raising law has neither effectively controlled nor limited contributions, but only decentralized the process, thereby increasing the difficulties of monitoring it. Finally, the LDP primary election system reform not only failed to broaden and democratize the selection of the party president, but further increased the costs of the election by stimulating each Diet member to secure more *koenkai* members in order to enter them into the party roles by paying the party dues for them, thereby increasing the voting power of his faction. Curtis, *The Japanese Way of Politics*, pp. 98–106, 176–191.

50. Sohyo was the union federation affiliated with the JSP until 1989 when it folded into the larger Rengo federation, which also includes the former Domei federated unions that have been affiliated with the DSP.

51. Peter Berton, "The Japan Communist Party: The 'Lovable' Party," in Hrebenar, ed., *The Japanese Party System*, pp. 116–144.

52. See Nathaniel B. Thayer, *How the Conservatives Rule Japan* (Princeton, N.J.: Princeton University Press, 1969); Haruhiro Fukui, *Party in Power: The Japanese Liberal-Democrats and Policy-Making* (Berkeley: University of California

Press, 1970); John C. Campbell, *Contemporary Japanese Budget Politics* (Berkeley: University of California Press, 1979).

53. *The Japan Times Weekly*, April 10, 1982, p. 4; December 2, 1978, p. 4; Taketsugu Tsurutani, "The LDP in Transition: Mass Membership Participation in Party Leadership Selection," *Asian Survey*, 20 (August 1980), pp. 844–859.

54. Gerald L. Curtis, *Election Campaigning Japanese Style* (New York: Columbia University Press, 1971); Curtis, *The Japanese Way of Politics*, pp. 165–175. Whether it is the campaign rules that disadvantage newcomers or the power of established incumbents' political machines, incumbency is a powerful source of electoral victories. In the seven Lower House elections held between 1972 and 1990, the LDP incumbents' rate of victory ranged from 80 to 96 percent averaging 86 percent, while the election rate of the incumbents of all other parties combined ranged from 71 to 85 percent, averaging 77 percent. These figures were provided by Steven R. Reed from his comprehensive, computerized Japanese electoral data set.

55. Scott C. Flanagan, "National and Local Voting Trends: Cross-Level Linkages and Correlates of Change," in Steiner et al., *Political Opposition*, pp. 131–184.

56. Scott C. Flanagan, Shinsaku Kohei, Ichiro Miyake, Bradley M. Richardson, and Joji Watanuki, *The Japanese Voter* (New Haven, Conn.: Yale University Press, 1991).

57. Ibid.; and Bradley Richardson, "Constituency Candidates Versus Parties in Japanese Voting Behavior," *American Political Science Review*, 82, September 1988, pp. 695–718.

58. *Asahi Shimbun*, February 17, 1990.

59. Curtis, *The Japanese Way of Politics*.

60. The term *jiban* refers to the tendency of many rural and even quite a few city politicians to carve out a political base in a particular section of an electoral district. See Curtis, *Election Campaigning Japanese Style* and Bradley M. Richardson, "Japanese Local Politics and Leadership Styles," *Asian Survey*, 7, pp. 231–253.

61. Akira Kubota, *Higher Civil Servants in Japan: Their Social Origins, Educational Backgrounds and Career Patterns* (Princeton, N.J.: Princeton University Press, 1969).

62. Richard Samuels, *The Politics of Regional Policy in Japan: Localities Incorporated?* (Princeton, N.J.: Princeton University Press, 1983).

63. See Curtis, *The Japanese Way of Politics*, pp. 49–61.

64. See Scalapino and Masumi, *Parties and Politics in Contemporary Japan* and David Apter and Nagayo Suwa, *Against the State: Politics and Social Protest in Japan* (Cambridge, Mass.: Harvard University Press, 1984).

65. Campbell, *Contemporary Japanese Budget Politics*, pp. 128–132.

66. See Eugene J. Kaplan, *Japan: The Government–Business Relationship* (Washington, D.C.: U.S. Department of Commerce, 1972), Ira Magaziner and Thomas S. Hout, *Japan's Industrial Policy* (London: Policy Studies Institute, 1980), pp. 82–87, and Richard J. Samuels, *The Business of the Japanese State* (Ithaca, N.Y. and London: Cornell University Press, 1987).

67. Aurelia George, "Japanese Interest Group Behavior: An Institutional Approach," in J.A.A. Stockwin et al., *Dynamic and Immobilist Politics in Japan* (Honolulu: University of Hawaii Press, 1988).

68. Michio Muramatsu and Ellis S. Krauss, "The Conservative Party Line and the Development of Patterned Pluralism," in Kozo Yamamura and Yasukichi Yasuba, eds., *The Political Economy of Japan: Vol. 1 — The Domestic Transformation* (Stanford, Calif.: Stanford University Press, 1987).

69. The prime minister or Cabinet also is empowered to report to the Diet on national affairs and foreign relations, conclude treaties, supervise the civil service, prepare the budget, enact Cabinet orders, and declare general amnesty.

70. Factions are themselves not usually policy oriented. But faction leaders may at times take policy positions simply to discredit an incumbent prime minister, and therefore hasten his downfall. Faction leaders are also called on by members to champion their favorite causes. As a result, factions sometimes function as a transmission belt for interest articulation.

71. The term *zoku* (tribe) is used to describe these clusters of LDP Diet members affiliated with a particular interest sector; see Takeshi Inoguchi and Tomoaki Iwai, *Zoku Giin no Kenkyu* [Research on Parliamentarian Tribes] (Tokyo: Nihon Keizai Shinposha, 1983).

72. Michael Donnelly, "Setting the Price of Rice: A Case Study in Political Decision Making," in Pempel, ed., *Policymaking in Contemporary Japan*, pp. 171–172 and "Conflict over Government Authority and Markets: Japan's Rice Economy," and Ellis S. Krauss, Thomas P. Rohlen, and Patricia G. Steinhoff, *Conflict in Japan* (Honolulu: University of Hawaii Press, 1984).

73. See Campbell. *Contemporary Japanese Budget Politics*, pp. 43–70.

74. T. J. Pempel, "The Bureaucratization of Policymaking in Postwar Japan, *American Journal of Political Science*, 18 (1977), pp. 647–674.

75. Chalmers Johnson, "MITI and Japanese International Economic Policy," in Robert A. Scalapino, ed., *The Foreign Policy of Modern Japan* (Berkeley and Los Angeles: University of California Press, 1977), pp. 253–255.

76. Richardson and Flanagan, *Politics in Japan*, p. 349.

77. John Creighton Campbell, "Bureaucratic Primacy: Japanese Policy Communities in an American Perspective," *Governance*, 2:1 (1989), pp. 5–22.

78. The information on major bills is from our analysis data in Asahi Shimbunsha, *Asahi Nenkan*, 1960 through 1979, a period of important transition.

79. John Creighton Campbell, "Compensation for Repatriates: A Case-Study of Interest Group Politics and Party-Government Negotiations in Japan" and Michael W. Donnelly, "Setting the Price of Rice: A Study in Political Decision Making," cited in notes 17 and 33, respectively. See also Haruhiro Fukui, *Party in Power: The Japanese Liberal Democrats and Policymaking* (Berkeley and Los Angeles: University of California Press, 1970), ch. 7, pp. 173–197.

80. Nathaniel Thayer, *How the Conservatives Rule Japan* (Princeton, N.J.: Princeton University Press, 1969).

81. Shigeo Misawa, "An Outline of the Policymaking Process in Japan," in Hiroshi Ito, ed., *Japanese Politics: An Inside View* (Ithaca, N.Y.: Cornell University Press, 1972), pp. 12–48.

82. Ellis Krauss, "Conflict in the Diet: Toward Conflict Management in Diet Politics," in Krauss, Rohlen, and Steinhoff, *Conflict in Japan*.

83. Policy communities are discussed in Campbell, "Bureaucratic Primacy." The closely related concept of "subgovernments" was introduced by Douglass Cater in *Power in Washington* (New York: Random House, 1964) to describe the informal alliances between interest groups, congressional committees and their leadership, and elements of the administrative bureaucracy in the American political system. See also Campbell, *Contemporary Japanese Budget Politics*, pp. 123–128 and 268–272.

84. Hugh Patrick and Henry Rosovsky, *Asia's New Giant: How the Japanese Economy Works* (Washington, D.C.: Brookings Institution, 1976), especially ch 11 by Philip Trezise and Yukio Suzuki. See also Tsunehiko Watanabe, "National Planning and Economic Growth in Japan," in Bert. G. Hickman, ed., *Quantitative Planning of Economic Policy: A Conference of the Social Science Research Council Committee on Economic Stability* (Washington, D.C.: Brookings Institution, 1965), pp. 233–251.

85. For information on technology funding in the 1960s and early 1970s, see Patrick and Rosovsky, *Asia's New Giant*, p. 656. For up-to-date figures, see Keizai Koho Center, *Japan 1990 — An International Comparison* (Tokyo: 1990), p. 26. Documentation of industrial "targeting" effects by Bradley Richardson is reported with commentary in United States International Trade Commission, Foreign Industrial Targeting and Its Effects on U.S. Industries, Phase I: Japan (Washington, D.C.: USITC Publication 1437, October 1983).

86. Gabriel Almond and G. Bingham Powell, Jr., *Comparative Politics: System, Process and Policy* (Boston: Little, Brown, 1978), p. 298.

87. Keizai Koho Center, *Japan 1990: An International Comparison.*

88. By 1968 farm households were receiving 92 percent of the average incomes received by workers' families. Japan Institute of International Affairs, *White Papers of Japan, 1970–71*, p. 141.

89. In both the 1970s and the 1980s income distribution in Japan was more equal than in most other industrialized countries including the United States. See Martin Bronfenbrenner and Yasukichi Yasuba, "Economic Welfare," in Kozo Yamamura and Yasukichi Yasuba, eds., *The Political Economy of Japan: Vol. I.*

90. Japan Economic Institute, "Japanese Income Distribution," *Report* 33A, August 1987.

91. UNESCO, *Statistical Yearbook*, 1977. Japan had 526 newspapers per 1,000 persons in the population and was surpassed only by Sweden which had 572 daily general interest newspapers per 1,000 persons. More recent figures indicate 740 daily papers per 1,000 persons. In 1988, over 17 million weekly and monthly magazines were also published. See Medeiya Risachi Senta, *Zasshi-Shimbun Sokatalogo (A General Catalog of Newspapers and Magazines)* (Tokyo, 1988).

92. Keizai Koho Center, *Japan 1990: An International Comparison*.

93. Foreign Press Center, *Facts and Figures of Japan* (Tokyo, 1980), p. 24. Persons over sixty-five are expected to constitute 19 percent of the population by the year 2010, according to the *Japan Times Weekly*, September 17, 1983, p. 6.

94. Foreign Press Center, *Facts and Figures of Japan*, p. 114.

95. Japan Press Center, p. 103.

96. Japan Economic Institute, *Report* 17A, May 1, 1987, "Implications of Contrasting U.S. and Japanese Saving Behavior."

97. Prime Minister's Office, *Japan Statistical Yearbook*, various editions, and Shinsuke Kishida, ed., *Zusetsu Nihon no Zaisei* [Financial Politics in Japan] (Tokyo: Toyo Keizai Shinposha, 1978), p. 97.

98. See also John Creighton Campbell, "The 'Old People Boom' and Japanese Policymaking," *Journal of Japanese Studies*, 5:2 (1979), pp. 321–357. Actual per capita payments in some program areas in Japan were already equivalent to those in the United States.

99. Shinsuke Kishida, ed., *Zusetsu Nihon no Zaisei*, p. 91, and OECD, *Revenue Statistics of OECD Member Countries 1965–79* (Paris, 1980), p. 43.

100. Keizai Koho Center, *Some Data about Japanese Economy in Comparison with Foreign Countries* (Tokyo, 1979).

101. See Curtis, *The Japanese Way of Politics*.

UNION OF SOVIET SOCIALIST REPUBLICS

ARCTIC OCEAN

NORWAY

DENMARK

SWEDEN

FINLAND

Barents Sea

Baltic Sea

Tallinn

ESTONIA

POLAND

LITHUANIA

Vilnius

LATVIA

Riga

Leningrad

Minsk

BELORUSSIAN S.S.R.

Moscow ★

RUSSIAN SOVIET FEDERATED SOCIALIST REPUB

(R. S. F. S. R.)

Yakutsk

Lena R.

Kiev

ROMANIA

MOLDAVIA

Kishinev

UKRAINIAN S.S.R.

Volga R.

Ob R.

Irtysh R.

Omsk

Tomsk

Novosibirsk

Krasnoyarsk

Irkutsk

Lake Baikal

Black Sea

TURKEY

GEORGIA

Tbilisi

ARMENIAN S.S.R.

Erevan

AZERBAIJAN S.S.R.

Baku

Caspian Sea

KAZAKH S.S.R.

Aral Sea

Lake Balkash

PEOPLE'S REPUBLIC OF MONGOLIA

IRAQ

IRAN

Ashkhabad

TURKMEN S.S.R.

UZBEK S.S.R.

Tashkent

Frunze

KIRGIZ S.S.R.

Alma Ata

PEOPLE'S REPUBLIC OF CHINA

Dushanbe

TADJIK S.S.R.

500   1000

Scale of Miles

AFGHANISTAN

PAKISTAN

INDIA

────── borders of republics that have declared full independence of the Soviet Union.

CHAPTER 13

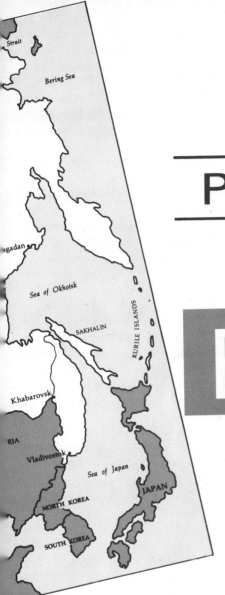

THOMAS F. REMINGTON
AND
FREDERICK C. BARGHOORN

POLITICS IN THE USSR

THE GORBACHEV REVOLUTION

FEW COUNTRIES in peacetime have undergone as profound a process of transformation as has the Soviet Union since the accession of Mikhail Sergeevich Gorbachev to power. The program of "restructuring"—*perestroika*—which he enacted has helped set in motion a train of events that have resulted in the dissolution of communist rule in Eastern Europe and deep change in the Soviet Union itself. Named general secretary of the *Communist party of the Soviet Union* (CPSU) on March 11, 1985, Gorbachev brought youth, vigor, and determination to a post that had been held most recently by a series of ailing and feeble individuals: Leonid Brezhnev, who held the general secretary's position from October 1964 until his death on November 10, 1982[1]; Yuri Andropov, who succeeded Brezhnev and ruled until he died on February 9, 1984; and Konstantin Chernenko, who occupied the position until his death on March 10, 1985.

Quickly grasping the powers that communist rule traditionally granted the party leader, Gorbachev soon distinguished himself from his cautious and conservative predecessors. Initially his program was rather conventional, emphasizing the need for moderate economic reform, greater discipline in society, openness (*glasnost*) in relations between regime and populace, technological modernization, and improved living standards.[2] But with time the course of political and economic change he launched grew increasingly radical and became, in effect, a revolution against communist rule itself. In turn, the bureaucratic structures created to govern the Soviet state found their political power fatally weakened. Their bitter opposition to Gorbachev's program found its expression in the unsuccessful attempt by a small group of hard-liners to seize power on August 19, 1991, remove Gorbachev from office, and declare a state of emergency. The dramatic turnabout two days later, when the coup collapsed and Gorbachev returned to office, reflected the massive outpouring of support for democratic principles among the Soviet population. The conspiracy's failure was evidence of the irreversibility of the democratizing trends Gorbachev had set in motion.

How did Gorbachev succeed in using the powers of the communist regime to destroy the very foundations of that regime? One answers lies in the fact that the party general secretary traditionally had extensive control over the system of filling leadership positions in all spheres of state and society, the "nomenklatura" system. Acting cautiously at first, and then with increasing decisiveness, Gorbachev removed opponents and promoted supporters. By the middle of 1986, he had replaced one-third of the powerful regional first secretaries and two-thirds of the party's senior staff officials in Moscow (Central Committee secretaries and department heads). By June 1987 he had replaced two-thirds of all USSR ministers and state committee chiefs and over half of the regional party first secretaries.[3] In April 1989 he engineered a mass resignation of 110 members from the party Central Committee. Perhaps most significant was the fact that Gorbachev's closest advisers and the government's senior ministers — including the prime minister — were left off the new Politburo of the CPSU when it was formed at the end of the Twenty-eighth Party Congress in July 1990. Power had not only been stripped from the Brezhnev-era old guard, but was increasingly moving away from the Communist party entirely.

Similarly, Gorbachev made use of the party's control of national policy to set new directions in domestic and foreign policy. In the economic sphere, he demanded "acceleration" of technological progress and economic growth through an infusion of capital, including stepped-up foreign investment. He also promised a loosening of the suffocating bureaucratic controls that discouraged innovation and risk on the part of enterprise managers. He called for invigoration of the democratic forms that shaped Soviet political life — elections and public debate. In the sphere of foreign policy he followed a new, active diplomacy in Europe and Asia, offered a series of disarmament proposals, and offered greater flexibility and understanding in relations with the West.

These early policy initiatives resembled those pursued by Nikita Khrushchev, who succeeded Stalin as party leader in 1953 and liberalized somewhat the harsh and bleak Soviet regime. Like Gorbachev, Khrushchev assumed the leadership at a time of economic stagnation and widespread political apathy, and tried to break the

impasse of mutual hostility in East – West relations by a series of gestures, some for show, some substantive, aimed at defusing some of the confrontational atmosphere of the cold war.[4] Khrushchev, however, remained faithful to the Marxist-Leninist heritage of the regime and was in turn its victim when he was deposed by a conspiracy of senior party leaders in 1964.

Western and Soviet observers alike were, therefore, startled by the radical turn Gorbachev took beginning around 1987. He not only called for political democratization, but he also pushed through a reform bringing about the first contested elections for local soviets in many decades.[5] He initiated a Law on State Enterprise that was intended to break the stranglehold that industrial ministries held over enterprises through their powers of plan-setting and resource allocation. He legalized private, market-oriented enterprise for individual and cooperative businesses and encouraged them to fill the many gaps in the economy left by the inefficiency of the state sector. He called for a "law-governed state" (*pravovoe gosudarstvo*) in which state power — including the power of the Communist party — would be subordinate to law. He welcomed the explosion of informal social and political associations that formed. He made major concessions to the United States in the sphere of arms control, resulting in a treaty that, for the first time in history, stipulated the destruction of entire classes of nuclear missiles.

In 1988, Gorbachev proposed still more far-reaching changes at an extraordinary gathering of party members from around the country, where in a nationally televised address he outlined a vision of a democratic, but still socialist, political system where legislative bodies made up of deputies elected in open, contested races would exercise the main policymaking power in the country; where the Supreme Soviet would become a genuine parliament, debating policy, overseeing government officials, and adopting or defeating bills. Moreover, the judiciary would be separated from party control, and at the top of the system there would be a body called on to adjudicate the constitutionality of legislative acts. The party conference itself treated the Soviet public to an unprecedented display of open debate among the country's top leaders. Using to the full the general secretary's authoritarian powers, Gorbachev quickly railroaded his proposals for democratization through the Supreme Soviet, and in 1989 and 1990 the vision Gorbachev laid out before that party conference was realized as elections were held, deputies elected, and new soviets formed at the center and in every region and locality. When nearly half a million coal miners went out on strike in the summer of 1989, Gorbachev declared himself sympathetic to their demands.

Gorbachev's radicalism received its most dramatic confirmation through the astonishing developments of 1989 in Eastern Europe. All the regimes making up the socialist bloc collapsed and gave way to multiparty parliamentary regimes in virtually bloodless popular revolutions (only in Romania was the ouster of the ruling communist elite accompanied by widespread bloodshed) — and the Soviet Union stood by and supported the revolutions![6] The overnight dismantling of communism in Eastern Europe meant that the elaborate structure of party ties, police cooperation, economic trade, and military alliance that had developed since Stalin imposed communism on Eastern Europe after World War II had vanished. Divided Germany was allowed to reunite, and, after initial reluctance, the Soviet leaders even sanctioned the admission of the reunited Germany to the North Atlantic Treaty Organization (NATO). Meanwhile, in the Soviet Union itself the Communist party was facing massive popular hostility and a critical loss of authority. Gorbachev forced it to renounce the principle of the "party's leading role" and to accept the legitimacy of private property and free markets. Real power in the state was being transferred to the elective and executive bodies of government — marked, above all, by the powerful new office of state president that Gorbachev created for himself in March 1990.[7] The newly elected governments of the national republics making up the Soviet state were one by one declaring their sovereignty within the union; and the three Baltic republics had declared their intention to secede altogether from the union. Everywhere, within and without the Soviet Union, Communist party rule was breaking down.

It would be a mistake to ascribe all the changes that occurred in the Gorbachev era to a plan or strategy. Gorbachev's early successes as leader owed to his brilliant skill at keeping opposing political forces in delicate balance. His reform measures had the effect of stimulating demands for further change among the Soviet population. As in the case of previous reform movements in the USSR and Eastern Europe, the pressure of popular demands snowballed. In response Gorbachev adopted ever more radical positions until confronted with the breakdown of the ties that bound the republics into a common political and economic union. At that point, in late 1990, he shifted course sharply, siding with the conservative forces opposing decentralization, then, in spring 1991, veering back to an acceptance of a new framework for a loose federation.

The tension caused by the collision of the declining structures of the old regime with the rising new popular movements for republican independence and democratic rule reached a climax in August 1991. A group of the government's most powerful officials — including the premier and the heads of the KGB, defense ministry, and interior ministry — conspired to remove Gorbachev and transfer power to a "state committee for a state of emergency." Within three days the coup collapsed and Gorbachev was restored to office. The aftermath of the coup intensified the collapse of the Communist party and of central authority. Gorbachev himself resigned as general secretary of the Communist party and the USSR Supreme Soviet voted to suspend the activity of the CPSU until the degree of its complicity in the coup attempt had been established. Through intensive negotiations with the presidents of ten republics, Gorbachev reached an agreement on an interim set of arrangements that preserved a framework for cooperation among the republics for trade and defense. Whether the former union would be succeeded by a federal or confederal state, or simply a commonwealth of independent nations, and what role might be left for Gorbachev as president of a dissolved union were questions left unanswered in the turmoil of the immediate aftermath of the failed coup.

BACKGROUND TO THE GORBACHEV REVOLUTION

The transformation of politics in the Soviet Union is the product of many forces. Gorbachev's early strategy was overtaken by the unexpected intensity of popular demands for ethnonational rights, individual liberties, decentralization of power, party competition, and rejection of the power and privileges of the old ruling elite. As engrossing as Gorbachev's personality is, and as profound as his impact has been, he might simply have remained one more Soviet leader offering a program of reform if a number of interacting pressures had not made reform so imperative, or popular pressure for change so urgent. Therefore, the student of comparative politics must try to step back from the flow of events in order to attempt to identify the factors that have shaped Gorbachev's agenda and the consequences of his reforms. We would emphasize six points in particular.

The Changing Environment of National Security

Although the international environment in the 1980s was relatively benign from the standpoint of Soviet national security, a look at the long-term perspective revealed that the Soviet Union was lagging behind the West in the new arenas of international technological rivalry, such as computers, robotics, and telecommunications, which were increasingly central to national security. The combination of Soviet successes and American setbacks in the Third World in the 1970s had helped to bring about the election of a vehemently anticommunist president in the United States. In his first term President Reagan launched a rapid buildup of American military power and presented a vision of a secure defensive shield that would undermine the Soviet nuclear arsenal as a deterrent force. Moreover, Soviet troops were mired in a brutal, debilitating war in Afghanistan, where Soviet ground forces invaded at the end of December 1979 to prop up a failing communist client regime faced with a massive popular insurrection. In striking imagery, Gorbachev characterized the Afghan war as "a bleeding wound" in his address to the Twenty-seventh Party Congress in 1986, and in early 1988 he promised the withdrawal of Soviet forces by early 1989, a commitment that was met by mid-February 1989. Soviet spokesmen assured the world that the original invasion had been a mistake of the Brezhnev era, brought about by the undemocratic foreign policy approaches of the past, declaring that in the future, Soviet troops would never be sent abroad without the approval of the Soviet legislature.

Despite the harsh tone of East–West relations in the early 1980s, the threat of general war was remote. Gorbachev, as Seweryn Bialer wrote, "took control of foreign and military policies in odd circumstances. He inherited awesome military power. He is the first leader to begin his rule in a position of strategic parity with the United States. Yet he also inherits a recent legacy of passive or reactive policies."[8] The USSR enjoyed the use of advantageous strategic naval bases in client states such as Cuba and Vietnam, and could project its military power at great distance.[9] Militarily, the Soviet Union had never been so strong, but economically and technologically the country was falling far behind the rest of the developed world. Not only was Afghanistan a quagmire for Soviet power, but it had become evident that the United States was in a position to challenge the Soviet Union in a new round of competition for military advantage by mobilizing its superiority in developing and adopting new technologies of warfare. For the Soviet leadership, therefore, it became clear that the search for strategic superiority was not only futile, but even counterproductive.[10]

The Quiet Revolution

The decades after Stalin's death brought about significant changes in Soviet society. While it would be foolish to assume that these changes made Gorbachev's ascent inevitable, it is evident that the strength of attachments to liberal and democratic values is at least partly a product of the maturation of Soviet society. As Lucian Pye writes, "the forces of modernization have made it harder for political willpower to mobilize and dominate a society."[11]

Among these changes we may cite four in particular:

a. *The rapid spread of access to the media of communication, including print media and radio and television broadcasting.* As a major party resolution in 1979 noted, a majority of Soviet families were now receiving three newspapers, listening to radio, and watching television.[12] Television, in particular, is almost universally available to the Soviet population, and has rapidly become the dominant medium through which the populace receives images and information about their world. But the saturation of Soviet society, long an objective of the Soviet leadership, has had some unintended consequences. Ellen Mickiewicz argues that "the television revolution in the Soviet Union, though initiated and administered under tight central control, has created a new and mobilized public" and one that is especially focused on information about the West.[13] Television's greatest effect may be concentrated among the least educated groups of the population, for whom newspapers and other sources of information may be hard to understand or inaccessible, and whom television has, in effect, "brought into the modern world."[14] Studies of the patterns of information receiving and opinion formation in the Soviet Union have shown that the effort to surround Soviet citizens with a stream of politically directed messages left a deficit of knowledge and understanding owing to the weaknesses and low credibility of official sources. This created an active hunger for news from unofficial sources, such as conversations with friends, family, and co-workers.[15]

b. *The transformation of the occupational structure, specifically the rapid increase in the number of individ-*

Boris Yeltsin, president of the Russian Republic, rallied popular resistance to the attempted coup of August 1991. He is seen here on the day the coup collapsed, waving to the crowd from the balcony of the Russian Republic parliament building.

uals employed in professional and specialist occupations. The massive industrialization drive was accompanied by an equally vast educational program aimed at turning out engineers and other technical specialists in huge numbers. Through a large network of specialized secondary schools and technically oriented higher educational institutions, the Soviet Union has brought about an enormous expansion in the ranks of qualified specialists — engineers, planners, recordkeepers, economists, scientific researchers, and professionals of many other profiles. The result is that Soviet society has a "professional class that is, numerically, the largest in the world."[16]

c. *The urbanization of society.* Although old village mentalities and habits have retreated only slowly, Soviet society has become predominantly urban in a very short span of time. By the end of the 1980s, two-thirds of the Soviet population lived in cities. As recently as 1961, however, the society was half urban, half rural. From 1950 to 1980 the urban population of the Soviet Union increased by nearly 100 million people — most of them immigrants from the countryside, which suffers from a continuing flight of population.[17] This growth of the urban population has had some significant but subtle effects on Soviet political culture, according to Moshe Lewin. It has tended to focus the attention of policymakers on problems of individual personality and human needs more directly than when the society was composed of large, seemingly homogeneous social blocs such as "workers" and "peasants." In addition, urbanization has facilitated the formation of informal and cross-cutting social ties that tend to nurture independent sources of public opinion and mediate the political messages sent out by the rulers.[18] These new, articulate, self-aware social units have begun to create the basis of a civic culture and a civil society.[19]

d. *The rise in educational attainments.* Over the 1960s, 1970s, and 1980s, the proportion of the population who were fifteen years of age and older and who had attained *at least* complete secondary education rose to over 60 percent. Moreover, a significant part of this growth has occurred among those with higher education. By 1989 over 10 percent of Soviet citizens aged fifteen and over had higher educational degrees, approaching the U.S. level.[20] As various studies have shown, precisely the most educated strata of the society were the most dissatisfied with the Brezhnev-era system. For example, the important study of Soviet immigrants to the United States in the 1970s, the SIP (Soviet Interview Project), found that critical and individualistic outlooks were strongest among the most highly educated groups.[21]

These changes in society made the political transformation wrought by Gorbachev both necessary and possible, since changes in the critical parameters of the society's organization must ultimately, though with a lag, bring about corresponding changes in political beliefs and values and the behavior of political institutions.[22] Indeed, according to the political scientist Jerry F. Hough, it is the state bureaucracy itself that is, albeit with ambivalence, the new social base for Gorbachev's opening of the Soviet system. Its members' aspirations, shaped by Western styles and tastes, now "center on a freer press, on greater access to western culture, on greater freedom to travel abroad, and, of course, a better selection of goods and services." Hough believes that the new urban educated classes have a vital interest in the security provided by private property.[23]

We should not assume that social change of the pre-Gorbachev era led smoothly or inevitably to Gorbachev's political revolution. (Among other things, we need to recall the struggles of dissidents for the rule of law and for human rights, the intensification of ethnonational feeling, the spread of liberal values, and the importance of political leadership.) Nevertheless, the modernization of Soviet society certainly helped prepare the way for its democratization. Compared with the revolutionary period, for example, the Soviet population today is far less susceptible to the sway of utopian dreams and illusions. In times past, encouraged by a combination of Russian cultural isolation and economic desperation, broad strata of the society believed that the revolution would usher in a "new age" of brotherhood, freedom, and prosperity.[24] Today's Soviet population, owing to its seven decades of experience with socialist forms of economic organization, its contact with the West, and its greater educational and knowledge base, is much less subject to utopian fantasy.

Ideological Bankruptcy

A third factor is the failure of the party's ideological efforts to infuse a common political faith or commitment into a society divided by class, regional, generational, ethnonational, and cultural differences. By the end of the 1970s, the party's own confidential polls, as well as the evidence of declining social discipline and productivity, indicated that the vacuum left by the exhaustion of ideology was filled with a variety of responses: indifference, apathy, cynicism, and corruption, as well as the growing strength of a number of competing value systems, such as nationalism, religion, and liberal democracy.[25] As the universalism and optimism of the Marxist theory came to be discredited by the deterioration of socialist societies and the prosperity and technological dynamism evident in the capitalist democracies, only through manipulation of hollow phrases about "developed socialism" and the "scientific-technical revolution" could Soviet propagandists maintain that their society possessed inherent advantages over that of the West. Meanwhile, the doctrine remained silent on the evident realities of the socialist system, unable to account for the immobilism and bureaucratism of the state, the political elite's clinging to privileges, the lingering poverty and backwardness of daily life. Gradually under Gorbachev, the political leaders realized that not only the particular policy prescriptions of the Brezhnev leadership, but also the core doctrines themselves of the party's vanguard role and state monopoly on property were deficient. Any new public faith sufficiently deep and widespread to inspire dedicated effort for the common good would have to be based on an ideology recognizing the value of individual freedom, effort, and reward.

Social Malaise

By the end of the 1970s, evidence mounted that Soviet society was experiencing a crisis of moral purpose. Gail Lapidus noted a "decline in civic morale" in which she identified three elements: "loss of optimism, loss of purpose, and disintegration of internal controls and self-discipline."[26] While the evidence for the shift in values was often impressionistic and anecdotal — relying on emigré testimony and the observations of Western journalists — its effects were palpable both in such behavioral trends as rising alcohol abuse and mortality rates, and in Soviet published sources such as sociological surveys, scholarly debate, and the fine arts. When *glasnost* under Gorbachev opened virtually all previously taboo topics to public scrutiny, the severity of the malaise was amply confirmed.

Perhaps the first clear indication of a deterioration in social well-being was the finding that, from around the mid-1960s through the end of the 1970s, mortality (death) rates had risen among infants and among most age groups of the male population.[27] This trend — unique among developed countries — reversed the improvement in public health that had marked the first decades of Soviet rule, and seemed to be related in part to increasing levels of alcohol abuse and disease.[28] Alcohol abuse, according to Soviet publications, was rising quickly among women as well as being endemic among men, and was linked to rising deaths from accidents, poisonings, and injuries as well as from heart disease.[29] Indeed, from 1974 until Gorbachev began the *glasnost* campaign, Soviet statistical handbooks simply ceased to report infant mortality data and much other social data. The computations of Soviet health statistics by Western scholars were the product of painstaking reconstruction from secondary and indirect sources.

These alarming trends were accompanied by a serious rise in official corruption. As is now fully documented in Soviet press reports and court proceedings, high-level abuses went well beyond occasional illegal private enrichment and became systematic. At a conference of the procuracy of the USSR in the spring of 1987, it was reported that, in the previous two years, over 240,000 ranking officials from throughout the Soviet Union had been charged with crimes such as theft, negligence, fraud, and other abuses of position.[30]

Under *glasnost* a number of other social pathologies were also revealed to the Soviet public, including drug addiction, prostitution, youth gangs, crime, suicide, elite privileges, poverty, and homelessness. News of the existence of such phenomena shocked Soviet citizens, not because Soviet society was unique in suffering from them, but because the media had covered them up in the past. Within a year, data on these and many other topics began being published. But because the concealment of these topics during the "era of stagnation" had prevented public awareness, let alone public debate, the country was poorly equipped to deal with the deepening decay of its social fabric.

Economic Gridlock

Before Gorbachev came to power, both Soviet and Western observers agreed that the Soviet economy's rate of growth was showing a long-term tendency to decline, although official Soviet estimates of year-to-year performance were substantially higher than the estimates of Western scholars. By the end of the 1970s, per capita Soviet economic growth, according to Western calculations, had fallen nearly to zero. From the early 1970s forward, Soviet leaders had demanded that the country's economic development move to an intensive rather than extensive growth strategy. That is, instead of emphasizing the mobilization of new resources and labor for production, the economy must drastically improve the efficiency with which resources were used. But no matter how often Brezhnev and other Soviet political leaders held forth on the need for intensification, the half-hearted policy measures that were enacted were incapable of altering economic performance. The system creaked along with an administrative structure that had been largely established in the 1930s. Gorbachev himself later characterized the mentality of the Brezhnev leadership as wanting to improve matters without changing anything.

The full severity of the economy's crisis only became evident under *glasnost* when Soviet economists produced figures challenging the official picture of economic progress under the five-year plans. The critics argued that published statistics on economic performance grossly overstated actual output growth by systematically failing to correct for price increases and by other statistical manipulations and distortions.[31] According to a respected Swedish economist, the real level of Soviet GNP per capita was less than one-third that of the United States by 1985. This means that the actual share of gross economic output devoted to the military sector was around 25 percent, not 14 to 15 percent, as most Western analysts previously believed.[32]

This trend represented a crisis, the economists explained, because the economy was increasingly working for itself: capital had to be invested at ever larger rates simply to maintain existing stock. The economy resembled a squirrel in a cage, running faster to stay in place. Each new effort to increase aggregate growth had successively less impact on living standards or technological development: the addition of new production capacity, although it consumed as much as a quarter of national income, barely managed to replace depreciated stock. It was therefore at the point where it no longer increased national wealth. Unrecouped expenditures, depleting existing reserves of labor, fuel, and raw materials, and swollen personal savings pushed up the state budget deficit and fueled inflation. Tremendous sums were locked up in unfinished construction projects, rising repair costs, and obsolete technology. The country produced more steel, tractors, fuel, and other goods than any other country, yet materials were constantly in short supply. As many as three in ten new tractors went unbought by farms, even though the price was set at half of production cost. As many as one-quarter of the workplaces in industry were vacant. Thus, much capital was simply wasted, having seemingly fallen into a black hole. For this reason, economists argue that the leadership's early strategy of acceleration — the effort to raise growth rates by raising investment rates — would only consume the country's productive potential all the more quickly, plundering the future for the sake of the present.[33] Instead, they argued, a radical turn to market relations was the only way to restore health to the economy.

Immobilism in the State

As many Soviet writers have recently argued, simply tinkering with the administrative structures inherited from the past could not have improved economic performance because the center had largely lost control of the economy.[34] Apart from setting a few high-priority plan goals, its attention was mainly on coping with crises. Its decision-making and information-processing facilities were overloaded, and its capacity to enforce its will was weak. But since the Soviet economy lacked either open market competition or tight discipline, self-coordination by units within the state's bureaucracy had pathological consequences. State structures became leaky and corrupt. Regardless of the planner's will, resources tended to go not to where the future economic benefit was greatest but where political influence was strongest.

Therefore, the declining performance of the Soviet economy represented less a failure of policy than a failure of the policymaking system: the complex of institutions for responding to demands, communicating problems that needed policy solutions, making coherent, timely, and relevant policy decisions, delegating power, and carrying out and enforcing the decisions. The system was very powerful when viewed from below, and it was certainly able to crush individual acts of opposition. Yet, viewed from above, it was weak and unable to carry out even modest policy measures, much as it was incapable of suppressing widespread private alienation.

The paralysis of central control stemmed from the basic logic of the command economy. The state's monopoly on productive property was converted into operational decisions on all basic resource allocation issues: quantity and quality of production, supply and distribution, pricing, and investment. As the economy grew larger and more complex, the administrative leviathan required to carry out the planners' will developed beyond the center's ability to manage. Bureaucratic organizations that ran branches of the economy and territorial regions acquired considerable autonomy. Moreover, the central leadership itself grew dependent on the political support of powerful regional and institutional elites. The policymaking process encouraged consultation and coordination among multiple interested agencies, with the result that any serious attempts at reform were distorted or watered down before being enacted. The implementation process provided yet more opportunities to subordinates to delay or sidetrack policy initiatives by issuing various directives and instructions that contradicted the measure's original intent. Public life revealed only distant echoes of the intense backstage struggles for turf, status, and resources that absorbed Soviet institutions. The political elite itself was increasingly insulated from checks on its power and privileges. As we have seen, many parts of the political elite gave way to corruption.

The self-interested collusion of bureaucratic organs with the various watchdog organizations that the system created to oversee them — the police, the mass media, scientific experts, public "kontrol" committees, and even the party itself — created a political system composed of numerous powerful political fiefdoms, with their own networks of vassalage and tributes. Invoking the leaders' fears of the consequences of real ideological pluralism, they intervened to choke off public scrutiny of their performance. The space program prohibited critical publicity; the Ministry of Health banned all mention of the problem of drug addiction in the Soviet Union; the water resources ministry spawned its own degree-granting research institutes that graduated the experts who then approved the ministry's plans.

As Gorbachev and his advisers became increasingly aware that it was impossible to force any reform through the state and party bureaucracy that opposed its interests, they turned to forces outside it, creating new institutional counterweights. *Glasnost* encouraged the intelligentsia and the general population to cast the light of publicity and debate on the deepest problems of society. Under the democratization strategy, new elective institutions took form, buttressed by new independent political associations, newspapers, enterprises, and political parties. But, of course, real political pluralism not only weakens the vast bureaucratic empire that the Soviet state has spawned, but it also destroys the Communist party's monopoly of power and, with it, the power of the party's leader to keep the country on the course he has set.

SOVIET POLITICAL CULTURE IN TRANSITION

The political culture of any large modern national society is both diverse and changing. Understood as the predispositions, including beliefs, values, and affective attachments that influence political behavior, the concept of political culture assumes that the attitudes held by members of a society interact with memories of the past and expectations about the future, with the evolving interests of groups and individuals, and with the cultures of other nations. There may be wide differences on certain dimensions of political culture among social groups. As Almond and Verba showed in their pioneering study, *The Civic Culture*, some attitudinal differences associated with groups of different educational levels in one society may be wider than average differences between societies.[35] However, studies of national political cultures consistently demonstrate that, even after taking into account the influence of such factors as education, occupation, sex, and generation, patterned differences among the cultures of political communities remain. These reflect the dense network of interaction among members of national societies and their collective interaction with the world environment.[36]

The political culture of Soviet society reflects a variety of influences, including the prerevolutionary culture of the Russian state, the cultures of the many non-Russian ethnic groups and nations incorporated into the Soviet state, the revolutionary ideology of the Russian communists, and the effects of industrialization and modernization. The Soviet state was brought into being through a revolution led by a radical wing of the Russian Marxist movement, which dedicated itself to the goal of taking power in the state and employing it to construct a new socialist society. Using terror and other forms of coercion, intense propaganda and suppression of alternative ideologies, and expropriation of capitalists and the landed gentry, the Bolsheviks[37] carried out a massive effort at social engineering. Through conquest and revolution, they restored Moscow's rule over most of the territories that had formed part of the old multiethnic tsarist empire, but sought in the process to change the political identity of the state from the Russian Empire to that of a nonethnic, ideologically defined, Soviet and socialist union of national republics.[38]

Moreover, the Soviet leaders attempted, sometimes with varying intensity, to construct a new *national* identity focused on the Soviet state, so that Soviet citizens would regard themselves not only as Russians, Ukrainians, Kazakhs, Georgians, and so on, but also as members of a larger Soviet nationality with its own culture and values. In 1971 Leonid Brezhnev, then the leader of the Soviet Communist party, went so far as to claim that "a new historical community of people — the Soviet people (sovetskii narod)" had developed in the Soviet Union. This new community was united, according to Brezhnev, by Marxist-Leninist ideology and by its common historical experience.[39] It is apparent today that Brezhnev was considerably overstating the degree to which the many ethnic-national cultures in the Soviet Union had come to think of themselves as parts of a single, ideologically defined, national culture, and that he chose to ignore the serious frictions dividing ethnic communities from one another and from Moscow. Members of the non-Russian nationalities were aware that the image of a common "Soviet" national culture that Soviet leaders presented was largely based on a Russian model. Russian national consciousness, in turn, often thought of itself as having a universalizing, civilizing, assimilating mission of bringing together the many disparate ethnic minorities in the state into a single, integrated society. Appeals to "Soviet" patriotism and "Soviet" national pride are thus, in part, implicit appeals to *Russian* patriotism and *Russian* national pride. Yet they do not entirely satisfy Russian national feeling — Solzhenitsyn speaks for many Russian nationalists in believing that the Soviet communist regime has exploited and victimized the Russian people more than any other in its drive for state power — and they exacerbate tensions between the Soviet state and the non-Russian peoples.[40]

Despite the destruction of many of the social and cultural institutions that had preserved national cultures among the peoples making up the Soviet state (such as the outlawing of both the Ukrainian Orthodox Church and the Uniate Roman Catholic Church in the Ukraine), national self-consciousness has endured. Modernization has tended to increase the size of the educated and articulate portion of each national society, while the liberalization of political life under Gorbachev has permitted the articulation of a range of national grievances and demands. Soviet nationality policy has always tried to balance acceptance of the many disparate ethnic-national cultures with the effort to meld them into a single overarching Soviet culture. In practice, this has meant that the regime has made certain concessions to the desires of ethnic-national communities for a measure of power and autonomy. Spokespersons for various national groups have been able to articulate muted demands for greater cultural freedom, such as the ability to honor past national heroes and promote the use of the national language, as well as to improve the material position of their peoples. In this effort, as Teresa Rakowska-Harmstone, Gregory Gleason, and other scholars have pointed out, the federal structure of the state has been a major facilitating factor.[41] The fact that the state has preserved territorial boundaries for ethnic-national communities enabled state and party institutions to become a channel for the articulation of nationalist interests as long as they did not challenge the hegemony of the central leadership. Rakowska-Harmstone points out that, as in India, Canada, Yugoslavia, and other multiethnic federal polities, in the Soviet Union "the convergence of ethnic and administrative boundaries results in politicization of ethnicity and in the emergence of nationalism. The identification of ethnic with political and socioeconomic structures sharpens the perception of each group's relative position in the competition for the allocation of social values. The demands are aggregated on ethnic rather than functional lines, for reasons of strategic efficacy as much as ethnicity's affective value."[42] In the more open political environment of the Gorbachev period, ethnic political mobilization has produced movements for national independence and national sovereignty that Moscow cannot repress except at an enormous cost in lives.

Just as the Soviet political culture is heterogeneous across territory, reflecting the distinct historical identities of the more than one hundred European and Asian peoples making up the state, so it also evolves over time. For many years, scholars have debated whether the absolutist heritage of the Russian state left a legacy of popular support for authoritarian rule that would impede the development of democratic institutions.[43] As the discussion of the "quiet revolution" in the introductory section suggests, the steady, gradual effects of urbanization, rising educational attainments, and exposure to the outside world are believed by many scholars to have wrought fundamental changes in the Soviet people's hopes, expectations, and values. Jerry F. Hough, for example, sees an important psychological change among the Soviet population since the revolution. In a deliberately provocative argument, Hough compares the Russian Revolution of 1917 with the Nazi movement or, to take a more contemporary example, the Khomeini revolution in Iran, in its nativist rejection of pluralist, secular, and democratic influences from the global civilization spreading from the West. That is, according to Hough, the early effects of industrialization in Russia created fear and disorientation among the newly urban and semi-urbanized workers, many of whom still retained strong ties to village society and the rural culture. They responded to an extremist revolutionary movement that closed Russia off to the economic and political development of the West. Now, however, social change has reduced the insecurities associated with early industrialization. As Hough puts it, "the lives of today's youth in a large Soviet city are far closer to the lives of the young in a large American city than to that of their great-grandparents in a rural Russian village."[44] These changes and the incipient consolidation of autonomous social structures have created a constituency for democratic government.

Finally, one additional feature of the Soviet political culture should be mentioned, besides that of the diversity across ethnic-national communities and the effects of social change. A persistent element in the political cultures of the prerevolutionary and Soviet societies has been the gap between the world of the political elite and that of the general population. This duality distinguishes the outlook and habits of the officials tied to the state's power from the values and practices of ordinary people — the *narod*. This "image of dual Russia," as Robert Tucker called it, refers to the mutual estrangement and alienation between the state's rulers, agents, symbols, doctrines, customs, and institutions and the vast, largely rural, folk society. A recurrent theme in Russian and Soviet history is the attitude taken by the rulers and officials of the state that the society must be conquered and placed in harness to achieve some overriding national purpose, such as modernization; and the characteristic attitude by the general population toward the state that sees in it an alien, predatory, and occupying power.[45]

The weakness of representative institutions, such as interest groups, competitive political parties, legislative assemblies, and autonomous local governments, historically reinforced the duality between state and society. Although the Communist party set itself the task of overcoming this division and mobilizing the population through its organizational, ideological, and recruitment efforts, the evidence of surveys indicates that the duality has remained a strong and durable feature of Soviet political culture. The major survey of emigrés from the Soviet Union after World War II, the Harvard Project, found that by far the most profound social distinction in Stalinist society was between "the party" or "party people" and "nonparty people."[46] A related attitude was very strongly expressed in the elections to the all-union and local soviets in 1989 and 1990, when the single most intense and universal theme among voters was the desire to remove those identified with the ruling establishment.[47] The challenge for the new democratic structures taking form in the Soviet Union today will be to establish their legitimacy as effective, responsible governing institutions while distinguishing themselves in the popular consciousness from the traditionally scorned and mistrusted institutions of the state.

The Soviet political system has sought to overcome the duality between state and society in several ways. A good example is *democratic socialism*, the formula Vladimir Lenin, the founder of the Soviet state, developed for the organization of the Communist party. Under democratic centralism, party members were supposed to enjoy wide freedom to discuss and influence policy, but once policy decisions were made, they were to be carried out and supported unhesitatingly. In practice, centralism in the party has always outweighed democratic elements. There was no effective way lower party organizations could hold higher level leaders to account for their actions. Although the party preserved the façade of elections of its leadership, in reality higher level officials named individuals to fill lower level positions, and the democratic elements in party practice of reports, elections, and debate were almost entirely ceremonial. The formula "democratic centralism" came to represent the party's insistence on unity and discipline at the expense of democratic accountability.

In other sectors of Soviet society, the tension between democracy and centralism has been reconciled in other ways. Although Russian and Soviet history provide many illustrations of autocratic leadership, they are also rich in examples of localized, decentralized self-rule, particularly based on face-to-face, communal forms of social organization. Decision making, both in the workplace and in government, often reveals a distinctive combination of centralized authority with deliberation, consultation, and consensus-building from below.

In the Soviet enterprise, for example, management is expected to harmonize the two conflicting principles of single-person management and collegiality.[48] Under single-person management, which Soviet leaders since Lenin have insisted on (and which was introduced into Russian public administration from military models as early as the eighteenth century), the chief executive is held solely and singly responsible for running the enterprise. Under Stalin, according to Moshe Lewin, the bosses were told to consider themselves commanders in a battle: "The party wanted the bosses to be efficient, powerful, harsh, impetuous, and capable of exerting pressure crudely and ruthlessly and getting results 'whatever the cost.'"[49]

Yet at the same time, collectivism and collective leadership have also been absorbed into the Soviet political culture from earlier Russian roots. Under collective leadership, decisions are supposed to be made by consensus, and discussion and consultation are used to achieve the necessary consensus. Formal mechanisms for ensuring wide consultation between the workforce and management were employed extensively in the 1960s and 1970s, and were often cited by Soviet propagandists as evidence of the strength of mass participation in society. For the most part, these forms — workplace meetings, councils of the labor collective, permanent production conferences, and so on — were part of the ceremonial backdrop to the reality of highly centralized decision-making power. They were never entirely defunct, however, and under Gorbachev, and especially since the adoption of the Law on the State Enterprise in 1987, they have been somewhat strengthened. In many workplaces, Soviet employees vote to elect their director. Both formal and informal groups provide advice and information to managers, and managers are expected to deal with a broad range of their subordinates' concerns.

Many other examples can be cited to show the duality of centralized leadership and grass-roots participation in Soviet political culture. These include the mass discussion campaigns held to publicize important policy decisions as well as to solicit popular reaction and create the appearance of a broadly participatory, democratic approach to politics. In his analysis of the media campaign surrounding the publication of the draft Soviet constitution in 1977, Robert Sharlet has identified three distinct phases: a short period of largely ceremonial commentary, followed by a longer period of extensive substantive debate, and then finally a statement from the commission charged with preparing the constitution which indicates that the discussion is now over and the commission is forwarding its proposals to the Supreme

Soviet for enactment. As Sharlet observes, this sort of mass discussion campaign is a "leadership technique for mobilizing the population and encouraging citizen participation in policy implementation, while the party uses the occasion for a mass political socialization campaign at the same time."[50]

As these examples indicate, in Soviet political practice centralism has been the dominant motif, and democracy has been relegated to largely ceremonial forms. Through the decades of Soviet rule, the leadership has found many justifications for the insistence on popular unity, discipline, and solidarity: the encirclement of the revolutionary socialist state by powerful and hostile imperialist enemies; the devious machinations of traitors and saboteurs who were generally portrayed as being in league with external enemies; the relentless momentum of the arms race which according to Soviet propaganda was forced on the Soviet people by the imperialists; the necessity of mobilizing all resources in order to overcome Russia's age-old backwardness and weakness; and, more subtly, appeals to the fear, particularly among intellectuals, that the Soviet people were not sufficiently mature to rule themselves and required a firm hand to guide them and educate them until society could begin to assume some of the burden of self-government. The traumatic influences of World War I, revolution, civil war, repeated famine, terror, and World War II undoubtedly left a powerful legacy in Soviet political consciousness of appreciation for a stern and powerful authority capable of preserving order and national security.

Yet the democratic and collegial elements in the political culture have repeatedly generated impulses for decentralization. As Stephen Cohen has argued, Soviet political life has always been characterized by a kind of dialogue between the "friends and foes of change," in which the foes of change — conservatives believing in strong, central authority — have usually had the dominant voice. Periods when the reformers — who have wanted to fight bureaucratization by expanding democratic institutions — were ascendant have been short-lived and have been followed by periods of conservative restoration.[51] Therefore, it is not a radical departure from Soviet political culture when a leader such as Mikhail Gorbachev attacks the bureaucratic distortions in socialism characteristic of the period of stagnation preceding his leadership, and calls for the revival of democratic principles in state and society.[52] What marks a significant discontinuity is the institutionalization of

democratic institutions and lasting constitutional constraints on the power of the state. Like earlier reformers in Soviet and Russian history, Gorbachev has appealed to the antibureaucratic, grass-roots democracy strain in the political culture for support against his political enemies and the entrenched interests blocking change. The challenge for him, as for other leaders seeking to introduce a certain limited, controlled liberalization into an authoritarian state, has been to maintain the initiative as power passed to a radicalized, mobilized, and increasingly institutionalized array of popular movements and political organizations. Gorbachev's embrace of the popular antagonism to the power and privileges of the ruling elite is risky. As the divisions in society deepen through the mobilization of ethnic and other social cleavages, the integrity of the Soviet state becomes increasingly difficult to sustain, and the state may fragment along ethnic and territorial lines. As Robert Dahl wrote, "[T]he price of polyarchy may be a breakup of the country. And the price of territorial unity may be a hegemonic regime."[53] Gorbachev may well have to choose between preserving the territorial unity of the Soviet Union and advancing the democratic aspirations of *perestroika*.

THE DYNAMICS OF SOCIAL STRUCTURE

Ethnicity and Social Stratification

Modernization has wrought profound changes in Soviet society. As we noted in the introductory section, some of the social processes set in motion under Stalin and his successors continue quietly to transform the face of society. The vast majority of Soviet youth now receive a complete secondary education. In a matter of thirty years, the ratio of urban to rural population has changed from half and half to two-thirds to one-third (see Table 13.1).

The specific pattern of industrialization, however, shows the distinctive mark of the Stalinist model of growth, which stressed development of heavy industry (metalworking, machine building, energy, power, extraction and chemicals) over light industry and consumer goods.[54] Moreover, the Stalinist model emphasized the mobilization of new resources to feed an expanding industrial plant at the expense of economy and productivity gains. Finally, the legacy of agricultural collectivization, when the state forced peasants to merge their private landholdings into state-controlled collec-

TABLE 13.1
SOVIET URBAN AND RURAL POPULATION GROWTH, 1959–1989

Year	Total Population (millions)	Urban	Rural	Pct. of total Urban	Rural
1959	208.8	100	108.8	48	52
1970	241.7	136.0	105.7	56	44
1979	262.4	163.6	98.8	62	38
1989	286.7	188.8	97.9	66	34

Source: "The 1989 Census: A Preliminary Report," *Current Digest of the Soviet Press* (CDSP), 41:17 (1989), p. 17.

tive farms, a process accompanied by massive violence and famine, has left a heritage of low agricultural productivity that Soviet leaders are still struggling to overcome. Thus, modernization has been the consequence of the imposition of a common Soviet social pattern on all sections of the country, a process that included the dispossession, and in some cases violent destruction, of alien social classes.

Industrialization has affected different parts of the Soviet Union differently. Some regions are still mainly agricultural and rural, while others are heavily industrial. Like every aspect of Soviet society and politics, patterns of social change also have an ethnic dimension. Some of the ethnic nationalities of the country show rates of modernization—that is, high levels of education, urban residence, and engagement in industrial occupations. Others have populations that are still predominantly involved in nonindustrial livelihoods. Overall, not quite half (47 percent) of the employed population of the Soviet Union is employed in manufacturing, construction, transportation, and communications branches, or what might be called the industrial sector.[55] This figure has remained roughly constant over the last two decades as the slow decline in the size of the workforce employed in agriculture has roughly equaled the rise in the proportion of the population occupied in science, health, education, and other service branches. What is striking is the wide variation in the levels of the industrially employed population across the different union republics. At 51 percent (i.e., 51 percent of the employed population is employed in manufacturing, construction, transportation, and communications), the Russian republic is a little above the national average. In fact, because of the overwhelming size and weight of the Russian republic in the union, most union-wide per capita statistics are heavily influenced by the patterns of the Russian republic. Estonia's population is also 51 percent industrial. Several of the republics, however, especially those in Central Asia, are well below the national average: 34 percent in Kirgizia; 31 percent in Uzbekistan; 29 percent in Turmenia; 28 percent in Tadjikistan; 38 percent in Georgia; 35 percent in Moldavia; 34 percent in Azerbaijan. The unequal diffusion of industrial growth leaves wide gaps between the republics in their levels of development, and, more broadly, their access to influence within the union as well as the levels of education and material well-being of their populations. *Within* republics, significant occupational, income, educational, and other status differences are often associated with ethnicity. These differences are reflected in the disparities in the percentages of the titular nationalities of each union republic which are engaged in industrial occupations (manufacturing, construction, communications, and transportation).

Table 13.2 shows that in some republics only a small proportion of the industrial workforce is composed of members of the indigenous nationality. For example, only a quarter of employees in manufacturing in Kirgizia are Kirgiz, and only a fifth of those in manufacturing in Kazakhstan are Kazakh. What these figures show is the degree to which the industrial workforce in each republic is ethnically diverse. In particular, although figures are hard to come by on this point, where members of the indigenous nationality comprise only a small proportion of the workforce in "modern" branches such as manufacturing, construction, transportation, and communications, Russians are in most cases the ethnic group making up the industrial sector. Members of the indigenous nationality are likely to be concentrated in traditional sectors such as agriculture. As a result, the stratification

TABLE 13.2
ETHNIC COMPOSITION OF THE WORKFORCE OF SOVIET REPUBLICS, BY INDUSTRIAL SECTOR, 1987 (IN PERCENT)

Republic and Nationality	Manufacturing	Transport and Communications	Construction
RSFSR (Russians)	83	85	78
Ukraine (Ukrainians)	68	71	69
Belorussia (Belorussians)	77	78	76
Uzbekistan (Uzbeks)	53	55	50
Kazakhstan (Kazakh)	21	28	21
Georgia (Georgians)	61	68	70
Azerbaijan (Azerbaijani)	69	74	73
Lithuania (Lithuanians)	71	84	81
Moldavia (Moldavians)	48	54	52
Latvia (Latvians)	38	38	46
Kirgizia (Kirgiz)	25	35	26
Tadjikistan (Tadjik)	48	57	48
Armenia (Armenians)	93	96	95
Turkmenia (Turkmen)	53	48	54
Estonia (Estonians)	43	47	61

Source: E. D. Igitkhanian, I. Iu. Petrushina, and F. R. Filipov, ''Industrial'nyi otriad trudiashchikhsia [The Industrial Detachment of the Toilers],'' *Sotsiologicheskie issledovaniia*, no. 3 (1990), p. 6.

of society by socioeconomic status partly overlaps with stratification by ethnicity, with members of the dominant Russian nationality found disproportionately concentrated in better paying and more prestigious occupations and members of the local nationality clustered in low-wage, low-status jobs.[56]

In all the non-Russian republics, the Russian population is significantly more urbanized than the titular nationality. This fact is attributable to the Russian migrants' patterns of settlement in the national republics, where they have tended to occupy positions in industry and administration. Similarly, Russians living in the national republics are almost always more highly educated than the indigenous populations.[57] Their predominance in important control positions in the society of national republics in turn exposes them to hostility and resentment from the nationally conscious local populations. Contributing to this tension is the longstanding expectation that all ethnic minorities of the country should master the Russian language, while Russians residing in the national republics rarely feel an equivalent obligation to learn the local language.

That there is an ethnic stratification that partly co-

incides with the stratification of society by social status is also indicated in the findings of a study reported by the informal organization, Tatar Social Center (a group pressing for greater rights for the Tatar nationality). The study examined the ethnic composition of the employees of the gigantic Kama River automotive works, an industrial conglomerate located in the Tatar autonomous republic of the Russian republic. Overall, ethnic Tatars comprise 44.2 percent of the workforce. But at higher levels of the administrative ladder, Tatars comprise smaller and smaller proportions (while Russians comprise larger and larger shares). Of the shift managers, only 23 percent are Tatars; of the shop chiefs, only 16 percent; of the eighty-nine deputy directors and chief engineers, only 11 percent are Tatars; and finally, of the twelve directors of factories in the association, only one is a Tatar.[58]

Broadly speaking, scholars distinguish two phases in the history of the migration of Russians outward into the national republics under Soviet rule. From the 1920s through the 1950s, Russians experienced a high growth rate of their own population and a high level of geographic mobility. This period saw high levels of migration of ethnic Russians from the European to the Asian parts of the Soviet Union. But in the 1960s, 1970s, and 1980s, this trend was reversed. The growth rate of Russians fell sharply, to a point that may be below maintenance rate. Their influence on other ethnic groups decreased, while the nationalities in Central Asia experienced very high rates of natural population increase. Outmigration of Russians to Central Asia fell substantially, and a large reverse migration from the south and east back to the north and west occurred. These trends, in turn, contributed to a slowing or reversal of interethnic integration. Increasingly, Russians in the national republics see themselves as a beleaguered minority, faced with potentially discriminatory language and political rights legislation. This issue has been considerably exacerbated by the strengthening of nationalist political movements claiming sovereignty for the national republic and its principal ethnic group.[59]

In addition to the shifts in the position of Russians within the multinational Soviet population, and the differential adaptation of ethnic groups to sovietization, another dimension of social change needs to be identified — the consolidation of larger nationalities.[60] With time, smaller nationalities have tended to disappear through assimilation into larger nationalities, while major nationalities have generally developed more self-conscious and fully developed national cultures, national intelligentsias and political elites, and institutional infrastructures that have enabled them to bargain with Moscow for concessions in cultural, political, and economic spheres.[61]

Changing demographic trends and the differential effects of modernization on different groups and regions are important factors in understanding the tense and tangled relations among ethnic groups in the Soviet population. Industrialization and other forms of social change have had an uneven effect on Soviet society. In some regions, ethnic minorities occupy a disproportionately large share of the lower status occupations or have even been left out of the industrial drive. Through migration, each region has a heterogeneous mix of nationalities, but there are often occupational and regional clusters, creating ethnic "ghettos" for some and pockets of relative privilege for others. As a result, a great deal of tension arising from the unequal distribution of benefits such as mobility, resources, influence, status, and prestige among ethnic groups leads to ethnic political mobilization. Soviet people tend to be intensely aware of ethnic nationality, and in a period of open politics, eth-

nically based political movements mobilize around demands for autonomy, sovereignty, and even independence for regions identified with national communities. Sometimes such movements take the form of violent resentments against domination by Russians, as well as against neighboring nationalities. The federal structure of the state, which provides nominal autonomy — including, according to the constitution, "sovereignty" for each republic making up the union — has fostered the identification of national minorities with territories that they regard as their homelands and in which they seek freedom and independence for the nation.

Rise and Fall of the "New Class"

The establishment of the Soviet model shifted the patterns of allocation of power and status in society. Dispossessing and in some cases bloodily eliminating the old dominant classes — landowners, industrialists, cultural intelligentsia, religious clergy, prosperous peasants, leaders of independent political parties and movements — the new Soviet state created its own ruling elite. The core of the new regime was the party of revolutionaries that seized power in the October Revolution of 1917. As it changed from a party dedicated to overthrowing the state to one committed to ruling it, it needed to broaden its base of support. The Communist party itself grew rapidly — roughly doubling its total size in the 1920s, again in the 1930s, and still again in the 1940s. Its rate of growth then slowed somewhat, but at its high point, in 1988, the party had 19.5 million members (including both full and "candidate," that is, probationary, members). Since then, party membership has declined at an accelerating rate as millions of members have formally quit or have ceased paying dues (see Table 13.3).

As it squeezed out the old social elites, the young Soviet regime put politically loyal cadres in their places to run the expanding industrial economy, the collective and state farms, the burgeoning ministries of government, and other positions of influence and prestige. Party membership quickly became an essential credential for career success since the regime's leaders treated the party as a transmission belt for extending Soviet policy and ideology outward into government and society. Although weakened by poor organization, local or regional sympathies, and especially by Stalin's terror, the party was the indispensable organizational instrument for binding together the large, diverse, multinational, and rapidly changing Soviet society.

TABLE 13.3
GROWTH OF SOVIET COMMUNIST PARTY MEMBERSHIP, 1917–1987 (IN THOUSANDS)

Year	Full Members	Candidate Members	Total
1917 (March)	24	—	24
1917 (October)	350	—	350
1927	786.3	426.2	1,212.5
1937	1,453.8	527.9	1,981.7
1947	4,774.9	1,277.0	6,051.9
1957	7,001.1	493.5	7,494.6
1967	12,135.1	549.0	12,684.1
1977	15,365.6	628.9	15,994.5
1987	18,566.8	700.9	19,267.7
1990 (January)			19,228.2
1991 (January)			16,516.1

Source: "KPSS v tsifrakh," *Partiinaia zhizn'*, no. 21 (1987), p. 6; *Tochka zreniia* (March 1991), p. 4.

With time party recruitment strategies centered on a few basic objectives. All individuals in certain key professions and occupations were expected to be party members. For example, virtually all flag officers in the armed forces and the vast majority of the officer corps generally are party members. Members of some occupations, such as factory directors, prosecutors, judges, historians, city mayors, and many others, were overwhelmingly likely to be party members, and usually party membership was a prerequisite for appointment to the job. Membership in the Communist party thus overlapped with all important spheres of social and political influence and prestige. In recent decades the Communist party has also sought to ensure that a majority of new members were manual workers (around 60 percent) and that only around one quarter were members of the engineering and managerial strata.[62] Another objective in party recruitment policy has been to secure a rising share for women; around one-third of new members in the 1980s were women. The purpose of these policies was to keep the party at least somewhat representative of society in its social makeup.

Soviet leaders have in the past always rejected any accusation that the political power of the Communist party gave rise to a new ruling class in place of the old ruling classes of prerevolutionary society. Nevertheless, many observers both within and outside Soviet society believe that that is precisely what happened. The first full statement of this position was offered by a former communist, one of the most powerful figures in the Yugoslav communist movement, who broke with the Communist party in the early 1950s and published a book accusing his former comrades of having become part of a *new class*. This new class, according to Milovan Djilas, controlled all the productive property that had been seized from the bourgeoisie and the landed classes, and used this power to maintain its own position of political and social dominance. The rhetoric of socialism merely concealed the real power and interests of the new class, but it was in fact a new exploiting class that lived off the labor of others by entrenching itself in the state bureaucracy that controls the economy. It used socialist ideology to prevent any opposition to its power from forming, it turned Marxist theory into a quasireligious dogma to legitimate itself, and it used its control over the media to keep its privileges and powers hidden from public view. Living in constant fear of popular opposition, it developed a framework of law to mask its tyranny over society. Eventually, Djilas argued, the new class became so powerful and independent that it was no longer the creature of the Communist party that created it, but used the Communist party to preserve its domination.[63]

Although the theory of the new class exaggerated the degree of commonality of members of the political elite in Soviet society, understating ethnic, regional, sectoral, generational, ideological, and other differences, it captured an important element of truth. Until the Gorbachev revolution, the Communist party maintained its power by controlling the process of selection of individuals to leading positions in the state and society through a system called *nomenklatura*. The nomenklatura system consisted of a series of lists of individuals and positions. Every territorial party organization maintained a list of job positions in its jurisdiction which it had the right of filling or appointments which it could veto. Many of these were managerial and administrative posts, such as party secretaries, government executives, enterprise managers, judges, police chiefs, newspaper editors, trade union officials, school directors, and even church leaders. Others were nominally elective positions, such as deputies to the soviets. Individuals were named to these positions only if they had been approved by, and often recommended by, the appropriate party officials. By controlling eligibility for nomenklatura jobs, the party ensured that only politically reliable persons were named to sensitive leadership positions in society.[64] In turn, individuals in the nomenklatura system often thought of themselves, and were thought of by the public, as forming a separate and distinct social group, with their own privileges and style of life.

This social division between the nomenklatura stratum and the rest of society was reinforced by the apparent job security enjoyed by political appointees. Especially under Brezhnev, once an individual was on the nomenklatura list, he was usually assured of tenure for life, barring serious incompetence, flagrant political errors, or close involvement with a disgraced leader. With time, popular resentment came to focus on the powers and privileges of the nomenklatura as an elite group.[65] In the last few years, one of the most explosive themes in the Soviet media was that of the privilege, corruption, and conservatism of the nomenklatura. Just before the Twenty-seventh Party Congress in 1986, an article appeared in the party's main daily newspaper, *Pravda*, that quoted several ordinary citizens' letters of resentment against the unjustified privileges of the party–state bureaucracy.[66] With time, media treatment of the subject grew more daring, discussing the nomenklatura by name and exposing the hidden perks and benefits its members enjoyed.

In the late 1980s popular frustration with the failure of the promised wholesale restructuring of society spilled out into a widespread movement to turn out the old privileged political elite. As in Eastern Europe, where the former party state was swept away with stunning rapidity once the regime lost its control over the popular movement, throughout the Soviet Union citi-

zens formed movements and organizations aimed less at reforming communist rule than at eliminating it. Above all, the popular movements focused on attacking the power of the ruling bureaucracy, who are generally thought of as a distinct social stratum.

The much more open, tense, and fluid political environment in the Soviet Union in the late 1980s has thus been influenced by the rising salience of two types of social cleavage: the ethnic dimension, which as we have seen is related to the existing divisions of occupational status and prestige; and a kind of new class warfare focused on the vividly conceived and widely detested party–state bureaucracy. These conflicts have resulted in the breakdown of many of the old integrating and coordinating structures that the old regime provided. At the same time, they have tended to prevent stable new institutions from forming, partly because of the same populist suspicion of *any* organized center of power. As a result, the breakdown of the old system has proceeded much more quickly than the consolidation of new, democratic, and law-governed institutions.

POLITICAL PARTICIPATION AND RECRUITMENT

Democratization from Above
The mobilization of popular political movements along nationality lines and other social cleavages, and the expression of public resentment of the privilege, corruption, and conservatism of the party–state bureaucratic elite, help to explain the explosive quality of the demands made on the regime and the discontinuous nature of the transition of the political system. Rather than being incorporated into an expanding political arena, newly politicized groups are seeking to replace the Communist party–state itself. In many parts of the country, the new political movements are intent on democratic change, but in some, new movements are replacing a communist form of authoritarianism with nationalistic and bureaucratic authoritarianism.

The abruptness of the transition process and the difficulty for the Gorbachev leadership in managing it stem from the highly integrated nature of the political elite in the old system. The core of the elite has been made up of executives in the key control bureaucracies of the political system — the party, the government, the Komsomol, the military, the KGB, and the mass media. Political executives were distinguished from specialist members of the political elite by the breadth of their functions, which concerned the aggregation of demands, policymaking, and policy implementation. Through co-optation, specialist elites were sometimes drawn into full-time political executive positions; in other cases, political executives were recruited from among activists in Komsomol and other political organizations who possessed the necessary skills, experience, and reliability. Some political executives became generalists, while others tended to acquire a particular career profile in industry, agriculture, ideology, or personnel.[67] Gorbachev himself had a career that began in youth work in the Komsomol before becoming a party leader in Stavropol, a predominantly agricultural region. In 1978 he was named a secretary of the Central Committee of the party specializing in agriculture. His is the narrowest career background of any general secretary in Soviet history. His meteoric rise is therefore a testament to his exceptional political skills.

Regardless of the particular function performed or career specialization, political executives in the party, government, and other centers of power have in the past tended to form a closely interlocking leadership. This pattern is visible in a number of practices that used to be standard and that now are breaking down. The first is incorporation of the political elite in territorial committees of the Communist party.

In every territorial subdivision of the state, the Communist party organization is headed by a committee comprising the most important Communist party members of the region. Thus, in the past the party maintained a governing committee for each rural district, each city, each province, and each republic, as well as the whole Soviet Union. In the republics, including autonomous republics, and at the level of the Soviet Union as a whole, the party's committee is called a Central Committee. Party committees have performed both a representative and a deliberative function. In their makeup they represented the most important political executives in the jurisdiction (all of them, of course, party members), and at the same time, they were the main arena in which interests were aggregated and policy decisions set, and they oversaw the implementation of policy. As a representative institution, party committees linked elites both horizontally and vertically. That is, all the chief political executives of the particular territory were represented on the committee: the party's own full-time executives, called party secretaries, as well as the head of government, the directors of leading facto-

ries, the chief of the trade union council, the head of the KGB branch, the heads of the main media organizations, and so on. In that sense, the party committee acted as a kind of hub of authority, the spokes of which radiated out into all other important organizations and bureaucracies in the area.

The horizontal interlocking of leadership was reinforced by vertical integration. Vertical links were those in which heads of organizations lower in the hierarchy were named as members of higher level committees. Vertically, each party committee also included the main political executives of the subordinate jurisdictions. A provincial party committee (*oblastnoi komitet*, or obkom) typically included the first secretaries of the party committees of the cities in the province, for example. The all-union Central Committee comprised the first secretaries of the major obkoms of the country. The same pattern applied to governmental and other organizations as well. In this way, the interlocking of the Soviet political elite had both horizontal and vertical elements that functioned to integrate major territorial and sectoral interests, helping to create a common outlook and understanding of policy across institutional sectors, and always preserving the party's primacy as the site where basic policy decisions were worked out. In turn, because of the party's role as the chief policymaking and coordinating force in the political system, the party's own full-time executives were always the most powerful officials in each territorial unit. At the top of the pyramid, the party's general secretary was therefore not only the head of the party, but the effective leader of the Soviet state, since all lines of political authority ultimately converged in him.

The party committees at each level have functioned as coordinating and integrating mechanisms more than as decision-making centers. Decision-making power was traditionally vested in a much smaller committee, called the *bureau*, consisting of the party's secretaries plus several other ranking political executives. At the all-union level of the party, the bureau is called the *Politburo*. Until Gorbachev pushed through radical changes in 1990, it consisted of the most powerful party and government officials in the country: the general secretary, who served as chairman; several other powerful central and territorial party secretaries; the chairman of the Council of Ministers, who is the equivalent of a prime minister; and, in recent years, the chairman of the KGB, the defense minister, and the foreign minister. In a pattern replicated at every lower rung of the party hierarchy, the small size and influential membership of the party's top decision-making body made it the final seat of actual authority in the political system. One of the most radical changes Gorbachev has made in the Soviet political system, therefore, was to strip the Politburo of its power to decide basic issues of domestic and foreign policy and to transfer that power to the new office of the president.

The interlocking of leadership across institutional sectors has also been evident in other domains besides the party's own organization. The Soviet political system has always contained an abundance of elective institutions for group deliberation and decision, although these institutions have generally been decorative and ceremonial rather than authoritative and effective. Every territorial unit in the country, down to the level of neighborhoods, apartment buildings, and university dormitories, have elective councils (soviets). At the republic and federal levels, the councils are called *Supreme Soviets*. In the past, soviets served largely as democratic window-dressing. Elections were treated in official propaganda as a pageant of democracy, where high turnouts and a festive atmosphere were seen as a token of the unshakeable unity between the Soviet people and their leaders. In virtually all races, however, only one candidate was running. The vote was treated as an endorsement of a selection process over which the ordinary citizen had no control. The party devoted considerable effort to ensuring that the deputies were socially representative of the population, so that at each level quotas were handed down that governed the share of workers, women, youth, white-collar employees, nonparty members, ethnic minorities, and other categories of the population who were to serve as deputies. A deliberately stage-managed tokenism was treated by propaganda as evidence of the popular and democratic character of the soviets.

In a recent book, Stephen White cites several examples of the old system for nominating candidates for the local soviets. A local party secretary reported that he had been instructed on the proper makeup of the deputies in his jurisdiction: 4.6 percent were to be enterprise directors, 1.1 percent were to be drawn from the sphere of culture and the arts, 0.8 percent should be party officials, and 45.9 percent were to be elected for the first time. In another case, a worker was nominated by his fellow workers for a second term as deputy to the regional soviet. But the workers were then informed that he was not eligible: " 'Stop', the collective was told. 'Our

thanks to Vasilii Stepanovich, but he's not included on the list because of his age and the need to elect new deputies. What we need is a woman, a Komsomol member and a leading worker. Find one!' " Another instance cited by White was a case in which a notorious prostitute was nominated as a candidate for deputy to a local soviet because she was the only person in the area who fit the prescribed criteria: female, a factory worker, and between thirty-five and forty years of age.[68]

Not surprisingly, the status of deputies was largely honorific, and the soviets themselves were not authoritative either in articulating and aggregating interests or in making policy. Greater stress was placed on the symbolic functions of the soviets as channels of popular representation and participation, in which 2 million Soviet citizens served — all on a part-time basis — as people's deputies. Deputy status was treated officially as an honor conferred on people who were held up as model citizens. Together with many manual workers, nearly all members of the nomenklatura also served as deputies, in many cases in districts far away from their places of work and residence. Party and government executives were normally members of soviets, and soviets elected executive organs from their own membership. As ceremonial bodies, the old soviets represented the principle not of the *separation* of legislative from executive authority, but rather their *unity*. But because there was no effective way in which soviets could set policy or oversee its implementation, the executive apparatus of the party and government dominated all phases of the policy process.

Over and over in Soviet political life, the same pattern was symmetrically repeated: full-time political executives took on spare-time, voluntary duties as members of elective bodies of their own and other organizations. The close linkage of institutional and territorial elites that resulted from this pattern of integration helped to ensure the coordination of policy in the principal organized spheres of social life and to build a sense of common interest and responsibility that undercut bureaucratic, ethnic, or other lines of division. This pattern also facilitated the party's overall control over the selection of elites, since the party's personnel managers routinely rotated officials across institutional spheres or promoted them to successively higher levels of responsibility in the same organization. The party's nomenklatura system governed both appointive and elective positions; as a result, the political elite tended to be a self-recruiting, self-perpetuating group, and the party controlled the key to membership. It follows that since access to command posts in all important spheres of social and political life was controlled by the same set of party officials rather than through electoral processes within mutually independent organizations, a successful career depended largely on such factors as personal and organizational ties to political patrons. Thus, Soviet elites often cultivated clientelistic relationships with powerful superiors, enjoying promotions when their patrons prospered and suffering declines when they fell from favor.

The changes under Gorbachev have altered this model and have begun to push the political system in the direction of democracy and pluralism. Democratization began as a campaign launched by Gorbachev in 1987 and 1988, but it acquired its own snowballing momentum in 1989 and 1990. Gorbachev's intent was to weaken the obstructive power of the party and state bureaucracy, which was resisting the moderate economic reforms he promoted in his first two years in power. As Gorbachev outlined democratization in his speeches and articles through 1987 and 1988, the concept entailed three areas of political reform. The first was the invigoration of meaningful popular participation in the soviets, workplaces, and other institutions; the second was a devolution of power within the Communist party from the bureaucracy to the rank-and-file members; and the third was a shift of power away from the party and toward the government.

Gorbachev signalled his interest in democratization in a major address to the Central Committee plenum (a plenum is a meeting of the full membership of the party's Central Committee) in January 1987. There he denounced the deformations that had been allowed to accumulate in the model of socialism in the Soviet Union.[69] Socialist values such as *collectivism* and patriotism had declined, he stated, while consumerism, parasitism, and social ills such as alcohol abuse and crime had increased. In some cases certain members of the party – state leadership itself had degenerated to the point where they were "accomplices in — if not organizers of — criminal activities."[70] The restructuring of the whole society, not just successful economic reform, depended on carrying out a "deep democratization." "Democracy," Gorbachev said in his concluding remarks at the plenum, "is as necessary to us as air."[71]

What did Gorbachev mean by democracy? As became clear over the next two years, Gorbachev intended and carried out profound changes in the political system.

As far as the party was concerned, he called for breathing new life into the purely ceremonial forms of party elections, so that especially at lower levels party executives would be elected by party committees and would answer to them. Yet Gorbachev did not offer to give up the party's nomenklatura system or his own power to remove uncooperative opponents. He also demanded an end to the common practice by which party officials tended to usurp the proper sphere of authority of government and managerial executives through excessive and unwarranted interference in their activity. Such meddling, Gorbachev declared, reduced the party's ability to exercise broader strategic leadership. But this idea was hardly radical either, since every party leader from Lenin's time forward had denounced the habitual tendency for local party officials to step in and intervene in the activity of administrators and line managers. Since party officials bore ultimate responsibility for the performance of officials under their jurisdiction, it was difficult for them to stand aside, given the parallelism of party and government organization.

Two of Gorbachev's policy initiatives associated with the democratization campaign did, however, have important consequences. The first was the stepping up of the *glasnost* campaign. *Glasnost*, or openness in public discussion and mass communications, was a policy entitling journalists and the public generally to reveal information and express opinions more freely than in the past. It opened party and governmental operations to greater — though certainly not complete — public scrutiny. It thus had the effect of rendering officials more accountable to the public, who were better able to judge for themselves the system's performance. In calling for wider *glasnost*, Gorbachev also cautioned the media to exercise discretion and responsibility: "The press must support *glasnost* in the country and inform our people," he declared. "But it must do so responsibly — this wish we would articulate. The press must not get distracted by sensationalism and the search for hot news."[72] But by granting newspaper editors, journalists, writers, scientists, and ordinary citizens far wider freedom to express themselves, Gorbachev was setting in motion a dynamic of continuous pressure to push back the limits of tolerated expression.

The other change Gorbachev presented beginning in January 1987, and continuing through the constitutional amendments enacted at the end of 1988, was a fundamental alteration of the system of soviets. Gorbachev pointed out that throughout the Soviet political system, administrative power had tended to replace elective institutions. Elective bodies tended to be purely formal and were overshadowed by executive organs. As a result, accountability to the citizenry had declined. This was true, he declared, in the government, the party, and other social institutions. One consequence of the loss of democratic accountability was the officials' abuse of power. As a result, it was necessary to increase the role of elective institutions in the party and government. To make elections more meaningful and to improve the democratic accountability of elected officials, he called for wider use of competition, where more candidates would run for election than there were seats.

Gorbachev stepped up the pressure for democratization in his remarkable address to the general party conference held in June–July 1988. There he laid out a vision of a political system with genuine parliamentary institutions: competitively elected soviets at all levels which would have meaningful budgetary and policy-making powers; a state governed by law in which a Committee on Constitutional Supervision would serve as guardian of the supremacy of the constitution; and, at the top, a new two-tiered legislative structure with a large, broadly representative Congress of People's Deputies, which would in turn elect a smaller working parliament (for which the old name of Supreme Soviet would be retained). This newly created parliament would have the power to discuss and decide basic policy questions; would determine the composition of government; and would oversee the state bureaucracy. These proposals were accepted by the party conference, subjected to a brief nationwide publicity campaign, and enacted with minor changes by the old Supreme Soviet in December 1988. In turn, the creation of a new constitutionally mandated system of competitive elections and working soviets generated further pressures from the public for opportunities for political participation and interest articulation.

As Figure 13.1 indicates, the new legislative system created by the constitutional changes of 1988 resulted in a parliamentary structure virtually identical to Gorbachev's plan. The Congress of People's Deputies, with 2,250 seats, of which two-thirds were filled by direct popular elections and one-third by a group of all-union social organizations that included the Communist party, the Komsomol, the trade unions, the Academy of Sciences, and other groups, elects the members of a smaller, working parliament called the Supreme Soviet. The Supreme Soviet, with 542 members, is in session eight to nine months of the year and has the main responsibility for debating and adopting legislative acts. The Supreme Soviet has been considerably more active than the purely ceremonial Supreme Soviet which it replaced, but has not fulfilled its promise of addressing the

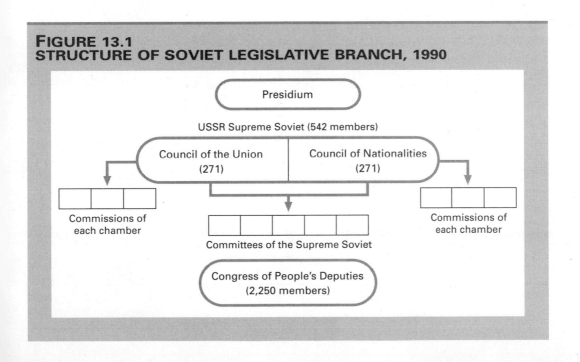

FIGURE 13.1
STRUCTURE OF SOVIET LEGISLATIVE BRANCH, 1990

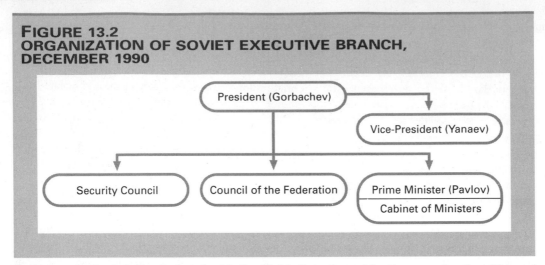

FIGURE 13.2
ORGANIZATION OF SOVIET EXECUTIVE BRANCH, DECEMBER 1990

Note: The president heads the Security Council and the Council of the Federation, and directly oversees the prime minister and Cabinet of Ministries. The vice-president has no executive duties but replaces the president in the event of the president's death or incapacitation.

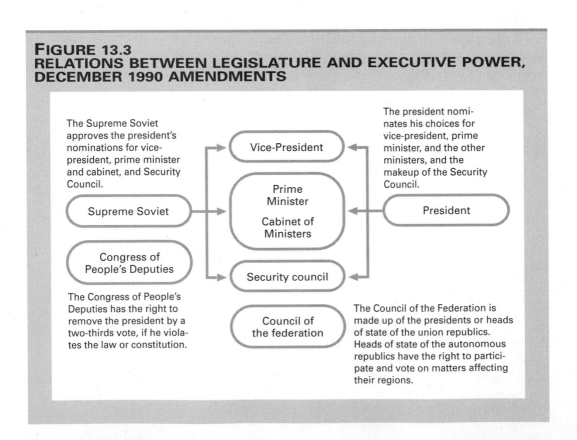

FIGURE 13.3
RELATIONS BETWEEN LEGISLATURE AND EXECUTIVE POWER, DECEMBER 1990 AMENDMENTS

The Supreme Soviet approves the president's nominations for vice-president, prime minister and cabinet, and Security Council.

The president nominates his choices for vice-president, prime minister, and the other ministers, and the makeup of the Security Council.

The Congress of People's Deputies has the right to remove the president by a two-thirds vote, if he violates the law or constitution.

The Council of the Federation is made up of the presidents or heads of state of the union republics. Heads of state of the autonomous republics have the right to participate and vote on matters affecting their regions.

country's major economic and political problems. One of its sorest weaknesses has been its inability to enforce compliance with its laws on the part of the vast state bureaucracy. Members of the Supreme Soviet have virtually no independent resources for developing legislative initiatives or monitoring the executive branch, and there are only the barest outlines of a system of parliamentary parties. Administration and staff work for the Supreme Soviet are handled by its Presidium, which most observers consider to be more a creature of the state bureaucracy than of the legislature itself.

In early 1990 and again at the end of the year, Gorbachev proposed plans for reorganizing the executive branch. Under the December 1990 scheme (Figure 13.2), approved by the Congress of People's Deputies, executive power in the USSR is overseen by the president. The president heads three bodies: a Security Council (responsible for national security policy and related issues); the Council of the Federation (which is made up of the heads of state of all the union republics and is charged with coordinating the relations between the union government and the republics); and the Cabinet of Ministers. The Cabinet is a smaller successor to the old Council of Ministers and is directed by a prime minister, who in turn is responsible to the president. In addition, Gorbachev created a vice-presidency which, much as in the United States, is an office with little direct responsibility or power and exists principally to ensure a smooth succession in the event of the president's demise or incapacitation.

The new Soviet system thus created is a peculiar amalgam of elements of parliamentary and presidential-type systems and might best be compared to the hybrid system of the French Fifth Republic. The Soviet Parliament is at least formally similar to that of other parliamentary regimes in that the legislature has the right to approve the composition of the government (Figure 13.3) and to force its resignation through a vote of no confidence. On the other hand, the executive branch itself is overseen by a powerful, independent chief executive in the person of the president.[73] The president serves for a five-year term and can be reelected once. His powers are very broad, although there are some limits on it. He can declare a state of emergency in a region or entire republic and impose a regime of "presidential rule" that suspends the powers of the civil authorities. (He must, however, have the agreement of the government of the region concerned or, failing that, the approval of the USSR Supreme Soviet.) He can veto

laws of the Supreme Soviet, although his veto can be overridden by a two-thirds vote of the Supreme Soviet. He can be removed by the Congress of People's Deputies if two-thirds of the deputies find that he has violated Soviet law or the constitution.

In addition to his wide constitutional powers, Gorbachev sought and received a grant of special temporary power from the Supreme Soviet in September 1990 to adopt whatever measures he deemed necessary to overcome the economic crisis and to preserve public order. This action followed a lengthy deadlock over economic policy between the Russian republic's government under Boris Yeltsin, the state economic bureaucracy, and the reform-minded economic advisers around Gorbachev. Unable to reach any agreement itself on policy, the Supreme Soviet in effect surrendered its power to make economic policy. In fact, neither the legislative nor the executive structures created by Gorbachev have been able to reverse the accelerating breakdown of the economy.

The weakness of the new legislative and executive organs in the face of the country's overwhelming problems illustrates the point that, in the struggle between a declining but resilient old system and the forces unleashed by *glasnost* and democratization, the power of newly created formal institutions at the all-union level is very tenuous. Gorbachev evidently hoped that, by creating a new framework of parliamentary institutions, he could channel popular energies into support for his policies. This strategy failed, however. Many of the popular movements centered on demands that could not be met or that Gorbachev was unwilling to grant, such as the demands for secession by several union republics. The state bureaucracy, on the other hand, has continued to resist meaningful reform. The political crisis that has resulted demonstrates the impossibility of adapting old institutions to the explosion of participatory demands from society awakened by *perestroika*. As many observers have commented, the situation is reminiscent of the short interval between the February Revolution of 1917, when, under the impact of World War I and widespread mass discontent, the tsarist dynasty collapsed and power passed to a weak democratic regime, and the October Revolution of 1917, when the Marxist revolutionaries of the Bolshevik party capitalized on the growing chaos and popular disillusionment, and seized power in the name of the working class.[74]

"In countries governed by authoritarian regimes," Robert Dahl has observed, "pressures for organizational autonomy are like coiled springs precariously restrained by the counterforce of the state and ready to unwind whenever the system is jolted." [75] The transition from authoritarian rule, therefore, is better conceptualized as two streams of change that overlap, rather than a single process. [76] The first is a *liberalization* of the political system that grants greater political rights — such as expression and association — to citizens and groups. This phase may be understood as a limited opening of the regime where the rulers tolerate a certain degree of public opposition in the expectation that popular demands can be vented and modest policy reforms accepted, without shaking the foundations of the rulers' power. Under some circumstances, however, such as when powerful pressures for participation and change have accumulated, when the regime itself is divided by hardliners and moderates, or when there is strong external pressure on the regime, a cycle of *popular mobilization* may rapidly follow the initial, halting steps by the regime toward a controlled liberalization. Social groups spring up, activating followers, and take to the streets to demand further changes. As society grows politicized and mobilized, it demands the ouster of the old rulers and their replacement: to avoid being overthrown, the rulers may seek some negotiated agreement on the transfer of power. This was the case, for example, in the "velvet revolution" in Czechoslovakia in November 1989. In other cases, a recalcitrant, unyielding ruler may be forcibly overthrown, as was Nicolae Ceausescu in Romania in December 1989.

In some important respects, the Soviet transition has followed this pattern: that is, Gorbachev's program of democratization — intended as a guided, controlled, but nonetheless genuine opening of the political system to greater participation and competition. The *glasnost* campaign and the efforts to open soviet elections to competitive races had the effect of expanding political rights, because they stimulated the widening and deepening of public debate about the basic tenets of Soviet socialism. [77] From Gorbachev's standpoint, they undoubtedly had an instrumental value in helping him to overcome the power and resistance of the inherited bureaucracy to his reforms. Never did he suggest, in 1987 and 1988, as he offered an increasingly far-reaching vision of democratization, that he intended to jettison the all-important principle of party rule itself, or even to encourage the formation of opposition parties. Indeed, in February 1989, addressing a conference of blue-collar workers, he derided the very idea of a multiparty democracy

under socialism as "nonsensical." His idea was that pluralism at the level of public debate and expression did not necessarily have to lead to a fuller democratization of political power.

Popular Political Mobilization

The dynamic of limited liberalization from above followed by an increase in the organized pressure from society for more rights and freedoms, resulting in further concessions from above, in turn leading to still more politicization and activation of mass politics, soon acquires a momentum of its own that cannot be controlled by the regime except at the price of enormous bloodshed (and its high cost to the regime's international reputation). The process of democratization results in a peaceful transition (1) if the leadership is willing to concede power without resorting to coercive suppression of its opponents (and this depends on the civilian leadership's ability to preserve the support of the military and secret police) *and* (2) if the opposition is sufficiently united and cohesive as it tests the limits of the regime's tolerance to prevent popular demands from spilling out of the limits of acceptable political behavior. Often in such revolutionary settings, mass frustrations and grievances, having accumulated over a long period, sweep away the more moderate and liberally minded leadership that could mediate between regime and opposition, and instead thrust forward maximalist or demagogic leaders, with the result that confrontation results in new violence and repression. A willingness and capacity to compromise on both sides is thus required if the transition is to be negotiated peacefully and result in a democratic outcome.

In the case of the Soviet Union, new channels of participation and recruitment quickly sprang up in response to the new opening that Gorbachev's democratic reforms provided. In 1986 and especially 1987 and 1988, an explosion of associational activity in society occurred. [78] Much of this activity was not explicitly political, and it took form in rock music groups, bodybuilding and martial arts clubs, loose associations of pacifists, hippies, religious mystics, and cultural and environmental preservation movements. Even groups that have no political agenda as such, however, are *implicitly* political in a communist system, because they are outside the network of party controls over ideology and personnel selection. They therefore may become nuclei of opposition ideas and organization. Moreover, in a rapidly changing environment, the clash between groups seeking to preserve their independence and the party – state bureaucracy often tends to politicize and radicalize society. With time, therefore, and particularly as opportunities opened up for forms of political expression, such as mass demonstrations, publication of independent newsletters and leaflets, and electoral campaigning, which did not incur repression from the authorities, more and more groups were drawn into politics. This politicization of the informal groups seems to have been given its greatest impetus in the spring of 1988, as society was drawn into the debate over democratization.[79] Broadly speaking, two processes occurred simultaneously over the 1987 – 1989 period: the proliferation of independent social associations (Soviet authorities estimated that 30,000 unofficial groups had formed in 1988, and perhaps as many as 60,000 by 1989); and the aggregation of smaller groups into larger movements and organizations.

One of the most common forms of independent, organized political activity in the 1988 – 1989 period was the *popular front*. Typically, the popular front is a broad popular movement with a democratic orientation that aggregates several overlapping causes: environmental preservation, the expansion of political freedoms, and, when they are organized along national lines, greater rights for a national society and territory. The first to form were those in the Baltic republics, Estonia, Latvia, and Lithuania, where over the 1988 – 1989 period they quickly grew from loose groupings of the cultural and scientific intelligentsia into broad movements with mass followings and organized branches in every town. Their power to mobilize support from the population (including — significantly — substantial elements of the Russian minorities living in the Baltic republics) was demonstrated most impressively in the March 1989 elections to the new Congress of People's Deputies.

The popular fronts and other grass-roots political organizations that sprang up in the 1987 – 1990 period have provided new channels of mass political participation. Often they have gone beyond the limits of what the authorities are willing to tolerate. Some peaceful demonstrations have ended in violence and bloodshed. One of the most shocking incidents occurred in Tbilisi, capital of the Georgian republic, in April 1989, when troops broke up a peaceful rally for Georgian independence and sovereignty with brutal force, leaving at least nineteen people dead. The Tbilisi killings in turn strengthened Georgian demands for independence. A similar incident

occurred in Kazakhstan in December 1986, in one of the first nationality-related mass political demonstrations of the Gorbachev period. Moscow engineered the removal of the first secretary of the Communist party of Kazakhstan, an ethnic Kazakh named Dinmukhamed Kunaev, and replaced him with an ethnic Russian, Gennadii Kolbin. As news of the decision spread through the capital city of the republic, Alma-Ata, thousands of people, most of them young Kazakhs, gathered on the main square of Alma-Ata to protest the firing of a Kazakh and the appointment of a Russian in his place. Although the Moscow authorities claimed that the crowd attacked the police who were there to maintain order, all eyewitnesses agree that the police moved in to break up the demonstration with violence and that, as a result, dozens of people were killed and many hundreds seriously injured.[80] In the eyes of many Kazakh people, according to Martha Brill Olcott, "the violent repression of the peaceful demonstration is seen as but another manifestation of official Russia's long history of harsh retaliation against the Kazakhs' efforts at political self-expression." One of the people who have emerged as leaders of the Kazakh national movement, the writer Olzhas Suleimenov, has indicated that the incident forced him to rethink his own political and personal goals, spurring him to become a champion of the Kazakh national cause.[81]

The popular fronts did not initially conceive their role as opposition parties, nor were their early demands particularly radical. With time, however, as their popularity grew and the opportunities for political expression expanded, they became the primary channel for articulating national and regional interests. The response of local Communist party officials was varied: in the Baltic republics, the party generally adopted a cooperative and conciliatory attitude toward the new movements, whereas in most other republics and regions, party officials took a repressive line. Generally speaking, the popular fronts reflected liberal democratic values, expressing support for market-oriented economic reform, multiparty competition, and political decentralization. At the same time, in the union republics, popular fronts were always vehicles for advancing national interests. In some republics, such as Moldavia, there was considerable tension between the moderate and intellectual-dominated leadership of the popular front and the more extremist popular base of support.[82]

Nationalist demands in a multinational state such as the Soviet Union are extremely sensitive, and not just

Lithuanians stand in front of a tank as Red Army soldiers take over the main printing house in Vilnius on January 11, 1991.

because national movements demand greater independence for their territories. Still more destabilizing are the implications of national sovereignty by a dominant group for ethnic minorities within their borders. In many cases regions populated by minorities counter a declaration of sovereignty by the titular nationality of a republic with declarations of sovereignty of their own. In Moldavia, for example, two internal minority populations — a Turkic group called the Gagauz and a group of Russians —countered the Moldavian national movement with declarations of independence for their own territories. By the end of 1990 all fifteen of the union republics had either adopted declarations of sovereignty or were close to doing so, and dozens of smaller internal territories had responded to these with similar declarations of their own. Some regions and cities closed themselves off economically to others; some prevented anyone from outside the region from purchasing goods within it, while others adopted laws on language use that discriminated against members of minority groups. Nearly all declarations of sovereignty asserted exclusive legal claims of property rights over all natural resources within a particular territory, further exacerbating the country's severe economic difficulties. By the end of 1990 over 600,000 people had fled their homes because of interethnic violence and discrimination and were living in other parts of the Soviet Union, and as many as half a million more in 1990 alone had emigrated from the Soviet Union.[83] The spiral of claims and counter-claims to sovereign rights threatened to undermine all bases of Soviet state power, including the traditional claim that all Soviet citizens were entitled to equal protection under the law. The struggle between central authority and the claims to sovereignty by republican and local governments, which some called the war of laws, led to deadlock and paralysis in a number of policy areas. For example, a decree issued by the USSR Council of Ministers on November 15, 1990, raising prices on a number of luxury goods was immediately countered by a decision of the legislature of the Russian republic declaring the decree invalid on the territory of the Russian republic.[84] But political measures such as trade restrictions were unable to stem the critical decline in economic output. A measure of the severity of the crisis in the fall of 1990 was the bitter fact that, in the face of the most abundant grain crop in many years, much grain would be left to rot in the fields because of the shortage of fuel, labor, farm machinery, and transportation to bring in the harvest.

Soviet workers have also been active in voicing their demands for better working conditions and greater control over their enterprises. In the most massive demonstration of labor unity since the days of the civil war, some 400,000 Soviet coal miners in the Ukraine, the Far North, and Siberia walked out in the summer of 1989. The strike committees and independent labor unions they formed have since become powerful political organizations, and the independent coal miners union has replaced the old official union as the voice of organized miners. Strikes have become widespread: in the spring of 1990, the Soviet press reported that an average of 130,000 workers per day were on strike in the first quarter of the year.[85] Representatives of independent strike committees won a number of races to national and local soviets in races in 1990 and have had some success in bargaining with the regime for improved conditions. Yet many of the newly empowered labor groups have found that against the backdrop of a general economic crisis, the lives of workers have continued to deteriorate. One twenty-eight-year-old chairman of a strike committee and regional miners union in Karaganda, in the republic of Kazakhstan, bitterly commented: "The truth is that for all the gains we appeared to make during the strike in July 1989, life now is a lot worse. Now that the state stores are completely empty, the only way to buy things is on the private market, or even on the black market. And that costs a lot more than anything we ever got in raises." Asked whether socialism should be discarded in favor of capitalism, he replied: "Hell, yes, I'm for capitalism. The first thing I did when I took over at the union was take Lenin's picture down from the office wall. When the relative success of the West stares you in the face, why should you be afraid of the word we learned to hate in school? Yes, I'm ready to be a capitalist. The question is, how?"[86]

The consolidation of new political parties, labor unions, popular fronts, and elected legislatures thus proceeded in the face of overwhelming economic and political problems. Many of the informal organizations that had sprung up during the heyday of *glasnost* in 1987 and 1988 focused their energies on capturing seats in the newly democratized legislative organs established

by Gorbachev's constitutional reforms of 1988. The 1989 elections for the Congress of People's Deputies of the USSR galvanized many of the new organizations into electoral competition. In the Baltic republics especially, the popular fronts recorded remarkable victories, winning two-thirds of all the seats they contested.[87] Very quickly the popular fronts became the dominant political organizations of the Baltic republics, displacing the Communist parties. In other cities, especially over the winter and spring of 1990, the strength of the new informal groups was reflected in the strong showing for insurgent groups in city soviets. In some cities, as in Moscow, Leningrad, Sverdlovsk, and elsewhere, coalitions of candidates identified with liberal democratic views won majorities of seats. In the newly elected legislatures, quasi-party blocs formed, gradually defining the ideological lines and creating the basis for the eventual emergence of full-blown political parties.

The mobilization of popular political participation has also generated new leadership. In many areas it has forced former Communist party and government executives to adapt to a pluralized political environment that they can no longer control. Some have been swept away, some have managed to hold on to their power, and a few have emerged as champions of reform. A prominent example of the latter is Boris Yeltsin. Yeltsin, who like Gorbachev was born in 1931, had a conventional political career for a provincial party boss. One month after Gorbachev's selection as party leader, Yeltsin was transferred to Moscow and early in 1986 was named first secretary of the Moscow city party organization — a vital and also extremely visible post. Shortly afterward, he was also brought into the party Politburo as a candidate (nonvoting) member. He lasted as Moscow party chief until he was formally removed in November 1987 for speaking out against Gorbachev at the October 1987 Central Committee plenum. Long before that, he had antagonized most of the leading party politicians by his heavy-handed, confrontational methods and his radical policy line. Firing most of the district party committee leaders, he became an advocate of the cause of the long-suffering Soviet consumer and railed against the privileges of bureaucrats. Impatient with the slow pace with which *perestroika* was being implemented, he attacked conservative opponents of reform and criticized Gorbachev for failing to fight hard enough for change. The final straw was his demand that the party accept his resignation from the Moscow post at the Central Committee plenum in October 1987, which was supposed to be devoted to the more ceremonial business of preparing for the celebration of the seventieth anniversary of the October Revolution. This move provoked an outpouring of public criticism of Yeltsin by his colleagues in the party leadership, and he was removed from his position as Moscow city party chief and member of the Politburo (although he was given a position as deputy minister of construction and remained a member of the Central Committee).[88]

Political disgrace such as this would traditionally have ended a Soviet party politician's career; in Stalin's time it would also have ended his life. But skillfully positioning himself as a populist democrat who had been made a martyr by the party establishment, Yeltsin mounted a remarkable political comeback. In the 1989 elections to the Congress of People's Deputies, he ran as a candidate for a Moscow-wide seat. In a stunning landslide, Yeltsin won his race with nearly 90 percent of the vote. His victory gave him a new mantle of democratic legitimacy which none of the other top party leaders possessed: Gorbachev, in glaring contrast, had never subjected himself to a popular vote for a political job. Yeltsin's immense prestige and authority were further heightened the following year, when he ran for the Russian Republic Congress of People's Deputies from his old political base of Sverdlovsk. Here he defeated a field of twelve rivals and won his seat with 70 percent of the vote. Subsequently, when the Congress convened in June 1990, he was elected its chairman. He further flaunted his independence in July 1990 by quitting the Communist party entirely. In June 1991 he won a convincing first-ballot majority in his Russia-wide race for the new post of president of the Russian republic. His enormous popularity, Russia's importance within the union, and his courage in rallying resistance to the August 1991 coup d'état made Yeltsin a powerful rival to Gorbachev.[89]

For the most part, however, examples of successful adaptation by political figures from the old establishment to the new pluralistic and democratic political environment are rare. Most of the old nomenklatura officials have either been swept aside or have resisted democratization from their bureaucratic strongholds. The greatest share of the new political elites has therefore emerged from outside the old political establishment. Many are members of the "prestige elite," especially the cultural and scientific intelligentsia. Writers, musicians, poets, physicians, professors, and journalists make up a striking proportion of the new political elite.

POLITICAL SOCIALIZATION AND PUBLIC OPINION

Propaganda and Communist Ideology

Traditionally, communist leaders in the Soviet Union assigned high priority to maintaining a comprehensive program for shaping the beliefs and values of the population. The system of formal political socialization embraced virtually every setting of education and communication in society — from schools and youth activity, to the mass media, the arts, and popular culture, and to collective activity in the workplace, place of residence, and avocational groups. As much as possible, influences that contradicted Marxist-Leninist doctrine were excluded, while the rhetoric of public life constantly reaffirmed the doctrine of the leading role of the Communist party, the superiority of socialism, devotion to the Soviet fatherland, and the correctness of the party's general policies at home and abroad. Because of the importance the regime assigned to the means of mass communications as agencies of political socialization and of mass mobilization, it saturated Soviet society with multiple channels of print and broadcast communications.[90]

The doctrine that guided political socialization — the doctrine called *Marxism-Leninism* — was based on the ideas of Karl Marx and Friedrich Engels as interpreted and applied by Vladimir Lenin and the Soviet Communist party leaders. Each new leadership that came to power reinterpreted Marxist-Leninist ideas to serve its policy interests, often discarding concepts promulgated by the preceding leaders. The doctrine was highly flexible and was interpreted to justify the preferences and decisions of the party leadership. Ideological doctrine and political authority were always closely linked, because power and ideology legitimated one another. This pattern was a source of strength as long as there was no serious challenge to the leaders' power or policy. But it also gave rise to a dogmatic intolerance of any criticism of the tenets of the doctrine itself, or of the leaders' interpretation of it. Dogmatism in the Brezhnev period, as under Stalin, stifled innovation and serious discussion of the trends affecting society.

The party's demand for full loyalty to the party and its doctrines prohibited any alternative doctrines from being aired in public life. In foreign policy, the doctrine of peaceful coexistence with the capitalist world referred to the possibility that conflicting social systems, socialism and capitalism, might have correct and even cooperative relations at the level of diplomacy, trade and cultural, and scientific contacts, but that at the fundamental level of ideas, the two ideologies were ultimately incompatible and that socialism would in the end triumph over capitalism because of its intrinsic superiority. Soviet leaders, especially the more conservative of them, have always been suspicious of any notion that the struggle between the world system of capitalism and the world system of socialism should be put aside in favor of a convergence of ideologies. They often quoted Lenin to the effect that any weakening of socialist ideology would inevitably lead to a strengthening of bourgeois ideology. The state's propaganda system thus had a twofold purpose: to persuade Soviet people of the correctness of party doctrine, and to prevent hostile ideologies from winning adherents.

The elaborate machinery for propagating and defending ideology included the following basic features:

1. Efforts to persuade parents to make the family an instrument for raising children steeped in communist morality, firm faith in the party and its leadership, a positive attitude toward labor, confidence in the socialist future, and intolerance toward hostile worldviews, such as religion. Because the family was the least amenable to control by the party authorities, however, and because it tended to protect value systems at odds with the official ideology, the family has long been the most important agency of transmission of liberal democratic values, national awareness, and religious faith.

2. School. The impact of schooling on political socialization entailed both the curriculum, where lessons in history, social studies, literature, and other subjects were used to reinforce political doctrines, and a system of organized youth activities, divided into three age categories. Each combined play, recreation and basic socialization with political indoctrination appropriate to the age level.

    a. The Young Octobrists was an organization that provided organized activities for children just starting school, from seven to nine years of age.

    b. The Pioneers, for children from ten to fourteen, sponsored after-school groups and summer camps where children learned a spirit of collectivism and regimentation; were taught reverence for the country, Lenin, the party, and other values; and were prepared for admission to the next and last group, the Komsomol.

    c. *Komsomol* was the organization for youth from ages fifteen to twenty-eight. It operated as an auxiliary organization to the Communist party and was organized along almost identical lines. It took in nearly all children after Pioneers, but most dropped out after finishing school and military service. It aimed at inculcating an attitude of political responsibility, readiness to serve the party and the country, and a knowledgeable and convinced mastery of political doctrine. In reality, it functioned as a kind of ministry of youth, because Komsomol frequently controlled access to desirable recreational activities, such as camping trips, dances, and discotheques.

3. The mass media. Officially, the broadcast and print media were to serve as instruments of political socialization in addition to their roles as conduits of needed information, exhortation to work hard and well, criticism of problems, and some feedback from the public through letters. They were thus called on to mold the consciousness of the population while at the same time combatting the system's inefficiencies. All mass media organizations were under the ideological authority of the party through its department of propaganda and similar departments charged with ideological oversight in every lower party committee.

4. Oral political indoctrination. The party managed a large and differentiated network of channels for communicating with people on a face-to-face basis. Most of this effort was conducted by spare-time activists who took on an assignment as a speaker or lecturer to fulfill their obligation to the party to carry out some form of social work on a voluntary basis. Over time the party developed a complex array of settings for oral indoctrination and political education.

Despite the enormous spread of newspapers, radio, and television as channels of information, the party in the Brezhnev era made every effort to increase the scope of oral propaganda. As many as 11 million people were recruited to serve as activists and take on work in agitation, political education, delivering lectures and reports, and related tasks. Yet studies showed that the impact of this effort was extremely low and even counterproductive. Why then was so much attention given to propaganda? Scholars have offered various reasons. One is inertia. The section of the party concerned with ideological propaganda and control justified its existence by ever greater displays of quantitative success, increasing the number of people reached and activists recruited. A second reason is fear. The leadership behaved as though it genuinely believed its claim that any weakening of socialist ideology must necessarily lead to a rise of hostile counter-ideologies. However ineffective the party's ideological effort may have been, it helped to prevent alternative ideologies from arising. A third reason may have been the awareness that the Soviet people continued to rely very heavily on word-of-mouth communication to gather information and to form opinion. Study after study showed that, despite the saturation of society by the mass media, direct interpersonal conversation among friends, family, and co-workers continued to be one of the main sources of information transmission and the shaping of public opinion.[91] Oral propaganda was intended to combat the power of the "unmedia" by helping to set a climate of opinion that favored party doctrine. For that reason, oral propaganda concentrated heavily on the workplace, where daily interaction among workers created a milieu conducive to the formation of group opinion. In any event, no Soviet leader until Gorbachev was willing to relinquish the party's monopoly on ideology. Even Gorbachev, when he first came to office, used the traditional powers of the general secretary to reprogram and redirect party propaganda, rather than to dismantle the system itself.

Gorbachev very quickly set his own stamp on the propaganda system, declaring that society was in need of an "acceleration" of the tempo of socioeconomic progress. This was to be achieved by a campaign to upgrade the technological level of Soviet industry, and especially by introducing computers and information technology widely into the economy. Another of Gorbachev's early policy themes, around which an old-fashioned ideological campaign was mounted, was his assault on alcohol abuse. Within two months of his coming to power, officials were forbidden to drink in public, numerous liquor stores were closed, hours for purchases of liquor were limited, and a number of plants producing wines and spirits were closed or turned to other purposes. Yet another of the new policy themes was the encouragement of more honest and open criticism of problems in society—a policy identified by the term *glasnost*.

For many of the institutions charged with propagating ideological doctrine and guarding against discordant ideas, adaptation to the new line set by Moscow required a simple and familiar response. Newspaper editorials repeated the new themes. Lecturers, political information speakers, party school instructors, factory agitators, teachers in school, professors in institutions of higher education, resolutions adopted at public meetings, and officials addressing ordinary working people —all echoed the pronouncements of the party leadership, as if a new tape cassette had been dropped into a machine and countless loudspeakers began broadcasting the new message.

At a still more basic level, primary political socialization, the reformist line of the new leadership in the mid-1980s did not alter either the forms or content of "communist upbringing." In day care facilities and in schools, teachers continued to teach children to revere Lenin as one who loved humankind and embodied its highest ideals. As in the past, basic moral education was identified with inculcating communist convictions. Even in secondary school and higher educational institutions, until around 1989, the curriculum was little affected by the ideological ferment occurring in society. Students continued to be required to pass courses reflecting memorization of Lenin's and the party's teachings. A scandal occurred in history education in the spring of 1988 when, all across the Soviet Union, history exams in secondary schools had to be canceled because the old history textbooks were considered inaccurate (they glossed over the magnitude of Stalin's terror) and new textbooks were not available. Yet on the whole, the old structures of ideological indoctrination and control continued to soldier on in a traditional spirit until 1989–1990, when the radical changes in the leadership's thinking and behavior finally provoked a crisis at all levels of the propaganda and socialization system.

The mass media also reflect the power of inertia and the slowness with which the ideological changes made at the top ripple out across the hierarchy of media organizations. The mass media had always been subject to a variety of cross-cutting controls. The supply of newsprint was controlled by a state monopoly. All printing equipment had to be licensed by the government. Selection of all senior editorial personnel was approved under the party nomenklatura system. All editorial content was subject to the party's ideological sector. Although unofficial, independent publications existed (called *samizdat*, or "self-publishing"), these were illegal, and their publishers and distributors could be arrested and charged with spreading anti-Soviet propaganda.

Therefore, in the beginning the *glasnost* campaign had all the earmarks of another shift in the ideological line: new targets were authorized for public criticism, past leaders were criticized for their mistakes, new promises were made to the people about the "acceleration" of economic progress, a more liberal attitude was adopted to discussions of material incentives and the need to activate "the human factor" to raise productivity. A sweeping wave of replacements of heads of media establishments occurred (just as there were very high levels of turnover among party and government officials, ambassadors, and military commanders). The content changed somewhat, but the party's methods of control over ideology and propaganda remained intact in Gorbachev's early years.

The *glasnost* campaign had far-reaching consequences, however, that eventually produced a significant feedback effect on the party's socialization program itself by discrediting socialism both in theory and practice. By late 1990 public opinion polls revealed that no more than 10 to 20 percent of the population professed support for the socialist principles on which the state was founded.[92] A poll of nearly 2,700 people throughout the Soviet Union in December 1989 found that 48 percent considered themselves religious believers, but only 6 percent thought that Marxism-Leninism had the answers to the country's problems.[93] Another countrywide survey in 1989 found that 61 percent of the respondents supported the principle of legalizing private property and only 11 percent opposed it.[94] In 1989 and 1990 there were many other indications of the power and speed of popular rejection of communist ideology.

At the same time, the position taken by Gorbachev and the party leadership grew progressively more unorthodox, until by 1990 almost nothing of the old Marxist-Leninist doctrine remained. The theory of the international class struggle between capitalism and socialism was gone; the party's leading role had been abandoned in favor of support for multiparty competition and parliamentary politics; and Gorbachev called his domestic program a transition to a "social market economy." By the end of 1990 Marxism-Leninism as such was essentially defunct. The doctrine had been abandoned in all essential points by the Communist party, and the party itself had lost its power to rule the country's ideological life.

Counterideologies and Political Pluralism

Over the 1987–1990 period, as the party's ideological controls broke down, public discussion grew increasingly free. Positions that had formerly been confined to private conversations or were considered illegal dissent could now be the basis for a letter to the editor, a protest demonstration, or a group manifesto. A variety of alternative ideologies fought for acceptance, mobilizing support for candidates for soviets or demanding the right to publish their own newspapers. For the most part, the newly articulate movements were voicing ideas that long had circulated in unofficial political culture. What were the main ideological alternatives in Soviet public opinion which emerged into the open under the impact of *glasnost* and liberalization? Broadly speaking, two sets of political values dominated public life in the late 1980s: ethnonationalism and liberal democracy. In many cases, these were mutually reinforcing currents of thought.

Both were given an impetus by the liberalization of political life following Stalin's death. Nikita Khrushchev's strategy following his dramatic denunciation of Stalin's crimes at the Twentieth Party Congress in 1956 was to redirect party ideology by attacking Stalin's "cult of personality" and its many harmful consequences, while holding out the promise of a renewed, cleansed socialism that would triumphantly achieve the highest form of social organization, communism. For many, however, particularly members of non-Russian nationalities where national culture and leadership had been destroyed under Stalin, the de-Stalinization campaign led to the rehabilitation of national symbols and, implicitly, attitudes of resentment toward and rejection of Soviet — and Russian — rule. For example, a generation of Ukrainian writers began to commemorate the victims of Stalin's terror (including the brutal and imposed famine of 1932–1933, when millions of Ukrainians died of starvation as a result of Stalin's collectivization campaign[95]) and the heroes of Ukrainian national culture. While not rejecting all values associated with socialism, they rejected the "Russification" of Ukrainian culture in the name of socialism. By Russification they meant the progressive elimination of Ukrainian language and culture by the spread of Russian linguistic and cultural assimilation.

The 1960s and 1970s stimulated a reassertion of national identities and ideologies throughout the Soviet Union, although the process affected different groups in different ways. The Tatars who had been forcibly resettled from their homeland on the Crimean Peninsula by Stalin during World War II agitated for a return to their homeland. Among Soviet Jews, who are officially classified as a nationality, a strong movement for the right to emigrate was stimulated by the Israeli victory in the 1967 war against Israel and Syria. As discrimination against Soviet Jews intensified in the 1970s, Soviet Jews actively campaigned against both anti-Semitism and restrictions on their freedom to emigrate. Among Georgians and Armenians, the rewriting of the constitutions of their republics in 1978 occasioned mass protest when the initial drafts threatened to eliminate the articles that had granted the status of state language to the native languages. After large-scale popular demonstrations, the authorities relented and retained state language status for the Georgian and Armenian languages in their respective republics (while giving Russian equal status in each republic). Soviet persecution of religion was the object of protest among the Lithuanian Catholics, evangelical Protestants, Jews, Ukrainian Uniate Catholics, and Russian Orthodox believers. It is important to remember that in the Soviet Union, religious adherence is closely linked with national identity, so that movements for religious rights were often associated with national revivals.

In the 1960s, 1970s, and 1980s, despite severe sanctions, groups of activists were willing to collect signatures on petitions, organize demonstrations, and seek international support. This evidence of protest movements indicates the hardiness of national feeling despite the enormous propaganda efforts by the regime to inculcate attachment to a generalized Soviet national identity. Although Soviet ideology attempted to create a bicultural and bilingual consciousness—that is, affiliation with a national language and culture plus mastery of Russian and identification with the Soviet state—many groups regarded their national culture as a victim of repression under Soviet and Russian rule.

It would be incorrect to suppose that national feeling among the non-Russian peoples is directed only against Moscow, although that is a powerful and persistent current of the political cultures of the national minorities. National consciousness in the Soviet Union, as in many other countries, also harbors strong sentiments about neighboring peoples. In some cases peoples resent the loss of parts of what they consider their national homeland, particularly when the area is populated by members of their own nationality. Since 1988 a state approaching civil war has existed between Armenia and Azerbaijan over a number of grievances, including the status of the territory of Nagorno-Karabakh, a predominantly Armenian territory controlled by Azerbaijan. Similarly, many Tadjiks believe that Samarkand and other parts of what is presently Uzbekistan should be returned to their republic. In a number of areas, groups resent what they regard as the intrusion of ethnically alien populations onto territories they regard as their own. In Central Asia, violent riots have broken out over resentments among a native group that a settler group had usurped land, housing, jobs, and other benefits. In June 1989, for example, several thousand Kazakhs set upon several hundred Lezgi, Chechen, Ingush and other North Caucasian groups in the belief that these groups were spiriting away food from the state retail distribution system and selling it at inflated prices at cooperatives, using their profits to bribe corrupt officials to obtain apartments, jobs, and residence permits. Similar factors —economic decline, high unemployment among the native population, and worsening consumer conditions —helped to spark the massacre of Meskheti Turks by an Uzbek mob in the same month.

Characteristic of many ethnic-national conflicts that have become acute in recent years in the Soviet Union is a struggle over incompatible claims for control of the same national territory. A common theme in many of the national movements, in the Soviet Union as in the Middle East and many other countries, is the identification of a nation with an ancestral homeland.[96] National groups regard pressure for assimilation to the dominant culture as a form of repression of their national identity.[97] In response, groups with claims to particular territories have asserted their rights to be sovereign masters within their borders against Moscow. In doing so, however, they are also claiming power over ethnic-national minorities within their territories, which react through protest and counter-claims of sovereignty. Throughout the Soviet Union, over 60 million people are living outside the territory where their national group is dominant or have no national territory at all. The potential for further conflict between dominant majorities and oppressed national minorities, leading to large-scale flights of refugees, is considerable.[98]

Nationalism in the Soviet Union thus takes many forms. Some national movements have embraced the goal of sovereignty of the national territory with the aim of universalizing individual rights, the rule of law, and an open, market-oriented economy. Other movements, however, have been directed primarily at settling accounts with neighboring peoples or asserting a cultural monopoly for the indigenous nationality. Nationalism can support both democratic and authoritarian political ideologies, and undoubtedly, as the heterogeneity of Soviet society increasingly replaces centralization, both types of rule will emerge in different republics.

Liberal democratic ideology is often thought to be a monopoly of the intelligentsia and to have only weak support among the majority of the population. Recent public opinion polls have confirmed, however, that support for multiparty competition, the rule of law, parliamentary democracy, individual rights, and market competition in the economy is much more widespread than previously believed.

Although polls reveal a considerable base of mass support for liberal democratic principles, the most active and articulate exponents of democracy were intellectuals, who followed an older Russian tradition of believing that it was their civic obligation to the society to stand up for ethical principles of justice and truth. Perhaps the most celebrated example of this tradition was Andrei Sakharov. Sakharov, who died in December 1989, was one of the most brilliant of the group of Soviet physicists who developed the Soviet hydrogen bomb. At the age of only thirty-two, he was elected a member of the Soviet Academy of Sciences, an extraordinary and unprecedented honor for so young a scholar. But Sakharov, like such American scientists as Robert Oppenheimer, became beset with doubts about the threat that atomic weapons could pose to humankind's peace and security. First cautiously, and later more publicly, Sakharov criticized regime policies initially on issues such as education and science policy and then on the more sensitive question of nuclear weapons testing. In the late 1960s, as the more conservative climate of the Brezhnev regime replaced the open and de-Stalinizing policies of Khrushchev, Sakharov began to play a leading role in the broader fight against restrictions on civic rights and freedoms. In 1966, together with twenty-four other celebrated figures from the worlds of science and the arts, Sakharov signed an appeal against rehabilitating Stalin and Stalinism. In 1968 he issued what became his most famous essay, "Progress, Coexistence, and Intellectual Freedom," in which he outlined his philosophy. Humankind must unite to save itself against the threats of nuclear annihilation and environmental disaster, he said. To ensure peaceful cooperation across national boundaries, governments must respect freedom of thought and action and free themselves of the deadening power of bureaucracy and ideology.

Sakharov never deviated from his principles. He became the most famous champion of the democratic movement in Soviet society and through the 1970s took up the cause of countless individuals and groups who had been repressed by the regime for peaceful political activity. In 1970, with two fellow physicists, he founded the Moscow Human Rights Committee, which inspired many later groups seeking to protect the cause of democratic freedoms and human rights in the Soviet Union. For his work he was awarded the Nobel Peace Prize in 1975; in response, the Soviet regime mounted a campaign of denunciations and slander against him. In 1980, after he had spoken out against the invasion of Afghanistan, the government forced him into exile in the closed city of Gorky, where he was almost entirely cut off from his friends and from Western sources of information. Nonetheless, despite harassment and privations, he continued his human rights work. Because of his reputation as the most outstanding symbol of the moral opposition to Soviet regime repression, Gorbachev's personal appeal to him in December 1986 to return to Moscow and to his work in science represented a stunning vindication of Sakharov's position. He continued to press for democratization and freedom. In the radically changed climate of the late 1980s, Sakharov's immense prestige enabled him to play a leading role in the democratization of Soviet society. He was elected to the Congress of People's Deputies in 1989, and he soon assumed a position as de facto head of the group of democratically oriented deputies. The outpouring of public grief, affection, and admiration following his death in December 1989 was a powerful testimonial to Sakharov's enormous stature as the embodiment of the spirit of humane and democratic values.

Sakharov was the most prominent example of a deep tradition among the Russian intelligentsia of a humanistic and democratic spirit, and through his integrity, courage, and devotion he became its most important representative in modern Soviet society. Sakharov and the many other activists who sacrificed themselves to defend democratic principles helped to activate latent strains in the Soviet and Russian political culture of civic responsibility and self-government, and, especially through their unequal struggle against the state's repressive power, they inspired further support from much broader strata of the population for liberal and democratic principles. Perhaps most importantly, they worked to demonstrate the universality of democratic ideas, especially by taking up the cause of national rights. The Soviet human rights movement in the 1960s and 1970s united activists from Moscow and other cities in the Russian republic with leaders from the movements for national self-determination from the Ukraine, the Baltic republics, and other national groups.[99]

The funeral procession for Andrei D. Sakharov brings 8,000 mourners, as it wound its way through Moscow to Lenin Stadium, where prominent Soviets paid tribute. Sakharov, a brilliant physicist, was also a tireless campaigner for human rights.

The emergence of strong popular support for values such as individual rights, tolerance, multiparty politics, parliamentary government, private property, and market competition, together with the resurgence of nationalist movements among ethnic-national populations, testify to the underlying strength of alternative ideologies, despite the efforts of Communist party propaganda to replace them with socialist ideology. They suggest that the agencies of political socialization, particularly the family, but also the arts, foreign radio and television broadcasting, and travel, have had effects independent of the regime's intentions or desires. Ellen Mickiewicz observes that the Soviet media have presented messages and images whose effects in many cases were unanticipated because of the interaction between the message and the audience: "What goes out on Soviet television bumps up against reality." In particular, with rising levels of educational attainment, media audiences have become more critical and independent in their interpretation of the content of the media. Soviet television has been successful, she suggests, in focusing attention on the West and on the United States in particular; but the impact of the images of the West that are projected is contradictory and often subverts the very lessons that the party had hoped to convey.[100]

As older civic, democratic, and nationalist traditions revive, and are reinforced by positive examples such as Sakharov, Yeltsin, and the new generation of democratic political leaders, the formal agencies of socialization are adapting to reflect and reinforce them. New textbooks are being written, and new youth groups are taking form. The present trends reflect the breakdown of the state-controlled, party-managed system of political socialization. Commercialism and partisan competition are becoming stronger influences. There is evidence of backlash phenomena, such as disenchantment with politics, moral disorientation, and a nostalgia for the simpler times when there were fewer choices. The Soviet citizen, once exposed to an intensive program of communist indoctrination, has entered a far more open and pluralistic world.

THE POLICY PROCESSES

The CPSU and Political Leadership

When we contrast the radical changes in Soviet politics that have occurred under Gorbachev with the stability that prevailed under Brezhnev, it is easy to forget that the basic directions of Soviet policy have changed repeatedly since the October Revolution. In fact, the eighteen years of Brezhnev's rule as general secretary of the CPSU were exceptional for the extremely cautious and restricted nature of policy change. The political system's capacity to recognize and respond to decay in the economy and society was so weak that by the time Brezhnev died in 1982 few inside or outside the country recognized the gravity of the country's problems. The ultracautious Brezhnev leadership evidently feared that major reform carried the risk of political destabilization and made it virtually impossible for political activists or the media to criticize the existing state of affairs.

The vigor and radicalism of Gorbachev's reform policy, however, have analogies in earlier phases of Soviet history, when leaders flexibly adapted policies and structures to new needs. Indeed, a longer look at Soviet political history reveals a wide diversity of relations between the top leader, the party hierarchy, the state bureaucracy, and the society, depending on the leaders' judgment as to the tasks of the day. For much of the first decades of the state's existence, the rulers' principal aim was to harness the revolutionary energies that had brought down the old regime and engage them in building a new society and state under the banner of socialism. Under *Vladimir Ilyich Lenin* (1870–1924), the Bolsheviks consolidated political power in the soviets —popularly elected councils performing government functions at every jurisdictional level of the state — and in the Communist party. Lenin's conception of a highly centralized state directed by a single vanguard party was innovative for the early twentieth century and became the model for many other modern authoritarian and totalitarian regimes, including those adopting fascist and Nazi ideologies.

Lenin recognized that, in order to create an organizational framework for mobilized mass participation in the running of the new state, the party would have to be separated from the day-to-day management of the affairs of state. Instead, the party would monitor, oversee, and guide decision making and policy implementation by government officials and economic functionaries. The party would serve as a check on the state bureaucracy's ability to grow too powerful, self-interested, or corrupt. The party retained formidable levers of power at its disposal in order to exercise its leadership and supervisory duties: its control over the guidelines and limits of public expression through its monopoly of ideology; its control of the elite recruitment function through the nomenklatura system; and its monopoly of final decision-making authority in all spheres of political life.[101] Lenin's conception of a division of functions between party and state organs proved to be adaptable to the very different policy and political imperatives of the early revolutionary period; the New Economic Policy of 1921–1928, Stalin's purges and terror, as well as his industrialization and collectivization campaigns, wartime and postwar reconstruction periods, Khrushchev's reforms, as well as the consolidation of power under Brezhnev. For this reason, it is worthwhile discussing the basic outlines of the Communist party's role in the political system as it existed for most of the Soviet period.

The party conceived itself as simultaneously providing political leadership in society and serving as a link between populace and regime. In each workplace, a primary party organization (PPO) — comprising all members of the party who were employed in the organization —was charged with keeping tabs on the collective mood of the workers, maintaining morale and a sense of common purpose, and intervening in operational problems. Until very recently, Soviet citizens considered it normal to approach local party activists with requests for help with a variety of problems, because the party was considered a potentially effective intermediary between ordinary citizens and the vast, often inefficient, state apparatus. Similarly, in each territorial jurisdiction, the party committee and its small staff of regular officials served as liaison between higher party headquarters and the activity of virtually every organized sector of society —factories, government, schools, farms, courts, newspapers, hobby groups, and many other institutions. The party served as a kind of nerve center from which a vast number of communications links radiated that sought to coordinate the diverse functions of a heavily bureaucratized society. Because the party attempted to avoid taking direct responsibility for managing the society, preferring instead to supervise and guide those charged with direct responsibility, the party claimed for itself the right to speak for the society at large. Sometimes the party would mount a campaign to generate public pressure on the bureaucracy to improve its performance or concentrate on a particular priority task. Similarly, within every organization of society and state, the party maintained a separate group of its members. Even in the smallest organization those members of the collective who were party members met separately to determine their political mission within the larger organization. In the soviets, deputies who were party members met before each session to acquaint themselves with the agenda and the correct way to decide each issue. Through these caucuses, groups, PPOs, and other primary-level units, the party sought to fulfill the ambitious claim for its role set forth in Article 6 of the 1977 Soviet constitution:

> The Communist Party of the Soviet Union is the leading and guiding force of Soviet society, the nucleus of its political system and of state and public organizations. The CPSU exists for the people and serves the people.
>
> Armed with the Marxist-Leninist teaching, the Communist Party determines general prospects for the development of society and the lines of the USSR's domestic and foreign policy, directs the great creative activity of the Soviet people, and gives their struggle for the victory of communism a planned, scientifically substantiated nature.
>
> All Party organizations operate within the framework of the USSR Constitution.[102]

It was this article, with its constitutional mandate to lead the entire state and society, and the peculiar contradiction of its last sentence that subordinated it to the constitution, which was radically revised in March 1990 to eliminate the principle of the party's leading role from the constitution.

Although Soviet doctrine assigned the Communist party the leading role in society, under Lenin and still more under Stalin, other great hierarchical social organizations were also formed to serve as "transmission belts" — to use the language of the Stalin era — between the leadership and the society. The two most important of these were the Komsomol (the Leninist Communist Youth League) and the trade unions. Neither the Komsomol nor the trade unions constituted a significant vehicle for articulating the interests of their members, who had very little opportunity to influence their activity. Nor could members quit and join a competing group since both Komsomol and trade unions, like the Communist party, held monopolies in their spheres of activity.

Because the party controlled the political activity of all other state and public political organizations, con-

trol over the party itself was the object of intense political rivalry among Soviet leaders. Within the party, a leader at any level had enormous potential influence to select subordinates, who in turn supported him through pro forma votes in party meetings and adherence to the policy line he espoused. At the top, the general secretary of the party sought to appoint loyal followers to important positions in the central party bureaucracy and to the party's regional party committees as first secretaries. These individuals then had substantial power to decide who would attend the party congresses that met every five years to ratify a new Central Committee, which in turn approved the composition of the party's leadership. This self-reinforcing relationship of power and support between the leader and lower officials has been called *the circular flow of power*.[103] This model helps us to explain many features of the old, pre-Gorbachev political system, including the high degree of autonomy the party leader enjoyed in policymaking, the lack of institutional or legal constraints on his political power, the dependence of individual officials on powerful patrons in high places, and the fact that a well-prepared conspiracy of rival leaders could remove the top leader if that leader had alienated most of his former supporters. Such a conspiracy in fact was successful when a group of Nikita Khrushchev's colleagues in the party leadership plotted to remove him, forcing him into retirement in 1964.[104]

The importance of the "circular flow" illustrates the weakness of institutionalization in Soviet politics. New leaders traditionally sought to clean house by removing a large proportion of their predecessors' appointees and replacing them with their own. They then faced the problem of controlling their own appointees.

The same phenomenon — the weakness of institutionalization of political structures — may be observed in the authority-building and power-consolidation pattern established by the general secretaries. Until Gorbachev removed the party from its former pivotal position in the political system, a general secretary sought to establish himself among his fellow leaders as the principal spokesman for the country in domestic and foreign affairs. Through a combination of policy proposals and political maneuvers, a leader tried to position himself as the *primus inter pares* (first among equals) among the other senior party leaders. Leaders reinforced their hold on power by providing solutions to pressing problems.[105] When their policies failed, their support among followers weakened. Lacking well-institutionalized decision-making structures, the Soviet political system has traditionally placed extensive powers in the hands of individual leaders — from factory directors all the way up to the party general secretary. The immense personal power Gorbachev has claimed for himself in his new capacity as president thus conforms to an older tradition in Soviet politics and to an even older tradition of tsarist autocracy in the Russian state.

Lenin exercised leadership over the ruling party mainly by virtue of prestige, moral authority, and experience. He was ruthless in suppressing opposition when he considered it subversive. He deprived non-Bolshevik socialists, not to mention groups representing the old "ruling class," of freedom of speech and of life itself if in his opinion their activities threatened Soviet power. An important part of the political legacy which Lenin bequeathed to his successors was the dread system of political police informants, jailers, and executioners known in his time as the Cheka and later as the GPU, the NKVD, and the KGB. In relations with communists whose opinions differed from his own, however, Lenin, unlike Stalin, resorted less to coercion than to debate and persuasion.

Joseph Stalin established himself as sole leader through a combination of political machinations and brutal terror. Initially, he gained power by using his considerable talent for administration as well as his skill in political intrigue, and also by presenting himself to the party and society as Lenin's most faithful disciple.[106] Once in power, he launched his "revolution from above." The major features of this coercive campaign were collectivization of agriculture and forced-draft industrialization. Stalin laid the foundations of Soviet economic and military power and led the USSR to victory over Nazi Germany. The Soviet people paid an incalculable price in fear, suffering, and tens of millions of lives for Stalin's successes, although there continue to be Soviet citizens who look back on Stalin's era as a time of discipline and purpose and faith in a socialist future.[107] One of the most damaging consequences of Stalin's rule was that it led to the establishment of patterns of economic development and administration that have tended to strangle the system's capacity to innovate and evolve. For his part, Khrushchev in turn launched a campaign to denounce the cult of Stalin, a radical policy turn that both discredited other party officials who had loyally served under Stalin and legitimated new and reformist policy ideas in the economy, culture, and many other spheres of life.

Soviet political history thus reveals a pattern of sharp and radical turns in policy. New leaders usually repudiate their predecessors and try to set their own mark on policy and power relations. The difference under Gorbachev is that Gorbachev has put in motion a broad shift away from the concentration of power in a single party and has legitimated a search for multiparty parliamentary democracy. Two fundamental difficulties with Gorbachev's strategy, however, have led to serious, and perhaps ultimately insurmountable, contradictions in *perestroika*.

First, Gorbachev has employed highly undemocratic means to attain his political ends. Consistently since 1985, Gorbachev has strengthened his own power as leader even as he has weakened the party and state bureaucracy that he evidently regarded as stubborn obstacles to the success of his reforms.

Gorbachev used high-handed parliamentary manipulation to push through the constitutional amendment creating a powerful presidency in March 1990.[108] Mistrust of Gorbachev's intentions, both among conservatives dissatisfied with the breakdown of the old order and among reformers demanding a stronger commitment to democracy, sapped his ability to command acceptance of his decisions and hindered the institutionalization of the new institutions created to replace old policymaking and executing agencies.[109] At the same time it reinforced the old pattern of the system's dependency for initiative and authority in policymaking on the supreme leader.

The other basic flaw in Gorbachev's reform strategy has been the weakness of new structures for aggregating demands, policymaking, and policy implementation. Gorbachev has been far more effective in undermining the power of the old system than in transferring power to new structures. He has acted as though he thought it possible to restructure socialism incrementally, preserving a leading position for a reformed, democratized Communist party, which was to lead society through the power of persuasion rather than command, while transferring more power to the newly elected soviets. Perhaps this strategy was necessary if he was to stay in office and not alienate the existing blocs of power too quickly. But, as the examples of Eastern Europe have vividly shown, such coexistence between the old system and a democratic system is impossible. No ruling Communist party has succeeded in making a transition to a new role as a competitive, democratically oriented party while still retaining control of government. The transition from the old system in which the party maintained a monopolistic position in the political system to a new system of competitive party politics has been accompanied throughout the communist world by a massive, sometimes violent, popular repudiation of the power and privilege of the party apparatus. But the momentum of rejection of the old institutions of communist rule does not lead to the legitimation of new democratic institutions. Powerful groups, such as the military, the secret police, the economic bureaucracy, party apparatchiki, and elements of the working class, have opposed movement to liberal democratic politics on the West European model. Perhaps the greatest threat from conservative opponents of democratization is not from their public statements, but from countless small acts — some private but some probably the product of conspiracy — that subvert the implementation of reform policies.

Even among those favoring democracy, the new institutional arrangements are sometimes also weakened by the democrats' inability to take advantage of the new freedoms to lay the basis for strong, confident interest groups and political parties. One reformer observed that it is far easier to rally many thousands of people to a pro-democracy demonstration than to get a few dozen people to do the laborious behind-the-scenes organizational work necessary to build an enduring political party. Many reformers believe that the new structures of parliamentary power are fatally weakened by the continuing power of the old bureaucracy wielded from behind the scenes. And, among nationalists in the union republics, new all-union structures are regarded with a suspicion that sometimes amounts to a total rejection of all union-level authority.[110]

Future scholars will debate whether Gorbachev had a radical plan for democratic transformation from the start, or whether he found that radical democratization served his tactical interests in attempting to defeat his opponents in the party and state bureaucracy. Either interpretation, however, lends itself too easily to an overappreciation of Gorbachev's importance as the author of the democratization program associated with his name. In fact, as Joel Moses has shown, "Philosophically, the reform movement of Gorbachev clearly draws its inspiration, vision, and even specific proposals from a home-grown corps of Soviet social scientists and jurists, whose open, if constrained espousals of the very same positions antedate Gorbachev by three decades, constituting something of a quasi-democratic reformist tend-

ency or impulse in the political twilight between the Soviet dissident movement and the official establishment." During the Brezhnev period, these reformers had little opportunity to articulate their ideas openly, and they tended to confine themselves to offer guarded suggestions for change, often in rather obscure or veiled language and often in specialized academic publications. They sought to sponsor limited "experiments" when a full-blown reform was politically impossible, and they advanced cautious arguments for a more just, decentralized, and participatory society.[111] Many of the most important political and economic reforms introduced under Gorbachev were developed by these reform-minded intellectuals from policy think tanks such as the Institute of State and Law of the Academy of Sciences; the Institute of Economics of the World Socialist System; the Institute of World Economics and International Relations; the Siberian Division of the Academy of Sciences; the Soviet Sociological Association; as well as certain important media organs, such as *Kommunist*, the theoretical organ of the party, and *EKO*, the journal of the Institute of Economics and Organization of Industrial Production.

Although the ideas themselves proposed in the first few years of Gorbachev's leadership were far more radical than any discussed in the Brezhnev era, the pattern of articulation is similar. That is, policy advocates tended to be dependent on the favor or sponsorship of policymakers for the opportunity to advance their ideas. Generally, innovative ideas needed the hospitable soil of a sympathetic institute or journal in order to gain access to a wider hearing. Policymakers could commission studies from experts, who then in turn might draw on the research of like-minded scholars to buttress a policy recommendation. By the same token, the same policymakers were free to ignore the advice they received and even to forbid further discussion of the ideas.[112]

Policy Performance and the Crisis of Governance

Gorbachev's program for restructuring Soviet society has failed to extricate the Soviet economy from its long-term decline or to alter the basic structure of state control of resources. Moreover, the economy lost ground between 1985 and 1991. Shortages of basic foodstuffs and consumer goods grew acute. Rationing was introduced on subsistence goods such as milk, meat, eggs, butter, sugar, and oil, while prices of food on the farm markets skyrocketed. Economic production was falling:

output declined by a total of about 5 percent in 1990 over 1989, and the slide was accelerating. Yet the country's total wage bill kept increasing (by 8 percent in 1988 and 12 percent in 1989) as the center in effect covered the gap between revenues and expenditures by printing rubles. In 1989 alone the country's money supply rose by 56 percent. Thus, the volume of money in circulation burgeoned, while official prices on most goods hardly changed. The tremendous "monetary overhang" — that is, the excess of money in circulation over goods to buy — fueled enormous inflationary pressure that would produce severe social tension if prices were allowed to float. No near-term solutions were in sight, because neither the state nor the new forms of enterprise outside the plan system such as cooperatives and joint ventures were investing new capital to replace the country's worn-out, obsolete productive infrastructure.[113] The economy was locked in a spiral of falling output and rising deficits.

The traditional Soviet economic model had concentrated power over policymaking in a closely linked set of highly centralized party and state structures. Most decisions about the allocation of resources and the balance of coercive and material incentives to be used to obtain resources were made by decision makers at the top of the party and state hierarchies. They set general output targets for the economy as well as directions of future development. In turn, they had decided how national product should be distributed between capital investment, military needs, consumption, and other uses. With time, as we have seen, the bureaucratized structures of planning and administration became overloaded and functioned with extreme inefficiency, but were still able to prevent private entrepreneurs from competing with the state in the use of the state's resources. Gorbachev's *perestroika* was unable to reverse the deteriorating performance of the state-controlled economy and also failed to transfer economic power to institutions outside the state. As Gorbachev's own economic advisers recognized, meaningful restructuring of the economy would require a radical devolution of power to regional governments and rapid steps toward establishing a market system.

The traditional instruments for enforcing compliance with policy designs had lost their effectiveness because of the general revolt against the power of the old bureaucracy. Yet in practice republics and regional governments were finding it extremely difficult to exercise power independently of the old central bureaucracy, be-

cause it continued to control many scarce resources. The outcome of the crisis of governance appeared to depend on two trends. One was the continuing concentration of both decision-making and implementing power in the hands of Mikhail Gorbachev as president. Protesting the drift toward what he called dictatorship, Eduard Shevardnadze, Gorbachev's formerly close ally and his foreign minister since July 1985, resigned unexpectedly on December 20, 1990. Many feared that Shevardnadze's departure, together with other indications of Gorbachev's readiness to turn to authoritarian measures to enforce central authority, signalled that Gorbachev would soon be unwilling or unable to tolerate independent political activity. Some predicted that Gorbachev — or some other figure — would declare a state of national emergency and rule by presidential decree, as did Poland's President Jaruzelski when he declared martial law in December 1981. Some recalled the coup by Chile's President Pinochet in 1973.

The spring of 1991 brought renewed waves of unrest as the old command-oriented, administered economy continued to break down and living standards fell. Harsh economic stabilization measures — including a steep across-the-board increase of consumer prices — adopted by Gorbachev's new prime minister, Valentin Pavlov, exacerbated social tension. Polls revealed a sharp decline in public confidence in all central institutions. Through March and April 1991 coal miners in all the major coal-mining regions of the Soviet Union walked out, coupling their demands for improved living and working conditions with demands for Gorbachev's resignation. The strikes spread to other industries and regions as workers throughout the country demanded an immediate transfer of their enterprises to the jurisdictions of the republics rather than the federal union.

The miners' strikes reflected the general crisis of political authority in the country, the most intractable element of which was the growing confrontation between the union authorities and the increasingly assertive, independence-oriented governments of the republics. Although a referendum in March 1991 held in most republics demonstrated that three quarters of the populace still supported some form of union, the battle for sovereignty among the regions paralyzed political authority and made it impossible to negotiate a general agreement on a new form of union that would satisfy all the national republics while preserving a dominant role for the federal center. Against this background of political and economic disorder, many feared that the contest between President Gorbachev and his bitter rival, Boris Yeltsin, for preeminence could provoke a new period of dictatorship.

At the same time, a trend toward the institutionalization of local and regional power was gaining strength. As republics and cities claimed autonomous control over their economies, they began developing new commercial relationships with each other and the outside world independent of the central government. Boris Yeltsin actively promoted the establishment of political, economic, and other ties among the union republics on the basis of the sovereign equality of the republics. Cities such as Moscow and Leningrad established mayoralties in the hopes of increasing the power and self-sufficiency of local government. Eventually, Gorbachev had little choice but to bow to the new political realities in the country. On April 23, 1991, he met with the presidents of nine union republics—the three Slavic republics (Russia, Ukraine, and Belorussia) and the six Muslim republics (Kazakhstan, Uzbekistan, Kirgizia, Tadzhikistan, Turkmenistan, and Azerbaijan) and agreed with them on a series of principles that would govern the new treaty of union defining the division of powers between the center and the republics.

The agreement amounted to a surrender to the republics' demands for independence, although it also authorized the central government to enforce order in basic industries with harsh measures. It endorsed the republics' demands for real sovereignty over their economies and opened a new phase of political development: in a looser, more confederal type of union, the Russian republic—and Yeltsin as its president—would inevitably be the dominant force and Gorbachev's role as federal president would diminish. Some observers in Moscow believed that Gorbachev had broken the political impasse by finding a formula under which he preserved the formal existence of the union but relinquished most policymaking power to the republics.

RULE ADJUDICATION: TOWARD THE PRIMACY OF LAW

One of the most important goals of the restructuring program is to establish a *law-governed state* (*pravovoe gosudarstvo*) in place of the arbitrary, often illegal, exercise of political power by the state. One high-ranking legal authority, Vladimir Kudryavtsev, quotes Immanuel Kant in defining the concept of the law-governed state: "an association of many people subordinated to laws."[114] Other scholars employ the concept of the law-governed state more broadly, usually emphasizing two basic points: the primacy of individual rights over the power of the state, and the need to separate the powers of the executive, judicial, and legislative branches of the state instead of, as in the past, fusing them. Thus, in a truly law-governed state, the judicial branch would guarantee observance of citizens' rights by the state. Although the concept is sometimes defined as "the rule of law," this is misleading: *pravovoe gosudarstvo* should be seen rather as a condition in which the state acts only through the law and will observe its own laws, but it does not mean that there is a sphere of law higher than the state from which the state derives its right to rule.[115] Even the limited concept of a state bound by the laws that its duly constituted lawmakers have enacted is a step toward greater respect for law and away from the doctrines that have traditionally been used to justify various abuses of law by the Soviet state. One of the most enduring is the concept that "revolutionary justice" is higher than any written law, so that the rights and obligations of rulers and citizens must be subordinate to the political interests of the regime. One of the most radical implications of a law-governed state is therefore that the Communist party, as the embodiment of the revolutionary cause, itself must obey the law.

The struggle for the primacy of law did not begin with Gorbachev.[116] After Stalin, Soviet political leaders and members of the legal professions attempted with mixed results to place the extrajudicial powers of the secret police and other law enforcement agencies under stricter legal control. Extrajudicial trials, judgments, and sentences—once a common practice in the time of Stalin's terror—were prohibited, and criminal defendants were granted important rights. New codes of criminal law and criminal process were adopted in the union republics, and official policy promoted a concept of socialist legality. Like many Soviet doctrines (such as democratic centralism), it was a mixture of contradictory principles. Through the post–Stalin period and until the most recent time, legality was expected to uphold socialist principles and practices. In fact, this doctrine meant that the party and police could use legal procedures as a way of legitimating actions taken in the interests of the regime's power and security. The criminal codes themselves contained articles providing legal penalties for "anti-Soviet agitation and propaganda" and for "circulation of fabrications known to be false which defame the Soviet state or social system." In the post–Stalin period these articles were frequently used against individuals whom the regime considered to be political dissidents.[117] Alternatively, the authorities sometimes resorted to the practice of declaring a particular individual mentally incompetent and forcibly incarcerating him in a mental hospital, where he could be further punished by administering mind-altering drugs.[118] The continuation of these practices for purposes of political repression until the late 1980s attests to the law's inability to protect the rights of individuals whom the party and KGB for any reason decided to suppress.

Full establishment of a law-governed state would mean that such abuses would end and that no arm of the state would be able to bend or violate the law for political ends. In turn, this would require that the judiciary be independent of political influence. As many recent Soviet articles have shown, judges have been susceptible to various forms of pressure that have interfered with the impartial administration of justice. At times these pressures are direct and overt; at other times they are simply part of a political climate set by political officials. One of the most notorious forms of political influence is called telephone justice — the practice whereby a party official or some other powerful individual would privately communicate advice or instructions to a judge on a particular case.[119] "Telephone justice" was symptomatic of a prevalent pattern in which the law was held in relatively low repute and legal institutions possessed little autonomy of the policy-implementing organs of government. The party might direct judges to be especially harsh in passing sentences on a particular class of criminals if it was attempting to conduct a propaganda campaign against a social problem, such as alcoholism, hooliganism, or economic crimes. A party official might direct prosecutors to crack down on some previously tolerated activity, or to gather incriminating evidence on someone it wished to punish. As Robert Sharlet has noted, pressures such as these often pushed adjudication in the past over the line from full and vigorous enforcement of the law into abandonment of the law in pursuit of political ends.[120] By the same token, an unwritten but firmly observed norm made it impossible to prosecute a high-ranking member of the political elite without the party's consent. Even where improper political influence was not involved, many judges routinely accepted the prosecutor's case for a defendant's guilt, since the norm that a defendant is innocent until proven in court to be guilty

was only weakly rooted in law and practice. In 1989, in keeping with the effort to bring the legal system closer to the ideal of a law-governed state, legal reformers succeeded in winning adoption of principles of legal procedure that provided greater rights for defendants, including a declaration that a defendant was to be considered innocent until proven guilty, granting a defendant a right to a defense lawyer from the moment of detention, and authorizing union republics to mandate jury trials in certain categories of cases.[121] These principles are aimed at reducing the possibility of political abuses as well as limiting the tendency for legal proceedings to be biased in favor of the prosecution.

The Soviet legal system has vested a great deal of power in the procuracy; the procuracy is traditionally considered to be the most prestigious of the legal professions. The procurator (the official corresponding to a prosecutor in U.S. practice) is assigned great leeway in fighting crime, corruption, and abuses of power in the bureaucracy, both instigating investigations of criminal wrongdoing among private citizens and responding to complaints about official malfeasance. One of the procuracy's assigned tasks is to ensure that all state officials and public organizations observe the law. Moreover, the procuracy is charged with overseeing the entire system of justice, including the penal system. The procuracy, more than the judiciary, has traditionally been seen as the principal check on illegal activity by officials and curbing abuses of power. The procuracy has usually been inadequately equipped to meet the sweeping responsibilities that Soviet law assigns to it, because of the difficulty of effectively supervising the vast economic bureaucracy and overcoming the entrenched political machines of party and state officials. Lacking independence of the state which it is called on to supervise, it is not an effective substitute either for full marketplace competition in the economy or of democratic accountability by officeholders to the citizenry. Moreover, in cases where especially grave economic or political crimes are involved, the KGB is assigned jurisdiction for the investigation.

The vast majority of trials are conducted by the people's courts which are presided over by a judge and two lay assessors, who are ordinary citizens performing roles as co-judges as a form of community service. The judge and lay assessors have equal votes in deciding on the verdict and sentence, but in practice lay assessors tend to defer to the superior legal knowledge and experience of judges. Regional and republican courts hear appeals from lower level courts, as well as certain cases as courts of the first instance. Presiding over the entire judicial system is the USSR Supreme Court, which hears cases referred from the Supreme Courts of the republics and also issues instructions to lower courts on judicial matters. The Supreme Court does not have the power to challenge the constitutionality of laws and other normative acts adopted by legislative and executive bodies. Thus, it is not a check on the other branches of government.

Partly because there was no legal institution to ensure that legislative and administrative acts of the state conformed with the Soviet constitution, legal reformers advocated the creation of a constitutional court, equivalent to the Constitutional Council in the French Fifth Republic or the Constitutional Court in Germany, which would rule on the constitutionality of laws and would adjudicate disputes between the union and the republics. A constitutional amendment creating a body called the committee on constitutional supervision (*komitet konstitutsionnogo nadzora*) was passed in December 1988. Its twenty-three members were elected in 1989, and the committee's powers took effect as of January 1, 1990. One of its early decisions was that there would be no Communist party organization within it—a small symbolic indication that it considered the law superior to the dictates of the party. Its first official ruling, in September 1990, found that Gorbachev had acted unconstitutionally when he had decreed earlier in the year that he as president had the power either to forbid or allow demonstrations within Moscow. Gorbachev did not respond to the committee's ruling. Still more significantly, the committee found itself powerless to overcome the paralyzing effects of the "war of laws" between union, republican, and local government authorities. Moreover, since it was not a court, the committee could not adjudicate cases. Nevertheless, the committee's creation, and the care it exercised to avoid taking decisions that would be flagrantly ignored, indicated that an important precedent had been established.

Change of another sort has been occurring among members of that branch of the legal profession who represent individual citizens in both criminal and civil matters: advocates (*advokaty*). Comparable to defense attorneys in the United States, Soviet advocates often oppose procurators and other state bodies in judicial proceedings. They have long enjoyed a certain autonomy through their self-governing associations, called colleges, through which they elect officers and govern the

admission of new practitioners. In the past, their ability to make effective use of the nominal autonomy given them was limited, but in recent years, their independence and prestige have risen markedly, partly as a result of the new emphasis on legality under Gorbachev. Together with other professional groups, they have begun organizing their own professional association and codifying corporate ethical standards, often struggling with the Ministry of Justice to free themselves of interference from the state. One of the most telling indicators of a change in the status of advocates was the revision of the previous rules limiting an advocate's earnings. As of September 1988, an advocate was theoretically free to take on as many cases as he or she wished and to charge any fee agreed on with the client. With the new freedom to form cooperatives, some lawyers have begun forming legal cooperatives and competing with the colleges of advocates in dispensing legal assistance to citizens; the colleges of advocates have begun to organize their own for-profit legal cooperatives in response. Advocates have become popular guests on national television programs and have contributed a number of articles on legal subjects to mass periodicals, suggesting widespread popular interest in learning about the law.[122]

How close has the Soviet system come to realizing the ideal of a "law-governed state"? While substantial change has occurred, above all in the airing of problems and proposals for remedies, structural barriers to the full triumph of law remain. Two will be singled out.

The first is the continuing power of the Committee for State Security, better known by the initials *KGB*. In stark contrast to the MVD (the Ministry of Internal Affairs, which oversees the uniformed police as well as special security troops), the military, and virtually every other sector of the state, the KGB has not been subjected to a sweeping turnover of personnel under Gorbachev.[123] This fact has suggested to many observers that Gorbachev has relied on its immense power as a base of support for his rule. The KGB is the institutional successor to the powerful instruments of coercion that the regime has used since the revolution to eliminate its political enemies, including the Cheka (created within six weeks of the October Revolution), the GPU, and the NKVD. Today, according to its spokesmen, the KGB has nothing in common with these predecessor organizations, and it is dedicated to upholding the law while carrying out its mission of defending the security of the state and its citizens. Often KGB press representatives discuss the modern efforts of the organization in combating drug trafficking and terrorism. Evidently keen to be portrayed in a positive light in the media, the KGB has promoted itself as a heroic organization, the victim under Stalin of terror and lawlessness, and today a body performing its difficult duties with scrupulous respect for the law as well as considerable ingenuity and courage. The KGB continues to hold the same general responsibilities as before *perestroika*: namely, the investigation and prevention of dangerous crimes against the state and violations of the state's sovereignty. (The country's border guards, for example, are a specialized force under KGB command.) In addition, Gorbachev assigned it a number of important new functions in late 1990 and early 1991, including monitoring food distribution and supervising all state and private enterprises to prevent "economic sabotage." As in the past, the KGB combines both foreign espionage (and clandestine operations) duties with its domestic surveillance mission. The KGB also continues to rely on a network of informers to extend its reach into society. Only its efforts in suppressing political dissent have been abandoned, at least for the time being.

Glasnost and the pluralization of power have reduced some of the KGB's power and autonomy. A number of critical articles and exposés of the organization, revealing that its clandestine activities were continuing even in the late 1980s, have appeared in the press. A remarkable event was the Kalugin affair. Oleg Kalugin was a career office in the KGB who rose to head its counter-espionage branch. In 1990 he retired with full honors at the rank of general. Shortly after retiring, he published blistering exposés of continuing abuses of the law by the KGB. He was punished by being stripped of his state orders and awards by President Gorbachev, but he became a popular hero for his outspokenness and courage. After a seat in the USSR Congress of People's Deputies was vacated by the new head of the breakaway Russian Communist party, he successfully ran for the Congress and has continued to use his deputy's mandate to call for reform.

Nevertheless, many observers believe that the KGB has been more concerned with improving its image than relinquishing its power. In December 1990 Vladimir Kriuchkov, chairman of the KGB since 1988, went on a media offensive against "enemies" of the country, domestic and foreign. He began to appear often on television and in the press. Using language equivalent to that used under Stalin and Brezhnev, Kriuchkov warned in a television broadcast on December 11 that

the Soviet Union was in the grip of "extremist radical groups . . . supported morally and politically from abroad." In a lengthy address to the Congress of People's Deputies on December 22, Kriuchkov warned that some of the Soviet Union's trading partners were using trade and assistance for purposes of espionage, subversion, and sabotage.[124] Kriuchkov's clear hostility to the deep changes occurring in the Soviet political system culminated in his complicity in the August 1991 coup attempt. Following the coup's collapse, the union and republican governments undertook a radical reorganization of the KGB. The KGB was stripped of its military formations and its domestic surveillance powers. Most important, its territorial organs were subordinated to the national republics. Its new chairman, Vadim Bakatin, known as a reformer committed to the rule of law, vowed to prevent the destruction of the KGB's vast archive of records but promised not to publish the names of the agency's many secret informers.

The other impediment to the primacy of law was of a different order, reflecting less the repressive extrajudicial legacy of a once-revolutionary regime than the immense inertia of a heavily bureaucratized state. As Eugene Huskey has argued, the lawmaking authority of the USSR Supreme Soviet is frequently vitiated by the administrative agencies' issuance of normative acts — decrees, regulations, instructions, orders, directives, circular letters, and many other kinds of official and binding rules — which apply not only to subordinates in the same agency but, often, to other governmental agencies and to Soviet citizens generally. Some indication of the magnitude of this practice is suggested by the fact that over the first seventy years of Soviet power, the USSR legislature adopted fewer than 800 laws and decrees, whereas over the same period, the union-level government issued hundreds of thousands of decrees and other normative acts.[125] The profusion of rules and regulations, complementing, interpreting, and often contradicting one another, creates ample opportunities for evasions, and generates pressures for intervention through the authority of powerful individuals to cut through the jungle of red tape. Patronage and protection often serve to compensate for the paralyzing effects of anonymous bureaucratic power.

Moreover, as Huskey shows, two other features of the Soviet rulemaking system reduce still further the subordination of state power to law: the tendency for much of the rulemaking by bureaucratic agencies to be secret, and the fact that rulings issued by lower levels of the bureaucracy often take precedence over the law. As he observes, the bureaucratic hierarchy "may also be conceived of as an iceberg. A small portion is visible, but obscured from view is that vast body of departmental instructions that gives direction to Soviet life. As one goes further down the pyramid, *glasnost* lessens. There is, to put it in an American context, no *Federal Register*."[126] Most regulations are issued in numbered copies to a small list of authorized personnel, with most of them being classified "for internal use only." Even the procuracy, which has official responsibility for ensuring the legality and consistency of governmental regulations, lacks full access to all legal acts of the bureaucracy or the power to annul those it finds illegal.[127] The other element of government rulemaking, according to Huskey, that undermines legality is the tendency for laws passed by the Supreme Soviet to remain dead letters until the bureaucrats in state agencies "interpret" them and give them concrete, binding content. Although the rules and regulations that the departments issue are supposed to be consistent with both the language and spirit of the law, in practice they frequently gut it, so that reform adopted by the legislature may be eviscerated and weightless by the time they reach the level where they are supposed to be acted on.

These patterns not only contradict the primacy of law, but also hamper the ability of a reforming central leader to ensure the implementation of his wishes. For this reason, Gorbachev has been keen to restrain the state bureaucracy's vast power to distort and water down his reform policies. After the Law on State Enterprise was passed in 1987 (this law, it will be recalled, attempted to expand the freedom of productive enterprises to plan their own production and trade with other producers), a commission was formed to review all relevant government instructions and to annul those that were found to contradict the law. Over 1,000 legal acts had been fully or partially rescinded by the beginning of 1989, and another 3,500 were being scheduled for action.[128] Nonetheless, the abject failure of the Law on State Enterprise, conceived as a centerpiece of Gorbachev's early economic reforms to alter significantly the relations between enterprises and ministries, suggested the state bureaucracy's continuing ability to subvert intended reforms that would strip it of its power.

The concept of a law-governed state is an essential feature of the reform program initiated under the rubric of *perestroika*. The precedence of law over political and administrative power in the state would reduce the ability of officials in the Communist party, the economic bureaucracy, the secret police, and other sectors of the state to behave arbitrarily from the standpoint of both citizens' rights and the interests of the state's rulers. Moreover, like *glasnost* and pluralism, a real rule of law would help stimulate innovation and responsibility on the part of citizens, which as Soviet leaders have frequently stated is essential to reinvigorating Soviet society. Perhaps these are among the reasons why the Gorbachev leadership has actively propagated the ideal of the *pravovoe gosudarstvo* and has taken several steps to put the ideal into practice. Like many other efforts that *perestroika* has begun, however, progress toward a law-governed state would ultimately require changes that would permanently alter the political system of a Communist party state. It would provide legal recourse for individuals and organizations whose rights had been violated by action of state agencies, including the party and police. It would separate the powers previously combined in the centralized, sovereign state, and provide for independent review of the actions of officials by both judicial and legislative branches. It would ultimately vest political power in the citizenry rather than the leadership or the bureaucracy, and this, in the end, would make the course of policy unpredictable and uncontrollable.

Perhaps the radical political implications of a move to a fully law-governed state are one reason why the leadership has been hesitant to move more decisively toward it. The continuing hold among the population of the traditionally skeptical attitude toward the law — the view of the law as an instrument of those in power — may also impede movement in this direction. Yet the central importance of the concept of legal rights in public discussion and the intense popular interest in legal issues, together with the significant developments in legal reform and constitutionalism, suggest that a substantial base of support exists for the concept of law as an impartial and autonomous domain to which state power is subordinate.

THE USSR AND THE WORLD: NEW THINKING AND NEW BEHAVIOR

In no realm have the changes initiated by Mikhail Gorbachev been as profound as in foreign policy. As in his economic and political reforms, it is difficult to separate intention from pragmatic adaptation in the evolution of the radical policy program that has taken the Soviet

Union, over less than five years, from a position as the bulwark of a world socialist system locked in ideological enmity with Western capitalist democracy to a partnership with the West in the consolidation of democracy and collective security throughout Europe and the developing world. Robert Legvold does not exaggerate the magnitude of this change when he writes of a "revolution" in Soviet foreign policy.[129] Since the collapse of the socialist commonwealth in Eastern Europe — including the breakdown of communist rule in every state of Eastern Europe as well as the collapse of the multilateral organizations linking the East Europeans with the Soviet Union in economic and military alliance — the gravity of this revolution has been unmistakable. In turn, the radical turn in the Soviet posture in the world created serious dissensions among Soviet policymakers which, by the end of 1990, led to the resignation of Foreign Minister Shevardnadze and a pause in the momentum of progress.

The revolution in foreign policy grew out of a fundamental reappraisal of the nature of state security in the contemporary era. Although the analysis that undergirded this reappraisal had been developing for many years in Soviet foreign policy institutes, not until Gorbachev took power did policymakers themselves accept the radical consequences for Soviet strategic policy that the *new thinking* logically implied.[130] Undoubtedly, the pressure of the arms race helped precipitate the Soviet decision to look for a less enervating and less dangerous relationship with the West, one that strengthened rather than sapped Soviet national power. Gorbachev has repeatedly stressed that he believes the military dimension is only one aspect of a country's national security. Military power by itself, he declared early on in his tenure as general secretary, cannot overcome other threats to security, including grave economic and political problems, particularly in an era when humankind is linked in relations of interdependence as never before.

As time went on, Soviet official assessments of international relations grew increasingly innovative and self-critical. Gorbachev's accession to power occurred within several weeks after U.S. President Ronald Reagan began his second term, and American official receptivity to arms agreements and other actions relaxing the extremely tense, hostile climate of relations of the first half of the 1980s contributed to the success of Gorbachev's initiatives. By 1988 the evolution of official Soviet thinking about international peace and security led the Gorbachev leadership to break with one of the cornerstones of the old ideology by declaring that the international class struggle was no longer the principal determinant of relations among nations. That is, international relations was moved by considerations of national interest and by the need for cooperation to overcome common threats to humankind's well-being, such as environmental degradation, hunger, and poverty. What united humankind across national boundaries was to be considered primary, whereas the divisions and conflicts between capital and labor, imperialism and socialism, were of declining significance.[131]

With respect to the arms race, Soviet new thinking posited a different conceptual framework for evaluating military needs. Whereas Soviet behavior in the past had appeared to reflect the pursuit of absolute security, now Gorbachev asserted that no nation could be totally secure if other nations were insecure. Hence, security must be shared and indivisible among the community of nations. The accumulation of nuclear weapons was therefore detrimental to national security if it provoked a similar response in other powers. The only reasonable goal of security was "sufficiency" — meaning that beyond the level of armaments needed to assure destruction of any enemy that attacked the Soviet Union, further force was meaningless and often destabilizing.[132] One of the most remarkable indications that the new thinking had real behavioral consequences was the success of the negotiations between the United States and Soviet Union on a treaty providing for the elimination of all intermediate-range nuclear weapons (INF) from Europe.[133] After a little over a year of intense negotiations, the two countries signed the INF treaty in December 1987. The treaty set several momentous precedents. One was the fact that, unlike nuclear arms control treaties in the past, the INF treaty required the *elimination of entire classes* of nuclear weapons rather than setting maximum allowable limits. Second was the agreement on monitoring compliance with the treaty, which allowed each side to send teams of military and technical experts to weapons production and deployment sites of the other country, an unprecedentedly intrusive form of verification. Third, two-thirds of the 2,695 missiles that the treaty covered were Soviet: in order to win the removal of all American short- and medium-range missiles from Europe, the Soviet Union agreed to destroy twice as many of its own weapons. Similarly, in July 1991, Presidents Bush and Gorbachev signed a treaty reducing the two sides' arsenals of strategic, or long-range, nuclear weapons by around 30%.

The revolution in Soviet foreign policy affected all domains of Soviet international behavior, not only its relations with the United States. Gorbachev and his foreign minister actively promoted improvement of relations with Western Europe, China, Japan, the ASEAN countries, and the United Nations, while seeking a diplomatic framework for withdrawing from the long and destructive war in Afghanistan. Results have been mixed. Gorbachev succeeded in improving relations with China substantially, to the point that he became the first top Soviet leader to visit China. His visit, however, occurred at a time of massive student-led demonstrations demanding democracy, in June 1989, when hundreds of thousands of students demanded for China substantial political reforms similar to those identified with Gorbachev in the Soviet Union. Shortly after his visit, the Chinese authorities suppressed the demonstrations with conspicuous brutality. As far as Japan was concerned, Soviet desires for a breakthrough in relations, which might bring with them commitments of Japanese aid and trade, were frustrated by the impasse over the Kurile Islands issue.[134] Despite many hints that the Soviet Union was willing to make major concessions over the issue, it was clear that the Soviet authorities were reluctant to cede territory to Japan for fear of encouraging claims by other neighboring countries to Soviet territory.

In the case of a number of regional conflicts in Central America, Africa, and Asia, the Soviet Union changed policy fundamentally. It offered full support for democratic elections in Nicaragua in 1990, and greeted the electoral defeat of the revolutionary Sandinista junta by offering economic aid to the victorious Chamorro government. It contributed to political settlement of the civil wars in Angola and Cambodia and welcomed negotiations between the African National Congress and the white government in South Africa. Meanwhile, relations with its formerly close ally, Castro's Cuba, grew tense and bitter as the Soviet Union began cutting back on its shipments of oil and its economic subsidies to the unrepentantly militant Castro regime.

In Europe, the Soviet Union under Gorbachev revived the concept that the Soviet Union was part of a common European home. In the Brezhnev era this slogan had been part of a longstanding Soviet policy of seeking to improve Soviet relations with Western Europe by fanning European resentments against American power and presence. Therefore, when the rhetoric of the common European home returned under Gorba-

chev, many in the West were skeptical, despite Gorbachev's assurances that "we are not conducting a Metternichian 'balance of power' policy, setting one state against another, knocking together blocs and counterblocs, . . . but a policy of global detente, strengthening world security and developing international cooperation everywhere."[135] By 1988 and 1989, however, it became clear that the shift in Soviet policy was real. The Soviet Union began seeking improved ties not just with individual European countries, but with the European Economic Community. In the summer of 1989 Gorbachev reaffirmed Soviet support for a broader conception of European security in which both the United States and Soviet Union would have a place, and once again assured the West that the Soviet Union renounced the "Brezhnev doctrine" — the policy formalized under Brezhnev following the invasion of Czechoslovakia in 1968 which claimed that the Soviet Union had the right and duty to intervene whenever the "gains" of socialism were in jeopardy.

Still, many still doubted that, if put to the test of political revolution in Eastern Europe, Gorbachev could or would allow Eastern Europe to choose its own fate. The summer and fall of 1989 brought this test. First, Poland held national elections in June in which Solidarity swept nearly all the races in which it ran candidates against communist officials, forcing the communists to negotiate with it over the shape of a new government. The Soviet Union watched with approval as a Solidarity leader became prime minister. Then, in the late summer and fall of 1989, massive protests in East Germany forced the regime of the German Democratic Republic (GDR) first to open the border with West Germany and permit free emigration and then to negotiate with the opposition over free elections and the formation of a new government. Almost immediately, popular protest in Czechoslovakia forced a negotiated surrender of power by the communist regime to an opposition movement whose recognized leader was the playwright and rights activist Vaclav Havel. Soon after, popular uprisings in Romania forced the dictatorial president, Nicolae Ceausescu, from power. By the end of 1990, every formerly communist regime in Europe, even the staunchly Stalinist regime of Albania, had taken steps toward instituting parliamentary democracy.

Still more stunning was the rapidity with which the population of East Germany embraced the goal of unification with West Germany, giving a decisive legislative victory to the political parties favoring early reunification, first in the elections to a newly constituted East German Parliament in March 1990 and then in general Germany-wide elections in December 1990. By the end of the year, full political and legal unification of the two Germanies had occurred. This was a difficult enough pill for Soviet policymakers to swallow, given the historic Soviet sensitivity to German power; but it was compounded by the question of the united Germany's foreign policy alignment. After its initial refusal to accept the possibility that a united Germany might be a member of NATO, talks with the United States, Britain, France, and Germany itself finally yielded Soviet acceptance of this step as well, eased by the German government's far-reaching assurances that Germany would never again pose an offensive threat to Soviet interests as well as by generous commitments of economic aid. Among the implications of these extraordinary changes in the political complexion of Europe was that the security pact that had bound the communist regimes of Eastern Europe in a Soviet-dominated alliance structure, the Warsaw Treaty Organization, was a dead letter, whereas NATO continued to play a major role in linking American strategic power to Europe's security.

With the Iraq crisis in the summer of 1990, therefore it was not surprising that Soviet behavior would conform to the universalistic principles it espoused as part of its new thinking. Indeed, many still failed to grasp how revolutionary the implications of Soviet new thinking were. First, in a major article in *Pravda* in September 1987, and then in an address before the United Nations General Assembly in December 1988, Gorbachev offered a vision of Soviet policy based on the doctrine of international collective security administered by the United Nations. Again, this represented a reversal of previous Soviet attitudes. Traditionally, the Soviets viewed the United Nations and other international multilateral bodies to which it belonged as purely instrumental organs. International organizations were useful platforms for propaganda and espionage; they enabled Soviet representatives to attack Western imperialism and cultivate clients in the Third World. Soviet citizens who were members of the permanent staff of the United Nations were expected to serve the Soviet government's interests despite explicit UN rules to the contrary.[136]

The conceptual revolution in Soviet foreign policy brought a basic change in the Soviet attitude to the United Nations and other bodies, however. An early sign was the decision in 1987 to pay off all its financial obligations to the UN despite other pressing needs for foreign exchange. (The Soviet Union committed itself to paying back nearly $200 million in old debts, making it all the more conspicuous that the United States was now well over $400 million in arrears on its obligations.)[137] The Soviet Union worked to make the United Nations the vehicle for resolving several international conflicts, including the Iran–Iraq War and its own extrication from Afghanistan. Soviet behavior began to substantiate Soviet rhetoric about the need for a "comprehensive system of international security" which would contribute to advancing "the supremacy of the common human idea over the countless multiplicity of centrifugal forces."[138]

Gorbachev used the occasion of the December 1988 speech to announce substantial unilateral reductions in Soviet armed forces — including a cut of half a million troops from active forces, and reductions in the deployment of Soviet troops and weapons from Eastern Europe. Like other high-profile gestures, this announcement served to demonstrate the seriousness of the Soviet commitment to lowering the salience of military power in Soviet foreign policy as well as to generate popular pressure in the West for equivalent gestures. Soviet behavior in the Gulf crisis of 1990 confirmed that these words and declarations were not meant simply for propagandistic effect. Despite considerable internal opposition, Soviet representatives worked closely with the United States to win Security Council support for strong resolutions demanding Iraq's withdrawal from Kuwait and threatening military action if it failed to comply. When the United States-led coalition launched war in January 1991 to force Iraq out of Kuwait, the Soviet Union generally supported the coalition effort, while seeking to keep a channel of communication open to Iraq in the hope of producing a political settlement. According to Robert Legvold, Soviet behavior in the Gulf crisis is explained by "a deep desire to be a part of a community mobilized against aggression, mostly as a first fragile step toward a different international order. This larger enterprise, after all, goes to the heart of Gorbachev's foreign policy vision."[139] Indeed, according to Legvold, under Gorbachev the Soviet Union has gone further in its support for collective security, the principle of a common international response to aggression, than any other major power: "Indeed, among the great powers, the Soviet Union may be the only one willing to entrust the general welfare to this principle. The only one willing to make this a rule of policy, rather than a course when convenient."[140]

The reversal of a decades-long policy of Soviet antagonism to what it termed world imperialism created deep and traumatic divisions within the Soviet leadership. The military raised new conditions in the negotiations with the United States and Europe on a treaty reducing conventional forces in Europe. Some Soviet officials opposed the policy of backing the United States and United Nations in the Gulf crisis at the expense of a long-term ally, Iraq, and a loss of influence in the Arab world. Many conservatives believed that Gorbachev and Shevardnadze had been too eager to accept Western economic assistance. In an interview in February 1991, Gorbachev's prime minister, Valentin Pavlov, declared that certain Western banks had been conspiring to destabilize the Soviet economy by creating a hyperinflation and then moving in to buy up Soviet assets cheaply. The killing of as many as twenty-five unarmed civilians in Lithuania and Latvia in January 1991 by Soviet "black beret" special forces demonstrated that Moscow was prepared to sacrifice much of the international goodwill toward the USSR that had developed over the previous five years in order to prevent the breakup of the union.

In view of the immense changes in the world system that were due either directly or indirectly to the new line in Soviet foreign policy after 1985, most observers agreed that Gorbachev deserved the Nobel Prize for Peace that he received in 1990. The unanswerable question hanging in the air, of course, as the economic and political deterioration in the Soviet Union worsened and fears of a reversion to authoritarian or military rule spread, was whether Gorbachev's new thinking in foreign policy was permanent.

AFTER *PERESTROIKA*

Throughout Russian and Soviet history, the state has played the dominant part in initiating phases of intense social change, and personal leadership has been critical in moving the state. Gorbachev, as we have seen, has not broken this pattern: his democratizing reforms can be interpreted as efforts to use *glasnost*, democratization, legal reform, economic decentralization, and foreign policy successes to increase his power and autonomy within the party and the government. Although his radical initiatives have fatally weakened the old party–state regime, they have not established a new institutional framework to replace it. Moreover, through the years since he entered office, Gorbachev has sought to expand his own legal powers, first as party general secretary and then as president. Each institutional reform has strengthened his own nominal control over policymaking and implementation. Yet at the same time, he has won acceptance by the Communist party and the new legislative institutions of the Soviet Union of the institutional guarantees of liberal democracy: respect for the supremacy of law, private property, the separation of government powers, a freely elected legislative branch, meaningful local power, ideological pluralism and tolerance, and political competition among freely organizing associations and parties. By the end of 1990 these ideals had begun to be embodied in a variety of new structures.

One of the striking lessons of Eastern Europe's overnight transformation was the totality of the collapse of communist regimes once popular opposition was sufficiently mobilized and organized, and the regime's capacity to suppress opposition sufficiently weakened, to confront state power successfully. For most East European polities, however, the identification of the nation with the state was close enough that loyalty to the ideal of national statehood contributed to maintaining cohesion within the popular opposition movement. Where national and state boundaries diverged substantially, the collapse of the regime also brought with it a massive repudiation of the state's very existence.

In East Germany, for example, the fundamental illegitimacy of the GDR regime stemmed from the fact that it possessed only its claim to socialist identity to justify its existence, rather than a German patrimony, which was claimed far more effectively by the larger and more prosperous Federal Republic of Germany across the border. Accordingly, when the wall dividing East and West Germany was breached, the momentum for the dissolution of East Germany entirely as a separate political entity became overwhelming. Yugoslavia and Czechoslovakia offer examples of a different kind. In each, the state was a federal system in which the major constituent parts were vehicles for *national* identity. Democracy brought powerful demands in each for a breakup of the federal union, and freedom and independence for the smaller, more vulnerable constituents. Counter-claims by members of the larger national communities in each state, the Czechs in Czechoslovakia and the Serbs in Yugoslavia, were generally interpreted as reflections of great-power imperialism by the more nationalistically minded members of the smaller nations.

The same tendency affects the Soviet Union. Gorbachev is unable to carry out a policy that democratizes the entire Soviet Union without awakening demands on the part of smaller national communities for freedom and independence. The very state boundaries of the Soviet Union are linked historically to the military victories of the Bolsheviks' Red Army, which extended Soviet, hence Moscow's, rule over virtually all the territories that had once made up the tsarist Russian Empire. Still more did the memory of independence and sovereignty stir members of the national republics that had been most recently annexed by force to the Soviet Union under Stalin: the Baltic republics, the western portions of the Ukraine, and Moldavia. Thus, Gorbachev faced the fundamental contradiction in his economic and political reforms that the populations of different republics would use the new freedoms for ends that in many cases contradicted Gorbachev's intentions.

The failure of the hard-liners' coup attempt in August 1991 hastened the collapse of the centralized structures governing the old union — the army, the KGB, the state economic bureaucracy, and the Communist party, and speeded the movement toward the dissolution of the union as its constituent republics gained independence. The formal independence of Lithuania, Latvia, and Estonia was recognized by a growing number of countries around the world, including the United States, and the republics of Georgia and Moldova (formerly Moldavia) were seeking international recognition as well. To preserve political and economic order until a constitutional basis for a new union could be found, Gorbachev, Yeltsin, and eight other republican presidents agreed on a set of interim arrangements that included a council of deputies elected by republican parliaments, an economic council, and a state council comprising Gorbachev and the republican presidents to coordinate foreign and defense policy. These superseded the earlier constitutional changes that had restructured the union government.

Over 1990 and 1991, the republics began establishing direct political and economic relations among themselves. In July 1991 a treaty signed by Boris Yeltsin for the Russian Republic and Vytautas Landsbergis for Lithuania provided for recognition of Lithuanian independence in exchange for concessions by the Lithuanian government to the interests of the Russian and other non-Lithuanian minorities residing in Lithuania. (For example, under the agreement, Lithuania promised to drop the requirement that ethnic minorities in the republic would have to learn Lithuanian as a condition for citizenship.) In the future similar direct treaties among republics may lay the foundation for a new federal union. For harmonious relations among the repubics to emerge, however, guarantees will have to be found to protect the interests of the many ethnic minorities living in each republic and to prevent war among republics over their territorial borders, since many of the frontiers delineating republics are contested.

In the wake of the failed August 1991 coup there are some grounds for cautious optimism about the future of democratic institutions in the Soviet Union and its successor states. The "era of stagnation" before Gorbachev took power created a potential for democratization by spreading the effects of modernization throughout the Soviet Union and thus creating a public receptive to liberal values. At the same time the decay of economic and political institutions generated enormous discontent, which spilled out under *glasnost* and *perestroika* into a generalized revolt against communist rule. Many observers wondered whether the young democratic institutions created under *perestroika* could succeed in consolidating themselves in the face of rapidly declining economic production and living standards. The new political elites have to defend democracy despite their inability to resolve the country's economic and social crisis. The legal system is not equipped to adjudicate the flood of constitutional disputes arising from the conflicting claims of competing governmental jurisdictions. Few entrepreneurs have the skills or confidence to take large risks in developing businesses. The network of independent civic associations, labor unions, communications media, and interest groups that could channel and aggregate popular political interests is still in its infancy, and many are tied to nationalist movements.

Still, the degree of popular support for democratic values that was demonstrated in the days of the August 1991 coup attempt is impressive. The widespread resistance to the coup testifies to the depth of the changes that have occurred in the Soviet Union since 1985. First, the elections of 1989, 1990, and 1991 mobilized popular participation in democratic politics, providing an impetus for new political movements, and generating leadership whose power rests not on patronage from above, but on popular electoral support. Second, a new legally constituted institutional order, above all elected presidents and legislatures, had become the legitimate source of political power in the state. Finally, the coup dramatized the impossibility of preserving the Soviet state through highly centralized rule over the union republics. Any federal union that succeeds the old party —

state will have to proceed from the equality and sovereignty of its members.

KEY TERMS

circular flow of power
collectivism
Communist party of the Soviet Union (CPSU)
democratic centralism
democratization
glasnost (openness)

KGB
Komsomol
law-governed state
Vladimir Ilyich Lenin
Marxism-Leninism
modernization
new class

new thinking
nomenklatura
perestroika (restructuring)
Politburo
popular fronts
procuracy
Russian Soviet

Federative Socialist Republic (RSFSR)
Joseph Stalin
Supreme Soviet
union republic
Boris Yeltsin

END NOTES

1. Note that Brezhnev was named first secretary of the CPSU upon Khrushchev's forced retirement in 1964. Brezhnev quickly began to build his own personal power base, marked by the change in the title of the party's leader to general secretary (the same title Stalin had held) in 1966, and subsequently by Brezhnev's supremacy within the ruling Politburo.

    On the patterns of succession and power-consolidation in the Khrushchev and Brezhnev leaderships, see George W. Breslauer, *Khrushchev and Brezhnev as Leaders: Building Authority in Soviet Politics* (London: Allen & Unwin, 1982).

2. Archie Brown, "Power and Policy in a Time of Leadership Transition," in Archie Brown, ed., *Political Leadership in the Soviet Union* (Bloomington: Indiana University Press, 1989), pp. 163–217.

3. Thane Gustafson and Dawn Mann, "Gorbachev's Next Gamble," *Problems of Communism*, 36:4 (July–August 1987), pp. 1–20.

4. Martin McCauley, ed., *Khrushchev and Khrushchevism* (Bloomington: Indiana University Press, 1987).

5. Stephen White, "Reforming the Electoral System," *Journal of Communist Studies*, 4:4 (1988), pp. 1–17.

6. The eyewitness reports by Timothy Garton Ash, *The Magic Lantern* (New York: Random House, 1990), are exceptionally valuable first-hand accounts as well as brilliant political analysis of the revolutions of 1989 in Eastern Europe.

7. On Gorbachev's autocratic methods in forcing through the constitutional amendments needed to create a powerful presidency, see David Shipler,

"Between Dictatorship and Anarchy," *The New Yorker*, June 25, 1990.

8. Seweryn Bialer, *The Soviet Paradox: External Expansion, Internal Decline* (New York: Alfred A. Knopf, 1986), p. 307.

9. On Soviet power projection, see Rajan Menon, *Soviet Power and the Third World* (New Haven, Conn.: Yale University Press, 1986); U.S. House of Representatives, Committee on Foreign Affairs, *The Soviet Union in the Third World, 1980–85: An Imperial Burden or Political Asset?* (Washington, D.C.: U.S. Government Printing Office, September 23, 1985).

10. Two very useful sources on the backgrounds to the shift in Soviet thinking about international relations are, first, Robert Legvold, "The Revolution in Soviet Foreign Policy," *Foreign Affairs*, 68:1 (1989), pp. 82–98; and David Holloway, "Gorbachev's New Thinking," *Foreign Affairs*, 68:1 (1989), pp. 66–81.

11. Lucian W. Pye, "Political Science and the Crisis of Authoritarianism," *American Political Science Review*, 84:1 (1990), p. 9. This article originated as the author's presidential address to the American Political Science Association.

12. Thomas F. Remington, *The Truth of Authority: Ideology and Communication in the Soviet Union* (Pittsburgh: University of Pittsburgh Press, 1988), p. 3.

13. Ellen Mickiewicz, *Split Signals: Television and Politics in the Soviet Union* (New York: Oxford University Press, 1988), pp. 4–5.

14. Ibid., p. 209.

15. Remington, *The Truth of Authority*, pp. 189–195.

16. Seweryn Bialer cited in Lucian Pye, "Political Science and the Crisis of Authoritarianism," p. 10.

17. Frederick C. Barghoorn and Thomas F. Remington, *Politics in the USSR*, 3rd ed. (Boston: Little, Brown & Co., 1986), p. 62.

18. Moshe Lewin, *The Gorbachev Phenomenon: A Historical Interpretation* (Berkeley: University of California Press, 1988), pp. 62–71.

19. S. Frederick Starr, "The Changing Nature of Change in the USSR," in Seweryn Bialer and Michael Mandelbaum, eds., *Gorbachev's Russia and American Foreign Policy* (Boulder, Colo.: Westview Press, 1988), pp. 3–36.

20. In 1980, 66.3 percent of Americans aged twenty-five or over had completed secondary school, and 16.3 percent had four or more years of college. See Andrew Hacker, *U/S: A Statistical Portrait of the American People* (New York: Viking, 1983), pp. 250–251.

21. Brian Silver, "Political Beliefs of the Soviet Citizen," in James R. Millar, ed., *Politics, Work, and Daily Life in the USSR* (Cambridge: Cambridge University Press, 1987), p. 127.

22. Lewin, *The Gorbachev Phenomenon*.

23. Jerry F. Hough, *Opening up the Soviet Economy* (Washington, D.C.: Brookings Institution, 1988), p. 22.

24. Richard Stites, *Revolutionary Dreams: Utopian Vision and Experimental Life in the Russian Revolution* (New York, Oxford: Oxford University Press, 1989).

25. On the crisis in ideology, see Remington, *The Truth of Authority*; Sylvia Woodby and Alfred B. Evans, Jr., eds., *Restructuring Soviet Ideology: Gorbachev's New Thinking* (Boulder, Colo.: Westview Press, 1990); David Wedgwood Benn, *Persuasion and Soviet Politics* (Oxford: Basil Blackwell, 1989).

26. Gail Warshofsky Lapidus, "Social Trends," in Robert F. Byrnes, ed., *After Brezhnev: Sources of Soviet Conduct in the 1980s* (Bloomington: Indiana University Press, 1983), p. 283.

27. Christopher Davis and Murray Feshbach, "Rising Infant Mortality in the USSR in the 1970's," Series P–25, no. 74 (Washington, D.C.: U.S. Bureau of the Census, September 1980); Nick Eberstadt, "The Health Crisis in the USSR," *New York Review of Books*, February 19, 1981.

28. Murray Feshbach, "Issues in Soviet Health Problems," in *Soviet Economy in the 1980s: Problems and Prospects*, vol. 2 (Washington, D.C.: Joint Economic Committee of the U.S.

Congress, 1982), pp. 203–227; see also Nick Eberstadt, "Overview," in the same volume, pp. 187–202.

29. See Murray Feshbach, Prepared Statement, in *Political Economy of the Soviet Union* (Washington, D.C.: Joint Economic Committee and House Committee on Foreign Affairs, 1984), pp. 127–137.

30. Nikolai Bykov, "Oko gosudarstvennoe," *Ogonek*, no. 25 (June 1987), p. 18.

31. The article that sparked the debate was published in February 1987. See Vasilii Seliunin and Grigorii Khanin, "Lukavaia tsifra," *Novyi mir*, no. 2 (1987), pp. 181–201.

32. Anders Åslund, "How Small Is Soviet National Income?" in Henry S. Rowen and Charles Wolf, Jr., eds., *The Impoverished Superpower: Perestroika and the Soviet Military Burden* (San Francisco: Institute for Contemporary Studies, 1990), p. 49.

33. Vasilii Seliunin, "Glubokaia reforma ili revansh biurokratii?" *Znamia*, no. 7 (1988), pp. 155–167; idem, "Chernye dyry ekonomiki," *Novyi mir*, no. 10 (1989), pp. 153–178.

34. Vasilii Seliunin, "Glubokaia reforma?"; Nikolai Petrakov, "Ekonomika i gosudarstvo," *Ogonek*, no. 10 (1989), pp. 14–15; Nikolai Shmelev, "Avansy i dolgi," *Novyi mir*, no. 6 (1987), pp. 142–158; E. Gaidar and V. Iaroshenko, "Nulevoi tsikl: k analizu mekhanizma vedomstvennoi ekspansii," *Kommunist*, no. 8 (1988), pp. 74–86.

35. Gabriel A. Almond and Sidney Verba, *The Civic Culture: Political Attitudes and Democracy in Five Nations* (Boston: Little, Brown & Co., 1965), pp. 164–165.

36. Karl W. Deutsch, *Nationalism and Social Communication* (Cambridge, Mass.: MIT Press and John Wiley & Sons, 1953).

37. "Bolsheviks" was the name used by the faction of the Russian Social Democratic Labor party — that is, Russia's Marxist party — led by Vladimir Ilyich Lenin. The Bolsheviks organized and led the uprising that succeeded in seizing governmental power in the October Revolution of 1917. Through the ensuing civil war (1918–1921) they suppressed rival socialist and other parties and all other opposing political forces. In 1918 the Bolsheviks took the name "Russian Communist party," and in 1925, upon the formation of a federal Union of Soviet Socialist

Republics, they renamed the party "All-Union Communist party." Since 1952 the party has been known as the Communist party of the Soviet Union, or CPSU.

38. Two excellent recent studies provide extensive documentation on the effects of Soviet rule on the peoples of Central Asia. See Martha Brill Olcott, *The Kazakhs* (Stanford, Calif.: Hoover Institution Press, 1987) and Edward A. Allworth, *The Modern Uzbeks* (Stanford, Calif.: Hoover Institution Press, 1990). An excellent comprehensive survey of Soviet nationality policy is Bohdan Nahaylo and Victor Swoboda, *Soviet Disunion: A History of the Nationalities Problem in the USSR* (New York: Free Press, 1990).

39. Nahaylo and Swoboda, *Soviet Disunion*, pp. 172–173.

40. Frederick C. Barghoorn, "Russian Nationalism and Soviet Politics: Official and Unofficial Perspectives," in Robert Conquest, ed., *The Last Empire: Nationality and the Soviet Future* (Stanford, Calif.: Hoover Institution Press, 1986), pp. 30–77.

41. Teresa Rakowska-Harmstone, "Minority Nationalism Today: An Overview," in Conquest, ed., *The Last Empire*, p. 239; Gregory Gleason, *Federalism and Nationalism: The Struggle for Republican Rights in the USSR* (Boulder, Colo., and London: Westview Press, 1990); and Thomas Remington, "Federalism and Segmented Communications in the USSR," *Publius*, 15:4 (1985), pp. 113–132.

42. Rakowska-Harmstone, "Minority Nationalism Today," in Conquest, ed., *The Last Empire*, p. 239.

43. See the important discussions of this issue in Stephen White, *Political Culture and Soviet Politics* (London: Macmillan, 1979), and Archie Brown, ed., *Political Culture and Communist Studies* (Armonk, N.Y.: M. E. Sharpe, 1985).

44. Hough, *Opening up the Soviet Economy*, pp. 19–20.

45. Robert C. Tucker, *The Soviet Political Mind: Stalinism and Post-Stalin Change*, rev. ed. (New York: W. W. Norton, 1971), ch. 6, "The Image of Dual Russia."

46. Alex Inkeles and Raymond Bauer, *The Soviet Citizen* (New York: Atheneum, 1968), p. 300.

47. Thomas F. Remington, "The March 1990 RSFSR Elections," in Darrell Slider, ed., *Elections and Political Change in the Soviet Republics* (forthcoming).

48. The discussion that follows draws heavily on a pioneering comparative study of management in Soviet and U.S. enterprises conducted by scholars at the Harvard Business School in collaboration with Soviet researchers. See Paul R. Lawrence and Charalambos A. Vlachoutsicos et al., *Behind the Factory Walls: Decision Making in Soviet and U.S. Enterprises* (Boston: Harvard Business School Press, 1990), pp. 74–80.

49. Moshe Lewin, *The Making of the Soviet System* (New York: Pantheon Books, 1985), p. 237.

50. Robert Sharlet, *The New Soviet Constitution of 1977: Analysis and Text* (Brunswick, Ohio: King's Court Communications, 1978), p. 27.

51. Stephen F. Cohen, *Rethinking the Soviet Experience* (New York: Oxford University Press, 1985), ch. 5, "The Friends and Foes of Change: Soviet Reformism and Conservatism."

52. Gorbachev's book, *Perestroika*, provides a broad overview of Gorbachev's views on domestic and foreign policy as of 1987. Since then, his positions have grown markedly more radical and a good deal more pessimistic in tone.

Mikhail Gorbachev, *Perestroika: New Thinking for Our Country and the World* (New York: Harper & Row, 1987).

53. Robert A. Dahl, *Polyarchy: Participation and Opposition* (New Haven, Conn.: Yale University Press, 1971), p. 121. Dahl employs the terms *polyarchy* and *hegemony* instead of the more familiar but imprecise terms, *democracy* and *authoritarianism*.

54. Gur Ofer, "Soviet Economic Growth; 1928–1985," *Journal of Economic Literature*, 25:4 (December 1987), pp. 1767–1833, offers a comprehensive review of Soviet economic growth patterns and the policy choices that can be inferred from a review of actual performance.

55. E. D. Igitkhanian, I. Iu. Petrushina, and F. R. Filippov, "Industrial'nyi otriad trudiashchikhsia [The Industrial Detachment of the Toilers]," *Sotsiologicheskie issledovaniia*, no. 3 (1990), p. 5. Figures pertain to 1987.

56. See the discussion of different models of social and ethnic stratification by Victor Zaslavsky, "Ethnic Group Divided: Social Stratification and Nationality Policy in the Soviet Union," in Peter J. Potichnyj, ed., *The Soviet Union: Party and Society* (Cambridge: Cambridge University Press, 1988), pp. 218–228.

57. Mark Beissinger and Lubomyr Hajda,

"Nationalism and Reform in Soviet Politics," in Lubomyr Hajda and Mark Beissinger, eds., *The Nationalities Factor in Soviet Politics and Society* (Boulder, Colo., San Francisco and Oxford: Westview Press, 1990), p. 307.

58. Paul Goble, "USSR—Ethnicity and Economic Reform," *Radio Liberty Research* (Munich, February 2, 1990).

59. Rakowska-Harmstone, "Minority Nationalism Today: An Overview," in Conquest, ed., *The Last Empire*, pp. 247–249.

60. Ronald Grigor Suny, "Transcaucasia: Cultural Cohesion and Ethnic Revival in a Multinational Society," in Hajda and Beissinger, eds., *The Nationalities Factor*, p. 248.

61. On the mediating role played by the national elites in the major republics, see Gregory Gleason, *Federalism and Nationalism: The Struggle for Republican Rights in the USSR* (Boulder, Colo., San Francisco, and London: Westview Press, 1990), especially ch. 5, "Bureaucratic Nationalism."

62. "KPSS v tsifrakh," *Partiinaia zhizn'*, no. 21 (1987), p. 8.

63. Milovan Djilas, *The New Class: An Analysis of the Communist System* (New York: Praeger, 1957).

64. Important information on the nomenklatura system will be found in Bohdan Harasymiw, *Political Elite Recruitment in the Soviet Union* (New York: St. Martin's Press, 1984).

65. An important book by a former high-level Soviet official that analyzes the nomenklatura stratum as a new ruling class is Michael Voslensky, *Nomenklatura: The Soviet Ruling Class*, trans. Eric Mosbacher (Garden City, N.Y.: Doubleday, 1984).

66. T. Samolis, "Ochishchenie," *Pravda*, February 13, 1986.

67. A valuable study of career patterns in the political elite is Joel C. Moses, "Functional Career Specialization in Soviet Regional Elite Recruitment," in T. H. Rigby and Bohdan Harasymiw, eds., *Leadership Selection and Patron–Client Relations in the USSR and Yugoslavia* (London: Allen & Unwin, 1983), pp. 15–61.

68. Stephen White, *Gorbachev in Power* (Cambridge: Cambridge University Press, 1990), p. 28.

69. On Gorbachev's democratization strategy, see White, *Gorbachev in Power*, ch. 2, "Democratizing the Political System."

70. Quoted in ibid., p. 24.

71. *Pravda*, January 30, 1987.

72. Ibid.

73. Some observers believe that Gorbachev made a serious tactical mistake when he created the presidency in March 1990 by not immediately running for the office himself and winning a popular mandate to rule. Instead, apparently wishing to put the new system in place as quickly as possible, Gorbachev had the Congress of People's Deputies elect him, stipulating that when his term expired in 1995 he or his successor would be elected in a direct election as the constitution required.

74. One of the first Soviet writers to make this alarming comparison was the sociologist Yuri Levada, "Dinamika sotsial'nogo pereloma: vozmozhnosti analiza," *Kommunist*, no. 2 (January 1989), pp. 34–45.

75. Robert A. Dahl, *Dilemmas of Pluralist Democracy: Autonomy vs. Control* (New Haven, Conn.: Yale University Press, 1982), p. 3.

76. Dahl, *Polyarchy*; Guillermo O'Donnell, Philippe C. Schmitter, and Laurence Whitehead, *Transitions from Authoritarian Rule: Prospects for Democracy* (Baltimore: Johns Hopkins University Press, 1986); Thomas F. Remington, "Regime Transition in Communist Systems: The Soviet Case," *Soviet Economy*, 6:2 (1990), pp. 160–190.

77. See Remington, "A Socialist Pluralism of Opinions," pp. 271–304.

78. Vladimir Brovkin, "Revolution from Below: Informal Political Associations in Russia, 1988–1989," *Soviet Studies*, 42:2 (April 1990), pp. 233–257; see also James Butterfield and Judith Sedaitis, eds., *New Social Movements in the Soviet Union* (Boulder, Colo.: Westview Press, 1991).

79. Brovkin, "Revolution from Below," p. 234.

80. Martha Brill Olcott, "Perestroyka in Kazakhstan," *Problems of Communism*, 39:4 (July–August 1990), pp. 66–67.

81. Olcott, "Perestroyka," p. 67.

82. For a discussion of the Moldavian case, see William Crowther, "The Politics of Mobilization: Nationalism and Reform in Moldavia," *Russian Review*, forthcoming.

83. Well over half of these were Armenians who had fled Azerbaijan and Azerbaijani who had fled Armenia. A sizable proportion were Russians, however, many of whom were leaving Central

Asia and other regions where anti-Russian sentiments were becoming increasingly powerful.

84. *Argumenty i fakty*, no. 46 (1990), p. 1.

85. *Izvestiia TsK KPSS*, no. 5 (1990), p. 132.

86. David Remnick, "Soviet Mining City a Model of 'Whole, Sick System'," *Washington Post*, October 21, 1990, pp. 1, 30.

87. Vladimir N. Brovkin, "The Making of Elections to the Congress of People's Deputies (CPD) in March 1989," *Russian Review*, 49:4 (1990), p. 441.

88. Seweryn Bialer, "The Yeltsin Affair: The Dilemma of the Left in Gorbachev's Revolution," in Bialer, ed., *Politics, Society, and Nationality Inside Gorbachev's Russia*, pp. 91–120.

89. For a vivid portrait of Yeltsin as a politician, see Bill Keller, "Boris Yeltsin Taking Power," *New York Times Magazine*, September 23, 1990.

90. On the impact of television in Soviet society, see Ellen Mickiewicz, *Split Signals: Television and Politics in the Soviet Union* (New York and Oxford: Oxford University Press, 1988); on propaganda and mass communications more generally, see Stephen White, *Political Culture and Soviet Politics* (London: Macmillan, 1979); Stephen White and Alex Pravda, eds., *Ideology and Soviet Politics* (London: Macmillan, 1988); Stephen White, "Propagating Communist Values in the USSR," *Problems of Communism*, 34:6 (November–December 1985), pp. 1–17; David Wedgwood Benn, *Persuasion and Soviet Politics* (Oxford: Basil Blackwell, 1989); and Thomas F. Remington, *The Truth of Authority: Ideology and Communication in the Soviet Union* (Pittsburgh: University of Pittsburgh Press, 1988). Major studies of propaganda in earlier periods include Gayle Durham Hollander, *Soviet Political Indoctrination* (New York: Praeger, 1972); and Alex Inkeles, *Public Opinion in Soviet Russia: A Study in Mass Persuasion*, 3rd ed. (Cambridge, Mass.: Harvard University Press, 1958).

91. Thomas Remington, "The Mass Media and Public Communication in the USSR," *Journal of Politics*, 43:3 (August 1981), pp. 803–817; also see idem, *The Truth of Authority*, pp. 189–207.

92. Bill Keller, "At Mrs. Gorbachev's School, Hardly a Communist in Sight," *New York Times*, November 4, 1990.

93. Yu. Levada et al., "Homo Sovieticus: A Rough Sketch," *Moscow News*, no. 11 (1990), p. 11.

94. Tatiana Zaslavskaia, "Vesti dialog s liud'mi," *Narodnyi deputat*, no. 2 (1990), pp. 25–27. Zaslavskaia is a distinguished sociologist who was one of the most important theorists of reform in the pre-Gorbachev and early Gorbachev periods. A member of the Academy of Sciences and a deputy to the Congress of People's Deputies, she is director of a new institute that conducts public opinion surveys throughout the Soviet Union.

95. The famine has become the object of intensive study by scholars in the West and now in the Ukraine as well. One of the most important works on the subject is Robert Conquest, *The Harvest of Sorrow: Soviet Collectivization and the Terror–Famine* (New York and Oxford: Oxford University Press, 1986).

96. Cf. Anthony D. Smith, *The Ethnic Origins of Nations* (Oxford: Basil Blackwell, 1986), pp. 212–213.

97. Cf. Walker Connor, "Nation-Building or Nation-Destroying?" *World Politics* (April 1972), p. 346.

98. Zbigniew Brzezinski, "Post-Communist Nationalism," *Foreign Affairs*, 68:5 (1989), p. 11.

99. On the democratic movement in relation to the policy of detente with the West, see especially Frederick C. Barghoorn, *Detente and the Democratic Movement in the USSR* (New York: Free Press, 1976).

100. E. Mickiewicz, *Split Signals*, pp. 224, 219–20.

101. Ronald J. Hill and Peter Frank, *The Soviet Communist Party*, 3rd ed. (Boston: Allen & Unwin, 1986); T. H. Rigby, *Communist Party Membership in the U.S.S.R., 1917–1967* (Princeton, N.J.: Princeton University Press, 1968); Jerry F. Hough, *The Soviet Prefects: The Local Party Organs in Industrial Decision-Making* (Cambridge, Mass.: Harvard University Press, 1969).

102. Robert Sharlet, *The New Soviet Constitution of 1977: Analysis and Text* (Brunswick, Ohio: King's Court Communication, 1978), p. 78.

103. Robert V. Daniels, "Office Holding and Elite Status: The Central Committee of the CPSU," in Paul S. Cocks, Robert V. Daniels, and Nancy Whittier Heer, eds., *The Dynamics of Soviet Politics* (Cambridge, Mass.: Harvard University Press, 1976), pp. 77–95; Jerry F. Hough and Merle Fainsod, *How the Soviet Union Is Governed* (Cambridge, Mass.: Harvard University Press, 1979), pp. 128–132, 454–455.

104. Myron Rush, *Political Succession in the USSR* (New York: Columbia University Press, 1968).

105. George W. Breslauer, *Khrushchev and Brezhnev and Leaders: Building Authority in Soviet Politics* (Boston: Allen & Unwin, 1982).

106. On Stalin's career, see the magisterial biography by Robert C. Tucker, two volumes of which have appeared covering his rise to power and his rule in the 1930s: *Stalin as Revolutionary, 1879–1929* (New York: W. W. Norton, 1973) and *Stalin in Power: The Revolution from Above, 1928–1941* (New York: W. W. Norton, 1990).

107. On the system of terror under Lenin and Stalin, the greatest documentary study remains Alexander Solzhenitsyn, *The Gulag Archipelago, 1918–1956: An Experiment in Literary Investigation* (New York: Harper & Row, 1973–1976).

108. David Shipler, "Between Dictatorship and Anarchy," *The New Yorker*, June 25, 1990.

109. Richard Sakwa, *Gorbachev and His Reforms, 1985–1990* (New York: Prentice Hall, 1990), pp. 166–167.

110. Thomas F. Remington, "Regime Transition in Communist Systems: The Soviet Case" *Soviet Economy*, 6:2 (January 1991), pp. 160–190.

111. Joel C. Moses, "Democratic Reform in the Gorbachev Era," *The Russian Review*, 48:3 (July 1989), pp. 241–242.

112. An excellent discussion of the relationship between specialists who are policy innovators and policymakers in the Brezhnev era is the chapter "Bringing New Ideas into Soviet Politics," by Thane Gustafson, *Reform in Soviet Politics: Lessons of Recent Policies on Land and Water* (Cambridge: Cambridge University Press, 1981), pp. 83–95.
   One of the most prominent of the "specialist-entrepreneurs" under Gorbachev, and a man responsible for shaping many of the economic reform proposals that were adopted, is Abel Aganbegyan. In his book *Inside Perestroika*, Aganbegyan cites a number of instances showing the tenuous and dependent relationship of specialists to policymakers in the past. When it was convenient, a leader might call on experts to legitimate a policy preference or to identify a solution to a problem. Often, however, when they offered unwanted advice or criticism, the leader rudely attacked the specialists as slanderers or fools, and might withhold certain privileges from them, such as the opportunity to travel abroad.
   See Abel Aganbegyan, *Inside Perestroika: The Future of the Soviet Economy*, trans. Helen Szamuely (New York: Harper & Row, 1989).

113. Two good overviews of Soviet economic performance are: "Survey: The Soviet Union," *The Economist*, October 20, 1990; "The Rise and Fall of Perestroika," *The Economist*, January 19, 1991.

114. Vladmimir N. Kudryavtsev, "Towards a Socialist Rule-of-Law State," in Abel Aganbegyan, ed., *Perestroika 1989* (New York: Scribner's, 1988), p. 110.

115. I am indebted to Professor Harold J. Berman for clarification of this point.

116. A seminal study of the influences on the development of law in the Soviet Union is Harold J. Berman, *Justice in the U.S.S.R.*, rev. ed. (Cambridge, Mass.: Harvard University Press, 1963).

117. Full texts of these articles of the RSFSR Criminal Code together with commentary will be found in Harold J. Berman, ed., *Soviet Criminal Law and Procedure: The RSFSR Codes*, 2nd ed. (Cambridge, Mass.: Harvard University Press, 1972). Analogous articles were contained in the criminal codes of other republics as well.

118. Sidney Bloch and Peter Reddaway, *Psychiatric Terror: How Soviet Psychiatry Is Used to Suppress Dissent* (New York: Basic Books, 1977).

119. One of the early products of *glasnost* was the exposure of "telephone justice" as a prevalent practice. See, for example, Arkadii Vaksberg, "Pravde v glaza," *Literaturnaia gazeta*, December 17, 1986, p. 13.

120. Robert Sharlet, "The Communist Party and the Administration of Justice in the USSR," in Donald D. Barry et al., eds., *Soviert Law after Stalin, Part III: Soviet Institutions and the Administration of Law* (Alpen aan den Rijn, The Netherlands and Germantown, Md.: Sijthoff & Noordhoff, 1979), pp. 321–392. In another article, Sharlet details several ways in which the regime acted to repress individuals for political acts, including administrative penalties such as job dismissal, officially sponsored acts of hooliganism, psychiatric internment, forced emigration, and criminal trials. See Robert Sharlet, "Party and Public Ideals in Conflict: Constitutionalism and Civil Rights in the

USSR," *Cornell International Law Journal*, 23:2 (1990), pp. 341–362.

121. Donald D. Barry and Carol Barner-Barry, *Contemporary Soviet Politics: An Introduction*, 4th ed. (Englewood Cliffs, N.J.: Prentice Hall, 1991), p. 160.

122. An informative article about the advocates, based on interviews in the winter of 1988–1989, is Michael Burrage, "*Advokatura:* In Search of Professionalism and Pluralism in Moscow and Leningrad," *Law and Social Inquiry*, 15:3 (Summer 1990), pp. 433–478. An article analyzing the statute of the Russian Republic that governs the activity of the advocates is Harold J. Berman and Yuri I. Luryi, "The Soviet *Advokatura:* The 1980 RSFSR Statute with Annotations," *Soviet Union/Union Sovietique*, 14:3 (1987), pp. 253–299.

123. On the role of the KGB in the current system, see "The New Soviet Policy-Makers," *The Economist*, February 9, 1991.

124. On Kriuchkov's warnings in the media and his Congress speech, see *The Economist*, December 22, 1990, p. 62; Bill Keller, "K.G.B. Chief Warns Against West's Aid to Soviet Economy," *New York Times*, December 23, 1990, pp. 1, 6.

125. Eugene Huskey, "Government Rulemaking as a Brake on Perestroika," *Law and Social Inquiry*, 15:3 (Summer 1990), p. 421.

126. Ibid., p. 424.

127. Ibid., pp. 424–425.

128. Ibid., p. 429.

129. Robert Legvold, "The Revolution in Soviet Foreign Policy," *Foreign Affairs*, 68:1 (1989), pp. 82–98.

130. Allen Lynch, *The Soviet Study of International Relations* (Cambridge: Cambridge University Press, 1989). The Introduction of this book is a very helpful analysis of the ideas that had been developed in Soviet think tanks before being adopted as official policy under the general rubric of "new thinking."

131. David Holloway, "Gorbachev's New Thinking," *Foreign Affairs*, 68:1 (1989), pp. 66–81.

132. Seweryn Bialer, "The Soviet Union and the West: Security and Foreign Policy," in Bialer and Mandelbaum, eds., *Gorbachev's Russia and American Foreign Policy.*

133. These are officially considered to be missiles with a range of between 500 and 5,500 kilometers, or about 300 to 3,400 miles.

134. Following World War II, the Soviet Union occupied four small islands or groups of islands just north of the Japanese main islands, called the Kurile Islands. The Japanese have never accepted Soviet possession of these islands as legitimate and have made their return a condition of significant improvement in political and economic relations.

135. *Pravda*, October 4, 1985, cited in Neil Malcolm, "The 'Common European Home' and Soviet European Policy." *International Affairs*, 65:4 (Autumn 1989), p. 659.

136. Jonathan Haslam, "The UN and the Soviet Union: New Thinking?" *International Affairs*, 65:4 (Autumn 1989), p. 679.

137. Ibid., p. 681.

138. Quoted from Gorbachev's September 1987 article and December 1988 address, in Robert Legvold, "The Gulf Crisis," and the Future of Gorbachev's Foreign Policy Revolution," *Harriman Institute Forum*, 3:10 (October 1990), p. 5, and Jonathan Haslam, "The UN and the Soviet Union," p. 683.

139. Legvold, "The Gulf Crisis," p. 7.

140. Ibid., p. 8.

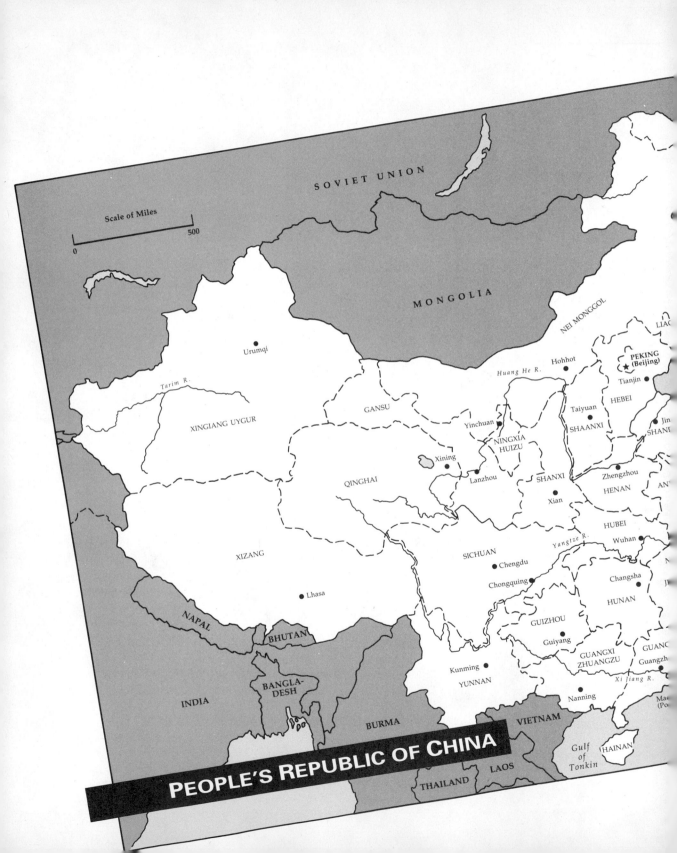

SOVIET UNION

Scale of Miles

0   500

MONGOLIA

NEI MONGGOL

LIAO

PEKING
(Beijing)

★

Urumqi

Hohhot

Tianjin

Huang He R.

Tarim R.

GANSU

Taiyuan

HEBEI

Yinchuan

NINGXIA
HUIZU

SHAANXI

Jin

SHAND

XINGIANG UYGUR

Xining

SHANXI

Zhengzhou

QINGHAI

Lanzhou

HENAN

AN

Xian

HUBEI

XIZANG

Yangtze R.

Wuhan

N

SICHUAN

Chengdu

Changsha

Lhasa

Chongquing

HUNAN

NAPAL

GUIZHOU

BHUTAN

Guiyang

GUANGXI
ZHUANGZU

GUANG

BANGLA-
DESH

Kunming

Guangzh

INDIA

YUNNAN

Xi Jiang R.

Nanning

Mac
(Po

BURMA

VIETNAM

Gulf
of
Tonkin

HAINAN

PEOPLE'S REPUBLIC OF CHINA

THAILAND

LAOS

CHAPTER 14

BRANTLY WOMACK
JAMES R. TOWNSEND

POLITICS IN CHINA

INTRODUCTION

I N THE spring of 1989, China experienced a momentous and tragic series of crises that brought Chinese politics to the forefront of world attention. For week after week, hundreds of thousands and eventually millions of demonstrators filled Tiananmen Square ("The Gate of Heavenly Peace") in the center of Beijing. Despite the government's official criticism of the "turmoil," the demonstrators camped in the square, staged a hunger strike, and broadcast to the world their demands for democratic reform. Even the government's declaration of martial law on May 20 did not end the demonstrations, and initial attempts to enforce martial law were peacefully frustrated by popular support for the demonstrators. In the meantime sympathetic demonstrations were occurring in most other Chinese cities. Not only were the demonstrations reported with approval and optimism by the Western press (and the Western response was immediately relayed back to China through Voice of America and BBC World Service), but even the official Chinese press was clearly sympathetic. Finally, however, the People's Liberation Army (PLA) shot its way into the center of the city to disperse the last demonstrators, leaving hundreds of dead civilians in its wake. At one stroke, the June 4 Massacre forced China in a new and dark direction.

As it became clear that the regime had apparently succeeded with its repression and the demonstrations were indeed over, world attention shifted to the more optimistic developments in Eastern Europe. The brutal massacre in Beijing led many governments and international organizations to adopt sanctions against China, and China's international trade and tourism dropped precipitously. But China was not ostracized for long. Sanctions began to soften six months after the massacre, and they were generally abandoned after Iraq's invasion of Kuwait required China's cooperation in the United Nations. As of early 1991, Chinese domestic politics appeared sullen but quiet, and its international position appeared shaken but basically stable. It was clear, however, that Chinese politics was in the eye of a storm. The eventual death of Deng

An unemployed worker and a street trader are about to be executed for arson in connection with demonstrations in June 1989. Demonstrations occurred not only at Tiananmen Square in Beijing, but in most cities in China. Violence and repression occurred in some locations.

until 1989, China experienced a decade of unparalleled prosperity under the leadership of Deng Xiaoping. Deng relaxed ideological tension, reduced state controls on economic activity, and permitted people to pursue profit. As a result, the lives of most Chinese were transformed from a monotonous routine tightly controlled by authorities to a more colorful existence with both new hopes and new anxieties, one in which the authorities played a more distant and ambiguous role. The students who demonstrated in Tiananmen were children of this decade of prosperity and decontrol. At bottom, they demanded that China's leaders acknowledge and guarantee the new diversity and freedom of society. But China's leaders saw the threat of chaos in such demands for diversity.

Both characteristics continue to be major influences on post–Tiananmen politics. On the one hand, the fear of chaos and the habit of revolutionary politics can be seen in the government's determination to keep control over society and not to compromise. Students and faculties at universities and workers at other organizations involved in the demonstrations have had to write personal accounts of their activities and to affirm their loyalty to the regime. On the other hand, Deng Xiaoping is reluctant to change the reform policies of the 1980s, and so a wholesale reversal of policy has not occurred. The regime remains committed to modernization and openness, but it is adamantly opposed to any challenges to its monopoly of political power. It is not clear, however, how long it can combine economic reform with political repression.

In order to understand the current situation of Chinese politics, we must grasp both its general pattern of development in the twentieth century and the new context of politics which emerged in the 1980s.

The *Chinese Communist party (CCP)* emerged in the 1920s as one of the forces attempting to save China from chaos, backwardness, and foreign oppression. China's situation was indeed desperate. Its territory was split up among warlords who were constantly scheming and fighting among themselves, while in the cities foreigners controlled much of the modern economy from self-governing enclaves. Nine-tenths of the population struggled to eke out a living by farming; in the words of one observer, their situation was "like that of a man standing permanently up to the neck in water, so that even a ripple is sufficient to drown him." [1] The CCP could succeed as a revolutionary movement because of the disunity of the country, the threats from

Xiaoping and the other octogenarians who reasserted control in 1989 will surely have massive but unpredictable repercussions.

The *Tiananmen* events demonstrated the continuing importance of two strands in Chinese politics. The first is the struggle for order and unified leadership in the face of chaos, a major characteristic of Chinese politics since the fall of the Chinese Empire in 1911. The second is the unfolding and diversification of society as it has progressed and modernized. The first strand is most evident in *Deng Xiaoping*'s power politics as reflected in the bloody suppression of the demonstrations, but it can also be seen in the student leaders' radicalism and refusal to compromise. Twentieth-century Chinese politics has been a turbulent and bitter struggle for power; the familiar style of politics is one of revolutionary struggle.

The second characteristic, the expression of a diversified society, was a minor and subordinate theme of Chinese politics until the 1980s. Only in the last decade were economic prosperity and individual material welfare acknowledged as basic social goals. From 1979

foreigners, especially Japan, and the misery of the people.

When the CCP came to power and founded the People's Republic of China (PRC) in 1949, it was determined to transform China into a unified, independent, and modern country along the lines of the Soviet Union. The PRC was set up as a party–state, a state where all significant resources are controlled by public authorities and where all political power is concentrated in the hands of party leadership. In just a few years it was clear that China was unified, independent, and beginning to make economic progress.

However, the initial successes of the PRC led to overly ambitious programs and new political turbulence. From 1957 to 1977 leftist ideology promoted by Mao Zedong brought political tensions into every aspect of life and led to two major disasters, the Great Leap Forward of 1958 and the Cultural Revolution of 1966. Although in general China's economic development continued, most Chinese lived lives of deprivation and anxiety. In contrast to the situation before 1949, the problem was not that of a central government that was too weak, but one of a party–state that was too strong, too intrusive, and too capricious. The death of Mao in 1976 presented the opportunity of swinging the pendulum away from the concentration of party–state power, and Deng Xiaoping took the lead.

The 1980s were generally a time of optimism and prosperity during which the party–state loosened its control over society. Practical results became more important than ideological purity, and families who got rich through hard work were praised. Massive changes occurred in the economy, in governmental policies, and in administrative personnel. Significant reforms were adopted even in the political system, although the CCP's monopoly of power was not questioned and there was not a firm, official commitment to *glasnost* as in the Soviet Union under Mikhail Gorbachev. China also opened its economy to the world market. The reforms were remarkably successful. China became one of the most rapidly developing economies in the world, and the nonstate sector developed especially rapidly. Consumer goods proliferated, and life-styles diversified. Of course, such phenomena as corruption, crime, and pornography also increased. All these changes appeared to signal the end of the revolutionary era and the beginning of a postrevolutionary era in which the party and state would play a defined and limited role.

In 1989 at Tiananmen, the optimism and societal changes of the 1980s collided with the political structure of the party–state formed in the crucible of revolution. The violence and tragedy of the collision was unexpected. Deng Xiaoping did not think that those who had benefited from the reforms he patronized would rise to challenge him, while the demonstrators thought that they were only demanding the next logical step in the process of reform. The massacre has not erased the 1980s, but it did profoundly confuse and unsettle China's immediate political future.

HISTORICAL AND ENVIRONMENTAL SETTING

In Chinese perspective, the PRC is a new political system. The old imperial order, which ended in 1911 with the overthrow of the Qing (Manchu) dynasty, had endured more than 2,000 years. This political tradition, with its remarkable power and longevity, continues to influence Chinese political thought and institutions. Historical orientations, analogies, and comparisons remain common in political discourse.

Personal experience reinforces the closeness and relevance of tradition. Most of the leaders who governed the PRC until recently were born before the fall of the Qing dynasty. Mao and his colleagues knew imperial society at first hand and were educated at least partly in the style followed by Chinese intellectuals for centuries. In the 1980s leadership shifted to younger figures without direct experience of the imperial past, but even they are aware of traditional ideas and social patterns that survived after 1911. More importantly, the identity of the CCP was set by three decades of revolutionary activity before it came to power in 1949, and even the younger leaders had come to political maturity during the party's struggle for victory. It is important, therefore, to take a closer look at the political tradition and revolutionary setting from which the CCP emerged. These sections will be followed by an overview of post–1949 political history, emphasizing changes in China's society, economy, and international environment.

The Chinese Political Tradition

The Chinese Empire was a centralized authoritarian system staffed by a scholar-bureaucracy.[2] In contrast to Western feudalism, there were no grants of authority to hereditary landed nobility, and entrance to the bureaucracy was gained by means of an examination system that was open, in principle, to anyone. Nevertheless, there was a strong cleavage between the elite and the rest of the population with regard to privileges and opportunities for advancement. The elite included officials of the imperial bureaucracy and the degree-holding scholars or gentry from whose ranks officials were chosen.

Supplementing the distinction between elite and commoner was a hierarchic structure of authority throughout society, an intricate network of superior-inferior relationships. Within the political elite, the emperor stood alone at the top of the hierarchy, with absolute power over all his officials and subjects. The bureaucracy was divided by ranks and grades, with each official's position fixed in a hierarchy descending from the emperor. Beneath the officials came degree holders not selected for official position, ranked according to the degree they held.

Ordinary subjects, who constituted most of the population, fell outside of this political hierarchy. But where the political hierarchy left off, a highly complex structuring of social relationships took over, with profound implications for the political system. Authority within a family or larger kinship group was held by the eldest male within generational lines; the older generation held sway over younger ones, and elder males were superior to females and younger males of the same generation. Of course, the family head was subordinate to the hierarchy extending downward from the emperor, and thereby brought those beneath him into an ordered relationship with political authority. Therefore, the pattern of hierarchic authority was dominant at both elite and popular levels; any kind of social action, political or not, had to take place within its framework. As a result, the rupture of authority that came with the collapse of the old political system traumatically affected all social relations, and Chinese attempts to reconstruct their political system have usually involved authoritarian and hierarchic authority structures.

The authority structure of traditional China gave the political system supreme power, since the emperor and the bureaucracy — the political leaders — sat at the top of the social hierarchy. Equally significant was the political system's relative independence from external influence or restraint.

One important aspect of the system's self-governing status was its handling of political recruitment and advancement. Individuals could prepare for a political career by acquiring knowledge or wealth, but formal certification came only from the government. Once there, an officeholder had no constituency that might dilute service to the emperor. Political representation was an unknown concept, although a quota system in the examinations encouraged distribution of degree holders among the provinces.

Just as it denied external claims to influence or to membership, the regime acknowledged no legal or institutional limitations on its actions. The government could initiate, manage, regulate, adjudicate, or repress as it saw fit. Elites admitted a moral obligation to provide just and responsive government, but enforcement of that obligation depended on recruitment, which allegedly chose only men of superior virtue, or on the bureaucracy's own mechanisms of control and supervision. That is, the obligation was enforceable only by elite self-regulation.

The ideal of government by a disinterested, educated elite, chosen through examinations without reference to class or wealth, profoundly affected traditional China, but it was never an unqualified reality. Wealth mattered, since officials and official status could be bought. Personal obligations and loyalties to family could erode an official's impartiality, as could those to the same clan, locality, or school. The system tolerated these discrepancies within bounds because it had little choice; but it never granted them legal or moral acceptance, and it frequently punished factional activity or favoritism toward friends and relatives.

Like its imperial predecessor, the communist elite has rejected claims to representation or recognition of partisan interests within the government. Competing political organizations are firmly suppressed in favor of the monolithic authority of the party. Factionalism within the ruling structure is anathema now, as it was under the emperor, although disapproval has failed in both cases to prevent the evil. In contrast to the past, the present system has extended its authority directly to the mass level, reducing sharply the limited local autonomy allowed under the Manchus. At the same time, by enlarging the size and responsibilities of the bureaucracy and by encouraging mass political mobilization, it has made the governmental process more complex and more open to societal pressures and demands.

The Chinese tradition contained from ancient times a number of philosophical-religious schools of thought, but Confucianism became the official ideology of the imperial system. Government officials were appointed mainly on the basis of superior performance in examinations that tested their knowledge of the Confucian classics. Through lifetime study of these classics, officials and other scholars internalized the Confucian beliefs that the role of government is to maintain social order and harmony and that successful performance of this role rests mainly on moral education and conduct. The legitimacy of political authority rested on observance of this moral doctrine, and Confucian ideology thus became an integrative force that justified political rule, defined the purposes of the state, provided the values of the elite, and harmonized diverse interests in society. To the extent that it was widely accepted, it would bring society and officialdom together in common loyalty to rightful imperial authority.

The indispensability of official ideology, carefully defined and studied, is also central to the Communist government, although the content of contemporary ideology is completely different. Indeed, the CCP has gone far beyond the imperial elite in exploiting the integrative benefits of ideology, using it with the masses as well. Although they are concerned about possible deviations from their ideology, their vigorous propagation of it encourages a consciousness of popular membership in the political system. Moreover, the current ideology stresses the virtues of the common people and their role in society, making it significantly more populist than the Confucian ethic.

The Revolutionary Setting

The PRC is part of a revolutionary era dominated by three major themes. Since the revolution had been in progress for decades before the CCP became a significant force in Chinese politics, a sense of how these themes merged with the history of the party is essential to understand the present system.

The first theme, nationalism, has been at the forefront throughout the revolution. Perhaps its clearest manifestation was the desire for independence from foreign influence and control. From 1900 to about 1925, virtually all political movements with significant popular support — the anti-Manchu struggles, the frequent boycotts of foreign goods and enterprises, the strikes and demonstrations of May Fourth (1919) and May Thirtieth (1925) — appealed directly to popular resentment of foreign involvement in Chinese affairs. Independence remained a prominent issue in the Nationalist Revolution of 1926 to 1928 and in the early years of the *Guomindang* (GMD, the Nationalist party, also called the Kuomintang or KMT) government, and with the Japanese invasion of 1937 it again became the paramount national objective. Although China largely regained its independent status in the postwar years, its

conflicts with the United States and the Soviet Union have continued the legacy of earlier anti-imperialist struggles.

China was never a full-fledged colony, but both Chinese and foreigners recognized that Chinese independence was only nominal. Although imperialism never directly affected most areas of Chinese life, its effects were highly visible to urbanized laborers, intellectuals, and businessmen who were influential in defining national political issues. Most politically conscious Chinese believed that foreign economic activities had damaged Chinese development, and virtually all Chinese exposed to the foreign presence resented its forced and privileged penetration of their country. The leaders of the CCP absorbed the anti-imperialist attitudes, used them in their rise to power, and have continued to nourish them since 1949.

A second theme of the Chinese revolution has been national unification under a central authority. After the Revolution of 1911, the basic form of Chinese government was *warlordism*. This term refers specifically to the years between 1916 and 1928, when control of the central government shifted frequently from one regional military leader to another. It also refers in a broader sense to the chronic political and military disunity that prevailed until 1949.

Military unification alone could not fully replace the imperial political system. Reunification required a new political structure, sensitive to the demands of a modern nation-state. Administratively, reunification required a new system of political recruitment and an expanded range of governmental activities at all levels. Ideologically, it called for a new doctrine that would not only justify the exercise of political authority but also seek the allegiance of ordinary citizens and integrate them into the political system.

Finally, no discussion of the Chinese revolution is complete without reference to socioeconomic conditions and demands for radical change in them. China's economic situation in the first half of the twentieth century imposed harsh burdens on a troubled and rebellious populace. High rates of tenancy and the presence of a few large landowners were obvious sources of peasant dissatisfaction and obvious targets for reformers and revolutionaries, although neither condition was typical of all China. High rents and taxes, usurious credit, small and fragmented farms, traditional farming methods, low productivity, illiteracy, and external disturbances all contributed to the poverty and vulnerability of most of the rural population. The cities afforded better opportunities for a small but growing industrial proletariat, but living conditions were scarcely an improvement. Low wages, long hours, unsafe working conditions, inadequate housing, high rates of female and child labor, and large pools of unemployed or irregular workers were the rule in China's emerging factory cities.

By the 1920s, the banner of socioeconomic reform had passed from scattered intellectuals to organized political parties, with increasing evidence that reform movements could gain mass support. The Nationalist Revolution of 1928 clung to the proven appeal of national independence and unification, but at least briefly from 1925 to 1927, its radical wing (which included the Communists) was able to organize a worker–peasant movement that brought class struggle to the fore. From that time on, social and economic reform was an unavoidable issue. It was also the most divisive of the three main revolutionary themes. Although there were strong demands for reform within the GMD, its ties with the old elite and its dependence on the support of former warlords for its military power made GMD leadership of a social revolution impossible. The CCP, on the other hand, saw social and economic change as central to its program, inseparable from its nationalist objectives. Ultimately, the victory of the CCP over the GMD depended on the popular support that it mobilized as a result of it social revolutionary policies. This fact was acknowledged by the GMD itself:

> It is impossible to crush the Communist bandits by relying only on the government and the army, without the help of the common people. The reason we were defeated on the mainland was precisely because we did not intimately join hands with the common people.[3]

CCP History

The appeal of communism in China arose from the success of the Russian Revolution in 1917. Marx's economic critique of capitalism seemed fairly remote from Chinese problems, but the example of the Bolshevik overthrow of the tsarist system, coupled with Lenin's condemnation of imperialism and call for world revolution, struck a responsive chord. The Bolsheviks were also willing to provide advice, funding, and leadership to revolutionary groups in other countries through the Communist International (Comintern).

Chen Duxiu and Li Dazhao, two of the most famous spokesmen for the anti-imperialist May Fourth Movement of 1919, became cofounders of the Chinese Communist party in 1921. *Mao Zedong* was a representative from Hunan Province at the founding meeting. At first the CCP followed the Bolshevik pattern of organizing workers (the proletariat), but a massacre of railway workers on February 27, 1923, proved that a party of the proletariat would be too weak to make a revolution on its own. By 1924 the CCP had concluded an alliance with the GMD in order to pursue their common goals of national reunification and the end of unequal treatment of China by the imperialists. The decision to enter this alliance was encouraged by Soviet advisers, who were also working with the GMD. This first United Front was a period of major growth and expansion for both the GMD and the CCP (see Table 14.1). It ended in 1927 when the GMD expelled the Communists and broke off its contacts with Soviet advisers.

The rupture of the first United Front left the CCP a fragmented, outlaw party. Small bands of armed and mobile Communists survived in relatively isolated rural areas. Gradually, these forces acquired loose territorial bases referred to as soviets after the Russian example. The most prominent soviet was in the mountains of Jiangxi, where Mao Zedong was a major political figure. Mao developed his ideas of rural revolution in the Jiangxi soviet, but he was criticized by the *Central Committee*, which was under the control of young ideologues recently returned from study in the Soviet Union. In late 1933 GMD leader Chiang Kai-shek launched the fifth in a series of campaigns against the Jiangxi soviet, and by the latter part of 1934 this campaign had forced the Communists to abandon their stronghold and set out on the *Long March*. During the Long March, Mao criticized the Central Committee's leadership and became the leading figure of the CCP, though major opposition to him, backed by the Comintern, continued until 1941.

While the Communists were on the way to Shaanxi, which their first units reached in October 1935 in greatly weakened condition, a second United Front with the GMD was taking shape in response to growing military pressure from the Japanese. With the beginning of full-scale war between China and Japan in 1937, the second United Front became a reality. This alliance was significantly different from the first, however, being essentially an armed truce in the interests of anti-Japanese unity. There was little cooperation between the two parties, aside from a loosely observed understanding that they would avoid open war on each other and that Communist-controlled territories and forces would retain de

TABLE 14.1
GROWTH OF THE CHINESE COMMUNIST PARTY, 1921−1989

Period and Year	Number of Members	Years Covered	Average Annual Increase
FIRST REVOLUTIONARY CIVIL WAR			
1921 (First Congress)	57	—	—
1922 (Second Congress)	123	1	66
1923 (Third Congress)	432	1	309
1925 (Fourth Congress)	950	2	259
1927 (Fifth Congress)	57,957	2	28,508
1927 (after GMD-CCP rupture)	10,000	—	−47,967
SECONDARY REVOLUTIONARY CIVIL WAR			
1928 (Sixth Congress)	40,000	1	30,000
1930	122,318	2	41,159
1933	300,000	3	59,227
1937 (after the Long March)	40,000	4	−65,000
ANTI-JAPANESE WAR			
1940	800,000	3	253,333
1941	763,447	1	−36,553
1942	735,151	1	−27,296
1944	853,420	2	58,635
1945 (Seventh Congress)	1,211,128	1	357,708
THIRD REVOLUTIONARY CIVIL WAR			
1946	1,348,320	1	137,192
1947	2,759,456	1	1,411,136
1948	3,065,533	1	306,077
1949	4,488,080	1	1,422,547
PEOPLE'S REPUBLIC OF CHINA			
1950	5,821,604	1	1,333,524
1951	5,762,293	1	59,311
1952	6,001,698	1	239,405
1953	6,612,254	1	610,556
1956 (Eighth Congress)	10,734,384	3	1,374,043
1957	12,720,000	1	1,985,616
1959	13,960,000	2	620,000
1961	17,000,000	2	1,520,000
1969 (Ninth Congress)	22,000,000	8	625,000
1973 (Tenth Congress)	28,000,000	4	1,500,000
1977 (Eleventh Congress)	35,000,000	4	1,750,000
1982	39,000,000	5	800,000
1986	44,000,000	4	1,250,000
1989	48,000,000	3	1,333,333
1991	50,000,000	2	1,000,000

Sources: The figures for 1921 to 1961 are reprinted from John Wilson Lewis, *Leadership in Communist China.* Copyright © 1963 by Cornell University. Used by permission of Cornell University Press. Figures from 1969 on are from official sources.

facto independence. Even this limited truce broke down by 1941, and CCP–GMD relations degenerated into active, if not open, hostility.

The CCP's strength grew remarkably during the second United Front, which lasted until Japan's defeat in 1945. From headquarters in Yanan, Mao Zedong consolidated his position as party leader and established his thought as the CCP's guide for the application of Marxism-Leninism to China. Although serious social reforms continued, the focus of the movement became patriotic defense against Japan rather than class struggle against landlords, and the Communists entered the postwar period as genuine competitors for national political power.

After the Japanese surrender in August 1945, the two major contenders for power briefly negotiated, with American mediation, for a peaceful solution to their conflict. The American role was compromised from the first, however, by its support for the Nationalist government, while profound suspicion and hostility between the GMD and CCP made a workable agreement unlikely. By 1946 a civil war had begun. The Nationalist armies had superior numbers and weapons and scored some initial successes, but the Communists soon demonstrated their superiority in the field and the strength of their popular support. The tide had turned by 1948, and within a year the Nationalist forces were defeated. The GMD retreated to the island of Taiwan, and the CCP established its new government on the mainland.

The CCP came to power with a conviction that mobilization and struggle are the essence of politics. Military virtues — enthusiasm, heroism, sacrifice, and collective effort — acquired great value. To the CCP elite, politics was not simply peaceful competition or management of material resources, but mobilizing and activating human resources in a crisis.

Closely related to these themes is the party's *mass line*, a principle that originated in the circumstances the CCP faced on the road to power. The mass line, a basic element of *Maoism*, is perhaps the most complicated and pervasive concept in CCP doctrine. In one dimension, it is a recognition of the fact that the movement cannot be sustained by party members alone, but depends on the support, intelligence, food supplies, new recruits, and even administrative skills of nonparty masses. In a second dimension, the mass line has a control function with respect to bureaucrats and intellectuals. By insisting that officials interact with the masses, the CCP hopes to uncover abuses and to reduce or dilute

the bureaucratic structure. Finally, with its exhortations to "eat, live, work and consult with the masses," the mass line is an expression of identification with and commitment to the welfare of the people. Developed during the soviet period, the mass line carries a strong orientation toward the peasants, simply because the Chinese Communists could not talk about their popular base or obligations without talking about the peasantry.

Self-reliance is a third element of the CCP's political style that draws strength from historical experience. The conditions encouraging it were the relative geographic, economic, and political isolation of the Communists' bases from 1927 on. Each soviet was largely on its own, depending for survival on military and economic self-sufficiency. The principle of self-reliance has both national and international implications. Nationally, it has fostered a preference for local units that are relatively self-sufficient. Internationally, the Chinese Communists remain sensitive to the way a foreign presence can lead to foreign interference and control. Although they welcome international support and will offer it themselves to other countries and movements with which they sympathize, they still insist that each must rely on its own resources to accomplish its goals.

The most difficult doctrinal problem the Chinese Communists have faced has been to create a socialist revolution and build a socialist society in an agrarian country close to its feudal past. How could this goal be reached in the absence of a proletarian base? The answer is that proletarian ideology can be created by education rather than by objective economic conditions. But the CCP has never assumed that this road to ideological purity would be easy, and they have warned repeatedly that powerful nonproletarian influences in their society can corrupt even those who seem to have been converted.

Political History of the PRC

The PRC's history falls into three periods. In the first (1949 to 1957), the CCP's desire to attain security and rapid industrialization by emulating the Soviet Union led it away from its own revolutionary principles (summarized at the end of the preceding section). The second period (1958 to 1976) saw the ascendancy of the Maoist model that revived indigenous revolutionary themes and sought to translate them into developmental policies. The third (1977–1989) which has emphasized socialist modernization based on a mixture of Chinese and foreign techniques was one of ambiguous reform. The leftist dogmatism of the preceding period was rejected, and China experienced sweeping changes under Deng Xiaoping's pragmatic leadership. However, the CCP was unwilling to give up its monopoly of power, and increasing tensions ultimately led to Tiananmen. Since the massacre the regime has been in a transitional phase politically, while remaining committed to economic and technological modernization.

THE SOVIET MODEL: RECONSTRUCTION AND THE FIRST FIVE-YEAR PLAN, 1949–1957 In January 1950 the PRC concluded a treaty of friendship and alliance with the Soviet Union. In the cold war climate, soon to be worsened by Sino-American military confrontation in Korea, Mao saw the treaty as China's best hope for national security and economic assistance. Despite previous conflicts between Chinese and Russian Communists, and obvious differences between the two societies in economic development and revolutionary history, the Soviet model seemed the best, indeed the only, guide for socialist development.

To reconstruct the economy, devastated by decades of war and disorder, was the first task. It was completed by 1952, with production restored to prewar highs, national finances stabilized, and the way prepared for socialization of the economy. The CCP was also consolidating its control over the administrative structure and extending its organizational apparatus to the mass level. Both efforts moved forward in conjunction with mass campaigns that served as vehicles both for party penetration of the villages and implementation of policy. Land reform (1949 to 1952) took land from large holders and gave it to small holders, tenants, and agricultural laborers, breaking the power of the landlords and leveling the rural economy and society. The marriage law campaign proclaimed the legal equality of women and initiated (though far from completed) important changes in kinship organization, social values, and sex roles. Suppression of counterrevolutionaries eradicated GMD supporters and other opponents of the new order, removing any doubts about the new government's willingness and capacity to deal harshly with its enemies. With its political authority consolidated, major social reforms underway, and the economy restored to an even keel, the CCP was ready to begin the transition to socialism.

The First Five-Year Plan, for 1953 to 1957, was a comprehensive program of planned economic development closely modeled on Soviet practice and emphasizing investment in heavy industry. Soviet aid provided many key industrial facilities and supplies. Russian advisers and engineers were instrumental in drafting and implementing the plan. Socialization of the economy proceeded rapidly, as all but the smallest enterprises were brought under state control. In the countryside, collectivization began with mutual aid teams that encouraged informal cooperation among small groups of peasant households, moved on to lower agricultural producers' cooperatives that collectivized production but left some ownership rights intact, and then — in a "high tide" proclaimed by Mao in 1955 — pushed ahead to the fully socialist higher agricultural producers' cooperatives, or collectives (see Table 14.2). By 1956 China's economy was basically socialized, with no private control of any significant assets or means of production.

The plan brought rapid industrialization and urbanization. The power and complexity of the central government kept pace, with a top-heavy bureaucracy emerging as the controlling force in Chinese society. Signs of institutionalization were evident in the CCP, in the state structure established in the constitution of 1954, and in the panoply of mass organizations. But a combination of factors diverted this modernization from its conventional course.

Sino-Soviet relations began to cool with Khrushchev's de-Stalinization speech in 1956 and the related disorders in Poland and Hungary, which the Chinese saw as symptoms of Russian irresponsibility at home and disregard of "fraternal" parties abroad. Soviet overtures to the United States and lack of enthusiasm for providing military backing or nuclear development aid to the PRC revealed increasingly divergent international interests between the two socialist powers. Domestically, Mao was concerned about the centralization, urbanization, and bureaucratization accompanying the plan. An outburst of criticism from intellectuals in the spring of 1957, in the *Hundred Flowers Campaign*, persuaded many Chinese leaders that it was no time to relax their guard against the "bourgeois" intellectuals, specialists, and technicians favored by modernization.[4] These complicated issues were debated at length between 1956 and 1958, but by late 1957 Mao had led his colleagues to reject the Soviet model and adopt a new, leftist approach to development. The *Anti-Rightist Campaign* was initiated in which those who had spoken out during the Hundred Flowers Campaign were condemned as "poisonous weeds" and punished.[5]

TABLE 14.2
DEVELOPMENT OF COLLECTIVIZED AGRICULTURE

Years	Household	Small Village or Village Section (20–40 households)	Large Village or Village Cluster (100–300 households)	Rural Marketing Area
1949–1952	Land reform ends large holdings and tenancy, destroys old rural elite.			
1952–1955		Mutual aid teams of 4–10 households lead into lower agricultural producers' cooperatives, which become BAU.[a]		
1955–1957	Households retain small private plots.	Early co-ops become production teams within higher co-ops.	Higher agricultural producers' cooperatives emerge, become BAU, full collectivization begins.	
1958–1959	Private plots absorbed by communes.	Become production teams within communes.	Become production brigades within commune.	
	Experimentation with highly collectivized communities; large-scale rural labor mobilization for water conservation and other construction projects.			People's communes formed and become BAU; early total of 25,000 large-scale communes, many exceeding marketing area in extent.
1960–1978	Private plots returned to household with limited free markets for household production.	Production team becomes BAU.	Production brigade runs primary schools, small rural industries; a few serve as BAU.	Communes reduced in size and increased in number (about 50,000 after 1970); roughly coterminous with marketing area.

"Agriculture as the Foundation" policy prevails: increased attention to rural areas with push for agricultural modernization (mechanization, use of chemical fertilizers, growth of small-scale rural industry) and, after Cultural Revolution, improved social services; rural institutions basically stable despite Cultural Revolution pressures to abolish private plots and raise BAU to a higher level.

Villages (formerly brigades) and townships (formerly communes) remain to manage large-scale economic activities in the countryside.

1979–present

Family farming and free marketing of surplus

Production team contracts to smaller groups, households, or even individuals. Long-term leasing of land.

"Responsibility System" appears: To increase agricultural production and raise peasant standards of living, production teams transfer use of land, draft animals, and tools to groups or households, which are then responsible for most decisions on production and earn profits when they exceed quotas contracted with the team. Three-level system of agricultural collectivization and collective ownership (of land and other major means of production) remain in principle, but reforms greatly expand the scope and profit incentives of household farming.

aBAU = basic accounting unit. This is the unit responsible for making work assignments, organizing agricultural production, and collecting and distributing the agricultural product; it handles its own accounting and is responsible for its own profits and losses; hence, it is an important indicator of the level of collectivization.

THE MAOIST MODEL: GREAT LEAP AND CULTURAL REVOLUTION, 1958–1976 The Maoist model emerged gradually from the debates of the mid-1950s, but its characteristics became clear only in the *Greap Leap Forward* of 1958 to 1960. The Great Leap was the pivotal issue in Chinese politics between 1958 and 1966, and the general principles it advanced held the political initiative until Mao's death in 1976. The Great Leap pulled China sharply away from the Soviet model, embarking the country on policies more in keeping with the CCP's revolutionary tradition and Mao's perception of China's priorities. The difficulties it soon encountered led to retreat from some of its features. The result was an increasingly tense debate between Maoists and their more moderate opponents, which erupted in the Cultural Revolution and continued throughout the next decade.

Four principles — drawn from a combination of Mao's thought, CCP experience, and dissatisfaction with the five-year plan — underlay the Great Leap. First was the idea of all-around development, that China could accelerate development on all fronts without leaving any sectors behind. Industry retained priority, but agricultural production, and the rural sector in general, were to catch up with it. The people's commune, which emerged in the summer of 1958, was the institution for promoting the Great Leap in the countryside. In 1958 the communes, a larger and more collectivized unit, replaced the cooperatives and simultaneously became the unit of local government in rural areas (see Table 14.2). They were to facilitate large-scale labor mobilization and projects, encourage mechanization and rural industrialization, and generally accelerate output in rural areas without diverting central funds from heavy industry. Mass mobilization, the second principle, indicated the resource base for the developmental surge. Greater utilization of personnel — through harder work, better motivation, larger organization, and mobilization of the unemployed — made China's population an asset to be substituted for scarce investment funds.

The third principle — that politics takes command — brought much greater emphasis on political unanimity and zeal, partly a reaction against the rightist criticism of 1956 to 1957, and shifted decision-making power away from state ministries toward party committees. Political cadres (party workers), not bureaucrats and experts, were to guide the process. Bureaucrats and intellectuals were pressured to mend their bureaucratic ways and engage in manual labor at the mass level. The fourth factor, decentralization, loosened central control and encouraged lower level units to exercise greater initiative. Decentralization also reflected the heavy stress on mass line and populist themes that characterized the rhetoric of the period.

The Great Leap achieved some production increases at first, but a crisis soon developed. Bad weather, withdrawal of Russian aid and technicians in 1960 as the Sino-Soviet conflict intensified, and problems in the leap itself combined to produce a downward economic trend and growing disenchantment. Flaws in the early leap strategy included weakening of planning and statistical controls, initiation of ill-conceived projects, overworking of the labor force, and general disruption of established work, marketing, and administrative patterns; the last was particularly acute, as the communes amalgamated units that had not previously worked together. Agricultural output declined precipitously in 1959 and 1960 while grain sales to the state increased, leading to a famine that cost more than 20 million lives. As the agricultural base of the economy shrank, other programs suffered drastic cutbacks.

In 1961 the CCP moderated the Great Leap. Political mobilization gave way to a cautious orientation toward restoring production. Planners, managers, technicians, and experts regained some of their lost status. Commune policy shifted in three fundamental ways (see Table 14.2). First, the basic accounting unit (the unit with prime responsibility for planning, collecting, and distributing the agricultural production), which had been raised from the higher cooperatives to the commune in 1958, was moved back, first to the production brigade and then to the production team, the lowest level of organization. The effect was decollectivization of rural accounting back to the mid-1950s level, although many more centralized features of commune life remained. Second, private plots — the small patches of land left for private cultivation — were returned to peasant households. Third, communes were made smaller, the number increasing from 25,000 in 1958 to 75,000 in the early 1960s (stabilizing at about 50,000 in 1970). Finally, the CCP adopted a new slogan "agriculture as the foundation," committing the government for the first time to the principle that development policies must serve the needs of the agricultural sector.

These reforms had widespread support but soon became controversial. For one thing, some moderates wanted to go further, to experiment with even more "capitalistic" formulas. Moreover, the leap had touched off debates questioning not only Mao's policies but also his leadership. Increasingly, the issue seemed not simply how to adjust the Great Leap, but whether the CCP was to remain committed to the Maoist model. The issue escalated to more general and potentially factional grounds, feeding on tensions generated by the now open Sino-Soviet hostility. Because the Maoists saw the Soviet Union as both hostile and an "incorrect" model, they looked more closely at domestic opponents for signs of similar tendencies. They found enough evidence to persuade them that their fears of capitalist restoration were justified. Meanwhile, American escalation in Vietnam revived Chinese fears of this old "number one enemy," even as the Soviet Union loomed more threateningly. For Mao, the danger to his image of the revolution was real and immediate.

The *Great Proletarian Cultural Revolution* was the second great effort to implement the Maoist model. Like the Great Leap, it began by asserting the model in dramatic, and extreme, terms, moved into a period of consolidation of central control, and ended with a debate over how much of the initial movement to retain. Unlike the Great Leap, the Cultural Revolution was not primarily an economic campaign — the post – Great Leap economic adjustments remained, despite some criticism — nor did it produce economic difficulties as severe as those of 1959 to 1961. It was far more violent and disruptive, however, and it posed far more sharply the question of how, and at what level, the Maoist model should be institutionalized.

The campaign began in the fall of 1965 with media criticism of some literary figures. In the spring of 1966, the attack shifted to some high party leaders, charging that *capitalist roaders* trying to install a revisionist system were opposing Mao. Simultaneously, it demanded thorough reform of culture — thought, attitudes, and behavior — to implant the Maoist ethic of struggle, mass line, collectivism, egalitarianism, and unstinting service to society. Soon students in Red Guard groups were carrying the struggle to the streets with fearless criticism of and sometimes violent action against those believed to be opposing Mao or representing bourgeois culture. The Cultural Revolution was thus at once a purge of the political elite, a drive for cultural reform in the broadest sense, and a mobilization of mass action that invited spontaneous organization and criticism. Of course, the Maoists in Beijing sought to control the movement, but their encouragement or at least tolerance of Red Guard activities — which included publication of uncensored

newspapers, formation of federations among the mass organizations, and direct action against rival groups and individuals — gave the campaign a degree of spontaneity unique in the history of communist systems.[6]

Between the summers of 1966 and 1967, the PRC slipped close to anarchy. Party and state offices were paralyzed, schools were closed, cadres at all levels were vulnerable to disgrace or dismissal, and mass organizations brought work stoppages, disrupted transportation and communications, and, in many cases, engaged in full-scale street fighting among rival groups, some of them armed. When the disorder began to involve units of the *People's Liberation Army (PLA)*, the Maoists pulled back. From the fall of 1967 on, order was restored. The PLA assumed control of much of the administrative apparatus, mass organizations were disbanded, economic functions were reemphasized, and the reconstruction of party and state offices began. The Ninth Party Congress in April 1969 proclaimed defeat of the capitalist roaders and initiation of new policies in accord with Chairman Mao's directives. Roughly half the party leadership was gone; the two highest victims were Liu Shaoqi (second to Mao in pre – 1966 party rankings) and Deng Xiaoping (perhaps fourth in power, after Mao, Liu, and Premier *Zhou Enlai*, and who later was to make two dramatic returns to prominence). Replacing these old revolutionary cadres were a large number of PLA commanders, radical party figures, and some new mass representatives who had achieved prominence in the campaign. Of course, there was also a substantial contingent of experienced leaders who had passed the test of the Cultural Revolution and remained in office.

The post – 1969 leadership was a coalition of three groupings: the most ardent Maoists, or radicals, who drew strength from close association with the chairman and their manipulation of his directives (Jiang Qing, Mao's wife, was perhaps most representative of this group); military figures who, though not united, benefited from Defense Minister Lin Biao's designation as second-in-command and Mao's chosen successor; and veteran administrators, led by Zhou Enlai, who represented what was left of the moderates.

This coalition proved unstable. Lin Biao's purge in 1971, for allegedly plotting a coup against Mao, was followed by reduction in PLA influence — a tendency fostered, too, by the policy of returning to normalcy. The radicals and moderates were left in uneasy balance, with mounting tension as Mao's health failed and Zhou sponsored restoration of many old cadres purged in the Cultural Revolution. Deng Xiaoping was the most prominent example. His return to power triggered an intense dispute, forced into the open in January 1976 when Zhou died, leaving Deng as his most likely successor as premier. Instead, the Maoists engineered Deng's second purge, with the premiership going to a relative newcomer and compromise choice, *Hua Guofeng.* But when Mao died in September, the tables were turned. Hua Guofeng arrested the *Gang of Four*—the epithet chosen for Jiang Qing and the three other leading radicals —and unleashed a vitriolic campaign against them for distorting Mao's thought, sabotaging the government and economy with the factionalism, and generally following a right-wing line under the guise of radicalism.

Sharp border clashes with the Soviet Union in 1969, coupled with the beginnings of American withdrawal from Vietnam, made Mao and Zhou more receptive to rapprochement with the United States, which was consummated with President Richard Nixon's visit and the Shanghai Communique early in 1972. Once this step had been taken, the logic of trade and cooperation with capitalist countries—to serve China's trade, technology, and security needs—was unmistakable. The radicals resisted this notion, as well as any diminution of post–Cultural Revolution reforms, but the latter were already slipping or become routine. The factional struggle sharpened, with labor disputes, intra-enterprise feuds, and lowered labor morale. An economic slowdown occurred from 1974 to 1976, caused by many factors but providing good ammunition for those who disliked the Maoist emphasis on struggle. Thus, when Mao died his model was less secure politically and institutionally than one would expect from the apparently unqualified support it had received over the previous decade.

MODERNIZATION MODEL: 1977–1989 A new model emphasizing socialist modernization began after Mao's death, passing through a transitional phase before assuming clearer form.[7] Modernization had been a goal of the PRC all along, but in contrast to Mao's leftism, the new model emphasized economic achievement over ideological purity. This historic shift away from a half century of revolutionary politics and toward a more stable, pragmatic regime has affected every area of policy, but policy change has been uneven, with both advances and retreats. The modernization model is similar to the Maoist model in that there was no general

blueprint for policy at the beginning, only a rather vague but determined commitment to a "path." Modernization has been the most successful path that the PRC has yet pursued, but by the second half of the 1980s it had given rise to tensions between conservative and reform groups within the leadership. The reforms also fostered the growth of societal forces such as intellectuals, students, and entrepreneurs whose interests were in tension with the party–state's continued monopoly of power. The tensions within the leadership and the demands of new societal forces for more citizen rights led to the Tiananmen crisis in 1989. Since the crisis, the regime still claims to pursue a modernization model and certainly does not want to return to the Maoist model, but the advanced age of the current leaders, uncertainties concerning succession, and the trauma of Tiananmen define the current situation as one of waiting for a new direction to consolidate itself.

In the transitional phase from Maoism to modernization, lasting from the fall of 1976 to December 1978, Hua Guofeng, who had followed Mao as CCP chairman while continuing as premier, proposed an ambitious development program that would realize the "four modernizations" (of agriculture, industry, national defense, and science and technology) by the year 2000 without discarding Maoist symbols. He proceeded by focusing all criticism on the Gang of Four, not on Mao or Maoism, and by glossing over the hard choices inherent in his call to accelerate economic growth. Hence, although much of the modernization rhetoric appeared, the new approach remained vague.

Deng Xiaoping reemerged as the advocate of a strong commitment to modernization and a break with the Maoist model. He returned to his old positions of party vice-chairman and governmental vice-premier in mid–1977 and mounted an increasingly severe attack on the Maoist model, coupled with indirect criticism of Hua's ties to it. In May 1978, Deng supported the slogan "Practice Is the Sole Criterion for Testing Truth," which suggested that Mao's opinions and writings should no longer be binding on PRC policy. The outraged leftists were provoked into a losing struggle with Deng's "practice faction." In December 1978, at the Third Plenum of the CCP's Eleventh Central Committee, Deng's forces triumphed. They criticized remaining Maoist leaders, who were among Hua's main supporters, and announced a "shift of focus" to socialist modernization that would go far beyond the initial post–Mao attacks on the Gang.

The Third Plenum is now considered the beginning of a new era in Chinese politics. Politically, the Maoist model was repudiated in a series of important decisions: posthumous rehabilitation in February 1980 of Liu Shaoqi, arch-foe of Cultural Revolution Maoism; Hua's loss of the premiership to Zhao Ziyang (September 1980) and of the party chairmanship to Hu Yaobang (June 1981), both new leaders being Deng's followers; and adoption in June 1981 of a CCP Resolution on Party History that explicitly criticized Mao's leadership during the period 1958 to 1976, reducing the late chairman to normal human dimensions as one who had both strengths and weaknesses, accomplishments and errors. In September 1982 the Twelfth CCP Congress affirmed Deng's program, dropped Hua from all higher posts, and abolished the post of party chairmanship associated with Mao's individual leadership.

Deng's repudiation of Maoist leftism was balanced by an affirmation of CCP leadership and Communist orthodoxy, leaving the regime in a middle position between leftism and positions considered too bourgeois.[8] Deng was supported in his struggles with Hua by posters put up on *Democracy Wall* in Beijing, but after he had consolidated his power, he closed Democracy Wall and outlawed spontaneous political posters. In March 1979 he declared that everyone must uphold the four fundamental principles: the socialist road, the leadership of the party, the dictatorship of the proletariat, and Marxism-Leninism, Mao Zedong Thought. Statements that officials deemed contrary to these principles became in effect political crimes, and thousands suffered administrative and criminal sanctions. Although the general abolition of class labels was declared in 1979, the notions of dangerous bourgeois elements, bourgeois spiritual pollution, and bourgeois liberalism remained in the CCP's ideological arsenal.

The core of the modernization model was economic policy. Although economic reforms took some steps backward as well as many forward, in general there was an unparalleled expansion in the use of material incentives and of market forces, resulting in the greatest economic growth in modern Chinese history. Individuals and families were encouraged to "enrich themselves," and they did so.

In many respects agricultural reforms set the pace. Poor peasants in Anhui experimented with the "responsibility system" (see Table 14.2) in which household production gradually replaced collective labor. By taking responsibility for production, households were allowed to retain profit, encouraging them to produce as much as possible. They were also allowed more discretion in deciding what to plant and more freedom in private marketing. The results were remarkable. Not only did peasant incomes more than double, but the number of peasants living in poverty was reduced drastically. There was a surge in productivity in both farm produce and rural industry. In 1984 the grain surplus exceeded the state's storage capacity. Such successes spurred further liberalization, including the abolition of mandatory grain production quotas in 1985. It turned out, however, that 1984 was the high point of success in grain production in the 1980s (see Figure 14.1). Grain production did not reach that level again until 1989. The drop led to criticism of the reforms because maintaining a sufficient supply of food is essential for modernization. As a result, a conflict arose between the government's need for grain and the farmers' desire to grow more profitable crops.

China's urban economy is both more complex and more deeply embedded in the Stalinist administrative model; so reforms here were not as early or as successful as in agriculture. Nevertheless, the abandonment of Maoist reservations concerning profit, bonuses, and marketing led to growth. The structural reform of the urban economy adopted in late 1984 was a major step toward replacing the Stalinist administrative economic system with a socialist commodity economy, one that, like the rural economy, depends more on producer autonomy and market mechanisms. Not only was state industry restructured but also private and cooperative enterprises were encouraged, and these enterprises increased astronomically throughout the 1980s. Both the rapid growth and decentralization contributed to occasional supply crises and to inflation, with inflation becoming a serious problem by 1987 for the first time since the aftermath of the Great Leap Forward.

The modernization model included an "open door" in foreign policy, reforms in education, and efforts to institutionalize the revolution. The open door involved closer relations with the international economy, especially with capitalist countries, to help China acquire foreign capital, technology, and vital goods (oil-drilling rigs, computers, grain). Vital elements here were normalization of diplomatic relations with the United States in December 1978, increased diplomatic and cultural exchanges, rapid expansion of foreign trade with a tourism and export drive to pay the import bill,

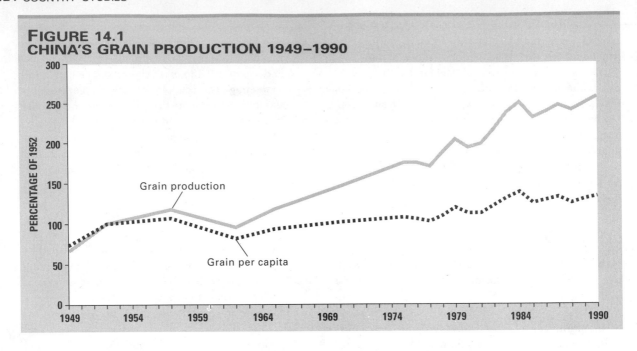

FIGURE 14.1
CHINA'S GRAIN PRODUCTION 1949–1990

Grain production

Grain per capita

and opening of "special economic zones" in China for foreign investment and manufacture.

New policies for education and the intellectuals included higher academic standards, expansion of higher education and research, and efforts to train a large cadre of specialists by identifying talented individuals and sending them to elite schools. Academic debate became more open, contacts with colleagues abroad more regular and productive. Publications became more numerous and varied, and political limits on art and literature were relaxed, though by no means abolished.

Institutionalization restored most organizations

A small wineshop run by six youths waiting for employment is doing a thriving business from 8 in the morning till 10 in the night.

weakened or destroyed during the Maoist period. It was accompanied by calls to observe regular procedures and strengthen the legal system. New constitutions were adopted for the state and party in 1982, and both emphasized that the state constitution was binding on the party. A significant development was initiation of popular election of county congresses, with approval of some competition among candidates for popularly elected positions.

The success of the modernization model in delivering economic benefits to most of China's population and in improving China's world stature ended any possibility of the return to power of Cultural Revolution leftism. However, modernization faced Deng's coalition of leaders with difficult choices: how far to go, how fast to go, how much social and political freedom to allow, how much centralization was necessary, and so forth. Opinions differed on every question and on every policy. When a daring policy, like the responsibility system in agriculture, succeeded, then the bolder options on other policies were strengthened. When difficulties with reform occurred, or when the leadership was scandalized by the appearance of crime or pornography, then voices spoke louder urging caution and tighter ideological control. As a result of these differing interpretations of modernization, two different camps gradually emerged among the leadership during the 1980s: the reformers, who favored more radical structural changes, and the conservatives, who wanted to protect the party's total political control and state control over the economy. Deng Xiaoping remained the final authority because he had a foot in each camp. He was the most prestigious of the veteran leaders, and the conservatives could be confident that he would not compromise the CCP's monopoly of power. Deng was also the chief patron of reform, and the new leaders of reform, *Hu Yaobang* and *Zhao Ziyang*, were his proteges.

Leadership Conflict, 1986–1989: The Road to Tiananmen

Although not officially acknowledged, serious conflict within the central leadership became obvious in 1987, with Hu Yuobang's resignation.

The course of events leading to Hu's resignation had begun in early 1986 with a failed attempt by the conservatives to discipline outspoken reformers. The conservatives were encouraged to make this attempt by the inflationary problems associated with the urban reforms; Hu Yaobang, however, not only rejected their

attack, but called for even greater freedom of discussion and a new "Hundred Flowers" campaign. Having been given the green light by Hu, the reformers took the offensive. They blamed the difficulties of the urban reform on feudal vestiges in the political system and said that that reform of economic institutions could succeed only if it were accompanied by reform of political institutions. The phrase "political structural reform" became a banner under which political reforms were discussed that were more radical than any hitherto considered. The party's interference in state affairs was criticized, and greater societal and even political pluralism was suggested. Excited by the political atmosphere, students in nineteen cities participated in peaceful demonstrations in December 1986.

The conservatives were of course outraged by the student demonstrations and even more so by the bold initiatives of the reformers. In January 1987 an enlarged *Politburo* meeting accepted Hu Yaobang's resignation and began a heated campaign to oppose "bourgeois liberalization." The conservatives, who appeared to have lost definitively in 1986, now removed their opponent. Hu was criticized for acting on his own without proper consultation, for speaking too freely in public, for encouraging bourgeois liberal intellectuals, and for responding too mildly to the student demonstrations. Many outspoken reformers were removed from their posts or criticized.

It was not a total conservative victory, however. Premier Zhao Ziyang, Hu's fellow reformer, replaced him as acting secretary, and conservative leaders joined Zhao in promising that basic modernization policies, including openness to the West, would not be affected. The campaign to oppose bourgeois liberalization was restricted to party members and to urban areas. Some prominent reformers were criticized and disciplined, especially the astrophysicist Fang Lizhi, who had advocated a Western-style democracy with scientists as the new political elite, but the disciplinary measures were very mild.

The Thirteenth Party Congress in October 1987, planned as the retirement congress for Deng and his elderly colleagues, turned out to be indecisive. The old leaders retired from their formal positions but remained active behind the scenes, and Deng Xiaoping retained his post as chair of the Military Affairs Commission. While the reformer Zhao was confirmed as party secretary, the conservative *Li Peng* replaced Zhao as premier. In his address to the congress, Zhao pledged to continue reform policies in every area, but economic difficulties and continued pressure from the conservatives frustrated his plans. The inflation and food supply problems of 1988 were blamed on the reforms, and an economic policy of austerity and strengthened central control was forced on Zhao by the conservatives in September 1988. By the beginning of 1989 Zhao was on the defensive, and there was little momentum behind further reforms.

Tiananmen

In the early months of 1989 the intellectuals and students were beginning to stir as they had in 1986, but the circumstances were different. Previously, they had assumed that the party leadership was on their side because of Hu Yaobang's support; now they felt that the government was deadlocked. The government was not very responsive either positively or negatively: petitions to grant amnesty to political prisoners were ignored, but the petitioners were not punished. People were quite open about expressing grievances and disagreements with the government, and students organized "democracy salons" in which they discussed ideas for reform.

Hu Yaobang's unexpected death on April 15 provided the catalyst for student demonstrations in Beijing in favor of reform. It was the perfect occasion because Hu had been removed for his tolerance of the students in 1986, but the authorities could hardly suppress processions commemorating a major party leader. The students made demands for reforms and evaded attempts to limit their demonstrations, but at this stage they were careful to be orderly and not to challenge the CCP's political leadership. They criticized corruption and petitioned for democracy and for the recognition of autonomous student organizations. Nevertheless, an authoritative editorial was published in the *People's Daily* on April 26 which accused the demonstrators of causing turmoil and claimed that a handful of counterrevolutionary instigators were responsible. The students and the Beijing public were outraged, and hundreds of thousands participated in new demonstrations calling for the repudiation of the editorial and announcing a boycott of classes.

Zhao Ziyang had been on a state visit to North Korea on April 26; he did not participate in drafting the editorial and did not see it in its entirety before its publication. When he returned to Beijing, he tried unsuccessfully to persuade Deng to repudiate the editorial. On May 4 Zhao gave an important speech in Beijing in

which he said that the students were acting out of patriotism, implicitly distancing himself from the editorial. This mollified the students somewhat and the class boycott dissipated, but it also encouraged other groups — journalists, social scientists, workers, even policeman's groups — to join in the demonstrations. Media publicity concerning the demonstrations became more favorable, and similar movements began to occur in most cities. As the occupation of Tiananmen continued, the student leadership became more and more radical. A massive hunger strike was initiated on May 13 which started with 400 participants and eventually involved thousands. On May 15 Mikhail Gorbachev visited Beijing, but Tiananmen had to be scratched from his itinerary because of the demonstrations. This was a major embarrassment for Deng Xiaoping, and the world press gathered for Gorbachev's visit brought even more attention to the demonstrators. While Zhao attempted through various emissaries to contact the demonstrators and to satisfy their original demands, the student leadership, heady from their success, refused to compromise or withdraw. The confrontation was vividly symbolized by a televised exchange between Premier Li Peng, who obviously wanted to squelch the demonstrations without making concessions, and a student, Wuerkaixi, who said that no one would leave Tiananmen until everyone was satisfied.

On May 19 Deng Xiaoping decided that harsh measures were needed to restore order. Zhao refused to be the spokesperson of the new policy and resigned as general secretary of the CCP. His last appearance in public was a tearful midnight visit to the students at Tiananmen. The following day martial law was declared and the demonstrators were ordered out of the square, but hundreds of thousands of Beijing residents went to major intersections to block the troops. By the end of May, the number camped out in Tiananmen had dwindled to a few thousand, but a statue called the "Goddess of Democracy" had been erected in the square and tensions were mounting. On the night of June 3 the army shot its way into the center of Beijing, killing hundreds of civilians as it approached Tiananmen from several directions. According to official accounts, more than 1,000 military vehicles were destroyed in the street fighting and more than 6,000 martial law forces were injured, with a few dozen killed. Unofficial estimates place the number of civilian fatalities between 700 and several thousand. The troops were much more careful in the square itself. After a tense confrontation between the soldiers and the remaining students in the square, the students were allowed to leave peacefully. Sporadic fighting between troops and citizens continued over the next few days in Beijing. On June 9 Deng Xiaoping thanked the troops and his conservative colleagues, the "veteran proletarian revolutionaries," for rallying around the party and beating back the "counterrevolutionary rebellion."

After Tiananmen

Tiananmen was a shattering experience for Chinese politics, even though on the surface order was restored. Both Chinese and foreigners had assumed that China was on a path toward reform and modernization that might have its ups and downs but was almost inevitable. Now the old leaders seemed to have turned on their country's future and shot it dead in the streets. The prestige and credibility of the party was badly damaged. Basic uncertainty was reintroduced into Chinese politics. Deng and his colleagues did not seem to know where to go. They were united in opposing the demonstrators, but Deng was more reluctant than his conservative friends to roll back reform and to dismiss reformers.

The Fourth Plenum of the Thirteenth Central Committee of the CCP held in late June was the first authoritative meeting after Tiananmen, and it confirmed the dismissal of Zhao Ziyang as general secretary and named *Jiang Zemin*, the party secretary of Shanghai, as Zhao's replacement. Jiang is a rather cautious person and not known as a reformer, but he does not have the blood of Tiananmen on his hands like Li Peng. Deng Xiaoping has thrown the weight of his prestige behind Jiang and has called on the entire leadership to accept him as his successor. In November 1989 Deng resigned from his post as chair of the Military Affairs Commission in favor of Jiang. With the removal of Zhao, the central leadership is composed of the Tiananmen conservatives and the moderate conservatives, with Deng occupying a small middle ground between them.

Despite the decisiveness of the removal of Zhao and some of his close associates in the central leadership, it is remarkable how few broad personnel and policy changes have been made since June 1989. Except for leadership positions in the central organs of the CCP, the rate of leadership turnover was lower in the first year after the massacre than it was for the preceding year. The lack of turnover is significant because the overwhelming majority of these subordinate leaders in the

Central Committee, National People's Congress, and provinces were appointed by Zhao and Hu Yaobang and are committed to reform. Indeed, during the crisis many of them acted in ways supportive of the students. The administrative pyramid that led China in reform is still fairly intact below the very top.

Post–Tiananmen policy has also stayed within the general parameters set in the 1980s. The leadership has continually reaffirmed its commitment to modernization and openness. Serious efforts have been made to encourage foreign investment and trade, and China has gradually succeeded in removing international sanctions that were adopted in response to the massacre. At the same time, however, the disruptions are blamed on bourgeois influence from the West, and warnings are given that capitalism is still trying to overthrow communism by peaceful means.

In economic policy, the regime continued and stiffened the policies of retrenchment and stronger central control begun in September 1988. These harsh policies stopped inflation, but they also led to a sharp recession. As a result, the retrenchment policies were gradually softened throughout 1990, and experimentation with further economic reform was resuming. Similarly, the regime continued to pass new laws (including one permitting the police to use weapons against unauthorized demonstrations), hold meetings and elections, and in general behave as it did in the 1980s.

But Chinese politics after Tiananmen faces a fundamental problem. Deng Xiaoping is older than Mao Zedong was when he died, and he is unlikely to be able to hold central power much longer. Jiang Zemin is his chosen successor, but the Tiananmen conservatives in the party and the army may oppose his power. Jiang does not have much personal prestige, and Deng cannot continue to support him from beyond the grave. Meanwhile, most of China's elite identifies with reform and feels threatened by continued conservative rule. Probably most of the high levels of the party and state leadership would favor a return to the path of reform symbolized by Zhao Ziyang and Hu Yaobang and a repudiation of the massacre. There are also many intellectuals who now would rather reject the CCP because of Tiananmen and set up a multiparty state along the lines of Eastern Europe. China's political spectrum is thus much broader than it has ever been in the past — from military conservatism to multiparty democracy — and there is no reliable mechanism for deciding which road China will take. By crushing the challenge of Tiananmen, Deng will leave China with a much more difficult and daunting challenge.

Socioeconomic Change

We conclude this survey of post–1949 history with a few general observations on the social and economic transformation that has accompanied four decades of CCP rule. In society, the most obvious change has been in class structure, with some social strata eliminated or neutralized and others expanded. The civil war and early campaigns not only destroyed the GMD governmental elite and its warlord allies, but also dispossessed landlords, merchants, industrialists, and other local political leaders. The new political elite, defined almost solely by CCP membership, differs significantly in ideology, political experience, and social origin. A new intermediate stratum of moderately privileged groups has emerged, consisting of skilled industrial workers, college and middle-school graduates, and professional, scientific, and technical workers. The 1980s also saw the emergence of an entrepreneurial class in response to the relaxation of central controls. This group, the individual households (*geti hu*), has a tainted reputation because it often makes large profits in the gray areas of Chinese society and economy, but considers itself the victim of state overregulation and corruption, and enthusiastically supported the demonstrations of 1989.[9] Although most peasants remain poor and by far the largest class —perhaps 75 percent of the population lives in rural areas, though not necessarily engaging in agriculture— they are now better educated and more secure economically.

The nuclear family remains the basic residential and kinship unit, and continues to be a key economic unit for personal income and expenditures. The larger kinship groups (lineages and clans) have lost the power they once held. Instead, the work unit (the village in rural areas, the factory in urban areas) has become the primary social unit above the family. Membership in the work unit is usually permanent, and the unit provides a comprehensive range of services to its members. Within the family, the domination of older males has weakened, with much greater opportunity and mobility for women and young people. Clear differences remain in sex roles, but the change from traditional patterns has been great.

Finally, there has been a major shift in the relationship between government and society, centering on expansion of the government's resources, personnel, operations, claims, and power. Although old indicators of economic and social status still have some relevance, increasingly it is government action that determines the citizen's social and economic role and defines favored and disfavored status. This concentration of power in the hands of the party–state–army bureaucracies has had some leveling effect on Chinese society, particularly in conjunction with the egalitarianism of the Maoist ethic. At the same time, the expanded scope and responsibilities of government have made the political process more receptive to claims from society, to competition for social and economic rewards. In short, the new government is both more powerful and more responsive, in relation to society, than its predecessors. Since 1978, the CCP's attempt to enlist all societal forces in the modernization effort has improved the prestige and strengthened the political influence of specialists and intellectuals.

As Tables 14.4 and 14.5 at the end of this chapter illustrate, China's economy has changed tremendously since 1949, and these changes have reshaped the state's resources and policy goals. The early economic goals of the regime were to reestablish a war-torn economy and to provide the necessities of life to a large population. Now the PRC has a fairly well-educated, healthy, and well-fed population with more sophisticated needs. Its industrial base has become quite impressive. In 1989 China was the world's fourth largest steel producer; in 1949 it ranked twenty-eighth. China is now the world's largest producer of coal, grain, cotton, and meat. It has also made impressive progress in technology. In 1986 American firms began to contract for Chinese rockets to launch their satellites, and in 1990 China became the world's third largest producer of computer diskettes, after the United States and Japan. But as the industrial base has become more sophisticated, the old Stalinist methods of economic management have become more and more inefficient. The economic reforms of the 1980s were to a great extent a response to the new level of complexity and sophistication that the Chinese economy has achieved.

The economic reforms of the post–Mao era loosened central controls, emphasized material incentives, and allowed individual entrepreneurship. Private markets and small businesses became common in the cities, and a great variety of industries sprang up in rural areas. These nonstate activities utilized the unemployed and the underemployed and added greatly to China's productivity and prosperity. A new level of society came into being which did not depend closely on state institutions, and the CCP's capacity for tight control of the economy began to slip. Inflation became a serious problem in 1985 and reached more than 20 percent in urban areas in 1988. The government's harsh retrenchment measures in 1989 brought down inflation, but they also depressed sales and production and increased unemployment. By the end of 1990 the economy was again prospering, but the threat of inflation was looming again.

The special problem of the Chinese economy remains that of the rural workforce and food production. Chinese agricultural growth must be intensive rather than extensive because of its land shortage. To give some comparative perspective on the problem, the United States would be in a situation similar to China's if the United States had a population of 2 billion people. Conversely, China achieved the current American ratio of population to arable land in approximately 1660 with a population of 123 million, roughly one-tenth of its current population. In contrast to Khrushchev's "virgin lands" development policy, the PRC has actually lost arable land because of urban growth. In 1978 each Chinese agricultural worker used three-quarters of an acre of arable land, compared to 1.5 acres in Japan, 4.8 acres in the Soviet Union, and 39.4 acres in the United States.[10] Intensive cultivation in China produces high yields per acre — 1,612 kilograms as against 1,417 kilograms in the United States, and 759 kilograms in the USSR — but the productivity of each farmer is limited by the land at his or her disposal. From 1960 to 1978 productivity per worker grew only 23 percent in China, compared to 215 percent in the United States and 247 percent in the USSR, and much of the growth during this period was the result of increasingly costly investments in fertilizer and irrigation. Since 1978 productivity per worker has doubled, partly because of the increased incentives of the responsibility system and partly because of commercialization and the growth of rural enterprises. The proportion of rural income earned in farming declined from 70 percent in 1978 to 50 percent in 1987. Nevertheless, the crushing pressure of people on arable land means that agricultural production and population control will remain key problem areas for the Chinese economy. China's total arable land may only be capable of supporting a total of 1.5 to 1.6 billion people, a figure that may well be reached in forty years even with strict family planning.

The effect of the land and population constraint on Chinese agriculture can be seen in Figure 14.1. China's grain production rose in the 1950s, dipped in 1959 – 1961 (with the loss of life of 20 to 30 million), rose through the 1960s and 1970s, and then rose sharply from 1979 to 1984. A plateau of production appeared to be reached in 1984, and the exceptional harvest of 1990 is very unlikely to be repeated in 1991. Meanwhile, because of population increases, per capita production of grain remained close to 1952 levels until the 1980s, and it is gradually lessening as grain production stagnates and population continues to grow. Given the size of its population and its relative poverty, China must continue to strive to grow its own food.

These broad social and economic parameters are politically significant in two respects. First, they suggest the extent and limits of revolutionary transformation in modern China and the political system's performance in guiding that transformation. Second, they emphasize the social and economic logic of the new policies after Mao's death. The PRC of the 1990s is vastly different from that of the 1950s, let alone of the 1930s when Maoism took shape. Now a budding international power — possessing nuclear weapons and space technology, deeply involved in global politics, and seeking foreign trade and technology — the PRC cannot sustain the earlier isolationist policy of self-reliance. Domestically, the increasing complexity and sophistication of Chinese society, and the dependence of economic growth on an accelerated technical revolution, and decentralized market forces, have made the political domination of the CCP more difficult and less justifiable.

CONSTITUTION AND POLITICAL STRUCTURE

The political structure of the PRC consists of two major organizational hierarchies — the state and the party — plus the army and a variety of mass organizations that provide additional links between these hierarchies and the citizenry. All these institutions have undergone significant changes since 1949, both internally and in relation to each other. In the Maoist era, politics took command of institutions, creating considerable uncertainty and fluidity in the political structure, whereas post – 1976 institutionalization has clarified the structure.

State
The PRC's initial state structure, from 1949 to 1954, was a temporary administrative system that relied heavily on regional military units to oversee reconstruction and early reforms. A constitution was adopted in 1954,

establishing a centralized government to administer the transition to socialism. Soon, however, the Great Leap Forward brought important changes, as decentralization and CCP assertiveness weakened central state organs, while the communes created new patterns of local administration. The Cultural Revolution further unsettled the 1954 system and, in effect, abolished the constitution. State structure remained in limbo, without effective guidelines, until a second constitution was adopted in 1975. The 1975 constitution incorporated many principles of the Cultural Revolution, but in 1978 another new constitution was adopted, which was somewhat closer to the 1954 model. In 1982 a new constitution was adopted, reflecting Deng's interest in legal and institutional reform. We discuss the 1982 constitution, but most of the terminology applies in earlier periods as well (see Figure 14.2).

According to the constitution, the *National People's Congress* (NPC) is the highest organ of state power. It is a large representative body, consisting of deputies elected by provincial-level congresses and army units. It meets once a year for five years. The constitution, however, allows NPC meetings to be advanced or postponed in emergencies; there was no meeting of the NPC between February 1965 and January 1975, for example. In any case, NPC meetings have been short and mostly ceremonial, for deputies hear and then ratify major reports and documents presented to them by party leaders. The NPC symbolizes the regime's popular base, but in practice it is not the highest organ of power. That power resides in the CCP, which exercises leadership over the state and all other organizations.

The NPC has extensive formal powers of amendment, legislation, and appointment. It elects the president and vice-president of the PRC, the chairman of the Central Military Commission (CMC), the president of the Supreme People's Court, and the chief procurator of the Supreme People's Procuratorate; decides (approves recommended choices) on the premier, vice-premiers, ministers and commissioners, and the members of the CMC; and may recall all these officials it has chosen. Except for the most important formalities, all these powers may be exercised by the NPC's Standing Committee, a much smaller body of high officials resident in Beijing and hence able to meet in regular working sessions throughout the year. The president of the PRC is executive and ceremonial head of state; because this post was abolished in 1966 (it had been held by Mao

from 1954 to 1959 and by Liu from 1959 to 1966) and restored only in 1982, its actual political role remains unclear. The current president is *Yang Shangkun*, one of the conservative old guard. The CMC is another new organ of state, because previous constitutions assigned top control of military affairs to the CCP, but at present its membership is identical with that of the party's Military Commission.

The *State Council* is the chief administrative organ of government. It includes the premier (Zhou Enlai, 1954–1976; Hua Guofeng, 1976–1980; Zhao Ziyang, 1980–1987; and Li Peng, 1987–present), several vice-premiers, and the ministers who head the ministries and commissions of the central government, and it meets once a month. The State Council consists mainly of high-ranking party members. As translator of party decisions into state decrees, with control over government action at all levels, it is the administrative center of state power. The core of the State Council is its Standing Committee, which meets twice a week.

The constitution entrusts judicial authority to a *Supreme People's Court* at the central level and to unspecified local people's courts. All courts are formally responsible to the congresses at their respective levels. The procuratorates, also formally responsible to the congresses at each level, are supervisory and investigative bodies set up to ensure observance of the constitution and the law. These organs were first established in the 1950s but were bypassed during the Maoist period. Their restoration in the 1978 constitution, which had expanded sections on the court system as well, coincided with the renewed interest in legality that has marked the post–Mao period. Even so, actual operation of the PRC's formal legal organs appears to be controlled by the political-administrative hierarchy.

Local state structure includes three levels of government: provincial, county, and basic. Each unit at the first three levels includes a people's congress defined as the "local organ of state power" and an administrative structure called the people's government. Like the NPC, local congresses meet rather briefly and irregularly. The standing committees of provincial and county congresses are a recent innovation to give representative organs more constant and thorough supervision over their governments, courts, and procuratorates. Nonetheless, local governments and their departments are the most significant local organs of state. They are part of a centralized administrative hierarchy in which higher governments supervise all those beneath them, with

FIGURE 14.2
STRUCTURE OF THE STATE, 1982 CONSTITUTION

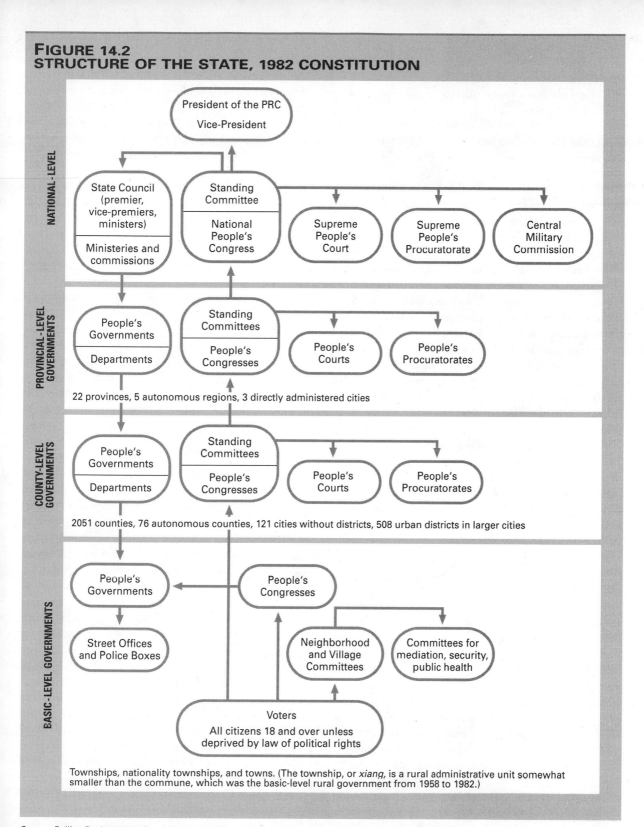

President of the PRC
Vice-President

NATIONAL-LEVEL

State Council (premier, vice-premiers, ministers)

Ministries and commissions

Standing Committee

National People's Congress

Supreme People's Court

Supreme People's Procuratorate

Central Military Commission

PROVINCIAL-LEVEL GOVERNMENTS

People's Governments

Departments

Standing Committees

People's Congresses

People's Courts

People's Procuratorates

22 provinces, 5 autonomous regions, 3 directly administered cities

COUNTY-LEVEL GOVERNMENTS

People's Governments

Departments

Standing Committees

People's Congresses

People's Courts

People's Procuratorates

2051 counties, 76 autonomous counties, 121 cities without districts, 508 urban districts in larger cities

BASIC-LEVEL GOVERNMENTS

People's Governments

Street Offices and Police Boxes

People's Congresses

Neighborhood and Village Committees

Committees for mediation, security, public health

Voters

All citizens 18 and over unless deprived by law of political rights

Townships, nationality townships, and towns. (The township, or *xiang*, is a rural administrative unit somewhat smaller than the commune, which was the basic-level rural government from 1958 to 1982.)

Source: *Beijing Review* 25:52 (December 27, 1982), pp. 10–29.

power to revise or annul lower level actions. Control from higher governments (ultimately the State Council) and local CCP bodies outweighs the limited supervision of local congresses.

Provincial congresses, including those of the three great cities (Beijing, Shanghai, and Tianjin) directly administered by the central government and the five autonomous regions, have five-year terms and are indirectly elected by the lower level congresses within their jurisdictions. The same rules apply to other cities large enough to be districted, although they are technically county-level units under provincial jurisdiction. Congresses at the county level have three-year terms and are elected directly by the voters. The term "autonomous" or "nationality" denotes units heavily populated by non-Chinese minorities. These units have constitutional guarantees for preserving minority culture and representation but differ little administratively from regular units.

Basic units are in the most direct contact with citizens. They include the township (called the commune from 1958 to 1982) and smaller towns, along with smaller, less formally organized neighborhood committees and villages. The township government is not as elaborately organized as the county and its people's congress does not have a standing committee, but it is charged with the oversight and implementation of most of the ordinary business of government as it affects people's lives. In rural areas the village (called the brigade or production brigade from 1958 to 1982) is an important unit of local decision making, but from the point of view of formal governmental structure it is a unit of self-management by the masses rather than a level of government.

The 1982 constitution gave formal expression to several new tendencies in Chinese politics. It increased congressional powers, specified the roles and autonomy of the state more clearly, limited most high officials to two terms, and extended direct election of deputies from the basic level to the county level. These attempts at structural clarification and reform of government were supported by a number of new laws, as well as by various efforts to promote the rule of law and the correct functioning of institutions. Greater attention was paid in the media to the meetings of people's congresses and the opinions of delegates, and occasionally cases would be reported in the 1980s in which a people's congress or standing committee successfully prevailed against the wishes of local party leadership. In general, however, it remained true that the party was in control of politics,

and the people's congresses had only an advisory role to play. Reformers hoped for more, and during the Tiananmen crisis a serious effort was made to have the National People's Congress take political control and revoke the declaration of martial law. The party reasserted its power without difficulty, but it is imaginable that a new reform phase or a new crisis could present the NPC with real political power.

Party

The CCP constitution adopted at the Twelfth Party Congress in September 1982 sets forth an organization roughly parallel to that of the state (see Figure 14.3). Positioning some form of party organization alongside most state organs strengthens CCP leadership of the state by encouraging party knowledge about and supervision of issues handled by state agencies. Whatever formal powers a state organ holds, the party organ at the corresponding level is the authoritative political voice. Although the 1982 constitution goes much further than previous ones in insisting that party members observe the state constitution and other laws, so that the CCP does not encroach on nonparty powers, it affirms the CCP's general leadership in all areas of Chinese life.

The 1982 party constitution, like its state counterpart, grants impressive powers to a hierarchy of party congresses. As in the state system, however, the congresses at various levels meet infrequently and briefly, and it is the committees elected by these congresses, or the standing committees and secretaries elected by the full committees, which actually wield the party's immense power. Party congresses are elected by the congresses immediately below them in the hierarchy; ordinary party members choose their representatives directly only at the lowest level. The National Party Congress is to meet every five years, although the constitution remarks that meetings may be advanced or postponed. Historically, CCP congresses have been irregular: the Seventh Party Congress met in 1945, the eighth in 1956, the ninth in 1969, the tenth in 1973, the eleventh in 1977, the twelfth in 1982 and the thirteenth in 1987. Despite the irregularity in convocation, congresses are important events. Each of those named has adopted a new constitution, elected a significantly altered Central Committee, and ratified changes in the CCP's general program.

In addition to formal approval of major policy changes, the National Party Congress elects the Central Advisory Commission, the Central Commission for Dis-

FIGURE 14.3
STRUCTURE OF THE CCP, 1982 CONSTITUTION

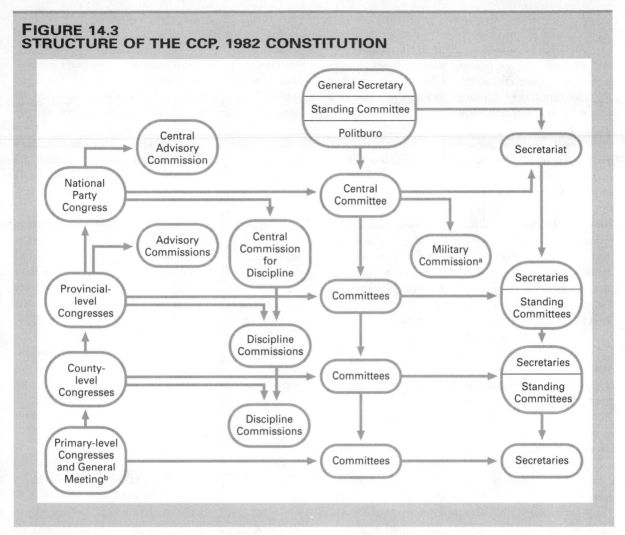

a—The official English translation of the 1982 constitution identifies this body as the Military Commission. In the past it was more commonly known as the Military Affairs Committe.
b—Primary-level organizations, including primary committees, general branches, and branches are set up in factories, shops, schools, offices, city neighborhoods, townships, towns and companies of the PLA. Party organization in the PLA above the company level presumably is regarded as county-level organization.
Source: "Constitution of the Communist Party of China," adopted September 6, 1982, *Beijing Review* 25:38 (September 20, 1982), pp. 8–21.

cipline Inspection, and the Central Committee. The Central Advisory Commission is a new organ created in 1982 to allow party elders (members must be established leaders with more than forty years of party service) to give advice and recommendations to other central party organs. Advisory Commissions with less senior members are also set up at the provincial level. The Discipline Commission (which had antecedents in the Control Commissions of the 1956 constitution that were abolished in the Cultural Revolution) was set up in 1977 to oversee party compliance with various laws and

regulations and to improve party discipline and effectiveness. It also has supervisory powers over the work of similar commissions at provincial and county levels.

The *Central Committee* (CC) acts for the Congress and is the most important representative body in the PRC. It is identified by the number of the congress that elected it, and its full meetings are known as *plenums* and also numbered sequentially. Thus, the first CC meeting following the Thirteenth Party Congress was the First Plenum of the Thirteenth CC. The constitution calls for plenums at least once a year, a provision followed closely since Mao's death, though not during the Maoist period. Many partial or informal CC meetings occur between plenums because most CC members are high-ranking officials holding important positions in Beijing or provincial capitals. Through plenums and other meetings, the CC provides a forum for discussing and ratifying major policies, if not actually initiating or deciding them.

The CC's most important duty is electing the party's top leadership, namely the *Politburo* and its *Standing Committee*, the general secretary, and the *Secretariat*; it is also said to decide on the membership of the party's Military Commission (more commonly known in the past as the Military Affairs Committee), although it is likely that top elites actually choose the members of this sensitive body. The Politburo, and particularly the Standing Committee, exercise all functions and powers of the CC between plenums and constitute the supreme political elite of China. Until 1982 they were headed by the party chairman, a position held by Mao from the 1930s until September 1976, by Hua Guofeng until June 1981, and by Hu Yaobang until September 1982. The 1982 constitution abolished the chairmanship, leaving the general secretary as effective chairman of the Politburo and head of the Secretariat. Although the general secretary is the highest ranking party leader, he is not all-powerful. Hu Yaobang was forced to resign by an enlarged meeting of the Politburo in January 1987. Premier Zhao Ziyang replaced him as acting general secretary until the Thirteenth Party Congress which confirmed the appointment. On May 19, 1989, an enlarged Politburo meeting deprived Zhao of his power, and in June a Central Committee plenum appointed Jiang Zemin in his stead. The enlarged Politburo meetings have been so powerful because in times of crisis they have been gatherings of all the old leaders, who then unite their prestige behind a decision.

Under the 1956 constitution, a staff agency known as the Secretariat supervised all the central party departments and committees responsible for particular lines of work. The 1973 and 1977 constitutions omitted reference to it in a bow to Maoist principles of bureaucratic simplicity. Although badly damaged by the Cultural Revolution, the party's powerful central bureaucracy survived and gradually assumed its former role. The Secretariat was reestablished at the Fifth Plenum of the Eleventh CC in February 1980 and was duly formalized in the 1982 constitution. Through it and its departments, presided over by the secretary general, the Polit-

buro supervises execution of its decisions by lower level secretaries and party committees in all localities and units in China.

The organizational principle of the party is *democratic centralism*. Democracy requires election of all leading bodies by their members or congresses, regular reports to members and representative bodies, and opportunities for discussion, criticism, and proposals from below. Centralism requires unified discipline throughout the party. As the constitution says, individuals are subordinate to the majority, lower levels are subordinate to higher levels, and all party members and organizations are subordinate to the National Congress and its CC. Centralism is also evident in committee powers to convene their congresses and in higher level powers of approval over all lower level decisions.

Both post–Cultural Revolution constitutions have contained strong language on the need to maintain party discipline and combat factionalism. The most concrete sign was creation of the discipline commissions in 1977. The 1982 constitution gave even more attention to the operation of these commissions and went into great detail on the conduct required of party members and circumstances under which they might lose their membership. Nevertheless, corruption at all levels within the party has been a growing problem in the post–Mao period.

Army

The *People's Liberation Army (PLA)* has always had a uniquely important role in Chinese Communist politics. From its founding in the late 1920s until 1949, the PLA organization was virtually inseparable from the party organization, and the army held major government responsibilities in the areas under CCP control. Since 1949 the PLA has continued to perform a variety of nonmilitary functions, including party recruitment and training, economic construction, and education. During the early reconstruction years and the Cultural Revolution it also assumed important administrative powers. Moreover, the salience of internal and external security issues in Chinese politics has placed the PLA, willingly or not, close to the center of many national policy debates. In the 1980s China's more peaceful international posture and the modernization needs of the civilian economy pushed the PLA more into the political background. Of course, the declaration of martial law and the massacre in Beijing returned the PLA to an active function in central politics, and it has been rewarded with a larger share of the budget. It is clear, however, that there were mixed emotions within the PLA about its repressive activities.

The PLA (including field armies, regional armies, and militia) lies administratively in the State Council's Ministry of National Defense, and the 1982 state constitution vests leadership of it in the new Central Military Commission; the previous constitution had named the CCP chairman commander of the armed forces. Despite this shift toward more formal state authority, the CCP has exercised and will probably continue to exercise de facto leadership of the PLA through the party CC's Military Affairs Commission and the system of political departments within the PLA. The Military Affairs Commission has always been one of the most important party organs and has held general responsibility for military affairs throughout PRC history.

Political departments, headed by commissars, are a regular part of each PLA unit's general headquarters down to the division level; below that, they are represented by a political office in the regiment and by political officers in battalions, companies, and platoons. Thus, a commissar (or political officer at lower levels) works alongside the commanding officer of every army headquarters or unit, and is responsible for implementing CCP policies and carrying out political education among the troops. Political departments and their commissars are subordinate, not to the military commanders in their military units, but to the next highest functionary in the CCP organization. Their chain of command within the army ascends through higher political departments to the General Political Department and the Military Affairs Committee. At the same time, each is responsible to the CCP committee in its own military unit.

Mass Organizations

Chinese political institutions also include many mass organizations that mobilize ordinary citizens, supplementing and supporting the two dominant institutions. In general, mass organizations are national in scale and have a hierarchy of units extending down to a mass membership defined by a common social or economic characteristic, such as youths, students, women, workers, or other occupational groups. These organizations play a large role in implementing the party's mass line, "coming from the masses and going to the masses." They provide a sounding board for popular opinion, channel representatives into the state and party structure, and mobilize support for CCP policies from different segments of the population. In some cases, they perform administrative and service functions for the groups they represent.

The most important mass organization before the Cultural Revolution was the *Communist Youth League (CYL)*. During the 1950s and early 1960s, the CYL was responsible for leadership of all youth activities and other youth organizations, was a major source of new recruits for the CCP, and generally assisted in implementing all policies at the basic level. Other important mass organizations before the Cultural Revolution included the Young Pioneers, for children aged nine to fifteen; the All-China Women's Federation; the All-China Federation of Trade Unions; and a variety of associations for occupational and professional groups. Closely related were the democratic parties, a collective name for eight minor parties that cooperated with the Communist-led United Front in the late 1940s and continued to operate after 1949 under CCP leadership. Their umbrella organization, the *Chinese People's Political Consultative Conference (CPPCC)*, was responsible for drafting the 1954 state constitution, and it continued to meet in conjunction with national and local people's congresses until the early 1960s.

All these mass organizations were suspended during the Cultural Revolution. They were replaced by the Red Guards (mainly student organizations) and "revolutionary rebels" (mainly organizations of workers and peasants), localized popular organizations that played a vigorous, militant, and sometimes independent role in the Cultural Revolution. Despite their early prominence, their evident urban strength, and their close ties with some Maoist leaders, Red Guards and rebels never established themselves as national organizations and were disbanded in the later stage of the Cultural Revolution.

The mass organizations began to revive after 1969. By the early 1970s the CYL, Women's Federation, Trade Union Federation, and Young Pioneers were reorganizing, as were some professional associations. Rebuilding was slow, however, suggesting that these forms of association remained controversial. Following the fall of the Gang of Four, which was blamed for wreaking havoc on mass organizations, reactivation accelerated. National congresses of the CYL, Women's Federation, and Trade Union Federation were held in late 1978. The professional associations became prominent again, and even the democratic parties — which had been portrayed in the Cultural Revolution as strongholds for China's "bourgeois intellectuals" — reappeared. The CPPCC has returned to its role as a symbol of a united front, now in the service of modernization, and has resumed its meetings in conjunction with people's congress meetings. Mass organizations including the CYL and the CPPCC were prominently in favor of reform, but they have continued normal functioning since Tiananmen. Their publications support the repression, but they contain many hints of opposition and critical distance. The CPPCC in particular might play a pivotal role in a future reform phase because of its multiparty structure.

POLITICAL CULTURE AND POLITICAL SOCIALIZATION

Two thousand years of imperial rule reinforced by Confucian orthodoxy had given traditional China a remarkably stable and sophisticated political culture that was moralistic in tone and centralized in direction. But in the twentieth century the collapse of traditional institutions led to a rejection of imperial Confucian ideology and thereby to a profound crisis in cultural orientation and values. The warlord period was a time of cultural chaos as well as political disunity. While the GMD responded by attempting to reinstitutionalize Confucian values, the CCP has always had as part of its mission the founding of a "new China" in a social and moral sense. It was eager to promote a complete socialist society and to do battle with what it considered the remnants of feudalism and the temptations of capitalism.

Since 1949 the policies and values of the CCP have had a massive effect on life in China. As we will see in this section, the family, the educational system, and the media have each been transformed several times. But the lingering influence of both the imperial past and the turbulence of the twentieth century can still be seen. Although the content of the culture has been changed, the CCP strives to instill a highly moralistic, centralized political culture as did its Confucian forebears. Unlike the long-established orthodoxy of traditional China, there have been numerous radical changes in the ideology of the PRC. As a result, political socialization in China is not simply the product of the party's new institutions and messages; it is also deeply affected by each individual's personal experience of political turbulence and ideological change.

Revolutionary Values

The CCP views its efforts to instill a revolutionary mortality in China as a constant struggle against remnants of feudalism, bourgeois temptations, and human weakness. The idealism and destructiveness of the struggle was most clear in the Cultural Revolution. At that time activities such as raising goldfish or collecting stamps were condemned, and the smallest failings of individuals were used to condemn them for "going the capitalist road." Red Guards even reversed traffic signals for a while, feeling that it was bourgeois to stop on red, the revolutionary color.

The fanaticism of the Cultural Revolution was followed by a general relaxation of political and ideological demands by the post–Mao regime. Pastimes and private money-making ventures were tolerated, and clothes became fashionable. There was considerable confusion among the public and within the party and the Communist Youth League as to what was enlightened and what was immoral. But the party did not forsake its role of moral leader and defender of orthodoxy. In 1979 it stipulated that everyone must uphold the four fundamental principles (as noted earlier, the socialist road, the leadership of the CCP, the dictatorship of the proletariat, and Marxism-Leninism Mao Zedong Thought). In 1981 a crack-down on crime began which involved thousands of executions, some of them public. And in 1983 there was a brief campaign to "oppose spiritual pollution," in which such things as pornography, Western hairstyles, and disco dancing were condemned. The campaign was halted when it became apparent that its spirit was contrary to modernization and openness to the West. In the aftermath of Tiananmen, there have been new campaigns to emulate revolutionary heroes, respect Chinese culture, oppose pornography and corruption, and cherish the PLA, but now many Chinese view such movements as empty rituals.

Agents of Socialization

THE FAMILY The traditional Chinese family has been a major object of reformers' attacks for the last hundred years. The traditional ideal was a multigenerational family under one roof, ruled absolutely by the senior male, with wives marrying into their husband's family and subordinated to their mother-in-law, and supplemented by concubines and bondservants. Beginning with campaigns against footbinding, progressives pressed for the end of arranged marriages, polygamy, and subjection of women within the family. The plays of Henrik Ibsen that dramatized the plight of Victorian women were a powerful inspiration to Chinese progressives in the 1920s. Women students and factory workers were major elements of early CCP membership, and in rural areas women's unions founded by the party were instrumental in transforming marital relations in the countryside. Nevertheless, the family, not the individual, remains the basic unit of Chinese society. Therefore, it is particularly important to understand the fate of the family since 1949.

Family policy might be divided into three main phases. The first occurred in the early 1950s and was the culmination of the progressive ideals of the CCP. Symbolized by the marriage law of 1950, freedom of marriage and divorce and equality of the sexes were recognized, while the power of lineages over local affairs was replaced by that of the party. Needless to say, habits did not change overnight, but tremendous grass-roots effort was put into reducing the violence and domination that had been an accepted part of family life. The second phase, from the mid-1950s to 1980, was one of the decline of family power under political and economic pressures. Politically, the turmoil of the Great Leap Forward and the Cultural Revolution subjected families to generational and ideological cross-pressures. Economically, the emergence of the production team in the countryside and the work unit in the city reduced the family's role as an independent unit of production, even though it remained the unit of residence and consumption. The third phase is marked by some important policies that are somewhat contrary in their effects. The policy of decollectivizing agriculture has again made the family a unit of production, a fact that puts more weight on the familial decision-making structure. At the same time, a new marriage law adopted in 1980 has further liberalized divorce, although obtaining a divorce remains a difficult process.

Probably the most important policy affecting family life is the "one child per family" birth control policy. This policy, introduced in the late 1970s, favors families with one child and, depending on local enforcement, penalizes or prohibits more than one child. The policy was adopted because of the unsupportable population increase that would occur if the current generation reaching childbearing age were to have more than one child. Given the great importance attached to carrying on the family name, the birth of a girl as the family's only child provoked serious crises in many households, and it led occasionally to abuse of child and wife, divorce, and even infanticide. All these actions were strenuously opposed by the government, but they occurred because of the collision between a strict population policy and China's strong and patriarchal family tradition.

ETHNICITY AND RELIGION   Only about 7 percent of China's population belongs to non-Chinese ethnic groups; therefore, China's ethnic problems are not as serious as those of the Soviet Union or Yugoslavia. Minority ethnic groups are usually concentrated in the border provinces, and areas with a significant minority population are designated as minority autonomous areas. Five whole provinces are autonomous areas: Inner Mongolia, Tibet, Guangxi, Yunnan, and Ningxia, and thirteen other provinces contain minority units. Despite the low population, minority areas are important to China because they comprise 64 percent of national territory, and contain 94 percent of China's pastureland, 38 percent of forests, and 51 percent of hydroelectric power.

There is a basic tension between the extreme centralism and ethnic homogeneity of Chinese politics and the ethnic identities and local interests of minorities. This problem has been compounded by the hostility of communists toward religion. Paradoxically, the reform of minority policies in the 1980s encouraged a greater assertiveness of ethnic interests, and this led to bloody confrontations in Tibet in 1988 and Xinjiang in 1989. However, as important as ethnicity and religion are to minorities, they are peripheral concerns to most Chinese.

EDUCATION   By and large, the educational policies of the PRC have been a tremendous success (see Figure 14.4), considering the size of the problem and the limitation resources. China's 250 million students comprise 40 percent of total school enrollment in the developing world. In 1949 primary and junior middle schools admitted 25 percent and 5 percent, respectively, of their cohort. In 1989 over 97 percent of young children attended primary school, and 70 percent of primary school graduates went on to high school. Not only has China transformed the educational opportunities of its population, but it is also providing educational services that are considerably broader and more effective than the average developing country. But education has not simply been a success story. The entire system was shut

FIGURE 14.4
SCHOOL ENROLLMENT IN CHINA

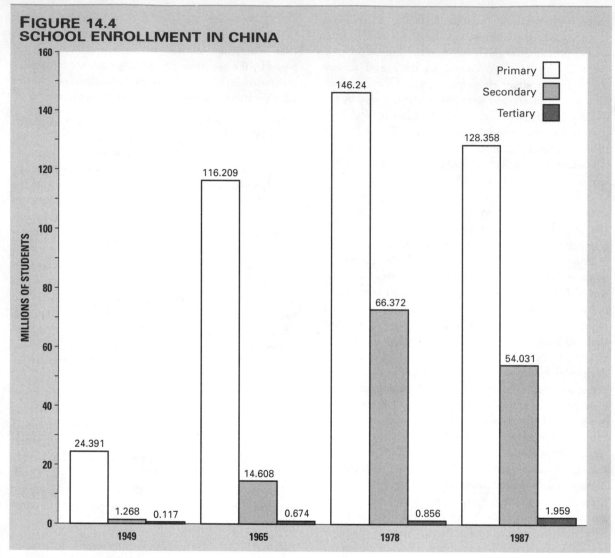

Source: Zhongguo tongji nianjian 1988.

down for a time during the Cultural Revolution, and students led the challenges to the regime in the 1980s. Despite accomplishments, educational policy has pursued a zigzag course and has occasionally posed acute political problems for the regime.

The first phase of educational development, 1949–1957, was characterized by rapid expansion at all levels, but especially at the university level. By 1957 there were more places available in universities than there were middle-school graduates. Also during this period the diverse collection of private and public schools that the regime inherited was reshaped into a uniform state educational system based on the Soviet model.

In the leftist phase, 1957–1976, the pattern of growth was reversed. University enrollment slowed and eventually declined, while the expansion of primary and junior middle schools in the countryside became the target. The educational system remained under central control, but many of the new schools were locally financed, and the teachers were recruited locally. The leftist period put primary education within the reach of virtually every child. Secondary education, which had been a rare chance to attend a boarding school in a rural town, now became a common part of the local school system. Perhaps inevitably, the overall quality of education declined.

The big event in education during the leftist period was of course the Cultural Revolution. In the universities, radical critiques of bourgeois tendencies in education played an important part in the early development of the movement, and student organizations of Red Guards in high schools and colleges were active in much of the destruction and chaos from 1966 to 1968. The entire school system was shut down by the end of 1966, and the universities did not reopen until 1970. Even after 1970 the colleges continued to be disrupted by various leftist experiments, including the abolition of entrance exams, the assignment of faculty and students to work in the countryside, and constant ideological and political activities. China's colleges did not resume normal functioning until 1977.

Educational policy of the post–Mao period has reversed leftist priorities and emphasized qualitative improvement rather than expansion. The shift of emphasis from quantity to quality was made possible by the achievement of near universal primary schooling and broad availability of secondary schooling during the leftist period. It was also encouraged by a shrinking cohort of school-age children as a result of birth control policies begun in the early 1970s. Universal compulsory education to the ninth grade remains a major goal, but the most spectacular changes occurred at the college level, partly because of the modernizing goals of the regime, but also partly because of the imbalance in the system created by the rapid expansion of the primary and secondary schools in the previous two decades. The imbalance can be illustrated by comparison with the United States. In 1982 China had five times as many primary school students, three times as many secondary students, and one-tenth as many college students as the United States.

The new emphasis on academic quality, higher education, and international openness transformed the educational world of the 1980s. To be sure, the CCP and the CYL continued to occupy central institutional roles, and open challenges to authority remained risky. But the requirement of ideological correctness became a more distant and intermittent influence on academic life. Faculty pushed for more control over academic matters, and promotions tended to be made on the basis of scholarly reputation rather than loyalty. Because admission to universities was based primarily on national

examinations starting in 1977, ambitious high school students concentrated on preparing for the exams. University students could dream of going to graduate school abroad: over 70,000 Chinese students were studying in the United States and Japan in 1991. Chinese students are the largest group of foreign students in the United States.

The shift in China's academic environment in the post–Mao period was the result of the CCP's own emphasis on modernization. In order for China to make progress in science and technology, universities had to be expanded, and experts had to be encouraged and respected. But there was a deep-seated contradiction between the new role of the universities as agents of modernization and their old role as agents of socialization into the party–state. The students who participated in the demonstrations of December 1986 and April and May 1989 had become part of a new world which was quite different from that of Deng Xiaoping.

Among the repressive measures adopted after the Tiananmen massacre were several which aimed at reintroducing the ideological discipline of the 1970s. Students were required to participate in military drills and study sessions. It is unlikely, however, that these measures have affected the basic political mood of the universities except to alienate them further from the CCP. Regardless of how the "good old days" might appeal to China's top leadership, the party has neither the credibility nor the strength to return to them.

THE COMMUNICATIONS SYSTEM China has only recently become a mass media society. The completion of the wired radio network in the early 1960s finally brought most residents into instant, direct touch with Beijing. The wired network was supplemented in the 1970s by the spread of transistor radios, and in the 1980s the television became the most desired consumer good. China is now the world's third largest manufacturer of televisions. The publication of newspapers and magazines has also increased enormously since 1949, although the Cultural Revolution led to a suspension of most periodicals. As Table 14.3 suggests, the post–Mao era has been a golden age of media, with the amount, quality, and variety available to the public expanding every year.

Domestic media in China can be divided into three categories: mass media (print, radio, and television), "internal" media, and specialized periodicals. Mass media are closely controlled by the CCP. *The People's*

TABLE 14.3
GROWTH OF MEDIA, 1950–1989

Year	Book titles	New book titles	Magazines	Newspapers	Radio stations	Television stations
1950	12,153	7,049	295	382	49 (1949)	—
1955	21,071	13,187	370	285	61 (1957)	—
1960	30,797	19,670	442	396	94 (1962)	14
1965	20,143	12,352	790	343	87	12
1968	3,694	2,677	22	49	—	—
1970	4,889	3,870	21	42	80	31
1975	13,716	10,633	476	180	88	32
1980	21,621	17,660	2,191	188	106	38
1985	45,603	33,743	4,705	698	213	219
1986	51,789	39,426	5,248	791	278	292
1987	60,193	42,854	5,687	850	386	366
1988	65,961	46,774	5,865	829	461	422
1989	74,973	55,475	6,078	852	531	469

Source: *Zhongguo Tongii Nianjian* (Statistical Yearbook of China), 1990 (Beijing: China Statistics Press, 1985), pp. 783–788.

Daily (Renmin Ribao) is the newspaper of the CCP Central Committee and therefore the most authoritative voice. All major newspapers are directly subordinate to their appropriate party committee; there is heavy editorial oversight of media contents; and there are no private mass media in China. There is also an extensive secret communications system, called *neibu* ("internal") media. The internal media include information too sensitive for public circulation, as well as discussions of issues on which the party position has not yet been decided, and information and views from the international press. Some internal material is closely guarded, but one publication of international news, *Reference News*, had a circulation of 8.7 million in 1981, considerably larger than the circulation of *The People's Daily* and larger than the combined circulations of the eight largest U.S. newspapers. The specialist media, which have mushroomed since 1978, consist of various newsletters, popular science periodicals, and workplace publications.

The news content of the Chinese mass media system has expanded and improved in the post–Mao era, but it still has a number of characteristics that distinguish it from familiar Western systems.[11] The most fundamental fact about the system is that it is almost exclusively an official state or party operation, controlled in content and management. The press, as Party Secretary Hu Yaobang reiterated in 1985, is the "mouthpiece of the party." Every news item is expected to relate positively to current policy. Criticism of negative phenomena and even of leadership failings is allowed, but there cannot be general criticism of the leadership or opposition to current policy.

A second characteristic that follows from the first is that the language of media in China is often slogan-bound, ideological, and obscure. The ideological language of the party is used to express party messages. Moreover, since the fact of conflict between leaders and divergent views on policies is suppressed, the discussion of politically sensitive issues often uses cryptic or vague language. This approach produces dull, ambiguous articles that even party cadres dislike reading.

Finally, the style of communications is pedagogical. The media persuade people to plant trees, to oppose bourgeois liberalization, to respect intellectuals — whatever the current policy calls for. The messages are often accompanied by descriptions of "typical" cases that illustrate either the benefits of correct behavior or the problems that need correction.

Despite these distinctive features of the Chinese media that result from party control, in the 1980s they became an impressive information, news, and entertainment system. Almost everyone listens to the radio. The rural elite and the urban population are avid newspaper readers. The quality of international news available to the average citizen has improved, and many listen to Voice of America, the BBC, and Radio Moscow. What an American reader would miss in a Chinese newspaper would be the political analysis and criticism, stories of crime and disasters, and consumer-oriented advertising. A Chinese reader in the United States might miss the variety and low price of newspapers, the availability of international news, the careful presentation of the government's position, and the time to read newspapers that many jobs in China allow.

One of the communication system's distinctive forms is face-to-face contact in meetings or small-group encounters organized primarily by the branch level of the party structure. Party members meet regularly to discuss policy implementation, the activities of their unit, and their own successes and failures. Party members are supposed to guide the political thinking of their nonparty colleagues and make sure that work and life in general meet the standards set by the party. During the leftist period everyone, including peasants, spent long hours each week in study groups reviewing and criticizing their performance. In the 1980s such activity was far less common outside the party and youth league, but it was revived after Tiananmen.

It is difficult to generalize about the overall effectiveness of the communications system in political socialization and ideological reeducation. As with any communications system, those in control have considerable leeway in presenting and shaping information. But the effectiveness of the system depends on its credibility, and credibility cannot be controlled so easily. During the Cultural Revolution the leftists manipulated the news at will, but few in China believed the stories. The mass media were studied as a barometer of national politics rather than as a news source.

In the 1980s the media remained subordinate to the CCP, but the party encouraged the development of journalism oriented toward information rather than propaganda. Investigative journalism became popular and influential. (One of the most famous political exiles, Liu Binyan, was once a star investigative reporter for the *People's Daily*.) New newspapers were founded with weaker links to the CCP and bolder editorial policies; one of these, reputed to be Zhao Ziyang's favorite newspaper, was closed down in the early days of the Tiananmen crisis. Older, stodgier newspapers lost circulation

and had to catch up by changing their editorial policies. Journalists gradually developed and expressed a feeling of professional identity and autonomy. On May 9, 1989, a petition with the signatures of more than a thousand journalists was given to the Journalists' Association demanding a dialogue with the government on press reform, and freedom of the press was one of the main demands of the Tiananmen demonstrations. Throughout the month of May 1989, the Chinese press became more open in reporting on the demonstrations in Beijing and elsewhere and more obviously supportive of the demonstrators.[12]

There was much subtle resistance in the media to reporting the government's version of the massacre and to propagandizing repressive measures. The press remains subordinate to the party, however, and its work is too visible to allow sustained resistance to the party's policies. Yet the party is not able to remove the entire cohort of reform-minded journalists because there is not a great reservoir of loyal conservatives to take their place. Thus, since June 1989 the media have been an unwilling mouthpiece for the party, and the tone of the press has been dull and depressed.

Socialization and Major Political Change

Although family, education, and communication are all vital agents of socialization, the political outlook of any individual is most strongly influenced by his or her own experience. Momentous variations in Chinese policies, such as the Cultural Revolution and the post–Mao shift to modernization, have brought major changes to the lives of most people and have been formative political experiences for several generations of young people. Major events such as the founding of the PRC in 1949, the death of Mao, or Tiananmen create historical watersheds that separate the political attitudes of the generations who experience the event from those who come afterward. As a result of so many major changes, different political experiences divide the Chinese population into many strata.

The founding of the People's Republic of China was perhaps the major political change. Until 1949 life for many Chinese had been characterized by chaos, uncertainty, foreign incursions, and undisguised exploitation and oppression. After 1949 a powerful and effective national political system was rapidly put into place, and the old elite was rooted out from top to bottom. The mandate of the new order was both revolutionary and convincing, and even such later policy failures as the

Great Leap Forward did not lead to widespread questioning of the party's right to rule. Thus, pre – 1949 generations have had a broader political experience but one haunted by disunity and chaos, while the children of the PRC have seen the party's policy changes against a constant background of a strong party – state. In the minds of more than 80 percent of its population, China is assumed to be unified, strong, and socialist.

Despite this common feature of "post – 49" generations, the wide variations in PRC policy have produced major differences in the life experiences and political behavior of everyone, as well as differences in the political socialization of youth.[13] A "good" high school student in the 1950s and early 1960s was one who studied hard, volunteered for a variety of service activities, and did well on examinations. Children whose parents were party members, workers, and poor peasants were favored, but the ultimate criterion was academic performance. As a result, the student bodies of colleges contained large percentages of middle-class youths who had done very well on examinations under the influence of a more academically oriented home environment. Students were cautious and orderly; the school environment was strict; and the memory of the Anti-Rightist Campaign discouraged political boldness. Although standards were different for different social classes, everyone except those from the worst family backgrounds could imagine a place for themselves in the new order. There was remarkable idealism and enthusiasm, even among middle-class students, and thousands volunteered to transfer to the countryside.

The Cultural Revolution challenged every aspect of the educational environment, dismissing the previous seventeen years as "bourgeois culture." Students were urged to criticize their teachers and administrators and to form Red Guard units to promote Mao Zedong Thought and oppose bourgeois influence. High school classes did not meet for two years, and universities were closed for four years. Academic values based on expertise were replaced by political values based on "redness." But the definition of "redness" was not clear. Students from good class backgrounds considered themselves "naturally red," while middle-class students worked hard to show that they were especially dedicated to Chairman Mao and the revolution. These differences were related to conflicts and eventually battles that broke out between different Red Guard factions. The initial idealism and excitement turned to chaos and terror, and eventually to disillusionment, as the army re-

stored party control and millions of youths were forcibly transferred to rural areas. The Red Guard generation lived through a violent and exciting time that generated close friends and strong enemies. They became cynical concerning party leadership and resentful of their own vain sacrifices. Despite their own participation in the Cultural Revolution, they were happy to see the leftist leadership fall in 1976.

The post – Mao generation of Chinese youth reflects a complex but, until Tiananmen, basically positive and optimistic situation. They are certainly not as ideological as the previous generation, but neither are they as docile as students before the Cultural Revolution. Somewhat like the post – Vietnam American youth they have been more concerned with personal success than they are with politics. But their individual futures are premised on the continuation of the party's commitment to modernization, and so by and large they support continued liberalization and openness to the West. The widespread demonstrations by college students in December 1986 were in part a response to a new climate of liberalization introduced by Hu Yaobang and in part an attempt to push the reforms further. Suppression of the 1986 demonstrations alienated students and intellectuals from the CCP, many for the first time, and contributed to the more critical and confrontational tone of the 1989 demonstrations. The massacre and the repressive atmosphere prevailing on campuses since Tiananmen must have increased student alienation from and resentment of the regime.

POLITICAL PARTICIPATION AND RECRUITMENT

The political process of the Chinese party – state is fundamentally different from the processes of the Western liberal democracies. As a result, the process functions —political participation, interest articulation, aggregation, and so forth — which are clearly present in industrial democracies are much more ambiguous and mixed in the case of China. We will therefore preface our attempt to describe Chinese politics in the general terms of process functions by stressing four characteristic features of the party – state.

The fundamental political reality in the PRC is the unitary nature of political, state, and even societal power. To a great extent Chinese society was recreated by the CCP after 1949, and all of its organizations, from the village and factory to the National People's Con-

华人民共和国万岁　　世界人民大团结万岁

Chinese students from various universities in Beijing gather beneath the giant portrait of China's best-known revolutionary, Mao Zedong, during their demonstration in front of Tiananmen Square on January 1, 1987. Such demonstrations led to the removal of Hu Yaobang and foreshadowed the demonstrations of 1989.

gress, were structured with the CCP at the core and the higher levels of the CCP in unquestioned command. Not only was opposition not allowed, but even organization independent of the CCP's internal control was not allowed. The students at Tiananmen demanded recognition of autonomous student associations, and Deng Xiaoping considered this to be in itself a threat to the party – state. The party – state allows nothing outside itself, and it is this total concentration of power which justifies the adjectives "totalitarian" or "totalistic." On the other hand, by including all of society the party – state necessarily contains many interests and conflicting tendencies within itself.

Second, participation is very important for the party – state, but it is mobilized participation sponsored by the CCP rather than participation generated independently by citizens. The CCP seeks broad, nearly universal participation in both occasional campaigns and in routine tasks and institutions in order to educate the masses, get grass-roots feedback, and help implement party policies. The assumption of such mobilization is that the party – state is close to the masses and has their interests at heart, and so the masses are supposed to respond enthusiastically to the party's call. From the party's perspective, mobilization is neither spontaneous nor commanded, but rather a natural interaction between the leaders and the masses. Those who respond consistently are considered activists and may be recruited into the party. Of course, participation does not always go as planned. Many times mobilization goes too far and is then corrected by a period of consolidation, producing a "campaign cycle" of mobilization and consolidation.

The third feature is that the current leadership expects unanimous support. There is no such thing as a loyal opposition even within the party, and the leadership controls the diversity of public opinion on any subject. Sometimes the arena for public discussion is set rather broadly, as in the Hundred Flowers movement in 1957, but caution is advised because one might be declared a "poisonous weed" afterward. On the other hand, standards may be turned upside down when the current leadership changes. People who were punished as class enemies at one time may be declared heroes in the future. Within the leadership disagreements are expressed privately and symbolically. It is only when the leadership changes that disagreements within the previous leadership are acknowledged. Since leadership does change, most people wait for a favorable political wind.

A fourth feature is that the Chinese party–state has had definite stages of development which can be compared to a life cycle, and the metaphor is strengthened by the fact that it corresponds to the life cycle of its top leadership. In its first stage, in its "youth" as a revolutionary movement before 1949, the CCP developed its approach to politics because of the necessity of mobilizing popular support against the government and the Japanese. The party and the people were indeed close because they depended on one another for survival. In its second stage, from 1949 to 1976, the party–state went through various successes and crises of maturity. It established an unusually strong state and attempted ambitious goals, but its power made it less dependent on the people and less guided by their concrete interests and capacities. Its solidarity and ideological self-confidence were destroyed by the excesses of the Great Leap Forward and the Cultural Revolution.

After the death of Mao Zedong the party–state entered a third stage, that of semiretirement. Great changes were wrought not through its collected energies but through its relaxation. It permitted the economy and society to diversify. It maintained its central position as patron of reforms, often in a passive role of privileged power rather than leadership. During the 1980s the control of the party–state began to deteriorate, and more common forms of citizen political participation began to emerge. Central control over the economy and the workplace was weakened by market forces, the party–state's ideological monopoly was threatened by the attractiveness of foreign ideas and its own intellectual narrowness, and the reform leadership of Hu Yaobang and Zhao Ziyang implicitly threatened its singleness of purpose and commitment to power. The conservative coup of 1989 reasserted the power of the party–state, but it cannot be rejuvenated. Nevertheless, the party–state will remain the major political heritage of whatever regime succeeds it.

Participation

The *mobilized political participation* characteristic of the party–state can be described in terms of three modes of participation. The first mode is participation in the formal institution of the state structure, essentially the election of deputies to rural commune and urban district congresses, and since 1979 to all county-level congresses as well. This mode involves widespread participation, with turnouts regularly exceeding 90 percent of eligible voters, but has been mainly symbolic because the congresses are weak and voters have usually just approved an official list of candidates. The reforms of 1979 to 1982 have increased congressional powers, added the county elections, and explicitly encouraged multiple candidates for positions. Despite these reforms, the party is ambivalent about encouraging electoral competition and certainly does not want to legitimate questioning of or opposition to its policies.

Participation in mass campaigns has been a more important mode over the years. It involves citizens in implementation of government programs, requires actions that have both socializing and symbolic functions for participants, and allows some popular influence on local decisions or decision makers through criticism of cadres and policy experimentation that are part of most campaigns. Deng Xiaoping's group has criticized the large-scale mass struggle campaign as an inappropriate "ultra-left" technique, but they have not renounced its use in organizing orderly support for their policies.

A third mode is participation in the internal affairs of primary units beneath the basic level of government, such as villages and teams, urban neighborhood organizations, schools, factories, and other units. This mode produces the most regular and significant forms of participation: the masses have greater say in the elections of unit leaders, they have more regular and influential contact with these leaders, and they are able to discuss issues that bear directly on their daily lives. Local units also recruit people into activist roles or lead them to serve the community by accepting assignments that contribute to collective welfare.

Mobilized mass political participation in China has little to do with decision making, except in primary units that have little leverage against the system, but it plays an important role in policy implementation, political socialization, and symbolic expression. As mentioned in the discussion of socialization, Chinese modes of participation have produced tension, hardship, and alienation for some citizens. The participant may be compelled to implement unpopular policies, to criticize self and others in cynical or destructive ways, or to spend dreary hours in the study of materials that have little personal meaning. The general pattern weakens or routinizes some conventional forms of participation (voting, for example), while sometimes encouraging unconventional forms that may bring psychological and physical violence (seen most clearly in the Cultural Revolution). With the semiretirement of the party–state in the 1980s, the level of mobilized participation dropped off considerably, and citizens gradually began to use some of their participatory opportunities for their own purposes. Occasionally, elections and assembly votes produced results the party had not intended. Although these occurrences were rare enough to be newsworthy in the 1980s, they highlight the possibility of an evolution of some party–state institutions toward citizen-based political functions.

Of course, the demonstrations at Tiananmen were examples of massive political participation that was not mobilized by the party–state. The broad support for these demonstrations showed the extent to which Chinese society in the 1980s had outgrown the control of the party–state. At bottom, the demonstrators were demanding to be treated as citizens who could express their own interests and form their own associations rather than as the masses under party tutelage. The form of participation, however, was quite similar to mobilized participation in that a few leaders assumed that they were spokesmen for everyone, and they tended to see their struggle with Li Peng as a revolutionary struggle for total victory rather than a search for an acceptable compromise.

Recruitment

Three important political roles — activist, *cadre*, and party member — dominate the staffing of the Chinese political system. Activists are ordinary citizens, not holding full-time official positions, who acquire special interest, initiative, or responsibility in public affairs. Cadres are those who hold a leadership position in an organization, normally as a full-time post. New members of the party are carefully selected by party branches, but they need not be cadres.

Becoming an activist is generally the first step in political recruitment, and it is from the ranks of activists that most new cadres and CCP members are drawn. Local party organizations keep track of activists within their jurisdiction, turning to them when political campaigns and recruitment are underway. In practice, activists are designated on the basis of self-selection, personal ability, and group support, with local officials watching closely to veto undesirables and to select the most promising candidates for more important roles.

Recruitment to cadre status is different. State cadres (full-time employees who staff state, party, and mass organization hierarchies above the primary level and who receive their salaries from the government) are appointed from within the bureaucracies, through the personnel sections of the state and the departments of the CCP. The most serious problem in cadre recruitment is tension between the dissimilar criteria of professional skills and political activism. In the leftist period, political activism received the primary emphasis. Since 1978 intellectual work has been considered respectable, and the status of specialists has been greatly improved. Nevertheless, a tension persists between the party's commitment to ideological leadership and the technocrats' preference for autonomy.

Admission to the CCP is the decisive act of political recruitment. Higher level units and some types of work (journalism, for instance) have a preponderance of party members, but in most of society the party is a dedicated and self-selecting minority.

Party membership provides entrance into a political career with significant opportunities for advancement and power. The party member is always in a position of relative political prominence. If an ordinary worker, the member is expected to have an activist role; among activists, members are the most likely to be selected as cadres; and among cadres, members have superior political status and opportunities.

From the late 1920s to the late 1940s, most party members were politically committed. Party members seldom joined the communist movement for security, material, or opportunistic reasons. Hardship, danger, and the threat of execution by the GMD were risks faced by party members and followers alike, and there was little assurance of ultimate victory until very late. A second pattern emerged in 1948–1953 as CCP power spread rapidly over all China, creating a great demand for political recruits to staff the new system. These new circumstances made it easier for opportunists and even "class enemies" to seek political office, so from 1953 on the CCP regularized and institutionalized recruitment through the PCA and the CYL. These key, politically reliable organizations helped to screen and train perspective cadres and party members, but institutionalization failed to eliminate opportunism and actually accelerated beauracratization of the party. In effect, recruitment was undermining Mao's revolutionary party.

Maoists recognized the shift from a revolutionary to a bureaucratic party and tried to combat it. There were attempts to reduce cadre members in the mid-1950s; initiation of *xia fang*, movements to recruit more peasant CCP and CYL members, and repoliticization of the PLA in the late 1950s; socialist education and cultivation of revolutionary successor campaigns in the early 1960s; and a new CYL recruitment drive to add worker–peasant members and rejuvenate league organization in 1964 and 1965. These measures checked the institutionalization of recruitment but did not reverse it. With the exception of the PLA, where Lin Biao's revival of the revolutionary political style had a marked influence, none of the institutions involved turned decisively away from the post–1953 pattern.

The Cultural Revolution produced many real and rhetorical attacks on the established recruitment process. The CCP proceeded to take in fresh blood, but how well it was absorbed is another matter. With an apparent loosening of admission standards, the party swelled to more than 35 million members in 1977 (see Table 14.1); nearly half the membership had joined since the Cultural Revolution. High turnover occurred as well, since numerous purges and other departures accompanied the Cultural Revolution. However, the old leadership began returning even before Mao's death, and most of the Central Committee members who had risen during the Cultural Revolution had been removed by the late 1970s. The personnel problem was far more difficult at the local and provincial levels. The problem of strengthening the party's ranks was addressed by a massive rectification campaign that began at the center in 1983 and worked its way down to the basic level by 1987.

Party recruitment in the post–Mao era has been very complex. First, the top leadership is hardly "new blood." Deng Xiaoping and his colleagues are now in their eighties, and although they claim to be turning power over to younger successors, the sacking of Hu Yaobang and Zhao Ziyang by Deng shows that ultimate power still remains in elderly hands.

Second, party discipline became quite lax in the 1970s and even more so in the 1980s. Party secretaries became excessively powerful in the early 1970s, and then modernization opened up many opportunities to profit from power. Reestablishing party discipline is therefore a major and continuing task. A system of "commissions for discipline inspection" was reestablished in 1979, and there have been a succession of campaigns to fight corruption, economic crime, to promote socialist spiritual civilization, to oppose bourgeois liberalism, and so forth. Some Chinese analysts say that the problem is not due to leftist or capitalist influence but to the feudal, patriarchal power structure that does not provide adequate democratic controls over those who hold power.

Third, although the party adopted modernization as its chief task in 1978, its personnel and its leadership style are more suited to political revolution and basic economic construction. The party has made an effort to recruit more intellectuals, as it did in the 1950s, but many perceive a latent tension between the pluralistic tendencies of a modern society and unquestioned political domination by the party. The problem is more complex than it appears, because the party has led the modernization reforms. But the massacre and the removal of the top reformers damaged, perhaps irretrievably, the CCP's credibility as a reform leader. No other political institutions exist which could challenge the CCP or replace it in its central political function, but one lesson of reform in Eastern Europe is that an alternative does not have to be fully formed in order to remove a party–state that has lost legitimacy.

INTEREST ARTICULATION

The central process in every political system is the conversion of demands, representing the interests, goals, and desires of individuals or groups within the society, into political decisions that are then applied and enforced by the government. The CCP's idea of how this process ought to work is contained in the mass line, stated in a directive written for the Central Committee in June 1943 by Mao Zedong:

> In all the practical work of our Party, all correct leadership is necessarily "from the masses, to the masses." This means: Take the ideas of the masses (scattered and unsystematic ideas) and concentrate them (through study turn them into concentrated systematic ideas), then go to the masses and propagate and explain these ideas until the masses embrace them as their own, hold fast to them and translate them into action, and test the correctness of these ideas in such action. Then once again concentrate ideas from the masses and once again go to the masses so that the ideas are persevered in and carried through. And so on, over and over again in an endless spiral, with the ideas becoming more correct, more vital and richer each time.[14]

Masses articulate interests (express their "scattered and unsystematic ideas"), while the party — and only the party—aggregates them (turns them into "concentrated and systematic ideas" that can become policy alternatives). There are, of course, organizations other than the CCP that have the capacity, in membership and scale, to pull together and synthesize the demands of particular groups in Chinese society. But these organizations are not autonomous. Their leadership is dominated by party members whose job is to protect the CCP's favored position in the formulation of policy proposals and to discourage demands that conflict with the CCP's general line.

The CCP's willingness to encourage political claims from the populace conflicts with its fear of organized competition or opposition. The result is that many such claims are put forward in an unorganized, fragmented way.

Since the articulation of one's own political interests and demands is restricted to informal pleading and pressure on party leadership, the two most important political assets for an individual are *access* and *connections*. Access is regular interaction with leadership. A person with access can make sure that the leadership is constantly aware of his interests and point of view. The party actively solicits the views of the masses, and those with regular access are in a good position to take advantage of such openness. Therefore, a position in the People's Congress or the Women's Union, though it may not be powerful in itself, is quite desirable because of the access it affords.

Connections are, simply, the people whom one knows. Connections can open the "back door" of the leadership when the "front door" is forbidding or is clogged with red tape. When faced with a problem, an individual sifts through his friends and family, and the friends of friends and family, to locate someone whose position or access might be useful. Of course, reciprocity is expected, and thus "connection networks" evolve. Some people build their careers on such exchanges of favors, a practice called "climbing the connection network." Although access and connections are important in every culture and have always been particularly important in China, it should be noted that the party's monopoly of interest articulation and the weakness of the legal system put the individual in a weak, suppliant position and thus encourage such behavior.

Popular demands are most frequently and easily expressed within basic-level government, especially within primary production and residential units. The smallest groups—villages in the countryside, work teams in factories, and residents' groups in cities—have frequent meetings and choose their own group leadership. The masses also have a direct voice in more inclusive groups—production brigades, factory-wide organizations, and neighborhood committees—through selection of representatives to managing committees or meetings of the entire constituency. Selection of leaders and representatives may stem from discussion and consensus rather than from contested elections, and individuals unacceptable to higher cadres are not likely to be chosen. The leaders chosen are themselves ordinary workers, however, and are in close association with their colleagues. In such a context, the leaders have the power of the state behind them, but they may also elicit the cooperation of the members. However, in the small group just as in society at large, no one is allowed to challenge the party openly.

Other means of expressing individual or deviant demands include writing letters to mass media and making personal visits to cadres' offices. Rectification campaigns give citizens special opportunities to review and criticize the performance of local elites; for all its abuses, the Cultural Revolution produced a great surge of popular interest articulation. Finally, popular demands make themselves known through acts of noncompliance or resistance, such as slowdowns or absenteeism at work, violation of regulations, and taking advantage of loopholes or ambiguities in policy.

A totally different sort of interest articulation occurred during the first three years of the Cultural Revolution.[15] Established mass organizations were banned, but students and workers were encouraged to form revolutionary mass organizations. Although these organizations did not view themselves as promoting the interests of their members, it is clear that students and workers who were disadvantaged by "the system" tended to form more radical groups, while the children of party cadres and workers with good jobs tended to form groups that defended the authorities. Beginning in 1967, Mao tried to incorporate the new mass organizations into normal politics, but the hostility among the groups prevented it. Finally, the power of the revolutionary mass organizations was suppressed by the army, and some of their leadership were given token political positions.

Organized articulation occurs when the group making the demand has members drawn from many units or localities and some means of communicating with its members and the larger public. Such organized articulation is the special function of mass organizations, the Women's Union, the All-China Federation of Trade Unions, the Writers' Union, and so on. All these groups in turn have members in the people's congresses and in the Chinese People's Political Consultative Conference. But the primary function of such groups is to inform and implement party policy in their respective social spheres, not to provide independent representation of an interest group. The level of activism in mass organizations is determined more by the party's willingness to listen than by the urgency of mass demands. The party is in firm control of the leadership of mass organizations, and they have no means of action that do not require party acquiescence.

Despite party leadership, mass organizations provide a variety of services for their members and serve as advocates of their interests within the limits of party policy. Most mass organizations were disbanded during the Cultural Revolution, but in the 1980s their advocacy functions were stronger than ever. The most interesting case is the Writers' Union, which in early 1985 was allowed to freely elect its national executive committee. One of those elected, Liu Binyan of The *People's Daily*, was expelled from the party in early 1987 for advocating bourgeois liberalization. Thus, the tension between group representation and party control continues.

In summary, popular articulation of interests tends to limit itself in normal times to unorganized expression of demands within the primary unit. Organized articulation is risky and likely to occur only when in conformity with official policy or when the group has high-level bureaucratic support; in such cases, it is difficult to tell whether the demand starts below and receives elite support or whether it appears only after elites solicit it as a weapon in higher level debate. In either case, elite allies are normally essential for wider dissemination of the demand and for any hopes of favorable response. The episodes in which popular demands have exceeded elite guidelines are significant exceptions to these generalizations, but, as we have seen, each episode brought suppression of dissidents and reaffirmation of the party's right to define the limits of popular political activity.

INTEREST AGGREGATION AND ELITE CONFLICT

In contrast to multiparty politics in the West, which sometimes gives an artificial sense of conflict and disunity, the monopoly of interest aggregation by the CCP in China often gives an artificial appearance of unity and harmony in the leadership. Since there is no legitimate opposition and the media are controlled by the party, leadership conflict in China only becomes obvious when the current leadership is displaced by a new leadership with a different direction. Even at such times the process of debate and displacement is not usually open to the public. Instead, the media are filled with criticisms and condemnations of the previous policy line. It is strange to see policies and leaders with apparently unanimous support suddenly be replaced by opposing policies and leaders, also with apparently unanimous support. This pattern, which was most clear in the Cultural Revolution and the transition to the post – Mao era, became more complex in the 1980s, and then reasserted itself in 1989.

The key to the paradox of unanimity and bitter conflict in Chinese politics lies in the tendency to view political conflict as an all-or-nothing struggle. There can be no open pluralism of viewpoints. Public political struggles are in reality not struggles between two sides, but rather attacks by the winners on the losers, in which the losers are not allowed to respond or to defend themselves. Therefore, those who differ with current policy avoid challenging it openly in normal times, but may suddenly appear as enthusiastic supporters of a new policy and critics of the old if a new leadership permits a change.

Although the prohibition of opposition and open challenge is the basic rule of the game, differing views on policy do exist, bureaucracies attempt to increase their budgets, and new policies are adopted. Since overt interest aggregation and constituency building are impossible, informal networks based on a number of factors, including mutual support, shared opinions, and patron-client ties form a strong but publicly invisible fabric of elite politics. In times of crisis and high vulnerability, the mutual protection provided by informal groups becomes crucial and the factional fabric of politics becomes more obvious. But even when factional politics has been at its most extreme — for instance, pitched battles between various Red Guard groups during the Cultural Revolution — factionalism itself has always been publicly condemned.

Informal associations are not the only trellis of political activity and interest aggregation. The major bureaucratic structures compete privately and indirectly for budget shares and for the attention of the top leadership. The Ministry of Agriculture, for example, might emphasize the importance of investment in chemical fertilizer plants, while the Railways Ministry might push for electrification of trunk lines. Besides the interbureaucratic differences at each level, there is also tension between central ministries and local governments concerning control over projects and investment. Moreover, the encouragement of foreign investment and trade in the 1980s has created a clear difference of interests between coastal provinces, whose natural advantages in foreign trade have been enhanced by special privileges, and inland provinces, which are poorer and therefore demand more redistributive developmental policies.

POLICYMAKING AND POLICY IMPLEMENTATION

The primary decision maker in the Chinese system is the CCP. The decision-making structure is narrow, based on party committees acting in closed session. There is little open legislative activity or issuance of public laws, although both have increased with recent reforms. Decisions usually take the form of general statements on policy or doctrine, or they emerge as administrative directives and regulations.

Although the government issues legal-sounding rules, implying implementation at a specific time and procedures to enforce compliance, its decisions on many important issues have a tentative and experimental quality. They are cast in the form of general statements, indicating models to be followed or goals to be attained but not specifying exact procedures, forms, and relationships. The meaning of such a decision emerges only in practice, as lower levels begin to develop concrete responses to the tasks demanded of them. In the midst of this practice, higher levels review and investigate the early results. They may decide to accelerate or decelerate the process, publicize new models, or even issue new directives that alter the initial thrust of the policy. Members of the party elite seem to regard the attendant shifts and variations as necessary for the development of viable policies. It is their way of practicing the mass line, of refining their views through practical experience.

Decision Making

Mao Zedong was long the central figure in Chinese decision making, initiating, approving, and legitimating many of the most important CCP policies. His knowledge of personalities and issues, his self-confidence and determination, his ability to persuade, and his sensitivity to tactics and strategy made him a formidable politician. As party chairman, he had ample power to shape the procedural and institutional context of elite politics. Above all, he held unique authority and prestige. His politics were occasionally criticized, resisted, or altered, but direct challenges to his leadership were doomed to failure.

For several reasons, however, it is a mistake to look on decision making under Mao as a dictatorial process. Although Mao's influence was greater than that of any other leader, his changing perceptions of priorities and his own personal style led him to exercise it unevenly. His authority over senior colleagues weakened at times, the years just before the Cultural Revolution being the best example. After the Cultural Revolution, declining vigor removed him from an active role in administration. He continued to have a decisive role in some key decisions — for example, the rapprochement with the United States, the purge of Lin Biao, and the 1976 demotion of Deng Xiaoping — but his domination of central politics was coming to a close well before his death.[16]

Since the death of Mao in 1976, Chinese decision making has necessarily been more collegial than it was before. Deng Xiaoping does not have as much personal authority as Mao had, and it is difficult to know whether any single policy decision expresses his personal preferences or is the result of a collective decision. Nevertheless, top Chinese leadership as a whole retains the unrestricted, personalistic ambience characteristic of Mao and of imperial times. Deng Xiaoping has twice removed a chosen successor, as Mao did twice. Although Deng has been active in imposing restrictions on the rest of the party and administrative hierarchy, the top of the hierarchy appears to feel that its own unrestricted power is a necessary condition for proper political guidance.

No central leadership, however, can simply do what it wants. The major restraint on their power is the limitation of human and natural resources. With the economy still depending heavily on the harvest and with popular compliance essential for the success of mass campaigns of social change, central plans may come up against unexpected and insuperable obstacles. The Great Leap Forward is probably the best example of what may happen when elites defy the objective limits of nature and humankind. Moreover, because of China's great size, a large amount of discretion and leeway must be delegated in applying policy, thereby putting central preferences at the mercy of local interpretations. This tendency is strengthened by administrative commitments to experimentalism and decentralization.

Another set of questions about Chinese decision making concerns its capacity to assess rationally a significant range of policy alternatives and their possible consequences. Some observers argue that concentration of power in a small group of party elites, combined with insistence on ideological orthodoxy, closes the process to needed unorthodox or nonparty views. Even Mao complained about this shortcoming. But although there is ample evidence of dogmatism, the process as a whole has not excluded consideration of a wide range of alternatives. The debates and conflicts discussed earlier indicate the contrary. The real problem seems to be the hazards associated with sponsoring a rejected alternative; these hazards lead to caution in taking a stand on an issue not yet decided. The veiled and frustrating language of Chinese political debate is best understood as a function of this desire to argue a position without appearing to deviate from orthodoxy.

The utilization of "models" illustrates both the capabilities and the limits of Chinese policymaking. Because of the discretion allowed to local levels, a unit occasionally is quite successful when it follows a variant of normal policy. The unit is studied closely, and if its initiative is successful, its experience may be propagandized for general study. National policy is often legitimated, validated, or amended on the basis of successful models. The classic case was the Dazhai Brigade, a very poor rural unit that in the early 1960s made itself into a success through good leadership and collective labor. Mao Zedong was so impressed with their success that he penned the slogan, "In agriculture, learn from Dazhai," and the Dazhai model became a policy lodestone for more than a decade. The problem with using models in this way is that the conditions of the successful model might not exist elsewhere, and the political attention directed at models distorts their performance. When Dazhai ceased to be a model in 1978, much of its success was attributed to state subsidies and dishonest leadership. The utilization of models allows policymaking to be empirically oriented without being dependent on experts, but it runs the risk of basing policy on unrepresentative and inappropriate evidence. Because of such problems, specialists and statistics are becoming more important in policymaking.

Finally, one might ask if the weakness of popular representation above the basic level and of independent political communication restricts policymakers' understanding of how decisions will be received. The answer must be yes, since the central elite relies on cadre reports filtered up through the bureaucracy for its impressions of popular mood. As in all bureaucracies, such reports reflect what bureaucrats think their superiors want to see as well as what is actually happening. Elites have some ways of guarding against serious miscalculations of popular response, however. One is the combination of mass line and decentralization that leaves implementation to units better informed of local conditions. Another is the experimental approach that permits altering initial policies on the basis of early results.

Administration

The Chinese political system entrusts the application of its rules to a variety of structures, including state, party, and army bureaucracies and the communications systems they control; the management organs of primary units; and a multitude of popular committees, organizations, and meetings that mobilize the population for direct action on government programs. It is the world's largest bureaucracy, governing a society with the world's longest experience with bureaucratic rule. Precisely because they know these things, and recognize the traditional and modern abuses of bureaucracies, the Chinese Communists have made many efforts to restrain the exercise of bureaucratic power. Although they accept the necessity for centrally directed organizational hierarchies, they have tried to ensure bureaucracy's responsiveness to political controls and to keep its structure simple and efficient. As a result, the history of bureaucracy in China since 1949 has been one of recurring tendencies to expand its role matched by counterpressures to limit it.

The basic problem of political control over the bureaucracy has expressed itself most forcefully in the relationship between the party and the state hierarchies. When the PRC was established, the party was in no position to take over the specialized responsibilities of running national level and urban bureaucracies, but by the early 1960s party committees were in control of the decision making of every public organ. Despite the initial attacks on the party, the Cultural Revolution strengthened party displacement of the state by establishing "unified leadership" under revolutionary committees. The post – Mao leadership has taken as a major task the reestablishment of some degree of state autonomy. The "feudalism" encouraged by party domination is criticized, and professionalism and the rule of law are encouraged. Nevertheless, the dilemma of party control and state autonomy is likely to remain as a basic policy tension.

A second major issue is ensuring that administrative personnel effectively fulfill their functions and serve the people. Campaigns against bureaucratism and cadre corruption have been launched periodically since the birth of the PRC. Harry Harding describes two different approaches to bureaucratic reform in Maoist China.[17] The first, rationalistic reform, accepts bureaucracy as necessary but attempts to discipline it internally. This approach was more characteristic of Liu Shaoqi. The second, radical reform, is more fundamentally antagonistic to bureaucracy and seeks to control it externally through mobilizing the masses, as in the Cultural Revolution. In the post–Mao era radical reform through mass mobilization has dropped out of the picture. New trends in bureaucratic reform in the 1980s included professionalization, mandatory retirement ages, legal and procedural improvement, and the strengthening of popular control through election mechanisms.

Decentralization is an important issue of Chinese administrative politics that can be used to illustrate the difference between the Maoist and post–Mao regimes. Some degree of decentralization is inevitable in China because of its size and diversity. Moreover, the party's guerrilla heritage inclines it to be flexible and to trust local leadership. But decentralization also entails a loss of central information and control, a loss that inevitably inconveniences and embarrasses top leadership. Because of China's unitary ethnic and political heritage, decentralization involves a delegation of decision making, but not a real segmentation of power as in a federal system. For these reasons both Mao and the current modernizers favored decentralization, but the kinds of decentralization they promoted were quite different.

Mao's decentralization stressed self-sufficiency of egalitarian communities. Each locality was supposed to raise its own food. Sideline occupations were often discouraged, and regional trade in agricultural products declined. Individuals were supposed to prosper through collective efforts. This version of decentralization is akin to a traditional peasant's idea of prosperity and security: to be independent of outsiders, to be united as a community, and to produce a sufficiency of basic goods.

The decentralization favored in the 1980s was quite different; indeed, it was almost the opposite of the Maoist ideal. Instead of self-sufficiency, decentraliza-

tion now stressed production of marketable commodities. Villages and families were allowed to produce what was profitable and to buy their own grain if necessary. Sideline enterprises were encouraged, and more and more peasants were employed in nonfarm tasks. Families were allowed to work for themselves and become rich before their neighbors. The current version of market decentralization is thus very modern. It stresses choices made for self-interest within a differentiated and interdependent economy. Its ideal is "more, better, faster" for both individual and society. The conservative post–Tiananmen regime is suspicious of market decentralization because it erodes central control, but it acknowledges that the general pattern of market decentralization established in the 1980s cannot be reversed.

Rule Enforcement and Adjudication

Examination of the way in which the political system enforces and adjudicates its rules begins with the formal legal system. In China, the institutions that do the work are the courts, whose function is to try cases, render verdicts, and assign sentences; the procuracy, which investigates and prosecutes possible violations of law; public security or police organs; local mediation committees; and the CCP, which is deeply involved in the entire legal process. The structure and activity of these institutions, and their relationships, set the tone of law enforcement in China. But the formal legal system plays a relatively modest role in social control. The CCP approach to law enforcement and adjudication is not highly legalistic, in the sense of reliance on statutes and institutionalized procedures for their application and interpretation. Rather, the party views social control from the perspectives of its ideology and the Chinese legal tradition, which weaken legal formalities and shift legal functions away from the structures designed to perform them.

The role of law in China differs from the role of law in the West in a number of important respects. First, a democratically elected legislature is the basis of legitimacy in the West, and the rule of law is superior to governmental and nongovernmental organizations. In China, the party's legitimacy derives from its successful leadership of the revolution and its commitment to Marxism-Leninism. The rule of law is secondary to the rule of the party, and the legislature, the National People's Congress, is definitely secondary to the party. A citizen must obey party decrees and officials as well as laws and state officials. This basic fact has not been changed by recent increases in legal codification, though it is important to note that the party is also bound by legislation.

Second, whereas citizens have equal legal and political rights in the West, the PRC is a "people's democratic dictatorship" that expects to treat class enemies differently from class allies. The distinction between friends and enemies is based not only on the revolutionary experience but also on the Marxist critique of Western law. So the legal and political systems actively discriminate against class enemies and favor workers, peasants, and party members. The class basis of law was taken to an extreme in the leftist period, when the Ministry of Justice ceased functioning and the party and mass groups took over legal functions. In reaction to such abuses, class labels have been virtually abolished, and the equality of citizens before the law was emphasized in the 1980s. However, unequal treatment, especially for political reasons, remains a severe problem, and such terms as "bourgeois spiritual pollution" and "bourgeois liberalization" suggest that the spirit of class struggle remains alive.

Third, law and the legal system are viewed as only a part of adjudication, mediation, and application of sanctions. As in traditional China, no one wants to go to court in the PRC. There are more than 900,000 mediation committees, and together they handle ten times the number of cases handled by the court system. A decision by a mediation committee can be appealed into the court system, and through the various levels of courts, but such litigiousness is not yet a habit. Even though a number of new law schools have been opened in the last ten years, the Chinese legal system is still, in the words of one expert, "law without lawyers."[18]

Besides the problems intercepted by the mediation committees, there are many administrative sanctions that do not fall under the jurisdiction of the courts and to which the legal rights of defendants apparently do not apply. For instance, thousands of youths were reportedly sentenced to two years in labor re-education camps in the early 1980s by public security organs. Moreover, most disciplinary action against party members, even for criminal offenses, takes place within the party, and the defendant may or may not be turned over to the courts afterward for normal criminal penalties.

Fourth, although careful investigative work may be done beforehand by the police and procuracy, courtroom procedure itself is occupied more with the hearing of confessions and with sentencing than with a "fair trial" of guilt or innocence. To consider the defendant innocent until proven guilty is still regarded as a bourgeois notion, though now defendants are entitled to lawyers and can appeal decisions.

Last, the community is far more active in the prevention of crime and in the rehabilitation of criminals than is common in the West. Not only is neighborhood security very close, but even slightly deviant behavior will be commented on and criticized. In most cases a returning criminal is expected to be taken back by his original work unit. Very few people are either let loose or cast off by society.

Despite these differences from Western legal systems, there have been important developments in Chinese law in the post–Mao period. Major legal codes have been introduced, including the first criminal code in 1979. The 1982 constitution is more carefully written than its predecessors, although it contains clauses that permit the avoidance of inconvenient provisions. The importance attached to law and the prestige of the legal profession have increased enormously. The rapid growth of economic contracts has prompted growth in civil law, an area that had been neglected. Major campaigns for public legal education have been launched. But law has never been a very vital or autonomous force in China, and social habits change slowly. In any case, the goal of the legal system is not to be like that of the West, but to handle the conflicts occurring in a socialist party–state in a regular, fair, and efficient manner.

PUBLIC POLICY: PERFORMANCE AND EVALUATION

In this concluding section we concentrate on the general policy strategies that China has pursued and the effects they have had on political and economic development. As we have seen, the Chinese themselves consider the course of public policy to have been a zigzag path, with the major phases being the Soviet-style policies of the 1950s, the leftist policies initiated in 1957 by Mao Zedong, and finally the modernization policies of the post–Mao era. We will examine how each of these phases affected the power and performance of the state, and we will end with a brief look at foreign policy.

Performance Capabilities

As indicated in Chapter Eight, the capabilities of a political system can be described in terms of its capacity to extract resources, distribute goods and services, regulate behavior, and symbolize goals. In general, the PRC has performed strongly in all categories, but not in all categories at once. A closer look at its policy history reveals that extraction and regulation dominated the 1950s, distributional and symbolic concerns dominated the leftist period, and the enhancement of the resource base of the state has preoccupied the post – Mao leadership. The shifts of policy focus have been due in part to perceptions of earlier mistakes and failings, but also in part to changes of policy context brought on by the success of earlier policies.

The PRC began with the historic distributional policies of land reform and the promotion of mass interests in the urban economy, but the major task of the 1950s was to establish political and economic control in order to build a modern state structure on the Soviet model. In the urban sector, the state established control of the marketing system and increasingly pressured remaining capitalists to become part of the state-controlled system. As a result, there was a rapid increase in state income led by a great increase in the profits of state-owned enterprises. Meanwhile, the rural economy, somewhat dispersed by land reform, was consolidated through cooperatization and the establishment of compulsory grain quotas in 1953. Agricultural taxes were reduced (they provided 29.3 percent of revenue in 1950 and only 9.6 percent by 1957), but resources were extracted from agriculture through low prices and compulsory deliveries.

Politically, the CCP's consolidation of power was much milder than that of the Bolsheviks, probably because of its tradition of United Front policies and its confidence in broad popular support. However, in line with Marxism-Leninism, the CCP felt no need to allow a pluralistic political system or seriously to guarantee political rights to the masses. Although there were many campaigns against bureaucratism and corruption among cadres, it was assumed that party leadership was correct. The criticism of the party voiced in the Hundred Flowers Campaign of 1957 was a shock to the leadership, and the critics were quickly condemned as rightists and treated as outcasts.

By 1957 the accomplishments of the PRC were the source of both pride and concern. China had completed the transition to a socialist political economy more rapidly and with better results than had its mentor, the Soviet Union. But the urban and central orientation of the Soviet model had produced imbalances. Educational and health resources were now developed in the cities but still primitive in the countryside. Agricultural production had improved, but it had trouble keeping ahead of population growth. Some sort of breakthrough was necessary, but agricultural mechanization, the solution suggested by the Soviet model, was too costly. In politics and ideology the PRC had moved beyond the need for a united front, and its erstwhile allies among the former bourgeoisie and intellectuals now appeared to be insidious class enemies of socialism. In the terms introduced earlier, extractive and behavioral capabilities were no longer the major focus, and attention shifted to distributional and symbolic development.

The leftist period from 1957 to 1976 was highlighted by two massive policy failures, the Great Leap Forward and the Cultural Revolution. Both of these campaigns, as well as the general trend of the period, concentrated on ideological motivation and distributional policies. The forced enthusiasm of the Great Leap Forward led to the falsification of results and eventually to administrative breakdown and famine, and the egalitarianism implicit in free mess halls and the establishment of communes proved unworkable. In the Cultural Revolution, Mao's call to "bombard the headquarters" led eventually to armed conflicts between factions, and the criticism of expertise dealt a heavy blow to Chinese intellectuals. Despite such spectacular failures, distributive policies had positive effects on national health care and education. As a result of leftist policies, basic health care and education reached almost every rural area. Urban incomes and rural incomes within villages became very equal, but there was an increase in the differences among villages and between rural and urban areas.

The extractive and regulatory capabilities of the earlier period were not abandoned by Mao. State revenue increased its dependence on enterprise profits, and expenditures included record levels of capital investment. Quotas and sanctions against sideline enterprises were applied in order to force rural areas to concentrate on raising grain. As Figure 14.5 makes clear, inflation was held to nearly zero, but at the cost of extensive rationing and a bleak consumer life-style. In the leftist period the party – state had become too strong for its own good and had held the reins of society too tightly. Despite the apparent spontaneity and chaos of the early years of the Cultural Revolution, Chinese society was in a cultural and political straitjacket for the twenty years of leftism.

When Mao Zedong died in 1976, the PRC was

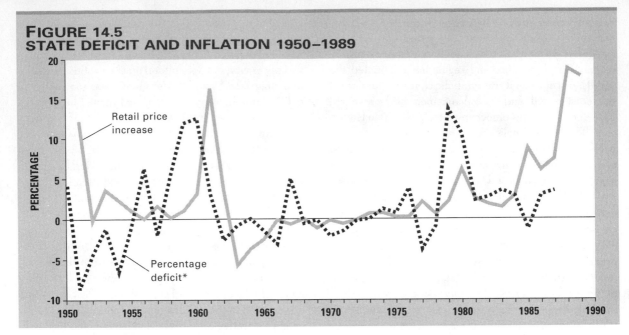

FIGURE 14.5
STATE DEFICIT AND INFLATION 1950–1989

* "Percentage deficit" refers to the annual deficit as a percentage of state expenditures; a negative deficit is a revenue surplus.
Source: Calculated from *1990 Zhongguo Tongji Nianjian.*

burdened with extractive policies and obsessed with behavioral conformity, and it had grown cynical toward symbols. Central control of investment, which had been effective during the basic construction of an industrial base, became more wasteful as the economy became more sophisticated. Leftist egalitarianism had distributed primary and secondary education and basic health care more widely, but the disdain for quality slowed further improvement and left higher education in a shambles.

The transition period from 1977 to 1979 was characterized by new goals for old policies. Hua Guofeng reoriented official enthusiasm toward the four modernizations, but his methods simply utilized different symbols, more capital investment, and a continuation of regulatory and distributive policies. As Deng Xiaoping became more prominent, a fundamental shift in Chinese public policy became apparent. The state's capabilities were restrained, and society was encouraged to develop its own capabilities. State revenues declined as a proportion of the total social product, and taxation replaced enterprise profits as the major source of revenue. Defense and capital construction expenditures declined, while housing and other consumer needs received more attention than ever before. The expansion of the nonstate economy was dramatic: in 1975 state enterprises

carried out 90 percent of retail sales; in 1985 the figure was 40 percent. Within state enterprises more control was shifted from the party committee to the manager, and in some factories the management was elected by the workers. Throughout the economy material incentives—bonuses, profits, contracts, piecework, and so on—replaced the collective moral and political persuasion of the Maoist era. Occasionally, conservatives have complained of the shift, and campaigns to learn from various paragons of selfless socialist virtue have become more common since Tiananmen, but no one argues for a return to the Maoist economic system.

The most important and successful policy initiatives have been in agriculture (Table 4.4). The World Bank has called China's new policies "the most far-reaching agricultural reforms [in the world] in the last decade."[19] Instead of constraining peasants to grow more grain by raising quotas and restricting other activities, the new policies raised the purchase price of grain, allowed crop diversification, and permitted peasant families to sell surplus produce privately. The success of these policies has been remarkable. Grain production increased at 5 percent per year until 1985, and commercial crops such as cotton have increased at rates near 20 percent per year. Market forces have introduced new fluctuations in yields: jute production, for instance, grew

TABLE 14.4
SELECTED ECONOMIC INDICATORS

	1987 as a percentage of: 1952	1978	Average annual increase 1953–1987	1979–1987
Population	183.0	112.3	1.8	1.3
Workers	254.6	139.1	2.7	3.1
Total social product	1,822.4	251.1	8.6	10.8
Agricultural output	371.6	176.8	3.8	6.5
Grain	246.9	132.8	2.6	3.2
Cotton	325.5	195.9	3.4	7.8
Meat	586.7	231.9	5.2	9.8
Industrial output	4,516.9	276.4	11.5	12.0
Cloth	451.7	156.8	4.4	5.1
Bicycles	51,459.0	482.0	19.5	19.1
Electricity	6,812.3	193.8	12.8	7.6
Steel	4,168.9	177.1	11.2	6.6
Cement	6,512.2	285.5	12.7	12.4
Rail freight volume	2,917.2	226.2	10.1	9.5
Medical personnel	523.0	146.5	4.8	4.3
Foreign trade	4,260.3	400.4	11.3	16.7

Source: 1988 Zhongguo Tongji Nianjian.

by 128 percent in 1985 and then declined by 65 percent in 1986.

Although the overall value of agricultural production continued to rise throughout the 1980s and the expansion of nonagricultural employment brought prosperity to rural areas, grain production reemerged as a major problem in 1985. It is likely to remain a serious concern (see Figure 14.2 for grain production). The bumper crop of 1990 is likely to be an exception because it was favored by unusually good weather, high grain prices, and the regime's emphasis on grain production. After the initial benefit of market activities in rural production, the regime must now cope with the problems of maintaining infrastructural investment in agriculture, guaranteeing producer prices in order to insure production, subsidizing consumer prices in order to avoid unrest and inflation, and balancing the budget.

The general impression of the regime's capabilities in the 1980s was that there was a tremendous response to the relaxation of central controls in the first half of the 1980s. This led to a strengthening of reformers within the leadership, a diminution of the party–state's control mechanisms, and a growth of parts of society and economy beyond the direct control of the government. In the second half of the 1980s problems of rapid growth became apparent, especially inflation, and the government was not in a position to exert its usual controls. This made Zhao Ziyang and the reformers look ineffective and contributed to their downfall. However, conservative economic policy has proven equally disastrous in the opposite direction, with low inflation but also low production and high unemployment. Thus, the conservatives have been forced to amend their policies. Moreover, the conservatives have attempted to strengthen the central power by increasing the subsidies to state industries and increasing the army's expenditures, thereby further imbalancing the budget.

Performance Outcomes
Charles Lindblom has characterized capitalist political economies as having "strong fingers but weak thumbs," while those of communist countries have "strong thumbs but weak fingers."[20] The "fingers" are the manifold responses of supply and demand in the marketplace, and the "thumbs" are the control and allocation of resources by public authority. Applying this

U.S. technician imparts the operational tenet of the JMR-4 satellite receiver to the technicians of the Chinese South China Sea Petroleum Company.

metaphor to China, the CCP rapidly developed strong thumbs in the 1950s and used its thumbs to try to shape society in the leftist phase. The 1980s have been characterized by a lessening of thumb pressure and an attempt to develop market "fingers."

With the exception of the Great Leap Forward and the Cultural Revolution, each policy phase has been remarkably successful in terms of its major goals. The major tasks of the 1950s were the creation of a modern industrial base and a strong state, and Soviet-style thumbs were applied very effectively. In a few years the PRC transformed a society that had suffered forty years of profound crisis and disarray. In the five years from 1952 to 1957, the industrial output index more than doubled, and heavy industry tripled. Steel output, the Stalinist benchmark of progress, increased by four times in five years. At the same time the educational and health systems were being restored and expanded, and inexpensive, state-managed media began to be widely available. Such developments were essential to China's political and economic independence and to its further growth as a modern power.

The leftist period continued the pattern of rapid growth in basic industry. Steel production increased sixfold from 1957 to 1978; the rail system increased its freight load by five times. But the period's most characteristic successes were in distributive and symbolic areas. The primary school system grew rapidly from 1957 to 1965, spurred on by rural self-financing schemes, and secondary enrollment grew at an annual rate of more than 25 percent for the thirteen years from 1965 to 1978. Meanwhile, the national wired radio system reached almost every village in China by the early 1960s, and the printing presses managed to deliver 2 billion volumes of Mao quotations during the Cultural Revolution.

Overall, the accomplishments of the PRC from 1949 to 1978 were quite impressive, but life had become drab, fearful, and hemmed in by restrictions. Moreover, the bureaucratized industrial system had become increasingly inefficient. While students huddled under forty-watt light bulbs to read, heavy industry used twice as much energy per unit of output as comparable countries. In agriculture, production barely kept ahead of population despite tremendous state pressure and large investments in irrigation and fertilizer. Food grain per capita did not climb significantly beyond its high point in the 1950s until 1978, and commercial crops stagnated. Urban consumers were fairly equal in the mid-1970s, but there was little to buy. By the time of Mao's death the thumbs of a strong state had resulted in an oppressive and stagnant atmosphere.

The astonishing economic successes of post–Mao policy are evident in Table 14.4, which shows that the total social product grew at an annual rate of more than 10 percent from 1979 to 1987. In the same period, retail sales increased by 15 percent annually, and imports and exports by more than 16 percent. Urban and rural economies have greatly diversified, and consumer incomes and goods have improved. Table 14.5 illustrates the improvement in consumer welfare. Urban and rural populations have both benefited, and the gap between the two is narrowing. From 1978 to 1987 urban income increased 237 percent, while rural income increased 345 percent. China's economy and society are becoming more complex and sophisticated.

The post–Mao leadership is paying less attention to areas emphasized during the first twenty-seven years of the PRC. Industry, especially heavy industry, is expanding less rapidly than before. Primary and secondary enrollments have actually declined, mostly in response to a diminishing age cohort, while university enrollment has thrived. The number of medical professionals and the amount of freight have expanded less rapidly than before. State revenues and expenses have risen less rapidly since 1979, and state indebtedness has increased.

This pattern of policy change does not mean a lack of interest in steel, health care, or basic education. Rather, it indicates that the current diversification of the political economy and utilization of market mechanisms

builds on the achievements of the first quarter-century of PRC rule, even while policy direction is being changed. For example, if primary and secondary education had not been vastly expanded during the leftist period, these would necessarily be high priorities for current leaders, and there would not be so much student pressure for the expansion of tertiary education. The policy change of the post–Mao period should not be seen simply as correcting previous mistakes, although there were certainly many of these. Current reforms are also a response to new opportunities created by the successful completion of the basic tasks of economic and state construction.

It is tempting to view Deng Xiaoping as a victim of his own success in the 1980s. The policies of the post–Mao era were intended to encourage initiative and diversity and raise China's level of prosperity. They were successful, and thereby they lowered the party–state's capacity to control society as well as reducing many of the functions formerly supplied by political leadership. Like the broom of the sorcerer's apprentice, modernization has acquired a momentum of its own, which has led not only to new demands on the party–state, but also to challenges to its exclusive role. Unfortunately, the challenge has been suppressed with force, but the society that generated the challenge remains, as do the policies encouraging further modernization.

China and the World

For the first half of the twentieth century, the primary concerns of Chinese politics were national reunification and the establishment of Chinese autonomy. It is a major tribute to the success of the PRC in these areas

TABLE 14.5
CONSUMER WELFARE: AN URBAN-RURAL COMPARISON, 1980 AND 1984 (CONSUMER GOODS PER HUNDRED FAMILIES)

Consumer good	1980			1984		
	Urban	Rural	Rural/Urban (percent)	Urban	Rural	Rural/Urban (percent)
Bicycles	126.77	36.87	29.0	162.67	74.48	45.8
Radios	84.90	33.54	39.5	103.11	61.13	59.2
Wristwatches	223.89	37.58	16.8	282.95	109.44	38.7
Sewing machines	65.57	23.31	35.5	77.52	42.37	54.7
Television sets	32.29	0.39	1.2	85.36	7.24	8.5

Source: Calculated from Li Chengrui, "Economic Reform Brings Better Life," *Beijing Review*, 28:29 (July 22, 1985), p. 19.

that our discussion of domestic policy has not been distracted by problems of regional dissension and division or by the intrusion or pressure of foreign powers. China, formerly pitied by its friends and despised by its enemies, has become a major power in world affairs. As the Chinese themselves like to say, China has stood up.

During the 1950s, however, China did not stand up straight but rather "leaned to one side," that of the Soviet Union. The Korean War of 1950–1953 confirmed a mutual hostility between the PRC and the United States, and the Soviet Union was able to provide developmental assistance and a nuclear umbrella. But even during the 1950s China's foreign policy was set more by a self-confidence in revolutionary strength than by a fearful dependence on a strong ally. Mao claimed that imperialism and even atom bombs were "paper tigers," and foreign policy should not be based on fear of them. China's failure to behave as a client state, together with its more risky and revolutionary posture, contributed to the breakdown in Sino-Soviet relations by 1960.

From 1960 to 1972 China stood straight and isolated. Foreign policy reflected the ideological dogmatism of domestic policy. Its hostility to the United States was heightened by American intervention in Vietnam and continued alliance with Taiwan. Openly hostile relations with the Soviet Union began with bitter condemnations of Khrushchev's "revisionism" in 1960, and China proceeded to split the international communist movement into pro-Moscow and pro-Beijing factions. Among communist countries, Albania was China's only unequivocal ally, but the radical policies of the Cultural Revolution attracted Western radicals into pro-Beijing groups. Relations with the Soviet Union reached their low point in 1969 with the deaths of hundreds of soldiers in incidents on the Sino-Soviet border. The Soviet Union began to explore the possibility of joint U.S.–Soviet actions against China and to prepare seriously for nuclear war with China.

The turn of China's foreign policy in 1972 toward normalization with the West was the product of a number of factors. First, the Soviet actions just mentioned were a major threat to China's security. Second, America's failure in Vietnam convinced China that American imperialism was in decline and no longer posed an active threat. Conversely, President Richard Nixon and his national security adviser, Henry Kissinger, were interested in improving relations with both China and the Soviet Union in order to isolate North Vietnam. If the

Taiwan issue could be resolved, normalization of relations with the United States would be possible. Third, China was concerned about the long-term consequences of Japanese rearmament. Fourth, China changed its policy on state-to-state relations, dropping all ideological inhibitions. It established relations with Francisco Franco in Spain before he died, and with the Shah in Iran.

Richard Nixon visited China, met with Mao Zedong and Zhou Enlai, and signed the Shanghai Communiqué in February 1972. The issue of Taiwan was finessed with the policy of "one China but not now": The United States recognized that Taiwan was a part of China, while the PRC provided assurances of peaceful reunification. Although normalization of U.S.–Chinese relations did not occur until December 1978, Chinese relations with the West began to improve rapidly. Japan normalized relations in 1972. Strident hostility toward the Soviet Union was maintained, so in effect China began to tilt slightly toward the West.

The modernization policies of the 1980s replaced earlier isolation with an open-door policy. Trade expanded rapidly; foreign investment and tourism were encouraged. The open door has brought some undesirable consequences: trade imbalances, corruption, and Western cultural influences. Meanwhile, Chinese economic and diplomatic relations with the Soviet Union and Eastern Europe gradually improved during the 1980s. Although China remained more committed to its Western relations, other doors were open as well. In 1989 relations were normalized between China and the Soviet Union. In 1991 China offered food aid to the Soviet Union, a gesture that contrasted China's economic success with Russia's economic difficulties.

The year 1989 was a crisis year for China's world position. Until Tiananmen, China watchers, politicians, and businesspeople throughout the world had become accustomed to thinking that China's reform policies would continue indefinitely. The massacre was a profound shock to such assumptions as well as being an outrage to international standards of human rights. Even if the repression of the reformers had taken place without the massacre, there would still have been a reevaluation of assumptions concerning China's future. The massacre provoked immediate condemnations, especially from the West, as well as suspensions of aid and diplomatic ostracism. Although the Chinese government also showed some isolationist tendencies, its first diplomatic priority became the removal of sanctions and the restoration of trade and investment. By 1991 it was largely successful in this effort, though relations with many countries, especially the United States, will remain very sensitive to the government's handling of popular protests in the future.

Because of its own struggle against foreign pressures, China has always felt called to a leadership role among developing countries. In 1955 at a conference in Bandung, Indonesia, Zhou Enlai enunciated the "five principles of peaceful coexistence," stressing relations of mutual benefit and noninterference in domestic affairs. However, China was also involved in aiding revolutionary movements in a number of countries. In 1964 Lin Biao declared that China was a model of how the world's countryside could encircle the world's cities. In the post – Mao period China has greatly reduced its support for revolutionary movements and enhanced its posture as a spokesperson for the interests of developing countries.

The exception in the peaceful trend of China's foreign relations in the 1980s is its relations with Vietnam, its former ally and the chief recipient of Chinese aid for twenty-five years. Vietnam invaded Pol Pot's Democratic Kampuchea, which was actively supported by China, in late 1978, and China retaliated by invading Vietnam in 1979. The Vietnamese Army remained in Kampuchea, and China supported 40,000 rebel soldiers based in Thailand. From the Chinese perspective, Vietnam's ingratitude, its treatment of ethnic Chinese, its alliance with the Soviet Union, and its occupation of Kampuchea justified continuing hostility. From Vietnam's point of view, China's patronizing attitude, support for the anti-Vietnamese and genocidal regime of Pol Pot in Kampuchea, continued support for Pol Pot's exile troops, and border hostilities showed that China was continuing its long tradition of threatening Vietnamese independence. With the pullout of Vietnamese troops from Cambodia in September 1989, the hostility began to lessen. Border traffic boomed, and China began to play a more positive role in international negotiations. Vietnam and China now expect to have peaceful, though not close, relations in the future.

A unique dimension of China's external relations is that some of its territory is under the administration of other governments. The PRC has always demanded the return of the Portuguese colony of Macao and the British colony of Hong Kong as well as the "liberation" of Taiwan, and in the 1980s significant steps were taken to resolve these issues. The British agreed to the reversion of Hong Kong to China in 1997, when a 100-year lease on part of the territory runs out, and Macao will revert to China as well. The Chinese for their part agreed to permit Hong Kong considerable autonomy and a special status for fifty years. In any case the colonies were militarily indefensible and intimately linked to China. Taiwan is a different matter. The GMD had withdrawn to Taiwan when they lost the mainland. They still officially consider their government, the Republic of China, the legitimate government of all of China and their residence in Taiwan to be temporary. Although Taiwan has become prosperous and was partly democratized in the 1980s, technically it was under martial law from 1947 to 1991. China made important peaceful overtures to Taiwan beginning in 1980, and in the second half of the 1980s Taiwan began to allow contacts with the mainland. Tourism and investment in China have snowballed, and the relationship between the two may move to a qualitatively new level in the 1990s.

PROSPECTS

It is difficult to conclude a chapter on Chinese politics without a discussion of what may happen next, but given the transitional nature of the current regime it is impossible to make predictions with any confidence. Any future reader armed only with his or her daily newspaper will know more than we can know right now.

The reason for uncertainty and anxiety about political leadership in China is, first, that Deng Xiaoping and his colleagues damaged the texture of Chinese politics and society by their bloody intervention; second, they upset the institutionalized transfer of power by removing Zhao Ziyang; and third, they set a repressive political course that will be both difficult to maintain and difficult to change. The current political situation is held together by the personal prestige of the party elders, and there is tension among them. Thus, the length of the current transitional period and the spin it gives to subsequent events will be set by time and the sequence of the deaths of Deng and his colleagues. It is therefore impossible to predict what will happen when, or to specify the mechanism of change.

It is imaginable that China could continue in its present conservative direction. But it is also possible that China could turn again in a reformist direction, repudiating the Tiananmen massacre and trying once again to encourage change. Finally, it is possible that China could move in a radical direction, repudiating the party – state and the leadership of the Chinese Communist party. Despite the example of Eastern Europe, the last alternative seems least likely, but the course of future change cannot be foreseen.

With three options that are so different, it is important to reflect on the points of agreement among them. All three would, over the long term, attempt to preserve China's unity and international self-respect and express commitment to popular welfare and prosperity. All three would retain the bulk of modernization reforms and at-tempt to maintain international openness, although the West would shun a repressive regime. All three would have to cope with the aftermath of the Tiananmen crisis, both the alienated and radicalized societal forces of the demonstrations and the fact of the repression. In other words, the historical development of Chinese politics, the policies of the post – Mao era, and the events of Tiananmen will remain important parameters of the immediate future of China whatever the specific political direction.

KEY TERMS

cadre
capitalist roader
Central Committee (CC)
Chinese Communist
  party (CCP)
Cultural Revolution
Democracy Wall
democratic centralism
Deng Xiaoping

Gang of Four
Great Leap Forward
Guomindang (GMD)
Hu Yaobang
Hua Guofeng
Hundred Flowers
  Campaign
Jiang Zemin

Li Peng
Long March
Mao Zedong
Maoism
mass line
mobilized participation
National People's
  Congress

Peoples Liberation Army
  (PLA)
Politburo
Tiananmen
warlordism
Yang Shangkun
Zhao Ziyang
Zhou Enlai

END NOTES

1. R. H. Tawney, *Land and Labour in China* (New York: Harcourt, Brace & Co., 1932), p. 77.
2. Brief descriptions of imperial institutions and the examination system can be found in S. van der Sprenkel, *Legal Institutions in Manchu China* (London: Athlone Press, 1977), and Ichisada Miyazaki, *China's Examination Hell,* trans. Conrad Schirokauer (New Haven, Conn.: Yale University Press, 1976).
3. Political Bureau of the Ministry of National Defense of the Republic of China (Taiwan), quoted in Lloyd Eastman, *Seeds of Destruction* (Stanford, Calif.: Stanford University Press, 1984), p. 171.
4. The Hundred Flowers Campaign was a brief period of liberalization, in which competing views were allowed. Its name comes from Mao's slogan "Let a hundred flowers bloom, a hundred schools of thought content." It was ended when the criticism got out of hand.
5. Roderick MacFarquhar, *Origins of the Cultural Revolution,* vol. 1 (New York: Columbia University Press, 1974).
6. Interesting personal accounts of the Cultural Revolution include Liang Heng and Judith Schapiro, *Son of the Revolution* (New York: Vintage, 1984), Yue Daiyun and Carolyn Wakeman, *To the Storm* (Berkeley: University of California Press, 1985), and Neale Hunter, *Shanghai Journal* (Boston: Beacon, 1969).
7. See Lowell Dittmer, *China's Continuous Revolution* (Berkeley: University of California Press, 1987), and Harry Harding, *China's Second Revolution* (Washington, D.C.: Brookings Institution, 1987).
8. Tang Tsou, "Political Change and Reform: The Middle Course," in his *The Cultural Revolution and Post – Mao Reforms* (Chicago: University of Chicago Press, 1986), pp. 219 – 258.
9. Anita Chan and Jonathan Unger, "Voices from the Protest Movement, Chongqing, Sichuan," *Australian Journal of Chinese Affairs,* no. 24 (July 1990), pp. 259 – 279.
10. Wu Dingguang, "Wo' guo nongye laodong renkou yu gengdi di guanxi" [The Relationship between the Agricultural Labor Population and Arable Land in Our Country], *Shehui kexue yanjiu,* 1985, no. 5.
11. Brantly Womack, ed., *Media and the Chinese Public* (Armonk, N.Y.: M. E. Sharpe, 1986).
12. For personal accounts by Chinese journalists of

the Tiananmen events, see Frank Tan, "The
People's Daily — Journalistic Defiance in China
During the Spring of 1989," *Pacific Affairs*, 63:2
(Summer 1990), pp. 151–169; Yi Mu and Mark
Thompson, *Crisis at Tiananmen* (San Francisco:
China Books, 1989).

13. Anita Chan, "Images of China's Social Structure,"
World Politics, 34:3 (April 1982), pp.
295–323.

14. "Some Questions Concerning Methods of
Leadership," *Selected Works of Mao Tse-tung*
(Peking: Foreign Languages Press, 1965), vol. 3,
p. 119.

15. Hong Yung Lee, *The Politics of the Chinese
Cultural Revolution* (Berkeley: University of
California Press, 1978).

16. Frederick Teiwes, "Mao and His Lieutenants,"
Australian Journal of Chinese Affairs, nos. 19–20
(January and July 1988), pp. 1–80.

17. Harry Harding, *Organizing China: The Problem of
Bureaucracy, 1949–1976* (Stanford, Calif.:
Stanford University Press, 1981), pp. 329–360.

18. Victor Li, *Law Without Lawyers* (Boulder, Colo.:
Westview Press, 1978).

19. *World Development Report, 1986* (New York:
Oxford University Press, 1986), p. 104.

20. Charles Lindblom, *Politics and Markets* (New
York: Basic Books, 1977).

MEXICO

CHAPTER 15

WAYNE A. CORNELIUS
ANN L. CRAIG

POLITICS IN MEXICO

THE MEXICAN POLITICAL SYSTEM: THE END OF AN ERA

ON JULY 7, 1988, Mexico's newly elected president, Carlos Salinas de Gortari, appeared before the television cameras to make a startling pronouncement: "The era of the virtual one-party system [in Mexico] has ended," giving way to a period of "intense political competition." Salinas's statement was intended both as a celebration of Mexico's maturing political system and as a thinly veiled warning to the leadership of his own party, the Partido Revolucionario Institucional (PRI), which had dominated all levels of the political system continuously since its creation in 1929. Henceforth, PRI leaders would be operating in a much more fluid and uncertain political environment. Given the strength demonstrated by opposition parties, the government could no longer guarantee the outcomes of the electoral process.

Although many PRI militants were clearly unpersuaded that the era of one-party dominance had ended, the results of the July 6 election vividly reflected the new political realities of which Salinas spoke: For the first time in history, a Mexican president had been elected with less than half of the votes cast (48.7 percent)—more than twenty percentage points below the vote share attributed to PRI presidential candidate Miguel de la Madrid in the 1982 election.[1] Also for the first time, a PRI presidential candidate had failed to carry several whole states: Baja California Norte, Estado de México, Michoacán, Morelos, and the Federal District, which includes most of the Mexico City metropolitan area. These five entities were won by ex-PRIista Cuauhtémoc Cárdenas, who was officially credited with 31.1 percent of the nationwide vote—far more than any previous opposition candidate.

The ruling party's control of the Congress was weakened significantly, setting the stage for a new era in executive-legislative relations. Sixty-six PRI candidates for seats in the lower house of Congress were defeated—nearly as many as the total of ruling party candidates defeated in all elections between

1946 and 1985. For the 1988–1991 period, the PRI was reduced to a bare working majority in the Chamber of Deputies (260 out of 500 seats), and for the first time since the ruling party was founded in 1929, opposition party candidates were elected to the Senate (four out of sixty-four seats). Because the PRI no longer commanded a two-thirds majority in the lower house, President Salinas would have to negotiate with the opposition party delegations to secure passage of key legislation amending the constitution.

Moreover, the Congress had ceased to function as a reliable instrument for the internal distribution of power and its perks within the ruling party. With the recognition of so many opposition victories for congressional seats in 1988, aspiring PRIistas had to face the reality that nomination by their party was no longer tantamount to election. The tradition of the *carro completo* (clean sweep) by PRI candidates was clearly threatened.

What happened after the 1988 election was nearly as extraordinary as the election results themselves. The validity of the presidential returns was immediately challenged by all opposition parties, which alleged massive fraud by the PRI and government election officials and refused to recognize the legitimacy of the Salinas government.[2] During the three-month period between the election and certification of the results by the newly elected Congress, acting as the Electoral College, Mexico would endure unprecedented uncertainty about whether the newly elected president would be able to assume office or whether the election results would be annulled by the Congress, in response to massive protest demonstrations led by a coalition of opposition parties. In the end, the opposition pulled back from its confrontational, antisystem strategy. Salinas's election was certified, but only with the votes of PRI members of Congress; not a single opposition party representative supported his confirmation.

Mexico's political earthquake of 1988 produced significant shifts in well-established patterns of electoral behavior. The emergence of a left-of-center, nonsocialist opposition movement outside of the ruling party, led by the son of Lázaro Cárdenas, Mexico's most revered president of the postrevolutionary era, undermined the PRI's electoral base in the most developed, urbanized parts of the country, while cutting into its formerly "safe" support in rural areas. The neo-Cardenista coalition drew relatively little support away from the Partido de Acción Nacional (PAN), Mexico's principal right-of-

center opposition party, which held its own in its traditional strongholds. The strong performance of opposition candidates of both right and left in several of the states where gubernatorial or municipal elections were held in 1989 proved that the previous year's results were no fluke. The PRI's sixty-year-old monopoly of state governorships was finally broken, with the overwhelming, officially recognized victory of PANista candidate Ernesto Ruffo in Baja California Norte. Finally, the low turnout in the 1988 presidential election (less than half of those eligible bothered to vote) and considerably lower turnout rates in most state and local elections held during 1989 and 1990 signalled a serious erosion of public confidence in the whole system of parties and elections.

Only a decade ago, such drastic changes in the Mexican political system would have seemed unthinkable. This regime had been the most stable in the modern history of Latin America, with a well-earned reputation for resilience, flexibility, and a high capacity for co-optation of dissidents. In the early 1970s concerns had been raised about the stability of the system, after the bloody repression of a student protest movement in Mexico City by President Gustavo Díaz Ordaz on the eve of the 1968 Olympic Games. Many analysts at that time suggested that Mexico was entering a period of institutional crisis, requiring fundamental reforms in both political arrangements and strategy of economic development. But the discovery of massive oil and natural gas resources during the last half of the decade gave the incumbent regime a new lease on life. The continued support of masses and elites could be purchased with an apparently limitless supply of *petro-pesos*, even without major structural reforms. The government's room for maneuver was abruptly erased by the collapse of the oil boom in August 1982, owing to a combination of adverse international economic circumstances (falling oil prices, rising interest rates, recession in the United States) and fiscally irresponsible domestic policies. Real wages and living standards for the vast majority of Mexicans plummeted, and the government committed itself to a socially painful restructuring of the economy, including a drastic shrinkage of the sector owned and managed by the government itself.

The economic crisis of the 1980s, unprecedented in depth and duration, placed enormous stress on Mexico's political system. Indeed, it could be argued that the serious divisions that emerged within the political elite in 1987–1988 and the PRI's electoral debacles of

1988–1989 were inevitable consequences of the multiple failures of government performance in managing the economy. It does not necessarily follow, however, that a recovery of economic health in the 1990s will reverse the decline of Mexico's hegemonic one-party regime. The PRI has managed to regain some of the electoral ground that it lost in 1988, but its image of invincibility has been shattered. The 1988 election results demonstrated, beyond all reasonable doubt, that the political system put in place by Lázaro Cárdenas in the 1930s has outlived its usefulness. In many ways, Mexican society—increasingly complex, heterogeneous, more urban, better educated, rapidly being integrated into the world economy—has simply outgrown that system. The main issues now are what set of political structures and arrangements will replace it, how rapidly the change will occur, and how conflictual the transition process will be.

HISTORICAL PERSPECTIVE

Legacies of Colonialism

Long before Hernán Cortés landed in 1519 and began the Spanish conquest of Mexico, its territory was inhabited by numerous Indian civilizations. Of these, the Maya in the Yucatán peninsula and the Toltec on the central plateau had developed the most complex political and economic organization. Both of these civilizations had disintegrated, however, before the Spaniards arrived. Smaller Indian societies were decimated by diseases introduced by the invaders or were vanquished by the sword. Subsequent grants of land and Indian labor by the Spanish Crown to the colonists further isolated the rural Indian population and deepened their exploitation.

The combined effects of attrition, intermarriage, and cultural penetration of Indian regions have drastically reduced the proportion of Mexico's population culturally identified as Indian. By 1990, according to census figures, 8.5 percent of the population spoke an Indian language.[3] The Indian minority has been persistently marginal to the national economy and political system. Today, the indigenous population is heavily concentrated in areas that the government classifies as the country's most economically depressed, located primarily in the southeast and the center of the country. They engage in rainfall-dependent subsistence agriculture using traditional methods of cultivation, are seasonally employed as migrant laborers in commercial

agriculture, or produce crafts for sale in regional and national markets. The Indian population is an especially troubling reminder of the millions of people who have been left behind by uneven development in twentieth-century Mexico.

The importance of Spain's colonies in the New World lay in their ability to provide the Crown with vital resources to fuel the Spanish economy. Mexico's mines provided gold and silver in abundance until the wars of independence began in 1810. After independence, Mexico continued to export these ores, supplemented in subsequent eras by hemp, cotton, textiles, oil, and winter vegetables.

The Crown expected the colony to produce enough basic food crops for its own sustenance. Agriculture developed, unevenly, alongside the resource-exporting sectors of the economy. Some farming was small-scale subsistence agriculture. Most large landholdings in the colonial era were farmed through combinations of sharecropping, debt peonage, and large-scale cultiva-

Cuauhtémoc Cárdenas, leader of the center-left opposition to the ruling PRI, being carried by supporters through a town in Michoacán State during the presidential campaign of 1988.

tion; they produced basic food grains and livestock for regional markets. Over the nineteenth century, some large landholders made significant capital investments in machinery to process agricultural products (grain mills and textile factories) and in agricultural inputs (land, dams, and improved livestock). These agricultural entrepreneurs produced commercial crops for the national or international market. Today, the relationship between subsistence agriculture on tiny plots (*minifundia*) and large-scale, highly mechanized commercial agriculture is far more complex; but the extreme dualism and the erratic performance that characterize Mexico's agricultural sector are among the most important bottlenecks in the country's economic development.

Church and State

Since the Spanish conquest, the Roman Catholic Church has been an institution of enduring power in Mexico, but the nature of its power has changed notably in the postcolonial era. Priests joined the Spanish invaders in an evangelical mission to promote conversion of the Indians to Catholicism, and individual priests have continued to play important roles in national history. Father Miguel Hidalgo y Costilla helped launch Mexico's war of independence in 1810, and Father José María Morelos y Pavón replaced Hidalgo as spiritual and military leader of the independence movement when Hidalgo was executed by the Crown in 1811.

During Mexico's postindependence period, institutional antagonisms between church and central government have occasionally flared into open confrontations on such issues as church wealth, educational policy, the content of public school textbooks, and political activism by the church. The constitutions of 1857 and 1917 formally established the separation of church and state and defined their respective domains. Constitutional provisions dramatically reduced the church's power and wealth by nationalizing its property, including large agricultural landholdings. The 1917 constitution makes church-affiliated schools subject to the authority of the federal government, denies priests the right to vote or speak publicly on political issues, and gives the government the right to limit the number of priests who can serve in Mexico.

Government efforts during the 1920s to enforce these constitutional provisions led the church to suspend religious services throughout the country. Church leaders also supported the Cristero rebellion of 1927 –

1929, as a last stand against the incursions of a centralizing state. Large landholders took advantage of the conflict, inciting devout peasants to take up arms against local dissidents who had begun to petition the government for land reform. Because the church also opposed redistribution of land, the landowners could depict themselves as faithful partners in the holy war against a state that espoused such policies. The rebellion caused 100,000 combatant deaths, uncounted civilian casualties, and economic devastation in a large part of central Mexico. The settlement of the conflict established, once and for all, the church's subordination to the state, in return for which the government relaxed its restrictions on church activities in nonpolitical arenas.

This accord inaugurated a long period of relative tranquility in church – state relations, during which many of the anticlerical provisions of the 1917 constitution (such as the prohibition on church involvement in education) were ignored by both the government and the church. The central church hierarchy — among the most conservative in Latin America — cooperated with the government on a variety of issues, and the church posed no threat to the official party's hegemony.

Today, the church retains considerable influence, particularly in Mexico's rural areas and small cities. But even though more than 80 percent of the country's population identify themselves as Catholics in sample surveys, this religious preference does not translate automatically into support for the church's positions on social or political issues. Formal church opposition to birth control, for example, has not prevented widespread adoption of family planning practices in Mexico since the government launched a birth control program in the mid-1970s. Nevertheless, the government respects and perhaps even fears the Catholic Church's capacity for mass mobilization, which was demonstrated dramatically during Pope John Paul II's visits to Mexico in 1979 and 1990. On each of those occasions, an estimated 20 million Mexicans participated in street demonstrations and other public gatherings held in connection with the papal visit. In 1990 a well-organized protest movement organized by the Catholic Church in response to a state law legalizing abortions in the southern state of Chiapas succeeded in overturning the law, virtually ending hopes for liberalizing abortion laws throughout Mexico. The Catholic Church has also been able to enlist the help of the federal government and the PRI in its drive to prevent the growth of evangelical Protestant sects in Mexico.

During the 1980s church–state relations were strained by the highly visible political activism of some church leaders in northern Mexico, who publicly criticized electoral fraud committed by the PRI and sided openly with the conservative opposition party, the Partido de Acción Nacional (PAN). In 1986 the archbishop of the state of Chihuahua ordered the temporary suspension of all church services, in protest of the fraud-ridden elections of July 1986 in his state. This and other episodes of overt political activism by church leaders and priests led the government in December 1986 to amend the federal electoral code to provide stiff fines and jail terms of up to seven years for clergy found to take sides in electoral campaigns.

In 1988 President Salinas began an unprecedented formal rapprochement with the church, as part of his project to "modernize" Mexican politics and win back some of the pro-clerical PAN's supporters for the official party. He invited several senior church leaders to attend his inauguration, met with the Pope during his visit to Mexico in 1990, and took the first steps toward establishing full diplomatic relations with the Vatican. Salinas was aware of the considerable public support for changes that would close the formal breech between church and state. Opinion polls show that a majority of Mexicans in large cities favor granting priests the same political rights as other citizens, including the right to vote in elections. By a smaller margin, the public is willing to allow private schools to teach religion. The average Mexican still has reservations, however, about lifting restrictions on political and economic activities by the church as an institution.[4]

Revolution and Its Aftermath

The civil conflict that erupted in Mexico in 1910 is often referred to as the first of the great "social revolutions" that shook the world early in the twentieth century, but Mexico's upheaval originated within the country's ruling class. The revolution did not begin as a spontaneous uprising of the common people against an entrenched dictator, Porfirio Díaz, and against the local bosses and landowners who exploited them. Even though hundreds of thousands of workers and peasants ultimately participated in the civil strife, most of the revolutionary leadership came from the younger generation of middle- and upper class Mexicans who had become disenchanted with three and a half decades of increasingly heavy-handed rule by the aging dictator and his clique. These disgruntled members of the elite saw their future opportunities for economic and political mobility blocked by the closed group surrounding Díaz.

Led by Francisco I. Madero, whose family had close ties with the ruling group, these liberal bourgeois reformers were committed to opening up the political system and creating new opportunities for themselves within a capitalist economy whose basic features they did not challenge. They sought not to destroy the established order but rather to make it work more in their own interest than that of the foreign capitalists who had come to dominate key sectors of Mexico's economy during the Porfirian dictatorship (a period called "the Porfiriato").

Of course, some serious grievances had accumulated among workers and peasants. Once the rebellion against Díaz got underway, leaders who appealed to the disadvantaged masses pressed their claims against the central government. Emiliano Zapata led a movement of peasants in the state of Morelos who were bent on regaining the land they had lost to the rural aristocracy by subterfuge during the Porfiriato. In the north, Pancho Villa led an army consisting of jobless workers, small landowners, and cattle hands, whose main interest was steady employment. As the various revolutionary leaders contended for control of the central government, the political order that had been created and enforced by Díaz disintegrated into warlordism — powerful regional gangs led by revolutionary *caudillos* (political-military strongmen) who aspired more to increasing their personal wealth and social status than to leading a genuine social revolution. In sum, "although class conflict was central to the Revolution, the Revolution cannot be reduced to class conflict. . . . [It] was a mix of different classes, interests, and ideologies," giving rise to a state that enjoyed considerable autonomy vis-à-vis specific class interests.[5]

The first decade of the revolution produced a new, remarkably progressive constitution, replacing the constitution of 1857. The young, middle-class elite that dominated the constitutional convention of 1916–1917 "had little if any direct interest in labor unions or land distribution. But it was an elite that recognized the need for social change. . . . By 1916, popular demands for land and labor reform were too great to ignore."[6] The constitution of 1917 established the principle of state control over all natural resources, subordination of the church to the state, the government's right to redistribute land, and rights for labor that had not yet been secured even by the labor movement in the United States. Nearly two decades passed, however, before most of these constitutional provisions began to be implemented.

Many historians today stress the continuities between prerevolutionary and postrevolutionary Mexico. The processes of economic modernization, capital accumulation, state-building, and political centralization that gained considerable momentum during the Porfiriato were interrupted by civil strife from 1910 to 1920, but they resumed once a semblance of order had been restored. During the 1920s, the central government set out to eliminate or undermine the most powerful and independent-minded regional *caudillos* by co-opting the local power brokers (known traditionally as *caciques*). These local political bosses became, in effect, appendages of the central government, supporting its policies and maintaining control over the population in their communities. By the end of this period, leaders with genuine popular followings like Zapata and Villa had been assassinated, and control had been seized by a new postrevolutionary elite bent on demobilizing the masses and establishing the hegemony of the central government.

The rural aristocracy of the Porfiriato had been weakened but not eliminated; its heirs still controlled large concentrations of property and other forms of wealth in many parts of the country. Most of the large urban firms that operated during the Porfiriato also survived, further demonstrating that the revolution was not an attack on private capital per se.[7]

The Cárdenas Upheaval

Elite control was maintained during the 1930s, but this was nevertheless an era of massive social and political upheaval in Mexico. During the presidency of Lázaro Cárdenas (1934–1940), peasants and urban workers succeeded for the first time in pressing their claims for land and higher wages; in fact, Cárdenas actively encouraged them to do so. The result was an unprecedented wave of strikes, protest demonstrations, and petitions for breaking up large rural estates.

Most disputes between labor and management during this period were settled, under government pressure, in favor of the workers. The Cárdenas administration also redistributed more than twice as much land as that expropriated by all of Cárdenas' predecessors since 1915, when Mexico's land reform program was formally initiated. By 1940 the country's land tenure system had been fundamentally altered, breaking the traditional domination of the large haciendas and creating a large

sector of small peasant farmers called *ejidatarios* — more than 1.5 million of them — who had received plots of land under the agrarian reform program. The Cárdenas government actively encouraged the formation of new organizations of peasants and urban workers, grouped the new organizations into nationwide confederations, and provided arms to rural militias formed by the *ejidatarios* who had received plots of land (*ejidos*) from the government. Even Mexico's foreign relations were disrupted in 1938 when the Cárdenas government nationalized oil companies that had been operating in Mexico under U.S. and British ownership.

The Cárdenas era proved to be a genuine aberration in the development of postrevolutionary Mexico. Never before or since had the fundamental "who benefits?" question been addressed with such energy and commitment by a Mexican government. Mexican intellectuals frequently refer to 1938 as the highwater mark of the Mexican revolution as measured by social progress, and characterize the period since then as a retrogression. Certainly, the distributive and especially the *re*distributive performance of the Mexican government declined sharply in the decades that followed, and the worker and peasant organizations formed during the Cárdenas era atrophied and became less and less likely to contest either the will of the government or the interests of Mexico's private economic elites. De facto reconcentration of landholdings and other forms of wealth occurred as the state provided increasingly generous support to the country's new commercial, industrial, and financial elites during a period of rapid industrialization.

Critics of the Cárdenas administration have laid much of the blame for this outcome on the kind of mass political organizing that occurred under Cárdenas. The resulting organizations were captives of the regime — tied so closely to it that they had no capacity for autonomous action. Under the control of a new group of national political leaders whose values and priorities were unfavorable to the working classes, these same organizations, after Cárdenas, functioned only to enforce political stability and limit lower class demands for government benefits.

During his last two years in office, Cárdenas himself backed away from a full-scale confrontation with domestic and foreign capitalists and moderated his redistributive policies. The changes introduced by his government had generated so much tension that a counterreform movement — led by a conservative military man and drawing support both from elites whose interests had been damaged by Cárdenas's policies and from disadvantaged groups who had not yet benefited from the reform programs — threatened the survival of his administration. To protect and consolidate the gains made for peasants and urban workers under his regime, Cárdenas moved to limit political polarization and prevent open class warfare.

Cárdenas represented a coalition of forces that was progressive but not committed to destroying the foundations of Mexican capitalism. While he was advised by left-wing Keynesian economists trained in England, Cárdenas himself was not a socialist. Cárdenas may have considered socialism a desirable long-term goal, but neither he "nor his associates believed it was a realistic possibility for the immediate future."[8] His government's large investments in public works (electricity, roads, irrigation projects) and its reorganization of the country's financial system laid the foundations for the post-1940 "Mexican miracle" of rapid industrialization and low inflation within a capitalist framework. In the long term, the principal beneficiaries of Cárdenas's economic project proved to be the middle classes and unionized industrial workers — not peasants and the unorganized urban poor.

The original Cardenista project — emphasizing redistribution of income, full employment, and state patronage for the weaker sectors of Mexican society — still has great influence among the Mexican people — even those born decades after Cárdenas's presidency. It was precisely the public's identification of *Cuauhtémoc Cárdenas* with his father's social reformism — together with anger over recent economic problems — that turned *neo-Cardenismo* into such a powerful political force in 1988.

Finally, the Cárdenas era left an institutional legacy: the presidency became the primary institution of Mexico's political structure, with sweeping powers exercised during a constitutionally limited six-year term with no possibility of reelection; the military was removed from overt political competition and transformed into one of several institutional pillars of the regime; and an elaborate network of government-sponsored peasant and labor organizations provided a mass base for the official political party and performed a variety of political and economic control functions, utilizing a multilayered system of patronage and clientelism.

By 1940 a much larger proportion of the Mexican population was nominally included in the national political system, mostly by their membership in peasant and labor organizations created under Cárdenas. No real democratization of the system resulted from this vast expansion of "political participation," however. Although working-class groups did have more control over their representatives in the government-sponsored organizations than over their former masters on the haciendas and in the factories, their influence over public policy and government priorities after Cárdenas was minimal and highly indirect. Policy recommendations, official actions, and nominations for elective and appointive positions at all levels still emanated from the central government and official party headquarters in Mexico City, filtering down the hierarchy to the rank-and-file for ratification and legitimation. Cárdenas's experiment with democratization was centered in the workplace.[9] Workers would participate in economic decision making in their *ejido* or industrial plant. The outcome was greater workplace democracy during Cárdenas's presidency, but hardly the workers' democracy that in 1938 he claimed would be the end result of his political institution-building.

INTERNATIONAL ENVIRONMENT

Since independence, Mexico's politics and public policies have always been influenced to some extent by proximity to the United States. Porfirio Díaz is widely reputed to have exclaimed, "Poor Mexico! So far from God and so close to the United States." Indeed, this proximity has made the United States a powerful presence in Mexico. The 2,000-mile land border between the two countries, Mexico's rich supplies of minerals, labor, and other resources needed by U.S. industry, and Mexico's attractiveness as a site for U.S. private investment made such influence inevitable.

Midway through the nineteenth century, Mexico's sovereignty as a nation was directly threatened when the United States' push for territorial and economic expansion met little resistance in northern Mexico. Emerging from a war for independence from Spain and plagued by chronic political instability, Mexico was highly vulnerable to aggression from the north. By annexing Texas in 1845 and instigating the Mexican-American War of 1846 to 1848 (Ulysses S. Grant later called it "America's great unjust war"), the United States was able to seize half of Mexico's national territory: disputed land in Texas, all the land that is now California, Nevada, and Utah, most of New Mexico and Arizona, and part of Colorado and Wyoming. This massive seizure of territory, along with several later military interventions and meddling in the politics of "revolutionary" Mexico that extended through the 1920s, left scars that have not healed. Even today, the average Mexican suspects that the United States has designs on Mexico's remaining territory, its oil, even its human resources.

The lost territory includes the U.S. regions that have been the principal recipients of Mexican immigrant workers in this century. This labor migration, too, was instigated mainly by the United States. Beginning in the 1880s, U.S. farmers, railroads, and mining companies, with U.S. government encouragement, obtained many of the workers needed to expand the economy and transport systems of the Southwest and Midwest by sending labor recruiters into northern and central Mexico.

By the end of the 1920s, the economies of Mexico and the United States were sufficiently intertwined that the effects of the Great Depression were swiftly transmitted to Mexico, causing employment, export earnings, and GNP to plummet. In response to these economic shocks, Mexico tried during the 1930s to reduce its dependence on the United States as a market for silver and other exports. The effort failed, and by 1940 Mexico was more dependent than before on the flow of goods, capital, and labor to and from the United States.

After 1940, Mexico relied even more heavily on U.S. private capital to help finance its drive for industrialization. It was also during the 1940s, when the United States experienced severe shortages of labor in World War II, that Mexico's dependence on the United States as a market for its surplus labor became institutionalized through the so-called *bracero* program of importing contract labor. Operating from 1942 to 1964, this program brought more than 4 million Mexicans to the United States to work in seasonal agriculture.

The United States' stake in Mexico's continued political stability and economic development has increased dramatically since World War II. Mexico is now the third largest trading partner of the United States (behind Canada and Japan), with the two-way trade between them exceeding $60 billion annually. Employment for hundreds of thousands of people in both Mexico and the United States depends on this trade. In 1982, when U.S. trade with Mexico fell by 32 percent because of Mexico's economic crisis, an estimated 250,000 jobs were lost in the United States.

Mexico has also become one of the preferred sites for investments by U.S.-based multinational corporations, especially for investments in modern industries like petrochemicals, pharmaceuticals, food processing, machinery, and transportation. Subsidiaries of U.S. companies produce half the manufactured goods exported by Mexico. Firms in Mexico's own private sector have actively sought foreign capital to finance new joint ventures and to expand plant facilities.

Beyond the more than $18 billion that U.S. firms have directly invested in Mexico, U.S. commercial banks have loaned huge sums to both the Mexican government and private companies in Mexico. By the end of 1988, Mexico had foreign debts of more than $100 billion, of which $70 billion came from 600 commercial banks. Most of this money flooded into Mexico during the oil boom years of 1978 to 1981, when the largest U.S. banks vigorously competed against one another to make loans to Mexico, whose vast oil collateral seemed to guarantee high profits and low risks to the lenders. Rising interest rates on those loans, a result of the United States' Federal Reserve Board's tight-money policies designed to combat inflation in the U.S. economy, were a major factor in the Mexican financial crisis that erupted in 1982.

In the late 1970s, to reduce dependence on the United States, Mexican policymakers embarked on a strategy of diversifying their country's international economic relations. A rapid increase in oil exports was to be the key instrument for achieving this goal. Mexico pushed hard to sell more oil to Japan and Western Europe, and succeeded in reducing the U.S. share of its oil exports from 80 percent in the 1975–1980 period to 50 percent in 1981–1987.[10] Nevertheless, Mexico's overall dependence on the United States—for capital investment, export markets, technology, tourism, and employment opportunities—continues to increase.

The Mexican government's principal strategy for recovering from the economic crisis of the 1980s was to stimulate the production of manufactured goods for export, mainly to the United States. This policy has been remarkably successful, with Mexico's nonoil exports rising from 21 percent of the total in 1982 to 65 percent in 1989. But reliance on the U.S. market for consumer electronics, auto parts, and other key manufactured exports leaves Mexico highly vulnerable to cyclical economic downturns in the United States. That country buys nearly 70 percent of Mexico's exports, and for each percentage decline in the U.S. gross domestic product, Mexico's exports fall by 2.5 percent.

Mexico's external economic dependence has often been cited by both critics and defenders of the Mexican system as an all-encompassing explanation for the country's problems. In fact, economic ties between Mexico and the United States usually explain only part of the picture. And these linkages do not necessarily predetermine the choices of policy and development priorities that are set by Mexico's rulers. But Mexico's economic relationships with the United States and with the international economy do limit the kinds and scope of changes that might be effected in Mexico's political system and development model; and international economic fluctuations have become the largest source of uncertainty in Mexico's planning and policymaking.

The crucial role played by foreign capital in Mexico's overall strategy of capitalist development makes it imperative for the Mexican state to maintain a favorable investment climate. Traditionally, it has done so by imposing discipline and wage restraint on Mexico's labor force (through government-controlled labor unions), providing generous fiscal incentives and infrastructure for investors (both foreign and domestic), keeping taxes low, and maintaining political stability.

More recently, foreign capital has been courted by liberalizing regulations for such investment (allowing up to 100 percent foreign ownership of many new firms, versus the traditional limit of 49 percent) and opening up more sectors of the economy to foreign investment —sectors formerly reserved for domestic investors or the government itself. Beginning in 1990, the Mexican government added to these incentives by proposing a U.S.–Mexico–Canada free trade agreement, which would make Mexico a more attractive investment site for U.S. firms seeking low-cost labor. While President Salinas opposed such an agreement during his electoral campaign, because "there is such a different economic level between the U.S. and Mexico,"[11] he soon found himself with no alternative to pursuing greater economic integration with the United States. With 1 million new job-seekers entering its labor force each year, Mexico desperately needs to increase its rate of economic growth, and the only way to do that while containing inflation is to stimulate a massive new infusion of investment capital from abroad.

As the U.S. and Mexican economies have become more closely linked, scrutiny of Mexico's political process by U.S. officials and the U.S. media has increased. The fiscal mismanagement symbolized by Mexico's economic crisis of the 1980s eroded U.S. confidence in the Mexican government and raised concern about its ability to maintain political stability. Simultaneously,

the United States' heightened preoccupation with illicit drugs—most of which now reach the United States via Mexico—has led members of the U.S. Congress and other officials to publicly criticize police and government corruption in Mexico, which is viewed as a significant facilitator of the drug traffic. Finally, as Mexican opposition parties increasingly turned to the U.S. media, the U.S. Congress, and international human rights organizations to voice complaints about electoral fraud by the PRI–government apparatus, the halting and incomplete character of Mexico's democratization has become an issue in U.S.–Mexican relations. International observation of elections has become common in Latin America in recent years, and all significant Mexican opposition parties and even some elements of the PRI have endorsed such scrutiny; but the Mexican government rejects international observers as an unacceptable dilution of national sovereignty. The transition to a more competitive political system in Mexico will make bilateral tensions over such issues increasingly unavoidable in the future.

POLITICAL STRUCTURE AND INSTITUTIONS

Mexico's political system has long defied easy classification. In the 1950s and 1960s some U.S. political scientists depicted the regime as a one-party democracy that was evolving toward "true" (North Atlantic-style) democracy. Certain imperfections were recognized, but in the view of these analysts, political development in Mexico was simply incomplete. After the government's massacre of student protesters in 1968, most analysts began describing the system as authoritarian, but even this characterization was subject to qualification. Mexico now seems to belong to that rapidly expanding category of hybrid, part-free, part-authoritarian systems that do not conform to classical typologies.[12] Such labels as selective democracy, hard-line democracy, *democradura* (a Spanish contraction of "democracy" and "dictatorship"), and modernizing authoritarian regime have been applied to such systems.[13] They are characterized by competitive (though not necessarily fair and honest) elections that install governments more committed to maintaining political stability and labor discipline than to expanding democratic freedoms, protecting human rights, or mediating class conflicts. Some regimes of this type are more likely to countenance undemocratic practices and procedures (e.g., electoral fraud, selective repression of dissidents) than others.

For most of the period since 1940, Mexico has had a pragmatic and moderate authoritarian regime, not the zealously repressive kind that emerged in Latin America's southern cone in the 1960s and 1970s. It has been an institutional system, not a personalistic instrument, which has dealt successfully with one of the most difficult problems for nondemocratic systems: elite renewal and executive succession. The Mexican system has been inclusionary, given to co-optation and incorporation rather than exclusion or elimination of troublesome political forces. It strives to incorporate the broadest possible range of social, economic, and political interests within the official party, its affiliated "mass" organizations, and opposition groups whose activities are sanctioned by the regime. As potentially dissident groups have appeared, their leaders usually have been co-opted into government-controlled organizations, or new organizations have been established under government auspices as vehicles for emerging interests. However, when confronted with unco-optable opposition groups or movements (e.g., students in 1968; the neo-Cardenistas since 1987), the regime has responded punitively.

On paper, the Mexican government appears to be structured much like the U.S. government: a presidential system, three autonomous branches of government (executive, legislative, judicial) and checks and balances, and federalism with considerable autonomy at the local (municipal) level. In practice, however, Mexico's system of government is far removed from the U.S. model. Decision making is highly centralized. The president, operating with relatively few restraints on his authority, completely dominates the legislative and judicial branches.[14] Both houses of the federal legislature have been dominated continuously by representatives affiliated with the ruling PRI. Opposition party members, who now comprise a significant portion of the lower house of Congress (240 out of 500 seats in the 1988–1991 period), can criticize the government and its policies vociferously; but their objections to proposals initiated by the president and backed by his party rarely affect the final shape of legislation. Courts and legislatures at the state level normally mirror the preferences of the state governors, who themselves are handpicked by the incumbent president. The sole exception to this pattern occurred in 1989 in the state of Baja California, where the candidate of the opposition National Action party was elected governor and the same party also gained control of the state legislature.

At all levels of the system, the overwhelming majority of those who are elected to public office are, in effect, appointed to their positions by higher-ups within the PRI–government apparatus. Until recently, selection as the candidate of the official party has been tantamount to election, except in some municipalities and a handful of congressional districts where opposition parties are so strong that they cannot be ignored. Those elected on the PRI ticket are accountable and responsive not primarily to the people who elected them but to their political patrons within the regime. Most citizens who bother to vote do so with little or no expectation that their votes will influence the outcome of the election. The winner, they recognize, has been predetermined by the selection process within the PRI, which until recently has had little grass-roots input. Instead, nominating conventions attended only by party activists have ratified the choices made secretively by officials at higher levels.

These and other features of the Mexican system are common to authoritarian regimes elsewhere: limited (not responsible) pluralism; low popular mobilization, with most citizen participation in the electoral process mobilized by the government itself; competition for public office and government benefits restricted mainly to those who support the system; centralized, often arbitrary decision making by one leader or small group; weak ideological constraints on public policymaking; extensive government manipulation of the mass media. As described above, however, the Mexican system is more complex than most of the authoritarian regimes that have ruled other Third World nations in recent decades.

Political Centralism

Despite the federalist structure of government that is enshrined in the Mexican constitution and legal codes, with their emphasis on the *municipio libre* (the concept of the free municipality, able to control its own affairs), Mexico has a highly centralized political system. Since the 1920s, the concentration of decision-making power at the federal level has been continuous. The resulting system of centralized control is generally considered to be one of the main factors underlying Mexico's long-term political stability.[15]

Mexico is divided into thirty-two states and federal territories, and each state is divided into *municipios*—politico-administrative units roughly equivalent in size and governmental functions to county governments in the United States. The *municipio* is governed by an *ayuntamiento*, or council, headed by a *presidente munic-*

ipal. Municipal officials are elected every three years. In practice, each presidente municipal has been hand-picked by higher-ups within the PRI – government apparatus, normally a federal congressman (*diputado*) and the state governor.

The absence of popular input into this candidate selection process has often led to the designation of municipal presidents who were intensely disliked by their constituents, and who embarrassed the PRI and the government by their inept handling of local problems. Such outcomes periodically provoke calls for open primary elections within the PRI, to compel the party's candidates to develop a popular support base. An abortive experiment with open primaries was conducted in the mid-1960s, but the idea was adamantly resisted by old-guard PRI leaders, and it was soon dropped. Carlos Madrazo, the PRI national chairman who instigated the reform, was removed from his position.

Another attempt to introduce a system of PRI primary elections at the *municipio* level was made in the mid-1980s by President Miguel de la Madrid. Implemented in just a few states, the system had mixed results. It worked adequately in some small *municipios*, but not in large cities, where PRI leaders feared that open primaries would be divisive and cost the party electoral support. In 1989 President Salinas began authorizing municipal and gubernatorial primaries in certain states where the PRI faced tough competition. At the PRI's Fourteenth General Assembly held in September 1990, Salinas pushed through a set of changes designed to "democratize" the party's candidate selection process throughout the country. Henceforth, aspiring candidates for municipal offices, congressional seats, and state governorships must demonstrate that they have the support of a specific percentage of the "directive committees" of PRI-affiliated organizations (25 to 30 percent, depending on the office) or of the registered voters in a given district (10 to 20 percent). The final selection of PRI candidates will be made at party conventions, to which delegates will be "elected democratically." It remains to be seen whether the new rules will, in fact, make elective positions accessible to all PRI members and reduce the incidence of candidate impositions from above.

These changes represent, at least in part, a response by the ruling elite to the public's growing resentment of centralism and to the resurgence of political regionalism during the 1980s. Regional particularism has been a constant in Mexican politics since the mid-

nineteenth century, but it has been especially potent during periods in which the central government is perceived as being less efficacious and legitimate.[16] The economic crisis that erupted in 1982 again focused provincial resentment on the capital and the highly centralized decision-making process, which was blamed for the economic debacle.

Regional pride, combined with the increasing rejection by business elites and the general public of control by a failing central government, became a major source of opposition party strength in municipal and gubernatorial elections held between 1983 and 1989 in the northern states. In 1983 the PAN swept to victory in all major cities of Chihuahua, containing more than 70 percent of the state's population. In the state of Baja California Norte in 1989, the vote for the PAN's gubernatorial candidate, Ernesto Ruffo, was so overwhelming that the federal government recognized his victory. This marked the first state governorship to be surrendered to an opposition candidate since the official party was founded in 1929.

The Mexico City-based political elite has not been oblivious to these trends. The federal government has been emphasizing economic policies — for example, deregulation, privatization, stimulation of *maquiladoras* (in-bond assembly plants) and other export-oriented industries — from which many entrepreneurs in the provinces have benefited and with which they are philosophically in tune. Some steps have been taken to rein in the federal security apparatus, especially the hated and feared federal judicial police, which traditionally has been run from Mexico City without regard for the sensibilities of state and local authorities. The Salinas government has taken a cooperative, nonconfrontational stance toward the PANista government of Baja California Norte State, hoping to demonstrate that Mexico City could work constructively with at least some kinds of opposition governments in the periphery.

Nevertheless, the consequences of political centralism remain dramatically evident in Mexico today. Each successive layer of government is substantially weaker, less autonomous, and more impoverished than the levels above it. Historically, the federal government has controlled about 85 percent of public revenues, the state governments have controlled less than 12 percent, and the *municipios* scarcely 3 percent. In recent years the *municipios'* share of total public spending has risen to 5 – 7 percent. The average municipal government depends on the federal and state governments for about 80

Baja California Governor Ernesto Ruffo is mobbed by enthusiastic supporters following his historic victory in 1989, the first ever officially recognized for an opposition party gubernatorial candidate.

percent of its income; only 20 percent comes from local sources.

Another manifestation of political centralism in Mexico is the growing predominance within the country's ruling elite of people born or raised in Mexico City.[17] The proportion of Cabinet members born in Mexico City has increased steadily since the 1940s; by 1990, *capitalinos* held nearly 60 percent of the Cabinet posts (see Figure 15.1). Politically ambitious individuals must gravitate to the center of the system or, prefer-

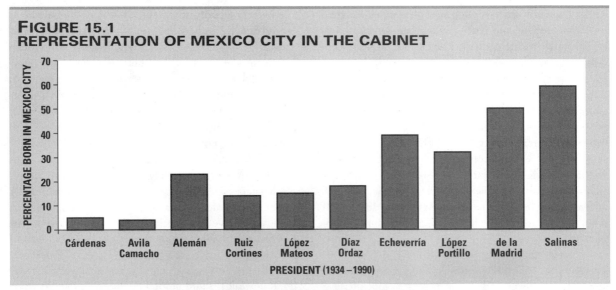

FIGURE 15.1
REPRESENTATION OF MEXICO CITY IN THE CABINET

Source: Miguel Angel Centeno, "The New Científicos: Technocratic Politics in Mexico, 1970–1990," Ph.D. dissertation, Yale University, 1990.

ably, be born there. This has been the case with Mexico's five most recent presidents, all of whom were either born or raised in Mexico City.

All five of these presidents entered office pledging to renew the "struggle against centralism," but serious efforts to decentralize have been made only since 1984. Under de la Madrid and Salinas, state and municipal authorities have been involved more fully in the planning of federal development programs affecting their jurisdictions; a limited form of revenue-sharing has been implemented and the federal constitution amended to enhance the capacity of local governments to raise their own revenues; partially successful efforts have been made to shift decision-making authority over public education and health care from the federal government to the states.[18] Nevertheless, the country's 2,378 *municipios* are still overwhelmingly dependent on the state and federal governments for the funds needed to finance essential public services. State governors retain control over resources transferred from the federal government. Effective administrative decentralization down to the *municipio* level would require state governors to relinquish a major portion of their political power — something that they have successfully resisted.

The Presidency

Mexico's political system is commonly described as a "presidentialist" or "presidentially centered" system. The Mexican president possesses a broad range of both constitutionally mandated and unwritten, informally recognized powers that assure his dominance over all of the country's other political institutions.[19]

The principle of executive control over the legislative and judicial branches has long been established in the Mexican system. Ratification of the president's policy choices by both houses of the federal Congress has been virtually automatic since the 1930s. The president has introduced most of the legislation considered by the Congress and, in his role as "supreme head" of the official party, secured its enactment. However, with the emergence of a strong opposition presence in Congress as a result of the 1988 elections, the president no longer commands the two-thirds majority required to pass constitutional amendments. Since the 1920s every Mexican president has used amendment of the constitution as a key instrument for implementing his administration's policy agenda and expanding the prerogatives of the presidency. (The 1917 constitution has been amended more than 300 times.) To revise the constitu-

tion now, the president must build coalitions with one or more opposition parties. In the first two years of his term, President Salinas obtained from the PAN the additional votes necessary for approval of two key constitutional amendments.

The Mexican federal judiciary remains firmly under the control of the president. On any issue that has national political significance, the federal judiciary can be expected to take its cue from the incumbent president. Presidential decrees or legislation enacted at the behest of the president are never found to be unconstitutional by the Mexican Supreme Court, and the Congress rubber-stamps presidential appointments to or dismissals from the federal judiciary.

The absence of a rigid, fully elaborated political ideology makes it possible for a Mexican president to have a pragmatic, flexible program and style of governance. The so-called ideology of the Mexican revolution is little more than a loosely connected set of goals or symbols: social justice (including agrarian reform), economic nationalism, restricting the influence of the church in public life, and freedom from self-perpetuating, dictatorial rule in the Porfirio Díaz style. There are a few tenets of "revolutionary" ideology that must still be scrupulously observed, such as the constitutionally mandated no-reelection principle: No official, at any level of the system, can be reelected to the same public office, at least for consecutive terms; the president himself is limited to a single, six-year term. But virtually all other elements of revolutionary ideology have been shaded or ignored, at one time or another, by the presidents holding office since 1940. President José López Portillo, for example, declared in 1977 that Mexico's land redistribution program was, for all practical purposes, at an end, because allegedly there was no more land left to distribute to landless peasants. Under Presidents de la Madrid and Salinas, the definition of economic nationalism has shifted from keeping U.S. interests at bay to achieving competitiveness and new markets for Mexico's exports in the world economy, through policies aimed at opening up the Mexican economy to more foreign-made products and direct foreign investment, and linking Mexico's economy even more closely to that of the United States.

Neither are Mexican presidents seriously constrained by the mass media. Although the government does not directly censor the media, there can be significant economic penalties for engaging in criticism or investigative reporting that seriously embarrasses the government. Government advertising can be withheld from offending publications. Recent presidents have also silenced criticism from some newspapers through government-orchestrated, hostile takeovers of their boards of directors. Finally, cash payments to journalists have traditionally been used to assure favorable treatment of a president and his policies — a practice that has been curtailed somewhat since 1982, as part of a general anticorruption campaign. But except for individual political columnists who often comment vituperatively on the failings of the president and his policies, editorial criticism of an incumbent president remains muted. Whatever they say about a president or his administration, the print media reach only a tiny fraction of the Mexican population (even the largest Mexico City newspapers are believed to have circulations under 100,000), and television is virtually monopolized by a huge private firm, Televisa, which has a notoriously close working relationship with the PRI–government apparatus.[20]

A great part of the Mexican president's power is derived from his ability to select and impose public officeholders at all levels of the system, including his own successor as president. All but a handful of public officeholders in Mexico serve at the pleasure of the president. State governors (except those belonging to an opposition party), the leaders of Congress and the PRI, some high-ranking military officers, the heads of state-owned industrial enterprises, and hundreds of other officeholders are handpicked by each incoming president. The president may even remove the leaders of large, government-affiliated labor unions, as Carlos Salinas demonstrated within several months of taking office by sacking two of Mexico's most powerful and corrupt labor chieftains.[21] Public officials whose actions have proven embarrassing, disruptive, or otherwise troublesome to the president or to his inner circle of advisers can be arbitrarily removed. Even popularly elected state governors who fall badly out of favor with the president are faced with almost instant dismissal, which the president can accomplish in a variety of ways. Sometimes a state governor is cashiered for failing to deliver a sufficiently large majority of votes for the PRI in his state; such was the fate of three governors of states carried by opposition candidate Cuauhtémoc Cárdenas in the 1988 presidential election. This absolute power to seat and unseat state governors has been a key element of presidential power in Mexico since the 1920s.

Even though the Mexican president wields great power, he does so within certain limits, perhaps the most important of which are unwritten, de facto constraints generally recognized and accepted within Mexico's political and economic elites. Sometimes these constraints have limited presidential autonomy in key policy areas. For example, President Luis Echeverría often blamed his economic policy failures on the machinations of the business elite centered in the city of Monterrey, and there is evidence that in 1972 big business forced Echeverría to drop his plan to increase the tax burden on the wealthy.[22] When some presidents went ahead and broke the established rules of the game in conspicuous ways — for example, by shooting the children of urban middle-class parents in the Tlatelolco massacre (Gustavo Díaz Ordaz in 1968); by expropriating large, prosperous landholdings in Sonora state (Luis Echeverría in 1976); and by running up the country's external debt irresponsibly and nationalizing the banks (José López Portillo, 1977–1982) — the moral and political authority of the presidency began to erode, and private sector confidence in the government was shaken. Miguel de la Madrid's failure to provide effective leadership after the devastating Mexico City earthquakes of September 1985 and his inability to engineer a sustained recovery from the economic crisis that he inherited from his predecessor further reinforced the image of a weakened and "devalued" presidency.[23]

By the end of de la Madrid's term, the conventional wisdom held that traditional Mexican *presidencialismo* — especially when defined as the ability of the president to take unilateral actions that may be damaging to the interests of key political and economic elites — was dead, the victim of the excesses of Díaz Ordaz, Echeverría, and López Portillo and the leadership failures of de la Madrid. Upon taking office in 1988, Carlos Salinas challenged this notion through a succession of bold strokes against the fiefdoms that had progressively challenged presidential prerogatives during the preceding four administrations (e.g., the oil workers' union), and by embracing new policies that entailed large political risks (e.g., a free trade agreement with the United States). These actions proved that the essential powers of Mexican *presidencialismo* were still intact and could be used to effect sweeping political and economic change.

Nevertheless, several developments are likely to reduce the power of the Mexican presidency in the long run. The shift since 1982 away from a statist model of development and toward market-oriented economic policies could have such an effect. Privatizing state-owned enterprises and dismantling government controls over large parts of the economy will inevitably reduce the state's role as "rector" (guide) of the economy and the president's power to influence the path of national development. Presidential prerogatives may also be eroded by steps toward political modernization. For example, Salinas's strategy to rejuvenate the PRI depends heavily on giving more autonomy to local party officials and committees in such matters as the selection of PRI candidates. This implies that the president must now negotiate with lower echelon party leaders rather than simply impose his own choices. If Salinas or his successors succeed in modernizing the PRI, they may lay the groundwork for a very different kind of *presidencialismo* —one that will have to rely more on skillful negotiation and alliance-building, with actors throughout the political system.[24]

It is generally believed that an incumbent president has the power to select his own successor. In September 1990 Luis Echeverría became the first former president to publicly acknowledge this crucially important, unwritten rule of the Mexican system. However, the actual process of selecting a new president remains shrouded in secrecy.[25] The man chosen is popularly referred to as *el tapado* (literally, the "hidden one," or the "hooded one"), until his identity is made public (an act known as the *destape*, or "unveiling") by PRI leaders to whom the president has communicated his choice (the *dedazo*, or pointing of the presidential finger).

Some analysts have argued (with no proof) that the outgoing president consults behind the scenes with former presidents, national level leaders of the government-affiliated labor movement and other PRI sectors, and key representatives of other groups like the military and the business community. The president may or may not choose to respect their views when he makes the final selection.[26] Other analysts contend that these consultations are mainly a means of co-opting the PRI leadership and discouraging dissident factions within the party from launching their own candidates; all that really counts in the selection process is the preference of the incumbent president.

The final choice is probably made through some highly idiosyncratic weighing of factors like personal relationships that the outgoing president has developed with potential successors over his entire career; which of these men is most likely to continue the basic policies of the outgoing president; the actual performance of various members of the presidential Cabinet (from whom the new president is likely to be chosen) during the administration now ending; the political and economic groups to which possible successors seem to be allied; and what is known as *la coyuntura* — the conjuncture of economic and political circumstances that Mexico confronts at home and abroad as the moment of presidential succession approaches. These circumstances indicate the kinds of problems that the next president may have to handle. For example, the financial crisis that began in 1981 is thought to have boosted the presidential prospects of Miguel de la Madrid, who had established his credentials as an expert on public finance, while diminishing the chances of several other Cabinet members who were perceived as traditional politicians.

By tradition, those who aspire to the presidency of Mexico cannot openly promote their candidacies or even admit that they are seeking the office. The supporters of the major contenders work diligently behind the scenes to advance the chances of their man and to discredit the other contenders. In 1987, in response to widespread criticism of the traditional, secretive selection process, Miguel de la Madrid, acting through the president of the PRI, publicly identified six "distinguished party members" as precandidates for the PRI's 1988 presidential nomination, and arranged for them to present their ideas to PRI notables at semipublic breakfast meetings. These appearances represented only a cosmetic change in the presidential succession process, however, since they provoked no real debate or public campaigning by the hopefuls, and the outgoing president remained firmly in control of the nomination process. "In accordance with tradition, virtually every member of the official party watched and waited for months for a signal 'from above' before deciding to support one of the six precandidates. When President de la Madrid gave that signal in favor of Carlos Salinas de Gortari, virtually the entire party jumped on the bandwagon."[27] In the end, de la Madrid's innovation only called attention to the closed, authoritarian nature of the presidential succession process and the highly circumscribed role of the PRI in that process, at least as it has operated in recent decades.[28]

Anticipating even stronger criticism of the traditional system when the next succession begins, Carlos Salinas in 1990 put into place a new mechanism for formally designating the PRI's presidential candidate. Rather than being so conspicuously handpicked by the outgoing president, the PRI's nominee for the 1994– 2000 term will have to win a majority of votes within a "national political council" consisting of 150 senior party officials. This procedure falls considerably short of an open, participatory selection process; nor does it force the outgoing president to relinquish control over the outcome. The selection committee is likely to be packed with party leaders personally loyal to Salinas, and their votes will undoubtedly reflect his preference.

However the selection is actually made, it is clear that the outgoing president chooses from a very short list: a handful of incumbent Cabinet members, which in recent transitions has included the secretaries of Gobernación (responsible for management of elections and internal security), planning and budget, finance, labor, education, and energy and state industries; and the mayor of Mexico City, who holds Cabinet rank. These men are the survivors of protracted and intense political and bureaucratic competition within the regime. In this sense, the power of the incumbent president to determine who will succeed him is circumscribed by the political system itself, and how it operates to thrust certain kinds of men to the top of the political pyramid.

Camarillas and Clientelism

The key to understanding the presidential succession process and elite political mobility in general lies in the clientage structures that permeate the Mexican political system. The entire system can be viewed as consisting of interlocking chains of *patron–client relationships*, in which the "patrons" — persons having higher political status — provide benefits such as protection, support in political struggles with rivals, and chances for upward political or economic mobility to their "clients" — persons having lesser political status. In exchange, the "clients" provide loyalty, deference, and useful services like voter mobilization, political control, and problem-solving to their patrons within the official party or governmental bureaucracy.[29]

The chains of patron–client relationships are interwoven, because patrons do not want to limit themselves to one client, and clients avoid pinning all their hopes on a single patron. Normally, these interweaving chains of clientage relationships come together at the apex of the national authority structure — the presidency. For all those who hold office during a given sexenio, the president is the supreme patron.

The vertical grouping of several different levels of patron–client relationships is popularly known in Mexico as a *camarilla* — roughly translated, a "political clique" (see Figure 15.2). Each camarilla has been assembled over a long period of time, through an elaborate process of personal alliance-building. Most of the truly important political conflict and competition in the Mexican system is related in some way to the constant struggle between rival camarillas. Especially at the cabinet level, the camarillas vie constantly for influence over national policymaking in key areas. They also struggle for control over strategically situated political offices, such as cabinet ministries. Above all, throughout the

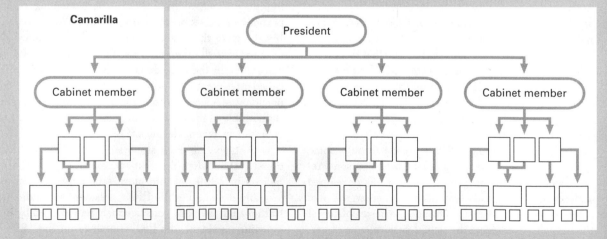

FIGURE 15.2
CLIENTAGE STRUCTURES WITHIN THE MEXICAN POLITICAL ELITE

sexenio they jockey for position in the race for the presidency itself. The cabinet ministers who lead the rival camarillas are often, themselves, aspirants to the presidency.

Because reelection to the presidency is prohibited, the Supreme Patron in this elaborate clientage structure is replaced every six years. The new president has his own camarilla, whose members, in turn, have different followers of their own, and so on down the system. The governmentwide shuffling of officeholders, at the beginning of each new presidential administration, actually amounts to substituting one major camarilla — the one that will now control the presidency — for another one (the one headed by the outgoing president).

The basic element that binds camarillas together is personal loyalty to the camarilla leader rather than ideology. The members of the winning camarilla may, indeed, share certain policy preferences or career experiences that distinguish them from previous administrations, but the essential bond is loyalty to the man who holds the presidency, from whom all policy and stylistic cues are taken.

One major consequence of this kind of political elite structure is that there is no room for political or policy innovation from below. No rational aspirant to power at lower levels of the system will take the risk of doing things that go beyond the well-recognized rules of the game. Thus, if the political system is to be reformed, it must be done "from the top," as a supreme exertion of presidential will. Another consequence is that the responsiveness and accountability of officials to the PRI's "mass constituencies" and to the general public is greatly diminished. Fervent, unquestioning loyalty and service to one's immediate superior in the PRI–government apparatus is the only promising route to upward political mobility. Even for elected officeholders like members of Congress, the official's only real constituency is his boss — his principal patron within the multilayered clientage structure. It is that person who will determine the officeholder's next position within the system.[30] Empirical analysis has demonstrated that camarilla membership — who one knows and services — is perhaps the best predictor of survival in the bureaucratic elite.[31]

To move up the hierarchy, a person must be concerned not only about joining the "right" camarilla but with building one's own. The larger and more diverse the camarilla, and the more tentacles it extends into all parts of the government bureaucracy and the PRI, the more powerful its leader is. The strongest camarillas built in recent sexenios have also linked several different generations of political leaders. For example, Carlos Salinas's camarilla links him, through family, school, or career ties, to practically every member of the economic cabinet who has held office since the 1940s.[32] When the camarilla leader moves vertically or horizontally within the political system, the key members of his team move with him. For example, Carlos Salinas followed his boss, Miguel de la Madrid, from the Treasury Ministry to the Ministry of Planning and Budget, when de la Madrid was promoted to Cabinet rank.

Joining the "wrong" camarilla can entail high career costs, but it is not necessarily fatal to one's long-term political prospects. All successful political leaders in Mexico are associated with multiple camarillas at different points in their careers.[33] It is acceptable to shift loyalties when the upward mobility of one's political mentor has been blocked. Politically agile individuals who have built personal alliances with some members of a rival camarilla can often jump directly from a losing camarilla to the winning one. For example, after Mario Moya Palencia lost out to José López Portillo in the 1976 presidential succession, many members of Moya Palencia's very large camarilla were able to gain positions in the López Portillo and de la Madrid administrations. One of them, Carlos Salinas, became president in 1988. Similarly, when Salinas's chief rival for the presidency, Jesús Silva Herzog, was forced to resign his Cabinet post in 1986, key members of his camarilla quickly switched to Salinas's team. One of them, Jaime Serra Puche, became Salinas's commerce secretary. Even disappointed presidential contenders sometimes receive Cabinet posts in the next administration, if they "discipline" themselves sufficiently. Providing jobs for losing camarilla leaders and their followers serves as a balancing and conciliating mechanism for the political system. It helps to ensure stability by providing even the losing factions with an incentive for remaining within the official fold, waiting out the current sexenio, and positioning themselves for the next one.

RECRUITING THE POLITICAL ELITE

What kinds of people gain entry into Mexico's national political elite, and who makes it to the top? At least since the days of the Porfiriato, the Mexican political elite has been recruited predominantly from the middle class. The 1910 revolution did not open up the political elite to large numbers of people from peasant or urban laborer backgrounds. That opening occurred only in the 1930s, during the Cárdenas administration, and then mainly at the local and state levels rather than the national level elite. A study of the national bureaucratic elite in power in 1984 found that 93 percent came from the middle to upper classes.[34]

The 1910 revolution did, however, increase rates of political mobility for the country's middle class, and it redistributed power within that class. Power shifted from those who had become entrenched in the Porfirian dictatorship to the politically dispossessed elements of the middle class: ambitious, well-educated people whose political aspirations had been blocked during the Porfiriato. The revolution opened up many public offices and created new routes to power for such people. Over the next sixty years, middle-class persons with literary skills (intellectuals, journalists) and those with military experience and backgrounds in electoral politics were gradually supplanted by middle-class people with different skills and professional training: lawyers, engineers, agronomists, planners, and, most recently, economists and professional public administrators—the so-called *técnicos* (technocrats) of recent presidential administrations.[35]

In recent sexenios, the national political elite has become more homogeneous in several important ways. As pointed out above (see Figure 15.1), its members have been drawn increasingly from the ranks of *capitalinos*—people born or raised in Mexico City. Most receive their undergraduate degrees at the National University in Mexico City (UNAM), which continues to serve as a crucial training and meeting ground for aspirants to political power, despite the increased importance in recent years of elite private institutions of higher learning. Luis Echeverría and José López Portillo were classmates at UNAM. Miguel de la Madrid was López Portillo's student in the UNAM law school. Carlos Salinas took public administration courses from Miguel de la Madrid at UNAM. Part-time teaching at UNAM or other universities is one of the most important ways in which an aspirant to political power can identify and recruit bright new talent for the camarilla he is assembling.

Postgraduate education has become a valuable asset in political career-building. More than one-third of the national bureaucratic elite in 1984 held master's degrees, and both the de la Madrid and Salinas administrations had ample representation of persons at the cabinet and subcabinet levels who had earned doctorates at elite U.S. and European universities.[36]

Since the 1970s, kinship ties have also become more important as a common denominator of those who attain positions of political power. Increasingly, such people are born into politically prominent families that have already produced state governors, cabinet ministers, federal legislators, and even presidents. In 1987 all three of the leading precandidates for the PRI's presidential nomination, as well as opposition leader Cuauhtémoc Cárdenas, were *cachorros* (cubs)—the offspring of earlier, nationally known political figures. Family connections can give an aspiring political leader a powerful advantage over rivals. In effect, he inherits the camarilla that has been assembled by his politically prominent relative, and the relative himself becomes a key mentor and opener of doors. In short, "politics in Mexico has become a 'family affair.'"[37]

Despite the privileged social background of Mexico's postrevolutionary political elite, relatively few of its members have come from the country's wealthiest families. The offspring of such families tended to pursue careers in private business rather than politics. Indeed, the upheaval of 1910–1920 seems to have engendered two fairly distinct national elites—a political elite and an entrepreneurial elite—rather than a single "power elite" dominating both the political and economic arenas.[38] While the representation of persons with family or career ties to private capital within the national political elite has been increasing over the past twenty years, the incidence of public/private sector elite interlocks is still relatively low.[39] The two elites have often shared important interests and objectives, and for most of the period since 1940 they have worked in tandem to develop Mexico within a mixed-economy framework. However, recent sexenios have demonstrated that the public policy preferences and agendas of Mexico's political and business elites can and do diverge.[40]

The growing importance of political family dynasties and other indicators of increasing homogeneity in personal backgrounds has caused some observers to worry that Mexico's political elite is becoming more closed and in-bred. While its social base may, indeed, be narrowing, the modern Mexican political elite still shows considerable fluidity; the massive turnover of officeholders every six years is proof of that. The circulation of political elites in Mexico is not just a game of musical chairs. According to one tabulation, 80 percent of the top 200 officeholders are replaced every twelve years, and 90 percent every eighteen years. At the end of each administration, nearly one-third of the top-level players actually drop out of political life.[41] This helps to explain why in Mexico, unlike other postrevolutionary countries such as China and (until recently) the Soviet Union, the regime has not become a gerontocracy. The major exception to this rule is the national level leadership of the government-controlled labor movement, which since the 1940s has been dominated by the same individuals.

The movement of thousands of persons into and out of the ruling elite at regular intervals has been a key source of political stability in Mexico, because it reinforces the idea of "giving everyone a turn." At least at the highest levels of the system, members of the political elite remain in power for only a certain length of time. The implied lesson is that politically ambitious individuals will get their chance to acquire power, status, and wealth — if they are patient, persistent, and self-disciplined.

Técnicos *versus* Políticos

In recent sexenios, this calculus of expectations has been upset somewhat by the rise of the so-called *técnicos*. Beginning in the Echeverría administration, but especially in the de la Madrid and Salinas sexenios, persons whose careers have been built mainly in the arena of electoral politics and in the labor unions and peasant organizations affiliated with the ruling party have been eclipsed in the competition for high office.

They have increasingly lost out to the técnicos, whose main ticket of admission to the national political elite is an advanced university degree, often acquired abroad, in such disciplines as economics and public administration. Typically, the técnicos come from upper class families and spend their entire career within the government bureaucracy, especially the financial and planning agencies. They generally lack substantial personal constituencies outside the bureaucracy, because they have not had the opportunity or need to develop such followings. The vast majority of técnicos who make it to the highest levels of the system have not run for elective office. Carlos Salinas is the fourth man in a row to become president of Mexico without having held an elective office. Like Salinas, the most upwardly mobile técnicos increasingly get their only experience in party politics through a brief stint in the PRI's think tank (IEPES), where they write the party's platform and help run a presidential campaign. The técnicos rise to power far more rapidly than the average traditional político, on

the strength of their expertise and problem-solving capacity in fields that are important to the government (e.g., public finance) and, especially, their camarilla ties.[42] Carlos Salinas, perhaps the quintessential técnico, was only thirty-four years old when he was appointed to a key Cabinet post by President de la Madrid, and thirty-nine when he was nominated for the presidency (Figure 15.3).

The so-called traditional políticos are conspicuously older when they attain positions of power, because they typically have spent many years doing service for the PRI and/or its affiliated sectoral organizations. With the rise of the técnicos, the traditional políticos have found their access to the most important posts in the government blocked. They have also been saddled with a set of "antipopular" economic policies favored by the technocrats in power and with the responsibility of maintaining political control and electoral support for the PRI in a period of economic crisis and government austerity. Meanwhile, the técnicos concentrated on fashioning new development strategies and negotiating foreign debt deals. Not surprisingly, during the 1980s this division of labor generated considerable tension between the técnicos and traditional politicians, especially since the career rewards for the políticos' efforts to win elections and mobilize mass support for the government's policies had been sharply diminished.

Traditional políticos have also been distressed by their lack of influence over the direction of public policy in recent sexenios. The técnicos have chosen to pursue an economic project emphasizing reduced government spending on subsidies to consumers, privatization of public enterprises, industrial "reconversion" or modernization, basing Mexican development more on a capacity to export, and timely servicing of the nation's external debt. Many traditional políticos objected to this *neo*liberal, outward-looking economic policy mix, arguing that its social costs were too high and that such policies would further undermine electoral support for the PRI. Fundamentally, the políticos have been apprehensive about the técnicos' preferred approach to development because it implies upsetting many of the internal economic and political arrangements that have evolved in Mexico since the 1930s under a more inward-looking, protectionist set of government policies. Finally, the políticos have been alarmed by the técnicos' plans to change the rules of the electoral game, in ways that would make it more difficult for the políticos to do their jobs and to retain their traditional share of public posi-

FIGURE 15.3
CAREER OF CARLOS SALINAS DE GORTARI

1948: Born in Mexico City

Father, Raúl Salinas, studied engineering at Mexico's National University (UNAM) and economics at Harvard University; served as secretary of industry and commerce under President Adolfo López Mateos (1958–1964).

1967–1971: Undergraduate study at UNAM

Majored in economics; took public administration courses from Miguel de la Madrid.

1970–1978: Part-time university teaching

Taught at UNAM, Autonomous Technological Institute of Mexico (ITAM), and Center for Latin American Monetary Studies (CEMLA).

1971–1974: Finance Ministry: Analyst, Office of International Financial Affairs

Appointed by Hugo Margáin (treasury secretary), who had been undersecretary in the Ministry of Industry of Commerce when that ministry was headed by Raúl Salinas Lozano.

1972–1974: Postgraduate study at Harvard and MIT

Earned M.A. in public administration; M.A. and Ph.D. in political economy, completing his doctoral dissertation in 1978 (topic: relationships among public investment, political participation, and mass support for the government in rural areas of Puebla and Tlaxcala states).

1974–1979: Finance Ministry

Held various positions, including Director, Dept. of Economic Studies, Office of International Financial Affairs; and Director-General of Financial Planning. Worked under Miguel de la Madrid (Undersecretary of the Treasury) and José López Portillo (Treasury Secretary).

1979–1981: Director of Economic and Social Policy, Ministry of Programming and Budget

Appointed by Miguel de la Madrid (Secretary of Programming and Budget).

1981–1982: Director, Institute of Political, Economic, and Social Studies (IEPES), PRI

Ran the PRI's think tank during Miguel de la Madrid's presidential campaign; campaigned with de la Madrid throughout the country.

1982–1987: Secretary of Programming and Budget

Appointed at age 34—youngest member of the de la Madrid Cabinet.

1987: Nominated as presidential candidate of the PRI

1988–1994: President of Mexico

tions. Old-guard PRI leaders feared a political opening and an increase in genuine competition, especially in the midst of an economic crisis, while some high-ranking técnicos — including, initially, Presidents de la Madrid and Salinas — pushed for "modernization" of the PRI and the electoral system. The resulting tensions contributed importantly to the breakdown in PRI unity that occurred in 1987–1988, which gave rise to the dissi-

dent candidacy of Cuauhtémoc Cárdenas and the PRI's electoral debacle of July 1988.

The dichotomy between técnicos and políticos undoubtedly has been overdrawn. The técnicos have been stereotyped as "number crunchers" whose abstract formulas for public policy do not take account of popular needs and frustrations, and who lack basic political skills. While some high-ranking technocrats could fairly be criticized for insensitivity to social realities, those who rise to the top of the government hierarchy today could not possibly achieve such positions by technical competence and administrative experience alone; they must be highly skilled political alliance-builders as well. Their bureaucratic responsibilities often require them to negotiate deals with state governors and other prominent members of the traditional political class, who may be incorporated into the técnico's personal network of supporters. "Political technocrats" who have engaged in political activity (however briefly) have an important edge over those who lack such experience, in the competition for higher office.

The técnico/político distinction is further blurred by the fact that many políticos perform management functions in the central PRI bureaucracy and general political control duties in Gobernación and other ministries. Like the técnicos, such political bureaucrats can make their careers without ever engaging directly in voter mobilization or representation of one of the PRI's sectoral constituencies (peasants, organized labor, middle-class professionals, etc).

Mexico's traditional politicians have clearly lost power in recent sexenios, but they have not been completely displaced. The cabinets chosen by Mexico's two most recent, technocratic presidents have been a blend of young técnicos (concentrated in the economic and planning ministries) and experienced politicians. The departments most critical to political control (such as Gobernación, Labor, and Education) have been left in the hands of older, career politicians regarded as hard-liners on matters of electoral politics and internal security. Salinas, in particular, made an effort to reach out to the traditional political class, choosing for his Cabinet a substantial number of men who are highly skilled political brokers and who, by virtue of both age and experience, could serve as a bridge between Salinas's technocratic inner circle and the PRI's old guard. The proportion of Salinas Cabinet members with some sort of political experience (especially having held state governorships) was more than double that of the preceding de la Madrid Cabinet (see Figure 15.4).

Through his Cabinet appointments and his go-slow approach to political reform, Salinas succeeded in reducing tensions within the national political elite. There is now a reasonably comfortable, symbiotic relationship between the two wings of the elite, rather than the barely concealed antagonism of the 1980s. The tra-

Fidel Velázquez, 91-year-old patriarch of the Mexican labor movement, and Carlos Salinas de Gortari, 43-year-old president of Mexico, applaud each other at a PRI congress.

ditional políticos need the technocrats to run the economy and negotiate complex arrangements with the outside world; the técnicos need the políticos to maintain political control. Nevertheless, a significant and probably irreversible shift of power has occurred within Mexico's political elite. Career politicians must now implement decisions made by technocrats, whose approach to the country's problems places much less emphasis on traditional populism and economic nationalism, and who are more preoccupied with economic problem-solving than with the health of the political system. Since further Mexican presidents are likely to be recruited from the ranks of the technocrats, there is little prospect of a return to government by traditional políticos.

INTEREST REPRESENTATION AND POLITICAL CONTROL

In the Mexican system, important public policies are initiated and shaped by the inner circle of presidential advisers before they are even presented for public discussion. Most interest representation therefore takes place within the upper levels of the government bureaucracy. The structures that aggregate and articulate interests in Western democracies (political parties, labor unions, and so on) actually serve other purposes in

FIGURE 15.4
POLITICAL EXPERIENCE OF THE CABINET

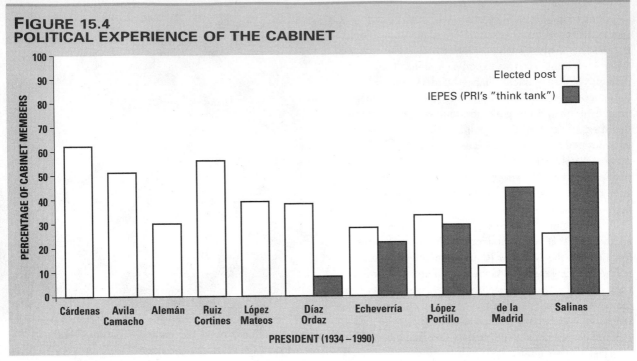

Source: Centeno, "The New Científicos."

the Mexican system: limiting the scope of citizens' demands on the government, mobilizing electoral support for the regime, helping to legitimate it in the eyes of other countries, distributing jobs and other material rewards to select individuals and groups. The principal vehicle for interest articulation and aggregation in the Mexican system, the official party PRI, has no independent influence on public policy; nor do the opposition parties in the system.

Since the late 1930s, Mexico has had a corporatist system of interest representation in which each citizen and societal segment should relate to the state through one structure "licensed" by the state to organize and represent that sector of society (peasants, urban unionized workers, businessmen, teachers, etc.). The official party itself is divided into three sectors: the peasant sector, the labor sector, and the "popular" sector (representing most government employees, small merchants, private landowners, and low-income urban neighborhood groups). Each sector is dominated by one mass organization: the *Confederación de Trabajadores de México (CTM)* in the labor sector; the Confederación Nacional Campesina (CNC) in the peasant sector; and the Confederación Nacional de Organizaciones Populares (CNOP) in the popular sector. Other organizations

are affiliated with each party sector, but their influence is dwarfed by that of the principal confederation.

A number of powerful organized interest groups —foreign and domestic entrepreneurs, the military, the Catholic Church — also are not formally represented in the PRI. These groups deal directly with the governmental elite, often at the presidential or cabinet level; they do not need the PRI to make their preferences known. These groups also have well-placed representatives within the executive branch who can be counted on to articulate their interests.

In addition, the business community is organized into several government-chartered confederations (CONCANACO, CONCAMIN, CANACINTRA), which take positions on public issues and have their preferences widely disseminated through the mass media. Since the Cárdenas administration, all but a handful of the country's industrialists and businessmen have been required by law to join one of these employers' organizations. In the 1980s, several businessmen's organizations independent of the state-sanctioned associations (most notably, COPARMEX, the Confederación Patronal de la República Mexicana) took a leading role in criticizing government economic policies.[43]

Because the party system and the national legislature do not effectively aggregate interests in the Mexican system, numerous conflicting claims must be resolved directly by the president or by one of the several "super ministries" (such as Planning and Budget) that have been created within the executive branch to serve as coordinating mechanisms. Large numbers of poorly aggregated and conflicting demands can at times threaten to overwhelm the decision-making apparatus and induce paralysis. But this pattern of interest mediation is also functional in maintaining the system's stability.

Individuals and groups seeking something from the regime often circumvent their nominal representatives in the PRI sectoral organizations and seek satisfaction of their needs through personal contacts — patrons — within the government apparatus. These patron–client relationships compartmentalize the society into discrete noninteracting, vertical segments that serve as pillars of the regime. Within the lower class, for example, unionized urban workers are separated from nonunion urban workers; ejidatarios from small private landholders and landless agricultural workers. The middle class is compartmentalized into government bureaucrats, educators, health care professionals, lawyers, economists, and so forth. Thus, competition between social classes is replaced by highly fragmented competition within classes.

The articulation of interests through patron–client networks assists the regime by reducing the number of potential beneficiaries for government programs and by limiting the scope of the demands made on the regime. It fragments popular demands into small-scale, highly individualized or localized requests that can be granted or denied case by case. Officials are rarely confronted with collective demands from broad social groupings. Rather than having to act on a request from a whole category of people (slum dwellers, ejidatarios, teachers), officials have easier, less costly choices to make (as between competing petitions from several neighborhoods for a piped water system).

The clientelistic structure not only provides a mechanism for distributing government benefits selectively; it also helps to legitimate such selectivity. It places the responsibility for outcomes on individual patrons and clients. If community X fails to receive its school, it must be because its patron in the state government has failed to do his job, or because community residents themselves have not been skillful or persistent

enough in cultivating enough patrons, or the right patrons, in the right government agencies — "the myth of the right connection."[44] This reasoning helps to limit citizens' frustration with government performance, while making it more difficult for dissident leaders to organize people on the basis of broadly shared economic grievances.

The appearance in recent years of independent organizations not tied into the regime's clientelistic networks has introduced new complexity and uncertainty into the political system. Numerous movements and organizations have emerged spontaneously among the urban poor, peasants, and even some middle-class groups like schoolteachers, which the PRI – government apparatus has generally failed to incorporate. These movements have developed partly in response to economic grievances created by the crisis, partly because of the declining responsiveness of existing state-chartered "mass" organizations to popular demands, and partly as a result of general societal modernization (expansion of mass communications, higher education levels, urbanization, changes in occupational structure, and the like). Because of the economic crisis and government austerity policies, state-affiliated organizations had little or nothing to deliver in terms of material benefits, and were increasingly viewed by the Mexican people as instruments of manipulation and corrupt, self-serving extensions of the state bureaucracy.

But the new popular movements have been equally distrustful of the traditional opposition political parties. Until the late 1980s, they avoided collaborating with all parties operating at the national level, preferring to focus their energies on localized struggles for land, water, housing, and other improvements in urban *barrios*.[45] In the 1988 election, many popular organizations supported the presidential candidacy of Cuauhtémoc Cárdenas, and a large portion of movement adherents probably voted for him; but the movements' support for the Partido de la Revolución Democrática (PRD), the political party established by Cárdenas after the 1988 election, has been limited and sporadic. In some parts of Mexico (e.g., Oaxaca, Durango, Baja California), leaders of popular movements have begun to compete directly in elections for local positions of power.

There is lively debate among scholars and political practitioners in Mexico about the long-term significance of the new popular movements and, more generally, the political awakening of civil society. Some view the recent organizational dynamism of civil society as a watershed in Mexican history, providing evidence of a fundamental crisis of representation in the Mexican political system. For example, some of the earliest peasant movements that challenged the CNC developed because it simply had failed to provide effective representation of the campesinos' interests. Thus, the emergence of numerous, highly localized popular movements that are seemingly apolitical (at least beyond the arena of municipal politics), and that pursue their own agendas is a symptom of the breakdown of corporatist controls and of the increasing inability of the state-chartered mass organizations to incorporate newly emerging social sectors and interests into the official fold.

While intra-elite conflict and the scarcity of patronage resources contributed greatly to the decline of the corporatist system in the 1980s, developments in civil society threatened it in other ways. The continued growth of the middle class and its increasing propensity to organize around issues like environmental pollution and inadequate urban services; the burgeoning of an unorganized, politically unincorporated, "informally" employed segment of the low-income urban population (often referred to as *los marginados*); and a peasantry enraged by the depredations of natural resource exploiters, encroaching urban development, and credit squeezes by government banks — all have served as catalysts for the gradual emergence of a qualitatively new, more participant political culture. Mexico's political leaders now confront a substantially larger number of interest groups, pursuing their goals in a less deferential, more independent manner. There appears to have been sufficient popular mobilization during the 1980s to capture the attention of political elites, who now recognize — however grudgingly — the growing pluralism of civil society and the need to respond to it, perhaps by revitalizing corporatist structures or bypassing them through new forms of leadership and representation.[46]

Nevertheless, it must be recognized that, while the Mexican regime's vaunted political control capabilities have been weakened by the economic and political crises of recent sexenios, the traditional instruments of control — patron–client relationships, *caciquismo* (local level boss rule), the captive labor movement, selective repression of dissidents by government security forces — remain in place and have not lost all of their former effectiveness. The low incidence of protest behavior, unauthorized strikes, and other forms of civil disobedience in Mexico during the post–1982 period of mounting social pain suggests that the PRI–

government apparatus remains highly skilled at dividing, buying off, co-opting and — if necessary — repressing protest movements before they get out of hand.

Partido Revolucionario Institucional (PRI)

Mexico's "official" party, the *Partido Revolucionario Institucional* (PRI), was founded in 1929 by President Plutarco Elías Calles to serve as a mechanism for reducing violent conflict among contenders for public office, and for consolidating the power of the central government, at the expense of the personalistic, local, and state level political machines that had passed for political parties during the decade following the 1910–1920 revolution. As historian Lorenzo Meyer has said, the official party "was a party that was born not to fight for power, but to administer it without sharing it."[47]

For more than half a century the ruling party served with impressive efficiency, as a mechanism for resolving elite conflicts, for co-opting newly emerging interest groups into the system, and for legitimating the regime through the electoral process. Potential defectors from the official party were deterred by the government's manipulation of electoral rules, which made it virtually impossible for any dissident faction to bolt the party and win an election. Dissident movements did emerge in 1940, 1946, 1952, and 1987–1988, but before the neo-Cardenista coalition contested the 1988 election, no breakaway presidential candidacy had been able to garner more than 16 percent of the vote (by official count).

In 1938 President Lázaro Cárdenas transformed the official party from an elite conflict-resolution/cooptation mechanism into a mass-based political party that could be used explicitly to build popular support for government policies and mobilize participation in elections. Cárdenas accomplished this by merging into the official party the local, state, and national level organizations of peasants and urban workers that had been created during his presidency.[48] This reorganization established the party's claim to be an inclusionary party, one that would seek to absorb into it as many as possible of the diverse economic interests and political tendencies that were represented in Mexican society. The official party and its affiliated mass organizations occupied so much political space that opposition parties and movements found it difficult to recruit supporters.

From the beginning, the official party was an appendage of the government itself, especially of the presidency. It was never a truly independent arena of political competition. A handful of nationally powerful party leaders, such as Fidel Velázquez, patriarch of the PRI-affiliated labor movement, occasionally constrained government actions, but the official party itself has never exerted any independent influence on government economic and social policies. Indeed, one of the key sources of the tensions that led to the breakdown of party unity and discipline in the late 1980s — culminating in the neo-Cardenista movement — was the PRI's lack of autonomy from unpopular government austerity policies, and the inability of the party's most entrenched leaders and cadres to influence the policy choices being made by the technocrats in the government.

During the 1940s and 1950s Mexico's ruling party became one of the world's most accomplished vote-getting machines, guaranteeing an overwhelming victory at the polls for all but a handful of its candidates in every election. None of the party's nominees for president has ever been officially defeated, and until 1988–1989 none of its candidates for federal senator or state governor had been denied victory. Only since the 1970s have opposition parties been able to win appreciable numbers of municipal presidencies and seats in the lower house of Congress. By 1990 opposition parties controlled only 5 percent of Mexico's nearly 2,400 municipal governments — up from 1 percent in 1985.

The official party has always had a number of major advantages over its electoral competitors. Privileged access to the mass media (and particularly, since the 1960s, television) is one of them. The media typically devote 90 percent or more of their coverage of electoral campaigns to the PRI's candidates, and the special political television broadcasts established by law to give opposition parties access to the media are scheduled at low-viewing hours, while the PRI invariably gets prime time.

The official party also enjoys essentially unlimited access to government funds to finance its campaigns. No one knows how much is actually transferred from government coffers to the PRI, since Mexico has no laws requiring the reporting of campaign income and expenditures. However, when an opposition government took power in the state of Baja California Norte, it found bank and legal records showing that more than (U.S.) $10 million in government funds had been channeled to the PRI for its 1989 gubernatorial campaign in that state. The PRI contends that it receives only the small government subsidy provided to all registered political parties under the terms of the federal electoral law, and dues from party members, which typically are automatically deducted from the salaries of government employees.

As the party in power, the PRI and its affiliated mass organizations have benefited from a vast network of government patronage, through which small-scale material benefits could be delivered to large segments of the population. The economic crisis of the 1980s and the government austerity measures provoked by it sharply reduced the resources that could be pumped through that national patronage system. One reason for the PRI's loss of voter support as the crisis wore on was that it had become increasingly ineffectual in delivering material rewards. The fiscally conservative Salinas administration's solution to this problem has been to concentrate the resources available for government patronage in a smaller number of politically strategic localities and neighborhoods, especially the vote-rich urban slums where the neo-Cardenista movement won much of its support in 1988. Salinas's highly visible National Solidarity Program (PRONASOL) invests mainly in infrastructure that low-income Mexicans badly need (piped water, electricity, sewage systems, paved streets, medical clinics, housing). It requires community self-help in obtaining, installing, and paying for these improvements. The program also emphasizes the linkage between the public goods provided and the government's policy of privatizing money-losing state-owned enterprises in order to free up revenues for PRONASOL and other social programs. Opposition politicians have criticized PRONASOL as selective neopopulism, but it represents a shrewd and potentially effective way to weaken the appeal of opposition parties and replenish the patronage resources of lower level PRI functionaries.

The PRI is the only political party in Mexico that possesses a truly nationwide network of campaign organizers, local representatives, and poll-watchers. It could count among its local cadres the 1 million members of the PRI-affiliated national teachers' union, who have played a particularly important role in securing the PRI's rural vote. The huge size and geographic dispersion of the ruling party's network of militants translate into great advantages at election time. For example, it would take over 100,000 poll-watchers to cover every polling place in the country during a presidential election. None of the opposition parties can come remotely close to fielding this number of poll-watchers. The PRI also has the personnel to get its voters to the polls — which is especially important in a period of rising abstentionism.

Historically, the official party's most potent advantage over the competition has been its ability to commit electoral fraud with relative impunity. A wide variety of techniques have been used: stuffing ballot boxes, intimidating potential opposition supporters by threatening to withdraw government benefits, disqualifying opposition party poll-watchers, relocating polling places at the last minute to sites known only to PRI supporters, manipulating voter registration lists (padding them with nonexistent or nonresident PRIistas while "shaving" those who might vote against the ruling party from the rolls), issuing multiple voting credentials to PRI supporters, organizing multiple voting by *carruseles* ("flying brigades" of PRI supporters, transported from one polling place to the next), and so forth. Moreover, with majority representation in all the local, state, and national government committees that control polling and vote counting, the PRI has always been able to count on "electoral alchemy" to nullify unfavorable election outcomes or manipulate the tallies to deny victory to opposition candidates. Final results have been determined from above, sometimes through secret negotiations with the opposition parties, more often by fiat.[49]

Fraud has become such an integral part of the electoral process over the years that its sudden removal could produce disastrous results for the PRI. During the first ten months of Miguel de la Madrid's presidency, the government followed a policy of recognizing municipal level victories by opposition party candidates wherever they occurred. The PRI was soon forced to concede defeat to PAN in seven major cities, including five state capitals. Under intense pressure from alarmed and angry state and local PRI leaders, de la Madrid abruptly suspended his policy of "electoral transparency," and during the remainder of his term only one relatively small city was allowed to pass into opposition control.

Until recently, the weakness of opposition parties made it possible for the PRI – government apparatus to control election outcomes without blatant rigging. Indeed, in most parts of the country, the PRI's candidates for president, governor, and federal senator would probably have won an absolute majority of the votes even if no doctoring of election results had occurred. Beginning in 1985, however, gubernatorial and municipal elections in a number of states (Sonora, Chihuahua, Baja California Norte, Michoacán, Guerrero, and Estado de

México) produced such an avalanche of opposition votes that tallies could not be adjusted so inconspicuously. The costs of "electoral alchemy" had gone up. Such tactics now provoked postelection protest demonstrations, violent clashes between PRI and opposition party militants, extensive criticism in the international media, rising public cynicism, and higher abstention in subsequent elections. In the case of Baja California Norte in 1989, national-level PRI and government authorities apparently concluded that the cost of blatant cheating would be excessive, and the PAN's historic state-level victory was recognized. In other states, heavy-handed electoral manipulations have persisted, with or without the sanction of central authorities.

While there was no effective opposition, the PRI's approach was to do everything possible to boost voter turnout, thus enabling the official party to roll up the huge majorities needed to validate its right to rule. With the emergence of strong opposition, blanket exhortations to register and vote have been replaced by a more targeted, block-by-block strategy aimed at mobilizing only those voters most likely to vote for the PRI. The presence of new opposition forces in the countryside — most notably, the neo-Cardenistas — has also constrained the PRI's ability to add votes to its totals, thereby artificially inflating voter participation. Such adding of votes to the PRI column, rather than taking votes away from opposition parties, has been the most common form of electoral fraud in rural areas. The effects of these changes can be seen in sharply reduced voter turnout rates since the late 1980s, even in hotly contested elections: no higher than 49.4 percent in the 1988 presidential election (see Table 15.1); and 15 to 33 percent in several key state and local elections held in 1989 and 1990.[50]

The share of the vote claimed by the PRI has been declining for nearly thirty years, but until recently the decline has been gradual and has not threatened the party's grasp on the presidency and state governorships (see Figure 15.5 and Table 15.2). The proportion of electoral districts dominated by the PRI dropped from 85 percent in 1964 to 35 percent in 1988 (see the first three columns of Table 15.3). In 1988 opposition parties officially defeated the PRI in nearly 23 percent of the country's 300 electoral districts. In terms of expressed party preference, opinion surveys suggest that the PRI had ceased to be a majority party by 1987, when less than 30 percent of a national sample of Mexicans identified themselves as PRI supporters.[51]

TABLE 15.1
VOTING IN PRESIDENTIAL ELECTIONS, 1934–1988

Year	Votes for PRI candidate[a] (%)	Votes for PAN candidate (%)	Votes for all others[b] (%)	Turnout (% voters among eligible adults)[c]
1934	98.2	—	1.8	53.6
1940	93.9	—	6.1	57.5
1946	77.9	—	22.1	42.6
1952	74.3	7.8	17.9	57.9
1958	90.4	9.4	0.2	49.4
1964	88.8	11.1	0.1	54.1
1970	83.3	13.9	1.4	63.9
1976[d]	93.6	—	1.2	59.6
1982	71.0	15.7	9.4	66.1
1988	50.7	16.8	32.5[e]	49.4[f]

[a]From 1958 through 1982, includes votes cast for the Partido Popular Socialista (PPS) and the Partido Auténtico de la Revolución Mexicana (PARM), both of which regularly endorsed the PRI's presidential candidate. In 1988 they supported opposition candidate Cuauhtémoc Cárdenas.

[b]Excludes annulled votes; includes votes for candidates of nonregistered parties.

[c]Eligible population base for 1934 through 1952 includes all males aged 20 and over (legal voting age: 21 years). Both men and women aged 20 and over are included in the base for 1958 and 1964 (women received the franchise in 1958). The base for 1970–1988 includes all males and females aged eighteen and over (the legal voting age was lowered to eighteen, effective 1970).

[d]The PRI candidate, José López Portillo, ran virtually unopposed because the PAN failed to nominate a candidate. The only other significant candidate was Valentín Campa, representing the Communist party, which was not legally registered to participate in the 1976 election. More than 5 percent of the votes were annulled.

[e]Includes 31.1 percent officially tabulated for Cuauhtémoc Cárdenas.

[f]Estimated using data from the Federal Electoral Commission. However, the commission itself has released two different figures for the number of eligible voters in 1988. Using the commission's larger estimate of eligible population, the turnout would be 44.9 percent.

Sources: Pablo González Casanova, *Democracy in Mexico* (New York: Oxford University Press, 1970), Table 1; Peter H. Smith, *Labyrinths of Power* (Princeton, N.J.: Princeton University Press, 1979), Table 2–7; Comisión Federal Electoral, *Procesos federales electorales, Cómputo de la votación por partido* (1964–1988).

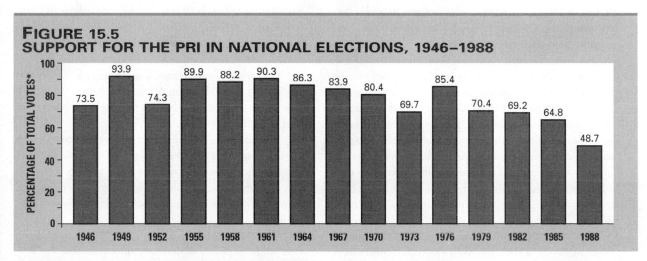

FIGURE 15.5
SUPPORT FOR THE PRI IN NATIONAL ELECTIONS, 1946–1988

*Percentage base includes annulled votes and those cast for nonregistered candidates.

Source: Data from Comisión Federal Electoral (Mexico), tabulated by Juan Molinar Horcasitas, Universidad Nacional Autónoma de México.

TABLE 15.2
REPRESENTATION OF POLITICAL PARTIES IN CHAMBER OF DEPUTIES, 1964–1988 (PERCENTAGE OF SEATS)

Party	Year of Congressional Elections								
	1964	1967	1970	1973	1976	1979	1982	1985	1988
Partido Revolucionario Institucional (PRI)	83.3	82.1	83.6	82.2	82.0	82.2	74.8	72.3	52.0
Partido de Acción Nacional (PAN)	9.5	9.4	9.4	10.8	8.5	10.0	12.5	10.3	20.2
Partido Popular Socialista (PPS)[a]	4.8	4.7	4.7	4.3	5.1	2.8	2.5	2.8	(see FDN)
Partido Auténtico de la Revolución Mexicana (PARM)[a]	2.4	2.4	2.3	3.0	3.8	3.0	0.0	2.8	(see FDN)
Partido Democrático Mexicano (PDM)	—	—	—	—	—	2.5	3.0	3.0	0.0
Partido Socialista de los Trabajadores (PST)[a] (which became:) Partido del Frente Cardenista de Reconstrucción Nacional (PFCRN)	—	—	—	—	—	2.5	2.8	3.0	(see FDN)
Partido Comunista Mexicano (PCM) (which became:) Partido Socialista Unificado de México (PSUM) (which became:) Partido Mexicano Socialista (PMS)[b]	—	—	—	—	—	4.5	4.3	3.0	3.8
Partido Revolucionario de los Trabajadores (PRT)	—	—	—	—	—	—	0.0	1.5	0.0
Frente Democrático Nacional (FDN)[c]	—	—	—	—	—	—	—	—	24.0

[a]Party allied with the PRI before 1988.
[b]Party allied with the Cardenista front (FDN) in 1988.
[c]Coalition consisting of the PARM, PFCRN, and PPS. While these parties supported the same presidential candidate in 1988, Cuauhtémoc Cárdenas, they have not necessarily voted as a bloc in the Chamber of Deputies, especially since the formation of the Partido de la Revolución Democrática (PRD), the new Cardenista party, in 1989.
Source: Juan Molinar Horcasitas, El tiempo de la legitimidad: *Elecciones, autoritarismo y democracia en México* (Mexico, D.F.: Cal y Arena, 1991).

One of the key factors accounting for the long-term decline in the official party's effectiveness as a vote-getting machine is the massive shift of population from rural to urban areas that has occurred in Mexico since 1950. In that year, 57 percent of the population lived in isolated rural communities of fewer than 2,500 inhabitants. By 1980 less than 34 percent lived in such localities, while 41 percent of all Mexicans lived in cities of 100,000 or more inhabitants. In large urban centers the regime's traditional mechanisms of political control work less efficiently. Education and income levels are higher, and the middle classes — which provide a considerable share of the opposition vote — are larger. The opposition parties are better organized and have more poll-watchers in these places, making it more difficult for the PRI to conceal vote fraud. The data assembled in Table 15.4 reveal that the PRI's electoral fortunes have declined most precipitously in the Mexico City metropolitan area (which now contains 25 percent of Mexico's total population) and other urban centers. In the 1988 presidential election, the would-be modernizer of Mexico, Carlos Salinas, derived his margin of victory from the most traditional, underdeveloped parts of the country. He received only one out of four votes cast in Mexico City, while Cuauhtémoc Cárdenas took 49 percent of the vote there. Even in rural areas, however, opposition forces — primarily the neo-Cardenistas — have cut into the PRI's formerly "safe" vote.

Elections held in the 1980s were also marked by the collapse of the PRI's so-called sectoral vote — votes supposedly controlled by the party's affiliated *campesino*, labor, and "popular" (urban middle class and slum-dweller) organizations. For the 1988 election, the national peasant confederation promised to deliver 10 million votes to the PRI's presidential candidate; the federation of public employees unions promised 2 million votes; and the national teachers union pledged that each of its 1 million members would mobilize a dozen or

TABLE 15.3
PATTERNS OF ELECTORAL COMPETITION, 1964–1988
(PERCENTAGE OF 300 FEDERAL ELECTORAL DISTRICTS)

Election year	Type of Competition[a]					
	PRI monopoly	Strong PRI hegemony	Weak PRI hegemony	Two-party competition	Multiparty competition	Opposition victory
1964	28.1	52.2	4.5	14.0	—	1.1
1967	24.2	61.2	3.6	9.7	—	1.2
1970	27.0	53.9	1.7	17.4	—	—
1973	18.7	51.3	4.1	21.8	1.0	3.1
1976	35.8	44.6	6.7	11.9	0.5	0.5
1979	9.4	48.0	12.3	6.3	22.7	1.3
1982	1.3	51.7	6.3	26.1	14.0	0.3
1985	3.3	41.7	9.0	21.0	21.3	3.7
1988[b]	1.0	19.0	15.0	8.3	34.0	22.7

[a]*PRI monopoly* = PRI vote >95 percent; *strong PRI hegemony* = PRI vote <95 percent but >70; *weak PRI hegemony* = PRI vote <70 percent, but the difference between PRI and second party in district is >40 percentage points; two-party competition = PRI vote <70 percent, difference between PRI and second party is <40 percentage points, second party vote >25 percent, and third party vote <10 percent; *multiparty competition* = PRI vote <70, difference between PRI and second party is <40 percentage points, and second party vote <25 percent or third-party vote >10 percent; *opposition victory* = any party's vote >PRI vote.
[b]For 1988, opposition victories include those won by the Cardenista coalition of parties.
Source: Leopoldo Gómez and John Bailey, "La transición política y los dilemas del PRI," *Foro Internacional*, 31:1 (July-September 1990), p. 69.

more voters for the PRI. The election results (Salinas was credited with a total of 9,687,926 votes, nearly 5 million fewer than PRI candidate Miguel de la Madrid received in 1982) dramatically demonstrated that the PRI could no longer rely on its sectoral organizations to deliver most of the votes needed to win strongly contested national elections in a convincing fashion.[52]

Another major part of the PRI's dilemma is a massive generational shift in the electorate. The median age of the Mexican population today is about seventeen years. With each election, there are fewer Mexicans who personally experienced the social reforms implemented in the 1930s, or even the post–1940 era of sustained economic growth and low inflation. Instead, today's

TABLE 15.4
SUPPORT FOR THE PRI BY TYPE OF CONGRESSIONAL DISTRICT (PERCENTAGE OF TOTAL VOTE)

Districts	Year				
	1979	1982	1985	1988	Average 1979–1988
Federal District (Mexico City)	46.7	48.3	42.6	27.3	41.2
Other Urban[a]	53.4	56.2	51.1	34.3	48.8
Mixed[b]	67.9	66.2	59.2	46.4	60.0
Rural[c]	83.5	80.9	77.3	61.3	75.8

[a]Urban districts are those in which 90 percent or more of the population lives in communities of 50,000 or more inhabitants. Total number: 40 in the Federal District and 56 in other urban areas.
[b]Districts in which more than 50 percent but less than 90 percent of the population lives in communities of 50,000 or more inhabitants. Total number: 44.
[c]Districts in which less than 50 percent of the population lives in communities of 50,000 inhabitants. Total number: 160.
Source: From Comisión Federal Electoral; tabulations by Juan Molinar Horcasitas, Universidad Nacional Autónoma de México.

under-thirty-five voters have experienced fifteen years of recurrent economic crises, declining living standards, increasing inequality in wealth distribution, and political stagnation within the PRI – government apparatus. As a result, one of the most formidable challenges facing the PRI is how to stimulate loyalty to the party among the millions of first-time voters, who are coming of age at a time of severely diminished rather than expanding economic opportunities.

The magnitude of the PRI's so-called generational problem is suggested by several public opinion surveys showing that the ruling party's support is concentrated increasingly in the older age groups, while the opposition parties draw considerably more of their support from younger voters. A national preelection survey in 1988 found that more than 50 percent of the Cardenista coalition's support base consisted of persons under thirty years of age, while 42 percent of the PANista base and only 35 percent of the PRIistas were in this age group.[53] In the state of Chihuahua, the PRI receives the bulk of its support from people above age forty-three, while the youngest age groups (eighteen to thirty-two years) are dominated by PAN supporters.[54] The already substantial segment of the population that is dissatisfied with the PRI and inclined to support an opposition party will grow in the years to come, as the PRIista "old guard" dies off, particularly in rural areas, where the average age of the remaining population is rising rapidly. This has major implications for the PRI, since today it is the rural areas that continue to provide the winning margin for its candidates in many states.

Finally, the deep divisions that emerged within Mexico's political elite during the 1980s have impaired the PRI's performance in recent elections. Executive power has fallen increasingly into the hands of technocrats whose political style and policy preferences differ sharply from those of old-line PRI bureaucrats. The designation of Carlos Salinas as the PRI's presidential candidate in 1987 was taken by the traditional, nationalist-populist wing of the PRI as evidence that the government's economic policies would continue to shift to the right of Mexico's "revolutionary creed," and as a signal that the party's left wing would be reduced to permanent obsolescence and irrelevance. The departure of the center–left Cardenistas from the PRI and their unexpectedly strong electoral showing in 1988 further polarized the situation, provoking a strong defensive response from the most conservative, politically hard-line elements within the PRI (represented by its labor sector). The hard-liners' demands for a crackdown on opposition groups and their insistence on winning elections at all costs exacerbated the long-running conflict within the political elite between those advocating some sort of political liberalization and those who favor the status quo. These developments have made it increasingly difficult for the PRI to function as a mechanism for elite conflict resolution, and they have handed the opposition parties by far their most effective campaign issue: persistent, highly visible vote fraud by the PRI.

Opposition Parties

Until recently, the opposition parties essentially performed a stabilizing function in the Mexican political system. They gave the regime a loyal opposition in the Congress; provided an outlet for the protest vote (people so dissatisfied with the government's performance that they could not bring themselves to vote for PRI candidates); and served as vehicles for dissident political leaders, keeping them within the government-sanctioned arena of political competition. Internally fragmented and organizationally weak, the opposition parties could not attract sufficient electoral support to challenge PRI hegemony at the state or national levels. Leaders of these parties accepted seats in the Congress, criticized occasional policy decisions, and negotiated election results with the PRI – government apparatus. Their most basic function was to give the PRI something to run against, thereby strengthening the government's claim to popular support and legitimate authority.

The regime's basic strategy for dealing with the opposition parties was to "carry a big stick, and offer small carrots."[55] The carrots took the form of periodic tinkering with the federal election laws, so as to guarantee some level of representation for opposition parties in the Congress, make it easier for them to qualify for legal registration, and provide modest amounts of public financing for their campaigns. By tolerating opposition parties and encouraging the formation of additional ones, the regime was able to channel most of the public discontent with its policies and performance through the electoral process, rather than risking violent, antisystem protests.

In the late 1970s, and especially since 1985, a less collaborationist electoral opposition emerged. Benefiting from the tidal wave of antigovernment sentiment provoked by the economic crisis of the 1980s, opposition parties of the right and left became more formidable competitors. Particularly on the right, the opposition sought mass support cutting across all social classes, hired full-time staff, and started conducting campaigns to win rather than simply educate the citizenry. Opposition parties of both right and left became more willing to adopt civil disobedience and other confrontational tactics in their dealings with the government, especially to protest electoral fraud. They began appealing to the international media, the Organization of American States, and even the U.S. Congress to validate their claims of victory. Their representatives in the Congress challenged key national policies, such as the nationalization of the banking system in 1982, the continued servicing of Mexico's huge external debt, and accelerated economic integration with the United States. In these ways they have disputed the government's legitimacy, embarrassed it abroad, and raised the cost of political control and co-optation.

Nevertheless, opposition parties in Mexico continue to operate under severe constraints. Limited access to the mass media, lack of control over patronage resources, and PRI–government control over the machinery of elections are among the most significant. It remains extremely difficult for opposition parties to "prove" electoral fraud; the evidentiary tests prescribed by the electoral code are severe. As a result, an opposition party cannot demand that its victories be recognized officially; it can only try to pressure the government (e.g., though public demonstrations) and *negotiate* particular victories behind closed doors.[56]

Electoral fraud works against the opposition parties in other ways, too. By campaigning mainly against vote fraud, the opposition parties leave themselves open to the charge that they have no credible, alternative program for solving the economic and social problems afflicting the electorate. The continued fixation on fraud also causes many potential opposition party supporters to stay home when elections are held; they become disillusioned, no longer believing that opposition candidates have any reasonable chance of winning. Public distrust of the electoral process hurts the opposition parties more than the PRI, which has the resources to get out its vote.

The principal opposition party on the right, the Partido de Acción Nacional (PAN), is the best equipped to overcome these handicaps. Established in 1939, PAN has worked diligently to develop a nationwide, mass following and a strong network of militants capable of closely monitoring the electoral process and defending its vote. In its regional strongholds — the northern border states, Jalisco and Guanajuato states, the Mexico City metropolitan area (Estado de México and Federal District), and the Yucatán — it is able to roll up convincing majorities in major cities, even with extensive fraud by the PRI. PAN is widely believed to have won or come very close to winning the gubernatorial elections in the states of Sonora in 1985 and Chihuahua in 1986. Its overwhelming, officially recognized gubernatorial victory in Baja California Norte in 1989 demonstrated that in at least some parts of the country, PAN is sufficiently popular and well organized to break PRI control over state governments. In these places, PAN has managed to create a de facto two-party system. Its candidates for the federal Congress have been increasingly successful, taking 101 out of the 240 seats in the Chamber of Deputies that went to opposition party representatives in the 1988 elections — the largest number of seats ever won by a single opposition party.

PAN was formed largely in reaction to the leftward drift of public policy under President Lázaro Cárdenas. Its founders included prominent Catholic intellectuals who espoused a Christian Democratic ideology, and the party has maintained its opposition to the anticlerical provisions of the 1917 constitution, especially the government's monopoly over public education. In some parts of the country, Catholic priests have sided openly with PAN, while criticizing electoral fraud committed by the ruling party. PAN's principal constituency is the urban middle class, but it has also attracted votes among socially conservative peasants and the urban working class.

While clearly the leader among Mexico's opposition parties in terms of organizational strength and ideological coherence, PAN is a party with several major weaknesses. Since the mid-1970s it has been divided into moderate-progressive and militant-conservative ("neo-PANista") factions, which have jockeyed for control of the party machinery and carried out purges of opposing faction members when they were in power. PAN has few leaders of national stature, and it has had difficulty defining a national project or set of policies that constitutes a clear alternative to the government's programs. This problem has been compounded by the rightward shift in government policies since 1982. Under de la Madrid and Salinas, PAN has seen many of its banners (free market-oriented economic policies, privatization of state-owned enterprises, closer ties with the United States, improved church – state relations) stolen by the government.

In recent years, the divisions within PAN have been widened by the willingness of the currently dominant (moderate) party leadership to make tactical alliances with the Salinas government in order to pass constitutional amendments on such issues as electoral law reform and reprivatization of the banks, in exchange for assurances of cleaner elections. The persistence of PRI fraud in PAN strongholds has denied the party many of its expected victories and made PAN's national leaders vulnerable to challenges from within their own party. Elections since 1988 have shown that PAN is holding onto its traditional constituency (now about 17 – 18 percent of the electorate) but not expanding it appreciably. In the 1988 presidential election, the neo-Cardenista movement cut deeply into PAN's usual antigovernment protest vote, especially among the urban poor.

Empirical research on PAN supporters has shown that the party has a well-scrubbed, relatively privileged clientele that wants to see the middle class recover from the ravages of the economic crisis of the 1980s, but is not much concerned about absolute poverty, social inequality, or even broader participatory democracy. By proportions ranging from 25 to 37 percent, PANistas interviewed in one study conducted in a middle-class neighborhood of Mexico City believed that illiterates, leftists, Indians, and the unemployed do not have the same rights as other citizens, because they are not sufficiently prepared for democracy.[57] It will be difficult for PAN to convince the masses that it is on their side until it begins to address the country's social problems much more aggressively and convincingly than it did in the 1988 election.

That election proved to be a dramatic turning point in the fortunes of the leftist opposition in Mexico. Before 1988, the Mexican left had spawned political parties like the Partido Popular Socialista (PPS), which for decades served as a home for moderate socialists and other left-of-center politicians willing to collaborate with the government and even to endorse the PRI's presidential candidates, in exchange for a seat in Congress. The more independent left — that is, those who did not collaborate openly with the ruling party — was traditionally represented by the Partido Comunista Mexicano (PCM). The Communists were allowed to compete legally in elections during the presidency of Lázaro Cárdenas, but their party was subsequently outlawed and did not regain its legal registration until 1979, when its

congressional candidates won 5 percent of the vote. During most of the 1980s, even in the face of Mexico's gravest economic crisis since the 1910 revolution, and despite a series of party mergers intended to reduce the fractionalization of the leftist vote, the parties to the left of the PRI lost ground electorally. They were hampered by constant internal squabbling (motivated by personalistic rivalries as well as ideological cleavages), an inability to do effective grass-roots organizing, and an identification with discredited statist policies, now blamed for Mexico's economic debacle.

The key to the left's rejuvenation in 1988 was a split within the PRI leadership — the most serious since the early 1950s. In August 1986 a number of nationally prominent PRI figures, all members of the party's center – left wing, formed a dissident movement within the PRI known as the Corriente Democrática (CD). They were led by Porfirio Múñoz – Ledo (former head of the PRI, runner-up candidate for the party's presidential nomination in 1976, former secretary of labor and secretary of education), and Cuauhtémoc Cárdenas, who was just finishing his term as governor of the state of Michoacán. The CD criticized the de la Madrid administration's economic restructuring program and sought a renewed commitment by the PRI to traditional principles of economic nationalism and social justice. Most urgently, CD adherents called for a thoroughgoing democratization of the PRI, beginning with the elimination of the *dedazo* (unilateral selection by the outgoing president) as the mechanism for determining the party's presidential candidates. The CD's proposals were widely interpreted as a last-ditch attempt by the PRI's traditional *políticos* to recover leadership of the party by influencing the outcome of the 1987 – 1988 presidential succession. The CD's demands for reform were resoundingly rejected by the PRI hierarchy, and they formally split from the party in October 1987.

Confronted with defeat within the PRI, Cuauhtémoc Cárdenas accepted the presidential nomination of the Partido Auténtico de la Revolución Mexicana (PARM), a conservative, nationalist party established by another group of dissident PRIstas in 1954. Later, four other parties — all to the left of PRI and including the remnants of the old Mexican Communist party — joined PARM to form a coalition, the Frente Democrático Nacional (FDN), to contest the 1988 presidential election, with Cárdenas as their candidate. In its decision to join the neo-Cardenista coalition, and subsequently to become part of the new political party established by Cárdenas after the 1988 election, Mexico's independent left subordinated ideology to pragmatic considerations. Cuauhtémoc Cárdenas is not a socialist but rather a European-style social democrat. Before joining this coalition, the leftist parties had been attracting only insignificant support in public opinion polls, and some were in danger of losing their legal registration. As members of a center – left coalition led by a political figure with broad popular appeal, they stood to gain a great deal.

The neo-Cardenista movement posed a much stronger challenge to the PRI than any defection from that party since 1940.[58] It was particularly threatening because Cárdenas had considerable appeal to rank-and-file labor union members and campesinos — two of the PRI's traditional mass constituencies, which had benefited greatly from the social reforms implemented by President Lázaro Cárdenas. Moreover, many of the PRI's lower echelon militants also sympathized with the nationalist-populist policies advocated by Cárdenas and his movement. There is even evidence that in the 1988 election old-guard PRI leaders in some regions worked to turn out the vote for Cárdenas, as a protest against the reign of technocrats like Salinas.

Following the 1988 presidential election, the left's deeply ingrained tradition of internal factionalism reasserted itself. Cárdenas invited his FDN coalition partners to merge themselves into a new political party, the Partido de la Revolución Democrática (PRD), but several of them chose not to join. The former coalition partners do not necessarily vote together in the Congress. And serious divisions have emerged within the PRD's top leadership over such issues as the degree of democracy in internal party governance and strategies for dealing with the government (dialogue versus permanent confrontation).

The PRD continues to take policy positions to the left of the ruling party on some issues (e.g., arguing for a moratorium or a cap on external debt service, and a go-slow approach to economic integration with the United States); but the PRD has had difficulty developing a general program that clearly differentiates it from its competitors. The PRD shares with the PRI and PAN an emphasis on improving social conditions through economic growth, as opposed to redistribution of wealth; and its differences with most of the incumbent government's policies are matters of degree and pacing rather than substance.[59]

Like PAN, PRD is much stronger in some regions than in others. Its strongholds are the states of Michoacán, Guerrero, Oaxaca, and the Mexico City metropolitan area. The PRD has retained the urban voters who supported the parties of the independent left, but as noted above it has also begun to take votes from the PRI in rural areas. It has begun to develop ties with the new popular movements that have emerged outside of the PRI-affiliated corporatist structures. The PRD's greatest challenge is to develop a well-institutionalized party structure, one that is not dependent on the personal charisma of Cuauhtémoc Cárdenas to mobilize PRD supporters and is strong enough to defend the PRD vote against PRI-government tactics of fraud and intimidation. State and local elections held since 1988 have shown that when Cárdenas himself is not on the ballot, support for the PRD falls off dramatically.[60] Under Salinas, the government has shown a greater willingness to recognize electoral victories of the PAN than those claimed by the PRD, except in Cárdenas's home state of Michoacán.

Barring a complete opening of the Mexican political system to permit unfettered competition between the PRI and its opposition, the strategic options available to the opposition parties appear limited to three. First, by protesting electoral fraud through mass demonstrations, civil disobedience, and appeals to international public opinion, each opposition party can raise incrementally the cost of fraud to the regime in terms of internal legitimacy and foreign investor confidence, while continuing to run candidates and negotiate election results with the government. Second, the opposition parties could attempt to form a national front to insist on clean elections and accelerated democratization. The PRD has already called for a National Accord for Democracy embracing all opposition parties and dissident groups within the PRI, to defend the vote in future national elections. Such a national front could not, however, run its own candidates, as the Cardenista coalition did in 1988; the revised electoral law enacted in 1989 – 1990 effectively prevents "fusion" candidacies. Finally, the opposition parties could adopt an abstentionist stance, refusing to participate in the PRI-dominated electoral process and devoting themselves to other forms of confrontation and resistance, public education, and support for social movements. The fact that the opposition parties have such a limited and less than attractive set of options is further evidence that Mexico's transition to a well-institutionalized, competitive, multiparty system is far from complete.

Political Reform Measures

Many times during the last four decades, segments of the Mexican political elite, including most incoming presidents, have called for reforms of the system of parties and elections.[61] Some reform projects have focused on the ruling party, especially the need to democratize its internal procedures of governance and candidate selection. Others have concentrated on the relationship between the PRI and the opposition parties, prescribing changes in electoral rules that would expand opportunities for the opposition. The two types of political reform are, of course, interrelated. Reforming the PRI is generally believed to be a necessary, though not sufficient, condition for broader political liberalization in Mexico.

The stimuli for political reform attempts have varied over time. Shocks to the system — the nationwide teachers' and railroad workers' strikes of 1958, the student protest movement and massacre of 1968, and the economic crises of 1975–1976 and 1982–1988 — have prompted efforts by political elites to create new safety valves for opposition activity and accumulated social tensions. Beginning in the mid-1970s, political reform projects were also fueled by the relentless climb of voter abstentionism and the continuing decline in voter support for the PRI. To some concerned members of the political elite, these indicators of rising political alienation and cynicism suggested that the electoral mechanism itself was being exhausted, as a vehicle for legitimating the regime and convincing private investors of its basic stability.

Since 1963 there have been five major revisions of the federal election laws. The thrust of these changes has been to bolster the PRI by giving it a more credible opposition to run against. A limited form of proportional representation was introduced to increase opposition party representation in the federal Congress, and the formation of new political parties was encouraged. The 1977 electoral law reforms made it possible for a party to qualify for legal registration by polling only 1.5 percent of the votes cast in a nationwide election or by enrolling at least 65,000 members. The 1989–1990 electoral code revisions ostensibly were aimed at reducing the PRI's advantages over the opposition parties, particularly by making it more difficult for PRI and government officials to commit electoral fraud. New, nationwide electoral rolls have been compiled, requiring the re-registration of more than 40 million eligible voters; new voting credentials bearing the holder's photograph are being issued to all voters; and the PRI will no longer

have majority control over the entity responsible for certifying final election results.

These changes, if fully and impartially implemented, would eliminate some, but not all, of the mechanisms traditionally used by the PRI–government apparatus to rig elections. However, the same revision of the electoral code included a "governability clause" that gives the party winning a plurality of votes, higher than 35 percent, in a national election an automatic majority in the Chamber of Deputies. This provision virtually guarantees continued control of Congress by the PRI and, through it, the president. The end result of these changes is likely to be a more competitive, multiparty system in which the PRI will be the dominant — but no longer hegemonic — party, with no significant diminution of presidential power.

Most attempts to reform the official party have taken the form of efforts to increase grass-roots participation in the PRI's candidate selection process (but mainly for municipal presidencies), and to dilute the power of the sectoral leaders — the old-guard party bosses who run the PRI-affiliated labor, campesino, and urban professional and slum-dweller (popular sector) organizations. Traditionally, the lists of PRI nominees for congressional seats and many other public offices have been the result of secret negotiations between the president and national level sectoral leaders. The candidate selections reflected the relative power of each of the three sectors within the ruling party.[62] Under new party statutes approved at the PRI's fourteenth national assembly in September 1990, citizens will be encouraged to affiliate with the PRI as individuals, without having to belong to one of the sectoral organizations. Moreover, in the future, relatively fewer of the PRI's candidates will be designated by the sectoral organizations. The party's territorially defined structures (local and state committees) will have a greater voice in candidate selection and other areas of decision making. The collapse of the PRI's "sectoral vote" in recent elections has given considerable impetus to these changes.[63]

While the new rules will reduce the discretionary power of PRI and government functionaries, there is no guarantee that they will translate into fundamentally different behavior in future elections. Previous reforms did nothing to insure respect for election results by PRI operatives, especially at the local and state levels. Ultimately, the holding of fair and clean elections still depends on the will of the president and other senior officials, as well as their ability to secure the cooperation of lower echelon PRI leaders. Would-be reformers within the PRI – government apparatus continue to encounter strong resistance from the so-called dinosaurs entrenched in the sectoral organizations and state and local PRI machines. These old-guard PRIista leaders have nothing to gain and a great deal to lose personally from a more rapid political opening with genuine contestation of elections at all levels. President Salinas has adopted a low-risk, gradualist approach to political reform, to prevent open ruptures within the PRI that might threaten the completion of his government's economic restructuring program.[64]

CAMPESINOS, ORGANIZED LABOR, AND THE MILITARY: PILLARS OF THE REGIME?

The Mexican state's relationships with three major sectors of society — *campesinos* (peasants), organized labor, and the military — have been central to the stability of the regime since the 1930s. Indeed, they are often referred to as pillars of the regime, in recognition of their crucial role in maintaining the political system. In this section we will sketch the basic terms of the relationships between Mexico's ruling elite and these three sectors, and identify some current sources of tension that might disrupt them.

State – Campesino Relations

From 1810 until 1929, the Mexican peasantry was among the most rebellious in Latin America, engaging in frequent armed uprising against both local and national elites.[65] After 1930, however, the rural poor became the largest support group of the Mexican government and of the official party. As a rule, this was the one segment of society that could always be counted on to vote for PRI candidates and to participate in electoral rallies and in public demonstrations supporting government policies. Perhaps more than any other segment of society, the low-income rural population believed in the ideals of the Mexican revolution and in the government's intention to realize those ideals.

The campesino sector includes three important subgroups: landless wage laborers (*jornaleros*), beneficiaries of land reform (*ejidatarios*), and owners of very small properties (*minifundistas*). Their support has been secured by two principal means: government policies which distribute vital resources (land, water, credit, fer-

tilizer, etc.) to the rural population, and mechanisms of political control in the countryside.

Traditionally, land has been the most important resource sought by campesinos, and land reform the most consistent government promise to them. Lázaro Cárdenas distributed more land more rapidly than any president before or since. In so doing, he secured campesino support for his policies in other areas, while extending the network of government-affiliated organizations whose members were actual or aspiring ejidatarios. The establishment of a nationwide confederation of campesino organizations, the Confederación Nacional Campesina (CNC), and its incorporation into the official party in 1938 institutionalized the relationship between the state and those campesinos who had received land under the agrarian reform program. (Other sectors of the campesino population — landless wage laborers and very small private landholders — were not included in the CNC.) Thenceforth, CNC officials would serve as intermediaries in most transactions between ejidatarios and the government ministries and banks that dispensed resources to the ejidos. The CNC has also been the organization through which the campesino sector endorses PRI candidates for public office and participates in electoral campaigns and other regime-supportive political activities.

The CNC's organizational dominance in the countryside has been contested increasingly by dissident groups. Three sets of grievances have fueled independent campesino organizations: unmet demands for land, especially in regions where large, undivided landholdings in excess of the legal size limit persist despite the existence of groups petitioning for land redistribution; complaints about low crop prices, limited access to markets, and inequitable distribution of agricultural inputs like water and credit by government agencies; and wage and employment problems affecting landless agricultural laborers. In addition, political grievances — usually rooted in the economic problems just mentioned — against caciques and municipal authorities have provoked campesino occupations of local government offices.

Despite the inroads made by autonomous movements since the late 1970s, most *organized* peasants in Mexico today are still members of CNC-affiliated organizations. However, the CNC's grip on the peasantry is increasingly tenuous, as demonstrated by the 1988 election. While Salinas's margin of victory came from the country's most rural electoral districts, analysis of the election results shows that the PRI had its greatest difficulties in those districts where the party's congressional candidate was affiliated with the CNC (as opposed to the labor or popular sector) *and* where the Cardenista front had a presence.[66] This suggests that when provided with an alternative to the PRI and the economic policies now associated with it, many campesinos will readily abandon their traditional allegiance to the official party.

The CNC's dilemma is partly of its own making. The CNC leadership has become increasingly divorced from the federation's social base. For many years, peasants have been manipulated, intimidated, and swindled by CNC leaders as well as by representatives of government agencies responsible for rural development programs.[67] Moreover, officials have often forged pernicious alliances with the *caciques* who control many ejido communities. These local bosses have amassed power and wealth by selling or renting ejido land to private farmers, with the acquiescence or active connivance of government officials. The CNC has become completely compromised by these transactions.

Rural support for the regime has also been undermined by major shifts in government policies affecting campesino interests. Each of Mexico's last three presidents has publicly declared that the land redistribution program, begun in 1917, has ended because allegedly there are no more large landholdings to be expropriated. The main function of the agrarian reform ministry has changed from processing peasants' petitions for land to granting certificates of "nonaffectability" to cattle ranchers and other private landowners whose holdings exceed the legal limits, thereby protecting them from expropriation.[68] Government policy in recent sexenios has emphasized the need to boost agricultural production by reorganizing the small ejido plots doled out through the agrarian reform program into larger, supposedly more efficient units of production—not to create additional small peasant producers.

The efficacy of clientelistic PRI controls over the peasantry also declined sharply during the economic crisis of the 1980s, as the government resources available for meeting the basic needs of landed campesinos contracted. Public spending on rural infrastructure, agricultural credit, and crop price supports declined drastically, even while other government policies were driving up the prices of fuel, fertilizer, and other necessary agricultural inputs. Government policy toward the rural sector now emphasizes linking "middle peasants" (farmers whose operations could become commercially viable with minimal government assistance—about 18 percent of all landholders) with domestic and international agribusinesses that can provide them with financing, technology, and marketing opportunities. For the subsistence farmers (80 percent of the total) who are too poor to meet that criterion, there are limited social welfare programs like PRONASOL. Clearly, the era of massive government subsidy programs aimed at small-scale peasant agriculture—programs initiated in the early 1970s and vastly expanded during the oil boom years of 1980–1982—has ended. Adjusting to these new realities, more and more residents of Mexico's rural communities are abandoning agricultural production altogether and turning to wage-labor (often in the United States) as their primary source of income.

Unless the CNC can expand the range of issues on which it can "deliver" beyond its traditional focus on land tenure, the PRI and the government may find their capacity for mobilization in the countryside permanently diminished. Despite its need to retain a "safe" rural electoral base, it is not at all clear what benefits a technocratic regime committed to fiscal discipline and letting market forces work will be able to offer the small farmer—much less Mexico's large population of landless rural workers—in the foreseeable future.

The State and Organized Labor

Since 1940, the Mexican government's control over organized labor has been essential to the strategy of economic development that the state has pursued. By tightly regulating the formation of new unions, wage increases, and strike activity, and even the resolution of individual worker grievances against employers, the government has been able to guarantee a disciplined and relatively cheap labor force, attractive to both foreign and domestic investors. Government control over labor strikes has been especially tight and has grown progressively tighter over time. During the 1938–1945 period, an average of 32 percent of all workers' petitions for strikes were authorized (recognized as legal strikes) by the federal government; only 2 percent of all strike petitions were approved during the 1963–1988 period. Between 1982 and 1988, despite high inflation and severe unemployment problems, the level of strike activity actually declined.[69]

Wage levels for most unionized workers are determined through behind-the-scenes negotiations between national level labor leaders and senior government officials—not between labor and management. The outcomes of these talks are ceilings on wage increases, which become negotiating guidelines for lower level union officials throughout the country. Since 1983, the Confederación de Trabajadores Mexicanos (CTM)—Mexico's largest and most politically influential labor organization—has been an active and essential partner in the government's economic stabilization program, settling for wage increases significantly below the rate of inflation. Since 1987, the CTM leadership has signed a series of economic solidarity pacts with the government and the business community which have kept wages under tight control, even while allowing many prices to rise. Unlike virtually all other labor federations in Latin America during the last ten years, the CTM has not opposed the government's policy of privatizing state-owned enterprises (often resulting in significant job losses) or other neoliberal policies intended to restructure the country's economy along free market lines.

The largely captive labor movement has also helped the government to maintain political control, by keeping lower class demand-making fragmented. From 1955 to about 1975, through a steady stream of government-orchestrated wage increases and expansions of nonwage benefits (subsidized food, clothing, housing, health care, transportation, etc.), the government created a privileged elite of unionized workers within the urban working class. These nonwage benefits served as a cushion during the economic crisis of the 1980s, partially insulating unionized workers from the ravages of high inflation and government austerity measures.

Of the three main sectors of the PRI, it has been the labor sector, dominated by the CTM and Fidel Velázquez, the undisputed leader of the government-affiliated labor movement since 1949, that has been the strongest and best organized for collective political action. Unionized workers could be mobilized quickly and on a national scale, for mass demonstrations to support government policies, campaign rallies, and voter registration drives. Organized labor's representatives—especially the members of the national teachers union—have also been very important to the PRI in mobilizing its vote in rural areas and small towns.

From the government's viewpoint, the high degree of continuity in CTM leadership has also been an important advantage. Although several of the eight presidents under whom Fidel Velázquez has served have had major policy disagreements with him, there is no question that his long reign and political dexterity have con-

tributed greatly to the stability of the Mexican political system. By the same reasoning, Velázquez's death (he was born in 1900) could release centrifugal forces within the labor movement that could complicate at least temporarily the government's relations with organized labor, since Velázquez's successor is unlikely to be as slavishly supportive of the regime and its policies as he has been. Over the past ten years, Velázquez has repeatedly backed down from threats to call a general strike, if the government failed to grant wage increases of the magnitude sought by the CTM. In every instance, organized labor has settled for less—usually much less.

Unable to secure significant concessions from the government on the wage front, the CTM has shifted its emphasis from wage increases to employment protection and safeguarding workers' purchasing power through the creation of union-owned retail stores, consumer cooperatives, and other social sector enterprises. Until 1991, the CTM also sought, and received, modest increases in political patronage. For example, the share of congressional seats allocated by the PRI leadership to the labor sector rose from 14 percent in 1976 to 22 percent in 1988. Although expanded political patronage is of limited benefit to rank-and-file union members, it has helped to maintain the support of the CTM leadership for government policies.

One paradox of organized labor is that, while professing to be the staunchest guardian of Mexico's revolutionary heritage, it has become the most conservative sector of the ruling coalition in recent years. The CTM hierarchy has advocated repression of most forms of political dissent and resisted any changes in the rules of electoral competition that would benefit opposition forces. The confederation's leaders apparently fear that the reformist impulse might spread beyond the electoral system to the *oficialista* labor movement itself, strengthening pressures for greater democracy within CTM-affiliated unions, which have been run like political machines.

Independent unionism gained a small foothold in the labor movement during the 1970s, mainly among university faculty and staff employees, and workers in the automobile, mining, electrical, telephone, and nuclear energy industries. Technological changes and deteriorating working conditions in these industries had created new worker grievances that were being ignored by established union organizations.[70] In 1979 a dissident movement emerged within the national teachers union, and by 1989 it had gained enough support to stage a nationwide strike by half a million teachers. This gave President Carlos Salinas a sufficient pretext to force the resignation of the union's long-entrenched president, Carlos Jonguitud Barrios.

Despite its sporadic triumphs, independent unionism has not progressed very far in Mexico. Widely detested union *caciques* like Jonguitud and Joaquín Hernández Galicia ("La Quina"), the head of the oil workers union also deposed by Salinas in 1989, have been replaced by leaders handpicked by the president who are less autocratic but more servile to presidential will than their predecessors. Independent unions have not won the ability to organize national level unions that could compete against the large, nationally organized, CTM-affiliated unions for the support of the working classes. Thus, the most militant independent union movements have remained localized and isolated. The government provides economic subsidies and political protection to its allies within the labor movement, while using its regulatory controls over union registration and strike activity to discipline potential opponents and create divisions within dissident movements.

As signalled by the 1988 elections, when millions of CTM-affiliated union members abandoned the PRI's candidates, organized labor's utility to the regime as an instrument of voter mobilization and political control will continue to decline. Recognizing this, the Salinas government sharply reduced the share of CTM-backed candidates among the PRI's nominees for congressional seats in the 1991–1994 term. However, as Mexico's economy is restructured and the nation's development strategy becomes increasingly dependent on export performance, the *oficialista* labor movement will become more important than ever as a pillar of support for the government's macroeconomic policies. Maintaining Mexico's comparative advantage in world markets (mainly owing to low wage scales), eliminating rigidities and inefficiencies that constrain productivity, privatizing or shutting down additional money-losing state-owned enterprises, preventing a resurgence of inflation — all will require continuing concessions from organized labor. In return, the ruling technocrats will continue to defer to the political preferences and sensibilities of *oficialista* labor leaders, including their fear of a more rapid transition to democracy.

The Military in Politics

By the end of the Cárdenas era, Mexico had a largely demilitarized political system: political activity by high-ranking military men had been confined to nonviolent competition and bargaining, within an institutionalized decision-making framework that was clearly dominated by civilian elites.

Beginning with Calles in the 1920s, Mexican presidents used three basic tools to achieve military disengagement from politics: frequent rotation of military zone commanders (to prevent them from building up large personal followings of troops and local politicians); generous material incentives for staying out of politics; and a policy of requiring military men who wanted to remain politically active to do so essentially as private individuals rather than as representatives of the military as an institution.

Since the 1940s the number of military men serving in high-level nonmilitary public offices has steadily declined. Up to 1964 it was traditional for the president to appoint a military man to serve in the post of PRI chairman; since then, that post has been held only by career politicians. Typically, the only Cabinet posts now held by active military officers are secretary of national defense and secretary of the navy.[71] State governorships held by career military officers dropped from 15 (out of 31) during the Alemán administration to one or two during the Echeverría, López Portillo, and de la Madrid sexenios, and none under Salinas. During the 1988–1991 congressional term, military officers held three of the sixty-four Senate seats and four of the five hundred seats in the Chamber of Deputies.

The most striking indicator of the military's decline as a political institution is its share of total government expenditures, which dropped from 17 percent in 1940, to 5–6 percent in the 1970s, to 1–3 percent in the 1980s. As a percentage of gross domestic product, Mexico's military expenditures averaged less than one percent during the 1960–1984 period — the lowest of any Latin American country, including Costa Rica, which has only a national police force. Spending on the military has increased moderately in recent years, partly in response to U.S. pressure on the Mexican government to step up its drug eradication and interdiction efforts. By 1990 Mexico had about 140,000 men under arms, over 25 percent of whom were engaged full-time in the antidrug campaign.[72]

While the Mexican military is relatively small and impoverished in terms of military hardware, successive governments have taken care to provide a steady flow of material benefits for military personnel. They have received regular salary increases (even during the worst years of economic crisis and government austerity budgets) and a variety of generous nonwage benefits (housing, medical care, loans, subsidized consumer goods) which added about 40 percent to base pay.

Despite the long-term decline in its influence on government policymaking, the Mexican military retains a capacity to influence important political events. Civilian presidents still call on the military for support in crisis situations. In recent sexenios such support has taken the form of armed repression of dissident groups (as in the 1968 massacre of student demonstrators in Mexico City, and the 1990 ejection of Cardenista militants from sixteen town halls in Michoacán State that they had occupied to protest electoral fraud); highly effective counterinsurgency campaigns against rural guerrillas during the 1960s and 1970s; the breaking of major, unauthorized labor strikes (such as a strike at Cananea, the country's largest mine, in 1989); and the arrest of major political figures accused of criminal offenses (e.g., "La Quina," head of the oil workers union). As the Echeverría and López Portillo sexenios drew to a close, amid fiscal chaos and erratic presidential behavior, rumors were widespread that the military would seize control of the government. In both cases, top-ranking military officers helped to bring an end to the rumor campaign and to guarantee a nonviolent transfer of power to a new civilian president by publicly reaffirming their loyalty to the nation's institutional order.

Since 1985, civilian authorities have called on the military to provide highly visible "security" for elections. Formerly, troops were deployed only in response to election-related disturbances if they occurred. Now, they can be seen before, during, and after the elections, particularly in states that are strongholds of the opposition parties. The opposition charges that the huge military presence in these places is intended to intimidate their supporters from going to the polls and from taking to the streets to protest fraudulent election practices. The routinized use of the military for such political control purposes could strain civil-military relations. "The military doesn't like to perform police functions," explained one general.[73]

Because the military is an important pillar of the regime, any decline in its previously strong support for civilian authorities could be destabilizing. Recognizing this, each new president has reaffirmed the longstanding policy of honoring the military effusively in public rhetoric, respecting its autonomy in promotions and other matters of internal governance, and maintaining the flow of material rewards to military personnel. Recent presidents have also supported a major upgrading of military education. By 1985 the military education system included a new National Defense College conferring a master's degree in national security and defense management, and twenty-two other schools that offered training in a wide range of professions and technical skills.

This expansion of educational opportunities has "increased the military's capacity to take on new political functions should Mexico suddenly experience a crisis of governability, or if civil-military relations deteriorated beyond a certain point."[74] Most observers, however, do not anticipate the reemergence of the military as an independent political actor, *unless* the country's civilian rulers fail completely to maintain law and order. An extremely widespread, totally uncontrolled mass mobilization — whatever its origins — might well provoke a military intervention, probably aimed at restoring order rather than installing a military government. It is the malfunctioning of civilian authority — rather than the military's own ambitions — that would be most likely to cause the military to assume an overt political role once again.[75]

POLITICAL CULTURE AND SOCIALIZATION

Most of what we know about Mexican political culture is based on research completed during the period of sustained economic growth and virtually unchallenged one-party rule in Mexico, from 1940 to the mid-1970s. There is now some sample survey-based research on mass political culture in the 1980s, but not yet enough to confidently document the changes in core values, attitudes, and behaviors that most observers assume have occurred during more than fifteen years of economic crises and government austerity.

The portrait of Mexican political culture that emerges from studies of previous decades can be summarized as follows:[76] Mexicans are highly supportive of the political institutions that evolved from the Mexican Revolution, and they endorse the democratic principles embodied in the constitution of 1917. However, they are critical of government performance, especially in creating jobs, reducing social and economic inequality, and delivering basic public services. Most government bureaucrats and politicians are viewed as distant, elitist, and self-serving, if not corrupt. Mexicans are deeply cynical about the electoral process and pessimistic about their ability to affect election outcomes. The average Mexican regards participation in electoral campaigns, attendance at rallies, voting, and affiliation with political parties as ritualistic activities. He or she believes that engaging in such activities may be necessary to extract benefits from the system, but they have little effect on the shape of public policy or the selection of public officials.

On the surface, this combination of attitudes and beliefs seems to be internally contradictory. How could Mexicans support a political system that they see as unresponsive or capricious at best? Historically, popular support for the Mexican political system has derived from three sources: the revolutionary origins of the regime, the government's role in promoting economic growth, and its performance in distributing concrete, material benefits to a substantial proportion of the Mexican population since the Cárdenas era. Each of these traditional sources of support has been undermined to some extent in the last decade.

The official interpretation of the 1910 revolution stresses symbols (or myths) such as social justice, democracy, the need for national unity, and the popular origins of the current regime. The government's identification with these symbols has been constantly reinforced by the mass media, public schools, and the mass organizations affiliated with the official party. Over the years, the party's electoral appeals were explicitly designed to link its candidates with agrarian reform and other revered ideals of the revolution, with national heroes like Emiliano Zapata and Lázaro Cárdenas, and with the national flag. (The PRI emblem conveniently has the same colors, in the same arrangement.) Beginning in 1987, the neo-Cardenista opposition mounted the first serious challenge to the PRI and government's claim to the revolutionary mantle.

Relatively few Mexicans have based their support for the system primarily on its revolutionary origins or symbolic outputs, however. For many sectors of the population, symbols were supplemented with particularistic material rewards: plots of land or titles to land that had been occupied illegally, schools, low-cost medical care, agricultural crop price supports, government-subsidized food and other consumer goods, and public sector jobs. For more than forty years, the personal receipt of some material "favor" from the official party – government apparatus, or the hope that such benefits might be received in the future, ensured fairly high levels of mass support for the system.

Despite their keen dissatisfaction with the government's recent economic performance, electoral corruption, and other irritations, the vast majority of Mexicans remain "system loyalists." Survey data collected during the 1980s demonstrated consistently the Mexican people's fundamental aversion to concepts of radical transformation, especially those promoted by the Marxist left.[77] A Gallup poll conducted in May 1988 showed that 61 percent of Mexicans thought that an opposition party victory at the national level would not enhance the country's economic prospects, and over half believed that an opposition victory would touch off social disorder.[78] In short, public opinion surveys in the late 1980s portrayed a citizenry still tethered to its traditional political moorings.

Nevertheless, Mexicans are increasingly willing to criticize the way in which the system often functions. Surveys show that Mexicans at all income levels are concerned about "bad government." Their assessments of politics, politicians, government bureaucrats, and the police are predominantly cynical and mistrustful.[79] Corruption is assumed to be pervasive, but historically most Mexicans tolerated it, within limits, as a price to be paid in order to extract benefits from the system.[80] Such tolerance may be declining, however. During the last ten years, corruption in the PRI – government apparatus has been one of the most successful campaign issues for the opposition parties, especially the PAN.

Mexicans increasingly blame their economic distress on failures of government performance. In previous decades, the government received much credit for stimulating and guiding the nation's economic development. The economic slowdowns, inflationary spirals, and currency devaluations of the 1970s and 1980s wiped out those positive perceptions. Particularly among middle-class Mexicans, many of whom saw their personal assets and living standards decline precipitously during the 1980s, loss of confidence in the government's ability to manage the economy was dramatic. Even among urban industrial workers, there is evidence of much dissatisfaction with the economic policies of recent Mexican administrations, and increasingly negative attitudes toward general features of the political system.[81]

The Mexican public's negativism toward the political process is reflected in attitudes toward political parties in general. A Gallup poll taken in July 1987 revealed that 38 percent of a national sample of Mexicans had no party preference. In another national survey, conducted in April 1990, nearly 51 percent of the respondents indicated that they did not support any political party.[82] These and other survey results suggest a sullen, cynical electorate, in which generalized "antiparty" attitudes are increasingly prevalent.

Moreover, all parties — including the PRI — have vague and confused images. As a result, Mexicans are more likely to identify with strong personalities like Cuauhtémoc Cárdenas and Carlos Salinas than with the political parties led by these figures. The lack of deeply rooted partisan attachments was demonstrated clearly in the 1988 election, when many of those who voted for the Cardenista front were found to be ex-PAN supporters who had originally been PRI voters! These floating protest voters were not ideologically committed to the left any more than they had been to the rightist opposition or the PRI in previous elections. Similarly, in the 1989 gubernatorial election in Baja California Norte, much of the support for victorious PANista candidate Ernesto Ruffo came from persons who had voted for Cuauhtémoc Cárdenas in the 1988 presidential election.

Mass Political Socialization

How do Mexicans form their attitudes toward the political system? In addition to the family, the schools and the Catholic Church are important sources of preadult political learning. All schools, including church-affiliated and lay private schools, must follow a government-approved curriculum and use the same set of free textbooks, written by the federal Ministry of Education. Although the private schools' compliance with the official curriculum is often nominal, control over the content of textbooks gives the government an instrument for socializing children to a formal set of political values. This learning supports the regime and stresses revolutionary symbols. Its impact is reflected in the beliefs of Mexican schoolchildren that their country has experienced a true social revolution; that, although this revolution is still incomplete, the government is working diligently to realize its goals; and that the president is an omnipotent authority figure, whose principal function is to "maintain order in the country."[83]

The Catholic Church is another key source of values that affect political behavior in Mexico. Private, church-run schools have proliferated in recent years, and along with secular private schools, they provide education for a large portion of children from middle- and upper class families. Religious schools and priests preach against socialism, criticize anticlerical laws and

policies, and promote individual initiative (as opposed to governmental action). They also stress the need for moral Christian behavior, which is seen as absent in the corrupt, self-serving, materialistic world of politics.

As adults, Mexicans learn about politics from their personal encounters with PRI and government functionaries and by participating in organizations, such as community improvement associations, that petition the government for collective benefits. Research shows that, in Mexico, attitudes such as political efficacy (a sense of competence to influence the political process), cynicism about politicians, and evaluations of government performance in delivering goods and services are strongly influenced by political learning that occurs after childhood and adolescence. The campesino who has been involved in years of inconclusive efforts to secure an all-weather road for his village is more likely to be aware of the inefficiency, corruption, and arbitrary interpretation of rules that characterize much of the Mexican public bureaucracy. Conversely, the resident of an urban squatter settlement who has participated in a well-organized movement that secured land titles for settlement residents is more likely to feel competent to influence government decisions, at least as part of an organized group.

Mexicans have been taught two sets of political values that increasingly seem to be in conflict.[84] On the one hand, mainly through the schools, they are formally taught a normative set of values about revolutionary institutions and objectives that identify the general public interest with the political system. On the other hand, adult experiences teach them how Mexican politics "really work." The PAN, and now the PRD, have sought to capitalize on the perceived gap between democratic-constitutional values and "real" politics. Support for the PRI has been declining among the better educated population. Education has increased criticism of the electoral system and reduced tolerance for human rights violations by the government and security forces. Higher levels of education are also associated with higher support for the right to dissent and other democratic liberties.[85]

Political Participation

Most political participation in Mexico has been of two broad types: ritualistic, regime-supportive activities (e.g., voting, attending campaign rallies), and petitioning or contacting of public officials to influence the allocation of some public good or service. Voting in national elections has been the most widespread form of participation. Until elections were strongly contested in the 1980s, Mexicans typically viewed them and electoral campaigns as purely symbolic events. They knew that they went to the polls not to select those who would govern but to ratify the choice of candidates made earlier by the PRI – government hierarchy. Some voted because they regarded it as their civic duty; others because they wished to avoid difficulty in future dealings with government agencies.[86] Some voted in response to pressures from local *caciques*, labor union representatives, or other agents of the regime. Despite these concerns, growing numbers of Mexicans have declined to participate in the ritual legitimation of the PRI's hold on public office. Even when elections became moments of genuine political confrontation in many parts of the country, the long-term trend toward lower voter participation persisted.

Mexicans participate in PRI campaign rallies and inaugurations of public works, primarily because participation in such government-sanctioned activities can have specific material payoffs. Many of the participants in these events are mobilized by local political leaders who "deliver" *acarreados* ("carted-in" participants), often using government-provided vehicles. The *acarreados* may receive chits redeemable for a free meal, tickets for a raffle, or simply free transportation to another town for the day. Others participate in such regime-supportive activities because they fear that failure to participate would have personal economic costs. Union members may be penalized a day's pay; some workers might even lose their jobs. Title to a plot of land or some keenly sought community benefit like a piped water system might be jeopardized.[87]

Such calculations link the two basic modes of citizen participation in Mexico. For most Mexicans, the reasons for engaging in nonelectoral forms of political activity are highly instrumental and particularistic: participants are usually bent on obtaining specific benefits from the government for themselves, their families, or their community or neighborhood. Participation strategies become ways of manipulating public agencies or officials more effectively on behalf of the individual or group of petitioners — or, increasingly, of protesting failure to benefit or be heard. Nonconfrontational styles of demand making have been the norm, because the government rarely rewards aggressive tactics.

The average Mexican harbors no illusions about the citizen's ability to influence the *content* of public policy or the ordering of government priorities. That kind of influence is exerted only by factions within the political-administrative elite itself and by the most powerful of the organized interest groups to which these factions respond (e.g., national and foreign entrepreneurs, organized labor, the military, and the church). Thus, the average citizen who seeks to influence public policy usually does so during the implementation stage, particularly at the local level. The goal is to obtain preferential application of specific policies or programs. The only governmental actions that can be influenced are low-level decisions on allocation of resources — who will get what under a specific policy.

GOVERNMENT PERFORMANCE

Economic Growth and Inequality

There is little debate about the importance of the state's contribution to the economic development of Mexico since 1940. Massive public investments in infrastructure (roads, dams, telecommunications, electrification) and generous, cheap credit provided to the private sector by Nacional Financiera and other government development banks made possible a higher rate of capital accumulation, stimulated higher levels of investment by domestic entrepreneurs and foreign corporations, and enabled Mexico to develop a diversified production capacity second only within Latin America to that of Brazil.

From 1940 until well into the 1970s, a strong elite consensus prevailed on the state's role in the economy. The state facilitated private capital accumulation and protected the capitalist system by limiting popular demands for consumption and redistribution of wealth; it established the rules for development; and it participated in the development process as the nation's largest single entrepreneur, employer, and source of investment capital. The state served as "rector" of this "mixed economy," setting broad priorities and channeling investment (both public and private) into strategic sectors. Acting through joint ventures between private firms and state-owned enterprises, the government provided resources for development projects so large that they would have been difficult or impossible to finance from internal (within-the-firm) sources or through borrowing from private banks.

From the mid-1960s to the mid-1970s, the result was the much-touted "Mexican miracle" of sustained

Much of Mexico's rural poverty has been transferred through migration to the capital, where more than one out of five Mexicans now live. This is one of the hundreds of squatter settlements in Mexico City inhabited mostly by migrants from the country's least developed areas. Most dwellings are made of laminated cardboard and other temporary materials. A dust storm swirls through the unpaved street at left. Electricity is pirated from lines in a more developed, adjacent neighborhood.

economic growth at annual rates of 6 to 7 percent, coupled with low inflation (5 percent per annum in the 1955–1972 period). By 1980 the gross national product had reached $2,130 per capita, placing Mexico toward the upper end of the World Bank's list of semi-industrialized or "middle-developed" countries. As proprietor of PEMEX, the state oil monopoly, the government was exclusively responsible for developing the crucial oil and natural gas sector of the economy, which by the end of the oil boom (1978–1981) was generating more than $15 billion a year in export revenues and fueling economic growth of more than 8 percent per year — one of the world's highest growth rates.

It is the *distributive* consequences of this impressive performance in economic development and, since the 1970s, the manner in which it was *financed* by the government, that have drawn most of the criticism. From Miguel Alemán (1946–1952) to the present, all but one or two of Mexico's presidents and their administrations reflected the private sector's contention that Mexico must first create wealth, and then worry about redistributing it; otherwise, the state would quickly be overwhelmed by popular demands that it could not satisfy. By the early 1970s, however, there was growing evidence that an excessively large portion of Mexico's population had been left behind in the drive for rapid industrialization.

This is not to say that some benefits of the development process did not trickle down to the poor. From 1950 to 1980, poverty in absolute terms declined. The middle class expanded to an estimated 29 percent of the population by 1970. From 1960 to 1980 illiteracy dropped from 35 to 15 percent of the population, infant mortality was reduced from 78 to 70 per 1,000 live births, and average life expectancy rose from fifty-five to sixty-four years. Clearly, the quality of life for many Mexicans — even in isolated rural areas — did improve during this period, although several other Latin American countries (Chile, Colombia, Costa Rica, Cuba, Ecuador, El Salvador, and Venezuela) achieved higher rates of improvement on indicators of social well-being than did Mexico during the same period.

There was, however, a dark side to Mexico's "economic miracle." From 1950 to the mid-1970s, ownership of land and capital (stocks, bonds, time deposits) became increasingly concentrated. Personal income inequality also increased, at a time when, given Mexico's level of development, the national income distribution should have been shifting toward greater equality. Indeed, Mexico appears to have had a higher overall concentration of income in the mid-1970s than it had in 1910, before the outbreak of the revolution.[88] By 1977 the poorest 70 percent of Mexican families received only 24 percent of all disposable income, while the richest 30 percent of families received 76 percent of income. A government survey indicates that the income distribution became slightly more equal between 1977 and 1984, but this may have been due to the extraordinarily large number of new jobs created during the oil boom years of 1978–1981, most of which were eliminated during the severe economic contraction of 1982–1988.[89]

Other social indicators mirrored the trends in income distribution. By 1975 nearly 60 percent of Mexico's people did not consume the minimum diet needed to prevent nutritional diseases. Only half of the children who started primary school finished it (barely 20 percent in the most impoverished rural areas). Among the dwellings included in the 1980 census, nearly half had no sewage connections, 29 percent had no piped water, and 25 percent no electricity. In Mexico City, 42 percent of the population was found to be living in squatter settlements.

On every indicator of economic opportunity and social well-being, there were also vast disparities among Mexico's regions and between rural and urban areas. Unemployment and underemployment were concentrated overwhelmingly in the rural population, and the rate of infant mortality in rural areas was nearly 50 percent higher than the national average. The central urban core (the Mexico City metropolitan area) had a per capita income that was double the national average, while the country's poorest, predominantly rural regions — containing nearly half the national population — had a smaller per capita income in 1970 than the central core region had in 1900.

The policies and investment preferences of Mexico's postrevolutionary governments contributed much to this pattern of inegalitarian development. At minimum, the public policies pursued since 1940 failed to counteract the wealth-concentrating effects of private market forces. Evidence is strong that some government investments and policies actually reinforced these effects. For example, during most of the post-1940 period, government tax and credit policies have worked primarily to the advantage of the country's large-scale agribusiness and industrial entrepreneurs. Government expenditures for social security, public health, and education remained relatively low by international standards. By the late 1970s Mexico was still allocating a smaller share of its central government budget to social services than countries like Bolivia, Brazil, Chile, and Panama. The slowness with which basic social services

were extended to the bulk of the population in Mexico was a direct consequence of the government's policy of keeping inflation low by concentrating public expenditures on subsidies and infrastructure for private industry, rather than on social programs.

Even during the period 1970–1982, when populist policies were allegedly in vogue and government revenues were expanding rapidly because of the oil export boom, public spending for programs like health and social security remained roughly constant, in real per capita terms.[90] The economic crisis that erupted in 1982, after an unprecedented runup in Mexico's domestic and externally held debt, made it impossible to maintain even that level of government commitment to social well-being. By 1986 debt service was consuming well over half of the total federal government budget (see Figure 15.6), necessitating deep cuts in spending for health, education, consumer subsidies, and job-creating public investments. Social welfare expenditures per capita fell to 1974 levels.

The residue of the economic crisis and austere government budgets of the 1980s is an even more acute social crisis. Minimum real wages fell by 66 percent between 1980 and 1990. By 1987, according to the government's own statistics, more than half of Mexico's total population fell below the official poverty line, and more than 20 percent were living in what the government defines as "extreme poverty."[91] As the "lost decade" of the 1980s ended, some 10 million Mexicans were suffering from what the government calls critical nutritional deficiencies.

The current government's neoliberal economic development model stresses the need to give much freer rein to market forces in order to attract more private investment (especially foreign capital), which is needed to push up Mexico's rate of economic growth. Spending on social programs like PRONASOL has increased each year since 1989, but the government argues that a significant increase in economic growth is the only way to make a major dent in Mexico's massive social deficit. Critics charge that "leaving it to the market," through such policies as reducing or eliminating government price subsidies for basic consumer goods and shrinking the role of the state as an employer, can only worsen the social crisis. Moreover, Mexico's experience with rapid economic growth during the "miracle" years suggests that without strong, sustained government action to correct for market failures and reduce inequality, income concentration will continue unabated.

FIGURE 15.6
GOVERNMENT BUDGETS, 1979-1989

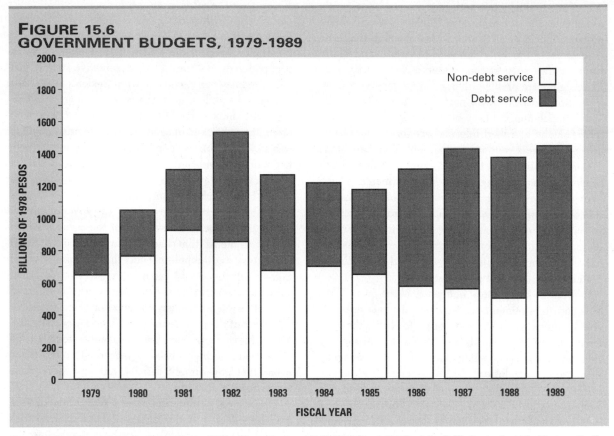

Source: Miguel Angel Centeno, *Mexico in the 1990s: Government and Opposition Speak Out* (La Jolla, Calif.: Center for U.S.–Mexican Studies, University of California–San Diego, Current Issue Briefs, No. 1, 1991), p. 12.

Population and Employment

The government can be credited with a major role in reducing Mexico's rate of population growth, which by the early 1970s was 3.5 percent per year—one of the world's highest growth rates. From the early nineteenth century through the 1930s, the Mexican population expanded at a relatively moderate rate. Around 1940 it began a sharp upward climb, as advances in public health reduced the mortality rate while the birth rate remained constant. The population grew from 20 million in 1940 to 35 million in 1960 to at least 81 million in 1990.[92] Entering office in 1970 with an endorsement of the traditional pronatalist policy of the Mexican government, President Luis Echeverría was convinced three years later by his advisers that the huge resources that would be needed to feed, educate, and provide productive employment for a population doubling in size every twenty years were beyond Mexico's possibilities.

A nationwide family planning program was launched in 1974, and within a few years the birth rate had begun to fall noticeably. By 1990 Mexico's population was growing at an estimated 1.9 to 2.1 percent per year.

Regardless of Mexico's recent success in limiting new births, the country's labor force is still growing by about 3.5 percent annually because of the high birth rates of the 1960s and early 1970s. This growth rate adds 1 million persons to the ranks of job seekers every year. Since nearly half of the nation's population is under the age of sixteen, the demand for new jobs will remain strong, well into the next century.

Unfortunately, the explosive growth of Mexico's labor force has coincided in recent years with a period of stagnation in job creation. By 1986 open unemployment had risen to an estimated 15.4 percent. The official unemployment rate fell below 6 percent in 1990, as the recovery from the economic crisis of the 1980s gained momentum; but both of these statistics greatly understate the magnitude of Mexico's employment problem. The government considers a person employed if he or she works only one hour per week, and World Bank studies suggest that underemployment is a far more significant problem than open unemployment, affecting perhaps 25 to 35 percent of the economically active population.[93] Many of these people have taken refuge in the so-called informal economy, working as unlicensed street vendors (up to 1 million of them in the Mexico City metropolitan area alone), washing windshields at busy intersections, sewing garments in their homes, and performing a wide variety of other tasks outside of the "formal" sector. This underground economy accounted for an estimated 28 to 35 percent of Mexico's gross domestic product in 1986.[94] Much of Mexico's underemployment is also being exported to the United States, through illegal immigration.

Perhaps the greatest deficiency of the post–1940 Mexican development strategy was the failure to develop an employment base adequate to absorb the labor force growth of the 1980s and 1990s. In the countryside, massive government investments in irrigation projects, "green revolution" technologies, infrastructure, and agricultural credit programs all benefited large producers far more than small farmers. This placed even greater capital resources in the hands of large landowners, who were able to mechanize their operations more rapidly. In agriculture as well as urban-based industry, government subsidies for acquisition of labor-saving machinery made it financially attractive for large-scale producers to substitute capital for labor.

An estimated 1.5 million jobs would have to be created annually until the year 2000 in order to absorb currently unemployed or severely underemployed Mexicans (the "backlog"), and to provide employment opportunities for the new entrants into the labor force.[95] Job creation on that scale would require the Mexican economy to grow extremely fast (at least 7 to 8 percent per annum, in real terms), risking hyperinflation. Moreover, businesses would have to be compelled to use much more labor-intensive technologies, at a time when they are under considerable pressure from the government and the marketplace to become highly efficient, globally competitive exporters. In short, coming fully to grips with Mexico's employment problem at this time would conflict with some of the key elements of the economic stabilization and restructuring project to which the government is committed.

Financing Development and Controlling Inflation

From 1940 to 1970 Mexico's public sector acquired an international reputation for sound, conservative monetary and fiscal policies. This conservative style of economic management, coupled with Mexico's long record of political stability, gave the country an attractive investment climate. By 1982 this image had been shattered; the public sector (and much of the private sector) was suffering from a deep liquidity crisis, and inflation had reached levels unheard of since the first decade of the Mexican Revolution, when paper currencies lost most of their value. What happened?

The basic difficulty was that the government had attempted to spend its way out of the social and economic problems that had accumulated since 1940, without paying the political cost that sweeping redistributive policies would have entailed. Instead, it attempted to expand the entire economic pie by enlarging the state's role as banker, entrepreneur, and employer. Throughout the period since 1940, and especially after 1970, Mexico's public sector expanded steadily while its revenue-raising capability lagged. The result was ever-larger government deficits, financed increasingly by borrowing abroad.

For most of the post–World War II period, Mexico's tax effort—its rate of taxation and its actual performance in collecting taxes—was among the lowest in the world. Officials feared that any major alteration in the tax structure would stampede domestic and foreign capital out of the country. Two modest attempts at tax reform, in 1964 and 1972, failed because of determined opposition from business elites. When the private sector refused to accede to higher taxes, the Echeverría administration opted for large-scale deficit financing, external indebtedness, and a huge increase in the money supply. The public sector itself was vastly enlarged, increasing the number of state-owned enterprises from 84 in 1970 to 845 in 1976. Fiscal restraint was finally forced on the government by depletion of its currency reserves in 1976.

Echeverría's successor, José López Portillo, at first attempted to reverse the trend toward larger government deficits, but the effort was abandoned when the treasury began to swell with oil export revenues. Again, the temptation was to address basic structural problems by further expanding the state sector, and López Portillo found it impossible to resist. Oil revenues seemed to be a guaranteed, limitless source of income for the government. Mexico borrowed heavily abroad, anticipating a steady rise in oil prices.

Although Mexico's long-term foreign debt (owed by both the government and private Mexican firms) had grown substantially during the Echeverría sexenio (from $12.1 billion in 1970 to $30.5 billion in 1976), the most rapid expansion occurred during López Portillo's oil boom administration. By the end of 1982 Mexico's external debt totaled nearly $82 billion, with annual interest payments of $16 billion (compared with $475 million paid to service the debt in 1970). In August 1982 the government was forced to suspend repayment of principal and begin a difficult renegotiation of the size and terms of the debt with Mexico's foreign creditors — the first of several such "restructurings," the most recent of which was completed in 1990. By the end of that year, Mexico had reduced its total long-term external debt to about $93 billion, but annual interest payments still totaled nearly $11 billion — considerably more than Mexico earns from its oil exports in an average year.

Deficit financing, especially in the context of the overheated economy of the oil boom years, also touched off a burst of inflation. The average annual inflation rate rose from 15 percent during Echeverría's presidency (nearly triple the average rate during the 1940–1970 period), to 36 percent under López Portillo and 91 percent in the de la Madrid sexenio (159 percent in 1987). Both the de la Madrid and Salinas administrations made reducing the inflation rate their top economic priority, but Salinas has been much more successful in bringing inflation under control than his predecessor. His principal instrument was price and wage controls, enforced by a formal, government – business – organized labor pact that has been renewed, with some adjustments, at twelve- to eighteen-month intervals. This form of shock therapy for inflation has proven more successful in Mexico than in any other country where it has been applied, bringing the inflation rate down to the 20–30 percent range in 1989–1990. The key to a successful economic stabilization program has been deep cuts in government spending coupled with unprecedented steps to boost revenues, including vigorous enforcement of the tax laws and the selling of hundreds of state-owned enterprises to private investors. Of the 1,171 state enterprises existing in 1982, only 344 had not been privatized, or liquidated, or were in process of divestment by the end of 1990. The Salinas administration has justified its policy of shrinking the public sector by arguing

that it is necessary to free up scarce resources, allowing the government to concentrate on meeting pressing social needs.[96]

MEXICO'S POLITICAL FUTURE: TRANSITION TO WHAT?

The progressive breakdown of the one-party hegemonic political system in Mexico raises the question of what will replace it. Below we sketch four possible scenarios for Mexico's future political evolution, taking into account the already observable changes, the political system's historic propensity for adaptation to changing realities in its environment, and the array of international constraints now weighing so heavily on political decision makers in Mexico.

Immobilism

In this scenario, Mexico's ruling elite will prove unable to adapt constructively to the country's new political environment. Responses to widespread demands for democratization will be too slow, too tentative, and too narrowly constrained by the state to satisfy the groups now pressing for a political opening. Democratization from above, even if pushed strongly by a reform-minded president, is no longer a realistic possibility. Either the "dinosaurs" will triumph in the struggle for control of the PRI, or the party will be irrevocably split, with the old-style corporatists and the modernizing technocrats going their own separate ways, taking whatever supporters they can muster. Less and less encumbered by presidential authority, intra-elite conflict may produce a series of political impasses to which the regime may be unable to respond effectively.

With increased fragmentation of the ruling elite, little could be done to halt further atrophy of the PRI and its sectoral organizations. The sectoral leaders' weakness will make them even more defensive and resistant to reform. Rather than a Spanish-style, relatively smooth, low-conflict transition to democracy guided from above, Mexico will be condemned to a Polish-style transition, in which each change is the result of an open and prolonged confrontation with the opposition, which ends with the regime making concessions.

The deep and difficult-to-repair cleavages within Mexico's ruling elite over political reform alone could be sufficient to induce immobilism. The probability of such a scenario would be greatly increased, however, if the economic recovery stalls (perhaps due to a prolonged, worldwide recession) or if the stabilization pact breaks down, initiating a new inflationary spiral. Without vigorous, sustained economic growth, the government could not meet its social objectives; absolute poverty, malnutrition, unemployment, and inequality in wealth distribution would continue to increase. Renewed economic grievances would provoke an upsurge in anti-PRI protest voting in future elections, further stiffening the resolve of the regime's "dinosaurs" to block any further changes in the rules of electoral competition that could benefit the opposition.

The opposition forces presently arrayed against the incumbent regime themselves appear to suffer a degree of immobilism in developing their own economic and political projects, beyond simple protest of PRI fraud and criticism of government policies. On the right, the construction of an alternative "legitimacy" is complicated by the coincidence of many policy views and interests between the PANistas and the governing technocrats. On the left, both the most prominent national leaders and many of their supporters are none other than "the authentic children of the PRI."[97] The ruling technocrats' economic restructuring project may fail to produce the promised social benefits; but building a broad societal consensus around an alternative model — based on realistic assumptions about Mexico's options at home and abroad — could prove very difficult for the leftist opposition.

Among both leftist and rightist opponents of the regime, the challenges of portraying themselves as a credible alternative and defending their vote against PRI–government fraud will be complicated by infighting. A highly fractious and disorganized opposition will not be able to exert the strong pressure on PRI and government hard-liners that would be needed to move the authoritarian system more rapidly toward democracy. Even though the PRI will continue to deteriorate, no opposition party will have the capacity to replace it in power, at least at the national level.

Immobilism in politics and public policymaking — the kind of political stalemate or "politics of social draw" that have regularly beset countries like Argentina and Italy[98] — could not be sustained indefinitely in contemporary Mexico. The accumulation of unresolved social problems during the 1970s and 1980s has been too great. The organized opposition to the regime is now too strong, and the recent changes in political consciousness among even unorganized segments of the Mexican population are irreversible — even if that consciousness

now manifests itself in nonvoting. The current inability of opposition forces to clearly articulate and advance counter-claims may provide breathing space for the PRI–government apparatus; but this advantage is likely to be fleeting. In short, the immobilism scenario would be a prescription for chronic crisis and a gradual unraveling of the coalition that has governed Mexico since the 1930s.

Political Closure

In this scenario, pressures for hardening of the regime will mount during Salinas's term, forcing him to abandon all attempts at political reform, in the interest of assuring a minimum level of elite cohesion and/or maintaining social order. Political retrenchment could result from a failure of the neoliberal economic model favored by Salinas and the technocrats in his Cabinet to produce a strong economic recovery. Thus, the government would have to rely increasingly on authoritarian means to impose its policies amid a continuing decline in living standards and job opportunities. Some see political hardening as a requirement of a *successful* neoliberal economic project, because of its high social costs. Reflecting on the implementation of this model in Chile during the 1970s, they predict the "Chileanization" of Mexico — a shift toward a significantly more authoritarian style of governance, with less respect for individual liberties and a rising level of government coercion. Unlike the Chilean case, there would be no overt interruption of constitutional processes, but rather a creeping, rightist *coup d'etat* within the regime itself, as the Soviet Union now appears to be undergoing.

Recourse to coercion would be even more likely in the event that opposition parties try to provoke social turmoil. Besieged political authorities, increasingly overwhelmed by events that seem to be spinning out of their control, may respond with mass repression. Even in less dramatic circumstances, old-guard PRI leaders and government bureaucrats who feel threatened by the emergence of new popular movements and organizations outside of existing corporatist structures may press for a "closing down" response. Since the PRI seems to have lost the capacity to incorporate such movements, there may be a strong temptation to simply repress them rather than try to build strategic alliances with them.

Increasing repression would be very costly for the regime's legitimacy, however, both at home and abroad. Indiscriminate use of coercion would divide the ruling political elite even more deeply than neoliberal economic policies have done. The country would become increasingly ungovernable, with the proliferation of bitter, unmediated conflicts. Foreign investment would be frightened away by the prospect of destabilization, and domestic capital would again flee the country. The loss of private sector confidence would effectively prevent the modernizing technocrats from carrying through their economic restructuring project. Moreover, it would be very difficult for the United States to live with a much more authoritarian regime in Mexico, thereby impeding major initiatives like a North American free trade agreement, which is central to the Mexican government's new export-oriented development strategy. For all these reasons, it seems likely that any hardening of the regime would stop well short of overt repression. Both the economic and political costs of a harsh, authoritarian closure would be prohibitively high.

Modernization of Authoritarianism with Selective Populism

The principal response by Mexico's political elite to emergent pluralism may be an energetic revival and remodeling of the existing corporatist system, rebuilt on a new set of organizations and alliances. In this "modernization-of-authoritarianism" scenario, Salinas's project to rebuild the PRI along territorial lines and to energize its grass roots through democratization of the party's local candidate selection process would be successful — within its carefully defined limits. Given the relatively low probability of a permanent, unified opposition party of the left in Mexico, and the rightist opposition's limitations in expanding its current largely middle- and upper class social base, a modernized PRI would not confront a serious opposition threat to its control of the presidency or most state governorships. The result would be more acceptable PRI candidates (at least at the municipal level), perhaps more lively debate within the PRI over public policy issues, but no truly effective opposition outside of the ruling party. The government would also take steps to expand freedom of expression (e.g., by relaxing controls on the electronic media) and to curb human rights abuses by the police and *caciques*.

To make the PRI more competitive against the opposition, and thereby reduce the necessity to resort to blatant and disruptive electoral fraud, a modernization of authoritarianism could be combined with a policy of selective populism. Pockets of popular discontent could be bought off with limited material benefits channeled through programs like National Solidarity, which also help the regime to maintain its socially "progressive" credentials and preempt leftist opposition groups.

This kind of carefully modulated, incremental, elite-initiated political liberalization would not necessarily pave the way for genuine democratization. There is virtually no evidence to suggest that the majority of PRI leaders accept the idea that their party will cease to be the "party of the state," much less cease to be the governing party. They may endorse a political opening, but without real risk of losing power.

Limited Power-Sharing: The Indian Congress Party Model

Recognizing the importance and durability of subnational variations in support for the PRI and its opposition, realists in the PRI – government apparatus may seek to transform the political system along the lines of the post-independence Indian experience. Before they took power in 1988, some of Salinas's more reform-minded advisers sometimes cited the Indian Congress party model as an acceptable and even desirable outcome of Mexico's transition from a hegemonic one-party system.

Acceptance of the Indian model implies a willingness to surrender control of municipal and state governments *routinely* to the rightist or leftist opposition in their regional strongholds, in the interest of staying in power at the national level. Under such a system, elections at the state and local levels in most parts of the country would be considerably more competitive than they have been, even in recent years. The PRI would retain control of the presidency and the Congress (as long as it won at least 35 percent of the votes in national elections). However, with truly competitive elections being held in a larger number of states and localities, the PRI's future presidential candidates would probably be elected by a plurality rather than a majority of the vote, and the ruling party would be unlikely to win the two-thirds majority of seats in the Chamber of Deputies that is needed to amend the constitution.

A shift from PRI hegemony at all levels to a situation of continued PRI domination of national politics combined with real, multiparty competition at the local and state levels would insure that political institutions at those levels would be considerably more responsive to the citizenry than in the present system. The level of mass political participation would rise, and elections would function once again as an important social and political safety valve. Finally, the need to become competitive in state and local elections would serve as a spur for internal reform and rejuvenation of the PRI itself, without risking the party's continued control of the truly important positions in the system.

A move to adopt the Congress party model would provoke strong resistance from entrenched, subnational PRI bosses. Elections for state and municipal offices held since mid-1988 in several parts of the country — most notably Baja California Norte — have been marked by sharp, public disputes between the national PRI organization and the party's state and local leaders, who are committed not to sharing power but to avoiding defeat, at any cost. As Mexican political scientist Federico Estévez has observed, lower echelon PRI officials "no longer align themselves automatically with dictates from the center."[99] The conflict of interest between such leaders and the modernizing national political elite is one of the most fundamental obstacles to a political opening that assures both the PRI and its opposition a share of power.

After the momentous developments of 1987–1988, it was widely assumed that none of the principal actors in the Mexican political system could return to "business as usual." This conventional wisdom has been upset by Carlos Salinas's determination to complete the restructuring of the economy, at the expense of more rapid political liberalization. Salinas and his most probable successors know, however, that a serious opening of the political system cannot be postponed indefinitely and that the PRI must be prepared for a period of greater political competition. They want to avoid another situation like 1988, in which the PRI's hold on the presidency may be seriously threatened by a wave of protest voting and the charisma of an opposition candidate. But they are unwilling to tear the PRI apart in order to reform it.

The Mexican public and most professional analysts of Mexican politics remain skeptical that the PRI can be rebuilt to function as a real political party, able and willing to compete everywhere for power on relatively equal terms with the opposition. Central control of the far-flung PRI apparatus, of its "mass" organizations, and local caciques is weakening, and it remains to be seen whether Salinas or any future PRI president can succeed in imposing drastic political reform on a resistant base.

Strong external pressure will continue to be needed to keep the reformist impulse alive within the PRI – government apparatus. Thus, the outcome of the political transition that began to unfold so dramatically in 1988 still depends to a very large extent on what happens with the opposition, especially to the left of the PRI. To influence that outcome, opposition forces would have to consolidate themselves into coherent, well-institutionalized political parties with credible alternative policies.

It is also possible that Mexico's ruling elite, with its vaunted pragmatism and flexibility intact, can muddle through a middle ground, in which there is no return to pre-1988 hegemonic control by the PRI, but a generally weak party system; elections are more competitive but their results continue to lack credibility; the president must operate under new limits, but remains firmly in control of the ruling party and the Congress; there is no recourse to widespread repression, but persisting human rights abuses in certain parts of the country; and no real movement is made toward unfettered, Western-style democracy.[100]

KEY TERMS

cacique
camarilla
Cuauhtémoc Cárdenas
Cardenismo
Confederación de
    Trabajadores
    Mexicanos (CTM)

governability clause
municipio
National Solidarity
    Program
    (PRONASOL)
neoliberal economics
Partido de Acción

Nacional (PAN)
Partido de la Revolución
    Democrática (PRD)
Partido Revolucionario
    Institucional (PRI)
partron – client relations
political centralism

presidencialismo
Carlos Salinas de Gortari
sectoral organizations (of
    the PRI)
sexenio
técnico
Fidel Velázquez

END NOTES

1. If the 695,042 annulled ballots and 14,333 votes cast for nonregistered presidential candidates in the 1988 election are *excluded* from the percentage base, Salinas's share rises to a bare majority (50.74 percent). If these votes are *included* in the tally, Salinas becomes the first Mexican president elected only by a plurality of the total votes cast.

2. The actual extent of irregularities in the tabulation of the 1988 presidential election will never be determined. Within a few hours after the polls closed, a "computer crash" in the National Registry of Voters allegedly interrupted the count, and six days would pass before even preliminary results for a majority of the country's polling places were announced. The government blocked "exit" surveys of voters leaving polling places. In subsequent months, government officials denied access to a large portion of the sealed ballot boxes that had been used in the election. Nevertheless, the official tally for Salinas was within a few percentage points of his showing in several of the most scientific preelection polls (see Miguel Basáñez, "Las encuestas y los resultados oficiales," *Perfil de La Jornada*, August 8, 1988). Based on detailed analyses of the partial, publicly released election results, most analysts have concluded that Salinas probably did win, but that his margin of victory over Cárdenas was considerably smaller than the nineteen-point spread indicated by the official results.

3. This represents an undercount, since the census counts only Indians over the age of five. Indians constitute an estimated 15 percent of the total population.

4. See, for example, "Encuestalía: ¿Quién quiere un Papa?" *Nexos*, No. 148 (April 1990).

5. Alan Knight, "Revolutionary Project, Recalcitrant People: Mexico, 1910–1940," in Jaime E. Rodríguez, ed., *The Revolutionary Process in Mexico: Essays on Political and Social Change, 1880–1940* (Los Angeles: UCLA Latin American Center Publications, 1990), pp. 228–229.

6. Peter H. Smith, "The Making of the Mexican Constitution," in William O. Aydelotte, ed., *The History of Parliamentary Behavior* (Princeton, N.J.: Princeton University Press, 1977), p. 219.

7. Stephen Haber, *Industry and Underdevelopment: The Industrialization of Mexico, 1890–1940* (Stanford, Calif.: Stanford University Press, 1988).

8. Nora Hamilton, *The Limits of State Autonomy: Post-Revolutionary Mexico* (Princeton, N.J.: Princeton University Press, 1982), p. 281.

9. Alicia Hernández, *Cardenismo and the Mexican Political System* (Berkeley: University of California Press, 1992).

10. Gabriel Székely, "Dilemmas of Export Diversification in a Developing Economy: Mexican Oil in the 1980s," *World Development*, 17:11 (1989), pp. 1177–1197.

11. *The New York Times*, March 28, 1990.

12. See Lucian W. Pye, "Political Science and the Crisis of Authoritarianism," *American Political Science Review*, 84:1 (March 1990), pp. 3–19.

13. Guillermo O'Donnell, Philippe C. Schmitter, and Laurence Whitehead, eds., *Transitions from Authoritarian Rule* (Baltimore: Johns Hopkins University Press, 1986); Catherine M. Conaghan and Rosario Espinal, "Unlikely Transitions to Uncertain Regimes? — Democracy without Compromise in the Dominican Republic and Ecuador," *Journal of Latin American Studies*, 22:3 (October 1990), pp. 553–574; Peter H. Smith, "Crisis and Democracy in Latin America," *World Politics*, 43:4 (July 1991), pp. 608–634.

14. A particularly striking example of executive domination of the legislature occurred in 1990, when the majority bloc of PRI congressmen voted almost unanimously to reprivatize the country's banking system, which the PRI majority had voted to nationalize in 1982. On both occasions, the Congress was ratifying decisions already taken by the incumbent president.

15. See Richard R. Fagen and William S. Tuohy, *Politics and Privilege in a Mexican City* (Stanford: Stanford University Press, 1972), pp. 18–41.

16. See Paul W. Drake, "Mexican Regionalism Reconsidered," *Journal of Inter-American Affairs*, 12:3 (July 1970), pp. 411–420; and Edward J. Williams, "The Resurgent North and Contemporary Mexican Regionalism," *Mexican Studies*, 6:2 (Summer 1990), pp. 299–323.

17. Peter H. Smith, *Labyrinths of Power: Political Recruitment in Twentieth-Century Mexico* (Princeton, N.J.: Princeton University Press, 1979), p. 306.

18. See John J. Bailey, *Governing Mexico: The Statecraft of Crisis Management* (New York: St. Martin's Press, 1988), pp. 83–86; and Victoria Rodríguez, "The Politics of Decentralization in Mexico, 1970–1986," Ph.D. dissertation, University of California—Berkeley, 1987.

19. For a detailed discussion of the "metaconstitutional" powers of the Mexican president, see Luis Javier Garrido, "The Crisis of *Presidencialismo*," in Wayne A. Cornelius, Judith Gentleman, and Peter H. Smith, eds., *Mexico's Alternative Political Futures* (La Jolla, Calif.: Center for U.S.–Mexican Studies, University of California–San Diego, 1989), pp. 417–434.

20. Dismissing criticism of Televisa's numbingly one-sided, pro-PRI coverage of the 1988 presidential campaigns, the conglomerate's president publicly declared himself to be a PRIista and explained that "if Televisa does not cover the campaigns of the opposition politicians, it is because they are not saying anything new" (*Latin America Weekly Report*, February 11, 1988, p. 8).

21. They were the long-time leader of the petroleum workers union, Joaquín Hernández Galicia, alias "La Quina," who was forcibly removed from his house by army troops and imprisoned for illegal stockpiling of firearms; and Carlos Jonguitud Barrios, leader "for life" of the national teachers' union (Mexico's largest labor union), who "resigned after a private meeting with President Salinas," according to an official account (Presidencia de México, *Mexican Agenda: Background Information on Mexico*, April 1990, p. 7).

22. See Samuel S. Schmidt, *El deterioro del presidencialismo mexicano: los años de Luis Echeverría* (México, D.F.: EDAMEX, 1986); and Leopoldo Solís, *Economic Policy Reform in Mexico: A Case Study for Developing Countries* (New York: Pergamon, 1981), pp. 73–76. On the Monterrey business elite and its often contentious relationship with the central government, see Alex M. Saragoza, *The Monterrey Elite and the Mexican State, 1880–*

1940 (Austin: University of Texas Press, 1988).

23. The term "devalued" was used in late 1982 by José López Portillo to characterize his own presidency, which ended amid Mexico's gravest economic crisis since the Great Depression of the 1930s.

24. See Lorenzo Meyer, "Democratization of the PRI: Mission Impossible?" in Cornelius, Gentleman, and Smith, eds., *Mexico's Alternative Political Futures*, pp. 343–344.

25. For attempts to codify the informal rules of presidential succession in Mexico, see Smith, *Labyrinths of Power*, ch. 10; Peter H. Smith, "The 1988 Presidential Succession in Historical Perspective," in Cornelius, Gentleman, and Smith, eds., *Mexico's Alternative Political Futures*, ch. 17; and Luis Javier Garrido, "Las quince reglas de la sucesión presidencial," in Abrahám Nuncio, ed., *La sucesión presidencial en 1988* (México, D.F.: Grijalbo, 1988).

26. See, for example, Frank Brandenburg, *The Making of Modern Mexico* (Englewood Cliffs, N.J.: Prentice–Hall, 1964), pp. 145–150.

27. Meyer, "Democratization of the PRI," p. 343.

28. In the 1940s and 1950s, until the transfer of power from Ruiz Cortines to López Mateos in 1958, the presidential succession process was marked by considerably more open competition and debate within the ruling party.

29. Clientelistic relationships are by no means limited to the political system. For an analysis of the continuing importance of clientelism as a way of structuring interaction and control throughout Mexican society, see Luis Roniger, *Hierarchy and Trust in Modern Mexico and Brazil* (New York: Praeger, 1990).

30. In the case of Congress, the effects of the *camarilla* system are reinforced by the prohibition on immediate reelection introduced into the federal constitution in 1933. Members of the Chamber of Deputies and Senate must skip at least one term before they can run again for a congressional seat. Under this system, it is the president and his agents (senior PRI leaders) who decide where members of Congress will go after their terms expire—not their constituents. See Jeffrey A. Weldon, "No Reelection and the Mexican Congress," Ph.D. dissertation, University of California–San Diego, in progress.

31. Miguel Angel Centeno and Jeffery Weldon, "A Small Circle of Friends: Elite Survival in Mexico," paper presented at the International Congress of the Latin American Studies Association, Washington, D.C., April 1991.

32. Ibid. See also Roderic A. Camp, "Comparing Political Generations in Mexico: The Last One Hundred Years," paper presented at the VIII Conference of Mexican and North American Historians, San Diego, October 1990.

33. See Roderic A. Camp, "Camarillas in Mexican Politics: The Case of the Salinas Cabinet," *Mexican Studies*, 6:1 (Winter 1990), pp. 85–107.

34. Miguel Angel Centeno, "The New Científicos: Technocratic Politics in Mexico, 1970–1990," Ph.D. dissertation, Yale University, 1990. This analysis is based on a sample of 867 members of the federal government bureaucracy at the level of director-general or above.

35. See Peter S. Cleaves, *Professions and the State: The Mexican Case* (Tucson: University of Arizona Press, 1987), pp. 87–105.

36. Centeno, "The New Científicos."

37. Lorenzo Meyer, "Linajes políticos: las buenas familias," *Excelsior* (Mexico City), October 27, 1982. See also: Smith, *Labyrinths of Power*, pp. 307–310; Roderic Camp, "Family Relationships in Mexican Politics," *Journal of Politics*, 44 (August 1982), pp. 848–862.

38. Smith, *Labyrinths of Power*, pp. 213–215.

39. One study of a sample of prominent Mexican entrepreneurs from the 1920s through the mid-1980s found that 15 percent had held national political office, while only 10 percent of Cabinet-level public officials during the same period had had private sector career experiences at the managerial level (Roderic A. Camp, *Entrepreneurs and Politics in Twentieth Century Mexico*, New York: Oxford University Press, 1989, p. 82).

40. See Sylvia Maxfield, ed., *Government and Private Sector in Contemporary Mexico* (La Jolla, Calif.: Center for U.S.-Mexican Studies, University of California—San Diego, 1987); and Maxfield, *Governing Capital: International Finance and Mexican Politics* (Ithaca, N.Y.: Cornell University Press, 1990).

41. Smith, *Labyrinths of Power*, ch. 6.

42. On the widening generational gap within Mexico's political elite, see Peter H. Smith, "Leadership and Change: Intellectuals and Technocrats in Mexico," in Roderic A. Camp, ed., *Mexico's Political Stability: The Next Five Years* (Boulder, Colo.: Westview Press, 1986), pp. 101–117.

43. See Luis Felipe Bravo Mena, "COPARMEX and Mexican Politics," in Sylvia Maxfield and Ricardo Anzaldúa-Montoya, eds., *Government and Private Sector in Contemporary Mexico* (La Jolla, Calif.: Center for U.S.-Mexican Studies, University of California–San Diego, Monograph No. 20, 1987), pp. 89–104.

44. Evelyn P. Stevens, *Protest and Response in Mexico* (Cambridge, Mass.: MIT Press, 1974), p. 94.

45. See Joe Foweraker and Ann L. Craig, eds., *Popular Movements and Political Change in Mexico* (Boulder, Colo.: Lynne Rienner Publishers, 1990; and Neil Harvey, *The New Agrarian Movement in Mexico, 1979–1990* (London: Institute of Latin American Studies, Monograph No. 23, 1990).

46. See Wayne A. Cornelius, Judith Gentleman, and Peter H. Smith, "The Dynamics of Political Change in Mexico," in Cornelius, Gentleman, and Smith, eds., *Mexico's Alternative Political Futures* (La Jolla, Calif.: Center for U.S.-Mexican Studies, University of California—San Diego, 1989), pp. 28–30.

47. Lorenzo Meyer, "La democracia política: esperando a Godot," *Nexos*, No. 100 (April 1986), p. 42.

48. See Wayne A. Cornelius, "Nation-building, Participation, and Distribution: The Politics of Social Reform under Cárdenas," in Gabriel A. Almond, et al., *Crisis, Choice, and Change: Historical Studies of Political Development* (Boston: Little, Brown, 1973), pp. 392–498.

49. For examples, see Silvia Gómez-Tagle, "Democracia y poder en México: el significado de los fraudes electorales en 1979, 1982 y 1985," *Nueva Antropología*, 9:3 (1986): 127–157; and George Philip, "The Dominant Party System in Mexico," in Vicky Randall, ed., *Political Parties in the Third World* (Newbury Park, Calif.: Sage Publications, 1988), pp. 107–108.

50. Voter turnout in states and municipalities where

elections have been held since 1988 has been lower than in previous, subnational elections in the same states and localities. Of course, other factors have also contributed to lower turnout rates. For example, persistent, increasingly visible vote fraud undermines the credibility of the opposition parties' challenge and reinforces feelings of powerlessness and cynicism among the general public ("No matter who you vote for, the PRI always wins"). This makes it much more difficult for the opposition to get out its vote. Any explanation of the trend toward higher abstentionism must be speculative, however, since there has been virtually no systematic research on nonvoting in Mexico.

51. Miguel Basáñez, *El pulso de los sexenios: 20 años de crisis en México* (México, D.F.: Siglo Veintiuno, 1990), p. 276. In four subsequent national opinion surveys, conducted by Mexican and U.S. survey research organizations between June 1988 and June 1990, the proportion of respondents expressing a preference for the PRI ranged from 23 to 39 percent (data provided by Centro de Estudios de Opinión Pública, Mexico City).

52. Guadalupe Pacheco Méndez, "Estructura y resultados electorales," *Examen* (Consejo Ejecutivo Nacional, PRI), 2:15 (August 15, 1990), p. 20.

53. PEAC (Prospectiva Estratégica, A.C.), "Encuesta I: El país/Distrito Federal," *Perfil de La Jornada*, July 5, 1988.

54. Tonatiuh Guillén López, "Political Parties and Political Attitudes in Chihuahua," in Arturo Alvarado, ed., *Electoral Patterns and Perspectives in Mexico* (La Jolla, Calif.: Center for U.S.-Mexican Studies, University of California–San Diego, Monograph no. 22, 1987), pp. 225–245.

55. Juan Molinar Horcasitas, *El tiempo de la legitimidad: Elecciones, autoritarismo y democracia en México* (México, D.F.: Cal y Arena, 1991), p. 63.

56. Larissa A. Lomnitz, Claudio Lomnitz, and Ilya Adler, "El fondo de la forma: la campaña presidencial del PRI en 1988," *Nueva Antropología*, 11:38 (1990), p. 62.

57. María Luisa Tarrés, "La oposición política y la idea de democracia entre las clases medias en la coyuntura actual," in Soledad Loaeza and Claudio Stern, eds., *Las clases medias en la coyuntura actual* (México, D.F.: El Colegio de

México, Cuadernos del CES, No. 33, 1990), pp. 85–86.

58. The previous two breakaway movements ("Almazanismo" in 1940 and "Henriquismo" in 1952) won only 5.7 and 15.9 percent, respectively, of the presidential vote, according to official results.

59. Cuauhtémoc Cárdenas has summarized his party's differences with the Salinas government as follows: "The issue is not whether the economy should be modernized and opened up, nor whether many of the costlier programs of the Mexican welfare state should be made more cost-effective and efficient. . . . The real issue is at what speed, how deeply, and under what conditions these changes should be undertaken . . . [and] who should pay the unavoidable costs that a program of economic restructuring entails" (Cuauhtémoc Cárdenas, "Misunderstanding Mexico," *Foreign Policy*, Winter, 1989–1990, p. 115). See also Miguel Angel Centeno, *Mexico in the 1990s: Government and Opposition Speak Out* (La Jolla, Calif.: Center for U.S.-Mexican Studies, University of California–San Diego, Current Issue Briefs, No. 1, 1991).

60. For example, in the state of Mexico, which includes much of the Mexico City metropolitan area, the PRD's candidates for state and local office in the 1990 elections polled only one-fifth as many votes as presidential candidate Cuauhtémoc Cárdenas won in 1988.

61. For a more detailed review of these various political reform projects, dating back to the Miguel Alemán administration in 1946, see John J. Bailey, *Governing Mexico* (New York: St. Martin's Press, 1988), pp. 106–120. See also Wayne A. Cornelius, "Political Liberalization in an Authoritarian Regime: Mexico, 1976–1985," in Judith Gentleman, ed., *Mexican Politics in Transition* (Boulder, Colo.: Westview Press, 1988), pp. 15–39.

62. For example, in 1988, 18 percent of the PRI's nominations for congressional seats went to representatives of the party's campesino sector, 22 percent to the labor sector, and 60 percent to the "popular" sector. The campesino sector, which until 1964 had received half of the PRI's congressional nominations, has lost ground continuously to the labor and popular sectors.

63. See Wayne A. Cornelius, Judith Gentleman, and Peter H. Smith, eds., *Mexico's Alternative Political Futures* (La Jolla, Calif.: Center for U.S.-Mexican Studies, University of California— San Diego, 1989), pp. 26–36.

64. Salinas explained his position as follows: "When you are introducing such a strong economic reform, you must make sure that you build the [necessary] political consensus around it. If you are simultaneously introducing additional drastic political reform, you may end up with no reform at all. And we want to have reform, not a disintegrated country" (quoted in Nathan Gardels, "North American Free Trade: Mexico's Route to Upward Mobility," *New Perspectives Quarterly*, 8:1, Winter 1991, p. 8).

65. See Friedrich Katz, ed., *Riot, Rebellion, and Revolution: Rural Social Conflict in Mexico* (Princeton, N.J.: Princeton University Press, 1988).

66. Pacheco Méndez, "Estructura y resultados electorales," p. 20.

67. For examples, see Merilee S. Grindle, *Bureaucrats, Peasants, and Politicians in Mexico: A Case Study in Public Policy* (Berkeley: University of California Press, 1977), pp. 147–163.

68. Nevertheless, the hunger for land persists. Official statistics show that by the end of 1986 more than 43 percent of the economically active population in rural areas—some 3.2 million persons—were landless (Neil Harvey, *The New Agrarian Movement in Mexico*, London: Institute of Latin American Studies, 1990, p. 7).

69. Kevin J. Middlebrook, *Organized Labor and the State in Postrevolutionary Mexico* (forthcoming), ch. 5. See also Alberto Aziz Nassif, *El estado mexicano y la CTM* (México, D.F.: Ediciones de la Casa Chata, No. 32, 1989); and Kevin J. Middlebrook, ed., *Unions, Workers, and the State in Mexico* (La Jolla, Calif.: Center for U.S.-Mexican Studies, University of California– San Diego, 1991).

70. For a case study, see Kevin J. Middlebrook, "Union Democratization in the Mexican Automobile Industry," *Latin American Research Review*, 24:2 (1989), pp. 69–93.

71. Carlos Salinas's Gobernación minister, Fernando Gutiérrez Barrios, is the first graduate of the national military college to hold a nonmilitary Cabinet post since the Díaz Ordaz (1964–1970)

administration (Camp, "Camarillas in Mexican Politics," p. 104).

72. See Roderic A. Camp, *Generals in the Palacio: The Military in Modern Mexico* (New York: Oxford University Press, 1992).

73. General Luis Garfías, remarks at a research workshop on the Mexican military, Center for U.S.-Mexican Studies, University of California, San Diego, March 1984.

74. José Luis Piñeyro, "The Modernization of the Mexican Armed Forces," in Augusto Varas, ed., *Democracy under Siege: New Military Power in Latin America* (Westport, Conn.: Greenwood Press, 1989), p. 116.

75. See David Ronfeldt, ed., *The Modern Mexican Military: A Reassessment* (La Jolla, Calif.: Center for U.S.-Mexican Studies, University of California–San Diego, 1984); and Roderic A. Camp, "Civilian Supremacy in Mexico: The Case of a Post-revolutionary Military," in Constantine P. Danopoulos, ed., *Military Intervention and Withdrawal* (London: Routledge, 1990).

76. For a critical review of this literature, see Ann L. Craig and Wayne A. Cornelius, "Political Culture in Mexico: Continuities and Revisionist Interpretations," in Gabriel Almond and Sidney Verba, eds., *The Civic Culture Revisited* (Newbury Park, Calif.: Sage Publications, 1989).

77. The data supporting this generalization are summarized in John J. Bailey, "Reform of the Mexican Political System: Prospects for Change in 1987–1988," paper prepared for the Office of External Research, U.S. Department of State, July 1987.

78. Dan Williams, "Polls Becoming an Issue in Mexico's Campaign," *Los Angeles Times*, June 28, 1988.

79. A recent national survey found that the most trusted social institutions in Mexico were the schools and the Catholic Church; the least trusted were the legislature, bureaucrats, and elected public officials. See Alberto Hernández Medina and Luis Navarro Rodríguez, eds., *Cómo somos los mexicanos* (Mexico City: Centro de Estudios Educativos, 1987), p. 22.

80. In a 1979 survey of Mexico City residents, 90 percent agreed with the following statement: "If you really want something from the government, you can almost always get it with a bribe" (Lee

Dye, "What Mexicans Think: Their Trust Is in Themselves," *Los Angeles Times*, special supplement on Mexico, July 15, 1979).

81. Charles L. Davis, *Working-Class Mobilization and Political Control: Venezuela and Mexico* (Louisville: University Press of Kentucky, 1989).

82. Data provided by the Centro de Estudios Opinión Pública, S.C., Mexico City.

83. Rafael Segovia, *La politización del niño mexicano* (Mexico City: El Colegio de México, 1975), pp. 51–58.

84. For a fuller explication of this point, see Kenneth M. Coleman and Charles L. Davis, *Politics and Culture in Mexico* (Ann Arbor: Institute for Social Research, University of Michigan, 1988).

85. John Booth and Mitchell Seligson, "The Political Culture of Authoritarianism in Mexico: A Reexamination," *Latin American Research Review*, 19 (1984), pp. 106–124; and Joseph L. Klesner, "Changing Patterns of Electoral Participation and Official Party Support in Mexico," in Judith Gentleman, ed., *Mexican Politics in Transition* (Boulder, Colo.: Westview Press, 1987), pp. 95–127.

86. By law, voting is obligatory in Mexico, and evidence of having voted in the most recent election is sometimes required to receive public services.

87. See Wayne A. Cornelius, *Politics and the Migrant Poor in Mexico City* (Stanford, Calif.: Stanford University Press, 1975), pp. 158–160.

88. See David Felix, "Income Distribution Trends in Mexico and the Kuznets Curve," in Sylvia A. Hewlett and Richard S. Weinert, eds., *Brazil and Mexico: Patterns in Late Development* (Philadelphia: Institute for the Study of Human Issues, 1982), pp. 265–316.

89. Data from the National Survey of Household Income and Expenditures (1984), analyzed in Fernando Cortés and Rosa María Rubalcava, "Equidad via reducción: la distribución del ingreso en México, 1977–1984" (unpublished manuscript, Center for U.S.-Mexican Studies, University of California–San Diego, June 1990).

90. Peter Ward, *Welfare Politics in Mexico: Papering over the Cracks* (London: Allen & Unwin, 1986), pp. 9–10, 135–136.

91. Luis Donaldo Colosio [president of the PRI], "Un nuevo partido," *Examen* (P.R.I.), 2:13 (June 15, 1990), p. 4; John Sheahan, *Conflict and Change in Mexican Economic Strategy: Implications for Mexico and Latin America* (La Jolla, Calif.: Center for U.S-Mexican Studies, University of California–San Diego, 1991).

92. The official census count in 1990 was 81.1 million inhabitants, but this may have been affected by significant undercounting. Demographers estimate that the true population size in 1990 was about 84.9 million.

93. World Bank, *Mexico after the Oil Boom: Refashioning a Development Strategy* (Washington, D.C., June 1987).

94. Centro de Estudios Económicos del Sector Privado, *La economía subterránea en México* (México, D.F.: CEESP, 1986).

95. Leopoldo Solís, "Social Impact of the Economic Crisis," in Dwight S. Brothers and Adele E. Wick, eds., *Mexico's Search for a New Development Strategy* (Boulder, Colo.: Westview Press, 1990), p. 46.

96. Data from the Centro de Estudios Económicos del Sector Privado, Mexico City. See also Oscar Vera Ferrer, "The Political Economy of Privatization in Mexico," in William Glade, ed., *Privatization of Public Enterprises in Latin America* (San Francisco and San Diego: ICS Press/Center for U.S.-Mexican Studies, 1991), pp. 35–57.

97. Barry Carr, "The Left and Its Potential Role in Political Change," in Wayne A. Cornelius, Judith Gentleman, and Peter H. Smith, eds., *Mexico's Alternative Political Futures* (La Jolla, Calif.: Center for U.S.-Mexican Studies, University of California–San Diego, Monograph no. 30, 1989), p. 383.

98. As described by Torcuato Di Tella, "Argentina has been stagnating for many years as a result of political stalemate. The various contenders for power simply can't liquidate each other, although they have been trying hard for the last three decades. At times one or the other of those groups seems on the verge of succeeding, but somehow society resists strongly, and a 'social draw' is reestablished. Each group has just enough power to veto the projects originated by the others, but none can muster the strength to run the country as it would like" (Torcuato S. Di Tella, "An Introduction to the Argentine System," in Richard R. Fagen and Wayne A.

Cornelius, eds., *Political Power in Latin America: Seven Confrontations* [Englewood Cliffs, N.J.: Prentice–Hall, 1970], p. 108).

99. Federico Estévez, "Salinastroika Opens a Hornets' Nest," *Los Angeles Times*, July 15, 1990.

100. Many of the factors that make this kind of hybrid, semi-authoritarian regime the most probable outcome of Mexico's political transition are analyzed in Lorenzo Meyer, "México: los límites de la democratizacíon neoliberal," paper presented at the Research Seminar on Mexico and U.S.-Mexican Relations, Center for U.S.-Mexican Studies, University of California–San Diego, May 15, 1991. (Abridged version published in *Nexos*, No. 163 [July 1991], pp. 25–34.)

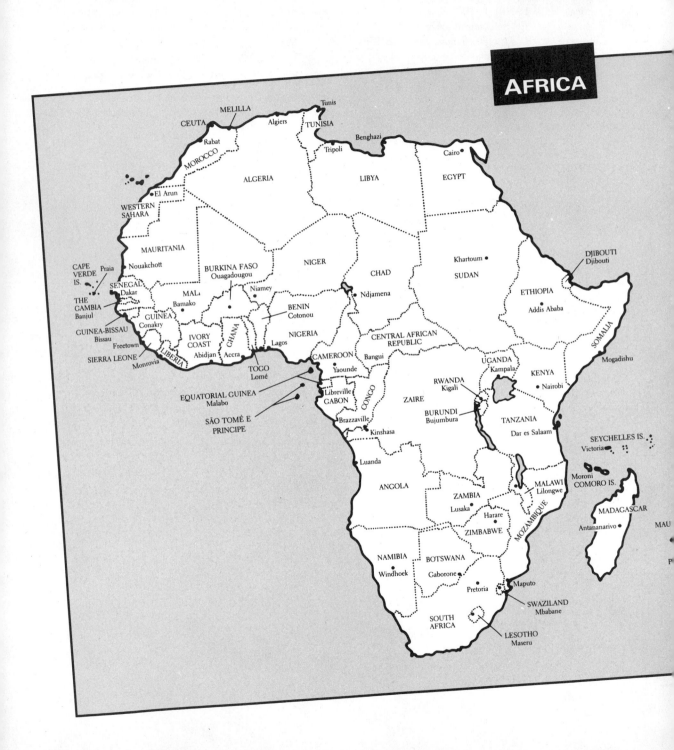

AFRICA

CEUTA
MELILLA
Tunis
Algiers
TUNISIA
Benghazi
Rabat
Tripoli
Cairo
MOROCCO

ALGERIA
LIBYA
EGYPT

El Arun
WESTERN
SAHARA

MAURITANIA
Nouakchott
BURKINA FASO
Ouagadougou
NIGER
CHAD
SUDAN
Khartoum
DJIBOUTI
Djibouti

CAPE
VERDE
IS.
Praia
SENEGAL
Dakar
MALI
Bamako
Niamey
Ndjamena
ETHIOPIA
Addis Ababa

THE
GAMBIA
Banjul
GUINEA
Conakry
BENIN
Cotonou
SOMALIA

GUINEA-BISSAU
Bissau
IVORY
COAST
GHANA
NIGERIA
CENTRAL AFRICAN
REPUBLIC
Freetown
Lagos
SIERRA LEONE
Monrovia
LIBERIA
Abidjan
Accra
TOGO
Lomé
CAMEROON
Bangui
UGANDA
Kampala
KENYA
Mogadishu

EQUATORIAL GUINEA
Malabo
Yaounde
RWANDA
Kigali
Nairobi

SÃO TOMÉ E
PRINCIPE
Libreville
GABON
CONGO
ZAIRE
BURUNDI
Bujumbura
TANZANIA

Brazzaville
Kinshasa
Dar es Salaam
SEYCHELLES IS.
Victoria

Luanda
Moroni
COMORO IS.

ANGOLA
MALAWI
Lilongwe
MADAGASCAR
MAU

ZAMBIA
Lusaka
Harare
MOZAMBIQUE
Antananarivo
P

ZIMBABWE
NAMIBIA
BOTSWANA
Windhoek
Gaborone
Pretoria
Maputo
SWAZILAND
Mbabane
SOUTH
AFRICA
LESOTHO
Maseru

CHAPTER 16

CRAWFORD YOUNG

POLITICS IN AFRICA

THE FIFTY-TWO STATES OF AFRICA

FRICA as a continent is the focus for this chapter. Unlike the other case study chapters which examine individual countries, this chapter explores comparatively all fifty-two sovereign states of contemporary Africa. This approach is necessary because the African political experience is not adequately conveyed by using any one country as a sustained example. Comparative analysis over so broad a political universe, encompassing so many units, presents its own problems; individual countries do have their unique features. Nonetheless, political development in Africa reveals many common themes, which offer a sufficient basis for adopting a broadly comparative approach.

In recent times, Africa has come to be seen, both by itself and by others, as more than a mere geographic entity. Its states share a history of foreign oppression, a sense of newly won independence and underdevelopment, and a desire for economic autonomy and development. Symbolic of their conviction of common heritage and destiny is their participation in the Organization of African Unity (OAU), as well as coordinated diplomatic action on issues affecting Africa as a whole.

Africa, politically defined, includes the physical continent and nearby island states that identify themselves with Africa[1] (see Tables 16.1 and 16.2). Although we do not specifically exclude any African states from our analysis, we will concentrate on those states that lie south of the Sahara Desert ("Black Africa"). The Arab tier of states to the north of the Sahara (Egypt, Libya, Tunisia, Algeria, and Morocco) has historical associations with the Mediterranean world and somewhat different cultural and social characteristics.

In 1415 Portuguese soldiers crossed the Strait of Gibraltar to establish small outposts on the Moroccan coast. From this modest beginning a momentous historical process of European subjugation of Africa was initiated. The forces of intrusion gathered momentum over the centuries, reaching their peak with the "scramble for Africa" late in the nineteenth century. Every

TABLE 16.1
BASIC POLITICAL DATA ON FIFTY-TWO AFRICAN STATES, 1990

State	Regime type[a]	Multi-party system now or promised[b]	Extended civil strife[c]	Successful coups since independence
Algeria	Single party, military	yes	no	1
Angola	Single party, liberation	yes	yes	0
Benin	Single party, military	yes	no	6
Botswana	Dominant party	yes	no	0
Burkina Faso	Military	no	no	6
Burundi	Single party, military	no	yes	3
Cameroon	Single party	no	yes	0
Cape Verde	Single party	yes	no	0
Central African Republic	Single party, military	no	no	3
Chad	Single party, insurgent faction	no	yes	4
Comoros	Single party	no	no	2
Congo	Single party, military	no	no	3
Djibouti	Single party	no	no	0
Egypt	Dominant party, military	yes	no	1
Equatorial Guinea	Military	no	no	1
Ethiopia	Single party, military	no	yes	3
Gabon	Single party	yes	no	0
Gambia	Dominant party	yes	no	0
Ghana	Military, populist movement	no	no	5
Guinea	Military	yes	no	1
Guinea-Bissau	Single party, liberation	no	no	1
Ivory Coast	Single party	yes	no	0
Kenya	Single party	no	no	0
Lesotho	Military	no	no	2
Liberia	Dominant party, military	yes	yes	1
Libya	Military, populist movement	no	no	1
Madagascar	Dominant party, military	yes	no	2
Malawi	Single party	no	no	0

continued

square inch of Africa fell at least briefly under foreign rule. After World War II, the tide of colonial domination began to recede, and rapidly from 1960 on. With the independence of Zimbabwe in 1980 and Namibia in 1990, only the original foreign beachheads, Ceuta and Melilla, remained under European rule.

THE EFFECTS OF COLONIALISM
The most important historical factor shaping contemporary African politics remains the encounter with imperial rule. Colonialism defined the boundaries of the contemporary political units; dominant political forces and leaders in many countries began as movements of nationalist resistance. The social map was changed beyond recognition, with novel categories of class stratification and transformation of lines of racial, ethnic, and religious differentiation. Economic infrastructure and production patterns were shaped by the interests and needs of the colonial powers.

From the sixteenth to the eighteenth century, the main form of European intervention in Africa was the slave trade. Perhaps 12 million Africans were landed in

TABLE 16.1 (*Continued*)

State	Regime type[a]	Multi-party system now or promised[b]	Extended civil strife[c]	Successful coups since independence
Mali	Single party, military	no	no	1
Mauritania	Military	no	no	3
Mauritius	Competitive party	yes	no	0
Morocco	Monarchy, multiparty	yes	no	0
Mozambique	Single party, liberation	yes	yes	0
Namibia	Dominant party	yes	no	0
Niger	Military	no	no	1
Nigeria	Military	yes	yes	5
Rwanda	Single party, military	no	no	1
São Tomé e Principe	Single party	yes	no	0
Senegal	Dominant party	yes	no	1
Seychelles	Single party	no	no	1
Sierra Leone	Single party	no	no	2
Somalia	Single party, military	yes	yes	1
South Africa	Dominant party, racial exclusion	yes	yes	0
Sudan	Military	no	yes	4
Swaziland	Monarchy	no	no	0
Tanzania	Single party	no	no	0
Togo	Single party, military	yes	no	2
Tunisia	Dominant party	yes	no	0
Uganda	Dominant party, insurgent faction	yes	yes	3
Zaire	Single party, military	yes	yes	2
Zambia	Single party	yes	no	0
Zimbabwe	Dominant party	yes	yes	0

[a]Major criteria are the nature of the party system and origins of the incumbent leadership. "Single party, liberation" refers to a party that originated in an armed liberation struggle. "Single party, military" refers to a party created by leaders who originally seized power in a military coup, and where the ruler came from the military. "Insurgent faction" refers to a party created by an armed faction that seized power.
[b]Classifications are by the author, based on development to the end of 1990.
[c]Prolonged, armed dissidence or civil war; classification by the author.

the Americas; many others perished en route.[2] This commerce was carried out from coastal establishments from Senegal to Angola; it began the remaking of African political geography, as its impetus led to mercantile African states formed around the supply of slaves.

Early in the nineteenth century, as the slave trade declined, European powers began to extend their influence into the interior. By degrees, this informal empire of zones of influence was supplanted by colonial annexation. In the last quarter of the nineteenth century, intensifying European rivalries and new military technolo-gies (especially the machine gun) brought rapid partition. Britain, France, Portugal, Germany, Belgium, Italy, and Spain divided nearly all of Africa among them.

Conquest was primarily a military undertaking. In its wake, colonizers were confronted with urgent tasks: structuring and institutionalizing their domination. Britain and France in particular had some experience in colonial rule, but African conditions were quite different. The shape of the colonial state responded to the imperatives of organizing alien rule over vast territories at minimal cost to imperial treasuries.

TABLE 16.2
BASIC INFORMATION ON FIFTY-TWO AFRICAN STATES

State	Capital city	Area (sq. miles)	Population (millions, 1988 est.)	Date of independence (month/day/year)
Algeria	Algiers	919,951	23.8	7/3/62
Angola	Luanda	481,351	9.4	11/11/75
Benin	Cotonou	43,483	4.4	8/1/60
Botswana	Gaborone	219,815	1.2	10/9/65
Burkina Faso	Ouagadougou	105,869	8.5	8/5/60
Burundi	Bujumbura	10,739	5.1	7/1/62
Cameroon	Yaounde	183,568	11.2	1/1/60
Cape Verde	Cidade Praia	1,557	0.3	7/5/75
Central African Republic	Bangui	241,313	2.9	8/13/60
Chad	Ndjamena	495,752	5.4	8/11/60
Comoros	Moroni	693	0.4	7/6/75
Congo	Brazzaville	132,046	2.1	8/15/60
Djibouti	Djibouti	8,800	0.4	6/27/77
Egypt	Cairo	386,872	50.2	2/28/22
Equatorial Guinea	Malabo	10,832	0.4	10/13/68
Ethiopia	Addis Ababa	457,142	47.4	5/5/41
Gabon	Libreville	102,317	1.1	8/17/60
Gambia	Banjul	4,003	0.8	2/18/63
Ghana	Accra	92,100	14.0	3/6/57
Guinea	Conakry	94,925	5.4	10/2/58
Guinea-Bissau	Bissau	13,948	0.9	9/10/74
Ivory Coast	Abidjan	124,503	11.2	8/7/60
Kenya	Nairobi	221,960	22.4	12/12/63
Lesotho	Maeru	11,716	1.7	10/4/66
Liberia	Monrovia	43,000	2.4	7/26/1847
Libya	Tripoli	679,536	4.2	12/24/51

continued

The first crucial goal was to consolidate colonial control over the territory. At the Berlin Conference in 1884 and 1885, where the imperial powers reached diplomatic agreement on the major outlines of the partition, the principle of effective occupation was enunciated. To confirm its title to a zone of African territory, a colonial power had to demonstrate to its European rivals that it exercised military control over the area; failing this, an imperial competitor might snatch it away.

Effective occupation was to be achieved, however, with small outlays. Finance ministers and parliaments in Europe insisted that military commitments be kept small and that the newly conquered territories pay for their own administration. Important consequences for the colonial state flowed from the twin imperatives of consolidating hegemony and generating revenue.

A grid of European administrative outposts was created in order to guarantee effective occupation. European personnel were costly, however, and only modest numbers could be covered by colonial budgets. In 1900 the colonial administration in Nigeria had only a few hundred British officers, and even later it never had more than a few thousand. African intermediaries were indispensable to complete the infrastructure of control. Often these were found by conferring colonial recognition on the ruler of an African state or community. In return for his collaboration in upholding the colonial order and his (or, rarely, her) participation in imple-

TABLE 16.2 (*Continued*)

State	Capital city	Area (sq. miles)	Population (millions, 1988 est.)	Date of independence (month/day/year)
Madagascar	Antanarivo	203,035	10.9	6/26/60
Malawi	Lilongwe	45,747	8.0	7/6/64
Mali	Bamako	464,873	8.0	9/22/60
Mauritania	Nouakchott	419,229	1.9	11/28/60
Mauritius	Port Louis	787	1.1	3/13/68
Morocco	Rabat	171,953	24.0	3/2/56
Mozambique	Maputo	303,373	14.9	6/25/75
Namibia	Windhoek	318,000	1.3	3/23/90
Niger	Niamey	489,206	7.3	8/3/60
Nigeria	Lagos	356,669	110.1	10/1/60
Rwanda	Kigali	10,169	6.7	7/1/62
São Tomé e Principe	São Tomé	372	0.1	7/12/75
Senegal	Dakar	76,124	7.0	8/25/60
Seychelles	Victoria	107	0.1	7/12/75
Sierra Leone	Freetown	27,925	3.9	4/27/69
Somalia	Mogardiscio	246,155	5.9	7/1/60
South Africa	Pretoria	471,819	34.0	6/31/10
Sudan	Khartoum	967,000	23.8	1/1/56
Swaziland	Mbabane	6,705	0.7	9/6/68
Tanzania	Dar es Salaam	363,708	24.7	11/9/61
Togo	Lome	21,853	3.4	4/27/60
Tunisia	Tunis	63,378	7.8	3/20/56
Uganda	Kampala	91,134	16.2	10/9/62
Zaire	Kinshasa	905,063	33.4	6/30/60
Zambia	Lusaka	290,724	7.6	10/24/64
Zimbabwe	Harare	150,333	9.3	4/18/80

menting its directives (collecting taxes, building roads, supplying labor), the ruler's own authority was confirmed and reinforced by the power of the colonial state. Superior power was the ultimate currency of colonial rule; with this as lever, intrigue, artifice, and diplomacy were inexpensive alternatives to sheer brute force for consolidating the framework of European hegemony.

As a result of the revenue imperative, the colonial state had to launch an early initiative to restructure the economy. The subsistence-oriented rural economies in most of Africa offered little extractable surplus for the colonial state. The discovery in South Africa of rich diamond deposits in 1869 and gold in 1885 aroused hopes of treasure troves elsewhere, but these were initially dis-

appointed. African oil deposits and much of its mineral wealth were to be discovered only after World War II.

The primary mobilizable resources in most territories were African labor and land. With direct or indirect coercion playing a central role in most areas, Africans were compelled to produce crops for sale. Because there was little internal market, these were mainly commodities salable on the international market: cotton, peanuts, palm oil, cocoa, and sisal, among others. In parts of north, east, and southern Africa where temperate climatic conditions prevailed, European settlement was encouraged. African land rights were extinguished by the colonial state, and fertile tracts were offered to prospective settlers for nominal payments. Access to low-wage labor was required for these farms to prosper; colonial administrations cooperated in its recruitment. African labor was also conscripted, with slender or even no remuneration, to create the basic infrastructure of roads and railways for communication.

The major policy instruments for mobilizing labor were imposition of some form of head tax on African peasants and regulations requiring labor service on such public works as roads. To earn the money required for the head tax, the African peasant had to cultivate a cash crop or seek temporary employment with a European enterprise. To enforce their hegemony, European administrators were armed with an array of arbitrary ordinances, permitting summary punishment for such offenses as disrespect for a chief or district officer and failure to comply with an administrative order.

By the 1920s the colonial order had been consolidated nearly everywhere. Taxation of external trade and African peasants provided a modest but sufficient basis for financing the colonial administration. The system of African intermediaries was institutionalized and maintained local order. An increasingly professional and almost exclusively European bureaucratic elite manned the policymaking levels of the administration and an apparatus of regional control and supervision. The more harshly coercive features of the colonial state were less visible.

After World War II, colonialism in Africa was placed on the defensive. Global politics were now dominated by the Soviet Union and the United States, who had no ultimate stake in perpetuating European rule. A rising tide of nationalist protest in Africa challenged the legitimacy of alien occupation. In response, the colonial powers made development a more explicit goal, with large-scale public investment programs. In addition, the welfare of the subject population became a significant state responsibility; for the first time, sizable public resources were committed to post-primary education, rural health facilities, safe water supplies, and other basic needs. As these needs were satisfied, the state expanded greatly. In the final decade of British colonial rule in Ghana, from 1947 to 1957, state expenditures rose tenfold. In Zaire (then the Belgian Congo), state outlays in 1960 were forty-five times higher than they had been in 1939.

Although broad similarities marked colonial influence, there were important variations. The several colonial powers in Africa applied somewhat different doctrines of administration. These reflected the political culture of the home country and the character of its own state institutions. For France, Germany, and Belgium the concept of the state was shaped by the absolutist tradition, which stressed centralization, hierarchy, and bureaucratic dominance. At home, this culture was overlain with nineteenth-century notions of constitutionalism, which were stripped away in designing state structures for conquered African domains. The British state had a distinctly different texture, with looser structure, greater diffusion of power, and more regional variation and autonomy.

These differences produced varied styles of African administration. The British, in seeking intermediaries, were more inclined to recognize and make use of existing African rulers, whose institutions were adapted to the purposes of the colonizer. This colonial ideology was known as *indirect rule*.[3] As a consequence, customary political structures retained more significance in areas formerly under British rule. Other colonizers, while often making use of existing chiefs as administrative intermediaries, treated them more as simple local agents of a centralized bureaucracy.

The centralized, bonapartist state ideology also had implications in the cultural sphere. Particularly in the French and Portuguese colonies, policy was aimed at permanent incorporation of the African domains. Ultimate assimilation of the subject population was proclaimed as the goal. Although this doctrine was applied sporadically and incompletely, it had significant influence in cultural policy and on the character of the African elite produced by the colonial experience. In the former French colonies, the first generation of postcolonial leaders, such as Leopold Senghor of Senegal or Felix Houphouet–Boigny of the Ivory Coast, were profoundly affected by French culture, and had developed intimate and durable ties in the upper echelons of French political society.[4] In the Portuguese colonies, an Afro-Portuguese class, which was Portuguese-speaking and often partly Portuguese in ancestry, had an important role both as intermediaries in colonial times and as leaders of the liberation movements that threw off metropolitan rule.

Legacy of the Colonial State

The contemporary African state system is affected in a number of ways by its colonial origins. To begin with, the territorial definition of the state reflects the administrative boundaries of the colonial partition. A handful of African states have historical continuity with a precolonial epoch,[5] but most originated as units of colonial administration. When the imperial powers divided up the continent, they paid little heed to African cultural or political units. As a consequence, African state boundaries frequently divide ethnolinguistic groups.[6] Moreover, African states, with few exceptions, have extensive internal diversity — ethnic, racial, linguistic, and religious.

A second major legacy of the colonial era is the nature of the state itself. The colonial state was organized as a structure of institutionalizing alien rule; its vocation was domination of a subjugated population. A command mentality, a paternalistic mode of rule, a hegemonic relationship with the populace — these attributes of the colonial state are deeply ingrained in the daily routines of administration. Legally and practically, the colonial state considered the indigenous populace as subjects, not citizens. The African leadership that succeeded to power has, to varying degrees, endeavored to eradicate this heritage. The inertia of the colonial state tradition is powerful, however, and continues to color state – society relationships.

A third legacy of the colonial state, related to the second, was a tradition of centralized, highly regulatory, and interventionist management of the economy. "Statism," so widely decried today, is rooted in the practices of colonial rule. Although the command role of the state as economic manager was greatly expanded after independence, its basic foundations were laid well before power transfer.

A final crucial effect of the colonial state lay in the process by which it yielded power to African successor regimes. One by one, in the three decades following World War II, colonial powers came to the conclusion that nationalism was an irresistible force. In a handful of cases, this conclusion was forced on the colonizer by prolonged armed struggle (Algeria, 1954 to 1962; Guinea – Bissau, 1961 to 1974; Mozambique, 1964 to 1975; Angola, 1961 to 1975; Zimbabwe, 1973 to 1979; Namibia, 1965 to 1989). In most instances, the withdrawing power recognized the need for accommodation with nationalist forces by negotiation. Once this conclusion was reached, the colonial power retained considerable means to influence the terms and method of decolonization.

The formula for decolonization generally called for creating political institutions closely modeled on the colonizing power's constitutional structure. The formal institutions of constitutional democracy — elected parliaments, competitive parties, and a politically recruited cabinet — were hastily grafted onto the authoritarian bureaucratic colonial state. The chapters in this book dealing with Britain, France, and Germany make clear how long and gradual was the institutionalizing of constitutional democracy in these countries. African states were asked to make an instantaneous transition from colonial subjugation to representative democracy. Enormous difficulties arose, and in most instances the initial constitutional structures failed to survive.

INDEPENDENCE AND AFTER

Resistance to colonial rule has a long history, and the first stirrings of nationalist response to foreign domination can be traced to the beginning of this century, stressing grievances over such issues as land expropriation, forced labor, conscription of African soldiers for European wars, and — more generally — oppression and exploitation of the African. In its early days, nationalist ideology had a pronounced pan-African current; it was stimulated and inspired by appeals to solidarity and uplift for all peoples of African ancestry, voiced by such American or Caribbean figures as W.E.B. Dubois and Marcus Garvey.

After World War II, nationalism came to focus more specifically on political liberation. The doctrine of self-determination as an inalienable right of all peoples was invoked. Before the right could be claimed, a crucial question needed an immediate answer: what political unit could advance such a demand? The answer was inevitable: self-determination could apply only to the territorial divisions of the colonial partition. The crazy-quilt pattern of imperial partition, and the logic of self-determination, brought to Africa an exceptionally large number of sovereign nation-states (fifty-two with one or two more in prospect in the 1990s — Eritrea, possibly Western Sahara or southern Sudan).

At the time of independence it was hoped that broader political units could be created. Only three amalgamations occurred: Tanganyika and Zanzibar joined in 1964 to form Tanzania; British and Italian Somaliland merged as Somalia; and part of British Cameroon joined the former French-mandated territory as independent Cameroon. Of the many independent states of Africa, a number are small and weak. Of the fifty-two, eighteen are smaller than New York State, and five are smaller than Rhode Island. Some twenty-one have fewer than 5 million citizens, and eight have less than a million.

In constructing an ideology of liberation, African nationalists sought to give moral content to the territorial entities for which self-determination was demanded. In 1947 a leading Nigerian nationalist and perennial presidential candidate, Obafemi Awolowo, declared that Nigeria was not a nation but "a mere geographical expression." At the time, such statements were common enough; a decade later, deprecatory references to colonial units were being supplanted by exaltation of these territories as nations-in-becoming.

In the transition, mainstream currents of African nationalism acquired a unitarian aspiration. Political unity, the argument ran, was crucial to anticolonial struggle. Otherwise, the colonizer could play on the divisions and manipulate the installation of groups that were particularly indulgent to their interests. Once independence was won, unity was even more necessary. Otherwise, the new rulers would consume all their energies in day-to-day parliamentary survival; the momentum of development would be lost in acrimonious conflict. Most importantly, consolidating the national personality of the new state made political unity crucial. Political competition was likely to follow ethnic, regional, or religious fault lines in civil society.

The Single-Party Formula

From such considerations rose the doctrine of the single party as a necessary formula for African governance. All the states shared the goals of independence and rapid development. African society, it was claimed, lacked pronounced class divisions that had served as a basis for political parties in Europe. With national unity and political stability ensured by a single party that brought all citizens together, true participation could safely occur within the party, without endangering the survival of the policy.[7]

In about a third of the African states, one political movement had achieved overwhelming dominance before full independence. Several movements, such as the Tanganyika African National Union (TANU) in Tanzania, the Parti Democratique de Guinée (PDG), or the Neo-Destour (later Destour Socialist) party in Tunisia, commanded wide prestige and served as influential models. In the period immediately after independence, there was a general tendency to impose the single-party formula of rule. Altogether, some forty-two of the fifty-two African states have experienced single-party rule at some point of their independent life.

The transition from nationalist movement articulating the many grievances produced by colonial rule to governing party bearing responsibility for popular well-being proved difficult. In building their constituencies, nationalist parties had promised swift and dramatic improvement in mass well-being. There were sharp increases in state expenditures for basic amenities — schools and clinics — in many countries, but the pace of change fell far short of expectations. The arbitrary measures to impose single-party rule generated friction. The conspicuous opulence in which many (though not all) rulers indulged soon bred resentment. Once a leader began to lose his popular standing, the potential shortcomings of the single-party formula became glaring. High office was seen as a lifelong prerogative. The anticolonial slogan "one man-one vote" was sardonically transformed into "one-man-one vote — once."

Military Intervention

This deterioration paved the way for a wholly unexpected development: widespread military intervention in politics. Until independence, the military had remained under tight colonial control, and it generally was held in low esteem. Most armed forces were small and lightly armed; their new African officers had played no part in the nationalist movement. But in states where the first-generation leadership had been widely unpopular and protest channels were closed, the road was open for military intervention.

The first military takeover in Africa occurred in Egypt in 1952. A second followed in neighboring Sudan in 1958. Military interventions changed from an isolated phenomenon to an epidemic in 1965 and 1966, when within a few months six regimes were overthrown by armies, including such key countries as Algeria, Nigeria, and Zaire. From that point, not until 1988 was there a year without an African military coup. From 1952 to 1990, seventy-four coups were successful (and many more failed) in thirty countries.[8] By the late 1960s about 40 percent of the African states were headed by a military ruler, a proportion that has remained fairly stable.[9]

The military regimes initially claimed that they were mere caretakers, driven to intervene by the calamitous state of political and economic affairs. Their role, they then argued, was simply to clean up the mess. Once the damage done by the ousted regime had been repaired, they would retire to the barracks and return power to civilians. In a few cases the military has peacefully withdrawn from power, as in Ghana in 1966 and

The ceremony marking promotion of President Mobutu Sese Seko to the rank of field marshal on the occasion of the ceremony of the establishment of his ruling political party, the M.P.R. At the far left is his second wife and in the center is the then commanding general of the Zairean armed forces, General Singa Boyenge.

1979, Nigeria in 1979, and Sudan in 1985. Most often, however, a ruling group of military origin has sought to perpetuate its hold on political power unless driven out by a popular uprising (Sudan, 1964), foreign intervention (France in the Central African Republic, 1979; Tanzania in Uganda, 1979), or — much more often — by another military coup.

To justify permanent consolidation of power, military rulers needed some form of political legitimacy. The ruler often deemphasized his military background by gradually ceasing to appear in public in uniform. Another source of legitimation for a military figure who wanted prolonged rule lay in ideology. The military rulers proclaimed radical populist or even Marxist-Leninist doctrines.

Personal Authoritarianism

A characteristic of many African regimes, both single party and military, has been their authoritarianism.[10] In such a system, ultimate legitimacy derives from the monopoly of power itself. Limited pluralism was sometimes permitted, but open opposition to the regime was not. Organized political competition outside the framework of the dominant party was excluded, though in some instances contests within the party somewhat analogous to those in American primary elections were permitted.

Another dominant feature of the African political system has been the ruler's preeminent role. In an authoritarian setting, final power lies in the hands of the ruler himself. Robert Jackson and Carl Rosberg have argued that the contemporary African political system is best described as personal rule. According to their analysis:

> Personal rule is a system of relations linking rulers not with the "public" or even with the ruled (at least not directly), but with patrons, associates, clients, supporters, and rivals, who constitute the "system." If personal rulers are restrained, it is by the limits of their personal authority and power and by the authority and power of patrons, associates, clients, supporters, and — of course — rivals. . . . The fact that it is ultimately dependent upon persons rather than institutions is its essential vulnerability.[11]

Democratization

By the end of the 1980s, there were growing signs that authoritarian formulas were losing their hold. Disaffected peasantries and impoverished urban poor withdrew into survival strategies based on the underground economy. Disgruntled youth took to the streets in South Africa in 1984 and 1985, and in Senegal and Algeria in 1988. Unrest was chronic in many African universities, which were frequently closed for prolonged periods to quell student dissidence. African intellectuals demanded, with increasing insistence, the opening of politics to legal opposition. A characteristic plea came from a leading Zairian intellectual, Nzongola Ntalaja, in his 1988 presidential address to the African Studies Association:

> There is . . . an imperative need for political change. The present crisis cannot be resolved, and development will never be realized, under corrupt and authoritarian regimes. . . . We must . . . support the popular struggle for pluralism, democracy and a more equitable distribution of wealth. Without a democratic state, without popular participation in decision-making, a people-oriented strategy of development is out of the question.[12]

In 1990 the pace quickened, pushed forward by stunning events in and out of Africa. The spectacular collapse of Soviet-type regimes in Eastern Europe had major repercussions for African autocracies; the assassination of Nicolae Ceausescu of Romania, who had been on close personal terms with several major African rulers, sounded a chilling note in a number of presidential palaces. The release of Nelson Mandela from his long imprisonment, and the movement toward some form of post-apartheid government in South Africa in which democratic rights long restricted to the white minority would be extended to all, also sent shock waves. A wave of popular protest in a number of countries shook long-established single-party systems to their foundations: the Ivory Coast, Gabon, Benin, Zaire, Zambia, Mali. Major foreign powers which had long supported or tolerated single-party regimes in Africa (France, the United States, and the Soviet Union) withdrew their backing. Even the World Bank, in a major 1989 document on the African economic crisis, now argued that political change in a democratic direction was an indispensable correlate of economic reform.[13]

The impact of these combined pressures was extraordinary. Competitive party systems had been few and far between; only in Mauritius (1982) had there been an unambiguous case of change of regime by electoral process. In a few other countries, freedom of organization existed, although the ruling party held power continuously (notably Senegal, Gambia, and Botswana). Short-lived democratic restorations had occurred in several other cases (the Sudan in 1965 and 1985, Ghana in 1969 and 1979, Nigeria in 1979, and Burkina Faso in the 1970s). But the present surge to democratization, propelled by powerful mass pressures, was altogether different in its scale and its broad-front nature. By 1991, movements toward a multiparty system were afoot or announced in more than two-thirds of the African states. The permanence of this trend remains to be tested, but the political geography of Africa appears to be undergoing profound transformation.

DEEPENING ECONOMIC CRISIS

The remarkable surge of democratization pressures at the beginning of the 1990s occurs in the context of a severe and prolonged economic crisis afflicting most African states. In assessing the prospects for successful political liberalization, we need to weigh carefully the difficulty of the circumstances. By any measure, Africa is the most poverty-stricken of the major world regions. Worse yet, it is the continent with the most disappointing rate of economic growth (see Table 16.3 and Table 16.4). With an annual population increase rate of 3 percent, per capita income stagnated in the 1970s and dropped steadily in the 1980s in the bulk of the continent. By 1990 many countries were poorer than they had been in 1960. Per capita food production for the continent as a whole has been in steady decline since 1970.

The 1980s were a devastating decade for most of Africa. Relentless population expansion intensified the pressures on environmental resources and made African states more dependent on imported food. In 1970 food imports were still negligible; by 1985, 40 percent of the continent's food needs were met by imports.[14] Prices for a number of Africa's traditional exports (such as cocoa and coffee) dropped sharply, particularly in the late 1980s. In 1990 African coffee — which a few years earlier had fetched nearly $6,000 per ton — had fallen to only $1,200. At the same time, Africa lost ground in world market trade share, which fell from 3 percent in 1960 to 1 percent in 1985. Environmental degradation emerged as a major issue. In this dismal decade, AIDS became a major epidemic, affecting above all a strip of countries in East and Central Africa; in the Zambian capital of Lusaka at the end of the 1980s, 25 percent of mothers giving birth in public hospitals tested seropositive.

In the 1980s debt also emerged as a crucial issue. External borrowing by African states was minimal until about 1970. However, the effort to sustain the momentum of state expansion and to supply the basic amenities

TABLE 16.3
REAL GROWTH OF GNP PER CAPITA, 1965–1985 (ANNUAL PERCENTAGE CHANGES)

Region	Africa Compared to Other Third World Regions		
	1965–1973	1973–1980	1980–1989
Sub-Saharan Africa	3.2	0.1	−2.2
East Asia	5.1	4.7	6.7
South Asia	1.2	1.7	3.2
Latin America and Caribbean	3.7	2.6	−0.6

Source: "Performance Indicators by Developing Regions, Selected Periods," *World Development Report 1990*, p. 11. Copyright © 1990 by The International Bank for Reconstruction and Development/The World Bank. Reprinted by permission of Oxford University Press, Inc.

outstripped domestic revenues and aid resources. Many states had recourse to large-scale borrowing, encouraged by the laxity of many public and private external lenders at the time. By 1980 there was a sobering recognition that Africa had accumulated an external debt that far exceeded its ability to pay. Furthermore, as the distressed condition of African economies became clear, by the mid-1980s the international banks had shut their doors to African borrowers, and private foreign investment all but dried up. At times by the end of the 1980s, debt repayments exceeded new flows of aid and credit.

In the 1980s the World Bank and the International Monetary Fund (IMF) became deeply involved in an effort to revive African economies through loans tied to reform programs known as *structural adjustment*. By the end of the 1980s about thirty countries had such programs. These packages normally involved such measures as devaluation of currencies, sharp curbs on government expenditure, elimination of price subsidies for basic consumer items (such as staple foods, cooking oil, and sugar), and privatization of many state enterprises. Structural adjustment has proved very controversial within Africa, for many of the reforms, at least in the short term, hit hard at lower and middle urban strata. Economic liberalization is slow to revitalize African economies, because indigenous capitalism is weak and foreign capital is wary of African involvement. The dramatic changes in Eastern Europe further complicated African recovery, as donors and investors seemed likely to see more opportunity in the desocialization of the former Soviet bloc.

CULTURAL PLURALISM: RACE, ETHNICITY, AND RELIGION

Under the colonial state, by far the most important cleavage was the racial divide. Europeans, whether or not directly associated with the colonial state, played the part of master. Africans of all social stations were subordinate. The alien domination was portrayed as racial; the colonial situation was saturated with racism.

The visibility and significance of this division radically diminished after independence, except in South Africa, where immigrants of European ancestry inherited exclusive political power. Elsewhere, except in a few French-speaking states of West Africa, Zimbabwe, Namibia and South Africa, the white population shrank. With the loss of colonial political power, most other overt racial barriers disappeared (except in South Africa).

With the triumph of nationalism, political conflict shifted from the racial to the ethnic arena. Ethnic consciousness was founded on cultural traits believed to be shared, usually language, common historical myths, rituals, and values. Ethnicity was politically activated by perception of shared interests. Issues of regional representation within the political institutions, perceptions of domination of one group by another, and allocations of public goods (state employment, access to schools, siting of amenities) rose to the surface. In a phrase heard widely, the time had come to "slice the national cake," and groups jostled jealously to ensure that their helping was the proper size. At the distribution, ethnic identities acquired new and urgent political meaning.[15]

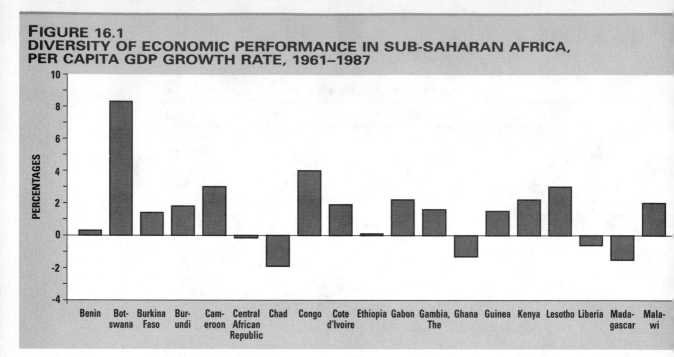

FIGURE 16.1
DIVERSITY OF ECONOMIC PERFORMANCE IN SUB-SAHARAN AFRICA,
PER CAPITA GDP GROWTH RATE, 1961–1987

Source: Sub-Saharan Africa: From Crisis to Sustainable Growth, p. 18. Copyright © 1989 The International Bank for Reconstruction and Development/The World Bank. Reprinted by permission.

The ethnic categories that became salient were by no means identical to those at the time of colonial penetration. The most important precolonial units were defined by political authority; these bore no necessary relationship to ethnicity. The larger precolonial African states usually incorporated a number of language groups. In areas such as much of the equatorial forest zone, where political communities were very localized, they were much smaller than zones of common language.

The colonial state itself had a powerful part in reordering the ethnic map. Despite very imperfect understanding of cultural maps, Africans were sorted and labeled.[16] Particularly in the British sphere, administrative districts were based on zones that the colonizer believed to be culturally similar. In time, the labels affixed to these administrative districts fed back into the social consciousness and became ethnic communities. Missionaries also had a major influence. In introducing schools for evangelical purposes and in developing linguistic vehicles for translating the Bible and religious communication, they organized closely related dialects into standardized languages. In so doing, they unwittingly created the basis for broader patterns of social consciousness and solidarity.

The substantial urban agglomerations that grew around the central places of colonial administration and production created novel arenas of social competition. In the urban setting, cultural heterogeneity brought a new consciousness of "we" and "they." In contrast to the generally homogeneous rural community, towns were places where ethnic affinity provided a valued basis for coping with the insecurities of urban life (finding jobs or housing, overcoming personal misfortune). At the same time, consciousness of competition with other groups for opportunities in social mobility took root. Through the intimate ties of kinship and home community that linked city and countryside, this coalescing social consciousness was diffused to the rural hinterland. In the final stage at the end of the colonial period, political competition appeared among those aspiring to high office. For the ambitious politician, the constituency most readily accessible to support his claim was that defined by ethnic affinity.

As we try to understand individual political behavior, it is useful to conceive of ethnicity as forming part of the repertory of social roles. The individual is not simply an ethnic person, but also has roles defined by occupation (teacher, civil servant, worker, farmer); by gender (male or female); by education ("old school tie," level

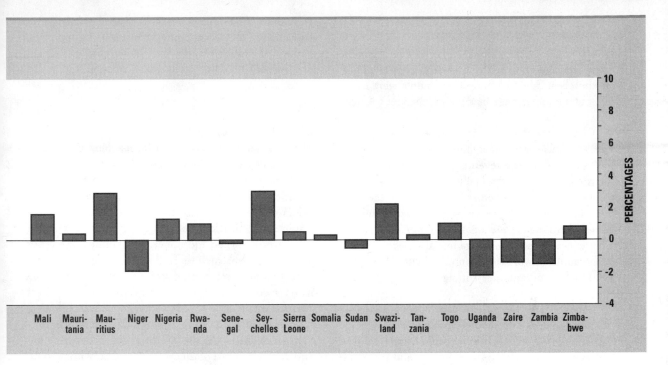

of schooling); by religious affiliation; by residence (neighborhood, town, or region), among others. Social class, too, may figure among the array of potential roles.

If we think of ethnicity as one of a number of possible social roles, we can then readily understand the importance of situation and context in determining which roles will govern behavior. In a dispute at the workplace pitting employees against managers, affinity to fellow workers would determine the individual's response. In a protest over poor food at the university restaurant, students would be likely to perceive and respond to the situation as students, not ethnics. In the framing of the Second and Third Republic Nigerian constitutions, discord arose over the place of Islamic courts in the judicial structure; Muslims and Christians aligned themselves on this issue according to their religion. Ethnicity comes into play as a determinant of behavior when the political situation is defined, in the eyes of those involved, as an ethnic contest. A heated election campaign in which the contending parties had primarily ethnic followings would illustrate such a situation.

Religion is another important dimension of social identity. Both Islam and diverse Christian churches have expanded rapidly in recent decades. Only the most isolated rural populations now lie outside the orbit of these two universal religions.

Although ancient Christian communities exist in Egypt and especially Ethiopia (the Coptic Christian church), the expansion of Christianity began on a large scale in Africa in the nineteenth century. Sharp rivalries between Catholic and Protestant missions were one factor in the scramble for Africa. With the colonial powers guaranteeing their security, usually providing some support, and leaving them a free hand in cultural policy, mission societies deployed numerous personnel in the task of creating Christian communities. Colonial powers usually excluded them from regions where Islam was dominant, but elsewhere by the 1920s Christian mission infrastructure had penetrated nearly everywhere.

Missions founded schools from an early stage, although at first these were only for religious instruction. Eventually, it became apparent that an opportunity for education was a strong attraction for potential converts. The school soon became the crucial agency for social mobility by young Africans, a pathway from village poverty to white-collar employment. At least nominal conversion was the price for entry into the mission schools. As the new class of educated Africans began to achieve prominence in social and later in political life, Christianity was associated with mobility, status, and power. Colonial powers favored the dominant church in the home country. In former British territories, Protestant churches were preeminent. In areas formerly under French and Belgian rule, Catholic missions had the edge. In many places, African separatist and prophet movements split off from the European-controlled mission churches. Some of these movements were short-lived, but a number have become independent African Protestant churches.

Islam is the dominant faith in seventeen African states, and Muslims are an important minority in a number of others. After the seventh-century Arab conquest of North Africa, Islam gradually spread southward, following the trade routes across the Sahara. In the eighteenth and nineteenth centuries, a number of militant Islamic reform states were created in inner West Africa. From the east coast, Muslim traders also began extending mercantile networks to the interior in the 1800s, and small Muslim communities sprang up around the outposts they created.

Paradoxically, the rate of Islam's spread increased dramatically during the colonial period, even though the imperial powers were generally hostile to it. Improved communications, easier transportation, and more settled conditions fostered the diffusion of Islam as well as of Christianity. Islam could not offer an equivalent to the opportunities for mobility provided by the Christian schools, but it had some advantages. Islam was not tainted by association with colonialism or with the pervasive racism embedded in the colonial situation. Its theology was simpler and more direct, and it was generally tolerant toward African religious practices persisting under the Islamic umbrella.

The spread of Islam and Christianity did not necessarily obliterate indigenous African religions. Patterns of religious belief associated with various African communities exhibited remarkable vitality. Frequently such beliefs continued even where formal conversion by one of the world religions had taken place. The shrines, religious figures, and beliefs associated with customary religion still retain their value for many Africans.

There is reason to believe that religious diversion is assuming growing importance. In Egypt, Tunisia, and Algeria, fundamentalist currents of Islam weigh more heavily in the political equation than they did a decade ago. In Sudan, renewed civil war broke out in 1983 when the Nimeiry regime imposed the "September laws" imposing *shari'a* (Islamic law) throughout the country, although the southern third of Sudan is not Muslim.[17] In Nigeria, tensions between Muslims and Christians have become far more serious than in the early postindependence years. In several countries, resurgence of religiosity among Christian communities, and a proliferation of independent churches, have been one response to the prolonged economic and social crisis.

SOCIAL CLASS

The colonial state introduced far-reaching changes in the class structure of the subjugated societies. Except for northern Africa and Ethiopia, most historical African societies lacked sharply differentiated social strata. When colonial rule was imposed, an alien ruling class was introduced. Along with it came a colonial capitalist class, which owned the mines, plantations, and other productive infrastructure. In the shadow of the colonial state grew mercantile intermediaries who came to dominate the commerce of the colonies: Levantines in West Africa, Greeks in the Sudan and the Belgian colonies, Indians and Pakistanis in East and Central Africa, Portuguese in Zaire. At the height of the colonial period Africans were most often excluded not only from political but also from economic ownership roles. The "foreign estate," as we name this group, was at once a ruling racial caste and a hegemonic economic class.

Among Africans a new category of persons appeared, whose status was above all derived from their Western education. Although they had negligible political power and little economic standing, their social and cultural skills earned them somewhat higher standing in colonial society than was accorded the mass of African subjects. They were fluent in the language of the colonizer and could thus win niches in the subaltern echelons of public and private bureaucracies. Some also entered the clergy of the Christian churches; others found a place in the liberal professions (lawyers, doctors, teachers). Particularly in the former Portuguese territories and South Africa, some were of racially mixed ancestry (mestizos in Portuguese usage, Coloureds in South Africa).

Another high-status group owed its position to leading rank in the historical political and religious structures of African society. Particularly where political structures were relatively centralized, ruling lineage remained an important source of societal rank. Where African rulers were incorporated as intermediaries in the colonial state structure, above all in nonsettler British territories, they retained significant prestige and authority.[18] The sons of royal families were often among the first to pass through the Western schools, enabling them to combine the status accruing to higher education with customary standing. In some areas, most notably Senegal and Sudan, the leading notables of influential Islamic religious orders (Ansar and Khatmiyya, in Sudan; Mourides and Tijaniyya in Senegal) also retained and even reinforced their high social rank.[19]

At the mass level, "worker" and "peasant" became meaningful sociological categories for the first time. In the early stages, mines, plantations, and construction of infrastructure (railways and roads) were carried out by highly labor-intensive methods and at very low wages. Substantial coercion was required to mobilize this labor force, which at first was mainly migratory or even seasonal. By the later decades of colonial rule, workforces became increasingly stabilized, as wage employment became a long-term commitment rather than a temporary interruption of a rural career. Until the 1950s, however, urban centers remained mostly small and dominated by the foreign estate. Proletarian consciousness of the sort that gave rise to socialist parties in late nineteenth-century Europe was still embryonic; it tended to be eclipsed by other forms of social consciousness (race and ethnicity).[20]

If by "peasant" we mean the rural persons whose primary goal in farming is to provide their own means of subsistence, based on family labor and hand tools, linked to a broader society as a subordinate component, then for most of Africa "peasantization" occurred during the colonial period. With a firm hegemony established over the countryside by the colonial state, African rural communities were linked to a broader system of control and exchange, ultimately extending to Europe and America. Some commercial production of export or food crops was grafted, often by force, onto the subsistence system.

Through its subordination to the colonial state and its partial incorporation in a wider capitalist economy, the peasantry lost its isolation and part of its autonomy. The loss of autonomy was by no means total, as argued in an influential work by Goran Hyden.[21] The peasantry retained some room for maneuver and possibilities for eluding the more vexatious impositions of the state. Beyond its market and political relationships, the peasantry remained partly governed by the system Hyden calls the "economy of affection." Local patterns of kinship obligation and community reciprocity and exchange provided crucial insurance for survival in times of distress. The economy of affection, outside the framework of state regulation before and after independence, imposed its own standards of solidarity, nurtured by ritual and exchange.

Further important changes in the configuration of social classes occurred after independence. The foreign estate lost its formal political power but generally retained its crucial economic position. At the same time, its composition changed. In colonial times, the dominant segment of the foreign estate was overwhelmingly drawn from the metropolitan (home) country. After independence, American and other multinational corporations entered the scene. So also did an international technocracy, composed of foreign assistance personnel, representatives of the United Nations and other international organizations, and diplomatic establishments. Although only a small part of the population, they are highly visible, particularly in the capital cities. Their opulent life-style sets consumption expectations for the dominant African class.

The lowest segment of the foreign estate, the Mediterranean and Asian immigrants who dominated commerce, have fared less well. In a number of countries — most dramatically, Uganda in 1972 — they have been forced either to leave the country or to withdraw from parts of the commercial economy, to make way for African merchants. Many, however, have found methods for forming combinations with African politicians in order to conserve an economic foothold. Such arrangements have been the target for opposition criticism in such countries as Sierra Leone, where clandestine partnerships between leading political figures and Lebanese businessmen are alleged to be a major source of corruption in public life.

The dominant African social class today is the array of politicians and top bureaucrats who control the state apparatus. The initial generation of political leaders came from the colonial African elite, their avenue to ascent being agitational politics and party activity. In the ranks of the public service, the rapid Africanization of bureaucracies that everywhere swiftly followed independence opened opportunities for spectacular promotion for those poised in the clerical ranks.

Recruitment changed after these one-time opportunities for promotion were seized. The decline of competitive politics and the consolidation of authoritarian patterns of rule foreclosed possibilities of ascent through populist politics. Political promotion was a favor that could be accorded by those in power to clients who had demonstrated their loyalty through faithful service. In the state bureaucracy, entry into the top ranks depends on holding a university diploma; working up from the lower clerical ranks has become almost impossible.

With the military coup a new element was added to the state class: the top military officers. As the military became part of the political process, interpenetration of the military, political, and bureaucratic groups followed. For all, the class rank depended on maintaining their control of the state apparatus.

Various labels have come into circulation to describe the African ruling class: bureaucratic bourgeoisie, administrative bourgeoisie, and political class, among others. All these imply recognition that political power is paramount in shaping emergent class relations. Many now agree with Richard Sklar that social class in Africa reflects power relations and not relations of production.[22] We will employ the phrase "state bourgeoisie" to connote the dependency of the dominant African class on its hold on state power.

The state bourgeoisie does tend to seek to transform its political preeminence into an economic base. Leading politicians and military officers usually develop business sidelines, which depend on special favors from the state (urban property speculation, import-export firms, taxi fleets, contracting companies supplying the state). Because there is no guarantee that individual members of the state bourgeoisie will long retain their high offices, these ventures are oriented toward ensuring quick returns on capital and opportunities for transferring funds abroad; the state bourgeoisie has generally not been attracted to long-term investments in manufacturing or mining.

Beyond parallel business ventures, carried on directly or through family intermediaries, corruption itself has been a major source of accumulation. Zaire and Nigeria have been most notorious in this respect, but state operations in most countries have been seriously affected by this phenomenon. Leaders such as Mobutu of Zaire (in power since 1965) have accumulated colossal wealth in office; Mobutu's holdings are widely estimated to approximate $5 billion.[23] West Indian economist Arthur Lewis detected this trend early in the game, commenting in 1965, "To be a Minister is to have a lifetime's chance to make a fortune."[24] The significance of the corruption phenomenon does vary in degree. In some countries, such as Botswana and Cape Verde, it has been far less pervasive. Leaders such as Julius Nyerere of Tanzania or Samora Machel of Mozambique were noted for their personal austerity.

In only a few states do we observe the emergence of a locally based capitalist class. Control of the economic infrastructure has usually been in the hands of the state and the foreign estate. Nigeria, Kenya, and Egypt, all of which possess an indigenous entrepreneurial group, are notable exceptions.[25] In Zimbabwe and especially South Africa, a strong capitalist class exists, but it is mostly limited to the white population.

Class consciousness is above all encountered among the state bourgeoisie. However, it would be erroneous to perceive the state bourgeoisie as a homogeneous or monolithic grouping. Viewed more closely, it is laced with factional divisions that are rooted in ethnicity, patron–client networks, sometimes ideology, and not infrequently competing external linkages.

Below the state bourgeoisie, foreign estate, and indigenous capitalist classes, the stratification pattern grows more complex. Two significant intermediate groups deserve our attention here: subaltern employees of the public and private bureaucratic structures, and new mercantile groups rooted in the swelling underground economies. The former are wholly tributary to the state; the latter grow up mainly outside the public domain.

Lower level state employees and their counterparts in large private sector firms may be called a petty bourgeoisie. This important group has greatly increased in number and diminished in status since independence. They include the clerks, teachers, lower ranks in the security forces, nurses, and similar occupational categories. Nearly everywhere since the 1950s, public employment has experienced explosive growth. In Kenya, the civil service employed 14,000 in 1945, a figure that increased to 170,000 in 1980. The Egyptian bureaucracy — which has served as employer of last resort for graduating university classes now numbering 100,000 — quadrupled in size between 1950 and 1970.[26]

Although the number of lower state employees has increased, their relative standing and material well-being have declined. A generation ago, those holding such posts, though of modest financial circumstances, were the highest ranking African social category. Furthermore, avenues for spectacular ascent were opening through politics and the Africanization of bureaucracies. Both pathways to social mobility are now closed. In many states, the petty bourgeoisie has become a vocal and volatile disaffected group, quick to welcome coups —and, today, democratization.

In the last two decades, a large underground economy has taken shape. In West Africa the phenomenon is known as *kalabule* (a Hausa word) and in East Africa, by the Swahili term *magendo*. In both cases, the term carries the connotation "black market." The underground economy is particularly large in countries such as Uganda, Zaire, and Ghana, which have experienced high inflation, and Tanzania or Sierra Leone, where foreign exchange shortages have compelled severe restrictions on imports. The large number and small scale of African states mean that some international frontier is usually not far away, and smuggling becomes highly profitable. Internally in many countries, the inadequacy of state marketing monopolies in agricultural or other products or artificially low state-imposed prices also provide strong incentives for black market dealings.

At the bottom of the social hierarchy are the urban and rural poor. In most African countries the ranks of the working class in the classic sense — manual laborers in wage employment — remain relatively small and have not increased in recent years. Much recent industrial and mineral development has been capital intensive, and it has provided only a modest number of jobs. Petroleum, for example, which accounts for as much as 90 percent of Nigerian state revenue and export earnings, employs no more than 20,000 persons out of a population of 110 million. Proletarian consciousness, weak in most countries, is clearly strongest in the most highly industrialized African state, South Africa, where labor protest has played a crucial role since the 1970s. Worker consciousness is somewhat stronger in the Arab tier of states in the north than in sub-Saharan Africa.

Much larger numerically than the worker category are the poor of the informal sector. These people lack access to regular wage employment and carry out a multitude of small-scale activities. Petty trade, small artisan activity, messenger service, personal services (standing in line in post offices, washing or watching cars), prostitution, pilferage — these are the survival pursuits of growing numbers of urban poor.[27] Such activities have always been a part of the urban scene; the new factor is their scale, which has made this sector a distinctive sphere of the economy, widely recognized as such only since the 1970s.

Survival niches grow up in the interstices of urban society for these huge numbers of persons without wage employment who must live by their wits. As one example among many, in the early 1980s Abidjan police developed a new strategy to combat an epidemic of illegal parking in the central city by letting the air out of the tires of offending vehicles. This practice immediately created a new informal-sector occupation; youths equipped with tire pumps appeared on the scene, ready to rescue parking violators with flattened tires for a dollar or two.[28]

Finally, we come to the peasantry. In most countries, rural populations have failed to benefit from independence. Only a handful of states can point to improving conditions in the countryside; Zimbabwe, Botswana, Cameroon, and Kenya would probably qualify. For most, a combination of such factors as heavy fiscal impositions (especially through export taxes on agricultural commodities), unfavorable prices (aimed at holding down food costs for urban consumers), and decline of rural infrastructure (roads, marketing facilities) have brought a decline in real income and a disincentive to produce for the official markets.[29] In the 1980s prices for a number of once profitable export crops went into a tailspin. Faced with disappointment in the hopes generated by independence, the peasantry — to an extent not anticipated by the political leadership — exercised the option of "exit," or silent withdrawal into the "economy of affection."[30]

Social class and cultural pluralism are the two most important dimensions of social cleavage, competition, and conflict. Linking them are the pervasive patron–client networks, with which society is honeycombed. The poor seek protection, access to government favor, and emergency aid from a more powerful patron in the event of misfortune, to whom they have a natural connection of kinship or community. The patron, in turn, expects service and support from his clients; he also fulfills customary value expectations of kinship obligation and solidarity.

POLITICAL CULTURE

Political culture in Africa is best seen as an amalgam of contradictory elements. The most important polarity is that between Western value systems introduced by the colonial state and Christian evangelization, and indigenous African cultural orientations. In the religious realm, Islamic, Christian, and African world-views contrast, with significant political implications. In the ideological sphere, differing forms of political philosophy have appeared, generally falling at the radical end of the spectrum and incorporating blends of nationalism, populist socialism, and Marxism. Finally, though less important, some differences in political culture are attributable to ethnic or regional distinction.

During colonial times, European hegemony resulted in a massive transfusion of Western values. African culture was generally held to be of slight value, and most administrators and missionaries had little interest in its nurture or preservation. From this perspective, African culture tended to be an impediment to the creation of disciplined workers, loyal subjects, and faithful converts. Thus, all aspects of colonial policy had the European behavioral model as their point of reference.

The influence of Western values was most strongly felt by those Africans who, by education and occupation, were closest to Europeans. Social mobility, beyond a very low ceiling, was available only to those who could demonstrate dexterity in meeting European behavioral expectations. To win admission to universities at home or overseas, a secondary school training equivalent to that in the home country was necessary.

In juxtaposition to the Western values linked with the state, the foreign state, and an important part of the state bourgeoisie stands the African cultural heritage. In northern Africa, this is inseparable from Islam as a world-view. A number of African political philosophers and religious thinkers assert that broad cultural similarities in sub-Saharan Africa transcend the particularities of specific ethnic communities. These arguments were particularly associated with such political leaders as Senghor, Kwame Nkrumah, and Nyerere, and such philosophers as Willie Abraham of Ghana, Joseph Ki-Zerbo of Burkina Faso, and John Mbiti of Kenya.

The common themes in African culture include a humanistic perspective, a value on community consensus and harmony, a synthesis of the material and nonmaterial worlds, and a view of the living community as an indissoluble part of a great chain of being incorporating the spirits of past ancestors and the generations yet to be born. According to those who have drawn on an African world-view as an ideological resource, it contrasts sharply with the materialism and rationalism of Western cultures. The value of consensus is embodied in the priority accorded in jurisprudence to reconciling the disputing parties. African political philosophy also views leadership as embodying the vitality of a community.

Within African states, some difference was observable between political cultures associated with various ethnic communities. In the political realm, perhaps the most important difference had to do with the attitudes toward authority visible in societies that had experienced a high order of precolonial political centralization, as contrasted to the large number of highly decentralized structures.[31] Compared with the contrast between African and Western values, however, these differences paled into relative insignificance.

In countries where Islam is the dominant faith, religion plays a significant and probably growing part in political culture. In these states, Islam is usually enshrined as the state religion. With the upsurge of integralist Islamic movements in the late 1970s, greater emphasis on Islamic heritage was frequent. The assassination of President Anwar Sadat of Egypt in 1981 was symptomatic of the pressures the religious vector of political culture placed on rulers; Sadat was accused by his slayers of having betrayed Islam. In 1990, in an astonishing upset, the fundamentalist *Front Islamique de Salut* (FIS) won a stunning victory in local and regional elections over the long-entrenched *Front de Liberation Nationale* (FLN), the secular and socialist movement that had led Algeria to independence in an epic eight-year struggle. The FIS, campaigning for an integral Islamic state, won 54.1 percent of the vote, against only 28.1 percent for the FLN.

Other examples of the vitality of popular Islam in folk culture have appeared in Nigeria. In five major cities in the northern, Islamic area, serious confrontations pitted the Nigerian security forces against the impoverished, zealous followers of the heterodox Islamic sect Maitatsine (Gombe, 1985; Kaduna, 1982; Kano, 1980; Maiduguri, 1982; Yola, 1984). Thousands of lives were lost in these battles.[32]

POLITICAL SOCIALIZATION

The concept of political socialization has been defined as "the process by which people acquire relatively enduring orientations toward politics in general and toward their own particular political systems."[33] Our understanding of political socialization has developed through research in Western countries, where political structures and processes have been relatively stable. Thus, the young acquire their orientations in a setting where the political system is a relatively fixed object, and society changes gradually. Even in the West, research suggests that gradual changes in socialization are brought about by dramatic events such as the Vietnam War or long-term changes such as the coming of age of generations with no recollection of the acute material deprivation of the Great Depression.

In Africa, political socialization occurs in a world of turbulent and dramatic change, both in the nature of society and in the structure of politics. In recent decades, socialization forces have been radically different for each succeeding generation. Adding to the complexity are several sharply different spheres of political learning: family, school, place of worship, the street. These various milieus may transmit highly contrasting lessons.

The family is the point of departure. There is no sense of "partisan" alignment or party identification to be transmitted, nor is it likely that ideological orientation will originate here. The child will, however, be taught aspects of his or her social identity that will play their part in defining future political orientation. A maternal language, an initial consciousness of ethnic affinity, originate here. So do a basic set of cultural beliefs and values that draw on the ancestral heritage of society.

The family structure, particularly in sub-Saharan Africa, is not directly comparable to the Western nuclear family. Many will spend part of their childhood with relatives, particularly if they are born in rural areas and wish to pursue their education beyond the first primary grades that may be available in the village. Family influences are likely to include exposure to the political knowledge of a wider circle of kinsmen than simply the biological parents.

Religious milieus may also be a means of acquiring political learning. Both Islam and Christianity possess powerful instruments for inculcating their perspectives in the young generation. Induction of the young into the faith is indispensable for the survival and expansion of the community of believers. Although both Islam and Christianity, in their instructional efforts, deal primarily with transmitting religious knowledge and belief, there are significant political implications in their labors.

Wherever established, Islam has centers of religious instruction, extending down into local communities. At the most rudimentary level, this teaching consists of rote recitation of the Koran in Arabic. But beyond memorization of Koranic verses, significant attitudes toward the state are transmitted in religious idiom: the obligation of obedience to constituted authority, unless the rule is impious and destructive of Islamic values; the duty of the state to promote a framework in which Islam may flourish; a comprehensive code of private and public behavior. One of the secrets of the vitality of contemporary Islam lies in the effectiveness of the socialization system.

The Christian churches often continue to play an important part in operating the formal educational system. Their action is still influenced by their missionary background; Christian communities are for the most part still of recent origin, and thus they are intensely preoccupied with deepening their roots in Africa. Though generally deferential to authority in their teachings, Christian clerics have often tried to promote ethical standards they feel are violated by state behavior, in countries as diverse as South Africa (condemning racism) and Zaire (denouncing corruption and oppression).

The independent state is very active in socialization efforts. African rulers are highly conscious of a need to build among the young a commitment to the new states as nations. At the same time, they stress fostering loyalty to the regime itself and to its leader. This goal is pursued through obligatory civics courses in school curricula, organization of youth branches of the dominant parties, and use of the state-controlled media (radio and press). Frequent public ceremonials — parades, dances, speeches — devoted to praise of the regime and appeals to national unity pursue the goal of socialization.

At the same time, the state is engaged in continuous socialization through its daily actions. Citizens, young and old, observe the operation of government and develop their own orientations toward politics and legitimacy of regime and state based on their perceptions of its behavior. There is good reason to believe that state-directed socialization has made important progress in consolidating acceptance of the idea of nation: "We are all Nigerians," or "We are all Tunisians." But where the state's public claims as to its policy goals and ideals are belied by its actual performance, the young will be quick to perceive the contradiction.

Surveys have demonstrated that African students combine a strong sense of commitment to their nation with striking cynicism about the integrity of the state and its representatives. As Table 16.4 demonstrates, in 1973 Nigerian students considered national unity far more important than economic development. At the same time, they were convinced that the behavior of political leaders and public servants was motivated primarily by ethnicity and corruption. The cynical disposition of youth toward the state and its rulers produced by the daily socialization of observed leader behavior found further confirmation in Nigeria in 1989 when a furor arose over reports that the May 1989 issue of the American magazine *Ebony* contained revelations that Presi-

TABLE 16.4
POLITICAL BELIEFS OF NIGERIAN UNIVERSITY STUDENTS: RESPONSES TO SURVEY QUESTIONS (PERCENTAGE CHOOSING EACH ALTERNATIVE)

Which is more important in a developing country? (Mark one of the pair of alternatives.)

	Ahmadu Bello University (1973)	Ibadan (1973)	Nsukka (1973)
Economic development	11.9%	14.0%	12.3%
National unity	88.1%	85.9%	87.7%

What were the greatest weaknesses of the First Nigerian Republic? (Choose three of the alternatives.)

	Ahmadu Bello University (1971)
Ethnic bitterness	77.7%
Financial corruption	50.4%
Poor calibre of politicians	41.0%
Unrestrained use of power against opponents	34.7%
Lack of ideology	33.7%
Constitutional balance between the regions	22.3%
Failure to promote rapid economic growth	12.7%
Failure to retain sympathy of educated elite groups	7.1%

What proportion of civil servants in most African countries are capable of putting national interests ahead of their own interests and family loyalties?

	Ahmadu Bello University (1970)	Ibadan (1972)	Lagos (1972)
Almost all	0.6%	3.2%	0.8%
Most but by no means all	10.8%	2.6%	12.0%
Relatively few	88.6%	94.2%	87.2%

Source: From *Education and Power in Nigeria* by Paul Beckett and James O'Connell. Copyright © 1977 by Paul Beckett and James O'Connell. Reprinted by permission of Hodder & Stoughton Publishers.

dent Ibrahim Babangida had embezzled $700 million. These rumors were without foundation; *Ebony* contained no such article. But the instant credence such a report could acquire well demonstrated the depth of suspicion concerning venality in the public realm.[34]

Much socialization occurs in informal settings, but it is somewhat different in rural and urban areas. In the countryside, where many people dwell in small communities, there is likely to be an organized set of social mechanisms through which social learning occurs. The elders and notables of the community, repositories of its wisdom, are influential in transmitting values to the young. Often some form of initiation ceremony marks the passage from childhood to adolescence and puberty; these are occasions for intensive instruction in the values of the group. Although much of this socialization is focused on the local lore of the community, it may well include more general orientations toward politics.

The dynamic of social learning is quite different in the towns and is much less under the control of the elders. Street-level society takes over as the primary focus for adolescents. The environment of poverty, the insecurity of urban life, and the ceaseless struggle for survival and employment form a crucible within which informal acquisition of political orientations takes place.

The rapidity of change and the complexity of political learning processes in Africa make it difficult to reach confident conclusions about the overall influence of socialization. We also lack the extensive body of research findings on this theme available for Western states. One may doubt whether African states enjoy the same reservoir of "diffuse support" that Western systems appear to acquire through the mechanisms of political socialization.[35]

In the new era that seems to be opening in the 1990s, where African states are groping toward more democratic forms of governance, the negative socializing effects on youth of regimes and rulers perceived as venal, inept, and oppressive constitute a major challenge. Nowhere is this more starkly illustrated than in South Africa in the search for a post-apartheid political order. Even an organization such as the African National Congress (ANC), respected for its long struggle against racial oppression, finds it difficult to capture the trust and channel the angry energies of a youth whose adolescent socialization has occurred in brutalizing and repressive conditions.

POLITICAL COMMUNICATION

The flow of information in Africa follows channels that contrast with those characterizing Western political systems. Political communication occurs through both formal and informal vehicles. What stands out in Africa is the relative importance of radio for formal communication, and the remarkable effectiveness of informal channels for filtering — and often distorting — information.

The authoritarian character of most African states, along with the leadership's fears about instability, has led the state to take close control of print, broadcast, and electronic media.[36] Governments generally seek to use the media as an instrument for political education of the public; frequently, the major newspapers are vehicles of the ruling party. In some countries, the press may have some latitude for discreet criticism, as long as it does not directly attack the ruler. Radio and television (as in most countries of the world) are invariably run by the state.

There are some exceptions to the limited freedom of expression of the press. Nigeria is the most important. The Nigerian press has a long tradition, dating from colonial times, of uninhibited expression. Even during the years of military rule (1966–1979, 1983–), Nigerian newspapers retained a degree of independence (even though most are now government-owned). In Senegal, a vigorous opposition press thrives, although the government daily enjoys evident financial advantages. Across the continent, the trend toward political opening at the beginning of the 1990s is felt at once in

the information field, as even state-run organs begin to engage in critical commentary.

Newspapers circulate mainly in the major cities; their readership is restricted by the poverty of the mass of the populace and relatively high illiteracy rates. The intellectual elite is likely to read news magazines and newspapers from abroad as well. In many countries, foreign publications, which circulate mainly in the capital cities, are likely to be seized if they contain commentary critical to the regime in question.

With the spread of the transistor radio in the 1960s, most of Africa has come within the reach of the broadcast media. Transistors are sufficiently cheap that even in rural communities some persons can afford them; because they are battery-powered, they do not depend on a supply of electricity. A handful of radios in a small community can bring the broadcast message within the reach of most residents.

Particularly important in considering the influence of radio is the diversity of information sources it makes possible. Most state-controlled national radio networks offer selective and sanitized reporting on domestic political affairs, but a number of international services blanket Africa with powerful signals easy to receive virtually everywhere in languages that are widely understood. The best of these, such as the British Broadcasting Corporation, enjoy a high reputation for accuracy and objectivity. France Inter and Voice of America also draw eager listeners. Although they do not provide detailed coverage of domestic events in particular African countries, major political events, which may be blacked out on the national radio because of their security implications, are likely to be reported on the international networks. Governments can effectively restrict the flow of information through the press, but it is virtually impossible to impede diffusion of information by radio. Even more uncomfortable for a number of states is the fact that the foreign broadcasts generally enjoy higher credibility than those of the domestic networks. Politically conscious Africans develop the habit of listening to several different foreign news reports daily.

Television has a much more limited effect. The cost of television sets is beyond the means of all but the most affluent citizens, who are limited to reception of the national network. Television broadcasting covers the capital city and a few larger provincial centers, but many rural citizens do not have access to this medium.

State-organized flows of political information are designed to elicit support for the incumbent regime. In countries where personalist rule has been pronounced, exaltation of the president and his achievements is daily fare. Much space is devoted to essentially didactic material, whose purpose is less to inform than to "educate" the reader in elementary civics.

Handling negative news becomes a delicate matter. The shortcomings of government policy may sometimes be criticized, but blame is placed on the inadequacies of subordinates or on ill fortune beyond the control of the regime. Above all, in most states the ruler has been exempt from criticism. Nor are continuing struggles among contending factions, symptoms of ethnic tensions, or other matters that could cast discredit on the regime likely to be reported.

But this by no means chokes off flows of information on the more scandalous or unflattering aspects of political life. The density and carrying capacity of informal channels of information are remarkable. In many African states, most parts of the country are within a day's road journey of the capital. Every morning at daybreak, assorted lorries, buses, and taxis set forth from a central bus park to all ends of the country. Drivers and passengers are laden with the latest news items on the system colloquially known as the "sidewalk radio." Truth, of course, is heavily laced with rumor and misinformation. Despite the distortions inherent in informal information flows, rural as well as urban citizens have a far more sophisticated understanding of politics than they might obtain if they relied solely on official information.

Marketplaces, bars, and cafes are important centers for informal political communication. Every town will have a central open marketplace, catering to those of modest means. The market is not only a place to obtain the necessities, but also an arena for social encounters. Especially in West Africa, the market vendors are generally women, whose wide range of customers make them a focal point for collecting and diffusing informal political news — and, in a number of countries, a potent political force in their own right.

The ubiquitous bars, with blaring music and copious consumption of beer, are not only places of entertainment, but also veritable unofficial newsrooms. The bar offers a relaxed ambiance for transmitting political gossip. Its informal mood loosens tongues and perhaps stokes the imaginations of those close enough to the passageways of power to have tales to bear.

Moments of political tension and crisis intensify the flow of informal information and enhance its distortion. In such situations, the official media are often silent, either because they do not wish to draw attention to the tensions or because they are uncertain how events should be presented to the public. Rumor has free rein; the popular mood of anxiety and uncertainty may lend momentary plausibility to reports that would normally strain the credulity of the most unwary citizen.

POLITICAL PARTICIPATION

Pressures for democratization which are sweeping the continent in the 1990s seem likely to produce important changes in the dynamic of political participation. The multiple mechanisms of political closure put in place by single-party and military regimes are beginning to crumble, as pressures for pluralization of politics from within and without build. The ultimate implications of these transformations are as yet unclear; what can be said with confidence is that important alterations in the role of participation are in course.

Large-scale participation occurred for the first time after World War II when nationalist political parties appeared.[37] At first, these parties were led by African notables who already had some access to the colonial authorities. But quickly there appeared populist leaders such as Nkrumah of Ghana, Sekou Toure of Guinea, and Nyerere of Tanzania, who saw that the most effective challenge to colonial rule lay in mass mobilization and agitational politics.

Weakening colonial administrations, having agreed to elections, had to accept their role. Aggressive political organization by nationalist parties in areas under British and French rule was generally tolerated by the 1950s, and frequent elections occurred in which these movements could display their strength. As independence neared, demonstration of numerical strength became indispensable to validate the claims of a nationalist movement to succeed to power. Thus, practical necessity as well as populist mood pushed parties toward organizing mass participation.

As parties extended their organizational efforts across the countryside, there was an era of turbulent — for many exhilarating — political participation. Central party organizations could encourage but not really direct and control the outburst of political activity. Particularly for ambitious young men, politics offered an unprecedented opportunity for leadership and self-expression. Political rallies and meetings across the country attracted large throngs. Agitational politics, bound to the

African National Congress leader Nelson Mandela tries to rally other African countries behind the struggle against South African apartheid after his release from prison in 1990. On the stage with him are his wife Winnie Mandela and Zimbabwe President Robert Mugabe.

simple themes of anticolonial protest and liberation, in many countries engendered a remarkably high order of mass participation.

Once in power, the new leaders sought to direct participation toward support and legitimation of their rule. It was soon apparent that it was hard to achieve the metamorphosis from opposition to support. For a number of reasons, regimes began to curb participation after independence. Opposition, rulers argued, led to disorder and instability, to a drain and waste of energies needed for national development. The high expectations created by the nationalist parties, their rulers recognized, could not be satisfied at once; thus, disappointed movements, factions, or leaders could easily stir their followers to renewed agitation. The general mass politicization attending the phase of nationalist organization had sharply raised not only national, but also ethnic, consciousness. As one writer put it, "departicipation" was a necessary strategy for taming the demons of ethnicity.[38]

Departicipation was a clear trend by the early 1960s. The single-party system was institutionalized in many countries, and military regimes began to appear. Arbitrary colonial legislation permitting the detention of

political foes without legal process was exhumed and widely used. Elections were transformed into ritualized plebiscites, with voters called on to approve a single list of candidates.

Beginning in 1969, the emergence of an explicitly Leninist state doctrine in several countries introduced a new normative code of participation. Full membership in the ruling party was restricted to the ideological elect, who could claim mastery of the Marxist-Leninist doctrine adopted by the state. Loosely modeled on Soviet theories of state organization, and most highly elaborated in Ethiopia, Leninist doctrine restricts full involvement in affairs of state to the ruler and his immediate entourage. Linkage with the mass of the population is to be sustained by party-directed ancillary organizations: unions, youth, women, and the like. In reality, participation through such channels, even in the orchestrated form desired, has been extremely limited, and Leninist regimes have fared no better than others in sustaining the vitality of state–civil society relationships.

Historically, restrictions on participation in South Africa have been unique in the utilization of racial criteria that deny political rights to the 71.5 percent of the population which is African. Whites enjoyed participation rights and competitive politics, although even they were subject to stringent security legislation. A new constitution in 1984 endeavored to co-opt the Coloured[39] and Indian communities by offering restricted participation rights. However, the condition attached to this participation — collaborating in a system that rigorously excluded black Africans — was unacceptable to many within these communities. In 1990 the release of African leader Nelson Mandela and the legalization of political movements representing the black majority, opened the door to possible future participation by all South Africans.

The trend toward departicipation did not reflect antipathy to all forms of participation. On the contrary, most rulers wished to find formulas whereby the populace could be involved in support of the regime. In this sense, state attitudes toward participation were in clear contrast to the attitudes of the colonial state. The colonial state sought apolitical domination; compliance and tranquility from the subject population sufficed. Postcolonial regimes felt the need to legitimate their rule through at least formal expressions of support.

This controlled, state-directed participation took several forms. One was the periodic conduct of plebiscitary elections. The electoral campaign, though devoid of competition, was not without significance. The incumbent regime used the occasion to organize meetings throughout the country, where its agents trumpeted the ruling party's accomplishments. State-controlled media were given over for a time to exaltation of the ruler.

Another pattern of imposed participation occurred through the continuing ritual of party activity. One form, developed in Zaire, Malawi, and Togo in particular, was the creation of party dance troupes. These teams, in colorful uniforms decorated with party and national symbols, performed dances combining African cultural themes and urban popular music. These were accompanied by praise songs, reciting the heroic qualities of the rule and the epic virtues of the party. Party luminaries punctuated the performances with discursive presentations of the same messages. Particularly when the form was novel, large crowds could be attracted to these sessions. Whatever one thought of the political messages, it was good entertainment.

The purposes of this form of participation are well expressed in the foreword to a collection of patriotic party songs published by the Ministry of Culture and Arts in Zaire.

The patriotic and revolutionary songs of the MPR [the Zairian ruling party] contain the teachings of the Guide of the Zairian Nation [President Mobutu], the core of his thought, the enumeration of his major achievements. The name of the Guide is sung with joy to render homage to him, to express to him the profound gratitude of the Zairian people, and to assure him the blessing of our ancestors to these prayers of invocation.[40]

A number of presidents employed the technique of direct dialogue with the populace with skill and effect. Particularly effective in using this form of participation was Houphouet – Boigny of the Ivory Coast and Nyerere of Tanzania. Periodic tours of the countryside were undertaken. The president not only addressed the large throngs that a chief of state can usually attract, but also engaged in question-and-answer exchanges. He would also receive individual petitioners and hear more individual grievances or learn about specific local needs: repair of a school, replenishment of a clinic's medical supplies, construction of a new communal well. Usually, the president could employ his control over state funds to provide immediate gratification of some of the requests: a few boxes of pharmaceuticals for the health center or cash on the spot to replace the leaking school roof. These "gifts" of the president are designed to create the impression of a direct channel from people to ruler and to symbolize the effectiveness of this form of participation.[41]

Africa's dramatically transformed political atmosphere, in the 1990s was well illustrated by the evidently declining efficacy of this form of participative link between ruler and ruled. The culminating event that led President Mobutu of Zaire to yield to demands for multiple parties was a dialogue tour in early 1990, where citizens expressed their anger at diminished well-being with remarkably audacious candor.

The local administration is also charged with continuously maintaining contact with the populace and securing its participation in public presentations of state policy. When any important new measures are announced, administrators are called on to organize public meetings to announce the policy and to secure expressions of acquiescence. The administration may also serve as a means of access for citizens in a less manipulative sense. Through the regional and local administration, the state is in face-to-face contact with its citizenry. For many categories of concerns and problems, the citizenry will first seek redress — individually or in delegations representing local communities or groups —

through contact with the state administrator. Local administrators are supposed to spend a good part of their time — half or more — on tour of their district (though in reality few meet these targets because of logistical problems — a vehicle may be out of order, there are no funds for gas — or personal disinclination to spend this amount of time in "the bush"). Much of their time on "safari" is consumed with hearing grievances and adjudicating local disputes. Henry Bienen contends that this access to administration is an important and meaningful form of participation in Kenya, a state whose administration enjoys a relatively high reputation for its competence. Many of the immediate concerns of the populace can be addressed at this level, without requiring any overall change in law or policy at the national level.[42]

The evident potential contradiction between the single-party system and effective participation was recognized in a growing number of states, even before the democratization surge in 1990. The first state to address the issue directly was Tanzania, under the inspiration of its first leader, President Nyerere. An original and innovative formula for permitting political competition and achieving some accountability while preserving the single-party structure was introduced in 1965, and has remained in place since that time. For parliamentary elections, in each constituency, voters were to be offered the choice of two candidates, both put forward by the ruling party. Virtually any party member could introduce his or her candidacy with a small number of supporting signatures on a petition. The local party organs screened the candidacies, eliminating those felt to lack commitment to the party program and goals and favoring those believed to have superior credentials for public office. Candidates were ranked at the local level, with the national executive committee making the final designations (usually, in practice, accepting the local rankings).

The party then organized the electoral campaign under strict rules designed to protect the integrity of the process and to place beyond challenge the party itself and its national program. Candidates could campaign only at public forums organized by the party. Informal canvassing, beer parties, and other popular forms of vote solicitation were forbidden. Debates had to take place in the national language, Swahili. References to race, religion, or ethnicity were outlawed, and basic party policy commitments were beyond debate. Thus, candidates were not expected to offer alternative programs. They were to compete on their personal qualifications, and, most importantly, to represent the local constituency to the national party and government.

Despite these restrictions, the electoral campaigns have generated real excitement. Participation rates have been relatively high, remaining at about 80 percent of those registered in the successive elections held under these rules in 1965, 1970, 1975, 1980, 1985, and 1990. Over this period, the outcome revealed a strikingly consistent pattern; roughly half the sitting members of Parliament were ousted. Electoral studies show that incumbent defeat reflects the voters' belief that the incumbents have grown "too fat" in office or have failed to defend constituency interests aggressively.[43] Whatever its limits, this form of participation has been more meaningful than state-controlled rituals celebrating the virtues of incumbent rulers. The Tanzanian model was copied in several other states in the 1970s and 1980s, usually with similar results. Zambia, Kenya, Sierra Leone, the Ivory Coast, and Zaire have all conducted competitive single-party elections to elect legislative members.

Through such mechanisms, the electoral process has shown more vitality in Africa than is commonly supposed. Careful studies of such elections in a number of countries demonstrate that the citizenry has a ready willingness to participate and attaches a real value to the process. The more widespread electoral competition now in prospect, with the trend toward democratization, offers the African state battered by the economic crises of the 1970s and 1980s and weakened by the cynicism of much of the populace an opportunity to repair the frayed relationship between state and civil society.

POLITICAL RECRUITMENT

Patterns of political recruitment have changed markedly over the years. In the colonial era, the few Africans who achieved some kind of preeminence did so by cooperation with the structures of alien rule. Some recognized customary rulers over large groups, such as the kings of Buganda in Uganda, the Ashanti in Ghana, or the emirs of northern Nigeria, had a significant role. A combination of pedigree in a royal lineage, official recognition by the colonizer, and sufficient Western schooling to function in the colonial state framework determined selection. A handful achieved leadership in professional fields or the civil service.

With the birth of nationalist parties, this older generation of African leaders was usually brushed aside.

Those who now rose to the surface were equipped with quite different skills: oratorical power, organizational flair, personal charisma, and a populist style. Fluent command of the state language imposed by the colonizer was necessary, but otherwise only modest educational attainments were requisite. Members of the political class produced by the nationalist surge of the 1950s were mostly young; relatively few had university degrees.

This generation succeeded to power when independence came, with every expectation of a long career in high political office. Some soon acquired sufficient assets to withdraw from politics into the relative safety of a commercial vocation. For many, perhaps most, politics was not only a calling, but also the only conceivable line of high-status employment.

The recruitment pattern was somewhat different in states that won independence through guerrilla struggle, such as Algeria, Zimbabwe, Mozambique, Angola, and Guinea-Bissau. In these states there was a clear division of function between the external leadership, operating in the diplomatic arena, and the guerrilla fighters, carrying out the actual struggle. Liberation struggle was a political environment in which toughness and even ruthlessness were required for effectiveness, rather than the coalition-building and bargaining skills crucial for nationalist leaders who won their spurs through electoral and agitational strategies.

After independence, the rules of the game changed decisively. Agitational politics were excluded; there was no place for the populist orator who could electrify an audience with his exposure of governmental abuse. Recognition and promotion depended on the favor of those at the political summit. Faithful service to those in power again determined ascension. Being labeled a rebel or a subversive incurred the risk of political ruin. The peaceful successions that took place following the death or retirement of an incumbent generally went to "dauphins" who had long served as faithful subordinates to the previous ruler (Abdou Diouf in Senegal, Quett Masire in Botswana, Joseph Momoh in Sierra Leone, Paul Biya in Cameroon, for example).

In most countries the end of open electoral competition removed one critical arena for achieving political visibility. In Nigeria, where full political competition was restored in 1979 after a thirteen-year military interlude, the immediate reemergence of the "old brigade" of politicians who had won fame in the 1950s was striking; no new faces could emerge in the political void of military rule. Two of the leading 1979 and 1983 presidential candidates, Obafemi Awolowo and Nnamdi Azikiwe, have dominated Nigerian politics since the 1940s. (Awolowo died in 1987, and Azikiwe is now over eighty years old.) One of the many uncertainties in Nigeria's transition to a promised full restoration of democratic politics by 1992 is the source of leadership. In framing the rules for Nigeria's "Third Republic," the military rulers have banned all "old politicians" from political roles, blaming their venality and unbridled personal ambition for the failure of Nigeria's first two experiments in constitutional democracy (1960–1966, 1979–1983).

The appearance by 1965 of the military coup as a major feature of African politics introduced new unpredictability into political recruitment. The disposition and ability to organize a coup has little relationship to the political skills required to govern. Indeed, the range of performance of military rulers in office is extremely wide. Some of Africa's most effective and reflective leaders have come from the military (Hosni Mubarak and Anwar Sadat of Egypt, Houari Boumedienne and Benjedid Chadli of Algeria, Yakubu Gowon and Muritala Mohammed of Nigeria), as have its most reviled tyrants (Idi Amin of Uganda and Jean-Bedel Bokassa of the Central African Republic).

Military leaders have come from all ranks of the hierarchy. In some cases, the military high command has seized power, as with Mobutu of Zaire. In many, the putsch leaders have been middle-ranking officers, such as Muammar Qadafy of Libya or Mengistu Haile Meriam in Ethiopia. In some cases, coups have been carried out by noncommissioned officers (e.g., Master Sergeant Samuel Doe of Liberia in 1980, who was subsequently assassinated in 1990 after ten years in power).

The backgrounds of military leaders are correspondingly diverse. Some, such as Gamal Abdel Nasser and Sadat of Egypt had been part of clandestine factions within the army that had long engaged in intensive political discussion and study. Others, like Mengistu and Doe, came from low-status backgrounds with slender educational credentials, but were propelled by circumstance and instinct for power when opportunity for top office presented itself. Ali Mazrui labels the latter category the "lumpenmilitariat"; their humble origin initially gives a populist aura to their rule. Their exercise of power is marked by cunning, ruthlessness, and latent distrust of the highly educated technocrats on whose collaboration they must rely to run government departments.[44]

The handful of surviving rulers of the independence generation, such as Hastings Banda of Malawi or Houphouet-Boigny of the Ivory Coast, are now passing from the scene. The likelihood of at least a degree of democratization in the 1990s will open new channels for political recruitment and bring to the fore a fresh infusion of leadership candidates. Doubtless their backgrounds will be more diverse than either those of the independence generation or the coup-makers from the military ranks. Wealthy entrepreneurs; university professors; successful professionals from law or medicine; religious notables — whatever their provenance, their political skills will be sorely tested by the continuing economic and social crisis in prospect for the 1990s.

INTEREST ARTICULATION

In the sphere of interest articulation, the characteristics that stand out are the weakness and lack of autonomy of associational groups. In the terminal colonial period, associational activity acquired some importance. For a time in the 1950s, the colonial regimes actively encouraged these forms of association, partly because they were viewed as an outlet for social energies alternative to the nationalist political parties that directly challenged colonial rule. After independence, however, consolidation of single-party or military rule was accompanied by imposition of state control and reduction of existing groups to ancillary organs of the party or the state.

The single party conceived of itself as the sole representative of civil society. This conception necessarily implied that associations seeking to articulate particular interests could do so only within the party framework. Any organization that sought to subsist outside the party was viewed as a direct threat to its hegemony. Once under party tutelage, the association was subject to political direction and was prevented from expressing views counter to party doctrine or interests.

In the heyday of associational activity, in the 1950s, there were several important forms: unions, rural cooperatives, alumni associations, student and youth unions, and ethnic associations. Probably the most important in the long run were the trade unions. Unions were given some encouragement in the postwar world and enjoyed significant support from overseas. This help initially came from the major trade union federations in the metropolitan countries. Participation in

government by socialist parties in the home country (Britain, Belgium, France) closely tied to the labor movement in Europe led to pressure on the colonial regime to promote establishment of African unions. Representatives of the metropolitan trade unions were dispatched to the colonies to provide technical and financial backing to colonial unions. Promising young African unionists were brought to labor training institutes to learn the techniques of organizing workers and managing unions.

As independence neared, the major union internationals, the World Federation of Trade Unions (WFTU) and the International Confederation of Free Trade Unions (ICFTU), both mounted major recruiting efforts in Africa. Cold war politics played a critical role in these activities. The WFTU was under Soviet control, and the ICFTU during this period received support from the American Central Intelligence Agency (CIA). Their vigorous competition for African affiliates introduced a factor of bitter division among African unions, which in countries such as Nigeria persists to this day.

As single parties forced union movements within their fold, the international factor tended to diminish. With the apparent end of the cold war, it seems likely to shrink further in the 1990s. The obligation to uphold state policies in the economic sphere, however, frequently placed the union leadership in a delicate position. To make matters more difficult, union strength was often concentrated in the state sector (teachers, public employees). However populist their ideology, ruling parties were inevitably hostile to union militancy and especially strike action within the state sector. Thus, even when unions are within the ruling party structure, confrontations with the regime have been frequent in countries such as Algeria, Tunisia, Tanzania, and Congo-Brazzaville.

Beyond their subjugation to party or state tutelage, union influence on political life is also limited by the small number of industrial wage-earners in most countries, their susceptibility to ethnic fragmentation, and their meager resources. With a huge reserve army of underemployed persons penned in the informal sector, unskilled workers are difficult to protect by collective action and hard to organize.

In a number of countries, however, a subculture of union militance is well rooted in certain sectors: public sector workers in Congo-Brazzaville, Benin, and Burkina Faso; mine workers in Zambia. Here unions have a base in member support that governments cannot easily subdue by legislated controls. South Africa is a particularly important case in this respect; in the 1970s and 1980s unions representing African workers played a crucial role in undermining the structures of apartheid. Although the union movement supported the liberation goals of the political movements such as the ANC, they were by no means subordinated to them. When the ANC and other resistance movements were legalized in 1990 within the country, the unions continued to insist on their autonomous role, not only in their combat for the material interests of their membership, but also in the political realm.

Youth and student associations have been a major challenge for many regimes, and considerable energies have been deployed in seeking to control, guide, or neutralize them. This is partly a consequence of the demographic structure of African societies. Very high birth rates and comparatively low average life expectancy result in age pyramids heavily skewed toward the young. In nearly all African states, more than half the population is under eighteen.

Beyond sheer demographic weight, youths stand at the threshold of their careers, at a moment when their expectations are highest and their concerns about their future mobility prospects are most intense. Their social and political behavior is not yet constrained by their family responsibilities and by the attendant fear of losing a position in reprisal for challenging the established order. These factors help explain why organized youth so frequently adopt a critical and oppositionist stance toward those holding power.

The wave of unrest in much of Africa in the late 1980s was in large measure a youth phenomenon. The implacable austerity programs forced by circumstance and external donors on African states produced particularly intense resentments among the young. University and secondary school graduates found their hard-won credentials devalued by the blockage of government employment, as states were compelled to reduce their wage bills. The anger and frustration over bleak future prospects were a primary motivating force in the wave of youth-led violence in Senegal and Algeria in 1988. In South Africa, an angry and embittered youth was a crucial force in challenging apartheid from within the country.

Students have particular impact through their intellectual mastery over contemporary world ideologies. Radical and anti-imperial doctrines, which focus blame for African poverty and dependency on the failings of the state bourgeoisie internally and Western capitalist powers externally, have particular plausibility to many. Students are a free-floating social category in their university years. Many enter the ranks of the state bourgeoisie and, once launched in their careers, fall into acquiescent compliance, but while they remain on the university benches the state has little leverage over them. Rarely have African regimes been able to enjoy student support for an extended period. Even though students usually have difficulty enlisting other sectors of the populace to their cause, their capacity to formulate a sophisticated ideological critique of the incumbents makes them a constant irritant to holders of power.

Regimes have used diverse strategies in dealing with the youth and student challenge. Single-party states have usually required that youth and student organizations be incorporated within the party structure, in the hope that they can then be brought under the doctrinal guidance of the party, and its leadership subjected to party discipline (by screening candidates or even appointing officers). This tactic does tend to neutralize the youth and student organizations as associational bases for confrontation, but it usually falls far short of imposing ideological acquiescence on the membership. More forceful tactics of intimidation have also been employed. In 1971 the entire student body at the Kinshasa campus in Zaire was conscripted into the army after a protest demonstration; regime thugs killed an estimated fifty students at the Lubumbashi campus to instill fear in a restive student body in 1990. Selective arrests may be made of alleged ringleaders. On a number of occasions, universities have simply been closed and all students expelled from campus; the students are readmitted individually only after signing pledges to withdraw from protest activity. In Senegal in 1988 and the Ivory Coast in 1990, entire university years were canceled because of the prolonged closings of the campuses.

Religious associations have played some role. In some countries, Islamic orders (*tariq*, or brotherhood) are a force to be reckoned with (e.g., in Senegal, Sudan, and Nigeria). The Roman Catholic Church is also significant in countries where its missionary efforts were extensive in the colonial era. Religious organizations are not easily brought within the framework of single-party systems. Although they are not primarily political in orientation, they can provide an important framework for social organization. On the Catholic side, the radical liberation theology that is an influential current in the

Latin American church is not operative in Africa. Yet a pastoral letter read during religious services, or a declaration by religious authorities, can have a powerful effect. When Zairian bishops in 1981 adopted a statement denouncing the state as "organized pillage for the profit of the foreigner and his intermediary," the Mobutu regime was both shaken and outraged. Similarly, the plethora of independent Christian churches that have sprung up in recent years represent a disguised channel for expressing popular frustrations. Christianity, in the eloquent phrase of Achille Mbembe, becomes an instrument appropriated by the African expressing "his historic capacity for indiscipline."[45]

Finally, the articulation of external interests deserves mention. Foreign business and financial interests that have a major stake in a country will seek private channels of influence and access to the incumbent regime. These, of course, cannot be based on overt organizational forms. Chambers of commerce or other business organizations are not usually significant. Reliable access often depends on well-cultivated personal relationships with the head of state or his entourage.[46] Corruption may well play a part in promoting these relationships. In addition, prominent political personalities may be rewarded with lucrative posts on company boards of directors, which place no burden on their time.

The major international financial institutions, the IMF and the World Bank, can usefully be seen as external interest groups that speak for the public and private Western economic system. In recent years, their vast influence in determining the international creditworthiness of indebted African states has provided them with potent leverage in pushing policies of structural adjustment and fiscal rectitude which they and the constituencies for which they speak perceive as requisite for African recovery.

INTEREST AGGREGATION

Interest aggregation, in theory, is primarily a function of political parties. In Africa at the time of independence, the parties seemed destined to have a crucial role. The bureaucratic structures of the state were a legacy of the colonial past. Because civil society in the colonial state was composed of subjects and not citizens, there was neither a place nor the need for political institutions that bound people to polity. The state itself was an alien imposition.

Political parties, the organizational expression of anticolonial nationalism, were, then, the first truly African institutions. In challenging the legitimacy of colonial domination, nationalist parties argued in effect that they were the sole authentic expression of the popular will. European rulers controlled the state, but African political parties spoke for the nation.

Parties, then, had a gargantuan task. The nationalist movements had brought down the colonial state, but now a new order had to be constructed. Parties were charged with creating a new legitimacy for the independent state by africanizing it and bending it to the populist purposes proclaimed in the crusade against colonialism. The alien colonial state was to be transformed into a nation-state; the party was charged with reweaving the unit of common resistance to foreign oppression into shared commitment to a national political community. The post-independence party was to express the "general will" of the citizenry.

In reality, this program was far too ambitious for parties to fulfill. Far more quickly than anyone foresaw at the moment of independence, the simple act of assuming power altered the very nature of parties. The state itself was the institutional framework through which the party was to exercise power. The faithful who had campaigned tirelessly in the wilderness of opposition were rewarded with attractive posts in the state apparatus. Party and state flowed together and became difficult to distinguish.

The party's higher purpose of maintaining a monopoly of political authority proved, in most instances, incompatible with its functions of political representation and interest aggregation. Single parties, whose primary task was to uphold the authority and legitimacy of those in power, tended to atrophy. Their activities became primarily ceremonial and ritualistic. The populace became indifferent and apathetic to their exhortations.[47]

Whatever their limitations, parties were never abandoned by holders of power. They were viewed as indispensable to sustain a claim to legitimacy. Only those who claimed the alternative legitimacy of a historical monarchy could contemplate doing without a political party (as in Swaziland and in Ethiopia until 1974).

Indeed, military leaders who seized power by coup and resolved to remain in office permanently found it expedient to create new parties as symbolic legitimation. A military ruler might claim that forcible seizure of power was temporarily justified by a national emergency or the corruption and ineptitude of its predecessors. A claim to permanent rule, however, could not be publicly justified by force alone; a political institution, as the expression of a ritualistic blessing of the people, was needed.

The formula was first devised in Egypt in 1958, when President Nasser created the National Union (subsequently renamed the Arab Socialist Union). Organized from the top *undergirded* by the state, the party was an effort to equip the regime with an effective political channel to its citizenry and to consolidate its legitimacy. In 1967 Mobutu in Zaire launched his own single party to civilianize his leadership and legitimacy. Subsequently, several other military regimes (such as Togo, Mali, Rwanda, Burundi, and Sudan) copied this formula.

A voting station for the 1983 presidential election in Nigeria. Note the voting clerk marking the voter's hand with indelible ink to prevent double voting. Despite such precautions, the electoral process was widely believed to have been distorted by fraud, one factor leading to a reimposition of military rule at the end of 1983.

Another significant type of single party appeared in 1969, when the first explicitly Marxist-Leninist regime was created in Congo-Brazzaville. The earlier versions of a single party had always insisted that the party represented the entire nation and that membership was open to — or even compulsory for — all citizens. The Leninist theory of party was quite different; although the party represented the "toiling masses," only ideologically

proven candidates could join it. The "vanguard" of the workers and peasants was to be recruited among the military officers, political cadres, state officials, and intellectuals who had demonstrated their mastery of and dedication to Marxist-Leninist doctrine and were free of capitalist connections. In countries that described themselves as Marxist-Leninist, such as Ethiopia, Benin, or Congo-Brazzaville, party membership was very small (3,000 in Congo-Brazzaville in 1979 and 30,000 in a population of over 40 million in Ethiopia in 1985).

As the 1990s opened, a great transformation of the political party scene had occurred: the disappearance of the Leninist model of party organization. The collapse of communist rule in Eastern Europe and the abandonment of the Leninist claim to the "leading role" for the Communist party in the Soviet Union itself had an undoubted impact. The claim to global respectability for this theory of Marxist-Leninist party rule vanished overnight. By 1990 in all the eight African states which at one point invoked Marxism-Leninism as the regime doctrine, the ideology had been abandoned, and with it the notion of an exclusive right to define policy monopolized by a small party elite guided by "scientific socialism." Symbolic of this development was the destruction of the giant statue of Lenin which dominated a central square in Addis Ababa, Ethiopia, in May 1991.

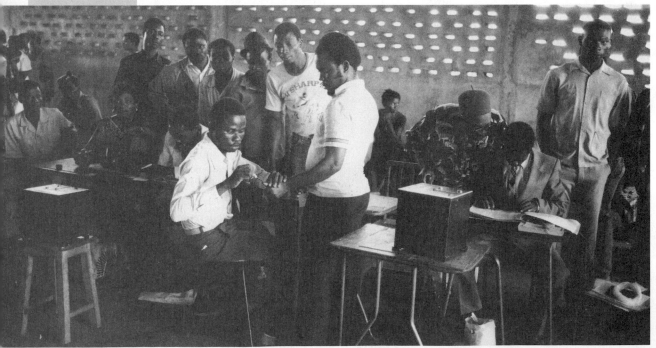

A political alternative to the party system was fashioned by Qadafy in Libya. After he seized power in 1969, Qadafy initially tried to create a single party influenced by the Nasser model from Egypt. Dissatisfied with his lifeless creation, in 1973 Qadafy proclaimed a *jamahiriya*, or "state of the masses," which was to be animated by people's committees in all workplaces and neighborhoods. The sovereignty of the mass was intended to be exercised by these popular committees, which then would send delegates to an annual General People's Congress. The popular committees do have an effervescent existence at the base; needless to say, power at the summit is closely held by Qadafy, together with a narrow circle of collaborators in his original military coup and persons from his clan. But the importance of the youth-dominated popular committees imparts a special flavor to the *jamahiriya*.

Jerry Rawlings of Ghana and Thomas Sankara of Burkina Faso experimented with similar formulas for legitimating and institutionalizing populist rule under military leadership during the 1980s. Neither had lasting success. There is reason to doubt the viability of such formulas for aggregating popular preferences without use of parties as intermediary agencies, particularly in the atmosphere of ferment that characterized the 1990s.

The overwhelming pressures for political openings were reshaping party systems across the continent. The first instinct of those regimes that had been long accustomed to rule through single parties was apparently to draw from the experience of such states as Tunisia, Senegal, Gambia, and Botswana, which have permitted opposition parties to contest elections, but have profited from control of the state apparatus and media to ensure that competing parties are confined to a minority role. Even this limited pluralization of the political process alters the chemistry of interest aggregation. The existence of a channel for criticism of state action and articulation of policy alternatives that is tolerated by the regime induces somewhat higher accountability and responsiveness. As the Eastern European experience of 1989 suggests, in some situations the momentum of events unleashed by a political opening may well escape the incumbents' control. The swift collapse of the eighteen-year dominance of Mathieu Kerekou in Benin in 1990 is a case in point.

A haunting fear of the dangers of electoral competition which divide African countries along ethnic, regional, or religious lines casts a large shadow over the debate on democratization formulas. Interests deriving from cultural pluralism are widely viewed as too dangerous to aggregate through political parties. A natural reflex is to forbid party organization on the basis of race, ethnicity, region, or religion. Senegal, for example, which permitted unlimited numbers of political parties in the 1980s, prohibits any reference to religion or ethnicity in name or program. This provision has been effective. Of the seventeen parties existing at the time of the 1988 elections, although a kaleidoscope of ideologies could be identified (there were no fewer than nine Marxist-Leninist parties), regional and religious divisions were not polarized by the electoral competition.

The risks, however, are real. In Sudan, where three efforts to govern within a competitive political party system have been made (1956–1958, 1965–1969, 1986–1989), on each occasion the parties' tendency to reflect religious and regional division undermined democracy. Nigeria, which experienced a bitter civil war after its First Republic (1960–1966) partisan divisions intensified regional antagonisms, has devoted great energies to constitutional engineering designed to avert a repetition of such a disaster. In the Second Republic (1979–1983), parties were required to meet exacting standards of nationwide organization and leadership before winning approval for registration. This reduced but did not wholly eliminate regionalism in party competition. For the Third Republic, scheduled for full launching by 1992, the military regime seeks to create two parties, a Social Democratic party (slightly left of center) and a National Republican Convention (slightly right of center). For this formula to succeed, these parties must avoid reflecting the country's north-south division.

In the unfolding drama of transformed patterns of interest aggregation, South Africa will be particularly crucial. By far the most industrial economy on the continent, South Africa has a complexity of structure and diversity of interests that are concealed by the sharpness of its racial polarization. One hotly debated issue in contemplation of a post-apartheid South Africa based on equal rights and participation by all South Africans has been "group rights," or entrenching in the constitutional structure institutions that aggregate interests in terms of racial community. The ANC, whose consent is indispensable to any new constitutional order, categorically rejects this approach. A stable and equitable form of governance in South Africa probably does require an institutional design that induces transracial interest aggregation, rather than a group rights racially rooted structure.[48]

For most of Africa, a period of change and flux in this functional domain is at hand. The single-party system as a device for interest aggregation has been thoroughly discredited. Nonetheless, the impulse of incumbent regimes to perpetuate their hold on power remains intact. Their efforts to navigate the tempestuous currents of democratization will be an absorbing spectacle in the 1990s.

THE POLICY PROCESS

In the years ahead, more open politics may alter the dynamics of policy in important ways. Until now, however, the character of the policymaking process has remained strongly influenced by concentration of power in the political ruler's hands. The very personal way in which power is exercised means that the various institutional sectors of the state have relatively little autonomy and do not play a strong independent part in the policy process. The vital center of the state is the presidency itself. Parties, legislatures, and courts are not important challenges.

The ruler himself, then, must make most of the important decisions. In his personal entourage, he needs to have a cadre of technically proficient and personally dedicated aides who can provide the minimum of staff support to make personal rule work in a complex contemporary state.

The need for unquestionably loyal subordinates extends beyond the presidency to the most sensitive sectors of state action: the finance ministry, central bank, security forces, foreign ministry, interior ministry, and party secretariat. Those holding office in the most crucial institutions of control and resource flow are likely to have close personal ties to the president. The ruler needs both competent performance and complete reliability in these functions. In one way or another, the most faithful servants of the ruler must count on generous rewards for their fidelity.

The personal character of rule also means that the ruler is relatively unconstrained by institutional formalities or law. He has wide discretion to respond to particular situations as his judgment dictates. Although few go as far as Mobutu in Zaire in claiming that his speeches have the force of law or introducing sweeping institutional changes without consultation by presidential declaration, nonetheless the ruler is not normally subject to legal challenge.

The centralized and personal character of policy decision has important implications. Those seeking a policy decision by the state must secure the ruler's attention, or that of a highly placed lieutenant who is willing to act in the ruler's name. Following the routine hierarchic channels of the administration is not always the most effective way of meeting this goal; one needs an entry to the state that is closer to where decisions on important matters will be made.

Public servants further down the bureaucratic ladder are often reluctant to assume responsibility for policy decisions that are not purely routine, even when they have the apparent legal authority to do so. Their caution is understandable; the wishes of the ruler are paramount and at times inscrutable. The costs for the official who makes a decision that displeases the ruler may be severe.

The policy machinery that the leader must inspire, direct, and control is very large. In addition to the conventional departments of government, which deal with such spheres as education, health, transportation, and information, a very large parastatal sector consists of public enterprises. These include not only such activities as electricity, water, railroads, and ports, but also many other ventures. The marketing and export of major cash crops is frequently handled by a state marketing board. Mines have been nationalized in a number of countries; new industries have frequently been created under state ownership. In comparison to other developing areas, the state sector in Africa is unusually large, and until recently it grew rapidly.

In the policymaking process, representative institutions — legislatures and party congresses — have generally not had an important part. Except for military regimes that claimed their role was merely transitional (thus justifying suspension of all political institutions), most states have had national assemblies of some sort. The single parties also held occasional national congresses. The sessions of both legislatures and congresses were generally brief and were summoned to ratify policies designed by the leadership.

The institutional sphere in which autonomy was greatest was the judiciary. Particularly in countries influenced by British concepts of the judiciary's independence, judges often exhibited remarkable dedication to the integrity of the legal process. Nowhere did the judicial branch have as much political influence as in the American system, where the doctrine of judicial review permits the courts to strike down legislative or executive acts and to adapt the Constitution to changing circumstances by its interpretation. But it could take part in curbing arbitrary state action in enforcing standards of due process in the administration of justice. On a number of occasions, judges displayed great personal courage when their verdicts were counter to the ruler's political interests.

POLICY PERFORMANCE

In the sphere of policy performance in Africa, the emphasis has shifted significantly in the last two decades. At the time of independence, political considerations tended to predominate. The African states' primary considerations at that time were to consolidate a national identity, define viable political structures, and reinforce their independence.

To some degree, these objectives were met. Despite the importance of ethnicity and religion in African politics, African states did not disintegrate. The national idea was more strongly rooted in the 1980s than it was when nationalist movements first challenged colonial rule.

Despite the frequency of military coups, instability was not endemic in Africa. In 1990 in forty of the fifty-two states, incumbents had held power for at least five years. By far the greatest disappointments of independence lay in the economic realm. Of all the major world regions, Africa has fared the worst since 1960, especially in the 1970s and 1980s (see Tables 16.3 and 16.5). By the late 1970s there was a growing sense of economic malaise in Africa, above all in the agricultural sector where the majority of the population earned their livelihood. The 1979 summit conference of the OAU took official note of these frustrations. A report for the assembled heads of state reached the candid conclusion that "Africa . . . is unable to point to any significant growth rate or satisfactory index of general well-being" after two decades of independence.

The situation worsened dramatically during the 1980s. Although part of the explanation for Africa's economic decline lies in external or uncontrollable factors — declining terms of trade, recurrent droughts — poor performance in economic policy must bear its share of the blame. No other region had such poor returns from public investment, which steadily dwindled during this decade. The extraordinary expansion of the state economic sector — agricultural marketing monopolies, many industries, and most mining enterprises — saddled African governments with many deficit-ridden enterprises. Excessive borrowing to sustain state consumption levels in the 1970s left an intolerable debt burden in the 1980s. Bloated state bureaucracies absorbed the bulk of the governments' operating budgets. A World Bank report in 1989 offers a biting judgment on policy performance in the economic domain:

> . . . the low return on investment is the main reason for Africa's recent decline. . . . Weak public sector management has resulted in loss-making public enterprises, poor investment choices, costly and unreliable infrastructure, price distortions (especially over-valued exchange rates, administered prices, and subsidized credit), and hence inefficient resource allocation. . . . Even more fundamental in many countries is the deteriorating quality of government, epitomized by bureaucratic obstruction, pervasive rent seeking, weak judicial systems, and arbitrary decisionmaking. . . . For the most part Africa is simply not competitive in an increasingly competitive world.[49]

Initially, African official opinion tended to stress external factors: Africa's weak and dependent situation on the margins of a Western-dominated world economic system that operated to Africa's economic disadvantage. This was the central motif of the 1980 Lagos Plan of Action, an economic policy document endorsed by African heads of state at an OAU meeting. By the mid-1980s African states had shifted to a more nuanced view, conceding that major policy errors as well as external factors explained Africa's plight. In a remarkable presentation, Senegalese President Abdou Diouf, speaking on behalf of all African states at a special session of the United Nations General Assembly devoted to the African economic crisis in May 1986, called for a compact for African recovery. Africa pledged to remedy policies that had proven ineffective and to raise half the required resources by its own efforts; the developed world was asked to participate in a major campaign of assistance, including debt relief, aid, and investment.[50]

Against this backdrop, we may briefly pose the issue of policy performance. The extraction process provides one major key to understanding. Above all, except in oil-producing states, the heavy weight of state fiscal policy on the rural sector placed the state and peasantry on a collision course.

Extraction

In Africa, to an unusual degree, the cost of colonial rule was placed squarely on the peasantry. Colonial subjects were compelled not only to accept the political authority

TABLE 16.5
ECONOMIC PERFORMANCE DATA ON FIFTY-TWO AFRICAN STATES

State	GNP per capita, 1988 ($)	Average annual growth rate, 1965–1988 (pct.)	Average annual inflation rate, 1980–1988 (pct.)	Adult illiteracy (pct.)	Life expectancy at birth, 1988 (years)
Algeria	2,360	2.7	4.4	50	64
Angola	840[a]	−5.7[b]	—	—	45
Benin	310	−0.6[c]	8.2[c]	—	—
Botswana	1010	8.6	10.0	29	67
Burkina Faso	210	1.2	3.2	87	47
Burundi	240	3.0	4.0	66	49
Cameroon	1,010	3.7	7.0	44	56
Cape Verde	500[d]	1.2[c]	13.9[c]	—	65[d]
Central African Republic	380	−0.5	6.7	60	50
Chad	160	−2.0	3.2	75	46
Comoros	370[d]	—	—	—	56
Congo	910	3.5	0.8	37	53
Djibouti	—	—	—	—	47
Egypt	660	3.6	10.6	56	63
Equatorial Guinea	—	—	—	—	46
Ethiopia	120	−0.1	2.1	38	47
Gabon	2,970	0.9	0.9	38	53
Gambia	220[d]	0.8[c]	13.8[c]	—	43[d]
Ghana	400	−1.6	46.1	47	54
Guinea	430	1.1	4.5	72	43
Guinea-Bissau	160[d]	0.8[c]	39.2[c]	—	39[d]
Ivory Coast	770	0.9	3.8	57	53
Kenya	370	1.9	9.6	41	59
Lesotho	420	5.2	12.2	26	56
Liberia	450[d]	−0.7[c]	1.5[c]	65	50
Libya	5,420	−2.7	0.1	33	61
Madagascar	190	−1.8	17.3	33	61
Malawi	170	1.1	12.6	59	47
Mali	230	1.6	3.7	83	47

continued

of the alien rulers, but also to pay the full cost of conquest and occupation. This extraction was accomplished through the early imposition of a head tax, coerced cultivation of export crops from which duties could be collected, forced supply of their labor at low cost to European enterprises, and — sometimes — expropriation of their land.

To provide the necessary revenue base for the expanding postwar state, effective rates of taxation on the rural sector again increased. To ensure the effectiveness of this extraction, state marketing monopolies were frequently created for the main export crops. Substantial export taxes — often 40 to 50 percent — were imposed. In addition, state-fixed prices were frequently well below those available on the black market. When all forms of direct and indirect extraction from the peasantry are put together, the effective extraction rate frequently exceeded half of the smallholders' income. This burden

TABLE 16.5 (*Continued*)

State	GNP per capita, 1988 ($)	Average annual growth rate, 1965–1988 (pct.)	Average annual inflation rate, 1980–1988 (pct.)	Adult illiteracy (pct.)	Life expectancy at birth, 1988 (years)
Mauritania	480	−0.4	9.4	—	46
Mauritius	1,800	2.9	7.8	17	67
Morocco	830	2.3	7.7	67	61
Mozambique	100	—	33.6	62	48
Namibia	—	—	—	—	—
Niger	300	−2.3	3.6	86	45
Nigeria	290	0.9	11.6	58	51
Rwanda	320	1.5	4.1	53	49
São Tomé e Principe	280[d]	−6.0[c]	4.9	—	65
Senegal	650	−0.8	8.1	72	48
Seychelles	3,120[d]	1.3[c]	3.7[c]	—	70
Sierra Leone	300[d]	−2.0[c]	50.0	71	42
Somalia	170	−2.1	56.1	88	47
South Africa	2,290	0.8	13.9	—	61
Sudan	480	0.0	33.5	—	50
Swaziland	700[d]	1.2[c]	10.2[d]	—	55[d]
Tanzania	160	−0.5	25.7	—	53
Togo	370	0.0	6.1	59	53
Tunisia	1,230	3.4	7.7	46	66
Uganda	280	−3.1	100.7	43	48
Zaire	170	−2.1	56.1	39	52
Zambia	290	−2.1	33.5	24	53
Zimbabwe	650	1.0	12.1	26	63

[a]Figures based on 1981.
[b]1970–1981.
[c]1980–1987.
[d]1987.
Source: World Bank, *World Development Report 1990* (New York: Oxford University Press, 1990); World Bank, *Sub-Saharan Africa: From Crisis to Sustainable Growth* (Washington, D.C.: World Bank, 1989).

contrasted with the extremely low tax rates in colonial times for European enterprises and residents. In the postcolonial period, the peasantry continue to pay far higher effective tax rates than the state bourgeoisie or the foreign estate.

The effects of these extraction patterns began to be visible in the 1970s. Smallholders did not revolt, though there were scattered uprisings, as in the Yoruba tax riots in the late 1960s in Nigeria. Rather, they sought means of "exit" — of withdrawal from crop sectors under gov-

ernment control through marketing board monopolies or other mechanisms. As black markets grew and smuggling opportunities expanded, many found ways to evade the state. In many countries, the state faces a real challenge in regaining the confidence of the rural sector.

Distribution
State expenditures have had some distributive influence. Since the 1950s pressure from the citizenry for rapid expansion in the supply of public amenities has

been enormous. The most important of these amenities are schools, health facilities, roads, and safe water supplies. Of these, education receives the largest allocation. In a number of countries, the school outlays run 25 to 35 percent of the operating budget. Almost everywhere, both parents and children perceive a close link between schooling and social mobility. A career as a small farmer means certain poverty; a secondary school diploma — or, much better, a university degree — creates the possibility of vastly more remunerative white-collar employment. The social tensions inherent in the very high inequality between the privileged social categories (foreign estate and state bourgeoisie) and the impoverished mass are partly absorbed by the widespread belief that social mobility across generations is possible through education. The power of this conviction is demonstrated in the tremendous sacrifices that peasant families will make to keep their children in school or that village communities will undertake to construct schools, in the hope that the state will then assign a teacher.

As the 1980s wore on, educational expansion as a distributive policy encountered two obstacles. First, the deepening economic crisis in many countries closed down white-collar employment opportunities for those emerging from the school system, particularly in the government bureaucracy. Second, the schools themselves suffered; basic supplies became impossible to obtain, and teachers were demoralized by salary arrearages often stretching for months. A deterioration in educational quality, particularly in rural schools, was a consequence in many countries.

Public investment in health is also highly valued and potentially has important distributive effects. Privileged social strata can afford much more sanitary residential conditions and can secure access to the basic medical supplies and services that counter the numerous dangerous maladies endemic in parts of Africa (bilharzia, river blindness, and malaria, among others). The poorer strata can be served only by state or mission-supplied clinical facilities.

Although most states make significant public expenditures on health, a fundamental philosophy of public choice determines its distributive effectiveness. A health policy based on providing costly high-technology medical services to capital cities will necessarily leave the rural areas inadequately served. A mass-based health program, amid the limited budgetary resources of most African states, will need to stress preventive medicine and low-cost paramedical services broadly distrib-

uted, at the price of delaying the introduction of the most expensive, specialized Western medical technology. The range of possible variation in health policy is extreme. Tanzania has resolutely opted for a broadly distributed network of basic health services. In Zaire, half the national health budget went to two well-equipped medical centers in the capital city, and an estimated 70 percent of the population was not effectively served by state health facilities.

Regulation

The regulatory capacity of African states has two important aspects: control over domestic and external markets, and enforcement of state directives. In recent years, in many African states a growing gap has opened between the regulatory ambitions of the state and its practical capacities. The increasing visibility of the state's overcommitment has led to the characterization of African governments as "soft states."

A legacy of far-reaching state regulatory action has come down from colonial times. Colonial states had sought to fix the prices of major agricultural commodities and many consumer goods, to control the flow of migrants into cities, and to manage the allocation of labor. Foreign trade in most colonial territories was closely regulated in order to maximize benefits to the ruling power. African subjects were enmeshed in a complex net of social controls.

A large part of the colonial legacy was absorbed into the regulatory role of the independent state. In many places, the conviction in the early years of independence that active development planning could accelerate economic growth, and in some cases commitment to socialist strategies, served to extend state regulation into yet additional domains. Nearly everywhere, parastatal organizations proliferated, charged with the management and direction of given sectors of economic and social life. The growing shortage of foreign exchange, exacerbated by the long-term downward tendency of the prices of African beverage, vegetable oil, and fiber export commodities in relation to the cost of industrial goods and fuel imports, had led many states into rationing imports through licensing systems. Both internal and external regulatory processes have encountered growing difficulties.

In domestic price regulation, the effort to hold prices low has led to a growing underground economy. By the 1980s the gigantic public enterprise sector was at bay; many of these corporations performed their functions poorly or not at all, and their cost was becoming an unbearable burden. Externally, import controls are difficult to administer effectively, and they are a frequent source of corruption. They also tend to create windfall profits for smugglers.

By the late 1980s the mood favored retrenchment of state regulation: a leaner, more efficient, less venal, less intrusive government apparatus. This trend was illustrated by Nigeria's sudden decision to abolish all its state agricultural marketing monopolies in 1986. It was reinforced by strong external pressure from the international financial agencies and Western governments, who were convinced that an expanded role for markets and a shrinkage of state regulation were indispensable to African recovery.

The severity of the economic crisis that had overtaken African states by the 1980s introduced a new dimension to regulation: a sharply increased external role. The desperate need for debt relief and economic assistance placed strong leverage in the hands of the IMF, the World Bank, Western governments, and private creditors, especially the major international banks. A consensus emerged among these external forces that structural adjustment was a necessary feature of African economic reforms. Among its prescriptions was the significant reduction in the regulatory mission of the African state; debt relief and assistance were conditioned on agreement to undertake such reforms.

In the sphere of symbolic capabilities, most states have lavished attention on promoting emblems of national identity and the regime's legitimacy. Although these ceremonial and ritual aspects of state action have helped consolidate the acceptance of national identity, there are important limits to symbolic and hortatory policy. If the material existence of the masses is visibly deteriorating, manipulative symbol-wielding is not likely to assuage popular discontent.

A DIFFICULT FUTURE

Difficult years lie ahead for the African state, both economically and politically. The vulnerability of African states to extend factors beyond their control or even influence creates painful dilemmas. The unwillingness of the economically more powerful outside states to make more than token efforts to alleviate the grip of Africa's poverty adds to the frustrations. African pleas for the cooperation of industrial states in stabilizing the commodity prices on which their economies depend

have fallen on deaf ears. For most outside states, foreign aid amounts are relatively small; since the early 1980s, American aid to Israel and Egypt alone was more than five times that extended to the rest of the continent. Furthermore, a significant portion of the aid was merely in the military field. Their economic fragility and an unfavorable international economic environment place tremendous pressures on African politics.

In the political realm, the African state has demonstrated a tenacious will to survive, and indeed the strength of its newly asserted national identity has surprised many observers. But both peril and promise lie within the pow-

Young Ethiopian soldier shows weapons and a few prisoners captured during fighting in the Horn of Africa.

erful trend to democratization which marked the beginning of the 1990s. The authoritarian legacy of the colonial state, and the predominant modes of patrimonial autocracy that characterized postcolonial governance, denied to African civil societies the opportunity to experiment with more open forms of political systems. The quest for a more pluralistic politics, with state power rendered more accountable and responsive, coincides with a period of deep economic distress. In extreme cases—Liberia, Mozambique, Sudan, Somalia, and Ethiopia—the ravages of civil strife left state and society virtually prostrate. In these circumstances, designing new institutional forms for governance rooted in the African cultural heritage and historical experience is a challenge of truly epic proportions.

Thus, the perils are evident enough, but so too is the promise. A new South Africa, truly representing all of its citizens and rid of the disfiguring legacy of apartheid, might serve as a potent political example and an economic stimulus to an entire region. Democratization everywhere opens the possibility of rebuilding the weakened linkages between state and society. A political will to rise to this challenge began to appear, epitomized by the solemn declaration adopted by African heads of state at the OAU summit in July 1990:

> We are fully aware that in order to facilitate this process of socio-economic transformation and integration, it is necessary to promote popular participation of our peoples in the process of government and development. A political environment which guarantees human rights and the observance of the rule of law, would assure high standards of probity and accountability particularly on the part of those who hold public office. In addition, popular-based political process would ensure the involvement of all, including in particular, women and youth in all the development efforts. We accordingly recommit ourselves to further democratization of our societies and to the consolidation of democratic institutions in our countries. We reaffirm the right of our countries to determine, in all sovereignty, their system of democracy on the basis of their socio-cultural values, taking into account the realities of each of our countries and the necessity to ensure development and satisfy the basic needs of our peoples. We therefore assert that democracy and development go together and should be mutually reinforcing.[51]

KEY TERMS

apartheid
Christianity
colonial situation
colonial state
cultural pluralism

democratization
dependency
ethnicity
foreign estate
informal sector

Islam
military intervention
nationalism
peasant

personal authoritarianism
single-party rule
state bourgeoisie
worker

END NOTES

1. Cape Verde, São Tomé e Principe, Madagascar, Comoros, Seychelles, Mauritius.
2. The precise number of slaves transported is a controversial topic. The best study remains Philip D. Curtin, *The Atlantic Slave Trade* (Madison: University of Wisconsin Press, 1969).
3. The classic statement of this ideology is in F. M. Lugard, *The Dual Mandate in Tropical Africa*, 4th ed. (London: William Blackwood, 1929).
4. This is well analyzed in the case of Senghor by Janet G. Vaillant, *Black, French, and African: A Life of Leopold Sedar Senghor* (Cambridge, Mass.: Harvard University Press, 1990).
5. Morocco, Tunisia, Egypt, Rwanda, Burundi, Swaziland, Lesotho, and Madagascar. Ethiopia,

only briefly under Italian rule (1936–1941), is a longstanding state that itself participated in the "scramble for Africa"; with British and French connivance, it roughly tripled in size at the end of the nineteenth century.
6. A. I. Asiwaju, *Partitioned Africans; Ethnic Relations across Africa's International Boundaries 1884–1984* (London: C. Hurst & Co., 1984).
7. The most thoughtful official document making this case comes from Tanzania, *Report of the Presidential Commission on the Establishment of a Democratic One-Party State* (Dar es Salaam: Government Printer, 1965). For a sophisticated scholarly defense of the idea, see Ruth Schachter Morganthau, *Political Parties in French-Speaking*

West Africa (Oxford: Clarendon Press, 1964), pp. 330–358.

8. Pat McGowan and Thomas H. Johnson, "African Military Coups d'Etat and Underdevelopment: A Quantitative Historical Analysis," *Journal of Modern African Studies*, 22:4 (December 1984), pp. 633–666.

9. Samuel Decalo, *Coups and Army Rule in Africa* (New Haven, Conn.: Yale University Press, 1976); Henry Bienen, *Armies and Parties in Africa* (New York: Africana Publishing Co., 1978); William J. Foltz and Henry Bienen, eds., *Arms and the African: Military Influences on Africa's International Relations* (New Haven, Conn.: Yale University Press, 1985). In 1990 twenty-eight countries were ruled by a leader of military origin.

10. For excellent portraits, see Jean-François Bayart, *L'Etat en Afrique: la politique du ventre* (Paris: Fayart, 1989); Achille Mbembe, *Afriques indociles: Christianisme, pouvoir, et Etat en Afrique post-coloniale* (Paris: Karthala, 1988).

11. Robert H. Jackson and Carl G. Rosberg, *Personal Rule in Black Africa* (Berkeley: University of California Press, 1982), pp. 17–19.

12. Illustrative of this trend are several recent volumes by African and other scholars devoted to democratization: Peter Anyang' Nyong'o, ed., *Popular Struggles for Democracy in Africa* (London: Zed Books, 1987); Walter O. Oyugi, E. S. Atieno Odhimbo, Michael Chege, and Afrifa E. Gitonga, eds., *Democratic Theory and Practice* (Portsmouth, N.H.: Heinemann, 1988); Larry Diamond, Juan J. Linz, and Seymour Martin Lipset, eds., *Democracy in Developing Countries: Africa* (Boulder, Colo.: Lynne Rienner Publishers, 1988).

13. World Bank, *Sub-Saharan Africa: From Crisis to Sustainable Growth* (Washington, D.C., 1989), pp. 60–61.

14. Jennifer Seymour Whitaker, *How Can Africa Survive?* (New York: Harper & Row, 1988), p. 18.

15. A vast literature on this topic has appeared in recent years. See especially Donald L. Horowitz, *Ethnic Groups in Conflict* (Berkeley: University of California Press, 1985).

16. Leroy Vail, ed., *The Creation of Tribalism in Southern Africa* (Berkeley: University of California Press, 1989).

17. Gabriel R. Warburg, "Islam and State in Numayri's Sudan," *Africa*, 55:4 (1985), pp. 400–413.

18. For some examples, see Rene Lemarchand, *African Kingships in Perspective* (London: Frank Cass, 1977).

19. Donal Cruise O'Brien, *Saints and Politicians: Essays in the Organization of a Senegalese Peasant Society* (Cambridge: Cambridge University Press, 1975); Christian Coulon, *Le marabout et le prince* (Paris: Pedone, 1981).

20. B. Freund, "Labor and Labor History in Africa: A Review of the Literature," *African Studies Review*, 27:2 (1984), pp. 1–59.

21. Goran Hyden, *Beyond Ujamaa in Tanzania* (Berkeley: University of California Press, 1980). See also Allen Isaacman, "Peasants and Rural Social Protest in Africa," *African Studies Review*, 30:2 (1990), pp. 1–120.

22. Richard Sklar, "The Nature of Class Domination in Africa," *Journal of Modern African Studies*, 17:4 (December 1979), pp. 531–552). For an excellent review of this issue, see Nelson Kasfir, ed., *State and Class in Africa* (London: Frank Cass, 1984).

23. For details bearing on Zaire, see David J. Gould, *Bureaucratic Corruption in the Third World* (New York: Pergamon Press, 1980); Crawford Young and Thomas Turner, *The Rise and Decline of the Zairian State* (Madison: University of Wisconsin Press, 1985).

24. W. Arthur Lewis, *Politics in West Africa* (New York: Oxford University Press, 1965), p. 32.

25. Nicole Swainson, *The Development of Corporate Capitalism in Kenya, 1918–1977* (Berkeley: University of California Press, 1980); John Sender and Sheila Smith, *The Development of Capitalism in Africa* (London: Methuen, 1986); John Iliffe, *The Emergence of African Capitalism* (London: Macmillan, 1983).

26. Nazih N. M. Ayubi, "Bureaucratic Inflation and Administrative Inefficiency: The Deadlock of Egyptian Administration," *Middle Eastern Studies*, 18:3 (July 1982), pp. 286–299. See also Larry Diamond, "Class Formation in the Swollen African State," *Journal of Modern African Studies*, 25:4 (1987), pp. 567–596.

27. John Iliffe, *The Urban Poor* (Cambridge: Cambridge University Press, 1987).

28. Ahmed Toure, *Les petits metiers à Abidjan* (Paris: Karthala, 1985).

29. Robert Bates gives a cogent analysis of these factors in *Markets and States in Tropical Africa* (Berkeley: University of California Press, 1981).

30. Albert O. Hirschman, *Exit, Voice and Loyalty: Response to Decline in Firms, Organizations and States* (Cambridge, Mass.: Harvard University Press, 1970).

31. Ali Mazrui and Omari Kokole, for example, argued that Uganda's tormented postcolonial history can be in good part explained by contrasting ancestral political cultures in the decentralized societies of the north, and the highly structured monarchies of the south. "Uganda: The Dual Policy and the Plural Society," in Diamond, Linz, and Lipset, *Democracy in Developing Countries*, pp. 259–298.

32. Paul M. Lubeck, "Islamic Protest under Semi-industrial Capitalism: 'Yan Tatsine Explained," *Africa*, 55:4 (1985), pp. 369–389.

33. Richard Merelman, "Resuscitating Political Socialization from Vertical to Lateral Theories of Society," in Margaret Hermann, ed., *Political Psychology*, 2nd ed. (San Francisco: Jossey–Bass, 1980), p. 279.

34. Larry Diamond, "Nigeria's Third Quest for Democracy," *Current History*, 90 (1991), p. 203.

35. David Easton and Jack Dennis, *Children in the Political System* (New York: McGraw–Hill, 1969).

36. William Hachten, *Muffled Drums* (Ames: Iowa State University Press, 1971); Frank Barton, *The Press in Africa* (New York: Africana Publishing, 1979).

37. There were a handful of older movements, most notably the ANC in South Africa, founded in 1912, and the nationalist Wafd party in Egypt, a major factor from the 1920s until the 1950s, then reappearing in the 1980s.

38. Nelson Kasfir, *The Shrinking Political Arena: Participation and Ethnicity in African Politics, with a Case Study of Uganda* (Berkeley: University of California Press, 1975).

39. Persons of racially mixed ancestry, many of whom now reject the Coloured label and identify with the African majority.

40. Quoted in Thomas M. Callaghy, "State-Subject Communication in Zaire," *Journal of Modern African Studies*, 18:3 (1980), p. 477.

41. The tactic of "presidential dialogue" in the Ivory Coast is well analyzed by Michael A. Cohen, *Urban Policy and Political Conflict in Africa* (Chicago: University of Chicago Press, 1974). The dwindling effectiveness of the presidential "gift" was illustrated in 1990 in the broad currents of indignation in the Ivory Coast at President Houpouet–Boigny's "present" to the country of a gigantic and sumptuous Basilica, larger than St. Peter's in Rome, estimated to cost $250 million. How, many asked in the first multiparty election, did the president accumulate the personal resources permitting such a costly "gift"?

42. Henry Bienen, *Kenya: The Politics of Participation and Control* (Princeton, N.J.: Princeton University Press, 1974).

43. The Tanzanian electoral experience is well summarized in Joel Samoff, "Single-Party Competitive Elections in Tanzania," in Fred M. Hayward, ed., *Elections in Independent Africa* (Boulder, Colo.: Westview Press, 1987), pp. 149–186.

44. Ali Mazrui, *Soldiers and Kinsmen in Uganda* (Beverly Hills, Calif.: Sage Publications, 1975).

45. Mbembe, *Afriques indociles*, pp. 148–149.

46. For a remarkable documentary study of the details of foreign business action in securing contracts and promoting development schemes, see Jean-Claude Willame, *Zaire: L'épopée d'Inga* (Paris: Harmattan, 1986).

47. For many examples, and evidence on the broader issue of disengagement of civil society, see Donald Rothchild and Naomi Chazan, eds., *The Precarious Balance: State & Society in Africa* (Boulder: Westview Press, 1988).

48. Donald L. Horowitz, *A Democratic South Africa? Constitutional Engineering in a Divided Society* (Berkeley: University of California Press, 1990).

49. World Bank, *Sub-Saharan Africa: From Crisis to Sustainable Growth* (Washington, D.C.: World Bank, 1989), p. 3.

50. The debate over the African development crisis and the concept of a compact for African recovery, combining African policy reform and major Western assistance, are examined in detail in Robert J. Berg and Jennifer Seymour Whitaker, eds., *Strategies for African Development* (Berkeley: University of California Press, 1986).

51. Cited in *West Africa*, 3925 (December 17–23, 1990), p. 3041.

ARCTIC OCEAN

Scale of Miles

0   400

ALASKA

Juneau

Gulf of Alaska

CANADA

WASHINGTON

Olympia

Salem

MONTANA

Helena

NORTH DAKOTA

Bismarck

MINNESOTA

St. Paul

WISCONSIN

Madison

MICHIGAN

Lansing

IDAHO

Boise

SOUTH DAKOTA

Pierre

WYOMING

Cheyenne

IOWA

Des Moines

Chicago

ILLINOIS

INDIANA

Indianapolis

OHIO

Columbus

Ohio R.

WE

VI

Charlest

NEVADA

Carson City

Salt Lake City

NEBRASKA

Lincoln

Springfield

Frankfort

KENTUCKY

N

Nashville

Sacramento

UTAH

Colorado R.

COLORADO

Denver

Missouri R.

MISSOURI

Jefferson City

Topeka

KANSAS

TENNESSEE

CALIFORNIA

ARIZONA

Santa Fe

OKLAHOMA

Oklahoma City

ARKANSAS

Little Rock

Mississippi R.

MISSISSIPPI

ALABAMA

Atlanta

GEOR

Los Angeles

NEW MEXICO

Phoenix

Montgomery

T

PACIFIC OCEAN

TEXAS

Austin

LOUISIANA

Jackson

Baton Rouge

Gulf of Mexico

MEXICO

UNITED STATES

Scale of Miles

0   500

HAWAII

Honolulu

Scale of Miles

0   100

AUSTIN RANNEY

POLITICS IN THE

UNITED STATES

And what should they
know of England
Who only England know?

Rudyard Kipling[1]

HY A CHAPTER on the United States in a book on comparative government? One reason is that most of its readers as well as its authors are Americans,[2] and politics in the United States impacts our lives far more than politics in any other country. Moreover, however feeble we may feel our power is to influence the actions of our government, it is certainly greater than our power to influence the actions of other nations' governments.

The question Rudyard Kipling asked about the English in the quotation above can be asked with equal justice about Americans. There are, of course, many excellent textbooks on the American political system written by Americans and intended for American students. But most of them make few references to, let alone systematic comparisons with, other political systems. Thus, viewing American politics with a special concern for how it resembles and differs from politics in other nations will help us better meet our version of Kipling's challenge. It may even give us some insight into how the special ways of American politics are likely to affect our country's ability to meet the enormous challenges it faces in the 1990s.

THE UNITED STATES AMONG THE WORLD'S NATIONS

History

The world today is divided among about 167 nations. (There is dispute about whether some of them, especially Vatican City and Monaco, are full-fledged nations.) The great majority of them are "new nations," that is, nations that have recently broken away from their former colonial masters and become independent sovereign nations. Indeed, no fewer than 70 percent of all modern nations have achieved their independence since the end of World War II in 1945.

Some of these nations have been able to establish and maintain political systems capable of meeting enough of their citizens' needs that their polities have remained relatively stable and solid. Unhappily, however, more of them have changed their political systems with some frequency since independence and have yet to find one that works well enough to stay in business very long. (For some of the sadder examples, see Crawford Young's chapter on governments in Africa in this book.)

Seymour Martin Lipset has argued that the United States was the world's "first new nation," in the sense that the problems it faced in its efforts to establish a stable and principled political system after winning its independence from Great Britain in 1783 were in many respects similar or identical to those faced by the nations created after 1945.[3] Thus, the United States, which is so often described as a young nation, is actually an old country — not as old as, say, Great Britain, France, or Japan, but much older than most other modern nations.[4] It has the world's oldest written constitution still in effect. It can fairly claim to have become a full-fledged democracy well before any other large modern nation. In the 1790s it developed the world's first modern political parties, and today's Democratic party is generally recognized as the world's oldest active political party.

We will consider many developments in American history throughout this chapter, but here we will emphasize only that the Civil War (1861–1865) is its great historical watershed.[5] Before 1861 it was a much-disputed question whether the United States was merely a convenient alliance among independent sovereign states, which had every right to secede whenever they wished, or a single sovereign nation whose people had divided governmental power among the national government and the state governments. After 1865, in both law and in fact it was established that the United States was, as every American schoolchild is drilled to know, "one nation, indivisible," not a federation of sovereign states.

Before 1861 many Americans, especially those in the eleven Southern states that seceded to form the Confederacy, felt that they were first and foremost citizens of their states and derived their American citizenship from the membership of their states in the union. Many of them felt that they owed their primary loyalty to their states, not to the United States. (The most famous example was Robert E. Lee: he strongly opposed both slavery and secession, and yet when Virginia seceded he refused command of the Union Army and cast his lot with Virginia because he felt he owed his primary loyalty to his state, not his nation.) The Fourteenth Amendment to the Constitution, ratified in 1868, removed all doubt by declaring that "All persons born or naturalized in the United States and subject to the jurisdiction thereof, are citizens of the United States and of the State wherein they reside." In short, all Americans are now primarily citizens of the United States, and derivatively become citizens of the state in which they reside.

Geography

The United States has jurisdiction over a territory totaling 3,618,768 square miles. This makes it the fourth largest nation in the world, smaller only than the Union of Soviet Socialist Republics (8,649,496 square miles), Canada (3,849,656 square miles), and the People's Republic of China (3,705,390 square miles).[6] The nation is bounded by the Atlantic Ocean on the east, the Pacific Ocean on the west, Canada on the north, and Mexico on the south. This secure location — great oceans on two sides, militarily weak nations on the other two sides — made feasible the foreign policy of isolation from alliances and wars with foreign countries that lasted until the end of the nineteenth century. In these days of intercontinental ballistic missiles and missile-firing submarines, however, no nation, including the United States, can count on its geographical location to keep it isolated from world politics.

Population

The 1990 census found that the United States has a total population of about 250 million.[7] This makes it the fourth most populous nation in the world; in the top three positions are the PRC with 1.1 billion, India with 850 million, and the Soviet Union with 290 million.[8] The U.S. rate of population increase has been phenomenal. The first census in 1790 showed a total population of 3,929,000, and so the 1990 figure represents a staggering increase of 615 percent in 200 years of nationhood. Over 50 million persons have moved from other parts of the world to the United States; as the British analyst H. G. Nicholas observes, it is "the greatest movement of population in western history."[9] Accordingly, one of the most important facts to recognize about the United States is that, more than any other nation in history, it is a nation of immigrants. The census classifies only 2.6 percent of the population as being of Native

American ancestry; the rest are immigrants or descendants of immigrants from all over the world.

According to the Bureau of the Census, the main areas of Americans' ancestral origins are: Western Europe and Scandinavia, 76.2 percent; Africa, 8.4 percent; Eastern Europe, 5.8 percent; Latin America, 5.3 percent; Asia, 1.4 percent; and the Middle East, 0.3 percent.[10] Most of these immigrants came in two historic waves: (1) 1840–1860, mainly from Western Europe and Scandinavia at an average annual rate of 8.9 per 1,000 of the existing population; and (2) 1870–1920, mainly from Eastern Europe at an average annual rate of 7.4. In the 1920s Congress imposed a ceiling on the number of immigrants allowed, and the rate dropped to below 1. Since the late 1970s the rate of immigration, mainly from Asia and Latin America, has risen to about 2.5 — which means that around 800,000 *legal* immigrants continue to arrive in America every year. Thus, annually the United States adds populations greater than those of such cities as San Francisco and Indianapolis.[11]

Hence, from its beginnings the United States has received far more immigrants than any other nation in history, and it has the most ethnically and culturally diverse population the world has ever seen. (Only India comes close.) Later, we will consider some of the consequences of this fact for the American way of politics.

The Economy

Despite the recent rise of the German and Japanese economies, at the beginning of the 1990s the United States still has the world's largest economy. In 1987 its gross national product (GNP), or the total value of all the goods and services it produces, was calculated at $4,527 billion, compared with Japan's $2,369 billion, the Soviet Union's $2,460 billion, and West Germany's $1,126 billion.[12] The American dollar continues to be the world's basic monetary unit, in that the value of all other nations' currencies is measured by how many pounds, francs, rubles, yen, and other units it takes to exchange for part or all of a dollar.

Some economists believe that the American economic dominance has ended. The United States, which for many years was the world's greatest creditor nation, has become the world's greatest debtor nation, in part because Americans continue to buy billions of dollars more foreign goods than foreigners buy of American goods, and in part because of the continuing enormous deficits in the federal government's budget. (From 1981 through 1989 the federal government spent $1,499.7 trillion more than it took in.)[13] Because of the deficit, the government has had to sell government bonds to foreign buyers to make up the difference between what it has been spending and what it has received in taxes and other revenues. Moreover, many analysts maintain that in 1992 when the European Economic Community, now strengthened by a reunited Germany, becomes a unified economy, the United States will clearly no longer be number one. We shall see.

America has long been regarded as the citadel of capitalist economic ideas and institutions, and the main enemy of people and nations who believe in socialism. If we measure the degree of capitalism in an economy by the proportion of economic enterprise that is privately owned and operated for profit, that characterization is quite correct. Even so, American institutions and practices have never come close to meeting the standards for truly free enterprise laid down by such laissez-faire economists as Adam Smith, Friedrich von Hayek, and Milton Friedman. These economists advocate the barest minimum of government interference in economic affairs, including no government regulation of the operations, profits, and wages paid by successful businesses *and* no government subsidies or "bail-outs" for unsuccessful businesses.

Yet governments in America have always helped American businesses in many ways. The Department of Agriculture, for example, does extensive research on the most efficient way to produce crops and gives farmers the free benefit of its findings; in addition, under the farm price support program, it buys up any surplus products that farmers cannot sell at "parity" prices. Congress imposes special tariffs and import quotas on certain foreign manufactured goods so as to prevent them from undercutting American manufacturers. Federal laws guarantee that all workers will be paid a certain minimum wage regardless of what they would get in a truly free market — and so on. Most of these goodies have come from political pressure by labor as well as farm and business pressure groups. Thus, it seems fair to say that, while most Americans say they believe in free enterprise, they prefer to practice safe enterprise.

America's Position in World Politics

As we noted above, until the end of the nineteenth century the United States followed an isolationist foreign policy and was only a minor player in world politics. The changeover came with the Spanish-American War (1898), Theodore Roosevelt's mediation of the Russo-Japanese War (1905), and America's belated entry (1917) into World War I (1914–1918). Since 1918 America has been a leading player on the world stage.

From 1945 to 1989 world politics was dominated by the cold war between the two great superpowers and their allies: the United States, leading an alliance of Western capitalist/democratic nations; and the Soviet Union, leading an alliance of Eastern communist/authoritarian nations. The cold war came to an end with Mikhail Gorbachev's introduction of *perestroika* and *glasnost* in the Soviet Union and the collapse of most of the other communist regimes in Eastern Europe. As the 1990s begin, the United States continues to be the world's most powerful nation, but a new international order is emerging. Whatever its final shape may be, the United States will continue to play an active and demanding role, though that new role is bound to be different from what it was during the cold war.

THE CONSTITUTIONAL SYSTEM

As in most modern nations (Great Britain and Israel are two notable exceptions), the basic structure of the American system of government is set forth in a written Constitution of the United States, drawn up in 1787, ratified in 1788, and instituted in 1789. As we noted above, it is the world's oldest written constitution still in force.

Of course, the Constitution of the 1990s differs from that of 1789 in a number of important ways. It has been formally amended twenty-six times, the most recent being the 1971 amendment lowering the voting age to eighteen.[14] Among the most important amendments are the following. The first ten, known collectively as the *Bill of Rights*, list the rights of individuals which the national government is forbidden to abridge; among these rights are freedom of speech, press, and religion, and due process of law guarantees of a fair trial for persons accused of crime. The Fourteenth Amendment, ratified just after the Civil War, makes national citizenship legally superior to state citizenship, and prohibits the states from violating the "privileges and immunities" of U.S. citizens—which, by judicial interpretation, has come to mean nearly all the rights guaranteed against the national government by the first ten amendments. Other major amendments have outlawed slavery (the Thirteenth), guaranteed the right to

vote to former slaves (the Fifteenth) and women (the Nineteenth), limited presidents to two elective terms (the Twenty-second), and spelled out the conditions under which the president can be replaced (the Twenty-fifth). Even with these amendments, most of the basic elements of the 1789 Constitution have remained in force, whereas the written constitutions in many other countries and in most of the American states have been replaced several times. Thus, if durability is a mark of constitutional strength, the Constitution of the United States is the strongest in history.

Yet the words in the Constitution do not tell all there is to be told about the basic structure of the American constitutional system. A number of customs, usages, and judicial decisions have significantly altered our way of governing without changing a word in the Constitution. Examples are the addition of judicial review; the development of political parties; and the conversion of the presidential selection process from one of choices made behind closed doors by small cliques of insiders to one of popular elections open to all citizens. We will say more about each of these changes below.

Taken together, the provisions of the written Constitution of the United States and their associated customs and usages add up to a constitutional system that has three distinctive features: federalism, separation of powers, and judicial review.

Federalism

Federalism is a system in which governmental power is divided between a national government and several subnational governments, each of which is legally supreme in its assigned sphere. This system has some ancient precursors, notably the Achaean League of Greek city-states in the third century B.C. and the Swiss Confederation of the sixteenth century; but the men who wrote the American Constitution established the first modern form of federalism. They did so because they had to. The 1787 convention in Philadelphia was called because its members felt that the new nation needed a much stronger national government than the Articles of Confederation provided, but the representatives from the small states refused to join any national government that did not preserve most of their established powers. Thus, the framers divided power between the national and the state governments, and gave each state equal representation in the national Senate, because it was the only way they could get a new Constitution.

Even so, some of the farmers regarded federalism

as more than a political expedient. James Madison in particular believed that the greatest threat to human rights in a popular government is the majority tyranny that results when one faction seizes control of the entire power of government and uses it to advance its own selfish interests at the expense of all other interests. He believed that dividing power among the national and the state governments, combined with separation of powers, was the best way to prevent such a disaster.

Federalism has been widely praised as one of the great American contributions to the art of government. A number of different nations have adopted it as a way of enabling different regions with sharply different cultures and interests to join together as one nation. The clearest examples of such nations today are Australia, Canada, Germany, and Switzerland, but significant elements of federalism are also found in systems, as disparate as those of Brazil, India, Mexico, and the Soviet Union.[15]

The American federal system divides government power in the following principal ways:

Powers specifically assigned to the federal[16] government, such as the power to declare war, make treaties with foreign nations, coin money, and regulate commerce between the states.

Powers reserved to the states by the Tenth Amendment, which says, "The powers not delegated to the United States by the Constitution, nor prohibited by it to the States, are reserved to the States respectively, or to the people." The main powers in this class are those over education, marriage and divorce, intrastate commerce, regulation of motor vehicles, and so on. However, the federal government often grants money to the states to help them build and operate schools, make and repair highways, make welfare payments to the poor and the sick, and so on. The states do not have to accept the money, but if they do they also have to accept federal standards governing how the money is to be spent and federal monitoring to make sure it is spent that way.[17]

Powers that can be exercised by either the federal government or the states, such as imposing taxes, and defining and punishing crimes.

Powers forbidden to the federal government, mainly those in the first eight amendments, such as abridging freedom of speech, press, and religion and various guarantees of fair trials for persons accused of crimes.

Powers forbidden to the state governments; some of these are in the body of the Constitution, but the main ones are the Fourteenth Amendment's requirements that no state shall "abridge the privileges or immunities of citizens of the United States; nor shall any State deprive any person of life, liberty, or property without due process of law; nor deny to any person within its jurisdiction the equal protection of the laws." A series of Supreme Court decisions have interpreted these general phrases to mean that almost all the specific liberties guaranteed against the federal government in the first eight amendments are also guaranteed against the state governments.

When all is said and done, however, perhaps the most important single point to note about the nature of American federalism is made in Article VI of the original Constitution:

> This Constitution, and the laws of the United States which shall be made in Pursuance thereof; and all Treaties made, or which shall be made, under the Authority of the United States, shall be the supreme Law of the Land; and the Judges in every State shall be bound thereby, any Thing in the Constitution or Laws of any State to the Contrary notwithstanding.

In short, while the federal government cannot constitutionally interfere with the powers assigned exclusively to the states, whenever a state constitution or law is inconsistent with a law or treaty the federal government has adopted in accordance with its proper powers, the conflicting state constitution and law must yield. Moreover, note that it is the Supreme Court of the United States, which is an organ of the federal government and not of the state governments, that decides precisely which acts of the federal government are within its legitimate powers. Thus, to the extent that the American federal system is a competition between the national government and the states, the chief umpire is a member of one of the two competing teams.

Separation of Powers

Since most analysts of the American system maintain that separation of powers is the most important single difference between the U.S. system (which is called a *presidential democracy*) and most other democratic systems (which are called parliamentary democracies),[18] let us be clear on the institution's main features.

MEANING *Separation of powers* means the constitutional division of government power among separate legislative, executive, and judicial branches. The Constitution of the United States specifically vests the legislative power in the Congress (Article I), the executive power in the president (Article II), and the judicial power in the federal courts, headed by the Supreme Court (Article III).

DISTINCT PERSONNEL The three branches are separated in several ways, the most important of which is the requirement in Article I, Section 6, that "No Person holding any Office under the United States, shall be a Member of either House during his Continuance in Office." This provision means that each branch is operated by persons entirely distinct from those operating the other two branches. Thus, when Representative Dick Cheney was appointed secretary of defense in 1989, he had to resign his seat in the House immediately. When Associate Justice Arthur Goldberg was named U.S. permanent representative to the United Nations in 1965, he had to resign his seat on the Supreme Court bench immediately. When Attorney General Robert Kennedy decided to run for senator from New York in 1964, he resigned his executive position before beginning his campaign. This, of course, is the direct opposite of the fusion of powers in most parliamentary democracies, according to which the political head of the executive (the Cabinet and Ministry) must be a member of Parliament.

The persons heading each branch are selected by different procedures for different terms.

Members of the House of Representatives are elected directly by the voters for two-year terms, with no limit on the number of terms they can serve.
Members of the Senate are elected directly by the voters for six-year terms with no limit on the number of terms they can serve, but their terms are staggered so that only one-third of the members of the Senate come up for reelection every two years.
The president is elected indirectly by the *Electoral College* (though actually by direct popular election) for a four-year term, and is limited to two full elected terms. Moreover, any president who has served more than two years by succeeding to the presidency on the death or resignation of an incumbent president is limited to one more elected term.
All federal judges, including the members of the Su-

preme Court, are appointed by the president with the approval of a majority of the Senate, and they hold office until death, resignation, or removal by the Congress.

CHECKS AND BALANCES The other main devices ensuring the separation of powers are the *checks and balances* by which each branch can keep the other two branches from invading its powers. For example, the Senate can disapprove top-level presidential appointments and refuse to ratify treaties. The two chambers of Congress acting together can impeach, convict, and remove the president and federal judges from office. They can (and often do) deny the president the legislation, appropriations, and taxes he asks for. The president, in turn, can veto any act of Congress, and the Constitution requires a two-thirds vote of both chambers to override the veto. The president also makes the initial appointments of all federal judges; presidents have almost always nominated only judges who are likely to agree with their own political philosophies and policy preferences.

The Supreme Court, through its power of judicial review, can declare any act of the president or Congress null and void on the ground that it violates the Constitution. Such a decision can be overturned only by a constitutional amendment or by the Court, usually with new members, changing its mind.

Some scholars believe that the American system is more accurately described as a system of "separated branches exercising shared powers," since getting government action usually requires some kind of joint action by the Congress and the president, with the acquiescence of the Supreme Court.[19] But separation of powers is what most political scientists have called this feature of the system since the time of the *Federalist Papers*. Whatever it is called, this constitutional feature, more than any other, makes the American system different from most other democratic systems.

Judicial Review

As we have noted before, *judicial review* can be defined as the power of a court to render an act of a legislature or an executive null and void on grounds of unconstitutionality. All American courts, including the lower federal courts and all levels of the state courts, exercise this power on occasion. But the final word on all issues involving an interpretation of the national Constitution, which, as we have seen, is "the supreme law of the land," belongs to the national Supreme Court.

Although every democracy has to determine who has the final word on what its constitution allows and does not allow, the United States is one of the few democracies in which that power is given to the top appellate court of the regular court system. Australia and Canada have similar systems, and some scholars feel that as many as twelve other countries have some form of judicial review. However, some (e.g., Austria and Italy) give the final word to special tribunals rather than to bodies in their regular court systems, while in others (e.g., Mexico and Switzerland) the power includes only the "federal umpire" power, and not the power to override decisions of the national executive and legislature.[20] Thus, judicial review is a prominent but not exclusive feature of the American system.

The American constitutional system, though an important part of the story of how Americans make political decisions, is not the whole story. To a considerable and perhaps unmeasurable degree, the American political system functions as it does because it is operated by Americans rather than by Britons, Italians, Mexicans, or Russians, and it does what it does because Americans have a distinctive political culture that underlies, animates, and controls all the formal institutions we have reviewed.[21]

POLITICAL CULTURE AND SOCIALIZATION

The editors of this book contend that "a political culture is a particular distribution of political attitudes, values, feelings, information, and skills" that provides the psychological environment within which a political system operates.[22] They, like most political scientists, believe that political culture is one of the most important elements of any political system, for, in Alexis de Tocqueville's wise words, "There is no country in which everything can be provided for by the laws, or in which political institutions can prove a substitute for common sense and public morality."[23]

Melting Pot or Patchwork Quilt?

As already noted, most Americans are immigrants or descendants of immigrants who came from many different cultures in Africa, Asia, Western and Eastern Europe, and Latin America. Thus, throughout most of its history America has had to deal with how best to fit the immigrants and their different cultures into American economic, social, and political life.

During most of our history the prevailing policy has been that of *the melting pot.* This policy sought

The New Immigrants: Mexicans crossing the Rio Grande to enter the United States

to blend all the different cultures into one uniquely American culture, which was to be conducted and passed on in one language, the American version of English. Some room was left for such special ethnic folkways as Polish weddings, Irish wakes, and Mexican food, but the basic task given to the regular schools, adult education and citizenship classes, English language classes, and the like was to turn everyone into an English-speaking American imbued with the main values and attitudes of the nation's existing political culture.[24]

Since the 1960s, the melting pot policy has been increasingly challenged by a number of ethnic groups, especially African-Americans, Hispanics, and Asians. More and more spokespersons for each group reject the idea that their ancient and special cultures should be homogenized into one prevailing new national culture —a culture which, they say, is not truly a blend of all cultures but rather the culture of Western Europe, especially Great Britain, which has always been the culture of the white ruling class and therefore an instrument for the oppression of minorities by the WASP (white Anglo-Saxon Protestant) majority. The only just policy, they say, is to make America a true cultural *patchwork quilt* (the phrase is Jesse Jackson's) — a piece-by-piece assembly of the languages, history, customs, and values of each of the nation's major ethnic groups, each to be given the same attention, respect, and importance as every other, with none dominant.

Among the policies advocated by this new movement are bilingual education — educating minority-group children in their native languages rather than forcing them to learn English as their primary language;

printing ballots and other official documents in several languages, not just English; and broadening school curricula so as to give full and fair attention to the contributions of African, Asian, and Latin cultures as well as of British and Western European cultures.

Some backlash has set in against this movement, as especially manifested in laws adopted by several states declaring English to be the state's official language. We have yet to see whether the patchwork quilt ideal will replace the melting pot ideal, and, if so, what its impact will be on American political culture.

Main Elements of the Traditional American Political Culture

TRUST THE PEOPLE; DISTRUST THE POLITICIANS. The first dimensions of political culture that political scientists usually consider are called trust in institutions, trust in government, and/or trust in leaders at one extreme and alienation and/or rejection at the other end. How do Americans compare with other peoples on this dimension? Some of the answers that have been provided are presented in Table 17.1, which compare the levels of popular trust in government in the United States and three Western European nations.

Table 17.1 shows that significantly smaller proportions of Americans than British, West Germans, and French believe that government benefits all the people or that one can trust the government to do what is right. On the other hand, higher proportions of Americans believe that officials stay in touch with the people, that they care about what people think, and that the parties are interested in public opinion. These findings do not show

TABLE 17.1
TRUST IN GOVERNMENT IN FOUR WESTERN NATIONS (IN PERCENT)

	United States	Great Britain	West Germany	France
Satisfied with working of democracy	32	13	35	32
Government benefits all	31	45	69	—
Trust government to do right	34	40	52	—
Officials care what people think	43	31	34	36
Parties interested in public opinion	37	29	39	—
Officials don't lose contact	30	26	22	—
Average	35	31	42	—

Source: Russell J. Dalton, *Citizen Politics in Western Democracies* (Chatham, N.J.: Chatham House Publishers, 1988), Table 11.1, p. 232.

that Americans are more "alienated" from their government than the other nationalities. Moreover, other studies have shown that more Americans say they are very proud of their country (80 percent) and willing to fight for it (71 percent) than the citizens of Great Britain, Spain, Italy, France, and Germany say about their countries (where the proportions range from 55 and 62 percent in Great Britain down to 21 percent and 35 percent in Germany).[25]

Thus, while Americans may trust their governments to do what is right less than Western Europeans do, they are nevertheless more proud of being Americans and more willing to fight for America than the Western Europeans are for their countries. How can we explain this paradox?

The answer may lie in the fact that throughout their history most Americans have strongly held two ideas that may be logically inconsistent. One is the idea that ordinary Americans are good, solid, reliable folks with plenty of that most valuable form of intelligence, common sense, and that America is a wonderful country. Conversely, they feel that the *government*, which is not the same thing as the country, is, as Ronald Reagan so often put it, "the problem, not the solution." They feel that the professional politicians who fill its offices, lead its parties, and conduct its business are self-seeking lightweights more interested in winning votes and getting reelected than in making courageous and forward-looking policies to solve the nation's problems.[26]

Leaving aside such apocalyptic notions as alienation and rejection, then, it is clear that most Americans are proud of their country, willing to fight for it, and think well of other ordinary Americans. At the same time, they are now, as they have always been, wary of government as an institution for solving social problems, and they take a dim view of most of the politicians who operate it.

POLITICAL EFFICACY   These findings are consistent with those on another dimension of political culture —the degree to which ordinary people believe that their preferences have a significant influence on what public officials do. One of the findings of the first great comparative study of political cultures, presented in Table 17.2, was that Americans score higher on this dimension than people in Great Britain, West Germany, Italy, and Mexico, and that in all five countries better educated people score higher than less-educated people.[27] Subsequent comparable studies have confirmed that

Americans generally feel more "politically efficacious" in this sense than do the citizens of most other nations.

THE ROLE OF IDEOLOGY   Political scientists usually think of ideology as a comprehensive and intensively held set of convictions about how governments ought to make their decisions and/or what those decisions ought to be.[28] The ideologies that receive the most attention in discussions of the political cultures of other nations are socialism and capitalism, the left (leaning more toward socialism) and the right (leaning more toward capitalism), democracy and authoritarianism, and constitutionalism and totalitarianism. Almost every comparative study of political cultures concludes that ideology plays a smaller role in American political culture than in many others. A typical study is reported in Table 17.2.

RIGHTS AND LITIGIOUSNESS   Many foreign commentators on America have been especially impressed by the depth of conviction among most Americans —black and white, women and men, young and old— that they have certain basic rights and that often the best way to make sure they get their rights is not to wait for executives, legislatures, and bureaucrats to do the right thing but to file lawsuits to force public officials — and other private individuals — to honor their rights. For example, two recent British commentators on America were struck by the *litigiousness* of Americans — that is, by their tendency to file suits against government officials and private citizens for violating their rights, and by the consequent central role this tendency gives to law-

TABLE 17.2
LEVELS OF IDEOLOGICAL AWARENESS IN SEVEN DEMOCRACIES (IN PERCENT)

Nation	Active use of Ideology	Recognition/ understanding left and right	Left/right self-placement
West Germany	34	56	92
Netherlands	36	48	90
Great Britain	21	23	82
Switzerland	9	39	79
Austria	19	39	75
Italy	55	54	74
United States	21	34	67

Source: Russell J. Dalton, *Citizen Politics in Western Democracies* (Chatham, N.J.: Chatham House Publishers, 1988), Table 2.2, p. 25.

yers in America. They note that America has one lawyer for every 440 of its people, as compared with one lawyer for every 10,000 people in Japan. They cite the comments of Arthur Burns, the former chairman of the Federal Reserve Board, that if more talented Americans went into business and fewer into law, the country's economy would be a lot healthier. They conclude, however, that America has so many lawyers because so many Americans are insistent on demanding their rights.[29]

Political Socialization

Political socialization is the process by which people acquire their basic political orientations — their notions of what the political world is like and which people, policies, and institutions are good and bad. That process in America is much the same as in every other modern large-scale industrialized democracy. Political socialization begins in children as young as three or four and continues until old age and death. Children typically begin by perceiving some political figures, notably the president and the local policeman, as important persons outside their own families. As they grow older their perceptions broaden and deepen, and they learn about political parties, legislators, judges, and public issues and policies.

The main agencies shaping their political socialization are their families, especially their parents, their schoolteachers, friends, schoolmates, and work associates, and the mass communications media. Most recent studies agree that parents continue to have the most powerful impact on most people's political socialization, but that in recent years their impact has lessened somewhat while the influence of the mass communications media has increased.[30] This finding should not surprise us, for most analysts of political life in America and the other large-scale industrial democracies agree that the mass media, especially television, have become one of the most important forces — many would say *the* most important — affecting people's political socialization, attitudes, and behavior. In most aspects of this development, the United States, for better or worse, has led the world.

THE MASS COMMUNICATIONS MEDIA

The term *mass communications media*[31] includes all the devices used to convey the ideas of a communicator to mass audiences who do not see the communicator face to face. They fall into two categories: the print media (newspapers, magazines, books, and pamphlets), in which the printing press is the basic communicating device; and the electronic media (radio, broadcast television, and cable television), in which the basic communicating device is the broadcasting of electromagnetic waves from communicator to audience over the air or by cable.

The relative political importance of these media in America is shown in Table 17.3.

Table 17.3 shows that television is both the primary and the most trusted source of information about politics for most Americans, with newspapers a distant second in both respects and all the other mass media politically much less important.

TABLE 17.3
THE AMERICAN MASS MEDIA AS TRUSTED SOURCES OF POLITICAL INFORMATION

"I'd like to ask you where you usually get most of your news about what's going on in the world today — from the newspapers or radio or television or magazines or talking to people or where?"

Source of most news	Percentage
Television	64
Newspapers	40
Radio	14
Magazines	4
People	4

"If you got conflicting or different reports of the same news story from radio, television, the magazines, and the newspapers, which of the four versions would you be most inclined to believe?"

Most believable	Percentage
Television	53
Newspapers	24
Radio	8
Magazines	7
Don't know, no answer	8

Source: Austin Ranney, "Broadcasting, Narrowcasting, and Politics," in Anthony King, ed., *The New American Political System*, second version (Washington, D.C.: AEI Press, 1990), Table 6–1, p. 181.

Ownership and Operation

The United States, like most other industrialized democracies, has a mixture of publicly owned and privately owned broadcast and cable television. The privately owned stations are businesses operated for profit, and they get most of their revenues from the sale of airtime to advertisers for broadcasting commercial messages. Cable television operators usually also charge their subscribers monthly viewing fees, but most of their revenue comes from advertising. Most newspapers make small charges to their readers, but their revenue comes mainly from the sale of space for printing advertisements. Public radio and television stations get about 30 percent of their revenues from direct state and local government subsidies, 23 percent from viewer/listener contributions, 18 percent from the federal government, 16 percent from grants by private businesses, and 13 percent from foundations and other sources.[32]

In most respects the privately owned media are much more important than the publicly owned. There are three times as many private as public broadcasting stations, and the public stations usually have only about 10 percent of the viewers.

Regulation

In the United States, the political content of newspapers, books, magazines, and the other print media is almost entirely unregulated by government because of the provision in the Constitution's First Amendment that "Congress shall make no law. . . . abridging the freedom . . . of the press."[33] About the only restriction on what they print are libel and slander laws, but in the landmark case of *New York Times v. Sullivan* (1964) the Supreme Court held that public officials and public figures cannot collect damages for remarks made about them in the print media unless those comments are (1) knowingly false or made with a "reckless disregard" for their truth and (2) made with provable "malice" as a deliberate attempt to damage the victim's public reputation and standing—something that, in practice, is very difficult to prove.[34]

Radio and television stations are much more closely regulated than the print media. They can operate only if they are granted a license by the Federal Communications Commission (FCC). That license, which must be renewed every five years, not only assigns broadcasting frequency, power of the transmitter, hours of broadcasting, and even the height of the transmitting antenna, but also requires that the political content of programs meet certain standards. For example, the stations must make available to all candidates for a particular political office an equal opportunity to make their appeals; they don't have to *give* any of them free time, but if they do give time to one candidate they must give it to all, and if they sell time to one candidate they must sell it to all at the same rates and at comparably desirable times. Even if they would rather not carry any political advertising at all (it usually bores their viewers), they still must sell a reasonable amount of time for political advertisements to any candidate or party that wishes to buy. They cannot charge political advertisers higher rates than they charge regular commercial advertisers. If in the course of a broadcast someone makes a personal attack on the moral integrity of a political figure, she or he must be given free time in which to reply to the charges.

The Supreme Court has consistently upheld the government's power to impose such restrictions on the electronic media while denying government any comparable power over the print media. The reason has to do with what is generally called the *scarcity doctrine*. The Supreme Court has ruled that there is no limit, other than economic, on the number of newspapers, books, magazines, or pamphlets that can be printed and circulated. But there is a physical limit on the number of broadcasting stations that can operate, because if two stations are broadcasting on the same frequency in the same viewing area, their signals will jam each other and no broadcasting will be possible. Accordingly, says the Court, in order to make possible the public good of broadcasting, the government must, in its licensing of stations, allocate particular frequencies to particular stations. Thus, broadcasting is a public resource, much like the national park system or navigable rivers; this gives the government the right not only to allocate frequencies, but also to set standards to ensure that their use will promote "the public convenience, interest, or necessity."[35]

The Paid Media and Free Media in American Politics

In assessing the role of the mass media in American politics, most political analysts distinguish between two kinds of media, each of which has its special advantages and disadvantages for political candidates, parties, and pressure groups. *Paid media* are political advertisements, in which the candidate, party, or pressure group, just like a commercial advertiser, prepares written and pictorial advertisements designed to make people support their cause ("positive ads") or reject the opposition ("negative ads"). They buy space in newspapers and time on television (usually in the form of 15- to 30-second "spots") to send their messages to readers and viewers.

A few countries, notably Great Britain, do not permit paid political advertising in any mass medium. Most democracies allow a certain amount of political advertising, but they restrict the amount of money that can be spent on it. The United States is in this second category, and there are many federal and state laws regulating such matters as who can contribute money to political campaigns, how much they can contribute, how much money can be spent, and the like. Some critics think these laws are far too lax, that the big spenders "buy" victories over the small spenders, and that the whole system of political finance in the United States is a national disgrace. Others disagree, pointing out that what Americans spend on political advertising is a tiny fraction of what they spend on product advertising, that the bigger spenders in political campaigns lose more often than they win, and that the main need is to establish "floors" that will guarantee every candidate and cause enough money at least to get its case before the voters —not to put ceilings on how far campaigns can go beyond that necessary minimum.[36]

From the standpoint of the political contender, paid media have one enormous advantage: the contenders control the message and, therefore, can use the arguments and images that their well-paid professional *campaign consultants* think are best calculated to defeat the opposition.[37] Paid media also have one great disadvantage: Americans, who watch commercial television more than they do anything else except work and sleep, are constantly bombarded with advertisements which they know are intended to make them buy a particular brand of detergent or beer or automobile. Most of them develop a certain skepticism about the truth value of advertisements in general, and their low opinion of politicians makes them even more skeptical of paid political advertisements. (The law requires that all political ads be labeled as such.) Consequently, it is far from clear that the paid media are worth their enormous cost.[38]

Many democratic nations provide party political broadcasts, in which some free time on television and radio is given to each of the leading parties to present its case to the voters in any manner it chooses. The United States provides no such free time, but the term *free media* also includes the extensive coverage candidates and issue advocates are given in newspaper reports and television and radio news and talk shows. From the standpoint of the political contestant, the free media have two great advantages: they cost nothing; and they have much greater credibility than the paid media. They also have one enormous disadvantage: the media, not the political contender, control what is said and shown. Thus, political candidates typically complain that television crews will videotape an entire 30-minute speech, but the network news will air only 10- or 15-second "videobytes" of the speech. Moreover, the news show producers, not the candidate, select what will be shown, and they love to feature a candidate's slip of the tongue or weeping or other loss of control rather than his or her stands on the issues. But if the producers think that the one bad moment is more newsworthy than the rest of the speech, that is what they will put on the air. Most politicians feel, quite correctly, that one bad showing on the nightly news outweighs hundreds of the most expensive and well-produced paid advertisements.

Consequently, while most American candidates, parties, and pressure groups raise and spend as much money as they can on paid political ads, the success or failure of their campaigns often depends more on how clever they are at presenting their speeches, rallies, and other political events in such a way that the free media will choose items to report that help rather than hurt their causes.[39]

Politicians depend heavily on exposure in the "free media:" Jesse Jackson being interviewed by NBC.

POLITICAL PARTICIPATION AND RECRUITMENT

Participation by Voting

Ordinary citizens can participate in a nation's politics in various ways, but voting is widely regarded as the most important form of participation. Indeed, some analysts argue that having regular, free, and competitive elections for public office is the most important difference between democratic and nondemocratic systems.

Most political scientists believe that since voting in elections is the main or only way in which ordinary citizens in all democracies actually participate in their nations' governing processes, *voting turnout* — the percentage of all the people eligible to vote who actually do vote — is one of the most important indicators of any democratic system's health. Studies of voting turnout in the world's democracies usually find that the turnout is lower in the United States than in any other country except Switzerland, and many view this finding as an alarming symptom of a deep sickness in America. They say it reflects a widespread popular feeling that election outcomes don't really matter, that the whole governmental system is rigged against ordinary people, and so there is no good reason why they should bother with it.

Other analysts argue that when the voting turnout is counted in exactly the same way in the United States as it is in other democracies, the American record looks much better (see below). The point, though technical, is important.

In America, as in most of the world's other democracies, citizens' names must appear on voting registers in advance of an election before they can legally vote in that election. But the United States differs from other nations in one important respect: in most other countries, getting on the register requires no effort by the voter. Public authorities take the initiative and do the work to get all eligible citizens enrolled, and as a result almost every citizen of voting age is on the register. In the United States, on the other hand, each state regulates *voting registration*, and in most states would-be voters must take the initiative to get on the register; no public official will do it for them. Moreover, in most democratic countries when voters move from one part of the country to another, they are automatically struck off the register in the place they leave and are added to the register in the place to which they move, all with no effort on their part. In contrast, in the United States when people move from state to state, they are struck off

the register in the state they leave, but they are not automatically added to the register in their new state of residence.

As a result, voting turnout can be measured in two ways, and they give markedly different results. One is to take a percentage of all persons of voting age, which, in most democracies, is nearly identical with the number of registered voters. The other, which is used in the United States, is to take a percentage of all persons of voting age — including not just unregistered persons and persons who moved but have not re-registered, but even noncitizens of voting age. The difference found when we use one measure or the other enables us to see how voting turnout in the United States compares with that in other democracies (see Table 17.4).

The statistics in Table 17.4 show that when voting turnout in America is measured by exactly the same measure as that used for other democratic countries — the percentage of *registered* voters who actually vote — turnout in the United States compares very favorably with that of all the countries that do not have compulsory voting laws, and there is no reason to believe that Americans are any more "turned off" from voting than the citizens of most other democracies.

AMERICAN VOTERS WORK HARDER Another explanation for America's "low" voting turnout arises from the fact that American voters are called on to cast far more votes than the citizens of any other country. (Only Switzerland comes close.) In the parliamentary democracies, the only national elections are those for the national Parliament, in which voters vote for one candidate among several choices in single-member district systems or for one party in party-list proportional systems. They also vote periodically for a candidate or a party in the elections for the city or rural district in which they live. In the other federal systems, they vote for a member of their state or provincial parliament. Hence, in most democracies other than the United States, the typical voter makes a total of only four or five voting decisions over a period of four or five years.

In the United States, the combination of separation of powers, federalism, and, at the state and local level, the *long ballot*, the *direct primary*, and the initiative and referendum requires that citizens make several *hundred* decisions in a period of four years. At the national level, voters are called on to vote in the presidential primaries of their parties, and in the general election to decide between the Democratic and Republican can-

TABLE 17.4
VOTING TURNOUT IN DEMOCRATIC NATIONS ACCORDING TO TWO MEASURES[a]

Rank	Vote as percentage of persons 18 and over	Rank	Vote as percentage of registered voters
1. Belgium[b]	94.6	1. Belgium[b]	94.6
2. Australia[b]	94.5	2. Australia[b]	94.5
3. Austria	91.6	3. Austria	91.6
4. Sweden	90.7	4. Sweden	90.7
5. Italy	90.4	5. Italy	90.4
6. Iceland	89.3	6. Iceland	89.3
7. New Zealand	89.0	7. New Zealand	89.0
8. Luxembourg	88.9	8. Luxembourg	88.9
9. West Germany	88.6	9. West Germany	88.6
10. Netherlands	87.0	10. Netherlands	87.0
11. France	85.9	11. *United States*	86.8
12. Portugal	84.2	12. France	85.9
13. Denmark	83.2	13. Portugal	84.2
14. Norway	82.0	14. Denmark	83.2
15. Greece[b]	78.6	15. Norway	82.0
16. Israel	78.5	16. Greece[b]	78.6
17. Great Britain	76.3	17. Israel	78.5
18. Japan	74.5	18. Great Britain	76.3
19. Canada	69.3	19. Japan	74.5
20. Spain[b]	68.1	20. Canada	69.3
21. Finland	64.3	21. Spain[b]	68.1
22. Ireland	62.2	22. Finland	64.3
23. *United States*	52.6	23. Ireland	62.2
24. Switzerland	48.3	24. Switzerland	48.3

[a] Most recent national election prior to 1981.
[b] Compulsory voting laws.
Source: David Glass, Peverill Squire, and Raymond Wolfinger, "Voter Turnout: An international Comparison," *Public Opinion* (December/January 1984), pp. 49–55.

didates. They are also expected to vote in primary elections and general elections every two years for members of the House of Representatives and two out of four years for members of the Senate. At the state and local level not only are the leading executive officials (governors and mayors) and members of the legislatures nominated in primary elections and elected in general elections, but in most states and localities a considerable number of other offices that are appointed offices in most other democracies — for example, state secretaries of state, attorneys general, treasurers, superintendents of education, judges of the higher and lower courts, and members of myriad local school boards, school superintendents, sanitary commissions, park commis-

sions, and so on and on — are selected by the same primary-plus-general election procedures. In addition, about half the states regularly hold elections on popular *initiatives* and *referendums*, in which the voters vote directly on questions of public policy.[40]

I make this point with a strong personal sense of what it means. Like every Californian, in the general election of November 6, 1990, I was called on to make choices for the following offices: one national office (member of the House of Representatives); nine state offices (governor, lieutenant governor, secretary of state, controller, treasurer, attorney general, insurance commissioner, state board of equalization, and member of the state assembly); fourteen nonpartisan state judicial offices; one county office (assessor); eleven city offices (mayor, council, auditor, three school directors, five members of the rent stabilization commission); one transit district commissioner; and one utilities district commissioner.

But when I finished making these choices among candidates, I was less than half done: I still had to vote on twenty-eight state initiative and referendum measures; one school district measure; two county measures; and three city measures (a slow year for Berkeley). In short, in a year without an election for president or U.S. senator, Berkeley voters were called on to make a grand total of seventy-two decisions in the general election—and there had already been a primary election in the preceding June for most of these offices and a number of initiative and referendum measures. Thus, in one year I had voted far more often than a citizen of almost any other democracy votes in a lifetime.

The opportunity to vote in free, fair, and competitive elections is a sine qua non of democratic government, and therefore surely a good thing. But a familiar American saying is that there can be too much of a good thing, and, while staggering out of the polling place in 1990, I concluded that the sheer number of voting decisions in America is a classic case in point.

Participation by Other Means

Voting, of course, is only one of several ways to participate in a nation's politics. Citizens can also serve in office, work in political parties, donate money to candidates, parties, and causes, attend rallies, take part in street demonstrations, send letters and telegrams (and these days, no doubt faxes) to their elected representatives, write letters to newspapers and op-ed columns, call in on radio talk shows, try to persuade their families and friends, file lawsuits against public officials, and so on. These other forms of participation have not been studied as extensively as voting, but Russell Dalton has collected some interesting comparative data on conventional and unconventional forms of participation in the United States and some Western European countries (see Table 17.5).

The responses summarized in Table 17.5 show that citizens of France are substantially more likely than citizens of the United States, Great Britain, and West Germany to join in boycotts and political strikes, whereas Americans are as likely or more likely than the others to sign petitions and participate in demonstrations, and much more likely to work with groups in the local community and directly contact public officials.

Several other studies have found that the form of

TABLE 17.5
NONVOTING FORMS OF POLITICAL PARTICIPATION IN FOUR DEMOCRACIES, 1981 (IN PERCENT)

Activity	United States	Great Britain	West Germany	France
VOTING				
Voted in last election	68	73	90	81
CAMPAIGN ACTIVITY				
Convince others how to vote	19	9	22	—
Attend meeting/rally	18	9	22	—
Work for party/candidate	14	5	8	—
COMMUNAL ACTIVITY				
Sign petitions	61	63	46	74
Work with group to solve community problem	37	17	14	—
Contact officials	27	11	11	—
PROTEST ACTIVITY				
Participate in lawful demonstrations	12	10	14	26
Join in boycott	14	7	7	11
Participate in unofficial strike	3	7	2	10

Source: Russell J. Dalton, *Citizen Politics in Western Democracies* (Chatham, N.J.: Chatham House Publishers, 1988), Table 3.4, p. 47, and Table 4.1, p. 65.

participation most frequently claimed by Americans is voting in elections (53 percent), followed by stating their political opinions to others (32 percent), contributing money to campaigns (12 percent), displaying political bumper-stickers and signs (9 percent), and attending political meetings or rallies (8 percent). Only 4 percent report belonging to a political club or working for a political party.[41]

In short, Americans participate in politics in ways other than voting in elections as much or more than the citizens of the handful of other Western democracies for whom we have reliable information. These data certainly do not support the conclusion that Americans are in any way more alienated or lazier than the citizens of other democracies.

Recruitment of Leaders

Leadership recruitment is the process whereby, out of the millions of a nation's citizens, emerge the few hundreds or thousands who hold elective and appointive pubic office, play leading roles in parties and pressure groups, decide how the mass communications media will portray politics, and, within the limits permitted by the general public, make public policy.

As Chapter Four points out, many scholars have studied leadership recruitment in many countries and have found certain general tendencies also evident in American politics. For instance, American leaders, like all leaders, are drawn disproportionately from people in the middle and upper ranges of wealth and status. The reason lies not in the existence of any conspiracy to oppress the lower classes but in the kinds of knowledge and skills a person must have to win the support needed for leadership selection: these skills are more likely to be acquired and developed by well-educated people rather than the poorly educated. For example, people's chances to climb in a political party or a pressure group, to be nominated for and elected to public office, or to be appointed to higher administrative offices, are considerably enhanced if they have the ability to speak well in public, if they get along well with and are liked by other people, and, for elected officials increasingly, if they look and sound good on television.

Under the "spoils system" that dominated the recruitment of lesser administrative officials in the United States until after the Civil War, these skills were less important than a record of loyalty and service to the winning political party. With the passage of the Pendleton Civil Service Reform Act in 1883, however, the federal government began to choose some of its administrative employees by merit system standards. In this system initial selection was made according to the applicants' abilities to score well on standardized examinations, and salary increases and promotions depended on job performance rather than on party connections.[42] Since then more and more federal positions have been placed under the merit system, and today only about 1 percent are available for purely political appointment.

Accordingly, in most respects elite recruitment in the United States differs very little from its counterpart in other advanced industrialized democracies. But in one aspect of that process — the nomination of candidates for elective office — the United States is unlike any other nation in the world.

The Unique Direct Primary

Most political scientists divide the process of electing public officials into three parts: (1) candidate selection, the mostly informal process by which political parties decide what persons to name as their standard-bearers and campaign for; (2) nomination, the mostly formal process through which public authorities decide what persons' names will be printed on the official ballots; and (3) election, the mostly formal process by which the voters register their choices among the nominees.

Many political scientists believe that candidate selection is the most important of the three processes. After all, the recruitment of public officials is essentially one of narrowing the choices from many to one. For example, in 1988 about 105 million Americans satisfied all the constitutional requirements for being elected president. Theoretically, all 105 million names could have been printed on the ballot and each voter could have had an absolutely free choice among them. But, of course, no voter can possibly make a meaningful choice among 105 million alternatives, and so a meaningful democratic election requires that the choices be narrowed down to a manageable number. The same is true for democratic elections to all offices in all countries.

In the United States, as in every other democracy, the narrowing process is accomplished mainly or entirely by the political parties. Each party chooses its candidates, gives their names to the election authorities, and those names appear on the ballot.[43] Accordingly, in 1988 the Democrats decided that their presidential candidate would be Michael Dukakis rather than Jesse Jackson, Al Gore, or Paul Simon, and the Republicans decided that theirs would be George Bush rather than

Robert Dole, Pat Robertson, or Jack Kemp. This made it relatively easy for the voters to make the final choice between Bush and Dukakis, but in fact the bulk of the 1988 presidential recruitment process had already been accomplished by the two major parties' selections of their candidates.

Given the crucial role of candidate selection in democratic elections, then, it is important to understand that the United States is the only nation in the world which makes most of its nominations by direct primaries. In all the parliamentary democracies, the parties' candidates for parliament are chosen by the parties' leaders or by small groups of card-carrying, dues-paying party members. A few countries, such as Belgium, Finland, Norway, and Germany, require that the parties choose their candidates by the secret votes of local party members in procedures that resemble but, strictly speaking, are not direct primaries. Consequently, in every nation except the United States the candidates are selected by only a few hundred, or at most a few thousand, party insiders.[44]

In the United States, nominations for almost all major elective public officers are made by direct primaries, in which candidates are selected directly by the voters in government-supervised elections rather than indirectly by party leaders in caucuses and conventions. Moreover—and this is the key difference between America's direct primaries and the primary-like procedures in other countries mentioned above—public law, not party rules, determines who is qualified to vote in a particular party's primary. Twenty-five states presently have *closed primaries*, in which only persons pre-registered as members of a particular party can vote in that party's primary; fourteen states have *crossover primaries*, which are the same as closed primaries except that voters do not have to make a public choice of the party primary in which they will vote until election day; nine states have *open primaries*, in which there is no party registration of any kind, and voters can vote in whichever party primary they choose (they can, however, vote in only one party's primary at a time) with no public disclosure of their choice; two states have *blanket primaries*, in which voters can switch back and forth between the parties in voting for nominees for particular offices, and do not disclose their switches or their choices.

Direct primaries make candidate selection in the United States by far the most open and participatory in the world. As noted above, in all other countries at most only a few thousand dues-paying party members participate in choosing candidates; in the United States they are chosen by any registered voter who wants to participate, and millions do in every election cycle. To give just one example: although American presidential candidates are formally selected by national nominating conventions, a great majority of the delegates to both conventions are chosen by direct primaries; and in 1988, a grand total of 35,127,051 votes were cast in the Democratic and Republican presidential primaries.[45]

The American system for choosing its presidents may be wiser or more foolish than the way other democracies select their top political leaders, but it is incomparably more participatory.

INTEREST ARTICULATION: PRESSURE GROUPS AND PACs

As we have seen throughout this book, every society has a number of different and conflicting political interests,[46] and the more advanced the economy and the more heterogeneous the society the more individuals and groups there are with interests that to some degree conflict with other interests. The inevitable clash of these interests generates the political process, which consists of two main parts: (1) interest articulation, by which the persons and groups make known their desires for government action or inaction; and (2) interest aggregation, by which various demands are mobilized and combined to press for favorable government policies. That is why most political scientists agree with Harold D. Lasswell's statement that the essence of government is deciding "who gets what, when, and how."[47]

In most democracies interests are articulated mainly by pressure groups and political parties, and the parties also aggregate interests in the formulation and implementation of their programs. In the United States, however, the political parties are much weaker and less cohesive than those in any other democratic system. Consequently, the pressure groups play a greater role in both interest articulation and aggregation than in most democracies.

Many foreign observers of America's peculiar politics have been especially struck by the great variety and power of the nation's organized political groups.[48] Today they are even more numerous and important than they were in the past. They take two main forms, each of which specializes in a particular technique for influencing government: (1) political action committees and campaign contributions, and (2) pressure groups and lobbying.

PACs and Campaign Contributions

THE NATURE AND GROWTH OF PACs Strictly speaking, a *political action committee* (PAC) is any organization that is not directly affiliated with a particular party or candidate that spends money to influence the outcome of elections.[49] PACs differ from political parties in two main respects: (1) unlike parties, they do not themselves nominate candidates and put them on ballots with PAC labels; rather, they support or oppose candidates nominated by the parties; and (2) they are interested mainly in the policies public officials make, and not in the party labels those officials bear. Hence, they usually support candidates of both major parties who are sympathetic to the PACs' particular policy preferences.

Such organizations have operated in American politics at least since the Civil War, and some of them have had considerable success. For example, the Anti-Saloon League was founded in 1893 to support both Democratic and Republican candidates for Congress pledged to support a constitutional amendment outlawing the manufacture and sale of alcoholic beverages. Most historians believe that it was an important force in the adoption of the Eighteenth Amendment in 1919.[50] For another example, the National Guard Association was founded in 1878 to lobby for more federal support for the equipment and training of state militia units and their closer integration with the nation's regular army; the modern structure of the National Guard is due largely to its efforts.[51] One of the most powerful organizations in the second half of the twentieth century has been the Committee on Political Education (COPE) of the AFL–CIO, which has supplied millions of dollars and thousands of election workers for candidates (mostly but not entirely Democrats) sympathetic to organized labor.

The greatest increase in the number and activity of PACs in American history has come since 1974 as an unanticipated (and, by many, unwanted) result of that year's amendments to the Federal Election Campaign Act. The amendments set low limits on the amount of money individuals could contribute to a candidate or a party, but considerably higher limits on what organizations could contribute. They also stipulated that, although labor unions and business corporations could not themselves contribute money to election campaigns, they could sponsor PACs. Their PACs could make such contributions, they stated, as long as the funds came from voluntary contributions by sympathetic individuals rather than by direct levies on union and corporation funds.

In ruling on the constitutionality of these rules, the Supreme Court upheld the limits on direct contributions, but said that limiting the amounts of money that an individual or an organization can spend on behalf of a candidate (that is, by broadcasting or publishing ads *not* controlled by candidates or parties) was a violation of the First Amendment's guarantee of free speech.[52]

These changes in the substance and interpretation of the campaign finance laws led most politically active interests to conclude that forming a PAC was the best way to influence election outcomes, and that is just what they have done. In 1974 there were only 608 PACs operating in national elections; by the end of 1988 the number had exploded to 4,268.

THE PRESENT STATUS OF PACs At present each PAC must register with the Federal Election Commission and periodically report its receipts (what persons contributed and how much) and its expenditures (to what candidates it gave contributions and how much, and how much it spent on its own independent campaigning). Individuals are allowed to contribute no more than $5,000 in a calendar year to a particular PAC and no more than $25,000 a year to all candidates, party committees, and PACs. A PAC can contribute $5,000 to a particular candidate in a primary election and another $5,000 in the general election. However, there is no limit on the total amount it can contribute to all candidates and party committees. There is also no limit on the amount it can spend on behalf of a particular candidate or party as long as its beneficiaries have no say in how the money is spent.

Although many PACs take some part in presidential election campaigns, the federal government finances most of the costs of those campaigns. Thus, most PACs make most of their contributions to House and Senate campaigns. It is estimated that they now contribute about one-third of all the funds for those campaigns.[53]

MAIN TYPES OF PACs The most important PACs can be classified in one of three main categories:[54]

1. Narrow material interest PACs. These PACs are concerned mainly with backing candidates who will

support legislation that favors a particular business or type of business: for example, Chrysler, Coca-Cola, General Electric, General Motors, Texaco, and many other corporations have their own PACs, as do many labor unions, including the Air Line Pilots Association, the American Federation of Government Employees, and the American Federation of Teachers. In addition, a number of PACs represent the interests of whole industries, such as the Dallas Energy Political Action Committee (oil), Edison Electric Institute (electric power), and the National Association of Broadcasters (radio and television).

2. Single, nonmaterial interest PACs. These PACs promote candidates who favor their positions on a particular nonmaterial issue. For example, the National Abortion Rights Action League (pro-choice) and the National Right to Life Committee (anti-abortion) are concerned with the abortion issue, and the National Rifle Association (anti-control) and Handgun Control, Inc. (pro-control) focus on the gun control issue.

3. Ideological PACs. Finally, a number of PACs support candidates committed to strong liberal or conservative ideologies and issues. Liberal PACs include the National Committee for an Effective Congress and the Hollywood Women's Political Committee. Conservative PACs include the National Conservative Political Action Committee and the Conservative Victory Committee.

Pressure Groups and Lobbying

Electioneering by PACs, as we have seen, is one kind of effort by organized interest groups to induce public officials to promote their interests. This effort concentrates on ensuring that candidates sympathetic to their interests and/or grateful for their support will, when they take office, vote as the groups wish on the issues that matter to them. The other kind of effort is lobbying through Washington representatives. This effort concentrates on inducing public officials already in office to support government action (including administrative and judicial rulings as well as legislative acts) the groups favor and to block those the groups oppose.[55]

LOBBYING TACTICS   In the bad old days, to induce members of Congress to vote their way, pressure groups often used straight bribes in the form of cash payments or guarantees of well-paid jobs after retirement. Sadly, bribes still occur on occasion, but the laws against them are strict and the mass medias' investigative reporters love nothing better than to expose bribe-taking. Consequently, most interest groups and public officials have decided that giving and taking bribes is either too immoral or too risky, or both, and bribery has become quite rare.

The main tactic of lobbyists is now *persuasion* — convincing members of Congress (and their staffs, who play key roles in making most members' decisions) that the legislation the lobbyist seeks is in the best interests of the nation as a whole and of the member's particular district or state. After all, almost all the members of Congress feel that their job is to do the best they can for the interests of their particular constituents. Since it is those constituents rather than the rest of the nation that determine whether or not they will stay in office, their likely reactions must be the members' first concern. Accordingly, lobbyists for all interests use the most persuasive evidence and arguments they can think of to convince a particular member that the actions their groups want will be in everyone's best interest — the voters in the particular district or state, the member's own welfare, and the national welfare. Lobbyists who work for interest groups that also have PACs will sometimes say that if the member fails to see the light their PACs will contribute money to his or her challenger at the next election. Surprisingly, however, most lobbyists and PACs work quite independently of one another, and lobbyists concentrate mainly on persuading members already in office.

OTHER TACTICS, ESPECIALLY LITIGATION
Although American interest groups most frequently employ electioneering and lobbying, they sometimes use tactics that are widely used in other countries, such as mass political propaganda, demonstrations, strikes and boycotts, nonviolent civil disobedience, and sometimes even violence. There is one tactic, however, in which the United States leads the world: the use of *litigation* for political purposes. Tocqueville wrote in 1835, "Scarcely any political question arises in the United States that is not resolved, sooner or later, into a judicial question."[56] Political scientists Benjamin Ginsberg and Martin Shefter note that from 1955 to 1985 the number of civil cases brought in federal district courts increased from 50,000 a year to over 250,000 a year. One main reason for that enormous increase, they say, is the fact that a growing number of interest groups that have done

poorly in elections and in lobbying have filed suits in the courts to reverse their losses in other arenas:

> Civil rights groups, through federal court suits, launched successful assaults on Southern school systems, state and local governments, and legislative districting schemes. . . . Environmental groups used the courts to block the construction of highways, dams, and other public projects that not only threatened to damage the environment but also provided money and other resources to their political rivals. Women's groups were able to overturn state laws restricting abortion as well as statutes discriminating against women in the labor market.[57]

Conservative groups have countered by trying to ensure that persons with conservative rather than liberal or feminist philosophies are appointed to the Supreme Court and other federal judgeships.

The fact that this tactic is used by interest groups far more in America than in any other democracy should not surprise us, for we learned earlier that pursuing one's individual rights through litigation is one way in which the political culture of America differs significantly from the political cultures of most other countries.

The most important special trait of interest articulation and aggregation in the United States, however, is the very different party environment in which they take place. In most of the democracies discussed in this book, most interests operate mainly within political parties. (Indeed, in several instances particular interest groups are formally associated with particular parties: the trade unions with the British Labour party and farmers' and business associations with the Austrian People's party.) Their main tactic is to persuade the parties in which they operate to give their demands prominent places in the parties' programs and actions in government.

In contrast, in the United States the parties are so much weaker and so much less important players in the policymaking process that the interest groups operate largely outside the parties and are little concerned about whether they are helping or hurting the parties. In 1980, for example, the National Organization for Women (NOW) fought for a rule in the Democratic party that prevented the party from helping to elect any Democratic candidate who opposed the Equal Rights Amendment. In 1984 NOW said that it would refuse to support the party's national ticket unless a woman was nominated for the vice presidency.

The same observation applies to the Republican party. For some time now many business PACs have contributed much more campaign money to incumbent Democrats than to their Republican challengers, even though the Republican political philosophy is much closer to that of business. The national leaders of the Republican party have complained bitterly about what they regard as treason to the party and to conservatism, but Doug Thompson, the leader of the National Association of Realtors, has rejected the Republicans' complaints and has spelled out his PAC's political priorities:

> We are a special interest group. Our interest is real estate and housing issues; it is not contra aid, it is not abortion, it is not the minimum wage. . . . Our members are demanding a lot more accountability. Gone are our free-spending days when we poured money into a black hole called "challenger candidates." Our marching orders on PAC contributions are very clear: Stop wasting money on losers.[58]

In short, interest articulation and aggregation are in many respects different in the United States because its political parties are in most respects very different from those in any other democracy.[59]

THE SPECIAL CHARACTERISTICS OF AMERICAN POLITICAL PARTIES

A Two-Party System

The American party system is almost a pure two-party system: that is, one in which two major parties are highly competitive with one another and together win almost all the votes and offices in every election.[60] Thus, in the 1988 presidential election candidates were nominated by nineteen different parties, including such minor socialist parties as the Socialist, Socialist Workers, and Peace and Freedom parties and such minor right-wing parties as the Libertarian, American, and Right to Life parties. However, together the Democratic and Republican candidates received 99.01 percent of the votes, and all the others combined received only 0.09 percent.[61] In the 1990 congressional elections all 100 members of the Senate and 434 of the 435 members of the House were Democrats or Republicans. (The odd man out was Socialist Bernard Sanders, the first candidate other than a Democrat or a Republican to be elected to either house of Congress since 1954.)

Differences between the Major Parties

Many foreign observers (and not a few Americans) often ask just what are the differences between the Democratic and Republican parties. One well-known response is that there are no real differences — that they are "like bottles with different labels but equally empty." A more accurate response is that while there is no philosophical principle or policy preference that *all* Democrats hold that is sharply different from what *all* Republicans hold, there are a number of respects in which most Democrats differ from most Republicans. Here we will note just two: the social composition of the parties' "identifiers" (that is, the people who say that to some degree they prefer one party to the other); and some issues on which most Democrats differ from most Republicans. The first is shown in Table 17.6.

As seen in Table 17.6, the Democrats have greater support among women than men, among blacks and Hispanics than whites, among people with lower incomes, education, and occupations than upper status people, and among Catholics and Jews than Protestants, especially evangelical Protestants. With the exception of the overwhelming rejection of the Republicans by African-Americans, both parties draw signifi-

TABLE 17.6
SOCIAL COMPOSITION OF AMERICAN MAJOR PARTY IDENTIFIERS[a]

Social Group	Democrat (43%)	Republican (29%)	Independent (28%)
Female	45	29	26
Male	40	30	30
Black	75	8	17
Hispanic	51	23	26
White	38	32	30
College graduate	34	36	30
Some college	39	33	28
High school graduate	44	28	28
Less than high school graduate	52	22	26
Age 18–29	38	32	30
Age 30–49	43	26	31
Age 50 and over	45	31	24
Income $40,000 and over	34	37	29
Income $25,000–39,999	41	30	29
Income $15,000–24,999	43	28	29
Income under $15,000	51	22	27
Protestants	41	32	27
Catholics	46	26	28
Jews	60	10	32
Evangelicals	43	31	26
Nonevangelicals	41	30	29
Professional and business	37	35	28
Other white collar	42	27	31
Skilled workers	42	29	29
Unskilled workers	49	22	29
Labor union members	52	22	26
Nonunion members	40	31	29

[a] The figures cumulate horizontally across each row to 100 percent minus apoliticals.
Source: The Gallup Poll, *Public Opinion 1988* (Wilmington, Del.: Scholarly Resources, 1989), pp. 130–132.

cant support from every major demographic group. Neither party, unlike some parties in some other countries, represents only farmers or industrial workers or members of a particular ethnic or linguistic interest.

In terms of political philosophy, both parties have the support of some *liberals* and some *conservatives*, although the Democrats have a higher proportion of liberals and the Republicans a higher proportion of conservatives. The same is true of the two parties' members of Congress, as is illustrated by the roll call votes on some significant issues in both houses in 1989 (see Table 17.7).

Table 17.7 shows that there are significantly more liberals than conservatives among the Democrats in both houses of Congress and significantly more conservatives than liberals among the Republicans — although on most issues some Democrats vote for conservative positions and some Republicans vote for liberal positions.

Generally, Democrats tend to believe that govern-

ment should take a major and active role in dealing with the nation's problems, while most Republicans tend to agree with Ronald Reagan that "big government *is* the problem." Thus, most Democrats favor higher levels of government spending than Republicans on aid for the poor and homeless, education, medical care, public housing, and the like. On the so-called social issues, Democrats tend to favor minimum government intervention in people's moral, religious, and intellectual lives, while Republicans favor greater government intervention in such matters as prohibiting the exhibition of obscene films and art and encouraging prayer in the public schools.

Democrats also tend to be more egalitarian than Republicans. That is, Republicans tend to support measures for equal opportunity (giving every citizen an equal chance to engage in a fair competition for material riches and the other good things in life), whereas Democrats tend to support measures for "equal conditions" (giving all citizens at least a guaranteed minimum of the good

TABLE 17.7
SELECTED VOTES IN CONGRESS, 1989

House and issue	Democrats			Republicans		
	Yes	No	Cohesion index[a]	Yes	No	Cohesion index
House						
Raise minimum wage	226	24	80	22	147	74
Reinstate TV fairness doctrine	207	43	66	54	119	38
Toughen oil-spill liability standards	150	71	36	35	126	56
Give military aid to El Salvador	58	188	52	162	10	88
Decrease funding for "Star Wars" program	132	120	4	6	166	94
Continue funding Stealth bomber program	53	194	60	123	50	51
Permit use of federal funds for abortions after rape or incest	173	71	42	39	136	56
Continue funding Civil Rights Commission	243	2	98	35	133	58
Senate						
Require new oil tankers to have double hulls	39	16	42	9	35	58
Remove limits on oil-spill liability	23	32	16	25	20	10
Stop funding Stealth bomber	27	28	2	2	43	90
Require drug testing for certain welfare recipients	1	54	96	23	21	4
Permit NEA and NEH to refuse grants to projects judged obscene	11	43	60	24	19	12
Allow paying subminimum wages to certain migrant workers	5	48	80	30	15	34

[a]See the text for the definition of cohesion index.
Source: Congressional Quarterly Almanac, 45 (Washington, D.C.: Congressional Quarterly, 1990).

things in life even if they cannot earn them by their own efforts).

Although there are more differences in political philosophies and policy preferences within each of the major parties in the United States than in their counterparts in most other nations, enough differences remain between most leaders and identifiers of the two parties to offer the voters meaningful choices in policies as well as candidates in elections.

Decentralized Organization

Most political parties in most democracies are organized as *hierarchies*, with a national leader and national organization at the top holding the power to supervise the activities of local and regional party organizations. In sharp contrast, the American Democratic and Republican parties are organized, in Samuel Eldersveld's apt phrase, as *stratarchies*.[62] That is, their organizations at the national, state, and local levels have no power, legal or extralegal, over the organizations at the other levels. Moreover, within each level most parties have an executive organization and a legislative organization, and neither has any power over the other.

At the national level, for example, the Democrats and Republicans each have a *presidential party* and a *congressional party*. For the party that holds the presidency, the presidential party consists of the president, the national committee, the national chairman, and the national nominating conventions. The party that does not hold the presidency has no single person as its universally acknowledged leader, although it has the other agencies.

Each party in each house of Congress has a caucus, consisting of all the party's members in the particular chamber (and thus equivalent to what in most democracies is called the parliamentary party); a floor leader, who is selected by the caucus to serve as the main coordinator of the party's legislative strategy and tactics; a policy committee, chosen by the caucus to advise the floor leader and the caucus on matters of substantive policy and legislative tactics; the whips, chosen by the caucus to serve as channels of communication between the leaders and the ordinary members; and the campaign committees, chosen by the caucus to raise money and distribute it among the campaigns of selected candidates for the particular chamber.

We should emphasize, however, that the presidential party has little formal connection with the congressional party, and any effort by the president (to say

nothing of the national committee or the national chairman) to intervene in the congressional party's selection of its leaders or the determination of its policies or strategy is resented and rejected as "outside interference."

At the state level, both parties usually have a gubernatorial party and a legislative party. The gubernatorial party consists of the governor (the other party has no single, acknowledged leader), the state central committee, the state chair, and the state conventions. The legislative parties, like the congressional parties, usually have caucuses, elected floor leaders, policy committees, and whips. But each state's gubernatorial and legislative parties have no power over one another, and the national parties have no power over any part of any of the state parties; the national and state parties are simply different strata, not higher and lower levels in a chain of command headed by the national agencies.

At the various local levels there are congressional district committees, county committees, city committees, ward and precinct committees, and others too numerous to list here. In most states the local party committees and conventions are, both in law and in fact, independent of both the state and the national party agencies. Hence, they constitute a third stratum, which is just as independent from the state agencies as the state agencies are from the national agencies.

Far more than almost any major party in any other modern democratic nation, then, American party organizations are agglomerations of many hundreds of different leaders and committees distributed among various organizational strata, each of which has little or no power to command or obligation to obey any other agency in its own stratum, let alone any agency in any other stratum.

Low Cohesion

The parliamentary parties in most modern democratic nations have very high *cohesion*, a term used by political scientists to denote the degree to which the members of a legislative party vote together on issues of public policy. Abstentions and even votes against the party leaders' wishes are not unknown in those parties, and in some countries their frequency has increased, though very slowly, in recent years. But these are, at most, minor deviations from the norm, whereby all the members of parliamentary parties in other countries vote solidly together in most parliamentary votes.

By sharp contrast, the only matters in either chamber of Congress on which all Democrats regularly vote one way and all Republicans vote the other way relate to "organizing" the chamber — that is, selecting the Speaker of the House, the President Pro Tem of the Senate, and the chairs of the leading standing committees. On all other issues they almost never vote unanimously. See, for example, the votes in Congress arrayed in Table 17.7.

The cohesion index figures shown in Table 17.7 come from a measure developed by Stuart Rice to show precisely the degree of internal party division on a legislative issue. A score of 100 means all the party members voted on one side, a score of 0 means that half of them voted one way and half the other way, and a score of 50 means that three-quarters voted one way and one-quarter the other way.

On the fourteen issues shown in the table, party cohesion was generally higher in both parties in the House than in the Senate, and on some issues one party or the other approached the cohesion levels of most major parties in other democracies. For example, the House Democrats' support for raising the minimum wage and continuing to fund the Civil Rights Commission was almost unanimous, while the House Republicans were nearly as solid in their support of military aid to El Salvador and funding the "Star Wars" defense program. On the other hand, the House Democrats split almost evenly on funding "Star Wars" and the Senate Democrats on funding the Stealth bomber, while the Republicans split evenly on removing the limits on oil-spill liability and on requiring drug testing for welfare recipients.

Consequently, some party cohesion exists in Congress on most issues. It is especially high on such issues as higher spending for social welfare measures, higher spending for defense, and greater regulation of business —with the Democrats usually voting predominantly, but not unanimously, Yes, and the Republicans usually voting predominantly, but not unanimously, No. On the other hand, on issues that cut sharply across party lines, especially moral issues such as abortion, capital punishment, and the regulation of pornography, both parties regularly split relatively evenly. But in comparison with the major parliamentary parties in most other democratic nations, the American congressional Democrats and Republicans have low cohesion on most issues.

This situation has important consequences for the role of American parties in the policymaking process, which we will note later. It also has several causes, the most important of which is the fact that, compared with most other democratic parties, the leaders of the Democrats and the Republicans have very weak disciplinary powers.

Weak Discipline

The leaders of most major parties in the world's democracies have a number of weapons to ensure that the public officials bearing their parties' labels support the parties' policies in the national parliaments. For one, they can make sure that no unusually visible or persistent rebel against the party's positions is given a ministerial position or preferment of any kind. If that fails to bring the fractious member into line, they can expel him or her from the parliamentary party altogether. Many parties in many countries give their leaders the ultimate weapon: the power to deny the rebel re-selection as an official party candidate at the next election.

In Israel, for example, the entire list of each party's candidates for the Knesset (Parliament) is chosen by a small group of party leaders, who also determine the order of the candidates' listing on the ballot (which controls which candidates have excellent chances to get seats and which candidates have no chance). They may as a matter of comity and prudence listen to suggestions from party leaders of their regional and local organizations, but they have the unchallenged power to deny re-selection to a rebellious party member. Leading parties in India, Japan, Sri Lanka, the Netherlands, and Italy use much the same systems.[63]

In Great Britain, the parliamentary candidates of both the Labour and Conservative parties are selected by their local organizations in the constituencies. However, no person so chosen can be publicly designated as the party's official candidate until he or she has been approved by a national party agency. Each party has used its veto power sparingly, but every constituency party knows that if it selects a candidate unacceptable to the national party leaders, they will have to choose another candidate, and so they almost always consider only persons whom they know will be acceptable to the national leaders.[64] Similar systems are used in Australia, Belgium, Canada, Denmark, Finland, Ireland, New Zealand, Germany, and Turkey.

By sharp contrast, in the United States any person who wins a party's primary for the House or Senate in any congressional district or state automatically becomes the party's legal candidate for that office, and no national party agency has any power to veto the nomination. On one notable occasion, called by historians "the purge of 1938," Franklin D. Roosevelt, being an unusually popular and powerful national party leader, tried to intervene in the primary elections of several states to prevent the re-selection of Democratic senators who had fought his New Deal policies. He failed in twelve of thirteen attempts, and most people have since concluded that any effort by a national party leader to interfere in candidate selection at the state and local levels is bound to fail.

To be sure, presidents and their parties' leaders in Congress can and often do plead with their fellow partisans to support the president's policies for the sake of party loyalty and/or to increase the party's chances at the next election or to keep the party from looking foolish. Unless they have some strong reason to do otherwise, most members of Congress go along. However, unlike the leaders of most parties in most other countries, neither the president nor his party's congressional leaders have any effective disciplinary power to compel their members in Congress to vote in ways contrary to their consciences — or to what they perceive to be the interests and wishes of their constituents.

A Special Consequence: Divided Party Control of Government

In the parliamentary democracies one party cannot control the legislature while another party controls the executive. If the Parliament refuses a Cabinet request, the Cabinet either resigns and a new Cabinet acceptable to the Parliament takes over; or the Parliament is dissolved, new elections are held, and a new Cabinet is formed that has the support of the parliamentary majority. But there can never be more than a short interim period in which the parliamentary majority and Cabinet disagree on any major question of public policy.

In the United States, separation of powers and the separate terms and constituencies for the president, the members of the House, and the members of the Senate make it possible for one party to win control of the presidency and the other party to win control of one or both houses of Congress. How often does it actually happen? From the election of 1832 (when most historians say the modern electoral and party systems began) through the election of 1990, there have been a total of eighty presidential and midterm elections. Each of these elections could have resulted in either divided party control or unified party control. In fact, forty-nine (61 percent) produced unified control, and thirty-one (39 percent) produced divided control.

Even more noteworthy is the fact that since the death of Franklin D. Roosevelt in 1945, *divided party control* has occurred so frequently that many observers feel it has become normal, not exceptional. In the period from 1946 through 1990 there have been twenty-three elections. Only nine (39 percent) have produced unified control (all with Democratic presidents and congresses), and fourteen (61 percent) have produced divided control (all but one with Republican presidents and Democratic congresses). Thus, of the five postwar Republican presidents — George Bush, Ronald Reagan, Gerald Ford, Richard Nixon, and Dwight Eisenhower — only Eisenhower enjoyed a brief period (1953–1955) in which both houses of Congress were controlled by his party. All the others so far (we will see about Bush) have served their entire terms dealing with a Congress in which at least the House of Representatives and often the Senate as well were controlled by the Democrats.

The most obvious cause for this situation, which is both unknown and impossible in parliamentary democracies, is the fact that the chief executive and the members of both houses of Congress are, as we have seen, elected separately by overlapping constituencies and with different terms. The constitutional structure thus makes it possible for American voters to do something that voters in the parliamentary democracies cannot do, namely, "split their tickets" — that is, vote for a member of one party for president and for a member of the other party for Congress.

Ticket splitting explains the increasing frequency of divided party control. Table 17.8 summarizes the voting patterns of all the voters who have been respondents in the National Election Studies of all presidential and congressional elections from 1952 through 1988.

THE POLICYMAKING PROCESS IN AMERICA

The Founding Fathers' Intentions and Design

When we discuss the policymaking process in the United States, the first point we must understand is that the constitutional framework within which it operates was carefully designed to keep government from doing bad things, not to make it easier for government to do good things. To be sure, in writing the Constitution, the men of Philadelphia hoped to get a more effective national government than that provided by the Articles of

TABLE 17.8
STRAIGHT AND SPLIT-TICKET VOTING, 1952–1988

Voting pattern	Number	Percent
Democrat for President, Democrat for House	3,702	41
Republican for President, Republican for House	3,507	39
Democrat for President, Republican for House	505	5
Republican for President, Democrat for House	1,340	15
Totals	9,054	100

Source: National Election Studies of Presidential and Midterm Elections, 1952–1988; data aggregated by the Computer-assisted Survey Methods Program, University of California, Berkeley.

Confederation. But making and implementing effective, coherent, and forceful national policies was not their prime goal.

They believed that government should never be regarded as some kind of benevolent mother, doing whatever is necessary to keep all her children well fed and feeling good. We should never forget, they warned, that government is a powerful and dangerous institution created by fallible human beings, and that its prime objective — indeed, its only legitimate reason for exist-

ing and being obeyed — is to secure every person's God-given right to life, liberty, and property. Anything that government does beyond that, they believed, was not only less important, but it was not even acceptable if it in any way abridged those basic rights.

The best way to make a government strong enough to secure the rights of its citizens without becoming so powerful that it overrode them, they believed, was to fragment its power and disperse it among many different agencies — among the federal and state governments

The oldest written constitution still in force: Celebrating the 200th birthday of the U.S. Constitution at its Philadelphia birthplace, 1987.

by federalism, and within the federal government by separation of powers. The power should so be divided, they felt, that no single faction would likely ever get control of the whole power of government to promote its interests at the expense of all the others.[65]

Accordingly, they did not think that policy deadlocks, in which the government could not act because one of its parts blocked action by other parts, were some kind of terrible failure that should be avoided wherever possible and unblocked as soon as possible. Rather, they regarded such deadlocks as highly preferable to any government action that rode roughshod over the interests and objections of any significant part of the community. Consequently, whenever a deadlock paralyzes the government of the 1990s from making effective policies to deal with budget deficits, mounting national debt, crime, and deterioration of the environment, the crisis in the Persian Gulf, or any other public problem, the least we can say is that the policymaking process is operating as its framers intended.

Traditional Ways of Avoiding Deadlocks

Alexis de Tocqueville wrote: "I have never been more struck by the good sense and the practical judgment of the Americans than in the manner in which they elude the numberless difficulties resulting from their Federal Constitution."[66] He had a point. From the opening of the First Congress in 1789 to the 1990s, Americans have found that, however dangerous to human rights it may be, the government of the United States has to make and implement at least some policies. It has to regulate interstate and foreign commerce, increase or decrease the supply of money, conduct relations with foreign nations, levy taxes, make expenditures, and so on. As Tocqueville rightly observed, Americans have developed ways of getting policies made despite the constitutional system's many roadblocks and general tendency toward inertia. One set of ways has been traditionally used in ordinary times, and the other set has been called on in times of great crisis.

IN ORDINARY TIMES: PUTTING TOGETHER AD HOC COALITIONS
In ordinary times public policies in America have been made mainly by putting together ad hoc, issue-specific coalitions of interests by bargaining and cutting deals among their representatives.[67] The main coalition builders have included public officials of all kinds, including presidents and their chief political aides in the Cabinet and the Executive

Office of the President; members of Congress and their professional staffs; political heads and permanent civil servants in the executive departments and the independent agencies; and federal judges and their clerks. At least as active and often as powerful as these inside players are the outside players, especially the lobbyists representing the major organized interest groups that feel they have major stakes in the policy outcomes. The usual result is that, while each contest over each policy produces winners and losers, it never produces total victory or total defeat for any highly involved interest. Each contestant gets something of what it wants but never all; and each manages to stave off total disaster.[68]

Many commentators, past and present, have been highly critical of this process. They claim that it usually takes far too long to get anything done, and that what is done is usually messy, full of inconsistencies, self-defeating, and in constant need of repair. They are also struck by how difficult it is get closure on any major policy: typically, they say, when a coalition loses in the presidency, it tries in the Congress; when it loses in the Congress, it tries in the bureaucracy; when it fails to persuade incumbent elected and appointed officials, it tries to replace them; and when it loses everywhere else, it turns to the courts to upset or water down policies made by the other agencies.

In recent years, for example, when the coalition that wanted to support the Contra rebels in Nicaragua failed to get enough support from Congress, they turned to secret machinations in the National Security Agency to provide the funds. As another example, when the civil rights movement in the 1950s failed to get Congress to abolish racial segregation in the schools, they turned to the Supreme Court and won their victory in its landmark decision in *Brown* v. *Board of Education* (1954). In more recent times the coalitions of feminists, gays, and lesbians, after losing in elections and among elected officials and bureaucrats, have often turned to the courts rather than give up.

Without doubt the ordinary-times process falls far short of the neat, orderly, and swift policymaking process that parliamentary democracies are widely thought to provide because of their fusion of powers and the consequent impossibility of deadlock between the executive and the legislature. Yet it has undeniably produced a large number of major policies, many of them quite successful: for example, the establishment of Alexander Hamilton's economic development program in the 1790s, the western expansion of the country in the nineteenth century, the absorption of millions of immigrants, the Progressive reforms of the early 1900s, the New Deal, the constant, though to some too slow, advance in the status of African-Americans since the end of slavery, the drastic overhaul of the tax system in 1986, and so on.[69]

Even at its best, however, the ordinary-times process has always taken some time to produce results, and there have been occasions in American history when the danger that it would not work fast enough made the nation turn to another kind of policymaking process.

IN TIMES OF CRISIS: PRESIDENTIAL DICTATORSHIP In 1889, James Bryce wrote:

> In troublous times . . . immense responsibility is thrown on one who is both the commander-in-chief and the head of the civil executive. Abraham Lincoln wielded more authority than any single Englishman has done since Oliver Cromwell. It is true that the ordinary law was for some purposes practically suspended during the War of Secession. But it will always have to be similarly suspended in similar crises, and the suspension ensures to the benefit of the President, who becomes a sort of dictator.[70]

Bryce was right about Lincoln, who, when the Southern states started seceding in 1861, took a number of steps that were far outside the ordinary policymaking process. By executive proclamations he suspended the writ of habeas corpus, called for volunteers to join the Union Army, spent government money to buy them food, uniforms, and arms, and made the fateful decision to provision Fort Sumter, even though he expected the action would start a civil war. Then, after having done all this, he summoned Congress into session, told them what he had done, and asked for retroactive authority—which they had no choice but to give him.

Since then, presidents have often taken the view that when the national interest requires prompt action, they either should do it on their own, as Lincoln did, or persuade Congress to rush through their radical reform measures, as Franklin D. Roosevelt did in the 1930s when it seemed clear that in the absence of extraordinary measures the economy would collapse under the stress of the Great Depression.

Presidents usually exert these extraordinary powers in foreign rather than domestic crises, as when Truman ordered American troops into Korea in 1950, Kennedy and Johnson followed suit in Vietnam in the 1960s, and Bush ordered troops to Panama and then to the Persian Gulf early in his administration. The War Powers Act of 1974 is designed to limit the president's power to take this kind of action without congressional approval, but in fact it has restrained presidents very little since it was enacted. No one doubts that in any future crisis, especially in foreign affairs, presidents will again bypass the ordinary policymaking process and do what they feel needs to be done.

The U.S. experience in Korea and Vietnam, however, makes it clear that the *presidential-dictatorship* escape valve does not stay open indefinitely. When the action accomplishes its mission quickly, there are few American casualties, and we get out in a few weeks, it works well. But when it drags on for months and years with huge expense, many casualties, and little hope of a clean-cut final victory—Korea and Vietnam are so far the leading examples—the president eventually loses the popular and then the congressional support he needs, and the nation returns to the ordinary process. In any case, a leader who is held to account for his actions in free elections every two years is no dictator.

POLICY PERFORMANCE

Extractive Policies

When considering policy performance in the United States, it is important to remember that we are dealing with the outputs of many governments, not just the one in Washington.[71] At present there are over 80,000 governmental units in America, including the federal government, 50 states, 3,042 counties, 19,200 municipalities, 16,691 townships, 14,721 local school districts, and 29,532 special districts—each of which has some constitutional or statutory power to make policies.[72]

Of these 83,237 authorities, the federal government extracts the greatest number of resources: it collects 69 percent of all taxes and 57 percent of revenues from all sources. Its share is, of course, smaller than the shares taken by the national governments of unitary nations, such as Great Britain, Japan, and Sweden, but it is larger than those taken by the national governments in any of the federal systems except Austria.[73]

TYPES OF TAXES Table 17.9 shows the main types of taxes as percentages of total revenue in the United States and other Organization for Economic Cooperation and Development (OECD) countries[74] in 1985. Table 17.9 shows that the United States relies more on individual income taxes than any other nation except

TABLE 17.9
TAX SOURCES AS PERCENTAGES OF TOTAL REVENUE, 1985

Country	Personal income	Corporate income	Employees' soc. sec.	Employers' soc. sec.	Sales and consumption	Property and wealth
Austria	23.1	3.3	13.2	15.9	32.6	2.4
Britain	26.0	12.9	8.1	8.8	31.6	12.0
Denmark	50.2	4.8	1.9	1.9	34.2	4.3
France	12.7	4.3	12.2	28.2	29.4	4.6
Germany	28.7	6.1	15.8	19.0	25.6	3.0
Italy	26.7	9.2	6.8	24.8	25.4	2.5
Japan	24.8	21.0	10.7	15.4	14.0	9.7
Netherlands	19.5	7.0	19.0	17.5	25.8	3.5
Norway	22.5	17.0	5.6	14.3	37.5	1.7
Sweden	38.5	3.5	0.0	23.7	26.4	2.3
United States	35.7	7.1	11.1	17.3	17.7	10.1
OECD Average	31.5	8.2	7.9	13.9	30.1	5.0

Source: Arnold J. Heidenheimer, Hugh Heclo, and Carolyn Teich Adams, *Comparative Public Policy*, 3rd ed. (New York: St. Martin's Press, 1990), Table 6.3, p. 190.

Sweden, while its reliance on corporate income taxes is slightly lower than the OECD average. Social security taxes paid by both employees and employers in America are higher than average. The United States relies less on sales and other taxes on consumption than any other OECD country except Japan, while it depends on taxes on property and wealth more than any country except Great Britain. Part of the reason is that, unlike most European governments, the U.S. national government has never levied a sales tax or a value added tax, although most American states levy both sales taxes and income taxes. Accordingly, the tax structure in the American federal system as a whole is more progressive (in the sense of placing the heaviest burden on people with the greatest ability to pay) than that in most but not all of the OECD nations.

THE TAX BURDEN Americans frequently complain about the great and debilitating tax burden they have to bear, and both Ronald Reagan and George Bush made cutting taxes the cornerstones of their economic programs (although Bush later retreated from his pledge of no new taxes). Just how great is the tax burden of Americans compared with those borne by the residents of other industrialized democracies?

The answer depends on what measure is used. Ex-

pressed as a percentage of gross domestic product (GDP), American taxes take a total of 29 percent, the lowest figure among the OECD nations. (Sweden, at 51 percent, is the highest.) Moreover, its take from GDP has increased at a lower rate than in any other industrialized democracy since 1965. (Again, Sweden leads with the highest rate of increase.)[75] However, expressed as a percentage of gross family earnings, the tax burden of the average American worker, both for single persons and for two-child families, is the third highest among eleven leading OECD nations, and from 1981 to 1985 (the first term of antitax President Ronald Reagan), the burden on individual workers dipped only from 23.5 percent to 22.8 percent, and for two-child families it actually rose from 14.4 percent to 15.3 percent.

In summary, compared with the tax systems of most other industrialized countries, the American system is one of the more progressive in its structure, one of the more burdensome in direct taxes on individuals and corporations, but second only to Japan in taking the lowest proportion of GDP.

Distributive Performance

U.S. GOVERNMENT EXPENDITURES Of the total expenditures by all American governments in

1987, the federal government spent almost half (49.1 percent), and the state (26.7 percent) and local (24.2 percent) governments each spent about one quarter. An overview of what they spent it on is shown in Table 17.10.

Not surprisingly, Table 17.10 shows that the main differences between the federal government and the state and local governments is that the federal government spends 29 percent of its budget on defense-related activities, while the state and local governments spend the most on education and on public welfare.

Among the democratic governments, only Israel spends as high a proportion of its budget on defense as the government of the United States. (Some Third World countries, such as Iraq, North Korea, Oman, and Saudi Arabia spend even higher proportions.)[76] Many Americans argue that defense spending is far too high, especially now that the cold war has ended. Others counter that the Persian Gulf crisis in the early 1990s

demonstrates that the world is still a dangerous place and America still needs to keep its powder dry and well-stocked. Whatever the merits of these positions, the trend in recent years has been toward lower proportions of federal spending on defense and higher proportions on domestic welfare programs. In 1989, as Table 17.10 shows, 47 percent of the federal budget was spent on welfare programs, while only 26 percent was spent on direct defense programs, with another 3 percent spent on veterans' benefits.

Regulative Performance

Like all modern industrialized democracies, the United States is a *welfare state* in the sense that many of its policies proceed from the conviction that government has an obligation to guarantee certain minimum levels of the good things in life to all its citizens, especially to those who cannot provide them for themselves. However, nations differ markedly both in the particular items

TABLE 17.10
GOVERNMENT EXPENDITURES BY FUNCTION, 1989

Category	Federal		State and Local	
	Total outlays ($billions)	Pct. of total	Total outlays ($millions)	Pct. of total
Domestic welfare-related				
Social security and medicare	319.1	28	—	—
Income security	136.9	12	91.8	14
Health	49.3	4	79.3	12
Education	36.4	3	226.7	34
(Total domestic welfare)	(541.7)	(47)	(397.8)	(60)
Defense-related				
Defense	298.3	26	—	—
Veterans' benefits	29.2	3	—	—
(Total defense)	(327.5)	(29)	—	—
Other				
Interest on debt	168.7	15	41.8	6
Police and fire	—	—	52.1	8
Transportation	28.5	2	52.2	8
Environment	16.5	1	20.7	3
Science and space technology	12.6	1	—	—
Intergovernmental payments	11.2	1	18.3	2
Other	41.5	4	89.8	13
	1,148.2	100	672.7	100

Source: Statistical Abstract of the United States, 1990 (Washington, D.C.: Bureau of the Census, 1990), Table 499, pp. 310–311; and Table 456, p. 274.

of the good life that government should provide and the levels at which they should be provided. In this section we will briefly review the major policies adopted by American governments in three main problem areas.

INCOME DISTRIBUTION AND MAINTENANCE

The United States was among the last of the modern industrialized nations to embrace fully the goals of the welfare state, and, as we noted above, even today the proportion of the nation's GDP spent on public welfare programs is lower than that in most industrialized nations. Even so, the federal, state, and local governments together provide a wide range of policies intended to put a floor beneath the income and living conditions of the poor. For that purpose it uses two main instruments:

Social Insurance. This category includes programs to protect citizens against the risk of loss of income due to old age, retirement, sickness, industrial accidents, and unemployment. The basic federal legislation is the Social Security Act of 1935, which establishes a fund from mandatory contributions by employees and employers from which all wage-earners are entitled to receive cash payments at retirement or on reaching a certain age. Since the program is contributory and has little means-testing, most Americans regard its benefits as entitlements, no stigma attaches to receiving social security checks, and most Americans of all income levels approve the program.

Public Assistance. This category includes both direct cash and in-kind payments to poor people, such as cash aid to families with dependent children, food stamps, free milk for young children, and day care for children of working mothers with low incomes. Unlike social security, these programs are noncontributory and thus constitute obvious income transfers from upper income people to lower income people. As a result, much more social stigma attaches to receiving public assistance benefits, and these welfare programs are much more controversial than the social insurance programs.

EDUCATION

In the United States as in other industrialized nations, education is provided mainly by government-financed and -operated schools, although there are more privately owned and operated schools, especially universities (including such famous institutions as Columbia, Harvard, Princeton, Stanford, and Yale) in America than in most other countries. (They are also important in Japan and Great Britain.)

What sets the American school system apart from systems in other countries is its high degree of decentralization. Most schools, from kindergarten through universities, are locally financed and regulated, although the federal government provides considerable subsidies for many special programs, each of which carries restrictions on how the money is to be spent. For example, in awarding federally funded scholarships and other forms of financial aid, schools may not discriminate against applicants because of their race or gender. The local financing and regulation of schools have many consequences, not the least of which is the fact that schools in poor states and poor districts generally spend considerably less money per pupil than schools in richer states and districts.

Whatever the consequences of these differences, the United States still has a higher proportion of its youth enrolled in schools than any other nation. It has the second highest (to Japan) proportion of seventeen year olds in secondary schools, the highest proportion of twenty-one year olds in colleges and universities, and the highest proportion of college graduates going on to graduate and professional schools.[77]

A number of industrial nations operate on the theory that higher education should be reserved for only the most talented and accomplished students. They therefore require that only those students who do well in demanding nationally administered tests after finishing one level may advance to a school at the next higher level. The United States, on the other hand, operates on the theory that as many people as possible should be given a chance at a college education, even those whose academic prospects are poor. As educational sociologist Martin Trow sums it up, "If Europe's slogan for higher education has been 'nothing if not the best,' America's has been 'something is better than nothing.'"[78] Consequently, it is much easier for American eighteen year olds to enter some kind of postsecondary education — a four-year college or university, or a two-year community college — than for their peers in any other country, and many more do so.

What about the *quality* of American education? Many scholars, school administrators, and politicians in America have long and inconclusively debated that question, and the literature on the subject is far too vast and complicated to survey in detail here. We will note only that many commentators, both in America and abroad, have concluded that American pupils in primary and secondary schools (ages five to seventeen) do not score as well on cross-national standardized tests as their counterparts in Western Europe, Scandinavia, and especially Japan. Nor are they as well equipped with such basic skills as reading and writing, foreign languages, mathematics, and science.

As we look higher on the educational pyramid, however, the performance and reputation of American schools get better. Undergraduate students in American colleges and universities come closer to matching the skills and performance of their counterparts in other countries, and, at the top, the quality of graduate and professional programs in law, medicine, engineering, and perhaps even the humanities and social sciences, are as good as any in the world and better than most. The proof is that many more foreign students come to America for advanced training than Americans go abroad for it.[79]

At present there is a widespread and growing feeling in the United States that American schools, especially at the primary and secondary levels, are doing a poor job of giving their pupils the kinds of basic skills the nation's labor force must have if its industries are to compete successfully with their competitors, especially Japan and Western Europe. Since the late 1950s many commissions have studied the schools, and many reports have been issued recommending many reforms. Many of their recommendations have actually been put into practice; yet the pupils' skills do not seem to have improved very much.

Intensifying the turmoil surrounding the schools are the growing demands to increase the proportions of Americans of African, Hispanic, and Asian descent among the students and faculties at all levels of the system and to add more studies of non-Western cultures to the curriculum rather than perpetuate the traditional focus on Western, white culture. Education policy has often been highly controversial in the United States, but seldom more so than in the 1990s. The final resolution will, of course, have a profound effect on the nation's future.

ENVIRONMENTAL PROTECTION Of the policy areas considered here, environmental protection is the most recent to take center stage, not only in the United States but in most other industrialized nations as well. From the beginning of the Industrial Revolution in the late eighteenth century until well after World War II,

one of the greatest goals of every nation was economic growth — constantly increasing the nation's production of goods and services, both for home consumption and for sale abroad. Indeed, most political scientists during the 1950s and 1960s classified the world's nations as developed or developing, depending not only on the existing per capita size of their GDPs but also on their rates of economic growth.

For many purposes that goal remains highly desirable today. After all, economic growth is the best instrument nations have yet found for getting the resources their governments need to achieve their other policy goals, whether the goals be increasing military strength and diplomatic clout, providing more food, shelter, and medical care for the poor, or increasing the coverage and improving the quality of education. Moreover, political scientists generally believe that many of the difficult problems involved in dividing a nation's economic "pie" fairly are much easier to handle when the total "pie" is steadily increasing than when it is constant or shrinking.

In recent years, however, policymakers in many nations, including the United States, have come to realize that economic growth, especially unrestrained and rapid growth, has great costs. Nowhere is this cost greater than in the area of the toxic emissions and solid wastes, toxic and nontoxic, that have been the by-products of large-scale industrialization. Those wastes are contaminating the food we eat, the water we drink, and the very air we breathe. As a result, policymakers in the United States, Western Europe, Eastern Europe, and Japan — and even in industrializing nations such as Brazil, Nigeria, and the People's Republic of China — have become increasingly aware that they must grapple with the problems of how to regulate the emissions of cars and factories into the air and the discharges of factories and farms into rivers and lakes, how to dispose of the growing mountains (or barge-loads) of solid waste, and how much economic growth they can afford to forego in order to protect and restore their environments.

Heidenheimer and his colleagues point out that some nations, especially Japan and Great Britain, have approached this problem by relying less on government regulations than on encouraging corporations and labor unions to work together to develop and implement their own plans for dealing with pollution. The United States has taken a quite different approach. It has enacted a series of stringent laws, beginning with the Clean Air Act of 1970, that require manufacturers to reduce sharply their emissions that pollute the air and water by installing such expensive devices as smoke scrubbers and water purifiers, to recycle solid wastes, and to clean up, mostly at their own (and/or their insurance companies') expense, the toxic waste dumps they have previously created. The federal government has established a special agency, the Environmental Protection Agency (EPA), to make sure that these laws are strictly enforced.

These laws also provide that businesses that have been ordered to stop polluting and/or clean up the results of past pollution can appeal those orders in the courts. As a result, many of the final decisions on environmental issues are being made, with little speed and great difficulty and expense, in extended litigation.[80]

That should not surprise us, since, as we noted earlier, one of the most persistent strains in American political culture has been the conviction that one of the highest of all political values is to protect the rights of private individuals, political and religious minorities, and even corporations against the built-in tendencies of governments to abridge them. That idea has undoubtedly had great benefits in protecting those rights, but it has also had great costs in making and implementing effective public policies. The current conflict over how to preserve and renew the environment without causing too great a loss of economic growth which supports so many other policies will continue to be one of the most difficult policy problems in the years to come, not only in the United States but in all industrialized and industrializing nations.

AMERICAN EXCEPTIONALISM: MYTH OR REALITY?

The Idea in History

During much of its history, many of the United States' leaders and citizens — and some foreign commentators and many of the millions of immigrants who left their native countries to become Americans — have regarded the nation as not just another polity in a world of many polities, but as significantly different from other political systems. Some have viewed it as a great social experiment from which all political systems can and should learn many lessons relevant to founding and reforming their own systems.

Thus, in his first Inaugural Address, George Washington said: "The preservation of the sacred fire of

liberty, and the destiny of the republican model of government, are justly considered as deeply, perhaps as finally staked, on the experiment intrusted to the hands of the American people."[81]

In December 1862, when the very existence of the American system was in great jeopardy, Abraham Lincoln said to the Congress: "We of this Congress and this administration, will be remembered in spite of ourselves. . . . The fiery trial through which we pass, will light us down, in honor or dishonor, to the latest generation. . . . We shall nobly save, or meanly lose, the last, best hope of earth.[82]

How True Is It?

It seems altogether fitting and proper that we should end this chapter by asking not whether the idea of *American exceptionalism* is noble or ridiculous, but rather how true it is. That is, in what respects and to what degree does the American system resemble and differ from the world's other political systems?

HOW THE AMERICAN SYSTEM CLOSELY RESEMBLES OTHER SYSTEMS   It is a government. It has jurisdiction over a certain territory and peoples. It makes laws governing their behavior and enforces them with means up to and including capital punishment. Its society is composed of many different groups with different interests, and its political process is essentially a contest among them to advance their interests. Few if any policies benefit all groups and interests equally, and most political decisions have, relatively speaking, some winners and some losers. This book's basic theoretical scheme for comparing governments is as applicable to the United States as to any other nation.

HOW THE AMERICAN SYSTEM RESEMBLES SOME NATIONS BUT DIFFERS FROM MANY OTHERS

1. It is a democracy.
2. It is based on the principle of constitutionalism.
3. It is a presidential democracy rather than a parliamentary democracy, based on the separation of powers rather than on the fusion of powers.
4. The head of government is elected rather than hereditary.
5. The roles of chief of state and head of government are performed by the same official.
6. It is a federal system rather than a unitary system.
7. The presiding officers of its legislative chambers are partisan rather than neutral.

8. Its legislative committees play a critical role in the legislative process.

9. Its legislators are largely free of party discipline and control their own votes.

10. Its legal system is based on the common law rather than on the civil law.

11. It has judicial review: its highest court has the power to declare acts of other government officials and agencies unconstitutional and thereby render them null and void.

12. A high proportion of its public officials are elected directly; therefore, it has far more elections than most countries.

13. Its elections use the single-member, plurality system rather than proportional representation.

14. Its elections are held on fixed dates, and there is no power of dissolution.

15. The practice is well established by law and custom that members of the national legislature must live in the states and districts they represent.

16. Particularly in some states and localities, though not at the national level, there is extensive use of popular initiatives and referendums.

17. It has a great variety of ethnic groups, and ethnicity plays a major role in political conflict.

18. Until recently, it has followed a melting pot rather than a patchwork quilt policy toward the assimilation of immigrants.

HOW THE UNITED STATES IS UNIQUE OR NEARLY SO

1. It has a truly bicameral legislature, in which on most matters the two chambers must act together.

2. It is closer to having its electoral politics dominated by two and only two political parties than almost any other country.

3. Not only can different parties control different branches of government at the same time, but they often do.

4. Its systems for registering voters are largely decentralized and put most of the burden on the voters.

5. By some measures, its voting turnout is among the lowest in the world.

6. It chooses most of its nominees for office by direct primaries conducted and regulated by public law, not by party rules.

7. Its political parties are closely regulated by law.

8. Its major political parties do not control who can become and remain their members, and are extremely uncohesive, undisciplined, and decentralized.

9. Because candidates run as individuals rather than as local representatives of national party teams, and because no publicly financed free media time is given to parties or candidates, the raising and spending of large amounts of money is far more important in American elections than in most other democracies.

10. A higher proportion of political issues are settled in the courts than in any other democracy. Consequently, lawyers play a more important role in the American political system than in any other.

CONCLUSION

It seems fitting to end this chapter comparing the American political system to the world's other systems with a quotation from one of its greatest foreign observers, the English scholar and statesman, Lord Bryce:

> All governments are faulty; and an equally minute analysis of the constitutions of England, or France, or Germany would disclose mischiefs as serious . . . as those we have noted in the American system. To any one familiar with the practical working of free governments it is a standing wonder that they work at all. . . . What keeps a free government going is the good sense and patriotism of the people . . . and the United States, more than any other country, are governed by public opinion, that is to say, by the general sentiment of the mass of the nation, which all the organs of the national government and of the State governments look to and obey.[83]

KEY TERMS

American exceptionalism	Congressional party	Electoral College	initiatives
Bill of Rights	conservatives	fairness doctrine	judicial review
campaign consultants	direct primaries	federalism	liberals
checks and balances	divided party control	free media	litigation

litigiousness
lobbyists
long ballot
melting pot versus
   patchwork quilt

national supremacy
paid media
party cohesion
political action committee
presidential democracy

presidential dictatorship
presidential party
referendum
scarcity doctrine
separation of powers

stratarchies
ticket splitting
voting registration
voting turnout
welfare state

END NOTES

1. "The English Flag," in *Barrack-room Ballads and Other Verses* (London: Methuen, 1892), stanza 1.

2. Geographically speaking, "America" means all the nations located in the Western Hemisphere, including Canada and the countries in Central America, the Caribbean, and South America. Yet, for better or worse, most people here and abroad use "American" to mean anything connected with just one of those nations, the United States of America. With apologies to the citizens of those other nations, I will follow this common, though technically incorrect, usage in this chapter.

3. Seymour Martin Lipset, *The First New Nation: The United States in Historical and Comparative Perspective* (New York: Basic Books, 1963).

4. The point is stressed by several recent foreign commentators on America; see, for example, Louis Heren, *Selections from the New American Commonwealth* (New York: Oxford University Press of America, 1968), p. xiii.

5. There is a vast literature on the causes, conduct, and consequences of the Civil War. For a recent and superbly written single-volume history, see James M. McPherson, *Battle Cry of Freedom: The Civil War Era* (New York: Oxford University Press, 1988).

6. *Statistical Abstract of the United States, 1990* (Washington, D.C.: Bureau of the Census, 1990), Table 1436, pp. 831–833.

7. By law, the United States has taken a census of its population every ten years beginning in 1790. Since many good things—representation in the House of Representatives, electoral votes for the presidency, and federal grants of money to the states—are allocated according to population, almost every census in the twentieth century has been followed by bitter complaints from many states and cities that their populations were badly undercounted, especially the blacks, Hispanics, and the homeless living in their inner cities. The 1990 census produced even more complaints than usual, but most demographers feel that the figure of "about" 250 million is a reasonable estimate.

8. The estimated populations of the United States and the world's other nations are given in *Statistical Abstract of the United States, 1990*, Table 1438, pp. 831–833.

9. H. G. Nicholas, *The Nature of American Politics*, 2nd ed. (New York: Oxford University Press, 1986), p. 4.

10. *Statistical Abstract of the United States, 1990*, Table 48, p. 42.

11. For immigration figures and rates from 1820 to 1988, see *Statistical Abstract of the United States, 1990*, Table 5, p. 9.

12. *Statistical Abstract of the United States*, Table 1446, p. 840.

13. *Statistical Abstract of the United States, 1990*, Table 497, p. 309.

14. The Twenty-First Amendment repeals the Eighteenth (prohibition) Amendment, so there are effectively only twenty-four operating amendments.

15. Useful comparisons of the American federal system with other federal systems include William H. Riker, *Federalism: Origin, Operation, Significance* (Boston: Little, Brown, 1964); Daniel J. Elazar, *Explaining Federalism* (University: University of Alabama Press, 1987); and K. C. Wheare, *Federal Government*, 4th ed. (London: Oxford University Press, 1963).

16. A word about this usage: strictly speaking, the government in Washington is the "national" government, and the whole divided-powers system of government is the "federal" government. However, most Americans use the terms *national* and *federal* interchangeably to mean the government in Washington. I will do the same, but the reader should be aware of the ambiguity of this usage.

17. A useful discussion of how the federal government has used grants-in-aid to increase its power over a number of matters technically reserved to the

states is Deil S. Wright, *Understanding Intergovernmental Relations*, 2nd ed. (North Scituate, Mass.: Duxbury, 1982).

18. There are far more parliamentary than presidential democracies in the modern world. Presently, about 110 nations have democratic systems, and of those only about 15 — the United States, Finland, France, and a number of Latin American democracies — have presidential systems; all the rest are parliamentary.

19. The point is most forcefully made in Richard E. Neustadt, *Presidential Power: The Politics of Leadership from FDR to Reagan* (New York: John Wiley, 1990).

20. For a useful, though somewhat outdated, international survey, see Joseph Tanenhaus, "Judicial Review," in *The International Encyclopedia of the Social Sciences* (New York: Crowell Collier and Macmillan, 1968), Vol. 8, pp. 303–307.

21. The oldest, and in several ways still the most influential study of American political culture is Alexis de Tocqueville, *Democracy in America* translated by Henry Reeve and published in 1835. A recent edition, edited by Philips Bradley, was published in New York by Alfred A. Knopf in 1945. The other great classic commentary by a foreign observer is James Bryce, *The American Commonwealth*, 2 vols. (London: Macmillan Co., 1889).

    Some more recent illuminating studies include: Samuel P. Huntington, *American Politics: The Promise of Disharmony* (Cambridge, Mass.: Harvard University Press, 1981); Herbert McClosky and Alida Brill, *Dimensions of Tolerance: What Americans Believe about Civil Liberties* (New York: Russell Sage Foundation, 1983); and Herbert McClosky and John Zaller, *The American Ethos: Public Attitudes toward Capitalism and Democracy* (Cambridge, Mass.: Harvard University Press, 1984).

22. See Chapter Three.

23. *Democracy in America*, Vol. I, p. 122.

24. Two leading accounts of the melting pot policy, how the nation and the states tried to implement it, and how immigrant groups coped with it are: Oscar Handlin, *The Uprooted: The Epic Story of the Great Migrations That Made the American People* (New York: Grosset & Dunlap, 1951); and Nathan Glazer and Daniel Patrick Moynihan,

Beyond the Melting Pot (Cambridge, Mass.: MIT Press, 1963).

25. James Q. Wilson, *American Government*, 4th ed. (Lexington, MA: D.C. Heath & Co., 1989), Table 4.3, p. 81.

26. I have written elsewhere: "Recent Gallup polls show that the only kinds of people who are thought to have even lower ethical standards than politicians are labor union leaders, advertisers, and car salespeople; and only 23 percent of Americans would like to see their children go into politics as a life's work. And Roget's trusty *Thesaurus* lists such unflattering synonyms for *politician* as *grafter, spoilsmonger, influence peddler, wheeler-dealer, finagler,* and *wire-puller*": *Governing: An Introduction to Political Science*, 5th ed. (Englewood Cliffs, N.J.: Prentice Hall, 1990), p. 25.

27. Gabriel A. Almond and Sidney Verba, *The Civic Culture: Political Attitudes and Democracy in Five Nations* (Princeton, N.J.: Princeton University Press, 1962), p. 186.

28. See the definition in Roy C. Macridis, *Contemporary Political Ideologies* (Glenview, Ill.: Scott, Foresman/Little, Brown, 1988), ch. 1.

29. Edmund Fawcett and Tony Thomas, *America and the Americans* (London: Fontana/Collins, 1983), pp. 333, 347, 351.

30. Some leading studies of political socialization in America include: Richard E. Dawson, Kenneth Prewitt, and Karen B. Dawson, *Political Socialization: An Analytic Study*, 2nd ed. (Boston: Little, Brown, 1977); Robert Coles, *The Political Life of Children* (New York: Atlantic Monthly Press, 1986); and M. Kent Jennings and Richard G. Niemi, *Generations and Politics: A Panel Study of Young Adults and Their Parents* (Princeton, N.J.: Princeton University Press, 1981).

31. The literature on mass communications in America is as vast as the subject is important. For more extended statements of my views, see *Channels of Power: The Impact of Television on American Politics* (New York: Basic Books, 1983). A useful general survey of mass communications and politics is Doris A. Graber, *Mass Media and American Politics*, 3rd ed. (Washington, D.C.: Congressional Quarterly Press, 1989).

32. *Statistical Abstract of the United States, 1990*, Table 922, p. 553. A useful and nontechnical

discussion of the organization and operation of private television stations and the commercial networks is still Les Brown, *Televi$ion: The Business Behind the Box* (New York: Harcourt Brace Jovanovich, 1971).

33. A useful introductory survey of the subject is Harvey L. Zuckman and Martin J. Gaynes, *Mass Communications Law in a Nutshell*, 2nd ed. (St. Paul, Minn.: West Publishing, 1983).

34. *New York Times v. Sullivan*, 376 U.S. 254 (1964).

35. The two key cases are: *National Broadcasting Company v. United States*, 319 U.S. 190 (1943) and *Red Lion Broadcasting Company v. Federal Communications Commission*, 395 U.S. 367 (1969).

36. For statements of the two opposing views, see Elizabeth Drew, *Politics and Money: The New Road to Corruption* (New York: Macmillan, 1983); and Herbert E. Alexander, *Financing Politics: Money, Elections, and Political Reform* (Washington, D.C.: Congressional Quarterly Press, 1984).

37. During much of the nation's history, American political campaigns were planned and conducted mainly by professional politicians — the candidates themselves, party leaders, and advocacy-group leaders, all coming out of backgrounds in active politics. In the past thirty years, however, most campaigns have come to be designed and executed by campaign consultants — people trained mainly in commercial advertising who use their technical expertise in taking public opinion polls, designing political advertisements, purchasing newspaper space and airtime, and other professional skills not possessed by most regular politicians. Two books that describe in detail the rise of the campaign consultants and their impact on American campaigning are: Dan D. Nimmo, *The Political Persuaders* (Englewood Cliffs, N.J.: Prentice-Hall, 1970); and Larry J. Sabato, *The Rise of Political Consultants* (New York: Basic Books, 1981).

38. See Edwin Diamond and Stephen Bates, *The Spot: The Rise of Political Advertising on Television* (Cambridge, MA: M.I.T. Press, 1984).

39. Some observers note that the rapid growth of cable and satellite television has greatly increased the number and variety of programs available to most American viewers and that producers increasingly follow a strategy of "narrowcasting" — aiming television and radio programming at well-defined *segments* of the population. This strategy makes it much easier for people interested in news and politics to get a great deal of each from such outlets as CNN and C-SPAN, and for people bored by politics to avoid entirely programs with political information and discussion. See, for example, my "Broadcasting, Narrowcasting, and Politics," in Anthony King, ed., *The New American Political System*, second version (Washington, D.C.: AEI Press, 1990), pp. 175–202.

40. The United States has never held an initiative or referendum election at the national level, but a majority of the states regularly have some initiative and referendum elections. In about twelve states there are regularly fifteen to thirty measures on the ballot in any particular election. Space does not permit a more extended description here, but the reader who wishes a full account of the conduct and the impact of these "direct legislation" elections can consult two excellent recent works: David B. Magleby, *Direct Legislation* (Baltimore: Johns Hopkins University Press, 1984); and Thomas E. Cronin, *Direct Democracy* (Cambridge, Mass.: Harvard University Press, 1989). For a comparative study of direct legislation in many countries, see David Butler and Austin Ranney, *Referendums: A Comparative Study of Practice and Theory* (Washington, D.C.: American Enterprise Institute, 1978).

41. Robert S. Erikson, Norman R. Luttbeg, and Kent L. Tedin, *American Public Opinion*, 3rd ed. (New York: Macmillan, 1988), Table 1.2, p. 5.

42. For an informative account of the causes and consequences of the civil service reform movement, see Stephen Skowronek, *Building a New American State: The Expansion of National Administrative Capacities, 1877–1920* (Cambridge: Cambridge University Press, 1982).

43. Many democratic countries also allow the voters to write on the ballots names other than the parties' nominees, but few voters do so and write-in candidates almost never get more than a handful of votes.

44. For a review of the candidate selection process in twenty-eight modern democratic nations, see my "Candidate Selection," in David Butler, Howard R. Penniman, and Austin Ranney, eds., *Democracy at the Polls: A Comparative Study of Competitive National Elections* (Washington, D.C.:

American Enterprise Institute for Public Policy Research, 1981), pp. 75–106. For more detailed information on the process in nine selected countries, see Michael Gallagher and Michael Marsh, eds., *Candidate Selection in Comparative Perspective: The Secret Garden of Politics* (Beverly Hills, Calif.: Sage Publications, 1988).

45. Richard M. Scammon and Alice V. McGillivray, eds., *America Votes 1988* (Washington, D.C.: Congressional Quarterly Press, 1989), pp. 48–49.

46. I take the term *political interest* to mean the stakes that different individuals and groups have in different policies—the values they hold that can be helped or hurt by what government does or fails to do.

47. Harold D. Lasswell, *Politics: Who Gets What, When, How* (New York: Meridian Books, 1936).

48. See, for example, Alexis de Tocqueville, *Democracy in America*, vol. I, pp. 191–193; and Michel Crozier, *The Trouble with America*, translated by Peter Heinegg (Berkeley: University of California Press, 1984), p. 81.

49. A useful short survey of the matter is Herbert E. Alex and Brian A. Haggerty, *PACs and Parties* (Los Angeles, Calif.: Citizens' Research Foundation, 1984).

50. The story is well told in Peter H. Odegard, *Pressure Politics: The Story of the Anti-Saloon League* (New York: Columbia University Press, 1928).

51. See Martha Derthick, *The National Guard in Politics* (Cambridge, Mass.: Harvard University Press, 1965); and Jim Dan Hill, *The Minute Man in Peace and War: A History of the National Guard* (Harrisburg, Pa.: Stackpole, 1964).

52. *Buckley v. Valeo*, 424 U.S. 1 (1976).

53. Frank J. Sorauf and Paul Allen Beck, *Party Politics in America*, 6th ed. (Glenview, Ill.: Scott, Foresman & Co., 1988), p. 377.

54. By far the most complete source of current information about PACs is Edward Zuckerman, ed., *Almanac of Federal PACs: 1990* (Washington, D.C.: Anward Publications, 1990), which lists the names, addresses, receipts, and expenditures of all federal PACs contributing a total of $50,000 or more to campaigns for the House and Senate. It is updated every two years.

55. Two useful works on lobbying are: Norman J. Ornstein and Shirley Elder, *Interest Groups, Lobbying and Policymaking* (Washington, D.C.: Congressional Quarterly Press, 1978); and Kay Lehman Schlozman and John T. Tierney, *Organized Interests and American Democracy* (New York: Harper & Row, 1986).

56. *Democracy in America*, Vol. I, p. 280.

57. Benjamin Ginsberg and Martin Shefter, *Politics by Other Means: The Declining Importance of Elections in America* (New York: Basic Books, 1990), pp. 151–152.

58. *New York Times*, November 21, 1988, p. A10.

59. The most comprehensive recent study of how American parties differ from the parties in other nations is Leon D. Epstein, *Political Parties in the American Mold* (Madison: University of Wisconsin Press, 1986). Two recent excellent surveys of the American party system are: Samuel J. Eldersveld, *Political Parties in American Society* (New York: Basic Books, 1982); and Frank J. Sorauf and Paul Allen Beck, *Party Politics in America*, 6th ed.

60. Arend Lijphart puts the United States at the top of his list of democratic nations with the smallest number of effective parliamentary parties, closely followed by New Zealand, the United Kingdom, and Austria: *Democracies: Patterns of Majoritarian and Consensus Government in Twenty-One Countries* (New Haven, Conn.: Yale University Press, 1984), Table 7.3, p. 122. My own ranking of "two-partyness," based on the somewhat different measure of "party fractionalization," which includes both the number of effective parties and the closeness of competition between them, ranks the U.S. parties third, behind New Zealand and Canada: *Governing: An Introduction to Political Science*, 5th ed. (Englewood Cliffs, N.J.: Prentice Hall, 1990), Table 10.2, p. 240.

61. Scammon and McGillivray, *America Votes, 1988*, pp. 6–7.

62. Eldersveld, *Political Parties in American Society*, pp. 133–136.

63. For a review of the power of national leaders over candidate selection in various countries, see Butler, Penniman, and Ranney, *Democracy at the Polls*, ch. 5.

64. For detailed discussions of how the British candidate selection process operates, see: Austin Ranney, *Pathways to Parliament* (Madison: University of Wisconsin Press, 1965); and Michael Rush, *The Selection of Parliamentary Candidates* (London: Thomas Nelson & Sons, 1969).

65. The fullest exposition of this philosophy is, of

course, *The Federalist Papers*, especially the tenth paper, by James Madison. See Rossiter, ed., *The Federalist Papers*.

66. *Democracy in America*, Vol. I, p. 167.
67. There are many excellent accounts of the American policymaking process in ordinary times. Some of the leading scholarly accounts include: John Kingdon, *Agendas, Alternatives, and Public Policies* (Boston: Little, Brown, 1984); Guy Peters, *American Public Policy*, 2nd ed. (Chatham, N.J.: Chatham House, 1986); and King, *The New American Political System*. For two leading journalistic accounts of policymaking in the Reagan administration, see Hedrick Smith, *The Power Game: How Washington Works* (New York: Random House, 1988); and "How Washington Works," a special issue of *The National Journal*, June 14, 1986.
68. Political scientists Benjamin Ginsberg and Martin Shefter have suggested that in recent years America has changed its ordinary policymaking process to one in which the election outcomes play little or no role, and policymaking takes place almost entirely *between* elections in such arenas as congressional investigations, bargaining among nonelected presidential aides and congressional staff, revelations of wrongdoing in the mass media, and by civil suits and criminal prosecutions in the courts. They feel that the root cause of this change is the weakening of the voters' party loyalties and their apparently permanent tendency to elect a president of one party and a Congress of the other party: see *Politics by Other Means*.
69. For detailed accounts of some instances in which the "ordinary system" has produced major policy innovations, see Nelson W. Polsby, *Political Innovation in America* (New Haven, Conn.: Yale University Press, 1984); and Jeffrey H. Birnbaum and Alan S. Murray, *Showdown at Gucci Gulch: Lawmakers, Lobbyists, and the Unlikely Triumph of Tax Reform* (New York: Random House, 1987).
70. *The American Commonwealth*, Vol. I, p. 61.
71. Hundreds of books have been written comparing American public policies with their counterparts in other nations. I have drawn heavily on two: Arnold J. Heidenheimer, Hugh Heclo, and Carolyn Teich Adams, *Comparative Public Policy*, 3rd ed. (New York: St. Martin's Press, 1990); and Harold Wilensky and Lowell Turner, *Democratic Corporatism and Policy Linkages* (Berkeley, Calif.: Institute of International Studies, University of California at Berkeley, 1987).
72. The figures are for 1987: *Statistical Abstract of the United States, 1990*, Table 454, p. 272.
73. *Comparative Public Policy*, Table 6.5, p. 198.
74. The OECD was established in 1961 as an association of twenty-five industrialized Western nations to promote economic growth and global trade. Headquartered in Paris, it is one of the best sources of information available about the economic policies and performance of its member nations.
75. *Comparative Public Policy*, Table 6.1, p. 187.
76. *Statistical Abstract of the United States, 1990*, Table 1486, p. 862.
77. *Comparative Public Policy*, Table 2.1, p. 30.
78. Quoted in *Comparative Public Policy*, p. 29.
79. Cf. R. Burton Clark, ed., *The School and the University: An International Perspective* (Berkeley: University of California Press, 1985).
80. Cf. *Comparative Public Policy*, pp. 323–324.
81. *The Addresses and Messages of Presidents of the United States*, compiled by Edwin Williams (New York: Edward Walker, Publisher, 1846), Vol. I, p. 32.
82. Address to Congress, December 1, 1862, in Roy P. Basler, ed., *The Collected Works of Abraham Lincoln* (New Brunswick, N.J.: Rutgers University Press, 1953), Vol. V, p. 537.
83. *The American Commonwealth*, Vol. I, pp. 300–301.

ANALYTIC APPENDIX
A GUIDE TO COMPARATIVE ANALYSIS IN COMPARATIVE POLITICS TODAY

Comparative analysis is a powerful and versatile tool. It enhances our ability to describe and understand politics in any country, by offering the concepts and reference points of a broader perspective. It stimulates the formation of general theories of political relationships through the comparative consideration of different types of political systems. It encourages us to test the theories we have about politics by confronting them with the experience of many institutions and settings. It helps expand our awareness of human possibilities in politics, taking us out of the network of assumptions and familiar arrangements within which we all operate.

In the text *Comparative Politics Today* we attempt to make use of comparative analysis in all these ways. The initial chapters introduce a set of concepts for discussing and comparing the system, process, and policy aspects of different political systems. The theoretical discussions in Chapters 3 to 8 expand on these concepts and present some general theories for describing and analyzing various aspects of political life. The nine country studies build on these concepts and theories in describing and analyzing politics in a wide range of situations.

This appendix is designed to facilitate further the use of comparative analysis by the readers of *Comparative Politics Today*. We hope to make it easier to go back and forth between the general discussion of concepts and theories and their application to specific countries. Perhaps more important, we want to encourage readers to ask and try to answer their own comparative questions, engaging in comparative analysis of their own by confronting the abstract concepts and theories with the evidence of the countries, or the explanations of events in one nation with the political experiences of other nations.

Although the authors of the analytic and country chapters of this book have adopted a common analytic framework, the country discussions presented are far from identical, and not all topics treated in the general introductory chapters are discussed in the country chapters. General headings differ somewhat; subheadings differ substantially; extensiveness of treatment of topics varies greatly. There are good reasons for such differences: the processes and problems of politics in these nine countries are quite different.

The authors wish to bring out some of the unique features of their countries, as well as characteristics they have in common. One way to give the reader a feel for the special configuration of structures, policy problems, and political resource balances in each country is to stress different key elements in the larger picture. Hence, we see the emphasis on the accumulated layers of political tradition in France, the Gorbachev revolution in the USSR, the search for nation building and economic development in Africa.

Although these divergences from chapter to chapter are both desirable and necessary, the reader will also find it helpful to have a comparative guide to the presentation of concepts in the analytic chapters and descriptions in the country chapters. The three tables in this appendix can serve as such a guide. By listing headings and subheadings in the text (often in abbreviated form) and page numbers, the tables indicate where discussions of the major concepts associated with the three general levels of the political system — system, process, and policy — can be found. They also show where these concepts are applied in the discussions of politics in each of the country analyses: England, France, Germany, Japan, the USSR, China, Mexico, the African region, and the United States. All the tables are organized in the same way. In the column at the far left of the table we find the major analytic topics, including the most significant functions and structures of the political system. Reading across the table we can find the location of the theoretical and country-specific discussions of each concept.

For example, political socialization is one of the major concepts associated with the system level — it is a critical system function in all political systems. In Table A.1 we see political socialization listed as the third topic. Reading across the table, we see first where the theoretical discussion of this function is to be found (Chapter 3), and under what subheadings. Then, reading farther to the right across the table, we see the subheadings and page numbers where political socialization in each of the countries is discussed. The similarities and differences in the subheadings themselves are interesting, for they reveal aspects of socialization that the author of each country study emphasizes. We see, for example, the emphasis on communication networks in the USSR and China, where the government makes specific efforts to shape citizen attitudes by controlling information. Further, most of the authors discuss education or schools as a distinct topic, and similarly devote special attention to the family in political socialization.

Table A.1 lists six separate analytic topics, covering both comparative analysis in general and the system level in particular. The reader can check the ideas put forth in the analytic chapter against the facts and interpretations presented later in the specific country chapters.

Table A.1 can be used to seek the answers, or promote discussion about, questions like these:

1. Comparative Analysis

    What are the major obstacles to comparing political systems that are very different in language, size, customs, organization, and policy? How and to what extent can these be overcome?

    Why have the authors of the country studies chosen the subheadings and emphases that appear in their chapters? What do these tell us about each country?

2. Environment of the Political System

    What are the effects of the level of social and economic development on the processes in the political system? On the problems faced by citizens and leaders?

    How does the international environment shape national political life?

    How may ethnic, religious, or linguistic divisions in a political system affect its processes and problems?

3. Political Socialization

    What are the agents in a society that contribute to political socialization?

    Under what conditions and to what extent can the images and ideas acquired in childhood be modified in later life?

4. Political Culture

    How is the legacy of the past transmitted to the present? Under what conditions can such a legacy be a burden to contemporary politics? Under what conditions can it help achieve political goals?

    What are political subcultures? When are they stabilizing or destabilizing influences?

    How does the political culture work to constrain the processes and policies of a society?

5. Political Recruitment: Citizen Participation

    What are the major types of citizen participation?

    When does citizen participation "make a difference" in politics?

    How can levels of citizen participation be modified or their composition altered?

6. Elite Recruitment

    What types of citizens are likely to become "elites"? How do they choose themselves and how are they chosen in different types of political systems?

    Why is recruitment of leaders a major means for controlling public policies?

    How is this control attempted and by whom in democracies? In one-party systems? What are the limitations on such control?

In Table A.2 we find the major analytic concepts associated with the process level of the political system — the major structures and functions involved in the expression of political interests, the mobilizing of political resources around those interests, and the making and implementation of public policies.

Table A.2 can be used to seek the answers, or promote discussion about, questions like these:

1. Interest Articulation and Groups

    What different types of interest groups predominate in different political systems?

What types of access channels do different groups find effective? Under what conditions?

How is access to the influential policymakers different in democratic and authoritarian systems?

What is the role of political protest in interest articulation? Of political violence?

2. Interest Aggregation and Political Parties

    Why are political parties so important in political systems and societies as different as those in England, France, Germany, Japan, the USSR, China, Mexico, and the United States?

    In what different ways do competitive party systems shape interest aggregation?

    What types of interest aggregation structures predominate in different political systems?

    How do the interest aggregation structures affect the types of interests taken seriously in the policymaking process?

3. Policymaking: Decision Rules

    Why do some decision rules make it easy to adopt new policies, though others make new policies the exception?

    What structures act to create change-oriented or status quo-oriented decision rules?

    Under what conditions are citizens likely to favor various decision rules?

4. Policymaking: Structures and Functions

    Why have executives become more important and legislatures less so, even in the democratic countries?

    Why are bureaucracies so important everywhere? How can they be controlled and by whom?

    How can leadership play a role in overcoming the constraints of decision rules?

In Table A.3 we find the major analytic concepts associated with the policy level of the political system: the different ways in which political systems attempt to achieve chosen goals by extracting resources, regulating behavior, and so forth; the successful and unsuccessful outcomes of these performance efforts; and the different strategies of organization and performance used to seek achievement of various political "goods."

Table A.3 can be used to seek answers for, or promote discussions about, questions like these:

1. Policy Performance

    How do political systems extract resources with which to implement policies.

    What differences in the size and role of the political system do we find in extraction and distribution of resources in different societies?

    What different areas of life are regulated in different kinds of political systems?

2. Policy Outcomes

    Why are some political systems oriented to equality, and others to seeking economic growth? How does the role of government vary in this regard?

    Why must some political systems make much greater demands on their citizens than other systems do to achieve the same policy outcome?

Why do policy efforts — policies and outputs — often fail to achieve desired policy outcomes?

3. Policy Evaluation and Strategy

What different types of "political goods" are desired by people in different societies?

How may the search for one kind of political good affect other political goods in positive and negative ways?

What kinds of strategies have preindustrial nations attempted in efforts to achieve their goals? How have these worked in practice?

By asking these and other questions in the context of the analytic chapters and the appropriate sections of country chapters, the reader can enhance his or her understanding of the issues of comparative politics today.

TABLE A.1
A GUIDE TO ANALYSIS IN COMPARATIVE POLITICS TODAY: THEORY AND SYSTEM LEVEL

Theoretical discussion	England	France	Germany	Japan
		1. Comparative analysis		
Chapter 1 Comparative analysis 3–4 Comparative systems 4–6 Political structures 6–8 Structure and function 8–10 The policy level 13–14	*All of Chapter 9* (131–186)	*All of Chapter 10* (189–237)	*All of Chapter 11* (239–294)	*All of Chapter 12* (297–348)
		2. Environment of the political system		

Chapter 2
 	
Historical setting 16–17
 	
Size 18
 	
Economic development 19–21
 	
Inequality 21–22
 	
Cultural heterogeneity 22
 	
International interdependence 22–28
	Constraints of history 132–136
	  Making of modern England 132–136
	  Mixed inheritance 136
	Constraints of place 136–140
	  Insularity and involvement 136–138
	  One Crown and many nations 138–140
	  Multiracial England 140
		Historical perspective 189–190
		Economy and society 190–192
		France and the new architecture of Europe 233–234
			The historical legacy 240–242
			  Second Empire 240
			  Weimer Republic 240–241
			  Third Reich 241–242
			  Occupation period 242
			Following two paths 242–247
			Social forces 247–249
				Introduction 297–298
				Occupation reforms and postwar political structure 298–302
				  Socioeconomic reforms 302
				Political culture and cleavages 311–312
				Foreign trade 338–339

TABLE A.1 *(continued)*

USSR	China	Mexico	Africa	United States
	1. Comparative analysis
All of Chapter 13 (351–406)	*All of Chapter 14* (409–461)	*All of Chapter 15* (463–519)	*All of Chapter 16* (521–560)	*All of Chapter 17* (562–601)

2. Environment of the political system

USSR	China	Mexico	Africa	United States
Background to the Gorbachev revolution 353–359	Introduction 409–411	Historical perspective 465–469	The fifty-two states of Africa 521–522	U.S. among the world's nations 563–
Changing national security 354	Historical setting 411–429	Legacies of colonialism 465–466	Effects of colonialism 522–527	History 563–564
Quiet revolution 354–356	Chinese political tradition 411–413	Church and state 466–467	Legacy of colonial state 526–527	Geography 564
Ideological bankruptcy 356	Revolutionary setting 413–414	Revolution and aftermath 467–468	Independence and after 527–530	Population 564–565
Social malaise 356–357	CCP history 414–416	Cárdenas upheaval 468–469	Single-party formula 528	Economy 565
Economic gridlock 357–358	History of PRC 416–426	International environment 469–471	Military intervention 528–529	World position 565–566
State immobilism 358–359	Tiananmen 426–427		Personal authoritarianism 529	
Dynamics of social structure 362–367	After Tiananmen 427–428		Democratization 529–530	
Ethnicity and social stratification 362–365	Socioeconomic change 428–429		Deepening economic crisis 530–531	
The new class 365–367			Cultural pluralism 531–534	
			Social class 534–537	

(table continued on next page)

TABLE A.1 (continued)

Theoretical discussion	England	France	Germany	Japan
		3. Political socialization		
Chapter 3 Political socialization 33–34 Resocialization 34–36 Agents of socialization 36–39 Family 36 School 36 Religious organizations 36–37 Occupation 37 Mass media 37 Parties 37–38 Contacts 38–39 Environment 39	Political socialization 156–160 Influence of family 156–157 Gender 158 Schooling 157–159 Class 159–160 Cumulative effect 160 Political communication 163–165	Political socialization 198–199 Family 199 Class and status 198 Associations 199–200 Education 200–201 Communications 201–202	Learning and communication 261–265 Family 262 Education 262–264 State actions 264 Mass media 264–265 Remaking political cultures 255–261 Nation and state 256–258 Democratic norms 258–259 Social values and the new politics 259–260	Political culture 309–311 Campaigns and voting behavior 316–319
		4. Political culture		
Chapter 3 Political culture 39–43 System propensities 39–40 Process propensities 40–41 Policy propensities 41–42 Consensual and conflictual 42–43 Change in political culture 43–44	Political culture and political authority 151–155 Allegiance to authority: legitimacy of the system 151–152 The role of law 152–153 Whose authority? 153–154 Culture as constraint 154–155	Themes of political culture 194–198 Burden of history 194 Abstractions and symbolism 194 Religious and antireligious traditions 196–198 Class and status 198 Distrust of government and politics 194–196	Remaking political cultures 255–261 Nation and state 256–258 Democratic norms 258–259 Social values and new politics 259–260 Two peoples in one nation? 260–261 Elite orientations 268–269	Political culture 309–311 Culture and cleavages 311–312 Political attitudes and involvement 312–313

TABLE A.1 (*continued*)

USSR	China	Mexico	Africa	United States
3. Political socialization				
The quiet revolution 354–356	Agents of socialization 436–441	Mass political socialization 503 Participation 503–504	Political socialization 538–541	Political socialization 572
Political socialization and public opinion 378–384	Socialization and major political change 441–442		Political communication 541–542	Mass communications media 572–574
Propaganda and communist ideology 378–381				
Counterideology and pluralism 381–384				
4. Political culture				
Ideological bankruptcy 356	The Chinese political tradition 411–413	Political culture 501–504	Political culture 537–538	Melting pot or patchwork quilt 569–570
Soviet political culture in transition 359–362	Political culture and socialization 436–441			Main elements of traditional political culture 570–572
Ethnicity and stratification 362–365	Revolutionary values 436			
Counterideology and pluralism 381–384	Socialization and major political change 441–442			

(table continued on next page)

TABLE A.1 (*continued*)

Theoretical discussion	England	France	Germany	Japan
5. Political recruitment: citizen participation				
Chapter 4 Recruitment of citizens 48–52 Types of citizen involvement 48–50 Who participates? 50–51 Citizens as subjects 51–52 How much participation? 52–53	Popular participation 155–156 (Also see 151, 163)	Electoral participation and abstention 208–209 Voting in parliamentary elections 209–210 Voting in referendums and presidential elections 210–212	Citizen participation 265–267	Political attitudes and involvement 312–313 Campaigns and voting behavior 316–319
6. Political recruitment of elites				
Chapter 4 Eligibility biases 53–54 Selection of elites 54–56 Control of elites 56–57 Democratic and authoritarian structures 57–58	Recruitment into political roles 160–164 Cabinet ministers 162 Higher civil servants 162–163 Intermittent public persons 163 Selective recruitment 163–164	Recruitment and style of elites 202–204	Politics at the elite level 267–268 Paths to the top 268 Elite orientations 268–269 Party government 280	Political recruitment in Japan 319–322 The Diet 320–321 The Cabinet 321 Educational elitism 321–322

TABLE A.1 (*continued*)

USSR	China	Mexico	Africa	United States
5. Political recruitment: citizen participation				
Political participation and political recruitment 367–378 Democratization from above 367–374 Popular political mobilization 374–378	Participation 444–445	Political participation 503–504	Political participation 542–545	Participation by voting 575–577 Participation by other means 577–579
6. Political recruitment of elites				
Rise and fall of the new class 365–367 Democratization from above 367–374 CPSU and political leadership 385–388	Recruitment 445–446	The presidency 475–478 Camarillas and clientelism 478–479 Recruiting the political elite 479–483 Técnicos vs. políticos 481–483	Political recruitment 545–547	Recruitment of leaders 578 Unique direct primary 578–579

TABLE A.2
A GUIDE TO ANALYSIS IN COMPARATIVE POLITICS TODAY: POLITICAL PROCESS LEVEL

Theoretical discussion	England	France	Germany	Japan
1. Interest articulation and interest groups				

Chapter 5
Types of groups 61–67
  Individuals and networks 62
  Anomic groups 62–63
  Nonassociational groups 63
  Institutional groups 63–64
  Associational groups 64–65
  Interest group systems 65–67
Legitimate access 67–69
Coercive tactics 69–70
Policy perspectives 70–71
Interest group development 71–73
	Articulating group pressures 165–168
	  What interest groups want 166
	  Organizing for political action 166–167
	  Political values as constraints 167
	  From pluralism and corporatism 167–168
		Interest groups 204–208
		  Expression of interests 204–206
		  Means and styles of action 206–208
			Interest groups 269–272
			  Business 270
			  Labor 270–271
			  Church 271
			  New politics movements 271–272
				Interest articulation and aggregation 322–328
				  Broad principles as interests 322–323
				  Quest for government aid 323
				  Demand for regulation 323
				  Group resources 323–324
				  Representation 324–325
				  Clientelism 325
				  Petitions and activism 325–326
				  Corporatism versus pluralism 326–328

2. Interest aggregation and political parties				

Chapter 6
Interest groups 76–77
Competitive parties and elections 78–80
Competitive parties in government 80–81
Competitive party systems 81–83
Authoritarian party system 83
  Exclusive governing parties 83–84
  Inclusive governing parties 84–85
Military forces 85–86
Trends in interest aggregation 86–87
Significance of aggregation 87–88
	The party system: aggregation and choice 168–173
	  Electoral choice 168–170
	  Control of organization 170–172
	  Policy preferences 172–173
	Prime minister 142–145
	Cabinet 145–146
	House of Commons 148–150
		Voting in parliamentary elections 209–210
		Voting in presidential elections 210–212
		Political parties 212–222
		  Traditional party system 212–213
		  Right and center 213–219
		  The left 219–222
		The executive 222–224
			Party system and electoral politics 272–280
			  Christian Democrats 273–274
			  Social Democrats 274–275
			  Free Democrats 275–276
			  The Greens 276–277
			  Communists to PDS 277
			  Electoral system 278
			  Electoral connection 278–280
			  Party government 280
			Initiating policy 281
			Legislating policy 282–284
				Interest articulation and aggregation 322–328
				Parties and elections 313–319
				Party system and context of competition 302–309
				Liberal Democratic party 331–332
				Opposition parties 332

TABLE A.2 (continued)

USSR	China	Mexico	Africa	United States

1. Interest articulation and interest groups

USSR	China	Mexico	Africa	United States

Popular political mobilization 374–378
 	
Counterideology and political pluralism 381–384
 	
CPSU and political leadership 385–388
	Mass organizations 435–436
	
	Interest articulation 446–448
		Camarillas and clientelism 478–479
		
		Interest representation and political control 483–486
		
		Campesinos, labor, the military 497–501
		
		  State-campesino relations 497–498
		
		  State and labor 498–500
		
		  Military in politics 500–501
			Interest articulation 547–549
			
			(See also cultural pluralism 531–534; social class 534–537)
				Interest articulation 579–582
				
				PACs 580–581
				
				Pressure groups 581–582

2. Interest aggregation and political parties

USSR	China	Mexico	Africa	United States
The Gorbachev revolution 351–353 CPSU and political leadership 385–388 Crisis of governance 388–390	Interest aggregation and elite conflict 448–449	Presidency 475–478 Camarillas and clientelism 478–479 Interest representation and political control 483–497 The PRI 486–492 Opposition parties 492–495 Political reform measures 496–497	Personal authoritarianism 529 Single-party formula 528 Military intervention 528–529 Democratization 529–530 Interest aggregation 549–552	American political politics 582–587 Two-party system 582 Party differences 583–585 Decentralization 585 Low cohesion 585–586 Weak discipline 586–587 Divided party control of government 587

(table continued on next page)

TABLE A.2 (*continued*)

Theoretical discussion	England	France	Germany	Japan
		3. Policymaking: decision rules		
Chapter 7 Policymaking 91–92 Rules for policymaking 92–97 Making constitutions 92–93 Geographic power distribution 93–94 Separation of powers 94–95 Limitations on power 95–96 Democratizing trends 97	One Crown and many nations 138–140 The constitution of the Crown 140–148 The prime minister 142–145 Cabinet and ministers 145–146 The role of law 152–153 Limits of centralization 173–174 Limits of decentralization 175–176	Constitution and governmental structure 192–193 Policy processes 222–231 The executive 222–224 Parliament 224–227 Checks and balances 227–229 State and territorial relations 229–231	Institutions and structure of government 249–255 Federal system 250–251 Parliamentary government 251–252 Federal chancellor and cabinet 252–254 Federal president 254 Judicial system 254–255	Occupation reforms and postwar political structure 298–302 Constitution 298–299 Emperor 299 National Diet 299–300 Executive 300–301 Judiciary 301 Local government 301–302
		4. Policymaking: structures and functions		
Chapter 7 Assemblies 96–99 Functions of assemblies 97–98 Structures of assemblies 98–99 Executives 99–102 Functions of executives 100–102 Bureaucracies 102–105 Structures of bureaucracies 102–103 Functions of bureaucracies 103–105	Making and delivering government policies 173–178 Limits of centralization 173–174 Limits of decentralization 175–176 The constitution of the Crown 140–148 Prime minister 142–145 Cabinet and ministers 145–146 The civil service 146–147 The role of parliament 148–151 Government as a network 147–148	Policy processes 222–231 The executive 222–224 Parliament 224–227 Checks and balances 227–229	Party government 280 The policy process 281–284 Initiating policy 281 Legislating policy 282–284 Policy administration 284 Judicial review 284	Policymaking 328–333 Central executive elite 328–329 Bureaucratic dominance? 329–330 Diet 330–331 Liberal Democratic party 331–332 Opposition parties 332 Policymaking and conflict 332–333

TABLE A.2 (*continued*)

USSR	China	Mexico	Africa	United States
3. Policymaking: decision rules				
The Gorbachev revolution 351–353	Constitution and political structure 429–436	Political structure and political institutions 471–479	The fifty-one states of Africa 521–522	The constitutional system 566–569
Democratization from above 367–374	The state 429–432	Political centralism 472–475	Single-party formula 528	Federalism 566–567
CPSU and political leadership 385–388	The party 432–434	Presidency 475–478	Military intervenes 528–529	Separation of powers 567–568
Crisis of governance 388–390	The army 434–435		Personal authoritarianism 529	Judicial review 568–569
Toward a rule of law? 390–394			Democratization 529–530	
			The policy process 552–553	
4. Policymaking: structures and functions				
The Gorbachev revolution 351–353	The state 429–432	Political structure and political institutions 471–479	The policy process 552–553	Policymaking process in America 587–590
Democratization from above 367–374	The party 432–434	Political centralism 472–475		Founders' intentions 587–589
CPSU and political leadership 385–388	The army 434–435	Presidency 475–478		Ways of avoiding deadlocks 589–590
Crisis of governance 388–390	Mass organizations 435–436	Camarillas and clientelism 478–479		
	Policymaking and implementation 449–452	Political participation 503–504		
	Decision making 449–450			
	Administration 450–451			
	Rule enforcement and adjudication 451–452			

TABLE A.3
A GUIDE TO ANALYSIS IN COMPARATIVE POLITICS TODAY: POLICY LEVEL

Theoretical discussion	England	France	Germany	Japan
1. Policy performance				
Chapter 8 Extraction 108–110 Distribution 110–113 Regulation 113–114 Symbolic performance 114–115	Making and delivering government policies 173–178 Limits of centralization 173–174 Growth of government 174–175 Limits of decentralization 175–176 Mix of state and market 176–178 Policy outputs 178–179	Performance and prospects 231–233 Welfare state 231 Nationalization and regulation 231–233	Policy performance 284–289 Policy record 285–287 Paying the costs 287–289	Political performance 333–339 What the government does 333 Political outputs 1952–1969 334–337 Recent political outputs 337–338 Foreign trade 338–339 Macro-Performance 339–342
2. Policy outcomes				
Chapter 8 Outcomes of performance 116–121 Domestic welfare 116–118 Domestic security 118–119 Outcomes in the international arena 119–121, 22–28	Policy outcomes 179–180 Popular evaluation 180–182	Performance and prospects 231–233 Welfare state 231 Nationalization and regulation 231–233	Policy performance 284–289 Policy record 285–287 Paying the costs 287–289	Performance of the economy 335–336 Benefits of high growth 336 Negative consequences of growth 336–337 Foreign trade 338–339
3. Policy evaluation and strategy				
Chapter 8 Political goods and productivity 121–123 Strategies for producing goods 123–126 Tradeoffs and opportunity costs 126	England is different 131–132	Performance and prospects 231–234	Policy challenges of unification 289–291 After the revolution 291–292	Macro-performance under LDP hegemony 339–342

TABLE A.3 (*continued*)

USSR	China	Mexico	Africa	United States
1. Policy performance				
The Gorbachev revolution 351–353 Ideological bankruptcy 356 Immobilism in the state 358–359 The policy process 385–390 CPSU and political leadership 385–388 Crisis of governance 388–390 USSR and the world 394–398	Political history of the PRC 416–429 Soviet model 417–419 Maoist model 420–422 Modernization model 422–425 Performance capabilities 452–455 China and the world 457–459	The presidency 475–478 Government performance 504–509 Economic growth and inequality 504–506 Population and unemployment 507–508 Financial development and inflation 508–509	The policy process 552–553 Policy performance 553–557 Extraction 553–555 Distribution 555–556 Regulation 556–557	Policy performance 590–595 Extractive policies 590–591 Distributive performance 591–592 Regulative performance 592–595
2. Policy outcomes				
Ideological bankruptcy 356 Social malaise 356–357 Economic gridlock 357–358 Immobilism in the state 358–359 USSR and the world 394–398	Socioeconomic change 428–429 Performance outcomes 455–457 China and the world 457–459	End of an era 463–465 Economic growth and inequality 504–506 Population and unemployment 507–508 Financial development and inflation 508–509	Policy performance 553–557 Extraction 553–555 Distribution 555–556 Regulation 556–557 (Also see deepening economic crisis 530–531)	Policy performance 590–595 Extractive policies 590–591 Distributive performance 591–592 Regulative performance 592–595
3. Policy evaluation and strategy				
The Gorbachev revolution 351–353 After *perestroika* 398–400	Introduction 409–411 Performance and evaluation 452–459 Prospects 459–460	Transition to what? 509–512	A difficult future 557–558	American "exceptionalism": myth or reality? 595–596

SELECTED BIBLIOGRAPHY

PREFACE

Castles, Francis. *The Comparative History of Public Policy.* Cambridge: Polity Press, 1989.

Dahl, Robert A. *Democracy and Its Critics.* New Haven, Conn.: Yale University Press, 1989.

Dalton, Russell, Scott Flanagan, and Paul Allen Beck, eds., *Electoral Change in Advanced Industrial Democracies: Realignment or Dealignment?* Princeton, N.J.: Princeton University Press, 1984.

Flora, Peter, and Arnold Heidenheimer. *The Development of Welfare States in Europe and America.* New Brunswick, N.J.: Transaction Books, 1981.

Heidenheimer, Arnold, et al. *Comparative Public Policy: The Politics of Social Choice in America, Europe and Japan.* New York: St. Martin's, 1990.

Inglehart, Ronald. *Culture Shift in Advanced Industrial Society.* Princeton, N.J.: Princeton University Press, 1990.

Lijphart, Arend. *Democracies.* New Haven, Conn.: Yale University Press, 1984.

Lindblom, Charles E. *Politics and Markets.* New York: Basic Books, 1977.

Marty, Martin. *Fundamentalism Observed.* Chicago: University of Chicago Press, 1991.

O'Donnell, Guillermo, and Philippe Schmitter. *Transitions from Authoritarian Rule; Tentative Conclusions about Uncertain Democracies.* Baltimore: Johns Hopkins University Press, 1986.

Powell, G. Bingham. *Contemporary Democracies.* Cambridge, Mass.: Harvard University Press, 1982.

Sartori, Giovanni. *The Theory of Democracy Revisited.* Chatham, N.J.: Chatham House Publishers, 1987.

CHAPTER 1
The Study of Comparative Politics

Almond, Gabriel A., and G. Bingham Powell, Jr. *Comparative Politics: System, Process, Policy,* 2nd ed. Boston: Little, Brown, 1978.

Collier, David, "New Perspectives in the Comparative Method," in Dankwart Rustow, ed., *Comparative Political Dynamics.* New York: Harper Collins, 1991.

Dogan, Mattei, and Dominique Pelassy. *How to Compare Nations: Strategies in Comparative Politics,* 2nd ed. Chatham, N.J.: Chatham House Publishers, 1990.

Easton, David. *A Systems Analysis of Political Life.* New York: Wiley, 1965.

Eckstein, Harry. "Case Studies in Political Explanation," in F. I. Greenstein and N. W. Polsby, eds., *Handbook of Political Science.* Reading, Mass.: Addison–Wesley, 1975.

————, and David Apter. *Comparative Politics: A Reader.* London: Free Press of Glencoe, 1963.

Holt, Robert, and John Turner, eds. *The Methodology of Comparative Politics.* New York: Wiley, 1970.

Lijphart, Arend. "Comparative Politics and Comparative Method," *American Political Science Review,* September 1971.

Przeworski, Adam, and James Teune. *The Logic of Comparative Social Injury.* New York: Wiley, 1970.

Sartori, Giovanni. "Concept Misformation in Comparative Politics," *American Political Science Review,* December 1970.

CHAPTER 2
Environment of the Political System

Cardoso, Fernando, and Enzo Faletto. *Dependency and Development in Latin America.* Berkeley: University of California Press, 1979.

Chenery, Hollis, et al. *Redistribution with Growth.* London: Oxford University Press, 1974.

Emerson, Rupert. *From Empire to Nation.* Cambridge, Mass.: Harvard University Press, 1960.

Enloe, Cynthia. *Ethnic Conflict and Development.* Boston: Little, Brown, 1973.

Evans, Peter, Dietrich Rueschemeyer, and Theda Skocpol. *Bringing the State Back In.* London: Cambridge University Press, 1985.

Fishlow, Albert. *Rich Nations, Poor Nations in the World Economy.* New York: McGraw–Hill, 1978.

Gilpin, Robert. *The Political Economy of International Relations.* Princeton, N.J.: Princeton University Press, 1987.

Janos, Andrew C. *Politics and Paradigms: Changing Theories of Change in Social Science.* Stanford, Calif.: Stanford University Press, 1986.

Rustow, Dankwart. *A World of Nations.* Washington, D.C.: Brookings Institution, 1967.

Tilly, Charles, ed. *The Formation of Nation States in Western Europe.* Princeton, N.J.: Princeton University Press, 1975.

Weiner, Myron, and Samuel Huntington. *Understanding Political Development.* Boston: Little, Brown, 1986.

Wiarda, Howard, ed. *New Directions in Comparative Politics.* Boulder, Colo.: Westview Press, 1986.

World Bank. *World Development Report* 1990. New York: Oxford University Press, 1990.

Young, Crawford. *The Politics of Cultural Pluralism.* Madison: University of Wisconsin Press, 1978.

CHAPTER 3
Political Socialization and Political Culture

Aberbach, Joel D., Robert D. Putnam, and Bert A. Rockman. *Bureaucrats and Politicians in Western Democracies.* Cambridge, Mass.: Harvard University Press, 1981.

Almond, Gabriel A., and Sidney Verba. *The Civic Culture.* Princeton, N.J.: Princeton University Press, 1963.

————, eds. *The Civic Culture Revisited.* Boston: Little Brown, 1980.

Baker, Kendall, Russell Dalton, and Kai Hildebrandt. *Germany Transformed: Political Culture and the New Politics.* Cambridge, Mass.: Harvard University Press, 1981.

Brown, Archie, and Jack Gray. *Political Culture and Political Change in Communist States.* New York: Holmes and Meier, 1977.

Dawson, Richard K., Kenneth Prewitt, and Karen S. Dawson. *Political Socialization,* 2nd ed. Boston: Little Brown, 1977.

Horowitz, Donald. *Ethnic Groups in Conflict.* Berkeley: University of California Press, 1985.

Inglehart, R. *Culture Shift in Advanced Industrial Society.* Princeton, N.J.: Princeton University Press, 1990.

Jennings, M. Kent, and Richard Niemi. *The Political Character of Adolescence.* Princeton, N.J.: Princeton University Press, 1974.

Kavanagh, Dennis A. *Political Culture.* London: Macmillan, 1972.

Putnam, Robert. *The Beliefs of Politicians.* New Haven, Conn.: Yale University Press, 1973.

————, R. Leonardi, R. Nanetti, and F. Pavoncello. "Explaining Institutional Success: The Case of Italian Regional Government." *American Political Science Review* 77:55–74, 1983.

Pye, Lucian W., and Sidney Verba, eds. *Political Culture and Political Development.* Princeton, N.J.: Princeton University Press, 1965.

Sears, David O. "Political Socialization," in F. I. Greenstein and N. W. Polsby, *Handbook of Political Science,* Vol. 2, Ch. 2. Reading, Mass.: Addison–Wesley, 1975.

Wylie, Laurence. *Village in the Vaucluse.* Cambridge, Mass.: Harvard University Press, 1957.

CHAPTER 4
Political Recruitment and Political Structure

Barnes, Samuel H., and Max Kaase. *Political Action: Mass Participation in Five Western Democracies.* Beverly Hills, Calif.: Sage Publications, 1979.

Bendix, Reinhard. *National-Building and Citizenship.* New York: Anchor, 1969.

Burling, Robbins. *The Passage of Power: Studies in Political Succession.* New York: Harcourt Brace Jovanovich, 1974.

Butler, David, Howard R. Penniman, and Austin Ranney, eds. *Democracy at the Polls.* Washington, D.C.: American Enterprise Institute, 1981.

Dahl, Robert A. *Polyarchy: Participation and Opposition.* New Haven, Conn.: Yale University Press, 1971.

————. *After the Revolution.* New Haven, Conn.: Yale University Press, 1971.

————. Democracy and Its Critics. New Haven, Conn.: Yale University Press, 1989.

Dalton, Russell J. *Citizen Politics in Western Democracies.* Chatham, N.J.: Chatham House, 1988.

Gurr, Ted Robert. *Why Men Rebel.* Princeton, N.J.: Princeton University Press, 1970.

Hibbs, Douglas A. *Mass Political Violence.* New York: Wiley, 1973.

Hirschman, Albert. *Exit, Voice, and Loyalty.* Cambridge, Mass.: Harvard University Press, 1970.

Huntington, Samuel. *Political Order in Changing Societies.* New Haven, Conn.: Yale University Press, 1968.

————. "Will More Countries Become Democratic?" *Political Science Quarterly* 99:193–218, 1984.

Lijphart, Arend. *Democracies: Patterns of Majorities and Consensus Governments in Twenty-One Countries.* New Haven, Conn.: Yale University Press, 1984.

Linz, Juan. "Totalitarian and Authoritarian Regimes, in F. I. Greenstein and N. W. Polsby, *Handbook of Political Science.* Reading, Mass.: Addison–Wesley, 1975.

Lipset, Seymour M. *Political Man.* London: Mercury 1963.

Marshall, T. H. *Class, Citizenship and Social Development.* New York: Doubleday, 1964.

O'Donnell, Guillermo, Philippe C. Schmitter, and Laurence Whitehead. *Transitions from Authoritarian Rule: Prospects for Democracy.* Baltimore: Johns Hopkins University Press, 1986.

Pastor, Robert A., ed. *Democracy in the Americas: Stopping the Pendulum.* New York: Holmes and Meier, 1989.

Pateman, Carole. *Participation and Democratic Theory.* New York: Cambridge University Press, 1970.

Perlmutter, Amos. *Modern Authoritarianism: A Comparative Institutional Analysis.* New Haven, Conn.: Yale University Press, 1981.

Powell, G. Bingham, Jr. *Contemporary Democracies: Participation, Stability and Violence.* Cambridge, Mass.: Harvard University Press, 1982.

Putnam, Robert D. *The Comparative Study of Political Elites.* Englewood Cliffs, N.J.: Prentice–Hall, 1976.

Verba, Sidney, Norman H. Nie and Jae-on Kim. *Participation and Political Equality.* Cambridge: Cambridge University Press, 1978.

CHAPTER 5
Interest Groups and Interest Articulation

Ash, Timothy Garton. *The Magic Lantern.* New York: Random House, 1990.

Beer, Samuel H. *British Politics in the Collectivist Age.* New York: Knopf, 1965.

Berger, Suzanne, ed., *Organizing Interests in Western Europe.* New York: Cambridge University Press, 1981.

Dalton, Russell J., and Manfred Kuechler. *Challenging the Political Order: New Social and Political Movements in Western Democracies.* New York: Oxford University Press, 1990.

Denardo, James. *Power in Numbers: The Political Strategy of Protest and Rebellion.* Princeton, N.J.: Princeton University Press, 1985.

Ehrmann, Henry W. *Interest Groups on Four Continents.* Pittsburgh: University of Pittsburgh Press, 1958.

Goldthorpe, John H., ed. *Order and Conflict in Contemporary Capitalism.* Oxford: Clarendon Press, 1984.

Katzenstein, P. *Small States in World Markets.* Ithaca, N.Y.: Cornell University Press, 1985.

Olson, Mancur. *The Logic of Collective Action.* Cambridge, Mass.: Harvard University Press, 1965.

Sabel, Charles. *Work and Politics.* New York: Columbia University Press, 1982.

Schmitter, Philippe, ed. "Corporatism and Policy-Making in Contemporary Western Europe." *Comparative Political Studies,* April 1977.

Scott, James C. *The Moral Economy of the Peasant: Rebellion and Subsistence in Southeast Asia.* New Haven, Conn.: Yale University Press, 1976.

Skilling, H. Gordon, and Franklyn Griffiths. *Interest Groups in Soviet Politics.* Princeton, N.J.: Princeton University Press, 1971.

Weiner, Myron. *The Politics of Scarcity: Public Pressure and Political Response in India.* Chicago: University of Chicago Press, 1962.

Wilkinson, Paul. *Political Terrorism.* London: Macmillan Press, 1974.

Wilson, James Q. *Political Organizations.* New York: Basic Books, 1973.

CHAPTER 6
Political Parties and Interest Aggregation

Converse, Philip E., and Roy Pierce. *Political Representation in France.* Cambridge, Mass.: Harvard University Press, 1986.

Dahl, Robert A., ed. *Regimes and Oppositions.* New Haven, Conn.: Yale University Press, 1973.

Dalton, Russell, Scott Flanagan, and Paul Allen Beck, eds. *Electoral Change in Advanced Industrial Societies.* Princeton, N.J.: Princeton University Press, 1984.

Dodd, Lawrence C. *Coalitions in Parliamentary Government.* Princeton, N.J.: Princeton University Press, 1976.

Downs, Anthony. *An Economic Theory of Democracy.* New York: Harper and Row, 1957.

Duverger, Maurice. *Political Parties.* New York: Wiley, 1955.

Gastil, R. D., ed. *Freedom in the World: Political Rights and Civil Liberties 1987–88.* New York: Freedom House, 1988.

Huntington, Samuel, and Clement Moore. *Authoritarian Politics in Modern Society.* New York: Basic Books, 1970

Jackson, Robert H., and Carl G. Rosberg. *Personal Rule in Black Africa.* Berkeley: University of California Press, 1982.

Laver, Michael, and Norman Schofield. *Multiparty Government.* New York: Oxford University Press, 1990.

Lijphart, Arend. *Democracy in Plural Societies.* New Haven, Conn.: Yale University Press, 1977.

Linz, Juan J., and Alfred Stepan, eds. *The Breakdown of Democratic Regimes.* Baltimore: Johns Hopkins University Press, 1978.

Lipset, Seymour M., and Stein Rokkan. *Party Systems and Voter Alignments.* New York: Free Press, 1967.

Michels, Robert. *Political Parties.* New York: Collier, 1962.

Nordlinger, Eric A. *Soldiers in Politics: Military Coups and Governments.* Englewood Cliffs, N.J.: Prentice–Hall, 1976.

O'Donnell, Guillermo, Philippe C. Schmitter, and Laurence Whitehead. *Transitions from Authoritarian Rule: Prospects for Democracy.* Baltimore: Johns Hopkins University Press, 1986.

Ostrogorski, M. J. *Democracy and the Organization of Political Parties.* New York: Anchor, 1964.

Powell, G. Bingham, Jr. *Contemporary Democracies: Participation, Stability and Violence.* Cambridge, Mass.: Harvard University Press, 1982.

Rae, Douglas. *The Political Consequences of Electoral Laws.* New Haven, Conn.: Yale University Press, 1971.

Riker, William H. *Liberalism Against Populism.* San Francisco: W. H. Freeman, 1982.

Rokkan, Stein. *Citizens, Elections, Parties.* New York: McKay, 1970.

Sartori, Giovanni. *Parties and Party Systems.* Cambridge: Cambridge University Press, 1976.

Strom, Kaare. *Minority Government and Majority Rule.* New York: Cambridge University Press, 1990.

Von Beyme, Klaus. *Political Parties in Western Europe.* New York: St. Martin's, 1985.

Ware, Alan. *Citizens, Parties and the State.* Princeton, N.J.: Princeton University Press, 1988.

CHAPTER 7
Government and Policy Making

Armstrong, John A. *The European Administrative Elite.* Princeton, N.J.: Princeton University Press, 1973.

Blondel, Jean. *Comparative Legislatures.* Englewood Cliffs, N.J.: Prentice–Hall, 1973.

———. *Government Ministers in the Contemporary World.* Beverly Hills, Calif.: Sage Publications, 1985.

———. *The Organization of Governments: A Comparative Analysis of Government Structures.* Beverly Hills, Calif.: Sage Publications, 1982.

———. *World Leaders: Heads of Government in the Post-War Period.* Beverly Hills, Calif.: Sage Publications, 1980.

Crozier, Michael. *The Bureaucratic Phenomenon.* Chicago: University of Chicago Press, 1963.

Dahl, Robert A. *Polyarchy: Participation and Opposition.* New Haven, Conn.: Yale University Press, 1971.

Duchacek, Ivo. *Power Maps.* Santa Barbara, Calif.: ABC Clio Press, 1973.

———. *Rights and Liberties in the World Today.* Santa Barbara, Calif.: ABC Clio Press, 1973.

Friedrich, Carl J. *Limited Government: A Comparison.* Englewood Cliffs, N.J.: Prentice–Hall, 1974.

King, Anthony. "Executives," in F. I. Greenstein and N. W. Polsby, eds., *Handbook of Political Science.* Reading, Mass.: Addison–Wesley, 1975.

La Palombara, Joseph, ed. *Bureaucracy and Political Development.* Princeton, N.J.: Princeton University Press, 1964.

Lijphart, Arend. *Democracies: Patterns of Majoritarian and Consensus Governments in Twenty-One Countries.* New Haven, Conn.: Yale University Press, 1984.

Linz, Juan J., and Alfred Stepan, eds. *The Breakdown of Democratic Regimes.* Baltimore: Johns Hopkins University Press, 1978.

Loewenberg, Gerhard, and Samuel Patterson. *Comparing Legislatures.* Boston: Little, Brown, 1979.

March, James, and Shaun Olsen. *Rediscovering Institutions.* New York: Free Press, 1989.

Neustadt, Richard E. *Presidential Power: The Politics of Leadership.* New York: Wiley, 1960.

O'Donnell, Guillermo, Philippe C. Schmitter, and Laurence Whitehead. *Transitions from Authoritarian Rule: Comparative Perspectives and Tentative Conclusions.* Baltimore: Johns Hopkins University Press, 1987.

Powell, G. Bingham, Jr. *Contemporary Democracies: Participation, Stability and Violence.* Cambridge, Mass.: Harvard University Press, 1982.

Putnam, Robert. *The Comparative Study of Political Elites.* Englewood Cliffs, N.J.: Prentice–Hall, 1976.

Strom, Kaare. *Minority Government and Majority Rule.* Cambridge: Cambridge University Press, 1990.

Vile, M.J. *Constitutionalism and the Separation of Powers.* New York: Oxford University Press, 1967.

Wheeler, Harvey. "Constitutionalism," in F.I. Greenstein and N.W. Polsby, eds., *Handbook of Political Science.* Reading, Mass.: Addison–Wesley, 1975.

CHAPTER 8
Public Policy

Almond, Gabriel A., Scott Flanagan, and Robert Mundt. *Crisis, Choice and Change.* Boston: Little, Brown, 1973.

Almond, Gabriel A., and G. Bingham Powell, Jr. *Comparative Politics: System, Process, Policy,* 2nd ed. Boston: Little, Brown, 1978.

Binder, Leonard, et al. *Crises and Sequences in Political Development.* Princeton, N.J.: Princeton University Press, 1971.

Cameron, David. "Social Democracy, Labor Quiescence, and the Representation of Economic Interest in Advanced Industrial Societies," in John Goldthorpe, ed., *Order and Conflict in Contemporary Capitalism.* London: Cambridge University Press, 1984.

Chenery, Hollis, et al. *Redistribution with Growth.* London: Oxford University Press, 1974.

Dahl, Robert A. *Democracy and Its Critics.* New Haven, Conn.: Yale University Press, 1990.

Eckstein, Harry. *The Evaluation of Political Performance: Problems and Dimensions.* Beverly Hills, Calif.: Sage Publications, 1971.

Flora, Peter, and Arnold Heidenheimer, eds. *The Welfare State in Europe and North America.* New Brunswick, N.J.: Transaction Press, 1981.

Grew, Raymond, ed. *Crises of Political Development in Europe and the United States.* Princeton, N.J.: Princeton University Press, 1978.

Gurevich, Peter. *Politics in Hard Times.* Ithaca, N.Y.: Cornell University Press, 1986.

Heclo, Hugh. *Modern Social Politics in Britain and Sweden.* New Haven, Conn.: Yale University Press, 1974.

Heidenheimer, Arnold, Hugh Heclo, and Carolyn T. Adams. *Comparative Public Policy,* 3rd ed. New York: St. Martin's, 1990.

Jackman, Robert W. *Politics and Social Equality.* New York: Wiley, 1975.

Jackson, Robert H., and Carl Rosberg. *Personal Rule in Black Africa.* New Haven, Conn.: Yale University Press, 1990.

Katzenstein, Peter. *Small States and World Markets.* Ithaca, N.Y.: Cornell University Press, 1985.

Lindblom, Charles E. *Politics and Markets.* New Haven, Conn.: Yale University Press, 1978.

Olson, Mancur. *The Rise and Decline of Nations.* New Haven, Conn.: Yale University Press, 1982.

Rawls, John. *A Theory of Justice.* Cambridge, Mass.: Harvard University Press, 1971.

Schmitter, Phillippe, and Gerhard Lehmbruch. *Trends Toward Capitalist Mediation.* Beverly Hills, Calif.: Sage Publications, 1979.

Singer, J. David, and Melvin Small. *The Wages of War 1816–1965.* New York: Wiley, 1972.

Tilly, Charles, ed. *The Formation of Nation States in Western Europe.* Princeton, N.J.: Princeton University Press, 1975.

Wilensky, Harold. *The Welfare State and Equality.* Berkeley: University of California Press, 1975.

Wilensky, Harold, et al., *Comparative Social Policy: Theories, Methods, Findings.* Berkeley, Calif.: Institute of International Studies, 1985.

Wilson, James Q., ed. *The Politics of Regulation.* New York: Basic Books, 1980.

CHAPTER 9
Politics in England

Anwar, Mohammed. *Race and Politics.* London: Tavistock, 1989.

Bogdanor, Vernon. *Multi-Party Politics and the Constitution.* New York: Cambridge University Press, 1983.

Butler, D. E. and D. E. Butler. *British Political Facts, 1900–1985,* 6th ed. London: Macmillan, 1986.

———, and Dennis Kavanagh. *The British General Election of 1987.* London: Macmillan, 1988.

Craig, F. W. S. *British Electoral Facts, 1832–1987.* Aldershot: Parliamentary Research Services/Dartmouth, 1989.

Drewry, Gavin, and Tony Butcher. *The Civil Service Today.* Oxford: Basil Blackwell, 1988.

Grant, Wyn. *Pressure Groups, Politics and Democracy in Britain.* Hemel Hempstead: Philip Allan, 1989.

Halsey, A. H., ed. *British Social Trends since 1900,* 2nd ed. London: Macmillan, 1988.

Hennessy, Peter. *Whitehall.* London: Fontana Books, 1990.

Jenkins, Peter. *Mrs. Thatcher's Revolution.* Cambridge, Mass.: Harvard University Press, 1987.

Kavanagh, Dennis. *Thatcherism and British Politics,* 2nd ed. Oxford: Oxford University Press, 1990.

Levacic, Rosalind. *Economic Policy-Making: Its Theory and Practice.* Brighton, Sussex: Wheatsheaf, 1987.

Marshall, Geoffrey. *Constitutional Conventions.* Oxford: Clarendon Press, 1984.

Norton, Philip, ed. *Parliament in the 1980s.* Oxford: Basil Blackwell, 1985.

Rose, Richard. *Do Parties Make a Difference?* 2nd ed. Chatham, N.J.: Chatham House, 1984.

———. *Ministers and Ministries.* New York: Oxford University Press, 1987.

———. *Ordinary People in Public Policy.* Newbury Park, Calif.: Sage Publications, 1989.

———. *The Territorial Dimension in Government: Understanding the United Kingdom.* Chatham, N.J.: Chatham House, 1982.

———, and Ian McAllister. *The Loyalties of Voters.* Newbury Park, Calif.: Sage Publications, 1990.

Seldon, Anthony, ed. *UK Political Parties since 1945.* Hemel Hempstead: Philip Allan, 1990.

Social Trends. London: Her Majesty's Stationery Office, annual.

Whitaker's Almanack. London: J. Whitaker & Sons, annual.

CHAPTER 10
Politics in France
Ambler, John, ed. *The Welfare State in France.* New York: New York University Press, 1991.

Ashford, Douglas E. *Policy and Politics in France.* Philadelphia: Temple University Press, 1982.

Bell, D. S., and Byron Criddle. *The French Socialist Party: The Emergence of a Party of Government.* Oxford: Clarendon Press/Oxford, 1988.

Birnbaum, Pierre. *The Heights of Power: An Essay on the Power Elite in France.* Chicago: University of Chicago Press, 1982.

Cerny, Philip G., and Martin A. Schain, eds. *Socialism, the State and Public Policy in France.* New York: Methuen, 1985.

Gallie, Duncan. *Social Inequality and Class Radicalism in France and Britain.* London: Cambridge University Press, 1983.

Godt, Paul. *Policy-Making in France.* London: Pinter Publishers, 1989.

Hall, Peter. *Governing the Economy: The Politics of State Intervention in Britain and France.* New York: Oxford University Press, 1986.

———, Jack Hayward, and Howard Machin. *Developments in French Politics.* London: Macmillan, 1990.

Hayward, Jack. *The State and the Market Economy: Industrial Patriotism and Economic Intervention in France.* New York: New York University Press, 1986.

Holifield, James, and George Ross, eds. *In Search of the New France.* New York: Routledge, 1991.

Keeler, John T.S. *The Politics of Neocorporatism in France.* New York: Oxford University Press, 1987.

Kesselman, Mark, ed. *The French Workers' Movement.* London: George Allen and Unwin, 1984.

Lauber, Volkmar. *The Political Economy of France: From Pompidou to Mitterrand.* New York: Praeger, 1983.

Ross, George, Stanley Hoffmann, and Sylvia Malzacher. *The Mitterrand Experiment.* New York: Oxford University Press, 1987.

Schmidt, Vivien. *Democratizing France.* New York: Cambridge University Press, 1990.

Smith, Rand W. *Crisis in the French Labor Movement: A Grassroots Perspective.* New York: St. Martin's, 1988.

Suleiman, Ezra. *Elites in French Society.* Princeton, N.J.: Princeton University Press, 1978.

Wilson, Frank L. *French Political Parties Under the Fifth Republic.* New York: Praeger, 1982.

———. *Interest Group Politics in France.* New York: Cambridge University Press, 1987.

Wright, Vincent. *The Government and Politics of France,* 3rd ed. London: Unwin Hyman, 1989.

CHAPTER 11
Politics in Germany
Bark, Dennis, and David Gress. *A History of West Germany,* 2 vols. London: Basil Blackwell, 1988.

Beyme, Klaus von, and Manfred Schmidt, eds. *Policy and Politics in the Federal Republic of Germany.* London: Gower, 1985.

Broszat, Martin. *Hitler and the Collapse of Weimar Germany.* New York: St. Martin's, 1987.

Bulmer, Simon, ed. *The Changing Agenda of West German Public Policy.* Brookfield, Vt.: Gower Publishing, 1989.

Childs, David. *The GDR: Moscow's German Ally,* 2nd ed. London: Hyman, 1988.

Craig, Gordon. *Germany 1866–1945.* New York: Oxford University Press.

Dalton, Russell. *Politics in West Germany.* Glenview, Ill.: Scott–Foresman, 1989.

Fest, Joachim. *Hitler.* New York: Random House, 1975.

Hanreider, Wolfram. *Germany, America, Europe: Forty Years of German Foreign Policy.* New Haven, Conn.: Yale University Press, 1989.

Katzenstein, Peter. *Policy and Politics in West Germany: The Growth of a Semisovereign State.* Philadelphia: Temple University Press, 1987.

————, ed. *Industry and Politics in West Germany: Toward the Third Republic.* Ithaca, N.Y.: Cornell University Press, 1989.

Krisch, Henry. *The German Democratic Republic: The Search for Identity.* Boulder, Colo.: Westview Press, 1985.

Merkl, Peter, ed. *The Federal Republic at Forty.* New York: New York University Press, 1989.

Orlow, Dietrich. *A History of Modern Germany.* Englewood Cliffs, N.J.: Prentice–Hall, 1987.

Padgett, Stephen, and Tony Burkett. *Political Parties and Elections in West Germany.* New York: St. Martin's, 1966.

Smith, Gordon, et al. *Developments in West German Politics.* London: Macmillan, 1989.

Turner, Henry. *The Two Germanies since 1945.* New Haven, Conn.: Yale University Press, 1987.

CHAPTER 12
Politics in Japan

Allinson, Gary D. *Suburban Tokyo: A Comparative Study in Politics and Social Change.* Berkeley: University of California Press, 1979.

Baerwald, Hans H. *Party Politics in Japan.* Boston: Allen and Unwin, 1986.

Bestor, Theodore C. *Neighborhood Tokyo.* Stanford, Calif.: Stanford University Press, 1989.

Calder, Kent E. *Crisis and Compensation: Public Policy and Political Stability in Japan, 1949–1986.* Princeton, N.J.: Princeton University Press, 1988.

Campbell, John Creighton. *Contemporary Japanese Budget Politics.* Berkeley: University of California Press, 1977.

————. *How Policies Change: The Japanese Government and the Aging Society.* Princeton, N.J.: Princeton University Press, 1991.

Curtis, Gerald L. *Election Campaigning Japanese Style.* New York: Columbia University Press, 1971.

————. *The Japanese Way of Politics.* New York: Columbia University Press, 1988.

Dore, Ronald. *Taking Japan Seriously: A Confucian Perspective on Leading Economic Issues.* Stanford, Calif.: Stanford University Press, 1987.

Flanagan, Scott C., Shinsaku Kohei, Ichiro Miyake, Bradley M. Richardson, and Joji Watanuki. *The Japanese Voter.* New Haven, Conn.: Yale University Press, 1991.

Fukui, Haruhiro. *Party in Power: The Japanese Liberal Democrats and Policymaking.* Berkeley, Calif.: University of California Press, 1970.

Fukutake, Tadashi. *The Japanese Social Structure.* Tokyo: University of Tokyo Press, 1989.

Hrebenar, Ronald J. *The Japanese Party System: From One-Party Rule to Coalition Government.* Boulder, Colo.: Westview Press, 1986.

Ike, Nobutaka. *A Theory of Japanese Democracy.* Boulder, Colo.: Westview Press, 1978.

Inoguchi Takashi, and Daniel Okimoto. *The Political Economy of Japan: Vol. 2, The Changing International Context.* Stanford, Calif.: Stanford University Press.

Ishida, Takeshi, and Ellis S. Krauss, eds. *Democracy in Japan.* Pittsburgh, Pa.: University of Pittsburgh Press, 1989.

Johnson, Chalmers. (1982). *MITI and the Japanese Miracle.* Stanford, Calif.: Stanford University Press, 1982.

Koh, B. C. *Japan's Administrative Elite.* Berkeley, Calif.: University of California Press, 1989.

Krauss, Ellis S., Thomas P. Rohlen, and Patricia G. Steinhoff. *Conflict in Japan.* Honolulu: University of Hawaii Press, 1984.

Lebra, Takie Sugiyama, and William P. Lebra, eds. *Japanese Culture and Behavior.* Honolulu: University Press of Hawaii, 1987.

Masumi Junnosuke. *Postwar Politics in Japan, 1945–1955.* Berkeley: University of California Center for Japanese Studies, Japan Research Monograph, No. 6, 1985.

McKean, Margaret A. *Environmental Protest and Citizen Politics in Japan.* Berkeley: University of California Press, 1981.

Mouer, Ross, and Yoshio Sugimoto. *Images of Japanese Society: A Study in the Social Construction of Reality.* London: Kegan Paul International, 1986.

Nakane, Chie. *Japanese Society.* Berkeley: University of California Press, 1970.

Okimoto, Daniel I. *Between MITI and the Market: Japanese Industrial Policy for High Technology.* Stanford, Calif.: Stanford University Press, 1989.

Okimoto, Daniel I., and Thomas P. Rohlen. *Inside the Japanese System: Readings on Contemporary Society and Political Economy.* Stanford, Calif.: Stanford University Press, 1988.

Ozaki, Robert S., and Walter Arnold. *Japan's Foreign Relations: A Global Search for Economic Security.* Boulder, Colo.: Westview Press, 1985.

Pempel, T. J., ed. *Policy and Politics in Japan.* Philadelphia: Temple University Press, 1982.

————. *Uncommon Democracies: The One-Party Dominant Regimes.* Ithaca, N.Y.: Cornell University Press, 1990.

Pharr, Susan J. *Losing Face: Status Politics in Japan.* Berkeley, Calif.: University of California Press, 1990.

Reed, Steven R. *Japanese Prefectures and Policymaking.* Pittsburgh: University of Pittsburgh Press, 1986.

Richardson, Bradley M., and Scott C. Flanagan. *Politics in Japan.* Boston: Little, Brown, 1984.

Samuels, Richard J. *The Business of the Japanese State: Energy Markets in Comparative and Historical Perspective.* Ithaca. N.Y.: Cornell University Press, 1987.

Steiner, Kurt, Ellis S. Krauss, and Scott C. Flanagan, eds. *Political Opposition and Local Politics in Japan.* Princeton, N.J.: Princeton University Press, 1980.

Stockwin, J. A. A., ed. *Dynamic and Immobilist Politics in Japan.* Honolulu: University of Hawaii Press, 1988.

Thayer, Nathaniel B. *How the Conservatives Rule Japan.* Princeton, N.J.: Princeton University Press, 1969.

Ward, Robert E., and Yoshikazu Sakamoto. *Democratizing Japan: The Allied Occupation.* Honolulu: University of Hawaii Press, 1987.

White, James W. *Migration in Metropolitan Japan.* Berkeley: Institute of East Asian Studies, University of California at Berkeley, 1982.

Wolferen, Karel van. *The Enigma of Japanese Power.* New York: Knopf, 1989.

Yamamura, Kozo, and Yasukichi Yasuba. *The Political Economy of Japan:* Vol. 1, *The Domestic Transformation.* Stanford, Calif.: Stanford University Press, 1987.

CHAPTER 13
Politics in the USSR

Aganbegyan, Abel. *Inside Perestroika: The Future of the Soviet Economy.* New York: Harper and Row, 1989.

Ash, Timothy Garton. *The Magic Lantern.* New York: Random House, 1990.

Barghoorn, Frederick. *Detente and the Democractic Movement in The USSR.* New York: Free Press, 1976.

———, and Thomas Remington. *Politics in the USSR,* 3rd ed. Boston: Little, Brown, 1986.

Bialer, Seweryn, ed. *Politics, Society, and Nationality Inside Gorbachev's Russia.* Boulder, Colo.: Westview Press, 1989.

Bloch, Sidney, and Peter Reddaway. *Psychiatric Terror: How Soviet Psychiatry Is Used to Suppress Dissent.* New York: Basic Books, 1977.

Brown, Archie, ed. *Political Culture and Communist Studies.* Armonk, N.Y.: M. E. Sharpe, 1985.

———. *Political Leadership in the Soviet Union.* Bloomington: Indiana University, 1989.

Butterfield, James, and Judith Sedaitis, eds. *New Social Movements in the Soviet Union.* Boulder, Colo.: Westview Press, 1991.

Conquest, Robert. *The Harvest of Sorrow: Soviet Collectivisation and the Terror-Famine.* New York and Oxford: Oxford University Press, 1986.

Gleason, Gregory. *Federalism and Nationalism: The Struggle for Republican Rights in the USSR.* Boulder, Colo.: Westview Press, 1990.

Gorbachev, Mikhail. *Perestroika: New Thinking for Our Country and the World.* New York: Harper and Row, 1987.

Harasimiw, Bohdan. *Political Elite Recruitment in the Soviet Union.* New York: St. Martin's, 1984.

Hill, Ronald, and Peter Frank. *The Soviet Communist Party,* 3rd ed. Boston: Allen and Unwin, 1986.

Hough, Jerry. *Opening up the Soviet Economy.* Washington, D.C.: Brookings Institution, 1988.

Lawrence, Paul R., et al. *Behind the Factory Walls: Decision Making in Soviet and U.S. Enterprises.* Boston: Harvard Business School Press, 1990.

Lynch, Allen. *The Soviet Study of International Relations.* Cambridge: Cambridge University Press, 1989.

Mickiewicz, Ellen. *Split Signals: Television and Politics in the Soviet Union.* New York and Oxford: Oxford University Press, 1988.

Nahaylo, Bohdan, and Victor Swoboda. *Soviet Disunion: A History of the Nationalities Problem in the USSR.* New York: Free Press, 1990.

Nove, Alec. *Glasnost in Action: Cultural Renaissance in Russia.* Boston: Unwin Hyman, 1989.

Remington, Thomas. *The Truth of Authority: Ideology and Communication in the Soviet Union.* Pittsburgh: University of Pittsburgh Press, 1988.

Rigby, Thomas H. *Leadership Selection and Patron Client Relations in the USSR and Yugloslavia.* London: Allen and Unwin, 1983.

Rowen, Henry, and Charles Wolf. *The Impoverished Superpower: Perestroika and the Soviet Military Burden.* San Francisco: Institute for Contemporary Studies, 1990.

Slider, Darrell, ed. *Elections and Political Change in the Soviet Republics.* Durham, N.C.: Duke University Press, 1991.

Voslensky, Michael. *Nomenklatura: The Soviet Ruling Class.* New York: Doubleday, 1984.

White, Stephen. *Gorbachev in Power.* Cambridge: Cambridge University Press, 1990.

———, and Alex Pravda, eds. *Ideology and Soviet Politics.* London: Macmillan, 1979.

CHAPTER 14
Politics in China

Blecher, Marc. *China: Politics, Economics and Society.* Boulder, Colo.: Lynne Rienner Publishers, 1986.

Chan, Anita, Richard Madsen, and Jonathan Unger. *Chen Village.* Berkeley: University of California Press, 1984.

Dittmer, Lowell. *Liu Shao-Chi'i and the Chinese Cultural Revolution.* Berkeley: University of California Press, 1974.

Eastman, Lloyd. *Seeds of Destruction.* Stanford, Calif.: Stanford University Press, 1984.

Harding, Harry. *China's Second Revolution: Reform after Mao.* Washington, D.C.: Brookings Institution, 1987.

Hinton, William. *Fanshen: A Documentary of Revolution in a Chinese Village.* New York: Monthly Review Press, 1966.

Jencks, Harlan. *From Muskets to Missiles: Politics and Professionalism in the Chinese Army, 1945–1981.* Boulder, Colo.: Westview Press, 1982.

Lee, Hong Yung. *The Politics of the Chinese Cultural Revolution.* Berkeley: University of California Press, 1978.

MacFarquhar, Roderick. *The Origins of the Cultural Revolution,* 2 vols. New York: Columbia University Press, 1974, 1983.

Oi, Jean. *State and Peasant in Contemporary China.* Berkeley: University of California Press, 1989.

Parish, William L., and Martin King Whyte. *Urban Life in*

Contemporary China. Chicago: Univeristy of Chicago Press, 1984.

————. *Village and Family in Contemporary China.* Chicago: University of Chicago Press, 1978.

Huang, Shu-Min. *The Spiral Road.* Boulder, Colo.: Westview Press, 1989.

Spence, Johnathan D. *The Gate of Heavenly Peace: The Chinese and Their Revolution, 1895–1980.* New York: Viking, 1981.

Teiwes, Frederick. *Leadership, Legitimacy and Conflict in China.* Armonk, N.Y.: M. E. Sharpe, 1983.

Townsend, James R., and Brantly Womack. *Politics in China,* 3rd ed. Boston: Little, Brown, 1986.

Tsou, Tang. *The Cultural Revolution and Post-Mao Reforms: A Historical Perspective.* Chicago: University of Chicago Press, 1986.

Walder, Andrew. *Communist Neo-Tradionalism: Work and Authority in Chinese Industry.* Berkeley: University of California Press, 1986.

Womack, Brantly, ed. *Contemporary Chinese Politics in Historical Perspective.* New York: Cambridge University Press, 1991.

————. *Foundations of Mao Zedong's Political Thought, 1917–1935.* Honolulu: University Press of Hawaii, 1982.

World Bank. *China: Socialist Economic Development,* 3 vols. Washington, D.C.: World Bank, 1983.

Yi Mu, and Mark Thompson. *Crisis at Tiananmen.* San Francisco: China Books, 1989.

CHAPTER 15
Politics in Mexico

Alvarado Mendoza, Arturo, ed. *Electoral Patterns and Perspectives in Mexico.* La Jolla, Calif.: Center for U.S.-Mexican Studies, University of California — San Diego, 1987.

Bailey, John J. *Governing Mexico: The Statecraft of Crisis Management.* New York: St. Martin's Press, 1988.

Barkin, David. *Distorted Development: Mexico in the World Economy.* Boulder, Colo.: Westview Press, 1990.

Bilateral Commission on the Future of U.S.-Mexican Relations. *The Challenge of Interdependence: Mexico and the United States.* Lanham, Md.: University Press of America, 1989.

Camp, Roderic A. *Entrepreneurs and Politics in Twentieth Century Mexico.* New York: Oxford University Press, 1989.

Cornelius, Wayne A. *Politics and the Migrant Poor in Mexico City.* Stanford, Calif.: Stanford University Press, 1975.

————, Judith Gentleman, and Peter H. Smith, eds. *Mexico's Alternative Political Futures.* La Jolla, Calif.: Center for U.S.-Mexican Studies, University of California — San Diego, 1989.

Cypher, James M. *State and Capital in Mexico: Development Policy Since 1940.* Boulder, Colo.: Westview Press, 1990.

Eckstein, Susan. *The Poverty of Revolution: The State and the Urban Poor in Mexico.* Princeton, N.J.: Princeton University Press, 1988.

Fagen, Richard R., and William S. Tuohy. *Politics and Privilege in a Mexican City.* Stanford, Calif.: Stanford University Press, 1972.

Foweraker, Joe, and Ann L. Craig, eds. *Popular Movements and Political Change in Mexico.* Boulder, Colo.: Lynne Rienner Publishers, 1990.

Gentleman, Judith, ed. *Mexican Politics in Transition.* Boulder, Colo.: Westview Press, 1987.

González de la Rocha, Mercedes, and Agustín Escobar Latapí, eds. *Social Responses to Mexico's Economic Crisis of the 1980s.* La Jolla, Calif.: Center for U.S.-Mexican Studies, University of California — San Diego, 1991.

Green, Rosario, and Peter H. Smith, series eds. *Dimensions of U.S.-Mexican Relations.* 5 vols. La Jolla, Calif.: Center for U.S.-Mexican Studies, University of California — San Diego, 1989.

Knight, Alan. *The Mexican Revolution.* 2 vols. London: Cambridge University Press, 1986.

Levy, Daniel, and Gabriel Székely. *Mexico: Paradoxes of Stability and Change,* 2nd ed. Boulder, Colo.: Westview Press, 1987.

Maxfield, Sylvia. *Governing Capital: International Finance and Mexican Politics.* Ithaca, N.Y.: Cornell University Press, 1990.

Middlebrook, Kevin, ed. *Unions, Workers, and the State in Mexico.* La Jolla, Calif.: Center for U.S.-Mexican Studies, University of California — San Diego, 1991.

Ronfeldt, David, ed. *The Modern Mexican Military: A Reassessment.* La Jolla, Calif.: Center for U.S.-Mexican Studies, University of California — San Diego, 1984.

Saragoza, Alex M. *The Monterrey Elite and the Mexican State.* Austin: University of Texas Press, 1988.

Smith, Peter H. *Labyrinths of Power: Political Recruitment in Twentieth-Century Mexico.* Princeton, N.J.: Princeton University Press, 1979.

Ward, Peter M. *Mexico City: The Production and Reproduction of an Urban Environment.* London: Bellhaven Press, 1990.

————. *Welfare Politics in Mexico: Papering Over the Cracks.* London: Allen and Unwin, 1986.

Wilkie, James W. *The Mexican Revolution: Federal Expenditure and Social Change Since 1910,* 2nd ed. Berkeley: University of California Press, 1970.

CHAPTER 16
Politics in Africa

Anyang' Nyong'o, Peter, ed. *Popular Struggles for Democracy in Africa.* London: Zed Books, 1987.

Bayart, Jean-Francois. *L'Etat en Afrique: la politique due ventre.* Paris: Fayart, 1989.

Berg, Robert J., and Jennifer Seymour Whitaker, eds. *Strategies for African Development.* Berkeley: University of California Press, 1986.

Carter, Gwendolyn M., and Patrick O'Meara, eds. *African Independence: The First Twenty-Five Years.* Bloomington: Indiana University Press, 1985.

Chabal, Patrick, ed. *Political Domination in Africa.* Cambridge: Cambridge University Press, 1986.

Chazan, Naomi, Robert Mortimer, John Ravenhill, and Donald Rothchild. *Politics and Society in Contemporary Africa.* Boulder, Colo.: Lynne Rienner Publishers, 1988.

Cruise O'Brien, Donal, John Dunn, and Richard Rathbone, eds. *Contemporary West African States.* Cambridge: Cambridge University Press, 1989.

Decalo, Samuel. *Coups and Army Rule in Africa.* New Haven, Conn.: Yale University Press, 1976.

Diamond, Larry, Juan J. Linz, and Seymour Martin Lipset, eds. *Democracy in Developing Countries: Africa.* Boulder, Colo.: Lynne Rienner Publishers, 1989.

Freund, Bill. *The Making of Contemporary Africa.* Bloomingtom: Indiana University Press, 1984.

Hayward, Fred M., ed. *Elections in Africa.* Boulder, Colo.: Westview Press, 1987.

Hyden, Goran. *Beyond Ujamaa in Tanzania.* Berkeley: University of California Press, 1980.

———. *No Shortcuts to Progress.* Berkeley: University of California Press, 1983.

Jackson, Robert H., and Carl G. Rosberg. *Personal Rule in Black Africa.* Berkeley: University of California Press, 1982.

Keller, Edmond J., and Donald Rothchild, eds. *Afro-Marxist Regimes.* Boulder, Colo.: Lynne Rienner Publishers, 1988.

Ottaway, David, and Marina Ottaway. *Afro-Communisn.* New York: Holmes and Meier, 1981.

Rothchild, Donald, and Victor A. Olorunsola, eds. *State Versus Ethnic Claims: African Dilemmas.* Boulder, Colo.: Westview Press, 1983.

Sandbrook, Richard. *The Politics of Africa's Economic Stagnation.* Cambridge: Cambridge University Press, 1986.

Tordoff, William. *Government and Politics in Africa.* Bloomington: Indiana University Press, 1984.

Vail, Leroy, ed. *The Creation of Tribalism in Southern Africa.* Berkeley: University of California Press, 1989.

Whitaker, Jennifer Seymour. *How Can Africa Survive?* New York: Harper and Row, 1988.

World Bank. *Sub-Saharan Africa: From Crisis to Sustainable Growth.* Washington, D.C., 1989.

Young, Crawford. *Ideology and Development in Africa.* New Haven, Conn.: Yale University Press, 1982.

———. *The Politics of Cultural Pluralism.* Madison: University of Wisconsin Press, 1976.

CHAPTER 17
Politics in the United States

Abraham, Henry J. *The Judiciary: The Supreme Court in the Governmental Process,* 6th ed. New York: Allyn and Bacon, 1983.

Davidson, Roger H., and Walter J. Oleszek. *Congress and Its Members,* 2nd ed. Washington, D.C.: Congressional Quarterly Press, 1985.

Epstein, Leon D. *Political Parties in the American Mold.* Madison: University of Wisconsin Press, 1986.

Ginsberg, Benjamin, and Martin Shefter. *Politics by Other Means: The Declining Importance of Elections in America.* New York: Basic Books, 1990.

Hamilton, Alexander, James Madison, and John Jay. *The Federalist Papers,* ed. by Clinton Rossiter. New York: New American Library, 1961.

Kernell, Samuel. *Going Public: New Strategies of Presidential Leadership.* Washington, D.C.: Congressional Quarterly Press, 1986.

King, Anthony S., ed. *The New American Political System.* Washington, D.C.: American Enterprise Institute, 1978.

Lindblom, Charles E. *The Policy-Making Process,* 2nd ed. Englewood Cliffs, N.J.: Prentice-Hall, 1980.

McClosky, Herbert, and John Zaller. *The American Ethos: Public Attitudes Toward Capitalism and Democracy.* Cambridge, Mass.: Harvard University Press, 1984.

Neustadt, Richard E. *Presidential Power and the Modern Presidents: The Politics of Leadership from Roosevelt to Reagan.* New York: Free Press, 1990.

Nicholas, Herbert G. *The Nature of American Politics,* 2nd ed. New York: Oxford University Press, 1986.

Page, Benjamin T. *Who Gets What from Government?* Berkeley: University of California Press, 1983.

Peltason, Jack W. *Corwin & Peltason's Understanding the Constitution,* 10th ed. New York: Holt, Rinehart and Winston, 1985.

Polsby, Nelson W. *Congress and the Presidency,* 4th ed. Englewood Cliffs, N.J.: Prentice–Hall, 1986.

Ranney, Austin. *Channels of Power: The Impact of Television on American Politics.* New York: Basic Books, 1983.

Robinson, Donald L., ed. *Reforming American Government: The Bicentennial Papers of the Committee on the Constitutional System.* Boulder, Colo.: Westview Press, 1985.

Rourke, Francis E. *Bureaucracy, Politics and Public Policy.* Boston: Little, Brown, 1983.

Schlozman, Kay Lehman, and John T. Tierney, *Organized Interests and American Democracy.* New York: Harper and Row, 1986.

Tocqueville, Alexis de. *Democracy in America,* 2 vols. The Henry Reeve text as revised by Francis Bowen and edited by Phillips Bradley. New York: Knopf, 1945.

Wildavsky, Aaron. *The Politics of the Budgetary Process,* 4th ed. Boston: Little, Brown, 1983.

INDEX

Mobutu, Sese Seko, 529, 536, 544, 546, 549, 552
Mohammed, Muritala, 546
Moldavia (Moldova), 363–364, 375–376, 399
Momoh, Joseph, 546
Monaco, 563
Monarchy, 100–101, 141–142
Monopolies Commission (Britain), 175
Montesquieu, Baron de, 189
Morelos y Pavón, José María, 466
Morocco, 521, 523, 525, 555
Moses, Joel, 388
Moya Palencia, Mario, 479
Mozambique, 523, 525, 527, 536, 546, 555, 558
Mubarak, Hosni, 546
Multiparty systems, 81–83
Múñoz-Ledo, Porfirio, 494
Murdoch, Rupert, 164
Muslims, 24, 37, 63, 83, 140, 198, 390, 533–535,
    538–539

Nadel, Mark, 104
Nader, Ralph, 104
Nakasone, Yasuhiro, 55
Namibia, 522–523, 525, 527, 531, 555
Napoleon I, 121, 190, 200–201, 210
Napoleon III, 190, 208, 210
Napoleonic Code, 199
Napoleonic wars, 120
Nasser, Gamal Abdel, 546, 550–551
National Action Party (Mexico), 464, 467, 472–473,
    475, 488–490, 492–495, 502–503, 510
National Assembly (France), 53, 93–94, 98–99,
    192–193, 195–196, 202–203, 206, 208, 210,
    213, 216, 218, 220, 222, 224–225, 227, 229,
    252
National Association of Realtors, 582
National Coal Board (Britain), 166, 175, 177
National Front (France), 218–219, 233–234
National Guard (United States), 581
National Health Service (Britain), 133, 146, 174–176,
    178–181
National Institutes of Health (United States), 103
Nationalism, 16–17, 138–140, 527–528
Nationalist Party (China). See Guomindang
Nationalist Revolution of 1928 (China), 413–414
Nationalization, 177
National Organization for Women, 582
National Party Congress (China), 432–434

National People's Congress (China), 6–8, 97–98,
    100, 427, 430, 432, 442–443, 447, 451
National Police Reserve (Japan), 303
National security, and interdependence, 24–25
National Security Council (United States), 99
National Socialist German Workers Party. See Nazis
National Solidarity Program (Mexico), 487, 506, 510
National Union of Mine Workers (Britain), 134, 166
National University (Mexico), 480
Nazis, 35, 190, 197, 210, 241–242, 249, 256, 264,
    268, 272, 360, 385, 387
Neocorporatism, 269
Neotraditional political systems, 125–126
Nepal, 4
Netherlands, 25–26, 337
    government power, 96
    interest groups, 65
    political parties, 76, 81, 586
    taxes, 110
New Caledonia, 208, 211
New Deal, 587, 590
New Economic Policy, 385
New Liberal Club (Japan), 307, 318
New Politics movement, 260–261, 266, 271–272,
    276–277, 280
Newspapers. See Mass media
New York Times v. Sullivan, 573
New Zealand, 65, 81, 95–96, 131, 136, 586
Nicaragua, 78, 120, 396, 589
Nicholas, H. G., 564
Niger, 523, 525, 555
Nigeria, 39, 136, 523–525, 528, 555, 557
    benefits/services, 111–112
    civil war, 41, 56
    democracy/authoritarianism in, 57–58, 530
    elections, 47, 56
    environmental protection, 594
    ethnic groups, 533
    GNP, 108–109, 111–112, 116, 118
    interest groups, 548, 550–551
    mass media, 541
    military, 85, 529
    political recruitment, 546
    political socialization, 539–540
    regulations, 114
    religious groups, 538
    social classes, 536–537
    taxes, 108–109
Nimeiry, Gaafar, 534

GREENLAND

ICELAND

CANADA

Alaska

SCOTLAND
N. IRELAND
IRELAND
WALES
ENGLAND
FRANCE
PORTUGAL   SPAIN

UNITED STATES

Hawaii

MEXICO

MOROCCO

AL

WESTERN
SAHARA

MAURITANIA

MA

CUBA
JAMAICA   HAITI
BELIZE   DOMINICAN REPUBLIC
GUATEMALA   HONDURAS
EL SALVADOR
NICARAGUA
COSTA RICA
PANAMA
COLOMBIA

SENEGAL
THE GAMBIA
GUINEA-BISSAU
GUINEA
SIERRA LEONE
LIBERIA
IVORY COAST
GHANA   TOGO
BENIN
CAMEROON
EQUAT. GUINE

UPP.
VOLT.

VENEZUELA
GUYANA
SURINAME
FRENCH GUIANA

ECUADOR

PERU

BRAZIL

A

BOLIVIA

PARAGUAY

CHILE

ARGENTINA

URUGUAY

THE WORLD